Name and Type of Organization as Focus Illustration of Each Chapter

| Chapter Title | Focus Company | Managerial Focus | Contrast Companies | Key Ratios |
|---|---|---|---|---|
| 8. Reporting and Interpreting Property, Plant, and Equipment; Natural Resources; and Intangibles | **Delta Air Lines**<br>Major international air carrier | Planning productive capacity | United Air Lines<br>U•S Airways<br>Singapore Airlines<br>Southwest Airlines<br>Sony<br>PepsiCo<br>Harley-Davidson | **Fixed Asset Turnover** |
| 9. Reporting and Interpreting Liabilities | **General Mills**<br>Manufacturer of popular food items | Capital structure | Kellogg<br>Quaker Oats<br>Southwest Airlines<br>Home Depot<br>Wal-Mart<br>Toyota<br>Ford Motor Company | **Current Ratio**<br>**Payables Turnover** |
| 10. Reporting and Interpreting Bonds | **Harrah's Entertainment, Inc.**<br>Operator of gambling casinos and hotels | Long-term debt financing | Mirage Resorts<br>Trump Casinos<br>Eastman Kodak<br>Southwestern Bell<br>Exxon<br>Halliburton Corp.<br>Kansas City Southern Industries | **Debt-to-Equity**<br>**Times Interest Earned** |
| 11. Reporting and Interpreting Owners' Equity | **Wal-Mart Stores, Inc.**<br>Retail industry | Corporate ownership | May Dept. Stores<br>Dollar General<br>JCPenney<br>Lone Star Ind.<br>Bally Manufacturing<br>DaimlerChrysler<br>Creative Learning Products | **Dividend Yield**<br>**Dividend Payout** |
| 12. Reporting and Interpreting Investments in Other Corporations | **Dow Jones** | Strategic investment in other companies | New York Times<br>Knight-Ridder<br>Disney<br>Harley-Davidson<br>Boston Beer<br>Papa John's International<br>IBM | **Return on Assets** |
| 13. Statement of Cash Flows | **Boston Beer**<br>Beer brewing company | Management of cash | Pete's Brewing Company<br>Foster's Brewing<br>Redhook Ale Brewery<br>General Mills<br>Papa John's International<br>Delta Air Lines<br>U•S Airways | **Quality of Income Ratio** |
| 14. Analyzing Financial Statements | **Home Depot**<br>Home improvement retailer | Financial statement analysis | Lowe's<br>Payless Cashways<br>Braniff International Corporation | **Ratio Summary** |

*Third Edition*

# FINANCIAL
# Accounting

**ROBERT LIBBY**
Cornell University

**PATRICIA A. LIBBY**
Ithaca College

**DANIEL G. SHORT**
Miami University

**McGraw-Hill
Irwin**

Boston   Burr Ridge, IL   Dubuque, IA   Madison, WI   New York   San Francisco   St. Louis
Bangkok   Bogotá   Caracas   Lisbon   London   Madrid
Mexico City   Milan   New Delhi   Seoul   Singapore   Sydney   Taipei   Toronto

# McGraw-Hill Higher Education

*A Division of The* **McGraw-Hill** *Companies*

FINANCIAL ACCOUNTING

Published by McGraw-Hill/Irwin, an imprint of The McGraw-Hill Companies, Inc. 1221 Avenue of the Americas, New York, NY, 10020. Copyright © 2001, 1998, 1996, by The McGraw-Hill Companies, Inc. All rights reserved. No part of this publication may be reproduced or distributed in any form or by any means, or stored in a database or retrieval system, without the prior written consent of The McGraw-Hill Companies, Inc., including, but not limited to, in any network or other electronic storage or transmission, or broadcast for distance learning.

Some ancillaries, including electronic and print components, may not be available to customers outside the United States.

This book is printed on acid-free paper.

domestic       2 3 4 5 6 7 8 9 0  VNH/VNH  0 9 8 7 6 5 4 3 2 1 0
international  1 2 3 4 5 6 7 8 9 0  VNH/VNH  0 9 8 7 6 5 4 3 2 1 0

ISBN 0-07-230035-3

Publisher: *Jeff Shelstad*
Senior vice president and editorial director: *Robin J. Zwettler*
Sponsoring editor: *Steve Hazelwood*
Developmental editor: *Tracey Douglas*
Senior marketing manager: *Rhonda Seelinger*
Project manager: *Kimberly D. Hooker*
Production supervisor: *Lori Koetters*
Senior designer: *Laurie Entringer*
Photo research coordinator: *Keri Johnson*
Supplement coordinator: *Carol Loreth*
New media: *Edward Przyeyciki*
Cover images: *Simon Pinto © SuperStock, Inc., Corbis Images, Photodisc*
Compositor: *GAC Indianapolis*
Typeface: *10.5/12 Times Roman*
Printer: *Von Hoffman Press, Inc.*

**Library of Congress Cataloging-in-Publication Data**

Libby, Robert
    Accounting/Robert Libby, Patricia A. Libby, Daniel G. Short—3rd ed.
        p. cm.
    Rev. Ed. of: Financial accounting/Robert Libby, Patricia A. Libby, Daniel G. Short. c1998.
    Includes bibliographical references and index.
    ISBN 0-07-230035-3 (alk. paper)
    1. Accounting. 2. Corporations—Accounting. 3. Financial statements. I. Libby, Patricia A. II. Short, Daniel G. III. Libby, Robert. Financial accounting. IV. Title.

HF5635. L684 2001
657—dc21

00-038322

International Edition ISBN 0-07-118053-2

Copyright ©2001. Exclusive rights by The McGraw-Hill Companies, Inc. for manufacture and export. This book cannot be re-exported from the country to which it is sold by McGraw-Hill. The International Edition is not available in North America.

www.mhhe.com

# About the Authors

### ROBERT LIBBY

Robert Libby is the David A Thomas Professor of Management at the Johnson Graduate School of Management at Cornell University. Bob teaches the introductory financial accounting course. He previously taught at the University of Illinois, Pennsylvania State University, the University of Texas, the University of Chicago, and the University of Michigan. He received his B.S. from Pennsylvania State University and his M.A.S. and Ph.D. from the University of Illinois; he is also a CPA. Bob is a widely published author specializing in behavioral accounting. He was selected as the AAA Outstanding Educator in 2000. His prior text, *Accounting and Human Information Processing* (Prentice Hall, 1981), was awarded the AICPA/AAA Notable Contributions to the Accounting Literature Award. He received this award again in 1996 for a paper. He has published numerous articles in the *Journal of Accounting Research; Accounting, Organizations, and Society;* and other accounting journals. He is an active member of the American Accounting Association and the American Institute of CPAs, and is a member of the editorial boards of the *Journal of Accounting Research; Accounting, Organizations, and Society; Journal of Accounting Literature;* and *Journal of Behavioral Decision Making.*

### PATRICIA A. LIBBY

Patricia Libby is Associate Professor of Accounting at Ithaca College where she teaches the undergraduate financial accounting course. She previously taught graduate and undergraduate financial accounting at Eastern Michigan University and the University of Texas. Before entering academe, she was an auditor with Price Waterhouse and a financial administrator at the University of Chicago. She received her B.S. from Pennsylvania State University, M.B.A. from DePaul University, and Ph.D. from the University of Michigan; she is also a CPA. Pat conducts research on how to use cases in the introductory course and in other parts of the accounting curriculum. She has published articles in *The Accounting Review, Issues in Accounting Education,* and *The Michigan CPA.* She also has conducted seminars nationally on active learning strategies, including cooperative learning methods.

### DANIEL G. SHORT

Dan Short is Dean of the Richard T. Farmer School of Business at Miami University. Previously, Dan was dean of the College of Business at Kansas State University and before that associate dean at the University of Texas at Austin, where he taught the undergraduate and graduate financial accounting courses. He also taught at the University of Chicago. He received his undergraduate degree from Boston University and his M.B.A. and Ph.D. from the University of Michigan. Dan has won numerous awards for his outstanding teaching abilities and has published articles in *The Accounting Review,* the *Journal of Accounting Research, The Wall Street Journal,* and other business journals. He has worked with a large number of Fortune 500 companies, commercial banks, and investment banks to develop and teach executive education courses on the effective use of accounting information. Dan has also served on the board of directors of several companies, including manufacturing, commercial banking, and medical services. He is currently chair of the audit committee of a large manufacturing company.

The first edition of *Financial Accounting* was written based on our belief that the subject is inherently interesting but most textbooks are not. Furthermore, we found that most financial accounting textbooks failed to demonstrate that accounting is an exciting choice of major or important to future careers in marketing, finance, and other areas of management and beyond. The second edition was written based on these same principles: **career relevance** served as the guide for selection of textual material, and the need to **engage the student** was our guide to style, pedagogy, and design. Because of the success of the first two editions we have benefited from feedback of many faculty and students who have used our textbook in their financial accounting course.

This third edition remains focused on career relevance and engaging the student. However, we have enhanced this focus based on vast market feedback. We have:

- Added new focus companies (Papa John's, Harrah's, and Dow Jones).
- Added a wider range and level of assignment material, including Internet and Student CD-ROM applications.
- Enhanced the ratio and cash flow analysis coverage.
- Improved the chapter layout and design.

We are excited by the results and hope that this third edition adds value to your course whether you are a teacher or student. As always, we welcome your feedback.

## TARGET AUDIENCE

This text is for students with career interests in marketing, management, finance, banking, manufacturing, human resources, and, of course, accounting. We assume the student has had no prior exposure to accounting and financial statements, and has had little exposure to the business world. We have carefully designed the scope and depth of the text with these students in mind and so that most or all of it can be covered in a single term.

To ensure accessibility of the material, we employ a building block approach; we carefully cover the basics before we address more complex issues. As the student's sophistication develops throughout the term, so does the sophistication of the focus company and contrasting company illustrations.

The technical material is conveyed with clear step-by-step presentations within the realistic examples. For example, Chapters 2, 3, and 4 follow Papa John's International, through each step of the basic accounting process, ensuring that students are prepared for the later material. The emphasis on contrasting company practices is conveyed through side-by-side illustrations that punctuate the effects of differences in financial statement presentations and accounting methods. Numerous exhibits and other visual aids are included to enhance comprehension and learning.

## ESTABLISHED FEATURES AND BENEFITS OF *FINANCIAL ACCOUNTING*

- **Integration of real-world business and accounting practices by writing each chapter around the operations and actual financial statements of an interesting, real *Focus Company.***

The introduction of the focus company concept to the market in the first edition proved to be highly successful. While many financial accounting textbooks rely on

**v**

contrived financial data combined with disjointed real-company vignettes, we strongly believe that students are best engaged through the integration of a single, real company's operations and financial disclosures to highlight important concepts. In addition to the **focus companies**, we reference **contrasting companies** when appropriate to illustrate the variety in real-world practices, and the effect of a company's particular circumstances on its accounting and reporting practices. Our selection of focus and contrast companies provides the proper balance of merchandising, manufacturing, and service companies because students need exposure to a variety of business settings. Studying accounting in the context of a real focus company's business decisions better prepares students, regardless of their major, to analyze and interpret real financial information to make better business decisions. Furthermore, they will view accounting as an interesting and important field of study.

- **Content selected for its managerial significance and its relevance to understanding and using real-company financial statements in a user orientation that benefits majors and nonmajors.**

In keeping with our philosophy that the first course should focus on the uses of accounting information, we have selected material based on its relevance to understanding real companies, financial statements, and actual management decisions. As a result, we have elected to omit unrealistic topics and minutiae that are rarely practiced in industry. LIFO applied on a perpetual basis has been eliminated. In keeping with the financial statement focus of the text, pure recordkeeping functions are provided on our website or reserved for future coursework. By eliminating the recordkeeping emphasis, we use basic transaction analysis, journal entries, and T-accounts to provide the structure for understanding the interplay between management decisions and the analysis of financial statements. We demonstrate how this structure is important to both future financial statement users as well as accountants.

The decision making focus encourages and develops critical thinking. At the same time, we cover the technical requirements for financial reporting format and content within a context that makes some of the most technical accounting material come alive. As a result, students will better remember the technical material and better understand its importance.

- **An early introduction to ratio analysis and cash flow analysis for better student comprehension through the use of *Key Ratio Analysis* and *Cash Flow Analysis* sections.**

Most financial accounting textbooks wait until the last few chapters to cover ratio analysis, which means that this important topic may receive incomplete coverage due to time constraints. Others introduce a barrage of ratios in the initial chapters before the students understand the numbers they are based on. We feel that both of these treatments are confusing to students because they are forced to absorb important ratio analysis all at once, if at all, so we have integrated ratio analysis throughout the text. The main benefit to the student is that they will learn ratio analysis in digestible parts and in the appropriate context.

We believe that students will be better prepared to use financial information if they learn to evaluate different elements of financial performance at the same time they are learning how to measure and report those elements. As a consequence, we introduce relevant key ratios in each chapter in **Key Ratio Analysis** sections.

Just as most textbooks slight the importance of ratio analysis, the same can be said for their coverage of cash flow analysis. This oversight means that students typically are not exposed to this important material until later in the text if at all. As with ratio analysis, we believe students should learn about the importance of cash flow analysis beginning in Chapter 1 and continuing throughout the text in the **Cash Flow Analysis** sections.

- **Inclusion of *Financial Analysis* sections to support the decision-making focus of the text.**

  The **Financial Analysis** sections have proven popular because they tie important concepts covered in the chapter to real-world decision-making examples. They also highlight alternative viewpoints that aid in student comprehension and add to the critical thinking and decision-making focus of the text.

- **Inclusion of *International Perspective* sections throughout the text to highlight the emergence of global competition and resulting business issues.**

  Because of the rapid increase in global competition, today's students must be aware of the differences in accounting methods used around the world. Understanding global accounting issues also increases student comprehension of domestic accounting practices. Because of the importance of international accounting issues, each chapter includes **International Perspective** sections. International issues are included in end-of-chapter problem material as well.

- **A *Question of Ethics* boxes throughout the chapters to convey the importance of acting responsibly.**

  In every business, decision-makers are occasionally confronted with ethical dilemmas that require them to make choices that will impact various groups of people differently. We incorporate accounting ethics into each chapter in **A Question of Ethics** boxes to convey to students the importance of acting responsibly in business practice. It is our belief that the more students are exposed to ethical dilemmas in their studies, the more likely they will be to consider the impact of their choices.

- **Incorporated active learning features to engage the student, provide interactivity, and promote critical thinking.**

  It has been our experience that students learn best when they are actively engaged in the learning process. Active learning creates attention and promotes retention. The integration of technical material in the real-world context produces major advantages under our approach. Unique **Self-Study Quizzes** have students pause at strategic points throughout each chapter to ensure they understand key points. These quizzes help students avoid reading the text in the same manner they would a novel; to understand accounting, students must be able to work with the numbers. Student feedback has indicated that in anticipation of the **Self-Study Quizzes**, they read the material more carefully, which enhances learning. The quizzes often require the student to prepare or use financial statement disclosures based on actual companies to reinforce what they are learning. The quizzes are part of our integrative approach and are followed by **Demonstration Cases** presented in the end-of-chapter materials. Students who have carefully worked with these two types of learning aids are ready to work the end-of-chapter homework assignments. Students are also encouraged throughout the textbook to explore actual Internet sites to experience the utilization of this powerful resource.

## NEW TO THE THIRD EDITION OF *FINANCIAL ACCOUNTING*

### (NEW!) FOCUS COMPANIES

In the third edition: Papa John's International, Inc. replaces Sbarro, Inc. in Chapters 2, 3, and 4, Harrah's Entertainment, Inc. replaces Showboat, Inc., in Chapter 10, and Dow Jones is the new focus company for Chapter 12, replacing General Electric.

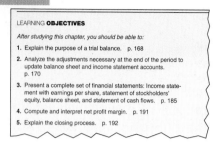

## (NEW!) LEARNING OBJECTIVES

Outlined at the beginning of each chapter, these new Learning Objectives are cross-referenced to the end-of-chapter material. This allows students to track their understanding of the concepts as they are presented in the chapter.

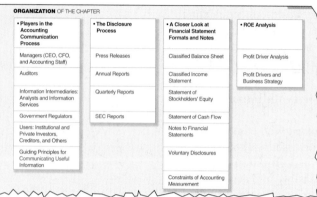

## (NEW!) ORGANIZATION OF THE CHAPTER SCHEMATIC

Now shown as a graphic at the beginning of each chapter, this visual framework is a quick reference guide that helps students easily find a topic in the chapter.

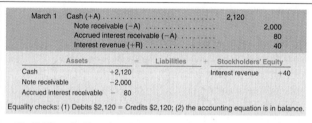

## (NEW!) ALL JOURNAL ENTRIES TIED TO THE ACCOUNTING EQUATION

Journal entries marked with (A), (L), (SE), (R), (E), or (X—if a contra-account) and plus and minus signs in early chapters assist students in transaction analysis. In addition, following each journal entry is a summary of the effects of the transaction on the fundamental accounting equation.

## (EXPANDED) UTILIZATION OF THE INTERNET

Throughout each chapter and its assignments, where appropriate, students are encouraged to explore actual Internet sites to experience how this powerful resource can be best utilized. At publication, all sites referenced were current and active. Because Internet sites are time and date sensitive, professors and students may need to use the Yahoo! search engine (http://www.yahoo.com) or a favorite search engine to locate the most current site.

## (UPDATED) FINANCIAL ANALYSIS SECTIONS

Nearly all of the **Financial Analysis** boxes in this edition have been rewritten to include up-to-date examples.

## (DRAMATICALLY ENHANCED) KEY RATIO ANALYSIS SECTIONS

The **Key Ratio Analysis** sections have been dramatically enhanced to help students understand and interpret ratios, and to allow professors the option of focusing more on decision analysis and less on bookkeeping procedures when teaching to non-accounting majors. Each **Key Ratio Analysis** box presents ratio analysis for the focus company in the chapter as well as for comparative companies. **Cautions** are also provided to help students understand the limitations of certain ratios. We use the KEY acronym to help structure use of financial ratios in performance assessment. The KEY indicates that there are three steps in ratio analysis:

**K**now the decision question that the ratio addresses. Each ratio measures a different financial attribute. The educated user must know which attribute each ratio measures, and how that attribute relates to particular decisions.

**E**xamine the ratio using two techniques: comparisons over time and comparisons with competitors. Ratios can be interpreted only in the context of prior period's ratios or ratios produced by similar companies.

**Y**ou interpret the results carefully. Simple rules of thumb rarely lead to accurate interpretation of ratios. As a consequence, you must carefully consider other related factors before drawing a conclusion.

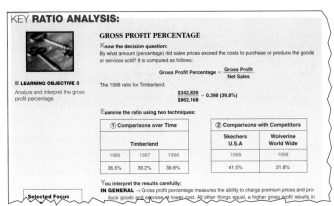

## (NEW!) FOCUS ON CASH FLOWS SECTIONS

Each chapter from one to twelve now includes a discussion and analysis of changes in the cash flow of the focus company and the decisions that caused those changes. The early and consistent coverage of cash flows encourages students to think more critically about the decisions they will be faced with as managers and the impact those decisions will have on the company's cash flow. This feature has been added to the third edition to further the discussion and importance of cash flows.

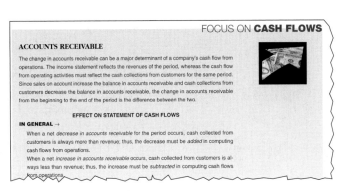

## (NEW!) END-OF-CHAPTER CONTENT AND ORGANIZATION

Each chapter is followed by an extensive selection of end-of-chapter assignments that examine single concepts or integrate multiple concepts presented in the chapter. To maintain the real-world flavor of the chapter material, they are often based on other real domestic and international companies, and require analysis, conceptual thought, calculation, and written communication. Assignments suitable for individual or group written projects and oral presentations are included in strategic locations. The end-of-chapter materials include the following:

- Chapter Take-Aways **(new to this edition)**: Created to replace the paragraph form chapter summaries in the second edition, these are bulleted end-of-chapter summaries that coincide with the learning objectives outlined at the beginning of the chapter. They have been created in response to professors and students' calls for a more succinct summary of chapter concepts and objectives.

- Key Ratios **(updated)**: Summary of the key ratios presented in the chapter.

- Key Terms (**new to this edition**): Key terms of the chapter page referenced to the chapter text; definitions also provided in the glossary.

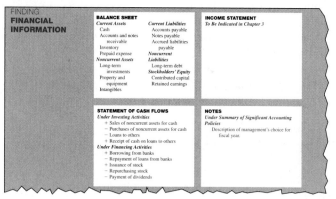

- Finding Financial Information (**new to this edition**); A **Finding Financial Information** section has been added at the end of each chapter to highlight the chapter's key concepts, numbers, and totals in an easy-to-review graphic. The graphic includes Balance Sheet, Income Statement, Statement of Cash Flows, and Note Information.

- Questions (**updated**)

- Mini-Exercises (**new to this edition**): Additional assignments illustrating the learning objectives of each chapter.

- Exercises (**updated**)

- Problems (**updated**): Cross-referenced in blue to the Alternative Problems.

- Alternate Problems (**new to this edition**): Provides professors and students with additional assignments similar in level and content to the end of chapter problems. Cross-referenced in blue to the Problems.

- Cases and Projects (**improved**): In most chapters, a project entitled **Interpreting the Financial Press** is presented to encourage students to look closely at various interpretations of accounting practices. Students are directed to a published article posted on our **Internet** website and are instructed to analyze this article. Also, in selected assignments, students are directed to **real company websites and other Internet resources** to gain experience in the utilization of this powerful tool. There are also one to three new cases/projects that utilize **Standard & Poor's ™ Market Insight Service.** Students will access **Excel** files housed on the **Student CD** and, using the real annual reports in the textbook appendices, will manipulate real-world data to solve problems. These assignments make the students experience problem solving as it truly happens in real companies.

  Also, in most chapters, a project entitled "Broadening Financial Research Skills" encourages students to access the internet and other sources to learn about and use several types of sources for analyzing financial information.

To assist instructors in identifying materials to use or assign and to provide students with information on similar assignments to work, at the end of each chapter we have:

- Added applicable Learning Objective numbers in the margin.

- Arranged assignments by level of difficulty in learning objective order.

- Included a number of assignments that do not rely on creating journal entries, but understanding the effects of transactions instead.

- Included an increased number of analytical user-oriented materials.

- Incorporated themes: International, ethics, cash flows, ratio analysis, real world, written communication, team project, broadening research skills, comparing companies within and across industries and over time, updating financial information on the focus company, finding financial information, and interpreting the financial press.

**LO5** | LO1: Learning Objective cross-reference.

 **International**: Assignments that include international perspective.

 **Ethics**: An ethical dilemma the student must resolve.

**Cash Flows**: Requires student to work cash flow analysis.

 **Ratio Analysis**: Assignment includes ratio analysis.

 **WWW**: Guides students to additional reference articles, exercises, and relevant Internet links.

 **Written Communication**: Assignment requires the student to do written work.

 **Team Project**: These assignments are done as a team.

 **GLAS**: General Ledger Applications Software solves end-of-chapter assignments that call for journal entries.

 **SPATS**: Spreadsheet Applications Template Software uses Excel templates to solve selected end-of-chapter assignments.

**STANDARD &POOR'S** **Standard & Poor's**: One to three end-of-chapter case/projects require the student to access and manipulate Excel files preloaded with Standard & Poor's data for Urban Outfitters and American Eagle.

## (ENHANCED) ADDITIONAL MARGINAL GRAPHICS TO SUPPORT CONCEPTS

For the third edition, approximately 250 new graphics and photos are used to help visually support the concepts presented.

## (NEW!) TWO ANNUAL REPORTS AT THE END OF THE BOOK TO ENHANCE ANALYSIS AND LEARNING

**American Eagle Outfitters** and **Urban Outfitters** annual reports are reprinted in the appendices for easy reference by the student, replacing the Toys R Us annual report used in the second edition.

## (NEW!) THE FORMAL RECORDKEEPING SYSTEM APPENDIX NOW PUBLISHED ONLY ON OUR WEBSITE

In keeping with the financial statement focus of the text, this material (formally Appendix C in the second edition) has been moved to our website for convenient accessibility if needed.

## CHAPTER REVISIONS FOR THE THIRD EDITION OF *FINANCIAL ACCOUNTING*

### CHAPTER 1

- Simplified Maxidrive example.
- Extensive instructions on how to use the features in the book.
- New improved **KEY** ratio feature.
- Simplified end-of-chapter material.

## CHAPTER 2

- Integrated new focus company—Papa John's International Inc.—throughout the chapter.

- Modified Exhibit 2.1 on the conceptual framework to be more concise while adding explanation of the concepts in the text for clarity and understanding by students.

- Introduced current asset and current liability classifications (in Chapter 5 in 2e) in a simple and straightforward manner.

- Added a financial analysis block introducing franchising as used by Papa John's and many other well-known businesses.

- Added the effects on the accounting equation (assets=liabilities+stockholders' equity) in all chapters, for every journal entry to help students learn appropriate accounts titles and classifications and to deepen their understanding of transaction analysis.

- Simplified the Transaction Analysis Model in Exhibit 2.4, using + and − symbols with the abbreviations for debit and credit.

- Simplified the transactions analyzed by including only those that are classified as investing and financing activities.

- Illustrated analysis of the KEY ratio financial leverage by comparing Papa John's ratio over time and to Uno Restaurant Corporation (Chicago Bar and Grill) and CEC, Inc. (Chuck E. Cheese).

- Enhanced the discussion in the Focus on Cash Flows block by illustrating the reporting of investing and financing activities on the statement and analysis and interpretation of the information.

## CHAPTER 3

- Integrated new focus company—Papa John's International Inc.—throughout the chapter.

- Shifted discussion of the operating cycle earlier in the chapter.

- Included marginal graphics on the primary operating activities generating revenue and expenses for Papa John's.

- Included marginal graphics summarizing cash basis versus accrual basis income measurement.

- Simplified the chapter by moving the discussion of the accounting cycle to Chapter 4.

- Expanded the new simplified graphic on the Transaction Analysis Model to include revenues and expenses.

- Added new financial analysis blocks on the effects of accounting information on stock prices, including an interesting Papa John's announcement.

- Illustrated the KEY ratio total asset turnover by comparing Papa John's ratio over time and to that of Pizza Hut and Domino's.

## CHAPTER 4

- Integrated new focus company—Papa John's International Inc.—throughout the chapter.

- Enhanced Exhibit 4.2 to explain the structure of the trial balance and the relationship of long-lived assets and accumulated depreciation.

- Included a marginal graphic of a timeline to provide a visual tool on adjusting entries.

- Clarified the steps used in identifying and measuring adjusting entries, including adding a more concise timeline.

- Revised discussion on financial statement preparation to include additional graphics.
- Illustrated the KEY ratio net profit margin by comparing Papa John's ratio over time and to that of Pizza Hut and Domino's.
- Expanded the closing process to include an adjusted trial balance and a post-closing trial balance.
- The end-of-book appendix on the formal recordkeeping process is now available to students as Appendix E on the Libby/Libby/Short website.

## CHAPTER 5

- Reorganized coverage of the accounting communication process including detailed analysis of Callaway's annual disclosure process.
- Updated discussion of web-based sources of company information.
- Illustrated analysis of KEY ratio return on equity (ROE) by comparing Callaway Golf ratio over time and to that of competitors and industry average.
- Added ROE profit driver analysis to summarize relationship among KEY ratios covered in Chapters 2 through 5 by tying ratios to business strategies aimed at improving ROE.
- Included new self-study quiz to take students through a step-by-step comparison of Dell and Gateway Computer's financial performance.
- Added many new exercises, cases and projects emphasizing company research, financial analysis, and writing skills.

## CHAPTER 6

- Changed coverage of sales and credit card discounts and returns and allowances to emphasize management decision making and reporting net sales. Moved journal entries to an end-of-chapter supplement.
- Illustrated analysis of KEY ratio gross profit percentage by comparing Timberland's ratio over time and to competitors Skechers and Wolverine World Wide.
- Added in all chapters, for every journal entry, the effects on the accounting equation (Assets = Liabilities + Stockholders' Equity) to help students learn appropriate accounts titles and classifications and to deepen their understanding of transaction analysis.
- Illustrated analysis of KEY ratio receivables turnover ratio by comparing Timberland's ratio over time and to that of competitors Skechers and Wolverine World Wide.
- Expanded Focus on Cash Flows feature to examine the effects of changes in accounts receivable on Timberland's cash flow from operating activities.
- Added new mini-exercises, exercises, and cases to emphasize financial statement analysis, understanding the financial press, and financial decision making.

## CHAPTER 7

- Simplified coverage of lower-of-cost-or-market method.
- Illustrated analysis of KEY ratio inventory turnover ratio by comparing Harley-Davidson's ratio over time and to that of competitors Titan Motorcycle and Honda Motor.
- Expanded Focus on Cash Flows feature examines the effects of changes in inventory and accounts payable on Timberland's cash flow from operating activities.
- Moved journal entries for purchase discounts and returns and allowances to end-of-chapter supplement.

- Added new mini-exercises, exercises, problems, and cases emphasizing finding financial information, financial statement analysis, web-based research, and understanding the financial press.

## CHAPTER 8

- Continued the Delta Air Lines focus company, updated for recent equipment purchases.
- Changed use of the term *operational assets* to *long-lived assets*.
- Updated amortization of intangible assets as outlined in a recent FASB exposure draft.

## CHAPTER 9

- Improved ratio analysis discussion using current ratio and accounts payable turnover.
- Better graphics showing reporting practices of actual companies.
- Updated real-world excerpts for comparison of companies.
- Refocused discussion of payroll liabilities.
- Emphasized accounting principles and measurement issues with discussion of liabilities, which are often ignored in introductory texts, such as environmental remediation.
- Improved discussion of working capital management and reporting of cash flows.
- Improved discussions of present and future value concepts to show the power of compounding.
- Increased number of real-world exercises and problems.

## CHAPTER 10

- New focus company, Harrah's.
- Improved discussion of ratios with comparison to major competitors.
- New graphics to illustrate reporting practices.
- Updated discussion of a new bond issue with real-world example of key players.
- Updated real-world examples of comparison companies.
- Expanded discussion of cash flows.
- Reduced procedural discussion, including the elimination of accounting for bonds sold between interest dates.
- New graphic compares straight-line and effective-interest amortization.

## CHAPTER 11

- New graphics to illustrate issues involving stock.
- Expanded discussion of the reporting of financing activities on the SCF.
- Discussion of the role of IPOs and stock options to appeal to students' interest in current business headlines.
- Improved discussion of ratio analysis.
- New end-of-chapter material based on real companies.

## CHAPTER 12

- Integrated new focus company—Dow Jones and Co.—throughout the chapter with significant revision of the chapter.
- Provided marginal graphics on passive investments, investments for significant influence, and investments for control.

- Discussed the accounting measurement and reporting issues for each type of investment in line with the graphic:
  - Securities available for sale and the market value method provide the focus; discussion of trading securities as a comparison of the differences with securities available for sale.
  - Investments for significant influence is organized similarly to securities available for sale.
- Revised the account titles used in the illustrative journal entries.
- Added exhibits summarizing the effects of the illustrations in T-account form.
- Illustrated the cash flow impact of buying, holding, and selling securities held as passive investments or for significant influence over another company in the new focus on cash flows block.
- Simplified the consolidation section by eliminating the discussion of consolidation in subsequent accounting periods, illustrating the consolidation worksheet as an Excel spreadsheet, and adding consolidated income statements.
- Illustrated the KEY ratio return on assets by comparing the Dow Jones ratio over time and to that of major competitors Knight-Ridder and *New York Times*.
- Expanded the demonstration case to include accounting for trading securities, on securities available for sale, applying the equity method, and one on consolidation.

## CHAPTER 13

- Simplified t-account illustration of cash flows from operating activities.
- Comparison of net income and cash flow from Operating Activities through KEY ratio quality of income by comparing Boston Beer over time and to that of its competitors Genesee and Coors.
- Illustrated business strategy differences illustrated through expanded KEY ratio illustration of capital acquisitions ratio comparing Boston Beer over time and to that of its competitors Minnesota Brewing and Redhook Ale.
- Added new financial analysis block on free cash flow analysis.

## CHAPTER 14

- New comparison companies.
- New discussion of the Du Pont model tied to a discussion of understanding business strategy.
- Simplification of return on investment ratios.
- New graphics used as financial analysis tool.
- Elimination of certain background information based on user suggestions.
- End-of-chapter material substantially revised to provide better balance of hypothetical and real-world companies.
- Expanded case material emphasizing use of the Internet.

## ENHANCED APPENDICES

Appendix A: Present and Future Value Tables
Appendix B: American Eagle Outfitters full Annual Report
Appendix C: Urban Outfitters Annual Report
Appendix D: Standard and Poor's Industry Ratio Report
Appendix E: The Formal Recordkeeping System available at
    **www.mhhe.com/business/accounting/libby3**

# SUPPLEMENTS FOR THE INSTRUCTOR

### Instructor's Resource Manual
ISBN 0-07-238292-9
All supplements, including the Test Bank, Videos, Study Guide, and PowerPoint, are topically cross-referenced in the IRM to help instructors direct students to specific ancillaries to reinforce key concepts.

### Solutions Manual
ISBN 0-07-238288-0
Provides solutions for end-of-chapter questions, mini-exercises, exercises, problems, and cases. Electronic files are available on the website.

### Ready Slides (Transparency Acetates)
ISBN 0-07-238587-1
These 4-color teaching transparencies, taken from the Ready Shows, are an upgraded version of traditional teaching acetates.

### Ready Shows (PowerPoint)
ISBN 0-07-238585-5
Ready Shows are completely customized PowerPoint presentations for use in your classroom.

### Solutions Acetates
ISBN 0-07-238295-3
These overhead transparencies provide both in-class visuals as well as solutions to most of the end-of-chapter material. Masters are available in the Solutions Manual.

### Test Bank (Print version)
ISBN 0-07-238290-2
This comprehensive Test Bank includes more than 3,000 true/false, multiple choice, essay, and matching questions.

### Computest (Brownstone)
Windows Test Bank ISBN 0-07-240828-6
Macintosh Test Bank ISBN 0-07-240829-4
Add and edit questions; create up to 99 versions of each test; attach graphic files to questions; import and export ASCII files; and select questions based on type, level of difficulty, or learning objective. This software provides password protection for saved tests and question databases, and is able to run on a network.

### Instructor CD-ROM
ISBN 0-07-240827-8
This integrated CD-ROM allows you to access most of the text's ancillary materials. You no longer need to worry about the various disk supplements that come with this text. Instead, everything is available on one convenient CD-ROM.

### Check Figures
ISBN 0-07-238296-1
Provide answers to select problems and cases. These figures are available for distribution to students.

### Instructor's Manual to Accompany Understanding Corporate Annual Reports by William R. Pasewark
ISBN 0-07-238716-5

### Instructor SPATS
ISBN 0-07-238583-9
Spreadsheet Applications Template Software allows students to develop important spreadsheet skills by using these templates to solve selected assignments.

### Website
www.mhhe.com/business/accounting/libby3
Instructor features include an Online Discussion Group for instructors, Active Learning/ Technology Integration suggestions from other instructors; links to focus companies; related readings to recent accounting news topics, and much more.

### Financial Accounting Video Library
ISBN 0-07-237616-3
Created to stimulate classroom discussion, illustrate key concepts, and review important material. Selected videos were produced and copyrighted by Dallas TeleLearning of the Dallas County Community College District © 1999. To acquire Accounting in Action as a Comprehensive Telecourse package, call Dallas TeleLearning at 972-669-6666 or FAX 972-669-6668 or visit their website at www.lecroy.dcccd.edu.

### Instructor Package for Interactive Financial Accounting Lab
ISBN 0-07-236134-4
This Instructor Package (prepared by Ralph E. Smith and Rick Birney of Arizona State University) contains a network CD-ROM, an Installation/Setup Manual, and instructions for the instructor grade book for the Interactive Financial Accounting Lab.

### PageOut
This exclusive McGraw-Hill product helps you create and customize a course website—hosted by McGraw-Hill and free of charge!
You can also use the content with WebCT, eCollege.com, Blackboard, or The McGraw-Hill Learning Architecture (powered by TopClass). To learn more about these digital solutions, visit www.mhhe.com/solutions.

### Online Learning Center/ eLearning Session
Study tools are placed strategically within the chapter outline to help students learn the concepts using different sources of information such as PowerPoint®, video clips, key terms, and critical concept checks. Also allows instructors to pull material into their PageOut course syllabus.

# STUDENT SUPPLEMENTS

### Working Papers
ISBN 0-07-238273-9
Selected by the authors, this booklet contains all the forms necessary for completing end-of-chapter materials.

### Study Guide
ISBN 0-07-238372-0
This guide gives students a deeper understanding of the presented material and reinforces what they are learning in the main text.

### Ready Notes
ISBN 0-07-238374-7
Derived from the Ready Shows, these notes help students focus on lectures and selectively annotate rather than scramble to take notes.

### Understanding Corporate Annual Reports by William R. Pasewark
ISBN 0-07-238714-9
This financial analysis project emphasizes the interpretation and analysis of financial statements. It contains extensive instructions for obtaining an annual report from a publicly traded corporation. Students gain hands-on experience with annual reports and so relate financial accounting concepts to the business world.

### Student CD-ROM
ISBN 0-07-240826-X
This CD-ROM includes the SPATS software, GLAS software, Tutorial Software, select PowerPoint slides, and the Excel files for solving the S&P case/problems.

### Website
www.mhhe.com/business/accounting/Libby3
The website contains web links, suggested readings, and study outlines organized by chapter that include PowerPoint, video clips, interactive quizzes, additional problems and exercises all linked to learning objectives.

### Interactive Financial Accounting Lab
ISBN 0-07-236136-0
The Interactive Financial Accounting Lab (developed by Ralph E. Smith and Rick Birney of Arizona State University) is Windows-based software that uses a multimedia setting to help students learn the fundamentals of the accounting cycle and its various procedures.

### Computerized Accounting Practice Sets
Business Simulations and practice sets using Microsoft® Windows® by Leland Mansuetti and Keith Weidkamp of Sierra College include:

|  | 3.5" Disks | CD-ROM |
| --- | --- | --- |
| Granite Bay Jet Ski, Level 1 | 0-256-22114-6 | 0-07-234088-6 |
| Granite Bay Jet Ski, Inc., Level 2 | 0-256-22098-0 | 0-07-234105-X |
| Wheels Exquisite, Inc., Level 1 | 0-07-561243-7 | 0-07-234111-4 |
| Thunder Mountain Snowmobile | 0-256-22112-X | 0-07-234114-9 |
| Gold Run Snowmobile, Inc. | 0-07-366098-1 | 0-07-234107-6 |

# ACKNOWLEDGMENTS

Writing a successful text requires a team effort, and we have enjoyed working with excellent teammates. Throughout the process of writing this text, many people stepped forward with tremendous efforts that allowed us to accomplish our stated goals. We would like to recognize the sincere and devoted efforts of the many people who added their input to the process of developing this text. As stated in the Development Story section, we received invaluable advice and suggestions during the manuscript development and revision process.

For this assistance, we thank the following colleagues:

## REVIEWERS AND FOCUS GROUP PARTICIPANTS

Susan Armstrong
*Inver Hills Community College*

Roderick Barclay
*University of Texas — Dallas*

Cecil Battiste
*El Paso Community College*

Paul Bayes
*East Tennessee State University*

Martin Birr
*Indiana University at Indianapolis*

Michael Capsuto
*Cypress College*

Barbara Cassidy
*St. Edward's University*

Nancy Cassidy
*Texas A&M University*

Ted Christensen
*Case Western University*

Anne Clem
*Iowa State University*

Rosalind Cranor
*Virginia Polytechnic Institute and State University*

Barbara Croteau
*Santa Rosa Junior College*

Bruce Dehning
*University of New Hampshire*

Manuel Dieguez
*Florida International University*

Patricia Doherty
*Boston University*

Tim Doupnik
*University of South Carolina*

David Durkee
*Weber State University*

Robert Egenolf
*University of Texas—Austin*

Thomas Evans
*University of Central Florida*

John Hatcher
*Purdue University*

Paul Healy
*Harvard University*

Kurt Heisinger
*Sierra College*

Afshad Irani
*University of New Hampshire*

Susan Kattelus
*Eastern Michigan University*

Howard Keller
*Indiana University at Indianapolis*

Cynthia Levick
*Austin Community College*

Gina Lord
*Santa Rosa Junior College*

Bobbie Martindale
*Dallas Baptist College*

Dawn Massey
*Fairfield University*

Paul McGee
*Salem State College*

Sarah Nutter
*George Mason University*

John O'Shaughnessy
*San Francisco State University*

Kanalis Ockree
*Washburn University*

Kathy Petroni
*Michigan State University*

Edwin Pinto
*San Jose State University*

Elizabeth Plummer
*Southern Methodist University*

Shirley Rockel
*Iowa Wesleyan College*

Kenneth Schwartz
*Boston College*

William Smith
*Xavier University*

Martin Taylor
*University of Texas—Arlington*

Suzanne Wright
*Penn State University*

Karen Taylor
*Butte Community College*

## SURVEY RESPONDENTS

Amwer Ahmed
*Syracuse University*

William Appleyard
*Salem State College*

Wendy Bailey
*University of Pittsburgh*

Robert Bloom
*John Carroll University*

Russell Briner
*University of Texas — San Antonio*

Kevin Brown
*Drexel University*

David Byrd
*Southwest Missouri State University*

Matthew Calderisi
*Farleigh Dickinson University*

Thomas Calderon
*University of Akron*

Mark Coffey
*Western New England College*

Michael Cornick
*University of North Carolina—Charlotte*

Gary Cunningham
*University of Minnesota*

Bruce Dehning
*University of New Hampshire*

Patricia Doherty
*Boston University*

Patricia Douglas
*Loyola Marymount University*

Allan Drebin
*Northwestern University*

Taylor Ernst
*Lehigh University*

Jack Ethridge
*Stephen Austin State University*

Kel-Ann Eyler
*Georgia State University*

Al Frakes
*Washington State University*

Joseph Galanate
*Millersville University*

Art Goldman
*University of Kentucky*

Russell Hardin
*Pittsburg State University*

Robin Hegedus
*Franklin University*

Jim Hood
*Mt. Hood Community College*

Chris Jones
*George Washington University*

Charles Klemstine
*University of Michigan*

John Koeplin
*University of San Francisco*

Gina Lord
*Santa Rosa Junior College*

Alan Mayer-Sommer
*Georgetown University*

Richard Muchow
*Palomar College*

Dennis Murphy
*California State University—
Los Angeles*

Sarah Nutter
*George Mason University*

Rosemarie Pilcher
*Richland College*

Peter Poznanski
*Cleveland State University*

Clayton Sager
*University of Wisconsin—Whitewater*

Shahrokh Saudagaran
*Santa Clara University*

Richard Scott
*University of Virginia*

Mary Alice Seville
*Oregon State University*

Franklin Shuman
*Utah State University*

Mike Slaubaugh
*Indiana University—Purdue University*

Bill Svihla
*Indiana State University*

Ben Trotter
*Texas Tech University*

Joan VanHise
*Fairfield University*

Paul Wertheim
*Pepperdine University*

L.K. Williams
*Morehead State University*

Linda Zucca
*Kent State University*

## FIRST EDITION REVIEWERS

D'Arcy Becker
*University of New Mexico*

Linda Bell
*William Jewell College*

Wayne Boutell
*University of California at Berkeley*

Patricia Doherty
*Boston University*

Allan Drebin
*Northwestern University*

Marie Dubke
*University of Memphis*

Gary Fish
*Illinois State University*

Paul Frishkoff
*University of Oregon*

Flora Guidry
*University of New Hampshire*

Marcia Halvorsen
*University of Cincinnati*

Leon Hanouille
*Syracuse University*

Peggy Hite
*Indiana University*

David Hoffman
*University of North Carolina at
Chapel Hill*

Kathy Horton
*University of Illinois at Chicago*

Sharon Jackson
*Auburn University at Montgomery*

Naida Kaen
*University of New Hampshire*

Sue Kattelus
*Eastern Michigan University*

Jim Kurtenbach
*Iowa State University*

David Lavin
*Florida International University*

Joan Luft
*Michigan State University*

Betty McMechen
*Mesa State College*

Greg Merrill
*California State University at Fullerton*

Brian Nagle
*Duquesne University*

Ron Pawliczek
*Boston College*

Don Putnam
*California State University Polytechnic
at Pomona*

Michael Ruble
*Western Washington University*

Mary Alice Seville
*Oregon State University*

Wayne Shaw
*Southern Methodist University*

Ken Smith
*Idaho State University*

Ralph Spanswick
*Catfornia State University at Los Angeles*

Kevin Stocks
*Brigham Young University*

Kathryn Sullivan
*George Washington University*

Michael Welker
*Drexel University*

T. Sterling Wetzel
*Oklahoma State University*

William Zorr
*University of Wisconsin—Oshkosh*

## SECOND EDITION REVIEWERS

Dawn Addington
*University of New Mexico*

Holly Ashbaugh
*University of Northern Iowa*

Ken Boze
*University of Alaska—Anchorage*

Anne Clem
*Iowa State University*

Carol Dicino
*University of Southern Colorado*

Jim Emig
*Villanova University*

Alan Falcon
*Loyola Marymount University*

Arthur Goldman
*University of Kentucky*

Tim Griffin
*University of Missouri—KC*

Donna Hetzel
*Western Michigan University*

Ken Hiltebeitel
*Villanova University*

Marge Hubbert
*Cornell University*

Frank Korman
*Mountain View College*

Jim Kurtenbach
*Iowa State University*

Larry Logan
*University of Massachusetts—Dartmouth*

Ron Mannino
*University of Massachusetts—Amherst*

Noel McKeon
*Florida Community College*

Betty McMechen
*Mesa State College*

Paul Mihalek
*University of Hartford*

Brian Nagle
*Duquesne University*

John Osborn
*California State University—Fresno*

Mawdudur Rahman
*Suffolk University*

Jane Reimers
*Florida State University*

Keith Richardson
*Indiana State University*

Bruce Samuelson
*Pepperdine University*

Gene Sauls
*Calfornia State University—Sacramento*

Wayne Shaw
*Southern Methodist University*

Blair Terry
*Fresno City College*

Laverne Thompson
*St. Louis Community College at Meramec*

Steven Wong
*San Jose City College*

In addition, we are deeply indebted to the following individuals who helped develop, critique, and shape the extensive ancillary package: Betty McMechen, Mesa State College; Jeannie Folk, College of DuPage; Jon Booker, Tennessee Technological University; Charles Caldwell, Tennessee Technological University; Susan Galbreath, Tennessee Technological University; Leland Mansuetti, Sierra College; Richard Rand, Tennessee Technological University; Barbara Schnathorst, The Write Solution, Inc.; Jack Terry, ComSource Associates, Inc.; Keith Weidkamp, Sierra College; Bruce Denning, University of New Hampshire; Deborah Jackson-Jones, Broadwork, Inc.; Diane Colwyn; Barbara Croteau; and Beth Woods.

We also received invaluable input and support from numerous colleagues and associates, in particular William Wright, University of California at Irvine; Marge Hubbard, Kristina Szafara, Steve Gallucci, Carol Marquardt, Susan Krische, Steve Smith, and Jennifer Bremner, all of Cornell University; and Susan Dahl, Kansas State University. Furthermore, we appreciate the additional comments, suggestions, and support of our students and our colleagues at Cornell University, Ithaca College, and Miami University.

Finally, the extraordinary efforts of a talented group of individuals at Irwin/McGraw-Hill made all of this come together. We would especially like to thank our sponsoring editor, Steve Hazelwood, for guiding us through the final stages of this revision; Jeff Shelstad, our publisher, for encouraging us to write the first edition and providing input and support during the writing of the subsequent editions; creative marketing ideas and support from our marketing manager, Rhonda Seelinger; Laurie Entringer, for outstanding design work; Kimberly Hooker, our tireless project manager; our production supervisor, Lori Koetters; Carol Loreth, our supplements coordinator and Tracey Douglas, Jane Ducham, Angela Jacobs, and Jackie Scruggs, for outstanding editorial development and feedback.

**Robert Libby**
**Patricia A. Libby**
**Daniel G. Short**

# Contents in Brief

# Contents

CHAPTER **TWO**

# Investing and Financing Decisions and the Balance Sheet 50

CHAPTER **THREE**

# Operating Decisions and the Income Statement 106

CHAPTER **FOUR**

# The Adjustment Process and Financial Statements   164

CHAPTER **FIVE**

# Communicating and Interpreting Accounting Information  236

CHAPTER **SIX**

# Reporting and Interpreting Sales Revenue, Receivables, and Cash 300

CHAPTER **SEVEN**

# Reporting and Interpreting Cost of Goods Sold and Inventory    360

HARLEY-DAVIDSON, INC.    361

## Business Background    362

## Nature of Inventory and Cost of Goods Sold    364

Items Included in Inventory    364

Inventory Cost    365

> FINANCIAL ANALYSIS:
> *Applying the Materiality Constraint in Practice    365*

Inventory Flows    365

> FINANCIAL ANALYSIS:
> *Modern Manufacturing Techniques and Inventory Costs    367*

Nature of Cost of Goods Sold    367

> FINANCIAL ANALYSIS:
> *Gross Profit Comparisons    368*

Errors in Measuring Ending Inventory    369

■ SELF-STUDY QUIZ    370

## Inventory Costing Methods    371

Applying the Four Methods    371

> INTERNATIONAL PERSPECTIVE:
> *Different Methods for Different Types of Inventory    374*

Choosing Inventory Costing Methods    375

> INTERNATIONAL PERSPECTIVE:
> *LIFO and International Comparisons    376*

> A QUESTION OF ETHICS:
> *LIFO Conflicts Between Managers' and Owners' Interests    376*

■ SELF-STUDY QUIZ    377

Inventory Costing Methods and Financial Statement Analysis    378

■ SELF-STUDY QUIZ    380

> KEY RATIO ANALYSIS:
> *Inventory Turnover    380*

> FINANCIAL ANALYSIS:
> *LIFO and Inventory Turnover Ratio    381*

> FOCUS ON CASH FLOWS:
> *Inventory    382*

■ SELF-STUDY QUIZ    383

Valuation at Lower of Cost or Market    384

## Keeping Track of Inventory Quantities and Costs    386

Perpetual and Periodic Inventory Systems    386

Perpetual Inventory Records in Practice    388

Methods for Estimating Inventory    389

## Demonstration Case A    389

## Demonstration Case B    391

> CHAPTER SUPPLEMENT A: LIFO LIQUIDATIONS    392

LIFO Liquidations and Financial Statement Analysis    393

> FINANCIAL ANALYSIS:
> *Inventory Management and LIFO Liquidations    394*

> CHAPTER SUPPLEMENT B: ADDITIONAL ISSUES IN MEASURING PURCHASES    394

Purchase Returns and Allowances    394

Purchase Discounts    395

*Chapter Take-Aways    395*

*Key Ratio    396*

*Finding Financial Information    397*

*Key Terms    397*

*Questions    397*

*Mini-exercises    398*

*Exercises    399*

*Problems    405*

*Alternate Problems    412*

*Cases and Projects    414*

CHAPTER **EIGHT**

# Reporting and Interpreting Property, Plant, and Equipment; Natural Resources; and Intangibles   420

CHAPTER **NINE**

# Reporting and Interpreting Liabilities  484

CHAPTER **TEN**

# Reporting and Interpreting Bonds  538

CHAPTER **ELEVEN**

# Reporting and Interpreting Owners' Equity   584

CHAPTER **TWELVE**

# Reporting and Interpreting Investments in Other Corporations   638

CHAPTER **THIRTEEN**

# Statement of Cash Flows   680

# FINANCIAL
# Accounting

# Financial Statements and Business Decisions

## CHAPTER ONE

LEARNING **OBJECTIVES**

*After studying this chapter, you should be able to:*

1. Recognize the information conveyed in each of the four basic financial statements and the way that it is used by different decision makers (investors, creditors, and managers).   p. 6

2. Identify the role of generally accepted accounting principles (GAAP) in determining the content of financial statements.   p. 21

3. Distinguish the roles of managers and auditors in the accounting communication process.   p. 24

4. Appreciate the importance of ethics, reputation, and legal liability in accounting.   p. 25

In January, Exeter Investors purchased Maxidrive Corp., a fast-growing manufacturer of personal computer disk drives, for $33 million. The price Exeter paid was decided by considering the value of the economic resources owned by Maxidrive, its debts to others, its ability to sell goods

# Maxidrive Corporation

### VALUING AN ACQUISITION USING FINANCIAL STATEMENT INFORMATION*

for more than the cost to produce them, and its ability to generate the cash necessary to pay its current bills. Much of this assessment was based on financial information provided by Maxidrive to Exeter. This financial information was presented in the form of financial statements. By July, Exeter discovered a variety of problems both in the operations of Maxidrive and in the financial statements that Maxidrive had provided. It then appeared that Maxidrive was worth only about half of what Exeter had paid. Furthermore, Maxidrive did not have enough cash to pay its debt to American Bank.

In response, Exeter filed a lawsuit against the previous owners and others responsible for Maxidrive's financial statements to recover the overpayment.

---

*The Maxidrive case is a realistic representation of an actual case of fraud. No names in the case are real. The actual fraud is discussed in the epilogue to the chapter.

## THE OBJECTIVES OF *FINANCIAL ACCOUNTING*

Determining the price that Exeter was willing to pay for Maxidrive is typical of the economic decisions that are made based on financial statements. Businesses use financial statements as the primary means to communicate financial information to parties outside the organization. The purpose of this text is to help you develop the ability to read and interpret financial statements of business organizations and understand the system that produces those statements. This book is aimed at two groups of readers: *future managers,* who will need to interpret and use financial statement information in business decisions, and *future accountants*, who will prepare financial statements for those managers. The book provides future managers with a firm basis for using financial statement information in their careers in marketing, finance, banking, manufacturing, human resources, sales, information systems, or other areas of management. It also provides future accountants with a solid foundation for further professional study.

Both managers and accountants must understand *financial statements* (what the statements tell you and what they do not tell you about a business enterprise), *business operations*, and *the use of financial statements in decision making* to perform their duties successfully. As a consequence, we integrate actual business practice in our discussions starting with Chapter 1. We examine the fundamentals of financial accounting in a variety of business contexts relevant to your future careers. Each chapter's material is integrated around a *focus company* (in this chapter, Maxidrive). The focus companies are drawn from 12 different industries, providing you with a broad range of experience with realistic business and financial accounting practices. When appropriate, the focus company's operations and financial statements are then compared to those of the *contrast companies*. When you complete this book, you will be able to read and understand financial statements of real companies.

The way that seasoned managers use financial statements in modern businesses has guided our selection of learning objectives and content. At the same time, our teaching approach recognizes that students using this book have no previous exposure to accounting and financial statements and often little exposure to the business world. The book also is aimed at helping you learn how to learn by teaching efficient and effective approaches for learning the material.

We begin this process with a brief but comprehensive overview of the four basic financial statements and the people and organizations involved in their preparation and use. This overview provides you with a context in which you can learn the more detailed material that is presented in the following chapters. We begin our discussion by returning to the Maxidrive acquisition. In particular, we focus on how two primary users of the statements, investors (owners) and creditors (lenders), relied on each of Maxidrive's four basic financial statements in their ill-fated decisions to buy and lend money to Maxidrive. Later in the chapter, we begin to discuss a broader range of uses of financial statement data in marketing, management, human resources, and other business contexts.

## BUSINESS BACKGROUND

### UNDERSTANDING THE PLAYERS

Maxidrive was founded by two engineers who had formerly worked for General Data, then a manufacturer of large computers. Predicting the rise in demand for personal computers with a hard disk drive, they started a company specializing in the manufacture of this important computer component (now called Maxidrive Corp.). To start the enterprise, the founders invested a major portion of their savings, becoming the sole owners of Maxidrive. As is common in new businesses, the founders also functioned as the managers of the business (they were *owner-managers*).

The founders soon discovered that they needed additional money to develop the business. Based on the recommendation of a close friend, they turned to American

Bank to borrow money. Maxidrive borrowed from others over the years, but American Bank continued to lend to it as the need arose, becoming its largest lender, or *creditor*. Early last year, one of the founders of the business became gravely ill. This event, plus the stresses of operating in their highly competitive industry, led the founders to search for a buyer for their company. In January of this year, they struck a deal for the sale of the company to the company's *new owners*, Exeter Investors, a small group of wealthy private investors. Both founders retired and a new manager was hired to run Maxidrive for the new owners. The new *manager* had formerly worked for another company owned by Exeter but was not an owner of the company.

Owners (often called *investors* or *stockholders*)—whether they are groups such as Exeter who recently bought all of Maxidrive Corp. or individuals who buy small percentages of large corporations—make their purchases hoping to gain in two ways. They hope to sell them in the future at a higher price than they paid and/or receive a portion of what the company earns in the form of cash payments called *dividends*. As the Maxidrive case suggests, not all companies increase in value or have sufficient cash to pay dividends. *Creditors*—whether they are individuals, business organizations, or financial institutions such as banks—lend money to a company for a specific length of time. They hope to gain by charging interest on the money they lend. As American Bank, Maxidrive's major creditor, has learned, some borrowers are not able to repay their debts.

## UNDERSTANDING THE BUSINESS OPERATIONS

To understand any company's financial statements, you must first understand its operations. As noted above, Maxidrive designs and manufactures hard disk drives for personal computers. The major parts that go into the drive include the disks on which information is stored, the motors that spin the disks, the heads that read and write to the disks, and the computer chips that control the operations of the drive. Maxidrive purchases the disks and motors from other companies, referred to as *suppliers*. It designs and manufactures the heads and chips and then assembles the drives. Maxidrive does not sell disk drives directly to the public. Instead, its *customers* are computer manufacturers such as Compaq and Apple Computer, which install the drives in machines they sell to retailers (businesses that sell to consumers) such as CompUSA. Thus, Maxidrive is a supplier to Compaq and Apple.

The hard disk drive business is very competitive. Maxidrive competes with much larger drive companies by investing a great deal of money in developing new and improved drives. It uses robots in its factory to keep labor costs low and ensure product quality. Among the employees working for Maxidrive are 36 engineers and technical staff who work in research and development to develop new disk drives.

Like all businesses, Maxidrive has an **accounting** system that collects and processes (analyzes, measures, and records) financial information about an organization and reports that information to decision makers. Maxidrive's managers (often called *internal decision makers*) and parties outside the firm such as investors like the managers at Exeter Investors and the loan officer at American Bank (often called *external decision makers*) use reports produced by this system. Exhibit 1.1 outlines the two parts of the accounting system. Internal managers typically require continuous detailed information because they must plan and manage the day-to-day operations of the organization. Developing accounting information for internal decision makers is called *managerial* or *management accounting* and is the subject of a separate accounting course. The focus of this text is accounting for external decision makers, called *financial accounting*, and the four basic financial statements and related disclosures that are the output of that system.

To determine the type of information reported in each statement, we now examine the financial statements that Maxidrive's former owner-managers presented to Exeter. Then we test what you have learned by trying to correct the errors in each of the statements and discuss the implications of the errors for Maxidrive's value. Finally, we discuss the ethical and legal responsibilities of various parties for those errors.

**ACCOUNTING** is a system that collects and processes (analyzes, measures, and records) financial information about an organization and reports that information to decision makers.

**ORGANIZATION** OF THE CHAPTER

| • Information Conveyed in Financial Statements |
| --- |
| Overview |
| The Balance Sheet |
| The Income Statement |
| Statement of Retained Earnings |
| Statement of Cash Flows |
| Notes |
| Using Financial Statements to Determine the Value of Maxidrive |
| Price/Earnings Ratio |

| • Responsibilities for the Accounting Communication Process |
| --- |
| Generally Accepted Accounting Principles |
| Management Responsibility and the Demand for Auditing |
| Ethics, Reputation, and Legal Liability |

# INFORMATION CONVEYED IN FINANCIAL STATEMENTS

Both Exeter Investors (Maxidrive's new owner) and American Bank (Maxidrive's largest creditor) used Maxidrive's financial statements to learn more about the company before making their purchase and lending decisions. In doing so, Exeter and American Bank assumed that the statements accurately represented Maxidrive's financial condition. As they soon learned and now have claimed in their lawsuits, however, the statements were in error. Maxidrive had (1) on its *balance sheet* overstated the economic resources it owned and understated its obligations to others, (2) on its *income statement* overstated its ability to sell goods for more than the costs to produce and sell them, and (3) on its *cash flow statement* overstated its ability to generate from those sales the cash necessary to meet its current debts. These three financial statements and the *retained earnings statement* are the four basic statements normally prepared by profit-making organizations for external reporting to owners, potential investors, creditors, and other decision makers.

The four basic statements summarize the financial activities of the business. They can be prepared at any point in time (such as the end of the year, quarter, or month) and can apply to any time span (such as one year, one quarter, or one month). Like most companies, Maxidrive prepares financial statements for investors and creditors at the end of each quarter (known as *quarterly reports*) and at the end of the year (known as *annual reports*).

EXHIBIT **1.1**

**The Accounting System and
Decision Makers**

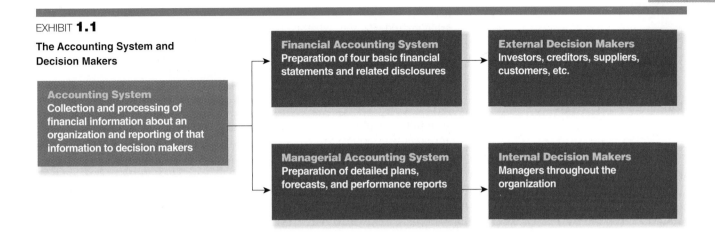

To understand the way that Exeter Investors used financial statements in its decision and the way it was misled, we must first understand what specific information is presented in the four basic financial statements for a company such as Maxidrive. Essential to this process is an emphasis on learning the *definitions* of key business and accounting terms that we rely on throughout the book and the key *relationships* among the terms used in financial statements. As is common with other professions, the terminology of accounting is technical because precision is necessary. In this chapter, we provide general definitions of these key terms; for certain key accounting terms, we add more detail to the definitions in later chapters.

## OVERVIEW

We present many new business and financial statement terms in this next section. Since so many terms will be new to you, the material that follows may seem overwhelming at first. This will be particularly true if you try to memorize the definitions of every term used in this chapter. Remember that the purpose of this overview is to provide a general context for the more detailed discussions that follow. Try to focus your attention on learning the general structure and content of the statements. Specifically, you should focus on these questions:

1. What categories of items (often called *elements*) are reported on each of the four statements? This will tell you what types of information the statements convey and where you as a statement reader can find each type.

2. How are the elements within a statement related? These relationships usually are described by an equation that tells you how the elements fit together.

3. Why are each of the elements important to an owner's or creditor's decisions? This will provide you with a general idea of how important financial statement information is to decision makers.

To provide feedback, we will test your ability to answer these questions in the *Self-Study Quizzes*, which occur throughout the chapter. After you complete the quizzes, you may check your answers against the solution provided in a footnote. If you are still unclear about any of the answers, you should refer back to the chapter material preceding the quiz before moving on.

The terms that are critical to understanding the answers to these questions are highlighted in bold print and repeated in the margins. You should pay special attention to the definitions of these terms. To be sure that you understand each definition, we repeat these key terms at the end of the chapter. If you are unsure of the definitions of other terms, please refer to the glossary at the back of the book. Also remember that since this chapter is an overview, each concept discussed here will be discussed again in Chapters 2 through 5.

## THE BALANCE SHEET

We can learn a great deal about what the balance sheet reports just by reading the statement from the top. The balance sheet of Maxidrive Corp., presented by its former owners to Exeter Investors, is presented in Exhibit 1.2. Notice that the *heading* specifically identifies four significant items related to the statement:

1. *the name of the entity*            Maxidrive Corp.

> An **ACCOUNTING ENTITY** is the organization for which financial data are to be collected.

Accounting requires a precise definition of the specific organization for which financial data are to be collected. When the organization is defined, it is called an **accounting entity.** For measurement purposes, the resources, debts, and activities of the entity are kept separate from those of the owners and other entities. This focus is called the *separate-entity assumption.*[1] The business entity itself, not the business owners, is viewed as owning the economic resources it uses and as owing its debts.

2. *the title of the statement*          Balance Sheet

> A **BALANCE SHEET** (statement of financial position) reports the financial position (assets, liabilities, and stockholders' equity) of an accounting entity at a point in time.

The purpose of the **balance sheet** is to report the financial position (assets, liabilities, and stockholders' equity) of an accounting entity at a point in time. Therefore, the balance sheet is sometimes called the *statement of financial position.* The meaning of financial position will become more evident when we read the body of the statement.

3. *the specific date of the statement*       At December 31, 20A

The heading of each statement indicates the *time dimension* of the report. The balance sheet is like a financial snapshot indicating the entity's financial position *at a specific point in time*—in this case, December 31, 20A—which is stated clearly on the balance sheet. Note that this book often uses the convention "20A" for the first year, "20B" for the second, and so forth. Thus, the sequence of years 20A, 20B, and 20C can be thought of as equivalent to any three-year sequence such as 2001, 2002, and 2003.

4. *unit of measure*                (in thousands of dollars)

Companies normally prepare reports denominated in the major currency of the country in which they are located, in this case U.S. dollars. Similarly, Canadian companies report in Canadian dollars and Mexican companies in pesos. Medium-sized companies such as Maxidrive and much larger companies such as Wal-Mart often report in thousands of dollars; that is, the last three digits are rounded to the nearest thousand. As a result, the listing of Cash $4,895 actually means $4,895,000.

After the statement heading, the three elements reported on a balance sheet are listed—assets, liabilities, and stockholders' equity.

**Assets**    Maxidrive lists five items under the category Assets:

| | | |
|---|---|---|
| Cash | $4,895 | *the amount of cash in the company's bank accounts* |
| Accounts receivable | 5,714 | *amounts owed by customers from prior sales* |
| Inventories | 8,517 | *parts and completed but unsold disk drives* |
| Plant and equipment | 7,154 | *factories and production machinery* |
| Land | 981 | *land on which the factories are built* |

These items called *assets* are economic resources owned by the entity that resulted from past transactions. The exact items listed as assets on a company's balance sheet depend on the nature of its operations. The five items listed by Maxidrive are the economic resources needed to manufacture and sell disk drives to companies such as Compaq. Each of these economic resources is expected to provide future benefits to the firm. To prepare to manufacture the drives, Maxidrive first needed *cash* to purchase *land* on which to build factories and install production machinery (*plant and*

---

[1]The separate-entity assumption is used for all types of business entities (corporations as well as sole proprietorships and partnerships, which we discuss later in the chapter).

EXHIBIT **1.2**

**Balance Sheet**

| MAXIDRIVE CORP. | | name of the entity |
| :--: | :--: | :-- |
| Balance Sheet | | title of the statement |
| At December 31, 20A | | specific date of the statement |
| (in thousands of dollars) | | unit of measure |

**Assets**

| Cash | | $ 4,895 | the amount of cash in the company's bank accounts |
| :-- | :-- | --: | :-- |
| Accounts receivable | | 5,714 | amounts owed by customers from prior sales |
| Inventories | | 8,517 | parts and completed but unsold disk drives |
| Plant and equipment | | 7,154 | factories and production machinery |
| Land | | 981 | land on which the factories are built |
| Total assets | | $27,261 | |

**Liabilities**

| Accounts payable | $7,156 | | amounts owed to suppliers for prior purchases |
| :-- | --: | --: | :-- |
| Notes payable | 9,000 | | amounts owed on written debt contracts |
| Total liabilities | | $16,156 | |

**Stockholders' Equity**

| Contributed capital | $2,000 | | amounts invested in the business by stockholders |
| :-- | --: | --: | :-- |
| Retained earnings | 9,105 | | past earnings not distributed to stockholders |
| Total stockholders' equity | | 11,105 | |
| Total liabilities and stockholders' equity | | $27,261 | |

The notes are an integral part of these financial statements.

*equipment*). Maxidrive then began purchasing parts and producing disk drives, which led to the balance assigned to *inventories*. When Maxidrive sells its disk drives to Compaq and others, it sells them on credit and receives promises to pay called *accounts receivable*, which are collected in cash later. Maxidrive lists as cash the amount of cash in its bank accounts on the balance sheet date, which it will use to pay its own bills.

Every asset is initially measured on the balance sheet by the total cost incurred to acquire it. For example, the balance sheet for Maxidrive reports Land, $981; this is the amount paid (in thousands) for the land when it was acquired. Even if the market value of the land increases, the balance sheet reports the land at its *original acquisition cost* (this is called the *cost principle*). Balance sheets *do not purport to show the current market value* of the assets listed. If Maxidrive attempted to sell the land, it might receive more or less than the amount listed.

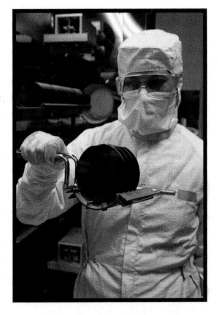

FINANCIAL **ANALYSIS**

## INTERPRETING ASSETS ON THE BALANCE SHEET

Assessment of Maxidrive's assets was important to its creditor, American Bank, and to its prospective investor, Exeter, because assets provide a basis for judging whether sufficient resources are available to operate the company. Assets also are important because they could be sold for cash in the event that Maxidrive goes out of business. As indicated, however, if the assets were sold, there is no assurance that the amount listed on the balance sheet would be the amount received from the sale. Some unsophisticated users of financial statements do not understand this point and can easily misinterpret the financial position of a business.

**BASIC ACCOUNTING EQUATION (BALANCE SHEET EQUATION):** Assets = Liabilities + Stockholders' Equity.

**Liabilities and Stockholders' Equity**   Maxidrive's balance sheet next lists its liabilities and stockholders' equity. They are the sources of financing or claims against the company's economic resources. Financing provided by creditors creates a liability. Financing provided by owners creates owners' equity. Since Maxidrive is a corporation, its owners' equity is designated as *stockholders' equity.*[2] Since the acquisition of each asset must have a source of financing, a company's assets must, by definition, always be equal to the company's liabilities and stockholders' equity. This **basic accounting equation,** often called the **balance sheet equation,** is restated here:

$$\text{Assets} \quad = \quad \text{Liabilities} + \text{Stockholders' Equity}$$

**Economic resources**          **Sources of financing for the economic resources**
**(e. g., cash, inventory)**                  **Liabilities: From creditors**
                                    **Stockholders' Equity: From stockholders**

The basic accounting equation shows what we mean when we refer to the company's *financial position,* the economic resources that the company owns and the sources of financing for those resources.

Under the category Liabilities, Maxidrive lists two items:

| | | |
|---|---|---|
| Accounts payable | $7,156 | *amounts owed to suppliers for prior purchases* |
| Notes payable | 9,000 | *amounts owed on written debt contracts* |

*Liabilities* are the entity's obligations that result from past transactions. They arise primarily from the *purchase of goods or services* on credit and through *cash borrowings* to finance the business.

Many businesses purchase goods and services from their suppliers on credit without a formal written contract (a note). For example, for the disk drives it produces, Maxidrive purchases electric motors from Magnalite, Inc. This transaction creates a liability known as *accounts payable.* Since there is no formal written contract, such purchases are often described as being on *open account.* The amount of accounts payable listed by Maxidrive includes all of its debts to suppliers on open account.

Business entities often borrow money, primarily from lending institutions such as banks, by entering into a formal written debt contract. In this case, a liability called *notes payable* is created. A note payable specifies an amount to be repaid, a definite maturity or payment date, and the rate of interest charged by the lender. The amount listed as Maxidrive's notes payable ($9,000,000) is owed to American Bank, is due in five years, and requires a yearly (annual) interest payment of 5 percent of the debt every December 31 (5% × $9,000,000 = $450,000).

## FINANCIAL ANALYSIS

### INTERPRETING LIABILITIES ON THE BALANCE SHEET

Maxidrive's existing debts were relevant to American Bank's decision to lend it money because these existing creditors share American Bank's claim against Maxidrive's assets. If a business does not pay its creditors, the law may give the creditors the right to force the sale of assets sufficient to meet their claims. If Maxidrive does not find another source of funds to pay its debts, American Bank and its other creditors will likely take this action. Exeter Investors also was interested in information concerning Maxidrive's debts because of its concern for whether the company had sufficient sources of cash to pay its debts.

---

[2]A corporation is a business that is incorporated under the laws of a particular state. The owners are called *stockholders* or *shareholders.* Ownership is represented by shares of capital stock that usually can be bought and sold freely. The corporation operates as a separate legal entity, separate and apart from its owners. The stockholders enjoy limited liability; they are liable for the debts of the corporation only to the extent of their investments. Chapter Supplement A discusses forms of ownership in more detail.

*Stockholders' equity* indicates the amount of financing provided by owners of the business and earnings. Stockholders' equity comes from two sources: (1) *contributed capital*, the investment of cash and other assets in the business by the owners, and (2) *retained earnings*, the amount of earnings reinvested in the business (and thus not distributed to stockholders in the form of dividends).

In Exhibit 1.2, the Stockholders' Equity section reports the following:

| | | |
|---|---|---|
| Contributed capital | $2,000 | *amounts invested in the business by stockholders* |
| Retained earnings | 9,105 | *past earnings not distributed to stockholders* |

The two founding stockholders of Maxidrive invested a total of $2,000,000 in the business. Each stockholder received 10,000 shares of capital stock (20,000 shares in total). It should be noted that the amounts in contributed capital on Maxidrive's balance sheet did not change when the two founding stockholders sold their shares to Exeter Investors since the transaction did not involve an additional contribution of cash or other assets to Maxidrive. This transaction, which took place between Maxidrive's original owners and Exeter, occurred outside of the accounting entity Maxidrive and thus was not recorded by its accounting system.

The total amount of earnings (or losses incurred) less all dividends paid to the stockholders since formation of the corporation is reported as *retained earnings*. Thus, retained earnings includes the portion of earnings not distributed to owners. The computation is reported on the retained earnings statement discussed later. Total stockholders' equity of $11,105,000 equals the sum of the original owners' investment ($2,000,000) plus the retained earnings ($9,105,000).

## FINANCIAL **ANALYSIS**

### INTERPRETING SHAREHOLDERS' EQUITY ON THE BALANCE SHEET

The basic accounting equation (Assets = Liabilities + Stockholders' Equity) shows that stockholders' equity is equal to total assets minus total liabilities of the business. Stockholders' equity sometimes is called *net worth*. The amount of total stockholders' equity or net worth of Maxidrive is important to American Bank because creditors' claims legally come before those of owners. This is important if Maxidrive goes out of business and its assets are sold. In those circumstances, the proceeds of that sale must be used to pay back creditors such as American Bank before the owners receive any money. Thus, stockholders' equity is considered a "cushion" that protects creditors should the entity go out of business. When Exeter Investors was considering buying Maxidrive, it also looked at stockholders' equity. Recall, however, that the amount recorded on the balance sheet for assets (called the *book value*) could be more or less than the current prices for those assets (called *market value*). As a consequence, Exeter knew that the amount of stockholders' equity did not represent the market value of the company as a whole to its owners.

**A Note on Format**   A few additional formatting conventions are worth noting here. Assets are listed on the balance sheet by ease of conversion to cash. Liabilities are listed by their maturity (due date). Most financial statements include the monetary unit sign (in the United States, the $) beside the first dollar amount in a group of items (e.g., the cash amount in the assets). Also, it is common to place a single underline below the last item in a group before a total or subtotal (e.g., land). A dollar sign is also placed beside group totals (e.g., total assets) and a double underline below. The same conventions are followed in all four basic financial statements. We will discuss alternative balance sheet formats in more detail in Chapter 5.

## SELF-STUDY QUIZ

1. Maxidrive's *assets* are listed in one section and *liabilities* and *stockholders' equity* in another. Notice that the two sections balance in conformity with the basic accounting equation. In the following chapters, you will learn that the basic accounting equation is the basic building block for the entire accounting process. Your task here is to verify that the stockholders' equity of $11,105,000 is correct using the numbers for assets and liabilities presented in Exhibit 1.2 and the basic accounting equation in the form

$$\text{Assets} - \text{Liabilities} = \text{Stockholders' Equity}$$

2. Learning which items belong in each of the balance sheet categories is an important first step in understanding their meaning. Mark each balance sheet item in the following list as an asset (A), liability (L), or stockholders' equity (SE), without referring to Exhibit 1.2.

| | |
|---|---|
| _____ Accounts payable | _____ Inventories |
| _____ Accounts receivable | _____ Land |
| _____ Cash | _____ Notes payable |
| _____ Contributed capital | _____ Retained earnings |
| _____ Plant and equipment | |

After you have completed your answers, check them with the solutions presented at the bottom of this page.*

## THE INCOME STATEMENT

A quick reading of Maxidrive's income statement also indicates a great deal about its purpose and content. The income statement of Maxidrive Corp. is presented in Exhibit 1.3. The heading of the income statement again specifically identifies the name of the entity, the title of the report, and unit of measure used in the statement. Unlike the balance sheet, however, which reports as of a certain date, the income statement reports for a *specified period of time* (for the year ended December 31, 20A). The time period covered by the financial statements (one year in this case) is called an **accounting period.**

The ACCOUNTING PERIOD is the time period covered by the financial statements.

The **income statement (statement of income, statement of earnings, or statement of operations)** reports the accountant's primary measure of performance of a business, the revenues less the expenses of the accounting period. The term *profit* is used widely in our language for this measure of performance, but accountants prefer to use the technical terms *net income* or *net earnings.* Maxidrive's net income measures its success in selling disk drives for more than it cost to generate those sales.

The INCOME STATEMENT (STATEMENT OF INCOME, STATEMENT OF EARNINGS, STATEMENT OF OPERATIONS) reports the revenues less the expenses of the accounting period.

Notice that Maxidrive's income statement has three major captions: *revenues, expenses,* and *net income.*[3] The income statement equation that describes their relationships is

$$\text{Net Income} = \text{Revenues} - \text{Expenses}$$

**Revenues**    *Revenues* are earned from the sale of goods or services to customers (in Maxidrive's case, its sale of disk drives). Revenues normally are reported on the income statement when the goods or services are sold to the customer who has either paid for them or promised to pay in the future. When a business sells goods or renders services, it may receive cash immediately. This is a rare occurrence, however, with the exception of retail stores such as Wal-Mart or McDonald's. Goods or services are normally sold on credit. When Maxidrive sells its disk drives to Compaq and Apple Computer, it receives a promise of future payment called an *account receivable,* which later is collected in cash. In either case, the business recognizes total sales (cash and credit)

---

*1. Assets ($27,261,000) − Liabilities ($16,156,000) = Stockholders' Equity ($11,105,000).

 2. L, A, A, SE, A, A, A, L, SE (reading down the columns).

[3]Other less commonly occurring elements of the income statement are discussed in later chapters.

EXHIBIT **1.3**

**Income Statement**

**MAXIDRIVE CORP.**

**Income Statement**

**For the Year Ended December 31, 20A**

**(in thousands of dollars)**

| | | | |
|---|---:|---:|---|
| Revenues | | | *name of the entity* |
| Sales revenue | $37,436 | | *title of the statement* |
| Total revenues | | $37,436 | *accounting period* |
| Expenses | | | *unit of measure* |
| Cost of goods sold expense | 26,980 | | *revenue earned from sale of disk drives* |
| Selling, general, and administrative expense | 3,624 | | |
| Research and development expense | 1,982 | | *cost to produce disk drives sold* |
| Interest expense | 450 | | *operating expenses not directly related to production* |
| Total expenses | | 33,036 | *expenses incurred to develop new products* |
| Pretax income | | 4,400 | *cost of using borrowed funds* |
| Income tax expense | | 1,100 | |
| Net income | | $ 3,300 | *income taxes on period's pretax income* |

The notes are an integral part of these financial statements.

as revenue for the period. *Revenue is normally reported in the period in which goods and services are sold. This may be different from the period in which cash is received since customers sometimes pay before or after the sale.* Revenue is measured in dollars as the cash-equivalent price agreed on by the two parties to the transaction. Various terms are used in financial statements to describe different sources of revenue (e.g., provision of services, sale of goods, rental of property). Maxidrive lists only one, *sales revenue*, for disk drives delivered to customers.

**Expenses**   Maxidrive lists five items as expenses on its income statement. *Expenses represent the dollar amount of resources the entity used up to earn revenues during a period of time. Cost of goods sold expense* is the total cost to Maxidrive to produce the disk drives delivered to customers during the year. These include the costs of parts used in production, wages paid to the factory workers, and even a portion of the cost of the factories and equipment used to produce the goods that were sold (called *depreciation*). *Selling, general, and administrative expense* (also called *operating expenses*) includes a wide variety of expenses, such as the salaries of management, the sales staff, and the internal company accountants, plus other general costs of operating the company not directly related to production.

Maxidrive is a high-technology company and must constantly spend money developing new products to keep ahead of competitors. These costs are listed as *research and development expense*. Maxidrive also reported *interest expense* for one year on the $9,000,000, 5 percent note payable to American Bank ($9,000,000 × 5% = $450,000), which was outstanding for all of 20A. Finally, as a corporation, Maxidrive must pay income tax at a 25 percent rate on pretax income.[4] Therefore, Maxidrive incurred *income tax expense* of $1,100,000 (pretax income of $4,400,000 × 25%).

Expenses may require the immediate payment of cash, a payment of cash in a later period, or the use of some other resource such as an inventory item, which may have been paid for in a previous period. For accounting purposes, *the period in which an expense is reported on the income statement is the period in which goods and services*

---

[4]Federal tax rates for corporations actually ranged from 15 percent to 35 percent at the time this book was written. State and local governments may levy additional taxes on corporate income, resulting in a higher total income tax rate.

*are used to earn revenues. This is not necessarily the period in which cash is paid for the expense item.* The expense reported in one accounting period may be paid for in another accounting period.

**Net Income**   *Net income* or net earnings (often called *profit* or *the bottom line* by nonaccountants) is the excess of total revenues over total expenses. If the total expenses exceed the total revenues, a net loss is reported. (Net losses are normally noted by parentheses around the income figure.) When revenues and expenses are equal for the period, the business has operated at breakeven. Alternative formats for the income statement are discussed in Chapter 5.

We noted earlier that revenues are not necessarily the same as collections from customers and expenses are not necessarily the same as payments to suppliers. As a result, net income is normally not equal to the net cash generated by operations. This latter amount is reported on the cash flow statement discussed later in the chapter.

## FINANCIAL **ANALYSIS**

### ANALYZING THE INCOME STATEMENT: BEYOND THE BOTTOM LINE

Investors such as Exeter and creditors such as American Bank closely monitor a firm's net income because it indicates the ability to sell goods and services for more than they cost to produce and deliver. The details of the statement also are important. For example, Maxidrive had to sell more than $37 million worth of disk drives to make just over $3 million. The disk drive industry is very competitive. If Maxidrive is forced to match a competitor that lowers prices just 10 percent or if Maxidrive needs to triple research and development to catch up to a competitor's innovative new product, its net income could easily turn into a net loss.

## SELF-STUDY **QUIZ**

1. Learning which items belong in each of the income statement categories is an important first step in understanding their meaning. Mark each income statement item in the following list as a revenue (R) or an expense (E) without referring to Exhibit 1.3.

   _____ Cost of goods sold              _____ Sales

   _____ Research and development        _____ Selling, general, and administrative

2. During the period 20A, Maxidrive delivered disk drives to customers for which the customers paid or promised to pay in the future amounts totaling $37,436,000. During the same period, it collected $33,563,000 in cash from its customers. Without referring to Exhibit 1.3, indicate which of the two numbers will be shown on Maxidrive's income statement as *sales revenue* for 20A. Why did you select your answer?

3. During the period 20A, Maxidrive *produced* disk drives with a total cost of production of $27,130,000. During the same period, it *delivered* to customers disk drives that had cost a total of $26,980,000 to produce. Without referring to Exhibit 1.3, indicate which of the two numbers will be shown on Maxidrive's income statement as *cost of goods sold expense* for 20A. Why did you select your answer?

After you have completed your answers, check them with the solutions presented at the bottom of this page.*

---

*1. E, E, R, E (reading down the columns).

2. Sales revenue in the amount of $37,436,000 is recognized because sales revenue is normally reported on the income statement when the goods or services have been delivered to the customer who has either paid or promised to pay for them in the future.

3. Cost of goods sold expense is $26,980,000 because expenses are the dollar amount of resources used up to earn revenues during the period. Only those disk drives delivered to customers are used up. Those disk drives still on hand are part of the asset inventory.

## STATEMENT OF RETAINED EARNINGS

The **statement of retained earnings** reports the way that net income and the distribution of dividends affected the financial position of the company during the accounting period. As we discussed in our look at the balance sheet, two major factors cause changes in retained earnings. The earning of net income during the year increases the balance of retained earnings, showing the relationship of the income statement to the balance sheet. The declaration of dividends to the stockholders decreases retained earnings.[5] The retained earnings equation that describes these relationships is

**Ending Retained Earnings = Beginning Retained Earnings + Net Income − Dividends**

Maxidrive prepares a separate statement of retained earnings, shown in Exhibit 1.4, which explains changes to the retained earnings balance that occurred during the year. Other corporations report these changes at the end of the income statement or in a more general statement of stockholders' equity, which we discuss in Chapter 4. Like the income statement, the statement of retained earnings reports for a specified period of time (the accounting period), which in this case is one year. It begins with Maxidrive's beginning-of-the-year *retained earnings*. The current year's *net income* reported on the income statement is added and the current year's *dividends* are subtracted from this amount.

During 20A, Maxidrive earned $3,300,000, as shown on the income statement (Exhibit 1.3). This amount was added to the beginning-of-the-year retained earnings in computing end-of-the-year retained earnings. A cash *dividend* pays an equal amount for each share of stock outstanding. During 20A, Maxidrive declared and paid a total of $1,000,000 in dividends to its two original stockholders. This amount was subtracted in computing end-of-the-year retained earnings on the balance sheet. The ending retained earnings amount is the same as that reported in Exhibit 1.2 on the Maxidrive balance sheet. Thus, the retained earnings statement indicates the relationship of the income statement to the balance sheet.

The **STATEMENT OF RETAINED EARNINGS** reports the way that net income and the distribution of dividends affected the financial position of the company during the accounting period.

---

EXHIBIT **1.4**

**Statement of Retained Earnings**

**MAXIDRIVE CORP.**
**Statement of Retained Earnings**
**For the Year Ended December 31, 20A**
**(in thousands of dollars)**

| | |
|---|---|
| Retained earnings, January 1, 20A | $6,805 |
| Net income for 20A | 3,300 |
| Dividends for 20A | (1,000) |
| Retained earnings, December 31, 20A | $9,105 |

*The notes are an integral part of these financial statements.*

name of the entity
title of the statement
accounting period
unit of measure

last period ending retained earnings
net income reported on the income statement
dividends declared during the period

ending retained earnings on the balance sheet

## FINANCIAL **ANALYSIS**

### INTERPRETING RETAINED EARNINGS

Reinvestment of earnings or retained earnings is an important source of financing for Maxidrive, representing more than one-third of its financing. Creditors such as American Bank closely monitor a firm's retained earnings statement because it indicates the firm's policy on dividend payments to the stockholders. This is important to American Bank because in this case every dollar Maxidrive pays to stockholders as dividends is not available to be used to pay back its debt to American Bank or the interest on that debt.

---

[5]Net losses are subtracted. The complete process of declaring and paying dividends is discussed in a later chapter.

## STATEMENT OF CASH FLOWS

Maxidrive's statement of cash flows is presented in Exhibit 1.5. As discussed earlier in this chapter, reported revenues do not always equal cash collected from customers because some sales may be on credit. Also, expenses reported on the income statement may not be equal to the cash paid out during the period because expenses may be incurred in one period and paid for in another. As a result, net income (revenues minus expenses) is usually *not* the amount of cash received minus the amount paid out during the period. In fact, many successful companies may earn large amounts of income and still have to borrow more money from the bank because they do not have sufficient cash to meet their other obligations. Because the income statement does not provide any information concerning cash flows, accountants prepare the **statement of cash flows** to report inflows and outflows of cash in the categories of operating, investing, and financing. Like the income statement, the cash flow statement reports for a specified period of time (the accounting period), which in this case is one year. Many bankers consider this the most important statement they use to estimate whether companies can afford to pay their debts.

The **STATEMENT OF CASH FLOWS** reports inflows and outflows of cash during the accounting period in the categories of operating, investing, and financing.

---

EXHIBIT **1.5**

**Statement of Cash Flows**

*name of the entity*
*title of the statement*
*accounting period*
*unit of measure*

*directly related to earning income*

*purchase/sale of productive assets*

*from investors and creditors*

*change in cash during the period*
*last period's ending cash balance*
*ending cash on the balance sheet*

| MAXIDRIVE CORP. Statement of Cash Flows For the Year Ended December 31, 20A (in thousands of dollars) | | |
|---|---:|---:|
| **Cash flows from operating activities** | | |
| Cash collected from customers | $33,563 | |
| Cash paid to suppliers and employees | (30,854) | |
| Cash paid for interest | (450) | |
| Cash paid for taxes | (1,190) | |
| Net cash flow from operating activities | | $1,069 |
| **Cash flows from investing activities** | | |
| Cash paid to purchase manufacturing equipment | $(1,625) | |
| Net cash flow from investing activities | | (1,625) |
| **Cash flows from financing activities** | | |
| Cash received from bank loan | $1,400 | |
| Cash paid for dividends | (1,000) | |
| Net cash flow from financing activities | | 400 |
| **Net decrease in cash during the year** | | $ (156) |
| **Cash at beginning of year** | | 5,051 |
| **Cash at end of year** | | $4,895 |

The notes are an integral part of these financial statements.

---

# FOCUS ON **CASH FLOWS**

## STATEMENT OF CASH FLOWS CLASSIFICATIONS

The statement divides Maxidrive's cash inflows and outflows (receipts and payments) into the three primary categories of cash flows in a typical business. *Cash flows from operating activities* are cash flows directly related to earning income (normal business activity including *interest paid* and *income taxes paid*). For example, when Compaq, Apple Computer, and other *customers* pay Maxidrive for disk drives that have previously been delivered to them, the amounts collected are listed as cash collected from customers. When Maxidrive pays salaries to its 36 *employees* involved in research and development or pays bills received from its parts *suppliers*, the amounts are included in cash paid to suppliers and employees. Alternative ways to present cash flows from operations are discussed in Chapter 5.

*Cash flows from investing activities* include cash flows related to the acquisition or sale of productive assets used by the company. This year, Maxidrive had only one cash outflow from investing activities, the *purchase of additional manufacturing equipment* to meet growing demand for its products. *Cash flows from financing activities* are directly related to the financing of the enterprise itself. They involve receipt or payment of money to investors and creditors (except for suppliers). This year, Maxidrive *borrowed* an additional $1,400,000 from the bank to purchase most of the new manufacturing equipment. It also paid out $1,000,000 in *dividends* to the founding stockholders before the company was sold.

The cash flow statement equation describes the causes of the change in cash reported on the balance sheet from the end of last period to the end of the current period:

$$\textbf{Change in Cash} = \textbf{Cash Flows from Operating Activities}$$
$$+ \textbf{ Cash Flows from Investing Activities}$$
$$+ \textbf{ Cash Flows from Financing Activities}$$

Note that each of the three cash flow sources can be positive or negative.

## FINANCIAL **ANALYSIS**

### INTERPRETING THE CASH FLOW STATEMENT

Many analysts believe that the statement of cash flows is particularly useful for predicting future cash flows that may be available for payment of debt to creditors and dividends to investors. Each section provides analysts with important information. Bankers often consider the Operating Activities section most important because it indicates the company's ability to generate cash from sales to meet current cash needs. Any amount left can be used to pay back the bank debt or expand the company.

Stockholders will invest in a company only if they believe that it will eventually generate more cash from operations than it uses because only this cash is available to pay dividends in the long run. The Investing Activities section tells us that Maxidrive is making heavy investments in new manufacturing capacity to meet the increasing demand for its products. This is a good sign if demand continues to increase. As the Financing Activities section indicates, however, if Maxidrive is not able to sell more drives, it may have trouble meeting the payments that the new bank debt will require.

## SELF-STUDY **QUIZ**

1. During the period 20A, Maxidrive delivered disk drives to customers that paid or promised to pay in the future amounts totaling $37,436,000. During the same period, it collected $33,563,000 in cash from its customers. Without referring to Exhibit 1.5, indicate which of the two numbers will be shown on Maxidrive's cash flow statement for 20A.

2. Learning which items belong in each cash flow statement category is an important first step in understanding their meaning. Mark each item in the following list as a cash flow from operating activities (O), investing activities (I), or financing activities (F), without referring to Exhibit 1.5. Also place parentheses around the letter only if it is a cash *outflow*.

    _____ Cash paid for dividends

    _____ Cash paid for interest

    _____ Cash received from bank loan

    _____ Cash paid for taxes

_____ Cash paid to purchase manufacturing equipment

_____ Cash paid to suppliers and employees

_____ Cash collected from customers

After you have completed your answers, check them with the solutions presented at the bottom of this page.*

### NOTES

**NOTES (FOOTNOTES)** provide supplemental information about the financial condition of a company, without which the financial statements cannot be fully understood.

At the bottom of each of Maxidrive's four basic financial statements is this statement: *"The notes are an integral part of these financial statements."* This is the accounting equivalent of the Surgeon General's warning on a package of cigarettes. It warns users that failure to read the **notes** (or **footnotes**) to these financial statements will result in an incomplete picture of the company's financial health. Footnotes provide supplemental information about the financial condition of a company, without which the financial statements cannot be fully understood.

There are three basic types of notes. The first type provides descriptions of the accounting rules applied in the company's statements. The second presents additional detail about a line on the financial statements. For example, Maxidrive's inventory note indicates the amount of parts, drives under construction, and finished disk drives included in its total inventory amount listed on the balance sheet. The third type of note presents additional financial disclosures about items not listed on the statements themselves. For example, Maxidrive leases one of its production facilities; terms of the lease are disclosed in a note. We will discuss many note disclosures throughout the book because understanding their content is critical to understanding the company.

## FINANCIAL **ANALYSIS**

### MANAGEMENT USES OF FINANCIAL STATEMENTS

In our discussion of financial analysis thus far, we have focused on the perspectives of *investors* and *creditors*. In addition, managers within the firm often make direct use of financial statements. For example, Maxidrive's *marketing managers* and *credit managers* use customers' financial statements to decide whether to extend them credit for their purchases of disk drives. Maxidrive's *purchasing managers* analyze parts suppliers' financial statements. This allows them to judge whether the suppliers have the resources necessary to meet Maxidrive's current demand for parts and to invest in the development of new parts in the future. Both the *employees' union* and Maxidrive's *human resource managers* use Maxidrive's financial statements as a basis for contract negotiations in determining what pay rates the company can afford. The net income figure even serves as a basis to pay *bonuses* not only to management but also to all employees through the profit-sharing plan. Regardless of the functional area of management in which you are employed, you will *use* financial statement data. You also will be *evaluated* based on the impact of your decisions on your company's financial statement data. Learning financial accounting now will benefit you in the future.

### USING FINANCIAL STATEMENTS TO DETERMINE THE VALUE OF MAXIDRIVE

**Correcting the Income Statement**   We next look at the errors that Exeter Investors later found in Maxidrive's statements to see whether we have learned enough to make

---

*1. $33,563,000 is recognized on the cash flow statement because this number represents the actual cash collected from customers related to current and prior years' sales.

2.  (F), (O), F, (O), (I), (O), O.

the necessary corrections. Then we discuss the responsibilities of various parties in the financial reporting process for the information in these financial statements. The article that began the chapter continues as follows:

# MAXIDRIVE CORP.

**Among Exeter's claims are that**

1. **Disk drives available for sale (part of inventories) included $1 million of obsolete drives that could not be sold and must be scrapped.**
2. **Reported sales to customers (and accounts receivable) for last year included $1,200,000 of overstatements. Maxidrive had cut the price of a certain type of disk drive by 40 percent. But Maxidrive personnel had created fake customer bills (called *invoices*) with the old higher prices to support these sales amounts.**

These two items together significantly overstate on the balance sheet the economic resources owned by Maxidrive (its assets) and overstate on the income statement Maxidrive's ability to sell goods for more than the cost of production (its net income).

For purposes of our discussion, we focus on these effects on the income statement because they were most relevant to Exeter Investors' evaluation of Maxidrive. The simplest way to determine the effects of these two errors on the income statement is to use the income statement equation we have just examined in this chapter. As we indicated earlier, one of the keys to understanding financial statements is to learn the elements of each of the basic financial statements and their relationships, which are represented in the basic equations. The top line in Exhibit 1.6 presents the income statement equation, followed by the amounts reported in Maxidrive's 20A income statement. Following them is each of the two errors that were subsequently discovered and the correction necessary to eliminate the effect of each error.

| | Revenues | – | Expenses | = | Pretax Income |
|---|---|---|---|---|---|
| As presented on Maxidrive's 20A income statement | $37,436 | | $33,036 | | $4,400 |
| Record expense for scrapping obsolete inventory | | | 1,000 | | (1,000) |
| Reduce sales revenue by amount of overstatement | (1,200) | | | | (1,200) |
| After correction of errors | $36,236 | | $34,036 | | $2,200 |

EXHIBIT **1.6**

**Correction of the Income Statement Amounts (in thousands of dollars)**

**Item 1:** Since the obsolete inventory items are held for sale, but now have no value, their cost should be added to this year's expenses. Accordingly, expenses should increase by $1,000,000.

**Item 2:** This involved recording the sales price of a certain type of disk drive at an amount too high, and, thus, total sales revenue is too high. Its correction requires a reduction of $1,200,000 of revenues.

Correcting the two errors, in total, reduces pretax income to $2,200,000. After we subtract 25 percent for income tax expense, we are left with a corrected net income equal to $1,650,000, just *half* of the $3,300,000 amount Maxidrive initially reported.

**Determining the Purchase Price for Maxidrive**   Even at this early stage of your study of accounting, we can provide some examples of the process Exeter Investors went through to determine the price it was willing to pay for Maxidrive Corp. This is a particularly interesting case for analysis because Exeter Investors has claimed that the financial statements it used to estimate the value of Maxidrive were in error. The price Exeter paid was decided by considering a variety of factors including the value of the economic resources owned by Maxidrive, its debts to others, its ability to sell goods for more than their production cost, and its ability to generate the cash necessary to pay its current bills. As we have now learned, these factors are the subject matter of financial statements: balance sheet, income statement, and cash flow statement.

Maxidrive's current and prior years' income statements played a particularly important part in Exeter's evaluation. Prior years' income statements (which were not presented to you) indicated that the company had earned income every year since its founding, except for the first year of operations. Many new companies do not become profitable this quickly. Further, both sales revenue and net income had been rising rapidly every year. One method for estimating the value of a company is with a *price/earnings ratio* (or *P/E ratio* or *P/E multiple*).

Managers, analysts, and investors often use financial ratios to assess different elements of a company's financial performance. We believe that you will be better prepared to use financial information if you learn to evaluate different elements of financial performance at the same time you are learning how to measure and report those elements. As a consequence, we will introduce relevant KEY *ratios* in each chapter. We will use the KEY acronym to help you structure your use of financial ratios in performance assessment. The KEY indicates that there are three steps in ratio analysis:

**Know the decision question that the ratio addresses.** Each ratio measures a different financial attribute. The educated user must know which attribute each ratio measures and how that attribute relates to particular decisions.

**Examine the ratio using two techniques: comparisons over time and comparisons with competitors.** Ratios can be interpreted only in the context of the prior period's ratios or ratios produced by similar companies.

**You interpret the results carefully.** Simple rules of thumb rarely lead to accurate interpretation of ratios. As a consequence, you must carefully consider other related factors before drawing a conclusion.

The KEY *RATIO ANALYSIS* feature will guide you through these three steps for each ratio.

# KEY **RATIO ANALYSIS:**

## PRICE/EARNINGS RATIO

**K**now the decision question:
How quickly will earnings grow in the future? It is computed as follows:*

$$\text{Price/Earnings Ratio} = \frac{\text{Market Price (of the Company)}}{\text{Net Income}}$$

Based on the price paid for the company of $33 million and the originally reported net income of $3.3 million, the 20A ratio for Maxidrive is

$$\frac{\$33,000,000}{\$3,300,000} = 10$$

**E**xamine the ratio using two techniques: comparisons over time and comparisons with competitors

**Comparisons over time:** An increase in the P/E ratio indicates that investors believe that earnings will grow more quickly in the future relative to the current level of earnings. Since Maxidrive was a private company in prior years, no market price was available on which the ratio could be computed.

**Comparisons with competitors,** either individual companies or the average of firms in the industry: The P/E ratio relative to competitors tells us how investors believe the company's growth opportunities stack up against similar companies.

---

*Note that this ratio can be computed on a per share basis with the same number resulting:

$$\text{Price/Earnings Ratio} = \frac{\text{Market Price per share}}{\text{Net Income per share}}$$

**Y**ou interpret the results carefully:

**IN GENERAL** → The price/earnings or P/E ratio measures how many times current year's earnings that investors are willing to pay for the company's stock. All other things equal, a high P/E ratio means that investors have confidence in the company's ability to produce higher profits in future years. As in the Maxidrive case, competitors' P/E ratios often serve as a starting point in analyzing the price that should be paid for a company or its stock.

**FOCUS COMPANY ANALYSIS** → A key to Exeter's decision to buy Maxidrive was the fact that other companies in the same industry with similar performance and past growth were selling for 12 times their current year's earnings. Accordingly, the opportunity to buy Maxidrive for 10 times its current earnings seemed to be an excellent one, particularly since economic forecasts suggested that the next five years would see continuing growth and profitability for disk drive manufacturers. The key calculation that determined the price Exeter paid was based on the following manipulation of the P/E ratio:

$$\text{Price/Earnings Ratio} = \frac{\text{Market Price}}{\text{Net Income}}$$

$$\text{Market (Purchase) Price} = \text{P/E Ratio} \times \text{Net Income}$$

$$\text{Market (Purchase) Price} = 10 \times \text{Net Income}$$

$$\$33,000,000 = 10 \times \$3,300,000$$

Using the same formula, the *corrected* net income figure suggests a much lower price for Maxidrive:

$\$16,500,000 = 10 \times \$1,650,000$

**A FEW CAUTIONS:** A difficult part of this analysis is deciding what price/earnings multiplier is appropriate for this situation. Exeter carefully considered this issue, and its analysis involved more than this simple formula. However, it provides a very real first approximation of Exeter's loss—a $16.5 million overpayment ($33 million paid minus $16.5 million estimated value using corrected earnings). This is the amount that Exeter hopes to recover from those responsible for the fraudulent financial statements it relied on in its analysis. The role of net income in determining the value of a company will be discussed in more detail in your corporate finance course and more advanced courses in financial statement analysis.†

---

†See E.g., K.R. Palepu, P.M. Healy, and V.B. Bernard, *Business Analysis and Valuation*. Cincinnati, OH: South-Western, 2000, Chapter 11.

---

# RESPONSIBILITIES FOR THE ACCOUNTING COMMUNICATION PROCESS

*Effective communication* means that the recipient understands what the sender intends to convey. For the decision makers at Exeter to use the information in Maxidrive's financial statements effectively, they had to understand what information each of the statements conveys. This is the reason that we began our discussion with the content of the four basic financial statements, yet the fraud suggests that this understanding is not sufficient.

Decision makers also needed to understand the *measurement rules* applied in computing the numbers on the statements, and they needed to know that the numbers in the statements represented what was claimed. The first point is a simple one in concept: a swim coach would never try to evaluate a swimmer's time in the 100 freestyle without first asking if the time was for a race in meters or in yards. Likewise, a decision maker should never attempt to use accounting information without first understanding the measurement rules that were used to develop the information. These measurement rules are called **generally accepted accounting principles**, or **GAAP.** The second point is equally important in concept: numbers that do not represent what they claim to are meaningless. For example, if the balance sheet lists $2,000,000 for a factory that does not exist, that part of the statement does not convey useful information. Actually developing a system of measurement rules for complex business transactions (GAAP)

**■ LEARNING OBJECTIVE 2**

Identify the role of generally accepted accounting principles (GAAP) in determining the content of financial statements.

**GENERALLY ACCEPTED ACCOUNTING PRINCIPLES (GAAP)** are the measurement rules used to develop the information in financial statements.

and a system for ensuring that statements fairly represent what they claim (called *auditing*) is much more complicated, however, as the Maxidrive fraud suggests.

## GENERALLY ACCEPTED ACCOUNTING PRINCIPLES

**How Are Generally Accepted Accounting Principles Determined?**   As the preceding discussion suggests, we must understand the measurement rules used to develop the information in the statements to understand the numbers in them. The accounting system that we use today has a long history. Its foundations are normally traced back to the works of an Italian monk and mathematician, Fr. Luca Pacioli. In 1494, he described an approach developed by Italian merchants to account for their activities as owner-managers of business ventures. Although many others wrote works on accounting after Pacioli, prior to 1933, each company's management largely determined its financial reporting practices. Thus, little uniformity in practice existed among companies.

The Securities Act of 1933 and The Securities Exchange Act of 1934 were passed into law by the U.S. Congress in response to the dramatic stock market decline of 1929. Part of these securities acts created the **Securities and Exchange Commission (SEC)** and gave it broad powers to determine the measurement rules for financial statements that companies must provide to stockholders. Contrary to popular belief, these rules are different from those that companies follow when filing their income tax returns. We discuss these differences further in later chapters.

> The **SECURITIES AND EXCHANGE COMMISSION (SEC)** is the U.S. government agency that determines the financial statements that public companies must provide to stockholders and the measurement rules that they must use in producing those statements.

Since its establishment, the SEC has worked with organizations of professional accountants to establish groups that are given the primary responsibilities to work out the detailed rules that become generally accepted accounting principles. The name of the current group that has this responsibility is the **Financial Accounting Standards Board (FASB)**. The Board has seven full-time voting members and a permanent staff who consider the appropriate financial reporting responses to ever-changing business practices. As of the date of publication of this book, the official pronouncements of the FASB (*Financial Accounting Standards*) and its predecessors total more than 4,700 pages of very fine print. Such detail is made necessary by the enormous diversity and complexity of current business practices.

> The **FINANCIAL ACCOUNTING STANDARDS BOARD (FASB)** is the private sector body given the primary responsibility to work out the detailed rules that become generally accepted accounting principles.

Stock of *privately held* corporations such as Maxidrive is owned by small groups of individuals and is not available for sale to the public at large. Like all prospective purchasers of shares of privately held companies, Exeter had to negotiate directly with the current owners to arrange the purchase. The stock of some corporations such as Maxidrive's largest customers, Apple Computer and Compaq, and other well-known companies such as General Motors, Wal-Mart, and McDonald's is *publicly traded*. This means that it can be bought and sold by investors on established stock exchanges (organized markets for stocks) such as the New York Stock Exchange. The SEC sets additional financial reporting requirements that only publicly traded companies must follow. We introduce some of these additional requirements later in the book.

Most managers do not need to learn all of the details included in these standards. Our approach is to focus on those details that have the *greatest impact on the numbers presented in financial statements* and are appropriate for a course at this level.

**Why Do Managers, Accountants, and Users Care What Is Generally Accepted?** You can be sure that what is included in generally accepted accounting principles (GAAP) is of great interest to the companies that must prepare the statements, to auditors, and to the readers of the statements. *Companies and their managers and owners* are most directly affected by the information presented in the statements and for that reason express the most interest. Companies incur the cost of preparing the statements and bear the major economic consequences of their publication. These economic consequences include, among others, *potential*

1. Effects on the selling price of a company's stock.
2. Effects on the amount of bonuses received by management and employees.
3. Loss of competitive advantage over other companies.

Recall that the amount that Exeter was willing to pay to purchase Maxidrive was determined in part by net income computed under GAAP. This presents the possibility that changes in GAAP can affect the price buyers are willing to pay for companies, either to the benefit or the detriment of the current owners. The business press often suggests this possibility. Regardless of the validity of these claims, owners and managers are concerned by these occurrences.

Managers and other employees often receive part of their pay based on reaching stated targets for net income. As a result, they are directly concerned with any changes in how net income is computed under GAAP. Managers and owners also often are concerned that publishing more information in financial statements will disclose the details of their successes and failures, which will help similar companies compete with them.

As a consequence of these and other concerns, changes in GAAP are actively debated, and the use of political muscle and lobbying often takes place. For example, owners and managers who were concerned about a proposed change in accounting for management pay let their elected representatives in government know about their concerns. In response, numerous senators and the Secretary of the Treasury sent letters to the FASB opposing this proposed change in GAAP. The result was a modification of the proposal, which was reported in the following *Accounting Today* headline:

**REAL WORLD EXCERPT**

*Accounting Today*

### POLITICS KILLS FASB STOCK OPTIONS PLAN

Norwalk, Conn.—Ending a decade of study and more than two years of increasingly acrimonious opposition, the Financial Accounting Standards Board has dropped its plan forcing companies to charge executive stock options against earnings.

SOURCE: *Accounting Today,* January 2–15, 1995, p. 1. © Faulkner and Gray, Inc., Republished with Permission.

# INTERNATIONAL **PERSPECTIVE**

## ARE GENERALLY ACCEPTED ACCOUNTING PRINCIPLES SIMILAR IN OTHER COUNTRIES?

While businesspeople compete in a single global economy, different sets of generally accepted accounting principles have developed within particular countries. Differences in political, cultural, and economic histories have produced a great number of cross-national differences in practice. These differences can have dramatic effects on the numbers presented in the financial statements. For example, the recent financial crisis in Korea and the accompanying dramatic drop in prices for Korean stocks have focused attention on its accounting rules. *The Asian Wall Street Journal* reported the following:

**REAL WORLD EXCERPT**

*The Asian Wall Street Journal*

### ACCOUNTING CHANGES LEAVE KOREA TELECOM UNFAZED

In Korea, corporate accounting policies seem to change with the wind. Understanding the changes can be tricky, but they can make a big difference to a company's reported results. . . .

Had it used U.S. accounting guidelines, Korea Telecom would have taken a big hit in 1997, recording a loss of 201 billion won,* rather than the 11 billion won in net earnings it reported using Korean guidelines. But it would have reported that net earnings bounced back to 388 billion won in 1998, compared with the gain of 195 billion won it reported using Korean guidelines. The big difference is largely because of foreign currency swings, which are reported differently in the U.S.

*The won is the currency of South Korea. At the time this chapter was written, $1 equaled 1,200 won.
SOURCE: *The Asian Wall Street Journal,* May 18, 1999, p. 13.

The International Accounting Standards Board (IASC) and others are attempting to eliminate these differences. But for now, managers and users of financial statements who cross national borders must be aware of the specific nature of these reporting differences to interpret financial statements successfully. Although our primary focus is on U.S. GAAP, we briefly discuss practice in other countries when appropriate.

## MANAGEMENT RESPONSIBILITY AND THE DEMAND FOR AUDITING

■ **LEARNING OBJECTIVE 3**

Distinguish the roles of managers and auditors in the accounting communication process.

Exeter's owners and managers were well aware of the details of U.S. GAAP, but they were still misled. Although the measurement rules that Maxidrive had used to produce its financial statements were consistent with GAAP, the underlying figures in the accounting system were fictitious; that is, they did not fairly represent reality. Any measurement system applied to underlying facts that do not match reality will produce unrepresentative measures. Who is responsible for the accuracy of the numbers in Maxidrive's financial statements? Two documents taken from Maxidrive's annual report provide us with much of the answer to this question.

The **REPORT OF MANAGEMENT** indicates management's primary responsibility for financial statement information and the steps to ensure the accuracy of the company's records.

The **report of management,** shown in Exhibit 1.7, makes two points clear. First, primary responsibility for the information in the financial statements lies with management, as represented by the highest officer of the company and the highest officer involved with the financial side of the company. Second, the managers take three important steps to ensure the accuracy of the company's records: (1) they maintain a system of controls over both the records and assets of the company, (2) they hire outside independent auditors to verify the fairness of the statement presentations, and (3) they have a committee of the board of directors whose job it is to review these other two safeguards. These safeguards failed in the case of Maxidrive, and those primarily responsible, whether directly involved or not, are listed in the report of management.

EXHIBIT **1.7**

**Report of Management**

### Report of Management

The management of Maxidrive is responsible for preparing the financial statements and other information contained in this annual report. Management believes that the financial statements fairly reflect, in all material respects, the form and substance of events and transactions and that the financial statements present the Company's financial position and results of operations in conformity with generally accepted accounting principles. Management has included in the Company's financial statements amounts that are based on informed judgments and estimates, which it believes are reasonable under the circumstances.

Maxidrive maintains a system of internal accounting policies, procedures and controls intended to provide reasonable assurance, at appropriate cost, that transactions are processed in accordance with Company authorization and are properly recorded and reported in the financial statements, and that assets are adequately safeguarded.

Smith and Walker, CPAs, the Company's independent auditing firm, audits the Company's financial statements in accordance with generally accepted auditing standards, which provide the basis of its report on the financial statements.

The Board of Directors of the Company has an Audit Committee composed of nonmanagement directors. The Committee meets with financial management and the independent auditors to review internal accounting controls and accounting, auditing, and financial reporting matters. In addition, Smith and Walker, CPAs, has full and free access to the Audit Committee, without management present, to discuss the results of its audits, the adequacy of the company's internal accounting controls, and the quality of its financial reporting.

Harold T. West
President and Chairman of the Board

Robert P. Malony
Chief Financial Officer

The role of the independent auditor is described in more detail in the second report (Exhibit 1.8), the **report of independent accountants,** or **audit report,** which describes the auditor's opinion of the fairness of the financial statement presentations and the evidence gathered to support that opinion. An accountant may be licensed as a *certified public accountant*, or *CPA*. This designation is granted only on completion of requirements specified by each state. Other accountants can offer various accounting services to the public, but only a licensed CPA can issue an audit report. In this role, accountants are known as *independent CPAs* (or *independent accountants*) because they have certain responsibilities that extend to the general public in addition to those to the specific business that pays for the services. Independent CPAs, although paid by their clients, are not employees of their clients.

The **REPORT OF INDEPENDENT ACCOUNTANTS (AUDIT REPORT)** describes the auditors' opinion of the fairness of the financial statement presentations and the evidence gathered to support that opinion.

EXHIBIT **1.8**

**Report of Independent Accountants**

---

**Report of Independent Accountants To the Stockholders and Board of Directors of Maxidrive Corp.**

We have audited the accompanying balance sheet of Maxidrive Corp. as of December 31, 20A, and the related statements of income, retained earnings and cash flows for the period ended December 31, 20A. These financial statements are the responsibility of the Company's management. Our responsibility is to express an opinion on these financial statements based on our audits.

We conducted our audits in accordance with generally accepted auditing standards. Those standards require that we plan and perform the audit to obtain reasonable assurance about whether the financial statements are free of material misstatement. An audit includes examining, on a test basis, evidence supporting the amounts and disclosures in the financial statements. An audit also includes assessing the accounting principles used and significant estimates made by management, as well as evaluating the overall financial statement presentation. We believe that our audits provide a reasonable basis for our opinion.

In our opinion, the financial statements referred to above present fairly, in all material respects, the financial position of Maxidrive Corp. at December 31, 20A, and the results of its operations and its cash flows for the period ended December 31, 20A, in conformity with generally accepted accounting principles.

Smith and Walker, CPAs

---

An **audit** involves the examination of the financial reports (prepared by the management of the entity) to ensure that they represent what they claim and conform with generally accepted accounting principles (GAAP). In performing an audit, the independent CPA examines the underlying transactions, including the collection, classification, and assembly of the financial data incorporated in the financial reports. To appreciate the magnitude of these responsibilities, consider the enormous number of transactions involving a major enterprise such as General Motors that total billions of dollars each year. The CPA does not examine each of these transactions, however; rather, professional approaches are used to ascertain beyond reasonable doubt that transactions were measured and reported properly. Many unintentional and, as we have learned in the Maxidrive case, intentional opportunities exist to prepare misleading financial reports. The audit function performed by an independent CPA is the best protection available to the public. When that protection fails, however, the independent CPA is often found liable for losses incurred by those who rely on the statements.

An **AUDIT** is an examination of the financial reports to ensure that they represent what they claim and conform with generally accepted accounting principles.

## ETHICS, REPUTATION, AND LEGAL LIABILITY

If financial statements are to be of any value to decision makers, users must have confidence in the fairness of the information. These users will have greater confidence in the information if they know that the people who were associated with auditing the financial statements were required to meet professional standards of ethics and competence.

**LEARNING OBJECTIVE 4**

Appreciate the importance of ethics, reputation, and legal liability in accounting.

The American Institute of Certified Public Accountants (AICPA) requires all of its members to adhere to a professional code of ethics. These broad principles are supported by specific rules that govern the performance of audits by members of the AICPA. Failure to comply with the rules of conduct can result in serious professional penalties. The potential economic effects of damage to reputation and malpractice liability, however, provide even stronger incentives to abide by professional standards.

CPAs' reputations for honesty and competence are their most important assets. If the Smith and Walker firm is found to be either negligent or dishonest in the audit of Maxidrive, American Bank and other lenders will refuse to lend money based on statements that firm has audited, and the firm's other clients will quickly choose new auditors. Financial statement fraud is a fairly rare event, due in part to the diligent efforts of practicing CPAs. In fact, many such frauds are first identified in the course of the annual audit. Even the most diligent audit, however, may not immediately uncover the results of fraud involving collusion of the top officers of a corporation, such as occurred with Maxidrive.

In case of malpractice in the audit function, the independent CPA is subject to potential liability that may extend to all parties (whether known to the CPA or not) who have suffered loss because they relied on financial statements examined by the CPA. Even if Smith and Walker was unaware that Exeter was using the statements as input to its decision to buy Maxidrive, if the CPAs' failure to detect the errors in the statements was a result of their malpractice, they could be liable for Exeter's loss.

As a result of the fraud, Maxidrive filed for bankruptcy and will likely be sold in an attempt to pay off creditors. Exeter Investors and American Bank claimed losses of $16.5 million and $9 million, respectively, in a civil lawsuit. It claimed that the officers of Maxidrive had "perpetrated a massive fraud" and the auditors had "overlooked the errors" in the audit.[6] Exeter and American Bank also have asked for punitive damages for gross negligence. The president and the chief financial officer of Maxidrive are under indictment by a federal grand jury for three counts of criminal securities fraud for which they face possible fines and prison terms.

## EPILOGUE

Although financial statement fraud is a fairly rare event, the misrepresentations in Maxidrive's statements aptly illustrate the importance of fairly presented financial statements to investors and creditors. It also depicts the crucial importance of the public accounting profession in ensuring the integrity of the financial reporting system. As noted at the beginning of the chapter, Maxidrive is not a real company but is based on a real company that perpetrated a similar fraud. The focus companies and contrasting examples in the remaining chapters are *real* companies except when indicated.

Maxidrive is loosely based on the infamous MiniScribe fraud. The size of the real fraud, however, was more than *10 times* as great as that in the fictional case, as were the losses incurred and the amounts in the lawsuits that followed. (Many of the numbers in the financial statements are simply one-tenth the amounts presented in MiniScribe's fraudulent statements.) The nature of the fraud also was quite similar. At MiniScribe, sales revenue was overstated by transferring nonexistent inventory between two of MiniScribe's own facilities and creating phony documents to make it look as though the inventory were transferred to customers. MiniScribe even packaged *bricks* as finished products, shipped them to distributors, and counted them as sold. Cost of goods sold was understated by activities such as counting scrap parts and damaged drives as usable inventory. Further, members of management even broke into the

---

[6]Even some accountants are confused about the auditor's responsibility to detect fraud. *Statement on Auditing Standards No. 82,* "Consideration of Fraud in a Financial Statement Audit" (and the earlier rules in *SAS No. 53*), requires that auditors design tests to ensure detection of fraud that materially affects financial statements. The statement notes, however, that no audit can guarantee the discovery of sophisticated collusive fraud.

auditors' locked trunks to change numbers on their audit papers. As a consequence, MiniScribe reported net income of $31 million, which was subsequently shown to be $9 million. Prior years' statements contained similar errors. MiniScribe's investors and creditors filed lawsuits asking for more than $1 billion in damages. Actual damages in the hundreds of millions were paid. Both the chairman and the chief financial officer of MiniScribe were convicted of federal securities and wire fraud charges and sentenced to jail. Although most managers and owners act in an honest and responsible fashion, this incident is a stark reminder of the economic consequences of lack of fair presentation in financial reports. Sales revenue and inventory frauds to this day are the most frequently occurring financial statement frauds.[7]

# DEMONSTRATION **CASE**

At the end of most chapters, one or more demonstration cases are presented. These cases provide an overview of the primary issues discussed in the chapter. Each demonstration case is followed by a recommended solution. You should read the case carefully and then prepare your own solution before you study the recommended solution. This self-evaluation is highly recommended.

The introductory case presented here helps you to start thinking in financial statement terms of some of the resource inflows and outflows of a business.

ABC Service Corporation was organized by Able, Baker, and Cain on January 1, 20A. On that date, the investors exchanged $36,000 cash for all of the stock of the company. On the same day, the corporation borrowed $10,000 from a local bank and signed a three-year note payable. The interest is payable each December 31. On January 1, 20A, the corporation purchased service supplies for $20,000 cash. Operations started immediately.

At the end of 20A, the corporation had completed the following additional business transactions (summarized):

(a) Performed services and billed customers for $100,500, of which $94,500 was collected in cash by year-end.
(b) Used up $5,000 of service supplies while rendering services.
(c) Paid $54,000 cash for other service expenses.
(d) Paid $1,500 in annual interest expense on the note payable.
(e) Paid $8,000 of income taxes in cash to the Internal Revenue Service (IRS).

## Required:
Complete the following two 20A financial statements by entering the correct amounts. The suggested solution follows the blank statements.

**ABC SERVICE CORPORATION**
**Income Statement**
_____ (date)
**(in dollars)**

| | | Computation |
|---|---|---|
| **Revenues** | | |
| Service revenue | $_____ | _____ |
| **Expenses** | | |
| Service expenses | $_____ | _____ |
| Interest expense | _____ | _____ |
| Total expenses | _____ | |
| Pretax income | $_____ | |
| Income tax expense | _____ | _____ |
| **Net income** | $_____ | |

[7]*Fraud Survey Results 1998*, KPMG Peat Marwick, 1998.

**ABC SERVICE CORPORATION**
**Balance Statement**
—————— (date)
**(in dollars)**

| | | Computation |
|---|---|---|
| **Assets** | | |
| Cash | $ _____ | _____ |
| Accounts receivable | _____ | _____ |
| Service supplies | _____ | _____ |
| Total assets | $ _____ | |
| **Liabilities** | | |
| Note payable (15%) | $ _____ | _____ |
| Total liabilities | $ _____ | |
| **Stockholders' Equity** | | |
| Contributed capital | $ _____ | _____ |
| Retained earnings | _____ | _____ |
| Total stockholders' equity | _____ | |
| Total liabilities and stockholders' equity | $ _____ | |

## SUGGESTED SOLUTION

**ABC SERVICE CORPORATION**
**Income Statement**
**For the Year Ended December 31, 20A**
**(in dollars)**

| | | | Computation |
|---|---|---|---|
| **Revenues** | | | |
| Service revenue | | $100,500 | Given (cash & on open account) |
| **Expenses** | | | |
| Service expenses | $59,000 | | $54,000 cash + 5,000 supplies |
| Interest expense | 1,500 | | |
| Total expenses | | 60,500 | |
| Pretax income | | $ 40,000 | |
| Income tax expense | | 8,000 | |
| **Net income** | | $ 32,000 | |

**ABC SERVICE CORPORATION**
**Balance Sheet**
**at December 31, 20A**
**(in dollars)**

| | | | Computation |
|---|---|---|---|
| **Assets** | | | |
| Cash | | $57,000 | $36,000 + $10,000 + $94,500 − $54,000 − $1,500 − $8,000 − $20,000 |
| Accounts receivable | | 6,000 | $100,500 − $94,500 |
| Service supplies | | 15,000 | $20,000 − $5,000 |
| Total assets | | $78,000 | |
| **Liabilities** | | | |
| Note payable | $10,000 | | Given, bank loan |
| Total liabilities | | $10,000 | |
| **Stockholders' Equity** | | | |
| Contributed capital | $36,000 | | Given |
| Retained earnings | 32,000 | | From income statement |
| Total stockholders' equity | | 68,000 | |
| Total liabilities and stockholders' equity | | $78,000 | |

## CHAPTER **TAKE-AWAYS**

1. **Recognize the information conveyed in each of the four basic financial statements and the way that it is used by different decision makers (investors, creditors, and managers). p. 6**

   The *balance sheet* is a statement of financial position that reports dollar amounts for the assets, liabilities, and stockholders' equity at a specific point in time.

   The *income statement* is a statement of operations that reports revenues, expenses, and net income for a stated period of time.

   The *statement of retained earnings* explains changes to the retained earnings balance that occurred during the reporting period.

   The *statement of cash flows* reports inflows and outflows of cash for a specific period of time.

   The statements are used by investors and creditors to evaluate different aspects of the firm's financial position and performance.

2. **Identify the role of generally accepted accounting principles (GAAP) in determining the content of financial statements. p. 21**
   GAAP are the measurement rules used to develop the information in financial statements. Knowledge of GAAP is necessary for accurate interpretation of the numbers in financial statements.

3. **Distinguish the roles of managers and auditors in the accounting communication process. p. 24**
   Management has primary responsibility for the accuracy of a company's financial information. Auditors are responsible for expressing an opinion on the fairness of the financial statement presentations based on their examination of the reports and records of the company.

4. **Appreciate the importance of ethics, reputation, and legal liability in accounting. p. 25**
   Users will have confidence in the accuracy of financial statement numbers only if the people associated with their preparation and audit have reputations for ethical behavior and competence. Management and auditors can also be held legally liable for fraudulent financial statements and malpractice.

In this chapter, we studied the basic financial statements that communicate financial information to external users. Chapters 2, 3, and 4 will provide a more detailed look at financial statements and examine how to translate data about business transactions into these statements. Learning how to translate back and forth between business transactions and financial statements is the key to using financial statements in planning and decision making. Chapter 2 will begin our discussion of the way that the accounting function collects data about business transactions and processes the data to provide periodic financial statements, with emphasis on the balance sheet. To accomplish this purpose, Chapter 2 will discuss key accounting concepts, the accounting model, transaction analysis, and analytical tools. We will examine typical business activities of an actual service-oriented company to demonstrate the concepts in Chapters 2, 3, and 4.

## Chapter Supplement A

### Types of Business Entities

This textbook emphasizes *accounting for profit-making business entities*. The three main types of business entities are sole proprietorship, partnership, and corporation. A *sole proprietorship* is an unincorporated business owned by one person; it usually is small in size and is common in the service, retailing, and farming industries. Often the owner is the manager. Legally, the business and the owner are not separate entities. Accounting views the business as a separate entity, however, that must be accounted for separately from its owner.

A *partnership* is an unincorporated business owned by two or more persons known as *partners*. Some partnerships are large in size (e.g., international public accounting firms and law firms). The agreements between the owners are specified in a partnership contract. This contract deals with matters such as division of income each reporting period and distribution of resources of the business on termination of its operations. A partnership is not legally separate from its owners. Legally, each partner in a general partnership is responsible for the debts of the business (each general partner has *unlimited liability*). The partnership, however, is a separate business entity to be accounted for separately from its several owners.

A *corporation* is a business incorporated under the laws of a particular state. The owners are called *stockholders* or *shareholders*. Ownership is represented by shares of capital stock that usually can be bought and sold freely. When an approved application for incorporation is filed by the organizers, the state issues a charter. This charter gives the corporation the right to operate as a separate legal entity, separate and apart from its owners. The stockholders enjoy *limited liability*. Stockholders are liable for the corporation's debts only to the extent of their investments. The corporate charter specifies the types and amounts of capital stock that can be issued. Most states require a minimum of two or three stockholders and a minimum amount of resources to be contributed at the time of organization. The stockholders elect a governing board of directors, which in turn employs managers and exercises general supervision of the corporation. Accounting also views the corporation as a separate business entity that must be accounted for separately from its owners.

In terms of economic importance, the corporation is the dominant form of business organization in the United States. This dominance is caused by the many advantages of the corporate form: (1) limited liability for the stockholders, (2) continuity of life, (3) ease in transferring ownership (stock), and (4) opportunities to raise large amounts of money by selling shares to a large number of people. The primary disadvantage of a corporation is that its income may be subject to double taxation (it is taxed when it is earned and again when it is distributed to stockholders as dividends). In this textbook, we emphasize the corporate form of business. Nevertheless, the accounting concepts and procedures that we discuss also apply to other types of businesses.

## Chapter Supplement B

### Employment in the Accounting Profession Today

Since 1900, accounting has attained the stature of professions such as law, medicine, engineering, and architecture. As with all recognized professions, accounting is subject to professional competence requirements, is dedicated to service to the public, requires a high level of academic study, and rests on a common body of knowledge. An accountant may be licensed as a certified public accountant, or CPA. This designation is granted only on completion of requirements specified by the state that issues the license. Although CPA requirements vary among states, they include a college degree with a specified number of accounting courses, good character, one to five years of professional experience, and successful completion of a professional examination. The CPA examination, scheduled in each state simultaneously on a semiannual basis, is prepared by the American Institute of Certified Public Accountants.

Accountants (including CPAs) commonly are engaged in professional practice or are employed by businesses, government entities, nonprofit organizations, and so on. Accountants employed in these activities may take and pass a professional examination to become a certified management accountant, or CMA (the CMA examination is administered by the Institute of Management Accountants), or a certified internal auditor, or CIA (the CIA examination is administered by the Institute of Internal Auditors).

### PRACTICE OF PUBLIC ACCOUNTING

Although an individual may practice public accounting, usually two or more individuals organize an accounting firm in the form of a partnership (in many cases, a limited liability partnership, or LLP). Accounting firms vary in size from a one-person office, to regional firms, to the Big Five firms (Arthur Andersen & Co., Deloitte & Touche, Ernst & Young, KPMG Peat Marwick, and PricewaterhouseCoopers), which have hundreds of offices located worldwide. Accounting firms usually render three types of services: assurance services, management consulting services, and tax services.

**Assurance Services**   Assurance services are independent professional services that improve the quality of information, or its context, for decision makers. The most important assurance service performed by the CPA in public practice is financial statement auditing. The purpose of an audit is to lend credibility to the financial reports, that is, to ensure that they fairly represent what they claim. An audit involves an examination of the financial reports (prepared by the management of the entity) to ensure that they conform with GAAP. Other areas of assurance services include electronic commerce integrity and security and information systems reliability.

**Management Consulting Services**   Many independent CPA firms offer *management consulting services*. These services usually are accounting based and encompass such activities as the design and installation of accounting, data processing, and profit-planning and control (budget) systems; financial advice; forecasting; inventory controls; cost-effectiveness studies; and operational analysis. This facet of public CPA practice is growing rapidly.

**Tax Services**   CPAs in public practice usually provide income tax services to their clients. These services include both tax planning as a part of the decision-making process and the determination of the income tax liability (reported on the annual income tax return). Because of the increasing complexity of state and federal tax laws, a high level of competence is required, which CPAs specializing in taxation can provide. The CPA's involvement in tax planning often is quite significant. Most major business decisions have significant tax impacts; in fact, tax-planning considerations often govern certain business decisions.

## EMPLOYMENT BY ORGANIZATIONS

Many accountants, including CPAs, CMAs, and CIAs, are employed by profit-making and nonprofit organizations. An organization, depending on its size and complexity, may employ from a few to hundreds of accountants. In a business enterprise, the chief financial officer (usually a vice president or controller) is a member of the management team. This responsibility usually entails a wide range of management, financial, and accounting duties.

In a business entity, accountants typically are engaged in a wide variety of activities, such as general management, general accounting, cost accounting, profit planning and control (budgeting), internal auditing, and computerized data processing. A primary function of the accountants in organizations is to provide data that are useful for internal managerial decision making and for controlling operations. The functions of external reporting, tax planning, control of assets, and a host of related responsibilities normally are also performed by accountants in industry.

## EMPLOYMENT IN THE PUBLIC AND NOT-FOR-PROFIT SECTOR

The vast and complex operations of governmental units, from the local to the international level, create a need for accountants. The same holds true for other not-for-profit organizations such as hospitals and universities. Accountants employed in the public and not-for-profit sector perform functions similar to those performed by their counterparts in private organizations. The General Accounting Office (GAO) and the regulatory agencies, such as the SEC and Federal Communications Commission (FCC), also use the services of accountants in carrying out their regulatory duties.

## KEY **RATIO**

**Price/earnings ratio** (P/E ratio; price/earnings multiplier) measures the relationship between current market price of a company and its net earnings and is a measure of expected company growth. It is computed as follows (p. 20):

$$\text{Price/Earnings} = \frac{\text{Market Price}}{\text{Net Income}}$$

## FINDING FINANCIAL INFORMATION

**BALANCE SHEET**
*Assets = Liabilities + Stockholders' Equity*

**INCOME STATEMENT**
*Revenues*
*− Expenses*
*Net Income*

**STATEMENT OF RETAINED EARNINGS**
*Retained Earnings, beginning of the period*
*+ Net Income*
*− Dividends*
*Retained Earnings, end of the period*

**STATEMENT OF CASH FLOWS**
*Cash Flow from Operating Activities*
*+ Cash Flow from Investing Activities*
*+ Cash Flow from Financing Activities*
*Net Change in Cash*

## KEY **TERMS**

**Accounting** p. 5

**Accounting Entity** p. 8

**Accounting Period** p. 12

**Audit** p. 25

**Balance Sheet (Statement of Financial Position)** p. 8

## QUESTIONS

1. Define *accounting*.
2. Briefly distinguish financial accounting from managerial accounting.
3. The accounting process generates financial reports for both internal and external users. Identify some of the groups of users.
4. Briefly distinguish investors from creditors.
5. What is an accounting entity? Why is a business treated as a separate entity for accounting purposes?
6. Complete the following:

   | Name of Statement | Alternative Title |
   | --- | --- |
   | *a.* Income statement | *a.* _____ |
   | *b.* Balance sheet | *b.* _____ |
   | *c.* Audit report | *c.* _____ |

7. What information should be included in the heading of each of the four primary financial statements?
8. What are the purposes of (*a*) the income statement, (*b*) the balance sheet, (*c*) the statement of cash flows, and (*d*) the statement of retained earnings?
9. Explain why the income statement and the statement of cash flows are dated "For the Year Ended December 31, 20X," whereas the balance sheet is dated "At December 31, 20X."
10. Briefly explain the importance of assets and liabilities to the decisions of investors and creditors.
11. Briefly define the following: *net income, net loss,* and *breakeven.*
12. Explain the accounting equation for the income statement. What are the three major items reported on the income statement?
13. Explain the accounting equation for the balance sheet. Define the three major components reported on the balance sheet.
14. Explain the accounting equation for the statement of cash flows. Explain the three major components reported on the statement.
15. Explain the accounting equation for the statement of retained earnings. Explain the four major items reported on the statement of retained earnings.
16. Financial statements discussed in this chapter are aimed at *external* users. Briefly explain how a company's *internal* managers in different functional areas (e.g., marketing, purchasing, human resources) might use financial statement information.
17. Briefly describe the way that accounting measurement rules (generally accepted accounting principles) are determined in the United States.
18. Briefly explain the responsibility of company management and the independent auditors in the accounting communication process.
19. (Supplement A) Briefly differentiate between a sole proprietorship, a partnership, and a corporation.
20. (Supplement B) List and briefly explain the three primary services that CPAs in public practice provide.

# MINI-EXERCISES

**LO1** **M1–1** **Matching Elements with Financial Statements**
Match each element with its financial statement by entering the appropriate letter in the space provided.

| Element | Financial Statement |
|---|---|
| _____ (1) Expenses | A. Balance Sheet |
| _____ (2) Cash Flow from Investing Activities | B. Income Statement |
| _____ (3) Assets | C. Statement of Retained Earnings |
| _____ (4) Dividends | D. Statement of Cash Flows |
| _____ (5) Revenues | |
| _____ (6) Cash Flow from Operating Activities | |
| _____ (7) Liabilities | |
| _____ (8) Cash Flow from Financing Activities | |

**LO1** **M1–2** **Matching Financial Statement Items to Financial Statement Categories**
Mark each item in the following list as an asset (A), liability (L), or stockholders' equity (SE) that would appear on the balance sheet or a revenue (R) or expense (E) that would appear on the income statement.

| | | | | |
|---|---|---|---|---|
| SE | (1) Retained earnings | | A | (6) Inventories |
| A | (2) Accounts receivable | | E | (7) Interest expense |
| R | (3) Sales revenue | | L | (8) Accounts payable |
| A | (4) Property, plant, and equipment | | A | (9) Land |
| E | (5) Cost of goods sold expense | | | |

**LO2** **M1–3** **Identifying Important Accounting Abbreviations**
The following is a list of important abbreviations used in the chapter. These abbreviations also are used widely in business. For each abbreviation, give the full designation. The first one is an example.

| Abbreviation | Full Designation |
|---|---|
| _____ (1) CPA | Certified Public Accountant |
| _____ (2) GAAP | _____ |
| _____ (3) CMA | _____ |
| _____ (4) AICPA | _____ |
| _____ (5) SEC | _____ |
| _____ (6) FASB | _____ |

# EXERCISES

**LO1, 2** **E1–1** **Matching Definitions with Terms or Abbreviations**
Match each definition with its related term or abbreviation by entering the appropriate letter in the space provided.

| Term or Abbreviation | Definition |
|---|---|
| K (1) SEC | A. A system that collects and processes financial information about an organization and reports that information to decision makers. |
| G (2) Audit | |
| I (3) Sole proprietorship | B. Measurement of information about an entity in the monetary unit—dollars or other national currency. |
| E (4) Corporation | |
| A (5) Accounting | C. An unincorporated business owned by two or more persons. |
| D (6) Separate entity | |

| Term or Abbreviation | Definition |
|---|---|
| __J__ (7) Audit report | D. The organization for which financial data are to be collected (separate and distinct from its owners). |
| __F__ (8) Cost principle | E. An incorporated entity that issues shares of stock as evidence of ownership. |
| __C__ (9) Partnership | F. Initial recording of financial statement elements at acquisition cost. |
| __O__ (10) AICPA | G. An examination of the financial reports to ensure that they represent what they claim and conform with generally accepted accounting principles. |
| __L__ (11) FASB | |
| __H__ (12) CPA | H. Certified Public Accountant. |
| __B__ (13) Unit of measure | I. An unincorporated business owned by one person. |
| __N__ (14) GAAP | J. A report that describes the auditors' opinion of the fairness of the financial statement presentations and the evidence gathered to support that opinion. |
| __M__ (15) Publicly traded | K. Securities and Exchange Commission. |
| | L. Financial Accounting Standards Board. |
| | M. A company that can be bought and sold by investors on established stock exchanges. |
| | N. Generally accepted accounting principles. |
| | O. American Institute of Certified Public Accountants. |

**E1–2  Matching Financial Statement Items to Financial Statement Categories**

LO1

Procter & Gamble

According to its annual report, "Procter & Gamble markets a broad range of laundry, cleaning, paper, beauty care, health care, food and beverage products in more than 140 countries around the world, with leading brands including Tide, Ariel, Crest, Crisco, Vicks and Max Factor." The following are items taken from its recent balance sheet and income statement. Note that different companies use slightly different titles for the same item. Mark each item in the following list as an asset (A), liability (L), or stockholders' equity (SE) that would appear on the balance sheet or a revenue (R) or expense (E) that would appear on the income statement.

_____ (1) Accounts payable

_____ (2) Accounts receivable

_____ (3) Cash and cash equivalents

_____ (4) Cost of products sold

_____ (5) Property, plant, and equipment

_____ (6) Income taxes

_____ (7) Interest expense

_____ (8) Inventories

_____ (9) Land

_____ (10) Marketing, administrative, and other operating expenses

_____ (11) Long-term debt

_____ (12) Net sales

_____ (13) Notes payable

_____ (14) Retained earnings

_____ (15) Taxes payable

**E1–3  Matching Financial Statement Items to Financial Statement Categories**

LO1

Tootsie Roll

Tootsie Roll Industries is engaged in the manufacture and sale of candy. Major products include Tootsie Roll, Tootsie Roll Pops, Tootsie Pop Drops, Tootsie Flavor Rolls, Charms, and Blow-Pop lollipops. The following items were listed on Tootsie Roll's recent income statement and balance sheet. Mark each item from the balance sheet as an asset (A), liability (L), or shareholders' equity (SE) and each item from the income statement as a revenue (R) or expense (E).

_____ (1) Accounts payable

_____ (2) Accounts receivable

_____ (3) Cost of goods sold

_____ (4) Distribution and warehousing

_____ (5) Dividends payable

_____ (6) General and administrative

_____ (7) Income taxes payable

_____ (8) Inventories

_____ (9) Investments

_____ (10) Buildings

_____ (11) Cash and cash equivalents

_____ (12) Land

_____ (13) Machinery and equipment

_____ (14) Marketing, selling, and advertising

_____ (15) Net sales

_____ (16) Notes payable to banks

_____ (17) Provision for income taxes*

_____ (18) Retained earnings

---

*In the United States, "provision for income taxes" is most often used as a synonym for "income tax expense."

■ **LO1**

**E1–4**

Honda Motor Co.

**Preparing a Balance Sheet**

Established less than 50 years ago, Honda Motor Co., Ltd. of Japan is a leading international manufacturer of automobiles and the largest manufacturer of motorcycles in the world. As a Japanese company, it follows Japanese GAAP and reports its financial statements in millions of yen (the sign for yen is ¥). Its recent balance sheet contained the following items (in millions). Prepare a balance sheet as of March 31, 20A, solving for the missing amount.

| | |
|---|---:|
| Cash and cash equivalents | ¥ 150,554 |
| Contributed capital | 281,208 |
| Accounts payable and other current liabilities | 1,308,748 |
| Inventories | 606,689 |
| Investments | 212,294 |
| Long-term debt | 569,479 |
| Net property, plant, and equipment | 1,008,196 |
| Other assets | 213,845 |
| Other liabilities | 94,485 |
| Retained earnings | 755,419 |
| Total assets | 3,009,339 |
| Total liabilities and stockholders' equity | ? |
| Trade accounts, notes, and other receivables | 817,761 |

■ **LO1**

**E1–5**

**Completing a Balance Sheet and Inferring Net Income**

Terry Lloyd and Joan Lopez organized Read More Store as a corporation; each contributed $50,000 cash to start the business and received 4,000 shares of common stock. The store completed its first year of operations on December 31, 20A. On that date, the following financial items for the year were determined: December 31, 20A, cash on hand and in the bank, $48,900; December 31, 20A, amounts due from customers from sales of books, $26,000; unused portion of store and office equipment, $48,000; December 31, 20A, amounts owed to publishers for books purchased, $8,000; one-year note payable to a local bank for $2,000. No dividends were declared or paid to the stockholders during the year.

***Required:***

1. Complete the following balance sheet as of the end of 20A.
2. What was the amount of net income for the year? *12,780*

**Read More Store**
**Balance Sheet**
**At December 31, 20A**

| Assets | | Liabilities | |
|---|---:|---|---:|
| Cash | $48,900 | Accounts payable | $ 8000 |
| Accounts receivable | 26,000 | Note payable | 2000 |
| Store and office equipment | 48,000 | Interest payable | 120 |
| | | Total liabilities | $10,120 |
| | | **Stockholders' Equity** | |
| | | Contributed capital | $100,000 |
| | | *Lifelong earnings kept* → Retained earnings | 12,780 |
| | | Total stockholders' equity | 112,780 |
| | | Total liabilities and | |
| Total assets | $122,900 | stockholders' equity | $122,900 |

■ **LO1**

**E1–6**

**Analyzing Revenues and Expenses and Preparing an Income Statement**

Assume that you are the owner of The Collegiate Shop, which specializes in items that interest students. At the end of January 20A, you find (for January only) this information:

*a.* Sales, per the cash register tapes, of $120,000, plus one sale on credit (a special situation) of $1,000.

*b.* With the help of a friend (who majored in accounting), you determined that all of the goods sold during January had cost $40,000 to purchase.

*c.* During the month, according to the checkbook, you paid $38,000 for salaries, rent, supplies, advertising, and other expenses; however, you have not yet paid the $600 monthly utilities for January on the store and fixtures.

*Required:*

On the basis of the data given, what was the amount of income for January (disregard income taxes)? Show computations. (*Hint:* A convenient form to use has the following major side captions: Revenue from Sales, Expenses, and the difference—Net Income.)

**E1–7 Preparing an Income Statement and Inferring Missing Values**

■ **LO1**

Wal-Mart

Wal-Mart Stores, Inc., is the largest retail chain in the United States, operating more than 2,000 stores. Its recent quarterly income statement contained the following items (in thousands). Solve for the missing amounts and prepare a condensed income statement for the quarter ended October 31, 20A. (*Hint:* First order the items as they would appear on the income statement and then solve for the missing values.)

| | |
|---|---|
| Cost of sales | $16,200,873 |
| Interest costs | 184,190 |
| Net income | ? |
| Net sales | 20,417,717 |
| Operating, selling, and general and administrative expenses | 3,340,263 |
| Provision for income taxes* | 339,422 |
| Rental and other income | 235,116 |
| Total costs and expenses | ? |
| Total revenues | ? |
| Pretax income | ? |

**E1–8 Analyzing Revenues and Expenses and Completing an Income Statement**

■ **LO1**

Home Realty, Incorporated, has been operating for three years and is owned by three investors. J. Doe owns 60 percent of the total outstanding stock of 9,000 shares and is the managing executive in charge. On December 31, 20C, the following financial items for the entire year were determined: commissions earned and collected in cash, $150,000, plus $16,000 uncollected; rental service fees earned and collected, $20,000; salaries expense paid, $62,000; commissions expense paid, $35,000; payroll taxes paid, $2,500; rent paid, $2,200 $200/mo (not including December rent yet to be paid); utilities expense paid, $1,600; promotion and advertising paid, $8,000; income taxes paid, $18,500; and miscellaneous expenses paid, $500. There were no other unpaid expenses at December 31. Also during the year, the company paid the owners "out-of-profit" cash dividends amounting to $12,000. Complete the following income statement:

Home Realty, Incorporated
Income Statement
For the Year Ended December 31, 20C

| | |
|---|---|
| Revenues | |
| Commissions earned | $166,000 |
| Rental service fees | 20,000 |
| Total revenues | $186,000 |
| Expenses | |
| Salaries expense | $62,000 |
| Commission expense | 35,000 |
| Payroll tax expense | 2,500 |
| Rent expense | 2,400 |
| Utilities expense | 1,600 |
| Promotion and advertising expense | 8,000 |
| Miscellaneous expenses | 500 |
| Total expenses (excluding income taxes) | 112,000 |
| Pretax income | $74,000 |
| Income tax expense | 18,500 |
| Net income | $ 55,500 |

**E1–9 Inferring Values Using the Income Statement and Balance Sheet Equations**

■ **LO1**

Review the chapter explanations of the income statement and the balance sheet equations. Apply these equations in each independent case following to compute the two missing amounts for each case. Assume that it is the end of 20A, the first full year of operations for the

*In the United States, "provision for income taxes" is a common synonym for "income tax expense."

company. (*Hint:* Organize the listed items as they are presented in the balance sheet and income statement equations and then compute the missing amounts.)

| Independent Cases | Total Revenues | Total Expenses | Net Income (Loss) | Total Assets | Total Liabilities | Stockholders' Equity |
|---|---|---|---|---|---|---|
| A | $100,000 | $82,000 | $ | $150,000 | $70,000 | $ |
| B | | 80,000 | 12,000 | 112,000 | | 60,000 |
| C | 80,000 | 86,000 | | 104,000 | 26,000 | |
| D | 50,000 | | 13,000 | | 22,000 | 77,000 |
| E | | 81,000 | (6,000) | | 73,000 | 28,000 |

**LO1**  **E1–10**  **Preparing an Income Statement and Balance Sheet**

Clay Corporation was organized by five individuals on January 1, 20A. At the end of January 20A, the following monthly financial data are available:

| | |
|---|---|
| Total revenues | $130,000 |
| Total expenses (excluding income taxes) | 80,000 |
| Income tax expense (all unpaid as of January 31) | 15,000 |
| Cash balance, January 31, 20A | 30,000 |
| Receivables from customers (all considered collectible) | 15,000 |
| Merchandise inventory (by inventory count at cost) | 42,000 |
| Payables to suppliers for merchandise purchased from them (will be paid during February 20A) | 11,000 |
| Contributed capital (2,600 shares) | 26,000 |

No dividends were declared or paid during 20A.

*Required:*
Complete the following two statements:

**CLAY CORPORATION**
**Income Statement**
**For the Month of January 20A**

| | |
|---|---|
| Total revenues | $_____ |
| Less: Total expenses (excluding income tax) | _____ |
| Pretax income | _____ |
| Less: Income tax expense | _____ |
| Net income | $_____ |

**CLAY CORPORATION**
**Balance Sheet**
**At January 31, 20A**

**Assets**

| | |
|---|---|
| Cash | $_____ |
| Receivables from customers | _____ |
| Merchandise inventory | _____ |
| Total assets | $_____ |

**Liabilities**

| | |
|---|---|
| Payables to suppliers | $_____ |
| Income taxes payable | _____ |
| Total liabilities | _____ |

**Stockholders' equity**

| | | |
|---|---|---|
| Contributed capital | $_____ | |
| Retained earnings | _____ | |
| Total liabilities and stockholders' equity | | $_____ |

**E1–11** **Analyzing and Interpreting an Income Statement and Price/Earnings Ratio**
■ LO1

Pest Away Corporation was organized by three individuals on January 1, 20A, to provide insect extermination services. At the end of 20A, the following income statement was prepared:

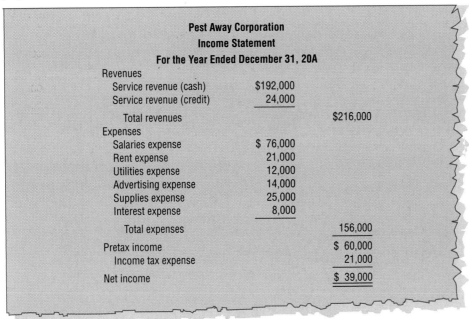

| Pest Away Corporation | | |
|---|---|---|
| Income Statement | | |
| For the Year Ended December 31, 20A | | |
| Revenues | | |
| Service revenue (cash) | $192,000 | |
| Service revenue (credit) | 24,000 | |
| Total revenues | | $216,000 |
| Expenses | | |
| Salaries expense | $ 76,000 | |
| Rent expense | 21,000 | |
| Utilities expense | 12,000 | |
| Advertising expense | 14,000 | |
| Supplies expense | 25,000 | |
| Interest expense | 8,000 | |
| Total expenses | | 156,000 |
| Pretax income | | $ 60,000 |
| Income tax expense | | 21,000 |
| Net income | | $ 39,000 |

*Required:*

1. What was the average monthly revenue amount?
2. What was the monthly rent amount?
3. Explain why supplies are reported as an expense.
4. Explain why interest is reported as an expense.
5. What was the average income tax rate for Pest Away Corporation?
6. Can you determine how much cash the company had on December 31, 20A? Explain.
7. If the company had a market value of $468,000, what is its price/earnings ratio?

**E1–12** **Focus on Cash Flows: Matching Cash Flow Statement Items to Categories**
■ LO1

Compaq Computer

Compaq Computer is a leading designer and manufacturer of personal computers. The following items were taken from its recent cash flow statement. Note that different companies use slightly different titles for the same item. Without referring to Exhibit 1.5, mark each item in the list as a cash flow from operating activities (O), investing activities (I), or financing activities (F). Also place parentheses around the letter only if it is a cash outflow.

_____ (1) Cash paid to suppliers and employees
_____ (2) Cash received from customers
_____ (3) Income taxes paid
_____ (4) Interest and dividends received
_____ (5) Interest paid
_____ (6) Proceeds from sale of investment in Conner Peripherals, Inc.
_____ (7) Purchases of property, plant, and equipment
_____ (8) Repayment of borrowings

**E1–13** **Preparing a Statement of Cash Flows**
■ LO1

NITSU Manufacturing Corporation is preparing the annual financial statements for the stockholders. A statement of cash flows must be prepared. The following data on cash flows were developed for the entire year ended December 31, 20D: cash inflow from operating revenues, $270,000; cash expended for operating expenses, $180,000; sale of unissued NITSU stock for cash, $30,000; cash dividends declared and paid to stockholders during the year, $22,000; and payments on long-term notes payable, $80,000. During the year, a tract of land was sold for $15,000 cash (which was the same price that NITSU had paid for the land in 20C), and $38,000 cash was expended for two new machines. The machines were used in the factory. The beginning-of-the-year cash balance was $63,000.

*Required:*

Prepare the statement of cash flows for 20D. Follow the format illustrated in the chapter.

■ LO1    E1–14    **Analyzing Cash Flows from Operations**

Paul's Painters, a service organization, prepared the following special report for the month of January 20A:

Service Revenue, Expenses, and Income

| | | |
|---|---:|---:|
| Service revenue | | |
|   Cash services (per cash register tape) | $105,000 | |
|   Credit services (per charge bills; not yet | | |
|     collected by end of January) | 30,500 | |
| | | $135,500 |
| Expenses: | | |
|   Salaries and wages expense (paid by check) | $ 50,000 | |
|   Salary for January not yet paid | 3,000 | |
|   Supplies used (taken from stock, purchased | | |
|     for cash during December) | 2,000 | |
|   Estimated cost of using company-owned truck | | |
|     for the month (called "depreciation") | 500 | |
|   Other expenses (paid by check) | 26,000 | 81,500 |
| Pretax income | | $ 54,000 |
|   Income tax expense (not yet paid) | | 13,500 |
| Income for January | | $ 40,500 |

*Required:*

1. The owner (who knows little about the financial part of the business) asked you to compute the amount by which cash had increased in January 20A from the operations of the company. You decided to prepare a detailed report for the owner with the following major side captions: Cash Inflows (collections), Cash Outflows (payments), and the difference—Net Increase (or decrease) in Cash.

2. See if you can reconcile the difference—net increase (or decrease) in cash—you computed in requirement (1) with the income for January 20A.

# PROBLEMS

■ LO1    P1–1    **Preparing an Income Statement and Balance Sheet** (AP1–1)

Assume that you are the president of Nuclear Company. At the end of the first year (December 31, 20A) of operations, the following financial data for the company are available:

| | |
|---|---:|
| Cash | $25,000 |
| Receivables from customers (all considered collectible) | 12,000 |
| Inventory of merchandise (based on physical count and priced at cost) | 90,000 |
| Equipment owned, at cost less used portion | 45,000 |
| Accounts payable owed to suppliers | 47,370 |
| Salary payable for 20A (on December 31, 20A, this was | |
|   owed to an employee who was away because of an emergency; | |
|   will return around January 10, 20B, at which time the payment | |
|   will be made) | 2,000 |
| Total sales revenue | 140,000 |
| Expenses, including the cost of the merchandise sold | |
|   (excluding income taxes) | 89,100 |
|   Income taxes expense at 30% × pretax income; all paid during 20A | ? |
| Contributed capital, 7,000 shares outstanding | 87,000 |
| No dividends were declared or paid during 20A. | |

*Required* (show computations):

1. Prepare a summarized income statement for the year 20A.

2. Prepare a balance sheet at December 31, 20A.

**P1–2 Analyzing a Student's Business and Preparing an Income Statement (AP1–2)**

■ **LO1**

During the summer between her junior and senior years, Susan Irwin needed to earn sufficient money for the coming academic year. Unable to obtain a job with a reasonable salary, she decided to try the lawn care business for three months. After a survey of the market potential, Susan bought a used pickup truck on June 1 for $1,500. On each door she painted "Susan's Lawn Service, Phone 471-4487." She also spent $900 for mowers, trimmers, and tools. To acquire these items, she borrowed $2,500 cash by signing a note payable promising to pay the $2,500 plus interest of $75 at the end of the three months (ending August 31).

At the end of the summer, Susan realized that she had done a lot of work, and her bank account looked good. This fact prompted her to become concerned about how much profit the business had earned.

A review of the check stubs showed the following: Bank deposits of collections from customers totaled $12,600. The following checks had been written: gas, oil, and lubrication, $920; pickup repairs, $210; mower repair, $75; miscellaneous supplies used, $80; helpers, $4,500; payroll taxes, $175; payment for assistance in preparing payroll tax forms, $25; insurance, $125; telephone, $110; and $2,575 to pay off the note including interest (on August 31). A notebook kept in the pickup, plus some unpaid bills, reflected that customers still owed her $800 for lawn services rendered and that she owed $200 for gas and oil (credit card charges). She estimated that the cost for use of the truck and the other equipment (called *depreciation*) for three months amounted to $500.

*Required:*

1. Prepare a quarterly income statement for Susan's Lawn Service for the months June, July, and August 20A. Use the following main captions: Revenues from Services, Expenses, and Net Income. Because this is a sole proprietorship, the company will not be subject to income tax.

2. Do you see a need for one or more additional financial reports for this company for 20A and thereafter? Explain.

**P1–3 Comparing Income with Cash Flow (A Challenging Problem)**

■ **LO1**

New Delivery Company was organized on January 1, 20A. At the end of the first quarter (three months) of operations, the owner prepared a summary of its operations as shown in the first row of the following tabulation:

| Summary of Transactions | Computation of | |
|---|---|---|
| | Income | Cash |
| *a.* Services performed for customers, $66,000, of which one-sixth remained uncollected at the end of the quarter. | +$66,000 | +$55,000 |
| *b.* Cash borrowed from the local bank, $30,000 (one-year note). | | |
| *c.* Small service truck purchased for use in the business: cost, $9,000; paid 30% down, balance on credit. | | |
| *d.* Expenses, $36,000, of which one-sixth remained unpaid at the end of the quarter. | | |
| *e.* Service supplies purchased for use in the business, $3,000, of which one-fourth remained unpaid (on credit) at the end of the quarter. Also, one-fifth of these supplies were unused (still on hand) at the end of the quarter. | | |
| *f.* Wages earned by employees, $21,000, of which one-half remained unpaid at the end of the quarter. | | |
| Based only on the above transactions, compute the following for the quarter: Income (or loss) Cash inflow (or outflow) | | |

*Required:*

1. For each of the six transactions given in this tabulation, enter what you consider the correct amounts. Enter a zero when appropriate. The first transaction is illustrated.

2. For each transaction, explain the basis for your dollar responses.

■ LO1    P1–4    **Evaluating Data to Support a Loan Application (A Challenging Problem)**

On January 1, 20A, three individuals organized West Company as a corporation. Each individual invested $10,000 cash in the business. On December 31, 20A, they prepared a list of resources owned (assets) and a list of the debts (liabilities) to support a company loan request for $70,000 submitted to a local bank. None of the three investors had studied accounting. The two lists prepared were as follows:

| Company resources | |
|---|---:|
| Cash | $ 12,000 |
| Service supplies inventory (on hand) | 7,000 |
| Service trucks (four practically new) | 68,000 |
| Personal residences of organizers (three houses) | 190,000 |
| Service equipment used in the business (practically new) | 30,000 |
| Bills due from customers (for services already completed) | 15,000 |
| Total | $322,000 |

| Company obligations | |
|---|---:|
| Unpaid wages to employees | $19,000 |
| Unpaid taxes | 8,000 |
| Owed to suppliers | 10,000 |
| Owed on service trucks and equipment (to a finance company) | 50,000 |
| Loan from organizer | 10,000 |
| Total | $ 97,000 |

*Required:*

Prepare a short memo indicating:

1. Which of these items do not belong on the balance sheet (bear in mind that the company is considered to be separate from the owners)?

2. What additional questions would you raise about measurement of items on the list? Explain the basis for each question.

3. If you were advising the local bank on its loan decision, which amounts on the list would create special concerns? Explain the basis for each concern and include any recommendations that you have.

4. In view of your response to (1) and (2), what do you think the amount of stockholders' equity (i.e., assets minus liabilities) of the company would be? Show your computations.

## ALTERNATE PROBLEMS

■ LO1    AP1–1    **Preparing an Income Statement and Balance Sheet (P1–1)**

Assume that you are the president of McClaren Corporation. At the end of the first year (June 30, 20C) of operations, the following financial data for the company are available:

| | |
|---|---:|
| ✓ Cash | $13,150 |
| ✓ Receivables from customers (all considered collectible) | 9,500 |
| ✓ Inventory of merchandise (based on physical count and priced at cost) | 57,000 |
| ✓ Equipment owned, at cost less used portion | 36,000 |
| ✓ Accounts payable owed to suppliers | 31,500 |
| ✓ Salary payable for 20C (on June 30, 20C, this was owed to an employee who was away because of an emergency; will return around July 7, 20C, at which time the payment will be made) | 1,500 |
| Total sales revenue | 90,000 |
| Expenses, including the cost of the merchandise sold (excluding income taxes) | 60,500 |
| Income taxes expense at 30% × pretax income; all paid during 20C | ? |
| ✓ Contributed capital, 5,000 shares outstanding | 62,000 |
| No dividends were declared or paid during 20C. | |

*Required* (show computations):

1. Prepare a summarized income statement for the year 20C.

2. Prepare a balance sheet at June 30, 20C.

**AP1–2  Analyzing a Student's Business and Preparing an Income Statement** (P1–2)

■ LO1

Upon graduation from high school, John Abel immediately accepted a job as an electrician's assistant for a large local electrical repair company. After three years of hard work, John received an electrician's license and decided to start his own business. He had saved $12,000, which he invested in the business. First, he transferred this amount from his savings account to a business bank account for Abel Electric Repair Company, Incorporated. His lawyer had advised him to start as a corporation. He then purchased a used panel truck for $9,000 cash and secondhand tools for $1,500; rented space in a small building; inserted an ad in the local paper; and opened the doors on October 1, 20A. Immediately, John was very busy; after one month, he employed an assistant.

Although John knew practically nothing about the financial side of the business, he realized that a number of reports were required and that costs and collections had to be controlled carefully. At the end of the year, prompted in part by concern about his income tax situation (previously he had to report only salary), John recognized the need for financial statements. His wife Jane developed some financial statements for the business. On December 31, 20A, with the help of a friend, she gathered the following data for the three months just ended. Bank account deposits of collections for electric repair services totaled $32,000. The following checks had been written: electrician's assistant, $8,500; payroll taxes, $175; supplies purchased and used on jobs, $9,500; oil, gas, and maintenance on truck, $1,200; insurance, $700; rent, $500; utilities and telephone, $825; and miscellaneous expenses (including advertising), $600. Also, uncollected bills to customers for electric repair services amounted to $3,000. The $200 rent for December had not been paid. The average income tax rate is 30 percent. John estimated that the cost of using on the truck and tools (depreciation) during the three months to be $1,200.

*Required:*

1. Prepare a quarterly income statement for Abel Electric Repair for the three months October through December 20A. Use the following main captions: Revenue from Services, Expenses, Pretax Income, and Net Income. (*Hint*: Complete the statement through the caption Pretax Income and multiply that amount by the tax rate to compute Income Tax Expense.)

2. Do you think that John may have a need for one or more additional financial reports for 20A and thereafter? Explain.

# CASES AND PROJECTS

## FINANCIAL REPORTING AND ANALYSIS CASES

**CP1–1  Finding Financial Information**

■ LO1, 3

American Eagle
Outfitters

Refer to the financial statements of American Eagle Outfitters in Appendix B at the end of this book, or open file AEOS10K.doc in the S&P directory on the student CD-ROM.

**STANDARD
&POOR'S**

*Required:*

1. What is the amount of net income for the current year?

2. What amount of revenue was earned in the current year?

3. How much inventory does the company have at the end of the current year?

4. By what amount did cash and cash equivalents* change during the year?

5. Who is auditor for the company?

**CP1–2  Finding Financial Information**

■ LO1, 3

Urban Outfitters

Refer to the financial statements of Urban Outfitters in Appendix C at the end of this book, or open file URBN10-K.doc in the S&P directory on the student CD-ROM.

**STANDARD
&POOR'S**

*Required:*

Read the annual report. Look at the income statement, balance sheet, and cash flow statement closely and attempt to infer what kinds of information they report. Then answer the following questions based on the report.

*Cash equivalents* are short-term investments readily convertible to cash whose value is unlikely to change.

1. What types of products does it sell?
2. Did the chief executive officer (CEO) believe that the company had a good year?
3. On what day of the year does its fiscal year end?
4. For how many years does it present complete
    - *a.* Balance sheets?
    - *b.* Income statements?
    - *c.* Cash flow statements?
5. Are its financial statements audited by independent CPAs? How do you know?
6. Did its total assets increase or decrease over the last year?
7. What was the ending balance of inventories?
8. Write out its basic accounting (balance sheet) equation in dollars at year-end.

 **LO1**    **CP1–3**

American Eagle
Outfitters vs.
Urban Outfitters

**STANDARD
&POOR'S**

### Comparing Companies Within an Industry

Refer to the financial statements of American Eagle Outfitters given in Appendix B and Urban Outfitters given in Appendix C and the Standard and Poor's Industry Ratio Report given in Appendix D at the end of this book, or open file CP1-3.xls in the S&P directory on the student CD-ROM.

*Required:*

1. Both companies report "basic" earnings per share on their income statements and the market price per share of their stock in a note near the end of the annual report. Using current year's earnings per share and the highest stock price per share reported for the last quarter of the most recent year, compute the price/earnings ratio. Which company provided the highest price/earnings ratio for the current year?
2. Which company do investors believe will have the higher growth in earnings in the future?
3. Examine the Standard and Poor's Industry Ratio Report. Compare the price/earnings ratio for each company to the industry average. Did you expect these two companies, which are relative newcomers to the industry, to have price/earnings ratios above or below the industry average? Why?

**LO1**    **CP1–4**

### Using Financial Reports: Identifying and Correcting Deficiencies in an Income Statement and Balance Sheet

Performance Corporation was organized on January 1, 20A. At the end of 20A, the company had not yet employed an accountant; however, an employee who was "good with numbers" prepared the following statements at that date:

**PERFORMANCE CORPORATION**
**December 31, 20A**

| | |
|---|---:|
| Income from sales of merchandise | $175,000 |
| Total amount paid for goods sold during 20A | (90,000) |
| Selling costs | (25,000) |
| Depreciation (on service vehicles used) | (10,000) |
| Income from services rendered | 52,000 |
| Salaries and wages paid | (62,000) |

**PERFORMANCE CORPORATION**
**December 31, 20A**

| | |
|---|---:|
| **Resources** | |
| Cash | $ 32,000 |
| Merchandise inventory (held for resale) | 42,000 |
| Service vehicles | 50,000 |
| Retained earnings (profit earned in 20A) | 30,000 |
|   Grand total | $154,000 |
| **Debts** | |
| Payables to suppliers | $ 22,000 |
| Note owed to bank | 25,000 |
| Due from customers | 13,000 |
|   Total | $ 60,000 |

| Supplies on hand (to be used in rendering services) | $15,000 | |
| Accumulated depreciation* (on service vehicles) | 10,000 | |
| Contributed capital, 6,500 shares | 65,000 | |
| Total | | 90,000 |
| Grand total | | $150,000 |

*Required:*

1. List all the deficiencies that you can identify in these statements. Give a brief explanation of each one.

2. Prepare a proper income statement (correct net income is $30,000) and balance sheet (correct total assets are $142,000).

**CP1–5  Using Financial Reports: Applying the Balance Sheet Equation to Liquidate a Company**   ■ **LO1**
On June 1, 20F, Bland Corporation prepared a balance sheet just prior to going out of business. The balance sheet totals showed the following:

| | |
| Assets (no cash) | $90,000 |
| Liabilities | 50,000 |
| Stockholders' equity | 40,000 |

Shortly thereafter, all of the assets were sold for cash.

*Required:*

1. How would the balance sheet appear immediately after the sale of the assets for cash for each of the following cases? Use the format given here.

| | | Balances Immediately after Sale | | | | |
| | Cash Received for the Assets | Assets | − | Liabilities | = | Stockholders' Equity |
| --- | --- | --- | --- | --- | --- | --- |
| Case A | $ 90,000 | $_____ | | $_____ | | $_____ |
| Case B | 80,000 | $_____ | | $_____ | | $_____ |
| Case C | 100,000 | $_____ | | $_____ | | $_____ |

2. How should the cash be distributed in each separate case? (*Hint:* Creditors must be paid in full before owners receive any payment.) Use the format given here:

| | To Creditors | To Stockholders | Total |
| --- | --- | --- | --- |
| Case A | $_____ | $_____ | $_____ |
| Case B | $_____ | $_____ | $_____ |
| Case C | $_____ | $_____ | $_____ |

## CRITICAL THINKING CASES

**CP1–6  Making Decisions as a Manager: Reporting the Assets and Liabilities of a Business**   ■ **LO1, 3**
Elizabeth Watkins owns and operates Liz's Boutique (a sole proprietorship). An employee prepares a financial report for the business at each year-end. This report lists all of the resources (assets) owned by Watkins, including such personal items as the home she owns and occupies. It also lists all of the debts of the business, but not her personal debts.

*Required:*

1. From the accounting point of view, in what ways do you disagree with what is being included in and excluded from the report of business assets and liabilities?

2. Upon questioning, Watkins responded, "Don't worry about it; we use it only to support a loan from the bank." How would you respond to this comment?

---

*Accumulated depreciation* represents the used portion of the asset and should be subtracted from the asset balance.

**LO3**    **CP1–7**

### Making Decisions as an Owner: Deciding about a Proposed Audit

You are one of three partners who own and operate Mary's Maid Service. The company has been operating for seven years. One of the other partners has always prepared the company's annual financial statements. Recently you proposed that the statements be audited each year because it would benefit the partners and preclude possible disagreements about the division of profits. The partner who prepares the statements proposed that his Uncle Ray, who has a lot of financial experience, can do the job and at little cost. Your other partner remained silent.

*Required:*

1. What position would you take on the proposal? Justify your response.
2. What would you strongly recommend? Give the basis for your recommendation.

**LO3, 4**    **CP1–8**

### Evaluating an Ethical Dilemma: Ethics and Auditor Responsibilities

A key factor that an auditor provides is independence. The *AICPA Code of Professional Conduct* states that "a member in public practice should be independent in fact and appearance when providing auditing and other attestation service."

*Required:*

Do you consider the following circumstances to suggest a lack of independence? Justify your position. (Use your imagination. Specific answers are not provided in the chapter.)

1. Jack Jones is a partner with a large audit firm and is assigned to the Ford audit. Jack owns 10 shares of Ford.
2. Jane Winkler has invested in a mutual fund company that owns 500,000 shares of Sears stock. She is the auditor of Sears.
3. Bob Franklin is a clerk/typist who works on the audit of AT&T. He has just inherited 50,000 shares of AT&T stock. (Bob enjoys his work and plans to continue despite his new wealth.)
4. Nancy Sodoma worked on weekends as the controller for a small business that a friend started. Nancy quit the job in midyear and now has no association with the company. She works full-time for a large CPA firm and has been assigned to do the audit of her friend's business.
5. Mark Jacobs borrowed $100,000 for a home mortgage from First City National Bank. The mortgage was granted on normal credit terms. Mark is the partner in charge of the First City audit.

## FINANCIAL REPORTING AND ANALYSIS PROJECTS

**LO1, 3**    **CP1–9**

### Broadening Financial Research Skills

Acquire the annual report of a public company you find interesting. We suggest you pick a company of local interest or a company whose products or services you often purchase. Library files, the SEC EDGAR service at www.sec.gov, Compustat CD, or the company's website are good sources. The Annual Report Gallery at www.reportgallery.com provides links to the websites of well-known companies.

*Required:*

Read the annual report. Look at the income statement, balance sheet, and cash flow statement closely and attempt to infer what kinds of information they report. Then answer the following questions based on the report.

1. What types of products or services does it sell?
2. Did the chief executive officer (CEO) believe that the company had a good year?
3. On what day of the year does its fiscal year end?
4. For how many years does it present complete
   *a.* Balance sheets?
   *b.* Income statements?
   *c.* Cash flow statements?
5. Are its financial statements audited by independent CPAs? How do you know?
6. Did its total assets increase or decrease over the last year?

7. What was the ending balance of inventories?

8. Write out its basic accounting (balance sheet) equation in dollars at year-end.

**CP1–10 Broadening Financial Research Skills**
Acquire the annual report of a public company you find interesting. We suggest you pick a company of local interest or a company whose products or services you often purchase. Library files, the SEC EDGAR service at www.sec.gov, Compustat CD, or the company's website are good sources. The Annual Report Gallery at www.reportgallery.com provides links to the websites of well-known companies.

■ **LO1, 3**

*Required:*

1. What is the amount of net income for the current year?

2. What amount of revenue was earned in the current year?

3. How much long-term debt does the company have at the end of the current year?

4. By what amount did cash and cash equivalents* change during the year?

5. Who is auditor for the company?

**CP1–11 Interpreting the Financial Press: Price/Earnings Ratio for Disk-Drive Companies from** *The Wall Street Journal*
Three of the largest producers of disk drives are Seagate Technology, Inc., Quantum Corporation, and Western Digital Corporation. All are public companies: Seagate and Western Digital are traded on the New York Stock Exchange and Quantum on the NASDAQ National Market. Obtain a recent copy of *The Wall Street Journal* from your library or a newsstand. Section C, "Money & Investing," lists a variety of facts about each of these companies. The column headings of the stock listing identify each of the listed facts. A box normally printed at the bottom of one of the early pages in the section "Explanatory Notes" explains the information provided.

■ **LO1**

The Wall Street Journal

*Required:*
Find the listing for one of the three disk drive companies. Then answer the following questions (refer to the "Explanatory Notes" box as necessary):

1. What was the closing price for one share of the stock?

2. What was the price/earnings (PE) ratio? (If the symbol "cc" or "dd" was reported, what does that mean?)

**CP1–12 Using Financial Reports: Cash Flow Statement**
Acquire the annual report of a company you find interesting. We suggest you pick a company of local interest or a company whose products or services you often purchase. (Library files, the SEC EDGAR service at www.sec.gov, Compustat CD, or the company's website are good sources.)

■ **LO1**

*Required:*
Look at the cash flow statement closely. Then answer the following questions based on the report.

1. Was cash flow from operating activities equal to net income? What causes the difference? (*Hint:* Consider the difference between cash inflows and outflows and revenues and expenses.)

2. List and explain two items listed under Cash Flows from Investing Activities and Cash Flows from Financing Activities.

**CP1–13 Evaluating an Ethical Dilemma: Analysis of an Accounting Irregularity**
Obtain a recent news story outlining an accounting irregularity. (Library files, *Wall Street Journal Index*, *Dow Jones Interactive*, and *Bloomberg Business News* are good sources. Search for the term *accounting irregularities*.) Write a short memo outlining the effect of the irregularity on reported net income, the impact of the announcement of the irregularity on the company's stock price, and any fines or civil penalties against the company and its officers.

■ **LO3, 4**

---

*Cash equivalents* are short-term investments readily convertible to cash whose value is unlikely to change.

■ **LO1, 3**

**CP1–14**

**Team Project: Examining an Annual Report**

As a team, select an industry to analyze. MarketGuide provides lists of industries and their makeup at <u>www.marketguide.com/mgi/INDUSTRY/INDUSTRY.html</u>. Each group member should acquire the annual report or 10-K for one publicly traded company in the industry, with each member selecting a different company. (Library files, the SEC EDGAR service at <u>www.sec.gov</u>, Compustat CD, or the company's website are good sources. The Annual Report Gallery at <u>www.reportgallery.com</u> provides links to the websites of well-known companies.) On an individual basis, each group member should write a short report answering the following questions about the selected company.

1. What types of products or services does it sell?
2. On what day of the year does its fiscal year end?
3. For how many years does it present complete
   *a.* Balance sheets?
   *b.* Income statements?
   *c.* Cash flow statements?
4. Are its financial statements audited by independent CPAs? If so, by whom?
5. Did its total assets increase or decrease over the last year?
6. Did its net income increase or decrease over the last year?

Discuss any patterns that you as a team observe. Then, as a team, write a short report comparing and contrasting your companies using the six attributes listed above.

# Investing and Financing Decisions and the Balance Sheet

## CHAPTER TWO

---

LEARNING **OBJECTIVES**

*After studying this chapter, you should be able to:*

1. Define the objective of financial reporting, the elements of the balance sheet, and the related key accounting assumptions and principles.   p. 53

2. Identify what constitutes a business transaction and identify common balance sheet account titles used in business.   p. 58

3. Apply transaction analysis to simple business transactions in terms of the accounting model: Assets = Liabilities + Stockholders' Equity.   p. 60

4. Determine the impact of business transactions on the balance sheet using two basic tools: journal entries and T-accounts.   p. 66

5. Prepare and analyze a simple balance sheet.   p. 72

6. Compute and interpret the financial leverage ratio.   p. 73

7. Identify investing and financing transactions and how they are reported on the statement of cash flows.   p. 74

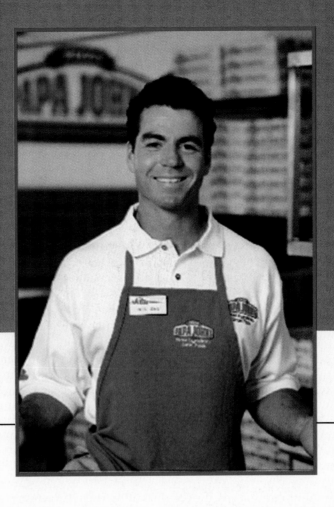

Although it is one-fifth the size of industry leader Pizza Hut, Papa John's shows it knows how to fight the battle "to become the No. 1 pizza brand in the world," taking on Pizza Hut as its primary target. *Time* magazine reports: "Papa John's scares Pizza Hut. That's because, since 1993, for every point Pizza Hut has lost in market share, Papa John's has gained one . . . So far, nothing Pizza Hut has tried has slowed Papa John's."*

FOCUS **COMPANY:**

# Papa John's International

### EXPANSION STRATEGY IN THE "PIZZA WARS"

In the pizza segment of the highly competitive restaurant business, Papa John's was ranked fourth in sales behind giants Pizza Hut, Domino's, and Little Caesars at the start of 1999. With more than 2,000 restaurants in the United States and international markets, the company has grown at a tremendous rate since its beginnings in 1983 when John Schnatter, founder and chief executive officer, knocked down walls in a broom closet where he was tending bar to install a pizza oven.

Ten years later, Papa John's became a public company with stock trading on the NASDAQ exchange (under the symbol PZZA). The company's balance sheets for two recent years (in thousands of dollars†) highlight its growth:

*John Greenwald, "Slice, Dice and Devour," *Time* magazine, October 26, 1998. © 1998 Time Inc. Reprinted by permission.

†These totals are rounded amounts from the actual financial statements for the respective years. Amounts used in illustrations throughout Chapters 2, 3, and 4 are realistic estimates of actual monthly amounts, which are not publicly available.

| | Assets | = | Liabilities | + | Stockholders' Equity |
|---|---|---|---|---|---|
| End of 1998 | $319,300 | | $56,600 | | $262,700 |
| End of 1997 | 253,200 | | 40,500 | | 212,700 |
| Change | + $ 66,100 | | + $16,100 | | + $ 50,000 |
| Percentage increase | 26% | | 40% | | 24% |

The company's plans were to add 400 new restaurants to the chain in 1999. The Pizza Wars continue.

## BUSINESS BACKGROUND

Pizza is a global commodity, generating more than $21 billion in sales annually. The business depends heavily on human capital, and companies can utilize high-technology marketing to compete. Papa John's strategy is to offer "Better Ingredients. Better Pizza." To do so requires an almost fanatical focus on testing ingredients and checking product quality, right down to the size of the black olive and fat content in the mozzarella cheese and meats. The company also keeps operations simple, offering a focused menu of pizza, breadsticks, cheesesticks, and soft drinks for pick-up or delivery.

To control quality consistency and increase efficiency, the company builds regional commissaries that make the dough and sell it to the stores. Building commissaries, opening new company-owned stores, and selling franchises explain most of the growth in Papa John's assets and liabilities from year to year.

To understand how the results of Papa John's growth strategy is communicated in the financial statements, we must answer the following questions:

- What business activities cause changes in balance sheet amounts from one period to the next?
- How do specific activities affect each of the balances?
- How do companies keep track of these balance sheet amounts?

Once we have answered these questions, we will be able to perform two key analytical tasks:

1. To analyze and predict the effects of our business decisions on our company's financial statements.
2. To use financial statements of other companies to identify and evaluate activities that other managers engaged in during a past period. These latter inferences are a key to *financial statement analysis.*

In this chapter, we focus on typical asset acquisition activities (often called *investing activities*) in which Papa John's engages, along with the related *financing activities* such as borrowing funds from creditors and receiving funds from investors to acquire the assets. We examine activities affecting only balance sheet amounts; we discuss operating activities affecting both income statement and balance sheet amounts in Chapters 3 and 4. Although these activities are all related, we separate them initially to aid your understanding.

**ORGANIZATION** OF THE CHAPTER

| • Overview of the Conceptual Framework | • What Business Activities Cause Changes in Financial Statement Amounts? | • How Do Transactions Affect Accounts? | • How Do Companies Keep Track of Account Balances? | • Balance Sheet Preparation |
|---|---|---|---|---|
| Elements of the Balance Sheet | Nature of Business Transactions | Transaction Analysis | The Direction of Transaction Effects and the Debit-Credit Framework | The Financial Leverage Ratio |
| | Accounts | | Analytical Tool The Journal Entry | Some Misconceptions |
| | | | Analytical Tool The T-Account | |
| | | | Transaction Analysis Illustrated | |

Let us begin our answers to the three questions by returning to the basic concepts introduced in Chapter 1.

# OVERVIEW OF THE CONCEPTUAL FRAMEWORK

We defined many key accounting terms and concepts in Chapter 1. These are part of a framework of accounting theory developed over many years and synthesized by the Financial Accounting Standards Board (FASB) in a series of publications called *FASB Statements of Financial Accounting Concepts*. These Statements make up the conceptual framework of accounting outlined in Exhibit 2.1 and will be discussed in each of the next four chapters (the relevant chapter is indicated beside each term or concept). An understanding of the accounting concepts will be helpful as you study. It is much easier to learn and remember *how* the accounting process works if you know *why* it works a certain way. A clear understanding will also help you in future chapters as we examine more complex business activities.

■ **LEARNING OBJECTIVE 1**

Define the objective of financial reporting, the elements of the balance sheet, and the related key accounting assumptions and principles.

## CONCEPTS EMPHASIZED IN CHAPTER 2

**Objective of Financial Reporting**    The top of the pyramid in Exhibit 2.1 indicates the **primary objective of external financial reporting,** which guides the remaining sections of the conceptual framework. The primary objective of financial accounting is to provide useful economic information about a business to help external parties, primarily investors and creditors, make sound financial decisions. The users of accounting information are identified as *decision makers*. These decision makers include average investors, creditors, and experts who provide financial advice. They are all expected to have a reasonable understanding of accounting concepts and procedures (this may be one of the reasons you are studying accounting). Of course, as we discussed in Chapter 1, many other groups, such as suppliers and customers, also use external financial statements.

The **PRIMARY OBJECTIVE OF EXTERNAL FINANCIAL REPORTING** is to provide useful economic information about a business to help external parties make sound financial decisions.

Users usually are interested in information to assist them in projecting a business's future cash inflows and outflows. For example, creditors and potential creditors need to assess an entity's ability to pay interest over time and pay back the principal on the loan. Investors and potential investors want to assess the entity's ability to pay dividends in the future. They also want to judge how successful the company might be so that the stock price rises and investors can then sell the stock for more than was paid.

EXHIBIT **2.1**

**Financial Accounting and Reporting Conceptual Framework**

**PRIMARY OBJECTIVE OF EXTERNAL FINANCIAL REPORTING** [Ch. 2]

To provide useful economic information to external users for decision making (for assessing future cash flows)

**QUALITATIVE CHARACTERISTICS OF FINANCIAL INFORMATION** [Ch. 5]

To be useful, information should possess:

**Relevancy**—be capable of making a difference in decisions
- Predictive value (extrapolate into the future)
- Feedback value (assess prior expectations)
- Timeliness (available to help with decisions)

**Reliability**—can be relied upon
- Verifiability (can be verified independently)
- Representational faithfulness (represents reality)
- Neutrality (unbiased)

Information should also be
**Comparable** across companies
**Consistent** over time

**ELEMENTS OF FINANCIAL STATEMENTS**

**Asset**—economic resource with probable future benefits. [Ch. 2]

**Liability**—probable future sacrifices of economic resources. [Ch. 2]

**Stockholders' Equity**—financing provided by owners and operations (residual interest to owners). [Ch. 2]

**Revenue**—increase in assets or settlement of liabilities from ongoing operations. [Ch. 3]

**Expense**—decrease in assets or increase in liabilities from ongoing operations. [Ch. 3]

**Gain**—increase in assets or settlement of liabilities from peripheral activities. [Ch. 3]

**Loss**—decrease in assets or increase in liabilities from peripheral activities. [Ch. 3]

**ASSUMPTIONS**

- **Separate entity**—activities of the business are separate from activities of the owners. [Ch. 2]

- **Continuity** (going concern)—entity will not go out of business in the near future. [Ch. 2]

- **Unit of measure**—accounting measurements will be in the national monetary unit. [Ch. 2]

- **Time period**—the long life of a company can be reported over a series of shorter time periods. [Ch. 3]

**PRINCIPLES**

- **Historical cost**—cash equivalent price on the transaction date is used initially to measure elements. [Ch. 2]

- **Revenue recognition**—record when *measurable, realizable* (transaction takes place and high probability of collection) and *earned* (substantially accomplished what is necessary to be entitled to benefits). [Ch. 3]

- **Matching**—record when expenses are incurred to generate revenues. [Ch. 3]

- **Full disclosure**—provide information sufficiently important to influence a decision (e.g., notes). [Ch. 5]

**CONSTRAINTS** [Ch. 5]

- **Cost benefit**—benefits to users should outweigh costs of providing information.

- **Materiality**—relatively small amounts not likely to influence decisions are to be recorded in the most cost-beneficial way.

- **Industry practices**—industry-specific measurements and reporting deviations may be acceptable.

- **Conservatism**—exercise care not to overstate assets and revenues or understate liabilities and expenses.

**SEPARATE-ENTITY ASSUMPTION** states that business transactions are separate from the transactions of the owners.

**UNIT-OF-MEASURE ASSUMPTION** states that accounting information should be measured and reported in the national monetary unit.

**CONTINUITY (GOING-CONCERN) ASSUMPTION** states that businesses are assumed to continue to operate into the foreseeable future.

**Underlying Assumptions of Accounting**   The assumptions of accounting are primarily based on the business environment in which accounting operates. They reflect the scope of accounting and the expectations that set certain limits on the way accounting information is reported. Three of these assumptions were discussed in Chapter 1. Under the **separate-entity assumption,** each business must be accounted for as an individual organization, separate and apart from its owners, all other persons, and other entities. Under the **unit-of-measure assumption,** each business entity accounts for and reports its financial results primarily in terms of the national monetary unit (dollars in the United States, yen in Japan, francs in France, etc.).

For accounting purposes, a business normally is assumed to continue operating long enough to meet contractual commitments and plans. This **continuity assumption** is sometimes called the *going-concern assumption* because we expect a business to continue to operate into the foreseeable future. Violation of this assumption means that assets and liabilities can be valued and reported on the balance sheet as if the company were to be liquidated (that is, discontinued with all assets sold and all debts paid). In all future chapters, unless indicated otherwise, we assume that businesses meet the continuity assumption.

As discussed in Chapter 1, assets, liabilities, and shareholders' equity are the key elements of a corporation's balance sheet. Let's review the definitions.

## ELEMENTS OF THE BALANCE SHEET

**Assets** are probable future economic benefits owned or controlled by the entity as a result of past transactions. In other words, these are the resources the entity has that it can use to operate in the future. When reporting conservative information to users, managers use judgment (and past experience) to determine the most likely future benefit. For example, a company may have a list of customers who owe $10,000. However, history suggests that only $9,800 will be collected. The lower, more probable figure is reported to users for projecting future cash flows.

Exhibit 2.2 presents the balance sheet of Papa John's International with amounts rounded to the nearest hundred thousand dollars. Notice that Papa John's year ends on the last Sunday in December, which in 1997 was December 28 and in 1998 was December 27. The choice of year-ends will be discussed in Chapter 4.

Assets are usually listed on the balance sheet *in order of liquidity*. Notice that several of the assets are categorized as **current assets**. Current assets are those resources that Papa John's will use or turn into cash within one year. Note that inventory is always considered a current asset, regardless of how long it takes to produce and sell the inventory. As indicated in Papa John's simplified balance sheet in Exhibit 2.2, its current assets include cash and cash equivalents (very short-term investments), accounts receivable (due from franchisees and others on account), inventories (of food, beverages, and paper supplies), prepaid expenses (such as rent paid in advance of the use of a building), and other current assets (a number of current assets with smaller balances).

All other assets are considered long term, to be used or turned into cash beyond the coming year. For Papa John's, that includes investments (marketable securities such as

**ASSETS** are probable future economic benefits owned by the entity as a result of past transactions.

**CURRENT ASSETS** are assets that will be used or turned into cash within one year. Inventory is always considered a current asset regardless of the time needed to produce and sell it.

| PAPA JOHN'S INTERNATIONAL, INC. AND SUBSIDIARIES<br>Consolidated Balance Sheets<br>(dollars in thousands) | | |
|---|---|---|
| | December 27,<br>1998 | December 28,<br>1997 |
| **Assets** | | |
| Current assets: | | |
| Cash and cash equivalents | $ 34,000 | $ 18,700 |
| Accounts receivable | 17,300 | 15,100 |
| Inventories | 9,700 | 9,100 |
| Prepaid expenses | 4,800 | 2,500 |
| Other current assets | 2,100 | 3,800 |
| **Total current assets** | 67,900 | 49,200 |
| Investments | 47,300 | 57,900 |
| Net property and equipment | 169,200 | 112,600 |
| Notes receivable | 12,500 | 15,100 |
| Other assets | 22,400 | 18,400 |
| **Total assets** | $319,300 | $253,200 |
| **Liabilities and stockholders' equity** | | |
| Current liabilities: | | |
| Accounts payable | $ 18,100 | $ 15,100 |
| Accrued expenses payable | 25,500 | 15,100 |
| Other current liabilities | — | 100 |
| **Total current liabilities** | 43,600 | 30,300 |
| Unearned franchise and development fees | 6,600 | 4,600 |
| Other long-term liabilities | 6,400 | 5,500 |
| Stockholders' equity: | | |
| Contributed capital | 164,500 | 149,700 |
| Retained earnings | 98,200 | 63,100 |
| **Total stockholders' equity** | 262,700 | 212,800 |
| **Total liabilities and stockholders' equity** | $319,300 | $253,200 |

stocks and bonds Papa John's purchased as investments of excess cash), net property and equipment, notes receivable from franchisees, and other assets (a number of assets with smaller balances that total the amount presented).

# FINANCIAL ANALYSIS

## UNRECORDED BUT VALUABLE ASSETS

Managers and analysts use the balance sheet as a basis for managing the company's assets and for valuing the firm. At the same time, they recognize that often a company's most valuable assets are not even listed on the balance sheet (they have no "book value").* One such asset is a firm's trademark or brand name. General Electric's balance sheet reveals no listing for the GE trademark. Its book value is zero because it was developed internally over time (created through research, development, and advertising); there was no identifiable exchange transaction (it was not purchased). Many valuable intangible assets, such as trademarks, patents, and copyrights that are developed inside the company, have no book value.

This same asset recognition rule (that assets are recorded at cost based on an exchange with an external party) suggests the circumstances in which trademarks and brand names are reported on the balance sheet. Several years ago, GE sold its television business to a French company, Thomson SA, which is the world's largest producer of televisions. Since the Thomson brand name has no value in the United States, it also purchased the right to use GE's trademark for 10 years at a cost of 250 million French francs (approximately $50 million). Thomson's balance sheet lists GE's trademark, which was initially recorded at its acquisition cost of 250 million francs.

*Book value is the amount reported on the balance sheet that is usually an asset's original acquisition cost minus amounts used in past operations.

**LIABILITIES** are probable debts or obligations of the entity that result from past transactions, which will be paid with assets or services.

**Liabilities** are an entity's probable debts or obligations that result from its past transactions, which will be paid with assets or services. Those entities that a company owes money to are called *creditors*. Creditors usually receive payment of the amount owed and sometimes interest on those amounts. Papa John's balance sheet includes five liabilities: Accounts Payable, Accrued Expenses Payable (a summary of payroll, rent, and other obligations), Unearned Franchise and Development Fees (amounts paid to Papa John's by franchisees who have not yet received promised services), and Other Long-Term Liabilities. These and other liabilities will be discussed in subsequent chapters.

**CURRENT LIABILITIES** are obligations that will be paid in cash (or other current assets) or satisfied by providing service within the coming year.

Liabilities are listed on the balance sheet *in order of maturity* (how soon an obligation is to be paid). Those liabilities that Papa John's will need to pay (in cash, services, or other current assets) within the coming year are classified as **current liabilities**. Providing information on current assets and current liabilities to external users of the financial statements assists them in assessing the amounts and timing of future cash flows. Most corporations separately report current assets and liabilities, even though classifying them as such is not required.

# A QUESTION OF ETHICS

## ENVIRONMENTAL LIABILITIES

Due to changing legal requirements and concerns for social responsibility, companies are facing significant pressure to estimate and disclose environmental liabilities, such as the cleanup of hazardous waste sites. Determining the amounts and likelihood of environmental obligations, though, can be very difficult. Effective in 1996, the AICPA issued its position on environmental accounting issues, stating that the probability criterion is met if the Environmental Protection Agency (EPA) has decided or probably will decide that a company must clean up a contaminated site.

"Once a liability is identified, its magnitude must be estimated. . . . Uncertainty about the magnitude of the liability should not keep a company from recognizing its best estimate of the liability, if the liability is probable and can be estimated within a range."* Past estimates of total costs to clean up air emissions, water quality, and remove asbestos exceed $250 billion per year (or approximately 2–5 percent of the gross domestic product). Given the significant magnitude of these issues, the accounting profession will need to continue to address the challenges of identifying, estimating, and reporting environmental liabilities.

*J. A. Hochman, "Cleaning Up Environmental Accounting," *National Public Accountant*, June 1998, pp. 20–23.

**Stockholders' equity (owners' equity or shareholders' equity)** is the financing provided by the owners and the operations of the business. **Contributed capital** results from owners providing cash (and sometimes other assets) to the business. When this occurs, we often say that owners invest in the business, or the company sells or issues its stock to owners. The major investor in Papa John's International, Inc., is John Schnatter, founder and CEO, who owns approximately 23 percent of the stock. Putnam Investments Inc. and FMR Corporation of Boston together own another 20 percent of the stock, with corporate employees, directors, and the general public owning the rest of the company. Owners invest (or buy stock) in a company in the hope of receiving two types of cash flows: dividends, which are a distribution of a company's earnings (a return on the shareholders' investment), and gains from selling their stock in the company for more than they paid (known as *capital gains*).

Earnings that are not distributed to the owners and are reinvested in the business by management are called **retained earnings**.[1] A look at Papa John's balance sheet (Exhibit 2.2) indicates that its growth has been financed by substantial reinvestment of earnings in the business; 37 percent of Papa John's stockholders' equity is retained earnings ($98,200 Retained Earnings ÷ $262,700 Total Stockholders' Equity).

**STOCKHOLDERS' EQUITY (OWNERS' EQUITY OR SHAREHOLDERS' EQUITY)** is the financing provided by the owners and the operations of business.

**CONTRIBUTED CAPITAL** results from owners providing cash (and sometimes other assets) to the business.

**RETAINED EARNINGS** refers to the cumulative earnings of a company that are not distributed to the owners and are reinvested in the business.

## FINANCIAL **ANALYSIS**

### GROWTH THROUGH FRANCHISING

Franchises are contracts in which a franchisor (in this case Papa John's) provides rights to franchisees (the restaurant operators) to sell or distribute a specific line of products or provide a particular service. The franchisees in return usually pay initial fees to obtain the franchise and make annual payments to receive ongoing services from the franchisor (such as accounting, advertising, and training assistance). Examples of other well-known franchises are Holiday Inn, McDonald's, and Dairy Queen.

About 75 percent of Papa John's stores are franchises. The company provides on-going management training, marketing, site selection, and restaurant design assistance. Franchisees must purchase dough and spice mix from Papa John's commissaries and equipment and supplies from the company or approved suppliers. Papa John's also monitors franchised operations to ensure adherence to company standards.

Papa John's does not include assets and liabilities of franchisees in its balance sheet in Exhibit 2.2. These would be included in the franchisees' financial statements.

**Basic Accounting Principle** The **historical cost principle** states that the cash-equivalent cost needed to acquire the asset on the date of the acquisition (the historical cost) should be used for initially recognizing (recording) all financial statement

The **COST PRINCIPLE** requires assets to be recorded at the historical cash-equivalent cost, which on the date of the transaction is cash paid plus the current dollar value of all noncash considerations also given in the exchange.

[1]Retained earnings can increase only from profitable operations. In addition, as we will learn in Chapter 3, a company's annual income from operations is usually not equal to the net cash flows for the year.

elements. Under the cost principle, cost is measured on the date of the transaction as the cash paid plus the current dollar value of all noncash considerations (any assets, privileges, or rights) also given in the exchange. For example, if you trade your computer plus cash for a new car, the cost of the new car is equal to the cash paid plus the market value of the computer. Thus, in most cases, cost is relatively easy to determine and can be verified. A disadvantage is that, subsequent to the date of acquisition, the continued use of historical cost on the balance sheet does not reflect any changes in market value.

Now that we have reviewed several of the basic accounting concepts and terms, we need to understand the economic activities of a business that result in changes in amounts reported in financial statements and the process used in generating the financial statements.

## WHAT BUSINESS ACTIVITIES CAUSE CHANGES IN FINANCIAL STATEMENT AMOUNTS?

### NATURE OF BUSINESS TRANSACTIONS

**■ LEARNING OBJECTIVE 2**

Identify what constitutes a business transaction and identify common balance sheet account titles used in business.

A **TRANSACTION** is (1) an exchange between a business and one or more external parties to a business or (2) a measurable internal event such as *adjustments* for the use of assets in operations.

Accounting focuses on certain events, although not all events, that have an economic impact on the entity. Those events that are recorded as a part of the accounting process are called **transactions.** The first step in translating the results of business events to financial statement numbers is determining which events are and are not reflected in the statements. Note that the definitions of *assets* and *liabilities* indicate that only economic resources and debts *resulting from past transactions* are recorded on the balance sheet. A broad definition includes two types of transactions:

1. *External events:* These are *exchanges* of assets and liabilities between the business and one or more other parties. Examples include the purchase of a machine, the sale of merchandise, the borrowing of cash, and the investment in the business by the owners. These types of transactions will be discussed in this chapter as they affect the balance sheet elements and in Chapter 3 as they affect the income statement elements.

2. *Internal events:* These are certain events that are not exchanges between the business and other parties but have a direct and measurable effect on the accounting entity. Examples include losses due to fire or other natural disasters and *adjustments* such as those to record the use of property, plant, and equipment in operations and

interest expense on money that was borrowed. Adjustments will be discussed in Chapter 4.

Throughout this textbook, the word *transaction* will be used in the broad sense to include both types of events.

At the same time, some important events that have an economic impact on the company are not reflected in Papa John's statements. In most cases, signing a contract, which involves no cash, goods, services, or property changing hands, is not considered to be a transaction because it involves only the exchange of promises, not of assets or liabilities. For example, if Papa John's hires a new regional manager and signs an employment contract, no transaction occurs from an accounting perspective because no exchange of assets or liabilities has occurred. Each party to the contract has made promises (the manager agrees to work; Papa John's agrees to pay in exchange for the manager's work). For each day the new manager works, however, the exchange of services by the employee results in a transaction that Papa John's must record (as an obligation to pay the manager's salary).

## ACCOUNTS

An **account** is a standardized format that organizations use to accumulate the dollar effects of transactions on each financial statement item. The resulting balances are kept separate for financial statement purposes. Each company must establish a chart of accounts to facilitate recording transactions. A *chart of accounts* is the list of all the account names, usually organized by financial statement element. That is, asset accounts are listed first (such as Cash, Inventory, Accounts Receivable, Equipment, and Land) followed by liability accounts (such as Accounts Payable, Notes Payable, and Taxes Payable), stockholders' equity accounts (Contributed Capital and Retained Earnings), revenue accounts (such as Sales Revenue), and expense accounts (such as Payroll Expense). The account names listed here are quite common and are used by most companies.

The chart of accounts also lists a unique number for each account that is used when entering data into the accounting system. For example, 1-111 could be the account number for Cash, 1-146 for Supplies Inventory, 2-221 for Long-Term Notes Payable, 3-111 for Contributed Capital, 4-235 for Rent Revenue, and 5-138 for Salaries Expense. In formal recordkeeping systems including computerized accounting systems, using appropriate account numbers is important.

The accounts you see in the financial statements are actually summations (or aggregations) of a number of more detailed accounts in a company's accounting system. For example, Papa John's keeps separate inventory accounts for paper supplies, food, and beverages but combines them as Inventories on the balance sheet. Since our aim is to understand financial statements, we focus on aggregated accounts as presented in the statements.

An **ACCOUNT** is a standardized format that organizations use to accumulate the dollar effects of transactions on each financial statement item.

# INTERNATIONAL **PERSPECTIVE**

## UNDERSTANDING THE MEANING OF ACCOUNT TITLES IN FOREIGN FINANCIAL STATEMENTS

Chapter 1 states that differences in the political, cultural, and economic environment of other countries have produced significant variations in accounting and reporting rules. Foreign companies often use different account titles than U.S. companies use. Some also use additional accounts for financial statement items not normally reported under U.S. accounting rules. For example, the Australian company, The News Corporation Limited, headed by K. Rupert Murdoch, follows A-GAAP (Australian generally accepted accounting principles). The principal activities of The News Corporation Limited include printing and publishing books, newspapers, and magazines, television broadcasting, and film production and distribution. U.S. corporations included in the news group include Fox Broadcasting Company and Twentieth Century

*The News Corporation Limited*

Fox Film Corporation. The titles of accounts in a recent financial report are similar to those used by U.S. companies, except for liabilities and stockholders' equity:

| Australian Accounts | U.S. Equivalents |
| --- | --- |
| **Liabilities** | |
|    Borrowings | Similar to Notes and Bonds Payable |
|    Creditors | Relates to what is owed to suppliers and others, similar to Accounts Payable |
|    Provision | A summary of payables for income tax, dividends, payroll, and other liabilities |
| **Shareholders' Equity** | |
|    Share Capital | Similar to Contributed Capital |
|    Retained Profits | Similar to Retained Earnings |

Every company has a different chart of accounts, depending on the nature of its business activities. For example, a small lawn care service may have an asset account called Lawn Mowing Equipment, but it is unlikely that General Motors would need such an account. These differences will become more apparent as we examine the balance sheets of many various companies.

Because each company has a different chart of accounts, you should *not* try to memorize a typical chart of accounts. When you prepare homework problems, either you will be given the account names the company uses or you should select appropriate descriptive names. Once a name is selected for an account, the exact name must be used in all transactions that affect the account.

## SELF-STUDY **QUIZ**

*Wendy's International*

The following is a list of accounts from a recent Wendy's International, Inc., balance sheet. Indicate on the line provided whether each of the following is an asset (A), liability (L), or stockholders' equity account (SE).

L Salaries and Wages Payable      L Long-Term Capital Lease Obligations

A Buildings      A Restaurant Equipment

A Notes Receivable      SE Retained Earnings

L Accounts and Drafts Payable      A Short-Term Investments

After you have completed the schedules, check your solutions with the answers in the footnote at the bottom of the page.*

## HOW DO TRANSACTIONS AFFECT ACCOUNTS?

**■ LEARNING OBJECTIVE 3**

Apply transaction analysis to simple business transactions in terms of the accounting model: Assets = Liabilities + Stockholders' Equity.

Managers make business decisions that often result in transactions affecting financial statements. Typical decisions are to expand the number of stores, advertise a new product, change employee benefit packages, and invest excess cash. Keeping a historical record (like a diary of important events) allows managers to evaluate the effects of past decisions and plan future business activities. In planning, managers are interested in how the implementation of their plans (their decisions) will be reflected on the financial statements. For example, the decision to purchase additional inventory for cash in anticipation of a major sales initiative increases the inventory and decreases cash. If the demand for the inventory does not occur, a lower cash balance reduces the company's

---

*Column 1: L; A; A; L. Column 2: L; A; SE; A.

flexibility and ability to pay other obligations. Business decisions often involve an element of risk that should be assessed. Therefore, it is necessary for business managers to understand how transactions impact the accounts on the financial statements. The process for determining the effects of transactions is called *transaction analysis* and is discussed next.

## TRANSACTION ANALYSIS

**Transaction analysis** is the process of studying a transaction to determine its economic effect on the entity in terms of the accounting equation (also known as the *accounting model*). We will outline the process in this section of the chapter and create a visual tool representing the process (the transaction analysis model). The basic accounting equation and two principles are the foundation for the transaction analysis model. You will recall from Chapter 1 that the basic accounting equation for a business organized as a corporation is as follows:

> **TRANSACTION ANALYSIS** is the process of studying a transaction to determine its economic effect on the business in terms of the accounting equation.

> ### Assets (A) = Liabilities (L) + Stockholders' Equity (SE)

The two principles underlying the transaction analysis process follow:

1.  Every transaction affects at least two accounts (duality of effects); it is critical to identify correctly the accounts affected and the direction of the effect (increase or decrease).
2.  The accounting equation must remain in balance after each transaction.

Success in performing transaction analysis depends on a clear understanding of how the transaction analysis model is constructed based on these concepts. Study this material well. You should not move on to a new concept until you understand and can apply all prior concepts. Now let's create the transaction analysis model from these basic principles.

**Duality of Effects** The first concept is that every transaction has *at least two effects* on the basic accounting equation. This is known as the *duality of effects*. (From this duality concept we have developed what is known as the *double-entry system* of recordkeeping.) Most transactions with external parties involve an *exchange* by which the business entity both gives up something and receives something in return. For example, suppose that Papa John's purchased some paper napkins (inventory) for cash.

| Transaction | Papa John's Received | Papa John's Gave |
|---|---|---|
| Purchased paper napkins for cash | Inventory | Cash |

In analyzing this transaction, we determined that the appropriate accounts affected were Inventory and Cash. Identifying the appropriate accounts affected and the direction of the effect on each is critical in transaction analysis. In the exchange, Papa John's received inventory (an increase in an asset) and gave up cash in return (a decrease in an asset).

As we discussed in Chapter 1, however, most inventory is purchased on credit (money is owed to suppliers). In this case, Papa John's engages in *two* transactions: (1) the purchase of an asset on credit and (2) the eventual payment. In the first, it receives inventory (an increase in an asset) and in return gives a promise to pay later called *accounts payable* (an increase in a liability). In the second, Papa John's eliminates (receives back) its promise to pay, accounts payable (a decrease in a liability), and gives up cash (a decrease in an asset).

| Transactions | Papa John's Received | Papa John's Gave |
|---|---|---|
| (1) Purchased paper napkins on credit | Inventory | Accounts payable (a promise to pay) |
| (2) Paid on its accounts payable | Accounts payable (the promise was reduced) | Cash |

As noted earlier, not all important business activities result in a transaction that affects the financial statements. Most important, signing a contract involving the exchange of two promises to perform does not result in an accounting transaction that is recorded. For example, consider the case in which Papa John's and Xerox sign an agreement with Xerox promising to provide repair service on Papa John's copy machines at a price of $50 for each visit during the next year and Papa John's promising to pay for the service when Xerox provides it. No accounting transaction has taken place here because Papa John's and Xerox have exchanged only promises. Any time Xerox provides service, however, a transaction occurs since service has been exchanged for a promise to pay.

Similarly, if Papa John's sent an order to its paper supplier for more napkins and the supplier accepted the order, which will be filled next week, no transaction has taken place for accounting purposes. Only two promises have been exchanged. From the supplier's perspective, the same holds true. No transaction has taken place, so the supplier's financial statements are unaffected. As soon as the goods are shipped to Papa John's, however, the supplier has given up inventory in exchange for a promise from Papa John's to pay for them, and Papa John's has exchanged its promise to pay for the goods that it received as ordered. Now *one promise* has been exchanged for *goods*, so a transaction has taken place, and both Papa John's and the supplier's statements will be affected.

**Balancing the Accounting Equation**    The accounting equation must remain in balance after each transaction. Total assets must equal total liabilities and stockholders' equity. If all of the correct accounts have been identified, and the appropriate direction of the effect on each account has been determined, the equation should remain in balance. Therefore, in performing the transaction analysis process, you should complete the following steps in this order:

1. *Accounts and effects*
   a. **Identify the accounts affected**, making sure that the duality principle is met (at least two accounts change). Ask yourself what is given and what is received.
   b. **Classify each account** as an asset (A), liability (L), or stockholders' equity (SE).
   c. **Determine the direction of the effect** (amount of increase [+] or decrease [−] on each A, L, and/or SE).

2. *Balancing*
   d. **Determine that the accounting equation (A = L + SE) remains in balance.**

Let us consider typical transactions of Papa John's, Inc., and most other businesses, as examples to illustrate the use of this process. As we stated earlier, only transactions affecting balance sheet accounts are presented in this chapter. Assume that Papa John's has the following transactions during January 1999 (the month following the balance sheet in Exhibit 2.2). The month will end on the last Sunday in January, which will be January 31. The chart of accounts to be used here and in Chapters 3 and 4 is provided in Exhibit 2.3. Remember that all amounts are in *thousands of dollars*:

EXHIBIT **2.3**

**Papa John's Chart of Accounts**

| Chart of Accounts (to be used in our Papa John's example) | To account for |
|---|---|
| **Assets (A)** | |
| Cash | — Cash on hand |
| Accounts Receivable | — Amounts owed by customers, franchisees, and affiliates |
| Inventories | — Food and paper products supplies on hand |
| Prepaid Expenses | — Benefits or rights to be received in the future (e.g., insurance coverage, rent) |
| Other Current Assets | — Summary of a number of accounts with smaller balances (current in nature) |
| Investments | — Amounts invested in securities of other entities |
| Property and Equipment | — The cost of land, buildings, and equipment to be used in operations in the future |
| Accumulated Depreciation | — The amount of buildings and equipment used to date |
| Notes Receivable | — Funds lent to others (e.g., affiliates, employees) |
| Other Assets | — Summary of a number of accounts with smaller balances (long term in nature) |
| **Liabilities (L)** | |
| Accounts Payable | — Amount owed to suppliers (e.g., for food deliveries, for utility usage) |
| Accrued Expenses Payable | — Amount to be paid to others (e.g., wages to employees, interest on debt) |
| Other Current Liabilities | — Summary of a number of accounts with smaller balances (current in nature) |
| Unearned Franchise and Development Fees | — Amount of future service owed by Papa John's to franchisees |
| Notes Payable | — Amounts borrowed from banks |
| Other Long-Term Liabilities | — Summary of a number of accounts with smaller balances (long term in nature) |
| **Stockholders' Equity (SE)** | |
| Contributed Capital | — Amount investors paid for the company's stock when issued by the company |
| Retained Earnings | — Accumulated net income not distributed to shareholders as dividends |
| **Revenues and Gains (R)** | |
| Restaurant Sales Revenue | — Sales of food service to customers |
| Franchise Related Revenue | — Amounts earned from franchisees through the franchise agreement |
| Commissary and Other Sales | — Amounts earned from selling dough, other pizza ingredients, and equipment |
| Investment Income | — Amounts earned on investments (e.g., dividends and interest) |
| **Expenses and Losses (E)** | |
| Cost of Sales | — Amount of food and paper products used to generate revenues |
| Salaries Expense | — Amount earned by the employees for work performed to generate revenues |
| Advertising Expense | — Amount incurred for advertising and promotions to generate revenues |
| Occupancy Expense | — Amount incurred for renting leased facilities during the period |
| General and Administrative Expense | — Amount of insurance and utilities used during the period |
| Depreciation Expense | — Estimated amount of buildings and equipment used during the period |
| Income Tax Expense | — Amount incurred on income generated during the period |

*(a)* **Papa John's issues $1,300 of additional common stock to new investors for cash.**

| 1. Identify and classify accounts and effects. | *Cash (A) is received + $1,300.* <br> *Additional stock certificates are given,* <br> *Contributed Capital (SE) + $1,300.* |
|---|---|
| 2. Is the accounting equation in balance? | *Yes. There is a $1,300 increase on the left side and a $1,300 increase on the right side of the equation.* |

| | Assets | = | Liabilities | + | Stockholders' Equity |
|---|---|---|---|---|---|
| | **Cash** | | | | **Contributed Capital** |
| *(a)* | +1,300 | = | | | +1,300 |

*(b)* **The company borrows $1,000 from its local bank, signing a promissory note to be paid in one year.**

| 1. Identify and classify accounts and effects. | *Cash (A) is received + $1,000.*<br>*A written promise to pay is given to the bank, Notes Payable (L) + $1,000.* |
| --- | --- |
| 2. Is the accounting equation in balance? | *Yes. There is a $1,000 increase on the left side and a $1,000 increase on the right side of the equation.* |

| | Assets | = | Liabilities | + | Stockholders' Equity |
| --- | --- | --- | --- | --- | --- |
| | **Cash** | | **Notes Payable** | | **Contributed Capital** |
| (a) | +1,300 | = | | | +1,300 |
| (b) | +1,000 | = | +1,000 | | |

Transactions *(a)* and *(b)* are *financing* transactions. Companies that need cash for *investing* purposes (to buy or build additional facilities as part of their plans for growth) often seek funds by selling stock to investors, as in Transaction *(a)* or borrowing from creditors, usually banks, as in Transaction *(b)*. *Operating* transactions also affect cash available to the business; this type of transaction will be discussed in Chapter 3.

*(c)* **For expansion, Papa John's opened eight new company-owned restaurants. The company purchased $5,700 of new ovens, counters, refrigerators, and other equipment (property and equipment), paying $1,500 in cash and the rest on a note payable to the equipment manufacturer in 60 days.**

| 1. Identify and classify accounts and effects. | *Property and Equipment (A) is received +$5,700.*<br>*Cash (A) −$1,500 is given and a written promise to pay is also given to the manufacturer, Notes Payable (L) +$4,200.* |
| --- | --- |
| 2. Is the accounting equation in balance? | *Yes, there is a $4,200 increase on the left side of the equation and a $4,200 increase on the right side.* |
| Notice that more than two accounts were affected by this transaction. | |

| | Assets | | = | Liabilities | + | Stockholders' Equity |
| --- | --- | --- | --- | --- | --- | --- |
| | **Cash** | **Property and Equipment** | | **Notes Payable** | | **Contributed Capital** |
| (a) | +1,300 | | = | | | +1,300 |
| (b) | +1,000 | | = | +1,000 | | |
| (c) | −1,500 | +5,700 | = | +4,200 | | |

The analysis of Transactions *(d)* through *(f)* follows. The effects are listed in the chart at the end of the Self-Study Quiz. For Transactions *(g)* and *(h)*, space is left on the chart for your answers to the quiz that follows Transaction *(f)*.

*(d)* **Papa John's lends $450 to new franchisees who sign notes agreeing to repay the loan in six months. The franchisees open 25 new restaurants.**

| 1. Identify and classify accounts and effects. | *Cash (A) is given −$450.*<br>*Written promises from the franchisees are received, Notes Receivable (A) +$450.* |
| --- | --- |
| 2. Is the accounting equation in balance? | *Yes. The equation remains the same because assets increase and decrease by the same amount.* |

*(e)* **Papa John's purchases $3,000 of stock in other companies as an investment.**

| 1. Identify and classify accounts and effects. | *Cash (A) is given −$3,000.*<br>*Stock certificates from the other companies are received, Investments (A) +$3,000.* |
| --- | --- |

| 2. Is the accounting equation in balance? | *Yes. The equation remains the same because assets increase and decrease by the same amount.* |
|---|---|

**(f)** **Papa John's board of directors has not declared dividends for shareholders. However, for illustration purposes, we will assume that the first dividend for $200 is declared and paid.**

| 1. Identify and classify accounts and effects. | *Cash (A) is given −$200.*  *In this transaction, earnings retained in the business are distributed to investors, Retained Earnings (SE) −$200.* |
|---|---|
| 2. Is the accounting equation in balance? | *Yes. There is a $200 decrease on the left side of the equation and a $200 decrease on the right side.* |

### SELF-STUDY **QUIZ**

The most effective way to develop your transaction analysis skills is to practice with many transactions. Therefore, beginning with the analysis in Transactions (*a*) through (*f*), complete the transaction analysis steps and following chart for Transactions (*g*) and (*h*). The key is repeating the steps until they become a natural part of your thought process.

**(g)** **Papa John's collects $500 cash on notes receivable from a number of franchisees. (*Hint:* Think about what is received and what is given back.)**

1. Identify and classify accounts and effects.
2. Is the accounting equation in balance?

**(h)** **Papa John's paid $400 on the promissory note owed to the local bank.**

1. Identify and classify accounts and effects.
2. Is the accounting equation in balance?

Complete the following chart.

| | Assets | | | | = | Liabilities | + | Stockholders' Equity | |
|---|---|---|---|---|---|---|---|---|---|
| | Cash | Investments | Property and Equipment | Notes Receivable | | Notes Payable | | Contributed Capital | Retained Earnings |
| (a) | +1,300 | | | | = | | | +1,300 | |
| (b) | +1,000 | | | | = | +1,000 | | | |
| (c) | −1,500 | | +5,700 | | = | +4,200 | | | |
| (d) | −450 | | | +450 | = | | | | |
| (e) | −3,000 | +3,000 | | | = | | | | |
| (f) | −200 | | | | = | | | | −200 |
| (g) | +500 | | | −500 | = | | | | |
| (h) | −400 | | | | = | −400 | | | |

After you have completed the schedule, check your solution with the answers in the footnote at the bottom of the page.*

---

*(*g*) Cash (A) is received +$500. The franchisees' written promises to pay are "given back" (paid off), Notes Receivable (A) −$500. The equation remains the same because assets increase and decrease by the same amount.

(*h*) Cash (A) is given −$400. Papa John's written promise to the bank is "given back" (paid off), Notes Payable −$400. There is a $400 decrease on the left side of the equation and a $400 decrease on the right side.

If your answers did not agree with ours, we recommend that you go back to each transaction to make sure that you have completed each of the steps for each transaction.

■ **LEARNING OBJECTIVE 4**

Determine the impact of transaction analysis using two basic tools: journal entries and T-accounts.

# HOW DO COMPANIES KEEP TRACK OF ACCOUNT BALANCES?

Because companies have significantly more transactions every day than those illustrated, recording transaction effects and keeping track of account balances in the manner used in the preceding illustration is impractical for most organizations. We will now expand the transaction analysis model and develop two very important tools that aid in reflecting the results of transaction analysis and performing other financial analysis tasks: journal entries and T-accounts.

These analytical tools are more efficient mechanisms for reflecting the effects of transactions and for determining account balances for financial statement preparation. These efficiencies are important from the standpoint of accounting systems design. As future business managers, you should develop your understanding and use of these tools in financial analysis. For those studying accounting, this knowledge is the foundation for understanding the accounting system and future coursework. After we learn to perform transaction analysis using these tools, we will illustrate their use in financial analysis.

## THE DIRECTION OF TRANSACTION EFFECTS AND THE DEBIT-CREDIT FRAMEWORK

As discussed earlier, assets, liabilities, and stockholders' equity account balances increase and decrease from the effects of transactions. To learn how to reflect the effects efficiently, the transaction analysis model first needs to be structured in a manner that shows the *direction* of the effects. This direction rule is critical for constructing the model as a tool for transaction analysis. The model follows. Notice

- The increase symbol + is written on the left when we are on the left side of the accounting equation and on the right when we are on the right side of the accounting equation.

**DEBIT** means the left side of an account.

- The concepts of *debit* and *credit* are now added to the model. **Debit** means the left side of an account, and **credit** means the right. We shorten the term debit to "dr" and credit to "cr."

**CREDIT** means the right side of an account.

The transaction analysis model now is constructed as shown in Exhibit 2.4.

EXHIBIT **2.4**

**Transaction Analysis Model**

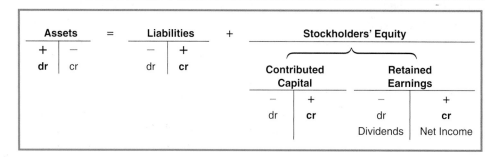

From this transaction analysis model, we can observe the following:

- Asset accounts have debit balances (their positive, or increase, side).
- Liabilities and stockholders' equity accounts have credit balances (their positive, or increase, side).

As we illustrated earlier for Transactions (*a*) through (*h*), each account (such as Cash and Notes Payable) in each of these categories can be increased (+) or decreased (−) by transactions, and each account has a balance. You may have noticed that no transactions affected net income under the Retained Earnings account in our illustration. We will introduce operating activities in Chapter 3. *As you are learning to perform transaction analysis, you should refer to this model often until you can construct it on your own without assistance.* We build on this model in Chapter 3 when we add transactions affecting operations.

Many students have trouble with accounting because they forget that the only meaning for *debit* is the left side of an account and the only meaning for *credit* is the right side of an account. Perhaps someone once told you that you were a credit to your school or your family. As a result, you may think that there is "goodness" attached to credits and perhaps a "badness" attached to debits. Such is not the case. Just remember that *debit means left* and *credit means right.*

It also should be easy to remember which accounts that debits increase and which accounts that credits increase. A debit (left) increases asset accounts because assets are on the left side of the accounting equation (A = L + SE). A credit (right) increases liability and stockholders' equity accounts because they are on the right side of the accounting equation.

If the correct accounts and effects have been identified through transaction analysis, the accounting equation will remain in balance. What will also be true is that *the total dollar value of all debits equals the total dollar value of all credits* in a transaction. Therefore, this equality check (Debits = Credits) should be added to the transaction analysis process.

## ANALYTICAL TOOL: THE JOURNAL ENTRY

In a bookkeeping system, transactions are initially recorded in chronological order in a *journal* (see our website at mhhe.com/business/accounting/libby3 (Appendix E) for an illustration of formal recordkeeping procedures). After analyzing the business documents that describe a transaction, the bookkeeper prepares the formal entry in the journal. Using debits and credits, the bookkeeper writes a journal entry for each transaction. The **journal entry** is an accounting method for expressing the effects of a transaction on accounts in a debits-equal-credits format. The journal entry for Transaction (c) in the Papa John's illustration is as follows:

A **JOURNAL ENTRY** is an accounting method for expressing the effects of a transaction on accounts in a debits-equal-credits format.

| (date or reference) | Property and equipment (+A) ......... | 5,700 | |
|---|---|---|---|
| | Cash (−A) ..................... | | 1,500 |
| | Notes payable (+L) ............. | | 4,200 |

Notice the following:

- Including a date or some form of reference for each transaction is useful.

- The debits are written first (on top); the credits are written below all of the debits and are indented to the right (both words and amounts). The order of the debits or credits doesn't matter, as long as the debits are on top and the credits are on the bottom and indented.

- Total debits ($5,700) equal total credits ($1,500 + $4,200).

- Any journal entry that affects more than two accounts is called a *compound entry.* Three accounts are affected by this transaction. Although this is the only transaction in the preceding illustration that affects more than two accounts, many transactions in future chapters will require a compound journal entry.

While you are learning to perform transaction analysis, use the symbols A, L, and SE next to each account title, as is done in the preceding journal entry, including all homework problems. Specifically identifying accounts as assets (A), liabilities (L), or stockholders' equity (SE) makes using the transaction analysis model clearer and journal entries easier. In the next few chapters, we will also include the direction of the effect with the symbol. For example, if Cash is to be increased, we will write Cash (+A).

We have found that many students try to memorize journal entries without understanding or using the transaction analysis model. The task becomes increasingly more difficult as new detailed transactions are presented in subsequent chapters. However, *memorizing, understanding, and using the transaction analysis model* presented and *following the steps in the transaction analysis process* will work for any transaction, including those in future chapters.

### ANALYTICAL TOOL: THE T-ACCOUNT

After the journal entries have been recorded, the bookkeeper posts (transfers) the dollar amounts to each account that was affected by the transaction to determine account balances. In most computerized accounting systems, this happens automatically upon recording the journal entry. As a group, the accounts are called a *ledger*. In a manual accounting system used by some small organizations, the ledger is often a three-ring binder with a separate page for each account. In a computerized system, accounts are stored on a disk.

The **T-ACCOUNT** is a tool for summarizing transaction effects for each account, determining balances, and drawing inferences about a company's activities.

Journal entries by themselves do not provide balances in accounts. One very useful tool for summarizing transaction effects and determining balances for individual accounts is called a **T-account,** which is a simplified representation of a ledger account.

The T-accounts for the Cash and Notes Payable accounts for Papa John's, based on Transactions (*a*) through (*h*) are presented in Exhibit 2.5. Notice that, for Cash, which is classified as an asset, increases are on the left and decreases are on the right side of the T-account. For Notes Payable, however, increases are on the right and decreases are on the left since the account is a liability. Also notice that the ending balance is indicated on the positive side and is double-underlined.

Handwritten or manually maintained accounts in the T-account format shown here may be used in small businesses. Computerized systems retain the concept of the account but not the T-account format.

EXHIBIT **2.5**

**T-Accounts Illustrated**

| | + Cash (A) – | | | – Notes Payable (L) + | |
|---|---|---|---|---|---|
| Beginning balance | 34,000 | | | Beginning balance | 0 |
| (a) | 1,300 | (c) 1,500 | –400 { (h) 400 | (b) | 1,000 |
| (b) | 1,000 | (d) 450 | | (c) | 4,200 |
| (g) | 500 | (e) 3,000 | | | |
| | | (f) 200 | | | |
| | | (h) 400 | | | |
| Ending balance | 31,250 | | | Ending balance | 4,800 |

+2,800 { (a)(b)(g)   −5,550 (c–h)   +5,200   

T-accounts can be written as equations that yield balances for financial statement purposes:

| | Beginning balance | + "+" side | – "–" side | = Ending balance |
|---|---|---|---|---|
| Cash | $34,000 | + 2,800 | – 5,550 | = $31,250 |
| Notes Payable | $   0 | + 5,200 | – 400 | = $ 4,800 |

The words *debit* and *credit* are used as verbs, nouns, and adjectives. For example, we can say that (1) Papa John's Cash account was debited (verb) when stock was issued to investors; (2) to credit (verb) an account means to put the amount on the right side of the T-account; (3) a debit (noun) is the left side of an account; and (4) Notes Payable is a credit account (adjective). These terms will be used instead of *left* and *right* throughout the rest of the textbook. The next section illustrates the steps you should follow in using the model to analyze the effects of transactions, record the effects in journal entries, and determine account balances by using T-accounts.

## TRANSACTION ANALYSIS ILLUSTRATED

The typical monthly transactions of Papa John's presented earlier will be used to demonstrate transaction analysis and the use of journal entries and T-accounts. We analyze each transaction, checking that the accounting equation remains in balance and debits equal credits. In the T-accounts, located together at the end of the illustration, the amounts from Papa John's December 27, 1998, balance sheet have been inserted as the beginning balances in each account. After reviewing or preparing each journal entry, trace the effects to the appropriate T-accounts using the transaction letters as a reference. The first transaction has been highlighted for you.

*You should study this illustration carefully* (including the explanations of transaction analysis). Careful study of the illustration is *essential* to the understanding of (1) the accounting model, (2) transaction analysis, (3) recording the dual effects of each transaction, and (4) the dual-balancing system. The most effective way to learn these critical concepts that affect material throughout the rest of the text is to practice, practice, practice.

*(a)* **Papa John's issues $1,300 of additional common stock to new investors for cash.**

| | | |
|---|---|---|
| Cash (+A) .................................. | 1,300 | |
| Contributed capital (+SE) ............... | | 1,300 |

| Assets | = | Liabilities | + | Stockholders' Equity | |
|---|---|---|---|---|---|
| Cash +1,300 | | | | Contributed capital | +1,300 |

Equality checks: (1) Debits $1,300 = Credits $1,300; (2) the accounting equation is in balance.

These effects were posted to the appropriate T-accounts at the end of the illustration (see the shaded amounts). To post, transfer or copy the debit or credit amount on each line to the appropriate T-account indicated to accumulate balances for each account. For example, the $1,300 debit is listed in the debit (increase) column of the Cash T-account.

*(b)* **The company borrows $1,000 from its local bank, signing a promissory note to be paid in one year.**

| | | |
|---|---|---|
| Cash (+A) .................................. | 1,000 | |
| Notes payable (+L) ..................... | | 1,000 |

| Assets | = | Liabilities | + | Stockholders' Equity |
|---|---|---|---|---|
| Cash +1,000 | | Notes payable +1,000 | | |

Equality checks: (1) Debits $1,000 = Credits $1,000; (2) the accounting equation is in balance.

*(c)* **For expansion, Papa John's opened eight new company-owned restaurants. The company purchased $5,700 of new ovens, counters, refrigerators, and other equipment (property and equipment), paying $1,500 in cash and the rest on a note payable to the equipment manufacturer in 60 days.**

| | | |
|---|---|---|
| Property and equipment (+A) ............... | 5,700 | |
| Cash (−A) ............................. | | 1,500 |
| Notes payable (+L) ..................... | | 4,200 |

| Assets | = | Liabilities | + | Stockholders' Equity |
|---|---|---|---|---|
| Property and equipment +5,700 | | Notes payable +4,200 | | |
| Cash −1,500 | | | | |

Equality checks: (1) Debits $5,700 = Credits $5,700; (2) the accounting equation is in balance.

*(d)* **Papa John's lends $450 to franchisees who sign notes agreeing to repay the loan in six months.**

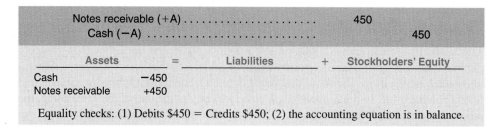

| | Notes receivable (+A) . . . . . . . . . . . . . . . . . . . . . | 450 | |
| | Cash (−A) . . . . . . . . . . . . . . . . . . . . . . . . . . | | 450 |

| Assets | | = | Liabilities | + | Stockholders' Equity |
|---|---|---|---|---|---|
| Cash | −450 | | | | |
| Notes receivable | +450 | | | | |

Equality checks: (1) Debits $450 = Credits $450; (2) the accounting equation is in balance.

*(e)* **Papa John's purchases $3,000 of stock in other companies as an investment.**

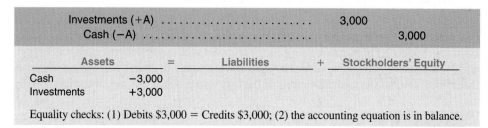

| | Investments (+A) . . . . . . . . . . . . . . . . . . . . . . . | 3,000 | |
| | Cash (−A) . . . . . . . . . . . . . . . . . . . . . . . . . . | | 3,000 |

| Assets | | = | Liabilities | + | Stockholders' Equity |
|---|---|---|---|---|---|
| Cash | −3,000 | | | | |
| Investments | +3,000 | | | | |

Equality checks: (1) Debits $3,000 = Credits $3,000; (2) the accounting equation is in balance.

*(f)* **Papa John's board of directors has not declared dividends for shareholders. However, for illustration purposes, we will assume that the first dividend for $200 is declared and paid.**

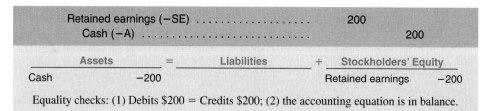

| | Retained earnings (−SE) . . . . . . . . . . . . . . . . . . | 200 | |
| | Cash (−A) . . . . . . . . . . . . . . . . . . . . . . . . . . | | 200 |

| Assets | | = | Liabilities | + | Stockholders' Equity | |
|---|---|---|---|---|---|---|
| Cash | −200 | | | | Retained earnings | −200 |

Equality checks: (1) Debits $200 = Credits $200; (2) the accounting equation is in balance.

## SELF-STUDY **QUIZ**

For Transactions *(g)* and *(h)*, fill in the missing information, including postings to the T-accounts. You can check your answers with the solution at the end of the illustration:

*(g)* **Papa John's collects $500 cash on notes receivable from a number of franchisees.**

Insert the journal entry →

| Cash (+A) | $500 | |
| Notes receivable (−A) | | $500 |

[Post to the T-accounts.]

| Assets | | = | Liabilities | + | Stockholders' Equity |
|---|---|---|---|---|---|
| Cash | +500 | | | | |
| Notes receivable | −500 | | | | |

Equality checks: (1) Debits $ 500 = Credits $ 500 ; (2) the accounting equation is in balance.

*(h)* **Papa John's paid $400 on the promissory note owed to the local bank.**

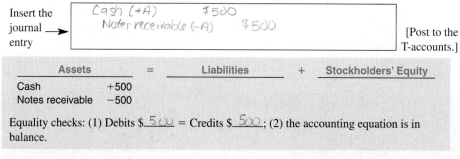

| | Notes payable (−L) . . . . . . . . . . . . . . . | 400 | |
| | Cash (−A) . . . . . . . . . . . . . . . . . . | | 400 |

[Post to the T-accounts.]

| Assets | = | Liabilities | + | Stockholders' Equity |
|--------|---|-------------|---|----------------------|
| | | Notes payable −400 | | |
| cash −400 | | | | |

Equality checks: (1) Debits $400 = Credits $400; (2) Is the accounting equation in balance?

The following are the T-accounts that changed during the period because of these transactions. The balances of all other accounts remained the same. The December 27, 1998, balances from Papa John's balance sheet have been included as the beginning balances:

**Cash (A)**

| + (dr) | | − (cr) | |
|--------|--------|--------|--------|
| Beg. bal. | 34,000 | | |
| (a) | 1,300 | (c) | 1,500 |
| (b) | 1,000 | (d) | 450 |
| (g) | 500 | (e) | 3,000 |
| | | (f) | 200 |
| | | (h) | 400 |
| End. bal. | 31,250 | | |

**Investments (A)**

| + (dr) | | − (cr) | |
|--------|--------|--------|---|
| Beg. bal. | 47,300 | | |
| (e) | 3,000 | | |
| End. bal. | 50,300 | | |

**Net Property and Equipment (A)**

| + (dr) | | − (cr) | |
|--------|---------|--------|---|
| Beg. bal. | 169,200 | | |
| (c) | 5,700 | | |
| End. bal. | 174,900 | | |

**Notes Receivable (A)**

| + (dr) | | − (cr) | |
|--------|--------|--------|-----|
| Beg. bal. | 12,500 | | |
| (d) | 450 | (g) | 500 |
| End. bal. | 12, 450 | | |

**Notes Payable (L)**

| − (dr) | | + (cr) | |
|--------|-----|--------|-------|
| | | Beg. bal. | 0 |
| (h) | 400 | (b) | 1,000 |
| | | (c) | 4,200 |
| | | End. bal. | 4,800 |

**Contributed Capital (SE)**

| − (dr) | | + (cr) | |
|--------|---|--------|---------|
| | | Beg. bal. | 164,500 |
| | | (a) | 1,300 |
| | | End. bal. | 165,800 |

**Retained Earnings (SE)**

| − (dr) | | + (cr) | |
|--------|-----|--------|--------|
| | | Beg. bal. | 98,200 |
| (f) | 200 | | |
| | | End. bal. | 98,000 |

You can verify that you posted the entries properly by adding the increase side and subtracting the decrease side and then comparing your answer to the ending balance given in each of the T-accounts. You can check your answers with the solutions below.

(g) Journal entry:

| Cash (+A) | 500 | |
| Notes receivable (−A) | | 500 |

Debits $500 = Credits $500.

(h) Effect on the Accounting Equation:

| Assets | = | Liabilities | + | Stockholders' Equity |
|--------|---|-------------|---|----------------------|
| Cash | −400 | Notes payable | −400 | |

The accounting equation is in balance.

---

# FINANCIAL **ANALYSIS**

## INFERRING BUSINESS ACTIVITIES FROM T-ACCOUNTS

T-accounts are useful primarily for instructional purposes and as a financial analysis tool. In many cases, we will use the T-account tool to determine what transactions a company engaged in during a period. For example, the primary transactions affecting Accounts Payable for a period are purchases of assets on account and cash payments to suppliers. If we know the

beginning and ending balances of Accounts Payable and all of the amounts that were purchased on credit during a period, we can determine the amount of cash paid. The T-account will include the following:

**Accounts Payable (L)**

| – (dr) | + (cr) | | |
|---|---|---|---|
| | Beg. bal. | 600 | |
| Cash | Purchases on | | |
| payments  ? | account | 1,500 | |
| | End. bal. | 300 | |

**SOLUTION:**

| Beginning balance | + Purchases | – Cash payments | = | Ending balance |
|---|---|---|---|---|
| $600 | + $1,500 | – ? | = | $300 |
| | $2,100 | – ? | = | $300 |
| | | ? | = | $1,800 |

# BALANCE SHEET PREPARATION

■ **LEARNING OBJECTIVE 5**

Prepare and analyze a simple balance sheet.

It is possible to prepare a balance sheet at any point in time from the balances in the accounts. The date January 31, 1999, is the last Sunday in January. With the new balances shown in the T-accounts in the preceding Papa John's illustration plus the original balances in the accounts that did not change, the balance sheet in Exhibit 2.6 compares the account balances at January 31, 1999, with those at December 27, 1998. Notice that when multiple periods are presented, the most recent balance sheet amounts are usually listed on the left, although this may vary.

EXHIBIT **2.6**

**Papa John's Balance Sheet**

**PAPA JOHN'S INTERNATIONAL, INC. AND SUBSIDIARIES**
**Consolidated Balance Sheets**
**(dollars in thousands)**

| | January 31, 1999 | December 27, 1998 |
|---|---|---|
| **Assets** | | |
| **Current assets:** | | |
| Cash and cash equivalents | $ 31,250 | $ 34,000 |
| Accounts receivable | 17,300 | 17,300 |
| Inventories | 9,700 | 9,700 |
| Prepaid expenses | 4,800 | 4,800 |
| Other current assets | 2,100 | 2,100 |
| **Total current assets** | 65,150 | 67,900 |
| Investments | 50,300 | 47,300 |
| Net property and equipment | 174,900 | 169,200 |
| Notes receivable | 12,450 | 12,500 |
| Other assets | 22,400 | 22,400 |
| **Total assets** | $325,200 | $319,300 |
| **Liabilities and stockholders' equity** | | |
| **Current liabilities:** | | |
| Accounts payable | $ 18,100 | $ 18,100 |
| Accrued expenses payable | 25,500 | 25,500 |
| Other current liabilities | — | — |
| **Total current liabilities** | 43,600 | 43,600 |
| Unearned franchise and development fees | 6,600 | 6,600 |
| Other long-term liabilities (including notes payable) | 11,200 | 6,400 |
| **Stockholders' equity:** | | |
| Contributed capital | 165,800 | 164,500 |
| Retained earnings | 98,000 | 98,200 |
| **Total stockholders' equity** | 263,800 | 262,700 |
| **Total liabilities and stockholders' equity** | $325,200 | $319,300 |

At the beginning of the chapter, we presented the changes in Papa John's balance sheets from the beginning of the year to the end of the year. We questioned what made the accounts change and what the process was for reflecting the changes. Now we can see that the accounts have changed again in one month due to the transactions illustrated in this chapter:

| | Assets | = | Liabilities | + | Stockholders' Equity |
|---|---|---|---|---|---|
| End of January 1999 | $325,200 | | $61,400 | | $263,800 |
| End of 1998 | 319,300 | | 56,600 | | 262,700 |
| Change | +$ 5,900 | | +$ 4,800 | | +$ 1,100 |

## KEY **RATIO ANALYSIS:**

### THE FINANCIAL LEVERAGE RATIO

**K**now the decision question:

How is management using debt to increase the amount of assets the company employs to earn income for stockholders? It is computed as follows:

$$\text{Financial Leverage Ratio} = \frac{\text{Average Total Assets}}{\text{Average Stockholders' Equity}}$$

The 1998 ratio for Papa John's:

$$\frac{(\$319,300 + \$253,200)/2}{(\$262,700 + \$212,800)/2} = 1.20$$

■ **LEARNING OBJECTIVE 6**

Compute and interpret the financial leverage ratio.

**E**xamine the ratio using two techniques:

| ① Comparisons over Time | | | ② Comparisons with Competitors* | |
|---|---|---|---|---|
| Papa John's International, Inc. | | | Uno Restaurant Corp. (& Chicago Bar & Grill) | Chuck E. Cheese (CEC, Inc.) |
| 1996 | 1997 | 1998 | 1998 | 1998 |
| 1.19 | 1.18 | 1.20 | 1.98 | 1.41 |

**Y**ou interpret the results carefully:

**IN GENERAL** → The financial leverage ratio measures the relationship between total assets and the stockholders' equity that finances the assets. As noted, companies finance their assets with stockholders' equity and debt. The higher the proportion of assets financed by debt, the higher the financial leverage ratio. Conversely, the higher the proportion of assets financed with stockholders' equity, the lower the ratio. Increasing debt (and the leverage ratio) increases the amount of assets the company employs to earn income for stockholders, which increases the chances of earning higher income. However, it also increases *risk*. Debt financing is riskier than financing with stockholders' equity because the interest payments on debt must be made every period (they are legal obligations), whereas dividends on stock can be postponed. An increasing ratio over time signals more reliance on debt financing and more risk.

Creditors and security analysts use this ratio to assess a company's risk level, while managers use the ratio in deciding whether to expand by adding debt. As long as the interest on

*You cannot always compare the closest competitors. Pizza Hut and Domino's, noted as primary competitors for Papa John's, were not used in this analysis because both were involved in a change in ownership in previous years, causing them to reflect negative amounts in stockholders' equity. The results would be unusual and, therefore, not useful as a basis for comparison.

borrowing is less than the additional earnings generated, utilizing debt will enhance the stock-holders' earnings.

**FOCUS COMPANY ANALYSIS** → Papa John's financial leverage increased slightly in 1998, al-though the ratio over the past three years has remained fairly constant. Papa John's approach to financing involves relatively little borrowing, a great deal of stockholders' equity, and heavy reinvestment of earnings. In fact, retained earnings is 37 percent of Papa John's total stock-holders' equity at December 27, 1998.

When compared against two other pizza restaurants, Papa John's 1998 financial leverage ra-tio indicates far less risk. This is in part due to the fact that the two competitors listed are eat-in restaurants that must invest more in facilities. Dun & Bradstreet reports that the average restau-rant chain has a leverage ratio of 1.87 (nearly twice as much debt as equity financing). This sug-gests that Papa John's at 1.20 is following a less risky (more conservative) financing strategy than are other companies in the restaurant industry.

**A FEW CAUTIONS:** A financial leverage ratio near 1:1 indicates a company that is choosing not to utilize debt to expand. This suggests the company has lower risk but is not enhancing the re-turn to stockholders. When comparing competitors, the ratio may be influenced by differences in business strategies, such as whether the company rents or buys facilities.

---

| SELECTED FOCUS COMPANY LEVERAGE RATIOS | |
|---|---|
| Delta Air Lines | 3.89 |
| Callaway Golf | 1.30 |
| Timberland | 1.85 |

---

## SELF-STUDY **QUIZ**

*Wendy's International*

Wendy's International, Inc., had the following balances on recent balance sheets (in thousands):

Beginning of year:   Assets—$1,941,680; Liabilities—$757,446; Stockholders' equity—$1,184,234
End of year:        Assets—$1,837,947; Liabilities—$769,880; Stockholders' equity—$1,068,067

Compute Wendy's leverage ratio:

What does this tell you about Wendy's financing strategy?

After you have completed the questions, check your solution with the answers at the bottom of the page.*

---

## FOCUS ON **CASH FLOWS**

■ **LEARNING OBJECTIVE 7**

Identify investing and financing transactions and how they are reported on the statement of cash flows.

### INVESTING AND FINANCING ACTIVITIES

Recall from Chapter 1 that companies report on cash inflows and outflows for a period in their statement of cash flows. This statement divides all transactions that affect cash into three cat-egories: Operating, Investing, and Financing activities. (Use the mnemonic "OIF" to remem-ber the order of the categories on the statement.)

We stated at the beginning of the chapter that we would focus on investing and financing activities in this chapter and operating activities in Chapter 3. Investing activities include buy-ing and selling noncurrent assets and investments. Financing activities include borrowing and repaying debt, issuing and repurchasing stock, and paying dividends. When cash is involved, these activities are reported on the statement of cash flows. When cash is not included in the transaction (such as acquiring a building with a long-term mortgage note payable), there is no cash effect to include on the statement.

---

*($1,837,947 + $1,941,680)/2 ÷ ($1,068,067 + $1,184,234)/2 = 1.68. Wendy's is following a slightly less risky financing strategy than other companies in the industry. The ratio is lower than the industry average, although it is higher than Papa John's. This appears reasonable since Wendy's builds and leases eat-in facilities, but Papa John's typically builds and leases smaller facilities for delivery service only.

### Effect on Statement of Cash Flows

| In General: | Effect on Cash Flows |
|---|---|
| **Operating activities** | |
| (No transactions in this chapter were operating activities.) | |
| **Investing activities** | |
| Purchasing long-term assets for cash | − |
| Selling long-term assets for cash | + |
| Lending cash to others | − |
| Receiving principal payments in cash on loans to others | + |
| **Financing activities** | |
| Borrowing cash from banks | + |
| Repaying in cash the principal on loans from banks | − |
| Issuing stock for cash | + |
| Repurchasing stock with cash | − |
| Paying cash dividends | − |

**Focus Company Analysis:** Exhibit 2.7 is the statement of cash flows for Papa John's based on the activities illustrated in this chapter. It reports the sources and uses of cash that created the $2,750 cash decrease (from $34,000 to $31,250) in our Papa John's example. Remember that only the transactions that affected cash are reported.

The pattern of cash flows in the statement in Exhibit 2.7 (net cash outflows in investing activities and net cash inflows in financing activities) is typical of Papa John's past several annual statements of cash flows. Companies that seek to expand usually report cash outflows in investing activities.

## SELF-STUDY **QUIZ**

*Lance, Inc.*

Lance, Inc., manufactures and sells snack products. From a recent annual statement of cash flows, indicate whether the transaction affected the cash flow as an investing (I) activity or a financing (F) activity and indicate the direction of the effect on cash (+ = increases cash; − = decreases cash):

| Transactions | Type of Activity (I or F) | Effect on Cash Flows (+ or −) |
|---|---|---|
| 1. Paid dividends. | _____ | _____ |
| 2. Sold property. | _____ | _____ |
| 3. Sold marketable securities (investments). | _____ | _____ |
| 4. Purchased vending machines. | _____ | _____ |
| 5. Repurchased its own common stock. | _____ | _____ |

After you have completed the schedule, check your solution with the answers in the footnote at the bottom of the page.*

## SOME MISCONCEPTIONS

Some people confuse bookkeeping with accounting. In effect, they confuse a part of accounting with the whole. Bookkeeping involves the routine, clerical part of accounting and requires only minimal knowledge of accounting. A bookkeeper may record the repetitive and uncomplicated transactions in most businesses and may

EXHIBIT **2.7**

**Papa John's Statement of Cash Flows**

Each is referenced to the transaction illustrated in the chapter.

Agrees with the amount on the balance sheet.

---

**PAPA JOHN'S INTERNATIONAL, INC.**
**Consolidated Statement of Cash Flows**
**For the month ended January 31, 1999**
**(in thousands)**

| | |
|---|---:|
| **Operating Activities** | |
| (None in this chapter.) | |
| **Investing Activities** | |
| Purchased property and equipment (c) | $(1,500) |
| Purchased investments (e) | (3,000) |
| Lent funds to franchisees (d) | (450) |
| Received payment on loans to franchisees (g) | 500 |
| Net cash used in investing activities | **(4,450)** |
| **Financing Activities** | |
| Issued common stock (a) | 1,300 |
| Borrowings (b) | 1,000 |
| Paid dividends (f) | (200) |
| Payments on borrowings (h) | (400) |
| Net cash provided by financing activities | **1,700** |
| Net decrease in cash | **(2,750)** |
| Cast at beginning of month | 34,000 |
| **Cash at end of month** | **$31,250** |

---

maintain the simple records of a small business. In contrast, the accountant is a highly trained professional, competent in the design of information systems, analysis of complex transactions, interpretation of financial data, financial reporting, auditing, taxation, and management consulting.

Another prevalent misconception is that all transactions are subject to precise and objective measurement and that the accounting results reported in the financial statements are exactly what happened that period. In reality, accounting numbers are influenced by estimates, as subsequent chapters will illustrate. Some people believe that financial statements report the entity's market value (including its assets), but they do not. To understand and interpret financial statements, the user must be aware of their limitations as well as their usefulness. One should understand what the financial statements do and do not try to accomplish.

Finally, financial statements are often thought to be inflexible because of their quantitative nature. As you study accounting, you will learn that it requires considerable *professional judgment* on the part of the accountant to capture the economic essence of complex transactions. Accounting is stimulating intellectually; it is not a cut-and-dried subject. It calls on your intelligence, analytical ability, creativity, and judgment. Accounting is a communication process involving an audience (users) with a wide diversity of knowledge, interest, and capabilities; therefore, it will call on your ability as a communicator. The language of accounting uses concisely written phrases and symbols to convey information about the resource flows measured for specific organizations.

To understand financial statements, you must have a certain level of knowledge of the concepts and the measurement procedures used in the accounting process. You should learn what accounting is really like and appreciate the reasons for using certain procedures. This level of knowledge cannot be gained by reading a list of the concepts and a list of the misconceptions. Neither can a generalized discussion of the subject matter suffice. A certain amount of involvement, primarily problem solving (similar to the requirement in mathematics courses), is essential in the study of accounting focused on the needs of the user. Therefore, we provide problems aimed at the desirable knowledge level for the user as well as the preparer of financial statements.

# DEMONSTRATION **CASE**

On April 1, 2000, three ambitious college students started Terrific Lawn Maintenance Corporation. Completed transactions (summarized) through April 30, 2000, for Terrific Lawn Maintenance Corporation follow:

(a) Issued $9,000 of common stock in total to the three investors in exchange for cash. Each investor received 500 shares of stock (totaling 1,500 issued shares).

(b) Acquired rakes and other hand tools (equipment) with a list price of $690 for $600; paid $200 cash and signed a note for the balance with the hardware store.

(c) Ordered three lawn mowers and two edgers from XYZ Lawn Supply, Inc., for $4,000.

(d) Purchased 4 acres of land as a future building site of a storage garage. Paid cash, $5,000.

(e) Received the mowers and edgers that had been ordered, signing a note to pay XYZ Lawn Supply in full in 30 days.

(f) Sold one acre of land to the city for a park. The city signed a note to pay Terrific Lawn Maintenance Corp. $1,250 by the end of the month.

(g) Paid $700 on the notes owed to XYZ Lawn Supply and the hardware store.

(h) Collected cash on note owed by the city.

(i) One of the owners borrowed $3,000 from a local bank for personal use.

### Required:

1. Set up T-accounts for Cash, Notes Receivable (from the city), Equipment (for hand tools and mowing equipment), Land, Notes Payable (to equipment supply companies), and Contributed Capital. Beginning balances are $0; indicate these beginning balances in the T-accounts. Analyze each transaction using the process outlined in the chapter. Prepare journal entries in chronological order. Enter the effects of the transactions on the accounting model in the appropriate T-accounts. Identify each amount with its letter in the preceding list.

2. Use the amounts in the T-accounts developed in requirement (1) to prepare a classified balance sheet for Terrific Lawn Maintenance Corporation at April 30, 2000. The April 30, 2000, balance sheet requires use of the account balances for all assets, liabilities, and stockholders' equity. The transaction analysis model is presented for your use:

3. Prepare the investing and financing sections of the statement of cash flows.

Now you can check your answers with the solution to these requirements in the following section.

## SUGGESTED SOLUTION

1.   **Transaction analysis, journal entries, and T-accounts:**

(a)      Cash (+A) .............................   9,000
             Contributed capital (+SE) ...........            9,000

| Assets | | = | Liabilities | + | Stockholders' Equity | |
|--------|--|---|-------------|---|---------------------|--|
| Cash | +9,000 | | | | Contributed capital | +9,000 |

Equality checks: (1) Debits $9,000 = Credits $9,000; (2) the accounting equation is in balance.

(b)      Equipment (+A) ........................   600
             Cash (−A) .........................            200
             Notes payable (+L) ................            400

| Assets | | = | Liabilities | | + | Stockholders' Equity |
|---|---|---|---|---|---|---|
| Equipment | +600 | | Notes payable | +400 | | |
| Cash | −200 | | | | | |

Equality checks: (1) Debits $600 = Credits $600; (2) the accounting equation is in balance.

The **cost principle** states that assets should be recorded at the amount paid on the date of the transaction. This is $600, not the $690 list price.

*(c)* **This is not an accounting transaction; no exchange has taken place. No accounts are affected.**

*(d)*    Land (+A) .................................. 5,000
             Cash (−A) ........................ 5,000

| Assets | | = | Liabilities | + | Stockholders' Equity |
|---|---|---|---|---|---|
| Land | +5,000 | | | | |
| Cash | −5,000 | | | | |

Equality checks: (1) Debits $5,000 = Credits $5,000; (2) the accounting equation is in balance.

*(e)*    Equipment (+A) ........................ 4,000
             Notes payable (+L) ................. 4,000

| Assets | | = | Liabilities | | + | Stockholders' Equity |
|---|---|---|---|---|---|---|
| Equipment | +4,000 | | Notes payable | +4,000 | | |

Equality checks: (1) Debits $4,000 = Credits $4,000; (2) the accounting equation is in balance.

*(f)*    Notes receivable (+A) ..................... 1,250
             Land (−A) ........................ 1,250

| Assets | | = | Liabilities | + | Stockholders' Equity |
|---|---|---|---|---|---|
| Notes receivable | +1,250 | | | | |
| Land | −1,250 | | | | |

Equality checks: (1) Debits $1,250 = Credits $1,250; (2) the accounting equation is in balance.

*(g)*    Notes payable (−L) ........................ 700
             Cash (−A) ........................ 700

| Assets | | = | Liabilities | | + | Stockholders' Equity |
|---|---|---|---|---|---|---|
| Cash | −700 | | Notes payable | −700 | | |

Equality checks: (1) Debits $700 = Credits $700; (2) the accounting equation is in balance.

*(h)*    Cash (+A) ................................ 1,250
             Notes receivable (−A) .............. 1,250

| Assets | | = | Liabilities | + | Stockholders' Equity |
|---|---|---|---|---|---|
| Cash | +1,250 | | | | |
| Notes receivable | −1,250 | | | | |

Equality checks: (1) Debits $1,250 = Credits $1,250; (2) the accounting equation is in balance.

*(i)*    **There is no transaction for the company. The separate-entity assumption states that transactions of the owners are separate from transactions of the business.**

| Cash (A) | | | | Notes Receivable (A) | | | | Equipment (A) | | | |
|---|---|---|---|---|---|---|---|---|---|---|---|
| **+ (dr)** | | **− (cr)** | | **+ (dr)** | | **− (cr)** | | **+ (dr)** | | **− (cr)** | |
| Beg. bal. | 0 | | | Beg. bal. | 0 | | | Beg. bal. | 0 | | |
| (a) | 9,000 | (b) | 200 | (f) | 1,250 | (h) | 1,250 | (b) | 600 | | |
| (h) | 1,250 | (d) | 5,000 | End. bal. | 0 | | | (e) | 4,000 | | |
| | | (g) | 700 | | | | | End. bal. | 4,600 | | |
| End. bal. | 4,350 | | | | | | | | | | |

| Contributed Capital (SE) | | | | Land (A) | | | | Notes Payable (L) | | | |
|---|---|---|---|---|---|---|---|---|---|---|---|
| **− (dr)** | | **+ (cr)** | | **+ (dr)** | | **− (cr)** | | **− (dr)** | | **+ (cr)** | |
| | | Beg. bal. | 0 | Beg. bal. | 0 | | | | | Beg. bal. | 0 |
| | | (a) | 9,000 | (d) | 5,000 | (f) | 1,250 | (g) | 700 | (b) | 400 |
| | | End. bal. | 9,000 | End. bal. | 3,750 | | | | | (e) | 4,000 |
| | | | | | | | | | | End. bal. | 3,700 |

2.  **Balance sheet:**

**TERRIFIC LAWN MAINTENANCE CORPORATION**
**Balance Sheet**
**At April 30, 2000**

| Assets | | Liabilities | |
|---|---|---|---|
| Current Asset: Cash | $ 4,350 | Current Liability: Notes payable | $ 3,700 |
| Equipment | 4,600 | | |
| Land | 3,750 | **Stockholders' Equity** | |
| | | Contributed capital | 9,000 |
| Total assets | $12,700 | Total liabilities and stockholders' equity | $12,700 |

Notice that balance sheets presented earlier in the text listed assets on the top and liabilities and stockholders' equity on the bottom. This is called the **report form**. Preparing a balance sheet with assets on the left side and liabilities and stockholders' equity on the right side, such as the preceding one, is called the **account form**. Both are used in practice.

3.  **Investing and financing effects of the statement of cash flows:**

**TERRIFIC LAWN MAINTENANCE CORPORATION**
**Statements of Cash Flows**
**For the Month Ended April 30, 2000**

| | |
|---|---|
| **Operating Activities** | |
| (none in this case) | |
| **Investing Activities** | |
| Purchased land (d) | $(5,000) |
| Purchased equipment (b) | (200) |
| Received payment on notes receivable (h) | 1,250 |
| Net cash used in investing activities | **(3,950)** |
| **Financing Activities** | |
| Issued common stock (a) | 9,000 |
| Payments on borrowings (g) | (700) |
| Net cash provided by financing activities | **8,300** |
| Change in cash | **4,350** |
| Beginning cash balance | 0 |
| **Ending cash balance** | **$4,350** |

Two common balance sheet forms:
**REPORT FORM** lists assets on top, liabilities and stockholders' equity on the bottom.

**ACCOUNT FORM** lists assets on the left, liabilities and stockholders' equity on the right.

## CHAPTER **TAKE-AWAYS**

1. **Define the objective of financial reporting, the elements of the balance sheet, and the related key accounting assumptions and principles.   p. 53**
   - The primary objective of external financial reporting is to provide useful economic information about a business to help external parties, primarily investors and creditors, make sound financial decisions.
   - Elements of the balance sheet:
     a. Assets—probable future economic benefits owned by the entity as a result of past transactions.
     b. Liabilities—probable debts or obligations of the entity as a result of past transactions, which will be paid with assets or services.
     c. Stockholders' equity—the financing provided by the owners and the operations of the business.
   - Key accounting assumptions and principles:
     a. Separate-entity assumption—transactions of the business are accounted for separately from transactions of the owner.
     b. Unit-of-measure assumption—financial information is reported in the national monetary unit.
     c. Continuity (going-concern) assumption—a business is expected to continue to operate into the foreseeable future.
     d. Historical cost principle—financial statements elements should be recorded at the cash-equivalent cost on the date of the transaction.

2. **Identify what constitutes a business transaction and identify common balance sheet account titles used in business.   p. 58**
   A transaction includes:
   - An exchange between a business and one or more external parties to a business.
   or
   - A measurable internal event such as adjustments for the use of assets in operations.
   An account is a standardized format that organizations use to accumulate the dollar effects of transactions of each financial statement item. Typical balance sheet account titles include the following:
   - Assets: Cash, Accounts Receivable, Inventory, Prepaid Expenses, and Property and Equipment.
   - Liabilities: Accounts Payable, Notes Payable, Accrued Liabilities, and Taxes Payable.
   - Stockholders' equity: Contributed Capital and Retained Earnings.

3. **Apply transaction analysis to simple business transactions in terms of the accounting model: Assets = Liabilities + Stockholders' Equity.   p. 60**
   To determine the economic effect of a transaction on the entity in terms of its accounting equation, each transaction is analyzed as to the accounts (at least two) that are affected. In an exchange, the company receives something and gives up something. If the accounts, direction of the effects, and amounts are correctly analyzed, the accounting equation must stay in balance. The transaction analysis model is

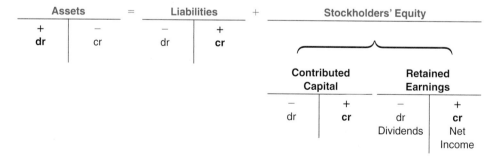

4. **Determine the impact of business transactions on the balance sheet using two basic tools: journal entries and T-accounts.   p. 66**
   - Journal entries express the effects of a transaction on accounts in a debits-equal-credits format. The accounts and amounts to be debited are listed first. Then the accounts and

amounts to be credited are listed below the debits and indented, resulting in debits on the left and credits on the right.

(date or reference) Account . . . . . . . . . . . . . . . . . . . . . . . . . . . . . .  xxx

                        Account . . . . . . . . . . . . . . . . . . . . . . .  xxx

- T-accounts summarize transaction effects for each account. These tools can be used to determine balances and draw inferences about a company's activities.

| + | Asset | − | | − Liability and Stockholders' Equity + | |
|---|---|---|---|---|---|
| Beginning balance | | | | | Beginning balance |
| Increases | | Decreases | Decreases | | Increases |
| Ending balance | | | | | Ending balance |

5. **Prepare and analyze a simple balance sheet.  p. 72**
   Classified balance sheets are structured with
   - Assets categorized as "current assets" (those to be used or turned into cash within the year with inventory always considered a current asset) and noncurrent assets such as long-term investments, property and equipment, and intangible assets.
   - Liabilities categorized as "current liabilities" (those that will be paid with current assets) and long-term liabilities.

6. **Compute and interpret the financial leverage ratio.  p. 73**
   The financial leverage ratio (Average Total Assets ÷ Average Stockholders' Equity) measures the relationship between total assets and the stockholders' capital that finances the assets. The higher the ratio, the more debt is used to finance assets. As the ratio (and thus debt) increases, risk increases.

7. **Identify investing and financing transactions and how they are reported on the statement of cash flows.  p. 74**
   A statement of cash flows reports the sources and uses of cash for the period by the type of activity that generated the cash flow: operating, investing, and financing. Investing activities are purchasing and selling long-term assets, making loans, and receiving payment from loans to others. Financing activities are borrowing and repaying loans to banks, issuing and repurchasing stock, and paying dividends.

In this chapter, we discussed the fundamental accounting model and transaction analysis. Journal entries and T-accounts were used to record the results of transaction analysis for investing and financing decisions that affect balance sheet accounts. In Chapter 3, we continue our detailed look at financial statements, in particular the income statement. The purpose of Chapter 3 is to build on your knowledge by discussing concepts for the measurement of revenues and expenses and by illustrating transaction analysis for operating decisions.

## KEY **RATIO**

**Financial leverage ratio** measures the relationship between total assets and the stockholders' capital that finances it. The higher the ratio, the more debt is assumed by the company to finance assets. It is computed as follows (p. 73):

$$\text{Financial Leverage Ratio} = \frac{\text{Average Total Assets}}{\text{Average Stockholders' Equity}}$$

**"Average" is (last year's value + this year's value) ÷ 2.**

## FINDING FINANCIAL INFORMATION

**BALANCE SHEET**

*Current Assets*
Cash
Accounts and notes
receivable
Inventory
Prepaid expense
*Noncurrent Assets*
Long-term
investments
Property and
equipment
Intangibles

*Current Liabilities*
Accounts payable
Notes payable
Accrued liabilities
payable
*Noncurrent*
*Liabilities*
Long-term debt
*Stockholders' Equity*
Contributed capital
Retained earnings

**INCOME STATEMENT**
*To Be Indicated in Chapter 3*

**STATEMENT OF CASH FLOWS**
*Under Investing Activities*
+ Sales of noncurrent assets for cash
− Purchases of noncurrent assets for cash
− Loans to others
+ Receipt of cash on loans to others
*Under Financing Activities*
+ Borrowing from banks
− Repayment of loans from banks
+ Issuance of stock
− Repurchasing stock
− Payment of dividends

**NOTES**
*Under Summary of Significant Accounting
Policies*
Description of management's choice for
fiscal year.

## KEY TERMS

## QUESTIONS

1. What is the primary objective of financial reporting for external users?
2. Define the following:
   a. Asset.
   b. Current asset.
   c. Liability.
   d. Current liability.
   e. Contributed capital.
   f. Retained earnings.
3. Explain what the following mean in accounting:
   a. Separate-entity assumption.
   b. Unit-of-measure assumption.
   c. Continuity assumption.
   d. Cost principle.
4. Why are accounting assumptions necessary?
5. How is the financial leverage ratio computed and how is it interpreted?

6. For accounting purposes, what is an account? Explain why accounts are used in an accounting system.
7. What is the fundamental accounting model?
8. Define a business transaction in the broad sense and give an example of the two different kinds of transactions.
9. Explain what *debit* and *credit* mean.
10. Briefly explain what is meant by *transaction analysis*. What are the two steps in transaction analysis?
11. What two equalities in accounting must be maintained in transaction analysis?
12. What is a *journal entry?*
13. What is a *T-account?* What is its purpose?
14. What transactions are classified as investing activities in a statement of cash flows? What transactions are classified as financing activities?
15. What is the difference between a bookkeeper and an accountant?

# MINI-EXERCISES

**M2–1**  **Matching Definitions with Terms**  ■ **LO1**

Match each definition with its related term by entering the appropriate letter in the space provided. There should be only one definition per term (that is, there are more definitions than terms).

| Term | Definition |
|---|---|
| _____ (1) Separate-entity assumption | A. = Liabilities + Stockholders' Equity. |
| | B. Reports assets, liabilities, and stockholders' equity. |
| _____ (2) Cost principle | C. Accounts for a business separate from its owners. |
| _____ (3) Credits | D. Increase assets; decrease liabilities and stockholders' equity. |
| _____ (4) Assets | |
| _____ (5) T-account | E. An exchange between an entity and other parties. |
| | F. The concept that businesses will operate into the foreseeable future. |
| | G. Decrease assets; increase liabilities and stockholders' equity. |
| | H. The concept that assets should be recorded at cash-equivalent cost. |
| | I. A standardized format used to accumulate data about each item reported on financial statements. |

**M2–2**  **Matching Definitions with Terms**  ■ **LO1**

Match each definition with its related term by entering the appropriate letter in the space provided. There should be only one definition per term (that is, there are more definitions than terms).

| Term | Definition |
|---|---|
| _____ (1) Journal entry | A. Accounting model. |
| _____ (2) A = L + SE, and Debits = Credits | B. Four periodic financial statements. |
| | C. The two equalities in accounting that aid in providing accuracy. |
| _____ (3) Assets = Liabilities + Stockholders' Equity | D. The results of transaction analysis in accounting format. |
| _____ (4) Liabilities | E. The account that is credited when money is borrowed from a bank. |
| _____ (5) Income statement, balance sheet, statement of retained earnings, and statement of cash flows | F. Probable future economic benefits owned by an entity. |
| | G. Cumulative earnings of a company that are not distributed to the owners. |
| | H. Every transaction has a least two effects. |
| | I. Probable debts or obligations to be paid with assets or services. |

■ **LO2**     **M2–3**     **Identifying Events as Accounting Transactions**

For each of the following events, which result in an exchange transaction for O'Brien Company (Y for yes and N for no)?

_Y_ (1) O'Brien purchased a machine that it paid for by signing a note payable.
_N_ (2) Six investors in O'Brien Company sold their stock to another investor.
_Y_ (3) The company lent $150,000 to a member of the board of directors.
_N_ (4) O'Brien Company ordered supplies from Office Max to be delivered next week.
_N_ (5) The founding owner, Meaghan O'Brien, purchased additional stock in another company.
_Y_ (6) The company borrowed $1,000,000 from a local bank.

■ **LO2**     **M2–4**     **Classifying Accounts on a Balance Sheet**

The following are several of the accounts of Gomez-Sanchez Company:

_____ (1) Accounts Payable                _____ (9) Long-Term Investments
_CA_ (2) Accounts Receivable           _NCL_ (10) Notes Payable (due in three years)
_____ (3) Buildings                            _____ (11) Notes Receivable (due in six months)
_CA_ (4) Cash                                    _CA_ (12) Prepaid Rent
_____ (5) Contributed Capital            _____ (13) Retained Earnings
_NCA_ (6) Land                                  _NCA_ (14) Supplies
_____ (7) Merchandise Inventory      _____ (15) Utilities Payable
_CL_ (8) Income Taxes Payable         _CL_ (16) Wages Payable

In the space provided, classify each as it would be reported on a balance sheet. Use the following code:

CA   = current asset          CL   = current liability          SE = stockholders' equity
NCA = noncurrent asset      NCL = noncurrent liability

■ **LO3**     **M2–5**     **Determining Financial Statement Effects of Several Transactions**

For each of the following transactions of Nardozzi Inc. for the month of January 20B, indicate the accounts, amounts, and direction of the effects on the accounting equation. A sample is provided.

a. *(Sample)* Borrowed $1,000 from a local bank.
b. Sold $3,000 additional stock to investors.
c. Purchased $500 in equipment, paying $100 cash and the rest on a note due in one year.
d. Declared and paid $100 in dividends to stockholders.
e. Paid $200 on a note payable.

| | Assets | = | Liabilities | + | Stockholders' Equity |
|---|---|---|---|---|---|
| a. *Sample:* | Cash      +1,000 | | Notes payable  +1,000 | | |

■ **LO3**     **M2–6**     **Identifying Increase and Decrease Effects on Balance Sheet Elements**

Complete the following table by entering either the word *increases* or *decreases* in each column.

| | Debit | Credit |
|---|---|---|
| Assets | | |
| Liabilities | | |
| Stockholders' equity | | |

**M2–7**   **Identifying Debit and Credit Effects on Balance Sheet Elements**     ■ **LO4**

Complete the following table by entering either the word *debit* or *credit* in each column.

| | Increase | Decrease |
|---|---|---|
| Assets | _____ | _____ |
| Liabilities | _____ | _____ |
| Stockholders' equity | _____ | _____ |

**M2–8**   **Recording Simple Transactions**     ■ **LO4**

For each of the transactions in M2–5 (including the sample), write the journal entry in good form.

**M2–9**   **Completing T-Accounts**     ■ **LO4**

For each of the transactions in M2–5 (including the sample), post the effects to the appropriate T-accounts and determine ending account balances. Beginning balances are provided.

| Cash | | Equipment | | Notes Payable | |
|---|---|---|---|---|---|
| Beg. bal. 2,000 | | Beg. bal. 16,300 | | | Beg. bal. 3,000 |

| Contributed Capital | | Retained Earnings | |
|---|---|---|---|
| | Beg. bal. 5,500 | | Beg. bal. 9,800 |

**M2–10**   **Reporting a Simple Balance Sheet**     ■ **LO5**

Given the transactions in M2–5 (including the sample), prepare a balance sheet for Nardozzi Inc. as of January 31, 20B.

**M2–11**   **Computing and Interpreting the Financial Leverage Ratio**     ■ **LO6**

Calculate the financial leverage ratio for Fullem Company based on the following data:

| | Assets | Liabilities | Stockholders' Equity |
|---|---|---|---|
| End of 20A | $245,600 | $ 90,300 | $155,300 |
| End of 20B | 278,100 | 110,200 | 167,900 |

What does the result suggest about the company? What can you say about Fullem's ratio when compared to Papa John's 1998 ratio?

**M2–12**   **Identifying Transactions as Investing or Financing Activities on the Statement of Cash Flows**     ■ **LO7**

For the transactions in M2–5, identify each as an investing (I) activity or financing (F) activity on the statement of cash flows.

# EXERCISES

**E2–1**   **Matching Definitions with Terms**     ■ **LO1**

Match each definition with its related term by entering the appropriate letter in the space provided. There should be only one definition per term (that is, there are more definitions than terms).

**Term**

E  (1) Transaction
F  (2) Continuity assumption
B  (3) Balance sheet
O  (4) Liabilities
J  (5) Assets = Liabilities + Stockholders' Equity

A  (6) Current assets
L  (7) Note payable
N  (8) Duality
M  (9) Retained earnings
D  (10) Debits

**Definition**

A. Economic resources to be used or turned into cash within one year.
B. Reports assets, liabilities, and stockholders' equity.
C. Accounts for a business separate from its owners.
D. Increase assets; decrease liabilities and stockholders' equity.
E. An exchange between an entity and other parties.
F. The concept that businesses will operate into the foreseeable future.
G. Decrease assets; increase liabilities and stockholders' equity.
H. The concept that assets should be recorded at cash-equivalent cost.
I. A standardized format used to accumulate data about each item reported on financial statements.
J. The accounting model.
K. The two equalities in accounting that aid in providing accuracy.
L. The account that is credited when money is borrowed from a bank.
M. Cumulative earnings of a company that are not distributed to the owners.
N. Every transaction has at least two effects.
O. Probable debts or obligations to be paid with assets or services.

**LO2**      **E2–2**      **Identifying Account Titles**

The following are independent situations.

a. A company orders and receives 10 personal computers for office use for which it signs a note promising to pay $25,000 within three months.

b. A company purchases a new delivery truck that has a list, or sticker, price of $24,000 for $21,000 cash.

c. A women's clothing retailer orders 30 new display stands for $300 each for future delivery.

d. A new company is formed and sells 100 shares of stock for $12 per share to investors.

e. A manufacturing company signs a contract for the construction of a new warehouse for $500,000. At the signing, the company writes a check for $50,000 as a deposit on the future construction.

f. A publishing firm purchases the copyright (an intangible asset) to a manuscript for an introductory accounting text from the author for $40,000.

g. A manufacturing firm pays stockholders $100,000 dividend in cash.

h. A company purchases 100 shares of Apple Computer common stock for $5,000 cash.

i. A company purchases a piece of land for $50,000 cash. An appraiser for the buyer valued the land at $52,500.

j. A manufacturing company purchases the patent (an intangible asset) on a new digital satellite system for television reception for $500,000 cash and a $400,000 note payable due in one year at 10 percent annual interest.

k. A local company is a sole proprietorship (one owner); its owner buys a car for $10,000 for personal use. Answer from the company's point of view.

l. A company signs a six-month note for a $1,000 loan on June 30, 20A to be paid back on December 31, 20A with 10 percent annual interest. Answer for the June 30, 20A date.

m. A company pays $1,500 principal on its note payable.

*Required:*

1. Indicate the appropriate account titles, if any, affected in each of the preceding events. Consider what is given and what is received.

2. At what amount would you record the truck in (*b*)? The land in (*i*)? What measurement principle are you applying?

3. For (*c*), what accounting concept did you apply? For (*k*), what accounting concept did you apply?

**E2–3** **Classifying Accounts and Their Usual Balances**

As described in a recent annual report, Polaroid Corporation designs, manufactures, and markets worldwide a variety of products primarily in instant image recording fields, including instant photographic cameras and films, electronic imaging recording devices, conventional films, and light polarizing filters and lenses.

■ **LO2, 4**

Polaroid Corporation

*Required:*

For each of the following accounts from Polaroid's recent balance sheet, complete the following chart by indicating whether the account is categorized as a current asset (CA), noncurrent asset (NCA), current liability (CL), noncurrent liability (NCL), or stockholders' equity (SE), and whether the account usually has a debit or credit balance.

| Account | Balance Sheet Categorization | Debit or Credit Balance |
|---|---|---|
| 1. Land | _____ | _____ |
| 2. Retained earnings | _____ | _____ |
| 3. Notes payable (due in 3 years) | _____ | _____ |
| 4. Prepaid expenses | _____ | _____ |
| 5. Long-term investments | _____ | _____ |
| 6. Contributed capital | _____ | _____ |
| 7. Machinery and equipment | _____ | _____ |
| 8. Accounts payable | _____ | _____ |
| 9. Short-term investments | _____ | _____ |
| 10. Taxes payable | _____ | _____ |

**E2–4** **Determining Financial Statement Effects of Several Transactions**

The following events occurred for Favata Company:

■ **LO3**

*a.* Received investment of cash by organizers, $20,000.

*b.* Borrowed cash from a bank, $6,000.

*c.* Purchased $12,000 in land; paid $1,000 in cash and signed a mortgage note with a local bank for the balance (due in 15 years).

*d.* Loaned $300 to an employee who signed a note due in three months. *Note receivable*

*e.* Paid bank $6,000, amount borrowed in (*b*).

*f.* Purchased $8,000 of equipment, paying $1,000 in cash and the rest on a note due to the manufacturer.

*Required:*

For each of the events (*a*) through (*f*), perform transaction analysis and indicate the account, amount, and direction of the effect (+ for increase and − for decrease) on the accounting equation. Check that the accounting equation remains in balance after each transaction. Use the following headings:

| Event | Assets | = | Liabilities | + | Stockholders' Equity |
|---|---|---|---|---|---|

**E2–5** **Determining Financial Statement Effects of Several Transactions**

Nike, Inc., with headquarters in Beaverton, Oregon, is one of the world's leading manufacturers of athletic shoes and sports apparel. The following activities occurred during a recent year. The amounts are rounded to millions of dollars.

■ **LO3**

Nike, Inc.

*a.* Purchased $216.3 in property, plant, and equipment; paid $5 in long-term debt and the rest in cash.

b. Issued $21.1 in additional stock for cash.

c. Declared $100 in dividends; paid $78.8 during the year with the rest due in the following year.

d. Several Nike investors sold their own stock to other investors on the stock exchange for $21.

e. Repaid $3.2 in principal on long-term debt obligations.

f. Sold $1.4 in investments in other companies for $1.4 cash.

*Required:*

1. For each of these events, perform transaction analysis and indicate the account, amount, and direction of the effect on the accounting equation. Check that the accounting equation remains in balance after each transaction. Use the following headings:

| Event | Assets | = | Liabilities | + | Stockholders' Equity |
|-------|--------|---|-------------|---|----------------------|
|       |        |   |             |   |                      |

2. Explain your response to Transaction (d).

**LO4    E2–6    Recording Investing and Financing Activities**
Refer to E2–4.

*Required:*
For each of the events in E2–4, prepare journal entries, checking that debits equal credits.

**LO4    E2–7    Recording Investing and Financing Activities**
Refer to E2–5.

*Required:*

1. For each of the events in E2–5, prepare journal entries, checking that debits equal credits.

2. Explain your response to Transaction (d).

**LO4    E2–8    Analyzing the Effects of Transactions in T-Accounts**
Mulkeen Service Company, Inc., was organized by Conor Mulkeen and five other investors. The following activities occurred during the year:

a. Received $60,000 cash from the investors; each was issued 1,000 shares of capital stock.

b. Purchased equipment for use in the business at a cost of $12,000; one-fourth was paid in cash, and the balance is due in six months (the company signed a note).

c. Signed an agreement with a cleaning service to pay it $120 per week for cleaning the corporate offices.

d. Lent $2,000 to one of the investors who signed a note due in six months.

e. Issued stock to additional investors who contributed $4,000 in cash and land valued at $10,000 in exchange for stock in the company.

f. Paid $2,000 principal on the note payable in (a).

g. Conor Mulkeen borrowed $10,000 for personal use from a local bank and signed a one-year note.

*Required:*

1. Create T-accounts for the following accounts: Cash, Note Receivable, Equipment, Land, Note Payable, and Contributed Capital. Beginning balances are zero. For each of the preceding transactions, record the effects of the transaction in the appropriate T-accounts. Include good referencing and totals for each T-account.

2. Using the balances in the T-accounts, fill in the following amounts for the accounting equation:

Assets $_____ = Liabilities $_____ + Stockholders' Equity $_____

3. Explain your response to Transactions (c) and (g).

**E2–9** **Inferring Investing and Financing Transactions and Preparing a Balance Sheet** ▪ **LO3, 5**

During its first week of operations, January 1–7, 20A, Fullem Fine Furniture Company completed seven transactions with the dollar effects indicated in the following schedule:

| Accounts | Dollar Effect of Each of the Seven Transactions | | | | | | | Ending Balance |
| | 1 | 2 | 3 | 4 | 5 | 6 | 7 | |
|---|---|---|---|---|---|---|---|---|
| Cash | $12,000 | $50,000 | $(4,000) | $(3,000) | $(7,000) | $(3,000) | $2,000 | |
| Short-term note receivable | | | | 3,000 | | | (2,000) | |
| Store fixtures | | | | | 7,000 | | | |
| Land | | | 12,000 | | | | | |
| Short-term note payable | | 50,000 | 8,000 | | | (3,000) | | |
| Contributed capital | 12,000 | | | | | | | |

*Required:*

1. Write a brief explanation of Transactions 1 through 7. Explain any assumptions that you made.
2. Compute the ending balance in each account and prepare a classified balance sheet for Fullem Fine Furniture Company on January 7, 20A.

**E2–10** **Inferring Investing and Financing Transactions and Preparing a Balance Sheet** ▪ **LO3, 5**

During its first month of operations, March 20B, Faye's Fashions, Inc., completed seven transactions with the dollar effects indicated in the following schedule:

| Accounts | Dollar Effect of Each of the Seven Transactions | | | | | | | Ending Balance |
| | 1 | 2 | 3 | 4 | 5 | 6 | 7 | |
|---|---|---|---|---|---|---|---|---|
| Cash | $50,000 | $(4,000) | $(4,000) | $(6,000) | $(3,000) | $2,000 | | |
| Short-term investments | | | | 6,000 | | (2,000) | | |
| Short-term note receivable | | | 4,000 | | | | | |
| Computer equipment | | | | | | | $4,000 | |
| Delivery truck | | 25,000 | | | | | | |
| Long-term note payable | | 21,000 | | | (3,000) | | | |
| Contributed capital | 50,000 | | | | | | 4,000 | |

*Required:*

1. Write a brief explanation of Transactions 1 through 7. Explain any assumptions that you made.
2. Compute the ending balance in each account and prepare a classified balance sheet for Faye's Fashions, Inc., at the end of March 20B.

■ **LO4**　　**E2–11**　**Recording Journal Entries**

Boyce Corporation was organized on May 1, 20A. The following transactions occurred during the first month.

a.　Received $60,000 cash from the three investors who organized Boyce Corporation.

b.　Borrowed $20,000 cash and signed a 12 percent note due in two years.

c.　Purchased $10,000 in equipment, paying $1,000 in cash and signing a six-month note for the balance.

d.　Ordered $16,000 in store fixtures.

e.　Paid $1,500 principal on the note signed in (c).

f.　Lent $1,000 to an employee who signed a note to repay the loan in three months.

g.　Received and paid for the store fixtures ordered in (d).

*Required:*

Prepare journal entries for each transaction. (Remember that debits go on top and credits go on the bottom, indented.) Be sure to use good referencing and categorize each account as an asset (A), liability (L), or stockholders' equity (SE). If a transaction does not require a journal entry, explain the reason.

■ **LO4**　　**E2–12**　**Recording Journal Entries**

Philippine Long Distance Telephone Company

In its recent annual report, Philippine Long Distance Telephone Company describes itself as "the largest of 63 entities furnishing telephone services in the Philippines. It has a network of 145 central office exchanges serving the Metro Manila area and 146 other cities and municipalities throughout the country." The stock is traded on the New York Stock Exchange and Pacific Stock Exchange. The monetary unit is the Philippine peso (₱). The following transactions were adapted from the annual report. Amounts are in millions of pesos.

a.　Declared ₱1,115.8 in dividends to be paid next month.

b.　Ordered ₱450 in equipment.

c.　Paid ₱1,115.8 in dividends previously declared in (a).

d.　Issued additional stock for ₱6,127.1 in cash.

e.　Sold land at its cost for cash, ₱3,549.9.

f.　Received the equipment ordered in Transaction (b), paying ₱120 in cash and signing a note for the balance.

g.　Purchased temporary investments for ₱745.6.

h.　Paid ₱4,642.6 in long-term debt.

*Required:*

Prepare journal entries for each transaction. (Remember that debits go on top and credits go on the bottom, indented.) Be sure to use good referencing and categorize each account as an asset (A), liability (L), or stockholders' equity (SE). If a transaction does not require a journal entry, explain the reason.

■ **LO4, 6**　　**E2–13**　**Analyzing the Effects of Transactions Using T-Accounts and Interpreting the Financial Leverage Ratio as a Manager of the Company**

Doane Company has been operating for one year (20A). You are a member of the management team investigating expansion ideas, all of which will require borrowing funds from banks. At the start of 20B, Doane's T-account balances were as follows:

*Assets:*

| Cash | | Short-Term Investments | | Property and Equipment | |
|---|---|---|---|---|---|
| 5,000 | | 2,000 | | 4,000 | |

*Liabilities:*

| Short-Term Notes Payable | | Long-Term Notes Payable | |
|---|---|---|---|
| | 300 | | 600 |

*Stockholders' Equity:*

| Contributed Capital | Retained Earnings |
|---|---|
| 8,100 | 2,000 |

*Required:*

1. Using the data from these T-accounts, determine the amounts for the following on January 1, 20B:

    Assets $_____ = Liabilities $_____ + Stockholders' Equity $_____.

2. Enter the following 20B transactions in the T-accounts:

    (*a*) Paid one-half of the principal on the long-term note payable.

    (*b*) Sold $1,500 of the investments for $1,500 cash.

    (*c*) Paid in full the principal on the short-term notes payable.

    (*d*) Sold one-fourth of the property and equipment for $1,000 in cash.

    (*e*) Borrowed $1,600 at 10 percent from the bank (signing a note); principal and interest are due in three years.

    (*f*) Paid $600 in dividends to stockholders.

3. Compute ending balances in the T-accounts to determine amounts for the following on December 31, 20B:

    Assets $_____ = Liabilities $_____ + Stockholders' Equity $_____.

4. Calculate the financial leverage ratio at December 31, 20B. If the industry average for the financial leverage ratio is 2.00, what does your computation suggest to you about Doane Company? Would you support expansion by borrowing? Why or why not?

**E2–14** **Preparing a Balance Sheet**          ▓ **LO5**
Refer to E2–13.

*Required:*
From the ending balances in the T-accounts in E2–13, prepare a classified balance sheet for December 31, 20B, in good form.

**E2–15** **Analyzing the Effects of Transactions Using T-Accounts, Preparing a Balance Sheet, and**     ▓ **LO4, 5, 6**
**Evaluating the Financial Leverage Ratio over Time as a Bank Loan Officer**
At the beginning of year 20F, Lee Delivery Company, Inc., which was organized in 20C, applied to your bank for a $100,000 loan to expand the business. The vice president of the bank asked you to review the information and make a recommendation on lending the funds. The following transactions occurred during year 20C (its first year of operations):

(*a*) Received the cash from the organizers, $40,000.

(*b*) Purchased land for $12,000 and signed a one-year note (at a 10 percent annual interest rate).

(*c*) Bought two used delivery trucks for operating purposes at the start of the year at a cost of $10,000 each; paid $2,000 cash and signed a promissory note due in three years for the rest (at 11 percent annual interest).

(*d*) Sold one-fourth of the land for $3,000 to Birkins Moving, which signed a six-month note.

(*e*) Paid $2,000 cash to a truck repair shop for a new motor for one of the trucks. (*Hint:* Increase the account you used to record the purchase of the trucks since the usefulness of the truck has been improved.)

(*f*) Traded the other truck and $6,000 cash for a new one.

(*g*) Stockholder Jonah Lee paid $22,000 cash for a vacant lot (land) for his personal use.

(*h*) Repurchased $5,000 of its capital stock from one of the investors.

(*i*) Collected $1,000 cash on the principal of the note due from Birkins Moving in (*d*).

(*j*) Paid one-third of the principal of the note due for the delivery trucks in (*c*).

*Required:*

1. Set up appropriate T-accounts with beginning balances of $0 for Cash, Note Receivable, Land, Equipment, Short-Term Notes Payable, Long-Term Notes Payable, and Contributed Capital. Using the T-accounts, record the effects of these transactions by Lee Delivery Company.

2. Prepare a classified balance sheet for Lee Delivery Company at the end of 20C.

3. At the end of the next two years, Lee Delivery Company reported the following amounts on its balance sheets:

|  | End of 20D | End of 20E |
| --- | --- | --- |
| Assets | $90,000 | $120,000 |
| Liabilities | 40,000 | 70,000 |
| Stockholders' Equity | 50,000 | 50,000 |

Compute the company's financial leverage ratio for 20D and 20E. What is the trend and what does this suggest about the company?

4. What recommendation would you make to the bank's vice president about lending the money to Lee Delivery Company?

**LO4**     **E2–16**     **Explaining the Effects of Transactions on Balance Sheet Accounts Using T-Accounts**

Heavey and Lovas Furniture Repair Service, a company with two stockholders, began operations on June 1, 20A. The following T-accounts indicate the activities for the month of June.

| | + Cash (A) − | | | + Notes Receivable (A) − | | | + Tools and Equipment (A) ⌒ | |
| --- | --- | --- | --- | --- | --- | --- | --- | --- |
| a. | 17,000 | (b) 10,000 | c. | 1,500 | d. 500 | a. | 3,000 | f. 800 |
| d. | 500 | (c) 1,500 | | | | | | |
| f. | 800 | (e) 1,000 | | | | | | |

| | + Building (A) − | | − Notes Payable (L) + | | ⌐ Contributed Capital (SE) + | |
| --- | --- | --- | --- | --- | --- | --- |
| b. | 50,000 | | e. 1,000 | (b) 40,000 | | a. 20,000 |

*Required:*

Explain Transactions (*a*) through (*f*), which resulted in the entries in the T-accounts. That is, what activity made the account increase and/or decrease?

**LO4**     **E2–17**     **Inferring Typical Investing and Financing Activities in Accounts**

The following T-accounts indicate the effects of normal business transactions:

| | Equipment | | | Note Receivable | | | Notes Payable | |
| --- | --- | --- | --- | --- | --- | --- | --- | --- |
| 1/1 | 300 | | 1/1 | 75 | | | 130 | 1/1 |
| | 250 | ? | | ? | 290 | ? | 170 | |
| 12/31 | 450 | | 12/31 | 50 | | | 180 | 12/31 |

*Required:*

1. Describe the typical investing and financing transactions that affect each T-account. That is, what economic events occur to make these accounts increase and decrease?

2. For each T-account, compute the missing amounts.

**LO7**     **E2–18**     **Identifying Investing and Financing Activities Affecting Cash Flows**

Woolworth
Corporation

Woolworth Corporation is a large global retailer with stores and related support facilities. It operates athletic and specialty footwear companies (Foot Locker family of businesses and Kinney shoe stores), specialty nonfootwear chains (After Thoughts, Accessory Lady, The San Francisco Music Box Company, and The Best of Times specialty stores), and clothing stores (Northern Reflections, Northern Elements, and Northern Getaway). The following are several of Woolworth's investing and financing activities that were reflected in a recent annual statement of cash flows.

*a.* Reduction of long-term debt.

*b.* Purchase of investments.

*c.* Issuance of common stock.

*d.* Capital expenditures (for property, plant, and equipment).

*e.* Issuance of long-term debt.

*f.* Proceeds from sales of assets and investments.

*g.* Dividends paid.

***Required:***

For each of these, indicate whether the activity is investing (I) or financing (F) and the direction of the effect on cash flows (+ = increases cash; − = decreases cash).

**E2–19** **Preparing the Investing and Financing Section of the Statement of Cash Flows**

■ **LO7**

Hilton Hotels Corporation constructs, operates, and franchises domestic and international hotel and hotel-casino properties. Information from the company's recent annual statement of cash flows indicates the following investing and financing activities during that year (simplified):

Hilton Hotels

| | |
|---|---|
| Additional borrowing from banks | $438.5 |
| Purchase of investments | 282.2 |
| Sale of property (assume sold at cost) | 5.4 |
| Issuance of stock | 2.9 |
| Purchase and renovation of properties | 274.5 |
| Payment of debt | 32.2 |
| Receipt of payment on a note receivable | 5.4 |

***Required:***

Prepare the Investing and Financing sections of the statement of cash flows for Hilton hotels. Assume that year-end is December 31, 20C.

**E2–20** **Finding Financial Information as a Potential Investor**

■ **LO2, 5, 7**

You are considering investing the cash you inherited from your grandfather in various stocks. You have received the annual reports of several major companies.

***Required:***

For each of the following, indicate where you would locate the information in an annual report. (*Hint:* The information may be in more than one location.)

1. Total current assets.

2. Amount of debt principal repaid during the year.

3. Summary of significant accounting policies.

4. Cash received from sales of noncurrent assets.

5. Amount of dividends paid during the year.

6. Short-term obligations.

7. Date of the statement of financial position.

## PROBLEMS

**P2–1** **Identifying Accounts on a Classified Balance Sheet and Their Normal Debit or Credit**

■ **LO1, 2**

**Balances** (AP2–1)

Chevron Corporation explores, produces, refines, markets, and supplies crude oil, natural gas, and petroleum products in the United States and 24 other countries. The following are several of the accounts from a recent balance sheet of Chevron Corporation:

Chevron
Corporation

(1) Cash and Cash Equivalents

(2) Accounts and Notes Receivable

(3) Contributed Capital

(4) Long-Term Debt

(5) Prepaid Expenses

(6) Patents (an intangible asset)

(7) Federal and Other Taxes Payable

(8) Material, Supplies, and Other Inventories

(9) Accounts Payable

(10) Marketable Securities

(11) Capital Lease Obligations

(12) Retained Earnings

(13) Crude Oil and Petroleum Products

(14) Long-Term Investments

(15) Property, Plant, and Equipment

*Required:*

For each account, indicate how it normally should be categorized on a classified balance sheet. Use CA for current asset, NCA for noncurrent asset, CL for current liability, NCL for noncurrent liability, and SE for stockholders' equity. Also indicate whether the account normally has a debit or credit balance.

**LO2, 3**   **P2–2**   **Determining Financial Statement Effects of Various Transactions** (AP2–2)

Lester's Home Healthcare Services was organized on January 1, 20A, by four friends. Each organizer invested $10,000 in the company and, in turn, was issued 8,000 shares of stock. To date, they are the only stockholders. During the first month (January 20A), the company completed the following six transactions:

a. Collected a total of $40,000 from the organizers and, in turn, issued the shares of stock.

b. Purchased a building for $65,000, equipment for $16,000, and three acres of land for $12,000; paid $13,000 in cash, with the balance due in 15 years on a 10 percent mortgage payable to the local bank. (*Hint:* Five different accounts are affected.)

c. One stockholder reported to the company that 500 shares of his Lester stock had been sold and transferred to another stockholder for a cash consideration of $5,000.

d. Purchased short-term investments for $3,000 cash.

e. Sold one acre of land for $4,000 to another company for cash.

f. Loaned one of the shareholders $5,000 for moving costs, receiving a signed note due in one year from the shareholder.

*Required:*

1. Was Lester's Home Healthcare Services organized as a sole proprietorship, a partnership, or a corporation? Explain the basis for your answer.

2. During the first month, the records of the company were inadequate. You were asked to prepare the summary of the preceding transactions. To develop a quick assessment of their economic effects on Lester's Home Healthcare Services, you have decided to complete the tabulation that follows and to use plus (+) for increases and minus (−) for decreases for each account. The first transaction is used as an example.

|  | Assets | | | | | | = | Liabilities | + | Stockholders' Equity | |
|---|---|---|---|---|---|---|---|---|---|---|---|
|  | Cash | Short-term Investments | Notes Receivable | Land | Building | Equipment |  | Notes Payable |  | Contributed Capital | Retained Earnings |
| (a) | +40,000 | | | | | | = | | | +40,000 | |

3. Did you include the transaction between the two stockholders—Transaction (c)—in the tabulation? Why?

4. Based only on the completed tabulation, provide the following amounts (show computations):

a. Total assets at the end of the month.

b. Total liabilities at the end of the month.

c. Total stockholders' equity at the end of the month.

d. Cash balance at the end of the month.

e. Total current assets at the end of the month.

**LO4, 5, 6**   **P2–3**    **Recording Transactions in T-Accounts, Preparing the Balance Sheet, and Evaluating the Financial Leverage Ratio** (AP2–3)

Patrie Plastics Company has been operating for three years. At December 31, 20C, the accounting records reflected the following:

| | | | |
|---|---|---|---|
| Cash | $ 35,000 | Intangibles | $ 5,000 |
| Short-term investments | 3,000 | Accounts payable | 25,000 |
| Accounts receivable | 5,000 | Accrued liabilities payable | 3,000 |
| Inventory | 40,000 | Short-term note payable | 12,000 |
| Long-term note receivable | 2,000 | Long-term note payable | 80,000 |
| Equipment | 80,000 | Contributed capital | 150,000 |
| Factory building | 150,000 | Retained earnings | 50,000 |

During the year 20D, the following summarized transactions were completed:

a. Purchased equipment that cost $30,000; paid $10,000 cash and signed a one-year note for the balance.

b. Issued an additional 2,000 shares of capital stock for $20,000 cash.

c. Lent $12,000 to a supplier who signed a two-year note.

d. Purchased $15,000 in investments.

e. Paid $5,000 on the note in Transaction (a).

f. Borrowed $20,000 cash on a 10 percent interest-bearing note from a local bank (on December 31, 20D), payable June 30, 20E.

g. Purchased a patent (an intangible asset) for $6,000.

h. Built an addition to the factory for $42,000; paid $15,000 in cash and signed a three-year note for the balance.

i. Hired a new president at the end of the year. The contract was for $85,000 per year plus *Not a transaction* options to purchase company stock at a set price based on company performance.

j. Returned defective equipment to the manufacturer, receiving a cash refund of $2,000.

*Required:*

1. Create T-accounts for each of the accounts on the balance sheet and enter the balances at the end of 20C as beginning balances for 20D.

2. Record each of the transactions for 20D in T-accounts (including referencing) and determine the ending balances.

3. Explain your response to Transaction (i).

4. Prepare a classified balance sheet at December 31, 20D.

5. Compute the financial leverage ratio for 20D. What does this suggest about Patrie Plastics?

**P2–4** **Identifying Effects of Transactions on the Statement of Cash Flows** (AP2–4)   ■ **LO7**
Refer to P2–3.

*Required:*
Using the transactions (a) through (j) in P2–3, indicate whether each transaction is an investing (I) or financing (F) activity for the year and the direction of the effect on cash flows (+ for increase and − for decrease). If there is no effect on cash flows, write NE.

**P2–5** **Recording Transactions, Preparing Journal Entries, Posting to T-Accounts, Preparing the Balance Sheet, and Evaluating the Financial Leverage Ratio** (AP2–5)   ■ **LO4, 5, 6**
Foster's Brewing Group Limited is an Australian corporation that brews beer, including the popular Foster's and Molson brands, and markets its products around the world. The following page presents Foster's balance sheet from a recent year.

Foster's Brewing

Assume that the following transactions occurred in July 19A:

a. Paid $134.1 in dividends owed to shareholders.

b. Paid $59.7 cash for additional intangibles.

c. Issued additional shares of stock for $1,203.1 in cash.

d. Repaid $150.0 of borrowings to banks.

e. Purchased property, plant, and equipment; paid $161.1 in cash and $479.4 with additional bank loans.

f. Acquired additional investments; paid $48.3 in cash.

**FOSTER'S BREWING GROUP LIMITED AND
CONTROLLING ENTITIES
Balance Sheet at 30 June 19A
(in millions of Australian dollars)**

### Assets

| | |
|---|---|
| Cash | $ 106.6 |
| Receivables | 1,129.8 |
| Inventories | 227.1 |
| Investments | 1,198.2 |
| Property, plant, and equipment | 2,030.3 |
| Intangibles | 717.8 |
| Other assets | 893.9 |
| Total assets | 6,303.7 |

### Liabilities

| | |
|---|---|
| Creditors | 928.9 |
| Borrowings | 1,958.9 |
| Other liabilities (includes income taxes and dividends due) | 596.6 |
| Total liabilities | 3,484.4 |
| Net assets | $2,819.3 |

### Shareholders' Equity

| | |
|---|---|
| Share capital | $3,267.4 |
| Reserves | 882.6 |
| Accumulated losses | (1,362.8) |
| Other | 32.1 |
| Total shareholders' equity | $2,819.3 |

*Required:*
1. Prepare a journal entry for each transaction.
2. Create T-accounts for each balance sheet account and include the June 30, 19A, balances. Post each journal entry to the appropriate T-accounts.
3. Prepare a balance sheet from the T-account ending balances for Foster's at July 31, 19A, based on these transactions. Use the same format as Foster's used.
4. Explain the meaning of "Accumulated losses."
5. Compute Foster's financial leverage ratio at the end of July. What does this suggest about Foster's?

■ **LO7**    **P2–6**    **Preparing the Investing and Financing Sections of a Statement of Cash Flows** (AP2–6)
Foster's Brewing    Refer to P2–5.

*Required:*
Based on the activities for the month of July, prepare the Investing and Financing sections of a statement of cash flows.

## ALTERNATE PROBLEMS

■ **LO1, 2**    **AP2–1**    **Identifying Accounts on a Classified Balance Sheet and Their Normal Debit or Credit Balances** (P2–1)

Hasbro, Inc.    According to a recent Form 10-K report of Hasbro, Inc., "The Company is a worldwide leader in the design, manufacture and marketing of toys, games, interactive software, puzzles and infant products." Hasbro produces products under several brands including Tonka, Milton Bradley, Playskool, and Parker Brothers. The following are several of the accounts from a recent balance sheet:

(1) Accounts Receivable          (4) Long-Term Debt
(2) Short-Term Borrowings        (5) Prepaid Expenses
(3) Contributed Capital          (6) Intangibles

(7) Property, Plant, and Equipment
(8) Retained Earnings
(9) Accounts Payable
(10) Cash and Cash Equivalents
(11) Accrued Liabilities Payable
(12) Deferred Long-Term Liabilities
(13) Inventories
(14) Income Taxes Payable

*Required:*
Indicate how each account normally should be categorized on a classified balance sheet. Use CA for current asset, NCA for noncurrent asset, CL for current liability, NCL for noncurrent liability, and SE for stockholders' equity. Also indicate whether the account normally has a debit or credit balance.

**AP2–2**     **Determining Financial Statement Effects of Various Transactions and Interpreting the Financial Leverage Ratio** (P2–2)

■ **LO2, 3**

Malamud Incorporated is a small manufacturing company that makes model trains to sell to toy stores. It has a small service department that repairs customers' trains for a fee. The company has been in business for five years. At the end of the most recent year, 20E, the accounting records reflected total assets of $500,000 and total liabilities of $200,000. During the current year, 20F, the following summarized transactions were completed:

*a.* Issued an additional 10,000 shares of capital stock for $100,000 cash.

*b.* Borrowed $120,000 cash from the bank and signed a 10-year 12 percent note.

*c.* Built an addition on the factory for $200,000 and paid cash to the contractor.

*d.* Purchased equipment for the new addition for $30,000, paying $3,000 in cash and signing a note due in six months for the balance.

*e.* Purchased $85,000 in long-term investments.

*f.* Returned a $3,000 piece of equipment, from (*d*), because it proved to be defective; received a reduction of its short-term note payable.

*g.* Paid $12,000 on principal due on note in (*b*).

*h.* Purchased a delivery truck (equipment) for $10,000; paid $5,000 cash and the remainder on a short-term note payable.

*i.* Loaned the company president, Jennifer Malamud, $2,000 cash. Ms. Malamud signed a note with terms showing the principal plus 10 percent annual interest due in one year.

*j.* A stockholder sold $5,000 of his capital stock in Malamud Incorporated to his neighbor.

*k.* Received $250 cash from Ms. Malamud on note due, Transaction (*i*).

*Required:*

1. During the first month, the records of the company were inadequate. You were asked to prepare the summary of the preceding transactions. To develop a quick assessment of their economic effects on Malamud Incorporated, you have decided to complete the tabulation that follows and to use plus (+) for increases and minus (−) for decreases for each account. The first transaction is used as an example.

| | Assets | | | | = | Liabilities | | + | Stockholders' Equity | |
|---|---|---|---|---|---|---|---|---|---|---|
| Cash | Notes Receivable | Long-Term Investments | Equipment | Building | | Short-Term Notes Payable | Long-Term Notes Payable | | Contributed Capital | Retained Earnings |
| (*a*) +100,000 | | | | | = | | | | +100,000 | |

2. Did you include Transaction (*j*) in the tabulation? Why?

3. Based on beginning balances plus the completed tabulation, provide the following amounts (show computations):

   *a.* Total assets at the end of the month.

   *b.* Total liabilities at the end of the month.

   *c.* Total shareholders' equity at the end of the month.

4. Compute the company's financial leverage ratio. What does this suggest to you about Malamud Incorporated?

■ **LO4, 5, 6**     **AP2–3**

Ethan Allen Inc.

**Recording Transactions in T-Accounts, Preparing the Balance Sheet, and Evaluating the Financial Leverage Ratio (P2–3)**

Ethan Allen Interiors Inc. is a leading manufacturer and retailer of home furnishings in 310 retail stores in the United States and abroad. The following is adapted from a recent annual financial report (assume the fiscal year ends on June 30, 20B). Dollars are in thousands.

| | | | |
|---|---:|---|---:|
| Cash and cash equivalents | $ 19,380 | Intangibles | $ 50,773 |
| Short-term investments | 0 | Other assets | 3,361 |
| Accounts receivable | 35,640 | Accounts payable | 51,135 |
| Short-term note receivable | 686 | Accrued expenses payable | 5,863 |
| Inventories | 114,364 | Other current liabilities | 16,614 |
| Prepaid expenses and | | Long-term debt | 45,191 |
|   other current assets | 17,829 | Contributed capital | 229,008 |
| Property, plant and equipment | 188,171 | Retained earnings | 85,312 |
| Long-term investments and | | | |
|   note receivable | 2,919 | | |

Assume that the following transactions occurred in the first quarter ended September 30, 20B:

a.  Received $630 on long-term receivables owed by affiliates.

b.  Paid $12,340 in principal on long-term debt.

c.  Purchased $3,400 in additional intangibles.

d.  Sold equipment at its cost for $4,020 cash.

e.  Purchased short-term investments of $2,980.

f.  Issued additional shares of stock for $1,020 in cash.

g.  Purchased property, plant, and equipment; paid $1,830 in cash and $9,400 with additional long-term bank loans.

h.  Sold at cost other assets for $310 cash.

i.  Declared and paid $300 in dividends.

*Required:*

1. Create T-accounts for each of the accounts on the balance sheet; enter the balances at June 30, 20B.

2. Record each of the transactions for the first quarter ended September 30, 20B, in the T-accounts (including referencing) and determine the ending balances.

3. Prepare a classified balance sheet at September 30, 20B.

4. Compute the financial leverage ratio for the quarter ended September 30, 20B. What does this suggest about Ethan Allen Inc.?

■ **LO7**     **AP2–4**

Ethan Allen Inc.

**Identifying Effects of Transactions on the Statement of Cash Flows (P2–4)**

Refer to AP2–3.

*Required:*

Using the transactions (*a*) through (*i*) in AP2–3, indicate whether each transaction is an investing (I) or financing (F) activity for the year and the direction of the effect on cash flows (+ for increase and − for decrease). If there is no effect on cash flows, write NE.

■ **LO4, 5, 6**     **AP2–5**

DaimlerChrysler Corporation

**Recording Transactions, Preparing Journal Entries, Posting to T-Accounts, Preparing the Balance Sheet, and Evaluating the Financial Leverage Ratio (P2–5)**

In 1998, Daimler-Benz and Chrysler merged to form DaimlerChrysler Corporation, a global manufacturer of automotive and transportation products and services. The following is DaimlerChrysler's (simplified) balance sheet from a recent year. Notice the different order of the accounts of this international company (based in Stuttgart, Germany).

**DAIMLERCHRYSLER CORPORATION**
**Balance Sheet at December 31, 20A**
**(in millions of Euros)**

| Assets | |
|---|---:|
| Intangible assets | € 2,561 |
| Property, plant and equipment | 29,532 |
| Long-term investments | 2,851 |
| Equipment on operating leases | 14,662 |
| **Fixed assets** | **49,606** |
| Inventories | 11,796 |
| Accounts and other receivables | 44,848 |
| Marketable securities | 12,160 |
| Cash and cash equivalents | 6,589 |
| **Current assets** | **75,393** |
| Prepaid expenses and other assets | 11,150 |
| **Total assets** | **136,149** |
| **Liabilities and Stockholders' Equity** | |
| Contributed capital | 9,835 |
| Retained earnings | 20,532 |
| **Stockholders' equity** | **30,367** |
| Accrued liabilities | 34,629 |
| Accounts payable | 12,848 |
| Other liabilities | 58,305 |
| **Total liabilities** | **105,782** |
| **Total liabilities and stockholders' equity** | **136,149** |

Assume that the following transactions occurred in 20B:

a.  Issued additional shares of stock for €1,200 in cash.

b.  Repaid €3,000 of borrowings to banks (included in other liabilities).

c.  Declared and paid €510 in dividends to shareholders.

d.  Purchased additional intangibles for €100 cash.

e.  Purchased property, plant, and equipment; paid €160.0 in cash and €580.0 with additional bank loans.

f.  Acquired additional investments; paid €3,000 in cash; one-half were long term.

g.  Lent €250 to affiliates, who signed a six-month note.

h.  Sold marketable securities costing €2,800 for €2,800 in cash.

*Required:*

1.  Prepare a journal entry for each transaction.

2.  Create T-accounts for each balance sheet account and include the December 31, 20A, balances. Post each journal entry to the appropriate T-accounts.

3.  Prepare a balance sheet from the T-account ending balances for DaimlerChrysler at December 31, 20B, based on these transactions. Use the same format that DaimlerChrysler uses.

4.  Compute DaimlerChrysler's financial leverage ratio at the end of 20B. What does this suggest about the company?

**AP2–6**  **Preparing the Investing and Financing Sections of a Statement of Cash Flows** (P2–6)
Refer to AP2–5.

■ **LO7**

DaimlerChrysler
Corporation

*Required:*
Based on the activities for 20B, prepare the investing and financing sections of a statement of cash flows.

# CASES AND PROJECTS

## FINANCIAL REPORTING AND ANALYSIS CASES

■ **LO1, 2, 3, 6, 7**

Urban Outfitters

**STANDARD &POOR'S**

**CP2–1**

### Finding Financial Information

Refer to the financial statements and accompanying notes of Urban Outfitters given in Appendix C at the end of this book or open file URBNF10K.doc in the S&P directory on the student CD-ROM.

**Required:**

1. Is the company a corporation, a partnership, or a proprietorship? How do you know?
2. Use the company's balance sheet to determine the amounts in the accounting equation (A = L + SE).
3. The company shows on the balance sheet that inventories are worth $21,881,000. Does this amount represent the expected selling price? Why or why not?
4. What is the company's fiscal year-end? Where did you find the exact date?
5. What are the company's long-term obligations?
6. Compute the company's financial leverage ratio and explain its meaning.
7. How much cash did the company spend on purchasing property, plant, and equipment each year (capital expenditures)? Where did you find the information?

■ **LO2, 6, 7**

American Eagle Outfitters vs. Urban Outfitters

**STANDARD &POOR'S**

**CP2–2**

### Comparing Companies within an Industry

Refer to the financial statements and accompanying notes of American Eagle Outfitters given in Appendix B, Urban Outfitters given in Appendix C, and the Standard and Poor's Industry Ratio Report given in Appendix D at the end of this book or open file CP2-2.xls in the S&P directory on the student CD-ROM.

**Required:**

1. Which company is larger in terms of total assets?
2. Compute the financial leverage ratio for both companies. Which company is assuming more risk? Why do you think that?
3. Compare the financial leverage ratio for both companies to the industry average from the Standard and Poor's Industry Ratio Report. Are these two companies financing assets with debt more or less than the industry average? How is the financial leverage ratio influenced by these companies' choice to rent space instead of buying it?
4. In the most recent year, what were the net cash flows (that is, the increases in cash minus the decreases in cash) related to the buying maturing, and selling of investments (marketable securities) for each company?
5. How much did each company pay in dividends for the most recent year?
6. What account title does each company use to report any land, buildings, and equipment it may have?

■ **LO5, 6**

Papa John's International

**CP2–3**

### Broadening Financial Research Skills: Locating Financial Information on the EDGAR Database

The Securities and Exchange Commission (SEC) regulates companies that issue stock on the stock market. It receives financial reports from public companies electronically under a system called *EDGAR* (Electronic Data Gathering and Retrieval Service). Using the Internet, anyone may search the database for the reports that have been filed.

Using your Web browser, access the EDGAR database at www.freeedgar.com. To search the database, type in "Papa Johns," click on "Search," and then click on "View Filings" when Papa John's International appears.

**Required:**

To look at SEC filings,

1. Click on the 10-Q (quarterly) report dated 8/11/99. Then skim down the Table of Contents to Item 1 and click on "Balance Sheet."
   a. What was the amount of Papa John's total assets for the most recent quarter reported?
   b. Did long-term debt increase or decrease for the quarter?
   c. Compute the financial leverage ratio. How does it compare to the ratio indicated for Papa John's in the chapter? What does this suggest about the company?

2. Click on "Cash Flow Statement."

   *a.* What amount did Papa John's spend on capital expenditures for the period?

   *b.* What was the total amount of cash flows from financing activities?

**CP2–4** **Interpreting the Financial Press**

The May 24, 1999, edition of *Fortune* magazine includes an article entitled "A Crash Course for Online Investors: The SEC Can't Always Protect You."* You can access the article on the Libby/Libby/Short website at www.mhhe.com/business/accounting/libby3.

*© 1999 Time Inc. All rights reserved.

Fortune

*Required:*

Read the article and then answer the following questions:

1. What is a cyberinvestor according to the article?

2. What investment risk do cyberinvestors face?

3. List the rules suggested in the article to minimize risk from investing online.

**CP2–5** **Using Financial Reports: Evaluating the Reliability of a Balance Sheet** ■ **LO1**

Betsey Jordan asked a local bank for a $50,000 loan to expand her small company. The bank asked Betsey to submit a financial statement of the business to supplement the loan application. Betsey prepared the following balance sheet.

**Balance Sheet**
**June 30, 20F**

| | |
|---|---:|
| **Assets** | |
| Cash and CDs (investments) | $ 9,000 |
| Inventory | 30,000 |
| Equipment | 46,000 |
| Personal residence (monthly payments, $2,800) | 300,000 |
| Remaining assets | 20,000 |
| **Total assets** | **$405,000** |
| **Liabilities** | |
| Short-term debt to suppliers | $ 62,000 |
| Long-term debt on equipment | 38,000 |
| Total debt | 100,000 |
| **Stockholder's equity** | **305,000** |
| **Total liabilities and stockholder's equity** | **$405,000** |

*Required:*

The balance sheet has several flaws. However, there is at least one major deficiency. Identify it and explain its significance.

**CP2–6** **Using Financial Reports: Analyzing the Balance Sheet** ■ **LO4, 5, 6**

Recent balance sheets of Gateway 2000, Inc. (producer and marketer of personal computers and PC-related products), follows the requirements.

Gateway 2000, Inc.

*Required:*

1. Is Gateway 2000 a corporation, sole proprietorship, or partnership? Explain the basis of your answer.

2. Use the company's balance sheet to determine the amounts in the accounting equation (A = L + SE) for 1998.

3. Calculate the company's financial leverage ratio. Interpret the ratio that you calculated. What other information would make your interpretation more useful?

4. Give the journal entry the company will make when it pays the principal on its long-term debt which is due at the end of 1998.

5. Does the company appear to have been profitable over its years in business? On what account are you basing your answer? Assuming no dividends were paid, how much was net income in 1998? If impossible to determine without an income statement, state so.

**Consolidated Balance Sheets**
**December 31, 1997 and 1998**
**(in thousands)**

| | 1997 | 1998 |
|---|---|---|
| **Assets** | | |
| Current assets: | | |
| Cash and cash equivalents | $ 593,601 | $1,169,810 |
| Marketable securities | 38,648 | 158,657 |
| Accounts receivable | 510,679 | 558,851 |
| Inventory | 249,224 | 167,924 |
| Other | 152,531 | 172,944 |
| Total current assets | 1,544,683 | 2,228,186 |
| Property, plant and equipment, net | 376,467 | 530,988 |
| Intangibles | 82,590 | 65,944 |
| Other assets | 35,531 | 65,262 |
| | $2,039,271 | $2,890,380 |
| **Liabilities and Stockholders' Equity** | | |
| Current liabilities: | | |
| Notes payable | $ 13,969 | $ 11,415 |
| Accounts payable | 488,717 | 718,071 |
| Accrued liabilities | 271,250 | 415,265 |
| Accrued royalties | 159,418 | 167,873 |
| Other current liabilities | 70,552 | 117,050 |
| Total current liabilities | 1,003,906 | 1,429,674 |
| Long-term obligations | 7,240 | 3,360 |
| Warranty and other liabilities | 98,081 | 112,971 |
| Total liabilities | 1,109,227 | 1,546,005 |
| Stockholders' equity: | | |
| Contributed capital | 310,024 | 367,552 |
| Retained earnings | 620,020 | 976,823 |
| Total stockholders' equity | 930,044 | 1,344,375 |
| | $2,039,271 | $2,890,380 |

**LO5, 6**     **CP2–7**

McDonald's
Corporation

### Using Financial Reports: Preparing a Classified Balance Sheet and Analyzing the Financial Leverage Ratio

The following accounts, in alphabetical order, are adapted from a recent McDonald's Corporation's balance sheet (amounts are in millions of dollars):

| | Current Year | Prior Year | | Current Year | Prior Year |
|---|---|---|---|---|---|
| Accounts and notes receivable | $ 609.4 | $ 483.5 | Long-term debt | $ 6,188.6 | $ 4,834.1 |
| Accounts payable | 621.3 | 650.6 | Notes payable (short-term) | 686.8 | 1,293.8 |
| Accrued liabilities | 783.3 | 503.5 | Notes receivable due after one year | 67.9 | 67.0 |
| Cash and equivalents | 299.2 | 341.4 | Other long-term liabilities | 1,574.5 | 1,491.0 |
| Contributed capital | 1,065.3 | 787.8 | Other noncurrent assets | 538.3 | 608.5 |
| Current maturities of long-term debt | 168.0 | 335.6 | Prepaid expenses and other current assets | 323.5 | 246.9 |
| Intangible assets | 973.1 | 827.5 | Property and equipment, net | 16,041.6 | 14,961.4 |
| Inventories | 77.3 | 70.5 | Retained earnings | 8,458.9 | 8,144.1 |
| Investments in and advances to affiliates (long-term) | 854.1 | 634.8 | Taxes payable | 237.7 | 201.0 |

*Required:*

1. Construct a classified balance sheet (with two years reported) for McDonald's Corporation in good form (assume that the current year ends on December 31, 20C).

2. Compute the company's financial leverage ratio for the current year.

3. In comparison to the ratio for the companies in the restaurant industry (as indicated in the chapter for Papa John's and others), how do you interpret this ratio for McDonald's?

# CRITICAL THINKING CASES

**CP2–8**  **Making a Decision as a Financial Analyst: Preparing and Analyzing a Balance Sheet**

 **LO1, 5**

Your best friend from home writes you a letter about an investment opportunity that has come her way. A company is raising money by issuing shares of stock and wants her to invest $20,000 (her recent inheritance from her great-aunt's estate). Your friend has never invested in a company before and, knowing that you are a financial analyst, asks that you look over the balance sheet and send her some advice. An *unaudited* balance sheet, in only moderately good form, is enclosed with the letter:

**DEWEY, CHEETUM, AND HOWE, INC.**
**Balance Sheet**
**For the Year Ending December 31, 20C**

| | |
|---|---:|
| Accounts receivable | $ 8,000 |
| Cash | 1,000 |
| Inventory | 8,000 |
| Furniture and fixtures | 52,000 |
| Delivery truck | 12,000 |
| Buildings (estimated market value) | 98,000 |
| **Total assets** | **$179,000** |
| Accounts payable | $ 16,000 |
| Payroll taxes payable | 13,000 |
| Notes payable | 15,000 |
| Mortgage payable | 50,000 |
| **Total liabilities** | **$ 94,000** |
| Contributed capital | $ 80,000 |
| Retained earnings | 5,000 |
| **Total stockholder's equity** | **$ 85,000** |

There is only one footnote, and it states that the building was purchased for $65,000, has been depreciated by $5,000 on the books, and still carries a mortgage (shown in the liability section). The footnote further states that, in the opinion of the company president, the building is "easily worth $98,000."

*Required:*

1. Draft a new balance sheet for your friend, correcting any errors you note. (If any of the account balances need to be corrected, you may need to adjust the retained earnings balance correspondingly.) If no errors or omissions exist, state so.

2. Write a letter to your friend explaining the changes you made to the balance sheet, if any, and offer your comments on the company's apparent financial condition based only on this information. Suggest other information your friend might want to review before coming to a final decision on whether to invest.

**■ LO2**

Leslie Fay

**CP2–9**

**Evaluating an Ethical Dilemma: Analyzing Management Incentives**
In 1993, Leslie Fay Companies, manufacturer of women's apparel, filed for Chapter 11 bankruptcy protection shortly after a scandal erupted over fraudulent accounting information. As reported in *The Wall Street Journal* (March 28, 1995, p. B1, B16), the company's audit committee report sharply criticized top management, suggesting that "it would have been difficult for senior management not to spot the extensive inventory and sales fraud."

There were numerous ways in which Leslie Fay committed the fraud, according to the report: To boost sales and lower costs, mid-level company officials forged inventory tags, ignored expected inventory shrinkage, multiplied the value of items in inventory, improperly inflated sales, and made up phantom inventory. These officials also constantly altered records to meet sales targets. In March 1995, Leslie Fay's independent auditors, BDO Seidman, filed charges against Leslie Fay management, suggesting a cause of the fraudulent activity was due to senior management's adoption of unrealistic budgets: "Senior management created an environment which encouraged and rewarded the cooking of Leslie Fay's books and records" (*The Wall Street Journal*, March 29, 1995).

*Required:*

1. Describe the parties who were harmed or helped by this fraud.
2. Explain how adopting unrealistic budgets may have contributed to the fraud.
3. Why do you think the independent auditor filed charges against its former client?

## FINANCIAL REPORTING AND ANALYSIS PROJECTS

**■ LO2**

**CP2–10**

**Comparing Balance Sheets across Industries**
Using your web browser, contact the websites of three companies within the same industry. Acquire the balance sheets from the annual reports or 10-K reports. Some companies do not share financial information on the Internet. If the companies file 10-K reports with the SEC electronically, you may also find the information from the SEC's archives at www.freeedgar.com.

*Required:*
Write a short report indicating any similarities and differences, if any, in the asset and liability accounts used by the three companies and their location on the balance sheet.

**■ LO6**

**CP2–11**

**Comparing Financial Leverage Ratio over Time**
Using your web browser, contact the website of Papa John's International (www.papajohns.com). Examine the three most recent years' balance sheets. You may also find the information from the SEC (www.freeedgar.com for the 10-K annual reports).

*Required:*
Write a short memo comparing the company's financial leverage ratio over the three years. Review the section of the annual report entitled "Management Discussion and Analysis" to identify what activities or strategies Papa John's suggests caused changes in the ratio.

**■ LO7**

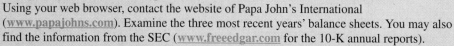

**CP2–12**

**Analyzing Investing and Financing Activities on the Statement of Cash Flows**
Using your web browser, contact the website of a company in the fast-food restaurant industry (such as Wendy's or McDonald's).

*Required:*
Write a short memo describing each of the major investing and financing activities for each year presented.

**■ LO2**

**CP2–13**

**Analyzing an Ethical Dilemma: Reporting Environmental Liabilities**
Obtain a recent news story concerning a company reporting or failing to report an environmental liability.

*Required:*
Write a short memo outlining the nature of the environmental incident and how it was or was not disclosed in the financial statements.

**CP2–14** **Team Project: Analysis of Balance Sheets and Ratios**

LO2, 6, 7

As a team, select an industry to analyze. Using your Web browser, each team member should acquire the annual report or 10-K for one publicly traded company in the industry, with each member selecting a different company.

*Required:*

1. On an individual basis, each team member should write a short report that lists the following information.

   *a.* The date of the balance sheet.

   *b.* The asset accounts.

   *c.* The major investing and financing activities for the most recent period.

   *d.* The financial leverage ratio for the most recent period.

2. Then, as a team, write a short report comparing and contrasting your companies using the preceding attributes. Discuss any patterns across the companies that you as a team observe, and provide potential explanations for any differences discovered.

# Operating Decisions and the Income Statement

## CHAPTER THREE

---

LEARNING **OBJECTIVES**

*After studying this chapter, you should be able to:*

Papa John's and Pizza Hut follow different operating strategies:

• Number one Pizza Hut regularly creates new pizza varieties, such as the New York pizza, the Bigfoot, and the Fiesta Taco pizza with bean sauce and chopped lettuce, to attract customers to its restaurants for eat-in, take-out, or delivery service. The company releases a new pizza, advertises like crazy, waits for the customers to rush in, and hopes they return.*

FOCUS **COMPANY**:

# Papa John's International

### SLINGING DOUGH, CHEESE, TOMATOES, AND PEOPLE IN THE "PIZZA WARS"

• Papa John's focuses on producing a limited variety of pizzas that customers may pick up or have delivered. Papa John's hopes to build strong customer brand loyalty for repeat business by advertising its simple slogan "Better Ingredients. Better Pizza."

Even with such different strategies, Papa John's has declared war on Pizza Hut, aiming to be the number one pizza brand in the world. Papa John's has taken the battle directly to Pizza Hut, running commercials comparing what it believes is the superior quality of its dough and tomatoes with those used by Pizza Hut. Another ad features one of its franchisees, Frank Carney, a co-founder of Pizza Hut, declaring he found a better pizza. Interestingly, Louisville is the hometown of both John Schnatter, founder of Papa John's, and David Novak, president of Pizza Hut's parent company Tricon Global. To rub salt in Pizza Hut's wounds, Papa John's and John Schnatter donated $5 million to name the University of Louisville's new stadium the Papa John's Cardinal Stadium.

But Pizza Hut is fighting back. Its new commercials show purported Papa John's employees pouring watery mushrooms out of a can, suggesting that Papa John's ingredients are inferior. Pizza Hut's full-page newspaper ads in Papa John's key markets declare that Papa John's is providing misinformation and taking cheap shots at Pizza Hut. Papa John's has responded with ads listing ingredients used by both companies.

Now the lawyers have been brought into the scene. In 1998, Pizza Hut filed a lawsuit in a federal court accusing Papa John's of deceptive advertising, asking for $12.5 million in damages and an order to stop using its "Better Ingredients. Better Pizza." slogan. As *Fortune* recently noted, "This is a dough- (and mud-) slinging fight with no truce in sight."*

---

*Roth, Daniel, "This Ain't No Pizza Party," *Fortune* Magazine, November 9, 1998. © 1998 *Time Inc.* All rights reserved.

## BUSINESS BACKGROUND

To become the number one pizza brand globally, Papa John's develops strategies, plans (or expectations), and measurable indicators of progress toward its goal. For example, its growth plan in 1999 was to add 400 new restaurants with two major advertising campaigns and continue to tell the Papa John's story of its fresh dough, tomato sauce, and high-quality cheese. In developing operating and growth strategies, companies such as Papa John's plan their companywide operations in terms of the elements of the income statement (specific revenues and expenses).

Financial analysts also develop their own set of expectations about Papa John's future performance. The published income statement provides the primary basis for comparing these plans or projections to actual results of operations. We discuss these comparisons and the stock market's reactions to Papa John's results throughout this chapter as we learn about income recognition and measurement. To understand how business plans and the results of operations are reflected on the income statement, we need to answer the following questions:

1. What business activities affect the income statement?

2. How are these activities recognized and measured?

3. How are these activities reported on the income statement?

In this chapter, we focus on Papa John's operating activities that involve the sale of food to the public and the sale of ingredients, equipment, and services to franchised restaurants. The results of these activities are reported on its income statement. First we discuss the operating cycle and relevant accounting terms and concepts. Then we examine key income recognition and measurement rules and demonstrate their application in an expanded transaction analysis illustration. From the results, we create an income statement from the operating activities. We also create a statement of retained earnings that links the income statement to the balance sheet and a statement of cash flows that lists operating, investing, and financing activities affecting cash. Finally, we discuss a key analytical ratio.

**ORGANIZATION** OF THE CHAPTER

| • What Business Activities Affect the Income Statement? | • How Are Operating Activities Recognized and Measured? | • Preparation of the Unadjusted Financial Statements |
|---|---|---|
| The Operating Cycle | Accrual Accounting | Unadjusted Income Statement |
| Elements of the Income Statement | The Revenue Principle The Matching Principle | Unadjusted Statement of Retained Earnings |
| | Transaction Analysis Illustrated | Unadjusted Balance Sheet |
| | The Expanded Transaction Analysis Model | The Total Asset Turnover Ratio |
| | Transaction Analysis Rules | |

# WHAT BUSINESS ACTIVITIES AFFECT THE INCOME STATEMENT?

In simple terms, the long-term objective for any business is *to turn cash into more cash*. For companies to stay in business, in the long run, this excess cash must be generated from operations (that is, from the activities for which the business was established, not from borrowing money or selling long-lived assets). Managers know that speeding up the time it takes to turn cash into more cash means more profit and growth. To understand operating activities and decisions to improve profits, you must first understand this *cash-to-cash* concept known as the *operating cycle*.

■ **LEARNING OBJECTIVE 1**

Understand a typical business operating cycle.

## THE OPERATING CYCLE

Exhibit 3.1 presents a typical operating cycle. The **operating cycle (cash-to-cash cycle)** is the *time* it takes for a company to purchase goods or services from suppliers, sell those goods or services to customers, and collect cash from customers. A merchandiser or manufacturer (1) purchases or manufactures and stocks the inventory, (2) pays cash to suppliers, (3) sells the product on credit (hopefully at a price exceeding costs), and (4) finally receives cash from the customer. Thus, cash is turned into more cash. For ongoing businesses, additional inventory is purchased or produced, and the cycle is repeated.

For service companies, the operating cycle is similar. Although spending cash on inventory is not necessary, other relevant costs are incurred in providing the service, such as rent, the use of necessary supplies and equipment, and employee wages. Then the service is provided on credit at a price exceeding costs. Finally, the cash is received from the customer.

In the example in Exhibit 3.1, $10,000 was expended and $17,000 was received for a net increase of $7,000 in cash. The net increase can be used to buy additional assets (resources for the business), pay off debt, and/or distribute to owners.

The length of time for a company's operating cycle depends on the nature of its business. Papa John's cycle should be shorter than that for a company producing consumer products such as refrigerators or clothing. Shortening the operating cycle by

The **OPERATING CYCLE (CASH-TO-CASH CYCLE)** is the time it takes for a company to purchase goods or services from suppliers, sell those goods and services to customers, and collect cash from customers.

EXHIBIT **3.1**

**A Typical Operating Cycle (cash-to-cash cycle)**

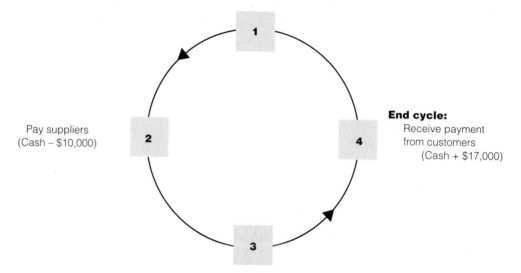

**Begin cycle:**
Purchase or manufacture products or supplies on credit
(e.g., buy $10,000 in inventory on account)

**1**

Pay suppliers
(Cash − $10,000)

**2**

**4**

**End cycle:**
Receive payment
from customers
(Cash + $17,000)

**3**

Deliver product or provide service to customers on credit
(e.g., sell inventory for $17,000 on account)

**What companies can do with excess cash:**

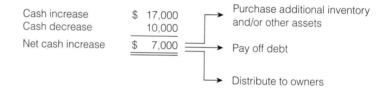

| | |
|---|---|
| Cash increase | $ 17,000 |
| Cash decrease | 10,000 |
| Net cash increase | $ 7,000 |

Purchase additional inventory
and/or other assets

Pay off debt

Distribute to owners

creating incentives to encourage customers to buy sooner and/or pay faster reduces costs and improves the company's financial position.

Although Exhibit 3.1 presents a typical operating cycle, it is important to note that in many instances cash is received (point 4) or paid (point 2) at other times. For example, companies that sell magazine subscriptions receive cash from customers well *before* they deliver any product. Insurance premiums also are usually paid *before* companies are covered for risk of loss, but utility bills usually are received for payment *after* the company has used electricity and gas. Papa John's receives cash from its pizza customers at the point of sale (point 3).

# FINANCIAL **ANALYSIS**

## SHORT-TERM DEBT FINANCING AND THE OPERATING CYCLE

From the timing of the cash outflows and inflows in Exhibit 3.1, we can see that many businesses must pay suppliers and employees before they receive cash from customers causing them to seek short-term financing. Then when the companies receive cash from customers, they pay off the liability. In addition, if a company plans to grow, say to sell twice as many goods as in the prior period, it may not have collected enough cash from the prior period's customers to purchase the amount of inventory needed in the next period. Sources of financing include suppliers through accounts payable and financial institutions (banks and commercial credit companies) through notes payable. Short- and long-term debt financing are discussed in Chapters 9 and 10.

**Underlying Accounting Assumption**    Until a company ceases activities, the operating cycle is repeated continuously. However, decision makers require periodic information about the financial condition and performance of a business. To address the need for "stopping" the operating cycle to measure periodic income, the **time period assumption** (see Exhibit 2.1 in Chapter 2 on the accounting conceptual framework) assumes that the long life of a company can be reported in shorter time periods, usually months, quarters, and years.[1] This assumption requires rules to answer two primary issues for reporting periodic income to users:

1. Recognition issues: *When* should the effects of operating activities be recognized (recorded)?

2. Measurement issues: *What amounts* should be recognized?

Although the time period assumption may appear to be of little consequence at first glance, many of the most difficult accounting problems we examine in this book involve issues in assigning business activities to time periods. Let's first discuss the elements of financial statements that are affected by operating activities.

The **TIME PERIOD ASSUMPTION** indicates that the long life of a company can be reported in shorter time periods.

## ELEMENTS ON THE INCOME STATEMENT

A recent income statement for Papa John's is presented in Exhibit 3.2. For purposes of this chapter, the income statement has been simplified by rounding the dollar amounts.[2] In addition, only one year's income statement is presented here. Publicly traded companies such as Papa John's are required to present income information for three years to help users assess trends over time.

■ **LEARNING OBJECTIVE 2**

Understand the time period assumption and the elements of the income statement.

As we discuss the elements of the income statement, you should refer to the accounting conceptual framework outlined in Exhibit 2.1 in Chapter 2. The concepts relevant to the income statement are discussed in this chapter as they apply to Papa John's.

**Revenues** result from selling goods or services as part of a company's normal ongoing operations (that is, what they are in business to do). When Papa John's sells pizza to consumers or equipment to franchisees, it has earned a revenue. When revenues occur, assets (usually cash or receivables) often increase. Sometimes, if a customer pays for goods or services in advance, a liability account is created (usually a deferred or unearned revenue). At this point, no revenue is earned. There is simply a receipt of cash (an asset) in exchange for a promise to provide a good or service in the future (a liability). When the company provides the promised goods or services to the customer, revenue is recognized and the liability is settled. We can say then that revenues are increases in assets or settlements of liabilities from *ongoing operations*.

**REVENUES** are increases in assets or settlements of liabilities from ongoing operations.

Papa John's generates revenues from three primary sources:

1. *Selling pizza in its company-owned restaurants.* Approximately 25 percent of its 2,000 stores are owned by the company, while 75 percent are franchises. The largest revenue on Papa John's income statement, Restaurant Sales, results from pizza sales in company-owned stores. Pizza sales for the franchised restaurants are reported in the franchisees' respective financial statements.

2. *Selling Papa John's franchises.* Approximately 5 percent of all revenues in 1998 were from selling franchises. *Initial fees* of $20,000 are paid by the franchisee to Papa John's for the right to open and operate within a defined period of time a specified number of Papa John's restaurants in a specified geographic area (the right extends for 10 to 20 years). Papa John's records these fees as a liability (Unearned Franchise and Development Fees) until it provides management training, site selection and restaurant design, and other promised services. As part of the franchise

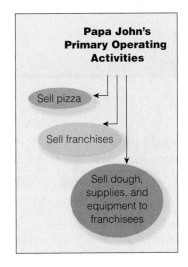

**Papa John's Primary Operating Activities**

Sell pizza

Sell franchises

Sell dough, supplies, and equipment to franchisees

---

[1]In addition to the audited annual statements, most businesses prepare quarterly financial statements (also known as *interim reports* covering a three-month period) for external users. The Securities and Exchange Commission requires public companies to do so.

[2]As another simplification, several accounts in the original statement have been combined with other accounts and/or shown in a different section of the statement in the exhibit.

EXHIBIT **3.2**

**Income Statement**

**PAPA JOHN'S INTERNATIONAL, INC. AND SUBSIDIARIES**
**Consolidated Statement of Income**
**(in thousands)**

| | Year Ended December 27, 1998 |
|---|---:|
| **Revenues**: | |
| Restaurant sales | $324,900 |
| Franchise royalties and development fees | 38,500 |
| Commissary, equipment and other sales | 306,400 |
| Investment income | 4,400 |
| Total revenues | 674,200 |
| **Costs and expenses**: | |
| Restaurant expenses: | |
| Cost of sales | 87,500 |
| Salaries and benefits | 87,000 |
| Advertising and related costs | 28,400 |
| Occupancy costs and other operating expenses | 58,500 |
| | 261,400 |
| Commissary, equipment and other expenses: | |
| Cost of sales | 240,700 |
| Salaries, benefits, and other operating expenses | 39,500 |
| | 280,200 |
| General and administrative expenses | 50,500 |
| Depreciation and amortization | 19,400 |
| Other costs and expenses | 5,300 |
| Total costs and expenses | 616,800 |
| Income before income taxes | 57,400 |
| Income tax expense | 22,200 |
| **Net income** | $ 35,200 |

agreement, franchisees are also required to remit weekly a fixed percentage of 4 to 5 percent of store sales to Papa John's as *franchise royalties*. Both the initial development fees and royalties earned during the year are reported on the income statement as Franchise Royalties and Development Fees.

3. *Selling dough, ingredients, supplies, and equipment to franchised stores from its regional commissaries.* As a strategy for reducing costs and controlling quality and consistency, Papa John's builds commissaries (that is, centralized kitchens and supply facilities) that provide all restaurants in their respective regions with necessary pizza supplies and equipment. Commissary, Equipment, and Other Sales is the second largest revenue source on Papa John's income statement.

Also, interest and dividends earned on investments during the year are included in Investment Income.

**GAINS** are increases in assets or decreases in liabilities from peripheral transactions.

**Gains**, on the other hand, result from *peripheral transactions* (that is, those that occur but are not the central operating focus for the business). For example, selling land for more than was paid would not result in a revenue for Papa John's since selling land is not part of Papa John's normal ongoing operation. Instead, the company recognizes a gain on the sale of the land.

**EXPENSES** are decreases in assets or increases in liabilities to generate revenues during the period.

**Expenses** are necessary to generate revenues. Some students confuse the term expenditures with expenses. An expenditure is any outlay of cash, including buying equipment or paying a bank loan (an investing activity and a financing activity, respectively). An expense results when a cost such as advertising is incurred or an asset such as inventory is used *to generate revenues during a period*. Therefore, not all expenditures are expenses. Papa John's pays employees to make and serve food, uses electricity to operate equipment and light facilities, advertises, and uses food and paper supplies. Without incurring these costs, Papa John's could not generate revenues; thus, these activities are examples of expenses, some of which may result from expenditures of cash at the time they are incurred. When an expense occurs, assets (such as supplies inventory and cash) decrease or are used up *or* liabilities (such as salaries payable or utilities payable) increase. We can say then that expenses are decreases in assets or increases in liabilities to generate revenues during the period (that is, what the business was created to do).

Likewise, **losses** are decreases in assets or increases in liabilities, but from peripheral transactions. If land with a recorded cost of $2,800 is sold for $2,500, Papa John's recognizes a loss of $300 on the sale. Papa John's occasionally purchases land for its new free-standing restaurants, but selling land is not one of its central operations. We will present transaction analysis for gains and losses in future chapters dealing with the valuation and disposition of specific assets and liabilities.

The following are Papa John's primary expenses:

1. *Cost of sales.* For restaurant operations, any ingredients or supplies, which are originally part of the asset Inventories and are used to produce pizza, breadsticks, or cheesesticks, are expensed as used. For commissary and equipment sales, any ingredients, supplies, and equipment, also originally part of Inventories, that are sold to franchisees are expensed as used or exchanged. In companies with a manufacturing or merchandising focus, cost of sales (or cost of goods sold) is usually the most significant expense.

2. *Salaries and benefits expense.* In service-oriented companies in which no products are produced or sold, the cost of using employees to generate revenues is usually the largest expense. In Papa John's restaurant operations, salaries and benefits expense to employees is as significant as its cost of sales.

3. *Occupancy costs.* Papa John's restaurant locations are often rented in strip shopping centers. Rent (occupancy cost) is paid on leases of shopping center locations.

4. *All other costs and expenses.* The remaining large expenses include Advertising and Related Expenses (including promotional costs), expenses for insurance, executive salaries, and rental of headquarters facilities (in General and Administrative Expenses), and expenses reflecting the use of a part of long-lived assets such as buildings, equipment (not held for sale to franchisees), and trademarks (in Depreciation and Amortization Expense).

Income Taxes is the last expense listed. All profit-making corporations are required to compute income taxes owed to federal, state, and foreign governments. Although we will add detail in Chapter 9, income tax expense is calculated as a percentage of the difference between revenues and expenses determined by applying IRS tax rates. Papa John's effective tax rate in 1998 was 38.7 percent (Income Tax Expense $22,200 ÷ Pretax Income $57,400). This indicates that for every dollar of profit that Papa John's made in 1998, the company paid almost $.39 to taxing authorities.

## HOW ARE OPERATING ACTIVITIES RECOGNIZED AND MEASURED?

Most of you determine your personal financial position by the cash balance in your bank account. Your financial performance is measured as the difference between your cash balance at the beginning of the period and the balance at the end of the period (that is, whether you end up with more or less cash). If you have a higher cash balance, cash receipts exceeded cash disbursements for the period. Measuring income in this manner is called **cash basis accounting.** Using this system, revenues are recorded when cash is received, and expenses are recorded when cash is paid, regardless of when the revenues are earned and expenses are incurred. Many small retailers, medical offices, and other small businesses use the cash basis of accounting. This basis

**LOSSES** are decreases in assets or increases in liabilities from peripheral transactions.

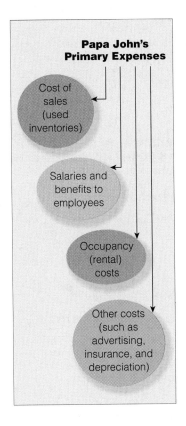

**Papa John's Primary Expenses**

Cost of sales (used inventories)

Salaries and benefits to employees

Occupancy (rental) costs

Other costs (such as advertising, insurance, and depreciation)

---

**CASH BASIS Income Measurement**

Revenues ( = cash receipts)
− Expenses ( = cash payments)
Net Income

**CASH BASIS ACCOUNTING** records revenues when cash is received and expenses when cash is paid.

is often quite adequate for these organizations that usually do not have to report to external users.

## ACCRUAL ACCOUNTING

**LEARNING OBJECTIVE 3**

Explain the accrual basis of accounting.

For publicly traded corporations and large private organizations, however, the cash basis is not considered appropriate for two main reasons. First, except for transactions involving cash, no assets or liabilities are recorded; therefore, a complete financial position is not available for analysis. In addition, cash basis net income, which is the difference between cash receipts and disbursements, can be misleading. For example, a company using the cash basis can report higher net income in one period simply because, for example, (1) a customer paid cash in advance of receiving a good or service or (2) the company postponed making utility payments until the next period. In the first case, the company has not performed the service or exchanged a good to earn a revenue. In the second case, the company has already used gas, electricity, and phone service to generate revenues (creating an expense), but the expense is not recorded because payment occurs in the next period.

---

**ACCRUAL BASIS**
**Income Measurement**

Revenues ( = when earned)
− Expenses ( = when incurred)

Net Income

---

Since financial statements created under the cash basis of accounting normally postpone or accelerate recognition of revenues and expenses long before or after goods and services are produced and delivered, these statements can be misleading and are less relevant to external decision makers. Therefore, generally accepted accounting principles require **accrual basis accounting** for financial reporting purposes. This means that assets, liabilities, revenues, and expenses should be recognized when the transaction that causes them occurs, not necessarily when cash is received or paid. *Revenues are recognized when earned and expenses when incurred.* Thus, a balance sheet and income statement prepared under the accrual basis, accompanied by a statement of cash flows for complete analysis, is more informative to decision makers.

**ACCRUAL BASIS ACCOUNTING** records revenues when earned and expenses when incurred, regardless of the timing of cash receipts or payments.

The two basic accounting principles that determine when revenues and expenses are to be recorded under the accrual basis of accounting are the *revenue principle* and the *matching principle*. These principles need to be understood clearly.

## THE REVENUE PRINCIPLE

**LEARNING OBJECTIVE 4**

Apply the revenue and matching principles to determine the timing and amount of revenues and expenses.

Under the **revenue principle,** three conditions normally must be met for revenue to be recognized (that is, recorded). If *any* of the following conditions is *not* met, revenue normally is *not* considered recognized and cannot be recorded.

1. *The earnings process is complete or nearly complete.* This means that the company has performed or substantially performed the promised acts (provided goods or services).

2. *An exchange transaction takes place.* In exchange for the company's performance, the customer provides cash or a promise to pay cash (a receivable).

3. *Collection is reasonably assured.* As discussed in more depth in Chapter 6, companies establish credit policies to reduce the risk of extending credit to customers who fail to pay. On the date of a sale on credit, assuming that the credit policies have been followed, collection is usually considered reasonably probable.[3]

The **REVENUE PRINCIPLE** states that revenues are recognized when the earnings process is complete or nearly complete, an exchange has taken place, and collection is probable.

In practice, these conditions are met for most businesses at the point of delivery of goods or services. In Exhibit 3.1, revenue is usually recorded on the date of delivery (point 3). As is typical in the fast-food industry, Papa John's receives most of its revenues from restaurant sales in cash at the time food products are sold to customers. The exchange is a receipt of cash for food service given. An exchange transaction has taken place, the earnings process is complete, and there is no uncertainty as to cash collected.

Papa John's also sells franchises from which it receives cash from new franchisees *before* it provides start-up services to them; the liability account Unearned Franchise

---

[3]We will learn in Chapter 6 that, even with strong credit policies, companies need to evaluate the likelihood that some accounts will not be collected. Probable bad debts will need to be estimated.

and Development Fees is created. This deferred or unearned revenue account represents the amount of goods or services owed to the franchisees. In this case, Papa John's has not provided service, so the earnings process is not complete. Later, when Papa John's provides the services, it earns and records revenues by reducing the liability account.

Revenue is recorded according to the revenue principle when the three conditions are met, *regardless of when cash is received*. Typical liabilities that are created when cash is received and later become revenues when earned include the following:

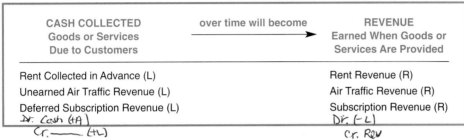

As time passes, the liability accounts should be adjusted to reflect the correct amounts earned and unearned. These accounts usually are adjusted at the end of a period. We will discuss the amounts and timing of adjustments in Chapter 4.

Franchisees must also pay royalties to Papa John's based on a percentage of their past week's sales revenues. By contract, Papa John's has earned the royalty and receives cash *after* it earns the revenue. Typical assets reflecting revenues earned but not yet received in cash are as follows:

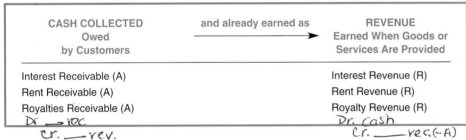

These asset accounts typically are recorded at the end of a period because revenue has been earned but has not been recorded. Cash will be received in the future. These adjustments (discussed in Chapter 4) ensure that revenues are recognized in the proper period.

Companies usually disclose their revenue recognition practices in a note to the financial statements. The following excerpt from Papa John's note describes how it recognizes its two forms of franchise related income:

**Papa John's International, Inc. and Subsidiaries**
**Notes to Consolidated Financial Statements**

**2. Significant Accounting Policies**

*Revenue Recognition*
Franchise fees are recognized when a franchised restaurant begins operations, at which time we have performed our obligations related to such fees. Fees received pursuant to development agreements which grant the right to develop franchised restaurants in future periods in specific geographic areas are deferred and recognized on a pro rata basis as the franchised restaurants subject to the development agreements begin operations. Both franchise and development fees are nonrefundable. Franchise royalties, which are based on a percentage of franchised restaurants' sales, are recognized as earned.

These practices follow the conditions of the revenue principle discussed earlier. In Chapter 6 we will discuss special generally accepted practices applied in certain circumstances when one of the conditions is not met (such as accounting for revenue under long-term construction contracts before the projects are completed).

## SELF-STUDY QUIZ

This self-study quiz allows you to practice applying the revenue principle under accrual accounting. We recommend that you refer back to the three *revenue recognition criteria* presented earlier as you answer each question. It is important to complete this quiz now to make sure you can apply this principle.

The following transactions are samples of typical monthly operating activities of Papa John's.

1. Indicate the account titles that are affected and the type of account for each (A for asset, L for liability, and R for revenue).

2. If a revenue is to be recognized in *January,* indicate the amount. If a revenue is not to be recognized in January, indicate which of the revenue recognition criteria are not met.

You should refer to the Papa John's chart of accounts presented in Exhibit 2.3 for account titles. *Note:* All dollars are in thousands.

| Activity | Accounts Affected and Type of Account | Amount of Revenue Earned in January OR Revenue Criteria Not Met |
|---|---|---|
| (a) In January, Papa John's company-owned restaurants sold food to customers for $35,200 cash. | | |
| (b) In January, Papa John's sold 25 franchises for $625 cash and provided $400 in services to these new franchisees during January; the remainder of services will be provided over the next three months. | | |
| (c) In January, franchisees paid Papa John's $3,450 in cash for royalties of which $750 related to December sales. | | |
| (d) In January, Papa John's commissaries sold sauce and dough to restaurants for $30,200 of which $20,200 was in cash and the rest was on account. | | |
| (e) In January, franchisees paid $1,200 on account to Papa John's (from December purchases of dough and sauce). | | |

After you have completed the quiz, check your solution with the answers in the footnote at the bottom of this page.*

---

| * | Accounts Affected and Type of Account | January Revenue Amount or Criteria Not Met |
|---|---|---|
| (a) | Cash (A) Restaurant Sales Revenue (R) | $35,200 earned. |
| (b) | Cash (A) Franchise-Related Revenue (R) Unearned Franchise and Development Fees (L) | $400 earned. 225 deferred; earnings process is not yet complete. |
| (c) | Cash (A) Franchise-Related Revenue (R) Accounts Receivable (A) | $2,700 earned in January. 750 earned in December. |
| (d) | Cash (A) Accounts Receivable (A) Commissary and Other Sales Revenue (R) | $30,200 ($10,000 of it earned but not yet received in cash). |
| (e) | Cash (A) Accounts Receivable (A) | No revenue earned in January; cash collections in January relate to earnings in prior periods. |

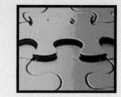

# A QUESTION OF ETHICS

## MANAGEMENT'S INCENTIVES TO VIOLATE THE REVENUE PRINCIPLE

The decisions of investors in the stock market are based on expectations of future earnings. When quarterly and annual earnings information is announced by the companies, investors evaluate how well the company met expectations and adjust their investing decisions accordingly. Companies that fail to meet expectations often experience a decline in the stock price. Management is thus motivated to produce earnings results that meet or exceed expectations. Sometimes this motivation leads managers to make unethical accounting and reporting decisions, as described in the August 2, 1999, issue of *Fortune*. Often the fraud involves falsifying revenues. The article includes a list of several recent revenue-related frauds and who went to jail:

| The CEO | What He Did | Conviction/Plea | The Outcome |
|---|---|---|---|
| **Donald Ferrarini**, 71 Underwriters Financial Group | Reported nonexistent revenues; made losing company look like profit maker. | Convicted, 2/99. | Sentenced to 12 years, one month. He is appealing. |
| **Richard Rubin**, 57 Donnkenny | Concocted false invoices and revenues to meet earnings goals. | Pleaded guilty, 2/99. | Sentence pending; faces maximum of 5 years. |
| **Chan Desaigoudar**, 61, California Micro Devices | Led staff to record sales for products not shipped—or even manufactured. | Convicted, 7/98. | Serving sentence of 36 months. |
| **Paul Safronchik**, 35 Home Theater Products Intl. | Invented customers and sales, showed profits when red ink was a reality. | Pleaded guilty, 12/96. | Serving sentence of 37 months. |

Besides those who end up in jail, many others are affected—stockholders lose stock value, employees may lose jobs, and customers and suppliers may become wary. As future managers, you may be faced with an ethical dilemma in the workplace; the ethical decision is the one you will be proud of 20 years later.

SOURCE: Carol J. Loomis, *Fortune*, August 2, 1999, "Lies, Damned Lies, and Managed Earnings: The Crackdown Is Here," pp. 75–90. © 1999 *Time, Inc.* All Rights reserved.

## THE MATCHING PRINCIPLE

Resources that are used to earn revenues are called *expenses*. The **matching principle** requires that when the period's revenues are properly recognized according to the revenue principle, all of the resources consumed in earning those revenues (such as inventory sold, amounts due to employees who worked, and the electricity used) should be recorded in that same period, *regardless of when cash is paid.* Thus, expenses are "matched" with revenues in the period incurred. When Papa John's records total restaurant sales revenue for the period, all of the related expenses (such as the cost of food and paper products from inventories, payroll expense, and occupancy expense) used to generate the revenues also should be recorded. The expenses should be matched with revenues for the same period.

As in the case of revenues and cash receipts, expenses and cash outlays are not necessarily recorded on the same date. For example, the acquisition of, and sometimes the cash outlay for, food and paper product supplies occurs *prior* to their use. They are recorded as inventory, an asset, when purchased, however, and are not expensed as the cost of food and paper products until they are used. Similarly, companies usually pay for rent in *advance* of using the property and record the cash outlay in an asset

The **MATCHING PRINCIPLE** requires that expenses be recorded when incurred in earning revenue.

account, Prepaid Expense, that represents future benefits to the company. The asset is allocated over time to Occupancy Expense as it is used. In addition, a part of the cost of long-lived assets, such as equipment used in operations, needs to be matched with the revenues generated by their use in a period. The used portion of the assets is allocated to Depreciation Expense. Typical assets and their related expense accounts are as follows:

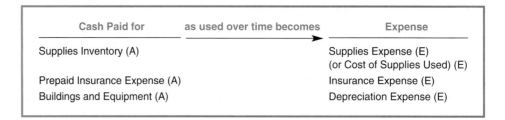

As time passes, the asset accounts should be adjusted to reflect the correct amounts used for the period (the expense) and the remaining future benefits (the asset). These accounts usually are adjusted at the end of a period. We discuss the amounts and timing of adjustments in Chapter 4.

In other cases, resources are used to generate revenues prior to the cash outlay. For Papa John's, payroll expense represents the amount earned by managers and employees who prepare and serve the food and is an expense of that period. Cash is usually paid to employees *after* the time when they provide their services. Expense should be recorded, however, when the service is provided. Typical liabilities and their related expense accounts are as follows:

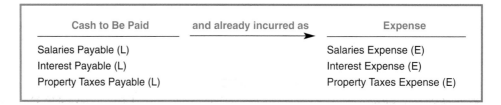

These liability accounts result from incurring expenses before cash is paid. Expense accruals typically are recorded at the end of a period as adjustments to ensure that expenses are recognized in the proper period.

## SELF-STUDY **QUIZ**

This self-study quiz allows you to practice applying the *matching principle* under accrual accounting. It is important to complete this quiz now to make sure you can apply this principle.

The following transactions are samples of typical monthly operating activities of Papa John's.

1. Indicate the account titles that are affected and the type of account for each (A for asset, L for liability, and E for expense).

2. If an expense is to be recognized in *January*, indicate the amount. If an expense is not to be recognized in January, indicate why.

You should refer to the Papa John's income statement presented in Exhibit 3.2 for account titles.

| Activity | Accounts Affected and Type of Account | Amount of Expense Incurred in January OR Why an Expense Is Not Recognized |
|---|---|---|
| (a) At the beginning of January, Papa John's company-owned restaurants paid $4,500 in rent for January, February, and March. | | |
| (b) In January, Papa John's paid $10,000 on account with suppliers for supplies received in December. | | |
| (c) In January, the cost of food and paper products sold to customers was $9,600. | | |
| (d) In late January, Papa John's received a utility bill for $500 that will be paid in February for electricity used in January. | | |

After you have completed the quiz, check your solution with the answers in the footnote at the bottom of this page.*

## TRANSACTION ANALYSIS ILLUSTRATED

Now that we have indicated what business activities affect the income statement and how they are measured, we need to complete the transaction analysis model to show how these business activities are recorded in the accounting system and reflected in the financial statements. Only investing and financing activities affecting assets, liabilities, and contributed capital were presented in Chapter 2. We now expand the transaction analysis model to include transactions involving revenues and expenses (from operating activities).

**■ LEARNING OBJECTIVE 5**

Apply transaction analysis to examine and record the effects of operating activities on the financial statements.

### THE EXPANDED TRANSACTION ANALYSIS MODEL

The complete transaction model presented in Exhibit 3.3 includes revenues and expenses. Recall that the Retained Earnings account is the accumulation of all past revenues and expenses minus any income distributed as dividends[4] to stockholders (that is, earnings not retained in the business). When net income is positive, Retained Earnings increases; when a net loss occurs, Retained Earnings decreases.

In constructing this complete model, we maintain the direction rule and the debit–credit framework described in Chapter 2:

| * | Accounts Affected | January Expense Amount or Why Not an Expense |
|---|---|---|
| (a) | Cash (A) Occupancy Expense (E) Prepaid Expenses (A) | $1,500 incurred in January. $3,000 not yet incurred until future months. |
| (b) | Cash (A) Accounts Payable (L) | December purchase paid in January; supplies expensed when used or sold. |
| (c) | Inventories (A) Cost of sales (E) | $9,600 (of used inventory) |
| (d) | Accounts Payable (L) General and Administrative Expense (E) | $500 incurred in January to be paid in the future. |

[4]Instead of reducing Retained Earnings directly when dividends are declared, companies may use the account Dividends Declared. It has a debit balance.

EXHIBIT **3.3**

**Transaction Analysis Model**

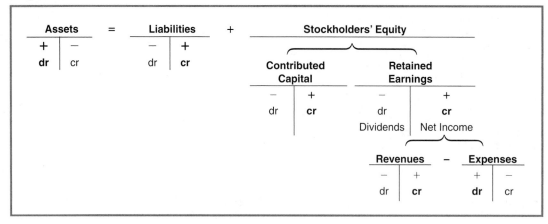

- For direction, the increase symbol + is written on the left when we are on the left side of the accounting equation and on the right when we are on the right side of the accounting equation.

- Debits (dr) are written on the left side of each element and credits (cr) are written on the right.

Before we illustrate the use of the transaction analysis model for these new elements, it is important to emphasize the following:

- Revenues increase Retained Earnings (SE) and therefore have *credit* balances.

- Expenses decrease Retained Earnings (SE) and therefore have *debit* balances (that is, to increase an expense, you debit it, but to do so decreases Retained Earnings). Students often have difficulty with this concept. As expenses increase, Retained Earnings and thus total stockholders' equity decrease.

When revenues exceed expenses, the company reports net income which increases Retained Earnings, a part of stockholders' equity. However, when expenses exceed revenues, a net loss results, which decreases Retained Earnings and thus stockholders' equity.

# FINANCIAL **ANALYSIS**

## THE FEEDBACK VALUE OF ACCOUNTING INFORMATION AND STOCK MARKET REACTION

A net loss does not have to occur for a company to recognize that it is experiencing difficulty. Any unexpected variance in actual performance from the operating plan, such as lower than expected quarterly earnings, needs to be explained. Stock market analysts and investors use accounting information to make investment decisions. The stock market, which is based on investors' expectations about future company performance, often reacts to operating deviations in negative ways (that is, with a reduction in the company's stock price).

On December 9, 1999, Papa John's announced that it anticipated it would report a lower than expected increase in sales for the fourth quarter. Prior to the announcement, its stock had been selling at $34.25 per share. Immediately, after the announcement, the price dropped by $7.375 to $26.875 per share,* a 22 percent decrease in one day. The explanation of the lower sales level was related to weaker than expected December sales and its recent decision to close its company-owned restaurants early on Christmas Eve.†

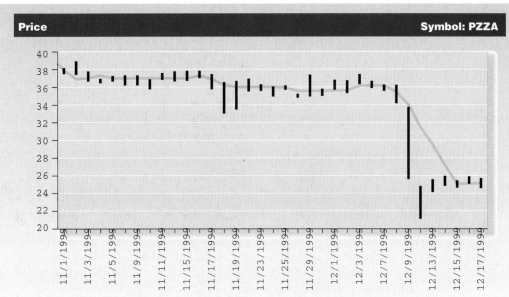

This is a clear example of how corporate decisions affect financial data and how internal and external users use the information. Accounting information has a pervasive effect on all forms of corporate decision making, as well as on the economic decisions that investors and creditors make.

*Dow Jones Interactive Quotes & Market Data, Pricing History Report.
†*Business Wire*, December 9, 1999, "Papa John's Revises 4th Quarter Comparable Sales Estimates and Announces $50 million Stock Repurchase Authorization."

## TRANSACTION ANALYSIS RULES

As presented in Chapter 2,

1. Every transaction affects at least two accounts (duality of effects); it is critical to identify correctly the accounts affected and the direction of the effect (increase or decrease).

2. The accounting equation must remain in balance after each transaction.

3. The total dollar value of the debits in the transaction should equal the total dollar value of the credits.

Since revenues are defined as inflows of net assets, then, by definition, to increase a revenue (a credit), an asset is usually increased or a liability is usually decreased (debited). In like manner, when increasing an expense (a debit), an asset is usually decreased or a liability is usually increased (credited). Revenues and expenses normally are not recorded in the same journal entry.

As we emphasized in Chapter 2, refer to the transaction analysis model until you can construct it on your own without assistance. You also should study this illustration carefully to make sure that you understand the impact of operating activities on the balance sheet and income statement.

We begin with Papa John's January 31, 1999, balance sheet constructed at the end of Chapter 2, which included the effects of the transactions illustrated in that chapter. We use the account titles listed in that balance sheet and those shown on the income statement in Exhibit 3.2 as we analyze operating activities. A list is also provided in Exhibit 2.3 (chart of accounts). Now let's apply the complete transaction analysis model and rules to our continuing Papa John's illustration. All amounts are in thousands of dollars.

(*a*) **Papa John's sold 25 franchises for $400 cash. The company earned $175 immediately by performing services for franchisees; the rest will be earned over the next several months.**

| Cash (+A) ................................. | 400 | |
|---|---|---|
| Franchise royalties and development fees | | |
| (+R → +SE) ......................... | | 175 |
| Unearned franchise and development fees (+L) | | 225 |

| Assets | | = | Liabilities | | + | Stockholders' Equity | |
|---|---|---|---|---|---|---|---|
| Cash | +400 | | Unearned franchise and development fees | +225 | | Franchise royalties and development fees | +175 |

Equality checks: (1) Debits $400 = Credits $400; (2) the accounting equation is in balance.

Notice that when the revenue is increased, we also indicate the effect on total stockholders' equity with the following notation: +R → +SE. Similar notation will be used for expenses, which decrease stockholders' equity.

These effects are posted to the appropriate T-accounts in Exhibit 3.4 (see the shaded amounts).

(b) **Papa John's company-owned restaurants received $35,200 in cash for pizza sales. The cost of the dough, sauce, cheese, and other ingredients for these sales was $9,600. [*Note:* This requires two entries, one for the revenue earned and one for the expense incurred in generating the revenue.]**

| Cash (+A) ................................. | 35,200 | |
|---|---|---|
| Restaurant sales revenue (+R → +SE) ..... | | 35,200 |
| Cost of sales—restaurants (+E → − SE) ....... | 9,600 | |
| Inventories (−A) ........................ | | 9,600 |

| Assets | | = | Liabilities | + | Stockholders' Equity | |
|---|---|---|---|---|---|---|
| Cash | +35,200 | | | | Restaurant sales revenue | +35,200 |
| Inventory | −9,600 | | | | Cost of sales | −9,600 |

Equality checks: (1) Debits $35,200 = Credits $35,200; (2) the accounting equation is in balance.
Equality checks: (1) Debits $9,600 = Credits $9,600; (2) the accounting equation is in balance.

(c) **Papa John's commissaries sold $30,200 in dough, sauce, and other ingredients to franchised restaurants; $20,200 was received in cash and the rest was due from the restaurants.**

| Cash (+A) ................................. | 20,200 | |
|---|---|---|
| Accounts receivable (+A) ................... | 10,000 | |
| Commissary, equipment, and other | | |
| sales revenue (+R → +SE) ............ | | 30,200 |

| Assets | | = | Liabilities | + | Stockholders' Equity | |
|---|---|---|---|---|---|---|
| Cash | +20,200 | | | | Commissary, equipment, | |
| Accounts receivable | +10,000 | | | | and other sales revenue | +30,200 |

Equality checks: (1) Debits $30,200 = Credits $30,200; (2) the accounting equation is in balance.

(d) **Papa John's paid a variety of other costs and expenses: $4,700 related to company-owned restaurants, $2,200 related to commissaries, and $410 in general. These were normal expenses for utilities, repairs, and gas for delivery vehicles.**

| Other operating expenses—restaurants (+E → −SE) ...... | 4,700 | |
|---|---|---|
| Other operating expenses—commissaries (+E → −SE) .... | 2,200 | |
| General and administrative expenses (+E → −SE) ....... | 410 | |
| Cash (−A) ................................. | | 7,310 |

| Assets | | = | Liabilities | + | Stockholders' Equity | |
|---|---|---|---|---|---|---|
| Cash | −7,310 | | | | Other operating expenses | −6,900 |
| | | | | | General and administrative expenses | −410 |

Equality checks: (1) Debits $7,310 = Credits $7,310; (2) the accounting equation is in balance.

(e) **Papa John's commissaries ordered and received $29,000 in supplies inventories; $9,000 was paid in cash and the rest was on account with suppliers.**

| | | |
|---|---|---|
| Inventories (+A) | 29,000 | |
| Cash (−A) | | 9,000 |
| Accounts payable (+L) | | 20,000 |

| Assets | | = | Liabilities | | + | Stockholders' Equity |
|---|---|---|---|---|---|---|
| Cash | − 9,000 | | Accounts payable | +20,000 | | |
| Inventories | +29,000 | | | | | |

Equality checks: (1) Debits $29,000 = Credits $29,000; (2) the accounting equation is in balance.

(f) **Papa John's paid $13,500 in cash to employees for work in January: $8,000 for restaurant employees, $1,500 for those in the commissaries, and $4,000 for employees in the corporate headquarters.**

| | | |
|---|---|---|
| Salaries expense—restaurants (+E → −SE) | 8,000 | |
| Salaries expense—commissaries (+E → −SE) | 1,500 | |
| General and administrative expense (+E → −SE) | 4,000 | |
| Cash (−A) | | 13,500 |

| Assets | | = | Liabilities | + | Stockholders' Equity | |
|---|---|---|---|---|---|---|
| Cash | −13,500 | | | | Salaries expense | −9,500 |
| | | | | | General and administrative expenses | −4,000 |

Equality checks: (1) Debits $13,500 = Credits $13,500; (2) the accounting equation is in balance.

(g) **Papa John's paid $7,400 for prepaid expenses: $1,600 for insurance for the next four months, $4,800 for rent in shopping centers for the next three months, and $1,000 for advertising in February.**

| | | |
|---|---|---|
| Prepaid expenses (+A) | 7,400 | |
| Cash (−A) | | 7,400 |

| Assets | | = | Liabilities | + | Stockholders' Equity |
|---|---|---|---|---|---|
| Cash | −7,400 | | | | |
| Prepaid expenses | +7,400 | | | | |

Equality checks: (1) Debits $7,400 = Credits $7,400; (2) the accounting equation is in balance.

### SELF-STUDY **QUIZ**

For transactions (h) through (k), fill in the missing information. Be sure to post journal entries to the T-accounts at the end of the illustration. When completed, you can check your answers with the solution at the end of the illustration:

(h) **Papa John's received $3,450 in royalties from franchisees; $750 of the amount was due from franchisees' sales in December and the rest from January sales.**

| | | |
|---|---|---|
| Cash (+A) | 3,450 | |
| Accounts receivable (−A) | | 750 |
| Franchise royalties and development fees (+R → +SE) | | 2,700 |

| | Assets | = | Liabilities | + | Stockholders' Equity |
|---|---|---|---|---|---|
| Indicate the effects → | | | | | |

Equality checks: (1) Debits $3,450 = Credits $3,450; (2) the accounting equation is in balance.

(i) Papa John's sold $4,300 in equipment inventory to franchisees who signed notes due in six months. The cost of the equipment was $3,800. (*Note:* This requires two entries, one for the revenue and one for the expense incurred in generating the revenue.)

Insert the journal entry → [blank]   [Post to the T-accounts.]

Insert the journal entry → [blank]   [Post to the T-accounts.]

| Assets | = | Liabilities | + | Stockholders' Equity | |
|---|---|---|---|---|---|
| Notes receivable +4,300 | | | | Commissary, equipment, | |
| Inventories −3,800 | | | | and other sales revenue | +4,300 |
| | | | | Cost of sales-commissaries | −3,800 |

Equality checks: (1) Debits $4,300 = Credits $4,300; (2) the accounting equation is in balance.

Equality checks: (1) Debits $_____ = Credits $_____; (2) Is the accounting equation in balance? _____

(j) Papa John's paid $10,000 on accounts owed to suppliers.

Insert the journal entry → [blank]   [Post to the T-accounts.]

| Assets | = | Liabilities | + | Stockholders' Equity |
|---|---|---|---|---|
| Cash −10,000 | | Accounts payable −10,000 | | |

Equality checks: (1) Debits $10,000 = Credits $10,000; (2) the accounting equation is in balance.

(k) Papa John's received $12,125 in cash; $125 was interest income earned on investments and $12,000 was payment made by franchisees on their accounts with Papa John's.

| | | |
|---|---|---|
| Cash (+A) .............................. | 12,125 | |
| Investment income (+R → +SE) .......... | | 125 |
| Accounts receivable (−A) .............. | | 12,000 |

| | Assets | = | Liabilities | + | Stockholders' Equity |
|---|---|---|---|---|---|
| Indicate the effects → | | | | | |

Equality checks: (1) Debits $_____ = Credits $_____; (2) Is the accounting equation in balance? _____

You can check your answers with the solutions at the bottom of this page.*

*(h)

| | Assets | | = | Liabilities | + | Stockholders' Equity | |
|---|---|---|---|---|---|---|---|
| | Cash | +3,450 | | | | Franchise royalties | |
| | Accounts receivable | − 750 | | | | and development fees | +2,700 |

(i)

| | | |
|---|---|---|
| Notes receivable (+A) | 4,300 | |
| Commissary, equipment, and other sales revenue (+R → +SE) | | 4,300 |
| Cost of sales − equipment (+E → −SE) | 3,800 | |
| Inventories (−A) | | 3,800 |

Equality checks: (1) Debits $3,800 = Credits $3,800; (2) The accounting equation balances.

EXHIBIT **3.4**

**T-Accounts**

## ASSETS

| + | Cash (A) | | − |
|---|---|---|---|
| Ch. 2 bal. | 31,250 | | |
| a | 400 | d | 7,310 |
| b | 35,200 | e | 9,000 |
| c | 20,200 | f | 13,500 |
| h | 3,450 | g | 7,400 |
| k | 12,125 | j | |
| End. bal. | 55,415 | | |

| + | Accounts Receivable (A) | | − |
|---|---|---|---|
| Ch. 2 bal. | 17,300 | | |
| c | 10,000 | h | 750 |
| | | k | 12,000 |
| End. bal. | 14,550 | | |

| + | Inventories (A) | | − |
|---|---|---|---|
| Ch. 2 bal. | 9,700 | b | 9,600 |
| e | 29,000 | i | |
| End. bal. | 25,300 | | |

| + | Prepaid Expenses (A) | | − |
|---|---|---|---|
| Ch. 2 bal. | 4,800 | | |
| g | 7,400 | | |
| End. bal. | 12,200 | | |

| + | Notes Receivable (A) | | − |
|---|---|---|---|
| Ch. 2 bal. | 12,450 | | |
| i | | | |
| End. bal. | 16,750 | | |

## LIABILITIES

| − | Unearned Franchise and Development Fees (L) | | + |
|---|---|---|---|
| | | Ch. 2 bal. | 6,600 |
| | | a | 225 |
| | | End. bal. | 6,825 |

| − | Accounts Payable (L) | | + |
|---|---|---|---|
| | | Ch. 2 bal. | 18,100 |
| j | | e | 20,000 |
| | | End. bal. | 28,100 |

## REVENUES

| − | Restaurant Sales Revenue (R) | | + |
|---|---|---|---|
| | | b | 35,200 |
| | | End. bal. | 35,200 |

| − | Franchise Royalties and Development Fees (R) | | + |
|---|---|---|---|
| | | a | 175 |
| | | h | 2,700 |
| | | End. bal. | 2,875 |

| − | Commissary, Equipment, and Other Sales Revenue (R) | | + |
|---|---|---|---|
| | | c | 30,200 |
| | | i | |
| | | End. bal. | 34,500 |

| − | Investment Income (R) | | + |
|---|---|---|---|
| | | k | 125 |
| | | End. bal. | 125 |

## EXPENSES

| + | Cost of Sales—Restaurants (E) | | − |
|---|---|---|---|
| b | 9,600 | | |
| End. bal. | 9,600 | | |

| + | Cost of Sales—Commissaries (E) | | − |
|---|---|---|---|
| i | | | |
| End. bal. | 3,800 | | |

| + | Other Operating Expenses— Restaurants (E) | | − |
|---|---|---|---|
| d | 4,700 | | |
| End. bal. | 4,700 | | |

| + | Other Operating Expenses— Commissaries (E) | | − |
|---|---|---|---|
| d | 2,200 | | |
| End. bal. | 2,200 | | |

| + | General and Administrative Expenses (E) | | − |
|---|---|---|---|
| d | 410 | | |
| f | 4,000 | | |
| End. bal. | 4,410 | | |

| + | Salaries Expense—Restaurants (E) | | − |
|---|---|---|---|
| f | 8,000 | | |
| End. bal. | 8,000 | | |

| + | Salaries Expense—Commissaries (E) | | − |
|---|---|---|---|
| f | 1,500 | | |
| End. bal. | 1,500 | | |

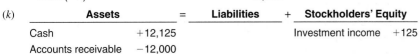

| (j) | Accounts payable (−L) | 10,000 | | |
|---|---|---|---|---|
| | Cash (−A) | | 10,000 | |

| (k) | Assets | = | Liabilities | + | Stockholders' Equity |
|---|---|---|---|---|---|
| | Cash +12,125 | | | | Investment income +125 |
| | Accounts receivable −12,000 | | | | |

Equality checks: (1) Debits $12,125 = Credits $12,125; (2) the accounting equation balances.

The T-accounts that changed during the period because of transactions (*a*) through (*k*) are illustrated in Exhibit 3.4. The balances of all other accounts remained the same. The amounts from Papa John's balance sheet at the end of Chapter 2 have been included as the beginning balances. At the beginning of every period, income statement accounts have zero beginning balances; therefore, no balances exist in the revenue and expense accounts at the beginning of the month.

You can verify that you posted the entries properly by adding the increase side and subtracting the decrease side and then comparing your answer to the ending balance given in each of the T-accounts.

## PREPARATION OF THE UNADJUSTED FINANCIAL STATEMENTS

**■ LEARNING OBJECTIVE 6**

Prepare unadjusted financial statements.

Based on the January transactions that have been posted in the T-accounts, we can now prepare financial statements reflecting operating activities recorded in January. Notice that the statements are called *unadjusted.* This is because the accounts have not been updated for revenues earned and expenses incurred in January when the receipt or payment of cash is at a different time. For example, many large expenses are not yet included, especially the cost of paper products used in January and the depreciation on equipment used during the month.

Also notice that we have not calculated income taxes. Because the income statement is unadjusted, the amount of taxes due is not yet determinable. These statements do not at this point reflect generally accepted accounting principles based on accrual accounting. We will adjust the accounts and prepare complete statements in Chapter 4.

### UNADJUSTED INCOME STATEMENT

**PAPA JOHN'S INTERNATIONAL, INC. AND SUBSIDIARIES**
**Unadjusted Consolidated Statement of Income**
**(dollars in thousands)**

| | Month Ended January 31, 1999 |
|---|---:|
| **Revenues:** | |
| Restaurant sales | $35,200 |
| Franchise royalties and development fees | 2,875 |
| Commissary, equipment, and other sales | 34,500 |
| Investment income | 125 |
| **Total revenues** | 72,700 |
| **Costs and expenses:** | |
| Restaurant expenses: | |
| Cost of sales | 9,600 |
| Salaries and benefits | 8,000 |
| Advertising and related costs | 0 |
| Occupancy costs and other operating expenses | 4,700 |
| | 22,300 |
| Commissary, equipment and other expenses: | |
| Cost of sales | 3,800 |
| Salaries, benefits, and other operating expenses | 3,700 |
| | 7,500 |
| General and administrative expenses | 4,410 |
| Depreciation and amortization | 0 |
| Other costs and expenses | 0 |
| **Total costs and expenses** | 34,210 |
| Income before income taxes | 38,490 |
| Income tax expense | 0 |
| **Unadjusted net income** | $38,490 |

This is the total of Salaries Expense and Other Operating Expenses related to the commissaries.

## FINANCIAL **ANALYSIS**

### REPORTING FINANCIAL INFORMATION BY GEOGRAPHIC AND OPERATING SEGMENTS

Many companies, especially very large ones, operate in multiple geographic segments. These companies are often called *multinationals.* The income statement just presented based on aggregated data may not prove as useful to investors seeking to assess possible risks and returns from companies operating in foreign markets. This is also true if a company operates in more than a single business. Therefore, additional summary information about geographic and operating segments is provided in footnotes to the financial statements. For example, an excerpt from the 1998 annual report of Harley-Davidson, Inc., follows:

**REAL WORLD EXCERPT**

*Harley-Davidson, Inc.*
ANNUAL REPORT

Notes to Consolidated Financial Statements

**12. BUSINESS SEGMENTS AND FOREIGN OPERATIONS**
**(A) BUSINESS SEGMENTS**
The Company operates in two business segments: Motorcycles and Related Products and Financial Services. . . .

*(In thousands)*

| Years ended December 31, | 1998 | 1997 | 1996 |
|---|---|---|---|
| Income from operations: | | | |
| Motorcycles and Related Products | $324,448 | $265,486 | $228,093 |
| Financial Services | 20,211 | 12,355 | 7,801 |
| General corporate expenses | (11,041) | (7,838) | (7,448) |
| | $333,618 | $270,003 | $228,446 |

**(B) GEOGRAPHIC INFORMATION**
Included in the consolidated financial statements are the following amounts relating to geographic locations:

*(In thousands)*

| Years ended December 31, | 1998 | 1997 | 1996 |
|---|---|---|---|
| Revenues: | | | |
| United States | $1,566,559 | $1,304,748 | $1,110,527 |
| Canada | 73,908 | 62,717 | 58,053 |
| Germany | 84,436 | 81,541 | 82,800 |
| Japan | 102,245 | 90,243 | 79,401 |
| Other foreign countries | 236,808 | 223,320 | 200,446 |
| | $2,063,956 | $1,762,569 | $1,531,227 |

Papa John's also reports on business segments. However, no geographic information is presented since the company operates primarily in the United States.

**Notes to Consolidated Financial Statements**

**14. Segment Information**
We have defined three reportable segments: restaurants, commissaries, and franchising. . . .
Through December 27, 1998, substantially all revenues for each business segment were derived
from business activities conducted with customers located in the United States. . . .

*(in thousands)*

|  | 1998 | 1997 | 1996 |
|---|---|---|---|
| Revenues from external customers: |  |  |  |
| Restaurants | $324,894 | $251,153 | $167,982 |
| Commissaries | 261,009 | 188,034 | 142,998 |
| Franchising | 38,499 | 29,645 | 22,113 |
| All others | 45,404 | 39,952 | 26,959 |
| **Total revenues from external customers** | **$669,806** | **$508,784** | **$360,052** |
| Intersegment revenues: |  |  |  |
| Commissaries | $102,292 | $ 77,596 | $ 54,619 |
| Franchising | 128 | 107 | 183 |
| All others | 15,570 | 14,869 | 12,354 |
| **Total intersegment revenues** | **$117,990** | **$ 92,572** | **$ 67,156** |

## UNADJUSTED STATEMENT OF RETAINED EARNINGS

Returning to our Papa John's illustration, we also can prepare a statement of retained
earnings that ties the information on the income statement to the balance sheet. Any
transactions affecting Retained Earnings (generating net income and declaring dividends) are summarized in the statement.

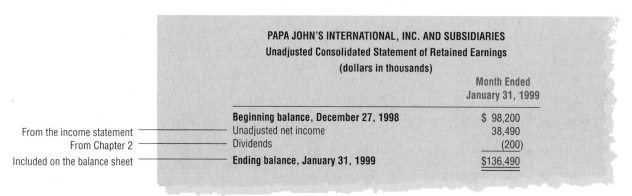

**PAPA JOHN'S INTERNATIONAL, INC. AND SUBSIDIARIES**
**Unadjusted Consolidated Statement of Retained Earnings**
**(dollars in thousands)**

| | Month Ended January 31, 1999 |
|---|---|
| **Beginning balance, December 27, 1998** | $ 98,200 |
| Unadjusted net income | 38,490 |
| Dividends | (200) |
| **Ending balance, January 31, 1999** | $136,490 |

From the income statement ─────── Unadjusted net income
From Chapter 2 ─────── Dividends
Included on the balance sheet ─────── Ending balance, January 31, 1999

## UNADJUSTED BALANCE SHEET

Now we can revise the balance sheet from Chapter 2 to reflect the effects of the operating activities discussed in this chapter. Notice that the ending balance in the statement of retained earnings flows into the Stockholders' Equity section of the balance
sheet. Revenue, expense, and dividend amounts are not included on the balance sheet
directly but are summarized in Retained Earnings. We explore the relationships among
each of the financial statements again in the next chapter.

**PAPA JOHN'S INTERNATIONAL, INC. AND SUBSIDIARIES**
**Unadjusted Consolidated Balance Sheet**
**(dollars in thousands)**

January 31, 1999

**Assets**

**Current assets:**

| | |
|---|---|
| Cash and cash equivalents | $ 55,415 |
| Accounts receivable | 14,550 |
| Inventories | 25,300 |
| Prepaid expenses | 12,200 |
| Other current assets | 2,100 |
| **Total current assets** | 109,565 |
| Investments | 50,300 |
| Net property and equipment | 174,900 |
| Notes receivable | 16,750 |
| Other assets | 22,400 |
| **Total assets** | $373,915 |

**Liabilities and stockholders' equity**

**Current liabilities:**

| | | |
|---|---|---|
| Accounts payable | $ 28,100 | |
| Accrued expenses payable | 25,500 | |
| Other current liabilities | — | |
| **Total current liabilities** | 53,600 | |
| Unearned franchise and development fees | 6,825 | |
| Other long-term liabilities (including notes payable) | 11,200 | |
| **Stockholders' equity:** | | |
| Contributed capital | 165,800 | |
| Retained earnings | 136,490 | ———— From the statement of retained earnings |
| **Total stockholders' equity** | 302,290 | |
| **Total liabilities and stockholders' equity** | $373,915 | |

# FOCUS ON **CASH FLOWS**

## OPERATING ACTIVITIES

In Chapter 2, we presented Papa John's statement of cash flows for the investing and financing activities for the month. Recall that investing activities relate primarily to transactions affecting long-term assets; financing activities are those from bank borrowings, stock issuances, and dividend payments to stockholders.

The final category of cash flows is from operating activities, actually reported first on the statement (remember the mnemonic "OIF"). The Operating Activities section of the statement of cash flows reports *cash from* operating sources and *cash to* suppliers and others involved in operations.* Usually current assets and current liabilities are those primarily used in operating activities with customers, suppliers, and employees.

*When operating cash inflows and outflows are presented, the company is using the *direct method* of reporting cash flows from operations. However, most companies report cash from operations using the *indirect method* that will be discussed in later chapters.

When cash is affected by a transaction, these activities are reported on the statement of cash flows. When cash is not included in a transaction (such as acquiring a building with a long-term mortgage note payable or selling goods on account to customers), there is no cash effect to include on the statement.

**Effect on Statement of Cash Flows**

| In General | | Effect on Cash Flows |
|---|---|---|
| **Operating activities** | | |
| Cash received from | Customers | + |
| | Investments | + |
| Cash paid to | Suppliers | − |
| | Employees | − |
| | Interest paid | − |
| | Income taxes paid | − |
| **Investing activities** (from Chapter 2) | | |
| **Financing activities** (from Chapter 2) | | |

**Focus Company Analysis:** The Operating Activities section of the following statement of cash flows for Papa John's is based on the transactions illustrated in this chapter; the investing and financing activities relate to Chapter 2 transactions. The statement reports the sources and uses of cash that created the overall $21,415 cash increase (from $34,000 to $55,415) in our Papa John's example. Remember that only the transactions that affect cash are reported.

For companies to remain in business, they must generate positive cash flows from operations in the long run. Cash is needed to pay suppliers and employees. When cash from operations is negative over a period of time, the only other ways to obtain the necessary funds are to (1) sell long-lived assets (which reduces future productivity), (2) borrow from creditors (at increasing rates of interest as risk of default rises), or (3) issue additional stock (where investor expectations about poor future performance drives the stock price down). There are clearly limits on how many of these activities companies can undertake.

Papa John's has not only realized positive operating cash flows over the years but has also reported a growth in the cash generated from operations as a percentage of net income earned (in 1996, $1.60 in cash for every dollar of net income; in 1997, $1.66; in 1998, $1.80). This represents a conservative approach to reporting revenues and expenses that builds analysts' confidence as to the reliability of the income information reported.

Each is referenced to the transaction illustrated in the chapter.

**PAPA JOHN'S INTERNATIONAL, INC.**
**Consolidated Statement of Cash Flows**
**For the Month Ended January 31, 1999**
**(dollars In thousands)**

| Operating Activities | | | |
|---|---|---|---|
| Cash received from: | Customers and franchisees (a, b, c, h, k) | | $71,250 |
| | Interest and dividends (k) | | 125 |
| | Operating cash inflows | | 71,375 |
| Cash paid to: | Suppliers (d, e, g, j) | | 33,710 |
| | Employees (f) | | 13,500 |
| | Operating cash outflows | | 47,210 |
| Net cash provided by operating activities | | | **24,165** |

*(continued)*

| Investing Activities | |
| --- | --- |
| Purchased property and equipment | $(1,500) |
| Purchased investments | (3,000) |
| Lent funds to franchisees | (450) |
| Received payment on loans to franchisees | 500 |
| Net cash used in investing activities | **(4,450)** |
| **Financing Activities** | |
| Issued common stock | 1,300 |
| Borrowings | 1,000 |
| Paid dividends | (200) |
| Payments on borrowings | (400) |
| Net cash provided by financing activities | 1,700 |
| Change in cash | **21,415** |
| Beginning cash balance | 34,000 |
| **Ending cash balance** | **$55,415** |

Agrees with amount on the balance sheet.

It is interesting to note that Papa John's has unadjusted net income of $38,490 based on the January transactions in this chapter. However, the balance in the Cash account increased by only $21,415. This is a very clear example of the effect of the accrual basis of accounting as compared to the cash basis. *Net income on an accrual basis is not equivalent to the change in cash.*

## SELF-STUDY **QUIZ**

*PETCO Animal Supplies, Inc.*

PETCO Animal Supplies, Inc. is a leading specialty retailer of premium pet food and supplies with nearly 500 stores across the United States. From a recent annual statement of cash flows, indicate whether the transaction affected cash flow as an operating (O), investing (I), or financing (F) activity and indicate the direction of the effect on cash (+ = increases cash; − = decreases cash):

| Transactions | Type of Activity (O, I or F) | Effect on Cash Flows (+ or −) |
| --- | --- | --- |
| 1. Distribution to shareholders | | |
| 2. Receipt of cash from customers | | |
| 3. Additions to property | | |
| 4. Payment of income taxes | | |
| 5. Payment of cash to suppliers | | |
| 6. Repayment of long-term debt | | |
| 7. Receipt of interest on investments | | |
| 8. Borrowings of long-term debt | | |
| 9. Issuance of common stock | | |
| 10. Payment of interest on debt | | |
| 11. Payment of cash to employees | | |
| 12. Sale of property | | |

After you have completed the schedule, check your solution with the answers in the footnote at the bottom of the page.*

*1. F −   2. O +   3. I −   4. O −   5. O −   6. F −
7. O +   8. F +   9. F +   10. O −   11. O −   12. I +

# KEY **RATIO ANALYSIS:**

**■ LEARNING OBJECTIVE 7**

Compute and interpret total asset turnover.

## THE TOTAL ASSET TURNOVER RATIO

**K**now the decision question:

How effective is management in generating sales from assets (resources)? It is computed as follows:

$$\text{Asset Turnover Ratio} = \frac{\text{Sales}}{\text{Average Total Assets}}$$

The 1998 ratio for Papa John's:

$$\frac{\$669,806}{(\$319,297 + \$253,243)/2} = 2.34$$

**E**xamine the ratio using two techniques:

| ① Comparisons over Time | | | ② Comparisons with Competitors | |
|---|---|---|---|---|
| Papa John's International, Inc. | | | Dominos' Inc. | Tricon Global* |
| 1996 | 1997 | 1998 | 1996 | 1998 |
| 2.11 | 2.19 | 2.34 | 3.79 | 1.76 |

*Tricon Global is the parent company of Pizza Hut, KFC, and Taco Bell.

**Selected Focus Company Total Asset Turnover Ratios**

| | |
|---|---|
| Delta Air Lines | 1.03 |
| Harley-Davidson | 1.17 |
| Boston Beer | 1.61 |

**Y**ou interpret the results carefully:

**IN GENERAL** → The total asset turnover ratio measures the sales generated per dollar of assets. A high asset turnover signifies efficient management of assets and a low asset turnover ratio signifies an inefficient one. A company's products and business strategy contribute significantly to its resulting ratio. However, when competitors are similar, management's ability to control the firm's assets is also vital in determining success. Financial performance improves as the ratio increases.

Creditors and security analysts use this ratio to assess a company's effectiveness at controlling current and noncurrent assets. In a well-run business, creditors expect fluctuations in the ratio due to seasonal upswings and downturns. For example, as inventory is built up preceding a high sales season, companies need to borrow funds. The asset turnover ratio will decline from the increase in assets. Then the high-season sales provide the cash needed to repay the loans. The asset turnover ratio accordingly increases from the increase in sales.

**FOCUS COMPANY ANALYSIS** → Papa John's asset turnover ratio increased slightly since 1996, suggesting an increase in management effectiveness in using assets to generate sales. In fact, Papa John's reported that, as the number of stores in a geographic area increases, regional commissaries show higher sales. Therefore, Papa John's management is able to utilize the commissary assets more efficiently.

When compared against its main competitors, Papa John's 1998 total asset turnover ratio falls in the middle. This is in part due to differences in operating strategy: Pizza Hut (and KFC and Taco Bell) operate primarily eat-in restaurants that must invest more in facilities (that is, they are more asset intensive). On the other hand, Domino's is the leading pizza delivery company, operating primarily from rented facilities (that is, it is less asset intensive).

**A FEW CAUTIONS:** The total asset turnover ratio may decrease due to seasonal fluctuation. However, a declining ratio may also be caused by changes in corporate policies, such as more lax collection efforts in accounts receivable, that cause assets to rise. A detailed analysis of the changes in the key components of assets provides additional information on the nature of the asset turnover ratio's change and thus management's decisions.

# DEMONSTRATION **CASE**

This case is a continuation of the Terrific Lawn Maintenance Corporation introduced in Chapter 2. The company was established with supplies, property, and equipment purchased ready for business. The balance sheet at April 30, 2000, based on investing and financing activities is as follows:

### TERRIFIC LAWN MAINTENANCE CORPORATION
### Balance Sheet
### At April 30, 2000

| Assets | | Liabilities | |
|---|---|---|---|
| Current Asset: Cash | $ 4,350 | Current Liability: Notes payable | $ 3,700 |
| Equipment | 4,600 | | |
| Land | 3,750 | **Stockholders' Equity** | |
| | | Contributed capital | 9,000 |
| Total assets | $12,700 | Total liabilities and stockholders' equity | $12,700 |

The following completed activities occurred during April 2000:
a. Purchased and used gasoline for mowers and edgers, paying $90 in cash at a local gas station.
b. In early April, received from the city $1,600 cash in advance for lawn maintenance service for April through July ($400 each month). The entire amount was recorded as Unearned Revenue.
c. In early April, purchased insurance costing $300 covering six months, April through September. The entire payment was recorded as Prepaid Expenses.
d. Mowed lawns for residential customers who are billed every two weeks. A total of $5,200 of service was billed in April.
e. Residential customers paid $3,500 on their accounts.
f. Paid wages every two weeks. Total cash paid in April was $3,900.
g. Received a bill for $320 from the local gas station for additional gasoline purchased on account and used in April.
h. Paid $100 on accounts payable.

*Required:*
1. a. On a separate sheet of paper, set up T-accounts for Cash, Accounts Receivable, Equipment, Land, Prepaid Expenses, Accounts Payable, Unearned Revenue (same as deferred revenue), Notes Payable, Contributed Capital, Retained Earnings, Mowing Revenue, Fuel Expense, and Wages Expense. Beginning balances for balance sheet accounts should be taken from the preceding balance sheet. Beginning balances for operating accounts are $0. Indicate these balances on the T-accounts.
   b. Analyze each transaction using the steps outlined in Chapter 2. Please refer to the expanded transaction analysis model presented in this chapter.
   c. On a separate sheet of paper, prepare journal entries in chronological order and indicate the effects on the accounting model (Assets = Liabilities + Stockholders' Equity). Include the equality checks: (1) Debits = Credits and (2) the accounting equation is in balance.
   d. Enter the effects of each transaction in the appropriate T-accounts. Identify each amount with its letter in the list of activities.
   e. Compute balances in each of the T-accounts.
2. Use the amounts in the T-accounts to prepare a full set of unadjusted financial statements: income statement, statement of retained earnings, balance sheet, and statement of cash flows for Terrific Lawn Maintenance Corporation at April 30, 2000. You will need to refer to the statement presented in Chapter 2 for the investing and financing activities. (Adjustments will be recorded in Chapter 4.)

Now you can check your answers to these requirements with the following solution.

## SUGGESTED SOLUTION

1. **Journal entries, effects on accounting equation, equality checks, and T-accounts:**

(a)
| Fuel expense (+E → −SE) | 90 | |
|---|---|---|
| Cash (−A) | | 90 |

| Assets | = | Liabilities | + | Stockholders' Equity | |
|---|---|---|---|---|---|
| Cash | −90 | | | Fuel expense | −90 |

Equality checks: (1) Debits $90 = Credits $90; (2) the accounting equation is in balance.

(b)
| Cash (+A) | 1,600 | |
|---|---|---|
| Unearned revenue (+L) | | 1,600 |

| Assets | = | Liabilities | + | Stockholders' Equity |
|---|---|---|---|---|
| Cash | +1,600 | Unearned revenue | +1,600 | |

Equality checks: (1) Debits $1,600 = Credits $1,600; (2) the accounting equation is in balance.

(c)
| Prepaid expenses (+A) | 300 | |
|---|---|---|
| Cash (−A) | | 300 |

| Assets | = | Liabilities | + | Stockholders' Equity |
|---|---|---|---|---|
| Cash | −300 | | | |
| Prepaid expenses | +300 | | | |

Equality checks: (1) Debits $300 = Credits $300; (2) the accounting equation is in balance.

(d)
| Accounts receivable (+A) | 5,200 | |
|---|---|---|
| Mowing revenue (+R → +SE) | | 5,200 |

| Assets | = | Liabilities | + | Stockholders' Equity | |
|---|---|---|---|---|---|
| Accounts receivable | +5,200 | | | Mowing revenue | +5,200 |

Equality checks: (1) Debits $5,200 = Credits $5,200; (2) the accounting equation is in balance.

(e)
| Cash (+A) | 3,500 | |
|---|---|---|
| Accounts receivable (−A) | | 3,500 |

| Assets | = | Liabilities | + | Stockholders' Equity |
|---|---|---|---|---|
| Cash | +3,500 | | | |
| Accounts receivable | −3,500 | | | |

Equality checks: (1) Debits $3,500 = Credits $3,500; (2) the accounting equation is in balance.

(f)
| Wages expense (+E → −SE) | 3,900 | |
|---|---|---|
| Cash (−A) | | 3,900 |

| Assets | = | Liabilities | + | Stockholders' Equity | |
|---|---|---|---|---|---|
| Cash | −3,900 | | | Wages expense | −3,900 |

Equality checks: (1) Debits $3,900 = Credits $3,900; (2) the accounting equation is in balance.

(g)
| Fuel expense (+E → −SE) | 320 | |
|---|---|---|
| Accounts payable (+L) | | 320 |

| Assets | = | Liabilities | + | Stockholders' Equity | |
|---|---|---|---|---|---|
| | | Accounts payable | +320 | Fuel expense | −320 |

Equality checks: (1) Debits $320 = Credits $320; (2) the accounting equation is in balance.

(h)
| Accounts payable (−L) | 100 | |
|---|---|---|
| Cash (−A) | | 100 |

| Assets | = | Liabilities | + | Stockholders' Equity |
|---|---|---|---|---|
| Cash | −100 | Accounts payable | −100 | |

Equality checks: (1) Debits $100 = Credits $100; (2) the accounting equation is in balance.

## T-Accounts

### ASSETS

| + | Cash (A) | | − |
|---|---|---|---|
| Ch. 2 bal. | 4,350 | | |
| b | 1,600 | a | 90 |
| e | 3,500 | c | 300 |
| | | f | 3,900 |
| | | h | 100 |
| End. bal. | 5,060 | | |

| + | Accounts Receivable (A) | | − |
|---|---|---|---|
| Ch. 2 bal. | 0 | | |
| d | 5,200 | e | 3,500 |
| End. bal. | 1,700 | | |

| + | Prepaid Expenses (A) | | − |
|---|---|---|---|
| Ch. 2 bal. | 0 | | |
| c | 300 | | |
| End. bal. | 300 | | |

| + | Equipment (A) | | − |
|---|---|---|---|
| Ch. 2 bal. | 4,600 | | |
| End. bal. | 4,600 | | |

| + | Land (A) | | − |
|---|---|---|---|
| Ch. 2 bal. | 3,750 | | |
| End. bal. | 3,750 | | |

### LIABILITIES

| − | Accounts Payable (L) | | + |
|---|---|---|---|
| | | Ch. 2 bal. | 0 |
| h | 100 | g | 320 |
| | | End. bal. | 220 |

| − | Unearned Revenue (L) | | + |
|---|---|---|---|
| | | Ch. 2 bal. | 0 |
| | | b | 1,600 |
| | | End. bal. | 1,600 |

| − | Notes Payable (L) | | + |
|---|---|---|---|
| | | Ch. 2 bal. | 3,700 |
| | | End. bal. | 3,700 |

### STOCKHOLDERS' EQUITY

| − | Contributed Capital (SE) | | + |
|---|---|---|---|
| | | Ch. 2 bal. | 9,000 |
| | | End. bal. | 9,000 |

| − | Retained Earnings (SE) | | + |
|---|---|---|---|
| | | Beg. bal. | 0 |

### REVENUES

| − | Mowing Revenue (R) | | + |
|---|---|---|---|
| | | Beg. bal. | 0 |
| | | d | 5,200 |
| | | End. bal. | 5,200 |

### EXPENSES

| + | Wages Expense (E) | | − |
|---|---|---|---|
| Beg. bal. | 0 | | |
| f | 3,900 | | |
| End. bal. | 3,900 | | |

| + | Fuel Expense (E) | | − |
|---|---|---|---|
| Beg. bal. | 0 | | |
| a | 90 | | |
| g | 320 | | |
| End. bal. | 410 | | |

## 2.  Unadjusted financial statements:

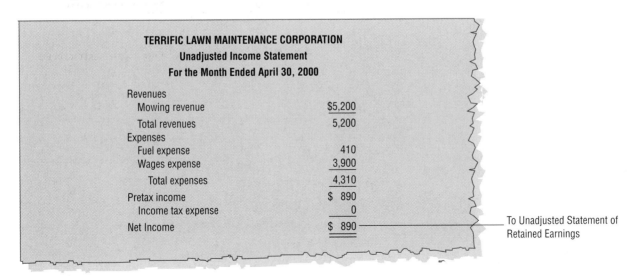

**TERRIFIC LAWN MAINTENANCE CORPORATION**
**Unadjusted Income Statement**
**For the Month Ended April 30, 2000**

| | |
|---|---|
| Revenues | |
| Mowing revenue | $5,200 |
| Total revenues | 5,200 |
| Expenses | |
| Fuel expense | 410 |
| Wages expense | 3,900 |
| Total expenses | 4,310 |
| Pretax income | $ 890 |
| Income tax expense | 0 |
| Net Income | $ 890 |

To Unadjusted Statement of
Retained Earnings

From Unadjusted Income Statement

Agrees with balance sheet

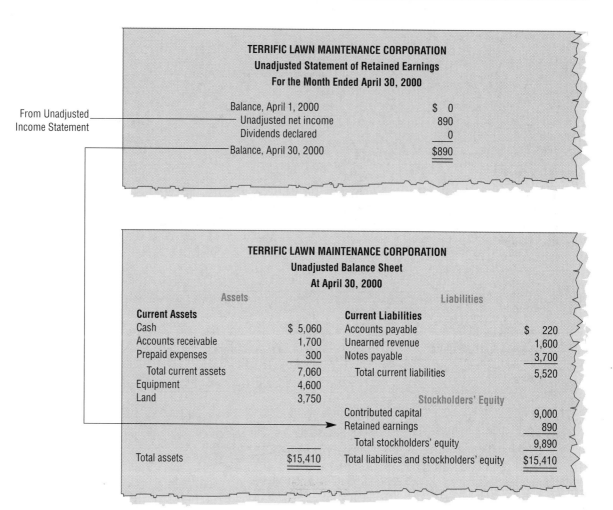

**TERRIFIC LAWN MAINTENANCE CORPORATION**
**Unadjusted Statement of Retained Earnings**
**For the Month Ended April 30, 2000**

| | |
|---|---|
| Balance, April 1, 2000 | $ 0 |
| Unadjusted net income | 890 |
| Dividends declared | 0 |
| Balance, April 30, 2000 | $890 |

**TERRIFIC LAWN MAINTENANCE CORPORATION**
**Unadjusted Balance Sheet**
**At April 30, 2000**

| Assets | | Liabilities | |
|---|---|---|---|
| **Current Assets** | | **Current Liabilities** | |
| Cash | $ 5,060 | Accounts payable | $ 220 |
| Accounts receivable | 1,700 | Unearned revenue | 1,600 |
| Prepaid expenses | 300 | Notes payable | 3,700 |
| Total current assets | 7,060 | Total current liabilities | 5,520 |
| Equipment | 4,600 | | |
| Land | 3,750 | **Stockholders' Equity** | |
| | | Contributed capital | 9,000 |
| | | Retained earnings | 890 |
| | | Total stockholders' equity | 9,890 |
| Total assets | $15,410 | Total liabilities and stockholders' equity | $15,410 |

**TERRIFIC LAWN MAINTENANCE CORPORATION**
**Unadjusted Statement of Cash Flows**
**For the Month Ended April 30, 2000**

| | | |
|---|---|---|
| **Operating Activities** | | |
| Cash from: Customers (b, e) | | $ 5,100 |
| Cash to: Suppliers (a, c, h) | | (490) |
| Employees (f) | | (3,900) |
| Net cash provided by operating activities | | 710 |
| **Investing Activities** | | |
| Purchased land | | $(5,000) |
| Purchased equipment | | (200) |
| Received payment on notes receivable | | 1,250 |
| Net cash used in investing activities | | (3,950) |
| **Financing Activities** | | |
| Issued common stock | | 9,000 |
| Payments on borrowings | | (700) |
| Net cash provided by financing activities | | 8,300 |
| Change in cash | | 5,060 |
| Beginning cash balance | | 0 |
| **Ending cash balance** | | $ 5,060 |

## CHAPTER **TAKE-AWAYS**

1. **Understand a typical business operating cycle.   p. 109**
   - Operating cycle—the cash-to-cash cycle is the time it takes to purchase goods or services from suppliers, sell the goods or services to customers, and collect cash from customers.

2. **Understand the time period assumption and the elements of the income statement.   p. 111**
   - Time period assumption—to measure and report financial information periodically, we assume the long life of the company can be cut into shorter periods.
   - Elements on the income statement:
     a. Revenues—increases in assets or settlements of liabilities from ongoing operations.
     b. Expenses—decreases in assets or increases in liabilities from ongoing operations.
     c. Gains—increases in assets or settlements of liabilities from peripheral activities.
     d. Losses—decreases in assets or increases in liabilities from peripheral activities.

3. **Explain the accrual basis of accounting.   p. 114**
   When applying accrual accounting concepts, revenues are recognized (recorded) when earned and expenses are recognized when incurred to generate the revenues.

4. **Apply the revenue and matching principles to determine the timing and amount of revenues and expenses.   p. 114**
   - Revenue principle—recognize revenues when the earnings process is complete or nearly complete, an exchange has taken place, and collection is probable.
   - Matching principle—recognize expenses when incurred in earning revenue.

5. **Apply transaction analysis to examine and record the effects of operating activities on the financial statements.   p. 119**
   The expanded transaction analysis model includes revenues and expenses:

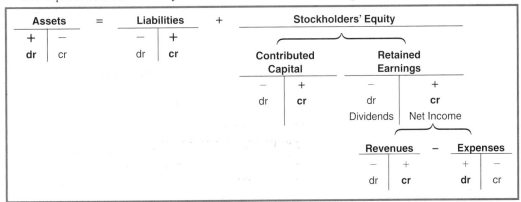

6. **Prepare unadjusted financial statements.   p. 126**
   Until the accounts are updated for all revenues earned and expenses incurred in a period (due to a difference in the time when cash is received or paid), the financial statements are titled "unadjusted":
   - Unadjusted income statement.
   - Unadjusted statement of retained earnings.
   - Unadjusted balance sheet.
   - Unadjusted statement of cash flows.

7. **Compute and interpret total asset turnover.   p. 132**
   The total asset turnover ratio (Sales ÷ Average Total Assets) measures the sales generated per dollar of assets. The higher the ratio, the more efficient the company is at managing assets.

In this chapter, we discussed the operating cycle and accounting concepts relevant to income determination: the time period assumption, definitions for the income statement elements (revenues, expenses, gains, and losses), the revenue principle, and the matching principle. These accounting principles are defined in accordance with the accrual basis of accounting, which requires revenues to be recorded when earned and expenses to be recorded when incurred in generating revenues during the period. The transaction analysis model introduced in Chapter 2 was expanded by adding revenues and expenses, and unadjusted financial statements were presented. In Chapter 4, we will build on your knowledge and discuss the activities at the end of the accounting period: the adjustment process, the preparation of adjusted financial statements, and the closing process.

## KEY **RATIO**

**Total asset turnover** measures the sales generated per dollar of assets. A high ratio suggests that the company is managing its assets (resources used to generate revenues) efficiently. It is computed as follows (p. 132):

$$\text{Total Asset Turnover} = \frac{\text{Sales}}{\text{Average Total Assets}}$$

**"Average" is (Last Year's Value + This Year's Value) ÷ 2.**

## FINDING **FINANCIAL INFORMATION**

**BALANCE SHEET**
*Current Assets*
 Cash
 Accounts and notes
  receivable
 Inventory
 Prepaid expense
*Noncurrent Assets*
 Long-term
  investments
 Property and
  equipment
 Intangibles

*Current Liabilities*
 Accounts payable
 Notes payable
 Accrued liabilities
  payable
*Noncurrent
Liabilities*
 Long-term debt
*Stockholders'
Equity*
 Contributed capital
 Retained earnings

**INCOME STATEMENT**
*Revenues*
 Sales (from various operating activities)
 Investment income
*Expenses*
 Cost of sales (used inventory)
 Rent, wages, interest, depreciation,
  insurance, etc.
*Pretax Income*
 Income tax expense
*Net Income*

**STATEMENT OF CASH FLOWS**
*Under Operating Activities*
 + Cash from customers
 + Cash from investments
 − Cash to suppliers
 − Cash to employees
 − Interest paid
 − Income taxes paid

**NOTES**
*Under Summary of Significant Accounting
Policies*
 Description of the company's revenue
  recognition policy.

## KEY **TERMS**

**Accrual Basis Accounting** p. 114
**Cash Basis Accounting** p. 113
**Expenses** p. 112
**Gains** p. 112
**Losses** p. 113
**Matching Principle** p. 117

**Operating Cycle (cash-to-cash
 cycle)** p. 109
**Revenues** p. 111
**Revenue Principle** p. 114
**Time Period Assumption** p. 111

## QUESTIONS

1. Explain a typical business operating cycle.
2. Explain what the time period assumption means in accounting.
3. Indicate the income statement equation and define each element.
4. Explain the difference between
   *a.* Revenues and gains.
   *b.* Expenses and losses.
5. Define *accrual accounting.* Contrast it with cash basis accounting.
6. What three conditions normally must be met for revenue to be recognized under the accrual basis of accounting?
7. Explain the matching principle.
8. Explain why stockholders' equity is increased by revenues and decreased by expenses.
9. Explain why revenues are recorded as credits and expenses as debits.

10. Complete the following matrix by entering either *debit* or *credit* in each cell:

| Item | Increase | Decrease |
|---|---|---|
| Revenues | | |
| Losses | | |
| Gains | | |
| Expenses | | |

11. Complete the following matrix by entering either *increase* or *decrease* in each cell:

| Item | Debit | Credit |
|---|---|---|
| Revenues | | |
| Losses | | |
| Gains | | |
| Expenses | | |

12. Identify whether each of the following transactions results in a cash flow effect from operating, investing, or financing activities, and indicate the effect on cash (+ for increase and − for decrease). If there is no cash flow effect, write "None":

| Transaction | Operating, Investing, or Financing Effect | Direction of the Effect |
|---|---|---|
| Cash paid to suppliers | | |
| Sale of goods on account | | |
| Cash received from customers | | |
| Purchase of investments | | |
| Cash paid for interest | | |
| Issuance of stock for cash | | |

13. What is the equation for the asset turnover ratio? Explain how it is interpreted.

# MINI-EXERCISES

## M3–1 Matching Definitions with Terms

LO1, 2, 3, 4

Match each definition with its related term by entering the appropriate letter in the space provided. There should be only one definition per term (that is, there are more definitions than terms).

| Term | Definition |
|---|---|
| _____ (1) Losses | A. Decreases in assets or increases in liabilities from ongoing operations. |
| _____ (2) Matching principle | B. Record revenues when earned and measurable (an exchange takes place, the earnings process is complete or nearly complete, and collection is probable). |
| _____ (3) Revenues | C. Report the long life of a company in shorter time periods. |
| _____ (4) Time period assumption | D. Record expenses when incurred in earning revenue. |
| _____ (5) Operating cycle | E. The time it takes to purchase goods or services from suppliers, sell goods or services to customers, and collect cash from customers. |
| | F. Decreases in assets or increases in liabilities from peripheral transactions. |
| | G. Increases in assets or decreases in liabilities from ongoing operations. |

## M3–2 Reporting Cash Basis versus Accrual Basis Income

LO3

Mostert Music Company had the following transactions in March:

*a.* Sold instruments to customers for $10,000; received $6,000 in cash and the rest on account.

b. Determined that the cost of the instruments sold was $7,000.

c. Purchased $4,000 of new instruments inventory; paid $1,000 in cash and the rest on account.

d. Paid $600 in wages for the month.

e. Received a $200 bill for utilities that will be paid in April.

f. Received $1,000 from customers as deposits on orders of new instruments to be sold to the customers in April.

Complete the following statements:

| Cash Basis Income Statement | | Accrual Basis Income Statement | |
|---|---|---|---|
| Revenues | | Revenues | |
| Cash sales | | Sales to customers | |
| Customer deposits | | | |
| Expenses | | Expenses | |
| Inventory purchases | | Cost of sales | |
| Wages paid | | Wages expense | |
| | | Utilities expense | _____ |
| | _____ | | |
| Net income | ====== | Net income | ====== |

■ **LO2, 3, 4**    **M3–3**    **Identifying Revenues**

The following transactions are July 20B activities of Bob's Bowling, Inc., which operates several bowling centers (for games and equipment sales).

1. Indicate the account titles that are affected and the type of account for each (A for asset, L for liability, and R for revenue).

2. If a revenue is to be recognized in July, indicate the amount. If a revenue is not to be recognized in July, indicate which of the revenue recognition criteria are not met.

| Activity | Accounts Affected and Type of Account | Amount of Revenue Earned in July OR Revenue Criteria Not Met |
|---|---|---|
| a. Bob's collected $10,000 from customers for games played in July. | Cash (+A) Game fees revenue (+R) | $10,000 |
| b. Bob's sold bowling equipment inventory for $5,000; received $3,000 in cash and the rest on account. [Ignore inventory cost.] | Cash (+A) Accounts receivable (+A) Equip. sales revenue (+R) | $5,000 |
| c. Bob's received $1,000 from customers on account who purchased merchandise in June. | Cash (+A) Accts. receivable (-A) | No revenue earned in July |
| d. The men's and ladies' bowling leagues gave Bob's a deposit of $1,500 for the upcoming fall season. | Cash (+A) Unearned revenue (+L) | No revenue earned in July, earnings process is not yet complete |

■ **LO2, 3, 4**    **M3–4**    **Identifying Expenses**

The following transactions are July 20B activities of Bob's Bowling, Inc., which operates several bowling centers (for games and equipment sales).

1. Indicate the account titles that are affected and the type of account for each (A for asset, L for liability, and E for expense).

2. If an expense is to be recognized in July, indicate the amount. If an expense is not to be recognized in July, indicate why.

| Activity | Accounts Affected and Type of Account | Amount of Expense Incurred in July OR Why an Expense Is Not Recognized |
|---|---|---|
| a. Bob's sold bowling merchandise costing $2,000. | | |
| b. Bob's paid $2,000 for the June electricity bill and received the July bill for $2,200, which will be paid in August. | | |
| c. Bob's paid $4,000 to employees for work in July. | | |
| d. Bob's purchased $1,200 in insurance for coverage from July 1 to October 1. | | |
| e. Bob's paid $1,000 to plumbers for repairing a broken pipe in the restrooms. | | |

**M3–5 Recording Revenues**   ■ **LO5**

For each of the transactions in M3–3, write the journal entry in good form.

**M3–6 Recording Expenses**   ■ **LO5**

For each of the transactions in M3–4, write the journal entry in good form.

**M3–7 Determining the Financial Statement Effects of Operating Activities Involving Revenues**   ■ **LO5**

The following transactions are July 20B activities of Bob's Bowling, Inc., which operates several bowling centers (for games and equipment sales). For each of the following transactions, complete the tabulation, indicating the amount and effect (+ for increase and − for decrease) of each transaction. (Remember that A = L + SE, R − E = NI, and NI affects SE through Retained Earnings). Write NE if there is no effect. The first transaction is provided as an example.

| | Balance Sheet | | | Income Statement | | |
|---|---|---|---|---|---|---|
| Transaction | Assets | Liabilities | Stockholders' Equity | Revenues | Expenses | Net Income |
| a. Bob's collected $10,000 from customers for games played in July. | +10,000 | NE | +10,000 | +10,000 | NE | +10,000 |
| b. Bob's sold $5,000 in bowling equipment inventory; received $3,000 in cash and the rest on account. | | | | | | |
| c. Bob's received $1,000 from customers on account who purchased merchandise in June. | | | | | | |
| d. The men's and ladies' bowling leagues gave Bob's a deposit of $1,500 for the upcoming fall season. | | | | | | |

**M3–8 Determining the Financial Statement Effects of Operating Activities Involving Expenses**   ■ **LO5**

The following transactions are July 20B activities of Bob's Bowling, Inc., which operates several bowling centers (for games and equipment sales). For each of the following transactions, complete the tabulation, indicating the amount and effect (+ for increase and − for decrease) of each transaction. (Remember that A = L + SE, R − E = NI, and NI affects SE through retained earnings). Write NE if there is no effect. The first transaction is provided as an example.

| | Balance Sheet | | | Income Statement | | |
|---|---|---|---|---|---|---|
| Transaction | Assets | Liabilities | Stockholders' Equity | Revenues | Expenses | Net Income |
| a. Bob's sold bowling merchandise costing $2,000. | −2,000 | NE | −2,000 | NE | +2,000 | −2,000 |
| b. Bob's paid $2,000 for the June electricity bill and received the July bill for $2,200 to be paid in August. | | | | | | |
| c. Bob's paid $4,000 to employees for work in July. | | | | | | |
| d. Bob's purchased $1,200 in insurance for coverage from July 1 to October 1. | | | | | | |
| e. Bob's paid $1,000 to plumbers for repairing a broken pipe in the restrooms. | | | | | | |

**M3–9 Preparing a Simple Income Statement**   ■ **LO6**

Given the transactions in M3–7 and M3–8 (including the examples), prepare an income statement for Bob's Bowling, Inc., for the month of July 20B.

**M3–10 Preparing the Operating Activities Section of a Statement of Cash Flows**   ■ **LO6**

Given the transactions in M3–7 and M3–8 (including the examples), prepare the operating activities section of the statement of cash flows for Bob's Bowling, Inc., for the month of July 20B.

**M3–11 Computing and Explaining the Total Asset Turnover Ratio**   ■ **LO7**

The following data are from annual reports of Justin's Jewelry Company:

| | 20C | 20B | 20A |
|---|---|---|---|
| Total assets | $ 60,000 | $ 50,000 | $ 40,000 |
| Total liabilities | 12,000 | 10,000 | 5,000 |
| Total stockholders' equity | 48,000 | 40,000 | 35,000 |
| Sales | 154,000 | 144,000 | 130,000 |
| Net income | 50,000 | 38,000 | 25,000 |

Compute Justin's total asset turnover ratio for 20B and 20C. What do these results suggest to you about Justin's Jewelry Company?

# EXERCISES

**LO1, 2, 3, 4**    **E3–1**    **Matching Definitions with Terms**

Match each definition with its related term by entering the appropriate letter in the space provided. There should be only one definition per term (that is, there are more definitions than terms).

| Term | Definition |
|---|---|
| _____ (1) Expenses | A. Report the long life of a company in shorter periods. |
| _____ (2) Gains | B. Record expenses when incurred in earning revenue. |
| _____ (3) Revenue principle | C. The time it takes to purchase goods or services from suppliers, sell goods or services to customers, and collect cash from customers. |
| _____ (4) Cash basis accounting | |
| _____ (5) Unearned revenue | D. A liability account used to record cash received before revenues have been earned. |
| _____ (6) Operating cycle | |
| _____ (7) Accrual basis accounting | E. Increases in assets or decreases in liabilities from peripheral transactions. |
| _____ (8) Prepaid expenses | F. Decreases in assets or increases in liabilities from ongoing operations. |
| _____ (9) Revenues − Expenses = Net Income | G. Record revenues when earned and measurable (an exchange takes place, the earnings process is complete or nearly complete, and collection is probable). |
| _____ (10) Ending Retained Earnings = Beginning Retained Earnings + Net Income − Dividends | H. Decreases in assets or increases in liabilities from peripheral transactions. |
| | I. Record revenues when received and expenses when paid. |
| | J. The income statement equation. |
| | K. An asset account used to record cash paid before expenses have been incurred. |
| | L. The retained earnings equation. |
| | M. Record revenues when earned and expenses when incurred. |

**LO2, 3, 4**    **E3–2**    **Identifying Revenues**

Revenues are normally recognized when the earnings process is complete or nearly complete, a transaction has taken place, and collection is reasonably assured. The amount recorded is the cash-equivalent sales price. The following transactions occurred in September 20A:

a. A customer orders and receives 10 personal computers from Gateway 2000; the customer promises to pay $25,000 within three months. Answer from Gateway's standpoint.

b. Sam Shell Dodge sells a truck with a list, or "sticker," price of $24,000 for $21,000 cash.

c. Hudson's Department Store orders 1,000 men's shirts from Arrow Shirt Company for $18 each for future delivery. The terms require payment in full within 30 days of delivery. Answer from Arrow's standpoint.

d. Arrow Shirt Company completes production of the shirts described in (c) and delivers the order. Answer from Arrow's standpoint.

e. Arrow receives payment from Hudson's for the order described in (c). Answer from Arrow's standpoint.

f. A customer purchases a ticket from American Airlines for $500 cash to travel the following January. Answer from American Airlines' standpoint.

g. General Motors issues $26 million in new common stock.

h. Penn State University receives $20,000,000 cash for 80,000 five-game season football tickets.

i. Penn State plays the first football game referred to in (h).

j. Hall Construction Company signs a contract with a customer for the construction of a new $500,000 warehouse. At the signing, Hall receives a check for $50,000 as a deposit on the future construction. Answer from Hall's standpoint.

k. On September 1, 20A, a bank lends $1,000 to a company. The loan carries a 12 percent annual interest rate, and the principal and interest are due in a lump sum on August 31, 20B. Answer from the bank's standpoint.

*l.* A popular ski magazine company receives a total of $1,800 today from subscribers. The subscriptions begin in the next fiscal year. Answer from the magazine company's standpoint.

*m.* Sears, a retail store, sells a $100 lamp to a customer who charges the sale on his store credit card. Answer from the standpoint of Sears.

*Required:*
For each of the September transactions,

1. Indicate the account titles that are affected and the type of account for each (A for asset, L for liability, SE for stockholders' equity, and R for revenue).

2. If a revenue is to be recognized in September, indicate the amount. If a revenue is not to be recognized in September, indicate which of the revenue recognition criteria are not met.

Use the following headings in structuring your solution:

| Activity | Accounts Affected and Type of Account | Amount of Revenue Earned in September OR Revenue Criteria Not Met |
| --- | --- | --- |

### E3–3 Identifying Expenses

LO2, 3, 4

Revenues are normally recognized when goods or services have been provided and payment or promise of payment has been received. Expense recognition is guided by an attempt to match the costs associated with the generation of those revenues to the same time period. The following transactions occurred in January 20B:

*a.* Gateway 2000 pays its computer service technicians $90,000 in salary for the two weeks ended January 7. Answer from Gateway's standpoint.

*b.* Turner Construction Company pays $4,500 in worker's compensation insurance for the first three months of the year.

*c.* McGraw-Hill Publishing Company uses $1,000 worth of electricity and natural gas in its headquarters building for which it has not yet been billed.

*d.* Arrow Shirt Company completes production of 500 men's shirts ordered by Bon Ton's Department Store at a cost of $9 each and delivers the order. Answer from Arrow's standpoint.

*e.* The campus bookstore receives 500 accounting texts at a cost of $50 each. The terms indicate that payment is due within 30 days of delivery.

*f.* During the last week of January, the campus bookstore sold 450 accounting texts received in (*e*) at a sales price of $80 each.

*g.* Sam Shell Dodge pays its salespersons $3,500 in commissions related to December automobile sales. Answer from Sam Shell Dodge's standpoint.

*h.* On January 31, Sam Shell Dodge determines that it will pay its salespersons $4,200 in commissions related to January sales. The payment will be made in early February. Answer from Sam Shell Dodge's standpoint.

*i.* A new grill is installed at a McDonald's restaurant. On the same day, payment of $12,000 is made in cash.

*j.* The University of Florida orders 60,000 season football tickets from its printer and pays $6,000 in advance for the custom printing. The first game will be played in September. Answer from the university's standpoint.

*k.* Carousel Mall had janitorial supplies costing $1,000 in storage. An additional $600 worth of supplies was purchased during January. At the end of January, $900 worth of janitorial supplies remained in storage.

*l.* An Iowa State University employee works eight hours, at $15 per hour, on January 31; however, payday is not until February 3. Answer from the university's point of view.

*m.* Wang Company paid $3,600 for a fire insurance policy on January 2. The policy covers the current month and the next 11 months. Answer from Wang's point of view.

*n.* Amber Incorporated has its delivery van repaired in January for $280 and charges the amount on account.

*o.* Ziegler Company, a farm equipment company, receives its phone bill at the end of January for $230 for January calls. The bill has not been paid to date.

*p.* Spina Company receives and pays in January a $1,500 invoice from a consulting firm for services received in January.

*q.* Felicetti's Taxi Company pays a $600 invoice from a consulting firm for services received and recorded in Accounts Payable in December.

*Required:*

For each of the January transactions,

1. Indicate the account titles that are affected and the type of account for each (A for asset, L for liability, and E for expense).

2. If an expense is to be recognized in January, indicate the amount. If an expense is not to be recognized in January, indicate why.

Use the following headings in structuring your solution:

| Activity | Accounts Affected and Type of Account | Amount of Expense Incurred in January OR Why An Expense Is Not Recognized |
|---|---|---|

**LO5**      **E3–4**    **Determining Financial Statement Effects of Various Transactions**

The following transactions occurred during a recent year:

*a.* Issued stock to organizers for cash (example).

*b.* Borrowed cash from local bank.

*c.* Purchased equipment on credit.

*d.* Earned revenue, collected cash.

*e.* Incurred expenses, on credit.

*f.* Earned revenue, on credit.

*g.* Paid cash on account.

*h.* Incurred expenses, paid cash.

*i.* Earned revenue, collected three-fourths in cash, balance on credit.

*j.* Experienced theft of $100 cash.

*k.* Declared and paid cash dividends.

*l.* Collected cash from customers on account.

*m.* Incurred expenses, paid four-fifths in cash, balance on credit.

*n.* Paid income tax expense for the period.

*Required:*

For each of the transactions, complete the tabulation, indicating the effect (+ for increase and − for decrease) of each transaction. (Remember that A = L + SE, R − E = NI, and NI affects SE through Retained Earnings). Write NE if there is no effect. The first transaction is provided as an example.

| | Balance Sheet | | | Income Statement | | |
|---|---|---|---|---|---|---|
| Transaction | Assets | Liabilities | Stockholders' Equity | Revenues | Expenses | Net Income |
| (*a*) (example) | + | NE | + | NE | NE | NE |

**LO5**      **E3–5**    **Determining Financial Statement Effects of Various Transactions**

Wolverine World Wide, Inc.

Wolverine World Wide, Inc., manufactures military, work, sport, and casual footwear and leather accessories under a variety of brand names, such as Hush Puppies, Wolverine, and Bates, to a global market. The following transactions occurred during a recent year. Dollars are in thousands.

*a.* Issued $48,869 in common stock to investors (example).

*b.* Purchased $299,794 of additional inventory of raw materials on account.

*c.* Borrowed $58,181 on long-term notes.

*d.* Sold $413,957 of products to customers on account; cost of the products sold was $290,469.

*e.* Paid cash dividends of $2,347.

*f.* Purchased $18,645 in additional property, plant, and equipment.

*g.* Incurred $85,993 in selling expenses with two-thirds paid in cash and the rest on account.

*h.* Earned $1,039 interest on investments, received 90 percent in cash.

*i.* Incurred $4,717 in interest expense.

*Required:*

For each of the transactions, complete the tabulation, indicating the effect (+ for increase and − for decrease) of each transaction. (Remember that A = L + SE, R − E = NI, and NI affects SE through Retained Earnings). Write NE if there is no effect. The first transaction is provided as an example.

| | Balance Sheet | | | Income Statement | | |
|---|---|---|---|---|---|---|
| Transaction | Assets | Liabilities | Stockholders' Equity | Revenues | Expenses | Net Income |
| (a) (example) | +48,869 | NE | +48,869 | NE | NE | NE |

### E3–6 Recording Journal Entries

Sysco, formed in 1969, is America's largest marketer and distributor of food service products, serving nearly 250,000 restaurants, hotels, schools, hospitals, and other institutions. The following summarized transactions are typical of those that occurred in a recent year.

a. Borrowed $80 million from a bank, signing a short-term note.

b. Provided $10.02 billion in service to customers during the year, with $9.5 billion on account and the rest received in cash.

c. Purchased plant and equipment for $127.9 million in cash.

d. Purchased $8.268 billion inventory on account.

e. Paid payroll, $1.02 billion during the year.

f. Received $410 million on account paid by customers.

g. Purchased and used fuel of $400 million in delivery vehicles during the year (paid for in cash).

h. Declared and paid $48.8 million in dividends for the year.

i. Paid $8.2 billion cash on accounts payable.

j. Incurred $20 million in utility usage during the year; paid $15 million in cash and the rest on account.

*Required:*

For each of the transactions, prepare journal entries. Determine whether the accounting equation remains in balance and debits equal credits after each entry.

### E3–7 Recording Journal Entries

Greek Peak Incorporated is a ski resort in upstate New York. The company sells lift tickets, ski lessons, and ski equipment. It operates several restaurants and rents townhouses to vacationing skiers. The following hypothetical December transactions are typical of those that occur at the resort.

a. Borrowed $500,000 from the bank on December 1 with a six-month note at 12 percent annual interest to finance the beginning of the new season. The principal and interest are due on the maturity date.

b. Purchased a new snow plow for $20,000 cash on December 1. The plow is estimated to have a five-year life and a $5,000 residual value.

c. Purchased and received $10,000 of ski equipment on account to sell in the ski shop.

d. Incurred $22,000 in routine maintenance expenses for the chair lifts; paid cash.

e. Sold $72,000 of season passes and received cash.

f. Sold daily lift passes for a total of $76,000 in cash.

g. Sold a pair of skis for $350 on account. (The cost of the pair was $250.)

h. Received a $320 deposit on a townhouse to be rented for five days in January.

i. Paid half the charges incurred on account in (c).

j. Received $200 on account from the customer in (g).

k. Paid $108,000 in wages to employees for the month of December.

*Required:*

1. Prepare journal entries for each transaction. (Remember to check that debits equal credits and that the accounting equation is in balance after each transaction.)

2. Assume that Greek Peak had a $1,200 balance in Accounts Receivable at the beginning of the year. Determine the ending balance in the Accounts Receivable account. Show your work in T-account format.

**LO5**

Sysco

**LO5**

Greek Peak

**LO5**

**E3–8**    **Recording Journal Entries**

Rowland & Sons Air Transport Service, Inc., has been in operation for three years. The following transactions occurred in February:

| February 1 | Paid $200 for rent of hangar space in February. |
|---|---|
| February 2 | Purchased fuel costing $450 on account for the next flight to Dallas. |
| February 4 | Received customer payment of $800 to ship several items to Philadelphia next month. |
| February 7 | Flew cargo from Denver to Dallas; the customer paid $900 for the air transport. |
| February 10 | Paid pilot $1,200 in wages for flying in January. |
| February 14 | Paid $60 for an advertisement in the local paper to run on February 19. |
| February 18 | Flew cargo for two customers from Dallas to Albuquerque for $1,700; one customer paid $500 cash and the other asked to be billed. |
| February 25 | Purchased spare parts for the planes costing $1,350 on account. |
| February 27 | Declared a $200 cash dividend to be paid in March. |

*Required:*

Prepare journal entries for each transaction. Be sure to categorize each account as an asset (A), liability (L), stockholders' equity (SE), revenue (R), or expense (E).

**LO3, 5**

**E3–9**    **Analyzing the Effects of Transactions in T-Accounts and Computing Cash Basis versus Accrual Basis Net Income**

Swanson's Piano Rebuilding Company has been operating for one year (20A). At the start of 20B, its income statement accounts had zero balances and its balance sheet account balances were as follows:

| | | | |
|---|---|---|---|
| Cash | $ 6,000 | Accounts payable | 8,000 |
| Accounts receivable | 25,000 | Deferred revenue (deposits) | 3,200 |
| Supplies | 1,200 | Note payable (due in three years | |
| Equipment | 8,000 |    with 12% annual interest) | 40,000 |
| Land | 6,000 | Contributed capital | 8,000 |
| Building | 22,000 | Retained earnings | 9,000 |

*Required:*

1. Create T-accounts for the balance sheet accounts and for these additional accounts: Rebuilding Fees Revenue, Rent Revenue, Wages Expense, and Utilities Expense. Enter the beginning balances.

2. Enter the following January 20B transactions in the T-accounts, using the letter of each transaction as the reference:

   *a.*   Received a $500 deposit from a customer who wanted her piano rebuilt.

   *b.*   Rented a part of the building to a bicycle repair shop; received $300 for rent in January.

   *c.*   Delivered 10 rebuilt pianos to customers who paid $14,500 in cash.

   *d.*   Received $6,000 from customers as payment on their accounts.

   *e.*   Received an electric and gas utility bill for $350 to be paid in February.

   *f.*   Ordered $800 in supplies.

   *g.*   Paid $1,700 on account in January.

   *h.*   Received from the home of Ms. Swanson, the major shareholder, a $600 tool (equipment) to use in the business.

   *i.* Paid $10,000 in wages to employees in January.

   *j.* Declared and paid a $3,000 dividend.

   *k.* Received and paid for the supplies in (*f*) in cash.

3. Using the data from the T-accounts, amounts for the following on January 31, 20B, were

     Revenues, $_____ − Expenses, $_____ = Net Income, $_____

     Assets, $_____ = Liabilities, $_____ + Stockholders' Equity, $_____

4. What is net income if Swanson used the cash basis of accounting? Why does this differ from accrual basis net income (in part 3 above)?

**E3–10** **Preparing an Income Statement, Statement of Retained Earnings, and Classified Balance Sheet** ▇ LO6
Refer to E3–9.

*Required:*
Use the ending balances in the T-accounts in E3–9 to prepare the following:

1. An unadjusted income statement for January 20B in good form.

2. An unadjusted statement of retained earnings for January 20B.

3. An unadjusted classified balance sheet as of January 31, 20B, in good form.

**E3–11** **Preparing a Statement of Cash Flows** ▇ LO6
Refer to E3–9.

*Required:*
Use the transactions in E3–9 to prepare a statement of cash flows in good form.

**E3–12** **Analyzing the Effects of Transactions in T-Accounts** ▇ LO5
Karen Gorewit and Pat Nally had been operating a catering business, Traveling Gourmet, for several years. In March 20C, the partners were planning to expand by opening a retail sales shop and decided to form the business as a corporation called Traveling Gourmet, Inc. The following transactions occurred in March 20C:

*a.* Received $10,000 cash from each of the two shareholders to form the corporation, in addition to $2,000 in accounts receivable, $5,300 in equipment, a van (equipment) appraised at a fair market value of $13,000, and $1,200 in supplies.

*b.* Purchased a vacant store for sale in a good location for $60,000 with a $9,000 cash down payment and a mortgage from a local bank for the rest.

*c.* Borrowed $25,000 from the local bank on a 10 percent, one-year note.

*d.* Purchased for cash and used food and paper supplies costing $8,830 in March.

*e.* Made and sold food at the retail store for $10,900 in cash.

*f.* Catered four parties in March for $3,200; $1,500 was billed, and the rest was received in cash.

*g.* Received a $320 telephone bill for March to be paid in April.

*h.* Paid $63 in gas for the van in March.

*i.* Paid $5,080 in wages to employees who worked in March.

*j.* Paid a $300 dividend from the corporation to each owner.

*k.* Purchased $15,000 of equipment (refrigerated display cases, cabinets, tables, and chairs) and renovated and decorated the new store for $10,000 (added to the cost of the building).

*Required:*

1. Set up appropriate T-accounts for Cash, Accounts Receivable, Supplies, Equipment, Building, Accounts Payable, Note Payable, Mortgage Payable, Contributed Capital, Retained Earnings, Food Sales Revenue, Catering Sales Revenue, Cost of Food and Paper Products, Utilities Expense, Wages Expense, and Gasoline Expense.

2. Record in the T-accounts the effects of each transaction for Traveling Gourmet, Inc., in March. Identify the amounts with the letters starting with (*a*).

**E3–13** **Preparing an Income Statement, Statement of Retained Earnings, and Classified Balance Sheet** ▇ LO6
Refer to E3–12.

*Required:*
Use the balances in the completed T-accounts in E3–12 to respond to the following:

1. Prepare an unadjusted income statement in good form for the month of March 20C.

2. Prepare an unadjusted statement of retained earnings for the month of March 20C.

3. Prepare an unadjusted classified balance sheet in good form as of March 20C.

4. What do you think about the success of this company based on the results of the first month of operation?

**LO6** **E3–14**

**Preparing a Statement of Cash Flows**
Refer to E3–12.

*Required:*
Use the transactions in E3–12 to prepare a statement of cash flows in good form.

**LO2, 3, 5, 6** **E3–15**

**Inferring Operating Transactions and Preparing an Income Statement and Balance Sheet**

Kiernan Kite Company (a corporation) sells and repairs kites from manufacturers around the world. Its stores are located in rented space in malls and shopping centers. During its first month of operations ended April 30, 20B, Kiernan Kite Company completed eight transactions with the dollar effects indicated in the following schedule:

| Accounts | (a) | (b) | (c) | (d) | (e) | (f) | (g) | (h) | Ending Balance |
|---|---|---|---|---|---|---|---|---|---|
| Cash | $50,000 | $(10,000) | $(5,000) | $ 7,000 | $(2,000) | $(1,000) | | $3,000 | |
| Accounts receivable | | | | 3,000 | | | | | |
| Inventory | | | 20,000 | (3,000) | | | | | |
| Prepaid expenses | | | | | $1,500 | | | | |
| Store fixtures | | 10,000 | | | | | | | |
| Accounts payable | | | 15,000 | | | | $1,200 | | |
| Unearned revenue | | | | | | | | 2,000 | |
| Contributed capital | 50,000 | | | | | | | | |
| Sales revenue | | | | 10,000 | | | | 1,000 | |
| Cost of sales | | | | 3,000 | | | | | |
| Wages expense | | | | | | 1,000 | | | |
| Rent expense | | | | | 500 | | | | |
| Utilities expense | | | | | | | 1,200 | | |

*Required:*

1. Write a brief explanation of Transactions (*a*) through (*h*). Explain any assumptions that you made.

2. Compute the ending balance in each account and prepare an income statement and a classified balance sheet for Kiernan Kite Company on April 30, 20B.

**LO5, 7** **E3–16**

**Analyzing the Effects of Transactions Using T-Accounts and Interpreting the Total Asset Turnover Ratio as a Financial Analyst**

Karcz Company, which has been operating for three years, provides marketing consulting services worldwide for dot-com companies. You are a financial analyst assigned to report on the Karcz management team's effectiveness at managing its assets efficiently. At the start of 20D (its fourth year), Karcz's T-account balances were as follows. Dollars are in thousands.

**ASSETS**

| Cash | | Accounts Receivable | | Long-Term Investments | |
|---|---|---|---|---|---|
| 4,000 | | 10,000 | | 8,000 | |

**LIABILITIES**

| Accounts Payable | | Unearned Revenue | | Long-Term Notes Payable | |
|---|---|---|---|---|---|
| | 3,000 | | 7,000 | | 2,000 |

**STOCKHOLDERS' EQUITY**

| Contributed Capital | | Retained Earnings | |
|---|---|---|---|
| | 6,000 | | 4,000 |

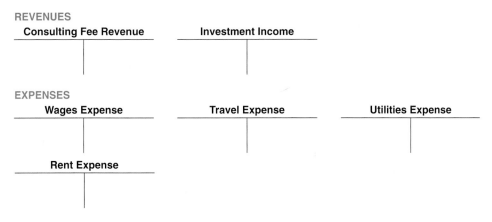

**REVENUES**

| Consulting Fee Revenue | Investment Income |
| --- | --- |

**EXPENSES**

| Wages Expense | Travel Expense | Utilities Expense |
| --- | --- | --- |

| Rent Expense |
| --- |

*Required:*

1. Using the data from these T-accounts, amounts for the following on January 1, 20D, were

     Assets \$_____ = Liabilities \$_____ + Stockholders' Equity \$_____.

2. Enter the following 20D transactions in the T-accounts:

   *a.* Received \$7,000 cash from clients on account.

   *b.* Provided \$70,000 in services to clients; received \$60,000 in cash and the rest on account.

   *c.* Received \$500 in income on investments.

   *d.* Paid \$20,000 in wages, \$20,000 in travel, \$12,000 rent, and \$2,000 on accounts payable.

   *e.* Received a utility bill for \$1,000.

   *f.* Paid \$600 in dividends to stockholders.

   *g.* Received \$2,000 in cash from clients in advance of services Karcz will provide next year.

3. Compute ending balances in the T-accounts to determine amounts for the following on December 31, 20D:

     Assets \$_____ = Liabilities \$_____ + Stockholders' Equity \$_____

     Revenues \$_____ − Expenses \$_____ = Net Income \$_____.

4. Calculate the total asset turnover ratio for 20D. If the company had an asset turnover ratio in 20C of 2.00 and in 20B of 1.80, what does your computation suggest to you about Karcz Company? What would you say in your report?

**E3–17** **Inferring Transactions and Computing Effects Using T-Accounts**

A recent annual report of Dow Jones & Company, the world leader in business and financial news and information (and publisher of *The Wall Street Journal*), included the following accounts. Dollars are in millions:

■ **LO5**

Dow Jones & Company

| Accounts Receivable | | Prepaid Expenses | | Unearned Revenue | |
| --- | --- | --- | --- | --- | --- |
| 1/1 | 313 | | 1/1 | 25 | | | 240 | 1/1 |
| | 2,573 | ? | | 43 | ? | ? | 328 | |
| 12/31 | 295 | | 12/31 | 26 | | | 253 | |

*Required:*

1. For each T-account, describe the typical transactions that affect each account (that is, what economic events occur to make these accounts increase and decrease).

2. For each T-account, compute the missing amounts.

**E3–18** **Finding Financial Information as an Investor**

You are evaluating your current portfolio of investments to determine those that are not performing to your expectations. You have all of the companies' most recent annual reports.

*Required:*

For each of the following, indicate where you would locate the information in an annual report. (*Hint:* The information may be in more than one location.)

1. Description of a company's primary business(es).
2. Income taxes paid.
3. Accounts receivable.
4. Cash flow from operating activities.
5. Description of a company's revenue recognition policy.
6. The inventory sold during the year.
7. The data needed to compute the total asset turnover ratio.

## PROBLEMS

■ **LO5**     **P3–1**     **Recording Nonquantitative Journal Entries** (AP3–1)

The following list includes a series of accounts for Heiss Corporation, which has been operating for three years. These accounts are listed and numbered for identification. Following the accounts is a series of transactions. For each transaction, indicate the account(s) that should be debited and credited by entering the appropriate account number(s) to the right of each transaction. If no journal entry is needed, write *none* after the transaction. The first transaction is used as an example.

| Account No. | Account Title | Account No. | Account Title |
|---|---|---|---|
| 1 | Cash | 9 | Wages payable |
| 2 | Accounts receivable | 10 | Income taxes payable |
| 3 | Supplies inventory on hand | 11 | Contributed capital |
| 4 | Prepaid expense | 12 | Retained earnings |
| 5 | Equipment | 13 | Service revenue |
| 6 | Patents | 14 | Operating expenses |
| 7 | Accounts payable | 15 | Income tax expense |
| 8 | Note payable | 16 | None of the above |

| | Transactions | Debit | Credit |
|---|---|---|---|
| a. | Example: Purchased equipment for use in the business; paid one-third cash and gave a note payable for the balance. | 5 | 1, 8 |
| b. | Issued stock to new investors. | | |
| c. | Paid cash for salaries and wages. | | |
| d. | Collected cash for services performed this period. | | |
| e. | Collected cash on accounts receivable for services previously performed. | | |
| f. | Performed services this period on credit. | | |
| g. | Paid operating expenses incurred this period. | | |
| h. | Paid cash on accounts payable for expenses previously incurred. | | |
| i. | Incurred operating expenses this period to be paid next period. | | |
| j. | Purchased supplies inventory to be used later; paid cash. | | |
| k. | Used some of the supplies inventory for operations. | | |
| l. | Purchased a patent (an intangible asset); paid cash. | | |
| m. | Made a payment on the equipment note in (*a*); the payment was part principal and part interest expense. | | |
| n. | Paid three-fourths of the income tax expense for the year; the balance will be paid next year. | | |
| o. | On the last day of the current period, paid cash for an insurance policy covering the next two years. | | |

**P3–2 Recording Journal Entries** (AP3–2)

■ **LO5**

Chad Polovick organized a new company, CollegeCaps, Inc. The company operates a small store in an area mall and specializes in baseball-type caps with logos printed on them. Chad, who is never without a cap, believes that his target market is college students. You have been hired to record the transactions occurring in the first two weeks of operations.

| | |
|---|---|
| May 1 | Issued 1,000 shares of capital stock for $30 per share. |
| May 1 | Borrowed $50,000 from the bank to provide additional funding to begin operations. The interest rate is 14 percent annually; principal and interest are due in 24 months. |
| May 1 | Paid $1,200 for the current month's rent and another $1,200 for next month's rent. |
| May 1 | Paid $2,400 for a one-year fire insurance policy (recorded as a prepaid expense). |
| May 3 | Purchased furniture and fixtures for the store for $15,000 on account. The amount is due within 30 days. |
| May 4 | Purchased a supply of University of Texas, Southern Methodist University, and Michigan State University baseball caps for the store for $1,800 cash. |
| May 5 | Placed advertisements in local college newspapers for a total of $250 cash. |
| May 9 | Sold caps totaling $400, half of which was charged on account. The cost of the caps sold was $150. |
| May 10 | Made full payment for the furniture and fixtures purchased on account on May 3. |
| May 14 | Received $50 from a customer on account. |

*Required:*

For each of the transactions, prepare journal entries. Be sure to categorize each account as an asset (A), liability (L), stockholders' equity (SE), revenue (R), or expense (E).

**P3–3 Determining Financial Statement Effects of Various Transactions and Identifying Cash Flow Effects** (AP3–3)

■ **LO5, 6**

Wendy's
International, Inc.

According to its annual report, Wendy's serves "the best hamburgers in the business" and other fresh food including salads, chicken sandwiches, and baked potatoes in more than 4,000 restaurants worldwide. The following activities were inferred from a recent annual report.

*a.* Purchased additional investments.

*b.* Served food to customers for cash. Ignore the using up of food supplies until (*h*).

*c.* Paid cash dividends.

*d.* Incurred restaurant operating costs in company-owned facilities; paid part in cash and the rest on account.

*e.* Sold franchises, receiving part in cash and the rest in notes due from franchisees.

*f.* Paid interest on debt.

*g.* Purchased food and paper products; paid part in cash and the rest on account.

*h.* Used food and paper products.

*Required:*

1. For each of the transactions, complete the tabulation, indicating the effect (+ for increase and − for decrease) of each transaction. (Remember that A = L + SE, R − E = NI, and NI affects SE through Retained Earnings). Write NE if there is no effect. The first transaction is provided as an example.

| | **Balance Sheet** | | | **Income Statement** | | |
|---|---|---|---|---|---|---|
| Transaction | Assets | Liabilities | Stockholders' Equity | Revenues | Expenses | Net Income |
| (*a*) (example) | +/− | NE | NE | NE | NE | NE |

2. For each transaction, indicate where, if at all, it would be reported on the statement of cash flows. Use O for operating activities, I for investing activities, F for financing activities, and NE if the transaction would not be included on the statement.

**LO5, 6, 7    P3–4    Analyzing the Effects of Transactions Using T-Accounts, Preparing Unadjusted Financial Statements, and Evaluating the Total Asset Turnover Ratio as a Manager (AP3–4)**

Paula Richardson, a connoisseur of fine chocolate, opened Paula's Passions in Collegetown on February 1, 20A. The shop specializes in a selection of gourmet chocolate candies and a line of gourmet ice cream. You have been hired as manager. Your duties include maintaining the store's financial records. The following transactions occurred in February 20A, the first month of operations.

a.  Received four shareholders' contributions of $16,000 to form the corporation.

b.  Paid three months' store rent at $800 per month (recorded as prepaid expenses).

c.  Purchased supplies for $300 cash.

d.  Purchased and received candy for $5,000, on account, due in 60 days.

e.  Negotiated a $10,000 loan at the bank, at 12 percent annual interest. The principal and interest are due in a lump sum in two years.

f.  Used the money from (e) to purchase a computer for $2,500 (for recordkeeping and inventory tracking) and the balance for furniture and fixtures for the store.

g.  Placed a grand opening advertisement in the local paper for $425 cash.

h.  Made sales on Valentine's Day totaling $1,800; $1,525 was in cash and the rest on accounts receivable. The cost of the candy sold was $1,000.

i.  Made a $500 payment on accounts payable.

j.  Incurred and paid employee wages of $420.

k.  Collected accounts receivable of $50 from customers.

l.  Made a repair on one of the display cases for $118 cash.

m. Made cash sales of $2,000 during the rest of the month. The cost of the goods sold was $1,100.

*Required:*

1.  Set up appropriate T-accounts for Cash, Accounts Receivable, Supplies, Merchandise Inventory, Prepaid Rent, Equipment, Furniture and Fixtures, Accounts Payable, Notes Payable, Contributed Capital, Sales Revenue, Cost of Goods Sold (Expense), Advertising Expense, Wage Expense, and Repair Expense. All accounts begin with zero balances.

2.  Record in the T-accounts the effects of each transaction for Paula's Passions in February, referencing each transaction in the accounts with the transaction letter. Show the unadjusted ending balances in the T-accounts.

3.  Prepare unadjusted financial statements at the end of February (income statement, statement of retained earnings, and balance sheet).

4.  Write a short memo to Paula offering your opinion on the results of operations during the first month of business.

5.  After three years in business, you are being evaluated for a promotion. One measure is how efficiently you managed the assets of the business. The following data are available:

| | 20C* | 20B | 20A |
|---|---|---|---|
| Total assets | $80,000 | $45,000 | $35,000 |
| Total liabilities | 45,000 | 20,000 | 15,000 |
| Total stockholders' equity | 35,000 | 25,000 | 20,000 |
| Total sales | 85,000 | 75,000 | 50,000 |
| Net income | 20,000 | 10,000 | 4,000 |

*At the end of 20C, Paula decided to open a second store, requiring loans and inventory purchases prior to the opening in early 20D.

Compute total asset turnover for 20B and 20C and evaluate the results. Do you think you should be promoted? Why?

**P3–5 Preparing a Statement of Cash Flows** (AP3–5)

Refer to P3–4.

*Required:*

For the transactions listed in P3–4, prepare a statement of cash flows for the month.

**P3–6 Analyzing the Effects of Transactions Using T-Accounts, Preparing Unadjusted Financial Statements, and Evaluating the Total Asset Turnover Ratio** (AP3–6)

The following are several May 31, 20A, account balances (in millions of dollars) from a recent annual report of Federal Express Corporation, followed by several typical transactions. The business is described in the annual report as follows:

LO5, 6, 7

Federal Express

> Federal Express Corporation offers a wide range of express services for the time-definite transportation of goods and documents throughout the world using an extensive fleet of aircraft and vehicles and leading-edge information technologies.

| Account | Balance | Account | Balance |
|---|---|---|---|
| Flight and ground equipment | $3,476 | Contributed capital | $ 702 |
| Retained earnings | 970 | Receivables | 923 |
| Accounts payable | 554 | Other assets | 1,011 |
| Prepaid expenses | 64 | Cash | 155 |
| Accrued expenses payable | 761 | Spare parts, supplies, and fuel | 164 |
| Long-term notes payable | 2,016 | Other noncurrent liabilities | 790 |

These accounts are not necessarily in good order and have normal debit or credit balances. The following transactions (in millions of dollars) occurred the next month (from June 1, 20A to June 30, 20A):

a. Provided delivery service to customers, receiving $7,200 in accounts receivable and $600 in cash.

b. Purchased new equipment costing $816; signed a long-term note.

c. Paid $744 cash to rent equipment and aircraft, with $648 for rental this year and the rest for rent in next year.

d. Spent $396 cash to maintain and repair facilities and equipment during the year.

e. Collected $6,524 from customers on account.

f. Borrowed $900 by signing a long-term note.

g. Issued additional stock for $240.

h. Paid employees $3,804 during the year.

i. Purchased for cash and used $492 in fuel for the aircraft and equipment.

j. Paid $384 on accounts payable.

k. Ordered $72 in spare parts and supplies.

*Required:*

1. Prepare T-accounts for June 30, 20A, from the preceding list; enter the respective balances. You will need additional T-accounts for income statement accounts; enter $0 balances.

2. For each transaction, record the effects in the T-accounts. Label each using the letter of the transaction. Compute ending balances.

3. Prepare an unadjusted income statement, unadjusted statement of retained earnings, unadjusted balance sheet, and statement of cash flows in good form.

4. Based on the unadjusted amounts, compute the company's total asset turnover ratio. What does it suggest to you about Federal Express?

**P3–7 Recording Journal Entries and Identifying Cash Flow Effects**

Cedar Fair, L. P. (Limited Partnership), owns and operates four seasonal amusement parks: Cedar Point in Ohio, Valleyfair near Minneapolis/St. Paul, Dorney Park and Wildwater Kingdom near Allentown, Pennsylvania, and Worlds of Fun/Oceans of Fun in Kansas City. The following are summarized transactions similar to those that occurred in a recent year (20A):

LO5, 6

Cedar Fair

a. Guests at the parks paid $89,664,000 cash in admissions.

b. The primary operating expenses (such as employee wages, utilities, and repairs and maintenance) for the year 20A were $66,347,000 with $60,200,000 paid in cash and the rest on account.

c. Interest paid on long-term debt was $6,601,000.

d. The parks sell food and merchandise and operate games. The cash received in 20A for these combined activities was $77,934,000.

e. The cost of products sold for cash during the year was $19,525,000.

f. Cedar Fair purchased and built additional buildings, rides, and equipment during 20A, paying $23,813,000 in cash.

g. The most significant assets for the company are land, buildings, rides, and equipment. Therefore, a large expense for Cedar Fair is depreciation expense (related to the using of these assets to generate revenues during the year). In 20A, the amount was $14,473,000 (credit Accumulated Depreciation).

h. Guests may stay at accommodations owned by the company at the parks. In 20A, Accommodations Revenue was $11,345,000; $11,010,000 was paid by the guests in cash and the rest was on account.

i. Cedar Fair paid $2,900,000 on notes payable.

j. The company purchased $19,100,000 in food and merchandise inventory for the year, paying $18,000,000 in cash and the rest on account.

k. The selling, general, and administrative expenses (such as the president's salary and advertising for the parks, those not classified as operating expenses) for 20A were $21,118,000; $19,500,000 was paid in cash and the rest was on account.

l. Cedar Fair paid $8,600,000 on accounts payable during the year.

*Required:*

1. For each of these transactions, record journal entries. Use the letter of each transaction as its reference.

2. Use the following chart to identify whether each transaction results in a cash flow effect from operating (O), investing (I), or financing (F) activities, and indicate the direction and amount of the effect on cash (+ for increase and − for decrease). If there is no cash flow effect, write *none*. The first transaction is provided as an example.

| Transaction | Operating, Investing, or Financing Effect | Direction and Amount of the Effect |
|:---:|:---:|:---:|
| (a) | O | +89,664,000 |

# ALTERNATE PROBLEMS

**LO5**     **AP3–1**     **Recording Nonquantitative Journal Entries** (P3–1)

The following is a series of accounts for Ortiz & Ortiz, Incorporated, which has been operating for two years. The accounts are listed and numbered for identification. Following the accounts is a series of transactions. For each transaction, indicate the account(s) that should be debited and credited by entering the appropriate account number(s) to the right of each transaction. If no journal entry is needed, write *none* after the transaction. The first transaction is given as an example.

| Account No. | Account Title | Account No. | Account Title |
|:---:|:---|:---:|:---|
| 1 | Cash | 9 | Wages payable |
| 2 | Accounts receivable | 10 | Income taxes payable |
| 3 | Supplies inventory | 11 | Contributed capital |
| 4 | Prepaid expense | 12 | Retained earnings |
| 5 | Buildings | 13 | Service revenue |
| 6 | Land | 14 | Operating expenses |
| 7 | Accounts payable | 15 | Income tax expense |
| 8 | Mortgage payable | | |

| Transactions | Debit | Credit |
|---|---|---|
| a. Example: Issued stock to new investors. | 1 | 11 |
| b. Performed services this period on credit. | ___ | ___ |
| c. Purchased (but did not use) supplies this period on credit. | ___ | ___ |
| d. Prepaid a fire insurance policy this period to cover the next 12 months. | ___ | ___ |
| e. Purchased a building this period with a 20 percent cash down payment and a mortgage loan for the balance. | ___ | ___ |
| f. Collected cash this year for services rendered and recorded in the prior year. | ___ | ___ |
| g. Paid cash this period for wages earned and recorded last period. | ___ | ___ |
| h. Paid cash for operating expenses charged on accounts payable in the prior period. | ___ | ___ |
| i. Paid cash for operating expenses charged on accounts payable in the current period. | ___ | ___ |
| j. Incurred and recorded operating expenses on credit to be paid next period. | ___ | ___ |
| k. Collected cash at the point of sale for services rendered. | ___ | ___ |
| l. Used supplies from inventory to clean the offices. | ___ | ___ |
| m. Recorded income taxes for this period to be paid at the beginning of the next period. | ___ | ___ |
| n). Declared and paid a cash dividend this period. | ___ | ___ |
| o. Made a payment on the building, which was part principal repayment and part interest. | ___ | ___ |
| p. This period a shareholder sold some shares of her stock to another person for an amount above the original issuance price. | ___ | ___ |

## AP3–2 Recording Journal Entries (P3–2)

■ LO5

Rhonda Bennett is the president of ServicePro, Inc., a company that provides temporary employees for not-for-profit companies. ServicePro has been operating for five years; its revenues are increasing with each passing year. You have been hired to help Rhonda in analyzing the following transactions for the first two weeks of April:

| | |
|---|---|
| April 2 | Purchased office supplies for $500 on account. |
| April 3 | Received the telephone bill for $245. |
| April 5 | Billed United Way $1,950 for temporary services provided. |
| April 8 | Paid $250 for supplies purchased and recorded on account last period. |
| April 8 | Placed an advertisement in the local paper for $400 cash. |
| April 9 | Purchased a new computer for the office costing $2,300 cash. |
| April 10 | Paid employee wages of $1,200. Of this amount, $200 had been earned and recorded in the prior period. |
| April 11 | Received $1,000 on account from United Way. |
| April 12 | Purchased land as the site of a future office for $10,000. Paid $2,000 down and signed a note payable for the balance. The note is due in five years and has an annual interest rate of 10 percent. |
| April 13 | Issued 2,000 additional shares of capital stock for $40 per share in anticipation of building a new office. |
| April 14 | Billed Family & Children's Service $2,000 for services rendered. |

*Required:*

For each of the transactions, prepare journal entries. Be sure to categorize each account as an asset (A), liability (L), stockholders' equity (SE), revenue (R), or expense (E).

## AP3–3 Determining Financial Statement Effects of Various Transactions and Identifying Cash Flow Effects (P3–3)

■ LO5, 6

Abercrombie & Fitch Co.

Abercrombie & Fitch Co. is a specialty retailer of quality casual apparel for men and women. The company was established in 1892, purchased by The Limited in 1988, and in 1996 a newly incorporated Abercrombie & Fitch Co. exchanged stock with The Limited, which now owns 84.2 percent of the stock of the company. The following activities were inferred from a recent annual report.

a. Example: Incurred expenses, paid part cash and part on credit.

b. Sold merchandise to customers on account. (*Hint*: Also reduce inventory for the amount sold.)

c. Declared and paid cash dividends.

d. Collected cash on account.

e. Used supplies.

f. Repaid long-term debt principal and interest.

g. Purchased equipment; paid part cash and part on credit.

h. Paid cash on account.

i. Issued additional stock.

j. Paid rent to mall owners.

k. Received dividends and interest on investments.

***Required:***

1. For each of the transactions, complete the tabulation, indicating the effect (+ for increase and − for decrease) of each transaction. (Remember that A = L + SE, R − E = NI, and NI affects SE through Retained Earnings). Write NE if there is no effect. The first transaction is provided as a sample.

| | Balance Sheet | | | Income Statement | | |
|---|---|---|---|---|---|---|
| Transaction | Assets | Liabilities | Stockholders' Equity | Revenues | Expenses | Net Income |
| (*a*) (example) | − | + | − | NE | + | − |

2. For each transaction, indicate where, if at all, it would be reported on the statement of cash flows. Use O for operating activities, I for investing activities, F for financing activities, and NE if the transaction would not be included on the statement.

■ **LO5, 6, 7**    **AP3–4**

**Analyzing the Effects of Transactions Using T-Accounts, Preparing Unadjusted Financial Statements, and Evaluating the Total Asset Turnover Ratio as a Manager**
(P3–4)

Green Stables, Inc., was established in Philadelphia on April 1, 20C. The company provides stables, care for animals, and grounds for riding and showing horses. You have been hired as the new Assistant Controller. The following transactions for April 20C are provided for your review.

a. Received contributions from five investors of $50,000 in cash ($10,000 each), a barn valued at $100,000, land valued at $60,000, and supplies valued at $2,000. Each investor received 3,000 shares of stock.

b. Built a small barn for $42,000. The company paid half the amount in cash and signed a three-year note payable for the balance on April 1, 20C.

c. Provided animal care services, all on credit, for $15,260.

d. Rented stables to customers who cared for their own animals and received cash payment of $13,200.

e. Received from a customer $1,500 to board her horse in April, May, and June (record as unearned revenue).

f. Purchased straw (a supply inventory) on account for $3,210.

g. Paid $840 in cash for water utilities incurred in the month.

h. Paid $1,700 on accounts payable for previous purchases.

i. Received $1,000 from customers on accounts receivable.

j. Paid $4,000 in wages to employees who worked during the month.

k. At the end of the month, purchased a two-year insurance policy for $3,600.

l. Received an electric utility bill for $1,200 for usage in April; the bill will be paid next month.

m. Paid $100 cash dividend to each of the investors at the end of the month.

***Required:***

1. Set up appropriate T-accounts. All accounts begin with zero balances.

2. Record in the T-accounts the effects of each transaction for Green Stables in April, referencing each transaction in the accounts with the transaction letter. Show the unadjusted ending balances in the T-accounts.

3. Prepare unadjusted financial statements at the end of April (income statement, statement of retained earnings, and balance sheet).

4. Write a short memo to the five owners offering your opinion on the results of operations during the first month of business.

5. After three years in business, you are being evaluated for a promotion to chief financial officer. One measure is how efficiently you managed the assets of the business. The following data are available:

|  | 20E* | 20D | 20C |
|---|---|---|---|
| Total assets | $480,000 | $320,000 | $300,000 |
| Total liabilities | 125,000 | 28,000 | 30,000 |
| Total stockholders' equity | 355,000 | 292,000 | 270,000 |
| Total sales | 450,000 | 400,000 | 360,000 |
| Net income | 50,000 | 30,000 | (10,000) |

*At the end of 20E, Green Stables decided to build an indoor riding arena for giving lessons year-round. The company borrowed construction funds from a local bank and the arena was opened in early 20F.

Compute total asset turnover and evaluate the results. Do you think you should be promoted? Why?

**AP3–5** **Preparing a Statement of Cash Flows** (P3–5)
Refer to AP3–4.

■ **LO6**

*Required:*
For the transactions listed in AP3–4, prepare a statement of cash flows for the month.

**AP3–6** **Analyzing the Effects of Transactions Using T-Accounts, Preparing Unadjusted Financial Statements, and Evaluating the Total Asset Turnover Ratio** (P3–6)
The following are the summary account balances from a recent balance sheet of Exxon Corporation. The accounts are followed by a list of hypothetical transactions for the month of January 20D. The following accounts are shown in millions of dollars.

■ **LO5, 6**

Exxon Corporation

| Cash | $ 1,157 | Marketable securities | $ 618 |
|---|---|---|---|
| Notes payable | 3,858 | Accounts payable | 13,391 |
| Accounts receivable | 8,073 | Income tax payable | 2,244 |
| Inventories | 5,541 | Prepaid expenses | 1,071 |
| Other debt | 30,954 | Investments | 5,394 |
| Property & equipment, net | 63,425 | Intangibles, net | 2,583 |
| Shareholders' equity* | 37,415 | | |

*This account is a combination of Contributed Capital and Retained Earnings.

The accounts have normal debit or credit balances, but they are not necessarily listed in good order.

*a.* Purchased new equipment costing $150 million on account.

*b.* Received $500 million on accounts receivable.

*c.* Received and paid the telephone bills for $1 million.

*d.* Earned $5 million in sales to customers on account; cost of sales was $1 million.

*e.* Paid employees $1 million for wages earned in January.

*f.* Paid half of the income taxes payable.

*g.* Purchased supplies inventory for $23 million on account.

*h.* Prepaid rent for February for a warehouse for $12 million.

*i.* Paid $10 million of other debt and $1 million in interest on the debt.

*j.* Purchased a patent (an intangible asset) for $8 million cash.

*Required:*

1. Prepare T-accounts for January 31, 20D, from the preceding list; enter the respective balances. You will need additional T-accounts for income statement accounts; enter $0 balances.

2. For each transaction, record the effects in the T-accounts. Label each using the letter of the transaction. Compute ending balances.

3. Prepare an unadjusted income statement, unadjusted statement of stockholders' equity (since contributed capital and retained earnings are not separately reported), unadjusted balance sheet, and unadjusted statement of cash flows in good form.

4. Based on the unadjusted amounts, compute the company's total asset turnover ratio. What does it suggest to you about Exxon?

# CASES AND PROJECTS

## FINANCIAL REPORTING AND ANALYSIS CASES

**▪ LO2, 5, 7    CP3–1**

Urban Outfitters

STANDARD
&POOR'S

**Finding Financial Information**
Refer to the financial statements and accompanying notes of Urban Outfitters given in Appendix C at the end of the book, or open file URBN10K.doc in the S&P directory on the student CD-ROM.

*Required:*

1. State the amount of the largest expense on the 1999 income statement and describe the transaction represented by the expense.

2. Give the journal entry for interest income for the year ended January 31, 1999 (for this question, assume that the amount has not yet been received).

3. Assuming that all net sales are on credit, how much cash did Urban Outfitters collect from customers? (*Hint:* Use a T-account of accounts receivable to infer collection.)

4. A shareholder has complained that "more dividends should be paid because the company had net earnings of $15.76 million. Since this amount is all cash, more of it should go to the owners." Explain why the shareholder's assumption that earnings equal net cash inflow is valid. If you believe that the assumption is not valid, state so and support your position concisely.

5. Describe and contrast the purpose of an income statement versus a balance sheet.

6. Compute the company's total asset turnover for 1999. Explain its meaning.

**▪ LO2, 7    CP3–2**

Urban Outfitters
versus
American Eagle
Outfitters

STANDARD
&POOR'S

**Comparing Companies within an Industry**
Refer to the financial statements of American Eagle Outfitters given in Appendix B, Urban Outfitters given in Appendix C, and the Standard and Poor's Industry Ratio Report given in Appendix D at the end of this book or open file CP3-2.xls in the S&P directory on the student CD-ROM.

*Required:*

1. What title does each company call its income statement? Explain what "Consolidated" means.

2. Which company had higher net income at the end of January 1999?

3. What does each company report were the primary causes of the change in sales from 1998 to 1999? (*Hint*: Look in the Management's Discussion and Analysis section of the annual report.)

4. Compute the total asset turnover ratio for both companies for 1999. Which company is utilizing assets more effectively to generate sales? Why do you think that?

5. Compare the total asset turnover ratio for both companies to the industry average. On average, are these two companies utilizing assets to generate sales better or worse than their competitors?

6. How much cash was provided by operating activities for 1999 by each company? What was the percentage change in operating cash flows (1) from the 1998 to 1999 and (2) from 1997 to 1998 for each company? (*Hint:* [Current Year Amount − Prior Year Amount] ÷ Prior Year.)

7. How much did each company pay in income taxes in 1999? Where did you find this information?

8. What segments does Urban Outfitters report in the notes? What does American Eagle report about segments?

**CP3–3 Comparing a Company over Time**

American Eagle
Outfitters

Refer to the annual report for American Eagle Outfitters (in Appendix B), or open file AEOS10K.doc in the S&P directory on the student CD-ROM.

STANDARD
&POOR'S

*Required:*

1. On page 2 of the annual report or on page 13 of the 10K, American Eagle Outfitters provides selected financial data for the past five years. Compute the total asset turnover ratio for 1996, 1997, 1998, and 1999.

2. In Chapter 2, we discussed the financial leverage ratio. Compute this ratio for 1996, 1997, 1998, and 1999.

3. What do your results from the trends in the two ratios suggest to you about American Eagle Outfitters?

**CP3–4 Interpreting the Financial Press**

The August 2, 1999, edition of *Fortune* presented numerous articles on accounting irregularities and fraud. One article entitled "Lies, Damned Lies, and Managed Earnings: The Crackdown Is Here" discusses the implications of unethical managerial decisions. You can access a portion of the article on the Libby/Libby/Short website at **www.mhhe.com/ business/accounting/libby3**.

*Required:*

Read the article and then answer the following questions:

1. From Chapter 1, what is the SEC and what is its role?

2. What are the three criteria for recording revenue under the revenue realization principle?

3. What fraudulent activities were committed by the three companies mentioned in the article? What accounting concepts were violated in each case?

**CP3–5 Using Financial Reports: Analyzing Changes in Accounts and Preparing Financial Statements**

Wilsey Painting Service Company was organized during January 20A by three individuals. On January 20, 20A, the company issued 5,000 shares of stock to each of its organizers. The following is a schedule of the cumulative account balances immediately after each of the first 10 transactions ending on January 31, 20A.

| Accounts | Cumulative Balances | | | | | | | | | |
|---|---|---|---|---|---|---|---|---|---|---|
| | *(a)* | *(b)* | *(c)* | *(d)* | *(e)* | *(f)* | *(g)* | *(h)* | *(i)* | *(j)* |
| Cash | $75,000 | $70,000 | $85,000 | $71,000 | $61,000 | $61,000 | $57,000 | $46,000 | $41,000 | $57,000 |
| Accounts receivable | | | 12,000 | 12,000 | 12,000 | 26,000 | 26,000 | 26,000 | 26,000 | 10,000 |
| Office fixtures | | 20,000 | 20,000 | 20,000 | 20,000 | 20,000 | 20,000 | 20,000 | 20,000 | 20,000 |
| Land | | | | 18,000 | 18,000 | 18,000 | 18,000 | 18,000 | 18,000 | 18,000 |
| Accounts payable | | | | | 3,000 | 3,000 | 3,000 | 10,000 | 5,000 | 5,000 |
| Note payable | | 15,000 | 15,000 | 19,000 | 19,000 | 19,000 | 19,000 | 19,000 | 19,000 | 19,000 |
| Contributed capital | 75,000 | 75,000 | 75,000 | 75,000 | 75,000 | 75,000 | 75,000 | 75,000 | 75,000 | 75,000 |
| Retained earnings | | | | | | | (4,000) | (4,000) | (4,000) | (4,000) |
| Paint revenue | | | 27,000 | 27,000 | 27,000 | 41,000 | 41,000 | 41,000 | 41,000 | 41,000 |
| Supplies expense | | | | | 5,000 | 5,000 | 5,000 | 8,000 | 8,000 | 8,000 |
| Wages expense | | | | | 8,000 | 8,000 | 8,000 | 23,000 | 23,000 | 23,000 |

*Required:*

1. Analyze the changes in this schedule for each transaction; then explain the transaction. Transactions (*a*) and (*b*) are examples:

   (*a*) Cash increased $75,000, and Contributed Capital (stockholders' equity) increased $75,000. Therefore, transaction (*a*) was an issuance of the capital stock of the corporation for $75,000 cash.

   (*b*) Cash decreased $5,000, office fixtures (an asset) increased $20,000, and note payable (a liability) increased $15,000. Therefore, transaction (*b*) was a purchase of office fixtures that cost $20,000. Payment was made as follows: cash, $5,000; note payable, $15,000.

2. Based only on the preceding schedule after transaction (*j*), prepare an unadjusted income statement, a statement of retained earnings, and a balance sheet.

3. For each of the transactions, indicate the type of effect on cash flows (O for operating, I for investing, F for financing, or None if there is no effect on cash flows) and the direction (+ for increase and − for decrease) and amount of the effect. The first transaction is provided as an example.

| Transaction | Operating, Investing, or Financing Effect | Direction and Amount of the Effect |
|---|---|---|
| (*a*) | F | +75,000 |

**LO5, 6**   **CP3–6**

Volkswagen

**Using Financial Reports: Interpreting Challenging International Financial Statements**

Your cousin, an engineering major, has inherited some money and wants to invest in an auto company. She has never taken an accounting course and has asked you to help her compare a U.S. automaker's financial statements to those of a German automaker. Your cousin has given you the income statement, asset section of the balance sheet (on the next page), and audit opinion for Volkswagen for a recent year.

---

### AUDIT CERTIFICATE

The consolidated financial statements, which we have audited in accordance with professional standards, comply with the German legal provisions. With due regard to the generally accepted accounting principles, the consolidated financial statements give a true and fair view of the Group's assets, liabilities, financial position and profit or loss. The Group management report is consistent with the consolidated financial statements.

Hanover, February 24, 20B
C&L TREUARBEIT
DEUTSCHE REVISION
Aktiengesellschaft

**Statement of Earnings of the Volkswagen Group for the Fiscal Year
Ended December 31, 20B—DM million—**

| | 20B | 20A |
|---|---|---|
| Sales | 85,403 | 76,315 |
| Cost of sales | 79,155 | 69,472 |
| Gross profit | + 6,248 | + 6,843 |
| Selling and distribution expenses | 5,661 | 5,414 |
| General administration expenses | 2,316 | 2,185 |
| Other operating income | 4,246 | 4,406 |
| Other operating expenses | 2,634 | 3,104 |
| Results from participations | + 55 | + 97 |
| Interest results | + 739 | + 1,228 |
| Write-down of financial assets and securities classified as current assets | 75 | 86 |
| Results from ordinary business activities | + 602 | + 1,785 |
| Taxes on income | 455 | 671 |
| Net earnings | **147** | **1,114** |

---

*Required:*
Review the excerpts of Volkswagen's financial statements. Write a letter to your cousin explaining the similarities and the dissimilarities you would expect to find if you compared Volkswagen's statements to those of a company in the United States. Offer your opinion on whether you would expect the underlying accounting principles of the two countries to be similar or dissimilar. On what are you basing your opinion?

| Balance Sheet of the Volkswagen Group, December 31, 20B—DM million— | | |
| --- | --- | --- |
| Assets | Dec, 31, 20B | Dec. 31, 20A |
| **Fixed assets** | | |
| Intangible assets | 631 | 372 |
| Tangible assets | 24,050 | 21,126 |
| Financial assets | 2,747 | 2,655 |
| Leasing and rental assets | 7,393 | 6,293 |
| | 34,821 | 30,446 |
| **Current assets** | | |
| Inventories | 9,736 | 9,049 |
| Receivables and other assets | 21,065 | 18,675 |
| Securities | 1,497 | 2,329 |
| Cash on hand, deposits at German Federal Bank and postal giro balances, cash in banks | 7,836 | 9,255 |
| | 40,134 | 39,308 |
| **Prepaid and deferred charges** | 329 | 336 |
| **Balance sheet total** | 75,284 | 70,090 |

# CRITICAL THINKING CASES

**CP3–7**  **Making a Decision as a Bank Loan Officer: Analyzing and Restating Financial Statements That Have Major Deficiencies (a Challenging Case)**

■ **LO3, 4, 5, 6**

Tom Martinez started and operated a small boat repair service company during 20A. He is interested in obtaining a $100,000 loan from your bank to build a dry dock to store boats for customers in the winter months. At the end of the year, he prepared the following statements based on information stored in a large filing cabinet:

### MARTINEZ COMPANY
#### Profit for 20A

| | | |
| --- | --- | --- |
| Service fees collected during 20A | | $55,000 |
| Cash dividends received | | 10,000 |
| Total | | $65,000 |
| Expense for operations paid during 20A | $22,000 | |
| Cash stolen | 500 | |
| New tools purchased during 20A (cash paid) | 1,000 | |
| Supplies purchased for use on service jobs (cash paid) | 3,200 | |
| Total | | 26,700 |
| Profit | | $38,300 |

#### Assets Owned at the End of 20A

| | |
| --- | --- |
| Cash in checking account | $ 29,300 |
| Service garage (at current market value) | 32,000 |
| Tools and equipment | 18,000 |
| Land (at current market value) | 30,000 |
| Stock in ABC Industrial | 130,000 |
| Total | $239,300 |

The following is a summary of completed transactions:

(*a*) Received the following contributions to the business from the owner when it was started in exchange for 1,000 shares of stock in the new company:

| | | | |
| --- | --- | --- | --- |
| Building | $21,000 | Land | $20,000 |
| Tools and equipment | 17,000 | Cash | 1,000 |

(*b*) Earned service fees during 20A of $87,000; of the cash collected, $20,000 was for deposits from customers on work to be done by Martinez in the next year.

(*c*) Received the cash dividends on shares of ABC Industrial stock purchased by Tom Martinez six years earlier.

(*d*) Incurred expenses during 20A, $61,000.

(*e*) Determined amount of supplies on hand (unused) at the end of 20A, $700.

*Required:*

1. Did Martinez prepare the income statement on a cash basis or an accrual basis? Explain how you can tell. Which basis should be used? Explain why.

2. Prepare an accrual-based income statement, balance sheet, and statement of cash flows. Explain (using footnotes) the reason for each change that you make to the income statement.

3. What additional information would assist you in formulating your decision regarding the loan to Mr. Martinez?

4. Based on the revised statements and additional information needed, write a letter to Mr. Martinez explaining your decision at this time regarding the loan.

■LO4    CP3–8    **Evaluating an Ethical Dilemma**

Mike Lynch is the manager of an upstate New York regional office for an insurance company. As the regional manager, his compensation package comprises a base salary, commissions, and a bonus when the region sells new policies in excess of its quota. Mike has been under enormous pressure lately, stemming largely from two factors. First, he is experiencing a mounting personal debt due to a family member's illness. Second, compounding his worries, the region's sales of new policies have dipped below the normal quota for the first time in years.

You have been working for Mike for two years, and like everyone else in the office, you consider yourself lucky to work for such a supportive boss. You also feel great sympathy for his personal problems over the last few months. In your position as accountant for the regional office, you are only too aware of the drop in new policy sales and the impact this will have on the manager's bonus. While you are working late at year-end, Mike stops by your office.

Mike asks you to change the manner in which you have accounted for a new property insurance policy for a large local business. A check for the premium, substantial in amount, came in the mail on December 31, the last day of the reporting year. The premium covers a period beginning on January 5. You deposited the check and correctly debited cash and credited an *unearned revenue* account. Ray says, "Hey, we have the money this year, so why not count the revenue this year? I never did understand why you accountants are so picky about these things anyway. I'd like you to change the way you have recorded the transaction. I want you to credit a *revenue* account. And anyway, I've done favors for you in the past, and I am asking for such a small thing in return." With that, he leaves for the day.

*Required:*

How should you handle this situation? What are the ethical implications of Mike's request? Who are the parties who would be helped or harmed if you complied with the request? If you fail to comply with his request, how will you explain your position to him in the morning?

# FINANCIAL REPORTING AND ANALYSIS PROJECTS

    CP3–9    **Broadening Financial Research Skills: Observing Stock Market Reaction to Company News**

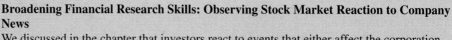

We discussed in the chapter that investors react to events that either affect the corporation directly or might do so indirectly by changing their expectations about the company's future performance. Their decisions affect the price of the company's stock.

*Required:*

1. Using your web browser, contact the website of a company of interest to you or scan business news retrieval services (such as Dow Jones or Bloomberg) to find an article about the company or announcement made by the company.

2. Using *The Wall Street Journal* or other source (for example, perhaps your institution has a center for analysis of financial instruments with connection to the stock exchanges), obtain the closing stock price for your company for five business days before, the day of, and five business days after the date of the article or announcement.

3. Graph the stock price data and write a short report on the nature of the article or announcement (that is, what was it about) and how investors reacted to the news as shown in the change, if any, in the stock price.

**CP3–10 Comparing Income Statements across Industries**

LO2, 6

Using your web browser, contact the websites of three companies within the same industry. Acquire the income statements from the annual reports or 10-Ks. Some companies do not share financial information on the Internet. If the companies file 10-K reports with the SEC electronically, you may also find the information from the SEC's archives at www.freeedgar.com.

*Required:*

Write a short report indicating any differences, if any, in the accounts used by the three companies and their location on the income statement.

**CP3–11 Analyzing Differences in Total Asset Turnover and Cash Flows among Competitors**

LO1, 2, 7

Papa John's SIC (Standard Industrial Classification) code is 5812—Retail Eating Places. Included in this classification are Outback Steakhouse, Boston Chicken, Cheesecake Factory, and Au Bon Pain. Using your web browser, contact the websites of Papa John's and two of these "competitors" (or others with a similar classification). Acquire the recent balance sheet and income statement for the companies. Some companies do not share financial information on the Internet. If the companies file 10-K reports with the SEC electronically, you may also find the information from the SEC's archives at www.freeedgar.com.

*Required:*

1. For the most recent year available, compute the total asset turnover ratio for each company (most recent year).
2. For the most recent year available, compute the percentage of cash from operating activities to total "change in cash" for each company.
3. Write a short memo comparing the companies' total asset turnover ratios and cash from operations-to-change in cash ratios. Indicate what differences in their businesses or operating cycles might account for any differences in the ratios.

**CP3–12 Analyzing an Ethical Dilemma: A Questionable Revenue Recognition Policy**

LO3, 4

Obtain a recent news story concerning the way that Boston Chicken records revenues and expenses related to franchises. Library files or other business news retrieval services are good sources.

*Required:*

Write a short memo outlining the nature of the revenue or expense recognition issue, how it compares to the revenue or matching principle, and who is hurt or helped by the recognition policy. Indicate your opinion on whether there is a question of ethics in this case.

**CP3–13 Team Project: Analysis of Income Statements and Ratios**

LO2, 3, 4, 7

As a team, select an industry to analyze. Using your Web browser, each team member should acquire the annual report or 10-K for one publicly traded company in the industry, with each member selecting a different company.

*Required:*

1. On an individual basis, each team member should write a short report that lists the following information:
   *a.* The major revenue and expense accounts on the most recent income statement.
   *b.* Computation of the total asset turnover ratio.
   *c.* Description of revenue recognition policy, if reported.
   *d.* The percentage of cash from operating activities to net income for each year presented. This measures how liberal (that is, speeding up revenue recognition or delaying expense recognition) or conservative (that is, taking care not to record revenues too early or expenses too late) a company's management is in choosing among various revenue and expense recognition policies. A ratio above 1.0 suggests more conservative policies and below 1.0, more liberal policies.

2. Then, as a team, write a short report comparing and contrasting your companies using these attributes. Discuss any patterns across the companies that you as a team observe. Provide potential explanations for any differences discovered.

# The Adjustment Process and Financial Statements

## CHAPTER FOUR

---

LEARNING **OBJECTIVES**

*After studying this chapter, you should be able to:*

1. Explain the purpose of a trial balance.   p. 168

2. Analyze the adjustments necessary at the end of the period to update balance sheet and income statement accounts.
   p. 170

3. Present a complete set of financial statements: Income statement with earnings per share, statement of stockholders' equity, balance sheet, and statement of cash flows.   p. 185

4. Compute and interpret net profit margin.   p. 191

5. Explain the closing process.   p. 192

Papa John's International, Inc., defines its fiscal year-end as the last Sunday in December of each year. Papa John's 1997 year ended on Sunday, December 28, 1997; the 1998 year ended on Sunday, December 27, 1998. As this focus company illustrates, a firm's annual accounting period does not have to

FOCUS **COMPANY:**

# Papa John's International

### THE BUSIEST TIME OF THE FISCAL YEAR

conform to the calendar year. In a recent survey of 600 companies, 223 (37 percent) did not use a December year-end.* In addition, 151 companies (25 percent) chose a fiscal year-end defined, for example, as "the last Saturday of the month" or "the Saturday closest to the end of the month," which results in financial information in some years covering 52 weeks and in other years 53 weeks.

Many companies use a natural business year-end, which occurs at the lowest point in their annual business cycle. Retail stores, for example, tend to experience much seasonal fluctuation in business activity. The holiday shopping period in November and December and merchandise returns in January are usually the months of highest activity followed immediately by several months of low activity. They often use a January 31 year-end. The following lists a number of well-known companies and their year-end dates:

---

*Accounting Trends & Techniques* (New York: American Institute of CPAs, 1999), p. 36.

| Company | Industry | Year-End |
|---------|----------|----------|
| Kmart Corporation | Retail | Last Wednesday in January |
| Land's End, Inc. | Direct marketing | Friday closest to January 31 |
| Woolworth Corporation | Retail | Last Saturday in January except European and Mexican operations, which end December 31 |
| Rex Stores Corporation | Electronics retailer | January 31 |
| Wendy's International, Inc. | Fast food | Sunday nearest December 31 |
| McDonald's Corporation | Fast food | December 31 |
| Campbell Soup Company | Foods | Sunday nearest July 31 |
| Ethan Allen Interiors, Inc. | Furniture | June 30 |
| U•S Airways | Airline | December 31 |
| Compaq Computer Corp. | Computer hardware | December 31 |
| Federal Express | Delivery | May 31 |
| Honda Motor Co., Ltd. | Automobiles | March 31 |

For any company, whatever fiscal year-end is chosen, it is the busiest and most critical time from an accounting standpoint—the time accounts are adjusted, financial statements are prepared, and the books are closed. It is also the point at which the external auditor completes audit work and issues an opinion on the fairness of the financial statements and the company makes the statements available to external users. For Papa John's, even though 1998 operations ended on December 27, 1998, the company's auditor, Ernst & Young, LLP, performed the audit and signed the opinion on February 26, 1999 (eight weeks later).*

*Reprinted from *Accounting Trends and Techniques*. Copyright © 2000 by the American Institute of Certified Public Accountants, Inc.

## BUSINESS BACKGROUND

Like all well-managed companies, Papa John's organizes its accounting system with recordkeeping efficiency in mind. As a consequence, it usually records external transactions when it processes the business documents supporting those transactions. For example, the sale of food is recorded at the end of each day based on the daily cash register total.

At the end of the accounting period (usually a month, quarter, or year), the asset, liability, revenue, and expense accounts may not be fully up-to-date following accrual accounting principles. That is, some revenues and expenses and the related changes in assets and liabilities may not be properly recorded in the correct accounting period. As a consequence, adjustments or corrections are necessary.

Exhibit 4.1 presents the fundamental steps in the **accounting cycle.** Phase 1 of the accounting cycle involves analyzing and recording transactions that occur *during* the accounting period. Primarily, these transactions result in exchanges between the company and other *external* parties, similar to our Papa John's illustrations in Chapters 2 and 3. In this chapter, we examine the *end-of-period* steps in Phase 2 that focus primarily on adjustments. These are *internal* transactions that do not result in an actual exchange between the business and others but do have a direct and measurable effect on the accounting entity, particularly for revenue and expense recognition. We need to understand the steps in the second phase of the accounting cycle because balance sheet valuation and income measurement are incomplete without updating accounts to ensure proper revenue recognition and expense matching for the period (the adjustment process).

The **ACCOUNTING CYCLE** is the recordkeeping process used during and at the end of the accounting period that results in financial statements.

EXHIBIT **4.1**

**Fundamental Steps in the Accounting Cycle**

**START OF ACCOUNTING PERIOD**

EXHIBIT **4.1**

**Fundamental Steps in the Accounting Cycle**

Phase 1:
**During the Accounting Period**
(discussed in Chapters 2 and 3)

Perform transaction analysis based on a review of source documents from each transaction.

Record journal entries for each transaction (in chronological order in the general journal).

Post amounts to the general ledger (pages are similar to T-accounts).

Phase 2:
**At the End of the Accounting Period**
(discussed in Chapter 4)

Prepare a trial balance (a list of accounts and balances to date) to verify the equality of debits and credits.

Analyze adjustments (to update all accounts for proper revenue recognition and expense matching).

Prepare and distribute financial statements (from adjusted balances).

Record and post adjusting and closing entries (to create zero balances in temporary accounts for use in the next period).*

*Temporary accounts are those that accumulate balances for the period. They are revenue and expense accounts.

**END OF ACCOUNTING PERIOD**

## FINANCIAL **ANALYSIS**

### MANAGEMENT'S JUDGMENT IN YEAR-END ADJUSTMENTS: SIGNALS FOR ANALYSTS AND AUDITORS

Unlike the fairly routine procedures followed to make entries based on supporting documentation during the accounting period, *knowledge* and *judgment* are primary inputs in determining end-of-period adjustments to revenues and expenses. As such, the accounts most subject to year-end adjustment are of considerable interest to external users of the financial statements. Analysts recognize that management's judgment plays the most important role in determining year-end adjustments and that these judgments may provide important signals of management's expectations for the future. At the same time, analysts recognize that these adjustments are therefore most subject to error and manipulation. As a result, auditors also scrutinize adjustments. You must understand the mechanics of the adjustment process before you can understand the information that adjustments contain and the errors that can occur.

Before you can fully understand the process of communicating accounting information to users (discussed in Chapter 5), you must understand the year-end process that results in producing the financial statements. In this chapter, we emphasize the use of the same analytical tools employed in Chapters 2 and 3 (T-accounts and journal entries) to understand how adjustments are analyzed and recorded. After these adjustments have been determined, financial statements can be prepared. In addition, certain accounts, such as revenues and expenses, need to be prepared for the beginning of the next accounting period. This step is called the *closing process*.

**ORGANIZATION** OF THE CHAPTER

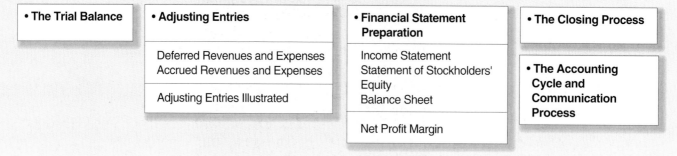

| • The Trial Balance | • Adjusting Entries | • Financial Statement Preparation | • The Closing Process |
|---|---|---|---|
| | Deferred Revenues and Expenses<br>Accrued Revenues and Expenses | Income Statement<br>Statement of Stockholders' Equity<br>Balance Sheet | • The Accounting Cycle and Communication Process |
| | Adjusting Entries Illustrated | Net Profit Margin | |

# THE TRIAL BALANCE

■ **LEARNING OBJECTIVE 1**

Explain the purpose of a trial balance.

A **TRIAL BALANCE** is a list of all accounts with their balances to provide a check on the equality of the debits and credits.

The first step normally taken at the end of the accounting period is to create a trial balance, also known as an *unadjusted trial balance*. A **trial balance** is a list of individual accounts, usually in financial statement order, with their ending debit or credit balances. In a two-column format, debit balances are indicated in the left column and credit balances are indicated in the right column. Then the two columns are totaled to provide a check on the equality of the debits and credits. In fact, that is all that the trial balance reflects. Many types of errors may still exist even though debits equal credits:

• Wrong accounts may have been used in journal entries.

• Wrong but equal amounts may have been used in journal entries.

• Wrong accounts may have been posted from correct journal entries.

• Wrong but equal amounts may have been posted from correct journal entries.

The trial balance does not indicate a problem due to these errors. If the two columns are not equal, however, errors have occurred in one or more of the following:

• In preparing journal entries when debits do not equal credits.

• In posting the correct dollar effects of transactions from the journal entry to the ledger.

• In computing ending balances in accounts.

• In copying ending balances in the ledger to the trial balance.

These errors can be traced and should be corrected before moving to the next step. Even though computerized accounting systems should reduce some of these potential errors, the use of improper accounts or equal but incorrect amounts in transaction analysis may still occur.

We ended Chapter 3 with incomplete, unadjusted financial statements for Papa John's because several internal transactions relating to revenue and expense items had still not been recorded in the proper period. The unadjusted balances in the Chapter 3 T-accounts are listed in the trial balance in Exhibit 4.2. A trial balance is a schedule prepared for internal purposes and is not considered a financial statement for external users. The schedule should be clearly labeled, however, for future reference as in Exhibit 4.2.

You will notice that the Property and Equipment account is stated at original cost of $223,100 in the trial balance but was stated at $174,900 (original cost minus the portion allocated to past operations) in the T-accounts in previous chapters. For long-lived assets such as equipment used in operations, individual account balances remain at original cost to preserve the historical information. To reflect the used-up portion of the assets' cost, a **contra-asset,** or offset, **account** is created. *Any contra-account is directly related to another account but has the opposite balance.* As a contra-account increases, the net amount (the account balance less the contra-account balance) decreases. For property and equipment, the contra-asset is called Accumulated Depreciation and Amortization.[1] It has a credit balance of $48,200. We will discuss many contra-accounts in other chapters and will designate contra-accounts with an *X* in front of the type of account to which it is related (e.g., Accumulated Depreciation and Amortization [XA] for contra-asset).

A **CONTRA-ACCOUNT** is an account that is an offset to, or reduction of, the primary account.

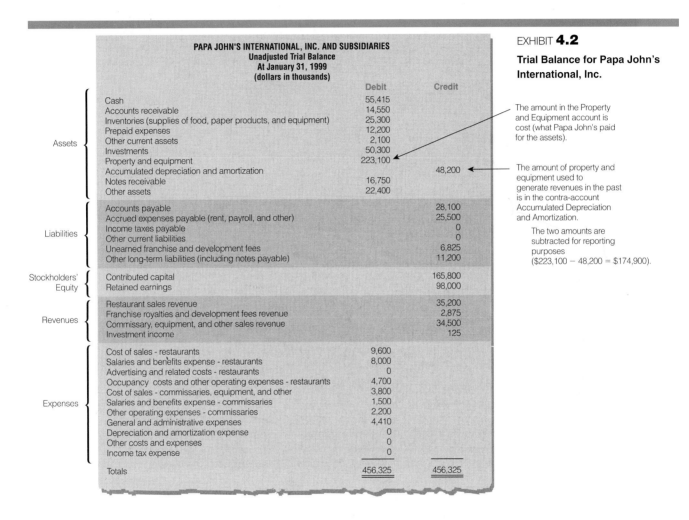

EXHIBIT **4.2**

**Trial Balance for Papa John's International, Inc.**

**PAPA JOHN'S INTERNATIONAL, INC. AND SUBSIDIARIES**
Unadjusted Trial Balance
At January 31, 1999
(dollars in thousands)

| | Debit | Credit |
|---|---|---|
| **Assets** | | |
| Cash | 55,415 | |
| Accounts receivable | 14,550 | |
| Inventories (supplies of food, paper products, and equipment) | 25,300 | |
| Prepaid expenses | 12,200 | |
| Other current assets | 2,100 | |
| Investments | 50,300 | |
| Property and equipment | 223,100 | |
| Accumulated depreciation and amortization | | 48,200 |
| Notes receivable | 16,750 | |
| Other assets | 22,400 | |
| **Liabilities** | | |
| Accounts payable | | 28,100 |
| Accrued expenses payable (rent, payroll, and other) | | 25,500 |
| Income taxes payable | | 0 |
| Other current liabilities | | 0 |
| Unearned franchise and development fees | | 6,825 |
| Other long-term liabilities (including notes payable) | | 11,200 |
| **Stockholders' Equity** | | |
| Contributed capital | | 165,800 |
| Retained earnings | | 98,000 |
| **Revenues** | | |
| Restaurant sales revenue | | 35,200 |
| Franchise royalties and development fees revenue | | 2,875 |
| Commissary, equipment, and other sales revenue | | 34,500 |
| Investment income | | 125 |
| **Expenses** | | |
| Cost of sales - restaurants | 9,600 | |
| Salaries and benefits expense - restaurants | 8,000 | |
| Advertising and related costs - restaurants | 0 | |
| Occupancy costs and other operating expenses - restaurants | 4,700 | |
| Cost of sales - commissaries, equipment, and other | 3,800 | |
| Salaries and benefits expense - commissaries | 1,500 | |
| Other operating expenses - commissaries | 2,200 | |
| General and administrative expenses | 4,410 | |
| Depreciation and amortization expense | 0 | |
| Other costs and expenses | 0 | |
| Income tax expense | 0 | |
| **Totals** | 456,325 | 456,325 |

The amount in the Property and Equipment account is cost (what Papa John's paid for the assets).

The amount of property and equipment used to generate revenues in the past is in the contra-account Accumulated Depreciation and Amortization.

The two amounts are subtracted for reporting purposes ($223,100 − 48,200 = $174,900).

The difference between an asset's acquisition cost and accumulated depreciation is called **book value** (**net book value** or **carrying value**). The book value does *not* represent the current market value of the asset because accounting for depreciation is a cost allocation process rather than a market valuation process (discussed later in the chapter and in Chapter 8). As do many other companies, Papa John's subtracts the balance in Accumulated Depreciation and Amortization from the cost in the Property and Equipment account, reporting the net amount on the balance sheet. The balance of each individual account is disclosed in a footnote to the financial statements. The note disclosure (with our clarification added in brackets) from a recent Papa John's annual report follows:

**BOOK VALUE (NET BOOK VALUE, CARRYING VALUE)** of an asset is the difference between its acquisition cost and accumulated depreciation, its related contra-account.

---

[1] Amortization is related to using up intangible assets over time in generating revenues, just as depreciation is related to using buildings and equipment over time. Intangible assets are typically rights owned by a business and include patents, trademarks, and copyrights. Long-lived assets are discussed in Chapter 8.

**4. Net Property and Equipment**
Net property and equipment consists of the following (in thousands):

|  | 1998 | 1997 |
|---|---|---|
| Land | $ 17,891 | $ 14,219 |
| Buildings and improvements | 18,871 | 13,478 |
| Leasehold improvements [modifications to rented property, such as installing new flooring and replacing an elevator or roof] | 47,322 | 35,406 |
| Equipment and other | 86,893 | 70,419 |
| Construction in progress [costs-to-date for facilities being constructed] | 46,430 | 11,790 |
|  | 217,407 | 145,312 |
| Less accumulated depreciation and amortization | (48,204) | (32,711) |
| Net property and equipment [reported on the balance sheet] | $169,203 | $112,601 |

# ADJUSTING ENTRIES

**ADJUSTING ENTRIES** are
entries necessary at the end of
the accounting period to measure
income properly, correct errors,
and provide for adequate
valuation of balance sheet
accounts.

We learned in Chapter 3 that under accrual accounting, revenues are recorded when earned and expenses are matched with the related revenues in the same period. Operating income for a period of time, therefore, is determined by measuring *all* revenues and expenses of that period. Often **adjusting entries** are necessary at the end of the accounting period to meet this objective. In reality, nearly all asset and liability accounts need to be analyzed and adjusted at year-end to measure income properly, correct errors, and provide for adequate valuation of accounts on the balance sheet. We introduce the adjustment process in this chapter for common adjusting entries. You will learn about additional adjustments in future chapters, most of which relate to the valuation of specific accounts (such as accounts receivable and investments) and the corrections of errors.

Adjusting entries are made at year-end to record revenues earned and expenses incurred in the proper period. The analysis involves determining whether (1) cash was received or paid *in the past* but over time has become earned or incurred or (2) cash will be received or paid *in the future* after revenues and expenses have been earned or incurred in the current period.

The types of transactions requiring adjustment are the following:

## A PAST CASH TRANSACTION

*Cash was received or paid in advance* of the related revenue or expense recognition.

**DEFERRED REVENUES** and
**DEFERRED EXPENSES** are
previously recorded assets,
liabilities, revenues, or expenses
that need to be adjusted at the
end of the period to reflect earned
revenues or incurred expenses.

**Deferred Revenues**   Cash received and recorded *in a liability account* until earned. Examples include the following:

- Rent collected by company in advance of occupancy by a tenant—Unearned Rent Revenue (L) is recorded when cash is received. Note that "Unearned" in the title means liability.

  - Cash received for magazine subscriptions before magazines are delivered—Deferred (or Unearned) Subscription Revenue (L) is recorded when cash is received.

**Deferred Expenses**   Cash paid and recorded *in an asset account* as a future benefit to the company until used. Examples include these:

- Cash paid for insurance coverage for a specified future time period— Prepaid Insurance Expense (A) is recorded when cash is paid. Note that "Prepaid" in the title signifies an asset.

- Supplies purchased before being used in the business—Supplies Inventory (A) is recorded when supplies are received.

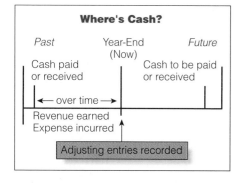

**Where's Cash?**

| Past | Year-End (Now) | Future |
|---|---|---|
| Cash paid or received | | Cash to be paid or received |

← over time →

Revenue earned
Expense incurred

Adjusting entries recorded

## A FUTURE CASH TRANSACTION

Revenues that have been earned or expenses that have been incurred by the end of the period but have not yet been recorded and for which *cash will be received or paid in the future.*

**Accrued Revenues**   Revenue earned before cash is received.

- Interest earned but not yet collected on a loan made to an affiliate—Since cash is owed to the company, Accrued Interest Receivable (A) (or simply Interest Receivable) is recorded at year end.
- Rent earned but not yet collected from lessees (i.e., renters)—Since cash is owed to the company, Accrued Rent Receivable (A) (or simply Rent Receivable) is recorded at year-end.

**Accrued Expenses**   Expense earned before cash is paid.

- Wages earned by employees but not yet paid—Since cash is owed to employees by the company, Accrued Wages Payable (L) (or simply Wages Payable) is recorded at year-end.
- Interest owed on outstanding loans—Since cash is owed by the company, Accrued Interest Payable (L) (or simply Interest Payable) is recorded at year-end.

**ACCRUED REVENUES** and **ACCRUED EXPENSES** are revenues that have been earned and expenses that have been incurred by the end of the current accounting period but that will not be collected or paid until a future accounting period.

The process for determining the proper adjusting entry in each case is slightly more complex for deferred revenues and expenses than accrued revenues and expenses. The primary tools used in the process are timelines, T-accounts, and journal entries.

To illustrate the process, let's assume that the fiscal year for a dental office ends on December 31. The dentist maintains her accounting records on an accrual basis. Upon reviewing her trial balance at the end of the year, she identifies four items that require adjustment:

1. Unearned dental fees she *received in the past* in advance from local businesses to provide dental care to their employees in the future (insurance coverage and dental services are assumed to occur evenly over time unless otherwise indicated)—a deferred revenue.
2. Professional liability insurance *paid in the past* that provides for insurance coverage in the future—a deferred expense.
3. Interest she will *receive in the future* from a loan made during the year to an employee—an accrued revenue.
4. Wages she *owes in the future* to employees who worked for her until year-end—an accrued expense.

We begin with deferred revenues and expenses.

## DEFERRED REVENUES AND EXPENSES

**Deferred Revenues**   On December 1, the dental office accepted a $2,400 payment from local businesses to provide dental care to their employees over the next three months. By December 31, the dentist had provided one month of service and thus had earned revenue. The process for adjusting the accounts is as follows:

### Step 1. For deferrals, what entry was made in the past?

On December 1, the amount received represents future obligations (dental service) owed by the dental office. This is the definition of a liability.

| | | |
|---|---|---|
| Cash (+A) . . . . . . . . . . . . . . . . . . . . . . . | 2,400 | |
| Unearned dental fee revenue (+L) . . . | | 2,400 |

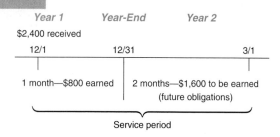

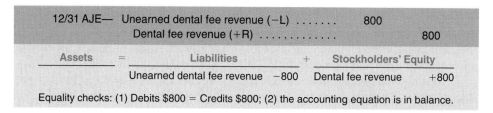

Equality checks: (1) Debits $800 = Credits $800; (2) the accounting equation is in balance.

### Step 2. Draw a timeline and, for deferrals, set up at least two T-accounts (one for the original asset or liability created and one for its related revenue or expense).

A good tool to help you visualize the events related to adjustments is a timeline. On it, indicate all relevant dates and amounts for each period involved. As time passes after receiving the fees, a portion of the liability is settled and revenue is earned.

### Step 3. Record the adjusting journal entry (AJE).

The effect needed to obtain the appropriate ending balances at year-end creates the adjusting journal entry. The earned portion ($800) of the liability Unearned Dental Fee Revenue is a revenue. The remaining unearned portion ($1,600) is service due in the future.

---

*AJE = adjusting journal entry

**Deferred Expenses**  Now we consider the second situation when, on November 1, the dentist paid $1,800 for six months of insurance coverage (from November 1 of this year to May 1 of next year). This results in $300 coverage each full month ($1,800 ÷ 6 months). Now, on December 31, two months have passed, and two of the six months of insurance coverage have been used during the year. To reflect incurring this expense in the current period, an adjusting entry is necessary. The process follows:

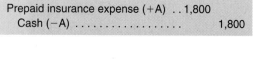

### Step 1. For deferrals, what entry was made in the past?

On November 1, the amount paid represents future benefits (insurance coverage) to the dental office. This is the definition of an asset.

### Step 2. Draw a timeline and, for deferrals, set up at least two T-accounts (one for the original asset or liability created and one for its related revenue or expense).

As time passes after paying for the insurance, a portion of the asset is used during the period representing coverage received by the dentist.

### Step 3. Record the adjusting journal entry (AJE).

The effect needed to obtain the appropriate ending balances at year-end creates the adjusting journal entry. The used-up portion ($600) of the asset Prepaid Insurance Expense is an expense. The remaining unused portion ($1,200) provides future benefits into next year.

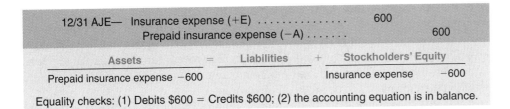

12/31 AJE— Insurance expense (+E) .............. 600
              Prepaid insurance expense (−A) ....... 600

| Assets | = | Liabilities | + | Stockholders' Equity | |
|---|---|---|---|---|---|
| Prepaid insurance expense −600 | | | | Insurance expense | −600 |

Equality checks: (1) Debits $600 = Credits $600; (2) the accounting equation is in balance.

By December 31 (the end of the fiscal period), the dentist will have received two months of coverage ($600). Therefore, for the current year, Insurance Expense (E) should be $600 with $1,200 in the Prepaid Insurance Expense (A) account on the balance sheet.

## FINANCIAL **ANALYSIS**

### AN OPTIONAL RECORDKEEPING EFFICIENCY

In the preceding examples, cash received or paid prior to revenue or expense recognition was recorded in a balance sheet account. This approach is consistent with accrual accounting since, on the cash exchange date, either an asset or liability exists. Payments or receipts are often recorded, however, as expenses or revenues on the cash transaction date. This is done to simplify recordkeeping since revenues or expenses are frequently earned or incurred by the end of the accounting period. When the full amount is not completely incurred or earned, an adjustment is necessary in these cases also. Note that regardless of how the original entry is recorded, the same correct ending balances in the Unearned Dental Fees and Dental Fees Revenue accounts result after the adjustment. The adjusting entry is different, however, in each case.

For example, for the December 1 illustration, the original entry could have been recorded in a revenue account and adjusted as follows:

***Step 1. For deferrals, what entry was made in the past?***

On December 1, the amount received could have been recorded as revenue.

***Step 2. Draw a timeline and, for deferrals, set up at least two T-accounts (one for the original asset or liability created and one for its related revenue or expense).***

As time passes after receiving the fees, only a portion of the fees are earned and the rest is due as service in the future.

Cash (+A) .................... 2,400
    Dental fee revenue (+R) ....... 2,400

| Year 1 | Year-End | Year 2 |
|---|---|---|
| $2,400 received | | |
| 12/1 | 12/31 | 3/1 |
| 1 month—$800 earned | 2 months—$1,600 to be earned (future obligations) | |

Service period

**Unearned Dental Fee Revenue (L)**

| | 0 | 12/1 |
|---|---|---|
| | 1,600 | AJE |
| | 1,600 | 12/31 |

***Step 3. Record the adjusting journal entry (AJE).***

The effect needed to obtain the appropriate ending balances at year-end creates the adjusting journal entry. The unearned portion ($1,600) of the revenue Dental Fee Revenue is a liability with service due in the future. The remaining portion ($800) is revenue earned in the current period.

**Dental Fee Revenue (R)**

| | | 2,400 | 12/1 |
|---|---|---|---|
| AJE | 1,600 | | |
| | | 800 | 12/31 |

12/31 AJE— Dental fee revenue (−R) ............. 1,600
              Unearned dental fee revenue (+L) ... 1,600

| Assets | = | Liabilities | + | Stockholders' Equity | |
|---|---|---|---|---|---|
| | | Unearned dental fee revenue +1,600 | | Dental fee revenue | −1,600 |

Equality checks: (1) Debits $1,600 = Credits $1,600; (2) the accounting equation is in balance.

## ACCRUED REVENUES AND EXPENSES

**Accruals** occur when *no cash* has been received or paid, but the company has undertaken activities that result in earning revenues or incurring expenses. Unlike deferrals, no original entry has been recorded. Therefore, the process for adjusting the accounts is simpler; Step 1 is eliminated, and T-accounts often do not need to be created. Here we compute the amount to be recorded directly.

Let us continue our example of the adjustment process for the dental office. Two activities that normally require an accrued revenue and an accrued expense adjustment are interest on a loan to an employee and wages to employees.

**Accrued Revenues**    We assume that the dental office loaned $2,000 to an employee on September 1 for which the employee signed a note to pay the principal and interest at a 12 percent annual rate in six months. Any borrowing or lending of money involves two cash flows; one for the principal and one for the interest. Interest is the cost of borrowing money; it is an expense to the borrower and revenue to the lender. As each day passes until the principal is paid, more interest accumulates.

On September 1, an entry is made to reflect the lending of cash (principal) to the employee, but no interest revenue is recorded since none is earned on the day the note is signed. By the end of the year, however, four months have passed, so the dental office has earned four months of interest revenue for which it will not be paid until March 1.

No entry was made for interest revenue earned in the past. However, when the money was loaned, the dental office increased the liability Note Payable for the principal.

*Step 1. What entry was made in the past?*

Since this is a revenue earned during the year that has not yet been collected (an accrual), there has been no entry yet.

*Step 2. Draw a timeline and set up at least two T-accounts (one for the original asset or liability created and one for its related revenue or expense).*

Interest is calculated by the following formula:

$$\text{Principal} \times \text{Annual Interest Rate} \times \frac{\text{\# of months to be computed}}{12}$$

$2,000 \times .12 \times 4/12 = $80$ interest earned in the first period.

*Step 3. Record the adjusting journal entry (AJE).*

To recognize revenues in the period earned, an adjusting journal entry is needed. The effect is an increase in an asset and an increase in a revenue related to interest.

T-accounts are not necessary since the amount is computed directly. They are presented here for illustration.

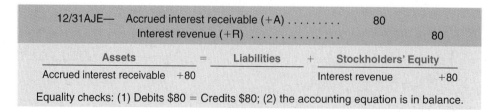

Since the accrued revenue has not yet been recorded until the end of the period, the adjusting entry increases a receivable and increases a revenue by the computed amount. When the employee pays the interest and principal on March 1 of the next period, the entry is as follows:

| March 1 | Cash (+A) ............................... | 2,120 | |
|---|---|---|---|
| | Note receivable (−A) ................. | | 2,000 |
| | Accrued interest receivable (−A) ......... | | 80 |
| | Interest revenue (+R) ................. | | 40 |

| Assets | | = | Liabilities | + | Stockholders' Equity | |
|---|---|---|---|---|---|---|
| Cash | +2,120 | | | | Interest revenue | +40 |
| Note receivable | −2,000 | | | | | |
| Accrued interest receivable | − 80 | | | | | |

Equality checks: (1) Debits $2,120 = Credits $2,120; (2) the accounting equation is in balance.

The $2,120 received in cash on March 1 includes $2,000 in principal repayment and $120 for interest. Four months of interest were recognized in the preceding year as interest revenue and the other two months of interest ($40) will be recognized in the next period.

**Accrued Expenses**   Now assume that all employees are paid a total of $3,000 biweekly. Payment for 10 working days (Monday through Friday) is made on the second Friday. The last payment for the year was on Friday, December 27. The employees continued to work through December 31, the end of the accounting period, but they will not be paid until January 10.

**Step 1. What entry was made in the past?**

Since this is for an expense incurred during the year that has not yet been paid (an accrual), there has been no entry.

**Step 2. Draw a timeline and set up at least two T-accounts (one for the original asset or liability created and one for its related revenue or expense).**

$3,000 paid for 10 working days = $300 owed to employees per workday. December 30 and 31 (Monday and Tuesday) are workdays not yet paid. Therefore, $300 × 2 days = $600 incurred.

**Step 3. Record the adjusting journal entry (AJE).**

To match expenses in the period when incurred to generate revenue, an adjusting journal entry is needed. The effect is an increase in a liability and an increase in an expense related to wages.

T-accounts are not necessary since the amount is computed directly. They are presented here for illustration.

No entry was made in the past

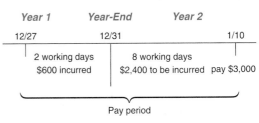

| | Accrued Wages Payable (L) | |
|---|---|---|
| | 600 | AJE |
| | 600 | 12/31 |

| Wages Expense (E) | | |
|---|---|---|
| AJE | 600 | |
| 12/31 | 600 | |

| 12/31 AJE— Wages expense (+E) .............. | 600 | |
|---|---|---|
| Accrued wages payable (+L) ..... | | 600 |

| Assets | = | Liabilities | | + | Stockholders' Equity | |
|---|---|---|---|---|---|---|
| | | Accrued wages payable | +600 | | Wages expense | −600 |

Equality checks: (1) Debits $600 = Credits $600; (2) the accounting equation is in balance.

To complete the analysis, consider what the January 10 payday entry will be in the next period:

| January 10 | Wages expense (+E) .............. | 2,400 | |
|---|---|---|---|
| | Wages payable (−L) .............. | 600 | |
| | Cash (−A) .................... | | 3,000 |

| Assets | = | Liabilities | + | Stockholders' Equity | |
|---|---|---|---|---|---|
| Cash | −3,000 | Wages payable | −600 | Wages expense | −2,400 |

Equality checks: (1) Debits $3,000 = Credits $3,000; (2) the accounting equation is in balance.

The $3,000 is paid, but only $2,400 relates to the expense incurred in the second period. The $600 was properly recorded as an expense in the prior period and is now paid (the liability is reduced). Because the year ended between paydays, a portion of the total paid in the second period is an expense in the first year and the rest is an expense in the second year. Thus, expenses were properly matched in the appropriate period.

The following summarizes this process.

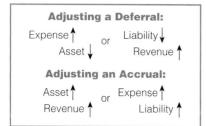

**Adjusting a Deferral:**

Expense ↑  or  Liability ↓
   Asset ↓         Revenue ↑

**Adjusting an Accrual:**

Asset ↑  or  Expense ↑
Revenue ↑         Liability ↑

**Deferrals:** Deferred accounts already exist at the end of the accounting period from a previous entry involving cash receipt or payment. At year-end due to the passage of time, an asset (usually, Prepaid Expenses, Supplies, Buildings, and Equipment) or a liability (Unearned Revenue) is overstated and must be *decreased;* its related revenue or expense account is understated and must be *increased.* We compute the corrected ending balance in the account and adjust the balance to that number. In each case, T-accounts and timelines can be quite useful.

**Accruals:** Since no previous entry has been made, expense accruals *increase* an expense and a payable, and revenue accruals *increase* a revenue and a receivable. As a consequence, we directly compute the amount of the needed adjustment.

**Overall:** It is important to note that adjusting entries *do not affect the Cash account.*

When adjustments are completed, the adjusted balances are used to prepare financial statements, which is the next step of the accounting cycle. Before we illustrate a complete set of financial statements, we need to adjust the accounts of Papa John's at the end of the month. Recall from the beginning of the chapter that Papa John's policy for fiscal year-end is the last Sunday of the month. Therefore, we adjust the accounts on January 31, the Sunday closest to month-end.[2]

# FINANCIAL **ANALYSIS**

## ACCRUALS AND DEFERRALS: THE KEYS TO FINANCIAL REPORTING STRATEGY

Most of the deferrals and accruals discussed in this chapter, such as the allocation of prepaid insurance or the determination of accrued interest revenue, involve direct calculations and require little judgment on the part of the company's accountants. In later chapters, we will discuss many other adjustments that involve difficult and complex estimates about the future. These include, for example, estimates of customers' ability to make payments to the company for purchases on account, the useful lives of new machines, and future amounts that a company may owe on warranties of products sold in the past. Each of these estimates and many others can have significant effects on the stream of net earnings that companies report over time.

When analysts attempt to value firms based on their balance sheet and income statement data, they also evaluate the estimates that form the basis for accruals and deferrals. Those

---

[2]Companies can choose fiscal periods other than actual month-ends, and financial statements can cover different accounting periods (month, quarter, or year). Adjusting entries may be prepared monthly, quarterly, and/or annually to ensure that proper amounts are included on the financial reports presented to external users.

firms that make relatively pessimistic estimates that reduce current income are judged to follow *conservative* financial reporting strategies, and their reports of performance are given more credence by experienced analysts. The earnings numbers reported by these companies are often said to be of "higher quality" because they are less influenced by management's natural optimism. Firms that consistently make optimistic estimates that result in reporting higher net income, however, are judged to be *aggressive*. Analysts judge these companies' operating performance to be of lower quality.

## ADJUSTING ENTRIES ILLUSTRATED

We illustrate common adjusting entries by updating the accounts of Papa John's based on the account balances and transactions in Chapters 2 and 3. As we review Papa John's trial balance in Exhibit 4.2, we can identify several deferral accounts that will need to be analyzed and may need to be adjusted:

| | |
|---|---|
| *Inventories* | A portion of food and paper products has been used during the month. |
| *Prepaid Expenses* | All or a portion of the prepaid rent, insurance, and advertising may have been used by month-end. |
| *Property and Equipment* | A portion has been used during the month to generate revenues. |
| *Unearned Franchise and Development Fees* | All or a portion may have been earned by month-end. |

In addition, we can see that several accruals need to be recorded for activities that have generated unrecorded revenues or expenses:

| | |
|---|---|
| *Accounts Receivable* | Franchisees may owe additional royalties to Papa John's for the last week's sales. |
| *Investments* | An investment in stocks and bonds usually produces investment income (dividends on stocks and interest on bonds). |
| *Notes Receivable* | Franchisees may owe interest on notes due to Papa John's. |
| *Accrued Expenses Payable* | Any wages due to employees for work during the last week and amounts due for utilities used during the month but not yet billed to Papa John's need to be recorded as expenses for the month. |
| *Notes Payable* | Papa John's owes interest on any borrowed funds. |
| *Income Taxes Payable* | Income tax expense needs to be recorded for the period. |

We use the three steps outlined earlier for deferrals and the simpler process for accruals. You should study the following illustration carefully to understand the steps in the adjustment process, paying close attention to the computation of the amounts in the adjustment and the effects on the account balances. First we adjust the deferred revenues and expenses and then the accrued revenues and expenses.

### ADJUSTING DEFERRED REVENUES AND EXPENSES

We adjust the identified deferred revenue and expense accounts utilizing the three-step process previously discussed: (1) identify the original entry, (2) create a timeline with relevant dates and amounts and T-accounts, and (3) identify the necessary adjusting entry.

(a) Inventories include food, paper products, and equipment for sale to franchisees. The balance of inventories at the beginning of the month totaled $9,700. During the month, Papa John's purchased $29,000 in inventories—recorded in Chapter 3, Transaction (e)—and sold or used inventories costing $13,400—recorded as Cost of Sales in Chapter 3, Transactions (b) and (i). At the end of the month, Papa John's counted $10,200 in inventories on hand. The difference ($15,100) is additional inventory used during the month by the commissaries.

| Inventories (+A) . . . . . . . . . . . . . . | 29,000 | |
|---|---|---|
| Cash (−A) . . . . . . . . . . . . . . . . . | | 29,000 |

**Step 1. For deferrals, what entry was made in the past?**

|  | Month 1 | Month-End | Month 2 and Beyond |
|---|---|---|---|

$29,000 paid
for inventories     1/31

Beginning—On hand— Ending
$9,700       $10,200

Previously Sold/Used = $13,400
Additionally Used = $15,100

**Step 2. Draw a timeline and, for deferrals, set up at least two T-accounts (one for the original asset or liability created and one for its related revenue or expense).**

**Inventories (A)**

| Beg. | 9,700 | | |
|---|---|---|---|
| Purchased | 29,000 | 9,600 | Used |
| | | 3,800 | Sold |
| | | 15,100 | Used AJE |
| End. | 10,200 | | |

**Cost of Sales—Commissaries (E)**

| Beg. | 0 | |
|---|---|---|
| Sold | 3,800 | |
| Used | 15,100 | |
| End. | 18,900 | |

**Cost of Sales—Restaurants (E)**

| Beg. | 0 | |
|---|---|---|
| Used | 9,600 | |
| End. | 9,600 | |

**Step 3. Record the adjusting journal entry (AJE).**

The effect needed to obtain the appropriate ending balance of $10,200 creates the adjusting journal entry. The additional used-up inventory by the commissaries ($15,100) is an expense. The remaining unused portion ($10,200) provides future benefits into the next period.

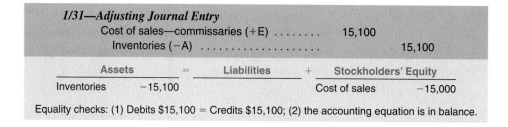

**1/31—Adjusting Journal Entry**

| Cost of sales—commissaries (+E) . . . . . . . . | 15,100 | |
|---|---|---|
| Inventories (−A) . . . . . . . . . . . . . . . . . . . | | 15,100 |

| Assets | = | Liabilities | + | Stockholders' Equity |
|---|---|---|---|---|
| Inventories    −15,100 | | | | Cost of sales    −15,000 |

Equality checks: (1) Debits $15,100 = Credits $15,100; (2) the accounting equation is in balance.

(b) From Chapter 3, Transaction (g), Prepaid Expenses, includes $1,600 for four months of insurance (three months remaining—a general expense), $4,800 for three months of rent (two months remaining), and advertising ($1,000 purchased in the current month and additional advertising prepaid in prior months, with $2,700 in advertising used during the month).

**Step 1. For deferrals, what entry was made in the past?**

| Prepaid expenses (+A) . . . . . . . . . | 7,400 | |
|---|---|---|
| Cash (−A) . . . . . . . . . . . . . . . . . | | 7,400 |

***Step 2.*** ***Draw a timeline and, for deferrals, set up at least two T-accounts (one for the original asset or liability created and one for its related revenue or expense).***

|  |  | Month 1 | Month-End | Month 2 and Beyond |
|---|---|---|---|---|
|  |  | During the month | 1/31 |  |
| Insurance | Expense incurred | $ 400 | To be incurred | $1,200 |
| Rent: | Expense incurred | $1,600 | To be incurred | $3,200 |
| Advertising: | Expense incurred | $2,700 |  |  |

***Step 3.*** ***Record the adjusting journal entry (AJE).***

As insurance, rent, and advertising are used, the asset Prepaid Expenses should reflect the remaining future benefits. In this case, three expenses were affected by the adjustment.

**Prepaid Expenses (A)**

| Beg. | 4,800 | | |
|---|---|---|---|
| Purchased | 7,400 | 4,700 | Used |
| End. | 7,500 | | |

**General and Administrative Expenses (E)**

| Ch. 3 bal. | 4,410 | |
|---|---|---|
| AJE | 400 | |
| End. | 4,810 | |

**Occupancy Costs and Other Operating Expenses (E)**

| Ch. 3 bal. | 4,700 | |
|---|---|---|
| AJE | 1,600 | |
| End. | 6,300 | |

**Advertising and Related Costs Expenses (E)**

| Ch. 3 bal. | 0 | |
|---|---|---|
| AJE | 2,700 | |
| End. | 2,700 | |

---

*1/31—Adjusting Journal Entry*

| General and administrative expenses (+E) ..... | 400 | |
|---|---|---|
| Occupancy costs and other operating expenses (+E) ........................ | 1,600 | |
| Advertising and related costs (+E) ............ | 2,700 | |
| Prepaid expenses (−A) ............... | | 4,700 |

| Assets | = | Liabilities | + | Stockholders' Equity | |
|---|---|---|---|---|---|
| Prepaid expenses  −4,700 | | | | General and administrative expenses | − 400 |
| | | | | Occupancy costs and other operating expenses | −1,600 |
| | | | | Advertising and related costs | −2,700 |

Equality checks: (1) Debits $4,700 = Credits $4,700; (2) the accounting equation is in balance.

(*c*) **Property and equipment with an historical cost of $223,100 and an accumulated depreciation and amortization (the used-up portion of the historical cost) of $48,200 has an average useful life of 10 years and an estimated residual value (the assets' estimated sales prices or scrap values at the end of their useful lives to the company) of $22,700.**

When long-lived assets are used over time, accountants say that they are *depreciated* (for tangible assets such as plant and equipment) or *amortized* (for intangible assets such as patents on inventions). The accounting process of depreciation and amortization involves the systematic and rational allocation of the cost of a long-lived asset over its useful life to the periods in which the asset is used to generate revenues.

A common misconception held by students and others unfamiliar with accounting terminology is that depreciation reflects the asset's decline in market

value. This concept of depreciation and amortization in an accounting context *does not necessarily match the change in the market value* of the asset. Thus, this concept differs from the layperson's usage in the statement that a new car "depreciates" when it is driven off the dealer's lot. In accounting, depreciation is a *cost allocation* concept, not a *valuation concept*. As previously discussed, a contra-account, Accumulated Depreciation, is used to accumulate the amount of the historical cost allocated to prior periods. It is directly related to the Property and Equipment account but has the opposite balance (a credit balance).

Depreciation and amortization will be discussed in much greater detail in Chapter 8. To simplify matters until we reach that chapter, we assume that long-lived assets used in operations provide benefits to the company evenly over time. Therefore, the historical cost is depreciated or amortized in equal amounts each period. This is known as the *straight-line* method.

| Property and equipment (+A) . . . . . | (many purchases) |
| Cash (−A) [or a liability] . . . . . . . | (many purchases) |

|  | Month 1 | Month-End | Month 2 and Beyond |
|---|---|---|---|
|  | One month used | 1/31 |  |

Depreciation expense = $1,670

($223,100 − 22,700) ÷ 10 years = $20,040 per year

$20,040 annual depreciation ÷ 12 months = $1,670 per month

**Accumulated Depreciation and Amortization (XA)**

|  | | |
|---|---|---|
|  | 48,200 | Ch. 3 bal. |
|  | **1,670** | **Used** |
|  | 49,870 | End. |

**Depreciation Expense (E)**

| Ch. 3 bal. | 0 | |
| **AJE** | **1,670** | |
| End | 1,670 | |

### Step 1. *For deferrals, what entry was made in the past?*

### Step 2. *Draw a timeline and, for deferrals, set up at least two T-accounts (one for the original asset or liability created and one for its related revenue or expense).*

The straight-line formula for computing the estimated amount of long-lived assets used during the period is as follows:

$$\frac{\text{(Cost − Residual value)}}{\text{Useful life}} = \textbf{Depreciation expense for the period}$$

### Step 3. *Record the adjusting journal entry (AJE).*

Note that increasing the contra-asset account decreases total assets.

**1/31—Adjusting Journal Entry**

| Depreciation expense (+E) . . . . . . . . . . . . . . . . . . | 1,670 | |
| Accumulated depreciation and amortization (+XA→−A) . . . . . . . . . . . | | 1,670 |

| Assets | = | Liabilities | + | Stockholders' Equity |
|---|---|---|---|---|
| Accumulated depreciation and amortization  −1,670 | | | | Depreciation expense  −1,670 |

Equality checks: (1) Debits $1,670 = Credits $1,670; (2) the accounting equation is in balance.

## ADJUSTING ACCRUED REVENUES AND EXPENSES

Now we adjust the identified accruals, those revenues and expenses that are not yet recorded. We use the three-step process previously discussed as modified for accruals that do not have an original entry: (1) identify the original entry (for accruals, there is only a past activity, no cash entry); (2) create a timeline with relevant dates, amounts, and T-accounts; and (3) identify the necessary adjusting entry. Income Taxes Payable and Income Tax Expense are determined after all other adjustments are made.

(*d*) **The franchisees reported that they owe Papa John's $900 in additional royalties for sales in the last week of the month.**

**Step 1. *What entry was made in the past?***

No past entry has been made.

**Step 2. *Draw a timeline and set up at least two T-accounts (one for the original asset or liability created and one for its related revenue or expense).***

| | Month 1 | Month-End | Month 2 and Beyond |
|---|---|---|---|
| | During the last week | 1/31 | |
| | $900 revenue earned | | To be collected |

**Step 3. *Record the adjusting journal entry (AJE).***

Since cash will be received in the future, both the receivable and revenue accounts increase.

**Accounts Receivable (A)**

| | | |
|---|---|---|
| Ch. 3 bal. | 14,550 | |
| **Earned** | **900** | |
| End. | 15,450 | |

**Franchise Royalties and Development Fees Revenue (R)**

| | | |
|---|---|---|
| | 2,875 | Ch. 3 bal. |
| | 900 | AJE |
| | 3,775 | End. |

*1/31—Adjusting Journal Entry*

| | | |
|---|---|---|
| Accounts receivable (+A) . . . . . . . . . . . . . . . . . . | 900 | |
|   Franchise royalties and | | |
|     development fees revenue (+R) . . . . . . . . | | 900 |

| Assets | = | Liabilities | + | Stockholders' Equity |
|---|---|---|---|---|
| Accounts receivable   +900 | | | | Franchise royalties and development fees revenue   +900 |

Equality checks: (1) Debits $900 = Credits $900; (2) the accounting equation is in balance.

(*e*) **Papa John's earned $250 on investments and $80 interest on notes receivable from franchisees for the month. The cash will be received next month. (Use Other Current Assets for the receivable instead of creating Interest Receivable.)**

**Step 1. *What entry was made in the past?***

No past entry has been made.

**Step 2. *Draw a timeline and set up at least two T-accounts (one for the original asset or liability created and one for its related revenue or expense).***

| | Month 1 | Month-End | Month 2 and Beyond |
|---|---|---|---|
| | During the month | 1/31 | |
| | $330 revenue earned | | To be collected |

**Step 3. *Record the adjusting journal entry (AJE).***

Since cash will be received in the future, both the receivable and revenue accounts increase.

**Other Current Assets (A)**

| | | |
|---|---|---|
| Ch. 3 bal. | 2,100 | |
| **Earned** | **330** | |
| End. | 2,430 | |

**Investment Income (R)**

| | | |
|---|---|---|
| | 125 | Ch. 3 bal. |
| | **330** | **AJE** |
| | 455 | End. |

*1/31—Adjusting Journal Entry*

| | | |
|---|---|---|
| Other current assets (+A) . . . . . . . . . . . . . . . . . . | 330 | |
|   Investment income (+R) . . . . . . . . . . . . . . . . | | 330 |

| Assets | = | Liabilities | + | Stockholders' Equity |
|---|---|---|---|---|
| Other current assets   +330 | | | | Investment income   +330 |

Equality checks: (1) Debits $330 = Credits $330; (2) the accounting equation is in balance.

(f) **On January 31, Papa John's received a utility bill for $500 for use of natural gas and electricity in the headquarters building during January. The bill will be paid in February.**

No past entry has been made.

| | | Month 2 |
| Month 1 | Month-End | and Beyond |

| During the month | 1/31 | |
| $500 expense incurred | | To be paid |

**Accrued Expenses Payable (L)**

| | | 25,500 | Ch. 3 bal. |
| | | 500 | Incurred |
| | | 26,000 | End. |

**General and Administrative Expenses (E)**

| Bal. From (b) 4,810 | |
| AJE | 500 | |
| End. | 5,310 | |

**Step 1. What entry was made in the past?**

**Step 2. Draw a timeline and set up at least two T-accounts (one for the original asset or liability created and one for its related revenue or expense).**

**Step 3. Record the adjusting journal entry (AJE).**

Since using utilities was necessary for the company to generate revenues in January, the amount should be recorded as a January expense.

**1/31—Adjusting Journal Entry**

| General and administrative expenses (+E) . . . . . | 500 | |
| Accrued expenses payable (+L) . . . . . . . . . . | | 500 |

| Assets | = | Liabilities | + | Stockholders' Equity |
|---|---|---|---|---|
| | | Accrued expenses payable +500 | | General and administrative expenses −500 |

Equality checks: (1) Debits $500 = Credits $500; (2) the accounting equation is in balance.

(g) **Papa John's owed its employees wages for the last week in the month: $1,200 for restaurant employees, $300 for commissary employees, and $1,600 to administrative employees working at the headquarters. The wages will be paid during the first week in February.**

No past entry has been made.

| | | Month 2 |
| Month 1 | Month-End | and Beyond |

| During the last week | 1/31 | |
| $3,100 expense incurred | | To be paid |

**Accrued Expenses Payable (L)**

| | | 26,000 | Bal. from (f) |
| | | 3,100 | Incurred |
| | | 29,100 | End. |

**Step 1. What entry was made in the past?**

**Step 2. Draw a timeline and set up at least two T-accounts (one for the original asset or liability created and one for its related revenue or expense).**

**Step 3. Record the adjusting journal entry (AJE).**

Since the employees worked and generated revenues during January, the amount owed to them should be recorded as a January expense.

**Salaries and Benefits Expense— Commissaries (E)**

| Ch. 3 bal. | 3,700 | |
| AJE | 300 | |
| End. | 4,000 | |

**Salaries and Benefits Expense— Restaurants (E)**

| Ch. 3 bal. | 8,000 | |
| AJE | 1,200 | |
| End. | 9,200 | |

**General and Administrative Expenses (E)**

| Bal. From (f) | 5,310 | |
| AJE | 1,600 | |
| End. | 6,910 | |

**1/31—Adjusting Journal Entry**

| Salaries and benefits expense—rest. (+E) . . . . . . | 1,200 | |
| Salaries and benefits expense—comm. (+E) . . . . | 300 | |
| General and administrative expenses (+E) . . . . . | 1,600 | |
| Accrued expenses payable (+L) . . . . . . . . . . | | 3,100 |

| Assets | = | Liabilities | + | Stockholders' Equity | |
|--------|---|-------------|---|----------------------|---|
| | | Accrued expenses payable +3,100 | | General and administrative expenses | −1,600 |
| | | | | Salaries and benefits expense—restaurants | −1,200 |
| | | | | Salaries and benefits expense—commissaries | −300 |

Equality checks: (1) Debits $3,100 = Credits $3,100; (2) the accounting equation is in balance.

## SELF-STUDY **QUIZ**

For transactions (*h*) and (*i*), fill in the missing information. When completed, you can check your answers with the solution at the end of the quiz:

(*h*) **Papa John's has provided $100 in additional services to new franchisees that had previously paid initial fees to Papa John's (unearned revenue at the time).**

**Step 1. What entry was made in the past?**

Because cash was paid in the past, the account to be adjusted is
(circle one)   an accrual   (a deferral)

**Step 2. Draw a timeline and set up two T-accounts (*one for the original asset or liability created and one for its related revenue or expense*).**

**Step 3. Record the adjusting journal entry (*AJE*).**

Cash (+A) . . . . . . . . . . . . . . . (many transactions)
  Unearned franchise and
  development fees (+L) . . . . .   (many transactions)

| | Month 1 | Month-End | Month 2 and Beyond |
|---|---|---|---|
| | | 1/31 | |
| | Revenue earned = $100 | | To be earned = $6,725 |

**Unearned Franchise and Development Fees (L)**

| | | 6,825 | Ch. 3 bal. |
|---|---|---|---|
| AJE | 100 | | |
| | | 6,725 | End. |

**Franchise Royalties and Development Fees Revenue (R)**

| | | 3,775 | Bal. from (*d*) |
|---|---|---|---|
| | | 100 | AJE |
| | | 3,875 | End. |

**1/31—Adjusting Journal Entry**

Record
the entry →

| Assets | = | Liabilities | + | Stockholders' Equity | |
|--------|---|-------------|---|----------------------|---|
| | | Unearned franchise and development fees −100 | | Franchise royalties and development fees revenue +100 | |

Equality checks: (1) Debits $100 = Credits $100; (2) the accounting equation is in balance.

(*i*) **At the beginning of the month, Papa John's borrowed $1,000 from a local bank (in Chapter 2, Transaction [*b*]) to be repaid in one year along with interest at an annual rate of 12 percent.**

**Step 1. What entry was made in the past?**

Because cash is to be paid in the future, the account to be adjusted is
(circle one)   (an accrual)   a deferral.

No entry for interest has been made.

Month 1    Month-End    Month 2 and Beyond

During the month    1/31

$ [____] expense incurred | To be paid

**Other Current Liabilities (L)***

| | | 0 | Ch. 3 bal. |
| | | *10* | Incurred |
| | | *10* | End. |

**Other Costs and Expenses (E)**

| Ch. 3 bal. | 0 | | |
| AJE | *10* | | |
| End. | *10* | | |

**Step 2. Draw a timeline and set up two T-accounts (*one for the original asset or liability created and one for its related revenue or expense*).**

**Step 3. Record the adjusting journal entry (*AJE*).**
Compute interest using the formula

$$\text{Principal} \times \text{Annual Rate} \times \frac{\text{\# of months}}{12}$$

*Common titles for the accounts related to interest are Interest Payable and Interest Expense. We use the titles illustrated, which are summary titles for several accounts with small dollar balances.

### 1/31—Adjusting Journal Entry

Record the entry → [_____]

| Assets | = | Liabilities | + | Stockholders' Equity |
| --- | --- | --- | --- | --- |
| | | Other current liabilities +[__] | | Other costs and expenses −[__] |

Equality checks: (1) Debits $[__] = Credits $[__]; (2) the accounting equation is in balance.

You can check your answers with the solution in the footnote at the bottom of this page.*

The final adjusting journal entry is to record the accrual of income taxes due (an unrecorded expense). This requires computing pretax income based on the adjusted balances:

| | | | |
| --- | --- | --- | --- |
| All revenues | $74,030 | Chapter 3 total | $72,700 + 900 + 330 + 100 |
| − All expenses | −59,290 | Chapter 3 total | $34,210 + 15,100 + 4,700 + 1,670 + 500 + 3,100 + 10 |
| Pretax income | $14,740 | | |

(*j*) **Papa John's average income tax rate is 37 percent.**

No past entry has been made.

***Step 1. What entry was made in the past?***

---

*(*h*) The account to be adjusted is a deferral.

| | | |
| --- | --- | --- |
| Unearned franchise and development fees (−L) .................... | 100 | |
| Franchise royalties and development fees revenue (+R) ........ | | 100 |

(*i*) The account to be adjusted is an accrual. Principal was recorded when the note was signed. However, the bank's money was used during the month. Using another's money is interest expense for the period of use until the principal is repaid.

**$1,000 principal × 12% annual interest rate × 1 month/12 = $10 interest expense**

Both Other Current Liabilities (L) and the related Other Costs and Expenses (E) are increased by $10; resulting in $10 balances for each. After recording the journal entry, Debits = Credits and the equation remains in balance.

| | | |
| --- | --- | --- |
| Other costs and expenses (+E) ................................ | 10 | |
| Other current liabilities (+L) ................................ | | 10 |

***Step 2.*** ***Draw a timeline and set up two T-accounts (one for the original asset or liability created and one for its related revenue or expense).***

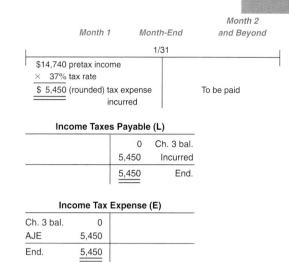

| | Month 1 | Month-End | Month 2 and Beyond |
|---|---|---|---|
| | | 1/31 | |

$14,740 pretax income
×   37% tax rate
$ 5,450 (rounded) tax expense incurred          To be paid

***Step 3.*** ***Record the adjusting journal entry (AJE).***

**Income Taxes Payable (L)**

| | | 0 | Ch. 3 bal. |
|---|---|---|---|
| | | 5,450 | Incurred |
| | | 5,450 | End. |

**Income Tax Expense (E)**

| Ch. 3 bal. | 0 | |
|---|---|---|
| AJE | 5,450 | |
| End. | 5,450 | |

*1/31—Adjusting Journal Entry*
Income tax expense (+E) . . . . . . . . . . . . . . . .          5,450
    Income taxes payable (+L) . . . . . . . . . . . . . .                    5,450

| Assets | = | Liabilities | + | Stockholders' Equity |
|---|---|---|---|---|
| | | Income taxes payable  +5,450 | | Income tax expense   −5,450 |

Equality checks: (1) Debits $5,450 = Credits $5,450; (2) the accounting equation is in balance.

From the balances in the adjusted T-accounts, we can now prepare a complete set of adjusted accrual-based financial statements at the end of the accounting period (January 31).

# FINANCIAL **ANALYSIS**

## END-OF-PERIOD ADJUSTMENTS AND AUDITING

Since end-of-period adjustments are the most complex portion of the annual recordkeeping process, they are prone to error. As noted in Chapter 1, external auditors (independent CPAs) examine the company's records on a test, or sample, basis. To maximize the chance of detecting any errors significant enough to affect users' decisions, CPAs allocate more of their testing to transactions most likely to be in error. A number of accounting research studies have documented the most error-prone transactions for medium-sized manufacturing companies. End-of-period accrual errors such as failure to provide adequate product warranty liability, failure to include items that should be accrued, and end-of-period transactions recorded in the wrong period (called *cut-off errors*) are in the top category and thus receive a great deal of attention from the auditors.

# FINANCIAL STATEMENT PREPARATION

The next step of the accounting cycle is to prepare a complete set of adjusted financial statements:

- Income statement.
- Statement of stockholders' equity (includes the statement of retained earnings).
- Balance sheet.
- Statement of cash flows.

First, we will illustrate the relationships between the statements, that is, how the numbers in one statement flow into the next statement.

**LEARNING OBJECTIVE 3**

Present a complete set of financial statements: income statement with earnings per share, statement of stockholders' equity, balance sheet, and statement of cash flows.

The transaction analysis model developed in Chapter 3 is presented in Exhibit 4.3. It illustrates how information flows from the income statement to the statement of stockholders' equity to the balance sheet. The portions of the model that relate to these three statements are indicated by overlapping circles.

EXHIBIT **4.3**

**Relationships of the Financial Statements Using the Transaction Analysis Model**

The **blue circle** highlights the information used on the income statement. The **red circle** highlights the components of the statement of stockholders' equity. Instead of a statement of retained earnings, most companies present a broader statement of stockholders' equity with separate columns for changes in contributed capital and changes in retained earnings. Changes in contributed capital include stock issuances and stock repurchases, which are discussed in more detail in Chapter 11 (along with other types of transactions affecting contributed capital). These changes can be represented by the following form for the statement of stockholders' equity. Notice that net income from the first equation is included in the second one. Then the ending balances in Retained Earnings, Contributed Capital, and Total Stockholders' Equity are included in the balance sheet equation (the **green circle**).

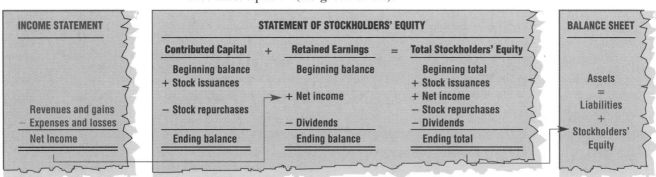

Now we prepare these three statements for Papa John's for the month ended January 31, 1999, based on the adjusted account balances.

## INCOME STATEMENT

Except that the amounts are for one month only, the following income statement based on adjusted balances more closely resembles the actual Papa John's annual income statement presented in Exhibit 3.2. Income statements prepared for external parties, as you may recall, are normally prepared quarterly and annually (presenting three years of data), although we have simplified this requirement in this chapter.

**PAPA JOHN'S INTERNATIONAL, INC. AND SUBSIDIARIES**
**Consolidated Statement of Income**
**(dollars in thousands)**

|  | Month Ended January 31, 1999 |
|---|---|
| **Revenues:** | |
| Restaurant sales | $35,200 |
| Franchise royalties and development fees | 3,875 |
| Commissary, equipment, and other sales | 34,500 |
| Investment income | 455 |
| **Total revenues** | 74,030 |
| **Costs and expenses:** | |
| Restaurant expenses: | |
| Cost of sales | 9,600 |
| Salaries and benefits | 9,200 |
| Advertising and related costs | 2,700 |
| Occupancy costs and other operating expenses | 6,300 |
| | 27,800 |
| Commissary, equipment and other expenses: | |
| Cost of sales | 18,900 |
| Salaries, benefits, and other operating expenses | 4,000 |
| | 22,900 |
| General and administrative expenses | 6,910 |
| Depreciation and amortization | 1,670 |
| Other costs and expenses | 10 |
| **Total costs and expenses** | 59,290 |
| Income before income taxes | 14,740 |
| Income tax expense | 5,450 |
| **Net income** | $ 9,290 |
| **Earnings per share** | $ .316 |

You will note that the ratio earnings per share (EPS) is reported on the income statement. It is widely used in evaluating the operating performance and profitability of a company and is the only ratio required to be disclosed on the statement or in the notes to the statements. Earnings per share is computed as follows:

$$\text{Earnings per Share} = \frac{\text{Net Income Available to the Common Stockholders}}{\text{Weighted-Average Number of Shares of Common Stock Outstanding during the Period}}$$

The calculation of the denominator is complex and is presented in other accounting courses. Based on Papa John's actual annual report for 1998, the weighted-average number of shares of stock outstanding was approximately 29,409,000. For simplicity, we use this same denominator in the computations of the earnings per share shown on the income statement. Additional EPS disclosures will be discussed in Chapter 5.

**EPS = $9,290,000 Net Income ÷ 29,409,000 Shares = $.316**

## STATEMENT OF STOCKHOLDERS' EQUITY

The final total from the income statement, net income, is carried forward to the Retained Earnings column of the statement of stockholders' (or shareholders') equity. To this, the additional elements of the statement are added. Relevant transactions from Chapter 2 are also included in the statement: dividends declared and an additional stock issuance.

**PAPA JOHN'S INTERNATIONAL, INC. AND SUBSIDIARIES**
**Consolidated Statement of Stockholders' Equity**
**For the Month Ended January 31, 1999**
**(dollars in thousands)**

|  | Contributed Capital | Retained Earnings | Stockholders' Equity |
|---|---|---|---|
| Beginning balance 12/27/98 | $164,500 | $ 98,200 | $262,700 |
| Stock issuance | 1,300 |  | 1,300 |
| Net income |  | 9,290 | 9,290 |
| Dividends |  | (200) | (200) |
| **Ending balance 1/31/99** | **$165,800** | **$107,290** | **$273,090** |

## BALANCE SHEET

The balances for contributed capital and retained earnings from the statement of shareholders' equity flow into the balance sheet. You will notice that the contra-asset account, Accumulated Depreciation, has been subtracted from the Property and Equipment account to reflect net book value (or carrying value) at month-end for balance sheet purposes. Detailed information on the cost of the equipment and the balance in the Accumulated Depreciation account could be provided in footnotes to the statements.

**PAPA JOHN'S INTERNATIONAL, INC. AND SUBSIDIARIES**
**Consolidated Balance Sheet**
**(dollars in thousands)**

|  | January 31, 1999 |
|---|---|
| **Assets** |  |
| **Current assets:** |  |
| Cash and cash equivalents | $ 55,415 |
| Accounts receivable | 15,450 |
| Inventories | 10,200 |
| Prepaid expenses | 7,500 |
| Other current assets | 2,430 |
| **Total current assets** | 90,995 |
| Investments | 50,300 |
| Net property and equipment | 173,230 |
| Notes receivable | 16,750 |
| Other assets | 22,400 |
| **Total assets** | $353,675 |
| **Liabilities and stockholders' equity** |  |
| **Current liabilities:** |  |
| Accounts payable | $ 28,100 |
| Accrued expenses payable | 29,100 |
| Income taxes payable | 5,450 |
| Other current liabilities | 10 |
| **Total current liabilities** | 62,660 |
| Unearned franchise and development fees | 6,725 |
| Other long-term liabilities (including notes payable) | 11,200 |
| **Stockholders' equity:** |  |
| Contributed capital | 165,800 |
| Retained earnings | 107,290 |
| **Total stockholders' equity** | 273,090 |
| **Total liabilities and stockholders' equity** | $353,675 |

$223,100 cost − 49,870 accumulated depreciation and amortization

FOCUS ON **CASH FLOWS**

## DISCLOSURE

As presented in the previous chapters, the statement of cash flows explains the difference be-tween the ending and beginning balances in the Cash account on the balance sheet during the accounting period. Put simply, the cash flow statement is a categorized list of all transac-tions of the period that affected the Cash account. The three categories are operating, invest-ing, and financing activities. For complete disclosure, however, companies are required to provide additional information on the statement or in notes to the statements.

### EFFECT ON STATEMENT OF CASH FLOWS

**IN GENERAL** →

|  | Effect on Cash Flows |
| --- | --- |
| Operating activities (from Chapter 3) | +/− |
| Investing activities (from Chapter 2) | +/− |
| Financing activities (from Chapter 2) | +/− |
| Change in cash | Total |
| + Beginning cash balance | + |
| Ending cash balance | Total |

**Supplemental Disclosure:** (1) Interest paid, (2) income taxes paid, and (3) a listing of the nature and amounts of significant noncash transactions (e.g., land exchanged for stock, acquisition of building by signing a long-term mortgage payable).

**FOCUS COMPANY ANALYSIS** → In Chapters 2 and 3, we analyzed and grouped the cash transactions into one of the three categories. Since no adjustments made in this chap-ter affected cash, the statement presented in Chapter 3 has not changed and is reproduced here. The beginning cash balance for the month ($34,000) and the ending cash balance for the month ($55,415) on the balance sheet are the same as those reported on the statement of cash flows. Information is provided on how Papa John's acquired and spent cash during the month.

**PAPA JOHN'S INTERNATIONAL, INC.**
**Consolidated Statements of Cash Flows**
**For the Month Ended January 31, 1999**
**(dollars in thousands)**

| Operating Activities | | |
| --- | --- | --- |
| Cash received from: Customers and franchisees | | $71,250 |
| Interest and dividends | | 125 |
| Operating cash inflows | | 71,375 |
| Cash paid to: Suppliers | | 33,710 |
| Employees | | 13,500 |
| Operating cash outflows | | 47,210 |
| Net cash provided by operating activities | | **24,165** |
| Investing Activities | | |
| Purchased property and equipment | | (1,500) |
| Purchased investments | | (3,000) |
| Lent funds to franchisees | | (450) |
| Received payment on loans to franchisees | | 500 |
| Net cash used in investing activities | | **(4,450)** |

*continued*

| Financing Activities | |
|---|---:|
| Issued common stock | 1,300 |
| Borrowings | 1,000 |
| Paid dividends | (200) |
| Payments on borrowings | (400) |
| Net cash provided by financing activities | **1,700** |
| Change in cash | 21,415 |
| Beginning cash balance | 34,000 |
| Ending cash balance | $55,415 |

Supplemental Disclosure:
No income taxes paid.
No interest paid.
There were no significant noncash transactions.

Agrees with amount on the balance sheet.

If these items are zero or insignificant, no disclosure is necessary. We included these lines to illustrate how disclosure on the face of the statement would be reported.

Papa John's disclosed $15.9 million in income taxes paid in the notes to its 1998 financial statements. No interest payments for the year or significant noncash transactions were noted; therefore, we can conclude that these items were immaterial (that is, were relatively small in amount and would not impact a user's decision).

**ONE FINAL NOTE:** The format we have shown for operating activities is known as the *direct method,* although most companies use the *indirect method.* We will provide an example of this form in the statement of cash flows for Callaway Golf, Inc., in Chapter 5. In addition, we provide more detailed information as to constructing and using the statement of cash flows in Chapter 13.

# FINANCIAL **ANALYSIS**

## CASH FLOW FROM OPERATIONS, NET INCOME, AND FINANCIAL ANALYSIS

Many standard financial analysis texts warn analysts to look for unusual deferrals and accruals when they attempt to predict future periods' earnings. They often suggest that wide disparities between net income and cash flow from operations is a useful warning sign. For example, Bernstein and Wild suggest that

> Cash flows are often less subject to distortion than is net income. Accounting accruals determining net income rely on estimates, deferrals, allocations, and valuations. These considerations typically admit more subjectivity than factors determining cash flows. For this reason we often relate cash flows from operations to net income in assessing its quality. Certain users consider earnings of higher quality when the ratio of cash flows from operations divided by net income is greater. This derives from a concern with revenue recognition or expense accrual criteria yielding high net income but low cash flows.*

*L. Bernstein and J. Wild, *Financial Statement Analysis* (Burr Ridge, IL: Irwin/McGraw-Hill, 1998), p. 366.

# A QUESTION OF **ETHICS**

## INCENTIVES, ACCRUAL, AND ETHICS

We noted in Chapter 1 that owners and managers of companies are most directly affected by the information presented in financial statements. If the financial performance and condition of the company appear strong, the company's stock price rises. Shareholders usually receive dividends and increase their investment value. Managers often receive bonuses based on the strength of a company's financial performance, and many in top management are compensated with options to buy their company's stock at prices below market.* The higher the market value, the more compensation they earn. When actual performance lags behind expectations, managers and owners may be tempted to manipulate accruals and deferrals to make up part of the difference. For example, managers may record cash received in advance of being earned as revenue in the current period or may fail to accrue certain expenses at year-end.

Evidence from studies of large samples of companies indicates that some do engage in such behavior. This research is borne out by enforcement actions of the Securities and Exchange Commission against companies and sometimes against their auditors. These SEC enforcement actions most often relate to accrual of revenue and receivables that should be deferred to future periods. In many of these cases, the firms involved, their managers, and their auditors are penalized for such actions. Furthermore, owners suffer because the company's stock price is affected negatively by news of an SEC investigation.

*P. Healy, and J. Whalen, "A Review of the Earnings Management Literature and Its Implications for Standard Setting," *Accounting Horizons*, December 1999, Vol. 13, No. 4.

## KEY **RATIO ANALYSIS:**

### NET PROFIT MARGIN

**K**now the decision question:

How effective is management in generating profit on every dollar of sales? It is computed as follows:

$$\text{Net Profit Margin} = \frac{\text{Net Income}}{\text{Net Sales*}}$$

The 1998 ratio for Papa John's:

$$\frac{\$35,165}{\$669,806} = .053 \ (5.3\%)$$

*Net sales is sales revenue less any returns from customers and other reductions discussed in Chapter 6. Since returns are not typically relevant in the restaurant industry, Papa John's total operating revenues equal net sales.

■ **LEARNING OBJECTIVE 4**

Compute and interpret net profit margin.

**E**xamine the ratio using two techniques:

| ① Comparisons over Time | | |
|---|---|---|
| **Papa John's International, Inc.** | | |
| 1996 | 1997 | 1998 |
| 5.2% | 5.3% | 5.3% |

| ② Comparisons with Competitors | |
|---|---|
| **Dominos' Inc.** | **Tricon Global†** |
| 1998 | 1998 |
| 6.5% | 5.3% |

†Tricon Global is the parent company of Pizza Hut, KFC, and Taco Bell.

**Y**ou interpret the results carefully:

**IN GENERAL** → Net profit margin measures how much of every sales dollar generated during the period is profit. A rising net profit margin signals more efficient management of sales and expenses and a declining margin of less-efficient management. Differences among industries result from the nature of the products or services provided and the intensity of competition. Differences among competitors in the same industry reflect how each company responds to changes in competition (and demand for the product or service) and changes in managing sales volume, sales price, and costs. Financial analysts expect well-run businesses to maintain or improve their net profit margin over time.

**FOCUS COMPANY ANALYSIS** → Papa John's net profit margin has increased slightly since 1996, suggesting an improvement in the control of sales and costs. As the regional commis-

| Selected Focus Company: Net Profit Margins | |
|---|---|
| General Mills | 7.0% |
| Harley-Davidson | 10.3% |
| Callaway Golf | 15.7% |

saries serve an increasing number of restaurants (operate closer to anticipated capacity), they become more efficient and costs per sale decrease.

Dominos', which is Papa John's main competitor in the delivery segment of the pizza business, has a 1.2 percent higher net profit margin. This may suggest greater efficiency in commissary activities. Papa John's has the same net profit margin as Tricon Global even though Tricon operates dine-in, take-out, and delivery restaurants that rely more heavily on facilities (a higher cost structure). These differences in business strategies and development stage explain differences in the ratio analysis.

**A FEW CAUTIONS:** The decisions that management makes to maintain the company's net profit margin in the current period may have negative long-run implications. Analysts should perform additional analysis of the ratio to identify trends in each component of revenues and expenses. This involves dividing each line on the income statement by net sales. Statements presented with these percentages are called common-sized income statements; they are discussed more fully in Chapter 14. Changes in the percentages of the individual components of net income provide information on shifts in management's strategies.

## THE CLOSING PROCESS

■ **LEARNING OBJECTIVE 5**

Explain the closing process.

**PERMANENT (REAL) ACCOUNTS** are the balance sheet accounts that carry their ending balances into the next accounting period.

**TEMPORARY (NOMINAL) ACCOUNTS** are income statement (and sometimes dividends declared) accounts that are closed to Retained Earnings at the end of the accounting period.

**CLOSING ENTRIES** are made at the end of the accounting period to transfer balances in temporary accounts to Retained Earnings and to establish a zero balance in each of the temporary accounts.

**INCOME SUMMARY** is a temporary account used only during the closing process to facilitate closing revenues and expenses.

You will notice in Exhibit 4.3 that a dashed line separates income statement accounts (revenues and expenses) and dividends from the balance sheet accounts (assets, liabilities, and stockholders' equity). The balance sheet accounts are updated continuously throughout the accounting period, and the ending balance for the current period becomes the beginning account balance for the next. These accounts are *not* closed (cleared to a zero balance) periodically; therefore, they are often called **permanent** or **real accounts.** To illustrate, the ending Cash balance of one accounting period must be the beginning Cash balance of the next accounting period. The only time a permanent account has a zero balance is when the item represented is no longer owned or owed.

In contrast, revenue, expense, gain, and loss accounts are often called **temporary** or **nominal accounts** because they are used to accumulate data for the current *accounting period only.* At the end of each period, their balances are transferred, or closed, to the Retained Earnings account. This periodic clearing of the balances of the income statement accounts into Retained Earnings is done by using closing entries.

The process of recording **closing entries** to transfer the balances of all temporary accounts to Retained Earnings is only a clerical phase. Closing entries have two purposes:

1. To transfer net income or loss to Retained Earnings.
2. To establish a zero balance in each of the temporary accounts to start the accumulation in the next accounting period.

Accounts with credit balances are closed by debiting the total amount; accounts with debit balances are closed by crediting the total amount. The other half of the entry is closed directly to Retained Earnings (although companies may close income statement accounts to a special temporary summary account, called **Income Summary,** which is then closed to Retained Earnings). In this way, the income statement accounts are again ready for their temporary accumulation function for the next period.

Referring to Exhibit 4.3, the process involves closing the lowest level of accounts in the model to the permanent account (Retained Earnings):

1. Close each revenue and gain account (income statement accounts with a credit balance) to Retained Earnings.
2. Close each expense and loss account (income statement accounts with a debit balance) to Retained Earnings.

Closing entries are dated the last day of the accounting period, entered in the usual debits-equal-credits format (in the journal), and immediately posted to the ledger (or T-accounts). We illustrate the closing process by preparing the closing entries for Papa John's at January 31, 1999, although most companies close their records only at the end of the fiscal year.

1. Close revenues and gains to Retained Earnings:

| | | |
|---|---|---|
| Restaurant sales revenue | 35,200 | |
| Franchise royalties and development fees | 3,875 | |
| Commissary, equipment, and other sales | 34,500 | |
| Investment income | 455 | |
| Retained earnings | | 74,030 |

2. Close expenses and losses to Retained Earnings:

| | | |
|---|---|---|
| Retained earnings | 64,740 | |
| Cost of sales—restaurants | | 9,600 |
| Salaries and benefits expenses—restaurants | | 9,200 |
| Advertising and related costs | | 2,700 |
| Occupancy costs and other operating expenses—restaurants | | 6,300 |
| Cost of sales—commissaries | | 18,900 |
| Salaries and benefits expenses—commissaries | | 2,500 |
| Other operating expenses—commissaries | | 1,500 |
| General and administrative expenses | | 6,910 |
| Depreciation and amortization expense | | 1,670 |
| Other costs and expenses | | 10 |
| Income tax expense | | 5,450 |

After the closing process is complete, all of the income accounts have a zero balance. These accounts are then ready for recording revenues and expenses in the new accounting period. The ending balance in Retained Earnings now is up-to-date (matches the amount on the balance sheet) and is carried forward as the beginning balance for the next period. As the last step of the accounting information processing cycle, a **post-closing trial balance** (Exhibit 4.4) should be prepared as a check that debits equal credits and that all temporary accounts have been closed.

A **POST-CLOSING TRIAL BALANCE** should be prepared as the last step of the accounting cycle to check that debits equal credits and all temporary accounts have been closed.

EXHIBIT **4.4**

**Post-Closing Trial Balance**

**Papa John's International, Inc. and Subsidiaries**
**Post-Closing Trial Balance**
**At January 31, 1999**
**(dollars in thousands)**

| | | Adjusted | | Post-Closing | |
|---|---|---|---|---|---|
| | | Debit | Credit | Debit | Credit |
| Permanent Accounts | Cash | 55,415 | | 55,415 | |
| | Accounts receivable | 15,450 | | 15,450 | |
| | Inventories (supplies of food, paper products, and equipment) | 10,200 | | 10,200 | |
| | Prepaid expenses | 7,500 | | 7,500 | |
| | Other current assets | 2,430 | | 2,430 | |
| | Investments | 50,300 | | 50,300 | |
| | Property and equipment | 223,100 | | 223,100 | |
| | Accumulated depreciation and amortization | | 49,870 | | 49,870 |
| | Notes receivable | 16,750 | | 16,750 | |
| | Other assets | 22,400 | | 22,400 | |
| | Accounts payable | | 28,100 | | 22,100 |
| | Accrued expenses payable (rent, payroll, and other) | | 29,100 | | 29,100 |
| | Income taxes payable | | 5,450 | | 5,450 |
| | Other current liabilities | | 10 | | 10 |
| | Unearned franchise and development fees | | 6,725 | | 6,725 |
| | Other long-term liabilities (including notes payable) | | 11,200 | | 11,200 |
| | Contributed capital | | 165,800 | | 165,800 |
| | Retained earnings | | 98,000 | | 107,290 |
| Temporary Accounts | Restaurant sales revenue | | 35,200 | | 0 |
| | Franchise royalties and development fees revenue | | 3,875 | | 0 |
| | Commissary, equipment, and other sales revenue | | 34,500 | | 0 |
| | Investment Income | | 455 | | 0 |
| | Cost of sales - restaurants | 9,600 | | 0 | |
| | Salaries and benefits expense - restaurants | 9,200 | | 0 | |
| | Advertising and related costs - restaurants | 2,700 | | 0 | |
| | Occupancy costs and other operating expenses - restaurants | 6,300 | | 0 | |
| | Cost of sales - commissaries, equipment, and other | 18,900 | | 0 | |
| | Salaries and benefits expense - commissaries | 2,500 | | 0 | |
| | Other operating expenses - commissaries | 1,500 | | 0 | |
| | General and administrative expenses | 6,910 | | 0 | |
| | Depreciation and amortization expense | 1,670 | | 0 | |
| | Other costs and expenses | 10 | | 0 | |
| | Income tax expense | 5,450 | | 0 | |
| | Totals | 468,285 | 468,285 | 403,545 | 403,545 |

## THE ACCOUNTING CYCLE AND COMMUNICATION PROCESS

Although the preparation of statements and the closing of books represent the final stage of the formal recordkeeping process, this stage represents only the beginning of the formal process of communicating financial statement information to external users. In the next chapter we take a closer look at the preparation of financial statements and related disclosures that appear in a company's annual report, quarterly reports, and, for public companies, additional reports filed with the Securities and Exchange Commission. We also examine the process by which this and related information is disseminated to professional analysts, investors, and the public.

# DEMONSTRATION **CASE**

We take our final look at the accounting activities of Terrific Lawn Maintenance Corporation by illustrating the activities at the end of the accounting cycle: the adjustment process, financial statement preparation, and the closing process. Chapter 2 presented investing and financing activities, and Chapter 3 presented operating activities. No adjustments had been made to the accounts to reflect all revenues earned and expenses incurred in April, however. The trial balance for Terrific on April 30, 2000, based on the unadjusted balances in Chapter 3 is as follows:

### TERRIFIC LAWN MAINTENANCE CORPORATION
#### Unadjusted Trial Balance
#### At April 30, 2000

| | Debit | Credit |
|---|---|---|
| Cash | 5,060 | |
| Accounts receivable | 1,700 | |
| Prepaid expenses | 300 | |
| Equipment | 4,600 | |
| Accumulated depreciation | | 0 |
| Land | 3,750 | |
| Accounts payable | | 220 |
| Unearned revenue | | 1,600 |
| Notes payable | | 3,700 |
| Accrued utilities payable | | 0 |
| Wages payable | | 0 |
| Interest payable | | 0 |
| Income tax payable | | 0 |
| Contributed capital | | 9,000 |
| Retained earnings | | 0 |
| Mowing revenue | | 5,200 |
| Fuel expense | 410 | |
| Wages expense | 3,900 | |
| Insurance expense | 0 | |
| Utilities expense | 0 | |
| Depreciation expense | 0 | |
| Interest expense | 0 | |
| Income tax expense | 0 | |
| Totals | 19,720 | 19,720 |

In reviewing the trial balance, three deferral accounts (Unearned Revenue, Prepaid Expenses, and Equipment) may need to be adjusted and additional accruals may be necessary related to the interest on Notes Payable, Wages Expense, income taxes, and others. The following information is determined at the end of the accounting cycle:

### Deferrals

a. $1,600 cash received from the city at the beginning of April (recorded as Unearned Revenue) for four months of service (April through July) has been partially earned by the end of April.

b. Insurance costing $300 for six months (April through September) paid by Terrific Lawn at the beginning of April (Prepaid Expenses) has been partially used in April.

c. Mowers, edgers, rakes, and hand tools (equipment) have been used and need to be depreciated. They have a total cost of $4,600 and an estimated useful life of 10 years. No residual value is expected. The company uses straight-line depreciation.

### Accruals

d. Wages have been paid through April 29. Wages earned in April by the employees but not yet paid accrue at $130 per day.

e. An extra telephone line was installed in April. The telephone bill for $52 including hookup and usage charges was received on April 30 and will be paid in May.

f. Interest accrued on the outstanding notes payable at an annual rate of 12 percent. The $3,700 in principal has been outstanding all month.

g. The estimated income tax rate for Terrific Lawn is 35 percent for state and federal income taxes.

### Required:

1. Analyze each deferral and each accrual using the process outlined in this chapter. Include T-accounts for both accruals and deferrals and compute ending balances.

2. Use the adjusted amounts from requirement 1 plus the accounts on the trial balance that did not need to be adjusted to prepare an income statement, statement of stockholders' equity, balance sheet, and statement of cash flows for the month ended April 30, 2000.

3. Prepare closing entries for April 30, 2000.

4. Compute the company's net profit margin for the month.

Now you can check your answers with the following solution to these requirements.


## SUGGESTED SOLUTION

1. Analysis of deferrals and accruals, adjusting entries, and T-accounts:

### Deferrals

(*a*) **$1,600 cash received from the city at the beginning of April (recorded as Unearned Revenue) for four months of service (April through July) has been partially earned by the end of April.**

**Step 1. For deferrals, what entry was made in the past?**

| | | |
|---|---|---|
| Cash (+A) .......................... | 1,600 | |
| Unearned revenue (+L) ............ | | 1,600 |

**Step 2. Draw a timeline and, for deferrals, set up at least two T-accounts (one for the original asset or liability created and one for its related revenue or expense).**

$1,600 ÷ 4 months = $400 earned each month

**Step 3. Record the adjusting journal entry (*AJE*).**

| | April | Month-End | Beyond April |
|---|---|---|---|
| $1,600 received | | | |
| | During the month | 4/30 | |
| | $400 revenue earned | | $1,200 to be earned |

**Unearned Revenue (L)**

| | | 1,600 | Bal. |
|---|---|---|---|
| Earned | 400 | | |
| | | 1,200 | End. |

**Mowing Revenue (R)**

| | 5,200 | Bal. |
|---|---|---|
| | 400 | AJE |
| | 5,600 | End. |

> **4/30—Adjusting Journal Entry**
> Unearned revenue (−L) . . . . . . . . . . . . . . . . . . . 400
> Mowing revenue (+R) . . . . . . . . . . . . . . . . . . . 400
>
> | Assets | = | Liabilities | + | Stockholders' Equity |
> |---|---|---|---|---|
> | | | Unearned revenue −400 | | Mowing revenue +400 |
>
> Equality checks: (1) Debits $400 = Credits $400; (2) the accounting equation is in balance.

**(b)** **Insurance costing $300 for six months (April through September) paid by Terrific Lawn at the beginning of April (prepaid expenses) has been partially used in April.**

Prepaid expense (+A) . . . . . . . . . . . . . . 300
 Cash (−A) . . . . . . . . . . . . . . . . . . . . . 300

| April | Month-End | Beyond April |
|---|---|---|
| $300 paid | | |
| During the month | 4/30 | |
| $50 expense incurred | | $250 to be incurred |

**Prepaid Expenses (A)**

| Bal. | 300 | | |
|---|---|---|---|
| | | 50 | Used |
| End. | 250 | | |

**Insurance Expense (E)**

| Bal. | 0 | |
|---|---|---|
| AJE | 50 | |
| End. | 50 | |

**Step 1.** *For deferrals, what entry was made in the past?*

**Step 2.** *Draw a timeline and, for deferrals, set up at least two T-accounts (one for the original asset or liability created and one for its related revenue or expense).*

$300 ÷ 6 months = $50 per month

**Step 3.** *Record the adjusting journal entry (AJE).*

> **4/30—Adjusting Journal Entry**
> Insurance expense (+E) . . . . . . . . . . . . . . . . . . 50
> Prepaid expenses (−A) . . . . . . . . . . . . . . . . . . 50
>
> | Assets | = | Liabilities | + | Stockholders' Equity |
> |---|---|---|---|---|
> | Prepaid expenses −50 | | | | Insurance expense −50 |
>
> Equality checks: (1) Debits $50 = Credits $50; (2) the accounting equation is in balance.

**(c)** **Mowers, edgers, rakes, and hand tools (equipment) have been used and need to be depreciated. They have a total cost of $4,600 and an estimated useful life of 10 years. No residual value is expected. The company uses straight-line depreciation.**

Lawn equipment (+A) . . . . . . . . . . . . . . 4,600
 Cash (−A) . . . . . . . . . . . . . . . . . . . . . 200
 Notes Payable (+L) . . . . . . . . . . . . . . 4,400

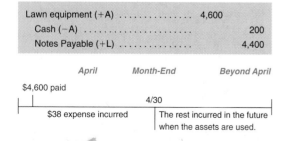

| April | Month-End | Beyond April |
|---|---|---|
| $4,600 paid | | |
| | 4/30 | |
| $38 expense incurred | The rest incurred in the future when the assets are used. | |

**Step 1.** *For deferrals, what entry was made in the past?*

**Step 2.** *Draw a timeline and, for deferrals, set up at least two T-accounts (one for the original asset or liability created and one for its related revenue or expense).*

$4,600 Cost ÷ 10 Years = $460 Annual Depreciation Expense
                        ÷ 12 months
                        $ 38 per Month (rounded)

*Step 3.  Record the adjusting journal entry (AJE).*

**Accumulated Depreciation (XA)**

| | | |
|---|---|---|
| | 0 | Bal. |
| | 38 | Used |
| | 38 | End. |

**Depreciation Expense (E)**

| | | |
|---|---|---|
| Bal. | 0 | |
| AJE | 38 | |
| End. | 38 | |

**4/30—Adjusting Journal Entry**
Depreciation expense (+E) . . . . . . . . . . . . . . . . .   38
    Accumulated depreciation (+XA→−A) . . . . . .       38

| Assets | = | Liabilities | + | Stockholders' Equity |
|---|---|---|---|---|
| Accumulated depreciation   −38 | | | | Depreciation expense   −38 |

Equality checks: (1) Debits $38 = Credits 38; (2) the accounting equation is in balance.

(*d*) **Wages have been paid through April 29. Wages earned in April by the employees but not yet paid accrue at $130 per day.**

*Step 1.  For deferrals, what entry was made in the past?*

This is an accrual; no entry was made.

| April | Month-End | Beyond April |
|---|---|---|
| 1 day worked | 4/30 | |
| $130 expense incurred | | To be paid |

*Step 2.  Draw a timeline and, for deferrals, set up at least two T-accounts (one for the original asset or liability created and one for its related revenue or expense).*

*Step 3.  Record the adjusting journal entry (AJE).*

**Wages Payable (L)**

| | | |
|---|---|---|
| | 0 | Bal. |
| | 130 | Incurred |
| | 130 | End. |

**Wages Expense (E)**

| | | |
|---|---|---|
| Bal. | 3,900 | |
| AJE | 130 | |
| End. | 4,030 | |

**4/30—Adjusting Journal Entry**
Wages expense (+E) . . . . . . . . . . . . . . . . . . . . .   130
    Wages payable (+L) . . . . . . . . . . . . . . . . . . . .       130

| Assets | = | Liabilities | + | Stockholders' Equity |
|---|---|---|---|---|
| | | Wages payable   +130 | | Wages expense   −130 |

Equality checks: (1) Debits $130 = Credits $130; (2) the accounting equation is in balance.

(*e*) **An extra telephone line was installed in April. The telephone bill for $52, including hookup and usage charges, was received on April 30 and will be paid in May.**

*Step 1.  For deferrals, what entry was made in the past?*

This is an accrual; no entry was made.

*Step 2.  Draw a timeline and, for deferrals, set up at least two T-accounts (one for the original asset or liability created and one for its related revenue or expense).*

| April | Month-End | Beyond April |
|---|---|---|
| | 4/30 | |
| $52 expense incurred | | To be paid |

**Accrued Utilities Payable (L)**

|        |    |          |
|--------|----|----------|
|        | 0  | Bal.     |
|        | 52 | Incurred |
|        | 52 | End.     |

**Utilities Expense (E)**

| Bal. | 0  |  |
|------|----|--|
| AJE  | 52 |  |
| End. | 52 |  |

*Step 3. Record the adjusting journal entry (AJE).*

**4/30—Adjusting Journal Entry**

Utilities expense (+E) . . . . . . . . . . . . . . . . . . . . .    52
    Accrued utilities payable (+L) . . . . . . . . . . . .    52

| Assets | = | Liabilities | + | Stockholders' Equity |
|--------|---|-------------|---|----------------------|
|  |  | Accrued utilities payable  +52 | | Utilities expense  −52 |

Equality checks: (1) Debits $52 = Credits $52; (2) the accounting equation is in balance.

(*f*)  **Interest accrued on the outstanding notes payable at an annual rate of 12 percent. The $3,700 in principal has been outstanding all month.**

The notes payable were recorded when signed. The interest incurred has not yet been recorded.

| April | Month-End | Beyond April |
|-------|-----------|--------------|
|       | 4/30      |              |
| $37 expense incurred | | To be paid |

**Interest Payable (L)**

|        |    |          |
|--------|----|----------|
|        | 0  | Bal.     |
|        | 37 | Incurred |
|        | 37 | End.     |

**Interest Expense (E)**

| Bal. | 0  |  |
|------|----|--|
| AJE  | 37 |  |
| End. | 37 |  |

*Step 1. For deferrals, what entry was made in the past?*

*Step 2. Draw a timeline and, for deferrals, set up at least two T-accounts (one for the original asset or liability created and one for its related revenue or expense).*

$3,700 Principal × 0.12 Annual Interest × 1 Month/12 = $37

*Step 3. Record the adjusting journal entry (AJE).*

**4/30—Adjusting Journal Entry**

Interest expense (+E) . . . . . . . . . . . . . . . . . . . . .    37
    Interest payable (+L) . . . . . . . . . . . . . . . . . . .    37

| Assets | = | Liabilities | + | Stockholders' Equity |
|--------|---|-------------|---|----------------------|
|  |  | Interest payable  +37 | | Interest expense  −37 |

Equality checks: (1) Debits $37 = Credits $37; (2) the accounting equation is in balance.

(*g*)  **The estimated income tax rate for Terrific Lawn is 35 percent for state and federal income taxes.**

This is an accrual; no entry has been made.

| April | Month-End | Beyond April |
|-------|-----------|--------------|
|       | 4/30      |              |
| $344 expense incurred | | To be paid |

*Step 1. For deferrals, what entry was made in the past?*

*Step 2. Draw a timeline and, for deferrals, set up at least two T-accounts (one for the original asset or liability created and one for its related revenue or expense).*

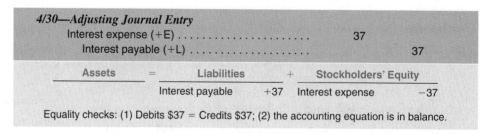

**Chapter 3 Totals + Adjustments**

| All revenues | $5,600 = $5,200 + 400 |
|--------------|------------------------|
| All expenses | −4,617 = 4,310 + 50 + 38 + 130 + 52 + 37 |
| Pretax income $ | 983 × 0.35 tax rate = $344 tax expense (rounded) |

## Step 3. Record the adjusting journal entry (AJE).

**Income Taxes Payable (L)**

| | | | |
|---|---|---|---|
| | | 0 | Bal. |
| | | 344 | Incurred |
| | | 344 | End. |

**Income Tax Expense (E)**

| | | | |
|---|---|---|---|
| Bal. | 0 | | |
| AJE | 344 | | |
| End. | 344 | | |

**4/30—Adjusting Journal Entry**

Income tax expense (+E) .................... 344

    Income taxes payable (+L) ............... 344

| Assets | = | Liabilities | + | Stockholders' Equity |
|---|---|---|---|---|
| | | Income taxes payable   +344 | | Income tax expense   −344 |

Equality checks: (1) Debits $344 = Credits $344; (2) the accounting equation is in balance.

2. Financial statements

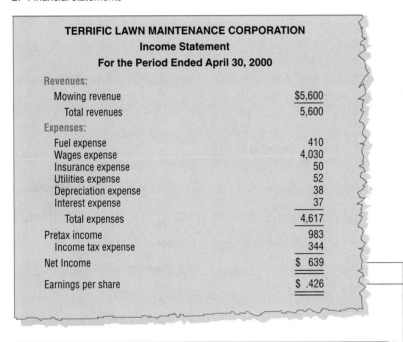

**TERRIFIC LAWN MAINTENANCE CORPORATION**
**Income Statement**
**For the Period Ended April 30, 2000**

Revenues:

| | |
|---|---|
| Mowing revenue | $5,600 |
| Total revenues | 5,600 |

Expenses:

| | |
|---|---|
| Fuel expense | 410 |
| Wages expense | 4,030 |
| Insurance expense | 50 |
| Utilities expense | 52 |
| Depreciation expense | 38 |
| Interest expense | 37 |
| Total expenses | 4,617 |
| Pretax income | 983 |
| Income tax expense | 344 |
| Net Income | $ 639 |
| Earnings per share | $ .426 |

$639 Net Income ÷ 1,500 Shares of Stock

**TERRIFIC LAWN MAINTENANCE CORPORATION**
**Statement of Stockholders' Equity**
**For the Period Ended April 30, 2000**

| | Contributed Capital | Retained Earnings | Total Stockholders' Equity |
|---|---|---|---|
| Beginning balance | $ 0 | $ 0 | $ 0 |
| Stock issuance | 9,000 | | 9,000 |
| Net income | | 639 | 639 |
| Dividends | | 0 | 0 |
| Ending balance | $9,000 | $639 | $9,639 |

To the balance sheet

**TERRIFIC LAWN MAINTENANCE CORPORATION**
**Balance Sheet**
**At April 30, 2000**

| Assets | | | Liabilities | |
|---|---:|---:|---|---:|
| **Current Assets:** | | | **Current Liabilities:** | |
| Cash | | $ 5,060 | Accounts payable | $   220 |
| Accounts receivable | | 1,700 | Unearned revenue | 1,200 |
| Prepaid expenses | | 250 | Wages payable | 130 |
| Total current assets | | 7,010 | Accrued utilities payable | 52 |
| Equipment | $4,600 | | Interest payable | 37 |
| Less: Accumulated depreciation | 38 | 4,562 | Income taxes payable | 344 |
| Land | | 3,750 | Notes payable | 3,700 |
| | | | Total current liabilities | 5,683 |
| | | | **Stockholders' Equity** | |
| | | | Contributed capital | 9,000 |
| | | | Retained earnings | 639 |
| | | | Total stockholders' equity | 9,639 |
| Total assets | | $15,322 | Total liabilities and stockholders' equity | $15,322 |

From the Statement of Shareholders' Equity

**TERRIFIC LAWN MAINTENANCE CORPORATION**
**Statement of Cash Flows**
**For the Month Ended April 30, 2000**

| | | |
|---|---|---:|
| **Operating Activities** | | |
| Cash from: | Customers | $5,100 |
| Cash to: | Suppliers | (490) |
| | Employees | (3,900) |
| Net cash provided by operating activities | | 710 |
| **Investing Activities** | | |
| Purchased land | | $(5,000) |
| Purchased equipment | | (200) |
| Received payment on notes receivable | | 1,250 |
| Net cash used in investing activities | | (3,950) |
| **Financing Activities** | | |
| Issued common stock | | 9,000 |
| Payments on borrowings | | (700) |
| Net cash provided by financing activities | | 8,300 |
| Change in cash | | 5,060 |
| Beginning cash balance | | 0 |
| **Ending cash balance** | | **$ 5,060** |

**Supplemental Disclosure:** No interest or income taxes were paid. There were no significant noncash transactions.

3. Closing entries
   The closing entries follow:

a. Close revenues and gains to Retained Earnings:

| | | |
|---|---:|---:|
| Mowing revenue (−R) | 5,600 | |
| Retained earnings (+SE) | | 5,600 |

*b.* Close expenses and losses to Retained Earnings:

| | | |
|---|---:|---:|
| Retained earnings (−SE) | 4,961 | |
| Fuel expense (−E) | | 410 |
| Wages expense (−E) | | 4,030 |
| Insurance expense (−E) | | 50 |
| Utilities expense (−E) | | 52 |
| Depreciation expense (−E) | | 38 |
| Interest expense (−E) | | 37 |
| Income tax expense (−E) | | 344 |

When these entries are posted to the temporary accounts, all now have zero balances to begin accumulating amounts for May activities.

4. Net Profit Margin:

$$\frac{\text{Net Income}}{\text{Net Sales}} = \$639 \div \$5,600 = 11.41\% \text{ for the month of April.}$$

# CHAPTER **TAKE-AWAYS**

1. **Explain the purpose of a trial balance.   p. 168**
   A trial balance is a list of all accounts with their debit or credit balances indicated in the appropriate column to provide a check on the equality of the debits and credits. The trial balance may be

   • Unadjusted—before adjustments are made.
   • Adjusted—after adjustments are made.
   • Post-closing—after revenues and expenses are closed to Retained Earnings.

2. **Analyze the adjustments necessary at the end of the period to update balance sheet and income statements accounts.   p. 170**
   • Adjusting entries are necessary at the end of the accounting period to measure income properly, correct errors, and provide for adequate valuation of balance sheet accounts. The analysis involves

   (1) Identifying deferrals (accounts created in the past when cash was received or paid before being earned or incurred) and accruals (revenues earned and expenses incurred before cash is to be received in the future).
   (2) Drawing a timeline and setting up at least two T-accounts with relevant dates, amounts, and any computations included for each deferral or accrual.
   (3) Recording the adjusting entry needed to obtain the appropriate ending balances in the accounts.

   The effect is summarized as follows:

   • Recording adjusting entries has no effect on the Cash account.

3. **Present a complete set of financial statements: Income statement with earnings per share, statement of stockholders' equity, balance sheet, and statement of cash flows. p. 185**
   Adjusted account balances are used in preparing the following financial statements:

   • Income Statement → Revenues − Expenses = Net Income (including earnings per share computed as net income available to the common stockholders divided by the weighted-average number of shares of common stock outstanding during the period).
   • Statement of Stockholders' Equity → (Beginning Contributed Capital + Stock Issuances − Stock Repurchases) + (Beginning Retained Earnings + Net Income − Dividends) = Ending Total Stockholders' Equity.
   • Balance Sheet → Assets = Liabilities + Stockholders' Equity.
   • Statement of Cash Flows → Change in Cash = Cash Flows from Operating Activities +/− Cash Flows from Investing Activities +/− Cash Flows from Financing Activities.

4. **Compute and interpret net profit margin. p. 191**

Net profit margin (Net Income ÷ Net Sales) measures how much of every dollar of sales generated during the period is profit. A rising net profit margin signals more efficient management of sales and expenses.

5. **Explain the closing process. p. 192**

Temporary accounts (revenues, expenses, gains, and losses) are closed to a zero balance at the end of the accounting period to allow for the accumulation of income items in the following period. To close these accounts:

- Debit each revenue and gain account to Retained Earnings (a credit).
- Credit each expense and loss account to Retained Earnings (a debit).

This chapter discussed the important steps in of the accounting process that take place at year-end. These include the adjustment process, the preparation of the four basic financial statements, and the closing process, which prepares the records for the next accounting period. This end to the internal portions of the accounting process, however, is just the beginning of the process of communicating accounting information to external users. In Chapter 5 we discuss the important players in this communication process, the many statement format choices available, the additional note disclosures required for both private and public companies, and the process, manner, and timing of the transmission of this information to users. At the same time, we discuss common uses of the information in investment analysis, debt contracts, and management compensation decisions. These discussions will help you consolidate much of what you have learned about the financial reporting process from previous chapters. It will also preview many of the important issues we will address later in the book.

## KEY **RATIO**

> **Net profit margin** measures how much of every sales dollar generated during the period is profit. A high or rising ratio suggests that the company is managing its sales and expenses efficiently. It is computed as follows (p. 191):
>
> $$\text{Net Profit Margin} = \frac{\text{Net Income}}{\text{Net Sales}}$$

## FINDING FINANCIAL INFORMATION

**BALANCE SHEET**

| *Current Assets* | *Current Liabilities* |
|---|---|
| Accruals include | Accruals include |
|   Interest receivable |   Interest payable |
|   Rent receivable |   Wages payable |
| Deferrals include |   Utilities payable |
|   Inventory |   Income tax |
|   Prepaid expenses |     payable |
| *Noncurrent Assets* | Deferrals include |
| Deferrals include |   Deferred revenue |
|   Property and | |
|     equipment | |
|   Intangibles | |

**INCOME STATEMENT**

*Revenues*
  Increased by adjusting entries
*Expenses*
  Increased by adjusting entries
*Pretax Income*
  Income tax expense
*Net Income*

**STATEMENT OF CASH FLOWS**

*Adjusting Entries Do Not Affect Cash*
  Interest paid
  Income taxes paid
  Significant noncash transactions

**NOTES**

*In Various Notes if Not on the Balance Sheet*
  Details of accrued expenses payable
  Interest paid, income taxes paid, significant noncash transactions (if not reported on the statement of cash flows)

## KEY **TERMS**

Accounting Cycle  p. 166

Accrued Revenues and Expenses  p. 171

Adjusting Entries  p. 170

Book Value (Net Book Value, Carrying Value)  p. 169

Closing Entries  p. 192

Contra-Account  p. 169

Deferred Revenues and Expenses  p. 170

Income Summary  p. 192

Permanent (Real) Accounts  p. 192

Post-Closing Trial Balance  p. 193

Temporary (Nominal) Accounts  p. 192

Trial Balance  p. 168

## QUESTIONS

1. Explain the accounting information processing cycle.
2. Identify, in sequence, the phases of the accounting information processing cycle.
3. What is a trial balance? What is its purpose?
4. Briefly explain adjusting entries. List the four types of adjusting entries, and give an example of each type.
5. Explain estimated residual value. Why is it important in measuring depreciation expense?
6. What is a contra-asset? Give an example of one.
7. Explain why adjusting entries are entered in the journal on the last day of the accounting period and then are posted to the ledger.
8. Explain how the financial statements relate to each other.
9. What is the equation for each of the following statements: (a) income statement, (b) balance sheet, (c) statement of cash flows, and (d) statement of stockholders' equity?
10. Explain the effect of adjusting entries on cash.
11. How is earnings per share computed and interpreted?
12. How is net profit margin computed and interpreted?
13. Contrast an unadjusted trial balance with an adjusted trial balance. What is the purpose of each?
14. What is the purpose of closing entries? Why are they recorded in the journal and posted to the ledger?
15. Differentiate among (a) permanent, (b) temporary, (c) real, and (d) nominal accounts.
16. Why are the income statement accounts closed but the balance sheet accounts are not?
17. What is a post-closing trial balance? Is it a useful part of the accounting information processing cycle? Explain.

## MINI-EXERCISES

**M4–1**  **Preparing a Trial Balance**                                                                      ■ LO1

Swanson Company has the following adjusted accounts and balances at year-end (June 30, 20B):

| | | | | | |
|---|---|---|---|---|---|
| Accounts payable | 200 | Contributed capital | 300 | Long-term debt | 1,300 |
| Accounts receivable | 350 | Cost of sales | 820 | Prepaid expenses | 40 |
| Accrued expenses payable | 150 | Depreciation expense | 110 | Salaries expense | 660 |
| | | Income taxes expense | 110 | Sales revenue | 2,400 |
| Accumulated depreciation | 250 | Income taxes payable | 30 | Rent expense | 400 |
| | | Interest expense | 80 | Retained earnings | 120 |
| Buildings and equipment | 1,400 | Interest income | 50 | Unearned fees | 100 |
| Cash | 120 | Inventories | 610 | | |
| | | Land | 200 | | |

*Required:*

Prepare an adjusted trial balance in good form for the Swanson Company at June 30, 20B.

**M4–2**  **Matching Definitions with Terms**                                                              ■ LO2

Match each definition with its related term by entering the appropriate letter in the space provided.

| | Definition | Term |
|---|---|---|
| _D_ 1. | A revenue not yet earned; collected in advance. | A. Accrued expense |
| _B_ 2. | Office supplies on hand to be used next accounting period. | B. Deferred expense |
| _D_ 3. | Rent revenue collected; not yet earned. | C. Accrued revenue |
| _C_ 4. | Rent not yet collected; already earned. | D. Deferred revenue |
| _A_ 5. | An expense incurred; not yet paid or recorded. | |
| _C_ 6. | A revenue earned; not yet collected. | |
| _B_ 7. | An expense not yet incurred; paid in advance. | |
| _A_ 8. | Property taxes incurred; not yet paid. | |

**LO2**    **M4–3**    **Matching Definitions with Terms**

Match each definition with its related term by entering the appropriate letter in the space provided.

| | Definition | Term |
|---|---|---|
| _____ 1. | At year-end, wages payable of $3,600 had not been recorded or paid. | A. Accrued expense |
| | | B. Deferred expense |
| _____ 2. | Supplies for office use were purchased during the year for $500, and $100 of the office supplies remained on hand (unused) at year-end. | C. Accrued revenue |
| | | D. Deferred revenue |
| _____ 3. | Interest of $250 on a note receivable was earned at year-end, although collection of the interest is not due until the following year. | |
| _____ 4. | At year-end, service revenue of $2,000 was collected in cash but was not yet earned. | |

**LO2**    **M4–4**    **Recording Adjusting Entries (Deferral Accounts)**

For each of the following transactions for Liner Company, give the adjusting entry required for the year ended December 31, 20C, using the process illustrated in the chapter:

a. Collected $900 rent for the period December 1, 20C, to March 1, 20D, which was credited to Deferred Rent Revenue on December 1, 20C.

b. Paid $2,400 for a two-year insurance premium on July 1, 20C; debited Prepaid Insurance for that amount.

c. Purchased a machine for $12,000 cash on January 1, 20A; estimated a useful life of five years with a residual value of $2,000.

**LO2**    **M4–5**    **Determining Financial Statement Effects of Adjusting Entries (Deferral Accounts)**

For each of the transactions in M4–4, indicate the amounts and direction of effects of the adjusting entry on the elements of the balance sheet and income statement. Using the following format, indicate + for increase, − for decrease, and NE for no effect.

| | Balance Sheet | | | Income Statement | | |
|---|---|---|---|---|---|---|
| Transaction | Assets | Liabilities | Stockholders' Equity | Revenues | Expenses | Net Income |
| a. | NE | − 300 | + 300 | +300 | NE | + 300 |
| b. | − 600 | NE | − 600 | NE | + 600 | − 600 |
| c. | − 2000 | NE | − 2000 | NE | + 2000 | − 2000 |

**LO2**    **M4–6**    **Recording Adjusting Entries (Accrual Accounts)**

For each of the following transactions for Liner Company, give the adjusting entry required for the year ended December 31, 20C, using the process illustrated in the chapter:

a. Received a $220 utility bill for electricity usage in December to be paid in January 20D.

b. Owed wages to 10 employees who worked three days at $120 each per day at the end of December. The company will pay employees at the end of the first week of January 20D.

c. On September 1, 20C, loaned $3,000 to an officer who will repay the loan in one year at an annual interest rate of 12 percent.

**M4–7** **Determining Financial Statement Effects of Adjusting Entries (Accrual Accounts)** ▪ LO2
For each of the transactions in M4–6, indicate the amounts and direction of effects of the
adjusting entry on the elements of the balance sheet and income statement. Using the
following format, indicate + for increase, − for decrease, and NE for no effect.

| | Balance Sheet | | | Income Statement | | |
|---|---|---|---|---|---|---|
| Transaction | Assets | Liabilities | Stockholders' Equity | Revenues | Expenses | Net Income |
| a. | NE | + 200 | −220 | NE | + 220 | − 220 |
| b. | NE | +3600 | − 3600 | NE | +3600 | − 3600 |
| c. | +120 | NE | +120 | +120 | NE | +120 |

**M4–8** **Reporting an Income Statement with Earnings per Share** ▪ LO3
Liner Company has the following adjusted trial balance at December 31, 20C. No dividends
were declared; however, 400 additional shares were issued during the year for $2,000:

| | Debit | Credit |
|---|---|---|
| Cash | $ 1,500 | |
| Accounts receivable | 2,000 | |
| Interest receivable | 120 | |
| Prepaid insurance | 1,800 | |
| Notes receivable | 3,000 | |
| Equipment | 12,000 | |
| Accumulated depreciation | | $ 2,000 |
| Accounts payable | | 1,600 |
| Accrued expenses payable | | 3,820 |
| Income taxes payable | | 2,900 |
| Deferred rent revenue | | 600 |
| Contributed capital (500 shares) | | 2,400 |
| Retained earnings | | 1,000 |
| R Sales revenue | | 42,000 |
| R Interest revenue | | 120 |
| R Rent revenue | | 300 |
| E Wages expense | 21,600 | |
| E Depreciation expense | 2,000 | |
| E Utilities expense | 220 | |
| E Insurance expense | 600 | |
| E Rent expense | 9,000 | |
| E Income tax expense | 2,900 | |
| Total | $56,740 | $56,740 |

Prepare an income statement in good form for 20C. Include earnings per share.

**M4–9** **Reporting a Statement of Stockholders' Equity** ▪ LO3
Refer to M4–8. Prepare a statement of stockholders' equity in good form for 20C.

**M4–10** **Reporting a Balance Sheet and Explaining the Effects of Adjustments on the Statement** ▪ LO3
**of Cash Flows**
Refer to M4–8. Prepare a classified balance sheet in good form at December 31, 20C. Then
explain how the adjustments in M4–4 and M4–6 affected the operating, investing, and
financing activities on the statement of cash flows.

**M4–11** **Analyzing Net Profit Margin** ▪ LO4
Compute net income based on the trial balance in M4–8. Then compute Liner Company's net
profit margin for the year.

**M4–12** **Recording Closing Entries** ▪ LO5
Refer to the adjusted trial balance in M4–8. Prepare closing entries on December 31, 20C.

# EXERCISES

**LO1**     **E4–1**     **Preparing a Trial Balance**

Latta Marketing Consultants, Inc., provides marketing research for clients in the retail industry. The company had the following unadjusted balances at September 30, 20A:

| Accumulated Depreciation | | Accrued Expenses Payable | |
|---|---|---|---|
| | 18,100 | | 25,650 |

| Cash | | General and Administrative Expense | | Supplies Inventory | |
|---|---|---|---|---|---|
| 173,000 | | 320,050 | | 12,200 | |

| Wages and Benefits Expense | | Prepaid Expenses | | Interest Expense | |
|---|---|---|---|---|---|
| 1,590,000 | | 10,200 | | 17,200 | |

| Accounts Receivable | | Consulting Fees Earned | | Retained Earnings | |
|---|---|---|---|---|---|
| 225,400 | | | 2,564,200 | | ? |

| Income Taxes Payable | | Travel Expense | | Building and Equipment | |
|---|---|---|---|---|---|
| | 2,030 | 23,990 | | 323,040 | |

| Utilities Expense | | Gain on Sale of Land | | Unearned Consulting Fees | |
|---|---|---|---|---|---|
| 25,230 | | | 5,000 | | 32,500 |

| Investment Income | | Accounts Payable | | Land | |
|---|---|---|---|---|---|
| | 10,800 | | 86,830 | 60,000 | |

| Other Operating Expenses | | Contributed Capital | | Professional Development Expense | |
|---|---|---|---|---|---|
| 188,000 | | | 233,370 | 18,600 | |

| Notes Payable | | Rent Expense (on leased computers) | | Investments | |
|---|---|---|---|---|---|
| | 160,000 | 152,080 | | 145,000 | |

*Required:*

Prepare in good form an unadjusted trial balance for Latta Marketing Consultants, Inc., at September 30, 20A.

**LO1, 2**     **E4–2**     **Identifying Adjusting Entries from Unadjusted Trial Balance**

Compaq Computer Corporation

As stated in its annual report, "Compaq Computer Corporation is a global information technology company, developing and marketing hardware, software, solutions, and services." Following is a trial balance listing accounts that Compaq uses. Assume that the balances are unadjusted at the end of a recent fiscal year ended December 31.

**COMPAQ COMPUTER CORPORATION**
**Unadjusted Trial Balance**
**At December 31, 20A**
**(millions of dollars)**

| | Debit | Credit |
|---|---|---|
| Cash | $ 4,091 | |
| Accounts receivable | 6,998 | |
| Inventories | 2,005 | |
| Prepaid expenses | 624 | |
| Property, plant, and equipment | 5,223 | |
| Accumulated depreciation | | $ 2,321 |
| Intangible assets | 3,641 | |
| Other assets | 3,414 | |
| Accounts payable | | 4,237 |
| Accrued liabilities | | 1,110 |
| Income taxes payable | | 282 |
| Pension obligations | | 545 |
| Other liabilities | | 5,104 |

*continued*

|                                              | Debit   | Credit  |
|----------------------------------------------|---------|---------|
| Contributed capital                          |         | 7,270   |
| Retained earnings                            |         | 8,633   |
| Product revenue                              |         | 27,372  |
| Services revenue                             |         | 3,797   |
| Cost of products sold                        | 21,383  |         |
| Cost of services sold                        | 2,597   |         |
| Selling, general and administrative expenses | 4,978   |         |
| Research and development costs               | 1,353   |         |
| Other operating expenses                     | 4,283   |         |
| Income tax expense                           | 81      |         |
|                                              | $60,671 | $60,671 |

*Required:*

1. Based on the information in the unadjusted trial balance, list the balance sheet deferral accounts that may need to be adjusted at December 31 and the related account for each (no computations are necessary).

2. Based on the information in the unadjusted trial balance, list the balance sheet accrual accounts that may need to be recorded at December 31 and the related account for each (no computations are necessary).

**E4–3 Recording Adjusting Entries**　　　　　　　　　　　　　　　　　　　　　■ **LO2**

Evans Company completed its first year of operations on December 31, 20A. All of the 20A entries have been recorded, except for the following:

*a.* At year-end, employees earned wages of $6,000, which will be paid on the next payroll date, January 6, 20B.

*b.* At year-end, the company had earned interest revenue of $3,000. The cash will be collected March 1, 20B.

*Required:*

1. What is the annual reporting period for this company?

2. Identify whether each transaction is a deferral or an accrual. Using the process illustrated in the chapter, give the required adjusting entry for transactions (*a*) and (*b*). Include appropriate dates and write a brief explanation of each entry.

3. Why are these adjustments made?

**E4–4 Recording Adjusting Entries and Reporting Balances in Financial Statements**　　　■ **LO2, 3**

Jenson Company is making adjusting entries for the year ended December 31, 20B. In developing information for the adjusting entries, the accountant learned the following:

*a.* Paid a two-year insurance premium of $7,200 on September 1, 20B for coverage beginning on that date.

*b.* At December 31, 20B, obtained the following data relating to shipping supplies from the records and supporting documents. The company uses a large amount of shipping supplies purchased in volume, stored, and used as needed.

| | |
|---|---|
| Shipping supplies on hand, January 1, 20B | $15,000 |
| Purchases of shipping supplies during 20B | 72,000 |
| Shipping supplies on hand, per inventory December 31, 20B | 11,000 |

*Required:*

1. What amount should be reported on the 20B income statement for Insurance Expense? For Shipping Supplies Expense?

2. What amount should be reported on the December 31, 20B, balance sheet for Prepaid Insurance? For Shipping Supplies Inventory?

3. Using the process illustrated in the chapter, record the adjusting entry at December 31, 20B, assuming that the premium was paid on September 1, 20B, and the bookkeeper debited the full amount to Prepaid Insurance.

4. Using the process illustrated in the chapter, record the adjusting entry at December 31, 20B, assuming that the purchases of shipping supplies were debited in full to Shipping Supplies Inventory.

**LO2, 3**   **E4–5**   **Determining Financial Statement Effects of Adjusting Entries**
Refer to E4–3 and E4–4.

*Required:*
For each of the transactions in E4–3 and E4–4, indicate the amount and direction of effects of the adjusting entry on the elements of the balance sheet and income statement. Using the following format, indicate + for increase, − for decrease, and NE for no effect.

| | Balance Sheet | | | Income Statement | | |
|---|---|---|---|---|---|---|
| Transaction | Assets | Liabilities | Stockholders' Equity | Revenues | Expenses | Net Income |
| E4–3 (a) | | | | | | |
| E4–3 (b) | | | | | | |
| E4–4 (a) | | | | | | |
| E4–4 (b) | | | | | | |

**LO2**   **E4–6**   **Recording Seven Typical Adjusting Entries**
Crawford's Department Store is completing the accounting process for the year just ended, December 31, 20B. The transactions during 20B have been journalized and posted. The following data with respect to adjusting entries are available:

a. Office supplies inventory at January 1, 20B, was $250. Office supplies purchased and debited to Office Supplies Inventory during the year amounted to $600. The year-end inventory showed $300 of supplies on hand.

b. Wages earned during December 20B, unpaid and unrecorded at December 31, 20B, amounted to $2,700. The last payroll was December 28; the next payroll will be January 6, 20C.

c. Three-fourths of the basement of the store is rented for $1,100 per month to another merchant, M. Riesman. Riesman sells compatible, but not competitive, merchandise. On November 1, 20B, the store collected six months' rent in the amount of $6,600 in advance from Riesman; it was credited in full to Unearned Rent Revenue when collected.

d. The remaining basement space is rented to Rita's Specialty Shop for $520 per month, payable monthly. On December 31, 20B, the rent for November and December 20B was not collected or recorded. Collection is expected January 10, 20C.

e. The store used delivery equipment that cost $30,000 and was estimated to have a useful life of four years and a residual value of $6,000 at the end of the four years. Assume depreciation for a full year for 20B. The asset will be depreciated evenly over its useful life.

f. On July 1, 20B, a two-year insurance premium amounting to $3,000 was paid in cash and debited in full to Prepaid Insurance. Coverage began on July 1, 20B.

g. Crawford's operates an alteration shop to meet its own needs. The shop also does alterations for M. Riesman. At the end of December 31, 20B, Riesman had not paid for alterations completed amounting to $750. This amount has not yet been recorded as Alteration Shop Revenue. Collection is expected during January 20C.

*Required:*
1. Identify each of these transactions as a deferred revenue, deferred expense, accrued revenue, or accrued expense.

2. Using the process illustrated in the chapter, record for each situation the adjusting entry that should be recorded for Crawford's at December 31, 20B.

**E4–7** **Determining Financial Statement Effects of Seven Typical Adjusting Entries**
Refer to E4–6.

■ **LO2, 3**

*Required:*
For each of the transactions in E4–6, indicate the amount and direction of effects of the
adjusting entry on the elements of the balance sheet and income statement. Using the
following format, indicate + for increase, − for decrease, and NE for no effect.

| | Balance Sheet | | | Income Statement | | |
|---|---|---|---|---|---|---|
| Transaction | Assets | Liabilities | Stockholders' Equity | Revenues | Expenses | Net Income |
| a. | −550 | NE | − 550 | NE | +550 | −550 |
| b. | NE | +2700 | −2700 | NE | + | −2700 |
| c. | NE | −2200 | +2200 | +2200 | NE | +2200 |
| d. | +1040 | NE | +1040 | +1040 | NE | +1040 |

**E4–8** **Recording Transactions Including Adjusting and Closing Entries (Nonquantitative)**
The following accounts are used by Kelsey's Kitchen, Inc.

■ **LO2, 5**

| Codes | Accounts | Codes | Accounts |
|---|---|---|---|
| A | Cash | J | Contributed capital |
| B | Office supplies inventory | K | Retained earnings |
| C | Revenue receivable | L | Service revenue |
| D | Office equipment | M | Interest revenue |
| E | Accumulated depreciation | N | Wage expense |
| F | Note payable | O | Depreciation expense |
| G | Wages payable | P | Interest expense |
| H | Interest payable | Q | Supplies expense |
| I | Unearned service revenue | R | None of the above |

*Required:*
For each of the following nine independent situations, give the journal entry by entering the
appropriate code(s) and amount(s).

| | Independent Situations | Debit Code | Debit Amount | Credit Code | Credit Amount |
|---|---|---|---|---|---|
| a. | Accrued wages, unrecorded and unpaid at year-end, $400 (example). | N | 400 | G | 400 |
| b. | Service revenue collected in advance, $800. | A I | 800 | L I | 800 |
| c. | Dividends declared and paid during year, $900. | K | 900 | A | 900 |
| d. | Depreciation expense for year, $1,000. | O | 1000 | E | 1000 |
| e. | Service revenue earned but not yet collected at year-end, $600. | C | 600 | L | 600 |
| f. | Office Supplies Inventory account at beginning of the year, $400; inventory of supplies on hand at year-end, $150. | Q | 250 | B | 250 |
| g. | At year-end, interest on note payable not yet recorded or paid, $220. | P | 220 | H | 220 |
| h. | Balance at year-end in Service Revenue account, $62,000. Give the closing entry at year-end. | | | | |
| i. | Balance at year-end in Interest Expense account, $420. Give the closing entry at year-end. | | | | |

**LO2, 3**

**E4–9** **Determining Financial Statement Effects of Three Adjusting Entries**

Oklahoma Company started operations on January 1, 20A. It is now December 31, 20A, the end of the annual accounting period. The part-time bookkeeper needs your help to analyze the following three transactions:

a. On January 1, 20A, the company purchased a special machine for a cash cost of $12,000. The machine has an estimated useful life of 10 years and no residual value.

b. During 20A, the company purchased office supplies that cost $1,400. At the end of 20A, office supplies of $400 remained on hand.

c. On July 1, 20A, the company paid cash of $400 for a two-year premium on an insurance policy on the machine that begins coverage on July 1, 20A.

*Required:*
Complete the following schedule of the amounts that should be reported for 20A:

| Selected Balance Sheet Amounts at December 31, 20A | Amount to Be Reported |
|---|---|
| *Assets* | |
| Equipment | $ 12,000 |
| − Accumulated depreciation | 1,200 |
| = Carrying value of equipment | 10,800 |
| Office supplies inventory | 400 |
| Prepaid insurance | 300 |
| **Selected Income Statement Amounts for the Year Ended December 31, 20A** | |
| *Expenses* | |
| Depreciation expense | $ 1,200 |
| Office supplies expense | 1,000 |
| Insurance expense | 100 |

**LO2, 3**

**E4–10** **Determining Financial Statement Effects of Adjustments for Interest on Two Notes**

**Note 1:** On April 1, 20B, Barken Corporation received a $10,000, 10 percent note from a customer in settlement of a $10,000 open account receivable. According to the terms, the principal of the note and interest are payable at the end of 12 months. The annual accounting period for Barken ends on December 31, 20B.

**Note 2:** On August 1, 20B, to meet a cash shortage, Barken Corporation obtained a $20,000, 12 percent loan from a local bank. The principal of the note and interest expense are payable at the end of 12 months.

*Required:*
For the relevant transaction dates of each note, indicate the amounts and direction of effects on the elements of the balance sheet and income statement. Using the following format, indicate + for increase, − for decrease, and NE for no effect. (*Reminder:* Assets = Liabilities + Stockholders' Equity; Revenues − Expenses = Net Income; and Net Income accounts are closed to Retained Earnings, a part of Stockholders' Equity.)

| | | Balance Sheet | | | Income Statement | | |
|---|---|---|---|---|---|---|---|
| Date | Transaction | Assets | Liabilities | Stockholders' Equity | Revenues | Expenses | Net Income |
| April 1, 20B | Receipt of Note 1 | | | | | | |
| December 31, 20B | Adjustment for Note 1 | | | | | | |
| March 31, 20C | Collection of Note 1 | | | | | | |
| August 1, 20B | Borrowing on Note 2 | | | | | | |
| December 31, 20B | Adjustment for Note 2 | | | | | | |
| July 31, 20C | Payment on Note 2 | | | | | | |

**E4–11 Inferring Transactions**

**LO2**

Deere & Company

Deere & Company is the world's leading producer of agricultural equipment; a leading supplier of a broad range of industrial equipment for construction, forestry, and public works; a producer and marketer of a broad line of lawn and grounds care equipment; and a provider of credit, managed health care plans, and insurance products for businesses and the general public. The following information was from a recent annual report (in millions of dollars):

| Income Taxes Payable | | | | Dividends Payable | | | | Interest Payable | | |
|---|---|---|---|---|---|---|---|---|---|---|
| | | Beg. bal. | 71 | | | Beg. bal. | 43 | | Beg. bal. | 45 |
| (a) | ? | (b) | 332 | (c) | ? | (d) | 176 | (e) 297 | (f) | ? |
| | | End. bal. | 80 | | | End. bal. | 48 | | End. bal. | 51 |

*Required:*

1. Identify the nature of each of the transactions (a) through (f). Specifically, what activities cause the accounts to increase and decrease?

2. For transactions (a), (c), and (f), compute the amount.

**E4–12 Analyzing the Effects of Errors on Financial Statement Items**

**LO2, 3**

Campbell and Long, Inc., publishers of movie and song trivia books, made the following errors in adjusting the accounts at year-end (December 31):

a. Did not record depreciation on the equipment costing $130,000 ($30,000 residual value, 10-year useful life).

b. Failed to adjust the Unearned Revenue account to reflect that $3,000 was earned by the end of the year.

c. Recorded a full year of accrued interest expense on a $15,000, 12 percent note payable that has been outstanding only since November 1.

d. Failed to adjust Insurance Expense to reflect that $400 related to future insurance coverage.

e. Did not accrue $750 owed to the company by another company renting part of the building as a storage facility.

*Required:*

1. For each error, prepare the adjusting journal entry (a) that was made, if any, and (b) that should have been made at year-end.

2. Using the following headings, indicate the effect of each error and the amount of the effect (that is, the difference between the entry that was or was not made and the entry that should have been made). Use O if the effect overstates the item, U if the effect understates the item, and NE if there is no effect. (*Reminder:* Assets = Liabilities + Stockholders' Equity; Revenues − Expenses = Net Income; and Net Income accounts are closed to Retained Earnings, a part of Stockholders' Equity.)

| | Balance Sheet | | | Income Statement | | |
|---|---|---|---|---|---|---|
| Transaction | Assets | Liabilities | Stockholders' Equity | Revenues | Expenses | Net Income |
| a. | | | | | | |
| b. | | | | | | |
| c. | | | | | | |
| etc. | | | | | | |

**E4–13 Analyzing the Effects of Adjusting Entries on the Income Statement and Balance Sheet**

**LO2, 3**

On December 31, 20B, Cohen and Company prepared an income statement and balance sheet and failed to take into account four adjusting entries. The income statement, prepared on this incorrect basis, reflected pretax income of $30,000. The balance sheet (before the effect of income taxes) reflected total assets, $90,000; total liabilities, $40,000; and stockholders' equity, $50,000. The data for the four adjusting entries follow:

a. Depreciation for the year on equipment that cost $85,000 was not recorded; estimated useful life, 10 years; residual value, $5,000.

b. Wages amounting to $17,000 for the last three days of December 20B were not paid and not recorded (the next payroll will be on January 10, 20C).

c. Rent revenue of $4,800 was collected on December 1, 20B, for office space for the period December 1, 20B, to February 28, 20C. The $4,800 was credited in full to Unearned Rent Revenue when collected.

d. Income taxes were not recorded. The income tax rate for the company is 30 percent.

***Required:***

Complete the following tabulation to correct the financial statements for the effects of the four errors (indicate deductions with parentheses):

| Items | Net Income | Total Assets | Total Liabilities | Stockholders' Equity |
|---|---|---|---|---|
| Balances reported | $30,000 | $90,000 | $40,000 | $50,000 |
| Effect of depreciation | _____ | _____ | _____ | _____ |
| Effect of wages | _____ | _____ | _____ | _____ |
| Effect of rent revenue | _____ | _____ | _____ | _____ |
| Adjusted balances | _____ | _____ | _____ | _____ |
| Effect of income taxes | _____ | _____ | _____ | _____ |
| Correct balances | _____ | _____ | _____ | _____ |

**■ LO2, 3**　**E4–14**　**Recording the Effects of Adjusting Entries and Reporting a Corrected Income Statement and Balance Sheet**

On December 31, 20C, the bookkeeper for Mesley Company prepared the following income statement and balance sheet summarized here but neglected to consider three adjusting entries.

| | As Prepared | Effects of Adjusting Entries | Corrected Amounts |
|---|---|---|---|
| **Income Statement** | | | |
| Revenues | $98,000 | _____ | _____ |
| Expenses | (72,000) | _____ | _____ |
| Income tax expense | _____ | _____ | _____ |
| Net income | $26,000 | | _____ |
| **Balance Sheet** | | | |
| **Assets** | | | |
| Cash | $20,000 | _____ | _____ |
| Accounts receivable | 22,000 | _____ | _____ |
| Rent receivable | | _____ | _____ |
| Equipment | 50,000 | _____ | _____ |
| Accumulated depreciation | (10,000) | _____ | _____ |
| | $82,000 | _____ | _____ |
| **Liabilities** | | | |
| Accounts payable | $10,000 | _____ | _____ |
| Income taxes payable | | _____ | _____ |
| **Stockholders' Equity** | | | |
| Contributed capital | 40,000 | _____ | _____ |
| Retained earnings | 32,000 | _____ | _____ |
| | $82,000 | | _____ |

Data on the three adjusting entries follow:

a. Depreciation on the equipment for 20C was not recorded; estimated useful life is 10 years with no residual value.

b. Rent revenue of $2,000 earned for December 20C was neither collected nor recorded.

c. Income tax expense for 20C was neither paid nor recorded; the amount was $6,900.

*Required:*

1. Prepare the three adjusting entries that were omitted. Use the account titles shown in the income statement and balance sheet data.

2. Complete the two columns to the right in the preceding tabulation to show the correct amounts on the income statement and balance sheet.

**E4–15** **Reporting a Correct Income Statement with Earnings per Share to Include the Effects of Adjusting Entries and Evaluating the Net Profit Margin as an Auditor**

■ **LO2, 3, 4**

Barton, Inc., completed its first year of operations on December 31, 20A. Because this is the end of the annual accounting period, the company bookkeeper prepared the following tentative income statement:

| Income Statement, 20A | | |
|---|---:|---:|
| Rental revenue | | $114,000 |
| Expenses: | | |
| Salaries and wages expense | $28,500 | |
| Maintenance expense | 12,000 | |
| Rent expense (on location) | 9,000 | |
| Utilities expense | 4,000 | |
| Gas and oil expense | 3,000 | |
| Miscellaneous expenses (items not listed elsewhere) | 1,000 | |
| Total expenses | | 57,500 |
| Income | | $ 56,500 |

You are an independent CPA hired by the company to audit the company's accounting systems and review the financial statements. In your audit, you developed additional data as follows:

a. Wages for the last three days of December amounting to $310 were not recorded or paid (disregard payroll taxes).

b. The $400 telephone bill for December 20A has not been recorded or paid.

c. Depreciation on rental autos, amounting to $23,000 for 20A, was not recorded.

d. Interest on a $20,000, one-year, 10 percent note payable dated October 1, 20A, was not recorded. The 10 percent interest is payable on the maturity date of the note.

e. The Unearned Rental Revenue account includes $4,000 rental revenue for the month of January 20B.

f. Maintenance expense includes $1,000, which is the cost of maintenance supplies still on hand (per inventory) at December 31, 20A. These supplies will be used in 20B.

g. The income tax expense is $7,000. Payment of income tax will be made in 20B.

*Required:*

1. What adjusting entry for each item *a.* through *g.* do you recommend Barton record at December 31, 20A? If none is required, explain why.

2. Prepare a correct income statement for 20A in good form including earnings per share, assuming that 7,000 shares of stock are outstanding. Show computations.

3. Compute net profit margin based on the corrected information. What does this ratio suggest? If the industry average net profit margin is 18 percent, what might you infer about Barton?

**E4–16** **Evaluating the Effect of Adjusting Unearned Subscriptions on Cash Flows and Performance as a Manager**

■ **LO3**

You are the regional sales manager for Weld News Company. Weld is making adjusting entries for the year ended March 31, 20C. On September 1, 20B, $18,000 cash was received from customers in your region for three-year magazine subscriptions beginning on that date. The magazines are published and mailed to customers monthly. These were the only subscription sales in your region during the year.

*Required:*

1. What amount should be reported as cash from operations on the statement of cash flows?
2. What amount should be reported on the 20C income statement for subscriptions revenue?
3. What amount should be reported on the March 31, 20C, balance sheet for unearned subscriptions revenue?
4. Give the adjusting entry at March 31, 20C, assuming that the subscriptions received on September 1, 20B, were recorded for the full amount in Unearned Subscriptions Revenue.
5. The company expects your region's annual revenue target to be $4,000.
    *a.* Evaluate your region's performance, assuming that the revenue target is based on cash sales.
    *b.* Evaluate your region's performance, assuming that the revenue target is based on accrual accounting.

**LO2**   **E4–17**   **Recording Four Adjusting Entries and Completing the Trial Balance Worksheet**

Cayuga Company prepared the following trial balance at the end of its first year of operations ending December 31, 20A. To simplify the case, the amounts given are in thousands of dollars.

| | Unadjusted | | Adjustments | | Adjusted | |
|---|---|---|---|---|---|---|
| Account Titles | Debit | Credit | Debit | Credit | Debit | Credit |
| Cash | 38 | | | | | |
| Accounts receivable | 9 | | | | | |
| Prepaid insurance | 6 | | | | | |
| Machinery (20-year life, no residual value) | 80 | | | | | |
| Accumulated depreciation | | 8 | | | | |
| Accounts payable | | 9 | | | | |
| Wages payable | | | | | | |
| Income taxes payable | | | | | | |
| Contributed capital (4,000 shares) | | 68 | | | | |
| Retained earnings | 4 | | | | | |
| Revenues (not detailed) | | 84 | | | | |
| Expenses (not detailed) | 32 | | | | | |
| Totals | 169 | 169 | | | | |

Other data not yet recorded at December 31, 20A:

*a.* Insurance expired during 20A, $5.
*b.* Depreciation expense for 20A, $4.
*c.* Wages payable, $7.
*d.* Income tax expense, $9.

*Required:*

1. Prepare the adjusting entries for 20A.
2. Complete the trial balance Adjustments and Adjusted columns.

**LO3**   **E4–18**   **Reporting an Income Statement, Statement of Stockholders' Equity, and Balance Sheet**

Refer to E4–17.

*Required:*

Using the adjusted balances in E4–17, complete the following income statement, statement of stockholders' equity, and balance sheet for 20A.

---

**Income Statement**
**For the Year Ended December 31, 20A**

| | |
|---|---|
| Revenues (not detailed) | $ _____ |
| Expenses (not detailed) | _____ |
| Pretax income | _____ |
| Income tax expense | _____ |
| Net income | $ _____ |
| EPS | $ _____ |

---

**Statement of Stockholders' Equity**
**For the Year Ended December 31, 20A**

| | Contributed Capital | Retained Earnings | Total Stockholders' Equity |
|---|---|---|---|
| Beginning balances, 1/1/20A | $ _____ | $ _____ | $ _____ |
| Stock issuance | _____ | _____ | _____ |
| Net income | _____ | _____ | _____ |
| Dividends declared | _____ | _____ | _____ |
| Ending balances, 12/31/20A | $ _____ | $ _____ | $ _____ |

---

**Balance Sheet**
**December 31, 20A**

| Assets | | Liabilities | |
|---|---|---|---|
| Cash | $ _____ | Accounts payable | $ _____ |
| Accounts receivable | _____ | Wages payable | _____ |
| Prepaid insurance | _____ | Income taxes payable | _____ |
| Machinery | _____ | Total liabilities | _____ |
| Accumulated depreciation | _____ | | |
| | | **Stockholders' Equity** | |
| | | Contributed capital | _____ |
| | _____ | Retained earnings | _____ |
| Total assets | $ _____ | Total liabilities and stockholders' equity | $ _____ |

---

**E4–19  Recording Closing Entries**                                       ■ **LO5**
Refer to E4–17.

*Required:*
Using the adjusted balances in E4–17, give the closing entries for 20A. What is the purpose of "closing the books" at the end of the accounting period?

## PROBLEMS

**P4–1  Preparing a Trial Balance** (AP4–1)                                ■ **LO1**
Dell Computer Corporation is the world's largest computer systems company selling directly          Dell Computer
to customers. Products include desktop computer systems, notebook computers, workstations,          Corporation
network server and storage products, and peripheral hardware and software. The following is a
list of accounts and amounts reported. The accounts have normal debit or credit balances and
the dollars are rounded to the nearest million. Assume the year ended on January 29, 20A, in
recent financial statements.

| | | | | | | |
|---|---|---|---|---|---|---|
| Accounts payable | $2,397 | Income tax expense | $ 624 | Property, plant, and equipment | $ | 775 |
| Accounts receivable | 2,094 | Inventories | 273 | Research and | | |
| Accrued expenses payable | 1,298 | Long-term debt | 512 | development expense | | 272 |
| Accumulated depreciation | 252 | Marketable securities | 2,661 | Retained earnings | | ? |
| Cash | 520 | Other assets | 806 | Sales revenue | | 18,243 |
| Contributed capital | 1,781 | Other expenses | 38 | Selling, general, and | | |
| Cost of sales | 14,137 | Other liabilities | 349 | administrative expenses | | 1,788 |

*Required:*

Prepare an adjusted trial balance at January 29, 20A. How did you determine the amount for retained earnings?

**LO2**      **P4–2**    **Recording Adjusting Entries** (AP4–2)

McGraw Company's annual accounting year ends on December 31. It is December 31, 20C, and all of the 20C entries except the following adjusting entries have been made:

a. On September 1, 20C, McGraw collected six months' rent of $4,800 on storage space. At that date, McGraw debited Cash and credited Unearned Rent Revenue for $4,800.

b. The company earned service revenue of $3,000 on a special job that was completed December 29, 20C. Collection will be made during January 20D; no entry has been recorded.

c. On November 1, 20C, McGraw paid a one-year premium for property insurance, $4,200, for coverage starting on that date. Cash was credited and Prepaid Insurance was debited for this amount.

d. At December 31, 20C, wages earned by employees not yet paid totaled $1,100. The employees will be paid on the next payroll date, January 15, 20D.

e. Depreciation must be recognized on a service truck that cost $12,000 on July 1, 20C (estimated useful life is six years with no residual value).

f. Cash of $1,500 was collected on November 1, 20C, for services to be rendered evenly over the next year beginning on November 1 (Unearned Service Revenue was credited).

g. On December 27, 20C, the company received a tax bill of $400 from the city for 20C property taxes on land; it is payable during January 20D.

h. On October 1, 20C, the company borrowed $10,000 from a local bank and signed a 12 percent note for that amount. The principal and interest are payable on maturity date, September 30, 20D.

*Required:*

1. Indicate whether each transaction relates to a deferred revenue, deferred expense, accrued revenue, or accrued expense.

2. Give the adjusting entry required for each transaction at December 31, 20C.

**LO3**      **P4–3**    **Determining Financial Statement Effects of Adjusting Entries** (AP4–3)

Refer to P4–2.

*Required:*

1. Indicate whether each transaction relates to a deferred revenue, deferred expense, accrued revenue, or accrued expense.

2. Using the following headings, indicate the effect of each adjusting entry and the amount of the effect. Use + for increase, − for decrease, and NE for no effect. (*Reminder*: Assets = Liabilities + Stockholders' Equity; Revenues − Expenses = Net Income; and Net Income accounts are closed to Retained Earnings, a part of Stockholders' Equity.)

| | Balance Sheet | | | Income Statement | | |
|---|---|---|---|---|---|---|
| Transaction | Assets | Liabilities | Stockholders' Equity | Revenues | Expenses | Net Income |
| a. | | | | | | |
| b. | | | | | | |
| c. | | | | | | |
| etc. | | | | | | |

**P4–4 Recording Adjusting Entries (AP4–4)**    ■ **LO2**

Handy Haulers Company is at the end of its accounting year, December 31, 20B. The following data that must be considered were developed from the company's records and related documents:

a. On July 1, 20B, a three-year insurance premium on equipment in the amount of $1,200 was paid and debited in full to Prepaid Insurance on that date. Coverage began on July 1.

b. During 20B, office supplies amounting to $800 were purchased for cash and debited in full to Supplies Inventory. At the end of 20A, the inventory count of supplies remaining on hand (unused) showed $200. The inventory of supplies on hand at December 31, 20B, showed $300.

c. On December 31, 20B, Bert's Garage completed repairs on one of the company's trucks at a cost of $800; the amount is not yet recorded and by agreement will be paid during January 20C.

d. In December 20B, a tax bill for $1,600 on land owned during 20B was received from the city. The taxes, which have not been recorded, are due and will be paid on February 15, 20C.

e. On December 31, 20B, the company completed a contract for an out-of-state company. The bill was for $8,000 payable within 30 days. No cash has been collected, and no journal entry has been made for this transaction.

f. On July 1, 20B, the company purchased a new hauling van at a cash cost of $23,600. The estimated useful life of the van was 10 years, with an estimated residual value of $1,600. No depreciation has been recorded for 20B (compute depreciation for six months in 20B).

g. On October 1, 20B, the company borrowed $10,000 from the local bank on a one-year, 12 percent note payable. The principal plus interest is payable at the end of 12 months.

h. The income before any of the adjustments or income taxes was $30,000. The company's federal income tax rate is 30 percent. Compute adjusted income based on a. through g. to determine income tax expense.

*Required:*

1. Indicate whether each transaction relates to a deferred revenue, deferred expense, accrued revenue, or accrued expense.

2. Give the adjusting entry required for each transaction at December 31, 20B.

**P4–5 Determining Financial Statement Effects of Adjusting Entries (AP4–5)**    ■ **LO2**

Refer to P4–4.

*Required:*

1. Indicate whether each transaction relates to a deferred revenue, deferred expense, accrued revenue, or accrued expense.

2. Using the following headings, indicate the effect of each adjusting entry and the amount of each. Use + for increase, − for decrease, and NE for no effect. (*Reminder:* Assets = Liabilities + Stockholders' Equity; Revenues − Expenses = Net Income; and Net Income accounts are closed to Retained Earnings, a part of Stockholders' Equity.)

| | Balance Sheet | | | Income Statement | | |
|---|---|---|---|---|---|---|
| Transaction | Assets | Liabilities | Stockholders' Equity | Revenues | Expenses | Net Income |
| a. | | | | | | |
| b. | | | | | | |
| c. | | | | | | |
| etc. | | | | | | |

**P4–6 Computing Amounts on Financial Statements and Finding Financial Information (AP4–6)**    ■ **LO3**

The following information was provided by the records of South Hill Apartments (a corporation) at the end of the annual fiscal period, December 31, 20B:

| Cash Receipts | |
|---|---:|
| *a.* Rent revenue collected in cash during 20B for occupancy in 20B | $512,000 |
| *b.* Rent revenue earned for occupancy in December 20B; not collected until 20C | 16,000 |
| *c.* In December 20B, collected rent revenue in advance for January 20C | 12,000 |
| **Cash Disbursements for Salaries** | |
| *d.* Cash payment in January 20B for employee salaries earned in December 20A | 4,000 |
| *e.* Salaries incurred and paid during 20B | 62,000 |
| *f.* Salaries earned by employees during December 20B that will be paid in January 20C | 3,000 |
| *g.* Cash advance to employees in December 20B for salaries that will be earned in January 20C | 1,500 |
| **Cash Disbursements for Supplies** | |
| *h.* Maintenance supplies inventory on January 1, 20B (balance on hand) | 3,000 |
| *i.* Maintenance supplies purchased for cash during 20B | 8,000 |
| *j.* Maintenance supplies inventory on December 31, 20B | 1,700 |

*Required:*

Using T-accounts, compute the amounts that should be reported in South Hill's 20B financial statements for the following items and indicate on which financial statement the item is located. For Cash, create one T-account and label each effect to determine the amounts affecting cash as indicated here (from renters, to suppliers, to employees):

1. Rent revenue
2. Salary expense
3. Maintenance supplies expense
4. Cash from renters
5. Rent receivable
6. Cash to suppliers
7. Receivables from employees
8. Maintenance supplies inventory
9. Unearned rent revenue
10. Salaries payable
11. Cash to employees

**LO1, 2, 4, 5**

**P4–7**    **Inferring Year-End Adjustments, Computing Earnings per Share and Net Profit Margin, and Recording Closing Entries** (AP4–7)

Willenborg Company is completing the information processing cycle at its fiscal year-end, December 31, 20B. Following are the correct balances at December 31, 20B, for the accounts both before and after the adjusting entries for 20B.

| | Trial Balance, December 31, 20B | | | | | | |
|---|---|---|---|---|---|---|---|
| | **Before Adjusting Entries** | | **Adjustments** | | **After Adjusting Entries** | | |
| Items | Debit | Credit | Debit | Credit | Debit | Credit |
| *a.* Cash | $ 9,000 | | | | $ 9,000 | |
| *b.* Service revenue receivable | | | | | 400 | |
| *c.* Prepaid insurance | 600 | | | | 400 | |
| *d.* Equipment | 120,200 | | | | 120,200 | |
| *e.* Accumulated depreciation, equipment | | $31,500 | | | | $ 40,000 |
| *f.* Income taxes payable | | | | | | 4,700 |
| *g.* Contributed capital | | 80,000 | | | | 80,000 |
| *h.* Retained earnings, January 1, 20B | | 14,000 | | | | 14,000 |
| *i.* Service revenue | | 46,000 | | | | 46,400 |
| *j.* Salary expense | 41,700 | | | | 41,700 | |
| *k.* Depreciation expense | | | | | 8,500 | |
| *l.* Insurance expense | | | | | 200 | |
| *m.* Income tax expense | | | | | 4,700 | |
| | $171,500 | $171,500 | | | $185,100 | $185,100 |

*Required:*

1. Compare the amounts in the columns before and after the adjusting entries to reconstruct the adjusting entries made in 20B. Provide an explanation of each.

2. Compute the amount of income assuming that it is based on the amounts (a) before adjusting entries and (b) after adjusting entries. Which income amount is correct? Explain why.

3. Compute earnings per share, assuming that 3,000 shares of stock are outstanding.

4. Compute net profit margin. What does this suggest to you about the company?

5. Record the closing entries at December 31, 20B.

**P4–8** **Recording Adjusting and Closing Entries and Preparing a Balance Sheet and Income Statement Including Earnings per Share** (AP4–8)

Mostert, Inc., a small service company, keeps its records without the help of an accountant. After much effort, an outside accountant prepared the following unadjusted trial balance as of the end of the annual accounting period, December 31, 20D:

| Account Titles | Debit | Credit |
|---|---|---|
| Cash | 60,000 | |
| Accounts receivable | 13,000 | |
| Service supplies inventory | 800 | |
| Prepaid insurance | 1,000 | |
| Service trucks (5-year life, no residual value) | 20,000 | |
| Accumulated depreciation, service trucks | | 12,000 |
| Other assets | 11,200 | |
| Accounts payable | | 3,000 |
| Wages payable | | |
| Income taxes payable | | |
| Note payable (3 years; 10% each December 31) | | 20,000 |
| Contributed capital (5,000 shares outstanding) | | 28,200 |
| Retained earnings | | 7,500 |
| Service revenue | | 77,000 |
| Remaining expenses (not detailed; exclude income tax) | 41,700 | |
| Income tax expense | | |
| Totals | 147,700 | 147,700 |

Data not yet recorded at December 31, 20D:

*a.* The supplies inventory count on December 31, 20D, reflected $300 remaining on hand to be used in 20E.

*b.* Insurance expired during 20D, $500.

*c.* Depreciation expense for 20D, $4,000.

*d.* Wages earned by employees not yet paid on December 31, 20D, $900.

*e.* Income tax expense was $7,350.

*Required:*

1. Record the 20D adjusting entries.

2. Complete the following financial statements (show computations) for 20D to include the effects of the preceding five transactions.

3. Record the 20D closing entries.

**Income Statement**
**For the Year Ended December 31, 20D**

| | | |
|---|---|---|
| Service revenue | | $ _____ |
| Supplies expense | $ _____ | |
| Insurance expense | _____ | |
| Depreciation expense | _____ | |
| Wages expense | _____ | |
| Remaining expenses (not detailed) | _____ | |
|   Total expenses | | _____ |
| Pretax income | | _____ |
| Income tax expense | | _____ |
| Net income | | $ _____ |
| EPS | | $ _____ |

**Balance Sheet**
**At December 31, 20D**

| Assets | | Liabilities | |
|---|---|---|---|
| Cash | $ _____ | Accounts payable | $ _____ |
| Accounts receivable | _____ | Wages payable | _____ |
| Service supplies inventory | _____ | Income taxes payable | _____ |
| Prepaid insurance | _____ | Note payable, long-term | _____ |
| Service trucks | _____ | Total liabilities | _____ |
|   Accumulated depreciation | _____ | **Stockholders' Equity** | |
| Other assets (not detailed) | _____ | | |
| | | Contributed capital | _____ |
| | | Retained earnings | _____ |
| | | Total stockholders' equity | _____ |
| | | Total liabilities and | |
| Total assets | $ _____ |   stockholders' equity | $ _____ |

**LO1, 2, 3, 4, 5**    **P4–9**

**Comprehensive Review Problem: From Recording Transactions (including Adjusting and Closing Entries) to Preparing a Complete Set of Financial Statements and Performing Ratio Analysis (see Chapters 2, 3, and 4) (AP4–9)**

Brothers Steve and Herman Hargenrater began operations of their tool and die shop (H & H Tool, Inc.) on January 1, 20A. The annual reporting period ends December 31. The trial balance on January 1, 20B, was as follows (the amounts are rounded to thousands of dollars to simplify):

| Account No. | Account Titles | Debit | Credit |
|---|---|---|---|
| 01 | Cash | 3 | |
| 02 | Accounts receivable | 5 | |
| 03 | Service supplies inventory | 12 | |
| 04 | Land | | |
| 05 | Equipment | 60 | |
| 06 | Accumulated depreciation (equipment) | | 6 |
| 07 | Remaining assets (not detailed to simplify) | 4 | |
| 11 | Accounts payable | | 5 |
| 12 | Notes payable | | |
| 13 | Wages payable | | |
| 14 | Interest payable | | |
| 15 | Income taxes payable | | |
| 21 | Contributed capital (65,000 shares) | | 65 |
| 31 | Retained earnings | | 8 |
| 35 | Service revenue | | |
| 40 | Depreciation expense | | |
| 41 | Income tax expense | | |
| 42 | Interest expense | | |
| 43 | Remaining expenses (not detailed to simplify) | — | — |
| | Totals | 84 | 84 |

Transactions during 20B (summarized in thousands of dollars) follow:

a. Borrowed $10 cash on a 12 percent note payable, dated March 1, 20B.

b. Purchased land for future building site, paid cash, $9.

c. Earned revenues for 20B, $160, including $40 on credit.

d. Sold 3,000 additional shares of capital stock for $1 cash per share (show dollars in thousands; number of share and price per share are as presented).

e. Recognized remaining expenses for 20B, $85, including $15 on credit.

f. Collected accounts receivable, $24.

g. Purchased additional assets, $10 cash (debit Remaining Assets).

h. Paid accounts payable, $13.

i. Purchased on account service supplies for future use, $18 (debit to Account No. 3).

j. Signed a $25 service contract to start February 1, 20C.

k. Declared and paid cash dividend, $17.

Data for adjusting entries:

l. Service supplies inventory counted on December 31, 20B, $14 (debit Remaining Expenses).

m. Equipment, useful life 10 years (no residual or scrap value).

n. Accrued interest on notes payable (to be computed).

o. Wages earned since the December 24 payroll not yet paid, $12.

p. Income tax expense was $8, payable in 20C.

### Required:

1. Set up T-accounts for the accounts on the trial balance and enter beginning balances.
2. Record transactions (a) through (k) and post them to the T-accounts.
3. Record and post the adjusting entries (l) through (p).
4. Prepare an income statement (including earnings per share), statement of stockholders' equity, balance sheet, and statement of cash flows.
5. Record and post the closing entries.
6. Prepare a post-closing trial balance.
7. Compute the following ratios for 20B:
   a. Financial leverage
   b. Total asset turnover
   c. Net profit margin

# ALTERNATE PROBLEMS

## AP4–1 Preparing a Trial Balance (P4–1)

▥ **LO1**

*Starbucks Corporation*

Starbucks Corporation purchases and roasts high-quality whole bean coffees and sells them along with fresh-brewed coffees, Italian-style espresso beverages, a variety of pastries and confections, coffee-related accessories and equipment, and a line of premium teas. In addition to sales through its company-operated retail stores, Starbucks also sells coffee and tea products through other channels of distribution. The following is a simplified list of accounts and amounts reported in recent financial statements. The accounts have normal debit or credit balances and the dollars are rounded to the nearest million. Assume the year ended on September 30, 20A.

| | | | | | |
|---|---|---|---|---|---|
| Accounts payable | $ 56 | Income tax expense | $ 62 | Other operating expenses | $ 51 |
| Accounts receivable | 48 | Interest expense | 1 | Prepaid expenses | 19 |
| Accrued liabilities | 131 | Interest income | 9 | Property, plant and equipment | 1,081 |
| Accumulated depreciation | 321 | Inventories | 181 | Retained earnings | ? |
| Cash | 66 | Long-term investments | 68 | Short-term bank debt | 64 |
| Contributed capital | 647 | Long-term liabilities | 40 | Short-term investments | 51 |
| Cost of sales | 741 | Net revenues | 1,680 | Store operating expenses | 544 |
| Depreciation | 98 | Other current assets | 21 | | |
| General and administrative expenses | 90 | Other long-lived assets | 38 | | |

*Required:*

Prepare an adjusted trial balance at September 30, 20A. How did you determine the amount for retained earnings?

**■ LO2    AP4–2    Recording Adjusting Entries** (P4–2)

Bryson Company's annual accounting year ends on June 30. It is June 30, 20B, and all of the 20B entries except the following adjusting entries have been made:

a. On March 30, 20B, Bryson paid a six-month premium for property insurance, $3,200, for coverage starting on that date. Cash was credited and Prepaid Insurance was debited for this amount.

b. At June 30, 20B, wages of $900 were earned by employees but not yet paid. The employees will be paid on the next payroll date, July 15, 20B.

c. On June 1, 20B, Bryson collected two months' maintenance revenue of $450. At that date, Bryson debited Cash and credited Unearned Maintenance Revenue for $450.

d. Depreciation must be recognized on a service truck that cost $15,000 on July 1, 20A (estimated useful life is four years with a $3,000 residual value).

e. Cash of $4,200 was collected on May 1, 20B, for services to be rendered evenly over the next year beginning on May 1 (Unearned Service Revenue was credited).

f. On February 1, 20B, the company borrowed $16,000 from a local bank and signed a 9 percent note for that amount. The principal and interest are payable on maturity date, January 31, 20C.

g. On June 15, 20B, the company received a $500 tax bill from the city for the first half of 20B property taxes on land that is payable during July 20B.

h. The company earned service revenue of $2,000 on a special job that was completed June 29, 20B. Collection will be made during July 20C; no entry has been recorded.

*Required:*

1. Indicate whether each transaction relates to a deferred revenue, deferred expense, accrued revenue, or accrued expense.

2. Give the adjusting entry required for each transaction at June 30, 20B.

**■ LO2    AP4–3    Determining Financial Statement Effects of Adjusting Entries** (P4–3)

Refer to AP4–2.

*Required:*

1. Indicate whether each transaction relates to a deferred revenue, deferred expense, accrued revenue, or accrued expense.

2. Using the following headings, indicate the effect of each adjusting entry and the amount of the effect. Use + for increase, − for decrease, and NE for no effect. (*Reminder*: Assets = Liabilities + Stockholders' Equity; Revenues − Expenses = Net Income; and Net Income accounts are closed to Retained Earnings, a part of Stockholders' Equity.)

| | Balance Sheet | | | Income Statement | | |
|---|---|---|---|---|---|---|
| Transaction | Assets | Liabilities | Stockholders' Equity | Revenues | Expenses | Net Income |
| a. | | | | | | |
| b. | | | | | | |
| c. | | | | | | |
| etc. | | | | | | |

**■ LO2    AP4–4    Recording Adjusting Entries** (P4–4)

Murphy's Catering Company is at its accounting year-end, December 31, 20B. The following data that must be considered were developed from the company's records and related documents:

a. During 20B, office supplies amounting to $1,200 were purchased for cash and debited in full to Supplies Inventory. At the beginning of 20B, the inventory count of supplies remaining on hand (unused) showed $350. The inventory of supplies on hand at December 31, 20B, showed $400.

*b.* On December 31, 20B, the company catered an evening gala for a local celebrity. The $75,000 bill was payable by the end of January 20C. No cash has been collected, and no journal entry has been made for this transaction.

*c.* On December 15, 20B, repairs on one of the company's delivery vans were completed at a cost of $600; the amount is not yet recorded and by agreement will be paid at the beginning of January 20C.

*d.* On October 1, 20B, a one-year insurance premium on equipment in the amount of $1,200 was paid and debited in full to Prepaid Insurance on that date. Coverage began on November 1.

*e.* In November 20B, Murphy's signed a lease for a new retail location, providing a down-payment of $2,100 for the first three months rent. The lease began on December 1, 20B.

*f.* On July 1, 20B, the company purchased new refrigerated display counters at a cash cost of $18,000. The estimated useful life of the equipment is five years, with an estimated residual value of $2,000. No depreciation has been recorded for 20B (compute depreciation for six months in 20B).

*g.* On November 1, 20B, the company loaned $4,000 to one of its employees on a one-year, 12 percent note payable. The principal plus interest is payable at the end of 12 months.

*h.* The income before any of the adjustments or income taxes was $22,400. The company's federal income tax rate is 30 percent. Compute adjusted income based on (*a*) through (*g*) to determine income tax expense.

***Required:***

1. Indicate whether each transaction relates to a deferred revenue, deferred expense, accrued revenue, or accrued expense.

2. Give the adjusting entry required for each transaction at December 31, 20B.

**AP4–5 Determining Financial Statement Effects of Adjusting Entries (P4–5)**  ■ **LO2**
Refer to AP4–4.

***Required:***

1. Indicate whether each transaction relates to a deferred revenue, deferred expense, accrued revenue, or accrued expense.

2. Using the following headings, indicate the effect of each adjusting entry and the amount of each. Use + for increase, − for decrease, and NE for no effect. (*Reminder:* Assets = Liabilities + Stockholders' Equity; Revenues − Expenses = Net Income; and Net Income accounts are closed to Retained Earnings, a part of Stockholders' Equity.)

| | Balance Sheet | | | Income Statement | | |
|---|---|---|---|---|---|---|
| Transaction | Assets | Liabilities | Stockholders' Equity | Revenues | Expenses | Net Income |
| *a.* | | | | | | |
| *b.* | | | | | | |
| *c.* | | | | | | |
| *etc.* | | | | | | |

**AP4–6 Computing Amounts on Financial Statements and Finding Financial Information (P4–6)**  ■ **LO3**
The following information was provided by the records of Deerfield Cleaning (a corporation) at the end of the annual fiscal period, December 31, 20C:

| Cash Receipts | |
|---|---|
| *a.* Collected cash in January 20C for the only cleaning contracts completed in past years that were not yet paid by customers. | $ 11,000 |
| *b.* Service revenue collected in cash during 20C for cleaning contracts in 20C. | 213,000 |
| *c.* Service revenue earned for contracts in December 20C; not collected until 20D. | 14,000 |
| *d.* In December 20C, collected contract revenue in advance for January 20D. | 19,000 |

---

**Cash Disbursements for Salaries**

*e.* Cash payment made in January 20C for employee salaries earned in 20B;
no other amounts were due to employees for past periods.    1,500

*f.* Salaries incurred and paid during 20C.    78,000

*g.* Salaries earned by employees during December 20C that will be paid
in January 20D.    1,900

**Cash Disbursements for Supplies**

*h.* Cleaning supplies inventory on January 1, 20C (balance on hand).    1,800

*i.* Cleaning supplies purchased for cash during 20C.    14,500

*j.* Cleaning supplies inventory on December 31, 20C.    2,700

---

*Required:*

Using T-accounts, compute the amounts that should be reported in Deerfield's 20C financial
statements for the following items and indicate on which financial statement the item is
located. For cash, create one T-account and label each effect to determine the amounts
affecting cash as indicated here (from renters, to suppliers, to employees):

1. Service revenue
2. Cash to employees
3. Cleaning supplies expense
4. Receivables from employees
5. Cash to suppliers

6. Cleaning supplies inventory
7. Wages expense
8. Cash from customers
9. Unearned revenue
10. Wages payable

■ **LO1, 2,**    **AP4–7**    **Inferring Year-End Adjustments, Computing Earnings per Share and Net Profit Margin,**
**4, 5**                  **and Recording Closing Entries** (P4–7)

Quillan Company is completing the information processing cycle at the end of its fiscal year,
December 31, 20B. Following are the correct balances at December 31, 20B, for the accounts
both before and after the adjusting entries for 20B.

| | Trial Balance, December 31, 20B | | | | | | |
| | Before Adjusting Entries | | Adjustments | | After Adjusting Entries | |
| Items | Debit | Credit | Debit | Credit | Debit | Credit |
| --- | --- | --- | --- | --- | --- | --- |
| *a.* Cash | $ 18,000 | | | | $ 18,000 | |
| *b.* Service revenue receivable | | | | | 1,500 | |
| *c.* Prepaid rent | 1,200 | | | | 800 | |
| *d.* Property, plant, and equipment | 210,000 | | | | 210,000 | |
| *e.* Accumulated depreciation, PP&E | | $52,500 | | | | $ 70,000 |
| *f.* Income taxes payable | | | | | | 6,500 |
| *g.* Deferred revenue | | 16,000 | | | | 8,000 |
| *h.* Contributed capital | | 110,000 | | | | 110,000 |
| *i.* Retained earnings, January 1, 20B | | 21,700 | | | | 21,700 |
| *j.* Service revenue | | 83,000 | | | | 92,500 |
| *k.* Salary expense | 54,000 | | | | 54,000 | |
| *l.* Depreciation expense | | | | | 17,500 | |
| *m.* Rent expense | | | | | 400 | |
| *n.* Income tax expense | | | | | 6,500 | |
| | $283,200 | $283,200 | | | $308,700 | $308,700 |

*Required:*

1. Compare the amounts in the columns before and after the adjusting entries to reconstruct
the adjusting entries made in 20B. Provide an explanation of each.

2. Compute the amount of income assuming that it is based on the amounts (a) before
adjusting entries and (b) after adjusting entries. Which income amount is correct?
Explain why.

3. Compute earnings per share, assuming that 5,000 shares of stock are outstanding.

4. Compute net profit margin. What does this suggest to you about the company?

5. Record the closing entries at December 31, 20B.

**AP4–8** **Recording Adjusting and Closing Entries and Preparing a Balance Sheet and Income Statement Including Earnings per Share (P4–8)**  ▇ **LO1, 2, 3, 5**

Vialdi, Co., a small service repair company, keeps its records without the help of an accountant. After much effort, an outside accountant prepared the following unadjusted trial balance as of the end of the annual accounting period, December 31, 20B:

| Account Titles | Debit | Credit |
|---|---|---|
| Cash | 19,600 | |
| Accounts receivable | 7,000 | |
| Supplies inventory | 1,300 | |
| Prepaid insurance | 900 | |
| Equipment (5-year life, no residual value) | 27,000 | |
| Accumulated depreciation, equipment | | 12,000 |
| Other assets | 5,100 | |
| Accounts payable | | 2,500 |
| Wages payable | | |
| Income taxes payable | | |
| Note payable (2 years; 12% each December 31) | | 5,000 |
| Contributed capital (4,000 shares outstanding) | | 16,000 |
| Retained earnings | | 10,300 |
| Service revenue | | 48,000 |
| Remaining expenses (not detailed; exclude income tax) | 32,900 | |
| Income tax expense | | |
| Totals | 93,800 | 93,800 |

Data not yet recorded at December 31, 20B:

*a.* Depreciation expense for 20B, $3,000.

*b.* Insurance expired during 20B, $450.

*c.* Wages earned by employees not yet paid on December 31, 20B, $1,100.

*d.* The supplies inventory count on December 31, 20B, reflected $600 remaining on hand to be used in 20C.

*e.* Income tax expense was $2,950.

*Required:*

1. Record the 20B adjusting entries.

2. Complete the following financial statements (show computations) for 20B to include the effects of the preceding five transactions.

3. Record the 20B closing entries.

**Income Statement**
**For the Year Ended December 31, 20B**

| | | |
|---|---|---|
| Service revenue | | $ _____ |
| Supplies expense | $ _____ | |
| Insurance expense | _____ | |
| Depreciation expense | _____ | |
| Wages expense | _____ | |
| Remaining expenses (not detailed) | _____ | |
| Total expenses | | _____ |
| Pretax income | | _____ |
| Income tax expense | | _____ |
| Net income | | $ _____ |
| EPS | | $ _____ |

**Balance Sheet**
**At December 31, 20B**

| Assets | | Liabilities | |
|---|---|---|---|
| Cash | $ _____ | Accounts payable | $ _____ |
| Accounts receivable | _____ | Wages payable | _____ |
| Service supplies inventory | _____ | Income taxes payable | _____ |
| Prepaid insurance | _____ | Note payable, long-term | _____ |
| Equipment | _____ | Total liabilities | _____ |
| Accumulated depreciation | _____ | **Stockholders' Equity** | |
| Other assets (not detailed) | _____ | | |
| | | Contributed capital | _____ |
| | | Retained earnings | _____ |
| | | Total stockholders' equity | _____ |
| | | Total liabilities and | |
| Total assets | $ _____ | stockholders' equity | $ _____ |

**LO1, 2, 3, 4, 5    AP4–9**

**Comprehensive Review Problem: From Recording Transactions (including Adjusting and Closing Entries) to Preparing a Complete Set of Financial Statements and Performing Ratio Analysis (see Chapters 2, 3, and 4) (P4–9)**

Sophie and Bill Davis began operations of their furniture repair shop (Rumours Furniture, Inc.) on January 1, 20A. The annual reporting period ends December 31. The trial balance on January 1, 20B, was as follows (the amounts are rounded to thousands of dollars to simplify):

| Account No. | Account Titles | Debit | Credit |
|---|---|---|---|
| 01 | Cash | 5 | |
| 02 | Accounts receivable | 4 | |
| 03 | Supplies inventory | 2 | |
| 04 | Small tools inventory | 6 | |
| 05 | Equipment | | |
| 06 | Accumulated depreciation (equipment) | | |
| 07 | Remaining assets (not detailed to simplify) | 9 | |
| 11 | Accounts payable | | 7 |
| 12 | Notes payable | | |
| 13 | Wages payable | | |
| 14 | Interest payable | | |
| 15 | Income taxes payable | | |
| 16 | Deferred revenue | | |
| 21 | Contributed capital (15,000 shares) | | 15 |
| 31 | Retained earnings | | 4 |
| 35 | Service revenue | | |
| 40 | Depreciation expense | | |
| 41 | Income tax expense | | |
| 42 | Interest expense | | |
| 43 | Remaining expenses (not detailed to simplify) | — | — |
| | Totals | 26 | 26 |

Transactions during 20B (summarized in thousands of dollars) follow:

*a.* Borrowed $20 cash on a 10 percent note payable, dated July 1, 20B.

*b.* Purchased equipment for $18 cash on July 1, 20B.

*c.* Sold 5,000 additional shares of capital stock for $1 cash per share (show dollars in thousands; numbers of shares and price per share are as presented).

*d.* Earned revenues for 20B, $65, including $9 on credit.

*e.* Recognized remaining expenses for 20B, $35, including $7 on credit.

*f.* Purchased additional small tools inventory, $3 cash.

*g.* Collected accounts receivable, $8.

   *h.* Paid accounts payable, $11.

   *i.* Purchased on account supplies for future use, $10 (debit to Account No. 3).

   *j.* Received a $3 deposit on work to start January 15, 20C.

   *k.* Declared and paid cash dividend, $10.

Data for adjusting entries:

   *l.* Service supplies inventory of $4 and small tools inventory of $8 counted on December 31, 20B (debit Remaining Expenses).

   *m.* Equipment, useful life four years ($2 residual value).

   *n.* Accrued interest on notes payable (to be computed).

   *o.* Wages earned since the December 24 payroll not yet paid, $3.

   *p.* Income tax expense was $4, payable in 20C.

*Required:*

1. Set up T-accounts for the accounts on the trial balance and enter beginning balances.
2. Record transactions (*a*) through (*k*) and post them to the T-accounts.
3. Record and post the adjusting entries (*l*) through (*p*).
4. Prepare an income statement (including earnings per share), statement of stockholders' equity, balance sheet, and statement of cash flows.
5. Record and post the closing entries.
6. Prepare a post-closing trial balance.
7. Compute the following ratios for 20B:

   *a.* Financial leverage

   *b.* Total asset turnover

   *c.* Net profit margin

# CASES AND PROJECTS

## FINANCIAL REPORTING AND ANALYSIS CASES

**CP4–1** **Finding Financial Information**

Refer to the financial statements and accompanying notes of Urban Outfitters given in Appendix C at the end of this book, or open file URBN10K.doc in the S&P directory on the student CD-ROM.

**LO2, 3, 4, 5**

Urban Outfitters

STANDARD &POOR'S

*Required:*

1. How much is in the Prepaid Expenses account at the end of the 1999 fiscal year?
2. What did the company report for Accrued Sales Taxes at January 31, 1999? Where did you find this information?
3. What is included in the liability Accrued Rent? In Accrued Compensation?
4. How much did the company pay in income taxes for the 1999 fiscal year? Where did you find this information?
5. To what account is Interest Income related?
6. What company accounts would not appear on a post-closing trial balance?
7. Give the closing entry for Prepaid Expenses.
8. What is the company's earnings per share (basic only) for the three years reported?
9. Compute the company's net profit margin for the three years reported. What does the trend suggest to you about Urban Outfitters?

**CP4–2** **Comparing Companies Within an Industry and over Time**

Refer to the financial statements of American Eagle Outfitters in Appendix B, Urban Outfitters given in Appendix C, and the Standard and Poor's Industry Ratio Report given in Appendix D at the end of this book or open file CP4-2.xls in the S&P directory on the student CD-ROM.

**LO2, 4**

Urban Outfitters
versus
American Eagle
Outfitters

STANDARD
&POOR'S

*Required:*

1. What was Advertising Expense for each company for 1999? Where did you find the information?

2. Compute the percentage of Advertising Expense to Net Sales for 1999 for both companies. Which company incurred the higher percentage? Show computations. Are you able to perform the same comparison for 1998 and 1997? If so, show the computations. If not, explain why not.

3. Compare the Advertising Expense to Net Sales ratio computed in requirement two to the industry average found in the Standard and Poor's Industry Ratio Report. Were these two companies spending more or less than their average competitor on advertising (on a relative basis)? What does this ratio tell you about the general effecctiveness of each companies' advertising strategy?

4. Both companies have a note to the financial statements explaining the accounting policy for advertising. How do the policies differ, if at all?

5. Compute each company's net profit margin for the three years reported. What do your results suggest to you about each company over time and in comparison to each other?

6. Compare each company's net profit margin for 1999 to the industry average net profit margin in the Standard and Poor's Industry Ratio Report. Were these two companies performing better or worse than the average company in the industry?

**CP4–3    Interpreting the Financial Press**

A January 18, 2000, article in *Motley Fool* discusses the results of the initial court case between Papa John's and Tricon Global (Pizza Hut's parent company).* You can access the article on the Libby/Libby/Short website at **www.mhhe.com/business/accounting/libby3**.
*© Copyright 2000. *The Motley Fool*. All rights reserved.

*Required:*
Read the brief article and answer the following questions:

1. What was the court's decision about Papa John's using the "Better Ingredients. Better Pizza." logo?

2. What did Papa John's estimate as the real cost of the lawsuit to the company?

3. What does the article suggest about the impact of the lawsuit on Papa John's stock price?

**■ LO1, 2, 5    CP4–4    Using Financial Reports: Inferring Adjusting Entries and Information Used in Computations and Recording Closing Entries**

The T-accounts of Longhorn Company at the end of the third year of operations, December 31, 20C (prior to the closing entries), follow. The 20C adjusting entries are identified by letters.

| Cash | |
|---|---|
| Bal.    20,000 | |

| Note Payable 8% | |
|---|---|
| | 1/1/20B    10,000 |

| Contributed Capital (8,000 shares) | |
|---|---|
| | Bal.    56,000 |

| Inventory, Maintenance Supplies | |
|---|---|
| Bal.    500 | (a)    300 |

| Interest Payable | |
|---|---|
| | (b)    800 |

| Retained Earnings | |
|---|---|
| | Bal.    9,000 |

| Service Equipment | |
|---|---|
| 1/1/20A    90,000 | |

| Income Taxes Payable | |
|---|---|
| | (f)    13,020 |

| Service Revenue | |
|---|---|
| (c)    6,000 | Bal.    220,000 |

| Accumulated Depreciation, Service Equipment | |
|---|---|
| | Bal.    18,000 |
| | (d)    9,000 |

| Wages Payable | |
|---|---|
| | (e)    500 |

| Expenses | |
|---|---|
| Bal.    160,000 | |
| (a)    300 | |
| (b)    800 | |
| (d)    9,000 | |
| (e)    500 | |
| (f)    13,020 | |

| Remaining Assets | |
|---|---|
| Bal.    42,500 | |

| Unearned Revenue | |
|---|---|
| | (c)    6,000 |

*Required:*

1. Develop three 20C trial balances of Longhorn Company using the following format:

| Account | Unadjusted Trial Balance | | Adjusted Trial Balance | | Post-Closing Trial Balance | |
|---------|-------|--------|-------|--------|-------|--------|
| | Debit | Credit | Debit | Credit | Debit | Credit |
| | | | | | | |

2. Write an explanation for each adjusting entry for 20C.

3. Record the closing journal entries.

4. What was the apparent useful life of the service equipment? What assumptions must you make to answer this question?

5. What was the average income tax rate for 20C?

6. What was the average issue (sale) price per share of the capital stock?

**CP4–5** **Using Financial Reports: Analyzing the Effects of Adjustments**                    ■ **LO2**

Seneca Land Company, a closely held corporation, invests in commercial rental properties. Seneca's annual accounting period ends on December 31. At the end of each year, numerous adjusting entries must be made because many transactions completed during current and prior years have economic effects on the financial statements of the current and future years. Assume that the current year is 20D.

*Required:*

This case concerns four transactions that have been selected for your analysis. Answer the questions for each.

**TRANSACTION (*a*):** On July 1, 20A, the company purchased office equipment costing $14,000 for use in the business. The company estimates that the equipment will have a useful life of 10 years and no residual value.

1. Over how many accounting periods will this transaction directly affect Seneca's financial statements? Explain.

2. Assuming straight-line depreciation, how much depreciation expense was reported on the 20A and 20B income statements?

3. How should the office equipment be reported on the 20C balance sheet?

4. Would Seneca make an adjusting entry at the end of each year during the life of the equipment? Explain your answer.

**TRANSACTION (*b*):** On September 1, 20D, Seneca collected $24,000 rent on office space. This amount represented the monthly rent in advance for the six-month period, September 1, 20D, through February 28, 20E. Unearned Rent Revenue was increased (credited), and Cash was increased (debited) for $24,000.

1. Over how many accounting periods will this transaction affect Seneca's financial statements? Explain.

2. How much rent revenue on this office space should Seneca report on the 20D income statement? Explain.

3. Did this transaction create a liability for Seneca as of the end of 20D? Explain. If yes, how much?

4. Should Seneca make an adjusting entry on December 31, 20D? Explain why. If your answer is yes, give the adjusting entry.

**TRANSACTION (*c*):** On December 31, 20D, Seneca owed employees unpaid and unrecorded wages of $7,500 because the employees worked the last three days in December 20D. The next payroll date is January 5, 20E.

1. Over how many accounting periods does this transaction affect Seneca's financial statements? Explain.

2. How would this $7,500 affect Seneca's 20D income statement and balance sheet?

3. Should Seneca make an adjusting entry on December 31, 20D? Explain why. If your answer is yes, give the adjusting entry.

**TRANSACTION (*d*):** On January 1, 20D, Seneca agreed to supervise the planning and subdivision of a large tract of land for a customer, J. Ray. This service job that Seneca will perform involves four separate phases. By December 31, 20D, three phases had been completed to Ray's satisfaction. The remaining phase will be done during 20E. The total price for the four phases (agreed on in advance by both parties) was $60,000. Each phase involves about the same amount of services. On December 31, 20D, Seneca had collected no cash for the services already performed.

1. Should Seneca record any service revenue on this job for 20D? Explain why. If yes, how much?

2. If your answer to part one is yes, should Seneca make an adjusting entry on December 31, 20D? If yes, give the entry. Explain.

3. What entry will Seneca make when it completes the last phase, assuming that the full contract price is collected on completion date, February 15, 20E?

■ **LO1, 2, 4, 5 CP4–6**

### Using Financial Reports: Inferring Adjusting and Closing Entries and Answering Analytical Questions

Rowland Company was organized on January 1, 20A. At the end of the first year of operations, December 31, 20A, the bookkeeper prepared the following trial balances (amounts in thousands of dollars):

| Account No. | Account Titles | Unadjusted Trial Balance Debit | Unadjusted Trial Balance Credit | Adjustments | | Adjusted Trial Balance Debit | Adjusted Trial Balance Credit |
|---|---|---|---|---|---|---|---|
| 11 | Cash | 40 | | | | 40 | |
| 12 | Accounts receivable | 17 | | | | 17 | |
| 13 | Prepaid insurance | 2 | | | | 1 | |
| 14 | Rent receivable | | | | | 2 | |
| 15 | Property, plant, and equipment | 46 | | | | 46 | |
| 16 | Accumulated depreciation | | | | | | 11 |
| 17 | Other assets | 6 | | | | 6 | |
| 18 | Accounts payable | | 27 | | | | 27 |
| 19 | Wages payable | | | | | | 3 |
| 20 | Income taxes payable | | | | | | 5 |
| 21 | Unearned rent revenue | | | | | | 4 |
| 22 | Note payable (10%; dated January 1, 20A) | | 20 | | | | 20 |
| 23 | Contributed capital (1,000 shares) | | 30 | | | | 30 |
| 24 | Retained earnings | 3 | | | | 3 | |
| 25 | Revenues (total) | | 105 | | | | 103 |
| 26 | Expenses (total including interest) | 68 | | | | 83 | |
| 27 | Income tax expense | | | | | 5 | |
| | Totals | 182 | 182 | | | 203 | 203 |

### Required:

1. Based on inspection of the two trial balances, give the 20A adjusting entries developed by the bookkeeper (provide brief explanations).

2. Based on these data, give the 20A closing entries with brief explanations.

3. Answer the following questions (show computations):

   a. How many shares of stock were outstanding at year-end?

   b. What was the estimated useful life of the property, plant, and equipment, assuming a $2,000 residual value and a purchase date of January 1, 20A?

   c. What was the amount of interest expense included in the total expenses?

   d. What was the balance of Retained Earnings on December 31, 20A?

   e. What was the average income tax rate?

   f. How would the two accounts Rent Receivable and Unearned Rent Revenue be reported on the balance sheet?

   g. Explain why cash increased by $40,000 during the year even though net income was comparatively very low.

  *h.* What was the amount of earnings per share for 20A?

  *i.* What was the average selling price of the shares?

  *j.* When was the insurance premium paid and over what period of time did the coverage extend?

  *k.* What was the net profit margin for the year?

**CP4–7** **Using Financial Reports: Analyzing Financial Information in a Sale of a Business—A Challenging Case**

 LO2, 3

John Place, a local massage therapist, decided to sell his practice and retire. He has had discussions with a therapist from another state who wants to relocate. The discussions are at the complex stage of agreeing on a price. Among the important factors have been the financial statements of Place's practice, Halcyon Stress Reduction. Place's secretary, Kelsey, under his direction, maintained the records. Each year they developed a statement of profits on a cash basis from the incomplete records maintained; no balance sheet was prepared. Upon request, Place provided the other therapist with the following statements for 20F prepared by Kelsey:

---

**HALCYON STRESS REDUCTION**

**Statement of Profits**

**20F**

| | | |
|---|---:|---:|
| Therapy fees collected | | $115,000 |
| Expenses paid: | | |
| Rent for office space | $13,000 | |
| Utilities expense | 360 | |
| Telephone expense | 2,200 | |
| Office salaries expense | 22,000 | |
| Office supplies expense | 900 | |
| Miscellaneous expenses | 2,400 | |
| Total expenses | | 40,860 |
| Profit for the year | | $74,140 |

---

Upon agreement of the parties, you have been asked to examine the financial figures for 20F. The other therapist said, "I question the figures because, among other things, they appear to be on a 100 percent cash basis." Your investigations revealed the following additional data at December 31, 20F:

  *a.* Of the $115,000 in therapy fees collected in 20F, $32,000 was for services performed prior to 20F.

  *b.* At the end of 20F, therapy fees of $9,000 for services performed during the year were uncollected.

  *c.* Office equipment owned and used by Place cost $5,000 and had an estimated useful life of 10 years.

  *d.* An inventory of office supplies at December 31, 20F, reflected $200 worth of items purchased during the year that were still on hand. Also, the records for 20E indicate that the supplies on hand at the end of that year were about $125.

  *e.* At the end of 20F, the secretary whose salary is $18,000 per year had not been paid for December because of a long trip that extended to January 15, 20G.

  *f.* The $1,400 phone bill for December 20F was not paid until January 11, 20G.

  *g.* The $13,000 office rent paid was for 13 months (it included the rent for January 20G).

*Required:*

  1. On the basis of this information, prepare a correct income statement for 20F. Show your computations for any amounts changed from those in the statement prepared by Place's secretary. (Suggested solution format with four-column headings: Items; Cash Basis per Halcyon's Statement, $; Explanation of Changes; and Corrected Basis, $.)

  2. Write a memo to support your schedule prepared in requirement (1). The purpose should be to explain the reasons for your changes and to suggest other important items that should be considered in the pricing decision.

## CRITICAL THINKING CASES

**LO2, 3, 4    CP4–8**    **Using Financial Reports: Evaluating Financial Information as a Bank Loan Officer**
Meadville Corporation has been in operation since January 1, 20A. It is now December 31, 20A, the end of the annual accounting period. The company has not done well financially during the first year, although revenue has been fairly good. The three stockholders manage the company, but they have not given much attention to recordkeeping. In view of a serious cash shortage, they have applied to your bank for a $20,000 loan. You requested a complete set of financial statements. The following 20A annual financial statements were prepared by a clerk and then were given to the bank.

---

### MEADVILLE CORPORATION

| Income Statement | | Balance Sheet | |
|---|---|---|---|
| **For the Period Ended December 31, 20A** | | **At December 31, 20A** | |
| Transportation revenue | $85,000 | *Assets* | |
| Expenses: | | Cash | $2,000 |
|   Salaries expense | 17,000 | Receivables | 3,000 |
|   Maintenance expense | 12,000 | Inventory of maintenance supplies | 6,000 |
|   Other expenses | 18,000 | Equipment | 40,000 |
|   Total expenses | $47,000 | Prepaid insurance | 4,000 |
| Net income | $38,000 | Remaining assets | 27,000 |
| | | Total assets | $82,000 |
| | | *Liabilities* | |
| | | Accounts payable | $9,000 |
| | | *Stockholders' Equity* | |
| | | Contributed capital (10,000 shares outstanding) | 35,000 |
| | | Retained earnings | 38,000 |
| | | Total liabilities and stockholders' equity | $82,000 |

---

After briefly reviewing the statements and "looking into the situation," you requested that the statements be redone (with some expert help) to "incorporate depreciation, accruals, inventory counts, income taxes, and so on." As a result of a review of the records and supporting documents, the following additional information was developed:

*a.* The inventory of maintenance supplies of $6,000 shown on the balance sheet has not been adjusted for supplies used during 20A. An inventory count of the maintenance supplies on hand (unused) on December 31, 20A, showed $1,800. Supplies used should be debited to Maintenance Expense.

*b.* The insurance premium paid in 20A was for years 20A and 20B; therefore, the prepaid insurance at December 31, 20A, amounted to $2,000. The total insurance premium was debited in full to Prepaid Insurance when paid in 20A.

*c.* The equipment cost $40,000 when purchased January 1, 20A. It had an estimated useful life of five years (no residual value). No depreciation has been recorded for 20A.

*d.* Unpaid (and unrecorded) salaries at December 31, 20A, amounted to $2,200.

*e.* At December 31, 20A, transportation revenue collected in advance amounted to $7,000. This amount was credited in full to Transportation Revenue when the cash was collected earlier during 20A.

*f.* Income tax expense was $3,650 (the tax rate is 25 percent).

*Required:*

1. Record the six adjusting entries required on December 31, 20A, based on the preceding additional information.

2. Recast the preceding statements after taking into account the adjusting entries. You do not need to use classifications on the statements. Suggested form for the solution:

| | Amounts | CHANGES | | Correct |
|---|---|---|---|---|
| Items | Reported | Plus | Minus | Amounts |
| (List here each item from the two statements) | | | | |

3. Omission of the adjusting entries caused:

   *a.* Net income to be overstated or understated (select one) by $ _____ .

   *b.* Total assets on the balance sheet to be overstated or understated (select one) by $ _____ .

4. For both of the unadjusted and adjusted balances, calculate these ratios for the company: (a) earnings per share and (b) net profit margin. Explain the causes of the differences and the impact of the changes on financial analysis.

5. Write a letter to the company explaining the results of the adjustments, your analysis, and your decision regarding the loan.

## FINANCIAL REPORTING AND ANALYSIS PROJECTS

**CP4–9  Broadening Financial Research Skills: Obtaining Stock Prices and Recent News Articles**
Yahoo provides financial information about numerous businesses at finance.yahoo.com.

*Required:*
Using your Web browser, contact finance.yahoo.com. Select "Research—By industry," then "Retail," and then "Restaurants." Under Papa John's, select "Chart." Specify that you want a chart for one year versus the S&P 500.

1. What is the trend in the stock price over the past year? How does the stock price compare to the S&P 500?

2. Below the chart is a list of recent news articles. What news services include a recent article related to the company?

3. Select at least one article, summarize its contents, and discuss how, if at all, the article affected the stock price or the stock price was related to the article.

**CP4–10  Comparing Accrual and Deferral Accounts between Industries**
Using your web browser, contact the websites of three companies in different industries. Acquire the balance sheets from the annual reports or 10-Ks of the three companies. (www.freeedgar.com is also a good source).

*Required:*

1. Identify the accounts that result from accruals and those that are deferrals.

2. Write a short report indicating any similarities and differences, if any, in the accounts used by the three.

**CP4–11  Comparing a Company's Net Profit Margin over Time**
Using your web browser, contact the website of Papa John's (www.freeedgar.com is also a good source). Acquire the income statements from the most recent annual reports or 10-Ks.

*Required:*

1. Compute the net profit margin for all years reported.

2. Write a short memo comparing these recent ratios with the company's net profit margin presented in the chapter. Indicate what might account for any difference in the ratio over time.

**CP4–12  Evaluating an Ethical Dilemma**
Using your Web browser, obtain a recent news story concerning a corporate financial fraud that discusses management's motivation for its fraudulent acts.

*Required:*

Write a short memo outlining the nature of the fraud, what management's motivation was, and who was hurt or helped by the fraudulent financial information.

**■ LO2, 3, 4 CP4–13**

**Team Project: Analysis of Accruals, Earnings per Share, and Net Profit Margin**

Using your Web browser, as a team select an industry to analyze. Each team member should then use the Internet to obtain the annual report or 10-K for one publicly traded company in the industry, with each member selecting a different company.

*Required:*

1. On an individual basis, each team member should write a short report listing the following:
   *a.* The company's earnings per share for each year.
   *b.* The company's net profit margin for each year.
   *c.* The amount of accrued expenses (a liability) on the balance sheet and the ratio of accrued expenses to total liabilities.
   *d.* Summaries of any notes to the financial statements that describe accrued expenses in detail.

2. Discuss any patterns that you as a team observe. Then, as a team, write a short report comparing and contrasting your companies according to the preceding attributes. Provide potential explanations for any differences discovered.

# Communicating and Interpreting Accounting Information

## CHAPTER FIVE

LEARNING **OBJECTIVES**

*After studying this chapter, you should be able to:*

1. Recognize the people involved in the accounting communication process (managers, auditors, information intermediaries, government regulators, and users), their roles in the process, and the guidance they receive from legal and professional standards.   p. 239

2. Identify the steps in the accounting communication process, including the issuance of press releases, annual reports, quarterly reports, and SEC filings as well as the role of electronic information services in this process.   p. 247

3. Recognize and apply the different financial statement and disclosure formats used by companies in practice.   p. 251

4. Analyze a company's performance based on return on equity and its components.   p. 265

In just 17 years, Ely [pronounced EE-lee] Callaway took a small manufacturer of specialty golf clubs with $500,000 in annual sales and built it into the industry leader with sales of more than $840 million. Callaway attributes this success to the innovative Big Bertha oversized clubs, created by a team of aerospace and metallurgical engineers, that make the game easier to learn and play. Both touring pros and average golfers including Bill Clinton and George Bush carry a Big Bertha driver in their golf bags. But industry insiders attribute an equal portion of Ely Callaway's success to his marketing skills. He spends hours each day talking to the pros who use his clubs at televised events and the dealers who sell his clubs. He even writes much of the company's ad copy.

## FOCUS **COMPANY:**

# Callaway Golf

### COMMUNICATING FINANCIAL INFORMATION AND CORPORATE STRATEGY

He and then chief financial officer (CFO) Carol Kerley applied that same personal marketing touch to the financial side of the business when they persuaded managers of the General Electric Pension Fund to invest $10 million in the company to provide the capital that fueled its initial growth in 1989. The same enthusiasm and clear approach to communication were apparent in the company's initial public offering (first stock issuance to the public, or IPO) in 1992. The CFO and her accounting staff worked tirelessly with the company's outside auditors, PricewaterhouseCoopers, and its investment bankers, Merrill Lynch, to prepare the detailed financial information necessary for the IPO. Callaway had prepared audited statements in the past. Now as a publicly traded company, it is required to provide even more information in regular filings with the Securities and Exchange Commission.

Clear communication with Callaway's four customer groups—professional endorsers, dealers, golfing consumers, and investors and other users of financial statements—continues to be a hallmark of its successful business strategy. Callaway drivers are now the most popular on the PGA tours and Callaway is the largest golf club company in the world. However, Southeast Asian economic problems, El Niño–induced weather changes, and increasing competition present new challenges for Callaway's business and communication strategy.

## BUSINESS BACKGROUND

Callaway Golf Company designs, manufactures, and markets high-quality innovative golf clubs that sell at premium prices. Its Big Bertha oversized stainless steel and titanium woods and irons account for most of its sales. Many judge these clubs to be the "friendliest" in the game because they are less sensitive to off-center hits. The company manufactures its metal woods and irons in its new Carlsbad, California, factories using clubheads, shafts, and grips supplied by independent vendors such as Coastcast Corporation, Aldila, True Temper, and others. The clubs are sold primarily at high-end pro shops. Callaway invests considerable amounts in research and development and is known for introducing new innovative products long before the end of its existing products' life cycles. Although it *manufactures* golf clubs, Callaway also sells other golf-related equipment, including bags and headcovers, that others manufacture. Thus, it is a *merchandiser* for this other equipment.

Successful companies such as Callaway learn to match their financial reporting strategies to their business strategies. Marketing and communication are fundamental to both strategies. Callaway values integrity in the communication of financial results as much as it does in its relationships with suppliers, customers, and employees. It deals honestly and candidly with the financial press, financial analysts, and the investing public. Also, to its credit, the financial statements and related disclosures provided in its annual report are a model of clarity. Callaway's management believes that such an approach eases the company's access to capital from lenders and investors. This approach lowers the costs of borrowing (interest rates) and lowers investors' perceptions of the riskiness of Callaway's stock. These policies, the fact that the company has recently changed from private to public financing, and its business success make Callaway Golf an excellent example through which we can focus our discussion of communicating and interpreting accounting information.

Chapters 2 through 4 focused on the mechanics of preparing the income statement, balance sheet, statement of stockholders' equity, and cash flow statement. In this chapter, we focus on the people involved and the sequential process that conveys accounting information to statement users during a typical year. We also discuss the exact statement formats and additional disclosures provided in annual reports and related reports to help you learn how to find relevant information in these reports. Finally, we examine a general framework for assessing a company's performance based on these reports.

## ORGANIZATION OF THE CHAPTER

| • **Players in the Accounting Communication Process** | • **The Disclosure Process** | • **A Closer Look at Financial Statement Formats and Notes** | • **ROE Analysis** |
|---|---|---|---|
| Managers (CEO, CFO, and Accounting Staff) | Press Releases | Classified Balance Sheet | Profit Driver Analysis |
| Auditors | Annual Reports | Classified Income Statement | Profit Drivers and Business Strategy |
| Information Intermediaries: Analysts and Information Services | Quarterly Reports | Statement of Stockholders' Equity | |
| Government Regulators | SEC Reports | Statement of Cash Flow | |
| Users: Institutional and Private Investors, Creditors, and Others | | Notes to Financial Statements | |
| Guiding Principles for Communicating Useful Information | | Voluntary Disclosures | |
| | | Constraints of Accounting Measurement | |

# PLAYERS IN THE ACCOUNTING COMMUNICATION PROCESS

Exhibit 5.1 summarizes the accounting communication process in terms of the people involved, their roles in the process, and the guidance they receive from legal and professional standards.

### MANAGERS (CEO, CFO, AND ACCOUNTING STAFF)

As noted in Chapter 1, the primary responsibility for the information in Callaway's financial statements and related disclosures lies with management as represented by the highest officer in the company, often called the *chairman and chief executive officer* (CEO) and the highest officer associated with the financial and accounting side of the business, often called the *chief financial officer* (CFO). These two officers normally sign the statement of management responsibility (as also discussed in Chapter 1) if one is included in the annual report. For public companies, the same officers are responsible for the principal reports filed with the Securities and Exchange Commission (SEC). At Callaway, Ely Callaway, chairman and CEO, and Carol Kerley, then the CFO, had that responsibility at the time of Callaway's initial public offering (IPO). They were responsible for the conformance of the statements and related disclosures with GAAP (generally accepted accounting principles). Although their legal responsibility is smaller, the members of the *accounting staff* who actually prepare the details of the reports also have professional responsibility for the accuracy of this information. Their professional success in the future depends heavily on their reputations for honesty and competence.

### AUDITORS

As we discussed in Chapter 1, the SEC requires publicly traded companies to have their statements audited by CPAs following generally accepted auditing standards.

■ **LEARNING OBJECTIVE 1**

Recognize the people involved in the accounting communication process (managers, auditors, information intermediaries, government regulators, and users), their roles in the process, and the guidance they receive from legal and professional standards.

EXHIBIT **5.1**

**The Accounting
Communication Process**

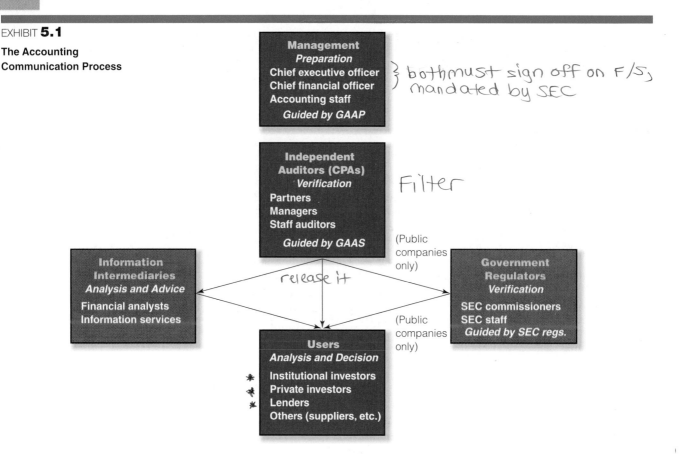

*[Handwritten annotations on figure: "both must sign off on F/S, mandated by SEC", "Filter", "release it"]*

Many privately owned companies also have their statements audited. By signing an **unqualified,** or **clean, audit opinion,** the CPA firm assumes financial responsibility for the fairness of the financial statements and related presentations. This opinion adds credibility to the statements and often is required by agreements with lenders and private investors who are not actively involved in management of the companies. Callaway Golf was initially financed through investments by Mr. Callaway and some of his close friends and loans from financial institutions (e.g., banks and commercial finance companies). By voluntarily subjecting the company's statements to independent verification, Callaway reduced the risk to the private investors and financial institutions that the company's condition was not as represented in the statements. As a consequence, rational investors and lenders should lower the rate of return (interest) they charge for providing capital.

PricewaterhouseCoopers (which along with KPMG Peat Marwick, Arthur Andersen, Ernst & Young, and Deloitte & Touche make up what are referred to as the "Big 5" CPA firms) is currently Callaway Golf's auditor. Each of these firms employs thousands of CPAs in offices scattered throughout the world. They audit the great majority of publicly traded companies and many privately held companies. Some public companies and most private companies are audited by CPA firms of smaller size. A list of well-known companies and their auditors at the time this chapter was written follows.

| Company | Industry | Auditor |
|---|---|---|
| The Boeing Company | Aircraft | Deloitte & Touche |
| Hilton Hotels Corporation | Hotels | Arthur Andersen |
| Honda Motor Co. Ltd. (Japan) | Automobiles | KPMG Peat Marwick |
| Singapore Airlines (Singapore) | Airline | Ernst & Young |
| Wendy's | Fast food | PricewaterhouseCoopers |

Carol Kerley, Callaway's CFO at the time of the initial public offering, and David A. Rane, current CFO, were senior managers with PricewaterhouseCoopers before moving to Callaway Golf. Companies often hire financial managers from their CPA firms because of their broad financial experience as well as their specific company knowledge gained during prior years' audits.

## INFORMATION INTERMEDIARIES: ANALYSTS AND INFORMATION SERVICES

**The Role of Financial Analysts**   Students often view the communication process between companies and financial statement users as involving a simple process of mailing the report to individual shareholders who read the report and then make investment decisions based on what they have learned. This simple picture is far from today's reality. Now sophisticated *financial analysts* use modern information technology to gather and analyze information. They receive accounting reports and other information about the company from electronic information services (discussed later). They also gather information through personal phone conversations with company executives and visits to company facilities. They then combine the results of these analyses with information about competitors, the overall economy, and even population trends to make predictions of future earnings and stock price. These predictions form the basis of their buy, hold, or sell recommendations for a company's stock.

Analysts often work in the research departments of brokerage and investment banking houses such as Merrill Lynch, mutual fund companies such as Fidelity Investments, and investment advisory services such as Value Line that sell their advice to others. Individual analysts often specialize in particular industries (such as sporting goods or energy companies) and in particular companies. For example, Hayley Kissel at Merrill Lynch and Timothy Conder of A.G. Edwards & Sons (both brokerage and investment banking companies) are among those who follow Callaway Golf. With other analysts at their firms, they write reports that analyze the company's future prospects.

Analysts' reports normally include their estimate or forecast of future quarterly and annual earnings per share for the company.[1] In making these **earnings forecasts,** the analysts rely heavily on their knowledge of the way the accounting system translates business events into the numbers on a company's financial statements.[2] This knowledge includes an understanding of the alternative accounting methods available to companies to account for different transactions and specialized industry practices that may be applied to a particular industry. Analysts are regularly evaluated based on the accuracy of their forecasts, as well as the profitability of their stock picks.[3] In 1999, Beth Burnson of ABN Amro topped *The Wall Street Journal*'s list of all-star forecasters in the leisure and recreation industry.

Analysts' employers either use the reports directly or sell them to other investors. As a consequence, the analyst is transferring his or her knowledge of accounting, the company, and the industry to others who lack this expertise. Many believe that decisions made based on analysts' advice cause stock market prices to react quickly to accounting information announcements. A quick, unbiased reaction to information is called *market efficiency* in finance.

It is highly unlikely that unsophisticated investors can glean more information from financial statements than the sophisticated analysts have already learned. Careful analysis does not lead all analysts to the same conclusions, however. These differences

**EARNINGS FORECASTS** are predictions of earnings for future accounting periods.

---

[1]For further discussion of analysts' forecasts, see K. Schipper, "Analysts' Forecasts," *Accounting Horizons,* December 1991, pp. 105–121.

[2]See G. J. Previts, R. J. Bricker, T. R. Robinson, and S. J. Young, "A Content Analysis of Sell-Side Financial Analyst Reports," *Accounting Horizons,* June 1994, pp. 55–70.

[3]See M. B. Mikhail, B. R. Walther, and R. H. Willis, "Does Forecast Accuracy Matter to Security Analysts?" *The Accounting Review,* April 1999, pp. 185–200.

of opinion are reflected in the following earnings (per share) forecasts and stock recommendations made by analysts at three investment firms for Callaway at the time this chapter was written.

**REAL WORLD EXCERPT**

*First Call Notes*

| | **COMPANY: CALLAWAY GOLF** | | |
| Firm | Stock Recommendation | Earnings Forecast for 12/98 | Earnings Forecast for 12/99 |
| --- | --- | --- | --- |
| ABN/Chicago Corp. | Buy | 1.20 | 1.80 |
| Raymond James and Associates | Neutral | 1.21 | 1.45 |
| Merrill Lynch | Neutral | 1.20–1.30 | 2.00 |

The information services discussed in the next section allow investors to monitor the recommendations of a variety of analysts.

# A QUESTION OF ETHICS

## IT PAYS TO BE A WARY INVESTOR

Recent events on Wall Street suggest that savvy investors should apply a healthy dose of skepticism along with their accounting knowledge when reading or listening to investment advice. Alleged ethical lapses, questionable business practices, and illegal activity by representatives of some of the largest, most highly respected brokerage and investment banking houses have recently made the news. These activities include the rigging of prices in securities auctions, excess trading of customers' accounts to generate higher commissions, insider trading, the sale of securities without full disclosure of their risks, and executing trades for some customers at more advantageous prices than others. Most analysts, brokers, and investment bankers act in an honest and ethical fashion; however, they earn profits by charging commissions on securities transactions. When brokers let their need to earn commissions cloud their investment advice, this can lead to unethical behavior.

**Information Services**   Financial analysts obtain much of the information they use from the wide variety of electronic information services available today. These services are normally either available on-line (via modem, computer networks, or satellite dish) or on CD-ROM (compact disk, read-only memory). Some of the services provide specialized information. For example, I/B/E/S, Inc., provides consensus (average) and analyst-by-analyst earnings forecasts for more than 18,000 domestic and foreign companies. More than 800 research analysts contribute earnings forecasts to the service. First Call provides a similar service. Samples of the consensus forecasts can be accessed on their websites:

> www.ibes.com
>
> www.firstcall.com

Services such as Lexis-Nexis, Compustat, and Disclosure provide broader access to financial statement and related news information. They also allow users to search the database by key words, including various terms in financial statements. Their websites describe their services in more detail:

> www.lexis-nexis.com
>
> www.compustat.com
>
> www.disclosure.com/dga_demo/

Companies actually can file SEC forms electronically with EDGAR (Electronic Data Gathering and Retrieval Service), sponsored by the SEC. This information is available to users through EDGAR within 24 hours of filing with the Commission, long before it is available through the mail in hard-copy form. EDGAR is currently a free service available on the Web at

www.sec.gov/cgi-bin/srch-edgar

To look at EDGAR, just type the address on your Web browser. Then, at the search prompt, enter "Callaway Golf" and you will be led to Callaway's latest filings. The 10-K and 10-Q forms (described later) include the financial statements and notes. Many of the financial statement examples used in this book were downloaded (electronically copied) from different services.

More general information services include the Dow Jones Interactive and Bloomberg Financial Markets and Commodities News. Dow Jones provides access to news stories about companies, as well as current and historical stock price and company press releases, including the initial announcements of annual and quarterly financial results. This information also is available electronically through the information service long before shareholders and others receive the hard-copy reports. The Bloomberg service also provides the ability to combine these sources of information in sophisticated analyses. The graph presented in Exhibit 5.2 plots Callaway's quarterly price per share and earnings per share over six years. Their websites describe their services in more detail:

www.dowjones.com

www.bloomberg.com

A growing number of other resources exist on the Web that offer a mixture of free and fee-based information on many companies. These include

www.marketguide.com

www.etrade.com

www.hoovers.com

www.yahoo.com

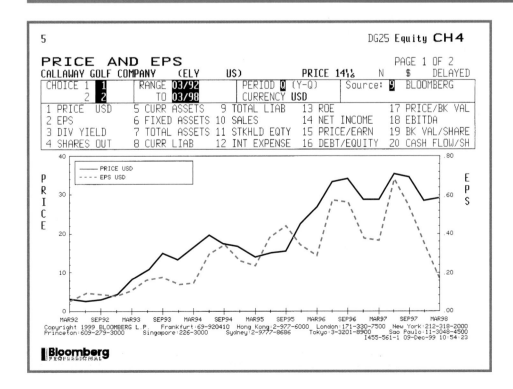

EXHIBIT **5.2**

**Price and Earnings per Share Graph from Bloomberg Terminal**

The most interesting new trend in information services is the provision of financial information in audio and video form. You can access recordings of conference calls and videos of meetings between financial analysts and company management on YAHOO!broadcast. Listening to these recordings is a good way to learn about a company's business strategy and its expectations for the future, as well as key factors that analysts consider when they evaluate a company.

**www.broadcast.com/business/**

Many companies also provide direct access to their financial statements and other information over the Web. You can contact Callaway at

**www.callawaygolf.com**

Readers should be aware that the definitions used to compute key ratios often differ across these sources.

# FINANCIAL ANALYSIS

## INFORMATION SERVICES: USES IN MARKETING, CLASSWORK, AND JOB SEARCHES

Information services have become the primary tools used not only by sophisticated analysts but also by marketing strategists to analyze competing firms. Sales representatives also use the services to analyze potential customers. These analyses allow the sales representative to determine which customers have growing needs for their products and which have the financial strength necessary to qualify for credit. Such companies are the most profitable targets for the sales representative's efforts.

The information services are an important source of information to students for their term papers and even their job searches. Potential employers expect top job applicants to be knowledgeable about their company before an interview. We suggest that you contact the business or reference librarian at your college or university library or visit a local brokerage house to learn more about these modern electronic information services and the usage fees they charge.

### GOVERNMENT REGULATORS

The *Securities and Exchange Commission* sets additional reporting standards for firms with publicly traded debt or equity securities. We discuss these requirements later in the chapter and throughout the text when relevant. The SEC staff reviews these reports for compliance with their standards, investigates irregularities, and punishes violators of their regulations. Current SEC Chairman Arthur Levitt has increased efforts in this area as indicated by the cover story from a recent issue of *Fortune* magazine.

**REAL WORLD EXCERPT**

*Fortune*

**The Crackdown Is Here**
The nation's top earnings cop has put corporate America on notice: *Quit cooking the books.* Cross the line, you may do time.

Source: *Fortune,* August 2, 1999, p. 75.

Research indicates that during a recent 11-year period, the SEC brought enforcement actions against nearly 300 firms for accounting-related violations.[4] In 72 percent of the cases, the CEO was implicated, and the company's auditors were also implicated in 29

---

[4]These statistics are reported in M. S. Beasley, J. V. Carcello, and D. R. Hermanson, "Fraudulent Financial Reporting: 1987–1997: An Analysis of U.S. Public Companies," *The Auditor's Report*, Summer 1999, pp. 15–17. See also E. H. Feroz, K. Parke, and V. S. Pastena, "The Financial and Market Effects of the SEC's Accounting and Auditing Enforcement Releases," *Journal of Accounting Research,* Supplement 1991, pp. 107–142.

percent of the cases. The *Fortune* article cited lists nine CEOs who have been sentenced to jail for accounting fraud during the last five years. Consequences to the company included bankruptcy or significant changes in ownership as well as financial penalties.

## USERS: INSTITUTIONAL AND PRIVATE INVESTORS, CREDITORS, AND OTHERS

**Institutional investors** include the managers of private pension funds (associated with unions and employees of specific companies); public pension funds (for state and municipal employees); mutual funds; and endowment, charitable foundation, and trust funds (such as the endowment of your college or university). These institutional stockholders usually employ their own analysts and use the information intermediaries just discussed. Institutional shareholders such as these control the majority of publicly traded shares of U.S. companies. For example, at the end of the current fiscal year, the following three institutional investors, along with the seven others owning between 1 and 1.5 million shares each, together owned more than 20 percent of Callaway's outstanding stock:

| Institution | Approximate Ownership |
| --- | --- |
| Neuberger & Berman | 2.5 million shares |
| Oppenheimer Management Corp. | 1.7 million shares |
| Alliance Capital Management | 1.6 million shares |

An additional 59 other institutional investors such as Mellon Bank, Bankers Trust, and the New York State Common Retirement Fund owned between 100,000 and 1 million shares each. Most small investors own stock in companies such as Callaway Golf *indirectly* through mutual and pension funds such as these.

**Private investors** include large individual investors such as Ely Callaway and his friends who invested directly in Callaway Golf before it became a public company and small retail investors who, like most individuals, buy a small number of shares of publicly traded companies through brokers such as Merrill Lynch and E*TRADE. Retail investors normally lack the expertise to understand financial statements and the resources to gather other important data efficiently. As a consequence, they often rely on the advice of information intermediaries or turn their money over to the management of mutual and pension funds (institutional investors).

**Lenders,** or **creditors,** include suppliers, banks, commercial credit companies, and other financial institutions that lend money to companies. Lending officers and financial analysts in these organizations use these same public sources of information in their analyses. In addition, when companies borrow money from financial institutions, they often agree to provide additional financial information (e.g., monthly statements) as part of the lending contract. Lenders are often the primary external user group for financial statements of private companies. Individuals and mutual funds also become creditors when they buy publicly traded bonds and debentures issued by a company.[5]

**INSTITUTIONAL INVESTORS** are managers of pension, mutual, endowment, and other funds that invest on the behalf of others.

**PRIVATE INVESTORS** include individuals who purchase shares in companies.

**LENDERS (CREDITORS)** include suppliers and financial institutions that lend money to companies.

## A QUESTION OF **ETHICS**

### CONFLICTING INTERESTS OF MANAGERS, STOCKHOLDERS, AND CREDITORS

The economic interests of managers, stockholders, and creditors often differ. For example, paying dividends to stockholders benefits the stockholders but leaves less money available to pay creditors; refurnishing the offices occupied by managers benefits the managers but leaves less

[5]*Debentures* are debt securities not secured with specific collateral (no specific assets are pledged as security for the debt). *Bonds* normally are secured by specific collateral such as investments in stock of other companies.

money to pay dividends. Expectations of ethical conduct and mutual trust play a major role in keeping these differing interests in balance.

Accounting and financial statements also play a major role in enforcing these relationships of trust. Later in the chapter we discuss how compliance with agreements (contracts) between managers and stockholders and between stockholders and creditors are monitored with financial statement data.* When the United States negotiates arms treaties with other countries, "trust but verify" is a common rule that is followed. Applying the same rule in business practice is prudent.

*Research that examines the use of accounting in contracting is called *agency theory.*

As noted in Chapter 1, these same financial statements play an important role in the relationships between customers and suppliers. Customers evaluate the financial health of suppliers to determine whether they will be able to provide a reliable, up-to-date source of supply. Suppliers evaluate their customers to estimate their future needs and ability to pay their debts to the suppliers. Competitors also attempt to learn useful information about a company from its statements. The potential loss of competitive advantage is one of the costs to the preparer of public financial disclosures. Accounting regulators consider these costs as well as the direct costs of preparation when they consider requiring new disclosures. They apply what is called the **cost-benefit constraint,** which suggests that the benefits of accounting for and reporting information should outweigh the costs. Other uses of financial statement information in labor–management relations and in government regulation were discussed in Chapter 1.

The **COST-BENEFIT CONSTRAINT** suggests that the benefits of accounting for and reporting information should outweigh the costs.

**RELEVANT INFORMATION** can influence a decision; it is timely and has predictive and/or feedback value.

**RELIABLE INFORMATION** is accurate, unbiased, and verifiable.

**CONSISTENT INFORMATION** can be compared over time because similar accounting methods have been applied.

**COMPARABLE INFORMATION** can be compared across businesses because similar accounting methods have been applied.

### GUIDING PRINCIPLES FOR COMMUNICATING USEFUL INFORMATION

For accounting information to be useful to any of these user groups, it must be relevant and reliable. **Relevant information** is capable of influencing decisions because it allows users to assess past activities (feedback value) and/or predict future activities (predictive value). **Reliable information** must be accurate, unbiased, and verifiable (independent parties can agree on the nature of the transaction and amount). Our discussions of ratio analysis emphasize the importance of comparing ratios produced by the same company over time as well as comparing the company's ratios with those of competitors. Such comparisons are valid only if the information is prepared on a consistent and comparable basis. **Consistent information** means that within a company, similar accounting methods have been applied over time. **Comparable information** means that similar accounting methods have been applied. These characteristics of useful information, along with the full-disclosure principle, are defined in the conceptual framework and guide the FASB in deciding what financial information should be reported.

## SELF-STUDY **QUIZ**

Match the players involved in the accounting communication process with their roles or the guiding principles for communicating information with their definitions.

1. Relevant information
2. CEO and CFO
3. Financial analyst
4. Auditor

5. Cost-benefit constraint

*a.* Management primarily responsible for accounting information.
*b.* An independent party who verifies financial statements.
*c.* Information that influences users' decisions.
*d.* Only information that provides benefits in excess of costs should be reported.
*e.* An individual who analyzes financial information and provides advice.

After you have completed the quiz, check your answers with those presented in the footnote at the bottom of this page. *

*1c, 2a, 3e, 4b, 5d.

# THE DISCLOSURE PROCESS

As noted in our discussion of information services and information intermediaries, the accounting communication process includes more steps and participants than one would envision in a world in which annual and quarterly reports are simply mailed to shareholders.

## PRESS RELEASES

Callaway and most public companies announce quarterly and annual earnings through a **press release** as soon as the verified figures (audited for annual and reviewed for quarterly earnings) are available to provide timely information to external users and to limit the possibility of selective leakage of information. Callaway normally issues its earnings press releases within four weeks of the end of the accounting period. The announcements are sent electronically to the major print and electronic news services including Dow Jones, the PR Newswire, and *Bloomberg Business News*, which make them immediately available to subscribers. The first page of a typical quarterly press release for Callaway is reprinted in Exhibit 5.3. It includes key financial figures and management's discussion of the results. Attached to the release are condensed income statements and balance sheets (unaudited) that will be included in the formal quarterly report to shareholders mailed after the press release.

■ **LEARNING OBJECTIVE 2**

Identify the steps in the accounting communication process, including the issuance of press releases, annual reports, quarterly reports, and SEC filings as well as the role of electronic information services in this process.

A **PRESS RELEASE** is a written public news announcement normally distributed to major news services.

---

**Callaway® Golf**

**Callaway Golf Reports Record Third Quarter Sales of $257.4 Million**

10/22/1997

CARLSBAD, Calif., Oct. 22—Callaway Golf Company (NYSE: ELY) today reported record net sales of $257.4 million for the third quarter ended September 30, 1997, an increase of 32 percent over net sales of $194.5 million reported in the third quarter of 1996, according to Ely Callaway, Founder and Chairman, and Donald H. Dye, President and CEO. Net income for the same period of $37.0 million ($0.52 fully diluted earnings per share) includes a one-time pretax charge of $12.0 million for the settlement of litigation between the Company and a former officer. Net income without the $12.0 million legal expense would have been $44.4 million compared to $38.4 million in the comparable quarter of 1996, an increase of 16 percent, and fully diluted earnings per share would have been $0.62 compared to $0.54 in the third quarter of 1996, an increase of 15 percent.

Mr. Dye stated, "The third quarter results reflect the continued success of the Company's products in the marketplace and the Company's commitment to continue building for the future. Where sales increased 32 percent, profits actually decreased because of a one-time payment for the settlement of litigation, early transitional costs associated with the Odyssey acquisition, and an increase in expenditures associated with research and development related to golf clubs, golf balls and interactive golf. Without these charges, earnings would have kept pace with sales."

Mr. Dye continued, "Callaway Golf had a record quarter with net sales of over $257 million. We are especially pleased that we were able to announce and complete the Odyssey acquisition during the third quarter and to have recognized $12.0 million in net sales of Odyssey products. Together with our Big Bertha®, Great Big Bertha®, and Biggest Big Bertha™ product lines, we feel that Odyssey's products add to our growing family of demonstrably superior and pleasingly different golf clubs, as well as adding a powerful brand name."

Net sales of $257.4 million for the third quarter were comprised of: $118.7 million of Great Big Bertha® and Biggest Big Bertha™ Titanium Metal Woods, $42.2 million of stainless steel Big Bertha® War Bird® Metal Woods, $52.1 million of Big Bertha® Irons, $20.8 million of Great Big Bertha® Tungsten-Titanium™ Irons, $11.5 million in Odyssey putter sales, and $12.1 million of other sales.

It was also announced that the Board of Directors has approved a quarterly dividend of $.07 per share payable November 18, 1997, to shareholders of record as of October 28, 1997.

For more information about Callaway Golf Company, please visit our website on the Internet at www.callawaygolf.com.

2285 Rutherford Road • Carlsbad, CA 92008-8815
Telephone: (619) 931-1771 • Outside California (800) 228-2767
FAX: (619) 931-9539

EXHIBIT **5.3**

**Earnings Press Release for Callaway Golf Company**

**REAL WORLD EXCERPT**

*Callaway Golf*

PRESS RELEASE

For actively traded stocks such as those of Callaway Golf, most of the stock market reaction (stock price increases and decreases from investor trading) to the news in the press release usually occurs quickly. Recall that a number of analysts follow Callaway and regularly predict the company's earnings. When the actual earnings are published, the market reacts *not* to the amount of earnings but to the difference between expectations of earnings and actual earnings. This amount is called *unexpected earnings.* For example, the *Bloomberg News Service* recently reported the following:

**REAL WORLD EXCERPT**

*The San Diego Union-Tribune*

**Callaway Stock Is Clubbed in Sell-off**
**Earnings Fail to Meet Hopes; Price Falls 10%**
Shareholders disappointed by Callaway Golf's lower-than-expected earnings whacked the stock yesterday, sending the price about 10 percent lower in a sell-off triggered by the company's first financial bogey. . . . The Carlsbad golf club maker posted fourth-quarter earnings of 34 cents a share, 3 cents below analysts' estimates and 2 cents below Callaway's earnings for the fourth quarter of 1996. It was the first time Callaway failed to meet or beat analysts' estimates.

SOURCE: *The San Diego Union-Tribune*, January 30, 1998, p. C-1. Reprinted with permission from the *San Diego Union-Tribune.*

Compared to the average estimate, unexpected earnings were minus 3 cents per share, and the share price dropped over $3. The following excerpt from a recent article in *Fortune* magazine points out the growing importance of meeting or beating the average or consensus analysts' estimate:

**REAL WORLD EXCERPT**

*Fortune*

**Learn to Play the Earnings Game (and Wall Street Will *Love You*)**
The simplest, most visible, most merciless measure of corporate success in the 1990s has become this one: Did you make your earnings last quarter?
  This is new . . . it's only in the past decade with the rise to prominence of the consensus earnings estimates compiled first in the early 1970s by I/B/E/S . . . and now also by competitors Zacks, First Call, and Nelson's, that those expectations have become so explicit.

SOURCE: *Fortune*, March 31, 1997, p. 77. © 1997 *Time Inc.* All rights reserved.

Companies such as Callaway issue press releases concerning other important events including new product announcements and new endorsement contracts with professional golfers. The stock market often appears to react to some of these important announcements. For example, a few years ago, Bloomberg reported the following:

**REAL WORLD EXCERPT**

*Bloomberg Business News*

**Callaway Shares Rise after Spokesman Wins Pro-Am**
New York, Feb. 7 (Bloomberg)—The shares of golf-club maker Callaway Golf Co. rose 6.6% today after Callaway's celebrity spokesman Johnny Miller won a California golf tournament yesterday . . . marking the 46-year-old golfer's first win in seven years.

SOURCE: *Bloomberg Business News*, New York, February 7, 1999. Copyright 1999 Bloomberg LP. All rights reserved.

Presumably, the stock market inferred that this would provide an impetus for future sales of the new product.

Press releases related to annual earnings and quarterly earnings often precede the issuance of the quarterly or annual report by 15 to 45 days. This time is necessary to prepare the additional detail and to print and distribute those reports.

## ANNUAL REPORTS

For privately held companies, *annual reports* are relatively simple documents photocopied on white bond paper. They normally include only the following:

1. Four basic financial statements: income statement, balance sheet, stockholders' equity or retained earnings statement, and cash flow statement.
2. Related footnotes or notes as described earlier.
3. Report of independent accountants (auditor's opinion).

The annual reports of public companies are significantly more elaborate, both because of additional SEC reporting requirements imposed on these companies and the fact that many companies use their annual reports as public relations tools to communicate nonaccounting information to shareholders, customers, the press, and others.

The annual reports of public companies are normally split into two sections: The first, "nonfinancial," section usually includes a letter to stockholders from the chairman and CEO; descriptions of the company's management philosophy, products, its successes (and occasionally its failures); and exciting prospects and challenges for the future. Beautiful photographs of products, facilities, and personnel often are included. The second, "financial," section, which is often printed on a different color of paper to make it easy to find, includes the core of the report. The SEC sets minimum disclosure standards for the financial section of the annual reports of public companies. The principal components of the financial section include these:

1. Summarized financial data for a 5- or 10-year period.
2. Management's Discussion and Analysis of Financial Condition and Results of Operations.
3. The four basic financial statements.
4. Notes (Footnotes).
5. Report of Independent Accountants (Auditor's Opinion) and sometimes the Report of Management Responsibility.
6. Recent stock price information.
7. Summaries of the unaudited quarterly financial data (described later).
8. Lists of directors and officers of the company and relevant addresses.

The order of these components varies.

Most of these elements except for Management's Discussion and Analysis have been discussed in earlier chapters. This element includes management's discussion and explanation of key figures on the financial statements and future risks the company faces. Complete annual reports from American Eagle Outfitters and Urban Outfitters, which include all of these sections, are reprinted in Appendices B and C, respectively, at the end of this book. As noted earlier, many companies make their annual report available on the web.

## QUARTERLY REPORTS

Quarterly reports normally begin with a short letter to shareholders. This is followed by a condensed income statement for the quarter, which often shows less detail than the annual income statement, and a condensed balance sheet dated at the end of the quarter (e.g., March 31 for the first quarter). These condensed financial statements are not audited and so are marked *unaudited*. Also, the cash flow statement, statement of stockholders' equity (or retained earnings statement), and some notes to the financial statements often are not included. Private companies also normally prepare quarterly reports for lenders. Callaway's quarterly reports are issued about five weeks after the end of each quarter.

## SEC REPORTS—10-K, 10-Q, 8-K

Public companies also must file periodic reports with the SEC. They include the annual report on Form 10-K, quarterly reports on Form 10-Q, and current event reports on Form 8-K. These reports are normally referred to by number (for example, the "10-K"). The SEC requires that the 10-K be filed within 60 days of the fiscal year-end and the 10-Q be filed within 35 days of the end of quarter. In general, the 10-K and 10-Q present all the information in the annual and quarterly

Sarbanes-Oxley Act of 2002

reports, respectively, along with additional management discussion and several required schedules.

The **FORM 10-K** is the annual report that publicly traded companies must file with the SEC.

**Form 10-K Annual Report**   In the **Form 10-K,** companies provide a more detailed description of the business including items such as their products, product development, sales and marketing, manufacturing, and competitors. It also lists properties owned and leased, any legal proceedings it is involved in, and significant contracts that the company has signed. This last point is particularly important given that, as we emphasized in Chapter 2, many important contracts between the company and other parties such as key employees, distributors, and others represent important economic assets and/or liabilities to the company. They are not included on the balance sheet, however. That is, they have no *book value.*

The 10-K also provides more detailed schedules concerning various figures on the income statement and balance sheet including bad debts, warranties, inventories, and advertising. We will discuss these disclosures in more detail in later chapters starting with the Chapter 6 discussion of bad debts.

# INTERNATIONAL **PERSPECTIVE**

**REAL WORLD EXCERPT**

*Callaway Golf*

FORM 10-K

### JUDGING INTERNATIONAL SALES STRATEGY FROM THE FORM 10-K

In its form 10-K, discussed above, Callaway disclosed a change in its international sales strategy:

> **Sales for Distribution Outside of the United States**
> Approximately 35%, 32% and 34% of the Company's net sales were derived from sales for distribution outside of the United States in 1997, 1996 and 1995, respectively. The majority of the Company's international sales are made through distributors specializing in the sale and promotion of golf clubs in specific countries or regions around the world. . . . In 1996, the Company acquired a majority interest in its distributor in Germany, Golf Trading GmbH, which sells and promotes the Company's products in Germany, Austria, the Netherlands and Switzerland. In February 1998, the Company purchased the distribution rights of its Korean distributor and began directly marketing its products in that country through its subsidiary, Callaway Golf Korea, Ltd. . . . The Company has established ERC International Company ("ERC"), a wholly- owned Japanese corporation, for the purpose of distributing Odyssey® products immediately, golf balls when ready and Callaway Golf clubs beginning January 1, 2000. . . . The Company's management believes that controlling the distribution of its products throughout the world will be an element in the future growth and success of the Company. . . . There can be no assurance that the acquisition of some or all of the Company's foreign distributors will be successful, and it is possible that an attempt to do so will adversely affect the Company's business.

While management believes that this change in strategy will be a source of future gains for Callaway, it clearly will also increase certain risks.

**FORM 10-Q** is the quarterly report that publicly traded companies must file with the SEC.

**Form 10-Q Quarterly Report**   The **Form 10-Q** report includes all the information included in the quarterly report to shareholders, along with a statement of shareholders' equity and a cash flow statement for the quarter, a variety of notes, and a management discussion. The amount of information disclosed in the 10-Q is very close to that included in the annual report to shareholders but less than that required by the Form 10-K. Like the quarterly report to shareholders, the information in the 10-Q is unaudited.

**FORM 8-K** is used by publicly traded companies to disclose any material event not previously reported that is important to investors.

**Form 8-K Current Report**   The **Form 8-K** Current Report is used to report any material event important to investors that has not been previously reported in the 10-Q or 10-K. It normally must be filed within 15 days of any event specified in the form. An example of an event requiring submission of a Form 8-K is a change of auditors.

# A CLOSER LOOK AT FINANCIAL STATEMENT FORMATS AND NOTES

We already know that the financial data contained in accounting reports are important factors in decisions made by investors, creditors, and analysts. To make financial statements more useful to decision makers, specific *classifications* of information are included on the statements.

A variety of classifications is used in practice. You should not be confused when you notice different formats used by different companies. You will find that each format is consistent with the principles discussed in this text. The following is a discussion of these classified financial statements.

■ **LEARNING OBJECTIVE 3**

Recognize and apply the different financial statement and disclosure formats used by companies in practice.

## CLASSIFIED BALANCE SHEET

The December 31, 1997, balance sheet for Callaway Golf is presented in Exhibit 5.4. First, notice the title of the statement, consolidated balance sheet. *Consolidated* means that the accounts of Callaway and the accounts of its wholly owned subsidiaries (e.g., Callaway Golf [U.K.] Limited) have been added together through a consolidation process that results in a single number being reported for each item. (We discuss the consolidation process further in Chapter 12.)

Callaway's balance sheet is shown in the report format (assets listed first and then liabilities and shareholders' equity accounts underneath in one column); others use an account format (assets on the left side and liabilities and shareholders' equity on the right). Like most, Callaway's balance sheet is *classified.* That is, assets and liabilities are listed in a particular order and are separated into current and noncurrent classifications. As noted in Chapter 2, *current assets* are defined as those that will be turned into cash or expire (be used up) within one year or by the end of the operating cycle, whichever is longer. In Chapter 3, we noted that the operating, or cash-to-cash, cycle varies by company and may be longer than one year. *Current liabilities* are defined as those obligations that will be paid with current assets, normally within one year. Typically a balance sheet is classified as follows:

**A.** Assets (by order of liquidity)
  1. Current assets (short term)
     *a.* Cash and cash equivalents
     *b.* Short-term investments (marketable securities)
     *c.* Accounts receivable
     *d.* Inventory
     *e.* Prepaid expenses (i.e., expenses paid in advance of use)
     *f.* Other current assets
  2. Noncurrent assets
     *a.* Long-term investments
     *b.* Property, plant, and equipment—at cost less accumulated depreciation
     *c.* Intangible assets
     *d.* Other (miscellaneous) assets
        Total assets

**B.** Liabilities (by order of time to maturity)
  1. Current liabilities (short-term)
     *a.* Accounts payable
     *b.* Accrued expenses payable
     *c.* Other short-term liabilities
  2. Long-term liabilities
     *a.* Notes and mortgages payable
     *b.* Lease obligations
     *c.* Bonds payable
        Total liabilities

*Ely Callaway, founder, chairman, and CEO of Callaway Golf*

EXHIBIT **5.4**

**Balance Sheet of Callaway Golf***

**REAL WORLD EXCERPT**

*Callaway Golf*

ANNUAL REPORT

**Consolidated Balance Sheet**
**December 31,**
**(in thousands, except share and per share data)**

| | 1997 | 1996 |
|---|---|---|
| **ASSETS** | | |
| Current assets: | | |
| Cash and cash equivalents | $ 26,204 | $108,457 |
| Accounts receivable, net | 124,470 | 74,477 |
| Inventories, net | 97,094 | 98,333 |
| Deferred taxes | 23,810 | 25,948 |
| Other current assets | 10,208 | 4,298 |
| Total current assets | 281,786 | 311,513 |
| | | |
| Property, plant and equipment, net | 142,503 | 91,346 |
| Intangible assets, net | 112,141 | 4,277 |
| Other assets | 25,284 | 21,292 |
| | $561,714 | $428,428 |
| | | |
| **LIABILITIES AND SHAREHOLDERS' EQUITY** | | |
| Current liabilities: | | |
| Accounts payable and accrued expenses | $ 30,063 | $ 14,996 |
| Accrued employee compensation and benefits | 14,262 | 16,195 |
| Accrued warranty expense | 28,059 | 27,303 |
| Income taxes payable | | 2,558 |
| Total current liabilities | 72,384 | 61,052 |
| Long-term liabilities (Note 7) | 7,905 | 5,109 |
| Commitments and contingencies (Note 9) | | |
| Shareholders' equity: | | |
| Preferred Stock, $.01 par value, 3,000,000 shares authorized, none issued and outstanding at December 31, 1997 and 1996 | | |
| Common Stock, $.01 par value, 240,000,000 shares authorized, 74,251,664 and 72,855,222 issued and outstanding at December 31, 1997 and 1996 (Note 4) | 743 | 729 |
| Paid-in capital | 182,513 | 123,189 |
| Accumulated other comprehensive income | (559) | 236 |
| Retained earnings | 298,728 | 238,113 |
| Total shareholders' equity | 481,425 | 362,267 |
| | $561,714 | $428,428 |

See accompanying notes to consolidated financial statements.

*To simplify, we have subtracted amounts for unearned compensation and grantor stock trust from the paid-in capital amounts. These amounts relate to the issuance of employee stock options, a topic beyond the scope of this text, and do not affect the interpretation of the balance sheet. We have also updated the statements for required disclosures of Accumulated other comprehensive income.

    **C.** Stockholders' equity (by source)
        1. Contributed capital (by owners)
        2. Retained earnings (accumulated earnings minus accumulated dividends declared)
            *a.* Total stockholders' equity
            *b.* Total liabilities and stockholders' equity
        3. Accumulated other comprehensive income

It should be emphasized again that each financial statement item is a combination of a number of accounts used in the company's accounting system. Under Current Assets, Callaway does not separately report any short-term investments or prepaid expenses. Any such amounts are included and combined in Other Current Assets. Deferred taxes, depending on the circumstances, can be listed in any of four places on the balance sheet: as a current asset, current liability, noncurrent asset, or noncurrent liability. The Deferred Taxes account represents the amount of income taxes that will most likely be paid or saved in the future based on differences in the application of tax laws and GAAP for recognizing revenues and expenses in the current period. If the amount is an asset (either current or noncurrent), future tax benefits (reductions) are expected. If the amount is a current or noncurrent liability, future tax payments are expected.

After the Current Asset section, *long-term investments* are reported. They include assets that are not used in operating the business. Examples include investments in real estate and stocks and bonds of other companies. Callaway does not separately report any long-term investments.

*Property, plant, and equipment* are often called *fixed assets*. This group includes tangible (physical) assets that were acquired for use in operating the business rather than for resale as inventory items or held as investments. The assets included are buildings; land on which the buildings sit; and equipment, tools, furniture, and fixtures used in operating the business. Property, plant, and equipment, with the exception of land, are depreciated as they are used. As discussed in Chapter 4, their initial cost is apportioned to depreciation expense over their estimated useful lives. Land is not depreciated because it does not wear. The amount of depreciation computed for each period is reported on the income statement as depreciation expense. The accumulated amount of depreciation expense for all past periods is deducted from the initial cost of the asset to derive the *book value* or *net book value* reported on the balance sheet (Cost − Accumulated Depreciation). To illustrate, assume that Callaway purchased a new computer system for $23,000. It had an estimated useful life of five years and a residual value of $1,000. Depreciation expense is computed as $22,000 ÷ 5 years = $4,400 per year. If this was the company's only fixed asset, the balance sheets developed during the five-year period would report the following, probably in a note to the financial statements:

|  | 20A | 20B | 20C | 20D | 20E |
|---|---|---|---|---|---|
| Computer system (at cost) | $23,000 | $23,000 | $23,000 | $23,000 | $23,000 |
| Less: Accumulated depreciation | 4,400 | 8,800 | 13,200 | 17,600 | 22,000 |
| Net book value | $18,600 | $14,200 | $ 9,800 | $ 5,400 | $ 1,000 |

*Intangible assets* have no physical existence and have a long life. Their value is derived from the *legal rights* and *privileges* that accompany ownership. Examples are patents, trademarks, copyrights, franchises, and goodwill from purchasing other companies. Intangible assets usually are not acquired for resale but are directly related to the operations of the business. The intangible assets that Callaway reports relate to trademarks and goodwill resulting from the purchase of Odyssey Sports, Inc., in 1997. As we discussed in Chapter 2, Callaway's internally developed intangible assets are not reflected on the balance sheet because they relate to no identifiable transaction; only those that are material and purchased from others are included. Yet the economic value of these unrecorded internally developed intangible assets is significant.

*Current liabilities* are expected to be paid out of the current assets listed on the same balance sheet normally within the coming year. Current liabilities include accounts payable, short-term notes payable, wages payable, income taxes payable, and other expenses incurred (used) but not yet paid. Callaway combines Accounts Payable and Accrued Expenses Payable and lists Accrued Compensation and Benefits, Accrued Warranty Expense, and Income Taxes Payable separately.

*Long-term liabilities* are a company's debts that are not classified as current liabilities. Long-term liabilities have maturities that extend beyond one year from the balance sheet date. Examples include long-term bank loans, bond liabilities, mortgages, pension liabilities, and lease obligations. In 1997, Callaway's balance sheet showed long-term liabilities made up of pension and other post-retirement liabilities.

*Stockholders' (Shareholders') equity* represents the residual claim of the owners (i.e., A − L = SE). This claim results from the initial contributions of the stockholders (contributed capital) plus retained earnings, which is the accumulated earnings of the company less the accumulated dividends declared. Retained earnings represents the amount of earnings that has been left in the company for growth. The account **Accumulated Other Comprehensive Income** includes accumulated amounts of three additional types of gains or losses not included in the computation of net income. These are unrealized gain or loss on securities, minimum pension liability adjustment, and foreign currency translation adjustment. The first item, unrealized gain or loss on securities, will be discussed in Chapter 12. The latter two items are discussed in intermediate accounting and advanced accounting courses, respectively. Each period the total amount of these gains and losses is directly credited or debited to this stockholders' equity account.

Until this chapter, we have identified the financing by investors as *contributed capital*. In practice, however, this account often is shown as two accounts: Common Stock and Contributed Capital in Excess of Par. Each share of common stock usually has a nominal (low) **par value** printed on the face of the certificate. Par value is a legal amount per share established by the board of directors; it has no relationship to the market price of the stock. Its significance is that it establishes the minimum amount that a stockholder must contribute. Callaway's common stock has a par value of $.01 per share, but the 1,039,000 shares were sold in its 1992 initial public offering at a market price of $15.84 per share (net of issuance costs).[6] When a corporation issues capital stock at net market value, the amount is recorded in part as Common Stock (Number of Shares × Par Value per Share) and the excess as **Capital in Excess of Par** (also called **Additional Paid-in Capital, Contributed Capital in Excess of Par**, or **Paid-in Capital**, which Callaway uses). The journal entry to record Callaway's 1992 initial public offering follows:

| | | |
|---|---|---|
| Cash (A) ($15.84 × 1,039,000 shares) . . . . . . . . . . . . . . . . . . . . . . 16,457,760 | | |
|     Common stock (SE) ($.01 per share × 1,039,000 shares) . . . . | | 10,390 |
|     Paid-in capital (SE) ($16,457,760 − 10,390) . . . . . . . . . . . . . . | | 16,447,370 |

| Assets | = | Liabilities | + | Stockholders' Equity | |
|---|---|---|---|---|---|
| Cash     +16,457,760 | | | | Common Stock | +10,390 |
| | | | | Paid-in Capital | +16,447,370 |

The face of Callaway's balance sheet (as is common for most companies) discloses information on the number of shares that the company is authorized to issue (240 million) and the number of shares "issued and outstanding" (74,251,664 at the end of 1997 issued to investors and not repurchased by the company). Callaway also has a second class of ownership called *preferred stock*. None of this type of stock has ever been issued, however. Additional discussion of accounting and reporting issues for owners' equity is presented in Chapter 11.

**ACCUMULATED OTHER COMPREHENSIVE INCOME** includes the net unrealized gains or losses on securities, net minimum pension liability adjustments, and net foreign currency translation adjustment, which are directly credited or debited to the stockholders' equity account.

**PAR VALUE** is a legal amount per share established by the board of directors; it establishes the minimum amount a stockholder must contribute and has no relationship to the market price of the stock.

**CAPITAL IN EXCESS OF PAR (ADDITIONAL PAID-IN CAPITAL, CONTRIBUTED CAPITAL IN EXCESS OF PAR, PAID-IN CAPITAL)** is the amount of contributed capital less the par value of the stock.

# FINANCIAL **ANALYSIS**

## BALANCE SHEET RATIOS AND DEBT CONTRACTS

When firms borrow money, they agree to make specific payments of interest and principal in the future. To provide protection for the creditors, they also often agree to other restrictions on their activities. For example, Callaway has a $50 million line of credit with its bank, which was

---

[6]These numbers are rounded.

increased to $150 for 1998. This line of credit is not secured by specific assets of the company as collateral; however, as part of the agreement with the bank, Callaway agrees to maintain a minimum specified current ratio and debt-to-equity ratio, which are defined as follows:

$$\text{Current Ratio} = \frac{\text{Current Assets}}{\text{Current Liabilities}} \qquad \text{Debt-to-Equity Ratio} = \frac{\text{Total Liabilities}}{\text{Stockholders' Equity}}$$

Maintaining a specified level of the current ratio assures the bank that the company has sufficient *liquidity* (liquid assets, after the payment of other current liabilities) to pay its current debts. The current ratio is discussed in more detail in Chapter 9. The debt-to-equity ratio measures the portion of the company that is financed with debt as opposed to equity. By limiting the debt-to-equity ratio, Callaway agrees to limit the amount of its additional borrowing, which limits additional demands by these new creditors on Callaway's cash. The debt-to-equity ratio is discussed in more detail in Chapter 10.

## CLASSIFIED INCOME STATEMENT

Callaway Golf's 1997 consolidated income statement is reprinted for you in Exhibit 5.5. Other common titles include *statement of earnings* and *statement of operations*. Income statements have up to five major sections:

1. Continuing operations.
2. Discontinued operations.
3. Extraordinary items.
4. Cumulative effect of changes in accounting methods.
   *Net income* (sum of 1, 2, 3, and 4)
5. Earnings per share.

EXHIBIT **5.5**

Income Statement of
Callaway Golf

**REAL WORLD EXCERPT**

*Callaway Golf*

ANNUAL REPORT

**Consolidated Statement of Income**
**(in thousands, except per share data)**
**Year Ended December 31,**

| | 1997 | | 1996 | | 1995 | |
|---|---|---|---|---|---|---|
| Net sales | $842,927 | 100% | $678,512 | 100% | $553,287 | 100% |
| Cost of goods sold | 400,127 | 47% | 317,353 | 47% | 270,125 | 49% |
| Gross profit | 442,800 | 53% | 361,159 | 53% | 283,162 | 51% |
| Selling expenses | 120,589 | 14% | 80,701 | 12% | 64,310 | 12% |
| General and administrative expenses | 70,724 | 8% | 74,476 | 11% | 55,891 | 10% |
| Research and development costs | 30,298 | 4% | 16,154 | 2% | 8,577 | 2% |
| Litigation settlement | 12,000 | 1% | | | | |
| Income from operations | 209,189 | 25% | 189,828 | 28% | 154,384 | 28% |
| Interest and other income, net | 4,576 | | 5,767 | | 4,017 | |
| Income before income taxes | 213,765 | 25% | 195,595 | 29% | 158,401 | 29% |
| Provision for income taxes | 81,061 | | 73,258 | | 60,665 | |
| Net income | $132,704 | 16% | $122,337 | 18% | $97,736 | 18% |
| Earnings per common share | | | | | | |
| Basic | $1.94 | | $1.83 | | $1.47 | |
| Diluted | $1.85 | | $1.73 | | $1.40 | |
| Common equivalent shares | | | | | | |
| Basic | 68,407 | | 66,832 | | 66,641 | |
| Diluted | 71,698 | | 70,661 | | 69,855 | |

See accompanying notes to consolidated financial statements.

All companies' income statements have sections 1 (continuing operations) and 5 (earnings per share). These are the two sections in Callaway's income statement. Depending on their particular circumstances, one or more of sections 2, 3, and 4 are reported. The amounts for section 1 and any of 2, 3, or 4 that are reported are summed to equal the bottom line *Net Income*. We first focus on the most common and important section, *Continuing Operations*.

**Continuing Operations**  This first section of an income statement presents the results of continuing operations. Companies such as Callaway that do not have any discontinued operations (discussed later) do not title this section separately. This section can be presented, however, using one of two common formats:

1. Single step.
2. Multiple step with cost of goods sold deducted from sales to show gross margin (or gross profit) as a subtotal and then other operating expenses deducted to show operating income as a second subtotal.

Callaway's income statement follows the multiple-step format with a subtotal for gross profit and a subtotal for income from operations before adding or subtracting other income, gains, expenses, and losses. In previous chapters, however, we illustrated a simplified format known as the *single-step* format in which all revenue, income, and gains were listed first, and then all costs, expenses, and losses were subtracted. About one-third of the companies in a recent survey used the single-step approach.[7] In Exhibit 5.6, we reorder the accounts in Callaway's income statement to show you how the same 1997 data would be displayed using the single-step format. Some companies also use a hybrid approach in which only one subtotal for operating income is presented.

EXHIBIT **5.6**

**Alternative Income Statement Formats for Continuing Operations**

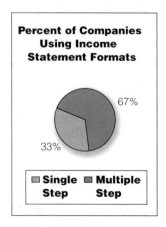

**Percent of Companies Using Income Statement Formats**

67%

33%

☐ Single   ☐ Multiple
  Step        Step

| Single Step | | Multiple Step | |
|---|---:|---|---:|
| Net sales | $842,927 | Net sales | $842,927 |
| Interest income and other income, net | 4,576 | Cost of goods sold | 400,127 |
| **Total revenues** | **847,503** | **Gross profit** | **442,800** |
| Cost of goods sold | 400,127 | Selling expenses | 120,589 |
| Selling expenses expenses | 120,589 | General and administrative expenses | 70,724 |
| General and administrative expenses | 70,724 | Research and development costs | 30,298 |
| Research and development costs | 30,298 | Litigation settlement | 12,000 |
| Litigation settlement | 12,000 | **Income from operations** | **209,189** |
| **Total expenses** | **633,738** | Interest income and other income, net | 4,576 |
| **Income before income taxes** | **213,765** | **Income before income taxes** | **213,765** |
| Provision for income taxes | 81,061 | Provision for income taxes | 81,061 |
| **Net Income** | **$132,704** | **Net Income** | **$132,704** |

[7]American Institute of Certified Public Accountants, *Accounting Trends & Techniques* (New York: AICPA, 1998).

No difference exists in the individual revenue, expense, gain, and loss items reported using the different formats. The differences relate only to the use of categories and subtotals, such as *Gross Profit* and *Income from Operations,* which are highlighted by shading in Exhibit 5.6. Note that, regardless of format, nearly all companies separate income tax expense (provision for income taxes) and report a subtotal Income before Income Taxes.

*Net sales* are gross sales minus any discounts, returns, and allowances during the period. These latter items are discussed in Chapter 6.

*Cost of goods sold* is the cost of inventory sold by a merchandiser (a company that buys products from manufacturers for resale) or a manufacturer (a company that produces goods for sale to wholesalers or retail merchandisers). For example, assume that Callaway sold golf club inventory costing $90,000 to Sumitomo Corporation (which imports and sells Callaway's golf clubs in Japan) for $200,000 on account. The journal entries are as follows:

| | | |
|---|---|---|
| Accounts receivable (A) .................................. | 200,000 | |
| Sales revenue (R) ................................ | | 200,000 |
| *To reflect the earning of revenue in exchange for a promise to pay from the customer.* | | |
| Cost of goods sold (E) ................................ | 90,000 | |
| Inventory (A) ................................ | | 90,000 |
| *To reflect the use of inventory to generate revenues in the period.** | | |

| Assets | | = | Liabilities | + | Stockholders' Equity | |
|---|---|---|---|---|---|---|
| Accounts receivable | +200,000 | | | | Sales revenue | +200,000 |
| Inventory | − 90,000 | | | | Cost of goods sold | − 90,000 |

*This example illustrates a perpetual inventory system. Alternative systems are illustrated in Chapter 7.

Any inventory that is purchased or produced but not sold during the period is included in the inventory on the balance sheet. We will present additional discussion of accounting for sales and cost of goods sold for merchandising and manufacturing companies in Chapters 6 and 7.

**Gross profit (gross margin)** is a subtotal, not an account. It is the difference between *Net Sales* and *Cost of Goods Sold*. Notice in Exhibit 5.5 that Callaway also reports income statement line items as a percentage of net sales, including the gross profit, which are often called *common-sized income statements*. Many analysts compute these common-sized statements as a first step in analysis, however, because they ease year-to-year comparisons.

**GROSS PROFIT (GROSS MARGIN)** is net sales less cost of goods sold.

*Operating expenses* are the usual expenses incurred in operating a business during an accounting period. Differences in the specific expense and revenue categories reported are common, depending on the nature of each company and industry. Significant unusual or infrequently occurring items are also often reported separately. Callaway reports one such item, the cost of the *Litigation Settlement* in 1997. Since this item relates to normal operations of the business, it is included in operating expenses. Another subtotal—**Income from Operations** (also called **Operating Income**)—is computed after subtracting operating expenses from gross profit.

**INCOME FROM OPERATIONS (OPERATING INCOME)** equals net sales less cost of goods sold and other operating expenses.

*Nonoperating (other) items* are income, expenses, gains, and losses that are not considered as resulting from the central operations of the business but are not unusual or infrequent in nature. Examples are interest income, interest expense, and gains and losses on the sale of fixed assets. Interest expense on debt is sometimes combined (netted) with interest revenue so that only a single amount is reported. These nonoperating items are added to or subtracted from income from operations to obtain **Income before Income Taxes,** which is also called **Pretax Earnings.**

**INCOME BEFORE INCOME TAXES (PRETAX EARNINGS)** is revenues minus all expenses except income tax expense.

# FINANCIAL ANALYSIS

## ACCOUNTING-BASED EXECUTIVE BONUSES

Callaway Golf believes in tying executives' compensation to the performance of the company as measured by accounting numbers. In addition to other compensation, Callaway pays its five executive officers bonuses up to 75 percent of base salary if pretax earnings growth (computed here) meets target amounts. Smaller growth statistics result in smaller bonuses. The current year target for maximum bonus was as follows:

**Target for Maximum Bonus**

$$\text{Pretax Earnings Growth \%} = \frac{\left( \begin{array}{c} \text{Current Year} \\ \text{Pretax Earnings} \end{array} - \begin{array}{c} \text{Last Year} \\ \text{Pretax Earnings} \end{array} \right)}{\text{Last Year Pretax Earnings}} = 30\%$$

Meeting this maximum goal in the current year will result in bonuses ranging from $300,000 to $562,500 for each of the five executive officers.

## SELF-STUDY QUIZ

1. Complete the following tabulation, indicating the sign (+ for increase, − for decrease, and NE for no effect) and amount of the effect of each transaction. Consider each item independently.

   a. Recorded and paid rent expense of $200.

   b. Recorded the sale of goods on account for $400 and cost of goods sold of $300.

| Transaction | Current Assets | Gross Profit | Income from Operations |
|---|---|---|---|
| a. | | | |
| b. | | | |

2. Callaway executives receive maximum bonuses if pretax earnings growth meets or exceeds the target of 30 percent. Use Exhibit 5.5 to see whether Callaway executives earned their maximum bonuses in the most recent year.

Computations _____

_____

Discuss why Callaway might choose to pay executives based on performance and why it uses the same accounting numbers in reports to shareholders to measure the executives' performance.

_____

Now check your answers to those in the footnote at the bottom of the page. *

**Discontinued Operations**  Any company that plans to dispose of a major segment of its business or customer line needs to present separate information on the income statement accompanied by disposal details written in a note. **Discontinued operations**

**DISCONTINUED OPERATIONS** result from the disposal of a major segment of the business and are reported net of income tax effects.

---

*1. a. −200, NE, −200; b. +100, +100, +100

2. Pretax earnings growth % = (213,765 − 195,595) ÷ 195,595 = 9.3% versus 30% target.

They did not earn their maximum bonuses. (In reality, they were eligible for bonuses of up to 40 percent of their base salaries.) The company believes that higher pretax earnings growth will result in higher prices for Callaway stock. Paying Callaway executives a bonus for increasing earnings growth thus helps align the interests of the executives with those of the shareholders. In addition, companies often pay shareholders bonuses based on the numbers in the annual report because the auditors have independently verified those numbers.

can result from abandoning or selling the major segment. Any operating income generated by the discontinued segment is disclosed separately from any gain or loss on the disposal (the difference between the book value of the net assets being disposed of and the sale price or the abandonment costs). The disclosure of each can be in a note or on the face of the income statement. Each line is to be reported net of the income tax effects. Separate reporting informs users that these results of discontinued operations are less useful as predictors of the company's future.

An example of a partial income statement that includes discontinued operations is presented in Exhibit 5.7 for Tenneco Inc., a global manufacturer of automotive parts and packaging. The note accompanying the income statement reported that during 1996, Tenneco formed separate companies for its energy and shipbuilding segments and distributed the shares in the new companies to its existing shareholders (called a *spinoff*). The results of the energy and shipbuilding operations, net of tax, are listed as discontinued operations.

**Extraordinary Items**   **Extraordinary items** are gains or losses incurred by the company that are considered both unusual in nature and infrequent in occurrence. Examples include losses suffered from natural disasters such as floods and hurricanes in geographic areas where such disasters rarely occur. These items must be reported separately on the income statement net of income tax effects. Separate reporting informs decision makers that the items are not likely to recur and for that reason are less relevant to predicting the company's future. Note disclosure is needed to explain the nature of the extraordinary item. In 1996, Tenneco Inc. also reported extraordinary losses due to the early retirement of long-term debt (Exhibit 5.7). Accounting for early retirement of debt is discussed in Chapter 10.

**EXTRAORDINARY ITEMS** are gains and losses that are both unusual in nature and infrequent in occurrence; they are reported net of tax on the income statement.

**Cumulative Effects of Changes in Accounting Methods**   The fourth section of the income statement reflects the income statement effects of any adjustment made to balance sheet accounts because of changing to a different acceptable accounting method. These amounts are called **cumulative effects of changes in accounting methods**. The goal is to determine what the balance sheet amount should be as if the new accounting method had always been applied, net of any tax effects. Often these changes are required by new FASB pronouncements, as is the case in the Tenneco example. At other times, corporate management determines that a change to an alter-

**CUMULATIVE EFFECTS OF CHANGES IN ACCOUNTING METHODS** are the amounts reflected on the income statement for adjustments made to balance sheet accounts when applying different accounting principles.

| TENNECO INC. AND CONSOLIDATED SUBSIDIARIES<br>Statements of Income<br>(millions except share and per share amounts) | | | |
| --- | --- | --- | --- |
| | **Years Ended December 31,** | | |
| | **1997** | **1996** | **1995** |
| Income from continuing operations | 361 | 218 | 258 |
| Income from discontinued operations, net of income tax | — | 428 | 477 |
| Income before extraordinary loss | 361 | 646 | 735 |
| Extraordinary loss, net of income tax | — | (236) | — |
| Income before cumulative effect of change in accounting principle | 361 | 410 | 735 |
| Cumulative effect of change in accounting principle, net of income tax | (46) | — | — |
| Net Income | 315 | 410 | 735 |

EXHIBIT **5.7**

**Partial Income Statements for Tenneco Inc.**

**REAL WORLD EXCERPT**

*Tenneco Inc.*

ANNUAL REPORT

native accounting method is necessary because of changes in business activities. The effects of accounting method changes are separated because they are normally not directly relevant to predicting the company's future. Note disclosure to explain the nature and effects of the change also is necessary.

Finally, we come to "the bottom line," Net Income. An income statement is not complete, however, without including earnings per share information for corporations.

**Earnings per Share**    As we discussed in Chapter 4, simple computations for earnings per share (EPS) are as follows:

$$\text{EPS} = \frac{\textbf{Net Income Available to Common Shareholders}}{\substack{\textbf{Weighted Average Number of Shares Outstanding} \\ \textbf{During the Reporting Period}}}$$

Callaway discloses this amount as illustrated in Exhibit 5.5 (called *basic EPS*). Any company that has a complex capital structure (that is, stock options or debt or equity securities convertible into common stock) must also compute the effect of these items as if they had been converted at the beginning of the period, or when initially issued if during the current reporting period (called *diluted EPS*). The computation of these amounts is beyond the scope of this text and is usually presented in advanced coursework for accounting majors. Any company that discloses discontinued operations, extraordinary items, or the cumulative effect of changes in accounting methods also must display these effects on a per share basis.

**A Note on Taxes**    One of the features of the first four sections of the income statement is that each section shows the amount of income tax expense related to that section. This is known as *intraperiod income tax allocation*. Items presented after continuing operations are reported net of the tax effect. For example, a $1,000 extraordinary loss is reported as $600 ($1,000 − 400 Tax Effect).

Before income from continuing operations is computed, the *provision (expense) for income taxes* is calculated and subtracted. For Callaway Golf, income tax expense is approximately 38 percent of pretax income. Income tax expense is incurred by a corporation but not by a sole proprietorship or partnership. Income taxes are payable each year (part in advance in quarterly estimates).

**COMPREHENSIVE INCOME** is net income plus unrealized gain or loss on securities, minimum pension liability adjustment, and foreign currency translation adjustment.

**Comprehensive Income**    **Comprehensive income** is net income plus or minus the three additional types of gains or losses discussed earlier, which are directly credited or debited to the stockholders' equity account, Accumulated Other Comprehensive Income. These are unrealized gains or losses on securities, minimum pension liability adjustment, and foreign currency translation adjustment. The computation can be disclosed as part of the income statement, the statement of changes in stockholders' equity, or on a separate statement. Most companies are using the statement of changes in stockholders' equity or separate statement formats. Callaway Golf had foreign currency losses from its foreign subsidiaries in 1997, which decreased Comprehensive Income and decreased Accumulated Other Comprehensive Income. Both Comprehensive Income and Accumulated Other Comprehensive Income are disclosed in its statement of stockholders equity.

## STATEMENT OF STOCKHOLDERS' EQUITY

The statement of stockholders' (shareholders') equity reports the changes in each of the company's stockholders' equity accounts during the accounting period. We will discuss this statement in more detail in Chapter 11.

## STATEMENT OF CASH FLOWS

We have introduced the statement of cash flow classifications in prior chapters. They are the following:

*Cash Flows from Operating Activities.* This section reports cash flows associated with earning income.

*Cash Flows from Investing Activities.* Cash flows in this section are associated with buying and selling productive assets (other than inventory) and investments in other companies.

*Cash Flows from Financing Activities.* These cash flows are related to financing the business through debt and equity issuances and payments or repurchases.

Callaway's 1997 consolidated statement of cash flows is presented in Exhibit 5.8. It follows the sections indicated in the preceding list. The first section (Cash Flows from Operations) can be illustrated using either the *direct* or *indirect* method. For Callaway, the first section (Cash Flows from Operating Activities) is reported using the indirect method as a reconciliation of net income on an accrual basis to cash flows from operations. This more common format is different from the presentation made in the statement prepared for Papa John's at the end of Chapter 4 that was constructed using the direct method.

## FOCUS ON **CASH FLOWS**

### OPERATING ACTIVITIES (INDIRECT METHOD)

The indirect method's Operating Activities section of the statement of cash flows helps the analyst understand the causes of differences between the net income and the cash flows of a business. The income of a company and its cash flows from operating activities can be quite different. Remember that the income statement is prepared under the accrual concept. Revenues are recorded when earned without regard to when the related cash flows occur. Expenses are matched with revenues and recorded in the same period as the revenues without regard to when the related cash flows occur.

The Operating Activities section starts with the net income number computed under the accrual concept and converts it to cash flow from operating activities. The items listed between these two amounts explain the reasons they are different. For example, since no cash is paid during the current period for Callaway's depreciation expense reported on the income statement, this amount is added back in the conversion process. Similarly, increases and decreases in current assets and liabilities also account for some of the difference between net income and cash flow from operations. Note that the buildup of accounts receivable accounted for the largest portion of the difference between Callaway's net income and cash flow from operations during 1997. As we cover different portions of the income statement and balance sheet in more detail in Chapters 6 through 12, we will also discuss the relevant sections of the cash flow statement. Then the complete cash flow statement will be discussed in detail in Chapter 13.

### NOTES TO FINANCIAL STATEMENTS

The numbers reported on the various financial statements provide important information to decision makers, but most users require additional details to facilitate their analysis. All financial reports include additional information in notes that follow the statements. Callaway's 1997 notes are categorized in the following discussion by type of note (key accounting policies, additional detail supporting reported numbers, and relevant financial information not disclosed on the statements). Examples are provided.

**Descriptions of Accounting Rules Applied in the Company's Statements**
The first note typically is a summary of significant accounting policies. As you will see in your study of subsequent chapters, generally accepted accounting principles (GAAP) permit companies to select alternative methods for measuring the effects of

EXHIBIT **5.8**

Cash Flow Statement of
Callaway Golf

**REAL WORLD EXCERPT**

*Callaway Golf*

ANNUAL REPORT

**Consolidated Statement of Cash Flows**
**(in thousands)**

| | Year ended December 31, | | |
|---|---|---|---|
| | 1997 | 1996 | 1995 |
| Cash flows from operating activities: | | | |
| Net income | $132,704 | $122,337 | $97,736 |
| Adjustments to reconcile net income to net cash provided by operating activities: | | | |
| Depreciation and amortization | 19,408 | 12,691 | 10,778 |
| Non-cash compensation | 8,013 | 4,194 | 2,027 |
| Tax benefit from exercise of stock options | 29,786 | 14,244 | 11,236 |
| Deferred taxes | 1,030 | (4,420) | 4,978 |
| Increase (decrease) in cash resulting from changes in: | | | |
| Accounts receivable, net | (36,936) | 3,510 | (43,923) |
| Inventories, net | 6,271 | (44,383) | 22,516 |
| Other assets | (6,744) | (12,817) | (6,518) |
| Accounts payable and accrued expenses | 13,529 | (15,395) | 9,227 |
| Accrued employee compensation and benefits | (2,437) | 2,031 | 1,322 |
| Accrued warranty expense | 756 | 3,534 | 5,587 |
| Income taxes payable | (2,636) | 626 | (9,845) |
| Other liabilities | 2,796 | 2,902 | 1,597 |
| Net cash provided by operating activities | 165,540 | 89,054 | 106,718 |
| Cash flows from investing activities: | | | |
| Capital expenditures | (67,938) | (35,352) | (29,510) |
| Acquisition of a business, net of cash acquired | (129,256) | (610) | |
| Net cash used in investing activities | (197,194) | (35,962) | (29,510) |
| Cash flows from financing activities: | | | |
| Issuance of Common Stock | 21,558 | 12,258 | 7,991 |
| Retirement of Common Stock | (52,985) | | (67,022) |
| Dividends paid, net | (19,123) | (16,025) | (13,350) |
| Net cash used in financing activities | (50,550) | (3,767) | (72,381) |
| Effect of exchange rate changes on cash | (49) | (25) | (26) |
| Net (decrease) increase in cash and cash equivalents | (82,253) | 49,300 | 4,801 |
| Cash and cash equivalents at beginning of year | 108,457 | 59,157 | 54,356 |
| Cash and cash equivalents at end of year | $26,204 | $108,457 | $59,157 |
| Supplemental disclosure: | | | |
| Cash paid for income taxes | $54,358 | $62,938 | $58,543 |

See accompanying notes to consolidated financial statements.

transactions. The summary of significant accounting policies tells the user which accounting methods the company has adopted. It is impossible to analyze a company's financial results effectively without first understanding the various accounting methods that have been used. The policy for accounting for property, plant, and equipment is as follows:

**REAL WORLD EXCERPT**

*Callaway Golf*

ANNUAL REPORT

**Note 1**
**The Company and Significant Accounting Policies**
PROPERTY, PLANT AND EQUIPMENT
Property, plant and equipment are stated at cost less accumulated depreciation. Depreciation is computed using the straight-line method over estimated useful lives of three to fifteen years. Repairs and maintenance costs are charged to expense as incurred.

FINANCIAL **ANALYSIS**

## ALTERNATIVE ACCOUNTING METHODS AND GAAP

Many people have a misimpression concerning the nature of the rules that make up generally accepted accounting principles (GAAP): that GAAP permit only one accounting method to be used to compute each value on the financial statements (e.g., inventory). Actually, GAAP often allow selection of an accounting method from a menu of acceptable methods. This permits a company to choose the methods that most closely reflect its particular economic circumstances (economic reality). This adds an additional complexity to the financial statement users' task, however—they also must understand how the company's choice of accounting methods affects its financial statement presentations. As Gabrielle Napolitano and Abby Joseph Cohen of the investment banking firm of Goldman, Sachs & Co. note in their recent research report,

**REAL WORLD EXCERPT**

*Goldman, Sachs & Co.*

ANALYSTS' REPORT

> There are numerous legitimate ways in which company accounts can be made obscure. Further, investors must be wary of the means by which reported earnings can be manipulated or smoothed. Users of financial statements (e.g., shareholders, creditors, and others) are often forced to wrestle with dramatic differences in reporting practices between firms.*

For example, before analyzing two companies' statements prepared using different accounting methods, one company's statements must be converted to the other's methods to make them comparable. Otherwise, the reader is in a situation analogous to comparing distances in kilometers and miles without conversion to a common scale. In later chapters, we will focus on developing the ability to make these conversions.

*Gabrielle Napolitano and Abby Joseph Cohen, "The Quality of Reported Earnings Has Improved, But . . . Pointers on What to Look for in Company Reports," *U.S. Research* (New York: Goldman, Sachs & Co., January 2, 1997).

**Additional Detail Supporting Reported Numbers**   The second category of notes provides supplemental information concerning the data shown on the financial statements. Among other information, these notes may show revenues broken out by geographic region or line of business, descriptions of unusual transactions, and expanded detail concerning a specific classification. For example, Callaway provides detail in Note 2 on cash; accounts receivable; inventory; property, plant, and equipment; intangible assets; accounts payable and accrued expenses; and accrued compensation and benefits. Note 12, which follows, shows sales information by geographic region:

**REAL WORLD EXCERPT**

*Callaway Golf*

ANNUAL REPORT

**Note 12**
**Sales Information**
The Company is engaged in domestic and international sales through retail customers and distributors located within the following geographic areas:

| (in thousands) | Year ended December 31, | | |
| --- | --- | --- | --- |
| | 1997 | 1996 | 1995 |
| United States | $547,256 | $460,611 | $367,359 |
| Japan | 84,634 | 58,156 | 60,971 |
| All others—individually less than 10% of net sales | 211,037 | 159,745 | 124,957 |
| | $842,927 | $678,512 | $553,287 |

Callaway provides a more detailed discussion of its international sales strategy in its form 10-K discussed earlier in the chapter.

**Relevant Financial Information Not Disclosed on the Statements** The final category includes information that impacts the company financially but is not specifically indicated on the statements. Examples include information on stock option plans, legal matters, and any material event that occurs subsequent to year-end but before the financial statements are published. Note 3 is as follows:

> **Note 3**
> **Bank Line of Credit**
> The Company had a $50,000,000 unsecured line of credit with an interest rate equal to the bank's prime rate (8.5% at December 31, 1997). The line of credit was renewed in February 1998 (Note 14). The line of credit has been primarily utilized to support the issuance of letters of credit, of which there were $4,046,000 outstanding at December 31, 1997, reducing the amount available under the Company's line of credit to $45,954,000.
> The line requires the Company to maintain certain financial ratios, including current and debt-to-equity ratios. The Company is also subject to other restrictive covenants under the terms of the credit agreement.

## VOLUNTARY DISCLOSURES

GAAP and SEC regulations set only a minimum level of required financial disclosures. Many companies, including Callaway, provide important disclosures beyond those required. For example, in its annual report, 10-K, and recent earnings press release (discussed earlier; see Exhibit 5.3), Callaway discloses sales by major product line, which helps investors track the success of new product lines. To our knowledge, it is the only major golf club company to provide such detailed sales information.

## CONSTRAINTS OF ACCOUNTING MEASUREMENT

Accurate interpretation of financial statements requires that the statement reader be aware of three important constraints of accounting measurement. First, although items and amounts that are of low significance must be accounted for, they do not have to conform precisely to specified accounting guidelines or be separately reported if they would not influence reasonable decisions. Accountants usually designate such items and amounts as *immaterial*. Determining **material amounts** is often very subjective.

**MATERIAL AMOUNTS** are amounts that are large enough to influence a user's decision.

Second, **conservatism** requires that special care be taken to avoid (1) overstating assets and revenues and (2) understating liabilities and expenses. This guideline attempts to offset managers' natural optimism about their business operations, which sometimes creeps into the financial reports that they prepare. This constraint produces more conservative income statement and balance sheet amounts.

**CONSERVATISM** suggests that care should be taken not to overstate assets and revenues or understate liabilities and expenses.

Finally, the educated financial statement reader must be aware of special industry practices or industry peculiarities due to long-standing and accepted accounting and reporting practices in various industries. For example, public utilities (an industry regulated by government) often present balance sheet information in what appears to be upside-down order. That is, property, plant, and equipment are listed first, followed by the more liquid assets (cash, accounts receivable, and supplies). The reason for this presentation is that regulatory commissions in many states require public utilities to use this format.

# RETURN ON EQUITY ANALYSIS: A FRAMEWORK FOR EVALUATING COMPANY PERFORMANCE

Evaluating company performance is the primary goal of financial statement analysis. Company managers, as well as competitors, use financial statements to better understand and evaluate a company's business strategy. Analysts, investors, and creditors use these same statements to evaluate performance as part of their stock valuation and credit evaluation judgments. Our discussion of the financial data contained in accounting reports has now reached the point where we can develop an overall framework for using that data to evaluate company performance. The most comprehensive framework of this type is called *return on equity* or *ROE analysis* (also called *return on stockholder's equity* or *return on investment*).

■ **LEARNING OBJECTIVE 4**

Analyze a company's performance based on return on equity and its components.

## KEY **RATIO ANALYSIS:**

## RETURN ON EQUITY

**K**now the decision question:

How well has management used the stockholders' investment during the period? It is computed as follows:

$$\text{Return on Equity} = \frac{\text{Net Income}}{\text{Average Stockholders' Equity*}}$$

*Average Stockholders' Equity = (Beginning Stockholders' Equity + Ending Stockholders' Equity) ÷ 2

The 1997 ratio for Callaway:

$$\frac{\$132,704}{(\$481,425 + 362,267) \div 2} = 0.315 \ (31.5\%)$$

**E**xamine the ratio using two techniques:

| ① Comparisons over Time | | | ② Comparisons with Competitors | |
|---|---|---|---|---|
| **Callaway Golf** | | | **S2 Golf** | **Recreational Products Industry** |
| 1995 | 1996 | 1997 | 1997 | 1997 |
| 47.5% | 41.7% | 31.5% | 27.9% | 17.1% |

**Y**ou interpret the results carefully:

**IN GENERAL** → ROE measures how much the firm earned for each dollar of stockholders' investment. In the long run, firms with higher ROE are expected to have higher stock prices than firms with lower ROE, all other things equal. Managers, analysts, and creditors use this ratio to assess the effectiveness of the company's overall business strategy (its operating, investing, and financing strategies).

**FOCUS COMPANY ANALYSIS** → ROE for large companies in the recreational products industry has averaged 17.1 percent over the last seven years.[8] The preceding computation indicates that

---

[8]Parker Center for Investment Research, Johnson Graduate School of Management, Cornell University, May 1999.

Callaway's ROE is well in excess of that amount. However, such high levels of ROE tend to be driven down over time by additional competition from new and existing competitors. Callaway is facing just such a situation as large companies such as American Brands–owned Cobra Golf and Adidas-owned Taylor-Made invest millions in marketing to unseat Callaway from the top of its market, while new entrants such as Orlimar attempt to develop more innovative clubs. As a result of this competition, Callaway's ROE has dropped from 47.5 percent to 31.5 percent in the last three years. While its ROE is still high compared to that of its competitors, further decreases will surely lead to declines in Callaway's stock price.

**A FEW CAUTIONS:** An increasing ROE can also indicate that the company is failing to invest in research and development or modernization of plant and equipment. While such a strategy will decrease expenses and thus increase ROE in the short run, it normally results in future declines in ROE as the company's products and plant and equipment reach the end of their life cycles. As a consequence, experienced decision makers evaluate ROE in the context of a company's business strategy.

## ROE PROFIT DRIVER ANALYSIS

Effective analysis of Callaway's performance also requires an understanding of *why* its ROE differs from prior levels and that of its competitors. ROE profit driver analysis (also called *ROE decomposition* or *DuPont analysis*) breaks down ROE into the three factors indicated in Exhibit 5.9. These factors are often called *profit drivers* or *profit levers* because they describe the three ways that management can improve ROE. They are measured by the key ratios we learned in the prior three chapters.

A. *Net profit margin.* Net profit margin is Net Income/Net Sales. It measures how much of every sales dollar is profit. It can be increased by
   1. Increasing sales volume.
   2. Increasing sales price.
   3. Decreasing expenses.

B. *Asset turnover (efficiency).* Asset turnover is Net Sales/Average Total Assets. It measures how many sales dollars the company generates with each dollar of assets. It can be increased by
   1. Increasing sales volume.
   2. Decreasing less productive assets.

C. *Financial leverage.* Financial leverage is Average Total Assets/Average Stockholders' Equity. It measures how many dollars of assets are employed for each dollar of stockholder investment. It can be increased by
   1. Increased borrowing.
   2. Repurchasing (decreasing) outstanding stock.

EXHIBIT **5.9**

**ROE Profit Driver Analysis**

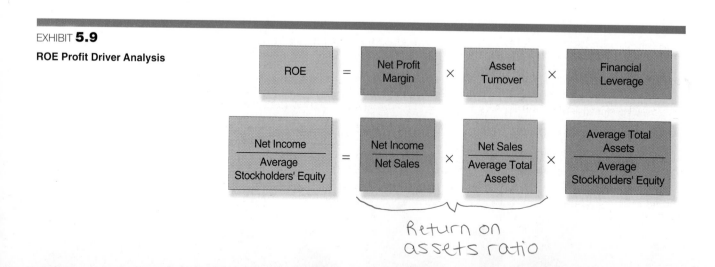

## PROFIT DRIVERS AND BUSINESS STRATEGY

Successful manufacturers often follow one of two business strategies. The first is a high-value or product-differentiation strategy. It relies on research and development and product promotion activities to convince customers of the superiority or distinctiveness of the company's products. This allows the company to charge higher prices and earn a higher net profit margin. The second is a low-cost strategy, which relies on efficient management of accounts receivable, inventory, and productive assets to produce high asset turnover.

Callaway Golf follows a classic high-value strategy. The ROE profit driver analysis presented in Exhibit 5.10 indicates the sources of Callaway's high ROE, as well as reasons for its decline over the last three years. The analysis indicates a steady decline in asset turnover, indicating that Callaway has had to employ increasing amounts of assets (in this case inventory, plant and equipment, and intangibles) to generate each dollar of sales. Callaway has also had to increase spending on research and development and promotional activities to maintain the perceived high value of its products in the face of increasing competition. This decreased its net profit margin in the most recent period from 18 to 16 percent. To limit risk to stockholders, Callaway has never relied heavily on financial leverage. It has reduced financial leverage over the last three years, further reducing the risk to stockholders if Callaway should face a particularly bad year in the future. Each of these changes has reduced Callaway's ROE.

| Fiscal Year Ending | 12/31/97 | 12/31/96 | 12/31/95 |
|---|---|---|---|
| Net Income/Net Sales | 0.16 | 0.18 | 0.18 |
| × Net Sales/Avg. Total Assets | 1.70 | 1.89 | 2.07 |
| × Avg. Total Assets/Avg. Stockholders' Equity | 1.17 | 1.22 | 1.30 |
| = Net Income/Avg. Stockholders' Equity | 0.32 | 0.42 | 0.48 |

EXHIBIT **5.10**

**Callaway Golf ROE Profit Driver Analysis**

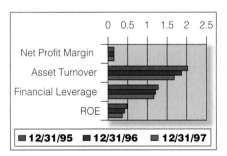

In such circumstances, companies often consider a variety of changes to increase ROE. These include

• Reducing promotional activities and fees paid to distributors to increase profit margin.

• Collecting accounts receivable more quickly, centralizing distribution to reduce inventory kept on hand, and consolidating production facilities in fewer factories to reduce the amount of assets necessary to generate each dollar of sales.

• Using more borrowed funds (financial leverage) so that more assets can be employed per dollar of stockholder investment.

Successful companies following a low-cost strategy such as Gateway and Dell Computer usually produce high ROE with higher asset turnover and higher leverage to make up for lower net profit margin. These companies' strategy is illustrated in the self-study quiz that follows this section.

As the preceding discussion indicates, companies can take many different actions to try to affect each of its profit drivers. To understand the impact of these actions, financial analysts disaggregate each of the profit drivers into more detailed ratios. For example, the asset turnover ratio is further disaggregated into turnover ratios for specific assets such as accounts receivable, inventory, and fixed assets. We will develop our understanding of these more specific ratios in the next eight chapters of the book. Then, in Chapter 14, we will bring these more specific ratios together in a comprehensive review.

## SELF-STUDY **QUIZ**

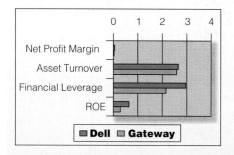

We used ROE analysis in Exhibit 5.10 to understand why Callaway's ROE had declined steadily over the last three years. This type of analysis is often called *time-series analysis*. ROE analysis can also be used to explain why a company has an ROE different from its competitors at a single point in time. This type of analysis is called *cross-sectional analysis*. The following is the current year's ROE analysis for Dell Computer and Gateway, the largest computer manufacturers employing mail-order/Internet distribution. Both of these companies have followed a low-cost strategy, developing reputations for good products and service at low prices. Dell has produced a higher ROE than Gateway over the last two years, and its stockholders have been amply rewarded with a 253 percent increase in the value of their shares, compared to 78 percent for Gateway's stockholders. Using ROE analysis, explain how Dell has produced its higher ROE.

| ROE Profit Drivers | Dell | Gateway |
|---|---|---|
| Net Income/Net Sales | 0.08 | 0.05 |
| × Net Sales/Average Total Assets | 2.65 | 2.58 |
| × Avg. Total Assets/Average Stockholders' Equity | 2.96 | 2.15 |
| = Net Income/Average Stockholders' Equity | 0.63 | 0.28 |

Now check your answers to those in the footnote at the bottom of the page. *

## EPILOGUE

In 1998, Callaway's sales were hit with a double-edged sword. Its continuing ability to produce higher than average ROE for its stockholders continued to attract more competition from old rivals and new entrants. While this was predictable, the crash of the Asian stock markets in late 1997 and the continuing crisis in 1998 were not. The resulting financial chaos in that part of the world led to declines in the sales of all high-end products, including Callaway clubs. As a result of the increasing competition and the decline in the Asian market, overall sales declined by 17 percent and Callaway reported its first loss since going public. This produced a dramatic drop in Callaway's asset turnover (efficiency) and a decline in the net profit margin to a negative number. The reduction in collections from customers also caused Callaway to increase its borrowing and thus its leverage. This multiplied the effect of the loss to its shareholders. This analysis is confirmed by the ROE analysis presented in Exhibit 5.11.

EXHIBIT **5.11**

**Callaway Golf 1998
ROE Analysis**

| Fiscal Year Ending | 12/31/98 |
|---|---|
| Net Income/Net Sales | −0.04 |
| × Net Sales/Average Total Assets | 1.15 |
| × Avg. Total Assets/Avg. Stockholders' Equity | 1.30 |
| = Net Income/Avg. Stockholders' Equity | −0.06 |

---

*Both Dell and Gateway are well known for the efficiency of their operations, and this efficiency is reflected in their high asset turnover ratios. Dell has the edge in asset efficiency, but the edge is small. Dell's major edge is its 60 percent higher net profit margin. This reflects Dell's success with its primary market segment, business customers. They purchase in higher quantity, which decreases order processing and production costs. They also often purchase higher-end, higher-net profit margin machines than customers in Gateway's primary market segment, individuals. The effect of this edge in net profit margin is multiplied further by Dell's greater reliance on leverage (debt financing). However, this greater leverage could come back to haunt Dell if there is a downturn in the personal computer market.

Callaway is now implementing a bold strategy of adjusting its profit drivers to its new operating environment. It has consolidated its manufacturing and distribution facilities to improve its asset turnover. More important, it has also turned to its perennial strong suit, introduction of innovative new products to boost sales volume and improve net profit margin. Based on what we have learned so far, we can assess the success of Callaway's new strategy by analyzing its future financial reports.

# DEMONSTRATION **CASE**

## MICROSOFT CORPORATION

Complete the following requirements before proceeding to the suggested solution. Microsoft Corporation, developer of a broad line of computer software including the Windows operating systems and Word (word processing) and Excel (spreadsheet) programs, is now the largest computer-related company in the world. Following is a list of the financial statement items and amounts adapted from a recent Microsoft income statement and balance sheet. These items have normal debit and credit balances and are reported in millions of dollars. For that year, 303 million (weighted average) shares of stock were outstanding. The company closes its books on June 30.

| | | | |
|---|---:|---|---:|
| Accounts payable | $ 239 | Net revenues | $3,753 ✓ |
| Accounts receivable | 338 | Other current assets | 95 |
| Accrued compensation | 86 | Other current liabilities | 111 |
| Cash and short-term investments | 2,290 | Other revenues and | |
| Common stock and paid-in capital | 1,086 | expenses (debit balance) | 7 |
| Cost of goods sold | 633 ✓ | Other noncurrent assets | 88 |
| General and administrative | 119 ✓ | Property, plant, and equipment (net) | 867 |
| Income taxes payable | 127 | Provision for income taxes | 448 |
| Interest income (net) | 82 | Research and development | 470 ✓ |
| Inventories | 127 | Retained earnings | 2,156 |
| | | Sales and marketing | 1,205 ✓ |

*Required:*
1. Prepare in good form a multiple-step income statement (showing both gross profit and operating income) and a classified balance sheet for the year.
2. Prepare an ROE profit driver analysis. Briefly explain its meaning and compare the result with that of Callaway Golf for 1997. (Microsoft's total assets and total shareholders' equity at the beginning of 20A were $2,640 million and $2,193 million, respectively.)

# SUGGESTED SOLUTION

1.

**MICROSOFT CORPORATION**
**Income Statement**
**For the Period Ended June 30, 20A**
**(in millions)**

| | |
|---|---:|
| Net revenues | $3,753 |
| Cost of goods sold | 633 |
| Gross profit | 3,120 |
| *Operating expenses:* | |
| Research and development | 470 |
| Sales and marketing | 1,205 |
| General and administrative | 119 |
| Total operating expenses | 1,794 |

| | |
|---|---:|
| **Operating income** | **1,326** |
| *Nonoperating income and expenses:* | |
| Interest income (net) | 82 |
| Other revenues and expenses | (7) |
| Income before income taxes | 1,401 |
| Provision for income taxes | 448 |
| Net income | $ 953 |
| **Earnings per share** | **$ 3.15** |

**MICROSOFT CORPORATION**
**Balance Sheet**
**June 30, 20A**
**(in millions)**

| | |
|---|---:|
| **Assets** | |
| *Current assets* | |
| Cash and short-term investments | $2,290 |
| Accounts receivable | 338 |
| Inventories | 127 |
| Other current assets | 95 |
| Total current assets | 2,850 |
| *Noncurrent assets* | |
| Property, plant, and equipment (net) | 867 |
| Other noncurrent assets | 88 |
| Total assets | $3,805 |
| **Liabilities** | |
| *Current liabilities* | |
| Accounts payable | $ 239 |
| Accrued compensation | 86 |
| Income taxes payable | 127 |
| Other current liabilities | 111 |
| Total current liabilities | 563 |
| *Noncurrent liabilities* | 0 |
| **Stockholders' equity** | |
| Common stock and paid-in-capital | 1,086 |
| Retained earnings | 2,156 |
| Total stockholders' equity | 3,242 |
| Total liabilities and stockholders' equity | $3,805 |

2.

| Fiscal Year Ending | June 30, 20A |
|---|---:|
| Net Income/Net Sales | 0.25 |
| × Net Sales/Average Total Assets | 1.16 |
| × Avg. Total Assets/Average Stockholders' Equity | 1.19 |
| = Net Income/Average Stockholders' Equity | 0.35 |

For the year ended June 30, 20A, Microsoft's shareholders earned an ROE of 35 percent. While the overall ROE is approximately the same as Callaway Golf's 1997 results, the detailed analysis shows that this is for very different reasons. In contrast to Callaway's 1997 results (see Exhibit 5.10), Microsoft maintains high profit margins, earning 25¢ of net income for every $1 of net sales but a lower asset efficiency with only $1.16 in sales generated for each $1 of assets. The analysis also indicates Microsoft's dominance of the computer software business, which allows the company to charge premium prices for its products. However, similar to Callaway, the financial leverage ratio indicates that Microsoft's capital is primarily equity (not debt) based. With $1.19 in assets for each $1 of shareholders' equity, Microsoft has chosen not to leverage (or borrow) as much, for example, as Dell Computer or Gateway, who face stiff competition in the computer hardware industry (see the Self-Study Quiz).

## CHAPTER **TAKE-AWAYS**

1. **Recognize the people involved in the accounting communication process (managers, auditors, information intermediaries, government regulators, and users), their roles in the process, and the guidance they receive from legal and professional standards.   p. 239**
   Management of the reporting company must decide on the appropriate format (categories) and level of detail to present in its financial reports. Independent audits increase the credibility of the information. Financial statement announcements from public companies usually are first transmitted to users through electronic information services. Analysts play a major role in making this and other information available to average investors through their stock recommendations and earnings forecasts.

2. **Identify the steps in the accounting communication process, including the issuance of press releases, annual reports, quarterly reports, and SEC filings as well as the role of electronic information services in this process.   p. 247**
   Earnings are first made public in press releases. Companies follow these announcements with annual and quarterly reports containing statements, notes, and additional information. Public companies must also file additional reports with the SEC, including the 10-K, 10-Q, and 8-K, which contain more details about the company. Electronic information services are the key source of dissemination of this information to sophisticated users.

3. **Recognize and apply the different financial statement and disclosure formats used by companies in practice.   p. 251**
   Most statements are classified and include subtotals that are relevant to analysis. On the balance sheet, the most important distinctions are between current and noncurrent assets and liabilities. On the income statement and cash flow statement, the separation of operating and nonoperating items are most important. The notes to the statements provide descriptions of the accounting rules applied and more information about items disclosed on the statements, as well as information about economic events not disclosed in the statements.

4. **Analyze a company's performance based on return on equity and its components.   p. 265**
   ROE measures how well management used the stockholders' investment during the period. Its three determinants, net profit margin, asset turnover, and financial leverage, indicate why ROE differs from prior levels or that of competitors; these determinants provide insights into strategies to improve ROE in future periods.

In Chapter 6, we begin our in-depth discussion of financial statements. We will begin with two of the most liquid assets, cash and accounts receivable, and transactions that involve revenue, adjustments to revenues, and certain selling expenses that relate to recording cash and accounts receivable. Many analysts and the SEC believe accuracy in revenue recognition and the related recognition of cost of goods sold (discussed in the next chapter) to be the most important determinants of the accuracy—and, thus, the usefulness—of financial statement presentations. We will also introduce concepts related to the management and control of cash and receivables, which is a critical business function. A detailed understanding of these topics is crucial to future managers, accountants, and financial analysts.

## KEY **RATIO**

**Return on equity** (ROE) measures how much the firm earned for each dollar of stockholders' investment. It is computed as follows (p. 265):

$$\text{Return on Equity} = \frac{\text{Net Income}}{\text{Average Stockholders' Equity}}$$

FINDING
**FINANCIAL**
**INFORMATION**

**BALANCE SHEET**
*Key Classifications*
    Current and noncurrent assets and
        liabilities
    Contributed capital and retained earnings

**INCOME STATEMENT**
*Key Subtotals*
    Gross profit
    Income from operations
    Net income
    Earnings per share

**STATEMENT OF CASH FLOWS**
*Under Operating Activities (indirect method)*
    Net Income
    ± Differences between Net Income and
        Cash Provided by Operating Activities
    Cash Provided by Operating Activities

**NOTES**
*Key Classifications*
    Descriptions of accounting rules applied in
        the statements
    Additional detail supporting reported
        numbers
    Relevant financial information not
        disclosed on the statements

## KEY **TERMS**

**Accumulated Other Comprehensive Income** p. 254

**Capital in Excess of Par (Additional Paid-in Capital, Contributed Capital in Excess of Par, Paid-in Capital)** p. 254

**Comparable Information** p. 246

**Comprehensive Income** p. 260

**Conservatism** p. 264

**Consistent Information** p. 246

**Cost-Benefit Constraint** p. 246

**Cumulative Effects of Changes in Accounting Methods** p. 259

**Discontinued Operations** p. 258

**Earnings Forecasts** p. 241

**Extraordinary Items** p. 259

**Form 8-K** p. 250

**Form 10-K** p. 250

**Form 10-Q** p. 250

**Gross Profit (Gross Margin)** p. 257

**Income before Income Taxes (Pretax Earnings)** p. 257

**Income from Operations (Operating Income)** p. 257

**Institutional Investors** p. 245

**Lenders (Creditors)** p. 245

**Material Amounts** p. 264

**Par Value** p. 254

**Press Release** p. 247

**Private Investors** p. 245

**Relevant Information** p. 246

**Reliable Information** p. 246

**Unqualified (Clean) Audit Opinion** p. 240

## QUESTIONS

1. Describe the roles and responsibilities of management and independent auditors in the financial reporting process.
2. Define the following three users of financial accounting disclosures and the relationships among them: *financial analysts, private investors,* and *institutional investors.*
3. Briefly describe the role of information services in the communication of financial information.
4. Explain why information must be relevant and reliable to be useful.
5. What basis of accounting do GAAP require on the (a) income statement, (b) balance sheet, and (c) statement of cash flows?
6. Briefly explain the normal sequence and form of financial reports produced by private companies in a typical year.
7. Briefly explain the normal sequence and form of financial reports produced by public companies in a typical year.
8. What are the five major classifications on the income statement?
9. Define *extraordinary items.* Why should they be reported separately on the income statement?

10. List the six major classifications reported on a balance sheet.
11. For property, plant, and equipment, as reported on the balance sheet, explain (a) cost, (b) accumulated depreciation, and (c) net book value.
12. Briefly explain the major classifications of stockholders' equity for a corporation.
13. What are the three major classifications on a statement of cash flows?
14. What are the three major categories of notes or footnotes presented in annual reports? Cite an example of each.
15. Briefly define *return on equity* and what it measures.

# MINI-EXERCISES

**M5–1  Matching Players in the Accounting Communication Process with Their Definitions**   ■ **LO1**

Match each player with the related definition by entering the appropriate letter in the space provided.

| Players | Definitions |
|---|---|
| _____ (1) CEO and CFO | A. Adviser who analyzes financial and other economic information to form forecasts and stock recommendations. |
| _____ (2) Independent auditor | B. Institutional and private investors and creditors (among others). |
| _____ (3) Users | C. Chief executive officer and chief financial officer who have primary responsibility for the information presented in financial statements. |
| _____ (4) Financial analyst | D. Independent CPA who examines financial statements and attests to their fairness. |

**M5–2  Identifying the Disclosure Sequence**   ■ **LO2**

Indicate the order in which the following disclosures or reports are normally issued by public companies.

| No. | Title |
|---|---|
| _____ | Annual report |
| _____ | Form 10-K |
| _____ | Earnings press release |

**M5–3  Finding Financial Information: Matching Financial Statements with the Elements of Financial Statements**   ■ **LO3**

Match each financial statement with the items presented on it by entering the appropriate letter in the space provided.

| Elements of Financial Statements | Financial Statements |
|---|---|
| _____ (1) Liabilities | A. Income statement |
| _____ (2) Cash from operating activities | B. Balance sheet |
| _____ (3) Losses | C. Cash flow statement |
| _____ (4) Assets | D. None of the above |
| _____ (5) Revenues | |
| _____ (6) Cash from financing activities | |
| _____ (7) Gains | |
| _____ (8) Owners' equity | |
| _____ (9) Expenses | |
| _____ (10) Assets owned by a stockholder | |

**M5–4  Determining the Effects of Transactions on Balance Sheet and Income Statement Categories**   ■ **LO3**

Complete the following tabulation, indicating the sign of the effect (+ for increase, − for decrease, and NE for no effect) of each transaction. Consider each item independently.

a. Recorded sales on account of $100 and related cost of goods sold of $60.

b. Recorded advertising expense of $10 incurred but not paid for.

| Transaction | Current Assets | Gross Profit | Current Liabilities |
|---|---|---|---|
| (a) | | | |
| (b) | | | |

**LO3**

**M5–5** **Determining Financial Statement Effects of Sales and Cost of Goods Sold and Issuance of Par Value Stock**

Using the following categories, indicate the effects of the following transactions. Use + for increase and − for decrease and indicate the accounts affected and the amounts.

a. Sales on account were $500 and related cost of goods sold was $360.

b. Issued 10,000 shares of $1 par value stock for $90,000 cash.

| Event | Assets | = | Liabilities | + | Stockholders' Equity |
|---|---|---|---|---|---|
| | | | | | |

**LO3**

**M5–6** **Recording Sales and Cost of Goods Sold and Issuance of Par Value Stock**

Prepare journal entries for each transaction listed in M5–5.

**LO3**

**M5–7** **Computing Net Book Value of Property, Plant, and Equipment**

May's Diner purchases new tables for $5,000 on January 1, 20A. The tables are expected to have a 10-year useful life and a $500 salvage value. What would be the net book value of the tables on December 31, 20C?

**LO4**

**M5–8** **Computing and Interpreting Return on Equity**

Chen, Inc., recently reported the following December 31 amounts in its financial statements (in thousands):

| | Current Year | Prior Year |
|---|---|---|
| Gross profit | $ 170 | $140 |
| Net income | 85 | 70 |
| Total assets | 1,000 | 900 |
| Total shareholders' equity | 800 | 750 |

Compute return on equity for the current year. What does this ratio measure?

## EXERCISES

**LO1**

**E5–1** **Matching Players in the Accounting Communication Process with Their Definitions**

Match each player with the related definition by entering the appropriate letter in the space provided.

| Players | Definitions |
|---|---|
| ＿＿ (1) SEC | A. Adviser who analyzes financial and other economic information to form forecasts and stock recommendations. |
| ＿＿ (2) Independent auditor | |
| ＿＿ (3) Institutional investor | |
| ＿＿ (4) CEO and CFO | B. Financial institution or supplier that lends money to the company. |
| ＿＿ (5) Creditor | |
| ＿＿ (6) Financial analyst | C. Chief executive officer and chief financial officer who have primary responsibility for the information presented in financial statements. |
| ＿＿ (7) Private investor | |
| ＿＿ (8) Information service | |

D. Independent CPA who examines financial statements and attests to their fairness.

E. Securities and Exchange Commission, which regulates financial disclosure requirements.

F. A company that gathers, combines, and transmits (paper and electronic) financial and related information from various sources.

G. Individual who purchases shares in companies.

H. Manager of pension, mutual, and endowment funds that invests on the behalf of others.

**E5–2** **Matching Definitions with Information Releases Made by Public Companies**  ■ **LO2**

Following are the titles of various information releases. Match each definition with the related release by entering the appropriate letter in the space provided.

| Information Release | Definitions |
|---|---|
| _____ (1) Annual report | A. Written public news announcement that is normally distributed to major news services. |
| _____ (2) Form 8-K | |
| _____ (3) Press release | B. Report containing the four basic statements for the year, related notes, and often statements by management and auditors. |
| _____ (4) Form 10-Q | |
| _____ (5) Quarterly report | C. Brief unaudited report for quarter normally containing summary income statement and balance sheet (unaudited). |
| _____ (6) Form 10-K | |
| | D. Annual report filed by public companies with the SEC that contains additional detailed financial information. |
| | E. Quarterly report filed by public companies with the SEC that contains additional unaudited financial information. |
| | F. Report of special events (e.g., auditor changes, mergers) filed by public companies with the SEC. |

**E5–3** **Finding Financial Information: Matching Information Items to Financial Reports**  ■ **LO2**

Following are information items included in various financial reports. Match each information item with the report(s) where it would most likely be found by entering the appropriate letter(s) in the space provided.

| Information Item | Report |
|---|---|
| _____ (1) Summarized financial data for 5- or 10-year period. | A. Annual report |
| _____ (2) Initial announcement of quarterly earnings. | B. Form 8-K |
| _____ (3) Announcement of a change in auditors. | C. Press release |
| _____ (4) Complete quarterly income statement, balance sheet, and cash flow statement. | D. Form 10-Q |
| _____ (5) The four basic financial statements for the year. | E. Quarterly report |
| _____ (6) Summarized income statement information for the quarter. | F. Form 10-K |
| _____ (7) Detailed discussion of the company's competition. | G. None of the above |
| _____ (8) Notes to financial statements. | |
| _____ (9) Description of those responsible for the financial statements. | |
| _____ (10) Initial announcement of hiring of new vice president for sales. | |

**E5–4** **Ordering the Classifications on a Typical Balance Sheet**  ■ **LO3**

Following is a list of classifications on the balance sheet. Number them in the order in which they normally appear on a balance sheet.

| No. | Title |
|---|---|
| _____ | Current liabilities |
| _____ | Long-term liabilities |
| _____ | Long-term investments |
| _____ | Intangible assets |
| _____ | Property, plant, and equipment |
| _____ | Current assets |
| _____ | Retained earnings |
| _____ | Contributed capital |
| _____ | Other noncurrent assets |

■ **LO3**

**E5–5**

Compaq Computer

### Preparing a Classified Balance Sheet

Compaq Computer Corporation began as the first manufacturer of portable computers compatible with the MS-DOS operating system. These sewing machine–size computers found their most important market niche with independent CPAs for whom portability was a must. Today, Compaq is one of the leading manufacturers of computers compatible with the Windows operating systems. Compaq sells a wide variety of desktop, portable, and home computers, as well as powerful servers that run business networks. Presented here are the items listed on its recent balance sheet (in millions) presented in alphabetical order:

| | |
|---|---|
| Accounts payable | $ 637 |
| Accounts receivable, net | 1,377 |
| Cash and cash equivalents | 627 |
| Common stock and capital in excess of par value | 586 |
| Deferred income taxes (noncurrent) | 186 credit |
| Income taxes payable | 69 |
| Inventories | 1,123 |
| Other current liabilities | 538 |
| Other noncurrent assets | 14 |
| Prepaid expenses | 164 |
| Property, plant, and equipment, less accumulated depreciation | 779 |
| Retained earnings | 2,068 |

*Required:*

Prepare a classified consolidated balance sheet for Compaq for the current year (ended December 31, 20A) using the categories presented in the chapter.

■ **LO3**

**E5–6**

Marvel Entertainment Group

### Preparing and Interpreting a Classified Balance Sheet with Discussion of Terminology (Challenging)

Marvel Entertainment Group is a leading entertainment company aimed at the youth market. Its products include Marvel Comics (X-Men, Captain America, Spider Man, Fantastic Four) and Fleer sports picture trading cards (baseball, basketball, hockey, football). At the time the statements were prepared, Marvel was 80 percent owned by billionaire Ronald O. Perelman; the remaining 20 percent of the stock was publicly traded on the New York Stock Exchange under the symbol MRV. Presented here are the items listed on its recent balance sheet (in millions) presented in alphabetical order:

| | |
|---|---|
| Accounts payable | $ 19.9 |
| Accounts receivable, net | 77.9 |
| Accrued expenses and other | 44.5 |
| Additional paid-in capital | 47.0 |
| Cash | 17.0 |
| Common stock, $.01 par value; 250,000,000 shares authorized, 97,642,992 shares issued and outstanding at December 31, 20A | 1.0 |
| Current portion of long-term debt | 45.1 |
| Deferred income taxes (current) | 8.3 debit |
| Due to former stockholders of Fleer (long term) | 0.1 |
| Goodwill, net | 274.6 |
| Inventories | 23.2 |
| Investment in and advances to Toy Biz | 14.2 |
| Long-term debt | 205.1 |
| Other assets (noncurrent) | 13.9 |
| Other long-term liabilities | 10.0 |
| Prepaid expenses and other | 6.1 |
| Property, plant, and equipment, net | 12.4 |
| Retained earnings (including cumulative translation adjustment) | 99.3 |
| Trademarks and other intangibles, net | 24.4 |

*Required:*

1. Prepare a classified consolidated balance sheet for Marvel Entertainment for the current year (ended December 31, 20A) using the categories presented in the chapter.

2. Four of the items end in the term *net.* Explain what this term means in each case.

**E5–7 Reporting Property, Plant, and Equipment on the Balance Sheet**
On January 1, 20B, Laura Anne's Bakery purchased a new oven for $6,800. The oven was expected to be used for four years and then to be sold for $2,000 on January 1, 20F. Prepare a schedule showing the amounts that would be reported on the balance sheets prepared at the end of 20B, 20C, 20D, and 20E for the oven (at cost), accumulated depreciation, and net book value.

■ LO3

**E5–8 Determining Financial Statement Effects of Stock Issuances with Par Value**
PolyGram Group, a Dutch company, is one of the three largest recorded music companies in the world. Its popular artists include Bryan Adams, Sting, U2, The Scorpions, Def Leppard, and many others. Its financial statements are denominated in Netherlands guilders (symbol NLG). To help finance its recent purchase of the legendary Motown recording label (Temptations, Boyz II Men), PolyGram issued 10 million additional shares (par value per share NLG 0.50) for NLG 599 million. Using the following categories, indicate the effects of this transaction. Use + for increase and − for decrease and indicate the accounts affected and the amounts.

■ LO3
PolyGram Group

|  Assets  | = | Liabilities | + | Stockholders' Equity |
| --- | --- | --- | --- | --- |
|  |  |  |  |  |

**E5–9 Recording Stock Issuances with Par Value**
In a recent year, Ben & Jerry's Homemade, Inc., maker of Ben & Jerry's ice cream and frozen yogurt, issued 12,000 shares of its $.033 par value stock for $96,000 (these numbers are rounded). These additional shares were issued under a stock purchase plan available to current shareholders that allowed them to purchase additional newly issued shares directly from Ben & Jerry's without paying a brokerage commission. Prepare the journal entry required to record the stock issuance.

■ LO3
Ben & Jerry's

**E5–10 Inferring Stock Issuances and Cash Dividends from Changes in Stockholders' Equity**
Callaway Golf recently reported the following December 31 balances in its stockholders' equity accounts (in thousands):

■ LO3
Callaway Golf

|  | Current Year | Prior Year |
| --- | --- | --- |
| Common stock | $ 169 | $ 140 |
| Paid-in capital | 57,807 | 31,948 |
| Retained earnings | 58,601 | 17,662 |
| Total shareholders' equity | $116,577 | $49,750 |

During the current year, Callaway reported net income of $42,862. Assume that the only other transactions that affected stockholders' equity during the current year were a single stock issuance and a single cash dividend that was declared and paid during the current year.

*Required:*
Recreate the two journal entries reflecting the stock issuance and dividend.

**E5–11 Matching Definitions with Income Statement-Related Terms**
Following are terms related to the income statement. Match each definition with its related term by entering the appropriate letter in the space provided.

■ LO3

| Terms | Definitions |
|---|---|
| _____ (1) Cost of goods sold | A. Sales Revenue − Cost of Goods Sold. |
| _____ (2) Interest expense | B. Item that is both unusual and infrequent. |
| _____ (3) Extraordinary item | C. Sales of services for cash or on credit. |
| _____ (4) Service revenue | D. Revenues + Gains − Expenses − Losses |
| _____ (5) Income tax expense on operations | including effects of discontinued operations, extraordinary items, and cumulative effects of accounting changes (if any). |
| _____ (6) Income before extraordinary items | E. Amount of resources used to purchase or produce the goods that were sold during the reporting period. |
| _____ (7) Net income | F. Income Tax on Revenues − Operating Expenses. |
| _____ (8) Gross margin on sales | G. Cost of money (borrowing) over time. |
| _____ (9) EPS | H. Net income divided by average shares outstanding. |
| _____ (10) Operating expenses | I. Income before unusual and infrequent items and the related income tax. |
| _____ (11) Pretax income from operations | J. Total expenses directly related to operations. |
| | K. Income before all income tax and before discontinued operations, extraordinary items, and cumulative effects of accounting changes (if any). |
| | L. None of the above. |

■ **LO3**   **E5–12**   **Inferring Income Statement Values**

Supply the missing dollar amounts for the 20B income statement of Ultimate Style Company for each of the following independent cases:

| | Case A | Case B | Case C | Case D | Case E |
|---|---|---|---|---|---|
| Sales revenue | $900 | $700 | $410 | $  ? | $  ? |
| Selling expense | ? | 150 | 80 | 400 | 250 |
| Cost of goods sold | ? | 380 | ? | 500 | 310 |
| Income tax expense | ? | 30 | 20 | 40 | 30 |
| Gross margin | 400 | ? | ? | ? | 440 |
| Pretax income | 200 | 90 | ? | 190 | ? |
| Administrative expense | 150 | ? | 60 | 100 | 80 |
| Net income | 170 | ? | 50 | ? | 80 |

■ **LO3**   **E5–13**   **Preparing a Multiple-Step Income Statement**

The following data were taken from the records of Village Corporation at December 31, 20B:

| | |
|---|---|
| Sales revenue | $70,000 |
| Gross profit | 24,500 |
| Selling (distribution) expense | 8,000 |
| Administrative expense | ? |
| Pretax income | 12,000 |
| Income tax rate | 30% |
| Shares of stock outstanding | 3,000 |

*Required:*

Prepare a complete multiple-step income statement for the company (showing both gross profit and income from operations). Show all computations. (*Hint:* Set up the side captions starting with sales revenue and ending with earnings per share; rely on the amounts and percentages given to infer missing values.)

**E5–14** **Preparing Single- and Multiple-Step Income Statements**

■ LO3

The following data were taken from the records of Kimberly Appliances, Incorporated, at December 31, 20D:

| | |
|---|---|
| Sales revenue | $120,000 |
| Administrative expense | 10,000 |
| Selling (distribution) expense | 18,000 |
| Income tax rate | 25% |
| Gross profit | 48,000 |
| Shares of stock outstanding | 2,000 |

*Required:*

1. Prepare a complete single-step income statement for the company. Show all computations. (*Hint:* Set up the side captions or rows starting with sales revenue and ending with earnings per share; rely on the amounts and percentages given to infer missing values.)

2. Prepare a complete multiple-step income statement for the company (showing both gross profit and income from operations).

**E5–15** **Determining the Effects of Transactions on Balance Sheet and Income Statement Categories**

■ LO3
Fruit of the Loom

Fruit of the Loom, Inc. is one of the largest domestic producers of underwear and activewear, selling products under the FRUIT OF THE LOOM®, BVD®, MUNSINGWEAR®, WILSON®, and other brand names. Listed here are selected aggregate transactions from the first quarter of 20B (in millions). Complete the following tabulation, indicating the sign (+ for increase, − for decrease, and NE for no effect) and amount of the effect of each transaction. Consider each item independently.

*a.* Recorded sales on account of $501.1 and related cost of goods sold of $360.4.

*b.* Borrowed $306.5 on line of credit with a bank with principal payable within one year.

*c.* Incurred research and development expense of $10, which was paid in cash.

| Transaction | Current Assets | Gross Profit | Current Liabilities |
|---|---|---|---|
| *a.* | | | |
| *b.* | | | |
| *c.* | | | |

**E5–16** **Determining the Effects of Transactions on Balance Sheet, Income Statement, and Statement of Cash Flows Categories**

■ LO3
Rowe Furniture

Rowe Furniture Corporation is a Virginia-based manufacturer of furniture. Listed here are selected aggregate transactions from the first quarter of 20B (in millions). Complete the following tabulation, indicating the sign (+ for increase, − for decrease, and NE for no effect) and amount of the effect of each additional transaction. Consider each item independently.

*a.* Recorded collections of cash from customers owed on open account of $32.2.

*b.* Repaid $2.1 in principal on line of credit with a bank with principal payable within one year.

| Transaction | Current Assets | Gross Profit | Current Liabilities | Cash Flow from Operating Activities |
|---|---|---|---|---|
| *a.* | | | | |
| *b.* | | | | |

**E5–17** **Preparing a Simple Statement of Cash Flows Using the Indirect Method**

■ LO3

Blackwell Corporation is preparing its annual financial statements at December 31, 20A. Listed here are the items on its statement of cash flows presented in alphabetical order. Parentheses indicate that a listed amount should be subtracted on the cash flow statement. The beginning balance in cash was $36,000 and the ending balance was $41,000.

| | |
|---|---:|
| Cash borrowed on three-year note | $25,000 |
| Decrease in inventory | 2,000 |
| Decrease in accounts payable | (4,000) |
| Increase in accounts receivable | (10,000) |
| Net income | 18,000 |
| Stock issued for cash | 22,000 |
| New delivery truck purchased | (12,000) |
| Land purchased | (36,000) |

*Required:*
Prepare the 20A statement of cash flows for Blackwell Corporation. The section reporting cash flows from operating activities should be prepared using the indirect method discussed in the chapter.

■ **LO4**        **E5–18**    **Analyzing and Interpreting Return on Equity**

Lands' End

Lands' End Inc. is a mail-order and Internet-based direct merchant of traditionally styled casual clothing accessories, domestics, shoes, and soft luggage. Presented here are selected income statement and balance sheet amounts (in thousands).

| | Current Year | Prior Year |
|---|---:|---:|
| Net sales | $1,371,375 | $1,263,629 |
| Net income | 31,185 | 64,150 |
| Average shareholders' equity | 349,211 | 338,092 |
| Average total assets | 913,647 | 848,551 |

*Required:*
1. Compute ROE for the current and prior years and explain the meaning of the change.
2. Explain the major cause(s) of the decline in Lands' End's ROE using ROE profit driver analysis.

■ **LO4**        **E5–19**    **Analyzing and Evaluating Return on Equity from a Security Analyst's Perspective**

Papa John's

Papa John's is one of the fastest-growing pizza delivery and carry-out restaurant chains in the country. Presented here are selected income statement and balance sheet amounts (in thousands).

| | Current Year | Prior Year |
|---|---:|---:|
| Net sales | $508,784 | $360,052 |
| Net income | 26,853 | 18,614 |
| Average shareholders' equity | 232,988 | 196,352 |
| Average total assets | 381,014 | 286,057 |

*Required:*
1. Compute ROE for the current and prior years and explain the meaning of the change.
2. Explain the major cause(s) of the improvement in Papa John's ROE using ROE profit driver analysis.
3. Would security analysts more likely increase or decrease their estimates of share value on the basis of this change? Explain.

## PROBLEMS

■ **LO1, 2**      **P5–1**    **Matching Transactions with Concepts**

Following are the concepts of accounting covered in Chapters 2 through 5. Match each transaction with its related concept by entering the appropriate letter in the space provided. Use one letter for each blank.

| Concepts | Transactions |
|---|---|
| _____ (1) Users of financial statements | A. Recorded a $1,000 sale of merchandise on credit. |
| _____ (2) Objective of financial statements | B. Counted (inventoried) the unsold items at the end of the period and valued them in dollars. |
| **Qualitative Characteristics** | C. Acquired a vehicle for use in operating the business. |
| _____ (3) Relevance | D. Reported the amount of depreciation expense because it likely will affect important decisions of statement users. |
| _____ (4) Reliability | E. Identified as the investors, creditors, and others interested in the business. |
| **Assumptions** | F. Used special accounting approaches because of the uniqueness of the industry. |
| _____ (5) Separate entity | G. Sold and issued bonds payable of $1 million. |
| _____ (6) Continuity | H. Paid a contractor for an addition to the building with $10,000 cash and $20,000 market value of the stock of the company ($30,000 was deemed to be the cash equivalent price). |
| _____ (7) Unit of measure | |
| _____ (8) Time period | |
| **Elements of Financial Statements** | I. Engaged an outside independent CPA to audit the financial statements. |
| _____ (9) Revenues | J. Sold merchandise and services for cash and on credit during the year; then determined the cost of those goods sold and the cost of rendering those services. |
| _____ (10) Expenses | |
| _____ (11) Gains | |
| _____ (12) Losses | K. Established an accounting policy that sales revenue shall be recognized only when ownership to the goods sold passes to the customer. |
| _____ (13) Assets | |
| _____ (14) Liabilities | |
| _____ (15) Stockholders' equity | L. To design and prepare the financial statements to assist the users in making decisions. |
| **Principles** | M. Established a policy not to include in the financial statements the personal financial affairs of the owners of the business. |
| _____ (16) Cost | |
| _____ (17) Revenue | N. Sold an asset at a loss that was a peripheral or incidental transaction. |
| _____ (18) Matching | |
| _____ (19) Full disclosure | O. The user value of a special financial report exceeds the cost of preparing it. |
| **Constraints of Accounting** | P. Valued an asset, such as inventory, at less than its purchase cost because the replacement cost is less. |
| _____ (20) Materiality threshold | |
| _____ (21) Cost-benefit constraint | Q. Dated the income statement "For the Year Ended December 31, 20B." |
| _____ (22) Conservatism constraint | R. Used services from outsiders—paid cash for some and the remainder on credit. |
| _____ (23) Industry peculiarities | S. Acquired an asset (a pencil sharpener that will have a useful life of five years) and recorded it as an expense when purchased for $1.99. |

T. Disclosed in the financial statements all relevant financial information about the business; necessitated the use of notes to the financial statements.

U. Sold an asset at a gain that was a peripheral or incidental transaction.

V. Assets of $500,000 − Liabilities of $300,000 = Stockholders' Equity of $200,000.

W. Accounting and reporting assume a "going concern."

**P5–2 Matching Definitions with Balance Sheet–Related Terms**  ▌**LO3**

Following are terms related to the balance sheet, which were discussed in Chapters 2 through 5. Match each definition with its related term by entering the appropriate letter in the space provided.

### Terms

| | | |
|---|---|---|
| _____ (1) Retained earnings | | _____ (10) Book value |
| _____ (2) Current liabilities | | _____ (11) Capital in excess of par |
| _____ (3) Liquidity | | _____ (12) Liabilities |
| _____ (4) Contra-asset account | | _____ (13) Fixed assets |
| _____ (5) Accumulated depreciation | | _____ (14) Shareholders' equity |
| _____ (6) Intangible assets | | _____ (15) Current assets |
| _____ (7) Other assets | | _____ (16) Assets |
| _____ (8) Shares outstanding | | _____ (17) Long-term liabilities |
| _____ (9) Normal operating cycle | | |

Definitions

| | |
|---|---|
| A. A miscellaneous category of assets. | K. Probable future economic benefits owned by the entity from past transactions. |
| B. Amount of contributed capital less the par value of the stock. | L. Liabilities expected to be paid out of current assets normally within the next year. |
| C. Total assets minus total liabilities. | M. The average cash-to-cash time involved in the operations of the business. |
| D. Nearness of assets to cash (in time). | |
| E. Assets expected to be collected in cash within one year or operating cycle, if longer. | N. Sum of the annual depreciation expense on an asset from its acquisition to the current date. |
| F. Same as carrying value; cost less accumulated depreciation to date. | O. All liabilities not classified as current liabilities. |
| G. Accumulated earnings minus accumulated dividends. | P. Property, plant, and equipment. |
| H. Asset offset account (subtracted from asset). | Q. Debts or obligations from past transactions to be paid with assets or services. |
| I. Balance of the Common Stock account divided by the par value per share. | R. None of the above. |
| J. Assets that do not have physical substance. | |

**LO3**    **P5–3**    **Preparing a Balance Sheet and Analyzing Some of Its Parts** (AP5–1)

King Jewelers is developing its annual financial statements for 20C. The following amounts were correct at December 31, 20C: cash, $42,000; accounts receivable, $51,300; merchandise inventory, $110,000; prepaid insurance, $800; investment in stock of Z corporation (long-term), $26,000; store equipment, $48,000; used store equipment held for disposal, $7,000; accumulated depreciation, store equipment, $9,600; accounts payable, $42,000; long-term note payable, $30,000; income taxes payable, $7,000; retained earnings, $86,500; and common stock, 100,000 shares outstanding, par $1 per share (originally sold and issued at $1.10 per share).

*Required:*

1. Based on these data, prepare a 20C balance sheet. Use the following major captions (list the individual items under these captions):

   *a.* Assets: Current Assets, Long-Term Investments, Fixed Assets, and Other Assets.

   *b.* Liabilities: Current Liabilities and Long-Term Liabilities.

   *c.* Stockholders' Equity: Contributed Capital and Retained Earnings.

2. What is the net book value of the

   *a.* Inventory?

   *b.* Accounts receivable?

   *c.* Store equipment?

   *d.* Note payable (long term)?

   Explain what these values mean.

**LO3**    **P5–4**    **Reporting Building, Land, and Depreciation Expense** (AP5–2)

Stewart Company is preparing its balance sheet at December 31, 20X. The following assets are to be reported:

*a.* Building, purchased 15 years ago (counting 20X): original cost, $450,000; estimated useful life, 25 years from date of purchase; and no residual value.

*b.* Land, purchased 15 years ago (counting 20X): original cost, $70,000.

*Required:*

1. Show how the two assets should be reported on the balance sheet. What is the total book value of the property, plant, and equipment?

2. What amount of depreciation expense should be reported on the 20X income statement? Show computations.

**LO3**    **P5–5**    **Reporting Stockholders' Equity on a Balance Sheet and Recording the Issuance of Stock** (AP5–3)

At the end of the 20A annual reporting period, Mesa Corporation's balance sheet showed the following:

**MESA CORPORATION**
**Balance Sheet**
**At December 31, 20A**

Stockholders' Equity

| | |
|---|---|
| Contributed capital | |
| Common stock (par $10; 7,000 shares) | $ 70,000 |
| Contributed capital in excess of par | 10,000 |
| Total contributed capital | 80,000 |
| Retained earnings | |
| Ending balance | 50,000 |
| Total stockholders' equity | $130,000 |

During 20B, the following selected transactions (summarized) were completed:

*a.* Sold and issued 1,000 shares of common stock at $15 cash per share (at year-end).

*b.* Determined net income, $40,000.

*c.* Declared and paid a cash dividend of $3 per share on the beginning shares outstanding.

*Required:*

1. Prepare the stockholders' equity section of the balance sheet at December 31, 20B.

2. Give the journal entry to record the sale and issuance of the 1,000 shares of common stock.

**P5–6 Preparing a Multiple-Step Income Statement with Discontinued Operations and Cumulative Effects of Accounting Changes (Challenging)**

■ **LO3**

Adolph Coors Company, established in 1873, is the third-largest brewer of beer in the United States. Its products include Coors, Coors Light, ZIMA, and many other malt beverages. Recently, Coors discontinued its ceramics, aluminum, packaging, and technology-based developmental businesses. In the same year, it reported two changes in accounting methods mandated by the FASB. The items reported on its income statement for that year (ended December 26, 20A) are presented here (in thousands) in alphabetical order:

| | |
|---|---|
| Cost of goods sold | $1,035,544 |
| Cumulative effect of change in accounting for income taxes | 30,500 |
| Cumulative effect of change in accounting for post-retirement benefits (net of tax) | (38,800) |
| Income tax expense | 22,900 |
| Interest expense | 16,014 |
| Interest income | 255 |
| Marketing, general and administrative | 429,573 |
| Miscellaneous income—net | 1,087 |
| Net loss from discontinued operations | 29,415 |
| Net sales | 1,550,788 |
| Research and project development | 12,370 |

*Required:*

1. Using appropriate headings and subtotals, prepare a multiple-step consolidated income statement (showing both gross profit and operating income).

2. What information does the multiple-step format emphasize that the single-step income statement does not?

**P5–7 Preparing Both an Income Statement and Balance Sheet from a Trial Balance** (AP5–4)

■ **LO3**

Thomas Real Estate Company (organized as a corporation on April 1, 20A) has completed the accounting cycle for the second year, ended March 31, 20C. Thomas also has completed a correct trial balance as follows:

**THOMAS REAL ESTATE COMPANY**
**Trial Balance**
**At March 31, 20C**

| Account Titles | Debit | Credit |
|---|---|---|
| Cash | 53,000 | |
| Accounts receivable | 44,800 | |
| Office supplies inventory | 300 | |
| Automobiles (company cars) | 30,000 | |
| Accumulated depreciation, automobiles | | 10,000 |
| Office equipment | 3,000 | |
| Accumulated depreciation, office equipment | | 1,000 |
| Accounts payable | | 20,250 |
| Income taxes payable | | 0 |
| Salaries and commissions payable | | 1,500 |
| Note payable, long term | | 30,000 |
| Capital stock (par $1; 30,000 shares) | | 30,000 |
| Contributed capital in excess of par | | 5,000 |
| Retained earnings (on April 1, 20B) | | 7,350 |
| Dividends declared and paid during the current year | 8,000 | |
| Sales commissions earned | | 77,000 |
| Management fees earned | | 13,000 |
| Operating expenses (detail omitted to conserve your time) | 48,000 | |
| Depreciation expense (on autos and including $500 on office equipment) | 5,500 | |
| Interest expense | 2,500 | |
| Income tax expense (not yet computed) | | |
| Totals | 195,100 | 195,100 |

*Required:*

1. Complete the financial statements, as follows:
   a. Income statement for the reporting year ended March 31, 20C. Include income tax expense, assuming a 30 percent tax rate. Use the following major captions: Revenues, Expenses, Pretax Income, Income Tax, Net Income, and EPS (list each item under these captions).
   b. Balance sheet at the end of the reporting year, March 31, 20C. Include (1) income taxes for the current year in income taxes payable and (2) dividends in retained earnings. Use the following captions (list each item under these captions).

**Assets**

Current Assets
Noncurrent Assets

**Liabilities**

Current Liabilities
Long-Term Liabilities

**Stockholders' Equity**

Contributed Capital
Retained Earnings

2. Give the journal entry to record income taxes for the year (not yet paid).

■ **LO3**   **P5–8**   **Inferring the Amounts on an Income Statement (Challenging)**
Following is a partially completed income statement of Reginold Corporation for the year ended December 31, 20B.

| Items | Other Data | Amounts |
|---|---|---|
| Net sales revenue | | $260,000 |
| Cost of goods sold | | |
| Gross margin on sales | Gross margin as percent of sales, 35% | |
| Expenses | | |
|   Selling expense | | |
|   General and administrative expense | | $28,000 |
|   Interest expense | | 4,000 |
|   Total expenses | | |
| Pretax income | | |
| Income tax on operations | | |
| Income before extraordinary items | | |
|   Extraordinary gain | | 12,000 |
|   Income tax effect | | |
|   Net extraordinary gain | | |
| Net income | | |
| EPS (on common stock) | | |
| Income before extraordinary gain | | 1.20 |
|   Extraordinary gain | | |
| Net income | | |

*Required:*

Based on these data and assuming (1) a 20 percent income tax rate on all items and (2) 25,000 common shares outstanding, complete the income statement. Show all computations.

**P5–9 Preparing a Simple Statement of Cash Flows Using the Indirect Method**

■ **LO3**

Following are the items on Srinivasan Company's 20B statement of cash flows presented in alphabetical order. Parentheses indicate that a listed amount should be subtracted on the cash flow statement. The beginning balance in cash was $40,000 and the ending balance was $27,000.

| | |
|---|---|
| Borrowing on long-term note | $20,000 |
| Increase in accounts payable | 6,000 |
| Increase in accounts receivable | (5,000) |
| Increase in inventories | (10,000) |
| Net income | 55,000 |
| Paid cash dividend | (15,000) |
| Paid long-term note | (12,000) |
| Purchased equipment | (80,000) |
| Purchased land | (8,000) |
| Sale of capital stock (3,000 shares × $12) | 36,000 |

*Required:*

Prepare the 20B statement of cash flows for Srinivasan Company using the indirect method presented in the chapter.

**P5–10 Determining and Interpreting the Effects of Transactions on Income Statement Categories and Return on Equity (AP5–5)**

■ **LO3, 4**

Apple Computer

Apple Computer popularized both the personal computer and the easy-to-use graphic interface. Today it is fighting for its life, however, against a bevy of companies that rely on Intel microprocessors and the Windows operating system. Presented here is its recent income statement (in millions).

| | |
|---|---:|
| Net sales | $5,941 |
| **Costs and expenses** | |
| Cost of sales | 4,462 |
| Research and development | 310 |
| Selling, general and administrative | 908 |
| Operating income (loss) | 261 |
| Interest and other income (expenses), net | 68 |
| Income (loss) before provision (benefit) for income taxes | 329 |
| Provision (benefit) for income taxes | 20 |
| Net income (loss) | $ 309 |

Its beginning and ending stockholders' equity was $1,200 and $1,642, respectively.

*Required:*

1. Listed here are hypothetical *additional* transactions. Assuming that they had *also* occurred during the fiscal year, complete the following tabulation, indicating the sign of the effect of each *additional* transaction (+ for increase, − for decrease, and NE for no effect). Consider each item independently and ignore taxes.

   *a.* Recorded sales on account of $500 and related cost of goods sold of $475.

   *b.* Incurred additional research and development expense of $100, which was paid in cash.

   *c.* Issued additional shares of common stock for $200 cash.

   *d.* Declared and paid dividends of $90.

| Transaction | Gross Profit | Operating Income (Loss) | Return on Equity |
|---|---|---|---|
| *a.* | | | |
| *b.* | | | |
| *c.* | | | |
| *d.* | | | |

2. Assume that next period, Apple does not pay any dividends, does not issue or retire stock, and earns the same income as during the current period. Will Apple's ROE next period be higher, lower, or the same as the current period? Why?

# ALTERNATE PROBLEMS

■ **LO3**    **AP5–1    Preparing a Balance Sheet and Analyzing Some of Its Parts** (P5–3)

Carpet Bazaar is developing its annual financial statements for 20C. The following amounts were correct at December 31, 20C: cash, $35,000; investment in stock of ABC corporation (long term), $32,000; store equipment, $51,000; accounts receivable, $47,500; carpet inventory, $118,000; prepaid insurance, $1,300; used store equipment held for disposal, $3,500; accumulated depreciation, store equipment, $10,200; income taxes payable, $6,000; long-term note payable, $26,000; accounts payable, $45,000; retained earnings, $76,100; and common stock, 100,000 shares outstanding, par $1 per share (originally sold and issued at $1.25 per share).

*Required:*

1. Based on these data, prepare a 20C balance sheet. Use the following major captions (list the individual items under these captions):

   *a.* Assets: Current Assets, Long-Term Investments, Fixed Assets, and Other Assets.

    *b.* Liabilities: Current Liabilities and Long-Term Liabilities.

    *c.* Stockholders' Equity: Contributed Capital and Retained Earnings.

2. What is the net book value of the

    *a.* Inventory?

    *b.* Accounts receivable?

    *c.* Store equipment?

    *d.* Note payable (long term)?

Explain what these values mean.

**AP5–2 Reporting Building, Land, and Depreciation Expense (P5–4)**        ▓ **LO3**

Richmond Inc. is preparing its balance sheet at December 31, 20X. The following assets are to be reported:

    *a.* Building, purchased 12 years ago (counting 20X): original cost, $630,000; estimated useful life, 20 years from date of purchase; and no residual value.

    *b.* Land, purchased 12 years ago (counting 20X): original cost, $112,000.

*Required:*

1. Show how the two assets should be reported on the balance sheet. What is the total book value of the property, plant, and equipment?

2. What amount of depreciation expense should be reported on the 20X income statement? Show computations.

**AP5–3 Reporting Stockholders' Equity on a Balance Sheet and Recording the**        ▓ **LO3**
**Issuance of Stock (P5–5)**

At the end of the 20A annual reporting period, Potamia Corporation's balance sheet showed the following:

**POTAMIA CORPORATION**
**Balance Sheet**
**At December 31, 20A**

| Stockholders' Equity | |
| --- | --- |
| Common stock (par $10; 9,500 shares) | $ 95,000 |
| Additional paid-in capital | 28,500 |
| Retained earnings—Ending balance | 70,000 |
| Total stockholders' equity | $193,500 |

During 20B, the following selected transactions (summarized) were completed:

    *a.* Sold and issued 1,500 shares of common stock at $17 cash per share (at year-end).

    *b.* Determined net income, $50,000.

    *c.* Declared and paid a cash dividend of $2 per share on the beginning shares outstanding.

*Required:*

1. Prepare the stockholders' equity section of the balance sheet at December 31, 20B.

2. Give the journal entry to record the sale and issuance of the 1,500 shares of common stock.

**AP5–4 Preparing Both an Income Statement and Balance Sheet from a Trial Balance (P5–7)**        ▓ **LO3**

ACME Pest Control Services (organized as a corporation on September 1, 20A) has completed the accounting cycle for the second year, ended August 31, 20C. ACME Pest Control also has completed a correct trial balance as follows:

**ACME PEST CONTROL SERVICES**
**Trial Balance**
**At August 31, 20C**

| Account Titles | Debit | Credit |
|---|---|---|
| Cash | 26,000 | |
| Accounts receivable | 30,800 | |
| Supplies inventory | 1,300 | |
| Service vehicles (company vans) | 60,000 | |
| Accumulated depreciation, automobiles | | 20,000 |
| Equipment | 14,000 | |
| Accumulated depreciation, equipment | | 4,000 |
| Accounts payable | | 16,700 |
| Income taxes payable | | 0 |
| Salaries payable | | 1,100 |
| Note payable, long term | | 34,000 |
| Capital stock (par $1; 10,000 shares) | | 10,000 |
| Contributed capital in excess of par | | 30,000 |
| Retained earnings (on September 1, 20B) | | 4,300 |
| Dividends declared and paid during the current year | 2,000 | |
| Sales revenue | | 38,000 |
| Maintenance contract revenue | | 17,000 |
| Operating expenses (detail omitted to conserve your time) | 27,000 | |
| Depreciation expense (on vehicles and including $2,000 on equipment) | 12,000 | |
| Interest expense | 2,000 | |
| Income tax expense (not yet computed) | | |
| Totals | 175,100 | 175,100 |

*Required:*

1. Complete the financial statements, as follows:

   a. Income statement for the reporting year ended August 31, 20C. Include income tax expense, assuming a 30 percent tax rate. Use the following major captions: Revenues, Expenses, Pretax Income, Income Tax, Net Income, and EPS (list each item under these captions).

   b. Balance sheet at the end of the reporting year, August 31, 20C. Include (1) income taxes for the current year in income taxes payable and (2) dividends in retained earnings. Use the following captions (list each item under these captions).

   **Assets**

   Current Assets
   Noncurrent Assets

   **Liabilities**

   Current Liabilities
   Long-Term Liabilities

   **Stockholders' Equity**

   Contributed Capital
   Retained Earnings

2. Give the journal entry to record income taxes for the year (not yet paid).

**AP5–5** **Determining and Interpreting the Effects of Transactions on Income Statement Categories and Return on Equity** (P5–10)

■ **LO3, 4**

Barnes & Noble

Barnes & Noble, Inc. revolutionized bookselling by making its stores public spaces and community institutions where customers may browse, find a book, relax over a cup of coffee, talk with authors, and join discussion groups. Today it is fighting increasing competition not only from traditional sources but also from on-line booksellers. Presented here is a recent income statement (in millions).

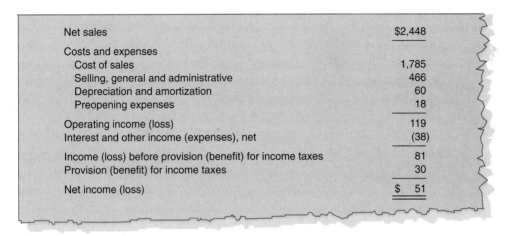

| | |
|---|---:|
| Net sales | $2,448 |
| Costs and expenses | |
|   Cost of sales | 1,785 |
|   Selling, general and administrative | 466 |
|   Depreciation and amortization | 60 |
|   Preopening expenses | 18 |
| Operating income (loss) | 119 |
| Interest and other income (expenses), net | (38) |
| Income (loss) before provision (benefit) for income taxes | 81 |
| Provision (benefit) for income taxes | 30 |
| Net income (loss) | $ 51 |

Its beginning and ending stockholders' equity was $400 and $446, respectively.

***Required:***

1. Listed here are hypothetical *additional* transactions. Assuming that they had *also* occurred during the fiscal year, complete the following tabulation, indicating the sign of the effect of each *additional* transaction (+ for increase, − for decrease, and NE for no effect). Consider each item independently and ignore taxes.

  *a.* Recorded and received additional interest income of $4.

  *b.* Purchased $25 of additional inventory on open account.

  *c.* Recorded and paid additional advertising expense of $9.

  *d.* Additional shares of common stock are issued for $50 cash.

| Transaction | Operating Income (Loss) | Net Income | Return on Equity |
|---|---|---|---|
| *a.* | | | |
| *b.* | | | |
| *c.* | | | |
| *d.* | | | |

2. Assume that next period, Barnes & Noble does not pay any dividends, does not issue or retire stock, and earns 20 percent more than during the current period. Will Barnes & Noble's ROE next period be higher, lower, or the same as in the current period? Why?

# CASES AND PROJECTS

## FINANCIAL REPORTING AND ANALYSIS CASES

**CP5–1** **Finding Financial Information**

■ **LO2, 3**

American Eagle Outfitters

Refer to the financial statements of American Eagle Outfitters given in Appendix B at the end of this book, or open file AEOS10K.doc in the S&P directory on the student CD-ROM. At the bottom of each statement, the company warns readers to "See notes to consolidated financial statements." The following questions illustrate the types of information that you can find in the financial statements and accompanying notes. (*Hint:* Use the notes.)

STANDARD
&POOR'S

*Required:*

1. Does the company present a single-step or multiple-step income statement?
2. The company spent $24,919,000 on capital expenditures (property, plant, and equipment) this year. Were operating activities or financing activities the major source of cash for these expenditures?
3. What was the company's largest asset (net) at the end of the year?
4. What was advertising expense for the most recent year?
5. Was women's apparel an increasing or decreasing percentage of its sales over the last three years?

**■ LO2, 3   CP5–2**

Urban Outfitters

**STANDARD &POOR'S**

**Finding Financial Information**

Refer to the financial statements of Urban Outfitters given in Appendix C at the end of this book, or open file URBN10K.doc in the S&P directory on the student CD-ROM. At the bottom of each statement, the company warns readers to "See accompanying notes." The following questions illustrate the types of information that you can find in the financial statements and accompanying notes. (*Hint:* Use the notes.)

*Required:*

1. What was the highest stock price for the company during the current year?
2. How much land did the company own at the end of the current year?
3. What was rent expense for the current year?
4. What amount of accrued expenses were accrued sales taxes at the end of the current year?
5. What amount of inventory relates to retail operations and what amount relates to wholesale operations?

**■ LO4   CP5–3**

American Eagle
Outfitters vs.
Urban Outfitters

**STANDARD &POOR'S**

**Comparing Companies within an Industry**

Refer to the financial statements of American Eagle Outfitters given in Appendix B, Urban Outfitters given in Appendix C, and the Standard and Poor's Industry Ratio Report given in Appendix D at the end of this book or open file CP5-3.xls in the S&P directory on the student CD-ROM.

*Required:*

1. Compute return on equity for the current year. Which company provided the highest return to shareholders during the current year?
2. Use ROE profit driver analysis to determine the cause(s) of any differences. How might the ownership versus the rental of property, plant, and equipment affect the total asset turnover ratio?
3. Compare the ROE profit driver analysis for American Eagle Outfitters and Urban Outfitters to the ROE profit driver analysis for their industry. Where does American Eagle Outfitters outperform or underperform the industry? Where does Urban Outfitters outperform or underperform the industry?

**■ LO1   CP5–4**

The Auditor's Report

**Interpreting the Financial Press**

The Committee of Sponsoring Organizations (COSO) recently published a research study that examined financial statement fraud occurrences between 1987 and 1997. A summary of the findings by M. S. Beasley, J. V. Carcello, and D. R. Hermanson, "Fraudulent Financial Reporting: 1987–1997: An Analysis of U.S. Public Companies," *The Auditor's Report*, Summer 1999, pp. 15–17 is available on the Libby/Libby/Short website at www.mhhe.com/business/accounting/libby3.* You should read the article and then write a short memo outlining the following:

1. The size of the companies involved.
2. The extent of top management involvement.
3. The specific accounting fraud techniques involved.
4. What might lead managers to introduce misstatements into the income statement near the end of the accounting period.

*Reprinted with permission from *The Auditor's Report,* copyright © 1999 by American Institute of Certified Public Accounts, Inc.

**■ LO2, 3   CP5–5**

**Using Financial Reports: Financial Statement Inferences**

The following amounts were selected from the annual financial statements for Genesis Corporation at December 31, 20C (end of the third year of operations):

From the 20C income statement:

| | |
|---|---:|
| Sales revenue | $275,000 |
| Cost of goods sold | (170,000) |
| All other expenses (including income tax) | (95,000) |
| Net income | $10,000 |

From the December 31, 20C, balance sheet:

| | |
|---|---:|
| Current assets | 90,000 |
| All other assets | 212,000 |
| Total assets | 302,000 |
| Current liabilities | 40,000 |
| Long-term liabilities | 66,000 |
| Capital stock (par $10) | 100,000 |
| Contributed capital in excess of par | 16,000 |
| Retained earnings | 80,000 |
| Total liabilities and stockholders' equity | $302,000 |

*Required:*
Analyze the data on the 20C financial statements of Genesis by answering the questions that follow. Show computations.

1. What was the gross margin on sales?
2. What was the amount of EPS?
3. If the income tax rate was 25 percent, what was the amount of pretax income?
4. What was the average sales price per share of the capital stock?
5. Assuming that no dividends were declared or paid during 20C, what was the beginning balance (January 1, 20C) of retained earnings?

**CP5–6 Using Financial Reports: Interpreting International Financial Statement Classifications (Challenging)**

■ **LO3**

Diageo

As the economy becomes more international in scope, users of financial statements may be expected to analyze companies that are not incorporated in the United States. Diageo is a major world corporation located in London. It owns many familiar U.S. businesses such as the Pillsbury Company, Burger King, and Häagen-Dazs ice cream.

*Required:*
Based on the concepts presented in this book, explain the meaning of the various account classifications shown on the portion of the Diageo annual report presented here. (*Note:* There are five reserve accounts. The middle three relate to topics that are discussed in advanced accounting courses.)

**DIAGEO**
**Consolidated Balance Sheet**
**At 30th September, 20B and 20A**

| | Notes | 20B £m | 20B £m | 20A £m | 20A £m |
|---|---|---:|---:|---:|---:|
| **Fixed assets** | | | | | |
| Intangible assets | 11 | | 2,652 | | 588 |
| Tangible assets | 12 | | 3,839 | | 3,280 |
| Investments | 13 | | 144 | | 206 |
| | | | 6,635 | | 4,074 |
| **Current assets** | | | | | |
| Stocks | 14 | 1,269 | | 761 | |
| Debtors | 15 | 1,451 | | 873 | |
| Cash at bank and in hand | | 215 | | 138 | |
| | | 2,935 | | 1,772 | |

| | | Current | Prior |
|---|---|---|---|
| **Creditors**—due within one year | | | |
| Borrowings | 17 | (362) | (187) |
| Other creditors | 19 | (2,316) | (1,301) |
| | | (2,678) | (1,488) |
| **Net current assets** | 15 | 257 | 284 |
| **Total assets less current liabilities** | | 6,892 | 4,358 |
| **Creditors**—due after more than one year | | | |
| Borrowings | 17 | (3,494) | (702) |
| Other creditors | 20 | (231) | (163) |
| | | (3,725) | (865) |
| **Provisions for liabilities and charges** | 21 | (325) | (55) |
| | | 2,842 | 3,438 |
| **Capital and reserves** | | | |
| Called-up share capital | 22 | 506 | 443 |
| **Reserves** | 23 | | |
| Share premium account | | 436 | 7 |
| Revaluation reserve | | (944) | 649 |
| Special reserve | | — | 282 |
| Related companies' reserves | | 10 | 16 |
| Profit and loss account | | 2,802 | 2,010 |
| | | 2,304 | 2,964 |
| | | 2,810 | 3,407 |
| **Minority interests** | | 32 | 31 |
| | | 2,842 | 3,438 |

**LO1, 2     CP5–7**
Callaway Golf

## Using Financial Reports: Analyzing Income Statement–Based Executive Bonuses

As noted in the chapter, Callaway Golf believes in tying executives' compensation to the company's performance as measured by accounting numbers. In a recent year, Callaway had agreed to pay its five executive officers bonuses of up to 200 percent of base salary if sales growth and pretax earnings as a percentage of sales (computed here) met or exceeded target amounts. Callaway's income statements for the relevant years are presented here.

| (in thousands, except per share data) | Year Ended December 31, | | | |
|---|---|---|---|---|
| | Current Year | | Prior Year | |
| Net sales | $254,645 | 100% | $132,058 | 100% |
| Cost of goods sold | 115,458 | 45% | 62,970 | 48% |
| Gross profit | 139,187 | 55% | 69,088 | 52% |
| Selling expenses | 38,485 | 15% | 19,810 | 15% |
| General and administrative expenses | 28,633 | 11% | 14,990 | 11% |
| Research and development costs | 3,653 | 1% | 1,585 | 1% |
| Income from operations | 68,416 | 27% | 32,703 | 25% |
| Other income (expense) | | | | |
| Interest income (expense), net | 1,024 | | 403 | |
| Other income, net | 160 | | 69 | |
| Income before income taxes and cumulative effect of accounting change | 69,600 | 27% | 33,175 | 25% |
| Provision for income taxes | 28,396 | | 13,895 | |
| Income before cumulative effect of accounting change | 41,204 | 16% | 19,280 | 15% |
| Cumulative effect of accounting change | 1,658 | | | |
| Net income | $42,862 | 17% | $19,280 | 15% |

Callaway executives will receive bonuses if *sales growth* and *pretax earnings as a percent of sales* meet or exceed target amounts (35.1 percent and 21.1 percent, respectively). Meeting these goals in the current year would result in bonuses ranging from $400,000 to $700,000 for each of the five executive officers.

*Required:*

1. Use the preceding information to determine whether Callaway executives earned their bonuses in the most recent year presented.

2. Sales increased three years later by 22.6 percent to $678,512. What might explain the slower growth rate in this later year compared to the current year presented here?

## CRITICAL THINKING CASES

**CP5–8** **Making Decisions as a Manager: Evaluating the Effects of Business Strategy on Return on Equity**

**LO4**

Sony is a world leader in the manufacture of consumer and commercial electronics as well as the entertainment and insurance industries. Its ROE has increased from 9 percent to 14 percent over the last three years.

Sony

*Required:*

1. Indicate the most likely effect of each of the changes in business strategy on Sony's ROE for the next period and future periods (+ for increase, − for decrease, and NE for no effect), assuming all other things are unchanged.

2. Explain your answer for each. Treat each item independently.

   *a.* Sony decreases its investment in research and development aimed at products to be brought to market in more than one year.

   *b.* Sony begins a new advertising campaign for a movie to be released during the next year.

   *c.* Sony issues additional stock for cash, the proceeds to be used to acquire other high-technology companies in future periods.

| Strategy Change | Current Period ROE | Future Periods' ROE |
|---|---|---|
| a. | | |
| b. | | |
| c. | | |

**CP5–9** **Making a Decision as an Auditor: Effects of Errors on Income, Assets, and Liabilities**

**LO1**

Megan Company (not a corporation) was careless about its financial records during its first year of operations, 20A. It is December 31, 20A, the end of the annual accounting period. An outside CPA examined the records and discovered numerous errors, all of which are described here. Assume that each error is independent of the others.

*Required:*

Analyze each error and indicate its effect on 20A and 20B income, assets, and liabilities if not corrected. Do not assume any other errors. Use these codes to indicate the effect of each dollar amount: O = overstated, U = understated, and NE = no effect. Write an explanation of your analysis of each transaction to support your response.

| | | Effect On | | |
|---|---|---|---|---|
| | Net Income | | Assets | | Liabilities | |
| Independent Errors | 20A | 20B | 20A | 20B | 20A | 20B |
| 1. Depreciation expense for 20A, not recorded in 20A, $950. | O $950 | NE | O $950 | O $950 | NE | NE |
| 2. Wages earned by employees during 20A not recorded or paid in 20A but will be paid in 20B, $500. | | | | | | |
| 3. Revenue earned during 20A but not collected or recorded until 20B, $600. | | | | | | |
| 4. Amount paid in 20A and recorded as expense in 20A but not an expense until 20B, $200. | | | | | | |
| 5. Revenue collected in 20A and recorded as revenue in 20A but not earned until 20B, $900. | | | | | | |
| 6. Sale of services and cash collected in 20A. Recorded as a debit to Cash and as a credit to Accounts Receivable, $300. | | | | | | |
| 7. On December 31, 20A, bought land on credit for $8,000, not recorded until payment was made on February 1, 20B. | | | | | | |

Following is a sample explanation of analysis of errors if not corrected, using the first error as an example:

1. Failure to record depreciation in 20A caused depreciation expense to be too low; therefore, income was overstated by $950. Accumulated depreciation also is too low by $950, which causes assets to be overstated by $950 until the error is corrected.

■ **LO3**      **CP5–10**      **Evaluating an Ethical Dilemma: Management Incentives and Fraudulent Financial Statements**

Mercury Finance

Mercury Finance Co. was a fast-growing auto-finance and insurance company. In January 1997, however, the auditors discovered that recently announced 1996 earnings had been grossly overstated and prior years' earnings had been overstated to a lesser extent. The estimated size of the earnings overstatement for 1996 is described in the following excerpt:

---

**Business Brief—Mercury Finance Co.**

Estimates for 1996 Revised Again, Now to a Big Loss
04/24/97 p. A8
The Wall Street Journal

Mercury Finance Co., which previously warned that it had grossly overstated earlier years' earnings, said it now expects to report up to a $55 million loss for 1996. In January, the Lake Forest, Ill., auto-finance company initially reported earnings of $120.7 million for 1996. Soon afterward, however, Mercury disclosed the accounting "irregularities" and estimated that last year's earnings probably would be about $56.7 million. Yesterday, Mercury said in an "update" that 1996 results will include an additional $125 million in loss provisions, as well as a $25 million reserve to cover the planned sale of its Lyndon insurance unit. As a result, the company anticipates a 1996 net loss of between $48 million and $55 million. In New York Stock Exchange composite trading, Mercury closed down 25 cents, or 13%, at $1.75.

---

*Required:*
Using more recent new reports (*Wall Street Journal Index, Dow Jones Interactive,* and *Bloomberg Business News* are good sources), answer the following questions.

1. Whom did the courts and regulatory authorities hold responsible for the misstated financial statements?

2. What were Mercury's closing stock prices on the day before (January 28, 1997) and the day after (January 30, 1997) the announcement of the misstatement?

3. How might executive compensation plans that tied bonuses to accounting earnings motivate unethical conduct in this case?

# FINANCIAL REPORTING AND ANALYSIS PROJECTS

**CP5–11 Comparing Companies over Time**

Using your web browser, contact Callaway Golf at its website (www.callawaygolf.com). Find the latest Callaway annual report. (*Note:* The necessary information also can be accessed from its Form 10-K through EDGAR.)

**LO4**
Callaway Golf

*Required:*

1. What was Callaway's ROE in the most recent year and how did it compare to the latest figures provided in the text? What was management's explanation for the change (if any)?

2. Use ROE profit driver analysis to determine what caused the bulk of the change.

**CP5–12 Comparing Companies across Industries**

Using your web browser, contact the websites of Microsoft, the leading computer *software* company (www.microsoft.com/msft/), and Dell Computer, a leading manufacturer of personal computer *hardware* (www.dell.com/us/en/gen/corporate/investor/investor.htm). On the basis of information provided in the latest annual reports, determine the return on equity for each company. Write a short memo comparing the companies' ratios. Indicate what differences in their businesses might account for any difference in the ratios.

**LO4**
Microsoft vs.
Dell Computer

**CP5–13 Broadening Financial Research Skills: Understanding the Disclosure Process through the Microsoft Website**

Using your web browser, contact Microsoft at its website (www.microsoft.com/msft/). Examine the most recent quarterly earnings press release and the related Form 10-Q, and the most recent Form 10-K.

**LO2**
Microsoft

*Required:*

Based on the information provided on the site, answer the following questions.

1. What were the release dates of the quarterly earnings press release and the Form 10-Q?

2. What additional information was provided in the Form 10-Q that was not reported in the earnings press release?

3. How do the statements and notes in the Form 10-K differ from those reported in the Form 10-Q?

**CP5–14 Broadening Financial Research Skills: Examining Library and Computer Resources**

Contact your school reference librarian and/or computer help desk.

**LO1**

*Required:*

Determine what information resources are available at your school for

1. Business-related news reports and announcements.

2. Company annual reports.

3. SEC reports.

4. Analyst forecasts.

Prepare a brief memo outlining the information available from one resource for each type of information. Also indicate its format (hard copy, website, CD-ROM, etc.).

**CP5–15 Broadening Financial Research Skills: Contacting Information Intermediaries on the Web**

Using your web browser, contact one of the information intermediaries at its website (listed in the text).

**LO1**

*Required:*

Determine what information that intermediary provides concerning

1. Business-related news reports and announcements.

2. Company annual reports.

3. SEC reports.

4. Analyst forecasts.

Prepare a brief memo outlining the information available from that resource for each of the four types of information. Also indicate its format (hard copy, website, CD-ROM, etc.).

**LO2, 3**    **CP5–16**

Microsoft

**Broadening Financial Research Skills: Information Provided on Company Websites**

Using your web browser, contact Microsoft at its website (www.microsoft.com/msft/).

*Required:*

Based on the information provided on the site, answer the following questions.

1. Which document(s) provided the most recent information on quarterly earnings?

2. For the most recent quarter, what was the change in sales revenue compared to the same quarter one year earlier? What was management's explanation for the change (if any)?

3. In what format is the latest income statement from the annual report provided?

4. What was the annual earnings per share, stock price per share, and price-earnings ratio (see Chapter 1) on the day of the most recent fourth quarter earnings press release?

**LO1**    **CP5–17**

**Ethics Project: Analyzing Irregularities and Management Compensation**

Obtain a recent news story outlining an accounting irregularity (misstatement) in which the reporter linked the motive for the misstatement to management compensation based on reported accounting earnings. (Library files, *Wall Street Journal Index, Dow Jones Interactive,* and *Bloomberg Business News* are good sources. Search for the terms *accounting irregularities* and *bonus.*)

*Required:*

Write a short memo outlining the nature of the irregularity, the size of the necessary correction of previously reported earnings, the impact of the announcement of the irregularity on the company's stock price, the impact of the irregularity on management compensation, and any fines or civil penalties against the company and its officers.

**LO2, 3**    **CP5–18**

**Team Project: Analyzing the Accounting Communication Process**

As a team, select an industry to analyze. MarketGuide provides lists of industries and their makeup at www.marketguide.com/mgi/INDUSTRY/INDUSTRY.html. Each team member should acquire the annual report or 10-K for one publicly traded company in the industry, with each member selecting a different company. (Library files, the SEC EDGAR service at www.sec.gov, Compustat CD, or the company itself are good sources.)

*Required:*

On an individual basis, each team member should write a short report answering the following questions about the selected company.

1. What formats are used to present the balance sheet and income statement?

2. Find one note that describes an accounting rule applied in the company's statements, one note that presents additional detail about a reported financial statement number, and one note that reports financial statement information not listed in the statements. What information is provided in each?

3. If an appropriate source is available at your school, using the company's website, *The Wall Street Journal Index,* or *Dow Jones Interactive* (or an instructor-assigned resource), find one article reporting the company's annual earnings announcement. How does the date of the announcement compare with the date on the annual report or 10-K?

4. Compute return on equity for the current year. Which company provided the highest return to shareholders during the current year?

5. Use ROE profit driver analysis to determine the cause(s) of any differences.

    Discuss any patterns across the three companies that you as a team observe. Then, as a team, write a short report comparing and contrasting your companies using these attributes. Provide potential explanations for any differences discovered.

**LO1, 2, 3**    **CP5–19**

**Comprehensive Project: Understanding Formats of Financial Statements and Earnings Announcements**

Using local library resources and company-provided information, your task is to understand the formats used for financial statements and notes in an annual report and to track the stock price reaction to the most recent annual earnings announcement for a public company. Your instructor may assign a particular company for you to analyze, or you may choose one of the focus companies in this text, a competitor company in the same industry, or a company in which you have career-related interests.

*Required:*

1. Contact the website or investor relations department of the company and obtain a copy of the most recent annual report. The Annual Report Gallery at www.reportgallery.com provides links to the websites of well-known companies. Alternatively, if your instructor so assigns, look in *The Wall Street Journal* stock price listings and select one company marked with the "♣" symbol. Call *The Wall Street Journal* Annual Reports Service at 1-800-654-2582 (check a recent issue to determine whether the number has been changed) or access its website at www.icbinc.com/cgi-bin/wsj.pl and request a copy of the most recent annual report for the selected company. (At publication time, this service was free.)

   *a.* Describe the formats used to present the balance sheet and the income statement.

   *b.* Describe the information contained in one note that describes an accounting rule applied in the company's statements, one note that presents additional detail about a reported financial statement number, and one note that reports financial statement information not listed in the statements.

2. Using the company's website, *The Wall Street Journal Index, Dow Jones Interactive,* or another service listed in the chapter (or an instructor-assigned resource), find one article reporting the company's annual earnings announcement. Using *The Wall Street Journal* or one of the websites listed in the chapter, locate the stock price listing for the company.

   *a.* Prepare a graph of the closing stock price for your company for the date of the earnings announcement and the five days preceding and following the announcement.

   *b.* Describe the apparent effect of the announcement on the company's stock price.

   *c.* Describe any explanations for the reported earnings or the stock price changes provided in the press article. Discuss whether you find the explanations convincing.

**CP5–20** **Comprehensive Project: Analyzing News Announcements and Financial Reporting (Extended)**

■ **LO1, 2, 3, 4**

Using local library resources and company-provided information, track the information announcement process for a public company for a three-month period following its most recent year-end. Your instructor may assign a particular company for you to analyze, or you may choose one of the focus companies in this text, a competitor in the same industry, or a company in which you have career-related interests.

*Required:*

1. Gathering the necessary information:

   *a.* Contact the investor relations department of the company by mail, phone, or the Internet and obtain copies of the most recent annual report, Form 10-K, and a recent earnings press release. The Annual Report Gallery at www.reportgallery.com provides links to the websites of well-known companies.

   *b.* Using *The Wall Street Journal Index, Dow Jones Interactive,* or another service listed in the chapter (or instructor-assigned resource), find one article reporting a nonearnings-related significant event (new product introduction, merger, etc.) that took place during the last year.

   *c.* Using *The Wall Street Journal* or another source, prepare two separate graphs: (1) the closing stock price for your company for the day of the earnings press release and the five days preceding and following the earnings press release and (2) the closing stock price for the week of the news article selected in part (*b*) and the five days preceding and following the news event.

2. Analyzing the information announcements:

   *a.* Based on the annual report and Form 10-K, determine the company's principal lines of business, CEO, CFO, auditors, and major competitors.

   *b.* Determine the format the company used to prepare its income statements and balance sheets in the annual report.

   *c.* Find one financial statement–related schedule that is included in the Form 10-K but not in the annual report.

   *d.* Compare the price-earnings ratio, leverage ratio, total asset turnover, net profit margin, and return on equity for the chosen year to the preceding year.

3. Presenting the results of your analysis: Prepare a written report including the following components:

   *a.* A brief description of the company and its operations, major players, and competitors.

   *b.* The formats used in the income statement and balance sheet and an example of additional information provided in the Form 10-K.

   *c.* The earnings press release and selected important news announcement, the apparent effect on the company's stock price, and any explanations for the reported events or the stock price changes provided in the press.

   *d.* A summary of your comparative analysis of the company's performance based on an ROE profit driver analysis.

# Reporting and Interpreting Sales Revenue, Receivables, and Cash

## CHAPTER **SIX**

### LEARNING **OBJECTIVES**

*After studying this chapter, you should be able to:*

1. Apply the revenue principle to determine the accepted time to record sales revenue for typical retailers, wholesalers, and manufacturers. p. 303

2. Analyze the impact of credit card sales, sales discounts, and sales returns on the amounts reported as net sales. p. 304

3. Analyze and interpret the gross profit percentage. p. 308

4. Estimate, report, and evaluate the effects of uncollectible accounts receivable (bad debts) on financial statements. p. 310

5. Analyze and interpret the accounts receivable turnover ratio and the effects of accounts receivable on cash flows. p. 316

6. Report, control, and safeguard cash. p. 319

Initially aimed at outdoorsmen, including hunters and hikers, Timberland's premium boots, casual shoes, sandals, and apparel are now as popular on the streets of New York City as they are on the 1,000-mile Iditarod Sled Dog Race in Alaska. Its footwear and apparel are sold through

# The Timberland Company

PRODUCT DEVELOPMENT, PRODUCTION, AND WORKING CAPITAL MANAGEMENT: KEYS TO GROSS PROFIT

quality department, retail, and specialty stores in more than 90 countries and through company-owned specialty and outlet stores in the United States and abroad. Though it is a publicly traded company with sales of more than $800 million, Timberland is also a family operation. Sidney Swartz (son of the company founder) and his son Jeffrey are the chairman and CEO of the company, respectively, and their family interests own about one-half of the company's stock.

An emphasis on comfort, style, high-quality construction, and protection from the elements has convinced customers of the superiority or distinctiveness of Timberland's products. This product differentiation strategy allowed Timberland to charge higher prices and earn higher gross margin on sales than many of its competitors, such as Wolverine World Wide and Rocky Shoes and Boots. In 1995, however, Timberland management changed marketing strategies, lowering prices and increasing advertising in an attempt to boost sales volume. This shift away from the company's core values led to the company's first net loss in its history as a public company.

By the end of 1995, Timberland recognized that to turn its growth into profits, it had to (1) continually refresh its product lines by introducing new technologies, new styles, and new product categories, (2) become a leaner manufacturer, taking advantage of lower cost production locations, and (3) focus more attention on inventory management and collections of accounts receivable since an uncollected account is of no value to the company. Each of these efforts is aimed at increasing net sales and/or decreasing cost of goods sold, thereby increasing gross profit.

## BUSINESS BACKGROUND

Planning Timberland's turnaround strategy requires careful coordination of marketing, production, and financing activities. The success of each element of Timberland's new strategy can be seen in the information presented in the comparative statements of income presented in Exhibit 6.1. Following the multiple-step format that we discussed in Chapter 5, Revenues (Sales Revenues) are reported first, and Cost of Goods Sold (an expense) is set out separately from the remaining expenses. Similar account titles sometimes used are Cost of Sales and Cost of Products Sold. Notice that the income statement then shows *gross profit* (*gross margin, gross profit margin*), which is net sales revenue minus cost of goods sold. Revenues, gross profit, and net income for 1998 are at an all-time high.

EXHIBIT **6.1**

**Consolidated Statements of Income**

**REAL WORLD EXCERPT**

*The Timberland Company*

ANNUAL REPORT

**For the Years Ended December 31, 1998, 1997 and 1996**
**(amounts in thousands, except per share data)**

|  | 1998 | 1997 | 1996 |
|---|---|---|---|
| Revenue | $862,168 | $796,458 | $689,973 |
| Cost of goods sold | 519,329 | 484,537 | 438,064 |
| Gross profit | 342,839 | 311,921 | 251,909 |
| Operating expense |  |  |  |
| Selling | 195,688 | 174,729 | 152,834 |
| General and administrative | 50,876 | 51,654 | 46,502 |
| Amortization of goodwill | 1,685 | 1,685 | 1,684 |
| Total operating expense | 248,249 | 228,068 | 201,020 |
| Operating income | 94,590 | 83,853 | 50,889 |
| Other expense (income) |  |  |  |
| Interest expense | 9,538 | 14,833 | 20,582 |
| Other, net | (1,942) | 1,419 | (631) |
| Total other expense | 7,596 | 16,252 | 19,951 |
| Income before income taxes | 86,994 | 67,601 | 30,938 |
| Provision for income taxes | 27,838 | 20,280 | 10,519 |
| Net income | $ 59,156 | $ 47,321 | $ 20,419 |
| Basic earnings per share | $ 5.18 | $ 4.20 | $ 1.84 |
| Weighted-average shares outstanding | 11,424 | 11,280 | 11,092 |
| Diluted earnings per share | $5.03 | $ 4.03 | $ 1.81 |
| Weighted-average shares outstanding | 11,759 | 11,737 | 11,255 |

The accompanying notes are an integral part of these consolidated financial statements.

To assess the effectiveness of its strategy, we need to know how net sales and cost of goods sold are determined. In this chapter, we will focus on the transactions that affect *net sales revenue* on the income statement and *cash* and *accounts receivable* on the balance sheet. We will also introduce the gross profit percentage ratio as a basis for evaluating changes in gross profit, as well as the receivables turnover ratio as a measure of the efficiency of credit-granting and collection activities. In the next chapter, we will discuss transactions related to cost of goods sold on the income statement and inventories on the balance sheet, as well as the inventory turnover ratio, which measures the efficiency of inventory management.

Generating operating cash flow is also one of Timberland's financial goals. As we discuss later in this chapter and in Chapter 7, the primary source of operating cash for most organizations is the collection of accounts receivable, and a primary use is payment for inventory. As a consequence, careful management of receivables and inventory can be the key to avoiding a business failure driven by cash shortages. Cash also is a tempting target for fraud and embezzlement, so accounting systems commonly include controls to prevent and detect these misdeeds.

Lenders, shareholders, and analysts also carefully monitor these accounts because of their importance as predictors of the future success of companies. Their importance is supported by the fact that the majority of shareholder lawsuits and SEC enforcement actions against companies for misleading financial statements relate to these accounts. We discuss an actual example of misleading statements later in the chapter.

**ORGANIZATION** OF THE CHAPTER

| • Accounting for Sales Revenue | • Measuring and Reporting Receivables | • Reporting and Safeguarding Cash |
|---|---|---|
| Sales to Consumers | Receivables Defined | Cash and Cash Equivalents Defined |
| Sales to Businesses | Accounting for Bad Debts | Internal Control of Cash |
| Sales Returns and Allowances | Reporting Accounts Receivable and Bad Debts | Reconciliation of the Cash Accounts and the Bank Statements |
| Reporting Net Sales | Methods for Estimating Bad Debts | |
| Gross Profit Percentage | Receivables Turnover Ratio | |

# ACCOUNTING FOR SALES REVENUE

As indicated in Chapter 3, the *revenue principle* requires recording revenues when earned (an exchange has taken place, the earnings process is nearly complete, and collection is probable). In most cases, these criteria are met when the goods pass from the seller to the buyer; the seller of goods records sales revenue on that date. Service companies most often record sales revenue when they have provided services to the buyer. Companies disclose the specific revenue recognition rule they follow in the footnote to its financial statements entitled Summary of Significant Accounting Policies. In that note, Timberland reports the following:

**NOTES TO CONSOLIDATED FINANCIAL STATEMENTS**
1. **Summary of Significant Accounting Policies**
*Recognition of Revenue*
 . . . Sales are recognized upon shipment of product to customers.

■ **LEARNING OBJECTIVE 1**

Apply the revenue principle to determine the accepted time to record sales revenue for typical retailers, wholesalers, and manufacturers.

**REAL WORLD EXCERPT**

*The Timberland Company*
ANNUAL REPORT

Like Timberland, many manufacturers, wholesalers, and retailers recognize revenue at shipment, regardless of whether title passes at shipment or delivery.[1] Companies follow this practice because it is easier to keep track of shipments than deliveries to customers. As long as the rule is applied *consistently*, recording sales revenue on the *shipping date* versus the *delivery date* usually has little effect on the financial statements. Other revenue recognition rules used in special circumstances are discussed later in an end-of-chapter supplement.

The appropriate *amount* of revenue to record is the *cash equivalent* sales price. Both the form of payment (cash, credit card, or credit) and returns and allowances affect the amount recorded as *net sales* on the income statement. If the sale involves the trade-in of a noncash asset (such as the trade-in of an old car for a new car), the amount of revenue is the cash equivalent of the goods received or given up, whichever is the more clearly determinable.

Some business practices concerning sales to businesses and consumers differ and, as a result, create accounting issues that are specific to one type of customer or the other. Timberland is a particularly useful example because it sells to both types of customers. It sells its footwear and apparel to other *businesses* (retailers) including stores such as Kaufmann's and The Shoe Dept., which then sell the goods to consumers. Timberland also operates its own factory outlet stores and specialty stores that sell footwear and apparel directly to *consumers*. Since most companies sell to either businesses or consumers, you will be able to apply what you have learned about Timberland to understand many different companies' statements.

Timberland uses a variety of methods to motivate customers to buy its products and make payment for their purchases. The principal methods include (1) allowing consumers to use credit cards to pay for purchases, (2) providing direct credit and discounts for early payment to business customers, and (3) allowing returns under certain circumstances to all customers. These methods, in turn, affect the way we compute net sales revenue.

$$\text{Net Sales} = \text{Sales Revenue} - \begin{cases} \textbf{Credit Card Discounts} \\ \textbf{Sales Discounts} \\ \textbf{Sales Returns and Allowances} \end{cases}$$

### SALES TO CONSUMERS

■ **LEARNING OBJECTIVE 2**

Analyze the impact of credit card sales, sales discounts, and sales returns on the amounts reported as net sales.

In Timberland's factory and specialty stores, sales to consumers are for cash or credit card (mainly Visa, MasterCard, and American Express). Timberland accepts credit cards as payment at its stores for a variety of reasons. First, it believes that offering this service increases the number of people who will shop at its stores. Second, Timberland avoids the costs of providing credit directly to consumers (recordkeeping and bad debts, discussed later). Third, accepting credit cards instead of checks avoids losses due to bad checks written by dishonest consumers. The credit card company (e.g., Visa) absorbs any losses from fraudulent credit card sales as long as Timberland follows the credit card company's verification procedure. Finally, Timberland receives its money faster than it would if it provided credit directly to consumers. It can deposit credit card receipts directly to its bank account.

The credit card company charges a fee for the service it provides. For example, when Timberland deposits its credit card receipts in the bank, it might receive credit for an amount equal only to 97 percent of the sales price. The credit card company is

---

[1]The point at which title (ownership) changes hands is determined by the shipping terms in the sales contract. When goods are shipped *F.O.B. shipping point,* title changes hands at shipment and the buyer normally pays for shipping. When they are shipped *F.O.B. destination,* title changes hands on delivery, and the seller normally pays for shipping. *Both* revenue recognition points meet the criterion that the "earnings process is *nearly* complete" and thus are in accordance with GAAP. Auditors expend a great deal of effort ensuring that revenue recognition rules are applied consistently and revenues are recognized in the proper period.

charging a 3 percent fee (the **credit card discount**) for its service. If credit card sales were $3,000 at a factory store for January 2, Timberland reports the following:

A **CREDIT CARD DISCOUNT** is the fee charged by the credit card company for services.

| | |
|---|---:|
| Sales revenue | $3,000 |
| Less: Credit card discounts (0.03 × $3,000) | 90 |
| Net sales (reported on the income statement) | $2,910 |

## SALES TO BUSINESSES

Most of Timberland's sales to businesses are credit sales on open account; that is, there is no formal written promissory note indicating the amount owed to Timberland by the customer. When Timberland sells footwear to retailers on credit, credit terms are printed on each sales document and invoice (bill) sent to the customer. Often credit terms are abbreviated using symbols. For example, if the full price is due within 30 days of the invoice date, the credit terms would be noted as *n/30*. Here, the *n* means the sales amount *net* of or less any sales returns. The terms *10, EOM,* mean the full price is due not later than 10 days after the end of the month (EOM) in which the sale was made.

In other cases, a **sales discount** (often called a **cash discount**) is granted to the purchaser to encourage early payment. For example, let's assume that Timberland offers standard credit terms of 2/10, n/30, which means that the customer may deduct 2 percent from the invoice price if cash payment is made within 10 days from the date of sale. If cash payment is not made within the 10-day discount period, however, the full sales price (less any returns) is due within a maximum of 30 days from date of sale.

A **SALES (OR CASH) DISCOUNT** is a cash discount offered to encourage prompt payment of an account receivable.

Timberland offers this sales discount to give its customers an incentive for fast payment of the accounts receivable. This benefits Timberland because prompt receipt of cash from customers reduces the necessity to borrow money from Morgan Guaranty Trust (and its other banks) to meet operating needs. Also, if a customer pays Timberland's bills earlier than the bills from other suppliers, it *decreases* the chances that the customer will run out of funds before Timberland's bill is paid.

## FINANCIAL **ANALYSIS**

### TO TAKE THE DISCOUNT, THAT IS THE QUESTION

Usually customers pay within the discount period because the savings are substantial. With terms 2/10, n/30, 2 percent is saved by paying 20 days early (the 10th day instead of the 30th), which is approximately 37 percent annual interest. This annual interest rate is obtained by first computing the interest rate for the discount period. When the 2 percent discount is taken, the customer pays only 98 percent of the gross sales price. Thus, the interest rate for the 20-day discount period is

**(Amount saved ÷ Amount paid) = Interest rate for 20 days**
**(2% of the bill ÷ 98% of the bill) = 2.04% for 20 days**

The annual interest rate is then computed in the following manner:

**Interest rate for 20 days x (365 days ÷ 20 days) = Annual interest rate**
**2.04% × (365 days ÷ 20 days) = 37.23% Annual interest**

Credit customers would save a great deal even if they had to borrow cash from a bank at 10 percent to take advantage of cash discounts. Normally, the bank's interest rate is less than the high interest rate associated with failing to take cash discounts.

Companies commonly record sales discounts taken by subtracting the discount from net sales if payment is made *within* the discount period (the usual case).[2] For example, if credit sales are recorded with terms 2/10, n/30 ($1,000 × 0.98 = $980) and payment is made within the discount period, net sales of the following amount would be reported:

| | |
|---|---|
| Sales revenue | $1,000 |
| Less: Sales discounts (0.02 × $1,000) | 20 |
| Net sales (reported on the income statement) | $ 980 |

If the payment is made after the discount period, the full $1,000 would be reported as net sales.

Note that both the purpose of sales discounts and the accounting for sales discounts are very similar to the purpose of and the accounting for credit card discounts. Both sales discounts and credit card discounts provide an attractive service to customers while promoting faster receipt of cash, reducing recordkeeping costs, and minimizing bad debts. Both are often reported as reductions of sales revenues (also known as *contra-revenues*), but may also be reported as expenses on the income statement. Accounting for sales discounts is discussed in more detail in Supplement B.

It is important not to confuse a cash discount with a trade discount. Vendors sometimes use a *trade discount* for quoting sales prices; the list or printed catalog price *less* the trade discount is the sales price. For example, an item may be quoted at $10 per unit subject to a 20 percent trade discount on orders of 100 units or more; thus, the price for the large order is $8 per unit. Similarly, the price on a slow-moving product line can be lowered simply by increasing the trade discount. Sales revenue should always be recorded net of trade discounts.

# A QUESTION OF **ETHICS**

## STRETCHING OUT THE PAYABLES

Hoffa Shoes has been incurring significant interest charges (12 percent) on short-term borrowing from its bank.* Hoffa normally purchases shoes from suppliers on terms 1/10, n/30. The annual rate of interest earned by taking the discount was 18.43 percent computed as follows:

$$\text{(Amount saved} \div \text{Amount paid)} = \text{Interest rate for 20 days}$$
$$(1\% \div 99\%) = 1.01\% \text{ for 20 days}$$
$$\text{Interest rate for 20 days} \times (365 \text{ days} \div 20 \text{ days}) = \text{Annual interest rate}$$
$$1.01\% \times (365 \text{ days} \div 20 \text{ days}) = 18.43\% \text{ annual interest}$$

Hoffa's policy had been to take all purchase discounts even if it had to borrow at 12 percent to make the early payment. Management reasoned that the company earned 6.43 percent more than it paid in interest (18.43 percent − 12 percent).

A new employee suggested a new plan. Records indicated that, even though the terms of Hoffa's agreement with its suppliers (1/10, n/30) required payment of the full amount within a maximum of 30 days, the suppliers would not complain as long as payment was made within 55 days of the purchase, since they normally did not send out a second bill until 60 days after the purchase. She reasoned that Hoffa would be better off forgoing the discount and paying on the 55th day after the purchase. She argued that since Hoffa would now be paying in

*Hoffa Shoes is a fictitious company, but most companies face this dilemma.

---

[2]We use the gross method in all examples in this text. Some companies use the alternative net method, which records sales revenue after deducting the amount of the cash discount. Since the choice of method has little effect on the financial statements, discussion of this method is left for an advanced course.

55 days instead of 10 days of the purchase, not taking the discount would be borrowing for 45 days, not the 20 days used in the former analysis. The analysis supporting the proposal is as follows:

$$\textbf{(Amount saved} \div \textbf{Amount paid)} = \textbf{Interest rate for 45 days}$$
$$\textbf{(1\%} \div \textbf{99\%)} = \textbf{1.01\% for 45 days}$$
$$\textbf{Interest rate for 45 days} \times \textbf{(365 days} \div \textbf{45 days)} = \textbf{Annual interest rate}$$
$$\textbf{1.01\%} \times \textbf{(365 days} \div \textbf{45 days)} = \textbf{8.19\% annual interest}$$

In effect, her plan allows Hoffa to borrow from suppliers at 8.19 percent instead of the bank's rate of 12 percent, saving 3.81 percent. When she presented this plan to the management for discussion, the purchasing manager agreed with the arithmetic presented but objected nonetheless. Since the plan violated its agreement with suppliers, the purchasing manager thought it was unethical. Many ethical dilemmas in business involve trade-offs between monetary benefits and potential violations of moral values.

## SALES RETURNS AND ALLOWANCES

For Timberland, prompt delivery of exactly what the customer ordered is a key to maintaining good relations with the retailers to whom it sells. Delivery of incorrect or damaged merchandise may cost the retailer sales and can destroy these relationships. When this occurs, the customers have a right to return unsatisfactory or damaged merchandise and receive a refund or an adjustment to their bill.

Such returns are often accumulated in a separate account called **Sales Returns and Allowances** and must be deducted from gross sales revenue in determining net sales. This account has an important purpose because it informs Timberland's management of the volume of returns and allowances and thus provides a measure of the quality of service provided to customers. Assume that Fontana Shoes of Ithaca, New York, bought 40 pairs of hiking boots from Timberland for $2,000 on account. Before paying for the boots, Fontana discovered that 10 pairs of boots were not the color ordered and returned them to Timberland. Timberland would compute net sales as follows:

> **SALES RETURNS AND ALLOWANCES** is a reduction of sales revenues for return of or allowances for unsatisfactory goods.

| | |
|---|---|
| Sales revenue | $2,000 |
| Less: Sales discounts (0.25 × $2,000) | 500 |
| Net sales (reported on the income statement) | $1,500 |

## REPORTING NET SALES

On the company's books, credit card discounts, sales discounts, and sales returns and allowances are accounted for separately to allow monitoring of the costs of the related activities (allowing use of credit cards, offering sales discounts, returns of incorrect or damaged merchandise, respectively). The amount of net sales reported on the income statement is computed in the following manner:

| |
|---|
| Sales revenue |
| Less: Credit card discounts (if treated as a contra-revenue) |
|       Sales discounts (if treated as a contra-revenue) |
|       Sales returns and allowances |
| Net sales (reported on the income statement) |

As illustrated later, however, it often is difficult even for the well-educated external user to determine the effects of these items since companies rarely disclose the determinants of net sales in the annual report. As we noted earlier, net sales less cost of goods sold equals the subtotal *gross profit* or *gross margin*. Analysts often examine gross profit as a percentage of sales or as the gross profit or gross margin percentage.

# KEY **RATIO ANALYSIS:**

■ **LEARNING OBJECTIVE 3**

Analyze and interpret the gross profit percentage.

## GROSS PROFIT PERCENTAGE

**K**now the decision question:

By what amount (percentage) did sales prices exceed the costs to purchase or produce the goods or services sold? It is computed as follows:

$$\text{Gross Profit Percentage} = \frac{\text{Gross Profit}}{\text{Net Sales}}$$

The 1998 ratio for Timberland:

$$\frac{\$342,839}{\$862,168} = 0.398 \ (39.8\%)$$

**E**xamine the ratio using two techniques:

| ① Comparisons over Time | | |
| --- | --- | --- |
| Timberland | | |
| 1996 | 1997 | 1998 |
| 36.5% | 39.2% | 39.8% |

| ② Comparisons with Competitors | |
| --- | --- |
| Skechers U.S.A | Wolverine World Wide |
| 1998 | 1998 |
| 41.5% | 31.8% |

**Selected Focus Company Comparisons**

Papa John's 31.7%

Harley-Davidson 34.1%

General Mills 59.01%

**Y**ou interpret the results carefully:

**IN GENERAL** → Gross profit percentage measures the ability to charge premium prices and produce goods and services at lower cost. All other things equal, a higher gross profit results in higher net income. Business strategy, as well as competition, affects gross profit percentage. Companies pursuing a product-differentiation strategy use research and development and product promotion activities to convince customers of the superiority or distinctiveness of the company's products. This allows them to charge premium prices, producing higher gross profit percentages. Companies following a low-cost strategy rely on more efficient management of production to reduce costs and increase the gross profit percentage. Managers, analysts, and creditors use this ratio to assess the effectiveness of the company's product development, marketing, and production strategy.

**FOCUS COMPANY ANALYSIS** → Timberland's gross profit percentage has risen from a 1995 low of 31 percent to nearly 40 percent in 1998 and is well above the industry average of 36.1 percent.* At the beginning of the chapter, we discussed key elements of Timberland's business strategy that focused on introducing new technologies, product lines, and styles, as well as managing production and inventory costs. According to Timberland's annual report, the increases in gross profit percentage "were due primarily to introduction of higher margin products and lower unit costs in footwear manufacturing and sourcing," indicating the success of the strategy.

**A FEW CAUTIONS:** Understanding the sources of any change in gross profit percentage is necessary to assess the company's ability to sustain its new gross margins. For example, an increase in margin resulting from increases in sales of high-margin boots during a hard winter would be judged less sustainable than one resulting from introducing new products. Also, higher prices must often be sustained with higher R&D and advertising costs, which can eat up any increase in gross margin. Finally, be aware that a small change in gross profit percentage can lead to a large change in net income.

*Market Guide, August 1999.

# FINANCIAL **ANALYSIS**

## CONTRA-REVENUES AND EVALUATING GROSS PROFIT PERCENTAGE

The computation of net sales is rarely reported on the financial statements. Note that if sales discounts and credit card discounts are recorded as contra-revenues, net sales is reduced, and thus both gross profit (and the gross profit percentage) and operating income are reduced. If they are treated as selling expenses, however, operating income is reduced, but gross profit is unaffected. Comparisons of gross profit percentages among firms using the alternative treatments can be distorted by this difference. For example, a comparison of the gross profit percentage of Kimberly-Clark, the manufacturer of Kleenex tissues and other paper products, and of its largest competitor, Scott Paper, based on numbers reported in their 1994 income statements yields the following results:

| | Kimberly-Clark | Scott Paper |
|---|---|---|
| Gross profit percentage | 33.4% | 29.9% |

When Kimberly-Clark acquired Scott in 1995, it disclosed that it had treated a variety of customer discounts as selling expenses while Scott had treated those same items as contra-revenues. Converting Scott's statements to Kimberly-Clark's accounting treatment revealed quite a different gross profit picture:

| | Kimberly-Clark | Scott Paper |
|---|---|---|
| Gross profit percentage | 33.4% | 41.0% |

Astute financial analysts should quiz company officials about the possible effects of such differences in accounting treatments before making comparisons between companies.

## SELF-STUDY **QUIZ**

1. Assume that Timberland sold $30,000 worth of footwear to various retailers with terms 1/10, n/30 and half of that amount was paid within the discount period. Gross sales at company-owned stores were $5,000 for the same period, 80 percent being paid with credit cards with a 3 percent discount, the rest in cash. Compute net sales for the period.

2. During the first quarter of 1999, Timberland's net sales were $176,897 and cost of goods sold was $103,768. Verify that its gross profit percentage was 41.3 percent.

After you have completed your answers, check them with the solutions presented in the footnote at the bottom of this page. *

---

*1. Gross Sales                                                    $35,000
    Less: Sales discounts $(0.01 \times \frac{1}{2} \times \$30,000)$           150
          Credit card discounts $(0.03 \times 0.8 \times \$5,000)$           120
    Net Sales                                                      $34,730
2. $176,897 - $103,768 = $73,129 gross profit.
    $73,129 \div $176,897 = 41.3% (rounded)

## MEASURING AND REPORTING RECEIVABLES

### RECEIVABLES DEFINED

**ACCOUNTS RECEIVABLE (TRADE RECEIVABLES, RECEIVABLES)** are open accounts owed to the business by trade customers.

Receivables may be classified in three common ways. First, the receivable may be either an account receivable or a note receivable. An **account receivable** is created when a credit sale on an open account occurs. For example, an account receivable is created when Timberland sells shoes on open account to Fontana Shoes in Ithaca, New York. A **note receivable** is a promise in writing (i.e., a formal document) to pay (1) a specified sum of money on demand or at a definite future date known as the *maturity date* and (2) specified interest at one or more future dates. A note often involves two distinctly different amounts: (1) *principal,* which is the amount that the interest rate is based on, and (2) *interest,* which is the specified amount charged for use of the principal. The notes also require periodic recording of interest revenue. We discuss the computation of interest when we discuss notes payable in a later chapter.

**NOTES RECEIVABLE** are written promises that require another party to pay the business under specified conditions (amount, time, interest).

Second, receivables may be classified as trade or nontrade receivables. A *trade receivable* is created in the normal course of business when a sale of merchandise or services on credit occurs. A *nontrade receivable* arises from transactions other than the normal sale of merchandise or services. For example, if Timberland loaned money to a new vice president for international operations to help finance a home at the new job location, the loan would be classified as a nontrade receivable. Third, in a classified balance sheet, receivables also are classified as either *current* or *noncurrent* (short term or long term), depending on when the cash is expected to be collected.

Like many companies, Timberland reports only one type of receivable account, Accounts Receivable from customers (trade receivables), and classifies the asset as a current asset (short term) because the accounts receivable are all due to be paid within one year. Timberland allows its business customers (the retail stores that buy and then resell its footwear) to purchase goods on open account because it believes that providing this service will result in more sales to this type of customer.

Providing this service to business customers also has a cost. Timberland must pay to maintain a credit-granting and collections system, and it must realize that not all customers will pay their debts. Credit policies should be set based on the *trade-off* between profits on additional sales and any additional bad debts. In fact, an extremely low rate of bad debts may not be good because it may indicate a too-tight credit policy. If the credit policy is too restrictive, the company will turn away many good credit customers, causing a loss of sales volume.

---

**Selected Foreign Currency Exchange Rates (in US$)**

Mexican Peso $0.11

Singapore Dollar $0.59

Swiss Franc $0.66

Euro $1.05

---

# INTERNATIONAL **PERSPECTIVE**

### FOREIGN CURRENCY RECEIVABLES

Export (international) sales are an increasing aspect of the U.S. economy. For example, international sales amounted to 29.2 percent of Timberland's revenues in 1998. As is the case with domestic sales to other businesses, most export sales to businesses are on credit. When the buyer has agreed to pay in its local currency instead of U.S. dollars, Timberland cannot add these accounts receivable, which are denominated in foreign currency, directly to its U.S. dollar accounts receivable. Timberland must first convert them to U.S. dollars using the end-of-period exchange rate between the two currencies. For example, if a French department store owed Timberland €20,000 (European currency units or Euros) on December 31, 1998, and each Euro was worth US$1.05 on that date, it would add US$21,000 to its accounts receivable on the balance sheet.

---

■ **LEARNING OBJECTIVE 4**

Estimate, report, and evaluate the effects of uncollectible accounts receivable (bad debts) on financial statements.

### ACCOUNTING FOR BAD DEBTS

Businesses that extend credit know that a certain amount of bad debts on credit sales occurs. The matching principle requires recording of bad debt expense in the *same* accounting period in which the related sales are made. However, Timberland may not learn that any particular customers will not pay until the *next* accounting period.

Timberland resolves this problem and satisfies the matching principle by using the **allowance method** to measure bad debt expense. The allowance method is based on *estimates* of the expected amount of bad debts. Two primary steps in employing the allowance method are (1) the end-of-period adjusting entry to record bad debt expense estimates and (2) writing off specific accounts determined to be uncollectible during the period.

**Recording Bad Debt Expense Estimates**  **Bad debt expense (doubtful accounts expense, uncollectible accounts expense, provision for uncollectible accounts)** is the expense associated with estimated uncollectible accounts receivable. An *adjusting journal entry at the end of the accounting period* records the bad debt estimate. For the year ended December 31, 1998, Timberland estimated bad debt expense to be $2,383,000 and made the following adjusting entry on December 31:

| Bad debt expense (E) | 2,383,000 | |
|---|---|---|
| Allowance for doubtful accounts (XA) | | 2,383,000 |

| Assets | = | Liabilities | + | Stockholders' Equity |
|---|---|---|---|---|
| Allowance for doubtful accounts −2,383,000 | | | | Bad debt expense −2,383,000 |

Timberland reported bad debt expense of $2,383,000 on the current year's income statement. It is normally included in the category Selling on the income statement (see Exhibit 6.1). The credit in the preceding journal entry was made to a *contra-asset account* called **Allowance for Doubtful Accounts** (also called **Allowance for Bad Debts** or **Allowance for Uncollectible Accounts**). Thus, the entry decreases net income and total assets. Accounts Receivable cannot be credited because there is no way to know which account receivable is involved. As a contra-asset, the balance in Allowance for Doubtful Accounts is *always* subtracted from the balance of Accounts Receivable. Thus, it is treated exactly like Accumulated Depreciation, the first contra-asset we discussed in Chapter 4.

**Writing Off Specific Accounts Determined to Be Uncollectible**  Write-offs of individual bad debts are recorded through *a series of journal entries made throughout the year* as soon as it is determined that the customer will not pay its debts (e.g., due to bankruptcy). The write-off removes the related Accounts Receivable account with an offsetting reduction of the contra-account Allowance for Doubtful Accounts. Timberland wrote off a total of $1,356,000 during 1998. The following journal entry summarizes the entries for these write-offs during the year:

| Allowance for doubtful accounts (XA) | 1,356,000 | |
|---|---|---|
| Accounts receivable (A) | | 1,356,000 |

| Assets | = | Liabilities | + | Stockholders' Equity |
|---|---|---|---|---|
| Allowance for doubtful accounts +1,356,000 | | | | |
| Accounts receivable −1,356,000 | | | | |

Notice that this journal entry *did not affect any income statement accounts*. It did not record a bad debt expense because the estimated expense was recorded with an adjusting entry in the period of sale and the related allowance account was established. Also, the entry *did not change the net book value of Accounts Receivable*, since the decrease in the asset account (Accounts Receivable) was offset by the decrease in the contra-asset account (Allowance for Doubtful Accounts) and thus did not affect total assets.

When a customer makes a payment on an account previously written off, the journal entry to write off the account is reversed for the amount to be collected and the collection of cash recorded.

**Actual Write-Offs Compared with Estimates**  The amount of uncollectible accounts actually written off seldom equals the estimated amount previously recorded. This situation is resolved when the next adjusting entry is made at the end of the

**The ALLOWANCE METHOD** bases bad debt expense on an estimate of uncollectible accounts.

**BAD DEBT EXPENSE (DOUBTFUL ACCOUNTS EXPENSE, UNCOLLECTIBLE ACCOUNTS EXPENSE, PROVISION FOR UNCOLLECTIBLE ACCOUNTS)** is the expense associated with estimated uncollectible accounts receivable.

**ALLOWANCE FOR DOUBTFUL ACCOUNTS (ALLOWANCE FOR BAD DEBTS, ALLOWANCE FOR UNCOLLECTIBLE ACCOUNTS)** is a contra asset account containing the estimated uncollectible accounts receivable.

accounting period (a higher or lower amount is recorded to make up for the previous period's error in estimate). When estimates are found to be incorrect, financial statement values for *prior* annual accounting periods are *not* corrected.

**Summary of the Accounting Process** It is important to remember that accounting for bad debts is a two-stage process:

1. *Bad Debt Expense* is recorded and the Allowance for Doubtful Accounts is increased in an *adjusting entry* (the bad debt adjustment) at the end of the accounting period. This stage affects both the income statement through the increase in Bad Debt Expense as well as the balance sheet, where the increase in the Allowance for Doubtful Accounts decreases the net book value of accounts receivable.

2. *Write-offs* are recorded, however, by decreasing both Accounts Receivable and the Allowance for Doubtful Accounts *throughout the period* as specific customer accounts are determined to be uncollectible. This stage does *not* affect the income statement, since no expense is recorded. It also does not affect the balance sheet, since the decrease in the Allowance for Doubtful Accounts combined with the decrease in Accounts Receivable does not change the net book value of accounts receivable.

Timberland's complete 1998 accounting process for bad debts can now be summarized in terms of the changes in Accounts Receivable and the Allowance for Doubtful Accounts:[3]

**Accounts Receivable (A)**

| | | | |
|---|---|---|---|
| Beginning balance | 79,535,000 | Collections on account | 856,554,000 |
| Sales on account | 862,168,000 | Write-offs | 1,356,000 |
| Ending balance | 83,793,000 | | |

**Allowance for Doubtful Accounts (XA)**

| | | | |
|---|---|---|---|
| | | Beginning balance | 3,742,000 |
| Write-offs | 1,356,000 | Bad debt expense adjustment | 2,383,000 |
| | | Ending balance | 4,769,000 |

## REPORTING ACCOUNTS RECEIVABLE AND BAD DEBTS

In Exhibit 6.2, Timberland reports accounts receivable, net of allowance for doubtful accounts (the *net book value*), of $79,024,000 and $75,793,000 for 1998 and 1997, respectively. It also reports the amount of the allowance for each year. Allowance for Doubtful Accounts has an end-of-period credit balance. The balance of the allowance account approximates the total amount of the accounts receivable estimated to be uncollectible. The balance of Accounts Receivable less the allowance account measures the *estimated net realizable value* (or how much Timberland expects to collect) of accounts receivable.

The amounts of bad debt expense included in selling expenses on the income statement and accounts receivable written off for the period are normally not disclosed in the annual report. If material, these amounts are reported on a schedule that publicly traded companies include in their Annual Report Form 10-K filed with the SEC (discussed in Chapter 5). Exhibit 6.3 presents this schedule from Timberland's 1998 filing. Write-offs are reported on Timberland's 10-K net of (less) reinstatements of previously written-off accounts.

## METHODS FOR ESTIMATING BAD DEBTS

The bad debt expense amount recorded in the end-of-period adjusting entry often is estimated in each accounting period based on either (1) the total credit sales for the period or (2) an aging of accounts receivable.

---

[3]This assumes that all sales to businesses (wholesale sales) are on account.

EXHIBIT **6.2**

Accounts Receivable on the
Balance Sheet

**REAL WORLD EXCERPT**

*The Timberland
Company*

ANNUAL REPORT

**CONSOLIDATED BALANCE SHEETS**
**As of December 31, 1998 and 1997**
**(dollars in thousands, except per share data)**

|  | 1998 | 1997 |
|---|---|---|
| Assets |  |  |
| Current assets |  |  |
| Cash and equivalents | $151,889 | $ 98,771 |
| Accounts receivable, net of allowance for doubtful accounts |  |  |
| of $4,769 in 1998 and $3,742 in 1997 | 79,024 | 75,793 |
| Inventory | 131,218 | 142,613 |
| Prepaid expense | 11,897 | 12,856 |
| Deferred income taxes | 13,538 | 11,973 |
| Total current assets | 387,566 | 342,006 |

EXHIBIT **6.3**

Accounts Receivable Valuation
Schedule (Form 10-K)

**REAL WORLD EXCERPT**

*The Timberland
Company*

FORM 10–K

**THE TIMBERLAND COMPANY**
**Valuation and Qualifying Accounts**
**(dollars in thousands)**

| Description | Additions | | | Deductions | |
|---|---|---|---|---|---|
|  | Balance at Beginning of Period | Charged to Costs and Expenses | Charged to Other Accounts | Write-Offs, Net of Recoveries | Balance at End of Period |
| Allowance for doubtful accounts: |  |  |  |  |  |
| Year ended |  |  |  |  |  |
| December 31, 1998 | $3,742 | $2,383 | — | $1,356 | $4,769 |
| December 31, 1997 | 3,540 | 3,605 | — | 3,403 | 3,742 |
| December 31, 1996 | 2,658 | 2,046 | — | 1,164 | 3,540 |

**Percentage of Credit Sales**   Many companies make their estimates using the **percentage of credit sales method,** which bases bad debt expense on the historical percentage of credit sales that result in bad debts. This method is also called the *income statement method* because it involves the direct computation of the income statement number *bad debt expense* based on the income statement number *credit sales.*

The average percentage of credit sales that result in bad debts can be computed by dividing total bad debt losses by total *credit* sales. A company that has been operating for some years has sufficient experience to project probable future bad debt losses. For example, assume that Rogers and Lambert (a hypothetical company) had experienced the following in three recent years:

**PERCENTAGE OF CREDIT SALES METHOD** bases bad debt expense on the historical perspective of credit sales that result in bad debts.

| Year | Bad Debt Losses | Credit Sales |
|---|---|---|
| 20A | $ 900 | $190,000 |
| 20B | 1,200 | 220,000 |
| 20C | 1,400 | 290,000 |
| Total | $3,500 | $700,000 |

$3,500 ÷ $700,000 = 0.5% average loss rate for the three-year period 20A–20C.

If net credit sales in the current year were approximately $268,000 and the company used this method, the amount

$$\textbf{Credit sales} \times \textbf{Bad debt loss rate} = \textbf{Bad debt expense}$$
$$\textbf{\$268,000} \times \textbf{0.5\%} = \textbf{\$1,340}$$

is directly recorded as Bad Debt Expense (and an increase in Allowance for Doubtful Accounts) in the current year. New companies often rely on the experience of similar companies that have been operating for a number of years. A company usually adjusts the historical average loss rate to reflect future expectations. For example, if retail sales were rising, the company might decrease its rate to 0.4 percent, reasoning that fewer of its business customers (retailers) will become bankrupt.

The sharp rise in Timberland's bad debt loss rate from 0.27 in 1993 to 0.56 percent in 1995 suggests that it fell into the trap of loosening credit policies as it tried to increase sales. In response, it has since instituted an organizational change, separating the credit and collections unit from the sales department to avoid these problems in the future. These changes reduced the bad debt percentage to 0.28 in 1998.

# FINANCIAL **ANALYSIS**

**REAL WORLD EXCERPT**

*The Wall Street Journal*

## JUDGING THE ACCURACY OF BAD DEBT ESTIMATES

Without access to detailed information concerning any changes in customer mix and credit terms, an outside financial analyst would have little basis for judging the accuracy of the current period's bad debt estimates. For example, *The Wall Street Journal* recently reported:

### FORMER T2 EXECUTIVES SETTLE SEC LAWSUIT OVER EARNINGS REPORTS

NEW YORK—Four former executives of T2 Medical Inc. agreed to pay a total of more than $456,000 to settle Securities and Exchange Commission allegations that they artificially inflated the company's reported earnings. . . . According to the suit, which the SEC filed against the four in federal court here, they improperly accelerated recognition of revenues and product-delivery schedules and deferred bad debt write-offs, all in order to overstate earnings.

In this case, the company had increased its recognized bad debt expense from 5.4 percent of sales in the prior year to 6.5 percent of sales in recognition of an increase in the risk of bad debts. After the accounting irregularities were investigated, however, the accurate bad debt rate was determined to be 11 percent of sales. Although the financial community expected an increase in the bad debt rate, a doubling of the rate surprised most analysts because they were not aware of the dramatic changes in the company's credit sales policies.

SOURCE: *The Wall Street Journal*, June 12, 1997, B12.

**AGING OF ACCOUNTS RECEIVABLE METHOD**
estimates uncollectible accounts based on the age of each account receivable.

**Aging of Accounts Receivable**   As an alternative to the percentage of credit sales method, many companies use the age that accounts receivable have been outstanding to estimate bad debt expense. This is called the **aging of accounts receivable method.** Older accounts receivable usually are less likely to be collectible. For example, a receivable due in 30 days that has not been paid after 60 days is more likely to be collected, on average, than a similar receivable that still remains unpaid after 120 days. Based on its prior experience, the company could estimate what portion of receivables of different ages will not be paid.

This method is also called the *balance sheet method* because it involves the direct computation of the balance sheet number *allowance for doubtful accounts* based on the

EXHIBIT **6.4**

**Aging Schedule**

**ROGERS AND LAMBERT**
**Aging Anaysis of Accounts Receivable,**
**December 31, 19A**

| Customer | Not Yet Due | 1-30 Days Past Due | 31-60 Days Past Due | 61-90 Days Past Due | Over 90 Days Past Due | Total |
|---|---|---|---|---|---|---|
| Adams, Inc. | $ 600 | | | | | $ 600 |
| Baker Stores | 300 | $ 900 | $ 100 | | | 1,300 |
| Cox Co. | | | 400 | $ 900 | $ 100 | 1,400 |
| Zoe Stores | 2,000 | | 1,000 | | | 3,000 |
| Total | $17,200 | $12,000 | $8,000 | $1,200 | $1,600 | $40,000 |
| Estimated % uncollectible | 1% | 3% | 6% | 10% | 25% | |
| Estimated uncollectible accounts | $ 172 | $ 360 | $ 480 | $ 120 | $ 400 | $ 1,532 |

balance sheet number *accounts receivable*. Suppose that Rogers and Lambert split its receivables into five age categories, as presented in Exhibit 6.4. Management of the company might then *estimate* the following probable bad debt loss rates: not yet due, 1 percent; 1 to 30 days past due, 3 percent; 31 to 60 days, 6 percent; 61 to 90 days, 10 percent; over 90 days, 25 percent. The total of the amounts estimated to be uncollectible under the aging method is the balance that *should be* in the allowance for doubtful accounts at the end of the period. This is called the *estimated balance.*

The approach to recording bad debt expense using the aging method is different from that for the percentage of credit sales method. Recall that using the percentage of credit sales, we *directly computed* the amount to be recorded as bad debt expense on the income statement for the period in the adjusting journal entry. Alternatively, when using the aging method, we are computing the *final ending balance* we would like to have in the allowance for doubtful accounts on the balance sheet after we make the necessary entry. Thus, the *difference* between the actual balance in the account and the estimated balance is recorded as the adjusting entry for bad debt expense for the period.

The amount of bad debt expense for the period is the difference between the estimated uncollectible accounts (just calculated) and the balance of the allowance for doubtful accounts at the end of the period *before the adjusting entry* has been made.

| Computation | |
|---|---|
| Estimated balance (from aging schedule) | $1,532 |
| Less: Current balance (preadjustment balance from ledger account) | 188 |
| Bad debt expense adjustment to be recorded for the current year (solve) | $1,344 |

This computation also can be illustrated in T-account form. The current credit balance in the allowance, before the end-of-period adjustment, is $188. We insert the new ending balance from the aging schedule and then solve for the current amount of bad debt expense.

**Allowance for Doubtful Accounts (XA)**

| | | | |
|---|---|---|---|
| | | Beginning balance | 1,455 |
| Write-offs (throughout the year) | 1,267 | | |
| | | Unadjusted balance | 188 |
| | | Bad debt expense adjustment (solve) | 1,344 ◄——— Step 2: Adjustment inferred |
| | | Estimated balance (from aging) | 1,532 ◄——— Step 1: Ending balance estimated from aging |

The end-of-period adjusting entry to Bad Debt Expense and Allowance for Doubtful Accounts is made on December 31 for $1,344.

The percentage of credit sales method focuses on an income statement valuation (bad debt expense matched to the period's sales); the aging method focuses on a balance sheet valuation (estimated net realizable value of accounts receivable). Both methods are acceptable under GAAP and are widely used in practice.

## FINANCIAL **ANALYSIS**

### SALES VERSUS COLLECTIONS—THE MARKETING/FINANCIAL MANAGEMENT CONFLICT

*Knight Ridder Tribune Business News* recently reported that many managers of sales- and marketing-oriented companies forget that "extending credit will increase your sales volume, but what good is that if you never get paid." The article points out that these companies that emphasize sales without monitoring the collection of credit sales will soon find much of their current assets tied up in accounts receivable. The following practices can help minimize bad debts:

1. Establish customers' credit history before allowing them to charge their purchases.
2. Age accounts receivable periodically and contact customers with overdue payments.
3. Reward both sales and collections personnel for speedy collections so that they work as a team.

SOURCE: *Knight Ridder Tribune Business News,* August 9, 1999.

To assess the effectiveness of overall credit granting and collection activities, managers and analysts often compute the receivables turnover ratio.

## KEY **RATIO ANALYSIS:**

### RECEIVABLES TURNOVER

**K**now the decision question:
How effective are credit-granting and collection activities? An answer to this question is computed as follows:

$$\text{Receivables Turnover} = \frac{\text{Net Sales*}}{\text{Average Net Trade Accounts Receivable}^\dagger}$$

*Since the amount of net credit sales is normally not reported separately, most analysts use net sales in this equation.
†Average Net Trade Accounts Receivable = (Beginning Net Trade Accounts Receivable + Ending Net Trade Accounts Receivable) ÷ 2

■ **LEARNING OBJECTIVE 5**

Analyze and interpret the accounts receivable turnover ratio and the effects of accounts receivable on cash flows.

The 1998 ratio for Timberland:

$$\frac{\$862,168}{(\$75,793 + 79,024) \div 2} = 11.1$$

**E**xamine the ratio using two techniques:

| ① Comparisons over Time | | |
|---|---|---|
| **Timberland** | | |
| 1996 | 1997 | 1998 |
| 7.0 | 9.0 | 11.1 |

| ② Comparisons with Competitors | |
|---|---|
| **Skechers U.S.A** | **Wolverine World Wide** |
| 1998 | 1998 |
| 9.6 | 4.6 |

**Y**ou interpret the results carefully:

**IN GENERAL** → The receivables turnover ratio reflects how many times average trade receivables were recorded and collected during the period. A higher ratio indicates faster collection of receivables. This benefits the company because it can invest the moneys collected, earning interest income, or reduce borrowings, reducing interest expense. Granting credit with later payment deadlines and using ineffective collection methods cause this ratio to be low. Analysts and creditors watch this ratio because a sudden decline in it may mean that a company is extending payment deadlines in an attempt to prop up lagging sales or even is recording sales that later will be returned by customers.

**FOCUS COMPANY ANALYSIS** → Timberland's receivables turnover has risen from a 1996 low of 7.0 to 11.1 in 1998 and is well above the industry average of 7.1.‡ At the beginning of the chapter, we discussed key elements of Timberland's turnaround strategy that focused in part on better asset management (receivables, inventory, and manufacturing facilities). Analysts Lee Backus and Larry Leeds at the *Buckingham Research Group* cited this dramatic improvement in receivables turnover (as well as inventory turnover—see Chapter 7) when they initiated their buy recommendation on Timberland's stock. As we will see shortly, this increase in receivables turnover also results in an increase in cash flow from operations.

**A FEW CAUTIONS:** Since differences across industries in the manner in which customer purchases are financed cause dramatic differences in the ratio, a particular firm's ratio should be compared only with its prior years' figures or with other firms in the same industry. Many managers and analysts compute the related number *average collection period* or *average days sales in receivables* which is equal to 365 ÷ Receivables Turnover Ratio, or 32.9 days for Timberland. It indicates the average time it takes a customer to pay its accounts.

‡*Dun and Bradstreet* Industry Norms and Key Business Ratios (1998–1999).

| Selected Industry Comparisons: Average Receivables Turnover | |
|---|---|
| Lumber and building materials | 10.9 |
| Malt beverages | 14.1 |
| Variety stores | 66.4 |

## FOCUS ON **CASH FLOWS**

### ACCOUNTS RECEIVABLE

The change in accounts receivable can be a major determinant of a company's cash flow from operations. The income statement reflects the revenues of the period, whereas the cash flow from operating activities must reflect the cash collections from customers for the same period. Since sales on account increase the balance in accounts receivable and cash collections from customers decrease the balance in accounts receivable, the change in accounts receivable from the beginning to the end of the period is the difference between the two.

#### EFFECT ON STATEMENT OF CASH FLOWS

**IN GENERAL** →

When a net *decrease in accounts receivable* for the period occurs, cash collected from customers is always more than revenue; thus, the decrease must be *added* in computing cash flows from operations.

When a net *increase in accounts receivable* occurs, cash collected from customers is always less than revenue; thus, the increase must be *subtracted* in computing cash flows from operations.

| | Effect on Cash Flows |
|---|---|
| **Operating activities** (indirect method) | |
| Net income | $xxx |
| Adjusted for | |
| *Add* accounts receivable *decrease* | + |
| or | |
| *Subtract* accounts receivable *increase* | – |

**Selected Competitor Comparisons: 3-Year Change in Cash Flows Related to Accounts Receivable Changes (in millions)**

| | |
|---|---|
| Skechers U.S.A. | −33.1 |
| Wolverine WW | −60.2 |
| Vans | −5.4 |

**FOCUS COMPANY ANALYSIS:** Exhibit 6.5 is the Operating Activities section of Timberland's statement of cash flows. When the accounts receivable balance increases during the period, as was the case at Timberland in 1996 and 1998, the company recorded more net sales than it collected in cash from customers during the period. Thus, the increase is subtracted in the computation of Timberland's cash flow from operations. Alternatively, when the accounts receivable balance decreases during the period, as was the case in 1997, the company collected more in cash from customers than it recorded as net sales during the period. Thus, the decrease is added in the computation of Timberland's cash flow from operations.*

When sales rise quickly, as they have at Timberland over the past three years, receivables usually rise, decreasing cash flow from operations. However, as part of its strategic plan, Timberland improved its credit-granting and collections activities, which improved its accounts receivable turnover ratio. The highlighted section of Exhibit 6.5 indicates that, as a result of these improvements, the change in accounts receivable actually produced a net increase in cash flow from operating activities of $16,477 (−2,781 + 24,799 − 5,541) during the period.

*For companies with receivables in foreign currency or business acquisitions/dispositions, the amount of the change reported on the cash flow statement will not equal the change in the accounts receivable reported on the balance sheet. This is true in the case of Timberland.

EXHIBIT **6.5**

**Accounts Receivable on the Cash Flow Statement**

**REAL WORLD EXCERPT**

*The Timberland Company*

ANNUAL REPORT

**Consolidated Statements of Cash Flows**
**For the Years Ended December 31, 1998, 1997 and 1996**
**(dollars in thousands)**

| | 1998 | 1997 | 1996 |
|---|---|---|---|
| Cash flows from operating activities: | | | |
| Net income | $ 59,156 | $ 47,321 | $20,419 |
| Adjustments to reconcile net income to net cash provided by operating activities: | | | |
| Deferred income taxes | (35) | (7,478) | 905 |
| Depreciation and amortization | 18,199 | 20,292 | 21,370 |
| Loss on disposal of property, plant and equipment | 1,303 | 1,564 | |
| Increase (decrease) in cash from changes in working capital: | | | |
| Accounts receivable | (2,781) | 24,799 | (5,541) |
| Inventory | 11,637 | 14,270 | 22,475 |
| Prepaid expense | 1,112 | (3,707) | 3,747 |
| Accounts payable | 5,083 | (454) | (4,000) |
| Accrued expense | (9,975) | 11,165 | 14,692 |
| Income taxes | 459 | 6,001 | 11,608 |
| Net cash provided by operating activities | 84,158 | 113,773 | 85,675 |

# SELF-STUDY **QUIZ**

1. Indicate whether *granting later payment deadlines* (e.g., 60 days instead of 30 days) will most likely *increase* or *decrease* the accounts receivable turnover ratio. Explain.

2. In an earlier year, Timberland's Form 10-K reported beginning and ending balances in the Allowance for Doubtful Accounts of $723 and $904, respectively. It also reported that write-offs of bad debts amounted to $648 (all numbers in thousands). Assuming that no previously written-off accounts had been collected (there were no reinstatements), what amount did Timberland record as bad debt expense for the period? (*Solution approach:* Use the Allowance for Doubtful Accounts T-account to solve for the missing value.)

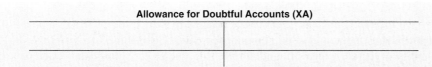

**Allowance for Doubtful Accounts (XA)**

3. In an earlier year, Timberland reported an increase of $6,098,000 in accounts receivable for the period. Was that amount added or subtracted on the (indirect method) cash flow statement in the computation of cash flow from operations? Explain your answer.

After you complete your answer, check it with the solution presented in the footnote at the bottom of this page.*

## REPORTING AND SAFEGUARDING CASH

### CASH AND CASH EQUIVALENTS DEFINED

**Cash** is defined as money or any instrument that banks will accept for deposit and immediate credit to the company's account, such as a check, money order, or bank draft. Cash excludes such items as notes receivable, IOUs, and postage stamps (a prepaid expense). Cash usually is divided into three categories: cash on hand, cash deposited in banks, and other instruments that meet the definition of cash.

*FASB Statement 95* defines **cash equivalents** as investments with original maturities of three months or less that are readily convertible to cash and whose value is unlikely to change (that is, are not sensitive to interest rate changes). Typical instruments included as cash equivalents are bank certificates of deposit and treasury bills that the U.S. government issues to finance its activities.

Even though a company may have several bank accounts and several types of cash equivalents, all cash accounts and cash equivalents are usually combined as one amount for financial reporting purposes. Timberland reports a single account, Cash and Equivalents. It also reports that the book values of cash equivalents on the balance sheet equal their fair market value, which we should expect given the nature of the instruments included as cash equivalents (investments whose value is unlikely to change).

Many businesses receive a large amount of cash, checks, and credit card receipts from their customers each day. Anyone can spend cash, so management must develop procedures to safeguard the cash it uses in the business. Effective cash management involves more than protecting cash from theft, fraud, or loss through carelessness. Other cash management responsibilities include these:

1. Accurate accounting so that reports of cash flows and balances may be prepared.
2. Controls to ensure that enough cash is on hand to meet (a) current operating needs, (b) maturing liabilities, and (c) unexpected emergencies.
3. Prevention of the accumulation of excess amounts of idle cash. Idle cash earns no revenue; therefore, it is often invested in securities to earn a revenue (return) pending future need for the cash.

**■ LEARNING OBJECTIVE 6**

Report, control, and safeguard cash.

**CASH** is money or any instrument that banks will accept for deposit and immediate credit to the company's account, such as a check, money order, or bank draft.

**CASH EQUIVALENTS** are short-term investments with original maturities of three months or less that are readily convertible to cash and whose value is unlikely to change.

---

*1. Granting later payment deadlines will most likely *decrease* the accounts receivable turnover ratio because later collections from customers will increase the average accounts receivable balance (the denominator of the ratio) and decrease the ratio.

2.                 **Allowance for Doubtful Accounts (XA)**

| | | | |
|---|---|---|---|
| | | Beginning balance | 723 |
| Write-offs | 648 | Bad debt expense (*solve*) | 829 |
| | | Ending balance | 904 |

**Beginning + Bad debt expense − Write-offs = Ending; $723 + X − 648 = $904; X = $829**

3. The amount would be subtracted because an increase in the Accounts Receivable account indicates that sales revenue was in excess of cash collected from customers for the period.

**INTERNAL CONTROLS** are the processes by which the company's board of directors, management, and other personnel provide reasonable assurance regarding the reliability of the company's financial reporting, the effectiveness and efficiency of its operations, and its compliance with applicable laws and regulations.

## INTERNAL CONTROL OF CASH

The term **internal controls** refers to the process by which the company's board of directors, management, and other personnel provide reasonable assurance regarding the reliability of the company's financial reporting, the effectiveness and efficiency of its operations, and its compliance with applicable laws and regulations. Internal control procedures should extend to all assets: cash, receivables, investments, operational assets, and so on. Controls that ensure the accuracy of the financial records are designed to prevent inadvertent errors and fraud like that described in the Maxidrive example discussed in Chapter 1.

Because cash is the asset most vulnerable to theft and fraud, a significant number of internal control procedures should focus on cash. You have already observed internal control procedures for cash, although you may not have known it at the time. At most movie theaters, one employee sells tickets and another employee collects them. It would be less expensive to have one employee do both jobs, but it would also be easier for that single employee to steal cash and admit a patron without issuing a ticket. If different employees perform the tasks, a successful theft requires participation of both.

## A QUESTION OF **ETHICS**

### ETHICS AND THE NEED FOR INTERNAL CONTROL

Some people are bothered by the recommendation that all well-run companies should have strong internal control procedures. These people believe that control procedures suggest that the company's management does not trust its employees. Although the vast majority of employees are trustworthy, an unfortunate fact of life is that employee theft costs businesses billions of dollars each year. Interviews with convicted felons indicate that in many cases they stole from their employers because they thought that it was easy and that no one cared (internal control procedures were not present).

Many companies give their employees a formal code of ethics that includes high standards of behavior in dealing with customers, suppliers, fellow employees, and the company's assets. Although each employee is ultimately responsible for his or her own ethical behavior, internal control procedures can be thought of as important value statements from management.

Effective internal control of cash should include the following:

1. Separation of duties.
   a. Complete separation of the jobs of receiving cash and disbursing cash.
   b. Complete separation of the procedures of accounting for cash receipts and cash disbursements.
   c. Complete separation of the physical handling of cash and all phases of the accounting function.
2. Responsibilities assigned to individuals.
   a. Require that all cash receipts be deposited in a bank daily. Keep any cash on hand under strict control.
   b. Require separate approval of the purchases and other expenditures and separate approval of the actual cash payments. Prenumbered checks should be used. Special care must be taken with payments by electronic funds transfers since the bank processes no controlled documents (checks).
   c. Assign the cash payment approval and the actual check-signing or electronic funds transfer transmittal responsibilities to different individuals.
   d. Require monthly reconciliation of bank accounts with the cash accounts on the company's books (discussed in detail in the next section).

The separation of individual responsibilities and the use of prescribed policies and procedures are important phases in the control of cash. Separation of duties deters theft because the collusion of two or more persons is needed to steal cash and then conceal the theft in the accounting records. Prescribed procedures are designed so that the work done by one individual is checked by the results reported by other individuals. For example, the amount of cash collected at the cash register by the sales clerk can be compared with the amount of cash deposited at the bank by another employee. Reconciliation of the cash accounts to the bank statements provides a further control on deposits.

All cash disbursements should be made with prenumbered checks. If prenumbered checks are not used, an employee could easily write a check to a friend and not record it. Cash payments should involve separate responsibilities for (1) payment approvals, (2) check preparation, and (3) check signing. When procedures similar to these are followed, concealing a fraudulent cash disbursement is difficult without the collusion of two or more persons. Again, the bank reconciliation provides an additional control on disbursements. The level of internal control, which is reviewed by the outside independent auditor, increases the reliability of the financial statements of the business.

## RECONCILIATION OF THE CASH ACCOUNTS AND THE BANK STATEMENTS

**Bank Statements**   Proper use of the bank accounts of a business can be an important internal control procedure for cash. Each month, the bank provides the company (the depositor) with a **bank statement** that lists (1) each deposit recorded by the bank during the period, (2) each check cleared by the bank during the period, and (3) the balance in the company's account. The bank statement also shows the bank charges or deductions (such as service charges) made directly to the company's account by the bank. The bank statement may include copies of the deposit slips and all checks that cleared through the bank during the period covered by the statement, although this practice is declining because it increases the bank's processing costs. A typical bank statement (excluding the deposit slips and canceled checks) is shown in Exhibit 6.6.

Exhibit 6.6 lists three items that need explanation. Notice that on June 20, listed under Checks and Debits, there is a deduction for $18 coded *NC*.[4] A check for $18 was received from a customer, R. Smith, and deposited by J. Doe Company with its bank, the Texas Commerce Bank. The bank processed the check through banking channels to Smith's bank. Smith's account did not have sufficient funds to cover it; therefore, Smith's bank returned it to the Texas Commerce Bank, which then charged it back to J. Doe Company. This type of check often is called an *NSF check* (not sufficient funds). The NSF check is now a receivable; consequently, J. Doe Company must make an entry to debit Receivables (R. Smith) and credit Cash for the $18.

Notice the $6 listed on June 30 under Checks and Debits and coded *SC*. This is the code for bank service charges. The bank statement included a memo by the bank explaining this service charge (which was not documented by a check). J. Doe Company must make an entry to reflect this $6 decrease in the bank balance as a debit to a relevant expense account, such as Bank Service Expense, and a credit to Cash.

Notice the $100 listed on June 12 under Deposits and the code *CM* for credit memo. The bank collected a note receivable owned by Doe and increased the company account of J. Doe Company. The bank service charge (SC) included the collection service cost. J. Doe Company must record the collection by making an entry to debit Cash and credit Note Receivable for the $100 (assume that interest on the note had been recorded).

A **bank reconciliation** is the process of comparing (reconciling) the ending cash balance in the company's records and the ending cash balance reported by the bank on the monthly bank statement. A bank reconciliation should be completed for each separate checking account (i.e., for each bank statement received from each bank) at the end of each month.

Usually, the ending cash balance as shown on the bank statement does not agree with the ending cash balance shown by the related Cash ledger account on the books

A **BANK STATEMENT** is a monthly report from a bank that shows deposits recorded, checks cleared, other debits and credits, and a running bank balance.

A **BANK RECONCILIATION** is the process of verifying the accuracy of both the bank statement and the cash accounts of a business.

---

[4]These codes vary among banks.

EXHIBIT **6.6**

**Example of a Bank Statement**

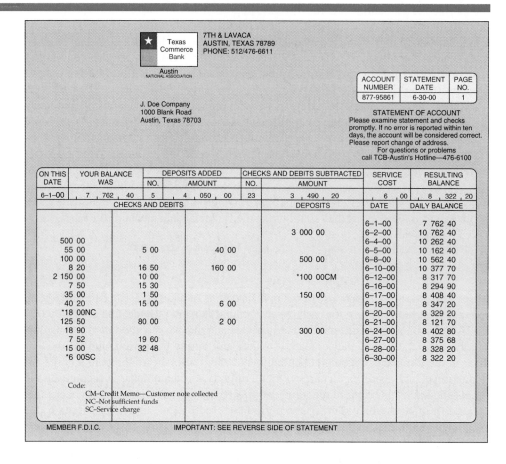

of the company. For example, the Cash ledger account of J. Doe Company showed the following at the end of June (Doe has only one checking account):

| Cash | | | |
|---|---|---|---|
| June 1 balance | 7,010.00 | June checks written | 3,800.00 |
| June deposits | 5,750.00 | | |
| Ending balance | 8,960.00 | | |

The $8,322.20 ending cash balance shown on the bank statement (Exhibit 6.6) is different from the $8,960.00 ending balance of cash shown on the books of the J. Doe Company. This difference exists because (1) some transactions affecting cash were recorded in the books of Doe Company but were not shown on the bank statement and (2) some transactions were shown on the bank statement but had not been recorded in books of the Doe Company. The general format for the bank reconciliation follows:

| | | | |
|---|---|---|---|
| Ending cash balance per books | $xxx | Ending cash balance per bank statement | $xxx |
| + Collections by bank | xx | + Deposits in transit | xx |
| − NSF Checks/Service charges | xx | − Outstanding checks | xx |
| ± Company errors | xx | ± Bank errors | xx |
| Ending correct cash balances | $xxx | Ending correct cash balance | $xxx |

The most common causes of differences between the ending bank balance and the ending book balance of cash are as follows:

1. *Outstanding checks.* Checks written by the company and recorded in the company's ledger as credits to the Cash account. These checks have not cleared the bank (they are not shown on the bank statement as a deduction from the bank balance). The

outstanding checks are identified by comparing the canceled checks that the bank returned with the record of checks (such as check stubs or a journal) maintained by the company.

2. *Deposits in transit.* Deposits sent to the bank by the company and recorded in the company's ledger as debits to the Cash account. The bank has not recorded these deposits (they are not shown on the bank statement as an increase in the bank balance). Deposits in transit usually happen when deposits are made one or two days before the close of the period covered by the bank statement. Deposits in transit are determined by comparing the deposits listed on the bank statement with the copies of the deposit slips retained by the company or other company records.

3. *Bank service charges.* An expense for bank services listed on the bank statement. This expense must be recorded in the company's ledger by making a debit to a relevant expense account, such as Bank Service Expense, and a credit to Cash.

4. *NSF checks.* A "bad check" that was deposited but must be deducted from the company's account. The company must make a journal entry to debit Accounts Receivable and credit Cash.

5. *Credit memo.* A note receivable collected by the bank for the company. It is recorded by making a debit to Cash and a credit to Notes Receivable.

6. *Errors.* Both the bank and the company may make errors, especially when the volume of cash transactions is large.

**Bank Reconciliation Illustrated**  The company should make a bank reconciliation immediately after receiving each bank statement. A bank reconciliation is an important element of internal control and is needed for accounting purposes. The bank reconciliation for the month of June prepared by J. Doe Company to reconcile the ending bank balance (Exhibit 6.6, $8,322.20) with the ending book balance ($8,960) is shown in Exhibit 6.7. On the completed reconciliation, Exhibit 6.7, the correct cash balance is $9,045. This balance is different from both the reported bank and book balances before the reconciliation with the bank statement. Space is provided for additions to and subtractions from each balance so that the last line shows the same correct cash balance (for the bank and the books). This correct balance is the amount that should be shown in the Cash account after the reconciliation. In this example, it is also the correct amount of cash that should be reported on the balance sheet (J. Doe Company has only one checking account and no cash on hand). J. Doe Company followed these steps in preparing the bank reconciliation:

1. *Identify the outstanding checks.* A comparison of the canceled checks returned by the bank with the company's records of all checks drawn showed the following checks still outstanding (not cleared) at the end of June:

| Check No. | Amount |
|---|---|
| 101 | $ 145.00 |
| 123 | 815.00 |
| 131 | 117.20 |
| Total | $1,077.20 |

This total was entered on the reconciliation as a deduction from the bank account. These checks will be deducted by the bank when they clear the bank.

2. *Identify the deposits in transit.* A comparison of the deposit slips on hand with those listed on the bank statement revealed that a deposit of $1,800 made on June 30 was not listed on the bank statement. This amount was entered on the reconciliation as an addition to the bank account. It will be added by the bank when it records the deposit.

3. *Record bank charges and credits:*
   a.  Proceeds of note collected, $100—entered on the bank reconciliation as an addition to the book balance; it already has been included in the bank

balance. A journal entry is needed to debit Cash and credit Note Receivable.

b. NSF check of R. Smith, $18—entered on the bank reconciliation as a deduction from the book balance; it has been deducted from the bank statement balance. A journal entry is needed to credit Cash and to debit Accounts Receivable.

c. Bank service charges, $6—entered on the bank reconciliation as a deduction from the book balance; it has been deducted from the bank balance. A journal entry is needed to credit Cash and to debit an expense account, Bank Service Expense.

4. *Determine the impact of errors.* At this point, J. Doe Company found that the reconciliation did not balance by $9. Because this amount is divisible by 9, a transposition was suspected. (A transposition, such as writing 27 for 72, always will cause an error that is exactly divisible by 9.) Upon checking the journal entries made during the month, a check written for $56 to pay an account payable was found. The check was recorded in the company's accounts as $65. The incorrect entry made was a debit to Accounts Payable and a credit to Cash for $65 (instead of $56). Therefore, $9 (i.e., $65 − $56) must be added to the book cash balance on the reconciliation; the bank cleared the check for the correct amount, $56. The following correcting entry must be made in the accounts: Cash, debit $9; Accounts Payable, credit $9.

EXHIBIT **6.7**

**Bank Reconciliation Illustrated**

**J. DOE COMPANY**

**Bank Reconciliation**

**For the Month Ending June 30, 2000**

| Company's Books | | Bank Statement | |
|---|---|---|---|
| Ending cash balance per books | $8,960.00 | Ending cash balance per bank statement | $ 8,322.20 |
| Additions | | Additions | |
| Proceeds of customer note collected by bank | 100.00 | Deposit in transit | 1,800.00 |
| Error in recording check No. 137 | 9.00 | | |
| | 9,069.00 | | 10,122.20 |
| Deductions | | Deductions | |
| NSF check of R. Smith | 18.00 | Outstanding checks | 1,077.20 |
| Bank service charges | 6.00 | | |
| Ending correct cash balance | $9,045.00 | Ending correct cash balance | $ 9,045.00 |

Note that in Exhibit 6.7 the Company's Books and the Bank Statement sections of the bank reconciliation now agree at a correct cash balance of $9,045. This amount will be reported as cash on a balance sheet prepared at the end of the period. If the company had cash on hand for making change, it would be added to the $9,045, and the total would be reported on the balance sheet.

A bank reconciliation as shown in Exhibit 6.7 accomplishes two major objectives:

1. Checks the accuracy of the bank balance and the company cash records, which involves developing the correct cash balance. The correct cash balance (plus cash on hand, if any) is the amount of cash that is reported on the balance sheet.

2. Identifies any previously unrecorded transactions or changes that are necessary to cause the company's Cash account(s) to show the correct cash balance. These transactions or changes need journal entries. The preceding explanations of the development of the bank reconciliation of J. Doe Company cite such transactions and changes. Therefore, the following journal entries based on the Company's Books side of the bank reconciliation (Exhibit 6.7), must be entered into the company's records.

## Accounts of J. Doe Company

| | | |
|---|---|---|
| (a) Cash (A) ........................................... | 100 | |
| Note receivable (A) ............................... | | 100 |
| To record note collected by bank. | | |
| (b) Accounts receivable (A) ............................... | 18 | |
| Cash (A) ........................................... | | 18 |
| To record NSF check. | | |
| (c) Bank service expense (E) .............................. | 6 | |
| Cash (A) ........................................... | | 6 |
| To record service fees charged by bank. | | |
| (d) Cash (A) ........................................... | 9 | |
| Accounts payable (L) .............................. | | 9 |
| To correct error made in recording a check payable to a creditor. | | |

| Assets | | = | Liabilities | + | Stockholders' Equity | |
|---|---|---|---|---|---|---|
| Cash (+100, −18, −6, +9) | +85 | | Accounts payable +9 | | Bank service expense | −6 |
| Accounts receivable | +18 | | | | | |
| Note receivable | −100 | | | | | |

**Cash Account of J. Doe Company**   The Cash account prior to reconciliation was given earlier in this chapter. After the preceding journal entries are posted, the Cash account is as follows:

**Cash (after recording results of bank reconciliation)**

| | | | | | |
|---|---|---|---|---|---|
| June 1 | Balance | 7,010.00 | June | Checks written | 3,800.00 |
| June | Deposits | 5,750.00 | June 30 | NSF check* | 18.00 |
| June 30 | Note collected* | 100.00 | June 30 | Bank service charge* | 6.00 |
| June 30 | Correcting entry* | 9.00 | | | |
| | Correct cash balance | 9,045.00 | | | |

*Based on the bank reconciliation.

Notice that all of the additions and deductions on the Company's Books side of the reconciliation need journal entries to update the Cash account. The additions and deductions on the Bank Statement side do not need journal entries because they will work out automatically when they clear the bank. The cash amount reported on the balance sheet and reflected in the Cash account will be the correct cash balance only if the proper journal entries are made after the bank reconciliation is completed.

SELF-STUDY **QUIZ**

Indicate which of the following items discovered while preparing a company's bank reconciliation will result in adjustment of the cash balance on the balance sheet.

1. Outstanding checks.
2. Deposits in transit.
3. Bank service charges.
4. NSF checks that were deposited.

After you complete your answer, check it with the solution presented in the footnote at the bottom of this page.*

## EPILOGUE

As we noted at the beginning of the chapter, Timberland recognized that to turn growth into profits, it had to (1) continually refresh its product lines by introducing new

---

*3. Bank service charges are deducted from the company's account; thus, cash must be reduced and an expense must be recorded. 4. NSF checks that were deposited were recorded on the books as increases in the Cash account; thus, cash must be decreased and the related account receivable increased if payment is still expected.

technologies, new styles, and new product categories, (2) become a leaner manufacturer, taking advantage of lower cost production locations, and (3) focus more attention on inventory management and collections of accounts receivable since an uncollected account is of no value to the company. It also recognized that, like its competitors, it could strengthen its brand identity through appropriate licensing agreements with other companies. Each of these efforts is aimed at increasing net sales and/or decreasing cost of goods sold, thereby increasing gross profit. The success of this strategy continues to be evident during the first half of 1999, with record sales and gross profits being reported.

Timberland is also well known for its contributions to the community. As Sidney and Jeffrey Swartz suggest in their letter to shareholders, "doing well and doing good are inextricably linked . . . We continue to believe that consumers prefer to do business with a brand that shares their values." Timberland's focus on community is also a key element of its business strategy.

# DEMONSTRATION **CASE A**

(Complete the requirements before proceeding to the suggested solutions.)

Wholesale Warehouse Stores sold $950,000 in merchandise during 20C, $400,000 of which was on credit with terms 2/10, n/30 (75 percent of these amounts were paid within the discount period), $500,000 was paid with credit cards (there was a 3 percent credit card discount), and the rest was paid in cash. On December 31, 20C, the Accounts Receivable balance was $80,000, and the Allowance for Doubtful Accounts was $3,000 (credit balance).

*Required:*
1. Compute net sales for 20C, assuming that sales and credit card discounts are treated as contra-revenues.
2. Assume that Wholesale uses the percentage of sales method for estimating bad debt expense and that it estimates that 2 percent of credit sales will produce bad debts. Record bad debt expense for 20C.
3. Assume that Wholesale uses the aging of accounts receivable method and that it estimates that $10,000 worth of current accounts are uncollectible. Record bad debt expense for 20C.

## SUGGESTED SOLUTION

1. Both sales discounts and credit card discounts should be subtracted from sales revenues in the computation of net sales.

| | |
|---|---:|
| Sales Revenue | $950,000 |
| Less: Sales Discounts (0.02 × 0.75 × $400,000) | 6,000 |
| Credit Card Discounts (0.03 × $500,000) | 15,000 |
| | $929,000 |

2. The percentage estimate of bad debts should be applied to credit sales. Cash sales never produce bad debts.

| | | |
|---|---:|---:|
| Bad debt expense (E) (0.02 × $400,000) . . . . . . . . . . . . . . . . . . . | 8,000 | |
| Allowance for doubtful accounts (XA) . . . . . . . . . . . . . . . . . . . | | 8,000 |

| Assets | = | Liabilities | + | Stockholders' Equity |
|---|---|---|---|---|
| Allowance for doubtful accounts   −8,000 | | | | Bad debt expense   −8,000 |

3. The entry made when using the aging of accounts receivable method is the estimated balance minus the unadjusted balance.

| | | |
|---|---:|---:|
| Bad debt expense (E) ($10,000 − $3,000) . . . . . . . . . . . . . . . . . | 7,000 | |
| Allowance for doubtful accounts (XA) . . . . . . . . . . . . . . . . . . . | | 7,000 |

| Assets | = | Liabilities | + | Stockholders' Equity |
|---|---|---|---|---|
| | | | | Bad debt expenses −7,000 |
| Allowance for doubtful accounts −7,000 | | | | |

# DEMONSTRATION **CASE B**

(Complete the requirements before proceeding to the suggested solution that follows.)

Heather Ann Long, a freshman at a large state university, has just received her first checking account statement. This was her first chance to attempt a bank reconciliation. She had the following information to work with:

| | |
|---|---|
| Bank balance, September 1 | $1,150 |
| Deposits during September | 650 |
| Checks cleared during September | 900 |
| Bank service charge | 25 |
| Bank balance, October 1 | 875 |

Heather was surprised that the deposit of $50 she made on September 29 had not been posted to her account and was pleased that her rent check of $200 had not cleared her account. Her checkbook balance was $750.

### Required:

1. Complete Heather's bank reconciliation.
2. Why is it important for individuals such as Heather and businesses to do a bank reconciliation each month?

## SUGGESTED SOLUTION

1. Heather's bank reconciliation:

| Heather's Books | | Bank Statement | |
|---|---|---|---|
| October 1 cash balance | $750 | October 1 cash balance | $875 |
| Additions | | Additions | |
| None | | Deposit in transit | 50 |
| Deductions | | Deductions | |
| Bank service charge | (25) | Outstanding check | (200) |
| Correct cash balance | $725 | Correct cash balance | $725 |

2. Bank statements, whether personal or business, should be reconciled each month. This process helps ensure that a correct balance is reflected in the customer's books. Failure to reconcile a bank statement increases the chance that an error will not be discovered and may result in bad checks being written. Businesses must reconcile their bank statements for an additional reason: The correct balance that is calculated during reconciliation is recorded on the balance sheet.

## Chapter Supplement A

### Applying the Revenue Principle in Special Circumstances

The revenue principle was introduced in Chapter 3. As noted earlier, application of this principle in the case of Timberland and similar companies was fairly straightforward. Such companies record revenue when goods or services are shipped or delivered. We now expand our discussion of the revenue principle and see how it is applied in business practice by companies other than typical manufacturers, wholesalers, and retailers.

## DELAYED REVENUE RECOGNITION: INSTALLMENT METHOD

Recall that to record revenue (1) an exchange must take place, (2) the earnings process must be nearly complete, and (3) collection must be probable. Failure to meet the third revenue recognition criterion (collection must be probable) requires that revenue recognition be delayed until after an initial exchange. When a great deal of uncertainty concerning the collectibility of the sales price exists, revenue recognition is postponed until *cash is collected from the customer*. This revenue recognition method, called the **installment method,** is considered to be a very conservative method since it postpones revenue recognition, sometimes until long after goods have been delivered. The most common applications are in certain types of *retail* and *real estate transactions* in which payment is made over a multiyear period and a large proportion of customers stop making payments long before the final payment is due. Certain types of expensive equipment, such as supercomputers, are sometimes sold under contracts calling for payment to be made over a multiyear period and giving the customers the right to return the equipment and cease making payments if they are dissatisfied. The installment method also is required here. Application of this specialized revenue recognition method is discussed in intermediate accounting courses.

## REVENUE RECOGNITION BEFORE THE EARNINGS PROCESS IS COMPLETE: LONG-TERM CONSTRUCTION CONTRACTS

An important exception to the usual criteria exists for companies involved in long-term construction projects such as building an office complex for a large corporation. These projects may take a number of years to complete. As a result, if the company recorded no revenue or expenses directly related to the project during the years that it worked on the project and then recorded a massive amount of revenue in the year that it delivered the product to the customer, the financial statements would not accurately represent the company's economic activities. This method of accounting is often referred to as the *completed contract method.*

To deal with this unique problem for long-term construction projects, many companies use the **percentage of completion method,** which records revenue based on the percentage of work completed during the accounting period, instead of the **completed contract method,** which records revenue when the completed product is delivered to the customer.

Under the percentage of completion method, revenues are based on the amount of work done each year. Typically, the amount of work accomplished each year is measured by the *percentage of total cost* that was incurred during the year. For example, assume that the total contract price was $50 million and the total cost for construction was $40 million. In 20A, the construction company spent $10 million, which was 25 percent of the contract cost ($10 million ÷ $40 million).[5] This percentage of completion is then multiplied by the total contract revenue to determine the amount of revenue to be reported in 20A ($25\% \times \$50,000,000 = \$12,500,000$).

The amount of expense reported each year is the actual cost incurred ($10,000,000 in 20A), and the amount of income is simply the difference between revenue and expense ($\$12,500,000 - \$10,000,000 = \$2,500,000$ in 20A). It is important to note that the total revenue, expenses, and income for the two methods over the life of the contract are exactly the same. The methods differ only in terms of the accounting periods in which the various revenues and expenses are reported (their timing). Percentage of completion recognizes income throughout the contract period; completed contract recognizes income only in the year of completion.

Notice that the percentage of completion method does not completely satisfy the second revenue recognition criterion because revenue is reported before the earnings process is complete. It is the preferred method, however, in cases such as this because the completed contract method makes it appear that the contractor was not able to gen-

The **INSTALLMENT METHOD** recognizes revenue on the basis of cash collection after the delivery of goods.

The **PERCENTAGE OF COMPLETION METHOD** records revenue based on the percentage of work completed during the accounting period.

The **COMPLETED CONTRACT METHOD** records revenue when the completed product is delivered to the customer.

---

[5]Cost overruns (underruns), which did not occur in this simple example, create additional accounting problems.

erate any profits for the initial years of the contract but then became very profitable in the final year. In reality, the company was active in all years. Thus, the percentage of completion method better represents this type of underlying economic activity.

Companies may use the percentage of completion method when progress toward completion and costs to complete the contract can be reasonably estimated and they have a firm contract that guarantees payment to satisfy the cash collectibility revenue recognition criterion. In a recent survey of 600 companies,[6] 85 of them were involved in long-term construction contracts. Only 6 did not use the percentage of completion or a closely related method.

## REVENUE RECOGNITION FOR SERVICE CONTRACTS

Companies that provide services over more than one accounting period often follow revenue recognition policies similar to those followed for long-term construction contracts. They may record revenue after all services have been provided (after the contract is completed) or may recognize revenue from the completed portion of the services. Since the individual size of the contracts involved often is small (compared to construction contracts) and companies often are engaged in many service contracts with different beginning and ending dates, the distortion caused by the completed contract method is usually smaller than that of long-term construction contracts. Yet many service companies, such as Federal Express, which provides air delivery service, employ the percentage of completion revenue recognition policy as indicated in the following note:

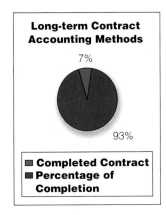

**Long-term Contract Accounting Methods**

7%

93%

■ **Completed Contract**
■ **Percentage of Completion**

**REAL WORLD EXCERPT**

*Federal Express*
ANNUAL REPORT

---

**FEDERAL EXPRESS CORPORATION AND SUBSIDIARIES**

Notes to Consolidated Financial Statements
NOTE 1. SUMMARY OF SIGNIFICANT ACCOUNTING POLICIES

Revenue recognition. Revenue is generally recognized upon delivery of shipments. For shipments in transit, revenue is recorded based on the percentage of service completed.

---

For the services in progress at the end of the accounting period, Federal Express uses the percentage of completion method for revenue recognition, recognizing only a percentage of the revenues and related costs of providing the services based on the degree of completion of the service. This method is also called the *proportional performance* method. This form of revenue recognition is very similar to Time Warner's accounting for its TV cable contracts and McDermott's accounting for its construction contracts. Each company recognizes revenues and expenses related to the *completed portion* of its contract with the customer. The major difference is that Time Warner is paid for the cable subscriptions in advance, McDermott receives progress payments throughout the contract period, and Federal Express receives payment from its business customers after it provides the service.

# FINANCIAL **ANALYSIS**

## REVENUE RECOGNITION AND FINANCIAL STATEMENT ANALYSIS

Financial analysts cannot evaluate the income earned by a company if they do not understand how it applied the revenue recognition criteria. As a result, all companies disclose any special revenue recognition issues in the notes to their financial statements. For example, General Motors' annual report states the following:

---

[6]*Accounting Trends & Techniques* (New York: AICPA, 1998).

Certain sales under long-term contracts, primarily in the defense business, are recorded using the percentage-of-completion (cost-to-cost) method of accounting. Under this method, sales are recorded equivalent to costs incurred plus a portion of the profit expected to be realized, determined based on the ratio of costs incurred to estimated total costs at completion.

This succinct explanation of the percentage of completion method is an adequate explanation for someone who has read this chapter, but it is doubtful that someone who has not studied accounting would understand its meaning. This is an excellent example of the importance of careful study of accounting even if you do not major in accounting.

# DEMONSTRATION **CASE C**

(Complete the requirements before proceeding to the suggested solution that follows.)

Assume that (1) Federal Express had shipments in transit involving fees totaling $20 million on December 31 of the current year, (2) none of the fees had been collected, and (3) on average, the shipments in transit were 60 percent completed.

*Required:*

1. Determine what amount related to the shipments in transit is recognized as revenue in the current year using the revenue recognition rule indicated in its footnote included in the prior section.

2. Indicate what asset(s) is(are) affected by recording revenue from the shipments in transit (accounts and amounts).

## SUGGESTED SOLUTION

1. Delivery revenue is recorded for $12,000,000.
2. Accounts Receivable increases by $12,000,000.

## Chapter Supplement B

### Recording Discounts and Returns

As noted earlier, both *credit card discounts* and *cash discounts* can be recorded either as contra-revenues or as expenses. For example, if the credit card company is charging a 3 percent fee for its service and credit card sales were $3,000 at a factory store for January 2, Timberland records the following:

| | | |
|---|---|---|
| Cash (A) | 2,910 | |
| Credit card discount (XR or E) | 90 | |
| Sales revenue (R) | | 3,000 |

| Assets | | = | Liabilities | + | Stockholders' Equity | |
|---|---|---|---|---|---|---|
| Cash | +2,910 | | | | Sales revenue | +3,000 |
| | | | | | Credit card discount | −90 |

Similarly, if credit sales are recorded with terms 2/10, n/30 ($1,000 × 0.98 = $980), and payment is made within the discount period, Timberland would record the following:

| Accounts receivable (A) | 1,000 | |
| Sales revenue (R) | | 1,000 |

| Assets | = | Liabilities | + | Stockholders' Equity | |
| --- | --- | --- | --- | --- | --- |
| Accounts receivable | +1,000 | | | Sales revenue | +1,000 |

| Cash (A) | 980 | |
| Sales discount (XR or E) | 20 | |
| Accounts receivable (A) | | 1,000 |

| Assets | = | Liabilities | + | Stockholders' Equity | |
| --- | --- | --- | --- | --- | --- |
| Cash | +980 | | | Sales discount | −20 |
| Accounts receivable | −1,000 | | | | |

*Sales returns and allowances* should always be treated as a contra-revenue. Assume that Fontana Shoes of Ithaca, New York, bought 40 pairs of hiking boots from Timberland for $2,000 on account. On the date of sale, Timberland makes the following journal entry:

| Accounts receivable (A) | 2,000 | |
| Sales revenue (R) | | 2,000 |

| Assets | = | Liabilities | + | Stockholders' Equity | |
| --- | --- | --- | --- | --- | --- |
| Accounts receivable | +2,000 | | | Sales revenue | +2,000 |

Before paying for the boots, Fontana discovered that 10 pairs of boots were not the color ordered and returned them to Timberland. On that date Timberland records:

| Sales returns and allowances (XR) | 500 | |
| Accounts receivable (A) | | 500 |

| Assets | = | Liabilities | + | Stockholders' Equity | |
| --- | --- | --- | --- | --- | --- |
| Accounts receivable | −500 | | | Sales returns and allowances | +500 |

## CHAPTER **TAKE-AWAYS**

1. **Apply the revenue principle to determine the accepted time to record sales revenue for typical retailers, wholesalers, and manufacturers.   p. 303**
   Revenue recognition policies are widely recognized as one of the most important determinants of the fair presentation of financial statements. For most merchandisers and manufacturers, the required revenue recognition point is the time of shipment or delivery of goods. For service companies, it is the time that services are provided.

2. **Analyze the impact of credit card sales, sales discounts, and sales returns on the amounts reported as net sales.   p. 304**
   Both *credit card discounts* and *cash discounts* can be recorded either as contra-revenues or as expenses. When recorded as contra-revenues, they reduce net sales. *Sales returns and allowances,* which should always be treated as a contra-revenue, also reduce net sales.

3. **Analyze and interpret the gross profit percentage.   p. 308**
   Gross profit percentage measures the ability to charge premium prices and produce goods and services at lower cost. Managers, analysts, and creditors use this ratio to assess the effectiveness of the company's product development, marketing, and production strategy.

4. **Estimate, report, and evaluate the effects of uncollectible accounts receivable (bad debts) on financial statements.   p. 310**
   When receivables are material, companies must employ the allowance method to account for uncollectibles. The steps in the process are

   1. The end-of-period adjusting entry to record bad debt expense estimates.

   2. Writing off specific accounts determined to be uncollectible during the period.

   The adjusting entry reduces net income as well as net accounts receivable. The write-off affects neither.

5. **Analyze and interpret the accounts receivable turnover ratio and the effects of accounts receivable on cash flows.** p. 316

   *Accounts receivable turnover ratio*—Measures the effectiveness of credit granting and collection activities. It reflects how many times average trade receivables were recorded and collected during the period. Analysts and creditors watch this ratio because a sudden decline in it may mean that a company is extending payment deadlines in an attempt to prop up lagging sales or even is recording sales that later will be returned by customers.

   *Effects on cash flows*—When a net decrease in accounts receivable for the period occurs, cash collected from customers is always more than revenue, and cash flows from operations increases. When a net increase in accounts receivable occurs, cash collected from customers is always less than revenue; thus, cash flows from operations declines.

6. **Report, control, and safeguard cash.** p. 319

   Cash is the most liquid of all assets, flowing continually into and out of a business. As a result, a number of critical control procedures, including the reconciliation of bank accounts, should be applied. Also, management of cash may be critically important to decision makers who must have cash available to meet current needs yet must avoid excess amounts of idle cash that produce no revenue.

Closely related to recording revenue is recording the cost of what was sold. Chapter 7 will focus on transactions related to inventory and cost of goods sold. This topic is important because cost of goods sold has a major impact on a company's gross profit and net income, which are watched closely by investors, analysts, and other users of financial statements. Increasing emphasis on quality, productivity, and costs have further focused production managers' attention on cost of goods sold and inventory. Since inventory cost figures play a major role in product introduction and pricing decisions, they also are important to marketing and general managers. Finally, since inventory accounting has a major effect on many companies' tax liabilities, this is an important place to introduce the effect of taxation on management decision making and financial reporting.

## KEY **RATIOS**

**Gross profit percentage** measures the excess of sales prices over the costs to purchase or produce the goods or services sold as a percentage. It is computed as follows (p. 308):

$$\text{Gross Profit Percentage} = \frac{\text{Gross Profit}}{\text{Net Sales}}$$

**Receivables turnover ratio** measures the effectiveness of credit-granting and collection activities. It is computed as follows (p. 316):

$$\text{Receivables Turnover} = \frac{\text{Net Sales}}{\text{Average Net Trade Accounts Receivable}}$$

FINDING
**FINANCIAL
INFORMATION**

**BALANCE SHEET**
*Under Current Assets*
    Accounts receivable (net of allowance for
      doubtful accounts)

**INCOME STATEMENT**
*Revenues*
    Net sales (sales revenue less discounts if
      contra-revenues and sales returns and
      allowances)
*Expenses*
    Selling expenses (including bad debt
      expense and discounts if treated as
      expenses)

**STATEMENT OF CASH FLOWS**
*Under Operating Activies (indirect method)*
    Net income
    + decreases in accounts receivable (net)
    − increases in accounts receivable (net)

**NOTES**
*Under Summary of Significant Accounting
Policies*
    Revenue recognition policy
*Under a Separate Note on Form 10-K*
    Bad debt expense and write-offs of bad
      debts

## KEY **TERMS**

**Accounts Receivable (Trade Receivables**
  or **Receivables)** p. 310
**Aging of Accounts Receivable**
  **Method** p. 314
**Allowance for Doubtful Accounts**
  **(Allowance for Bad Debts** or **Allowance**
  **for Uncollectible Accounts)** p. 311
**Allowance Method** p. 311
**Bad Debt Expense (Doubtful Accounts**
  **Expense, Uncollectible Accounts**
  **Expense,** or **Provision for Uncollectible**
  **Accounts)** p. 311
**Bank Reconciliation** p. 321
**Bank Statement** p. 321

**Cash** p. 319
**Cash Equivalents** p. 319
**Completed Contract Method** p. 328
**Credit Card Discount** p. 305
**Installment Method** p. 328
**Internal Controls** p. 320
**Note Receivable** p. 310
**Percentage of Completion Method** p. 328
**Percentage of Credit Sales Method** p. 313
**Sales (or Cash) Discount** p. 305
**Sales Returns and Allowances** p. 307

## QUESTIONS

1. Explain the difference between sales revenue and net sales.
2. What is gross profit or gross margin on sales? How is the gross profit ratio computed? In your explanation, assume that net sales revenue was $100,000 and cost of goods sold was $60,000.
3. What is a credit card discount? How does it affect amounts reported on the income statement?
4. What is a sales discount? Use 1/10, n/30 in your explanation.
5. What is the distinction between *sales allowances* and *sales discounts?*
6. Differentiate accounts receivable from notes receivable.
7. Which basic accounting principle is the allowance method of accounting for bad debts designed to satisfy?
8. Using the allowance method, is bad debt expense recognized in (a) the period in which sales related to the uncollectible were made or (b) the period in which the seller learns that the customer is unable to pay?

9. What is the effect of the write-off of bad debts (using the allowance method) on (a) net income and (b) accounts receivable, net?

10. Does an increase in the receivables turnover ratio generally indicate faster or slower collection of receivables? Explain.

11. Define *cash* and *cash equivalents* in the context of accounting. Indicate the types of items that should be included and excluded.

12. Summarize the primary characteristics of an effective internal control system for cash.

13. Why should cash-handling and cash-recording activities be separated? How is this separation accomplished?

14. What are the purposes of a bank reconciliation? What balances are reconciled?

15. Briefly explain how the total amount of cash reported on the balance sheet is computed.

16. (Supplement A) When is it acceptable to use the percentage of completion method?

17. (Supplement B) Under the gross method of recording sales discounts, is the amount of sales discount taken recorded (a) at the time the sale is recorded or (b) at the time the collection of the account is recorded?

# MINI-EXERCISES

**LO1** **M6–1** **Interpreting the Revenue Principle**

Indicate the *most likely* time you expect sales revenue to be recorded for each of the listed transactions.

| Transaction | Point A | Point B |
| --- | --- | --- |
| a. Airline tickets sold by an airline on a credit card | _____ Point of sale | _X_ Completion of flight |
| b. Computer sold by mail order company on a credit card | _X_ Shipment | _____ Delivery |
| c. Sale of inventory to a business customer on open account | _X_ Shipment | _____ Collection of account |

**LO2** **M6–2** **Reporting Net Sales with Sales Discounts**

Merchandise invoiced at $2,000 is sold on terms 2/10, n/30. If the buyer pays within the discount period, what amount will be reported on the income statement as net sales?

**LO2** **M6–3** **Reporting Net Sales with Sales Discounts, Credit Card Discounts, and Sales Returns**

Total gross sales for the period include the following:

| | |
| --- | --- |
| Credit card sales (discount 3%) | $8,000 |
| Sales on account (2/15, n/60) | $9,500 |

Sales returns related to sales on account were $500. All returns were made before payment. One-half of the remaining sales on account was paid within the discount period. The company treats all discounts and returns as contra-revenues. What amount will be reported on the income statement as net sales?

**LO3** **M6–4** **Computing and Interpreting the Gross Profit Percentage**

Net sales for the period was $56,000 and cost of sales was $48,000. Compute gross profit percentage for the current year. What does this ratio measure?

**LO4** **M6–5** **Recording Bad Debts**

Prepare journal entries for each transaction listed.

*a.* During the period, bad debts are written off in the amount of $17,000.

*b.* At the end of the period, bad debt expense is estimated to be $14,000.

**M6–6** **Determining Financial Statement Effects of Bad Debts**

■ **LO4**

Using the following categories, indicate the effects of the following transactions. Use + for increase and − for decrease and indicate the accounts affected and the amounts.

a. At the end of the period, bad debt expense is estimated to be $10,000.

b. During the period, bad debts are written off in the amount of $8,000.

| Assets | = | Liabilities | + | Stockholders' Equity |
|--------|---|-------------|---|----------------------|
|        |   |             |   |                      |

**M6–7** **Determining the Effects of Credit Policy Changes on Receivables Turnover Ratio**

■ **LO5**

Indicate the most likely effect of the following changes in credit policy on the receivables turnover ratio (+ for increase, − for decrease, and NE for no effect).

_____ a. Granted credit with shorter payment deadlines.

_____ b. Increased effectiveness of collection methods.

_____ c. Granted credit to less creditworthy customers.

**M6–8** **Matching Reconciling Items to the Bank Reconciliation**

■ **LO6**

Indicate whether the following items would be added (+) or subtracted (−) from the company's books or the bank statement during the construction of a bank reconciliation.

| Reconciling Item | + | − | Company's Books | Bank Statement |
|------------------|---|---|-----------------|----------------|
| a. Outstanding checks | | | | |
| b. Bank service charge | | | | |
| c. Deposit in transit | | | | |

**M6–9** **(Supplement B) Recording Sales Discounts**

A sale is made for $700; terms are 2/10, n/30. At what amount should the sale be recorded under the gross method of recording sales discounts? Give the required entry. Also give the collection entry, assuming that it is during the discount period.

## EXERCISES

**E6–1** **Reporting Net Sales with Credit Sales and Sales Discounts**

■ **LO2**

During the months of January and February, Bronze Corporation sold goods to three customers. The sequence of events was as follows:

Jan.  6   Sold goods for $1,000 to S. Green and billed that amount subject to terms 2/10, n/30.

      6   Sold goods to M. Munoz for $800 and billed that amount subject to terms 2/10, n/30.

     14   Collected cash due from S. Green.

Feb.  2   Collected cash due from M. Munoz.

     28   Sold goods for $500 to R. Reynolds and billed that amount subject to terms 2/10, n/45.

*Required:*

Assuming that Sales Discounts is treated as a contra-revenue, compute net sales for the two months ended February 28.

**E6–2** **Reporting Net Sales with Credit Sales, Sales Discounts, and Credit Card Sales**

■ **LO2**

The following transactions were selected from the records of Evergreen Company:

July  12   Sold merchandise to Customer R, who charged the $1,000 purchase on his Visa credit card. Visa charges Evergreen a 2 percent credit card fee.

| July | 15 | Sold merchandise to Customer S at an invoice price of $5,000; terms 3/10, n/30. |
|---|---|---|
| | 20 | Sold merchandise to Customer T at an invoice price of $3,000; terms 3/10, n/30. |
| | 23 | Collected payment from Customer S from July 15 sale. |
| Aug. | 25 | Collected payment from Customer T from July 20 sale. |

*Required:*
Assuming that Sales Discounts is treated as a contra-revenue, compute net sales for the two months ended August 31.

■ **LO2**    **E6–3**    **Reporting Net Sales with Credit Sales, Sales Discounts, Sales Returns, and Credit Card Sales**

The following transactions were selected from among those completed by Hailey Retailers in 20B:

| Nov. | 20 | Sold two items of merchandise to Customer B, who charged the $400 sales price on her Visa credit card. Visa charges Hailey a 2 percent credit card fee. |
|---|---|---|
| | 25 | Sold 20 items of merchandise to Customer C at an invoice price of $4,000 (total); terms 3/10, n/30. |
| | 28 | Sold 10 identical items of merchandise to Customer D at an invoice price of $6,000 (total); terms 3/10, n/30. |
| | 30 | Customer D returned one of the items purchased on the 28th; the item was defective, and credit was given to the customer. |
| Dec. | 6 | Customer D paid the account balance in full. |
| | 30 | Customer C paid in full for the invoice of November 25, 20B. |

*Required:*
Assume that Sales Discounts and Credit Card Discounts are treated as contra-revenues; compute net sales for the two months ended December 31, 20B.

■ **LO2**    **E6–4**    **Determining the Effects of Credit Sales, Sales Discounts, Credit Card Sales, and Sales Returns and Allowances on Income Statement Categories**

Rockland Shoe Company records sales returns and allowances as contra-revenues and sales discounts and credit card discounts as selling expenses. Complete the following tabulation, indicating the effect (+ for increase, − for decrease, and NE for no effect) of each transaction. Do not record related cost of goods sold.

| July | 12 | Sold merchandise to customer at factory store who charged the $300 purchase on her American Express card. American Express charges a 1 percent credit card fee. |
|---|---|---|
| July | 15 | Sold merchandise to Customer T at an invoice price of $5,000; terms 3/10, n/30. |
| July | 20 | Collected cash due from Customer T. |
| July | 21 | Before paying for the order, a customer returned shoes with an invoice price of $1,000. |

| Transaction | Net Sales | Gross Profit | Income from Operations |
|---|---|---|---|
| July 12 | | | |
| July 15 | | | |
| July 20 | | | |
| July 21 | | | |

■ **LO2**    **E6–5**    **Evaluating the Annual Interest Rate Implicit in a Sales Discount with Discussion of Management Choice of Financing Strategy**

Laura's Landscaping bills customers subject to terms 3/10, n/60.

*Required:*

1. Compute the annual interest rate implicit in the sales discount.

2. If his bank charges 15 percent interest, should the customer borrow from the bank so that he can take advantage of the discount? Explain your recommendation.

**E6–6 Analyzing Gross Profit Percentage on the Basis of a Multiple-Step Income Statement** ■ LO3

The following summarized data were provided by the records of Slate, Incorporated, for the year ended December 31, 20B:

| | |
|---|---|
| Sales of merchandise for cash | $220,000 |
| Sales of merchandise on credit | 32,000 |
| Cost of goods sold | 147,000 |
| Selling expense | 40,200 |
| Administrative expense | 19,000 |
| Sales returns and allowances | 7,000 |
| Items not included in above amounts: | |
| Estimated bad debt loss, 2.5% of credit sales | |
| Average income tax rate, 30% | |
| Number of shares of common stock outstanding, 5,000 | |

*Required:*

1. Based on these data, prepare a multiple-step income statement (showing both gross profit and income from operations). Include a Percentage Analysis column.

2. What was the amount of gross profit margin? What was the gross profit percentage ratio? Explain what these two amounts mean.

**E6–7 Analyzing Gross Profit Percentage on the Basis of a Multiple-Step Income Statement and Within-Industry Comparison** ■ LO3

Wolverine World Wide Inc. prides itself as being the "world's leading marketer of U.S. branded non-athletic footwear." It competes in many markets with Timberland, often offering products at a lower price point. The following data were taken from its recent annual report (in thousands):

Wolverine World Wide

| | |
|---|---|
| Sales of merchandise | $413,957 |
| Income taxes | 10,047 |
| Cash dividends declared | 2,347 |
| Selling and administrative expense | 85,993 |
| Cost of products sold | 290,469 |
| Interest expense | 3,678 |
| Other income | 297 |
| Items not included in above amounts: | |
| Number of shares of common stock outstanding, 17,114 | |

*Required:*

1. Based on these data, prepare a multiple-step income statement (showing both gross profit and income from operations). There were no extraordinary items. Include a Percentage Analysis column.

2. How much was the gross profit margin? What was the gross profit percentage ratio? Explain what these two amounts mean. Compare the gross profit percentage with that of Timberland. What do you believe accounts for the difference?

**E6–8 Recording Bad Debts** ■ LO4

During 20A, Gonzales Electronics, Incorporated, recorded credit sales of $720,000. Based on prior experience, it estimates a 0.5 percent bad debt rate on credit sales.

*Required:*

Prepare journal entries for each transaction:

*a.* The appropriate bad debt expense adjustment was recorded for the year 20A.

*b.* On December 31, 20A, an account receivable for $300 from a prior year was determined to be uncollectible and was written off.

**E6–9 Determining Financial Statement Effects of Bad Debts** ■ LO4

Using the following categories, indicate the effects of the transactions listed in E6–8. Use + for increase and − for decrease and indicate the accounts affected and the amounts.

| Assets | = | Liabilities | + | Stockholders' Equity |
|--------|---|-------------|---|----------------------|

**LO4**  **E6–10**    **Recording and Determining the Effects of Bad Debt Transactions on Income Statement Categories**

During 20A, Choi and Goldstein Furniture recorded credit sales of $650,000. Based on prior experience, it estimates a 2 percent bad debt rate on credit sales.

*Required:*

1. Prepare journal entries for each transaction below.
   a. The appropriate bad debt expense adjustment was recorded for the year 20A.
   b. On December 31, 20A, an account receivable for $1,600 from a prior year was determined to be uncollectible and was written off.
2. Complete the following tabulation, indicating the amount and effect (+ for increase, − for decrease, and NE for no effect) of each transaction.

| Transaction | Net Sales | Gross Profit | Income from Operations |
|-------------|-----------|--------------|------------------------|
| a. | | | |
| b. | | | |

**LO4**  **E6–11**    **Interpreting Bad Debt Disclosures**

DaimlerChrysler AG

DaimlerChrysler is the largest industrial group headquartered in Germany. Best known as the manufacturer of Mercedes-Benz and Chrysler cars and trucks, it also manufactures products in the fields of rail systems, aerospace, propulsion, defense, and information technology. In a recent filing pursuant to its listing on the New York Stock Exchange, it disclosed the following information concerning its allowance for doubtful accounts (in millions of German marks denoted DM):

| Balance at Beginning of Period | Charged to Costs and Expenses | Amounts Written Off | Balance at End of Period |
|--------------------------------|-------------------------------|---------------------|--------------------------|
| 1,933 | 92 | (52) | 1,973 |

*Required:*

1. Record summary journal entries related to bad debts for the current year.
2. If DaimlerChrysler had written off an additional DM10 million of accounts receivable during the period, how would receivables, net, and net income have been affected? Explain why.

**LO4**  **E6–12**    **Inferring Bad Debt Write-Offs and Cash Collections from Customers**

Microsoft

Microsoft develops, produces, and markets a wide range of computer software including the Windows operating system. On a recent balance sheet, Microsoft reported the following information about net sales revenue and accounts receivable.

| | 20B | 20A |
|---|-----|-----|
| Accounts receivable, net of allowances of $76 and $57 | $ 338 | $ 270 |
| Net revenues | 3,753 | 2,759 |

According to its Form 10-K, Microsoft recorded bad debt expense of $47 and did not reinstate any previously written-off accounts during 20B.

*Required:*

1. What amount of bad debts was written off during 20B?
2. Assuming that all of Microsoft's sales during the period were on open account, solve for cash collected from customers for 20B.

**E6–13 Determining the Impact of Uncollectible Accounts on Income and Working Capital**  ▪ LO4

A recent annual report for Sears contained the following information at the end of its fiscal year:  *Sears*

|  | Year 1 | Year 2 |
|---|---|---|
| Accounts receivable | $7,022,075,000 | $7,336,308,000 |
| Allowance for doubtful accounts | (86,605,000) | (96,989,000) |
|  | $6,935,470,000 | $7,239,319,000 |

A footnote to the financial statements disclosed that uncollectible accounts amounting to $55,000,000 were written off as bad during year 1 and $69,000,000 during year 2. Assume that the tax rate for Sears was 30 percent.

*Required:*

1. Determine the bad debt expense for year 2 based on the preceding facts.

2. *Working capital* is defined as current assets minus current liabilities. How was Sears's working capital affected by the write-off of $69,000,000 in uncollectible accounts during year 2? What impact did the recording of bad debt expense have on working capital in year 2?

3. How was net income affected by the $69,000,000 write-off during year 2? What impact did recording bad debt expense have on net income for year 2?

**E6–14 Computing Bad Debt Expense Using Aging Analysis**  ▪ LO4

Brown Cow Dairy uses the aging approach to estimate bad debt expense. The balance of each account receivable is aged on the basis of three time periods as follows: (1) not yet due $12,000, (2) up to 120 days past due $5,000, and (3) more than 120 days past due $3,000. Experience has shown that for each age group, the average loss rate on the amount of the receivable at year-end due to uncollectability is (1) 2 percent, (2) 10 percent, and (3) 30 percent, respectively. At December 31, 20F (end of the current year), the Allowance for Doubtful Accounts balance was $300 (credit) before the end-of-period adjusting entry is made.

*Required:*

What amount should be recorded as Bad Debt Expense for the current year?

**E6–15 Recording, Reporting, and Evaluating a Bad Debt Estimate**  ▪ LO4

Connor Company started business on January 1, 20A. During the year 20A, the company's records indicated the following:

| Sales on cash basis | $400,000 |
|---|---|
| Sales on credit basis | 150,000 |
| Collections on accounts receivable | 100,000 |

The company's manager is concerned about accounting for bad debts. At December 31, 20A, although no accounts were considered bad, several customers were considerably overdue in paying their accounts. A friend of the manager suggested a 1 percent bad debt rate on sales, which the manager decided to use at the start.

*Required:*

1. You have been employed on a part-time basis to assist with the company's recordkeeping. The manager told you to set up bad debt expense of $5,500. Give the required entry.

2. You are concerned about how the $5,500 was determined. The manager told you it was from another manager "who knew his business" and used 1 percent of sales. Do you agree with the estimate of bad debts? If you disagree, give the correct entry and explain the basis for your choice.

3. Show how the various accounts related to credit sales should be shown on the December 31, 20A, income statement and balance sheet.

**E6–16 Recording, Reporting, and Evaluating a Bad Debt Estimate**  ▪ LO4

During 20G, Martin's Camera Shop had sales revenue of $170,000, of which $85,000 was on credit. At the start of 20G, Accounts Receivable showed a $10,000 debit balance, and the

Allowance for Doubtful Accounts showed an $800 credit balance. Collections of accounts receivable during 20G amounted to $68,000.

Data during 20G follows:

a. On December 31, 20G, an Account Receivable (J. Doe) of $1,500 from a prior year was determined to be uncollectible; therefore, it was written off immediately as a bad debt.

b. On December 31, 20G, on the basis of experience, a decision was made to continue the accounting policy of basing estimated bad debt losses on 2 percent of credit sales for the year.

*Required:*

1. Give the required journal entries for the two items on December 31, 20G (end of the accounting period).

2. Show how the amounts related to Accounts Receivable and Bad Debt Expense would be reported on the income statement and balance sheet for 20G. Disregard income tax considerations.

3. On the basis of the data available, does the 2 percent rate appear to be reasonable? Explain.

**LO5**

**E6–17**

Federal Express

### Analyzing and Interpreting the Receivables Turnover Ratio

A recent annual report for Federal Express contained the following data:

|  | (in thousands) | |
| --- | --- | --- |
|  | Current Year | Previous Year |
| Accounts receivable | $1,034,608 | $805,495 |
| Less: Allowance for doubtful accounts | 36,800 | 38,225 |
| Net accounts receivable | $ 997,808 | $767,270 |
| Net sales (assume all on credit) | $7,015,069 | |

*Required:*

1. Determine the accounts receivable turnover ratio and average days sales in receivables for the current year.

2. Explain the meaning of each number.

**LO5**

**E6–18**

### Determining the Effects of Bad Debts on Receivables Turnover Ratio

During 20A, Leung Enterprises Corporation recorded credit sales of $650,000. Based on prior experience, it estimates a 1 percent bad debt rate on credit sales. At the beginning of the year, the balance in Net Trade Accounts Receivable was $50,000. At the end of the year, but *before* the bad debt expense adjustment was recorded and *before* any bad debts had been written off, the balance in Net Trade Accounts Receivable was $55,500.

*Required:*

1. Assume that on December 31, 20A, the appropriate bad debt expense adjustment was recorded for the year 20A and accounts receivable totaling $6,000 for the year were determined to be uncollectible and written off. What was the receivables turnover ratio for 20A?

2. Assume instead that on December 31, 20A, the appropriate bad debt expense adjustment was recorded for the year 20A and $7,000 of accounts receivable was determined to be uncollectible and written off. What was the receivables turnover ratio for 20A?

3. Explain why the answers to requirements (1) and (2) differ or do not differ.

**LO5**

**E6–19**

Stride Rite

### Interpreting the Effects of Sales Declines and Changes in Receivables on Cash Flow from Operations

Stride Rite Corporation manufactures and markets shoes under the brand names Stride Rite®, Keds®, and Sperry Top-Sider®. Three recent years produced a combination of declining sales revenue and net income culminating in a net loss of $8,430,000. Each year, however, Stride Rite was able to report positive cash flows from operations. Contributing to that positive cash flow was the change in accounts receivable. The current and prior year balance sheets reported the following:

| | (in thousands) | |
| --- | --- | --- |
| | Current Year | Previous Year |
| Accounts and notes receivable, less allowances | $48,066 | $63,403 |

*Required:*

1. On the current year's cash flow statement (indirect method), how would the change in accounts receivable affect cash flow from operations? Explain why it would have this effect.

2. Explain how declining sales revenue often leads to (a) declining accounts receivable and (b) cash collections from customers being higher than sales revenue.

**E6–20 Interpreting the Effects of Sales Growth and Changes in Receivables on Cash Flow from Operations**

**LO5**

Nike

Nike, Inc., is the best known sports apparel and equipment company in the world. Three recent years produced a combination of dramatic increases in sales revenue and net income. Cash flows from operations declined during the period, however. Contributing to that declining cash flow was the change in accounts receivable. The current and prior year balance sheets reported the following:

| | (in thousands) | |
| --- | --- | --- |
| | Current Year | Previous Year |
| Accounts receivable, less allowance for doubtful accounts | $1,346,125 | $1,053,237 |

*Required:*

1. On the current year's cash flow statement (indirect method), how would the change in accounts receivable affect cash flow from operations? Explain why it would have this effect.

2. Explain how increasing sales revenue often leads to (a) increasing accounts receivable and thus (b) cash collections from customers being lower than sales revenue.

**E6–21 Reporting Cash and Cash Equivalents When There Are Several Bank Accounts**

**LO6**

Strake Corporation has manufacturing facilities in several cities and has cash on hand at several locations as well as in several bank accounts. The general ledger at the end of 20A showed the following accounts: Cash on Hand—Home Office, $700; City Bank—Home Office, $58,600; Cash Held for Making Change, $300 (included in the regular Cash account balance); Cash on Hand—Location A, $100; National Bank—Location A, $3,350; Cash on Hand—Location B, $200; Southwest Bank—Location B, $785; Cash on Hand—Location C, $200; State Bank—Location C, $965; Metropolitan Bank—3-month Certificate of Deposit, $5,800; and Southwest Bank—6-month Certificate of Deposit, $850.

The bank balances given represent the current cash balances as reflected on the bank reconciliations.

*Required:*

What cash and cash equivalents amount should be reported on the company's 20A balance sheet? Explain the basis for your decisions on any questionable items.

**E6–22 Preparing Bank Reconciliation, Entries, and Reporting**

**LO6**

Jones Company has the June 30, 20B, bank statement and the June ledger accounts for cash, which are summarized here:

**Bank Statement**

|  | Checks | Deposits | Balance |
|---|---|---|---|
| Balance, June 1, 20B |  |  | $ 7,200 |
| Deposits during June |  | $17,000 | 24,200 |
| Checks cleared through June | $18,100 |  | 6,100 |
| Bank service charges | 50 |  | 6,050 |
| Balance, June 30, 20B |  |  | 6,050 |

**Cash**

| June 1 | Balance | 6,800 | June | Checks written | 18,400 |
|---|---|---|---|---|---|
| June | Deposits | 19,000 |  |  |  |

**Cash on hand**

| June 30 | Balance | 300 |  |
|---|---|---|---|

*Required:*

1. Reconcile the bank account. A comparison of the checks written with the checks that have cleared the bank shows outstanding checks of $700. Some of the checks that cleared in June were written prior to June. No deposits in transit were carried over from May, but a deposit is in transit at the end of June.

2. Give any journal entries that should be made as a result of the bank reconciliation.

3. What is the balance in the Cash account after the reconciliation entries?

4. What is the total amount of cash that should be reported on the balance sheet at June 30?

■ **LO6**     **E6–23**    **Preparing Bank Reconciliation, Entries, and Reporting**

The September 30, 20D, bank statement for Russell Company and the September ledger accounts for cash are summarized here:

**Bank Statement**

|  | Checks | Deposits | Balance |
|---|---|---|---|
| Balance, September 1, 20D |  |  | $ 6,300 |
| Deposits recorded during September |  | $27,000 | 33,300 |
| Checks cleared during September | $28,500 |  | 4,800 |
| NSF checks—Betty Brown | 150 |  | 4,650 |
| Bank service charges | 50 |  | 4,600 |
| Balance, September 30, 20D |  |  | 4,600 |

**Cash**

| Sept 1 | Balance | 6,300 | Sept. | Checks written | 28,600 |
|---|---|---|---|---|---|
| Sept. | Deposits | 28,000 |  |  |  |

**Cash on hand**

| Sept 30 | Balance | 400 |  |
|---|---|---|---|

No outstanding checks and no deposits in transit were carried over from August; however, there are deposits in transit and checks outstanding at the end of September.

*Required:*

1. Reconcile the bank account.

2. Give any journal entries that should be made as the result of the bank reconciliation.

3. What should the balance in the Cash account be after the reconciliation entries?

4. What total amount of cash should the company report on the September 30 balance sheet?

**E6–24** **(Supplement A) Determining Income Using the Percentage of Completion Method**
Jackson Construction Company entered into a long-term construction contract with the federal government to build a special landing strip at an Air Force base in Rapid City, South Dakota. The project took three years and cost the government $12 million. Jackson spent the following amounts each year: 20A, $2 million; 20B, $5 million; 20C, $3 million. The company uses the percentage of completion method. Cost estimates equaled actual costs.

*Required:*
Determine the amount of net income that Jackson can report each year for this project.

**E6–25** **(Supplement B) Recording Credit Sales, Sales Discounts, Sales Returns, and Credit Card Sales**
The following transactions were selected from among those completed by Hailey Retailers in 20B:

Nov. 20    Sold two items of merchandise to Customer B, who charged the $400 sales price on her Visa credit card. Visa charges Hailey a 2 percent credit card fee.

25    Sold 20 items of merchandise to Customer C at an invoice price of $4,000 (total); terms 3/10, n/30.

28    Sold 10 identical items of merchandise to Customer D at an invoice price of $6,000 (total); terms 3/10, n/30.

30    Customer D returned one of the items purchased on the 28th; the item was defective, and credit was given to the customer.

Dec.  6    Customer D paid the account balance in full.

30    Customer C paid in full for the invoice of November 25, 20B.

*Required:*
Give the appropriate journal entry for each of these transactions, assuming the company records sales revenue under the gross method. Do not record cost of goods sold.

# PROBLEMS

**P6–1** **Applying the Revenue Principle**                                                         ■ **LO1**
At what point should revenue be recognized in each of the following independent cases?

**Case A.** For Christmas presents, a McDonald's restaurant sells coupon books for $10. Each of the $1 coupons may be used in the restaurant any time during the following 12 months. The customer must pay cash when purchasing the coupon book.

**Case B.** Howard Land Development Corporation sold a lot to Quality Builders to construct a new home. The price of the lot was $50,000. Quality made a down payment of $100 and agreed to pay the balance in six months. After making the sale, Howard learned that Quality Builders often entered into these agreements but refused to pay the balance if it did not find a customer who wanted a house built on the lot.

**Case C.** In 20A, Smilor Construction Company started a long-term construction project to build a large office complex. The project was completed in 20C. At the end of 20C, Smilor had not yet sold the project because it was asking top dollar for the office space. Smilor was very confident that it could sell the building for the asking price because there was a serious shortage of office space in the area.

**Case D.** Driscoll Corporation has always recorded revenue at the point of sale of its refrigerators. Recently, it has extended its warranties to cover all repairs for a period of seven years. One young accountant with the company now questions whether Driscoll has completed its earning process when it sells the refrigerators. She suggests that the warranty obligation for seven years means that a significant amount of additional work must be performed in the future.

**P6–2** **Reporting Net Sales and Expenses with Discounts, Returns, and Bad Debts** (AP6–1)    ■ **LO2, 4**
The following data were selected from the records of May Company for the year ended December 31, 20C.

> Balances January 1, 20C
> 
> | Accounts receivable (various customers) | $120,000 |
> |---|---|
> | Allowance for doubtful accounts | 6,000 |

In the following order, except for cash sales, the company sold merchandise and made collections on credit terms 2/10, n/30 (assume a unit sales price of $500 in all transactions and use the gross method to record sales revenue).

### Transactions during 20C

a. Sold merchandise for cash, $228,000.
b. Sold merchandise to R. Jones; invoice price, $12,000.
c. Sold merchandise to K. Black; invoice price, $26,000.
d. Two days after purchase date, R. Jones returned one of the units purchased in (b) and received account credit.
e. Sold merchandise to B. Sears; invoice price, $24,000.
f. R. Jones paid his account in full within the discount period.
g. Collected $98,000 cash from customer sales on credit in prior year, all within the discount periods.
h. K. Black paid the invoice in (c) within the discount period.
i. Sold merchandise to R. Roy; invoice price, $17,000.
j. Three days after paying the account in full, K. Black returned seven defective units and received a cash refund.
k. After the discount period, collected $7,000 cash on an account receivable on sales in a prior year.
l. Wrote off a 20A account of $2,900 after deciding that the amount would never be collected.
m. The estimated bad debt rate used by the company was 1 percent of credit sales net of returns.

### Required:

1. Using the following categories, indicate the effect of each listed transaction, including the write-off of the uncollectible account and the adjusting entry for estimated bad debts (ignore cost of goods sold).

| Sales Revenue | Sales Discounts (taken) | Sales Returns and Allowances | Bad Debt Expense |
|---|---|---|---|
|  |  |  |  |

2. Show how the accounts related to the preceding sale and collection activities should be reported on the 20C income statement. (Treat sales discounts as a contra-revenue.)

**LO3**

**P6–3**    **Understanding the Income Statement Based on the Gross Profit Percentage**

The following data were taken from the year-end records of Nomura Export Company. You are to fill in all of the missing amounts. Show computations.

|  | Independent Cases | |
|---|---|---|
| Income Statement Items | Case A | Case B |
| Gross sales revenue | $160,000 | $232,000 |
| Sales returns and allowances | ? | 18,000 |
| Net sales revenue | ? | ? |
| Cost of goods sold | (68%)? | ? |
| Gross profit | ? | (30%)? |
| Operating expenses | 18,500 | ? |
| Pretax income | ? | 20,000 |
| Income tax expense (20%) | ? | ? |
| Income before extraordinary items | ? | ? |
| Extraordinary items | 10,000 (gain) | 2,000 (loss) |
| Less: Income tax (20%) | ? | ? |
| Net income | ? | ? |
| EPS (10,000 shares) | 3.00 | ? |

**P6–4** **Interpreting Disclosure of Allowance for Doubtful Accounts** (AP6–2)

■ **LO4**

Kimberly-Clark

Kimberly-Clark manufactures and markets a variety of paper and synthetic fiber products, of which the best known is Kleenex tissues. It recently disclosed the following information concerning the allowance for doubtful accounts on its Form 10-K Annual Report submitted to the Securities and Exchange Commission.

| | | | | | |
|---|---|---|---|---|---|
| **SCHEDULE VIII** | | | | | |
| **Valuation and Qualifying Accounts** | | | | | |
| **For the Years Ended December 31, 20C, 20B, and 20A** | | | | | |
| **(millions of dollars)** | | | | | |
| **Description: Allowances for Doubtful Accounts** | **Balance at Beginning of Period** | **Charged to Costs and Expenses** | **Charged to Other Accounts*** | **Write-Offs** | **Balance at End of Period** |
| December 31, 20C | $8.2 | $4.5 | $.2 | $2.7 | $10.2 |
| December 31, 20B | 7.1 | 4.8 | — | (?) | 8.2 |
| December 31, 20A | 6.4 | (?) | .2 | 3.3 | 7.1 |

*These are primarily bad debt recoveries. *Hint:* These require a reversal of the previous entry made when they were written off.

*Required:*

1. Record summary journal entries related to bad debts for 20C.

2. Supply the missing dollar amounts noted by (?) for 20A and 20B.

**P6–5** **Determining Bad Debt Expense Based on Aging Analysis** (AP6–3)

■ **LO4**

Green Pastures Equipment Company uses the aging approach to estimate bad debt expense at the end of each accounting year. Credit sales occur frequently on terms n/60. The balance of each account receivable is aged on the basis of three time periods as follows: (1) not yet due, (2) up to one year past due, and (3) more than one year past due. Experience has shown that for each age group, the average loss rate on the amount of the receivable at year-end due to uncollectability is (a) 1 percent, (b) 5 percent, and (c) 30 percent.

At December 31, 20F (end of the current accounting year), the Accounts Receivable balance was $41,000, and the Allowance for Doubtful Accounts balance was $1,020 (credit). To simplify, only five customer accounts are used; the details of each on December 31, 20F, follow:

| | | | | |
|---|---|---|---|---|
| **B. Brown—Account Receivable** | | | | |
| Date | Explanation | Debit | Credit | Balance |
| 3/11/20E | Sale | 14,000 | | 14,000 |
| 6/30/20E | Collection | | 5,000 | 9,000 |
| 1/31/20F | Collection | | 4,000 | 5,000 |
| **D. Donalds—Account Receivable** | | | | |
| 2/28/20F | Sale | 22,000 | | 22,000 |
| 4/15/20F | Collection | | 10,000 | 12,000 |
| 11/30/20F | Collection | | 8,000 | 4,000 |
| **N. Napier—Account Receivable** | | | | |
| 11/30/20F | Sale | 9,000 | | 9,000 |
| 12/15/20F | Collection | | 2,000 | 7,000 |
| **S. Strothers—Account Receivable** | | | | |
| 3/2/20D | Sale | 5,000 | | 5,000 |
| 4/15/20D | Collection | | 5,000 | 0 |
| 9/1/20E | Sale | 10,000 | | 10,000 |

*[handwritten annotations: "more than one 3 yr past due"; "2- up to one year past due"; "not yet due 1"; "3- more than one"]*

*continued*

| S. Strothers—Account Receivable (*continued*) | | | | |
|---|---|---|---|---|
| Date | Explanation | Debit | Credit | Balance |
| 10/15/20E | Collection | | 8,000 | 2,000 |
| 2/1/20F | Sale | 19,000 | | 21,000 |
| 3/1/20F | Collection | | 5,000 | 16,000 — *up to yr. due* |
| 12/31/20F | Sale | 3,000 — *not yet due* | | 19,000 |
| T. Thomas—Account Receivable | | | | |
| 12/30/20F | Sale | 6,000 | | 6,000 |

*Required:*

1. Set up an aging analysis schedule and complete it.

2. Compute the estimated uncollectible amount for each age category and in total.

3. Give the adjusting entry for bad debt expense at December 31, 20F.

4. Show how the amounts related to accounts receivable should be presented on the 20F income statement and balance sheet.

■ **LO2, 3, 4**    **P6–6**

**Preparing a Multiple-Step Income Statement and Computing the Gross Profit Percentage with Discounts, Returns, and Bad Debts** (AP6–4)

Builders Company, Inc., sells heavy construction equipment. There are 10,000 shares of capital stock outstanding. The annual fiscal period ends on December 31. The following condensed trial balance was taken from the general ledger on December 31, 20D:

| Account Titles | Debit | Credit |
|---|---|---|
| Cash | $ 42,000 | |
| Accounts receivable | 18,000 | |
| Inventory, ending | 65,000 | |
| Operational assets | 50,000 | |
| Accumulated depreciation | | $ 21,000 |
| Liabilities | | 30,000 |
| Capital stock | | 90,000 |
| Retained earnings, January 1, 20D | | 11,600 |
| Sales revenue | | 182,000 |
| Sales returns and allowances | 7,000 | |
| Cost of goods sold | 98,000 | |
| Selling expense | 17,000 | |
| Administrative expense | 18,000 | |
| Bad debt expense | 2,000 | |
| Sales discounts | 8,000 | |
| Income tax expense | 9,600 | |
| Totals | $334,600 | $334,600 |

*Required:*

1. Beginning with the amount for net sales, prepare a multiple-step income statement (showing both gross profit and income from operations). Treat sales discounts as a contra-revenue.

2. Compute the gross profit percentage and explain its meaning.

■ **LO5**    **P6–7**

**Evaluating the Effects of Credit Policy Changes on Receivables Turnover Ratio and Cash Flows from Operating Activities**

V. R. Rao and Company has been operating for five years as a software consulting firm specializing in the installation of industry standard products. During this period, it has experienced rapid growth in sales revenue and in accounts receivable. Ms. Rao and her associates all have computer science backgrounds. This year, the company hired you as its first corporate controller. You have put into place new credit-granting and collection procedures that are expected to reduce receivables by approximately one-third by year-end. You have gathered the following data related to the changes:

| | (in thousands) | |
|---|---|---|
| | Beginning of Year | End of Year (projected) |
| Accounts receivable | $1,000,608 | $660,495 |
| Less: Allowance for doubtful accounts | 36,800 | 10,225 |
| Net accounts receivable | $ 963,808 | $650,270 |
| | | Current Year (projected) |
| Net sales (assume all on credit) | | $7,015,069 |

*Required:*

1. Compute the accounts receivable turnover ratio based on two different assumptions:

   *a.* Those presented in the preceding table (a decrease in the balance in accounts receivable, net).

   *b.* No change from the beginning of the year in the accounts receivable balance.

2. Compute the effect of the projected change in the balance in accounts receivable on cash flow from operating activities for the year (the sign and amount of effect).

3. On the basis of your findings in requirements (1) and (2), write a brief memo explaining how an increase in accounts receivable turnover can result in an increase in cash flow from operating activities. Also explain how this increase can benefit the company.

**P6–8 Evaluating Internal Control**

LO6

Cripple Creek Company has one trusted employee who, as the owner said, "handles all of the bookkeeping and paperwork for the company." This employee is responsible for counting, verifying, and recording cash receipts and payments, making the weekly bank deposit, preparing checks for major expenditures (signed by the owner), making small expenditures from the cash register for daily expenses, and collecting accounts receivable. The owners asked the local bank for a $20,000 loan. The bank asked that an audit be performed covering the year just ended. The independent auditor (a local CPA), in a private conference with the owner, presented some evidence of the following activities of the trusted employee during the past year:

*a.* Cash sales sometimes were not entered in the cash register, and the trusted employee pocketed approximately $50 per month.

*b.* Cash taken from the cash register (and pocketed by the trusted employee) was replaced with expense memos with fictitious signatures (approximately $12 per day).

*c.* A $300 collection on an account receivable of a valued out-of-town customer was pocketed by the trusted employee and was covered by making a $300 entry as a debit to Sales Returns and a credit to Accounts Receivable.

*d.* An $800 collection on an account receivable from a local customer was pocketed by the trusted employee and was covered by making an $800 entry as a debit to Allowance for Doubtful Accounts and a credit to Accounts Receivable.

*Required:*

1. What was the approximate amount stolen during the past year?

2. What would be your recommendations to the owner?

**P6–9 Preparing a Bank Reconciliation and Related Journal Entries**

LO6

The bookkeeper at Hopkins Company has not reconciled the bank statement with the Cash account, saying, "I don't have time." You have been asked to prepare a reconciliation and review the procedures with the bookkeeper.

The April 30, 20D, bank statement and the April ledger accounts for cash showed the following (summarized):

|  | | Bank Statement | | |
| --- | --- | --- | --- | --- |
| | | **Checks** | **Deposits** | **Balance** |
| Balance, April 1, 20D | | | | $25,850 |
| Deposits during April | | | $36,000 | 61,850 |
| Notes collected for company (including $70 interest) | | | 1,070 | 62,920 |
| Checks cleared during April | | $44,200 | | 18,720 |
| NSF check—A. B. Wright | | 140 | | 18,580 |
| Bank service charges | | 50 | | 18,530 |
| Balance, April 30, 20D | | | | 18,530 |

| | Cash | | | | |
| --- | --- | --- | --- | --- | --- |
| Apr. 1 | Balance | 23,250 | Apr. | Checks written | 43,800 |
| Apr. | Deposits | 42,000 | | | |

| | Cash on hand | | |
| --- | --- | --- | --- |
| Apr. 30 | Balance | 100 | |

A comparison of checks written before and during April with the checks cleared through the bank showed outstanding checks at the end of April of $2,200. No deposits in transit were carried over from March, but a deposit was in transit at the end of April.

*Required:*

1. Prepare a detailed bank reconciliation for April.

2. Give any required journal entries as a result of the reconciliation. Why are they necessary?

3. What were the balances in the cash accounts in the ledger on May 1, 20D?

4. What total amount of cash should be reported on the balance sheet at the end of April?

■ **LO6**   **P6–10**   **Computing Outstanding Checks and Deposits in Transit and Preparing a Bank Reconciliation and Journal Entries (AP6–5)**
The August 20B bank statement for Martha Company and the August 20B ledger accounts for cash follow:

| | Bank Statement | | | |
| --- | --- | --- | --- | --- |
| **Date** | | **Checks** | **Deposits** | **Balance** |
| Aug. 1 | | | | $17,470 |
| 2 | | $ 300 | | 17,170 |
| 3 | | | $12,000 | 29,170 |
| 4 | | 400 | | 28,770 |
| 5 | | 250 | | 28,520 |
| 9 | | 900 | | 27,620 |
| 10 | | 300 | | 27,320 |
| 15 | | | 4,000 | 31,320 |
| 21 | | 400 | | 30,920 |
| 24 | | 21,000 | | 9,920 |
| 25 | | | 7,000 | 16,920 |
| 30 | | 800 | | 16,120 |
| 30 | | | 2,180* | 18,300 |
| 31 | | 100† | | 18,200 |

*$2,000 note collected plus interest.
†Bank service charge.

| Debit | | Cash | Credit | |
|---|---|---|---|---|
| Aug. 1 Balance | 16,520 | Checks written | | |
| Deposits | | Aug. 2 | | 300 |
| Aug. 2 | 12,000 | 4 | | 900 |
| 12 | 4,000 | 15 | 290 | OS-outstanding |
| 24 | 7,000 | 17 | 550 | OS |
| 31 | 5,000 | 18 | | 800 |
| | | 20 | | 400 |
| | | 23 | | 21,000 |

| Cash on hand | |
|---|---|
| Aug. 31 Balance | 200 |

Outstanding checks at the end of July were for $250, $400, and $300. No deposits were in transit at the end of July.

*Required:*

1. Compute the deposits in transit at the end of August.

2. Compute the outstanding checks at the end of August.

3. Prepare a bank reconciliation for August.

4. Give any journal entries that the company should make as a result of the bank reconciliation. Why are they necessary?

5. After the reconciliation journal entries are posted, what balances would be reflected in the cash accounts in the ledger?

6. What total amount of cash should be reported on the August 31, 20B, balance sheet?

**P6–11 (Supplement B) Recording Sales, Returns, and Bad Debts**
Use the data presented in P6–2, which was selected from the records of May Company for the year ended December 31, 20C.

*Required:*

1. Give the journal entries for these transactions, including the write-off of the uncollectible account and the adjusting entry for estimated bad debts. Do not record cost of goods sold. Show computations for each entry.

2. Show how the accounts related to the preceding sale and collection activities should be reported on the 20C income statement. (Treat sales discounts as a contra-revenue.)

## ALTERNATE PROBLEMS

**AP6–1 Reporting Net Sales and Expenses with Discounts, Returns, and Bad Debts** (P6–2)    ■ **LO2, 4**
The following data were selected from the records of Fluwars Company for the year ended December 31, 20B.

| | |
|---|---|
| Balances January 1, 20B: | |
| Accounts receivable (various customers) | $97,000 |
| Allowance for doubtful accounts | 5,000 |

In the following order, except for cash sales, the company sold merchandise and made collections on credit terms 3/10, n/30 (assume a unit sales price of $400 in all transactions and use the gross method to record sales revenue).

*Transactions during 20B*
a. Sold merchandise for cash, $122,000.
b. Sold merchandise to Abbey Corp; invoice price, $6,800.
c. Sold merchandise to Brown Company; invoice price, $14,000.
d. Abbey paid the invoice in (b) within the discount period.
e. Sold merchandise to Cavendish Inc; invoice price, $12,400.

*f.* Two days after paying the account in full, Abbey returned four defective units and received a cash refund.

*g.* Collected $78,000 cash from customer sales on credit in prior year, all within the discount periods.

*h.* Three days after purchase date, Brown returned two of the units purchased in (*c*) and received account credit.

*i.* Brown paid its account in full within the discount period.

*j.* Sold merchandise to Decca Corporation; invoice price, $9,000.

*k.* Cavendish paid its account in full after the discount period.

*l.* Wrote off a 20A account of $1,600 after deciding that the amount would never be collected.

*m.* The estimated bad debt rate used by the company was 2 percent of credit sales net of returns.

### *Required:*

1. Using the following categories, indicate the effect of each listed transaction, including the write-off of the uncollectible account and the adjusting entry for estimated bad debts (ignore cost of goods sold).

| Sales Revenue | Sales Discounts (taken) | Sales Returns and Allowances | Bad Debt Expense |
| --- | --- | --- | --- |
| | | | |

2. Show how the accounts related to the preceding sale and collection activities should be reported on the 20B income statement. (Treat sales discounts as a contra-revenue.)

■ **LO4**   **AP6–2**   **Interpreting Disclosure of Allowance for Doubtful Accounts** (P6–4)

Saucony, Inc.

Under various registered brand names, Saucony, Inc. and its subsidiaries develop, manufacture, and market bicycles and component parts, athletic apparel, and athletic shoes. It recently disclosed the following information concerning the allowance for doubtful accounts on its Form 10-K Annual Report submitted to the Securities and Exchange Commission.

**SCHEDULE II**

**Valuation and Qualifying Accounts**

**For the Years Ended January 1, 20C, January 2, 20B, and January 3, 20A**

**(dollars in thousands)**

| Allowances for Doubtful Accounts and Discounts | Balance at Beginning of Year | Additions Charged to Costs and Expenses | Deductions from Reserve | Balance at End of Year |
| --- | --- | --- | --- | --- |
| January 1, 20C | $2,032 | $4,908 | $5,060 | (?) |
| January 2, 20B | 1,234 | (?) | 4,677 | $2,032 |
| January 3, 20A | 940 | 5,269 | (?) | 1,234 |

### *Required:*

1. Record summary journal entries related to bad debts for 20C.

2. Supply the missing dollar amounts noted by (?) for 20A, 20B, and 20C.

■ **LO4**   **AP6–3**   **Determining Bad Debt Expense Based on Aging Analysis** (P6–5)

Briggs & Stratton Engines Inc. uses the aging approach to estimate bad debt expense at the end of each accounting year. Credit sales occur frequently on terms n/45. The balance of each account receivable is aged on the basis of four time periods as follows: (1) not yet due, (2) up to 6 months past due, (3) 6 to 12 months past due, and (4) more than one year past due. Experience has shown that for each age group, the average loss rate on the amount of the receivable at year-end due to uncollectability is (a) 1 percent, (b) 5 percent, (c) 20 percent, and (d) 50 percent.

At December 31, 20D (end of the current accounting year), the Accounts Receivable balance was $39,500, and the Allowance for Doubtful Accounts balance was $1,550 (credit). To simplify, only five customer accounts are used; the details of each on December 31, 20D, follow:

| Date | Explanation | Debit | Credit | Balance |
|------|-------------|-------|--------|---------|
| | **R. Devens—Account Receivable** | | | |
| 3/13/20D | Sale | 19,000 | | 19,000 |
| 5/12/20D | Collection | | 10,000 | 9,000 |
| 9/30/20D | Collection | | 7,000 | 2,000 |
| | **C. Howard—Account Receivable** | | | |
| 11/01/20C | Sale | 31,000 | | 31,000 |
| 06/01/20C | Collection | | 20,000 | 11,000 |
| 12/01/20D | Collection | | 5,000 | 6,000 |
| | **D. McClain—Account Receivable** | | | |
| 10/31/20D | Sale | 12,000 | | 12,000 |
| 12/10/20D | Collection | | 8,000 | 4,000 |
| | **T. Skibinski—Account Receivable** | | | |
| 05/02/20D | Sale | 15,000 | | 15,000 |
| 06/01/20D | Sale | 10,000 | | 25,000 |
| 06/15/20D | Collection | | 15,000 | 10,000 |
| 07/15/20D | Collection | | 10,000 | 0 |
| 10/01/20D | Sale | 26,000 | | 26,000 |
| 11/15/20D | Collection | | 16,000 | 10,000 |
| 12/15/20D | Sale | 4,500 | | 14,500 |
| | **H. Wu—Account Receivable** | | | |
| 12/30/20D | Sale | 13,000 | | 13,000 |

*Required:*

1. Set up an aging analysis schedule and complete it.

2. Compute the estimated uncollectible amount for each age category and in total.

3. Give the adjusting entry for bad debt expense at December 31, 20D.

4. Show how the amounts related to accounts receivable should be presented on the 20D income statement and balance sheet.

**AP6–4 Preparing a Multiple-Step Income Statement and Computing the Gross Profit Percentage with Discounts, Returns, and Bad Debts (P6–6)**     ■ LO2, 3, 4

Big Tommy Corporation is a local grocery store organized seven years ago as a corporation. At that time, 6,000 shares of common stock were issued to the three organizers. The store is in an excellent location, and sales have increased each year. At the end of 20G, the bookkeeper prepared the following statement (assume that all amounts are correct; note the incorrect terminology and format):

| | | |
|---|---|---|
| **BIG TOMMY CORPORATION** | | |
| **Profit and Loss** | | |
| **December 31, 20G** | | |
| | Debit | Credit |
| Sales | | $420,000 |
| Cost of goods sold | $279,000 | |
| Sales returns and allowances | 10,000 | |
| Selling expense | 58,000 | |
| Administrative and general expense | 16,000 | |
| Bad debt expense | 1,000 | |
| Sales discounts | 6,000 | |
| Income tax expense | 15,000 | |
| Net profit | 35,000 | |
| Totals | $420,000 | $420,000 |

*Required:*

1. Beginning with the amount of net sales, prepare a multiple-step income statement (showing both gross profit and income from operations). Treat sales discounts as an expense.

2. Compute the gross profit percentage and explain its meaning.

**AP6–5    Computing Outstanding Checks and Deposits in Transit and Preparing a Bank Reconciliation and Journal Entries (P6–10)**

The December 31, 20B, bank statement for Packer Company and the December 20B ledger accounts for cash follow.

| Bank Statement | | | |
|---|---|---|---|
| Date | Checks | Deposits | Balance |
| Dec.  1 | | | $48,000 |
| 2 | $400; 300 | $17,000 | 64,300 |
| 4 | 7,000; 90 | | 57,210 |
| 6 | 120; 180; 1,600 | | 55,310 |
| 11 | 500; 1,200; 70 | 28,000 | 81,540 |
| 13 | 480; 700; 1,900 | | 78,460 |
| 17 | 12,000; 8,000 | | 58,460 |
| 23 | 60; 23,500 | 36,000 | 70,900 |
| 26 | 900; 2,650 | | 67,350 |
| 28 | 2,200; 5,200 | | 59,950 |
| 30 | 17,000; 1,890; 300* | 19,000 | 59,760 |
| 31 | 1,650; 1,350; 150† | 5,250‡ | 61,860 |

*NSF check, J. Left, a customer.
†Bank service charge.
‡Note collected, principal, $5,000 plus interest.

| Cash | | | | |
|---|---|---|---|---|
| Dec.  1  Balance | 64,100 | Checks written during December: | | |
| Deposits | | 60 | 5,000 | 2,650 |
| Dec. 11 | 28,000 | 17,000 | 5,200 | 1,650 |
| 23 | 36,000 | 700 | 1,890 | 2,200 |
| 30 | 19,000 | 3,300 | 1,600 | 7,000 |
| 31 | 13,000 | 1,350 | 120 | 300 |
| | | 180 | 90 | 480 |
| | | 12,000 | 23,500 | 8,000 |
| | | 70 | 500 | 1,900 |
| | | 900 | 1,200 | |

| Cash on hand | |
|---|---|
| Dec. 31  Balance | 300 |

The November 20B bank reconciliation showed the following: correct cash balance at November 30, $64,100; deposits in transit on November 30, $17,000; and outstanding checks on November 30, $400 + $500 = $900.

*Required:*

1. Compute the deposits in transit December 31, 20B.

2. Compute the outstanding checks at December 31, 20B.

3. Prepare a bank reconciliation at December 31, 20B.

4. Give any journal entries that should be made as a result of the bank reconciliation made by the company. Why are they necessary?

5. After the reconciliation journal entries, what balances would be reflected in the cash accounts in the ledger?

6. What total amount of cash should be reported on the December 31, 20B, balance sheet?

# CASES AND PROJECTS

## FINANCIAL REPORTING AND ANALYSIS CASES

**CP6–1 Finding Financial Information**
Refer to the financial statements of American Eagle Outfitters given in Appendix B at the end of this book, or open file AEOS10K.doc in the S&P directory on the student CD-ROM.

*Required:*

1. How much cash and cash equivalents does the company hold at the end of the current year?

2. Does the company report an allowance for doubtful accounts on the balance sheet or in the notes? Explain why it does or does not. (*Hint:* Consider the makeup of its receivables.)

3. Compute the company's gross profit percentage for the most recent two years. Has it risen or fallen? Explain the meaning of the change.

4. Does the company disclose its revenue recognition policy? Given that it is a retailer, what recognition point do you believe that it uses?

LO1, 3, 4, 6

American Eagle
Outfitters

STANDARD
&POOR'S

**CP6–2 Finding Financial Information**
Refer to the financial statements of Urban Outfitters given in Appendix C at the end of this book, or open file URBN10K.doc in the S&P directory on the student CD-ROM.

*Required:*

1. What does the company disclose about the market value of its cash and cash equivalents? Would you expect this statement to be true given the securities included in cash equivalents?

2. The company sells to both consumers and business customers. What items would you expect to be subtracted from sales revenue in the computation of net sales?

3. What expenses does Urban Outfitters subtract from net sales in the computation of gross profit? How does this differ from Timberland's practice and how might it affect the manner in which you interpret the gross profit percentage?

4. Compute Urban Outfitters' receivables turnover ratio for the year ended January 31, 1999. What characteristics of its business might cause it to be so high?

5. What was the change in accounts receivable and how did it affect net cash provided by operating activities for the current year?

LO2, 5, 6

Urban Outfitters

STANDARD
&POOR'S

**CP6–3 Comparing Companies within an Industry**
Refer to the financial statements of American Eagle Outfitters given in Appendix B, Urban Outfitters given in Appendix C, and the Standard and Poor's Industry Ratio Report given in Appendix D at the end of this book or open file CP6-3.xls in the S&P directory on the student CD-ROM.

*Required:*

1. Compute gross profit percentage for both companies for the current year. Does Urban Outfitters' Management's Discussion and Analysis suggest a reason that its gross profit percentage might be lower?

2. Knowing that these two companies are specialty or niche retailers compared to some others in their industry (see the list of companies used in the industry ratio report), do you expect their gross profit percentage to be higher or lower than the industry average? Why?

3. Compare the gross profit percentage for each company to the industry average. Are these two companies doing better or worse than the industry average? Does this match your expectations from requirement 2 above?

4. On January 31, 1997, Urban Outfitters' balance in Accounts Receivable (net) was $2,827,000. Compute its accounts receivable turnover ratio for the most current two years. What accounts for its change?

LO3, 5

American Eagle
Outfitters versus
Urban Outfitters

STANDARD
&POOR'S

**CP6–4**

### Interpreting the Financial Press

*Knight-Ridder Tribune Business News* recently interviewed a number of managers and asked "How do you structure a credit policy that encourages sales without sending yourself to the poorhouse?"* The article is available on the Libby/Libby/Short website at www.mhhe.com/business/accounting/libby3.

*Reprinted with permission of Knight-Ridder/Tribune Information Services.

*Required:*
Read the article, organize the recommendations into categories, and write a short memo outlining the key recommended steps.

**■ LO4, 5**    **CP6–5**

### Using Financial Reports: International Bad Debt Disclosure

Foster's Brewing controls more than 50 percent of the beer market in Australia and owns 40 percent of Molson Breweries of Canada and 100 percent of Courage Limited of the United Kingdom. As an Australian company, it follows Australian GAAP and uses Australian accounting terminology. In the footnotes to its recent annual report, it discloses the information on receivables (all numbers are reported in thousands of Australian dollars).

| Note 3: Receivables | 20B | 20A |
| --- | --- | --- |
| *Current* | | |
| Trade debtors | 792,193 | 999,159 |
| Provision for doubtful debts | (121,449) | (238,110) |
| Other debtors | 192,330 | 130,288 |
| Provision for doubtful debts | (384) | (2,464) |
| | | |
| *Non-current* | | |
| Trade debtors | 164,808 | 200,893 |
| Other debtors | 15,094 | 16,068 |
| Provision for doubtful debts | (7,920) | (7,400) |
| | | |
| Note 15: Operation Profit | 20B | 20A |
| Amounts set aside to provisions for | | |
| Doubtful debts—trade debtors | (21,143) | (53,492) |
| Doubtful debts—other debtors | (228) | (2,570) |

*Required:*

1. The account titles used by Foster's are different from those normally used by U.S. companies. What account titles does it use in place of Allowance for Doubtful Accounts and Bad Debt Expense?

2. Sales on account for 20B were $9,978,875. Compute the accounts receivable (trade debtors) turnover ratio for 20B (ignore uncollectible accounts).

3. Compute the provision for doubtful debts as a percentage of current receivables separately for receivables from trade debtors and receivables from others. Explain why these percentages might be different.

4. What was the total amount of receivables written off in 20B?

## CRITICAL THINKING CASES

**■ LO6**    **CP6–6**

### Making Decisions as an Independent CPA

Lane Manufacturing Company is a relatively small local business that specializes in the repair and renovation of antique furniture. The owner is an expert craftsperson. Although a number of skilled workers are employed, there is always a large backlog of work to be done. A long-time employee who serves as clerk-bookkeeper handles cash receipts, keeps the records, and writes checks for disbursements. The owner signs the checks. The clerk-bookkeeper pays small amounts in cash, subject to a month-end review by the owner. Approximately 80 regular customers are extended credit that typically amounts to less than $1,000. Although credit losses are small, in recent years the bookkeeper had established an allowance for doubtful accounts, and all write-offs were made at year-end. During January 20E (the current year), the owner decided to start as soon as possible the construction of a building for the business that would provide many advantages over the presently rented space and would have space to expand facilities. As a part of the considerations in financing, the financing institution asked for 20D audited financial statements. The company statements never had been audited. Early in the audit, the independent CPA found numerous errors and one combination of amounts, in particular, that caused concern.

There was some evidence that a $2,500 job completed by Lane had been recorded as a receivable (from a new customer) on July 15, 20D. The receivable was credited for a $2,500 cash collection a few days later. The new account never was active again. The auditor also observed that shortly thereafter, three write-offs of accounts receivable balances had been made to Allowance for Doubtful Accounts as follows: Jones, $800; Blake, $750; and Sellers, $950—all of whom were known as regular customers. These write-offs drew the attention of the auditor.

*Required:*

1. Explain what caused the CPA to be concerned. Should the CPA report the suspicions to the owner?

2. What recommendations would you make with respect to internal control procedures for this company?

**CP6–7   Making a Decision as a Manager: Choosing among Alternative Recognition Points**

■ **LO1**

UPS, Federal Express, and Airborne

UPS, Federal Express, and Airborne are three of the major players in the highly competitive package delivery industry. Comparability is a key qualitative characteristic of accounting numbers that allows analysts to compare similar companies. The revenue recognition footnotes of the three competitors reveal three different revenue recognition points for package delivery revenue: package delivery, percentage of service completed, and package pickup. These points correspond to the end, continuous recognition, and the beginning of the earnings process.

---

**UNITED PARCEL SERVICE OF AMERICA, INC.**

Revenue is recognized upon delivery of a package.

---

**FEDERAL EXPRESS CORPORATION**

Revenue is generally recognized upon delivery of shipments. For shipments in transit, revenue is recorded based on the percentage of service completed.

---

**AIRBORNE FREIGHT CORP.**

Domestic revenues and most domestic operating expenses are recognized when shipments are picked up from the customer. . . .

---

The Airborne footnote goes on to say, however: "The net revenue resulting from existing recognition policies does not materially differ from that which would be recognized on a delivery date basis."

*Required:*

1. Do you believe that the difference between Airborne's and UPS's revenue recognition policies materially affects their reported earnings? Why or why not?

2. Assume that all three companies pick up packages from customers and receive payment of $1 million for services each day of the year and that each package is delivered the next day. What would each company's service revenue for a year be given its stated revenue recognition policy?

3. Given your answers to requirement (2), under what conditions would that answer change?

4. Which revenue recognition rule would you prefer as a manager? Why?

■ LO1    **CP6–8**

Platinum
Software

### Evaluating an Ethical Dilemma: Management Incentives, Revenue Recognition, and Sales with the Right of Return

Platinum Software was a fast-growing maker of accounting software. According to the federal charges, when business slowed and the company was unable to meet the stock market's expectation for continued growth, the former chairman and CEO (the company's founder), former CFO, and former controller responded by improperly recording revenue and allowances for returns resulting in overstatement of net income by $18 million. The three recently settled both federal charges brought by the SEC and a shareholder suit by paying nearly $2.8 million in restitution and fines and being suspended from practice for differing periods. The exact nature of the fraud is described in the following excerpt:

---

**Three Ex-Officers of O.C. Software Firm Sanctioned; SEC:**

**Platinum founder Gerald Blackie agrees to 10-year ban as officer of public company to settle suit over falsifying books. Two other former executives are fined.**

JOHN O'DELL TIMES STAFF WRITER

*Los Angeles Times* Orange County Edition 5/10/96

. . .

The SEC suit charged that Blackie, Tague and Erickson began falsifying sales records in 1993 and early 1994 in order to pump up Platinum's quarterly sales figures and make the company's financial situation appear stronger than it was.

For a period of at least nine months, ending early in 1994, the men backdated sales orders and reported as actual revenue fees that had not yet been received and were subject to secret cancellation agreements that the customers often exercised, the suit said.

In one case in 1993, the suit alleges, Blackie personally closed a $1.5-million software licensing deal with the Wackenhut Corp. on the day the fiscal year ended. He also executed a separate letter giving Wackenhut a 60-day right to cancel. Blackie then instructed Erickson to enter the $1.5 million as revenue in the just-completed fiscal year, even though the money had not been received.

Wackenhut later canceled the contract, the suit says, but Platinum did not disclose the cancellation or adjust for it when it later filed its annual report with the SEC.

In August 1993, with the company's stock price rising on the strength of the falsified financial reports, Blackie, Tague, and Erickson all sold large amounts of stock. Blackie profited again with a stock sale in November 1993, the SEC suit says. After the company revealed the accounting irregularities and announced Blackie's resignation in April 1994, the stock price plummeted 64 percent.

The suit also says Blackie received $128,125 in performance bonuses for the nine-month period in which he was falsifying financial reports; Erickson got $50,000 and Tague received $6,000. "If they had been any lower in the company they would never have gotten away with this for as long as they did," said SEC attorney Nathan.

---

Copyright 1996, *Los Angeles Times*. Reprinted by permission.

### *Required:*

1. What facts, if any, presented in the article suggest that Platinum violated the revenue principle?

2. Assuming that Platinum did recognize revenue when contracts were signed, how could it have properly accounted for the fact that customers had a right to cancel the contracts (make an analogy with accounting for bad debts)?

3. What do you think may have motivated management to falsify the statements? Why was management concerned with reporting continued growth in net income?

4. Explain who was hurt by management's unethical conduct.

5. Assume that you are the auditor for other software licensing firms. After reading about the fraud, what types of transactions would you pay special attention to in the audit of your clients in this industry?

# FINANCIAL REPORTING AND ANALYSIS PROJECTS

**CP6–9   Comparing Companies over Time: Gross Profit Percentage and Receivables Turnover Ratio**

■ **LO3, 5**

Timberland

Acquire the three most recent years' income statements and balance sheets for Timberland (contact Timberland investor relations at www.timberland.com or EDGAR service at www.sec.gov/cgi-bin/srch-edgar).

*Required:*

Write a short memo comparing the company's gross profit percentage and receivables turnover ratio over the three years. Indicate what differences in its operations might account for any differences in the ratios.

**CP6–10   Comparing Companies within Industries: Gross Margin Percentage and Receivables Turnover**

■ **LO3, 5**

Timberland vs. Competitors

Timberland's competitors in the shoe industry include Skechers, Wolverine World Wide, Brown Group, Reebok, Nike, Stride Rite, and others. Obtain the most recent income statement, balance sheet, and uncollectible accounts schedule (from the 10-K) for Timberland and two of its competitors. (Library files, the SEC EDGAR service at www.sec.gov, Compustat, or the companies' websites are good sources.)

*Required:*

Write a short memo comparing the companies' gross margin percentage and receivables turnover ratio. Indicate what differences in their products or business strategies might account for any differences in the ratios.

**CP6–11   Comparing Companies across Industries: Revenue Recognition Policies**

■ **LO2**

Acquire the revenue recognition note from the annual reports or 10-Ks of three companies from different industries. (Library files, the SEC EDGAR service at www.sec.gov, Compustat, or the companies' websites are good sources.)

*Required:*

Write a short report indicating any differences among the accounting policies. Consider whether the differences in policy lead to earlier, later, or no difference in timing of recognition of revenue and what differences in their lines of business may lead to the policy differences.

**CP6–12   Comparing Companies across Industries: Gross Profit Percentage**

■ **LO3**

Microsoft vs. Dell Computer

Using your web browser, contact the websites of Microsoft, the leading computer *software* company (www.microsoft.com/msft/), and Dell Computer, a leading manufacturer of personal computer *hardware* (www.dell.com/us/en/gen/corporate/investor/investor.htm).

*Required:*

1. On the basis of information provided in their latest annual reports, determine their gross profit percentage.
2. Write a short memo comparing the companies' ratios. Indicate what differences in their businesses might account for any difference in the ratios.

**CP6–13   Broadening Financial Research Skills: Analysts' Conference Calls on the Web**

Dell Computer

Contact Dell Investor Relations at www.dell.com/us/en/gen/corporate/investor/investor. htm. Choose "Video/Auditor Archives" followed by the most recent "Earnings Call." The call will include a formal presentation by Dell executives, as well as a question-and-answer period. Listen to the call and list the questions that the analysts ask. Categorize the questions by whether they relate to the (1) information in the latest earnings announcement (e.g., more details or explanations of the past period's performance), (2) future plans for the company (e.g., product introductions, forecasts of revenues or expenses), (3) competitor company activities, or (4) other. Write a brief report indicating the key issues raised in each category.

**CP6–14   Ethics Project: Analysis of Irregularities in Revenue Recognition**

■ **LO1**

Obtain a recent news story outlining an accounting irregularity related to revenue recognition. (Library files, *Wall Street Journal Index, Dow Jones Interactive,* and *Bloomberg Business News* are good sources. Search for the term "accounting irregularities.") Write a short memo outlining the nature of the irregularity, how it specifically violated the revenue principle, the size of the necessary correction of previously reported earnings, the impact of the announcement of the irregularity on the company's stock price, and any fines or civil penalties against the company and its officers.

**LO1, 4, 5**    **CP6–15**

**Team Project: Analyzing Revenues and Receivables**

As a team, select an industry to analyze (industry lists can be found at www.marketguide.com/mgi/INDUSTRY/INDUSTRY.html and www.hoovers.com; click on companies and industries). Each team member should acquire the annual report or 10-K for one publicly traded company in the industry, with each member selecting a different company. (Library files, the SEC EDGAR service at www.sec.gov/cgi-bin/srch-edgar, Compustat CD, or the company websites are good sources.) On an individual basis, each team member should then write a short report answering the following questions about the selected company.

1. What specific revenue recognition rule does the company follow?

2. What is the receivables turnover ratio?

3. If the 10-K is available, determine what additional disclosures are available concerning the allowance for doubtful accounts. If the necessary information is provided, what is bad debt expense as a percentage of sales?

4. What was the effect of the change in accounts receivable on cash flows from operations? Explain your answer.

Discuss any patterns across the companies that you as a team observe. Then, as a group, write a short report comparing and contrasting your companies using these attributes. Provide potential explanations for any differences discovered.

# Reporting and Interpreting Cost of Goods Sold and Inventory

## CHAPTER SEVEN

---

LEARNING **OBJECTIVES**

*After studying this chapter, you should be able to:*

1. Apply the cost principle to identify the amounts that should be included in inventory and the matching principle to determine cost of goods sold for typical retailers, wholesalers, and manufacturers.   p. 364

2. Analyze the effects of inventory errors on financial statements.   p. 369

3. Report inventory and cost of goods sold using the four inventory costing methods.   p. 371

4. Decide when the use of different inventory costing methods is beneficial to a company.   p. 375

5. Analyze and interpret the inventory turnover ratio and the effects of inventory on cash flows.   p. 380

6. Report inventory at the lower of cost or market (LCM).   p. 384

7. Keep track of inventory quantities and amounts in different circumstances.   p. 386

The Harley-Davidson eagle trademark was once known best as a popular request in tattoo parlors. Today its products are equally well known across the tattoo and necktie sets. The stunning popularity of its products has created a problem that most other companies envy. Though the Milwaukee-based company has more than doubled motorcycle production in the last six years, its major problem is meeting increases in customer demand. Many of its motorcycle models are sold out a year in advance. Harley has also dramatically expanded its riding and fashion apparel sales to bikers and nonbikers alike and even provides insurance and financing services for its dealers and customers.

# Harley-Davidson, Inc.

## FROM TURMOIL TO TRIUMPH AS A WORLD-CLASS MANUFACTURER

To close the gap between the supply and demand for its products, Harley-Davidson has opened a new engine plant near Milwaukee and a new assembly plant in Kansas City. However, increasing production quantities alone will not make this expansion successful. Harley must also continue to introduce new products to stay ahead of major competitors Honda, Yamaha, and BMW and control inventory quality and cost to maintain gross profit margin. As a result, the company also focuses on empowering, educating, and training both salaried and unionized employees to achieve personal growth, improvements in inventory quality, and reductions in the components of inventory cost: raw materials, labor, and overhead. Although Harley-Davidson does not manufacture the apparel it sells, it does work closely with apparel suppliers to maximize quality and minimize inventory costs. The provision of accurate and timely inventory accounting information is a key to many of these efforts. Furthermore, in a typical year, selection of appropriate accounting methods for inventory has a dramatic effect on the amount Harley-Davidson pays in income taxes. Continuous improvement in manufacturing and inventory management will be necessary for the Harley-Davidson eagle to continue its rise.

## BUSINESS BACKGROUND

Concerns about the cost and quality of inventory face all modern manufacturers and merchandisers and turn our attention to *cost of goods sold (cost of sales, cost of products sold)* on the income statement and *inventory* on the balance sheet. Exhibit 7.1 presents the relevant excerpts from Harley-Davidson's financial statements that present these accounts. Cost of goods sold is subtracted from net sales to produce gross profit on its multiple-step income statement. (The multiple-step format is discussed in Chapter 5.) Inventory is a current asset on the balance sheet; it is reported below cash and accounts receivable because it is less liquid than those two current assets.

EXHIBIT **7.1**

**Income Statement and Balance Sheet Excerpts**

**REAL WORLD EXCERPT**

*Harley-Davidson, Inc.*

ANNUAL REPORT

**HARLEY-DAVIDSON, INC.**
**CONSOLIDATED STATEMENTS OF OPERATIONS**
Years Ended December 31, 1998, 1997 and 1996
(in thousands, except per share amounts)

|  | 1998 | 1997 | 1996 |
|---|---|---|---|
| Net sales | $2,063,956 | $1,762,569 | $1,531,227 |
| Cost of goods sold | 1,373,286 | 1,176,352 | 1,041,133 |
| Gross profit | 690,670 | 586,217 | 490,094 |

**HARLEY-DAVIDSON, INC.**
**CONSOLIDATED BALANCE SHEETS**
December 31, 1998 and 1997
(in thousands, except share amounts)

| Assets | 1998 | 1997 |
|---|---|---|
| **Current assets:** | | |
| Cash and cash equivalents | $165,170 | $147,462 |
| Accounts receivable, net | 113,417 | 102,797 |
| Finance receivables, net | 360,341 | 293,329 |
| Inventories | 155,616 | 117,475 |
| Deferred income taxes | 29,076 | 24,941 |
| Prepaid expenses | 21,343 | 18,017 |
| Total current assets | 844,963 | 704,021 |

Harley-Davidson's successful expansion of production and management of cost of goods sold and inventory require a joint effort by human resource managers, engineers and production managers, marketing managers, and accounting and financial managers. It is truly a multidisciplinary task. The primary goals of inventory management are to have sufficient quantities of high-quality inventory available to serve customers' needs while minimizing the costs of carrying inventory (production, storage, obsolescence, financing, etc.). For example, purchasing or producing too *few* units of a hot-selling item causes stock-outs that mean lost sales revenue and decreases in customer satisfaction. Purchasing too *many* units of a slow-selling apparel item increases the storage costs and interest costs on short-term borrowings to finance the inventory purchases and may even lead to losses if the merchandise cannot be sold at normal prices. Low quality leads to customer dissatisfaction, returns, and a decline in future sales.

To meet these inventory management goals, marketing, financial, and production managers must work together to forecast customer demand for different motorcycle models or apparel items and provide feedback so that production or purchasing adjustments can be made. Production, human resource, and purchasing managers also must work to control the cost of goods sold to improve gross profit margin. Toward the end of the chapter, we discuss the way that faulty inventory purchasing decisions can even affect Harley's income tax liability. As a consequence, managers, investors, and financial analysts emphasize cost of goods sold and inventory because they are such important determinants of a company's success.

The accounting system plays three roles in the inventory management process. First, the system must provide accurate information necessary for preparation of periodic financial statements and reports to tax authorities.[1] Second, it must provide up-to-date information on inventory quantities and costs to facilitate ordering and manufacturing decisions. Third, since inventories are subject to theft and other forms of misuse, the system also must provide the information necessary to help protect these important assets. First we discuss the important choices management must make in the financial and tax reporting process. Then we will briefly discuss how accounting systems are organized to keep track of inventory quantities and costs for decision making and control. This topic will be the principal subject matter of your managerial accounting course.

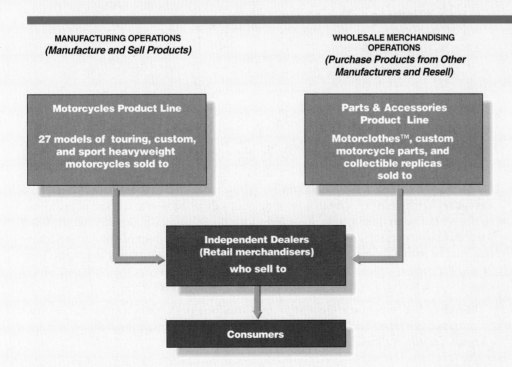

EXHIBIT **7.2**

**Harley-Davidson Motorcycle Division Product Lines**

Harley's successful production and inventory management strategy and its mix of product lines make it a particularly good example for this chapter. The organization of Harley-Davidson's Motorcycle Division is illustrated in Exhibit 7.2. Although best

---

[1]As we discuss later, tax reports often differ from the statements prepared for other external users.

known as a *manufacturer* of motorcycles, Harley also purchases and resells completed products such as its popular line of Motorclothes™ apparel. In the second case, it acts as a *wholesaler.* Both the motorcycle and Motorclothes™ product lines are sold to the public through a network of independent dealers who are the *retailers* for the products. From an accounting standpoint, these independent dealers are Harley-Davidson's customers. The inventory accounting problems faced by wholesalers and retailers (both often called *merchandisers*) are similar and are covered by discussing the Motorclothes™ line. The additional complexities that manufacturers face are discussed in the context of the motorcycle product line. We also will illustrate the application of these same inventory accounting principles to other companies that face different economic circumstances.

**ORGANIZATION** OF THE CHAPTER

| • Nature of Inventory and Costs of Goods Sold | • Inventory Costing Methods | • Keeping Track of Inventory Quantities and Costs |
|---|---|---|
| Items Included in Inventory | Applying the Four Methods | Perpetual and Periodic Inventory Systems |
| Inventory Flows | Choosing Inventory Costing Methods | Perpetual Inventory Records in Practice |
| Nature of Cost of Goods Sold | Inventory Costing Methods and Financial Statement Analysis | Methods for Estimating Inventory |
| Errors in Measuring Ending Inventory | Inventory Turnover Ratio | |
| | Valuation at Lower of Cost or Market | |

# NATURE OF INVENTORY AND COST OF GOODS SOLD

## ITEMS INCLUDED IN INVENTORY

**Inventory** is tangible property that (1) is held for sale in the normal course of business or (2) is used to produce goods or services for sale. Inventory is reported on the balance sheet as a current asset because it usually is used or converted into cash within one year or within the next operating cycle of the business, whichever is longer. The types of inventory normally held depend on the characteristics of the business. Merchandisers (wholesale or retail businesses) hold the following:

**Merchandise inventory** Goods (or merchandise) held for resale in the normal course of business. The goods usually are acquired in a finished condition and are ready for sale without further processing.

For Harley-Davidson, merchandise inventory includes the Motorclothes™ line and the other parts and accessories it purchases for sale to its independent dealers.

Manufacturing businesses hold the following:

**Raw materials inventory** Items acquired by purchase, growth (such as food products), or extraction (natural resources) for processing into finished goods. Such items are included in raw materials inventory until used, at which point they become part of work in process inventory.

**Work in process inventory** Goods in the process of being manufactured but not yet completed. When completed, work in process inventory becomes finished goods inventory.

**Finished goods inventory** Goods manufactured by the business, completed and ready for sale.

Inventories related to Harley-Davidson's motorcycle manufacturing operations are recorded in these accounts.

## INVENTORY COST

Goods in inventory are recorded in conformity with the *cost principle*. The primary basis of accounting for inventory is cash equivalent cost, which is the price paid or consideration given to acquire an asset. Inventory cost includes, in principle, the sum of the applicable expenditures and charges directly or indirectly incurred in bringing an article to usable or salable condition and location.

When Harley-Davidson purchases raw materials for the motorcycle line and merchandise inventory for the Motorclothes™ line, it follows similar accounting practices. Theoretically, the amount recorded for purchase of raw materials or merchandise should include the invoice price and indirect expenditures related to the purchase, such as freight charges to deliver the items to its warehouses (freight-in) and inspection and preparation costs. In general, the company should cease accumulating costs of purchases when the raw materials are *ready for use* or when the merchandise inventory is in a condition and location *ready for shipment* to the dealers. Any additional costs related to selling the merchandise inventory to the dealers, such as marketing department salaries and dealer training sessions, should be included in Selling, General, and Administrative Expenses of the period of sale to the dealers since they are incurred after the inventory is ready for use in the normal course of business.

FINANCIAL **ANALYSIS**

### APPLYING THE MATERIALITY CONSTRAINT IN PRACTICE

Incidental costs such as inspection and preparation costs often are not material in amount (see the discussion of the materiality constraint in Chapter 5) and do not have to be assigned to the inventory cost. Thus, for practical reasons, many companies use the invoice price, less returns and discounts, to assign a unit cost to raw materials or merchandise and record other indirect expenditures as a separate cost that is reported as an expense. Invoice price may or may not include transportation charges (freight-in) for shipment to the warehouse.

## INVENTORY FLOWS

The flow of inventory costs for merchandisers, both wholesalers and retailers, is relatively simple, as shown in Exhibit 7.3A. When merchandise is purchased, the merchandise inventory is increased. When the goods are sold, cost of goods sold is increased and the merchandise inventory is decreased.

The flow of inventory costs in a manufacturing environment is diagrammed in Exhibit 7.3B. For Harley-Davidson's motorcycle manufacturing operations, the flow of inventory costs is more complex. First *raw materials* (also called *direct materials*) must be purchased. These raw materials include steel and aluminum castings, forgings, sheet, and bars as well as certain motorcycle component parts including carburetors, batteries, and tires, which are produced by its small network of suppliers. When used, the cost of each material is removed from the raw materials inventory and added to the work in process inventory, along with two other components of manufacturing costs.

Direct labor and factory overhead costs also are added to the work in process inventory when incurred in the manufacturing process. **Direct labor** cost represents the earnings of employees who work directly on the products being manufactured. **Factory overhead** costs include all manufacturing costs that are not raw material or

EXHIBIT **7.3**

**Flow of Inventory Costs**

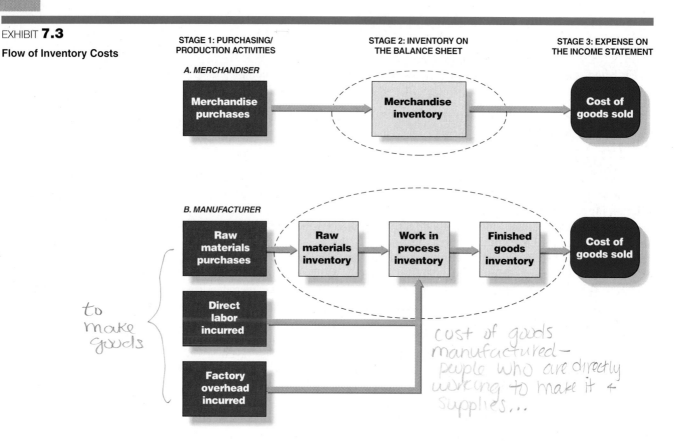

direct labor costs. For example, the salary of the factory supervisor and the cost of heat, light, and power to operate the factory are included in factory overhead. When the motorcycles are completed and ready for sale, the related amounts in work in process inventory are transferred to finished goods inventory. When the finished goods are sold, cost of goods sold is increased and the finished goods inventory is decreased.

Note in Exhibit 7.3 that for *both* merchandisers and manufacturers there are three stages to inventory cost flows. The first involves purchasing and/or production activities. In the second, these activities result in additions to inventory accounts on the balance sheet. At the third stage, the time of sale, these inventory amounts become cost of goods sold expense on the income statement.

Harley-Davidson's recent inventory note reports the following:

**REAL WORLD EXCERPT**

*Harley-Davidson, Inc.*

ANNUAL REPORT

**HARLEY-DAVIDSON, INC.**
**NOTES TO CONSOLIDATED FINANCIAL STATEMENTS**
2. ADDITIONAL BALANCE SHEET AND CASH FLOWS INFORMATION
(in thousands)

|  | December 31, | |
| --- | --- | --- |
|  | 1998 | 1997 |
| Inventories: | | |
| Components at the lower of FIFO cost or market: | | |
| Raw materials and work in process | $55,336 | $37,597 |
| Finished goods | 27,295 | 26,756 |
| Parts and accessories | 93,710 | 75,735* |

*These do not add up to the balance reported in Exhibit 7.1 because they do not include the LIFO adjustment discussed later.

Harley-Davidson combines the raw materials and work in process. Other companies separate these two components. The parts and accessories category includes purchased parts and Motorclothes™ and other accessories that make up merchandise inventory.

## FINANCIAL **ANALYSIS**

### MODERN MANUFACTURING TECHNIQUES AND INVENTORY COSTS

The flows of inventory costs diagrammed in Exhibit 7.3 represent the keys to manufacturing cost and quality control. Since the company must pay to finance and store raw materials and purchased parts, minimizing these inventories in keeping with projected manufacturing demand is the first key to the process. This requires that Harley-Davidson work closely with its suppliers in design, production, and delivery of manufactured parts and in planning raw materials deliveries; the related techniques often are called *just-in-time inventory.* Review and redesign of manufacturing operations and worker training and involvement programs are the keys to minimizing direct labor and factory overhead costs. New product designs often attempt to reduce manufacturing complexity, which leads to higher product quality and reduced scrap and rework costs. For example, at its Sportster assembly plant in York, Pennsylvania, three-person teams are responsible for assembly of a complete vehicle, a process that has resulted in both cost and quality improvements.

Harley-Davidson's management accounting system is designed to monitor the success of these changes and provide information to allow continuous improvements in these manufacturing efforts. Issues faced in the design of such systems are the subject matter of management accounting and cost accounting courses.

### NATURE OF COST OF GOODS SOLD

Cost of goods sold (CGS) is a major expense item for most nonservice businesses and is directly related to sales revenue. The amount of sales revenue during an accounting period is the number of units sold multiplied by the sales price. Cost of goods sold is the same number of units multiplied by their unit costs; it includes the cost of all merchandise and finished goods sold during the period. The measurement of cost of goods sold is an excellent example of the application of the matching principle.

The flow of inventory costs from merchandise inventory to cost of goods sold for the merchandiser and from finished goods inventory to cost of goods sold for the manufacturer involves similar processes. We focus on merchandise inventory to simplify the discussion.

Harley-Davidson starts each accounting period with a stock of inventory on hand called *beginning inventory* (BI) for sale to dealers. The merchandise and finished goods on hand at the end of an accounting period are called *ending inventory* (EI). The ending inventory for one accounting period automatically becomes the beginning inventory for the next period.

During the accounting period, the beginning inventory is increased by the purchase of more merchandise. The sum of the beginning inventory and the *purchases* of merchandise during the period (P) represents the **goods available for sale** during that period. The portion of goods available for sale that is sold becomes cost of goods sold on the income statement. Typically, not all of the goods available for sale are sold, so what remains becomes ending inventory on the balance sheet for the period. These relationships are represented visually in Exhibit 7.4

**GOODS AVAILABLE FOR SALE** refers to the sum of beginning inventory and purchases (or transfers to finished goods) for the period.

From these relationships, we can compute cost of goods sold as follows:

$$\underbrace{\begin{matrix}\text{Beginning}\\\text{Inventory}\end{matrix} + \begin{matrix}\text{Purchases of}\\\text{The Period}\end{matrix}}_{\begin{matrix}\text{Goods Available}\\\text{for Sale}\end{matrix}} - \underbrace{\begin{matrix}\text{Ending}\\\text{Inventory}\end{matrix}}_{\begin{matrix}\text{Goods}\\\text{Left Over}\end{matrix}} = \underbrace{\begin{matrix}\text{Cost of}\\\text{Goods Sold}\end{matrix}}_{\text{Goods Sold}}$$

Later in the chapter, this **cost of goods sold equation** serves as a basic tool for analyzing the effects of inventory errors and different accounting methods on the financial

**COST OF GOODS SOLD EQUATION:** BI + P − EI = CGS

EXHIBIT **7.4**

**Nature of Cost of Goods Sold for Merchandise Inventory**

\* Last period's ending inventory

statements. To illustrate the relationships represented by the equation for merchandise inventory, assume that for the Motorclothes™ line, Harley-Davidson began the period with $40,000 in beginning inventory, purchased additional merchandise during the period for $55,000, and had $35,000 in inventory at the end of the period. Using the inventory equation, we can determine that reported cost of goods sold would be $60,000, which was computed as follows:

| | |
|---|---:|
| Beginning inventory (January 1, 20F) | $40,000 |
| Add: Purchases of merchandise during 20F | +55,000 |
| Goods available for sale | $95,000 |
| Deduct: Ending inventory (December 31, 20F) | −35,000 |
| Cost of goods sold | $60,000 |

These same relationships can be represented in the merchandise inventory T-account as follows:

**Merchandise Inventory (A)**

| | | | | |
|---|---:|---|---|---:|
| Beginning inventory | $40,000 | | | |
| Add: Purchases of inventory | 55,000 | Deduct: Cost of goods sold | | 60,000 |
| Ending inventory | $35,000 | | | |

If three of these four values are known, either the equation or the inventory T-account can be used to solve for the fourth value. The process works similarly for finished goods inventory.

# FINANCIAL **ANALYSIS**

## GROSS PROFIT COMPARISONS

As we discussed in Chapter 6, gross profit percentage is calculated as Gross Profit ÷ Net Sales. Analysts use the gross margin percentage to compare similar companies and to compare the operations of the same company over time. Using similar companies for comparison is important because companies in different industries often have highly different gross margins. For example, until mid-1995, Harley-Davidson produced both motorcycles and motorhomes. Although they are related industries, the gross profit percentage on motorcycle sales was nearly twice as high as the gross profit percentage on motorhome sales. Because of the low margins, Harley-Davidson sold the motorhome division in 1995, which boosted the overall gross profit percentage. The importance of gross profit percentage to analysts is indicated by the fact that Harley's stock price rose from 26 7/8 to 31 1/2 the morning of the sale.

Expectation of an increasing gross profit percentage was a major factor determining Robinson-Humphrey analyst Dennis Van Zelfden's "long-term buy" recommendation on Harley-Davidson stock.* As production volume increases at Harley-Davidson's recently opened production facilities, he expects that certain components of manufacturing cost will decline and gross profit percentage will increase. This example illustrates how analysts can use accounting information to gain additional insight into the operations and competitiveness of a company.

*Dated February 12, 1999

## ERRORS IN MEASURING ENDING INVENTORY

As the cost of goods sold equation indicates, a direct relationship exists between ending inventory and cost of goods sold because items not in the ending inventory are assumed to have been sold. Thus, the measurement of ending inventory quantities and costs affects both the balance sheet (assets) and the income statement (cost of goods sold, gross profit, and net income). The measurement of ending inventory affects not only the net income for that period but also the net income for the *next accounting period*. This two-period effect occurs because the ending inventory for one period is the beginning inventory for the next accounting period.

*The Wall Street Journal*[2] recently reported that greeting card maker Gibson Greetings had overstated its current year profits by 20 percent because one division had overstated ending inventory for the year. You can compute the effects of the error on both the current year's and next year's pretax profits using the cost of goods sold equation. Assume that ending inventory is overstated by $10,000 due to a clerical error that is not discovered the next year. It would have the following effects:

**LEARNING OBJECTIVE 2**

Analyze the effects of inventory errors on financial statements.

### Current Year

$$\underset{\text{Inventory}}{\text{Beginning}} + \underset{\text{the Period}}{\text{Purchases of}} - \underset{\underset{\$10,000}{\text{Overstated}}}{\underset{\text{Inventory}}{\text{Ending}}} = \underset{\underset{\$10,000}{\text{Understated}}}{\underset{\text{Goods Sold}}{\text{Cost of}}}$$

Thus, income before taxes would be *overstated* by $10,000 in the *current year*. Since the current year's ending inventory becomes the next year's beginning inventory, it would have the following effects next year:

### Next Year

$$\underset{\underset{\$10,000}{\text{Overstated}}}{\underset{\text{Inventory}}{\text{Beginning}}} + \underset{\text{the Period}}{\text{Purchases of}} - \underset{\text{Inventory}}{\text{Ending}} = \underset{\underset{\$10,000}{\text{Overstated}}}{\underset{\text{Goods Sold}}{\text{Cost of}}}$$

Income before taxes would be *understated* by the same amount in the *next year*. Each of these errors would flow into retained earnings so that at the end of the current year, retained earnings would be overstated by $10,000 (less the related income tax expense). This error would be offset in the next year, and retained earnings and inventory at the end of next year would be correct.

---

[2] *The Wall Street Journal*, April 3, 1995, p. B5.

In this example, we assumed that the overstatement of ending inventory was inadvertent, the result of a clerical error. As we noted in Chapter 6, however, inventory fraud is one of the two most common forms of financial statement fraud. It occurred in the Maxidrive case discussed in Chapter 1 as well as in the real MiniScribe fraud. A similar fraud has been alleged at Nesmont, the Canadian gold refining and processing company as reported in the following article:

**REAL WORLD EXCERPT**

*Dow Jones News Service*

**SEC Sues Ex-Intl Nesmont Officers, Claiming Asset Inflation**

By Matthew Benjamin

WASHINGTON (Dow Jones)–The Securities and Exchange Commission filed a civil complaint Thursday against three former officers of International Nesmont Industrial Corp. (NESFE), accusing them of falsifying the company's financial results from 1992 through 1994.

Filed in federal court in New York, the suit alleges that the three engaged in a deliberate scheme to overstate income and inflate assets of the Canadian gold refining and processing company. Among their more creative schemes was a practice of passing off brass bars as gold in order to pump up inventory, the SEC said. They are also accused of creating phony documents and lying about earnings in press releases and documents filed with the SEC.

The defendants are Alexandra Montgomery, William Nestor and Frederick Burgess, all former executives at the Ladner, B.C., firm.

The company's shares rose significantly in 1994 on claims of soaring revenues and modest profits, but became almost worthless when the alleged inventory fraud was disclosed by new management and the stock was delisted from Nasdaq later that year. The stock is currently halted on the Vancouver exchange.

SOURCE: *Dow Jones News Service*, July 24, 1997.

## SELF-STUDY **QUIZ**

Assume the following facts for Harley-Davidson's Motorclothes™ leather baseball jacket product line for the year 20F:

Beginning inventory 500 units at unit cost of $75.

Ending inventory 600 units at unit cost of $75.

Sales 1,100 units at a sales price of $100 (cost per unit $75).

1. Using the cost of goods sold equation, compute the dollar amount of purchases of leather baseball jackets for the period.

$$\text{Beginning Inventory} + \text{Purchases of the Period} - \text{Ending Inventory} = \text{Cost of Goods Sold}$$

2. Prepare the first three lines of a multiple-step income statement (showing gross profit) for the leather baseball jacket line for the year 20F.

After you have completed your answers, check them with the solutions presented in the footnote at the bottom of this page.*

---

*1. BI = 500 × $75 = $37,500          BI + P − EI = CGS

EI = 600 × $75 = $45,000          37,500 + P − 45,000 = 82,500

CGS = 1,100 × $75 = $82,500                    P = 90,000

2.  Net sales                    $110,000

Cost of goods sold            82,500

Gross profit              $ 27,500

# INVENTORY COSTING METHODS

In the Motorclothes™ example presented in the self-study quiz, the cost of all units of the leather baseball jackets was the same—$75. If inventory costs normally do not change, this would be the end of our discussion of inventory costs. We are all aware, however, that the prices of most goods often change. The costs of many manufactured items such as automobiles and motorcycles have risen in recent years, but only at a moderate rate. In other industries, such as computers, however, costs of production (and retail prices) have dropped dramatically.

When inventory costs have changed, the determination of which inventory items to treat as sold and which as still remaining in ending inventory can turn profits into losses (and vice versa) and cause companies to pay or save hundreds of millions of dollars in taxes. Before we examine these complexities, we will use a simple example to discuss the mechanics of each accepted method for determining which goods to treat as sold. We will then look at which methods Harley-Davidson and other companies use and discuss the bases for their choices. Do not let the simplicity of our example mislead you. As you will see, the results of this example generalize broadly to actual company practices. The example is based on the following data.

New Company began operations on January 1, 20A. The following events took place during 20A:

| | | |
|---|---|---|
| Jan. | 15 | Purchased 1 unit of product A at $1. |
| April | 2 | Purchased 1 unit of product A at $3. |
| June | 27 | Purchased 1 unit of product A at $5. |
| Nov. | 5 | Sold 2 units for $7 each. |

Note that inventory costs are rising rapidly! On November 5, two units are sold for $7 each; revenues of $14 are recorded. What amount is recorded as cost of goods sold? The answer depends on which specific goods are assumed sold. Four generally accepted inventory costing methods are available for doing so:

1. First-in, first-out (FIFO).
2. Last-in, first-out (LIFO).
3. Weighted average.
4. Specific identification.

## APPLYING THE FOUR METHODS

The four inventory costing methods are *alternative allocation methods* for assigning the total dollar amount of goods available for sale (beginning inventory and purchases) between (1) ending inventory (reported as an asset at the end of the period) and (2) cost of goods sold (reported as an expense of the period). It is important to note at this point that the choice among the four inventory costing methods is *not based on the physical flow* of goods on and off the shelves. For example, the actual physical flow of goods at a supermarket is first-in, first-out (FIFO). A supermarket can use LIFO or any of the inventory costing methods, however, to report cost of goods sold and inventory in its financial statements. Generally accepted accounting principles (GAAP) require only that the inventory costing method used be rational and systematic. Since the inventory costing methods need not follow the actual physical flow of inventory, they are often called *cost flow assumptions.*

A useful visual learning tool for representing inventory cost flows is a bin, or container. The different inventory costing methods then can be visualized as flows of inventory in and out of the various bins. We use this concept to illustrate inventory flow throughout the following sections. Also, following practice, we apply the methods here (and in the end-of-chapter materials) *as if* all purchases during an accounting period take place before any sales and cost of goods sold are recorded. We discuss the importance of this assumption in more detail in Chapter Supplement A.

■ **LEARNING OBJECTIVE 3**

Report inventory and cost of goods sold using the four inventory costing methods.

The **FIRST-IN, FIRST-OUT (FIFO) METHOD** assumes that the oldest units (the first costs in) are the first units sold.

**First-In, First-Out Inventory Costing Method** The **first-in, first-out method,** frequently called **FIFO,** assumes that the oldest units (the first costs in) are the first units sold (the first costs out) and the newest units are left in ending inventory. Under FIFO, cost of goods sold and ending inventory are computed as if the flows in and out of the FIFO inventory bin in Exhibit 7.5 had taken place. First, each purchase is treated as if it were deposited in the bin from the top in sequence (one unit each at $1, $3, and $5). Each good sold is then removed from the *bottom* in sequence (one unit at $1 and one at $3); *first in is first out.* These goods totaling $4 become cost of goods sold (CGS). The remaining unit ($5) becomes ending inventory. These financial statement effects for a fictional company, New Company, are summarized in Exhibit 7.5. If any goods were in beginning inventory, they would be treated as if they were sold first. Then the units from the first purchase are sold next, and so on until the units left in the ending inventory all come from the most recent purchases. FIFO allocates the *oldest* unit costs to *cost of goods sold* and the *most recent* unit costs to the *ending inventory.*

EXHIBIT **7.5**

**FIFO and LIFO Inventory Flows—New Company, Year 1**

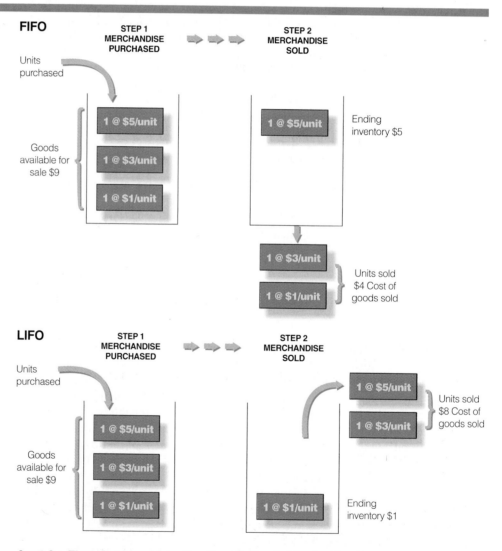

The **LAST-IN, FIRST-OUT (LIFO) METHOD** assumes that the most recently acquired units are sold first.

**Last-In, First-Out Inventory Costing Method** The **last-in, first-out method,** often called **LIFO,** assumes that the most recently acquired goods are sold first and the oldest units are left in ending inventory. This method can be visualized as involving a LIFO inventory bin such as that presented in Exhibit 7.5. As in the case of the FIFO bin, each purchase is treated as if it were deposited in the bin from the top in sequence ($1, $3, $5). Unlike the FIFO case, however, each good sold is then removed from the top in sequence ($5, $3). These goods totaling $8 become cost of goods sold (CGS). The remaining unit ($1) becomes ending inventory.

If any goods were in beginning inventory, they would be treated as if they were sold last. The units from the last purchase are always sold first, and so on until the units left in the ending inventory all come from the oldest purchases. Therefore, the unit costs of the beginning inventory and the earlier purchases remain in the ending inventory. LIFO allocates the *most recent* unit costs to *cost of goods sold* and the *oldest* unit costs to the *ending inventory.* The LIFO flow assumption is the exact opposite of the FIFO flow assumption. These relationships are summarized here:

|  | FIFO | LIFO |
|---|---|---|
| Cost of goods sold on income statement | Oldest unit costs | Most recent unit costs |
| Inventory on balance sheet | Most recent unit costs | Oldest unit costs |

**Weighted Average Inventory Costing Method**     The **weighted average method** requires computation of the weighted average unit cost of the goods available for sale.[3] The computed unit cost is multiplied by the number of units in inventory to derive the total cost of ending inventory. Cost of goods sold is determined by subtracting the ending inventory amount from the amount of goods available for sale. For the New Company data, the weighted average cost is computed as follows:

> The **WEIGHTED AVERAGE METHOD** uses the weighted average unit cost of the goods available for sale for both cost of goods sold and ending inventory.

$$\textbf{Number of Units} \times \textbf{Unit Cost} = \textbf{Total Cost}$$

| Number of Units | × | Unit Cost | = | Total Cost |
|---|---|---|---|---|
| 1 | × | $1 | = | $1 |
| 1 | × | $3 | = | 3 |
| 1 | × | $5 | = | 5 |
| 3 | | | | $9 |

$$\textbf{Average Cost} = \frac{\textbf{Cost of Goods Available for Sale}}{\textbf{Number of Units Available for Sale}}$$

$$\textbf{Average Cost} = \frac{\$9}{3 \textbf{ Units}} = \$3 \textbf{ per Unit}$$

In these circumstances, cost of goods sold and ending inventory are assigned the same weighted average cost per unit of $3. Cost of goods sold is $6 for two units sold, and ending inventory is $3 for one unit. These financial statement effects are summarized in Exhibit 7.6.

**Specific Identification Inventory Costing Method**     When the **specific identification method** is used, the cost of each item sold is individually identified and recorded as cost of goods sold. This method requires keeping track of the purchase cost of each item. This is done by either (1) coding the purchase cost on each unit before placing it in stock or (2) keeping a separate record of the unit and identifying it with a serial number. In the New Company example, any two of the items could have been sold. If we assume that the first and third items have been sold, the cost of those two items ($1 + $5) would become cost of goods sold ($6). The cost of the remaining item ($3) would be ending inventory.

> The **SPECIFIC IDENTIFICATION METHOD** identifies the cost of the specific item that was sold.

Given the way in which some inventory accounting systems are organized (discussed later in this chapter), the specific identification method is impractical when large numbers of different items are stocked. On the other hand, when dealing with expensive items such as automobiles or fine jewelry, this method is appropriate because each item tends to differ from the other items. The method may be manipulated when the units are *identical* because one can affect the cost of goods sold and the ending inventory accounts by picking and choosing from among the several available unit costs, even though the goods are identical in other respects.

---

[3]A weighted average unit cost rather than a simple average of the unit costs must be used. In most cases a simple average is incorrect because it does not consider the number of units at each unit cost. For example, if one unit were purchased at $1, one unit at $3, and two units at $5, the average cost is $3.50 ([$1 + $3 + $5 + $5] / 4 units).

EXHIBIT **7.6**

**Financial Statement Effects of Inventory Costing Methods**

| Cost of Goods Sold Calculation | FIFO | LIFO | Weighted Average |
|---|---|---|---|
| Beginning inventory | $ 0 | $ 0 | $ 0 |
| Add: Purchases | 9 | 9 | 9 |
| Goods available for sale | 9 | 9 | 9 |
| Deduct: Ending inventory (to balance sheet) | 5 | 1 | 3 |
| Cost of goods sold (to income statement) | $4 | $ 8 | $ 6 |
| | | | |
| **Effect on the Income Statement** | | | |
| Sales | $14 | $14 | $14 |
| Cost of goods sold | 4 | 8 | 6 |
| Gross profit | $10 | $ 6 | $ 8 |
| | | | |
| **Effect on the Balance Sheet** | | | |
| Inventory | $ 5 | $ 1 | $ 3 |

# INTERNATIONAL **PERSPECTIVE**

*Asahi Chemical Industry Co., Ltd.*

## DIFFERENT METHODS FOR DIFFERENT TYPES OF INVENTORY

Asahi Chemical Industry Co., Ltd., is a major Japanese manufacturer of chemicals, plastics, fibers and textiles, and housing and construction materials. Most of its inventories are accounted for using average cost, which is very common in Japan. In addition, its housing and construction materials division constructs and sells homes. It accounts for both residential lots and dwellings under construction, which are expensive, distinguishable items, by using specific identification.

**Comparison of the Inventory Costing Methods**   Each of the four alternative inventory costing methods is in conformity with GAAP and the tax law. Each method may produce significantly different income and asset (ending inventory) amounts, however. To illustrate this difference, the comparative results for New Company using FIFO, LIFO, and weighted average are presented in Exhibit 7.6. Notice that the difference in the *gross margin* among each of the methods is the same as the difference in the *ending inventory* amounts. The method that gives the highest ending inventory amount also gives the highest gross margin and income amounts and vice versa. The weighted average cost method gives income and inventory amounts that are between the FIFO and LIFO extremes.

Note that in the comparison in Exhibit 7.6, unit costs were increasing. When unit costs are *rising, LIFO* produces *lower income* and a *lower inventory valuation* than FIFO. Even though we may be experiencing general inflation, some companies' costs decline. When unit costs are *declining, LIFO* produces *higher income* and *higher inventory* valuation than FIFO. These effects, *which hold as long as inventory quantities are constant or rising,*[4] are summarized in the following table:

| Normal Financial Statement Effects of Rising Costs | | |
|---|---|---|
| | FIFO | LIFO |
| Cost of goods sold on income statement | Lower | Higher |
| Net income | Higher | Lower |
| Inventory on balance sheet | Higher | Lower |

---

[4]The impact of a decline in inventory quantity on LIFO amounts is discussed in Supplement A to this chapter.

| Normal Financial Statement Effects of Declining Costs | | |
|---|---|---|
| | FIFO | LIFO |
| Cost of goods sold on income statement | Higher | Lower |
| Net income | Lower | Higher |
| Inventory on balance sheet | Lower | Higher |

These effects occur because LIFO causes the new unit costs to be reflected in cost of goods sold on the income statement, which is a realistic measurement of the current cost of items that were sold; FIFO causes the older unit costs to be reflected in cost of goods sold on the income statement. In contrast, on the balance sheet, the ending inventory amount under LIFO is based on the oldest unit costs, which may be an unrealistic valuation, whereas FIFO ending inventory is a realistic measurement of their current cost.

Again, it is important to remember that regardless of the physical flow of goods, a company can use any of the inventory costing methods. Furthermore, a company is not required to use the same inventory costing method for all inventory items, and no particular justification is needed for the selection of one or more of the acceptable methods. Harley-Davidson, Asahi Chemical (discussed earlier), and most large companies use different inventory methods for different inventory items.

To enhance comparability, accounting rules require companies to apply their accounting methods on a consistent basis. A company is not permitted to use LIFO one period, FIFO the next, and then go back to LIFO. A change in method is allowed only if the change will improve the measurement of financial results and financial position. Changing from one inventory costing method to another is a significant event. Such a change requires full disclosure about the reason for the change and the accounting effects.

## CHOOSING INVENTORY COSTING METHODS

*Accounting Trends & Techniques* reported that although 326 (54 percent) of the 600 companies surveyed reported using LIFO for some portion of inventories, only 17 (3 percent) use LIFO for all inventories.[5] This raises an important question: What motivates companies to choose different inventory costing methods? Our discussion in Chapter 5 suggests that management should choose the method allowed by GAAP that most closely reflects its economic circumstances for its external financial statements (book purposes). Management must also make a second choice of accounting method to use on its tax return (tax purposes). The choice from among the acceptable methods for use on the company's tax return should be the one that allows payment of the least amount of taxes as late as possible—the "least-latest rule."

A business typically may use one set of accounting procedures for external financial statements and a different set of procedures for preparing its tax return. The choice of inventory costing methods is a special case, however, because of what is called the *LIFO conformity rule.* If LIFO is used on the income tax return, it must also be used to calculate inventory and cost of goods sold for the financial statements.[6] Since LIFO often minimizes taxes, the LIFO conformity rule leads many companies to adopt LIFO for *both* tax and financial reporting purposes. For most companies facing rising costs of inventory, LIFO is used for U.S. inventories. For inventory located in countries that do not allow LIFO for tax purposes or that do not have a LIFO conformity rule, FIFO or weighted average is mostly used. Similarly, when costs are falling, FIFO or weighted average is most often used. Since most companies in the same industry face similar cost structures, clusters of companies in the same industries often choose the same accounting method.

■ **LEARNING OBJECTIVE 4**

Decide when the use of different inventory costing methods is beneficial to a company.

---

[5]*Accounting Trends & Techniques* (New York: AICPA, 1998).

[6]Note that LIFO can be used for financial statement purposes along with FIFO or weighted average for tax purposes. However, this is rarely done.

# INTERNATIONAL **PERSPECTIVE**

## LIFO AND INTERNATIONAL COMPARISONS

The methods of accounting for inventories discussed in this chapter are used in most major industrialized countries. In several countries, however, the LIFO method is not generally used. In England, for example, LIFO is not acceptable for tax purposes, nor is it widely used in financial reporting. LIFO is also not used in Australia and Hong Kong but may be used in Singapore only if the difference between LIFO and FIFO is reported. These differences can create comparability problems when one attempts to compare companies across international borders. For example, General Motors and Ford use LIFO to value U.S. inventories and average cost or FIFO for non-U.S. inventories, while Honda (of Japan) uses FIFO.

The income tax effects associated with LIFO and FIFO for companies facing rising costs can be illustrated by continuing our simple New Company example. Using the data from Exhibit 7.6 and assuming that expenses other than cost of goods sold were $2 and the tax rate was 25 percent, the following differences in taxes result:

| Inventory Costing Method | | |
|---|---|---|
| | FIFO | LIFO |
| Sales revenue | $14 | $14 |
| Cost of goods sold | 4 | 8 |
| Gross profit | $10 | $ 6 |
| Other expenses | 2 | 2 |
| Pretax income | $ 8 | $ 4 |
| Income tax expense (0.25 × Pretax Income) | 2 | 1 |
| Net income | $ 6 | $ 3 |

In this situation, cost of goods sold and pretax income differed by $4, which was caused by the differences between the FIFO and LIFO methods. Costs were rising, and a significant difference existed between the old and new unit costs. When multiplied by the 25 percent income tax rate, the $4 difference in pretax income generates cash tax savings of $1. It is important to remember that this choice is independent of the actual physical flow of goods. This example illustrates the primary motivations for the choice of LIFO. In an inflationary world, most companies face cost increases. In the United States, the tax benefit in such circumstances plus the LIFO conformity rule explain the widespread use of the method.

This simple example illustrates the computations necessary to determine the tax savings but may not indicate the magnitude of the effect often faced in practice. Harley-Davidson is a fairly typical "mixed" LIFO company. The $155.6 million in inventory reported in Exhibit 7.1 included U.S. inventories of $111.9 million at LIFO. It has saved a total of approximately $7.7 million in taxes from the date it adopted the LIFO method through 1998. This is a significant benefit to Harley. It does not use LIFO for its non–U.S. motorcycle inventory either because LIFO is not acceptable for tax purposes or no LIFO conformity rule exists in those countries.

# A QUESTION OF **ETHICS**

## LIFO AND CONFLICTS BETWEEN MANAGERS' AND OWNERS' INTERESTS

As discussed earlier in this chapter, the selection of an inventory method can have significant effects on financial statements. Company managers may have incentives to select a particular method that may not be consistent with the objectives of the owners. For example, the use of LIFO during a period of rising prices may be in the best interests of the owners because LIFO often reduces the company's tax liability. On the other hand, managers may prefer FIFO because it typically results in higher profits, and the compensation of most managers is affected by reported profits.

A well-designed compensation plan should reward managers for acting in the best interests of the owners, but unfortunately, this is not always the case. Clearly, a manager who selects an accounting method that is not optimal for the company solely to increase his or her compensation has engaged in questionable ethical behavior.

In theory, LIFO cannot provide permanent tax savings because (1) when inventory levels drop or (2) costs drop, the income effect reverses and the income taxes deferred must be paid. The economic advantage of deferring income taxes in such situations is due to the fact that interest can be earned on the money that otherwise would be paid as taxes for the current year. Much of this amount is postponed for a very long period, however, and some is never paid because of accumulated losses preceding the end of the company's life.

Alternatively, many high-technology companies are facing declining costs. In such circumstances, the FIFO method, in which the oldest, most expensive goods become cost of goods sold, produces the largest cost of goods sold, the lowest gross profit, and thus the lowest income tax liability. For example, Apple Computer and Compaq Computer account for inventories at FIFO.

## SELF-STUDY **QUIZ**

Assume that a company began operations this year. Its purchases for the year included:

| | |
|---|---|
| Purchases January | 10 units @ $ 6 each |
| Purchases May | 5 units @ $10 each |
| Purchases November | 5 units @ $12 each |

During the year, 15 units were sold for $20 each and other operating expenses totaled $100.

1. Compute cost of goods sold and pretax income for the year under FIFO and LIFO accounting methods.

2. Which method would you recommend that the company adopt? Why?

After you have completed your answers, check them with the solutions presented in the footnote at the bottom of this page*

---

*1.

| | FIFO | LIFO |
|---|---|---|
| Sales revenue (15 × $20) | $300 | $300 |
| Cost of goods sold | 110 | 140 |
| Gross profit | 190 | 160 |
| Other expenses | 100 | 100 |
| Pretax income | 90 | 60 |

FIFO cost of goods sold = (10 × $6) + (5 × $10) = $110

LIFO cost of goods sold = (5 × $12) + (5 × $10) + (5 × $6) = $140

2. LIFO would be recommended because it produces lower pretax income and lower taxes.

## INVENTORY COSTING METHODS AND FINANCIAL STATEMENT ANALYSIS

Critics of GAAP charge that the existence of alternative accounting methods is inconsistent with the *comparability* characteristic of useful information. This quality is needed so that analysts can compare information for a company with that of other companies for the same time period. These types of comparisons are more difficult if companies use different accounting methods, since one company's statements must be converted to a comparable basis *before* meaningful comparisons can be made. However, careful readers of this text will be able to make many of the necessary adjustments.

Converting cost of goods sold and income before taxes from one inventory costing method to another is eased by the requirement that U.S. public companies using LIFO also report beginning and ending inventory on a FIFO, average cost, or related method basis in the notes if the LIFO and FIFO values are materially different. We can use this information along with the cost of goods sold equation to convert cost of goods sold and income before taxes to the FIFO basis. This process is similar to the manner in which we corrected errors in inventory earlier in this chapter. Recall the cost of goods sold equation:

$$\begin{matrix} \text{Beginning} \\ \text{Inventory} \end{matrix} + \begin{matrix} \text{Purchases of} \\ \text{the Period} \end{matrix} - \begin{matrix} \text{Ending} \\ \text{Inventory} \end{matrix} = \begin{matrix} \text{Cost of} \\ \text{Goods Sold} \end{matrix}$$

Recall also that the choice of a cost flow assumption affects how goods available for sale are allocated to ending inventory and cost of goods sold. It does not affect the recording of purchases. Ending inventory is affected, and, since last year's ending inventory is this year's beginning inventory, beginning inventory is also affected by the choice of a cost flow assumption. As a consequence, we can compute the effects of the *difference* in cost flow assumptions on cost of goods sold in the following manner:

$$\begin{matrix} \text{Difference in} \\ \text{Beginning Inventory} \end{matrix} - \begin{matrix} \text{Difference in} \\ \text{Ending Inventory} \end{matrix} = \begin{matrix} \text{Difference in Cost} \\ \text{of Goods Sold} \end{matrix}$$

| |
|---|
| Difference in Beginning Inventory (Excess of FIFO over LIFO) |
| Less: Difference in Ending Inventory (Excess of FIFO over LIFO) |
| Difference in Cost of Goods Sold (Excess of FIFO over LIFO) |

Harley-Davidson's 1997 annual report provides a typical disclosure of the differences between LIFO and FIFO values for beginning and ending inventory. The difference between its inventory valued using FIFO and LIFO is labeled "Excess of FIFO over LIFO inventory" and is often referred to as the **LIFO reserve.** Consequently, the preceding computation can also be thought of as

**LIFO RESERVE** is a contra-asset for the excess of FIFO over LIFO inventory.

| |
|---|
| Beginning LIFO Reserve (Excess of FIFO over LIFO) |
| Less: Ending LIFO Reserve (Excess of FIFO over LIFO) |
| Difference in Cost of Goods Sold (Excess of FIFO over LIFO) |

Companies that use a LIFO reserve keep their Inventory account during the accounting period using FIFO (or possibly average cost). At the end of the year, they convert the balances in inventory and cost of goods sold to LIFO through an adjusting entry to the LIFO Reserve, which is a contra-asset to the Inventory account. The approach taken is very similar to that used when adjusting the Allowance for Doubtful Accounts employing the aging method (discussed in Chapter 6).

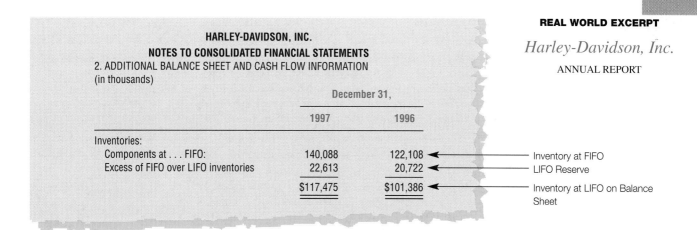

**HARLEY-DAVIDSON, INC.**
**NOTES TO CONSOLIDATED FINANCIAL STATEMENTS**
2. ADDITIONAL BALANCE SHEET AND CASH FLOW INFORMATION
(in thousands)

| | December 31, | |
| --- | --- | --- |
| | 1997 | 1996 |
| Inventories: | | |
| Components at . . . FIFO: | 140,088 | 122,108 |
| Excess of FIFO over LIFO inventories | 22,613 | 20,722 |
| | $117,475 | $101,386 |

Inventory at FIFO
LIFO Reserve
Inventory at LIFO on Balance Sheet

The LIFO Reserve (Excess of FIFO over LIFO inventories) provides the needed information for the conversion. Using our formula, we can compute the difference in cost of goods sold for the current year when we convert from LIFO to FIFO (a *decrease* of $1,891).

| | |
| --- | --- |
| Beginning LIFO Reserve (Excess of FIFO over LIFO) | $20,722 |
| Less: Ending LIFO Reserve (Excess of FIFO over LIFO) | 22,613 |
| Difference in Cost of Goods Sold (LIFO to FIFO) | $ (1,891) |

Since cost of goods sold decreases pretax income, the conversion's effect on pretax income is the opposite—an *increase* of $1,891. To compute the tax savings (postponement) from using LIFO instead of FIFO for the current year, multiply this increase by Harley's 37 percent total income tax rate, which yields approximately $700.

| | |
| --- | --- |
| Difference in pretax income (LIFO to FIFO) | $1,891 |
| Tax rate | × .37 |
| Difference in taxes (LIFO to FIFO) | $ 700 |

These Harley-Davidson computations are for 1997. It is important to note that even companies that usually face increasing costs occasionally face decreasing costs. For example, during 1998, Harley-Davidson's costs of new inventory declined. Consequently, when we convert from LIFO to FIFO, the difference in cost of goods sold for 1998 is actually an *increase* of $1,888, and the conversion's effect on pretax income is the opposite—a *decrease* of $1,888. As a result, even though LIFO usually *saves* it taxes, Harley paid $699 *extra* in taxes in 1998 (0.37 × $1,888). [7]

Users of financial statements must be certain that their decisions are based on real differences, not artificial differences created by alternative accounting methods. As a result, users must be knowledgeable about alternative accounting methods and how they affect statements. Remember that the choice of inventory costing method does not affect the physical attributes or economic value of the inventory.

---

[7] It is important to note that, even for companies that always face rising costs, LIFO does not lead to a reduction in pretax income and taxes in every year. When ending inventory quantities are lower than beginning inventory quantities (that is, the company sells more than it buys or produces), LIFO actually boosts pretax income and taxes. This situation, called a *LIFO liquidation,* is discussed in more detail in Chapter Supplement A.

## SELF-STUDY **QUIZ**

*Caterpillar Inc.*

1. In a recent year, Caterpillar Inc., a major manufacturer of farm and construction equipment, reported pretax earnings of $1,615 million. Its inventory note indicated "if the FIFO (first-in, first-out) method had been in use, inventories would have been $2,103 and $2,035 higher than reported at the end of the current and prior year, respectively." (The amounts noted are for the LIFO Reserve.) Convert pretax earnings for the current year from a LIFO to a FIFO basis.

> Beginning LIFO Reserve (Excess of FIFO over LIFO)  _____
>
> Less: Ending LIFO Reserve (Excess of FIFO over LIFO)  _____
>
> Difference in cost of goods sold (LIFO to FIFO)  _____
>
> Pretax income (LIFO)  _____
>
> Difference in pretax income (LIFO to FIFO)  _____
>
> Pretax income (FIFO)  _____

After you have completed your answers, check them with the solutions presented in the footnote at the bottom of this page.*

## KEY **RATIO ANALYSIS:**

■ **LEARNING OBJECTIVE 5**

Analyze and interpret the inventory turnover ratio and the effects of inventories on cash flows.

### INVENTORY TURNOVER

**K**now the decision question:

How efficient are inventory management activities? It is computed as follows:

$$\text{Inventory Turnover} = \frac{\text{Cost of Goods Sold}}{\text{Average Inventory*}}$$

*Average Inventory = (Beginning Inventory + Ending Inventory) ÷ 2

The 1998 inventory turnover ratio for Harley-Davidson:

$$\frac{\$1,373,286}{(\$117,475 + \$155,616) \div 2} = 10.1$$

**E**xamine the ratio using two techniques:

| ① Comparisons over Time | | | | ② Comparisons with Competitors | |
|---|---|---|---|---|---|
| **Harley-Davidson** | | | | **Titan Motorcycle** | **Honda Motor** |
| 1996 | 1997 | 1998 | | 1998 | 1998 |
| 11.2 | 10.7 | 10.1 | | 2.6 | 7.0 |

**Y**ou interpret the results carefully:

**IN GENERAL** → The inventory turnover ratio reflects how many times average inventory was produced and sold during the period. A higher ratio indicates that inventory moves more quickly through the production process to the ultimate customer. This benefits the company because it incurs lower storage and potential obsolescence costs. It also means that less money is tied up in inventory; the excess can be invested, earning interest income or used to reduce borrowings, reducing interest expense. More efficient purchasing and production techniques such as just-in-time inventory, as well as high product demand cause this ratio to be high. Inefficient purchasing and production techniques and declining product demand cause this ratio to be low. Analysts

---

| * 1. | Beginning LIFO Reserve | $2,035 | Pretax income (LIFO) | $1,615 |
|---|---|---|---|---|
|  | Less: Ending LIFO Reserve | 2,103 | Difference in pretax income | 68 |
|  | Difference in cost of goods sold | ($68) | Pretax income (FIFO) | $1,683 |

and creditors watch this ratio because a sudden decline in the ratio may mean that a company is facing an unexpected decline in demand for its products or is becoming sloppy in its production management. Many managers and analysts compute the related number *average days to sell inventory,* which is equal to 365 ÷ inventory turnover ratio, or 36.1 days for Harley-Davidson. It indicates the average time it takes the company to produce and deliver inventory to customers.

**FOCUS COMPANY ANALYSIS** → Harley-Davidson's inventory turnover has declined from a 1996 high of 11.2 to 10.1 in 1998. This is the result of opening two new plants that will not operate at full capacity until mid 1999. As we will see shortly, this decrease in inventory turnover also results in a decrease in cash flow from operations. However, Harley's ratio is much higher than its smaller U.S. rival (Titan) whose operations are much less efficient. Harley-Davidson benefits from what economists call "economies of scale." Harley's is even higher than the ratio of giant Japanese auto and motorcycle manufacturer Honda. At the beginning of the chapter, we discussed key elements of Harley's expansion strategy. According to analyst Dennis Van Zelfden at Robinson-Humphrey, more efficient management of inventory and productive capacity at the new production plants will be critical to its success.

**A FEW CAUTIONS:** Differences across industries in purchasing, production, and sales processes cause dramatic differences in the ratio. For example, restaurants such as Papa John's, which must turn over their perishable inventory very quickly, tend to have much higher inventory turnover. A particular firm's ratio should be compared only with its prior years' figures or with other firms in the same industry.

| **Selected Focus Company Inventory Turnover** | |
|---|---|
| Callaway Golf | 4.1 |
| Wal-Mart | 6.5 |
| Papa John's | 35.0 |

## FINANCIAL **ANALYSIS**

### LIFO AND INVENTORY TURNOVER RATIO

For many LIFO companies, the inventory turnover ratio can be deceptive. Remember that, for these companies, the beginning and ending inventory numbers that make up the denominator of the ratio will be artificially small because they reflect old lower costs. Consider Deere & Co., manufacturer of John Deere farm, lawn, and construction equipment. Its inventory note lists the following values:

**REAL WORLD EXCERPT**

*Deere & Company*

ANNUAL REPORT

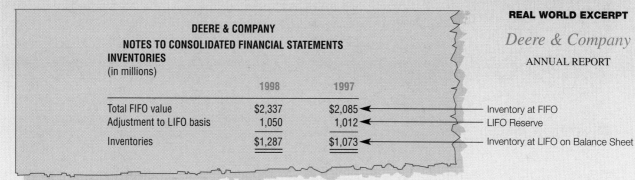

| **DEERE & COMPANY**<br>NOTES TO CONSOLIDATED FINANCIAL STATEMENTS<br>**INVENTORIES**<br>(in millions) | | | |
|---|---|---|---|
| | 1998 | 1997 | |
| Total FIFO value | $2,337 | $2,085 | Inventory at FIFO |
| Adjustment to LIFO basis | 1,050 | 1,012 | LIFO Reserve |
| Inventories | $1,287 | $1,073 | Inventory at LIFO on Balance Sheet |

John Deere's cost of goods sold for 1998 was $9,233.7 million. If the ratio is computed using the reported LIFO inventory values for the ratio, it would be

$$\text{Inventory Turnover Ratio} = \frac{\$9,233.7}{(\$1,287 + \$1,073) \div 2} = 7.8$$

Converting cost of goods sold in the numerator to a FIFO basis and using the more current FIFO inventory values in the denominator, it would be

$$\text{Inventory Turnover Ratio} = \frac{\$9,233.7 - 38}{(\$2,337 + \$2,085) \div 2} = 4.2$$

Note that the major difference is in the denominator. FIFO inventory values are nearly two times the LIFO values; the ratio is about one-half the LIFO amount. The LIFO beginning and ending inventory numbers are artificially small because they reflect old lower costs. Thus, the numerator in the first calculation does not relate in a meaningful way to the denominator. *

*Since the LIFO values for cost of goods sold on the income statement and the FIFO inventory numbers on the balance sheet are closer to current prices, they are often thought to be the most appropriate numerator and denominator, respectively, for use in this ratio.

# FOCUS ON **CASH FLOWS**

## INVENTORY

As with the change in accounts receivable, the change in inventories can be a major determinant of a company's cash flow from operations. The income statement reflects the cost of goods sold during the period whereas the cash flow statement should reflect the cash payments to suppliers for the same period. Cost of goods sold may be more or less than the amount of cash paid to suppliers during the period. Since most inventory is purchased on open credit (the borrowing from a supplier is normally called *accounts payable*), reconciling cost of goods sold with cash paid to suppliers requires consideration of the changes in both the Inventory and Accounts Payable accounts.

The simplest way to think about the effects of changes in inventory is that buying (increasing) inventory eventually decreases cash, and selling (decreasing) inventory eventually increases cash. Similarly, borrowing from suppliers, which increases accounts payable, increases cash; paying suppliers, which decreases accounts payable, decreases cash.

### EFFECT ON STATEMENT OF CASH FLOWS

**IN GENERAL** → When a net *decrease in inventory* for the period occurs, sales are more than purchases; thus, the decrease must be *added* in computing cash flows from operations.

When a net *increase in inventory* for the period occurs, sales are less than purchases; thus, the increase must be *subtracted* in computing cash flows from operations.

When a net decrease in *accounts payable* for the period occurs, payments to suppliers are more than new purchases; thus, the decrease must be *subtracted* in computing cash flows from operations.

When a net increase in *accounts payable* for the period occurs, payments to suppliers are less than new purchases; thus, the increase must be *added* in computing cash flows from operations.

| | Effect on Cash Flows |
|---|---|
| **Operating activities** (indirect method) | |
| Net income | $xxx |
| Adjusted for | |
| *Add* inventory *decrease* | + |
| or | |
| *Subtract* inventory *increase* | − |
| *Add* accounts payable *increase* | + |
| or | |
| *Subtract* accounts payable *decrease* | − |

**Selected Focus Company Comparisons: 3-Year Change in Cash Flows Related to Inventory Changes (in millions)**

| | |
|---|---|
| Timberland | +48.4 |
| Wal-Mart | −645.0 |
| Callaway Golf | −15.6 |

**FOCUS COMPANY ANALYSIS** → Exhibit 7.7 is the Operating Activities section segment of Harley-Davidson's statement of cash flows. When the inventory balance increases during the period, as was the case at Harley-Davidson in 1997 and 1998, the company purchased or produced more inventory than it sold during the period. Thus, the increase is subtracted in the computation of cash flow from operations. When the accounts payable balance increased during these periods, the company borrowed more from its suppliers than it paid back during the period. Thus, the increase is added in the computation of cash flow from operations.*

When sales rise quickly, as they have at Harley-Davidson over the past three years, inventories usually rise, decreasing cash flow from operations. However, the highlighted section of Exhibit 7.7 indicates that increases in borrowing from suppliers have offset that amount.

**CONSOLIDATED STATEMENTS OF CASH FLOWS**
**Years Ended December 31, 1998 and 1997**
**(in thousands)**

| | 1998 | 1997 |
|---|---|---|
| Cash flows from operating activities: | | |
| Net income | $213,500 | $174,070 |
| Adjustments to reconcile net income to net cash provided by operating activities: | | |
| Depreciation and amortization | 87,422 | 70,178 |
| Provision for credit losses | 10,338 | 6,547 |
| Deferred income taxes | 1,190 | 2,748 |
| Long-term employee benefits | 5,302 | 1,275 |
| Equity in net (income) loss of joint ventures | (27) | 1,290 |
| Other | 3,207 | 476 |
| Net changes in other current assets and current liabilities: | | |
| Accounts receivable | (8,606) | 38,518 |
| Inventories | (33,888) | (16,089) |
| Prepaid expenses | (3,295) | 125 |
| Accounts payable and accrued liabilities | 42,919 | 30,597 |
| Total adjustments | 104,562 | 135,665 |
| Net cash provided by operating activities | 318,062 | 309,735 |

EXHIBIT **7.7**

**Inventories on the Cash Flow Statement**

**REAL WORLD EXCERPT**

*Harley-Davidson, Inc.*

ANNUAL REPORT

*For companies with foreign currency or business acquisitions/dispositions, the amount of the change reported on the cash flow statement will not equal the change in the accounts reported on the balance sheet.

SELF-STUDY **QUIZ**

1. The Key Ratio Analysis for Harley-Davidson's inventory turnover was presented earlier in the chapter. Based on the computations for 1998, answer the following question. If Harley-Davidson had been able to manage its inventory more efficiently and *decrease* purchases and ending inventory by $10,000, would its inventory turnover ratio increase or decrease? Explain.

_____

_____

_____

2. Based on the Focus on Cash Flows section of the chapter, answer the following question. If Harley-Davidson had been able to manage its inventory more efficiently and *decrease* ending inventory, would its cash flow from operations increase or decrease?

_____

_____

After you have completed your answers, check them with the solutions presented in the footnote at the bottom of this page.*

## VALUATION AT LOWER OF COST OR MARKET

**LEARNING OBJECTIVE 6**

Report inventory at the lower of cost or market (LCM).

Inventories should be measured at their purchase cost in conformity with the cost principle. When the goods remaining in ending inventory can be replaced with identical goods at a lower cost, however, the lower cost should be used as the inventory valuation. Damaged, obsolete, and deteriorated items in inventory should be assigned a unit cost that represents their current estimated net realizable value if that is below cost. This rule is known as measuring inventories at the **lower of cost or market (LCM).**

**LOWER OF COST OR MARKET (LCM)** is a valuation method departing from the cost principle; it serves to recognize a loss when replacement cost or net realizable value drops below cost.

LCM is a departure from the cost principle because of the conservatism constraint (see Chapter 5) that requires special care to avoid overstating assets and income. It is particularly important for two types of companies: (1) high-technology companies such as Compaq Computer that manufacture goods for which the cost of production and the selling price are declining and (2) companies such as American Eagle Outfitters that sell seasonal goods such as clothing, the value of which drops dramatically at the end of each selling season (fall or spring).

**REPLACEMENT COST** is the current purchase price for identical goods.

For companies such as Compaq Computer, under LCM, a "holding" loss is recognized in the period in which the **replacement cost** of an item dropped rather than in the period in which the item is sold. The holding loss is the difference between purchase cost and the subsequent lower replacement cost and is added to the cost of goods sold of the period. To illustrate, assume that Compaq Computer had the following in the 20B ending inventory:

| Item | Quantity | Cost per Item | Replacement Cost (Market) per Item | Lower of Cost or Market per Item | Total Lower of Cost or Market |
|------|----------|---------------|-----------------------------------|----------------------------------|-------------------------------|
| Pentium chips | 1,000 | $250 | $200 | $200 | 1,000 × $200 = $200,000 |
| Disk drives | 400 | 100 | 110 | 100 | 400 × $100 = 40,000 |

The 1,000 Pentium chips should be recorded in the ending inventory at the current market ($200) that is lower than the cost ($250). Compaq makes the following journal entry to record the write-down:

| Cost of goods sold (E) (1,000 × $50) . . . . . . . . . | 50,000 | |
| Inventory* (A) . . . . . . . . . . . . . . . . . . . . . . . | | 50,000 |

| Assets | = | Liabilities | + | Stockholders' Equity | |
|--------|---|-------------|---|----------------------|---|
| Inventory    −50,000 | | | | Cost of Goods Sold | −50,000 |

*Some companies credit a contra-asset to inventory called a *reserve,* which is adjusted at the end of each accounting period.

---

*1. Inventory turnover will increase because the denominator of the ratio will decrease by $5,000.

$$\frac{\$1,373,286}{(\$145,616 + \$117,475) \div 2} = 10.4$$

2. A decrease in inventory would increase cash flow from operations. (See the Focus on Cash Flows section of the chapter.)

Since the cost of the disk drives ($100) is below market ($110), no write-down is necessary. They remain on the books at their cost of $100 per unit ($40,000 in total).

Several effects are caused by the write-down of the Pentium chips.

| Effects of LCM Write-Down | Current Period (20B) | Period of Sale (20C) |
|---|---|---|
| Cost of goods sold | Increase $50,000 | Decrease $50,000 |
| Pretax income | Decrease $50,000 | Increase $50,000 |
| Ending inventory on balance sheet | Decrease $50,000 | Unaffected |

First, LCM transfers the added expense from the period of sale (20C) back to the current period (20B). Consequently, pretax income is reduced by $50,000 in the period in which the replacement cost dropped (20B) rather than in the next period (20C) when the chips will be used in the production of computers and sold. Since the cost of goods sold for period 20B *increases* by $50,000 and the cost of goods sold for 20C *decreases* by $50,000, the total cost of goods sold expense (and net income before taxes) for the two periods (20B and 20C) combined does not change. Second, on the balance sheet, the $50,000 loss in 20B reduces the amount of inventory reported on December 31, 20B.

In contrast, the replacement cost of the disk drives has increased to $110 each; there is an economic holding gain. Recognition of holding gains is not permitted by GAAP except for certain marketable securities discussed in Chapter 12.

In the case of seasonal goods such as clothing, obsolete goods, or damaged goods, if the sales price less selling costs (or **net realizable value**) drops below cost, this difference is subtracted from ending inventory and added to cost of goods sold of the period. This has the same effect on current and future periods' financial statements as the write-down to replacement cost.

Under generally accepted accounting principles in the United States, the lower-of-cost-or-market rule can be applied to inventories the cost of which is determined using any of the four acceptable inventory costing methods. Note that in the two note examples that follow, both Harley-Davidson, which is a mixed LIFO company, and Compaq Computer, which is a FIFO company, report the use of lower of cost or market for financial statement purposes. For tax purposes, the lower-of-cost-or-market calculations may be applied with all inventory costing methods except LIFO.

**NET REALIZABLE VALUE** is the expected sales price less selling costs (e.g., repair and disposal costs).

---

**HARLEY-DAVIDSON, INC.**

**NOTES TO CONSOLIDATED FINANCIAL STATEMENTS**
**1. SUMMARY OF SIGNIFICANT ACCOUNTING POLICIES**
INVENTORIES - Inventories are valued at the lower of cost or market. Substantially all inventories located in the United States are valued using the last-in, first-out (LIFO) method. Other inventories totaling $43.7 million in 1998 and $33.3 million in 1997, are valued at the lower of cost or market using the first-in, first-out (FIFO) method.

**REAL WORLD EXCERPT**

*Harley-Davidson, Inc.*
ANNUAL REPORT

---

**COMPAQ COMPUTER**
**NOTES TO CONSOLIDATED FINANCIAL STATEMENTS**
**NOTE 1—DESCRIPTION OF BUSINESS AND SIGNIFICANT ACCOUNTING POLICIES:**
Inventories—Inventories are stated at the lower of cost or market, cost being determined on a first-in, first-out basis.

**REAL WORLD EXCERPT**

*Compaq Computer*
ANNUAL REPORT

# KEEPING TRACK OF INVENTORY QUANTITIES AND COSTS

To compute cost of goods sold, three amounts must be known: (1) beginning inventory, (2) purchases of merchandise (or transfers to finished goods) during the period, and (3) ending inventory. To simplify the discussion of how accounting systems keep track of these amounts, we will focus this discussion on the Motorclothes™ line for which Harley-Davidson is a wholesaler. Although the same general principles apply, the more complex details of manufacturing accounting systems are discussed in management accounting and cost accounting courses.

As noted earlier, the beginning inventory of one accounting period is the ending inventory of the previous period. The amount of purchases for the period is always accumulated in the accounting system. The amount of the ending inventory can be determined by using one of two different inventory systems: perpetual or periodic.

## PERPETUAL AND PERIODIC INVENTORY SYSTEMS

**Perpetual Inventory System**  A **perpetual inventory system** involves the maintenance of up-to-date inventory records in the accounting system during the period. For each type of merchandise stocked, a detailed record is maintained that shows (1) units and cost of the beginning inventory, (2) units and cost of each purchase, (3) units and cost of the goods for each sale, and (4) the units and cost of the goods on hand at any point in time. This up-to-date record is maintained on a transaction-by-transaction basis throughout the period. In a complete perpetual inventory system, the inventory record gives both the amount of ending inventory and the cost of goods sold amount at any point in time. Under this system, a physical count must be performed from time to time to ensure that records are accurate in case errors or theft of inventory occur.

This system typically involves a computer system. Whether the accounting system is manual or computerized, the data that are recorded and reported are the same. The maintenance of a separate inventory record for each type of good stocked on a transaction-by-transaction basis usually is necessary for purchasing, manufacturing, and distribution decisions. A company such as Harley-Davidson relies heavily on this system and even shares some of this information electronically with its suppliers.

All journal entries for purchase and sale transactions discussed in the text to this point have been recorded using a perpetual inventory system. In a perpetual inventory system, purchase transactions are directly recorded in an inventory account. In addition, when each sale is recorded, a companion cost of goods sold entry is made, decreasing inventory and recording cost of goods sold. As a result, information on cost of goods sold and ending inventory is available on a continuous (perpetual) basis.

**Periodic Inventory System**  Under the **periodic inventory system,** no up-to-date record of inventory is maintained during the year. An actual physical count of the goods remaining on hand is required at the *end of each period*. The number of units of each type of merchandise on hand is multiplied by their unit cost to compute the dollar amount of the ending inventory. Cost of goods sold is calculated using the cost of goods sold equation as follows:

$$\text{Beginning Inventory} + \text{Purchases of the Period} - \text{Ending Inventory} = \text{Cost of Goods Sold}$$

Thus, the amount of inventory is not known until the end of the period when the inventory count is taken. The amount of cost of goods sold cannot be determined reliably until the inventory count is completed. All of our discussions in this chapter of inventory errors and the application of different cost flow assumptions (FIFO, LIFO, etc.) have assumed a periodic system (all purchases for the period were recorded before any costs of goods sold were recorded).

Inventory purchases are debited to a temporary account called Purchases. Revenues are recorded at the time of each sale. However, cost of goods sold is not recorded until after the inventory count is completed. At other times, companies using a periodic system must estimate the amount of inventory on hand. We briefly discuss the estimation of inventory amounts later in the chapter.

Before affordable computers and bar code readers were available, the primary reason for using the periodic inventory system was its low cost. The primary disadvantage of a periodic inventory system is the lack of inventory information. Managers are not provided with any information concerning low stock or overstocked situations. Most modern companies could not survive without this information. As noted at the beginning of the chapter, cost and quality pressures brought on by increasing competition, combined with dramatic declines in the cost of computers, have made sophisticated perpetual inventory systems a minimum requirement at all but the smallest companies.

**Comparison of Perpetual and Periodic Systems** The differences between the perpetual and periodic inventory systems can be summarized using the basic inventory equation:

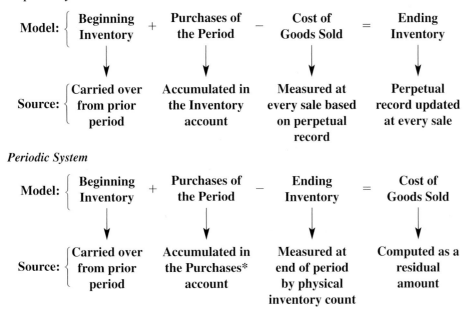

*Perpetual System*

| Model: | Beginning Inventory | + | Purchases of the Period | − | Cost of Goods Sold | = | Ending Inventory |
|---|---|---|---|---|---|---|---|
| Source: | Carried over from prior period | | Accumulated in the Inventory account | | Measured at every sale based on perpetual record | | Perpetual record updated at every sale |

*Periodic System*

| Model: | Beginning Inventory | + | Purchases of the Period | − | Ending Inventory | = | Cost of Goods Sold |
|---|---|---|---|---|---|---|---|
| Source: | Carried over from prior period | | Accumulated in the Purchases* account | | Measured at end of period by physical inventory count | | Computed as a residual amount |

*Purchases is a temporary account (T) closed to cost of goods sold at the end of the period.

Assume, for this illustration only, that Harley-Davidson stocks and sells only one item, its Eagle Harness Boots, and that only the following events occur in 20F:

Jan.    1  Beginning inventory: 800 units, at unit cost of $50.
April  14  Purchased: 1,100 additional units, at unit cost of $50.
Nov.  30  Sold: 1,300 units, at unit sales price of $83.

In the two types of inventory systems, the following sequential steps would take place as follows:

| Perpetual Records | Periodic Records |
|---|---|
| 1. Record all purchases in the *Inventory* account and in a detailed perpetual inventory record.<br>April 14, 20F:<br><br>Inventory (A) (1,100 units at $50)* ........ 55,000<br>    Accounts payable (L) (or Cash) .......     55,000<br><br>*Also entered in the detailed perpetual inventory record as 1,100 harness boots at $50 each. | 1. Record all purchases in an account called *Purchases*.<br>April 14, 20F:<br><br>Purchases[8] (T) (1,100 units at $50) ........ 55,000<br>    Accounts payable (L) (or Cash) .......     55,000 |
| 2. Record all sales in the Sales Revenue account and record the cost of goods sold.<br>November 30, 20F:<br><br>Accounts receivable (A) (or Cash) ........ 107,900<br>    Sales revenue (R) (1,300 units at $83) ...     107,900<br>Cost of goods sold (E) ................. 65,000<br>    Inventory (A) (1,300 units at $50)* .....     65,000<br><br>*Also entered in the perpetual inventory record as a reduction of 1,300 units at $50 each. | 2. Record all sales in a Sales Revenue account.<br>November 30, 20F:<br><br>Accounts receivable (A) (or Cash) ........ 107,900<br>    Sales revenue (R) (1,300 units at $83) ...     107,900 |
| 3. Use cost of goods sold and inventory amounts. At the end of the accounting period, the balance in the Cost of Goods Sold account is the amount of that expense reported on the income statement. It is not necessary to compute cost of goods sold because, under the perpetual inventory system, the Cost of Goods Sold account is up-to-date. Also, the Inventory account shows the ending inventory amount reported on the balance sheet. The sum of all the inventory balances in the various perpetual inventory records should equal the balance in the Inventory account in the ledger at any point in time. A physical inventory count is still necessary to assess the accuracy of the perpetual records and assess theft and other forms of misuse (called *shrinkage*).<br><br>No entry | 3. At end of period:<br>  *a.* Count the number of units on hand.<br>  *b.* Compute the dollar valuation of the ending inventory.<br>  *c.* Compute and record the cost of goods sold.<br><br>Beginning inventory (last period's ending)     $40,000<br>Add purchases (balance in the Purchases account)   55,000<br>Goods available for sale     $95,000<br>Deduct ending inventory<br>  (physical count—600 units at $50)     $30,000<br>Cost of goods sold     $65,000<br><br>December 31, 20F:<br>Transfer beginning inventory and purchases (GAS) to cost of goods sold:<br><br>Cost of goods sold (E) ................. 95,000<br>    Inventory (A) (beginning) ...........     40,000<br>    Purchases (T) .....................     55,000<br><br>Subtract the ending inventory amount from the cost of goods sold to complete its computation and establish the ending inventory balance:<br><br>Inventory (A) (ending) ................ 30,000<br>    Cost of goods sold (E) ..............     30,000 |

Note that the effects of the entries on the accounting equation are the same under both systems. Only the timing of the recording of amounts changes.

## PERPETUAL INVENTORY RECORDS IN PRACTICE

The decision to use a perpetual versus a periodic inventory system is based primarily on management's need for timely information for use in operating decisions and on the cost of the perpetual system. Further, the specific manner in which the perpetual system is designed will also be determined with these trade-offs in mind. Many inventory-ordering and production decisions require only exact information on inventory

[8]Purchases is a temporary account (T) closed to cost of goods sold at the end of the period.

quantities, not costs, which provides the information necessary for efficient management of inventory, providing delivery information to dealers, and quality control.

Systems that do keep track of the costs of individual items or lots normally do so on a FIFO or estimated average (or standard) cost basis, or for distinguishable high-value items using specific identification. Perpetual records are rarely kept on a LIFO basis for two reasons: (1) it is more complex and costly to do so and (2) doing so often causes LIFO liquidations, which can increase tax payments. The conversion to LIFO is made as an adjusting entry.

## METHODS FOR ESTIMATING INVENTORY

When a periodic inventory system is used and detailed perpetual inventory records are not kept, cost of goods sold and the amount of ending inventory can be directly computed only when a physical inventory count is taken. Because taking a physical inventory is expensive, it is normally done only once each year. In these circumstances, managers who wish to prepare monthly or quarterly financial statements for internal use often estimate the cost of goods sold and ending inventory using the *gross profit method*. The gross margin method uses the historical gross profit percentage (introduced in Chapter 6) to estimate cost of goods sold.

For example, we noted that Harley-Davidson's historical gross profit percentage on motorcycles was approximately 33.5 percent. If it sold $100,000,000 of motorcycles in January, it would estimate cost of goods sold to be $66,500,000 ($100,000,000 × [100% − 33.5%]) for the month. If Harley keeps track of purchases and other additions to inventory, it could then use the cost of goods sold equation to solve for an estimate of ending inventory. Retailers often take their physical inventory counts based on the retail price instead of cost and then use a similar method (called the *retail method*) to estimate cost. [9]

# DEMONSTRATION **CASE A**

(Complete the requirements before proceeding to the suggested solution that follows.)

Metal Products, Incorporated, has been operating for three years as a distributor of a line of metal products. It is now the end of 20C, and for the first time, the company will undergo an audit by an independent CPA. The company uses a *periodic* inventory system. The annual income statements (note which column is the current year) prepared by the company are as follows:

| | For the Year Ended December 31 | | | |
|---|---|---|---|---|
| | **20B** | | **20C** | |
| Sales revenue | | $750,000 | | $800,000 |
| Cost of goods sold | | | | |
| Beginning inventory | $ 45,000 | | $ 40,000 | |
| Add purchases | 460,000 | | 484,000 | |
| Goods available for sale | 505,000 | | 524,000 | |
| Less ending inventory | 40,000 | | 60,000 | |
| Cost of goods sold | | 465,000 | | 464,000 |
| Gross margin on sales | | 285,000 | | 336,000 |
| Operating expenses | | 275,000 | | 306,000 |
| Pretax income | | 10,000 | | 30,000 |
| Income tax expense (20%) | | 2,000 | | 6,000 |
| Net income | | $ 8,000 | | $ 24,000 |

During the early stages of the audit, the independent CPA discovered that the ending inventory for 20B was understated by $15,000.

---

[9]Methods for estimating inventory and cost of goods sold are discussed in detail in intermediate accounting texts and courses.

*Required:*

1. Based on the preceding income statement amounts, compute the gross profit percentage on sales for each year. Do the results suggest an inventory error? Explain.
2. Correct and reconstruct the two income statements.
3. Answer the following questions:
   a. What are the correct gross profit percentages?
   b. What effect did the $15,000 understatement of the ending inventory have on 20B pretax income? Explain.
   c. What effect did the inventory error have on the 20C pretax income? Explain.
   d. How did the inventory error affect income tax expense?

## SUGGESTED SOLUTION

1. Gross profit percentages as reported:
   20B: $285,000 ÷ $750,000 = 0.38
   20C: $336,000 ÷ $800,000 = 0.42
   The change in the gross profit percentage from 0.38 to 0.42 suggests the possibility of an inventory error in the absence of any other explanation.
2. Income statements corrected:

| | For the Year Ended December 31 | | | |
| --- | --- | --- | --- | --- |
| | **20B** | | **20C** | |
| Sales revenue | | $750,000 | | $800,000 |
| Cost of goods sold | | | | |
|   Beginning inventory | $ 45,000 | | $ 55,000* | |
|   Add purchases | 460,000 | | 484,000 | |
|     Goods available for sale | 505,000 | | 539,000 | |
|   Less ending inventory | 55,000* | | 60,000 | |
|     Cost of goods sold | | 450,000 | | 479,000 |
| Gross margin on sales | | 300,000 | | 321,000 |
| Operating expenses | | 275,000 | | 306,000 |
| Pretax income | | 25,000 | | 15,000 |
|   Income tax expense (20%) | | 5,000 | | 3,000 |
| Net income | | $ 20,000 | | $ 12,000 |

*Increased by $15,000.

3. a. Correct gross profit percentages:
   20B: $300,000 ÷ $750,000 = 0.400
   20C: $321,000 ÷ $800,000 = 0.401
   The inventory error of $15,000 was responsible for the difference in the gross profit percentages reflected in requirement (1). The error in the 20B ending inventory affected gross margin for both 20B and 20C—in the opposite direction but by the same amount, $15,000.

   b. Effect on pretax income in 20B: Ending inventory *understatement* ($15,000) caused an *understatement* of pretax income by the same amount.

   c. Effect on pretax income in 20C: Beginning inventory *understatement* (by the same $15,000 since the inventory amount is carried over from the prior period) caused an *overstatement* of pretax income by the same amount.

   d. Total income tax expense for 20B and 20C combined was the same ($8,000) regardless of the error. However, there was a shift of $3,000 ($15,000 × 20%) income tax expense from 20B to 20C.

**OBSERVATION** An ending inventory error in one year affects pretax income by the amount of the error and in the next year affects pretax income again by the same amount but in the opposite direction.

# DEMONSTRATION **CASE B**

(Complete the requirements before proceeding to the suggested solution that follows.)

This case reviews the application of the LIFO inventory costing method and the inventory turnover ratio.

Balent Appliances distributes a number of high-cost household appliances. One product, microwave ovens, has been selected for case purposes. Assume that the following summarized transactions were completed during the accounting period in the order given (assume that all transactions are cash):

|  | Units | Unit Cost |
|---|---|---|
| a. Beginning inventory | 11 | $200 |
| b. New inventory purchases | 9 | 220 |
| c. Sales (selling price, $420) | 8 | ? |

*Required:*

1. Compute the following amounts, assuming the application of the LIFO inventory costing method:

|  | Ending Inventory | | Cost of Goods Sold | |
|---|---|---|---|---|
|  | Units | Dollars | Units | Dollars |
| LIFO (costed at end of period) |  |  |  |  |

2. Compute the inventory turnover ratio for the current period. What does it indicate?

## SUGGESTED SOLUTION

1.

|  | Ending Inventory | | Cost of Goods Sold | |
|---|---|---|---|---|
|  | Units | Dollars | Units | Dollars |
| LIFO (costed at end of period) | 12 | $2,420 | 8 | $1,760 |

**Computations**

Goods Available for Sale = Beginning Inventory + (Purchases − Purchase Returns)
= (11 units × $200 = $2,200) + (9 units × $220 = $1,980)
= $4,180

**LIFO inventory (costed at end of period)**

Ending inventory: (11 units × $200 = $2,200) + (1 unit × $220 = $220) = $2,420.
Cost of goods sold: (Goods available, $4,180) − (Ending inventory, $2,420) = $1,760.

2. Inventory turnover ratio = Cost of Goods Sold ÷ Average Inventory
= $1,760 ÷ [($2,200+$2,420)÷2=$2,310]
= 0.76

The inventory turnover ratio reflects how many times average inventory was produced and sold during the period. Thus, Balent Appliances produced and sold its average inventory less than one time during the year.

## Chapter Supplement A

### LIFO Liquidations

A **LIFO LIQUIDATION** is a sale of a lower-cost inventory item from beginning LIFO inventory.

When a LIFO company sells more inventory than it purchases or manufactures, items from beginning inventory become part of cost of goods sold. This is called a **LIFO liquidation.** For companies facing rising inventory costs, these items in beginning inventory have lower costs, which produces a higher gross margin when they are sold. (People often call items purchased at the same price *LIFO layers.*) We illustrate this process by continuing our simple New Company example into its second year.

In its first year of operation, units were purchased for $1, $3, and $5 in sequence, and the $5 and $3 units were sold under LIFO, leaving the $1 unit in ending inventory. These events were represented using a LIFO inventory bin in Exhibit 7.5. We continue this illustration in Exhibit 7.8. The ending inventory from year 1 becomes the beginning inventory for year 2. In part a of the exhibit, we assume that in year 2, New Company purchased a total of *three* inventory units at the current $6 price before year-end, the sales price has been raised to $8, and three units are sold. Using LIFO, the three recently purchased $6 inventory items become part of cost of goods sold of $18, and the old $1 item from beginning inventory becomes ending inventory. Given that revenue is $8 per unit, the gross margin on the three newly purchased units is 3 units × $2 = $6.

Now assume instead, as we do in part b of Exhibit 7.8, that New Company purchased only *two* additional units at $6 each. Using LIFO, these two new $6 units and the old $1 unit would become cost of goods sold. Given that revenue is $8 per unit, the gross margin on the newly purchased units is 2 units × $2 = $4. Since the cost of the old unit is only $1, the gross margin on this one unit is $7 ($8 − $1) instead of $2, raising total gross profit to $11. This calculation is presented in Exhibit 7.8 part b.

Compared to part a, cost of goods sold decreases by $5 to $13, and gross profit and income before taxes increase by $5. This $5 change is the *pretax effect of the LIFO liquidation,* which took place in part b. Given the assumed tax rate of 25 percent, taxes paid are $1.25 (0.25 × $5) higher in this second situation.

In part a, the LIFO liquidation and extra tax payment are avoided even if the third purchase takes place *after* the sale of the third item because the tax law allows LIFO to be applied *as if* all purchases during an accounting period take place before any sales and cost of goods sold are recorded. Because of this feature, temporary LIFO liquidations can be eliminated by purchasing additional inventory before year-end. Most companies apply LIFO in this manner.

EXHIBIT **7.8**

**Inventory Flows—
New Company, Year 2**

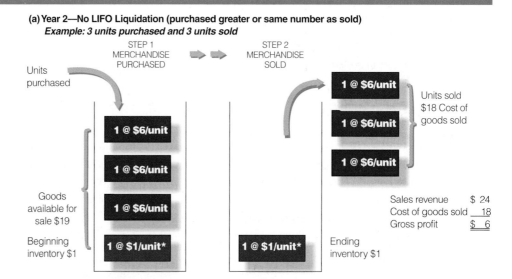

**(a) Year 2—No LIFO Liquidation (purchased greater or same number as sold)**
*Example: 3 units purchased and 3 units sold*

**(b) Year 2—LIFO Liquidation (purchased fewer than sold)**
*Example: 2 units purchased and 3 units sold*

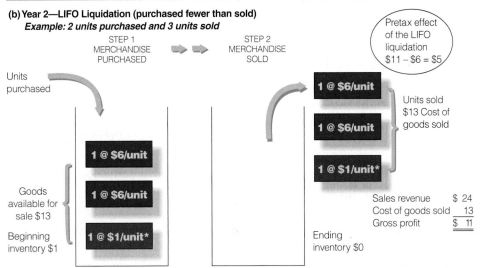

EXHIBIT **7.8**

(continued)

\* Beginning inventory = Ending inventory from year 1.

## LIFO LIQUIDATIONS AND FINANCIAL STATEMENT ANALYSIS

During the decade prior to 1993, Deere & Company and other companies in its industry faced declining demand and increasing competition in most major segments of their business. This reduced the inventory quantities necessary to meet customers' needs. Deere had also instituted modern manufacturing techniques that further decreased inventory levels. Deere, a long-time LIFO user, experienced continuing LIFO liquidations over this period. Companies must disclose the effects of LIFO liquidations in the notes when they are material, as Deere did in the note that follows. The second paragraph of the note explains the effect. The last sentence lists the pretax (after-tax) effects of the liquidations.

> **REAL WORLD EXCERPT**
>
> *Deere & Company*
>
> ANNUAL REPORT

**DEERE & COMPANY**
**NOTES TO CONSOLIDATED FINANCIAL STATEMENTS**

**INVENTORIES**

Substantially all inventories owned by Deere & Company and its United States equipment subsidiaries are valued at cost on the "last-in, first-out" (LIFO) method. . . .

Under the LIFO inventory method, cost of goods sold ordinarily reflects current production costs thus providing a matching of current costs and current revenues in the income statement. However when LIFO–valued inventories decline, as they did in 1993 and 1992, lower costs that prevailed in prior years are matched against current year revenues, resulting in higher reported net income. Benefits from the reduction of LIFO inventories totaled $51 million ($33 million or $.43 per share after income taxes) in 1993, $65 million ($43 million or $0.56 per share after income taxes) in 1992 and $128 million ($84 million or $1.11 per share after income taxes) in 1991.

Over the prior three years, LIFO liquidations have increased Deere's reported income before taxes by a total of $244 million ($51 + $65 + $128). (These numbers are the equivalent of the $5 effect of the liquidation computed in the New Company example.) To compute pretax income as if the liquidations had not taken place (as if current year's production were large enough so that no items from beginning inventory were sold), simply subtract the LIFO liquidation effect from pretax income.

| | |
|---|---|
| Pretax income on LIFO for 3 years (reported on the income statements) | $290 |
| Less: Pretax effect of LIFO liquidations (from note) | 244 |
| Pretax income on LIFO for 3 years basis as if no liquidations | $ 46 |

Fully 84 percent ($244 ÷ $290) of Deere's reported pretax profit over the three years is the result of LIFO liquidations. Since the $46 million pretax profit figure reflects Deere's current costs of production, educated analysts use this figure when comparing Deere's performance to that of other LIFO companies. It is important to emphasize that these numbers still are on a *LIFO* basis but are prepared *as if no liquidation took place.*

## FINANCIAL **ANALYSIS**

### INVENTORY MANAGEMENT AND LIFO LIQUIDATIONS

Several research studies have documented the year-end inventory purchasing decisions of firms that use LIFO. Many firms avoid LIFO liquidations and the accompanying increase in tax expense by purchasing sufficient quantities of inventory at year-end to ensure that ending inventory quantities are greater than or equal to beginning inventory quantities. While this practice increases the costs of carrying inventory (storage, financing, etc.), for these firms, the taxes saved exceed these amounts.

As noted earlier in the chapter, Harley-Davidson and many other firms have moved to more efficient just-in-time inventory techniques that greatly reduce the amount of inventory manufacturers keep on hand. When managers compare the savings in carrying costs against the costs of implementing the new system (new computers, training, etc.), they must also consider the added taxes they may pay if they account for the inventory using the LIFO method. When the company switches to the new just-in-time system, ending inventory quantity will normally decline below beginning inventory quantity, causing a LIFO liquidation and a one-time increase in taxes. This cost should be considered when deciding whether to adopt the new system. In this case the tax law provides an incentive for U.S. companies not to become more efficient.

SOURCE: M. Frankel and R. Trezevant, "The Year-End LIFO Inventory Purchasing Decision: An Empirical Test," *The Accounting Review* (April 1994), pp. 382–98.

## Chapter Supplement B

### Additional Issues in Measuring Purchases

#### PURCHASE RETURNS AND ALLOWANCES

Goods purchased may be returned to the vendor if they do not meet specifications, arrive in damaged condition, or otherwise are unsatisfactory. When the goods are returned or when the vendor makes an allowance because of the circumstances, the effect on the cost of purchases must be measured. The purchaser normally receives a cash refund or a reduction in the liability to the vendor for a return. Assume that Harley-Davidson returned to a supplier unsatisfactory harness boots that cost $1,000. The return would be recorded by Harley-Davidson as follows:

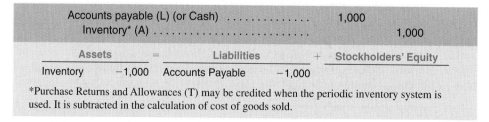

| Accounts payable (L) (or Cash) | 1,000 | |
| Inventory* (A) | | 1,000 |

| Assets | = | Liabilities | + | Stockholders' Equity |
|---|---|---|---|---|
| Inventory −1,000 | | Accounts Payable −1,000 | | |

*Purchase Returns and Allowances (T) may be credited when the periodic inventory system is used. It is subtracted in the calculation of cost of goods sold.

**PURCHASE RETURNS AND ALLOWANCES** are a reduction in the cost of purchases associated with unsatisfactory goods.

**Purchase returns and allowances** are a reduction in the cost of inventory purchases associated with unsatisfactory goods.

## PURCHASE DISCOUNTS

Cash discounts must be accounted for by both the seller and the buyer (accounting by the seller was discussed in Chapter 6). When merchandise is bought on credit, terms such as 2/10, n/30 are sometimes specified. This means that if payment is made within 10 days from date of purchase, a 2 percent cash discount known as the **purchase discount** is granted. If payment is not made within the discount period, the full invoice cost is due 30 days after purchase. Assume that on January 17, Harley-Davidson bought goods that had a $1,000 invoice price with terms 2/10, n/30. Assuming that it uses the gross method, the purchase should be recorded as follows:

A **PURCHASE DISCOUNT** is a cash discount received for prompt payment of an account

*Date of Purchase*

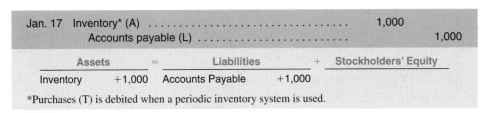

*Date of Payment, within the Discount Period*

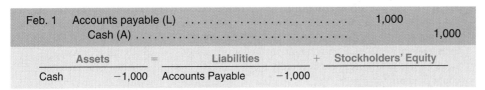

If for any reason Harley-Davidson did not pay within the 10-day discount period, the following entry would be needed:

| Feb. 1 | Accounts payable (L) ........................ | 1,000 | |
| | Cash (A) ................................... | | 1,000 |

| Assets | | = | Liabilities | | + | Stockholders' Equity |
|---|---|---|---|---|---|---|
| Cash | −1,000 | | Accounts Payable | −1,000 | | |

## CHAPTER **TAKE-AWAYS**

1. **Apply the cost principle to identify the amounts that should be included in inventory and the matching principle to determine cost of goods sold for typical retailers, wholesalers, and manufacturers. p. 364**

   Inventory should include all the items held for resale that the entity owns. Costs flow into inventory when goods are purchased or manufactured, and they flow out (as an expense) when the goods are sold or disposed of otherwise. In conformity with the matching principle, the total cost of the goods sold during the period must be matched with the sales revenue earned during the period.

2. **Analyze the effects of inventory errors on financial statements. p. 369**

   An error in the measurement of ending inventory affects cost of goods sold on the current period's income statement and ending inventory on the balance sheet. It also affects cost of goods sold in the following period by the same amount, but in the opposite direction, because this year's ending inventory becomes next year's beginning inventory. These relationships can be seen through the cost of goods sold equation (BI + P − EI = CGS).

3. **Report inventory and cost of goods sold using the four inventory costing methods. p. 371**

   When different unit cost amounts occur, a rational and systematic method must be used to allocate costs to the units remaining in inventory and to the units sold. The chapter discussed four different inventory costing methods and their applications in different economic circumstances. The methods discussed were FIFO, LIFO, weighted average cost, and specific identification. Each of the inventory costing methods is in conformity with GAAP. Public companies using LIFO provide note disclosures that allow conversion of inventory and cost of goods sold to FIFO amounts. It is important to remember that the cost flow assumption need not match the physical flow of inventory.

4. **Decide when the use of different inventory costing methods is beneficial to a company. p. 375**

   The selection of a method of inventory costing is important because it will affect reported income, income tax expense (and, hence, cash flow), and the inventory valuation reported on the balance sheet. In a period of rising prices, FIFO normally results in a higher income, and higher taxes, than does LIFO; in a period of falling prices, the opposite result occurs. The choice of methods is normally made to minimize taxes.

5. **Analyze and interpret the inventory turnover ratio and the effects of inventory on cash flows. p. 380**

   Inventory turnover measures the efficiency of inventory management. It reflects how many times average inventory was produced and sold during the period. Analysts and creditors watch this ratio because a sudden decline in this ratio may mean that a company is facing an unexpected decline in demand for its products or is becoming sloppy in its production management. When a net *decrease in inventory* for the period occurs, sales are more than purchases; thus, the decrease must be *added* in computing cash flows from operations. When a net *increase in inventory* for the period occurs, sales are less than purchases; thus, the increase must be *subtracted* in computing cash flows from operations.

6. **Report inventory at the lower-of-cost-or-market (LCM). p. 384**

   Ending inventory should be measured based on the lower of actual cost or replacement cost (LCM basis), which can have a major effect on the statements of companies facing declining costs. Damaged, obsolete, and deteriorated items in inventory also should be assigned a unit cost that represents their current estimated net realizable value if that is below cost. The LCM adjustment increases cost of goods sold, decreases income, and decreases reported inventory.

7. **Keep track of inventory quantities and amounts in different circumstances. p. 386**

   Two inventory systems were discussed for keeping track of the ending inventory and cost of goods sold for the period: (1) the perpetual inventory system, which is based on the maintenance of detailed and continuous inventory records for each kind of inventory stocked, and (2) the periodic inventory system, which is based on a physical inventory count of ending inventory and the costing of those goods to determine the proper amounts for cost of goods sold and ending inventory.

   In this and previous chapters, we discussed the current assets of a business. These assets are critical for the operations of a business, but many of them do not directly produce value. A business could not survive without cash, but cash does not produce goods or services that can be sold to customers. In Chapter 8, we will discuss the non-current assets property, plant, and equipment; natural resources; and intangibles that are the elements of *productive capacity*. Many of the noncurrent assets produce value, such as a factory that manufactures cars. These assets present some interesting accounting problems because they benefit a number of accounting periods.

## KEY **RATIO**

Inventory turnover ratio measures the efficiency of inventory management. It reflects how many times average inventory was produced and sold during the period. (p. 380):

$$\text{Inventory Turnover} = \frac{\text{Cost of Goods Sold}}{\text{Average Inventory}}$$

FINDING
**FINANCIAL
INFORMATION**

**BALANCE SHEET**
*Under Current Assets*
  Inventories

**INCOME STATEMENT**
*Expenses*
  Cost of goods sold

**STATEMENT OF CASH FLOWS**
*Under Operating Activities (indirect method):*
  Net income
    + decreases in inventory
    − increases in inventory
    + increases in accounts payable
    − decreases in accounts payable

**NOTES**
*Under Summary of Significant Accounting
Policies:*
  Description of management's choice of
    inventory accounting policy (FIFO,
    LIFO, LCM, etc)
*Under a Separate Note*
  If not listed on balance sheet, components
    of inventory (merchandise, raw
    materials, work in progress, finished
    goods)
  If using LIFO, LIFO reserve (excess of
    FIFO over LIFO)

## KEY **TERMS**

**Cost of Goods Sold Equation** p. 367

**Direct Labor** p. 365

**Factory Overhead** p. 365

**Finished Goods Inventory** p. 365

**First-In, First-Out (FIFO) Method** p. 372

**Goods Available for Sale** p. 367

**Inventory** p. 364

**Last-In, First-Out (LIFO) Method** p. 372

**LIFO Liquidation** p. 392

**LIFO Reserve** p. 378

**Lower of Cost or Market (LCM)** p. 384

**Merchandise Inventory** p. 364

**Net Realizable Value** p. 385

**Periodic Inventory System** p. 386

**Perpetual Inventory System** p. 386

**Purchase Discount** p. 395

**Purchase Returns and Allowances** p. 394

**Raw Materials Inventory** p. 364

**Replacement Cost** p. 384

**Specific Identification Method** p. 373

**Weighted Average Method** p. 373

**Work in Process Inventory** p. 365

## QUESTIONS

1. Why is inventory an important item to both internal (management) and external users of financial statements?
2. What are the general guidelines for deciding which items should be included in inventory?
3. Explain the application of the cost principle to an item in the ending inventory.
4. Define *goods available for sale.* How does it differ from cost of goods sold?
5. Define *beginning inventory* and *ending inventory.*
6. The chapter discussed four inventory costing methods. List the four methods and briefly explain each.
7. Explain how income can be manipulated when the specific identification inventory costing method is used.
8. Contrast the effects of LIFO versus FIFO on reported assets (i.e., the ending inventory) when (a) prices are rising and (b) prices are falling.
9. Contrast the income statement effect of LIFO versus FIFO (i.e., on pretax income) when (a) prices are rising and (b) prices are falling.
10. Contrast the effects of LIFO versus FIFO on cash outflow and inflow.
11. Explain briefly the application of the LCM concept to the ending inventory and its effect on the income statement and balance sheet when market is lower than cost.

12. When a perpetual inventory system is used, unit costs of the items sold are known at the date of each sale. In contrast, when a periodic inventory system is used, unit costs are known only at the end of the accounting period. Why are these statements correct?

13. The periodic inventory calculation is BI + P − EI = CGS. The perpetual inventory calculation is BI + P − CGS = EI. Explain the significance of the difference between these two calculations.

## MINI-EXERCISES

**LO1**  **M7–1**  **Matching Inventory Items to Type of Business**

Match the type of inventory with the type of business in the following matrix:

| Type of Inventory | Type of Business | |
|---|---|---|
| | Merchandising | Manufacturing |
| ✓Merchandise | ✗ | |
| Finished goods | | ✗ |
| Work in process | | ✗ |
| Raw materials | | ✗ |

**LO1**  **M7–2**  **Recording the Cost of Purchases for a Merchandiser**

Elite Apparel purchased 80 new shirts and recorded a total cost of $3,140 determined as follows:

| | |
|---|---|
| ✓ Invoice cost | $2,600 |
| ✓ Shipping charges | 165 |
| ✓ Import taxes and duties | 115 |
| Interest paid in advance (10%) on $2,600 Exp  borrowed to finance the purchase | 260 |
| | $3,140 |

*Required:*

Make the needed corrections in this calculation. Give the journal entry(ies) to record this purchase in the correct amount, assuming a perpetual inventory system. Show computations.

**LO1**  **M7–3**  **Identifying the Cost of Inventories for a Manufacturer**

Operating costs incurred by a manufacturing company become either (a) part of the cost of inventory to be expensed as cost of goods sold at the time the finished goods are sold or (b) expenses at the time they are incurred. Indicate whether each of the following costs belongs in category a. or b.

| | a. Part of Inventory | b. Expense as Incurred |
|---|---|---|
| 1. Wages of factory workers | | |
| 2. Sales salaries | | |
| 3. Costs of raw materials purchased | | |
| 4. Heat, light, and power for the factory building | | |
| 5. Heat, light, and power for the headquarters office building | | |

**LO1**  **M7–4**  
JCPenney

**Inferring Purchases Using the Cost of Goods Sold Equation**

JCPenney Company, Inc., is a major retailer with department stores in all 50 states. The dominant portion of the company's business consists of providing merchandise and services to consumers through department stores that include catalog departments. In a recent annual report, JCPenney reported cost of goods sold of $10,969 million, ending inventory for the current year of $3,062 million, and ending inventory for the previous year of $2,969 million.

*Required:*
Is it possible to develop a reasonable estimate of the merchandise purchases for the year? If so, prepare the estimate; if not, explain why.

**M7–5 Determining the Financial Statement Effects of Inventory Errors**    ■ **LO2**
Assume the 20A ending inventory was understated by $100,000. Explain how this error would affect the 20A and 20B pretax income amounts. What would be the effects if the 20A ending inventory were overstated by $100,000 instead of understated?

**M7–6 Matching Financial Statement Effects to Inventory Costing Methods**    ■ **LO3**
Indicate whether the FIFO or LIFO inventory costing method normally produces each of the following effects under the listed circumstances.

*a.* Rising costs
     Highest net income    _FIFO – lowest expense_
     Highest inventory    _FIFO – LISH_

*b.* Declining costs
     Highest net income    _LIFO_
     Highest inventory    _LIFO_

**M7–7 Matching Inventory Costing Method Choices to Company Circumstances**    ■ **LO4**
Indicate whether the FIFO or LIFO inventory costing method would normally be selected under each of the listed circumstances.

*a.* Rising costs      ~~FIFO~~ _LIFO_
*b.* Declining costs    ~~LIFO~~ _FIFO_

**M7–8 Determining the Effects of Inventory Management Changes on Inventory Turnover Ratio**    ■ **LO5**
Indicate the most likely effect of the following changes in inventory management on the inventory turnover ratio (+ for increase, − for decrease, and NE for no effect).

_____ *a.* Parts inventory delivered daily by suppliers instead of weekly.

_____ *b.* Shorten production process from 10 days to 8 days.

_____ *c.* Extend payments for inventory purchases from 15 days to 30 days.

**M7–9 Reporting Inventory under Lower of Cost or Market**    ■ **LO6**
Kinney Company had the following inventory items on hand at the end of the year.

| | Quantity | Cost per Item | Replacement Cost per Item | LCM |
|---|---|---|---|---|
| Item A | 50 | 3750 $75 | $100 5000 | 3750 |
| Item B | 25 | 1500 60 | 50 1250 | 1250 |
| | | 5250 | | 5000 |

Computing the lower of cost or market on an item-by-item basis, determine what amount would be reported on the balance sheet for inventory.

## EXERCISES

**E7–1 Inferring Missing Amounts Based on Income Statement Relationships**    ■ **LO1**
Supply the missing dollar amounts for the 20B income statement of Lewis Retailers for each of the following independent cases:

| Cases | Sales Revenue | Beginning Inventory | Purchases | Total Available | Ending Inventory | Cost of Goods Sold | Gross Profit | Expenses | Pretax Income or (Loss) |
|---|---|---|---|---|---|---|---|---|---|
| A | $ 650 | $100 | $700 | $ ? | $500 | $ ? | $ ? | $200 | $ ? |
| B | 900 | 200 | 800 | ? | ? | ? | ? | 150 | 0 |
| C | ? | 150 | ? | ? | 300 | 200 | 400 | 100 | ? |
| D | 800 | ? | 600 | ? | 250 | ? | ? | 250 | $100 |
| E | 1,000 | ? | 900 | $1,100 | ? | ? | 500 | ? | (50) |

■ **LO1**       **E7–2**    **Inferring Missing Amounts Based on Income Statement Relationships**

Supply the missing dollar amounts for the 20D income statement of Travis Company for each of the following independent cases:

|  | Case A | Case B | Case C |
|---|---|---|---|
| Sales revenue | $ 8,000 | $ 6,000 | $ ? |
| Sales returns and allowances | 150 | ? | 275 |
| Net sales revenue | ? | ? | 5,920 |
| Beginning inventory | 11,000 | 6,500 | 4,000 |
| Purchases | 5,000 | ? | 9,420 |
| Transportation-in | ? | 120 | 170 |
| Purchase returns | 350 | 600 | ? |
| Goods available for sale | ? | 14,790 | 13,370 |
| Ending inventory | 10,000 | 10,740 | ? |
| Cost of goods sold | ? | ? | 5,400 |
| Gross profit | ? | 1,450 | ? |
| Expenses | 1,300 | ? | 520 |
| Pretax income | $ 800 | $ (500) | $ 0 |

■ **LO1**       **E7–3**    **Inferring Merchandise Purchases**

The Gap, Inc.

The Gap, Inc., is a specialty retailer that operates stores selling clothes under the trade names Gap, GapKids, BabyGap, and Banana Republic. Assume that you are employed as a stock analyst and your boss has just completed a review of the new Gap annual report. She provided you with her notes, but they are missing some information that you need. Her notes show that the ending inventory for Gap in the current year was $243,482,000 and in the previous year was $193,268,000. Net sales for the current year were $1,586,596,000. Gross profit was $540,360,000; net income was $97,628,000. For your analysis, you determine that you need to know the amount of purchases for the year and cost of goods sold.

*Required:*

Do you need to ask your boss for her copy of the annual report, or can you develop the information from her notes? Explain and show calculations.

■ **LO2**       **E7–4**    **Analyzing the Effects of an Error in Recording Purchases**

Garraway Ski Company mistakenly recorded purchases of inventory on account received during the last week of December 20A as purchases during January of 20B (this is called a *purchases cutoff error*). Garraway uses a periodic inventory system, and ending inventory was correctly counted and reported each year. Assuming that no correction was made in 20A or 20B, indicate whether each of the following financial statement amounts will be understated, overstated, or correct.

1. Net Income for 20A.

2. Net Income for 20B.

3. Retained Earnings for December 31, 20A.

4. Retained Earnings for December 31, 20B.

■ **LO2**       **E7–5**    **Analyzing the Effect of an Inventory Error Disclosed in an Actual Note to a Financial Statement**

Gibson
Greeting Cards

Several years ago, the financial statements of Gibson Greeting Cards contained the following note:

> On July 1, the Company announced that it had determined that the inventory . . . had been overstated. . . . The overstatement of inventory . . . was $8,806,000.

Gibson reported an incorrect net income amount of $25,852,000 for the year in which the error occurred and the income tax rate was 39.3 percent.

*Required:*

1. Compute the amount of net income that Gibson reported after correcting the inventory error. Show computations.

2. Assume that the inventory error was not discovered. Identify the financial statement accounts that would have been incorrect for the year the error occurred and for the subsequent year. State whether each account was understated or overstated.

**E7–6 Analyzing and Interpreting the Impact of an Inventory Error**  ▉ **LO2**

Dallas Corporation prepared the following two income statements (simplified for illustrative purposes):

|  | First Quarter 20B | | Second Quarter 20B | |
| --- | --- | --- | --- | --- |
| Sales revenue |  | $15,000 |  | $18,000 |
| Cost of goods sold |  |  |  |  |
| Beginning inventory | $ 3,000 |  | *4400* ~~4,000~~ |  |
| Purchases | 7,000 |  | 12,000 |  |
| Goods available for sale | 10,000 |  | 16,000 *16400* |  |
| Ending inventory | 4,~~1~~00 |  | 9,000 |  |
| Cost of goods sold |  | *5600* ~~6,000~~ |  | *7400* ~~7,000~~ |
| Gross profit |  | 9,000 *9400* |  | *10600* 11,000 |
| Expenses |  | 5,000 |  | 6,000 |
| Pretax income |  | $ 4,000 *4400* |  | $ 5,000 *4600* |

During the third quarter, it was discovered that the ending inventory for the first quarter should have been $4,400.

*Required:*

1. What effect did this error have on the combined pretax income of the two quarters? Explain.

2. Did this error affect the EPS amounts for each quarter? (See Chapter 5 discussion of EPS.) Explain.

3. Prepare corrected income statements for each quarter.

4. Set up a schedule with the following headings to reflect the comparative effects of the correct and incorrect amounts on the income statement:

| Income Statement Item | 1st Quarter | | | 2nd Quarter | | |
| --- | --- | --- | --- | --- | --- | --- |
|  | Incorrect | Correct | Error | Incorrect | Correct | Error |

**E7–7 Analyzing and Interpreting the Financial Statement Effects of LIFO and FIFO**  ▉ **LO3**

Lunar Company uses a periodic inventory system. At the end of the annual accounting period, December 31, 20B, the accounting records provided the following information for Product 2:

| Transactions | Units | Unit Cost |
| --- | --- | --- |
| *a.* Inventory, December 31, 20A | 3,000 | $12 |
| For the year 20B: |  |  |
| *b.* Purchase, April 11 | 9,000 | 10 |
| *c.* Purchase, June 1 | 8,000 | 13 |
| *d.* Sale, May 1 ($40 each) | 5,000 |  |
| *e.* Sale, July 3 ($40 each) | 6,000 |  |
| *f.* Operating expenses (excluding income tax expense), $195,000 | | |

*Required:*

1. Prepare a separate income statement through pretax income that details cost of goods sold for

   *a.* Case A: FIFO.

   *b.* Case B: LIFO.

   For each case, show the computation of the ending inventory. (*Hint:* Set up adjacent columns for each case.)

2. Compare the pretax income and the ending inventory amounts between the two cases. Explain the similarities and differences.

3. Which inventory costing method may be preferred for income tax purposes? Explain.

■ **LO3, 4**   **E7–8**   **Evaluating the Choice among Three Alternative Inventory Methods Based on Cash Flow and Income Effects**

Courtney Company uses a periodic inventory system. Data for 20B: beginning merchandise inventory (December 31, 20A), 2,000 units at $35; purchases, 8,000 units at $38; expenses (excluding income taxes), $142,000; ending inventory per physical count at December 31, 20B, 1,800 units; sales price per unit, $70; and average income tax rate, 30 percent.

*Required:*

1. Prepare income statements under the FIFO, LIFO, and weighted average costing methods. Use a format similar to the following:

|  |  | Inventory Costing Method | | |
|---|---|---|---|---|
| **Income Statement** | **Units** | 8200 × $70 **FIFO** × 70 | for tax **LIFO** | **Weighted Average** |
| Sales revenue | 8200 | $574,000 | $574,000 | $574,000 |
| Cost of goods sold |  |  |  |  |
|  Beginning inventory | 2000 | 70,000 | 70,000 | 70,000 |
|  Purchases | 8000 | 304,000 | 304,000 | 304,000 |
|   Goods available for sale | 10000 | 374,000 | 374,000 | 374,000 |
|  Ending inventory | 1800 | 68,400 | 63,000 |  |
| Sales rev − Cost of goods sold | 8200 | 305,600 | 311,000 |  |
| Gross profit = | | 268,400 | 263,000 |  |
| Expenses | | 142,000 | 142,000 |  |
| Pretax income | | 126,400 | 121,000 |  |
|  Income tax expense × 30% | | 37,920 | 36,300 |  |
| Net income | | $88,480 | 84,700 |  |

2. Between FIFO and LIFO, which method is preferable in terms of (a) net income and (b) cash flow? Explain.

3. What would your answer to requirement 2 be, assuming that prices were falling? Explain.

■ **LO3, 4**   **E7–9**   **Evaluating the Choice among Three Alternative Inventory Methods Based on Cash Flow Effects**

Following is partial information for the income statement of Timber Company under three different inventory costing methods, assuming the use of a periodic inventory system:

|  | **FIFO** | **LIFO** | **Weighted Average** |
|---|---|---|---|
| Unit sales price, $50 |  |  |  |
| Cost of goods sold |  |  |  |
|  Beginning inventory (330 units) | $11,220 | $11,220 | $11,220 |
|  Purchases (475 units) | 17,100 | 17,100 | 17,100 |
|   Goods available for sale |  |  |  |
|  Ending inventory (510 units) |  |  |  |
|    Cost of goods sold |  |  |  |
| Expenses, $1,600 |  |  |  |

*Required:*

1. Compute cost of goods sold under the FIFO, LIFO, and weighted average inventory costing methods.

2. Prepare an income statement through pretax income for each method.

3. Rank the three methods in order of favorable cash flow and explain the basis for your ranking.

**E7–10 Analyzing Notes to Adjust Inventory from LIFO to FIFO**

The following note was contained in a recent Ford Motor Company annual report:

■ **LO4**

Ford Motor Company

> **Inventory Valuation—Automotive.** Inventories are stated at the lower of cost or market. The cost of most US inventories is determined by the last-in, first-out ("LIFO") method. The cost of the remaining inventories is determined substantially by the first-in, first-out ("FIFO") method.
>   If FIFO were the only method of inventory accounting used by the company, inventories would have been $1,235 million higher than reported this year and $1,246 million higher than reported last year.

The major classes of inventory for the company's automotive business segment at December 31 were as follows:

| | Inventory (in $ millions) | |
| --- | --- | --- |
| | Current Year | Previous Year |
| Finished products | $3,413.8 | $3,226.7 |
| Raw material and work in process | 2,983.9 | 2,981.6 |
| Supplies | 419.1 | 429.9 |
| Total | $6,816.8 | $6,638.2 |

*Required:*

1. Determine the ending inventory that would have been reported in the current year if Ford had used only FIFO.

2. The cost of goods sold reported by Ford for the current year was $74,315 million. Determine the cost of goods sold that would have been reported if Ford had used only FIFO for both years.

**E7–11 Analyzing and Interpreting the Inventory Turnover Ratio**

Dell Computer is the leading manufacturer of personal computers. In a recent year, it reported the following:

■ **LO5**

Dell Computer

| | |
| --- | --- |
| Net sales revenue | $12,327 |
| Cost of sales | 9,605 |
| Beginning inventory | 251 |
| Ending inventory | 233 |

*Required:*

1. Determine the inventory turnover ratio and average days to sell inventory for the current year.

2. Explain the meaning of each number.

**E7–12 Analyzing and Interpreting the Effects of the LIFO/FIFO Choice on Inventory Turnover Ratio**

The records at the end of January 20B for All Star Company showed the following for a particular kind of merchandise:

■ **LO5**

Inventory, December 31, 20A at FIFO 19 Units @ $14 = 266

Inventory, December 31, 20A at LIFO 19 Units @ $10 = 190

| Transactions | Units | Unit Cost | Total Cost |
|---|---|---|---|
| Purchase, January 9, 20B | 25 | 15 | $375 |
| Purchase, January 20, 20B | 50 | 16 | 800 |
| Sale, January 11, 20B (at $38 per unit) | 40 | | |
| Sale, January 27, 20B (at $39 per unit) | 28 | | |

*Required:*
Compute the inventory turnover ratio under the FIFO and LIFO inventory costing methods (show computations and round to the nearest dollar). Explain which you believe is the more accurate indicator of the liquidity of inventory.

**LO5**

First Team
Sports, Inc.

**E7–13**

**Interpreting the Effect of Changes in Inventories and Accounts Payable on Cash Flow from Operations**
First Team Sports, Inc., is engaged in the manufacture (through independent contractors) and distribution of in-line roller skates, ice skates, street hockey equipment, and related accessory products. Its recent annual report included the following on its balance sheet:

| CONSOLIDATED BALANCE SHEETS | | |
|---|---|---|
| February 29, 20B and February 28, 20A | | |
| | **20B** | **20A** |
| . . . . . . . | | |
| Inventory (Note 3) | 22,813,850 | 20,838,171 |
| . . . . . . . | . . . | . . . |
| Trade accounts payable | 9,462,883 | 9,015,376 |

*Required:*
Explain the effects of the changes in inventory and trade accounts payable in 20B on cash flow from operating activities for 20B.

**LO6**

**E7–14**

**Reporting Inventory at Lower of Cost or Market**
Peterson Company is preparing the annual financial statements dated December 31, 20B. Ending inventory information about the five major items stocked for regular sale follows:

| | Ending Inventory, 20B | | |
|---|---|---|---|
| Item | Quantity on Hand | Unit Cost When Acquired (FIFO) | Replacement Cost (Market) at Year-End |
| A | 50 | $15 | $13 |
| B | 75 | 40 | 40 |
| C | 10 | 50 | 52 |
| D | 30 | 30 | 30 |
| E | 400 | 8 | 6 |

*Required:*
Compute the valuation that should be used for the 20B ending inventory using the LCM rule applied on an item-by-item basis. (*Hint:* Set up columns for Item, Quantity, Total Cost, Total Market, and LCM Valuation.)

**LO7**

**E7–15**

**Recording Purchases and Sales Using a Perpetual and Periodic Inventory System**
Demski Company reported beginning inventory of 100 units at a unit cost of $25. It engaged in the following purchase and sale transactions during 20A:

Jan. 14   Sold 25 units at unit sales price of $45 on open account.

April 9   Purchased 15 additional units at unit cost of $25 on open account.

Sep. 2   Sold 50 units at sales price of $50 on open account.

At the end of the 20A, a physical count showed that Demski Company had 40 units of inventory still on hand.

*Required:*

Record each transaction, assuming that Demski Company uses (a) a perpetual inventory system and (b) a periodic inventory system (including any necessary entries at the end of the accounting period on December 31).

**E7–16 (Supplement A) Analyzing the Effects of a Reduction in the Amount of LIFO Inventory**

Standard Oil

An annual report of Standard Oil Company (Indiana) contained the following note:

> During this year and last year, the company reduced certain inventory quantities that were valued at lower LIFO costs prevailing in prior years. The effect of these reductions was to increase aftertax earnings this year by $71 million, or $0.24 per share, and $74 million, or $0.25 per share last year.

*Required:*

1. Explain why the reduction in inventory quantity increased after-tax earnings (net income) for Standard Oil.

2. If Standard Oil had used FIFO, would the reductions in inventory quantity during the two years have increased after tax earnings? Explain.

**E7–17 (Supplement B) Recording Sales and Purchases with Cash Discounts**

The Cycle Shop sells merchandise on credit terms of 2/10, n/30. A sale invoiced at $800 (cost of sales $500) was made to Missy Clemons on February 1, 20B. The company uses the gross method of recording sales discounts.

*Required:*

1. Give the journal entry to record the credit sale. Assume use of the perpetual inventory system.

2. Give the journal entry, assuming that the account was collected in full on February 9, 20B.

3. Give the journal entry, assuming, instead, that the account was collected in full on March 2, 20B.

On March 4, 20B, the company purchased bicycles and accessories from a supplier on credit, invoiced at $8,000; the terms were 1/15, n/30. The company uses the gross method to record purchases.

*Required:*

4. Give the journal entry to record the purchase on credit. Assume the use of the perpetual inventory system.

5. Give the journal entry, assuming that the account was paid in full on March 12, 20B.

6. Give the journal entry, assuming, instead, that the account was paid in full on March 28, 20B.

## PROBLEMS

**P7–1 Analyzing Items to Be Included in Inventory**

■ **LO1**

Reggie Company has just completed a physical inventory count at year-end, December 31, 20B. Only the items on the shelves, in storage, and in the receiving area were counted and costed on a FIFO basis. The inventory amounted to $70,000. During the audit, the independent CPA developed the following additional information:

 a. Goods costing $500 were being used by a customer on a trial basis and were excluded from the inventory count at December 31, 20B.

 b. Goods in transit on December 31, 20B, from a supplier, with terms FOB destination, cost $600. Because these goods had not arrived, they were excluded from the physical inventory count.

   *c.* On December 31, 20B, goods in transit to customers, with terms FOB shipping point, amounted to $1,000 (expected delivery date January 10, 20C). Because the goods had been shipped, they were excluded from the physical inventory count.

   *d.* On December 28, 20B, a customer purchased goods for cash amounting to $2,000 and left them "for pickup on January 3, 20C." Reggie Company had paid $1,200 for the goods and, because they were on hand, included the latter amount in the physical inventory count.

   *e.* On the date of the inventory count, the company received notice from a supplier that goods ordered earlier at a cost of $2,200 had been delivered to the transportation company on December 27, 20B; the terms were FOB shipping point. Because the shipment had not arrived by December 31, 20B, it was excluded from the physical inventory.

   *f.* On December 31, 20B, the company shipped $950 worth of goods to a customer, FOB destination. The goods are expected to arrive at their destination no earlier than January 8, 20C. Because the goods were not on hand, they were not included in the physical inventory count.

   *g.* One of the items sold by the company has such a low volume that the management planned to drop it last year. To induce Reggie Company to continue carrying the item, the manufacturer-supplier provided the item on a "consignment basis." This means that the manufacturer-supplier retains ownership of the item, and Reggie Company (the consignee) has no responsibility to pay for the items until they are sold to a customer. Each month, Reggie Company sends a report to the manufacturer on the number sold and remits cash for the cost. At the end of December 20B, Reggie Company had five of these items on hand; therefore, they were included in the physical inventory count at $1,000 each.

*Required:*

Assume that Reggie's accounting policy requires including in inventory all goods for which it has title. Note that the point where title (ownership) changes hands is determined by the shipping terms in the sales contract. When goods are shipped "F.O.B. shipping point," title changes hands at shipment and the buyer normally pays for shipping. When they are shipped "F.O.B. destination," title changes hands on delivery, and the seller normally pays for shipping. Begin with the $70,000 inventory amount and compute the correct amount for the ending inventory. Explain the basis for your treatment of each of the preceding items. (*Hint:* Set up three columns: Item, Amount, and Explanation.)

■ **LO2**

**P7–2**     **Analyzing and Interpreting the Effects of Inventory Errors** (AP7–1)

The income statements for four consecutive years for Clement Company reflected the following summarized amounts:

|  | 20A | 20B | 20C | 20D |
|---|---|---|---|---|
| Sales revenue | $50,000 | $51,000 | $62,000 | $58,000 |
| Cost of goods sold | 32,500 | 35,000 | 43,000 | 37,000 |
| Gross profit | 17,500 | 16,000 | 19,000 | 21,000 |
| Expenses | 10,000 | 12,000 | 14,000 | 12,000 |
| Pretax income | $ 7,500 | $ 4,000 | $ 5,000 | $ 9,000 |

*(handwritten annotations: GP% = .35, .31, .31/.306, .36; −300 near Cost of goods sold 20B; +3 near 20C 43,000)*

Subsequent to development of these amounts, it has been determined that the physical inventory taken on December 31, 20B, was understated by $3,000.

*Required:*

1. Recast the income statements to reflect the correct amounts, taking into consideration the inventory error.

2. Compute the gross profit percentage for each year (a) before the correction and (b) after the correction. Do the results lend confidence to your corrected amounts? Explain.

3. What effect would the error have had on the income tax expense assuming a 30 percent average rate?

**P7–3 Analyzing the Effects of Four Alternative Inventory Methods (AP7–2)** ■ LO3

Allsigns Company uses a periodic inventory system. At the end of the annual accounting period, December 31, 20E, the accounting records for the most popular item in inventory showed the following:

| Transactions | Units | Unit Cost |
|---|---|---|
| Beginning inventory, January 1, 20E | 400 | $30 |
| Transactions during 20E: | | |
| a. Purchase, February 20 | 600 | 32 |
| b. Sale, April 1 ($46 each) | (700) | |
| c. Purchase, June 30 | 500 | 36 |
| d. Sale, August 1 ($46 each) | (100) | |
| e. Sales return, August 5 (related to transaction d) | 20 | |

*Required:*

Compute the amount of (a) goods available for sale, (b) ending inventory, and (c) cost of goods sold at December 31, 20E, under each of the following inventory costing methods (show computations and round to the nearest dollar):

1. Weighted average cost.

2. First-in, first-out.

3. Last-in, first-out.

4. Specific identification, assuming that the April 1, 20E, sale was selected one-fifth from the beginning inventory and four-fifths from the purchase of February 20, 20E. Assume that the sale of August 1, 20E, was selected from the purchase of June 30, 20E.

**P7–4 Evaluating Four Alternative Inventory Methods Based on Income and Cash Flow** ■ LO3, 4

At the end of January 20B, the records of Atlanta Company showed the following for a particular item that sold at $18 per unit:

| Transactions | Units | Amount |
|---|---|---|
| Inventory, January 1, 20B | 500 | $2,500 |
| Sale, January 10 | (400) | |
| Purchase, January 12 | 600 | 3,600 |
| Sale, January 17 | (300) | |
| Purchase, January 26 | 160 | 1,280 |
| Purchase return, January 28 | (10) | Out of Jan. 26 purchase |

*Required:*

1. Assuming the use of a periodic inventory system, prepare a summarized income statement through gross profit on sales under each method of inventory: (a) weighted average cost, (b) FIFO, (c) LIFO, and (d) specific identification. For specific identification, assume that the first sale was out of the beginning inventory and the second sale was out of the January 12 purchase. Show the inventory computations in detail.

2. Of FIFO and LIFO, which method would result in the higher pretax income? Which would result in the higher EPS?

3. Of FIFO and LIFO, which method would result in the lower income tax expense? Explain, assuming a 30 percent average tax rate.

4. Of FIFO and LIFO, which method would produce the more favorable cash flow? Explain.

**P7–5 Analyzing and Interpreting Income Manipulation Under the LIFO Inventory Method** ■ LO3, 4

Pacific Company sells electronic test equipment that it acquires from a foreign source. During the year 20W, the inventory records reflected the following:

|  | Units | Unit Cost | Total Cost |
|---|---|---|---|
| Beginning inventory | 15 | $12,000 | $180,000 |
| Purchases | 40 | 10,000 | 400,000 |
| Sales (45 units at $25,000 each) | | | |

Inventory is valued at cost using the LIFO inventory method. On December 28, 20W, the unit cost of the test equipment was decreased to $8,000. The cost will be decreased again during the first quarter of the next year.

*Required:*

1. Complete the following income statement summary using the LIFO method and the periodic inventory system (show computations):

| Sales revenue | $_____ |
|---|---|
| Cost of goods sold | _____ |
| Gross profit | _____ |
| Expenses | 300,000 |
| Pretax income | $_____ |
| Ending inventory | $_____ |

2. The management, for various reasons, is considering buying 20 additional units before December 31, 20W, at $8,000 each. Restate the income statement (and ending inventory), assuming that this purchase is made on December 31, 20W.

3. How much did pretax income change because of the decision on December 31, 20W? Is there any evidence of income manipulation? Explain.

**LO4**      **P7–6**      **Evaluating the FIFO to LIFO Change from a Stockholder's Perspective**

Allendale Corporation reported the following summarized annual data at the end of 20X:

|  | (millions) |
|---|---|
| Sales revenue | $850 |
| Cost of goods sold* | 400 |
| Gross profit | 450 |
| Expenses | 310 |
| Pretax income | $140 |

*Based on ending FIFO inventory of $120 million. On a LIFO basis, this ending inventory would have been $75 million.

Before issuing the preceding statement, the company decided to change from FIFO to LIFO for 20X because "it better reflects our operating results." The company has always used FIFO.

*Required:*

1. Restate the summary income statement on a LIFO basis.

2. How much did pretax income change due to the LIFO decision for 20X? What caused the change in pretax income?

3. If you were a stockholder, what would be your reaction to this change? Explain.

**LO4**      **P7–7**      **Evaluating the LIFO and FIFO Choice When Costs Are Rising and Falling**

Income is to be evaluated under four different situations as follows:

a. Prices are rising:

1. Situation A: FIFO is used.

2. Situation B: LIFO is used.

b. Prices are falling:

    1. Situation C: FIFO is used.

    2. Situation D: LIFO is used.

The basic data common to all four situations are sales, 500 units for $12,500; beginning inventory, 300 units; purchases, 400 units; ending inventory, 200 units; and operating expenses, $4,000. The following tabulated income statements for each situation have been set up for analytical purposes:

| | Prices Rising | | Prices Falling | |
| --- | --- | --- | --- | --- |
| | Situation A<br>FIFO | Situation B<br>LIFO | Situation C<br>FIFO | Situation D<br>LIFO |
| Sales revenue | $12,500 | $12,500 | $12,500 | $12,500 |
| Cost of goods sold | | | | |
|   Beginning inventory | 3,600 | ? | ? | ? |
|   Purchases | 5,200 | ? | ? | ? |
|     Goods available for sale | 8,800 | ? | ? | ? |
|   Ending inventory | 2,600 | ? | ? | ? |
|     Cost of goods sold | 6,200 | ? | ? | ? |
| Gross profit | 6,300 | ? | ? | ? |
| Expenses | 4,000 | 4,000 | 4,000 | 4,000 |
| Pretax income | 2,300 | ? | ? | ? |
|   Income tax expense (30%) | 690 | ? | ? | ? |
| Net income | $ 1,610 | | | |

*Required:*

1. Complete the preceding tabulation for each situation. In Situations A and B (prices rising), assume the following: beginning inventory, 300 units at $12 = $3,600; purchases, 400 units at $13 = $5,200. In Situations C and D (prices falling), assume the opposite; that is, beginning inventory, 300 units at $13 = $3,900; purchases, 400 units at $12 = $4,800. Use periodic inventory procedures.

2. Analyze the relative effects on pretax income and on net income as demonstrated by requirement 1 when prices are rising and when prices are falling.

3. Analyze the relative effects on the cash position for each situation.

4. Would you recommend FIFO or LIFO? Explain.

**P7–8** **Evaluating the Choice between LIFO and FIFO Based on an Inventory Note** (AP7–3)

An annual report for General Motors Corporation included the following note:

    ■ **LO4**

General Motors

> Inventories are stated generally at cost, which is not in excess of market. The cost of substantially all domestic inventories was determined by the last-in, first-out (LIFO) method. If the first-in, first-out (FIFO) method of inventory valuation had been used by the Corporation for U.S. inventories, it is estimated that they would be $2,077.1 million higher at the end of this year, compared with $1,784.5 million higher at the end of last year.

For the year, GM reported net income (after taxes) of $320.5 million. At year-end, the balance of the GM retained earnings account was $15,340 million.

*Required:*

1. Determine the amount of net income that GM would have reported for the year if it had used the FIFO method (assume a 30 percent tax rate).

2. Determine the amount of retained earnings that GM would have reported at year-end if it always had used the FIFO method (assume a 30 percent tax rate).

3. Use of the LIFO method reduced the amount of taxes that GM had to pay for the year compared with the amount that would have been paid if it had used FIFO. Calculate the amount of this reduction (assume a 30 percent tax rate).

**LO5**　　**P7–9**　**Evaluating the Effects of Manufacturing Changes on Inventory Turnover Ratio and Cash Flows from Operating Activities (AP7–4)**

H.–T. Tan and Company has been operating for five years as an electronics component manufacturer specializing in cellular phone components. During this period, it has experienced rapid growth in sales revenue and in inventory. Mr. Tan and his associates have hired you as its first corporate controller. You have put into place new purchasing and manufacturing procedures that are expected to reduce inventories by approximately one-third by year-end. You have gathered the following data related to the changes:

|  | (in thousands) | |
|---|---|---|
|  | Beginning of Year | End of Year (projected) |
| Inventory | $463,808 | $310,270 |
|  |  | Current Year (projected) |
| Cost of goods sold |  | $7,015,069 |

*Required:*

1. Compute the inventory turnover ratio based on two different assumptions:

   *a.* Those presented in the preceding table (a decrease in the balance in inventory).

   *b.* No change from the beginning of the year in the inventory balance.

2. Compute the effect of the projected change in the balance in inventory on cash flow from operating activities for the year (the sign and amount of effect).

3. On the basis of the preceding analysis, write a brief memo explaining how an increase in inventory turnover can result in an increase in cash flow from operating activities. Also explain how this increase can benefit the company.

**LO6**　　**P7–10**　**Evaluating the Income Statement and Cash Flow Effects of Lower of Cost or Market**

Smart Company prepared its annual financial statements dated December 31, 20B. The company applies the FIFO inventory costing method; however, the company neglected to apply LCM to the ending inventory. The preliminary 20B income statement follows:

| | | |
|---|---:|---:|
| Sales revenue | | $280,000 |
| Cost of goods sold | | |
| Beginning inventory | $ 30,000 | |
| Purchases | 182,000 | |
| Goods available for sale | 212,000 | |
| Ending inventory (FIFO cost) | 44,000 | |
| Cost of goods sold | | 168,000 |
| Gross profit | | 112,000 |
| Operating expenses | | 61,000 |
| Pretax income | | 51,000 |
| Income tax expense (30%) | | 15,300 |
| Net income | | $ 35,700 |

Assume that you have been asked to restate the 20B financial statements to incorporate LCM. You have developed the following data relating to the 20B ending inventory:

| Item | Quantity | Acquisition Cost | | Current Replacement Unit Cost |
|---|---|---|---|---|
| | | Unit | Total | (Market) |
| A | 3,000 | $3 | $ 9,000 | $4 |
| B | 1,500 | 4 | 6,000 | 2 |
| C | 7,000 | 2 | 14,000 | 4 |
| D | 3,000 | 5 | 15,000 | 3 |
| | | | $44,000 | |

*Required:*

1. Restate this income statement to reflect LCM valuation of the 20B ending inventory. Apply LCM on an item-by-item basis and show computations.

2. Compare and explain the LCM effect on each amount that was changed in requirement 1.

3. What is the conceptual basis for applying LCM to merchandise inventories?

4. Thought question: What effect did LCM have on the 20B cash flow? What will be the long-term effect on cash flow?

**P7–11 (Supplement A) Analyzing LIFO and FIFO When Inventory Quantities Decline Based on an Actual Note**      General Electric

In a recent annual report, General Electric reported the following in its inventory note:

| December 31 (in millions) | 20B | 20A |
|---|---|---|
| Raw materials and work in progress | $5,603 | $5,515 |
| Finished goods | 2,863 | 2,546 |
| Unbilled shipments | 246 | 280 |
| | 8,712 | 8,341 |
| Less revaluation to LIFO | (2,226) | (2,076) |
| LIFO value of inventories | $6,486 | $6,265 |

It also reported a $23 million change in cost of goods sold due to "lower inventory levels."

*Required:*

1. Compute the increase or decrease in the pretax operating profit (loss) that would have been reported for the current year had GE employed FIFO accounting for all inventory for both years.

2. Compute the increase or decrease in pretax operating profit that would have been reported had GE employed LIFO but not reduced inventory quantities during the current year.

**P7–12 (Supplement B) Recording Sales and Purchases with Cash Discounts and Returns (AP7–5)**

Campus Stop, Incorporated, is a student co-op. On January 1, 20X, the beginning inventory was $150,000, the Accounts Receivable balance was $4,000, and the Allowance for Doubtful Accounts had a credit balance of $800. Campus Stop uses a perpetual inventory system and records inventory purchases using the gross method.

The following transactions (summarized) have been selected from 20X for case purposes:

| | | |
|---|---|---|
| *a.* | Sold merchandise for cash (cost of sales $137,500) | $275,000 |
| *b.* | Received merchandise returned by customers as unsatisfactory, for cash refund (cost of sales $800) | 1,600 |

Purchased merchandise from vendors on credit; terms 3/10, n/30 as follows:

| | | |
|---|---|---|
| *c.* | August Supply Company invoice price before deduction of cash discount | 5,000 |
| *d.* | Other vendors, invoice price before deduction of cash discount | 120,000 |
| *e.* | Purchased equipment for use in store; paid cash | 2,200 |

|   |   |   |
|---|---|---|
| f. | Purchased office supplies for future use in the store; paid cash | 700 |
| g. | Freight on merchandise purchased; paid cash | 400 |
|    | Paid accounts payable in full during the period as follows: | |
| h. | Paid August Supply Company after the discount period | 5,000 |
| i. | Paid other vendors within the 3% discount period | 116,400 |

*Required:*
Prepare journal entries for each of the preceding transactions.

# ALTERNATE PROBLEMS

■ LO2        AP7–1        **Analyzing and Interpreting the Effects of Inventory Errors** (P7–2)
The income statement for Sherwood Company summarized for a four-year period shows the following:

|  | 20A | 20B | 20C | 20D |
|---|---|---|---|---|
| Sales revenue | $2,000,000 | $2,400,000 | $2,500,000 | $3,000,000 |
| Cost of goods sold | 1,400,000 | 1,630,000 | 1,780,000 | 2,100,000 |
| Gross profit | 600,000 | 770,000 | 720,000 | 900,000 |
| Expenses | 450,000 | 500,000 | 520,000 | 550,000 |
| Pretax income | 150,000 | 270,000 | 200,000 | 350,000 |
| Income tax expense (30%) | 45,000 | 81,000 | 60,000 | 105,000 |
| Net income | $ 105,000 | $ 189,000 | $ 140,000 | $ 245,000 |

An audit revealed that in determining these amounts, the ending inventory for 20B was overstated by $20,000. The company uses a periodic inventory system.

*Required:*

1. Recast these income statements on a correct basis.

2. Did the error affect cumulative net income for the four-year period? Explain.

3. What effect would the error have had on the income tax expense assuming a 30 percent average rate?

■ LO3        AP7–2        **Analyzing the Effects of Four Alternative Inventory Methods** (P7–3)
Yalestone Company uses a periodic inventory system. At the end of the annual accounting period, December 31, 20C, the accounting records for the most popular item in inventory showed the following:

| Transactions | Units | Unit Cost |
|---|---|---|
| Beginning inventory, January 1, 20C | 1,800 | $2.50 |
| Transactions during 20C: | | |
| a. Purchase, January 30 | 2,500 | 3.10  7750 |
| b. Sale, March 14 ($5 each)  7250 | (1,450) | |
| c. Purchase, May 1 | 1,200 | 4.00  4800 |
| d. Sale, August 31 ($5 each)  9500 | (1,900) | |
| e. Sales return, September 5 (related to transaction [d]) | 150 | |
|    8750 | | |

*Required:*
Compute the amount of (a) goods available for sale, (b) ending inventory, and (c) cost of goods sold at December 31, 20C, under each of the following inventory costing methods (show computations and round to the nearest dollar):

1. Weighted average cost.

2. First-in, first-out.

3. Last-in, first-out.

4. Specific identification, assuming that the March 14, 20C, sale was selected two-fifths from the beginning inventory and three-fifths from the purchase of January 30, 20C. Assume that the sale of August 31, 20C, was selected from the remainder of the beginning inventory, with the balance from the purchase of May 1, 20C.

**AP7–3** **Evaluating the Choice between LIFO and FIFO Based on an Inventory Note** (P7–8)

The following note was contained in a recent DaimlerChrysler Corporation annual report:

**LO4**

DaimlerChrysler Corporation

**Inventories**

Inventories are valued at the lower of cost or market. The cost of approximately 44 percent and 50 percent of inventories for the current and previous years, respectively, is determined on a Last-In, First-Out (LIFO) basis. The balance of inventory cost is determined on a First-In, First-Out (FIFO) basis.

**Inventories and Cost of Sales**

Inventories are summarized by major classification as follows (in $ millions):

| | Current Year | Previous Year |
|---|---|---|
| Finished products, including service parts | $1,145 | $ 972 |
| Raw materials, finished production parts and supplies | 985 | 1,165 |
| Vehicles held for short-term lease | 760 | 336 |
| Total | $2,890 | $2,473 |

Inventories valued on the LIFO basis would have been $160 million and $123 million higher than reported had they been valued on the FIFO basis at December 31 of the current year and previous year, respectively.

Total automotive manufacturing cost of sales aggregated $27.2 billion and $26.3 billion for the current year and previous year, respectively.

*Required:*

1. Determine the ending inventory that would have been reported in the current year if DaimlerChrysler had used only FIFO.
2. Determine the cost of goods sold that would have been reported if DaimlerChrysler had used only FIFO for both years.
3. Explain why DaimlerChrysler management chose to use LIFO for certain of its inventories.

**AP7–4** **Evaluating the Effects of Failed Expansion Plans on Inventory Turnover Ratio and Cash Flows from Operating Activities** (P7–9)

Arctic Enterprises, Inc., was the world's second-largest manufacturer of snowmobiles and had experienced exceptional growth in recent years. It planned for a major increase in sales in the following period by increasing production dramatically. Unfortunately, North America experienced less snow that year than in any of the preceding 20 years. As a consequence, sales remained flat, and Arctic reported a small profit of $1.9 million. However, its inventory balance increased by $24 million. Based on the following information, answer the questions that follow:

**LO5**

Arctic Enterprises

| | (in thousands) | |
|---|---|---|
| | **Beginning of Year** | **End of Year** |
| Inventory | $23,808 | $47,270 |
| | | Current Year |
| Cost of goods sold | | $161,069 |

*Required:*

1. Compute the inventory turnover ratio based on two different assumptions:
   *a.* Those presented in the preceding table.
   *b.* No change from the beginning of the year in the inventory balance.

2. Compute the effect of the change in the balance in inventory on cash flow from operating activities for the year (the sign and amount of effect).

3. On the basis of your analysis, write a brief memo explaining how a decrease in inventory turnover can result in a decrease in cash flow from operating activities.

**AP7–5** **(Supplement B) Recording Sales and Purchases with Cash Discounts and Returns** (P7–12)

The following transactions were selected from those occurring during the month of January 20D for Dan's Store, Incorporated. A wide line of goods is offered for sale. Credit sales are extended to a few select customers; the usual credit terms are n/EOM. Cost of sales is always one-half of gross sales price.

- *a.* Sold to customers:

| | |
|---|---:|
| Cash | $228,000 |
| On credit | 72,000 |

- *b.* Unsatisfactory merchandise returned by customers:

| | |
|---|---:|
| Cash | 3,000 |
| Credit | 2,000 |

Purchased merchandise from vendors on credit; terms 2/10, n/30:

| | | |
|---|---|---:|
| *c.* | XYZ Supply Company, amount billed, before deduction of cash discount | 4,000 |
| *d.* | From other vendors, amount billed, before deduction of cash discount | 68,000 |
| *e.* | Freight paid on merchandise purchased; paid cash | 1,500 |
| *f.* | Collections on accounts receivable | 36,000 |

Paid accounts payable in full during the period as follows:

| | | |
|---|---|---:|
| *g.* | Paid XYZ Supply Company after the discount period | 4,000 |
| *h.* | Paid other vendors within the discount period | 66,640 |
| *i.* | Purchased two new typewriters for the office; paid cash | 1,000 |

*Required:*

Prepare journal entries for these transactions, assuming that a perpetual inventory system is in use. Record inventory purchases using the gross method.

# CASES AND PROJECTS

## FINANCIAL REPORTING AND ANALYSIS CASES

■ **1, 3, 5**    **CP7–1**

American Eagle
Outfitters

STANDARD
&POOR'S

**Finding Financial Information**

Refer to the financial statements of American Eagle Outfitters given in Appendix B at the end of this book, or open file AEOS10K.doc in the S&P directory on the student CD-ROM.

1. How much inventory does the company hold at the end of the current year?

2. Estimate the amount of merchandise that the company purchased during the current year. (*Hint:* Use the cost of goods sold equation and ignore "certain buying, occupancy, and warehousing expenses.")

3. What method does the company use to determine the cost of its inventory?

4. What was the change in inventory? How did it affect net cash provided by operating activities for the current year?

■ **1, 3, 5**    **CP7–2**

Urban Outfitters

STANDARD
&POOR'S

**Finding Financial Information**

Refer to the financial statements of Urban Outfitters given in Appendix C at the end of this book, or open file URBN10K.doc in the S&P directory on the student CD-ROM.

1. What method does the company use to determine the cost of its inventory?

2. What are the components of the company's inventory balance? What aspects of its operations might determine why the first component is much smaller than the second?

3. Compute Urban Outfitters' inventory turnover ratio for the year ended January 31, 1999.

## CP7–3 Comparing Companies within an Industry

Refer to the financial statements of American Eagle Outfitters given in Appendix B and Urban Outfitters given in Appendix C, and the Standard and Poor's Industry Ratio Report given in Appendix D at the end of this book or open file CP7–3.xls in the S&P directory on the student CD-ROM.

*Required:*

1. Compute the inventory turnover ratio for both companies for the current year. What would you infer from the difference?

2. Both companies measure inventory at the lower of cost or market. However, one of the companies determines cost of inventory using the average cost method while the other uses FIFO. Would you expect the different methods to cause a large difference in cost of goods sold? Why?

3. Compare the inventory turnover ratio for both companies to the industry average. Are these two companies doing better or worse than the industry average in turning over their inventory?

■ LO5

American Eagle
Outfitters vs.
Urban Outfitters

STANDARD
&POOR'S

## CP7–4 Interpreting the Financial Press

In an article entitled "Convenient Fiction: Inventory Chicanery Tempts More Firms, Fools More Auditors," *The Wall Street Journal* outlined a series of cases in which companies used inventory fraud to overstate earnings. The article is available on the Libby/Libby/Short website at www.mhhe.com/business/accounting/libby3. You should read the article and then write a short memo outlining the cases involved and how each of the inventory misstatements inflated earnings. Each case involved inflating ending inventory quantities or values. Indicate how doing so increases earnings. Also discuss the steps the author suggests that auditors should take to avoid such misstatements in the future.

■ LO2

*The Wall Street
Journal*

## CP7–5 Using Financial Reports: An International Perspective

As the economy becomes more international in scope, users of financial statements are often expected to analyze companies that are not incorporated in the United States. Diageo is a major world corporation located in London. It owns many U.S. businesses such as The Pillsbury Company, Burger King, and Hägen-Dazs ice cream.

Diageo

*Required:*

Based on the concepts presented in this book, explain the meaning of the various account classifications shown on the portion of the Diageo annual report presented here. *(Note:* "Share of profits of related companies" and "Minority interests and preference dividends" pertain to topics introduced in subsequent chapters.)

| DIAGEO<br>Consolidated Profit and Loss Account<br>For the Year Ended 30th September 20B | Notes | 20B £m | 20A £m |
|---|---|---|---|
| **Turnover** | 1 | 9,298 | 6,029 |
| Operating costs | 2 | (8,349) | (5,387) |
| | | 949 | 642 |
| Share of profits of related companies | 3 | 18 | 12 |
| **Trading profit** | | 967 | 654 |
| Profit on sale of property | | 80 | 39 |
| Reorganisation costs | | (35) | (25) |
| Interest | 4 | (280) | (93) |
| Profit on ordinary activities before taxation | | 732 | 575 |
| Taxation on profit on ordinary activities | | (216) | (155) |
| Profit on ordinary activities after taxation | | 516 | 420 |
| Minority interests and preference dividends | 5 | (8) | (8) |
| Profit attributable to ordinary shareholders | | 508 | 412 |
| Extraordinary items | 6 | 560 | 290 |
| Profit for the financial year | | 1,068 | 702 |
| Ordinary dividends | 7 | (167) | (129) |
| Transferred to reserves | | 901 | 573 |
| Earnings per share | 8 | 55.6p | 46.9p |

■**LO1**

*Dana Corporation*

**CP7–6**  **Using Financial Reports: Interpreting Effect of a Change in Accounting for Production-Related Costs**

Dana Corporation designs and manufactures component parts for the vehicular, industrial, and mobile off-highway original equipment markets. In a recent annual report, Dana's inventory note indicated the following:

> Dana changed its method of accounting for inventories effective January 1 . . . to include in inventory certain production-related costs previously charged to expense. This change in accounting principle resulted in a better matching of costs against related revenues. The effect of this change in accounting increased inventories by $23.0 and net income by $12.9.

*Required:*

1. Under Dana's previous accounting method, certain production costs were recognized as expenses on the income statement in the period they were incurred. When will they be recognized under the new accounting method?

2. Explain how including these costs in inventory increased both inventories and net income for the year.

■**LO3, 5**

*Caterpillar*

**CP7–7**  **Using Financial Reports: Interpreting Effects of the LIFO/FIFO Choice on Inventory Turnover**

In a recent annual report, Caterpillar, Inc., a major manufacturer of farm and construction equipment, reported the following information concerning its inventories:

> The cost of inventories is determined principally by the LIFO (last-in, first-out) method of inventory valuation. This method was first adopted for the major portion of inventories in 1950. The value of inventories on the LIFO basis represented approximately 90% of total inventories at current cost value on December 31, 1995, 1993, and 1992. If the FIFO (first-in, first-out) method had been in use, inventories would have been $2,103, $2,035, and $1,818 higher than reported at December 31, 1995, 1994, and 1993, respectively.

On its balance sheet, it reported:

|  | 1995 | 1994 | 1993 |
|---|---|---|---|
| Inventories | $1,921 | $1,835 | $1,525 |

On its income statement, it reported:

|  | 1995 | 1994 | 1993 |
|---|---|---|---|
| Cost of goods sold | $12,000 | $10,834 | $9,075 |

*Required:*

As a recently hired financial analyst, you have been asked to analyze the efficiency with which Caterpillar has been managing its inventory and to write a short report. Specifically, you have been asked to compute inventory turnover for 1995 based on FIFO and on LIFO and compare the two ratios with two standards: (1) Caterpillar for the prior year 1994 and (2) its chief competitor, John Deere. For 1995, John Deere's inventory turnover was 4.2 based on FIFO and 9.8 based on LIFO. In your report, include

1. The appropriate ratios computed based on FIFO and LIFO.

2. An explanation for the differences in the ratios across the FIFO and LIFO methods.

3. An explanation of whether the FIFO or LIFO ratios provide a more accurate representation of the companies' efficiency in use of inventory.

**CP7–8**

*General Motors*

**(Supplement A) Using Financial Reports: Analysis of the Effects of LIFO Liquidations**

Several years ago, General Motors reported the following in its inventory note:

> The cost of substantially all domestic inventories was determined by the last-in, first-out (LIFO) method. If the first-in, first-out (FIFO) method of inventory valuation had been used by the Corporation for U.S. inventories, it is estimated they would be $1,886.0 million higher at December 31, [current year] compared with $2,077.1 million at December 31, [prior year]. As a result of decreases in unit sales and actions taken to reduce inventories, certain LIFO inventory quantities carried at lower costs prevailing in prior years, as compared with the costs of current purchases, were liquidated. . . . These inventory adjustments favorably affected income (loss) before income taxes by approximately $305.0 million [current year].

In the current year, GM recorded a small pretax operating profit of $22.8 million.

*Required:*

1. Compute the amount of pretax operating profit (loss) that GM would have reported had it not reduced inventory quantities during the current year.

2. Compute the amount of pretax operating profit (loss) for the current year that GM would have reported had it employed FIFO accounting in both years.

3. What is the normal relationship between pretax operating profit computed using LIFO and FIFO when costs are rising? Why is this relationship not in evidence in this case?

## CRITICAL THINKING CASES

**CP7–9** **Making a Decision as a Financial Analyst: Analysis of the Effect of a Change to LIFO**

A recent annual report for Quaker Oats included the following information:

■ **LO4**

Quaker Oats

> The company adopted the LIFO cost flow assumption for valuing the majority of remaining U.S. Grocery Products inventories. The Company believes that the use of the LIFO method better matches current costs with current revenues. The cumulative effect of this change on retained earnings at the beginning of the year is not determinable, nor are the pro forma effects of retroactive application of LIFO to prior years. The effect of this change on the current year was to decrease net income by $16.0 million, or $0.20 per share.

*Required:*

As a new financial analyst at a leading Wall Street investment banking firm, you are assigned to write a memo outlining the effects of the accounting change on Quaker's financial statements. Assume a 34 percent tax rate. In your report, be sure to include the following:

1. In addition to the reason that was cited, why did management adopt LIFO?

2. As an analyst, how would you react to the $0.20 per share decrease in income caused by the adoption of LIFO?

**CP7–10** **Evaluating an Ethical Dilemma: Earnings, Inventory Purchases, and Management Bonuses**

Micro Warehouse is a computer software and hardware on-line and catalogue sales company. A recent *Wall Street Journal* article disclosed the following:

■ **LO2**

Micro Warehouse

> ### MICRO WAREHOUSE IS REORGANIZING TOP MANAGEMENT
>
> Micro Warehouse Inc. announced a "significant reorganization" of its management, including the resignation of three senior executives.
>
> The move comes just a few weeks after the Norwalk, Conn., computer catalogue sales company said it overstated earnings by $28 million since 1992 as a result of accounting irregularities. That previous disclosure prompted a flurry of shareholder lawsuits against the company. In addition, Micro Warehouse said it is cooperating with an "informal inquiry" by the Securities and Exchange Commission.
>
> SOURCE: Stephan E. Frank, *The Wall Street Journal,* November 21, 1996, p. B2.

Its Form 10–Q quarterly report filed with the Securities and Exchange Commission two days before indicated that inaccuracies involving understatement of purchases and accounts payable in current and prior periods amounted to $47.3 million. It also indicated that, as a result, $2.2 million of executive bonuses for 1995 would be rescinded. Micro Warehouse's total tax rate is approximately 40.4 percent. Both cost of goods sold and executive bonuses are fully deductible for tax purposes.

***Required:***
As a new staff member at Micro Warehouse's auditing firm, you are assigned to write a memo outlining the effects of the understatement of purchases and the rescinding of the bonuses. In your report, be sure to include the following:

1. The total effect on pretax and after-tax earnings of the understatement of purchases.

2. The total effect on pretax and after-tax earnings of the rescinding of the bonuses.

3. An estimate of the percentage of after-tax earnings management is receiving in bonuses.

4. A discussion of why Micro Warehouse's board of directors may have decided to tie managers' compensation to reported earnings and the possible relation between this type of bonus scheme and the accounting errors.

# FINANCIAL REPORTING AND ANALYSIS PROJECTS

■ **LO5**     **CP7–11**
Harley-Davidson

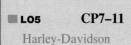

**Comparing Companies over Time: Inventory Turnover Ratio**
Acquire the three most recent years' income statements and balance sheets for Harley-Davidson (contact Harley-Davidson investor relations at www.harley-davidson.com, or obtain them from EDGAR service at www.sec.gov/cgi-bin/srch-edgar). Write a short memo comparing the company's inventory turnover ratio over the three years. Indicate what differences in its operations might account for any differences in the ratios.

■ **LO5**     **CP7–12**
Timberland
versus
Competitors

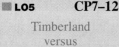

**Comparing Companies within Industries: Inventory Turnover Ratio**
Timberland's competitors in the shoe industry include Skechers, Wolverine World Wide, Brown Group, Reebok, Nike, and Stride Rite. Obtain the most recent income statement, balance sheet, and uncollectible accounts schedule (from the 10-K) for Timberland and two of its competitors. (Library files, the SEC EDGAR service at www.sec.gov/cgi-bin/srch-edgar, Compustat CD, or the company Web sites are good sources.) Write a short memo comparing the companies' inventory turnover ratio. Indicate what differences in their products or business strategies might account for any differences in the ratios. Consider the possible effect of use of the LIFO method.

■ **LO3, 4**     **CP7–13**

**Comparing Inventory Accounting Policies among Industries**
Acquire the inventory accounting note from the annual reports or 10-Ks of three companies from different industries (industry lists can be found at www.marketguide.com/mgi/INDUSTRY/INDUSTRY.html and www.hoovers.com, click on companies and industries). (Library files, the SEC EDGAR service at www.sec.gov/cgi-bin/srch-edgar, Compustat CD, or the company web sites are good sources.) Write a short report indicating any similarities or differences among the accounting policies. Consider what characteristics of the companies and their inventories may have led to the choices of methods. If the company used LIFO, indicate whether it paid higher or lower taxes as a result in the current year.

■ **LO5**     **CP7–14**

**Analyzing the Effects of Inventory and Accounts Payable on Cash Flows**
Acquire the three most recent years' cash flow statements for a single company. (Library files, the SEC EDGAR service at www.sec.gov/cgi-bin/srch-edgar, Compustat CD, or the company web sites are good sources.) Write a short memo describing the effect of the change in inventory and accounts payable on the difference between net income and cash flow from operations for each year.

■ **LO2**     **CP7–15**

**Ethics Project: Analysis of Irregularities in Inventory**
Obtain a recent news story outlining an accounting irregularity related to inventory. (Library files, *Wall Street Journal* Index, Dow Jones Interactive, and *Bloomberg Business News* are good sources. Search for the term *accounting irregularities*.) Write a short memo outlining the nature of the irregularity, the size of the necessary correction of previously reported earnings,

the impact of the announcement of the irregularity on the company's stock price, and any fines or civil penalties against the company and its officers.

**CP7–16    Broadening Financial Research Skills: Competitive Analysis on the Web**

A key to ratio analysis is the identification of similar companies (competitors) for comparison purposes. Your task is to use www.hoovers.com to identify competitors within the auto manufacturing industry. Go to its website, and click on "companies and industries." Work your way to the "auto manufacturing" industry and do the following: (1) determine the definition and SIC code for this industry, (2) list the companies for which there is a "profile" provided and the country in which they are headquartered, and (3) rank the companies by their most recent annual sales revenue.

**CP7–17    Team Project: Analyzing Inventories**

**LO4, 5**

As a team, select an industry to analyze (industry lists can be found at www.marketguide.com/mgi/INDUSTRY/INDUSTRY.html and www.hoovers.com, click on companies and industries). Each team member should acquire the annual report or 10-K for one publicly traded company in the industry, with each member selecting a different company. (Library files, the SEC EDGAR service at www.sec.gov/cgi-bin/srch-edgar, Compustat CD, or the company websites are good sources.) On an individual basis, each team member should then write a short report answering the following questions about the selected company.

1.  What inventory costing method is applied to U.S. inventories? What do you think motivated this choice?

2.  If the company used LIFO, how much higher or lower would net income before taxes be if it had used FIFO or a similar method instead?

3.  What is the inventory turnover ratio?

4.  What was the effect of the change in inventories on cash flow from operations? Explain your answer.

Discuss any patterns across the companies that you as a team observe. Then, as a team, write a short report comparing and contrasting your companies using these attributes. Provide potential explanations for any differences discovered.

# Reporting and Interpreting Property, Plant, and Equipment; Natural Resources; and Intangibles

## CHAPTER **EIGHT**

---

### LEARNING **OBJECTIVES**

*After studying this chapter, you should be able to:*

1. Define, classify, and explain the nature of noncurrent productive assets.   p. 424

2. Apply the cost principle to measure the acquisition of property, plant, and equipment.   p. 424

3. Understand the financial statement impact of management's decisions regarding ordinary and extraordinary repairs.
   p. 428

4. Apply various cost allocation methods and changes in estimates as assets are held and used over time.   p. 432

5. Explain the impact of cost allocation methods on cash flows and ratio analysis.   p. 442

6. Analyze the disposal of property, plant, and equipment.
   p. 444

7. Understand the measurement and reporting of natural resources and intangible assets.   p. 446

8. Explain the effect of asset impairment on the financial statements.   p. 450

Delta Air Lines is a major air carrier providing service to 148 domestic cities in 42 states and 46 international cities in 31 foreign countries. Delta is a capital-intensive company with more than $9,321,000,000 in property, plant, and equipment reported on its balance sheet. In fiscal year 1998,

FOCUS **COMPANY:**

# Delta Air Lines

## MANAGING PROFITS THROUGH CONTROL OF PRODUCTIVE CAPACITY

Delta acquired 29 aircraft and spent $1.86 billion on flight equipment. Demand for air travel is seasonal, with peak demand occurring during the summer months because of vacation time. Demand is very sensitive to general economic conditions. As a result, planning for optimal productive capacity in the airline industry is very difficult.

On March 20, 1997, Delta Air Lines signed a major long-term agreement with Boeing Co., the world's largest manufacturer of aircraft, to buy planes exclusively from Boeing over the next 20 years. The contract included an initial firm order to purchase 106 jets with list prices totaling $6.7 billion and a flexible agreement (options) "to buy as many as 644 planes from Boeing during the next two decades at prearranged discount prices."[1]

Twenty-eight new aircraft were on order for delivery in 1999 alone, including the Boeing 777-200, which carries more people than existing aircraft and is fuel efficient.

---

[1]J. Cole and M. Brannigan, "Delta's Pact to Buy Only Boeing Jets Draws Sharp Rebuke from Rival Airbus," *The Wall Street Journal,* March 21, 1997, p. A3.

The exclusive deal signaled a dramatic shift from traditional purchasing practices—a deal that effectively shuts out competitors. Delta hoped that a more modern fleet would attract additional passengers and reduce operating costs. Buying from a single supplier also should dramatically simplify maintenance of aircraft and employee training. Improved management of productive capacity will be a key to Delta's success in the 21st century.

## BUSINESS BACKGROUND

One of the major challenges facing managers of most businesses is forecasting the level of productive capacity (that is, the size of a company's plant and equipment) needed in the long term. If managers underestimate the need, the company will not be able to produce goods or services that are in demand and will miss the opportunity to earn revenue. On the other hand, if needed productive capacity is overestimated, the company will incur excessive costs that will reduce profitability.

The airline industry provides an outstanding example of the difficulty associated with planning for and analyzing productive capacity. If an airplane takes off from Kansas City, Missouri, en route to New York City with empty seats, the economic value associated with those seats is lost forever. There is obviously no way to sell the seat to a customer after the airplane has left the gate. Unlike a manufacturer, an airline cannot "inventory" seats for the future.

Likewise, if a large number of people want to board a flight, the airline must turn away customers if seats are not available. You might be willing to buy a television set from Sears even if you are told that it is out of stock and there will be a one-week delay in delivery. You probably wouldn't fly home for Thanksgiving on an airline that told you that you would have to wait one week because no seats were available on its flights. You would simply pick another airline or use a different mode of transportation.

The asset section of the balance sheet from Delta's annual report for the fiscal year ended June 30, 1998, is shown in Exhibit 8.1. Additional information about property, plant, and equipment is contained in Delta's 10–K report. The 10–K report shows the amount of new investment in equipment for the year, the amount of equipment that was sold or retired, and the specific number of each type of aircraft that Delta owns. We discuss some of these data in this chapter.

Delta has a number of large competitors with familiar names such as American, U•S Airways, United, and Southwest. The description of the business in Delta's 10–K report mentions that "all domestic routes served by Delta are subject to competition from new and existing carriers, and service over virtually all of Delta's domestic routes is highly competitive. . . . Service over most of Delta's international routes is highly competitive."

Much of the battle for passengers in the airline industry is fought in terms of property, plant, and equipment. Passengers want convenient schedules (which require a large number of aircraft) and to fly with new, modern equipment.

Because airlines have such a large investment in equipment with no opportunity to inventory unused seats, they work very hard to fill aircraft to capacity for each flight. The frequent fare wars that you read about in newspaper advertisements occur when airlines try to build customer demand to use their large investments in productive capacity. Delta's 10–K report contains a note addressing this issue.

**REAL WORLD EXCERPT**

*Delta Air Lines*

10–K REPORT

Delta expects that low-fare competition is likely to continue in domestic and international markets. If price reductions are not offset by increases in traffic or changes in the mix of traffic that improve the passenger mile yield, Delta's operating results will be adversely affected.

EXHIBIT **8.1**

**Delta Air Lines' Asset Section of the Balance Sheet**

**REAL WORLD EXCERPT**

*Delta Air Lines*

ANNUAL REPORT

**DELTA AIR LINES, INC.**
**CONSOLIDATED BALANCE SHEETS**
**June 30, 1998 and 1997**

| Assets *(in millions)* | 1998 | 1997 |
|---|---|---|
| **Current Assets:** | | |
| Cash and cash equivalents | $ 1,077 | $ 662 |
| Short-term investments | 557 | 508 |
| Accounts receivable, net of allowance for uncollectible accounts of $36 at June 30, 1998 and $48 at June 30, 1997 | 938 | 943 |
| Deferred income taxes | 464 | 413 |
| Prepaid expenses and other | 326 | 341 |
| Total current assets | 3,362 | 2,867 |
| **Property and Equipment:** | | |
| Flight equipment | 11,180 | 9,619 |
| Less: Accumulated depreciation | 3,895 | 3,510 |
| | 7,285 | 6,109 |
| Flight equipment under capital leases | 515 | 523 |
| Less: Accumulated amortization | 216 | 176 |
| | 299 | 347 |
| Ground property and equipment | 3,285 | 3,032 |
| Less: Accumulated depreciation | 1,854 | 1,758 |
| | 1,431 | 1,274 |
| Advance payments for equipment | 306 | 312 |
| Total property and equipment | 9,321 | 8,042 |
| **Other Assets:** | | |
| Marketable equity securities | 424 | 432 |
| Deferred income taxes | — | 103 |
| Investments in associated companies | 326 | 299 |
| Cost in excess of net assets acquired, net of accumulated amortization of $112 at June 30, 1998 and $102 at June 30, 1997 | 265 | 275 |
| Leasehold and operating rights, net of accumulated amortization of $209 at June 30, 1998 and $199 at June 30, 1997 | 124 | 134 |
| Other | 781 | 589 |
| Total other assets | 1,920 | 1,832 |
| Total assets | $14,603 | $12,741 |

As you can see from this discussion, issues surrounding property, plant, and equipment have a pervasive impact on a company in terms of strategy, pricing decisions, and profitability. Managers devote considerable time planning optimal levels of productive capacity, and financial analysts closely review statements to determine the impact of management decisions.

# CLASSIFICATION OF LONG-LIVED ASSETS

■ **LEARNING OBJECTIVE 1**

Define, classify, and explain the nature of noncurrent productive assets.

The resources that determine productive capacity are often called **long-lived assets.** They have different characteristics, depending on the nature of the business. These assets are listed as noncurrent on the balance sheet and have the following characteristics:

1. **Tangible assets** have physical substance; that is, they can be touched. The three kinds of long-lived tangible assets are

   a. *Land* (held for use in operations; not subject to depreciation). As is the case with Delta, land often is not shown as a separate item on the balance sheet.

   b. *Buildings, fixtures, and equipment* (held for use in operations; subject to depreciation). For Delta, this category includes aircraft, ground equipment to service aircraft, and office space.

   c. *Natural resources* (held for use in operations; subject to depletion). Delta does not report any natural resources on its balance sheet. However, examples for other industries include timber tracts and silver mines.

**LONG-LIVED ASSETS** are tangible and intangible resources owned by a business and used in its operations over several years.

**TANGIBLE ASSETS** (or fixed assets) have physical substance.

This classification usually is called *property, plant, and equipment* (or *fixed assets*).

**INTANGIBLE ASSETS** have special rights but not physical substance.

2. **Intangible assets** are long-lived assets without physical substance that the business holds because of specific rights to use the asset they confer on the owner. Examples are patents, copyrights, franchises, licenses, and trademarks. Leasehold and operating rights shown on the Delta balance sheet are intangible assets.

Following the natural life cycle of long-lived assets, we first discuss the measuring and reporting issues related to the acquisition of land, buildings, and equipment. Then we examine the variety of issues related to holding and using these assets over time. We also discuss the disposal of land, buildings, and equipment, and then we focus on measuring and reporting natural resources, intangible assets, and impaired assets.

**ORGANIZATION** OF THE CHAPTER

| • **Measuring and Recording Acquisition Cost** | • **Using Property, Plant, and Equipment after Acquisition** | • **Disposal of Property, Plant and Equipment** | • **Intangible Assets** |
| --- | --- | --- | --- |
| Various Acquistion Methods | Repairs, Maintenance, and Additions | Fixed Asset Turnover | Acquisition and Cost Allocation |
| | Depreciation Concepts | | Examples of Intangible Assets |
| | Alternative Depreciation Methods | | |
| | Managers' Selection Among Accounting Alternatives | • **Natural Resources** | • **Impaired Assets** |
| | Changes in Depreciation Estimates | Acquisition and Cost Allocation | |

# MEASURING AND RECORDING ACQUISITION COST

■ **LEARNING OBJECTIVE 2**

Apply the cost principle to measure the acquisition of property, plant, and equipment.

For the sake of illustration, let's assume that Delta received the first new 737 aircraft from Boeing under the new agreement on July 1, 1997 (the beginning of Delta's 1998 fiscal year). The list price was $63 million (the average price in the new contract). Under the *cost principle,* all reasonable and necessary costs incurred in acquiring a long-lived asset, placing it in its operational setting, and preparing it for use should be recorded in a designated asset account (that is, should be capitalized). These costs, including any sales taxes, legal fees, transportation costs, and installation costs, are added to the purchase price of the aircraft. Any special discounts or financing (interest) charges associated with the purchase should not, however, be included in the cost of the asset. Financing charges should be reported as interest expense.

Although details of the discounts negotiated by Boeing and Delta are not publicly available, we can make assumptions for illustration purposes. Let's assume that Boeing offered Delta a discount of $4 million for signing the exclusive agreement. That means the price of the new plane to Delta is $59 million. Let's also assume that Delta paid for transportation charges of $200,000 and preparation costs of $800,000 for the new plane to make it ready for use. The amount recorded for the purchase is called the **acquisition cost,** which is the net cash equivalent amount paid or to be paid for the asset. Delta calculates the acquisition cost of the new aircraft as follows:

The **ACQUISITION COST** is the net cash equivalent amount paid or to be paid for the asset.

| | |
|---|---:|
| Invoice price of the aircraft | $63,000,000 |
| Less: Special discount for the agreement | 4,000,000 |
| Net cash invoice price | $59,000,000 |
| Add: Transportation charges paid by Delta | 200,000 |
| Installation (preparation) costs paid by Delta | 800,000 |
| Cost—amount added to the asset account | $60,000,000 |

In addition to purchasing buildings and equipment, a company may acquire undeveloped land, typically with the intent to build a new factory or office building. When land is purchased, all of the incidental costs paid by the purchaser, such as title fees, sales commissions, legal fees, title insurance, delinquent taxes, and surveying fees, should be included in the cost of the land. Because land is not subject to depreciation, it must be recorded as a separate asset.

Sometimes an old building or used machinery is purchased for operational use in the business. Renovation and repair costs incurred by the purchaser prior to use should be included in the asset account as a part of the cost of the asset.

## VARIOUS ACQUISITION METHODS

**For Cash** Assuming that Delta paid cash for the aircraft, the transaction affects Delta's records as follows:

| | | |
|---|---:|---:|
| Flight equipment (A) ................... | 60,000,000 | |
| Cash (A) ........................... | | 60,000,000 |

| Assets | | = | Liabilities | + | Stockholders' Equity |
|---|---|---|---|---|---|
| Flight equipment | +60,000,000 | | | | |
| Cash | −60,000,000 | | | | |

**For Debt** It might seem unusual for Delta to pay cash to purchase new assets that cost $60 million, but this is often the case. When it acquires productive assets, a company may pay with cash that was generated from operations or cash that was recently borrowed. It also is possible for the seller to finance the purchase on credit.

Now let's assume that Delta signed a note payable for the new aircraft and cash for the transportation and preparation costs. Delta records the following journal entry; the effects on the accounting equation are also shown:

| | | |
|---|---:|---:|
| Flight equipment (A) ................... | 60,000,000 | |
| Cash (A) ........................... | | 1,000,000 |
| Note payable (L) .................... | | 59,000,000 |

| Assets | | = | Liabilities | | + | Stockholders' Equity |
|---|---|---|---|---|---|---|
| Flight equipment | +60,000,000 | | Note payable | +59,000,000 | | |
| Cash | − 1,000,000 | | | | | |

**For Noncash Consideration (Including Equity)**   Noncash consideration might be part of the transaction, such as a company's common stock or a right given by the company to the seller to purchase the company's goods or services at a special price over a specified period of time. When noncash consideration is included in the purchase of an asset, the cash-equivalent cost is measured as any cash paid plus the current market value of the noncash consideration given. Alternatively, if the market value of the non-cash consideration given cannot be determined, the current market value of the asset purchased is used for measurement purposes.

Now assume that Delta gave 400,000 shares of its common stock (par value of $3 per share) with a market value of $85 per share (the approximate stock price on the date of the transaction) and paid Boeing the balance in cash including cash for the transportation and preparation. The journal entry and transaction effects follow:

| | | |
|---|---|---|
| Flight equipment (A) . . . . . . . . . . . . . . . . . . . . . . . | 60,000,000 | |
| Cash (A) . . . . . . . . . . . . . . . . . . . . . . . . . . . . . | | 26,000,000 |
| Common stock (SE) ($3 par value × 400,000) . . | | 1,200,000 |
| Additional paid-in capital (SE) ($82 × 400,000) . . | | 32,800,000 |

| Assets | | = | Liabilities | + | Stockholders' Equity | |
|---|---|---|---|---|---|---|
| Flight equipment | +60,000,000 | | | | Common stock | + 1,200,000 |
| Cash | −26,000,000 | | | | Additional paid-in capital | +32,800,000 |

**By Construction**   In some cases, a company may construct an asset for its own use instead of buying it from a manufacturer. When a company does this, the cost of the asset includes all necessary costs associated with construction, such as labor and materials. In most situations, these costs also include interest incurred during the construction period. The amount that is included in the cost of an asset is called **capitalized interest.** Interest on self-constructed assets should be capitalized even when the company did not borrow funds directly to support the construction. The amount of interest capitalized is based on the amount of funds that actually are invested in the construction project. The complex computation of interest capitalization is discussed in detail in other accounting courses.

Delta Air Lines includes a note on capitalized interest in a recent annual report:

**CAPITALIZED INTEREST** represents interest expenditures included in the cost of a self-constructed asset.

**REAL WORLD EXCERPT**

*Delta Air Lines*

ANNUAL REPORT

**NOTES TO CONSOLIDATED FINANCIAL STATEMENTS**
1. Summary of Significant Accounting Policies:
. . .

*Interest Capitalized*—Interest attributable to funds used to finance the acquisition of new aircraft and construction of major ground facilities is capitalized as an additional cost of the related asset. Interest is capitalized at the Company's weighted average interest rate on long-term debt or, where applicable, the interest rate of specific borrowings. Capitalization of interest ceases when the property or equipment is placed in service.

**As a Basket Purchase of Assets**   When several long-lived assets, such as land, building, and equipment, are acquired in a single transaction and for a single lump sum, known as a **basket purchase,** the cost of each asset must be measured and recorded separately. This is true because land is not depreciated, but buildings and equipment are, although at different rates. The purchase price must be apportioned between the land, the building, and the equipment on a rational basis.

Relative market value of the several assets on the date of acquisition is the most logical basis on which to allocate the single lump sum. Appraisals or tax assessments often must be used to indicate the market values. Assume that Delta Air Lines paid $300,000 cash to purchase a building and the land on which the building is located.

**BASKET PURCHASE** is an acquisition of two or more assets in a single transaction for a single lump sum.

The separate, true market values of the building and land were not known; therefore, a professional appraisal was obtained. This appraisal, totaling $315,000, showed the following estimated market values: $189,000 for the building and $126,000 for the land. The apportioned purchase price based on a percentage of the relative market value is computed as follows:

| Building | Land |
|---|---|
| $\dfrac{\text{Market Value}}{\text{Total Market Value}} = \dfrac{\$189,000}{\$315,000} = 60\%$ | $\dfrac{\text{Market Value}}{\text{Total Market Value}} = \dfrac{\$126,000}{\$315,000} = 40\%$ |
| 60% × $300,000 Total Cost = $180,000 | 40% × $300,000 Total Cost = $120,000 |

The ratio of the market value of the land to the total market value ($126,000 ÷ $315,000 = 40 percent) is multiplied by the total cost to measure the cost of the land ($300,000 × 40 percent). Similarly, the ratio of the market value of the building to the total market value ($189,000 ÷ $315,000 = 60 percent) is multiplied by the total cost to measure the cost of the building ($300,000 × 60 percent). Assuming that Delta purchases the assets with cash, the entry and effects are as follows:

| | | |
|---|---|---|
| Land (A) ............................ | 120,000 | |
| Building (A) ........................ | 180,000 | |
| Cash (A) ............................ | | 300,000 |

| Assets | = | Liabilities | + | Stockholders' Equity |
|---|---|---|---|---|
| Land | +120,000 | | | |
| Building | +180,000 | | | |
| Cash | −300,000 | | | |

Perhaps the most common example of a basket purchase of assets occurs when one corporation buys another corporation. In this case, the basket includes all of the assets owned by the acquired corporation. We discuss corporate acquisitions in a subsequent chapter.

## SELF-STUDY QUIZ

*McDonald's Corporation*

In a recent year, McDonald's Corporation purchased property, plant, and equipment priced at $1.8 billion. Assume that the company also paid $70 million for sales tax; $8 million for transportation costs; $1.3 million for installation and preparation of the property, plant, and equipment before use; and $100,000 in maintenance contracts to cover repairs to the property, plant, and equipment during use.

1. Compute the acquisition cost for the buildings and equipment:

2. Under the various following assumptions, indicate the effects of this acquisition on the following financial statement categories. Use + for increase and − for decrease and indicate the accounts and amounts:

| | Assets | Liabilities | Stockholders' Equity |
|---|---|---|---|
| a. Paid 30% in cash and the rest by a note payable. | | | |

| | Assets | Liabilities | Stockholders' Equity |
|---|---|---|---|
| *b.* Issued 10 million shares of common stock ($.10 per share stated value) at a market price of $45 per share and the balance in cash. | | | |

After you have completed your answers, check them with the solutions presented in the footnote at the bottom of this page.*

# USING PROPERTY, PLANT, AND EQUIPMENT AFTER ACQUISITION

## REPAIRS, MAINTENANCE, AND ADDITIONS

Most assets require substantial expenditures during their lives to maintain or enhance their productive capacity. One of the major reasons that Delta is switching to a single supplier for its aircraft is to reduce these costs. These expenditures include ordinary repairs and maintenance, major repairs, replacements, and additions. Some unsophisticated investors assume that the terms *expenditure* and *expense* are synonymous, but such is not the case. An expenditure is the payment of money to acquire goods or services. These goods and services may be recorded as either assets or expenses, depending on whether they benefit future periods or only the current period. Expenditures made after an asset is acquired are classified as follows:

1. **Capital expenditures**—expenditures that provide benefits for one or more accounting periods beyond the current period. Therefore, they are added to the appropriate *asset* accounts.

2. **Revenue expenditures**—expenditures that provide benefits during the current accounting period only. Therefore, they are added to the appropriate current *expense* accounts when incurred.

In many cases, no clear line distinguishes capital expenditures (assets) from revenue expenditures (expenses). In these situations, managers must exercise professional judgment and make a subjective decision. Many managers prefer to classify an item as a capital expenditure for financial reporting because net income for the period is higher

* 1.

| Property, Plant, and Equipment (PPE) | |
|---|---|
| Acquisition cost | $1,800,000,000 |
| Sales tax | 70,000,000 |
| Transportation | 8,000,000 |
| Installation | 1,300,000 |
| Total | $1,879,300,000 |

The maintenance contracts are not necessary for making the assets ready for use and therefore are not included in the acquisition cost.

2.

| Assets | | Liabilities | | Stockholders' Equity | |
|---|---|---|---|---|---|
| *a.* PPE | +1,879,300,000 | Note payable | +1,315,510,000 | | |
| Cash | − 563,790,000 | | | | |
| *b.* PPE | +1,879,300,000 | | | Common stock | + 1,000,000 |
| Cash | −1,429,300,000 | | | Paid-in capital | +449,000,000 |

by not reporting the total amount as an expense in the current period. Of course, most managers prefer to classify the expenditure as a deductible expense on the income tax return to pay lower taxes in the current period. Because these decisions are subjective, auditors closely review the items reported as capital and revenue expenditures.

To avoid spending too much time on classifying capital and revenue expenditures, some companies develop simple policies that govern the accounting for these expenditures. For example, one large computer company expenses all individual items that cost less than $1,000. These policies are acceptable because of the *materiality constraint*. The following are various types of revenue and capital expenditures.

**Ordinary Repairs and Maintenance**    **Ordinary repairs and maintenance** expenditures are for normal maintenance and upkeep of long-lived assets and are necessary to keep the assets in their usual condition. These expenditures are recurring in nature, involve relatively small amounts at each occurrence, and do not directly lengthen the useful life of the asset. Cash outlays for ordinary repairs and maintenance are revenue expenditures. They are *recorded as an expense* in the accounting period in which they are incurred.

In the case of Delta Air Lines, examples of ordinary repairs include changing oil in engines, replacing lights in the control panels, and fixing torn fabric in a passenger seat. Although each expenditure for ordinary repairs is relatively small, in the aggregate these expenditures can be substantial. In a recent year, Delta paid $495 million for aircraft maintenance and repairs. This amount was reported as an expense on its income statement.

**Extraordinary Repairs**    **Extraordinary repairs** are classified as capital expenditures. The cost of an extraordinary repair is *added to the related asset account*. Extraordinary repairs occur infrequently, involve large amounts of money, and increase the economic usefulness of the asset in the future because of either increased efficiency or longer life. Examples are major overhauls, complete reconditioning, and major replacements and improvements. The complete replacement of an engine on an aircraft is an example of an extraordinary repair.

**Additions**    **Additions** are extensions to or enlargements of existing assets, such as the addition of a wing to a building. These additions are capital expenditures. Therefore, the cost of additions should be added to the existing account for the asset.

### DEPRECIATION

A long-lived asset that has a limited useful life (such as an airplane purchased by Delta Air Lines) represents the prepaid cost of a bundle of future services or benefits that will help earn future revenues. The matching principle requires that a portion of the cost of long-lived assets (other than land) be allocated as an expense in the periods in which revenue is earned as a result of using those assets. Thus, the cost of long-lived assets is matched in a systematic and rational manner with the revenues that are earned by

**ORDINARY REPAIRS AND MAINTENANCE** are expenditures for normal operating upkeep of long-lived assets.

**EXTRAORDINARY REPAIRS** are expenditures for major, high-cost, long-term repairs that increase the economic usefulness of the asset.

**ADDITIONS** are extensions to or enlargements of existing assets that increase the cost of the existing asset.

using the asset. Delta Air Lines earns revenue by flying its aircraft and incurs an expense by using up part of the limited life of its aircraft.

The term used to identify the matching of the cost of buildings and equipment with revenues generated by the assets is **depreciation.**

> **Depreciation:** The systematic and rational *allocation of the acquisition cost* of tangible long-lived assets, other than land, to future periods in which the assets contribute services or benefits to help earn revenue.

The amount of depreciation recorded during each period is reported on the income statement as an expense for the period. The amount of depreciation accumulated since the acquisition date is reported on the balance sheet as a contra-account, Accumulated Depreciation, and is deducted from the asset cost to which it pertains.

Students often are confused about the concept of depreciation as accountants use it. Depreciation in accounting is a process of *cost allocation.* It is not a process of determining the current market value or worth of the asset. When an asset is depreciated, the remaining balance sheet amount *probably does not* represent the current market value of the asset. The balance sheet amounts are called *book* or *carrying values.* The **book (or carrying) value** of a long-lived asset is its acquisition cost less the accumulated depreciation (accumulated allocated cost) from acquisition date to the date of the balance sheet.

Under the cost principle, the cost of a long-lived asset is recorded at its current market value only on the acquisition date. At subsequent balance sheet dates, the undepreciated cost is not measured on a market value basis. Instead, the acquisition cost is reduced by the accumulated depreciation.

### DEPRECIATION CONCEPTS

The purpose of depreciation is to allocate the cost of a tangible long-lived asset over its useful life. The need for depreciation can be illustrated with a simple example. If you were the president of Delta in a year when it acquired a new aircraft for $60 million in cash, you probably would object strongly if the accountant tried to charge the entire cost to expense in the year of acquisition. You would argue that the aircraft should produce revenue for several years, so the cost of the asset should be charged to expense over the period in which it will earn revenue. Failure to do so would understate income in the year of acquisition and overstate income in each year that the aircraft was used. This explains why accountants depreciate tangible long-lived assets and why depreciation is an important part of measuring a company's profitability.

The calculation of depreciation expense requires three amounts for each asset:

1. Acquisition cost.
2. *Estimated* useful life to the company.
3. *Estimated* residual (or salvage) value at end of the asset's useful life to the company.

Of these three amounts, two (useful life and residual value) are estimates. Therefore, *depreciation expense is an estimate.* To compute depreciation expense for the aircraft acquired by Delta Air Lines in our earlier illustration, we use the same estimates as described in a recent Delta annual report:

---

**DEPRECIATION** is the systematic and rational allocation of the cost of property, plant, and equipment (but not land) over their useful lives.

**BOOK (OR CARRYING) VALUE** is the acquisition cost of an asset less accumulated depreciation, depletion, or amortization.

**REAL WORLD EXCERPT**

*Delta Air Lines*

ANNUAL REPORT

---

**NOTES TO CONSOLIDATED FINANCIAL STATEMENTS**

1. Summary of Significant Accounting Policies:

. . .

*Depreciation and Amortization*—Effective July 1, 1998, the Company increased the depreciable life of certain new generation aircraft types from 20 to 25 years. Owned flight equipment is depreciated on a straight-line basis to a residual value equal to 5% of cost.

Therefore, the annual depreciation expense is measured by allocating 95 percent of the $60 million cost (or $57 million) over 25 years.

| Depreciation expense ($57,000,000 ÷ 25 years) (E) . . . | 2,280,000 | |
|---|---|---|
| Accumulated depreciation (XA) . . . . . . . . . . . . . . . | | 2,280,000 |

| Assets | = | Liabilities | + | Stockholders' Equity | |
|---|---|---|---|---|---|
| Accumulated depreciation  −2,280,000 | | | | Depreciation expense | −2,280,000 |

If the aircraft had been purchased and used during the year, say on April 1, instead of at the beginning of the year, the depreciation expense is computed for the part of the year in use. April 1 is three months before year-end. Therefore, depreciation expense is $570,000 ($2,280,000 annual expense × $\frac{3}{12}$ of a year).[2]

FINANCIAL **ANALYSIS**

## BOOK VALUE AS AN APPROXIMATION OF REMAINING LIFE

Some analysts compare the book value of assets to their original cost as an approximation of their remaining life. If the book value of an asset is 100 percent of its cost, it is a new asset; if the book value is 25 percent of its cost, the asset has about 25 percent of its estimated life remaining. In Delta's case, the book value of its flight equipment is 65 percent of its original cost. This compares with 80 percent for Continental Airlines and 72 percent for Southwest Airlines. This comparison suggests that the flight equipment used by Delta may have less of its estimated life remaining than that of some other major airlines, unless they tend to purchase used aircraft. This comparison is only a rough approximation and is influenced by some of the accounting issues discussed in the next section.

**Book Value/ Original Cost**

Continental 80%

Southwest 72%

Delta 65%

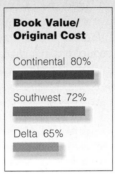

**Residual (or salvage) value** must be deducted from acquisition cost to compute depreciation expense. This value represents that part of the acquisition cost that is expected to be recovered by the user upon disposal of the asset at the end of its estimated useful life to the entity. The estimated net residual value is not necessarily the value of the asset as salvage or scrap. Rather, it may be the value to another user at the date on which the current owner intends to dispose of it. In the case of the aircraft owned by Delta Air Lines, it may be the amount it expects to receive when it sells the asset to a small regional airline that operates older equipment.

Residual value is the estimated amount to be recovered less any estimated costs of dismantling, disposal, and sale. In many cases, disposal costs may approximately equal the gross residual value. Therefore, many depreciable assets are assumed to have no residual value. In the case of Delta Air Lines, the notes to its financial statements indicate that it estimates residual value to be 5 percent of the cost of the asset.

**Estimated useful life** represents the useful *economic life* to the *present owner* rather than the total economic life to all potential users. In the Delta Air Lines example, the aircraft is able to fly for more than 25 years, but Delta wants to offer its customers a higher level of service by providing modern equipment. For accounting purposes,

**RESIDUAL (OR SALVAGE) VALUE** is the estimated amount to be recovered, less disposal costs, at the end of the company's estimated useful life of an asset.

**ESTIMATED USEFUL LIFE** is the expected service life of an asset to the present owner.

---

[2]Most of the examples that we discuss in this chapter assume that assets were acquired on the first day of the year and depreciated for the entire year. In practice, assets are purchased at various times during the year. Most companies adopt a policy to cover partial year depreciation, such as "to the nearest full month" or "half year in the year of acquisition."

Delta uses a 25-year estimated useful life, and the subsequent owner (the regional airline) uses an estimated useful life based on its own policies.

The determination of estimated useful life of a long-lived asset must conform to the *continuity assumption*. This assumption holds that the business will continue indefinitely to pursue its commercial objectives and will not liquidate in the foreseeable future.

## FINANCIAL **ANALYSIS**

### DIFFERENCES IN ESTIMATED LIVES WITHIN A SINGLE INDUSTRY

Notes to actual financial statements of companies in the airline industry reveal the following estimates for lives of flight equipment:

| Company | Estimated Life (in years) |
| --- | --- |
| Delta | 20 to 25 |
| TWA | 16 to 30 |
| U•S Airways | 11 to 20 |
| Singapore Airlines | 5 to 15 |
| Southwest | 20 to 25 |

The differences in estimated lives may be attributable to a number of factors such as type of aircraft used by each company, replacement plans, differences in operations, and degree of management conservatism. In addition, given the same type of aircraft, companies that plan to use the equipment over fewer years may estimate higher residual values than do companies that plan on a longer useful life. For example, Singapore Airlines uses a residual value of 20 percent over a relatively short useful life, as compared to 5 percent for Delta Air Lines over a 25-year useful life.

Differences in estimated lives and residual values of assets used by specific companies can have a large impact on the comparison of the profitability of the companies. Analysts must be certain that they identify the causes for the differences in depreciable lives.

## ALTERNATIVE DEPRECIATION METHODS

■ **LEARNING OBJECTIVE 4**

Apply various cost allocation methods and changes in estimates as assets are held and used over time.

Accountants have not been able to agree on a single, best method of depreciation because of significant differences among companies and the assets that they own. As a result, several different depreciation methods are commonly used in financial statements. The different depreciation methods are based on the same concept; each method allocates a portion of the cost of a depreciable asset to each future period in a systematic and rational manner. Nevertheless, each method allocates to each period a different portion of the cost to be depreciated. We discuss the following most common depreciation methods:

1. Straight line.
2. Units of production.
3. Accelerated depreciation method: declining balance.

The common set of facts and notations shown in Exhibit 8.2 will be used to illustrate these methods. This example is based on the assumption that Delta Air Lines acquired a service vehicle (ground equipment) with an estimated life of three years.

**STRAIGHT-LINE DEPRECIATION** is the method that allocates the cost of an asset in equal periodic amounts over its useful life.

**Straight-Line Method**    More companies, including Delta, use **straight-line depreciation** in their financial statements than all other methods combined. Under the

| DELTA AIR LINES | |
| --- | --- |
| Acquisition cost of repair truck, purchased on July 1, 20A | $62,500 |
| Estimated life (in years) | 3 |
| Estimated residual value | $2,500 |
| Estimated life in miles driven | 100,000 miles |
| Actual miles driven in: Year 20A | 30,000 miles |
| Year 20B | 50,000 miles |
| Year 20C | 20,000 miles |

straight-line method, an equal portion of the acquisition cost less the estimated residual value is allocated to each accounting period during the asset's estimated useful life. The formula to estimate annual depreciation expense follows:

**Straight-Line Method**

$$\underbrace{(\text{Cost} - \text{Residual Value})}_{\substack{\text{Depreciable} \\ \text{Amount}}} \times \underbrace{1/\text{Useful Life}}_{\substack{\text{Straight-Line} \\ \text{Rate}}} = \text{Annual Depreciation Expense}$$

"Cost minus residual value" is the depreciable amount. "$1 \div$ Useful life" is the straight-line rate. Using the data provided in Exhibit 8.2, the annual depreciation expense is measured as follows:

**($62,500 − $2,500) × 1/3 = $20,000 Annual Depreciation Expense**

Depreciation expense for Delta using the straight-line method is $20,000 per year. A *depreciation schedule* for the entire useful life of the machine is prepared:

| Year | Computations | Depreciation Expense (on the income statement) | Accumulated Depreciation (on the balance sheet at year-end) | Book Value (Cost − Accumulated Depreciation at year-end) |
| --- | --- | --- | --- | --- |
| At acquisition | | | | $62,500 |
| 20A | ($62,500 − $2,500) × 1/3 | $20,000 | $20,000 | 42,500 |
| 20B | ($62,500 − $2,500) × 1/3 | 20,000 | 40,000 | 22,500 |
| 20C | ($62,500 − $2,500) × 1/3 | 20,000 | 60,000 | 2,500 |
| | Total | $60,000 | | |

Notice that (1) depreciation expense is a constant amount for each year, (2) accumulated depreciation increases by an equal amount each year, and (3) book value decreases by the same amount each year. This is the reason for the designation of *straight line*. Also notice that, from this schedule, the adjusting entry can be prepared and the effect on the income statement and ending balance on the balance sheet are known. Delta Air Lines uses the straight-line method for all of its assets. Delta reported depreciation expense in the amount of $861,000,000 for 1998, which was 6.1 percent of the revenues earned for the year. Most companies in the airline industry use the straight-line method.

**Units-of-Production Method** **Units-of-production depreciation** relates depreciable cost to the total estimated productive output. The formula to estimate annual depreciation expense under this method follows:

**UNITS-OF-PRODUCTION DEPRECIATION** is the method that allocates the cost of an asset over its useful life based on its periodic output related to its total estimated output.

## Units-of-Production Method

Depreciation Rate
per Unit

$$\underbrace{\frac{\text{(Cost} - \text{Residual Value)}}{\text{Estimated Total Production}}} \times \frac{\text{Actual Annual}}{\text{Production}} = \text{Annual Depreciation Expense}$$

As before, "cost minus residual value" is the depreciable amount. By dividing the depreciable amount by estimated total production, the depreciation rate per unit of production also can be computed and then multiplied by the actual annual production to determine depreciation expense. Using the information in Exhibit 8.2, the computation of the depreciation rate per unit follows:

$$\frac{\$62,500 - \$2,500}{100,000 \text{ miles}} = \$0.60 \text{ Annual Depreciation Rate}$$

For every mile that the vehicle is driven, Delta records depreciation expense of $0.60. The depreciation schedule for Delta under the units-of-production method follows:

| Year | Computations | Depreciation Expense (on the income statement) | Accumulated Depreciation (on the balance sheet at year-end) | Book Value (Cost − Accumulated Depreciation at year-end) |
|---|---|---|---|---|
| At acquisition | | | | $62,500 |
| 20A | $.60 rate × 30,000 miles | $18,000 | $18,000 | 44,500 |
| 20B | .60 rate × 50,000 miles | 30,000 | 48,000 | 14,500 |
| 20C | .60 rate × 20,000 miles | 12,000 | 60,000 | 2,500 |
| | Total | $60,000 | | |

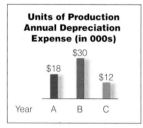

**Units of Production Annual Depreciation Expense (in 000s)**

$18   $30   $12
Year  A    B    C

**REAL WORLD EXCERPT**

*Exxon Corporation*

ANNUAL REPORT

Notice that depreciation expense, accumulated depreciation, and book value vary from period to period directly with the units produced. When the units-of-production method is used, depreciation expense is said to be a *variable expense* because it varies directly with production or use.

Exxon Corporation is in the energy industry with the worldwide exploration, production, transportation, and sale of crude oil and natural gas. The company uses the units-of-production method:

**1. Summary of Accounting Policies**

**Property, Plant and Equipment.** Depreciation, depletion, and amortization, based on cost less estimated salvage value of the asset, are primarily determined under either the unit of production method or the straight-line method. Unit of production rates are based on oil, gas and other mineral reserves estimated to be recoverable from existing facilities. The straight-line method of depreciation is based on estimated asset service life taking obsolescence into consideration.

The units-of-production method is based on an estimate of the total productive capacity of an asset. As you would expect, it is very difficult to estimate future output. This is another example of the degree of subjectivity that is inherent in accounting.

**Accelerated Depreciation—Declining-Balance Method** Accelerated depreciation means that in the early years of the useful life of an asset, depreciation expense amounts are higher, and in the later years, the amounts are lower. Accelerated depreciation is used for the following reasons:

**ACCELERATED DEPRECIATION** methods result in higher depreciation expense in the early years of an asset's life and lower expense in the later years.

1. A depreciable asset produces more revenue in its early life because it is more efficient in earlier years than in later years.
2. Repair costs increase in later years; therefore, total use cost per period should include decreasing depreciation expense to offset the increasing repair expense each period.

The relationship between accelerated depreciation expense, repair expense, and total use expense for Delta is in Exhibit 8.3.

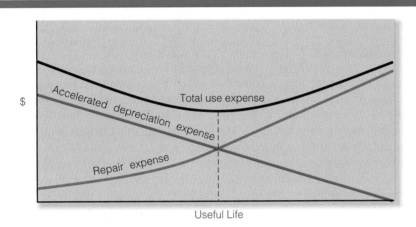

EXHIBIT **8.3**

**The Relationship between Depreciation Expense, Repair Expense, and Total Use Expense**

Accelerated methods are seldom used for financial reporting purposes. The accelerated method used more frequently than others is the declining-balance method, which is illustrated here. Another method, sum-of-the-years'-digits, is adopted less frequently and is described in higher-level accounting textbooks.

**Declining-balance depreciation** is based on applying an acceleration rate to the straight-line (SL) rate. The declining-balance (DB) rate is found by (1) computing the SL rate, ignoring residual value, and then (2) multiplying that SL rate by a selected acceleration rate, which may not exceed 200 percent. For example, if the estimated useful life is 10 years, the straight-line rate is 10 percent (1 ÷ 10), and the declining-balance rate at 200 percent is 20 percent (2 × the straight-line rate of 10 percent). Typical acceleration rates are 150 percent, 175 percent, and 200 percent. The 200 percent rate, often termed the *double-declining-balance (DDB) rate,* is adopted most frequently by companies utilizing the accelerated method and will be used in our illustration.

To calculate depreciation expense under the double-declining-balance method, the net book value of the asset is multiplied by the DDB rate as follows:

**DECLINING-BALANCE DEPRECIATION** is the method that allocates the cost of an asset over its useful life based on a multiple of (often two times) the straight-line rate.

| **Double-Declining-Balance Method** |
| :---: |

|                     | **Declining-Balance Rate** |
| :---: | :---: |
| **Net Book Value**  |                  |

**(Cost − Accumulated Depreciation) × 2/Useful Life = Annual Depreciation Expense**

Notice at this stage of the calculation, residual value is not used in computing depreciation expense (i.e., it is not subtracted from cost). An asset's book value cannot be depreciated below residual value, however. Therefore, if the annual computation creates an accumulated depreciation balance that is too high (and therefore a net book value that is below residual value), a lower amount of depreciation expense is recorded so that net book value equals residual value. Then no additional depreciation expense is computed in subsequent years. Computation of declining-balance depreciation expense is illustrated using the data given in Exhibit 8.2 and assuming an acceleration rate of 200 percent:

| Year | Computations | Depreciation Expense (on the income statement) | Accumulated Depreciation (on the balance sheet at year-end) | Book Value (Cost − Accumulated Depreciation at year-end) |
|---|---|---|---|---|
| At acquisition | | | | $62,500 |
| 20A | ($62,500 − $0) × 2/3 | $41,667 | $41,667 | 20,833 |
| 20B | ($62,500 − $41,667) × 2/3 | 13,889 | 55,556 | 6,944 |
| 20C | ($62,500 − $55,556) × 2/3 | 4,629 is too high; so record only 4,444 | 60,000 | 2,500 |
| | Total | $60,000 | | |

Notice that the calculated depreciation expense for year 20C ($4,629) is not the same as the amount actually reported on the income statement ($4,444). An asset should never be depreciated below its residual value. The asset owned by Delta has an estimated residual value of $2,500. If depreciation expense were recorded in the amount of $4,629, the book value of the asset would be less than $2,500. The correct depreciation expense for year 20C is $4,444 ($6,944 − $2,500), which is the amount that will reduce the book value to exactly $2,500. As you can see, it is necessary to check each year to be certain that the calculated amount of depreciation expense does not reduce the book value of the asset below its estimated residual value. In most cases when this occurs, depreciation expense is limited to the amount that reduces book value to the exact amount of the estimated residual value.

Companies in industries that expect fairly rapid obsolescence of equipment and many Japanese companies use the declining-balance method. Sony is one of the companies that uses this method.

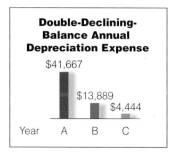

**Double-Declining-Balance Annual Depreciation Expense**

$41,667

$13,889

$4,444

Year     A     B     C

**REAL WORLD EXCERPT**

*Sony*

ANNUAL REPORT

**2. Summary of significant accounting policies:**

*Property, plant and equipment and depreciation*

Property, plant and equipment is stated at cost. Depreciation of property, plant and equipment is computed on the declining-balance method for the parent company and Japanese subsidiaries and on the straight-line method for foreign subsidiaries at rates based on estimated useful lives of the assets according to general class, type of construction and use.

As this note indicates, companies may use different depreciation methods for different classes of assets. Under the consistency principle, they are expected to apply the same methods over time.

The following summarizes the methods and computations and graphs the differences in depreciation expense over time between straight-line and declining-balance methods. The units-of-production method varies with the amount of actual production during the period; therefore, it is not on the graph in Exhibit 8.4.

| Method | Computation |
|---|---|
| Straight line | (Cost − Residual Value) × 1/Useful Life |
| Units of production | (Cost − Residual Value)/Estimated Total Production × Annual Production |
| Double declining balance | (Cost − Accumulated Depreciation) × 2/Useful Life |

# FINANCIAL **ANALYSIS**

## IMPACT OF ALTERNATIVE DEPRECIATION METHODS

Assume that you are analyzing two companies that are exactly the same except for the fact that one uses accelerated depreciation and the other uses the straight-line method. Which

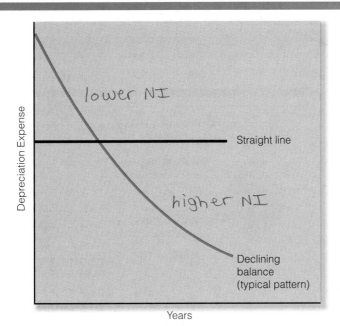

EXHIBIT **8.4**

**Differences in Depreciation over Time between Straight-Line and Declining-Balance Methods**

company would you expect to report higher net income? Actually, the question is a bit tricky. The answer is that you cannot say for certain.

The accelerated methods report higher depreciation during the early years of the life of an asset and therefore report lower net income. As the age of the asset increases, this effect reverses; therefore, companies that use accelerated depreciation report lower depreciation expense and higher net income during the later years of an asset's life. The preceding graph shows the pattern of depreciation over the life of an asset for the two methods discussed in this chapter. When the curve for the accelerated method falls below the curve for the straight-line method, the accelerated method causes higher net income to be reported compared to the straight-line method.

Users of financial statements must understand the impact of differences in the methods of accounting for depreciation and the way that the passage of time affects those differences. Significant differences in the reported net incomes of companies can be caused by differences in depreciation methods rather than by real economic differences.

## SELF-STUDY **QUIZ**

Assume that Delta acquired new computer equipment at a cost of $240,000. The equipment has an estimated life of six years (and an estimated operating life of 50,000 hours) with an estimated residual value of $30,000. Determine depreciation expense for the first full year under each of the following methods:

   1. Straight-line depreciation

   2. 200 percent declining-balance method

   3. Units-of-production method (assuming the equipment ran for 8,000 hours in the first year)

After you have completed your answers, check them with the solutions presented in the footnote at the bottom of this page.*

---

\*   1. ($240,000 − $30,000) × ⅙ = $35,000

   2. ($240,000 − 0) × ⅔ = $80,000

   3. [($240,000 − $30,000) ÷ 50,000] × 8,000 = $33,600

### MANAGERS' SELECTION AMONG ACCOUNTING ALTERNATIVES

The 1998 edition of *Accounting Trends & Techniques* (published by the AICPA) reported the depreciation methods used by 600 companies. Notice in the pie chart in Exhibit 8.5 that the number of methods exceeds the number of companies because some companies use more than one method for various asset categories.

EXHIBIT **8.5**

**Depreciation Methods
Commonly Used**

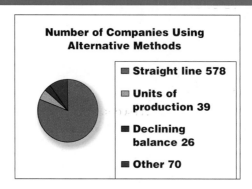

**Number of Companies Using
Alternative Methods**

- Straight line 578
- Units of production 39
- Declining balance 26
- Other 70

The method used by more than 95 percent of the companies for some or all of their assets is the straight-line method. Corporate managers find this method to be easy to use and to explain. During the early years of an asset's life, the straight-line method also reports higher income than the accelerated methods do.

**Depreciation and Federal Income Tax** Delta Air Lines, like most public companies, maintains two sets of accounting records. One set of records is prepared under GAAP for reporting to stockholders. The other set of records is prepared to determine the company's tax obligation under the Internal Revenue Code. When they first learn that companies maintain two sets of books, some people question the ethics or the legality of the practice. In reality, it is both legal and ethical to maintain separate records for tax accounting and financial reporting.

The reason that it is legal to maintain two sets of books is simple: The objectives of GAAP and the Internal Revenue Code differ.

| Financial Reporting (GAAP) | Tax Reporting (IRS) |
| --- | --- |
| Financial reporting rules following generally accepted accounting principles are designed to provide economic information about a business that is useful in projecting the future cash flows of the business. | The objective of the Internal Revenue Code is to raise sufficient revenues to pay for the expenditures of the federal government with many provisions designed to encourage certain behaviors that are thought to benefit our society (e.g., contributions to charities are tax deductible to encourage people to support worthy programs). |

It is easy to understand why two sets of accounting records are permitted, but perhaps the more interesting aspect concerns the reason that managers elect to go to the extra cost of maintaining two sets of books. In some cases, differences between the Internal Revenue Code and GAAP leave the manager no choice but to have separate records. In other cases, the explanation is an economic one. It is often called the *least and the latest rule.* All taxpayers want to pay the lowest amount of tax that is legally permitted, and they want to pay it at the latest possible date. If you had the choice of paying $100,000 to the federal government at the end of this year or the end of next year, you would choose the end of next year. By doing so, you would be able to invest the money for an extra year and earn a significant return on the investment.

By maintaining two sets of books, corporations are able to defer (delay) paying taxes in the amount of millions and sometimes billions of dollars. The following companies are entities that reported significant gross deferred tax obligations in a recent year by choosing accounting methods that delay tax payments. Much of the deferral is due to differences in asset cost allocation methods:

| Company | Deferred Tax Liabilities | Percentage Due to Applying Different Depreciation/Amortization Methods |
| --- | --- | --- |
| Delta Air Lines | $1,812 million | 80% |
| PepsiCo | 2,770 million | 76 |
| AT&T Corp. | 8,508 million | 86 |
| Kmart Corp. | 670 million | 55 |

Some of the depreciation methods discussed in the previous section are not acceptable for federal income tax reporting. Most corporations use the Modified Accelerated Cost Recovery System (MACRS) for calculating depreciation expense for their tax statement. MACRS is similar to the declining-balance method and is applied over relatively short asset lives, yielding high depreciation expense in the early years. It is not used for financial reporting purposes.

MACRS does not attempt to match the cost of an asset with the revenue it produces over its useful life in conformity with the matching principle. Instead, MACRS provides for rapid depreciation of an asset over a life that is usually much shorter than its estimated useful life. The intent of MACRS is to provide an incentive for corporations to invest in modern property, plant, and equipment to be competitive in world markets. The high depreciation expense reported under MACRS reduces a corporation's taxable income and therefore the amount it must pay in taxes.

INTERNATIONAL **PERSPECTIVE**

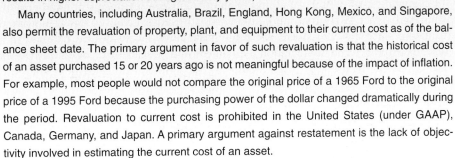

### DEPRECIATION METHODS IN OTHER COUNTRIES

The various depreciation methods discussed in this chapter are widely used by corporations in most countries. Some methods used in other countries are not generally used in the United States. German companies may depreciate based on the number of hours that an asset is used, and British companies may use the annuity method, which results in lower depreciation during the early years of the life of an asset (contrasted with accelerated depreciation, which results in higher depreciation during the early years).

Many countries, including Australia, Brazil, England, Hong Kong, Mexico, and Singapore, also permit the revaluation of property, plant, and equipment to their current cost as of the balance sheet date. The primary argument in favor of such revaluation is that the historical cost of an asset purchased 15 or 20 years ago is not meaningful because of the impact of inflation. For example, most people would not compare the original price of a 1965 Ford to the original price of a 1995 Ford because the purchasing power of the dollar changed dramatically during the period. Revaluation to current cost is prohibited in the United States (under GAAP), Canada, Germany, and Japan. A primary argument against restatement is the lack of objectivity involved in estimating the current cost of an asset.

### CHANGES IN DEPRECIATION ESTIMATES

Depreciation is based on two estimates—useful life and residual value. These estimates are made at the time a depreciable asset is acquired. One or both of these initial estimates may have to be revised as experience with the asset accumulates. In addition, extraordinary repairs and additions may be added to the original acquisition cost at some time during the asset's use. When it is clear that either estimate should be revised to a material degree or the asset's cost has been changed, the undepreciated asset balance less any residual value at that date should be apportioned, based on the new estimate, over the remaining estimated life. This is called a *change in estimate*.

For any of the depreciation methods described here, substitute the new cost for the original acquisition cost, the new residual value for the original amount, and estimated remaining life in place of the original estimated life. As an illustration, the computation using the straight-line method is as follows.

Assume the following for an aircraft owned by Delta:

| | |
|---|---|
| Cost of aircraft when acquired | $60,000,000 |
| Estimated useful life | 20 years |
| Estimated residual value | $ 3,000,000 |
| Accumulated depreciation through year 5 (assuming the SL method is used): | |
| ($60,000,000 − $3,000,000) × 1/20 = $2,850,000 per year × 5 years = $14,250,000 | |

Shortly after the start of year 6, Delta changed the initial estimated life to 25 years and lowered the estimated residual value to $750,000. At the end of year 6, the computation of the new amount for depreciation expense is as follows:

| | |
|---|---|
| Acquisition cost | $60,000,000 |
| Less: Accumulated depreciation (years 1–5) | 14,250,000 |
| Undepreciated balance | $45,750,000 |
| Less: New residual value | 750,000 |
| New depreciable amount | $45,000,000 |
| Annual depreciation based on remaining life: | |
| $45,000,000 ÷ 20 years (25 − 5 years) = | $ 2,250,000 per year |

The adjusting entry and effects at the end of year 6 (and future years) are as follows:

| | | |
|---|---|---|
| Depreciation expense (E) ................... | 2,250,000 | |
| Accumulated depreciation (XA) ............ | | 2,250,000 |

| Assets | = | Liabilities | + | Stockholders' Equity |
|---|---|---|---|---|
| Accumulated depreciation  −2,250,000 | | | | Depreciation expense  −2,250,000 |

Companies also may make a change in depreciation methods (for example, from declining balance to straight line), although such change requires significantly more disclosure since the consistency principle is violated. Under GAAP, changes in accounting estimates and depreciation methods should be made only when the new estimate or accounting method "better measures" the periodic income of the business. The *consistency principle* requires that accounting information reported in the financial statements be comparable across accounting periods. This principle places a significant constraint on changing depreciation estimates and methods unless the effect is to improve the measurement of depreciation expense and net income.

Delta Air Lines changed depreciation estimates twice in the 1990s. The financial statements contained the following note:

**REAL WORLD EXCERPT**

*Delta Air Lines*

1993 ANNUAL REPORT

Prior to the current year, substantially all of the Company's flight equipment was being depreciated on a straight-line basis to residual values (10% of cost) over a 15-year period from the dates placed in service. As a result of a review of its fleet plan, effective this year, the Company increased the estimated useful lives of substantially all of its flight equipment. Flight equipment that was not already fully depreciated is being depreciated on a straight-line basis to residual values (5% of cost) over a 20-year period from the dates placed in service. The effect of this change was a $34.3 million decrease in depreciation expense.

**REAL WORLD EXCERPT**

*Delta Air Lines*

1998 ANNUAL REPORT

Effective July 1, 1998, the Company increased the depreciable life of certain new generation aircraft types from 20 to 25 years. Owned flight equipment is depreciated on a straight-line basis to a residual value equal to 5% of cost.

Notice that Delta changed both the estimated life of its flight equipment and its estimated residual value in 1993. Why would Delta's management revise the estimates of useful life and residual value? The most likely explanation is found in other notes to the Delta financial statements. Delta and its competitors in the airline industry were managing in the face of an economic downturn in the early 1990s, one that caused losses or lowered operating profits for many. To improve financial performance at that time, management announced a number of cost control initiatives including "a $5.4 billion reduction in planned aircraft capital expenditures." As the result of planning to acquire fewer new aircraft, Delta decided to realize longer service from its existing equipment. Because of longer service, the equipment has less residual value when it is eventually sold.

In 1998, Delta received delivery of several new aircraft from Boeing including the Boeing 777. This popular and efficient jet is a type of "new generation aircraft." Delta suggests by the increase in estimated useful life to 25 years that such aircraft will be flown longer than prior jet purchases.

## FINANCIAL **ANALYSIS**

### INCREASED PROFITABILITY DUE TO AN ACCOUNTING ADJUSTMENT? READING THE FOOTNOTES

Financial analysts are particularly interested in changes in accounting estimates because they can have a large impact on a company's before-tax operating income. In Delta's case in 1993, the changes added $34.3 million because of reduced depreciation expense and would add a similar amount each year over the remaining life of the aircraft. Analysts pay close attention to this number because it represents increased profitability due to an accounting adjustment.

As another example, in May 1996, "Japan Airlines, the country's largest carrier, reported its first operating profit since 1991. The company attributed the improvement in the 12 months to March to its extensive restructuring and strong demand in growing Asian markets. But a change in its method of accounting for depreciation also improved JAL's results."* The company changed from the declining-balance method (higher depreciation expense) to the straight-line method (lower depreciation expense), and reported an increase in recurring profit compared with last year of ¥10.9 billion. "Although the move suggested the company would have recorded a large recurring loss for the year under the old principles, JAL said the change was a fairer reflection of the costs and benefits of the big outlays on new airports and other facilities recently made by JAL."

*SOURCE: Gerard Baker, *Financial Times*, May 30, 1996.

## SELF-STUDY **QUIZ**

Assume that Delta Air Lines owned a service truck that originally cost $100,000. When purchased, the truck had an estimated useful life of 10 years with no residual value. After operating the truck for five years, Delta determined that the remaining life was only two more years. Based on this change in estimate, what amount of depreciation should be recorded over the remaining life of the asset? Delta uses the straight-line method.

Check your answer with the footnote at the bottom of this page.*

* $50,000 (book value after 5 years) ÷ 2 years (remaining life) = $25,000 Depreciation Expense per Year.

# FOCUS ON **CASH FLOWS**

■ **LEARNING OBJECTIVE 5**

Explain the impact of cost allocation methods on cash flows and ratio analysis.

## PRODUCTIVE ASSETS AND DEPRECIATION

Depreciation expense is commonly called a *noncash expense* because it does not directly affect cash flows. The cash outflow associated with depreciation occurs when the related asset is acquired. Each period when depreciation is recorded, no cash payment is made (i.e., there is not a credit to Cash related to recording depreciation expense). Most other expenses cause an immediate or subsequent outflow of cash. The recording of salary expense, for example, is associated with either the immediate payment of cash or a subsequent payment when the Salaries Payable account is paid.

### EFFECT ON STATEMENT OF CASH FLOWS

**IN GENERAL** → Acquiring, selling, and depreciating long-term assets affect a company's cash flows as indicated in the following table:

|  | Effect on Cash Flows |
|---|---|
| **Operating activities** (indirect method) | |
| Net income | $xxx |
|     Adjusted for: Depreciation and amortization expense | + |
|                   Gains on disposition of long-term assets | − |
|                   Losses on disposition of long-term assets | + |
| **Investing activities** | |
|     Purchase of long-term assets | − |
|     Sale of long-term assets | + |

**FOCUS COMPANY ANALYSIS** → Exhibit 8.6 is Delta's statement of cash flows prepared using the indirect method. Buying and selling long-term assets are investing activities. In 1998, Delta used $2,291 million in cash to purchase flight equipment and ground property and equipment. Delta also sold flight equipment for $10 million in cash during the same period. Since selling long-term assets is not an operating activity, any gains (losses) on sales of long-term assets that are included in net income are deducted from (added to) net income in the operating activities section to eliminate the effect. Unless large, these gain and loss adjustments are normally not specifically highlighted on the statement of cash flows. Delta does not list any gains or losses in 1998.

EXHIBIT **8.6**

**Delta's Statement of Cash Flows**

**Delta Air Lines, Inc.**
**CONSOLIDATED STATEMENTS OF CASH FLOWS**
**For the Years Ended June 30, 1998, 1997 and 1996**

| *(in millions)* | 1998 | 1997 | 1996 |
|---|---|---|---|
| **Cash Flows from Operating Activities:** | | | |
| Net income | $1,001 | $ 854 | $ 156 |
| Adjustments to reconcile net income to cash provided by operating activities: | | | |
| Restructuring and other non-recurring charges | — | 52 | 829 |
| Depreciation and amortization | 861 | 710 | 634 |
| Deferred income taxes | 294 | 240 | (57) |
| Rental expense less than rent payments | (17) | (58) | (32) |
| Pension, postretirement and postemployment expense in excess of (less than) payments | 179 | 92 | (67) |
| Changes in certain current assets and liabilities: | | | |

EXHIBIT **8.6**
continued

| | 1998 | 1997 | 1996 |
|---|---:|---:|---:|
| Changes in certain current assets and liabilities: | | | |
| Decrease (increase) in accounts receivable | 5 | 25 | (213) |
| Decrease (increase) in prepaid expenses and other current assets | 15 | (31) | (47) |
| Increase in air traffic liability | 249 | 4 | 271 |
| Increase (decrease) in other payable and accrued expenses | 330 | 186 | (91) |
| Other, net | (1) | (35) | 8 |
| Net cash provided by operating activities | 2,916 | 2,039 | 1,391 |
| **Cash Flows from Investing Activities:** | | | |
| Property and equipment additions: | | | |
| Flight equipment, including advance payments | (1,760) | (1,598) | (639) |
| Ground property and equipment | (531) | (350) | (297) |
| Decrease (increase) in short-term investments, net | (43) | (1) | 22 |
| Proceeds from sale of flight equipment | 10 | 8 | 26 |
| Net cash used in investing activities | (2,324) | (1,941) | (888) |
| **Cash Flows from Financing Activities:** | | | |
| Payments on long-term debt and capital lease obligations | (307) | (196) | (440) |
| Cash dividends | (43) | (44) | (120) |
| Issuance of long term obligations | 125 | — | — |
| Issuance of Common Stock | 318 | 38 | 35 |
| Income tax benefit from exercise of stock options | 84 | — | — |
| Repurchase of Common Stock | (354) | (379) | (66) |
| Net cash used in financing activities | (177) | (581) | (591) |
| **Net Increase (Decrease) in Cash and Cash Equivalents** | 415 | (483) | (88) |
| Cash and cash equivalents at beginning of fiscal year | 662 | 1,145 | 1,233 |
| Cash and cash equivalents at end of fiscal year | $1,077 | $ 662 | $1,145 |

*The accompanying notes are an integral part of these consolidated statements.*

Finally, in capital-intensive industries such as airlines, depreciation is a significant noncash expense included in net income. In Delta's case, depreciation expense is the single largest adjustment to net income in determining cash flows from operations. It has averaged approximately 37 percent of operating cash flows over the past three years, although the percentage has steadily declined. Other focus companies that are less capital intensive, such as Timberland and Harley-Davidson, have significantly lower depreciation adjustments as a percentage of cash flows from operations.

| **Selected Focus Company Comparisons: Average Percentage of Depreciation to Cash Flows from Operations** | |
|---|---:|
| Timberland | 22% |
| Harley-Davidson | 30 |
| Delta Air Lines | 37 |

# FINANCIAL **ANALYSIS**

## A MISINTERPRETATION

Some analysts misinterpret the meaning of a noncash expense and often say that "cash is provided by depreciation." This may be caused by finding depreciation added in the operating section of the statement of cash flows. Depreciation is not a source of cash, however. Cash from operations can be provided only by selling goods and services. A company with a large amount of depreciation expense does not generate more cash compared with a company that reports a small amount of depreciation expense (assuming that they are exactly the same in every other respect). Depreciation expense reduces the amount of reported net income for a company, but it does not reduce the amount of cash generated by the company because it is a noncash expense. (Remember that the effects of recording depreciation are a reduction in stockholders' equity and a reduction in fixed assets, not cash.) That is why, on the statement of cash flows, depreciation expense is added back to net income (on an accrual basis) to compute cash flows from operations (income on a cash basis).

**Effect on Taxes**    Although depreciation is a noncash expense, depreciation policy for tax purposes can affect a company's cash flows. Depreciation is a deductible expense for income tax purposes (i.e., taxes are based on income, or revenues minus expenses). The higher the amount of depreciation recorded by a company for tax purposes, the lower the taxable income and the taxes that must be paid. Because taxes must be paid in cash, a reduction in the tax obligation of a company results in a reduction of cash outflows for the company.

## DISPOSAL OF PROPERTY, PLANT, AND EQUIPMENT

In some cases, a business may *voluntarily* decide not to hold a long-term asset for its entire life. The company may drop a product from its line and no longer need the equipment that was used to produce the product, or it may want to trade in a machine for a more efficient one. These disposals include sale, trade-in, or retirement. When it disposes of an old aircraft, Delta may sell it to a cargo airline or regional airline. A business may also dispose of an asset *involuntarily* as the result of a casualty, such as a storm, fire, or accident.

Disposals of long-term assets seldom occur on the last day of the accounting period. Therefore, the depreciation must be updated to the date of disposal. The disposal of a depreciable asset usually requires two entries: (1) an adjusting entry to update the depreciation expense and accumulated depreciation accounts and (2) an entry to record the disposal. Then the cost of the asset and any accumulated depreciation at the date of disposal must be removed from the accounts. The difference between any resources received on disposal of an asset and the book, or carrying, value of the asset at the date of disposal is a gain or loss on disposal of the asset. This gain (or loss) is reported on the income statement. It is not revenue (or expense), however, because it is from "peripheral or incidental" activities rather than from normal operations.

Assume that, at the end of year 17, Delta Air Lines sold an aircraft that was no longer needed because of the elimination of flight service to a small city. The aircraft was sold for $4,000,000 cash. The original cost of the flight equipment was $20 million and was depreciated using the straight-line method over 20 years with no residual value ($1,000,000 depreciation expense per year). The last accounting for depreciation was at the end of year 16; thus, depreciation expense must be recorded for year 17. The computations are as follows:

| | | |
|---|---|---|
| Cash received | | $4,000,000 |
| Original cost of flight equipment | $20,000,000 | |
| Less: Accumulated depreciation (1,000,000 × 17 years) | 17,000,000 | |
|     Book value at date of sale | | 3,000,000 |
|       Gain on sale of flight equipment | | $1,000,000 |

The entries and effects of the transaction on the date of the sale follow:

| | | |
|---|---|---|
| ① Depreciation expense (E) . . . . . . . . . . . . . . | 1,000,000 | |
|     Accumulated depreciation (XA) . . . . . . . . | | 1,000,000 |
| ② Cash (A) . . . . . . . . . . . . . . . . . . . . . . . . . | 4,000,000 | |
|     Accumulated depreciation (XA) . . . . . . . . . . | 17,000,000 | |
|       Flight equipment (A) . . . . . . . . . . . . . . . | | 20,000,000 |
|       Gain on sale of asset (R) . . . . . . . . . . . . | | 1,000,000 |

| Assets | | = | Liabilities | + | Stockholders' Equity | |
|---|---|---|---|---|---|---|
| ① Accumulated depreciation | − 1,000,000 | | | | ① Depreciation expense | −1,000,000 |
| ② Cash | + 4,000,000 | | | | ② Gain on sale of asset | +1,000,000 |
|     Accumulated depreciation | +17,000,000 | | | | | |
|     Flight equipment | −20,000,000 | | | | | |

A gain or loss on disposal occurs because (1) depreciation expense is based on estimates that may differ from actual experience and (2) depreciation is based on original cost, not current market value. Because the gain or loss on disposal is not part of the continuing operating activities of a company, it usually is shown as a separate line item on the income statement. In past years, for example, Delta Air Lines sold 18 DC-9 aircraft and reported a gain of $64,843,000 as a separate item on its income statement.

## FINANCIAL **ANALYSIS**

### TAKING A DIFFERENT STRATEGY TO SUCCESS

Singapore Airlines, formed in 1972, has recognized continued profitability as one of the world's largest operators of the most technologically advanced "jumbo jets," the Boeing 747-400. Unlike the rest of the airline industry with an average fleet age of more than 12 years, Singapore Airlines uses its aircraft for an average of just under six years. This strategy for managing the company's productivity has a dual effect. Depreciation expense is significantly higher due to the shorter estimated useful life, thus reducing net income. Singapore Airlines sells its used aircraft, however, an activity that has resulted in gains (entitled Surplus on Sale of Aircraft and Spares) reported on the income statement. Both the depreciation computations (through the use of estimates) and asset sales (through differences in the timing of the sales) provide management with the flexibility to manage earnings.

On October 28, 1996, *The Straits Times* (p. 48) reported that Singapore Airlines' six-month earnings were up 7.2 percent compared to the same period in the prior year. The surplus on sales of aircraft was up 734.7 percent, however. "Without the surplus in the six months ended Sept. 30, the national carrier's net earnings would have declined for the first time since 1994."

## KEY **RATIO ANALYSIS:**

### FIXED ASSET TURNOVER

**K**now the decision question:

How effectively is management utilizing fixed assets to generate revenues? It is computed as follows:

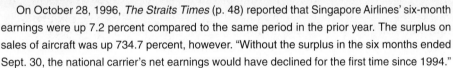

$$\text{Fixed Asset Turnover} = \frac{\text{Net Sales (or operating revenues)}}{\text{Average Net Fixed Assets}}$$

Beginning Fixed Asset Balance (net of accumulated depreciation)
+ Ending Fixed Asset Balance (net of accumulated depreciation)
————————————————————————————————
2

The 1998 ratio for Delta:

$14,138.5 operating revenues ÷ [($9,321 + $8,042) ÷ 2] = 1.63 times

**E**xamine the ratio using two techniques:

| ① Comparisons over Time | | |
|---|---|---|
| Delta Air Lines | | |
| 1996 | 1997 | 1998 |
| 1.81 | 1.83 | 1.63 |

| ② Comparisons with Competitors | |
|---|---|
| Southwest | United |
| 1998 | 1998 |
| 1.10 | 1.47 |

**Y**ou interpret the results carefully:

**IN GENERAL** → The fixed asset turnover ratio measures how many times average fixed assets generated revenues. A high rate normally suggests an effective management. An increasing rate over time signals more efficient fixed asset use. Creditors and security analysts use this ratio to assess a company's effectiveness in generating sales from its long-lived assets.

**FOCUS COMPANY ANALYSIS** → Delta's fixed asset turnover ratio decreased in the most recent year, suggesting a decline in asset efficiency. However, when compared to others in the industry, Delta appears to be relatively efficient. The notes to prior years' financial statements indicate that Delta has sold or written down flight equipment as part of its restructuring efforts. Selling equipment and maintaining productivity is an improvement in efficiency, whereas writing asset values down is a managerial judgment as to the assets' future earnings potential. In comparison, in 1998, Delta increased its possession of new aircraft, thereby reducing the turnover rate. In looking to the future, Delta's commitment to purchase $6.7 billion in new aircraft over the next 20 years should have the effect of reducing future turnover rates if not accompanied by a relative increase in revenues.

**A FEW CAUTIONS:** A lower or declining rate may indicate that a company is expanding (by acquiring additional productive assets) in anticipation of higher sales in the future. An increasing ratio could also signal that a firm has cut back on capital expenditures due to anticipation of a downturn in business. As a consequence, appropriate interpretation of the fixed asset turnover ratio requires an investigation of other related activities.

# NATURAL RESOURCES

**LEARNING OBJECTIVE 7**

Understand the measurement and reporting of natural resources and intangible assets.

**NATURAL RESOURCES** are assets that occur in nature, such as mineral deposits, timber tracts, oil, and gas.

You are probably most familiar with large companies that are involved in manufacturing goods (Ford, Black & Decker), distribution of goods (Sears, Home Depot), or performing a service (Federal Express, Holiday Inn). A number of large companies, some of which are less well known, develop raw materials and products from **natural resources,** which include mineral deposits (such as gold or iron ore), oil wells, and timber tracts. These resources are often called *wasting assets* because they are depleted (i.e., physically used). Companies involved with natural resources are critical to the economy because they produce such essential items as lumber for construction, fuel for heating and transportation, and food for consumption. Companies involved with natural resources also attract considerable attention because of the significant effect they can have on the environment. Concerned citizens often read financial statements from companies involved in exploration for oil, coal, and various ores to determine the amount of money spent to protect the environment.

## ACQUISITION AND COST ALLOCATION

When natural resources are acquired or developed, they are recorded in conformity with the *cost principle.* As a natural resource is used up, its acquisition cost, in conformity with the *matching principle,* must be apportioned among the various periods in which the resulting revenues are earned. The term **depletion** describes the process of periodic cost allocation over the economic life of a natural resource. The concept of depletion is exactly the same as depreciation; the only difference is the type of asset that is being accounted for.[3]

**DEPLETION** is the systematic and rational allocation of the cost of a natural resource over the period of exploitation.

> **Depletion:** The systematic and rational allocation of the acquisition cost of natural resources to future periods in which the use of those natural resources contributes to revenue.

> **Example:** Depletion of the $530,000 cost of a timber tract over the estimated period of cutting based on a "cutting" rate of approximately 20 percent per year:

| | | |
|---|---|---|
| Depletion expense (E) . . . . . . . . . . . . . . . . . . . . . | 106,000 | |
| Timber tract (A) . . . . . . . . . . . . . . . . . . . . . . . . | | 106,000 |
| (or Accumulated depletion XA) | | |

---

[3]Consistent with the procedure for recording depreciation, an accumulated depletion account may be used. In practice, most companies credit the asset account directly for the periodic depletion. This procedure is typically used for intangible assets, which are discussed in the next section.

| Assets | | = | Liabilities | + | Stockholders' Equity | |
| --- | --- | --- | --- | --- | --- | --- |
| Timber tract (or Accumulated depletion) | −106,000 | | | | Depletion expense | −106,000 |

A *depletion rate* is computed by dividing the total acquisition and development cost (less any estimated residual value, which is rare) by the estimated units that can be withdrawn economically from the resource. The depletion rate is multiplied each period by the actual number of units withdrawn during the accounting period. This procedure is the same as the units-of-production method of calculating depreciation.

When buildings and similar improvements are acquired for the development and exploitation of a natural resource, they should be recorded in separate asset accounts and *depreciated*—not depleted. Their estimated useful lives cannot be longer than the time needed to exploit the natural resource unless they have a significant use after the source is depleted.

The following is a partial asset section of the 1998 balance sheet for International Paper and the related footnote describing the accounting policies for its natural resource, forestlands:

**CONSOLIDATED BALANCE SHEETS (IN MILLIONS)**

| | 1998 | 1997 |
| --- | --- | --- |
| **Assets** | | |
| Cash | $ 477 | $ 398 |
| . . . | | |
| Forestlands | 2,795 | 2,760 |
| . . . | | |

**Note:**
**Forestlands**
Forestlands are stated at cost, less accumulated depletion representing the cost of timber harvested. Forestlands include owned property as well as certain timber harvesting rights with terms of one or more years. Costs attributable to timber are charged against income as trees are cut. The depletion rate charged is determined annually based on the relationship of remaining costs to estimated recoverable volume.

## INTANGIBLE ASSETS

An intangible asset, like any other asset, has value because of certain rights and privileges conferred by law on the owner of the asset. An intangible asset has no material or physical substance as do tangible assets such as land and buildings, however. Examples include patents, trademarks, and licenses. Most intangible assets, except for goodwill discussed later, usually are evidenced by a legal document.

### ACQUISITION AND COST ALLOCATION

Intangible assets are recorded in conformity with the *cost principle* only if they are purchased. If an intangible asset is developed internally, the cost of development normally is recorded as an expense. For example, Abbott Laboratories (a manufacturer of pharmaceutical and nutritional products) recently spent more than $1,202 million on research to discover new products. This amount was reported as an expense, not an asset; research and development expenditures typically do not possess sufficient probability of resulting in measurable future cash flows. If Abbott Labs had spent an equivalent amount to purchase patents for new products from other drug companies, it would have recorded the expenditure as an asset.

In a process similar to depreciation and depletion, intangible assets are amortized on a straight-line basis over the shorter of their legal life, useful life, or 20 years

**AMORTIZATION** is the systematic and rational allocation of the acquisition cost of an intangible asset over its useful life.

(the presumed maximum allowable allocation period under GAAP[4]). Most companies do not estimate a residual value for their intangible assets. **Amortization** expense is included on the income statement each period; intangible assets are reported at cost less accumulated amortization on the balance sheet.

> **Amortization:** The systematic and rational allocation of the acquisition cost of intangible assets to future periods in which the benefits contribute to revenue.

> **Example:** Amortization of the $850,000 purchase cost of a patent over its estimated economic useful (and legal) life to the entity of 17 years:

| | | |
|---|---:|---:|
| Amortization expense (E) . . . . . . . . . . . . . . . . . . . . . . | 50,000 | |
| Patents (A) (or Accumulated amortization XA) . . . . . | | 50,000 |

| Assets | = | Liabilities | + | Stockholders' Equity | |
|---|---|---|---|---|---|
| Patents (or Accumulated amortization) −50,000 | | | | Amortization expense | −50,000 |

### EXAMPLES OF INTANGIBLE ASSETS

The AICPA's 1998 *Accounting Trends & Techniques* summarizes intangible assets most frequently disclosed by the 600 companies surveyed:

| | Number of Companies | Percentage of 600 |
|---|---:|---:|
| Goodwill recognized in a business combination | 439 | 73% |
| Trademarks, brand names, copyrights | 83 | 14 |
| Patents, patent rights | 74 | 12 |
| Licenses, franchises, memberships | 28 | 5 |
| Noncompete covenants | 25 | 4 |
| Technology | 23 | 4 |
| Customer lists | 17 | 3 |
| Other—described in the annual report | 29 | 5 |

For accounting purposes, **GOODWILL (COST IN EXCESS OF NET ASSETS ACQUIRED)** is the excess of the purchase price of a business over the market value of the business's assets and liabilities.

**Goodwill**   By far, the most frequently reported intangible asset is **goodwill.** Goodwill, as used by most businesspeople, is the favorable reputation that a company has with its customers. Goodwill arises from such factors as customer confidence, reputation for good service or quality goods, and financial standing. From its first day of operations, a successful business continually builds goodwill. In this context, the goodwill is said to be *internally generated* and is not reported as an asset (i.e., it was not purchased).

The only way to report goodwill as an asset is to purchase another business. Often the purchase price of the business exceeds the fair market value of all of the assets minus liabilities owned or owed by the business. Why would a company pay more for a business as a whole than it would pay if it bought the assets individually? The answer is to obtain its goodwill. You could easily buy modern bottling equipment to produce and sell a new cola drink, but you would not make as much money as you would if you could acquire the goodwill associated with Coke or Pepsi.

---

[4]The proposed 20-year limit is effective beginning in the year 2000; intangibles purchased prior to 2000 may use a maximum limit of 40 years. The Financial Accounting Standards Board has indicated an exception to the recent 20-year limit: Intangible assets that are separable with useful economic lives exceeding 20 years may be amortized over periods exceeding 20 years if they have clearly identifiable cash flows that will continue for more than 20 years and are exchangeable or acquired through contractual agreement. Intangibles with indefinite lives and an observable market are not amortized until their lives become finite.

For accounting purposes, goodwill (often reported as cost in excess of net assets acquired) is defined as the difference between the purchase price of a company as a whole and the fair market value of all of its assets minus the fair market value of its liabilities.

> Purchase price
> − Fair market value of identifiable assets and liabilities
> Goodwill to be reported

Both parties estimate an acceptable amount for the goodwill of the business and add it to the appraised fair value of the business's assets and liabilities. Then the sale price of the business is negotiated. In conformity with the *cost principle,* the resulting amount of goodwill is recorded as an intangible asset only when it actually is purchased at a measurable cost.

A number of years ago, Delta Air Lines acquired Western Air Lines, a regional carrier. Delta purchased the entire company as an entity and paid a price in excess of the fair market value of the tangible assets owned by Western. The balance sheet prepared by Delta (Exhibit 8.1) includes the individual assets from Western and an item valued at $265 million called Cost in Excess of Net Assets Acquired (which is another term for goodwill). The notes to the statements include the following:

COST IN EXCESS OF NET ASSETS ACQUIRED. The cost in excess of net assets acquired (goodwill), which is being amortized over 40 years, is related to the Company's acquisition of Western Air Lines, Inc. in December 1986.

**REAL WORLD EXCERPT**

*Delta Air Lines*
1998 ANNUAL REPORT

Like other intangible assets, goodwill must be amortized to expense over its estimated economic life, usually on a straight-line basis. Because it is particularly difficult to estimate the life of goodwill, GAAP now requires goodwill to be amortized over a period not to exceed 20 years (or 40 years for acquisitions prior to the year 2000). Delta's income statement included amortization of cost in excess of net assets acquired (goodwill) of $9 million. When Delta records amortization of goodwill, it reduces the Goodwill account directly rather than creating a contra-account Accumulated Amortization. Most companies follow this practice. Additional discussion on goodwill and acquiring other companies is in Chapter 12.

**Trademarks**  A **trademark** is a special name, image, or slogan identified with a product or a company; it is protected by law. Trademarks are often some of the most valuable assets that a company can own. Most of us cannot imagine the Walt Disney Company without Mickey Mouse. You probably enjoy your favorite soft drink more because of the image that has been built up around its name. Many people can identify the shape of a corporate logo as quickly as they can recognize the shape of a stop sign. Trademarks are valuable assets, but they are rarely seen on balance sheets. The reason is simple; intangible assets are not recorded unless they are purchased. Companies often spend millions of dollars developing trademarks, but these expenditures usually are recorded as expenses and not capitalized.

A **TRADEMARK** is an exclusive legal right to use a special name, image, or slogan.

**Patents**  A **patent** is an exclusive right granted by the federal government for a period of 17 years. It is typically granted to an inventor who invents a new product or discovers a new process. The patent enables the owner to use, manufacture, and sell the subject of the patent and the patent itself. Without the protection of a patent, inventors likely would be unwilling to search for new products. The patent prevents a competitor from simply copying a new invention or discovery until the inventor has had a period of time to earn an economic return on the new product.

A **PATENT** is granted by the federal government for an invention; it is an exclusive right given to the owner to use, manufacture, and sell the subject of the patent.

A patent that is *purchased* is recorded at cost. An *internally developed* patent is recorded at only its registration and legal cost because GAAP require the immediate expensing of research and development costs. In conformity with the *matching principle,* the cost of a patent must be amortized over the shorter of its economic life or its remaining legal life. Amortization usually is recorded with a debit to Amortization Expense and a credit directly to the asset account instead of a contra-account Accumulated Amortization.

A **COPYRIGHT** is the exclusive right to publish, use, and sell a literary, musical, or artistic work.

**Copyrights**  A **copyright** gives the owner the exclusive right to publish, use, and sell a literary, musical, or artistic piece of work for a period not exceeding 50 years after the author's death. The book that you are reading has a copyright to protect the publisher and the authors. It would be against the law, for example, if an instructor copied several chapters from this book and handed them out in class. The same principles, guidelines, and procedures used in accounting for the cost of patents also are used for copyrights.

A **FRANCHISE** is a contractual right to sell certain products or services, use certain trademarks, or perform activities in a geographical region.

**Franchises**  **Franchises** may be granted by either the government or other businesses for a specified period and purpose. A city may grant one company a franchise to distribute gas to homes for heating purposes, or a company may sell franchises, such as the right for a local outlet to operate a KFC restaurant. Franchise agreements are contracts that can have a variety of provisions. Franchises usually require an investment by the franchisee to acquire them; therefore, they should be accounted for as intangible assets. The life of the franchise agreement depends on the contract and may be for a single year or an indefinite period. Blockbuster Video is a popular company in the home video rental business. To expand rapidly, the company enters into franchise agreements with local operators. The franchise agreement requires the payment of a franchise fee and covers a period of 20 years. Blockbuster has more than 750 stores under franchise agreements.

**LEASEHOLDS** are rights granted to a lessee under a lease contract.

**Leaseholds**  A **leasehold** is the right granted in a contract called a *lease* to use a specific asset. Leasing is a common type of business contract. For a consideration called *rent,* the owner (lessor) extends to another party (lessee) certain rights to use specified property. Leases may vary from simple arrangements, such as the month-to-month lease of an office or the daily rental of an automobile, to long-term leases having complex contractual arrangements.

The Delta balance sheet (Exhibit 8.1) shows an asset Leasehold and Operating Rights for $124 million. The leasehold rights are improvements to rented space at the airports where Delta provides services. The operating rights are authorized landing slots that are regulated by the government and are in limited supply at many airports. They are intangible assets that can be bought and sold by the airlines.

Lessees sometimes make significant improvements to a leased property when they enter into a long-term lease agreement. A company that agrees to lease office space on a 15-year lease may install new fixtures or move walls to make the space more useful. These improvements are called *leasehold improvements* and are recorded as an asset by the lessee despite the fact that the lessor usually owns the leasehold improvements at the end of the term of the lease. The cost of leasehold improvements should be amortized over the estimated useful life of the related improvements or the remaining life of the lease, whichever is shorter.

## IMPAIRED ASSETS

■ **LEARNING OBJECTIVE 8**

Explain the effect of asset impairment on the financial statements.

Under a recent FASB pronouncement, corporations must review long-lived assets and certain identifiable intangibles for impairment. *Impairment* occurs when events or changed circumstances cause the book value of these assets to be higher than estimates of future cash flows (future benefits). If the estimated future cash flows are less than the book value of the asset, an impairment loss should be recognized. We say the assets are *written down.* Delta Air Lines reported the following write-down in its 1996 annual report:

**REAL WORLD EXCERPT**

*Delta Air Lines*

1996 ANNUAL REPORT

The $829 million pretax charge for restructuring and other non-recurring charges recorded in fiscal 1996 includes a $452 million write-down of Delta's Lockheed L-1011 fleet and related assets. In connection with its decision to accelerate the replacement of its 55 L-1011 aircraft fleet, the Company performed an evaluation to determine, in accordance with SFAS 121 (see Note 1), whether future cash flows (undiscounted and without interest charges) expected to result from the use and the eventual disposition of the L-1011 fleet will be less than the aggregate carrying amount of the L-1011 aircraft and related assets. As a result of the evaluation, management determined that the estimated future cash flows expected to be generated by L-1011 assets will be less than their carrying amount, and therefore, the L-1011 assets are impaired as defined by SFAS 121. Consequently, the original cost basis of the L-1011 fleet was reduced to reflect the fair market value at the time of the evaluation, resulting in a $452 million non-recurring charge. In determining the fair market value of L-1011 assets, the Company considered recent transactions involving sales of L-1011 aircraft and market trends in aircraft dispositions.

Delta's L-1011 aircraft are among the oldest in its fleet. The planes are being retired and replaced with the flight equipment from the new Boeing order.

# A QUESTION OF **ETHICS**

## FIERCE PRESSURE TO REPORT SMOOTH, EVER HIGHER EARNINGS

Corporate executives have been under intense pressure over the past decade to keep earnings rising smoothly to meet the consensus expectations of analysts. As the expectations have become more explicit, so too have the mechanisms executives use to manage earnings and hit their targets. Long-lived assets can play a significant role in the ability of companies to meet or beat the estimates, as indicated in the financial press:

**REAL WORLD EXCERPT**

*Fortune*

**"Learn to Play the Earnings Game (and Wall Street will love you)"**

**How the pros do it**

**Plan ahead:** Time store openings or asset sales to keep earnings rising smoothly. In most cases, this is earnings management at its least controversial. The master of it is General Electric.

**Capitalize it:** Usually it's pretty clear which costs you capitalize and which you expense. But there are gray areas—software R & D is one—and you can get creative about the length of time an asset should be depreciated. America Online was, until it stopped in October, a noted aggressive capitalizer.

**Write it off:** Take a "big bath" and charge a few hundred million in restructuring costs, and meeting future earnings targets will be easier. Among the biggest restructurers in the 1990s: IBM.

SOURCE: *Fortune*, March 31, 1997, pp. 77–80. © 1997 *Time, Inc.* All rights reserved.

## EPILOGUE

By the 1990s, the airline industry faced excess capacity. Simply too many aircraft were competing for a limited number of customers. After losing nearly $2 billion between 1991 and 1994, Delta announced a campaign (Leadership 7.5) to slash $2 billion in expenses by eliminating 15,000 jobs. The company has since been profitable.

Wall Street analysts have been impressed with Delta's success in achieving greater productivity from its long-lived assets. When the major deal was signed with Boeing, however, Delta's stock slipped 12.5 cents a share to $84.375 as the market reacted warily to the announced shift in managing these assets.

In another setback, in spring 1999, *The Wall Street Journal* reported the following:

**REAL WORLD EXCERPT**

*The Wall Street Journal*

> **Delta Defers Delivery of 11 Boeing 777s as Contract Talks with Pilots Continue**
>
> Delta Air Lines, faced with the specter of assembling a fleet of pricey new jets that its pilots will refuse to fly, deferred delivery of all 11 Boeing 777-200 jets on order. The airline said it will sell or lease the two Boeing 777s that are already in its fleet.
>
> SOURCE: Branigan, Martha, *The Wall Street Journal,* June 14, 1999, p. B12.

Boeing 777 aircraft can carry more people and are more fuel efficient than previous aircraft. Deferring delivery effectively disarmed the pilots' union demands for pay increases significantly above the industry's top wages to fly Boeing 777s. At the time, most analysts predicted the union and the company would reach an accord eventually, but the announcement dampened Delta's plans to use the Boeing 777 as its premier aircraft to carry the company into the 21st century. Given the long life of Delta's productive assets, we will be well into the next century before we can assess the effects of these events and the success of Delta's plan.

# DEMONSTRATION **CASE**

(Resolve the requirements before proceeding to the suggested solution that follows.)

Diversified Industries has been operating for a number of years. It started as a residential construction company. In recent years, it expanded into heavy construction, ready-mix concrete, sand and gravel, construction supplies, and earth-moving services.

The following transactions were selected from those completed during year 20D. They focus on the primary issues discussed in this chapter. Amounts have been simplified for case purposes.

**20D**

Jan. 1 The management decided to buy a building that was about 10 years old. The location was excellent, and there was adequate parking space. The company bought the building and the land on which it was situated for $305,000. It paid $100,000 in cash and signed a mortgage note payable for the rest. A reliable appraiser provided the following market values: land, $126,000; and building, $174,000.

Jan. 12 Paid renovation costs on the building of $38,100 prior to use.

June 19 Bought a third location for a gravel pit (designated No. 3) for $50,000 cash. The location had been carefully surveyed. It was estimated that 100,000 cubic yards of gravel could be removed from the deposit.

July 10 Paid $1,200 for ordinary repairs on the building.

Aug. 1 Paid $10,000 for costs of preparing the new gravel pit for exploitation.

Dec. 31 Year-end adjustments:

a. The building will be depreciated on a straight-line basis over an estimated useful life of 30 years. The estimated residual value is $35,000.
b. During 20D, 12,000 cubic yards of gravel were removed from gravel pit No. 3 and sold.
c. The company owns a patent right that is used in operations. On January 1, 20D, the patent account had a balance of $3,300. The patent has an estimated remaining useful life of six years (including 20D).
d. At the beginning of the year, the company owned equipment with a cost of $650,000 and a book value of $500,000. The equipment is being depreciated using the double-declining-balance method, with a useful life of 20 years with no residual value.

e. At year-end, the company identified a piece of old excavation equipment with a cost of $156,000 and remaining book value of $120,000. Due to its smaller size and lack of safety features, the old equipment has limited use. The company reviewed the asset for possible impairment of value. The future cash flows are expected to be $40,000.

December 31, 20D, is the end of the annual accounting period.

### Required:

1. Indicate the accounts affected and the amount and direction (+ for increase and − for decrease) of the effect for each of the preceding events on the financial statement categories at year end. Using the following headings:

| Date | Assets | = | Liabilities | + | Stockholders' Equity |
|------|--------|---|-------------|---|----------------------|

2. Record the adjusting journal entries based on the information for December 31(*a* and *b* only).
3. Show the December 31, 20D, balance sheet classifications and amount for each of the following items:

   Fixed assets—land, building, equipment, and gravel pit

   Intangible asset—patent

4. Assuming that the company had sales of $1,000,000 for the year and a net book value of $500,000 for fixed assets at the beginning of the year, compute the fixed asset turnover ratio. Explain its meaning.

## SUGGESTED SOLUTION

1. Effects of events (with computations):

| Date | Assets | | Liabilities | | Stockholders' Equity | |
|------|--------|--|-------------|--|----------------------|--|
| Jan. 1 (1) | Cash<br>Land<br>Building | −100,000<br>+128,100<br>+176,900 | Note payable | +205,000 | | |
| Jan. 12 | Cash<br>Building | −38,100<br>+38,100 | | | | |
| June 19 | Cash<br>Gravel pit No. 3 | −50,000<br>+50,000 | | | | |
| July 10 | Cash | −1,200 | | | Repairs expense | −1,200 |
| Aug. 1 | Cash<br>Gravel pit No. 3 | −10,000<br>+10,000 | | | | |
| Dec. 31 *a* (2) | Accumulated depreciation | −6,000 | | | Depreciation expense | −6,000 |
| Dec. 31 *b* (3) | Gravel pit No. 3 | −7,200 | | | Depletion expense | −7,200 |
| Dec. 31 *c* (4) | Patent | −550 | | | Amortization expense | −550 |
| Dec. 31 *d* (5) | Accumulated depreciation | −50,000 | | | Depreciation expense | −50,000 |
| Dec. 31 *e* (6) | Accumulated depreciation | −80,000 | | | Loss due to asset impairment | −80,000 |

| (1) | Land | | Building | | Total |
|-----|------|--|----------|--|-------|
| Market | $126,000 | + | $174,000 | = | $300,000 |
| Percentage of total | 42% | + | 58% | = | 100% |
| Cost | $128,100 | + | $176,900 | = | $305,000 |

(2) **Cost of building**

| | | |
|---|---|---|
| Initial payment | $176,900 | |
| Repairs prior to use | 38,100 | |
| Acquisition cost | $215,000 | |

**Straight-line depreciation**

($215,000 cost − $35,000 residual value ) × 1/30 years = $6,000 annual depreciation

(3) **Cost of gravel pit**

| | | |
|---|---|---|
| Initial payment | $ 50,000 | |
| Preparation costs | 10,000 | |
| Acquisition cost | $ 60,000 | |

**Units-of-production depletion**

($60,000 cost/100,000 estimated production) × 12,000 actual production = $7,200 annual depletion

(4) **Straight-line amortization**

| | |
|---|---|
| Unamortized cost of patent | $3,300 |
| ÷ Remaining useful life | ÷ 6 years |
| | $ 550 |

(5) **Double-declining-balance depreciation**

($650,000 cost − $150,000 accumulated depreciation) × 2/20 = $50,000 annual depreciation

(6) **Asset impairment**

| | |
|---|---|
| Book value of old equipment | $120,000 |
| Expected future cash flows | 40,000 |
| Loss due to impairment | $ 80,000 |

2. Adjusting entries Dec. 31, 20D:

| | | | |
|---|---|---|---|
| a. | Depreciation expense, building (E) . . . . . . . . . . . . | 6,000 | |
| | Accumulated depreciation (XA) . . . . . . . . . . . . | | 6,000 |
| b. | Depletion expense (E) . . . . . . . . . . . . . . . . . . . . . . | 7,200 | |
| | Gravel pit No. 3 (A) . . . . . . . . . . . . . . . . . . . . | | 7,200 |

3. Balance sheet, December 31, 20D:

| Assets | | | |
|---|---|---|---|
| **Fixed assets** | | | |
| Land | | | $128,100 |
| Building | | $215,000 | |
| Less: Accumulated depreciation | | 6,000 | 209,000 |
| Equipment | | 650,000 | |
| Less: Accumulated depreciation ($150,000 + 50,000 + 80,000) | | 280,000 | 370,000 |
| Gravel pit | | | 52,800 |
| Total fixed assets | | | $759,900 |
| **Intangible asset** | | | |
| Patent ($3,300 − $550) | | | $ 2,750 |

4. Fixed asset turnover ratio:

$$\frac{\text{Sales}}{(\text{Beginning Net Fixed Asset Balance} + \text{Ending Net Fixed Asset Balance}) \div 2} = \frac{\$1,000,000}{(\$500,000 + \$759,900) \div 2} = 1.59$$

This construction company is capital intensive. The fixed asset turnover ratio measures the company's efficiency at using its investment in property, plant, and equipment to generate sales.

## CHAPTER **TAKE-AWAYS**

1. **Define, classify, and explain the nature of noncurrent productive assets.**   **p. 424**

   Noncurrent assets that a business retains for long periods of time for use in the course of normal operations rather than for sale; tangible assets (land, buildings, equipment, natural resources) and intangible assets (including goodwill, patents, and franchises).

2. **Apply the cost principle to measure the acquisition of property, plant, and equipment.**   **p. 424**

   The cash-equivalent purchase price plus all reasonable and necessary expenditures made to acquire and prepare the asset for its intended use; acquired with cash, debt, stock, as a basket purchase, and through self-construction.

3. **Understand the financial statement impact of management's decisions regarding ordinary and extraordinary repairs.   p. 428**
   a. *Capital expenditures:* Provide benefits for one or more accounting periods beyond the current period; amounts are debited to appropriate asset accounts and depreciated, depleted, or amortized over their useful lives.
   b. *Revenue expenditures:* Provide benefits during the current accounting period only; amounts are debited to appropriate current expense accounts when incurred.

4. **Apply various cost allocation methods and changes in estimates as assets are held and used over time.   p. 432**
   a. *Cost allocation methods:* In conformity with the matching principle, cost (less any estimated residual value) is allocated to periodic expense over the periods benefited; net book value of asset declines over time; net income is reduced by the amount of the expense. Common methods: straight-line (constant amount over time), units-of-production (variable amount over time), and double-declining-balance (decreasing amount over time).
   - Depreciation—buildings and equipment.
   - Depletion—natural resources.
   - Amortization— intangibles.
   b. *Changes in estimates:* Net book value less new salvage value is depreciated over remaining useful life in present and future periods.

5. **Explain the impact of cost allocation methods on cash flows and ratio analysis. p. 442**
   Depreciation expense is a noncash expense that has no effect on cash; add back to net income on statement of cash flows to determine cash from operations. The method used affects the amount of net property and equipment used in the computation of the fixed asset turnover ratio. Accelerated methods reduce net book value and increase the ratio as compared to the straight-line method.

6. **Analyze the disposal of property, plant, and equipment.   p. 444**
   (*a*) Make sure depreciation recognition is up to date. (*b*) Dispose of as a sale or abandonment; remove the cost of the old asset and the related accumulated depreciation, depletion, or amortization amount from the accounts. (*c*) Recognize the cash proceeds. (*d*) Gains or losses result when net book value is not equal to cash received.

7. **Understand the measurement and reporting of natural resources and intangible assets.   p. 446**
   Apply the cost principle upon acquisition; deplete natural resources (usually by the units-of-production method) and amortize intangibles (usually by the straight-line method over the shortest of economic life, legal life, or 20 years). Report at net book value on the balance sheet.

8. **Explain the effect of asset impairment on the financial statements.   p. 450**
   When events or changes in circumstances cause the book value of long-lived assets to be higher than estimated future cash flows; write down the asset (record a loss) to the estimated future cash flows.

In the previous chapters, we discussed business and accounting issues related to the assets a company holds. In Chapters 9, 10, and 11, we shift our focus to the other side of the balance sheet to see how managers finance the operations of their business and the acquisition of productive assets. We discuss various types of liabilities in Chapters 9 and 10 and examine owners' equity in Chapter 11.

## KEY **RATIO**

Fixed asset turnover ratio measures how efficiently a company utilizes its investment in property, plant, and equipment over time. Its ratio can be compared to the ratio of its competitors. It is computed as follows (p. 445):

$$\text{Fixed Asset Turnover} = \frac{\text{Operating Revenues}}{(\text{Beginning Net Fixed Asset Balance} + \text{Ending Net Fixed Asset Balance}) \div 2}$$

## FINDING
## FINANCIAL
## INFORMATION

### BALANCE SHEET
*Under Noncurrent Assets*

Property, plant, and equipment (net of accumulated depreciation)

Natural resources (net of accumulated depletion)

Intangibles (net of accumulated amortization)

### INCOME STATEMENT
*Under Operating Expenses*

Depreciation, depletion, and amortization expense or as part of

Selling, general, and administrative expenses and

Cost of goods sold (with the amount for depreciation expense disclosed in a note)

### STATEMENT OF CASH FLOWS
*Under Operating Activities (indirect method)*

Net income

+ Depreciation and amortization expense

− Gains on sales of assets

+ Losses on sales of assets

*Under Investing Activities*

+ Sales of assets for cash

− Purchases of assets for cash

### NOTES
*Under Summary of Significant Accounting Policies*

Description of management's choice for depreciation and amortization methods, including useful lives, and the amount of annual depreciation expense, if not listed on the income statement.

*Under a Separate Footnote*

If not specified on the balance sheet, a listing of the major classifications of long-lived assets at cost and the balance in accumulated depreciation, depletion, and amortization.

## KEY **TERMS**

**Accelerated Depreciation** p. 434

**Acquisition Cost** p. 425

**Additions** p. 429

**Amortization** p. 448

**Basket Purchase** p. 426

**Book (or Carrying) Value** p. 430

**Capital Expenditures** p. 428

**Capitalized Interest** p. 426

**Copyright** p. 450

**Declining-Balance Depreciation** p. 435

**Depletion** p. 446

**Depreciation** p. 430

**Estimated Useful Life** p. 431

**Extraordinary Repairs** p. 429

**Franchise** p. 450

**Goodwill (Cost in Excess of Net Assets Acquired)** p. 448

**Intangible Assets** p. 424

**Leaseholds** p. 450

**Long-Lived Assets** p. 424

**Natural Resources** p. 446

**Ordinary Repairs and Maintenance** p. 429

**Patent** p. 449

**Residual (or Salvage) Value** p. 431

**Revenue Expenditures** p. 428

**Straight-Line Depreciation** p. 432

**Tangible Assets** p. 424

**Trademark** p. 449

**Units-of-Production Depreciation** p. 433

## QUESTIONS

1. Define *long-lived assets*. Why are they considered a "bundle of future services"?
2. What are the classifications of long-lived assets? Explain each.
3. Relate the cost principle to accounting for long-lived assets. Under the cost principle, what amounts usually should be included in the acquisition cost of a long-lived asset?
4. Describe the relationship between the matching principle and accounting for long-lived assets.
5. What is a basket purchase? What measurement problem does it pose?
6. Distinguish between depreciation, depletion, and amortization.
7. In computing depreciation, three values must be known or estimated; identify and explain the nature of each.

8. Estimated useful life and residual value of a long-lived asset relate to the current owner or user rather than all potential users. Explain this statement.
9. What type of depreciation expense pattern is provided under each of the following:
   a. The straight-line method? When is its use appropriate?
   b. The units-of-production method? When is its use appropriate?
   c. The double-declining-balance method? When is its use appropriate?
10. Distinguish between
    a. Capital expenditures and revenue expenditures. How is each accounted for?
    b. Ordinary and extraordinary repairs. How is each accounted for?
11. Over what period should an addition to an existing long-lived asset be depreciated? Explain.
12. Define *intangible asset*. What period should be used to amortize an intangible asset?
13. Define *goodwill*. When is it appropriate to record goodwill as an intangible asset?
14. Distinguish between a leasehold and a leasehold improvement. Over what period should a leasehold improvement be amortized? Explain.
15. How is the fixed asset turnover ratio computed? Explain its meaning.
16. What is an *asset impairment?* How is it accounted for?
17. Why is depreciation expense added to net income on the statement of cash flows?

# MINI-EXERCISES

**M8–1 Classifying Long-Lived Assets and Related Cost Allocation Concepts**    ■ LO1
For each of the following long-lived assets, indicate its nature and related cost allocation concept. Use the following symbols:

| Nature | | Cost Allocation Concept | |
|---|---|---|---|
| L | Land | DR | Depreciation |
| B | Building | DP | Depletion |
| E | Equipment | A | Amortization |
| NR | Natural resource | NO | No cost allocation |
| I | Intangible | O | Other |
| O | Other | | |

| Asset | Nature | Cost Allocation | Asset | Nature | Cost Allocation |
|---|---|---|---|---|---|
| (1) Copyright | I | A | (6) Operating license | T | A |
| (2) Land held for use | L | NO | (7) Land held for sale | O | NO – investment |
| (3) Warehouse | B | DR | (8) Delivery vans | E | DR |
| (4) Oil well | NR | DP | (9) Timber tract | NR | DP |
| (5) New engine for old machine | E | DR | (10) Production plant | B | DR |

**M8–2 Determining Financial Statement Effects of Acquisition of Several Assets in a Basket Purchase**    ■ LO2
Kline Corporation acquired additional land and a building that included several pieces of equipment for $600,000. The assets were purchased with 20 percent cash, 20 percent no par common stock, and 60 percent long-term mortgage note with a local bank. An appraiser estimated the market values to be $200,000 for the land, $500,000 for the building, and $100,000 for the equipment. Using the following categories, indicate the effects of this acquisition. Use + for increase and − for decrease and indicate the accounts affected and the amounts.

| Assets | = | Liabilities | + | Stockholders' Equity |
|---|---|---|---|---|

■ LO3     **M8–3**     **Identifying Capital and Revenue Expenditures**

For each of the following items, enter the correct letter to the left to show the type of expenditure. Use the following:

Type of Expenditure

**C**     Capital expenditure

**R**     Revenue expenditure

**N**     Neither

Transactions

_____ (1) Paid $400 for ordinary repairs.

_____ (2) Paid $6,000 for extraordinary repairs.

_____ (3) Paid cash, $20,000, for addition to old building.

_____ (4) Paid for routine maintenance, $200, on credit.

_____ (5) Purchased a machine, $7,000; gave long-term note.

_____ (6) Paid $2,000 for organization costs.

_____ (7) Paid three-year insurance premium, $900.

_____ (8) Purchased a patent, $4,300 cash.

_____ (9) Paid $10,000 for monthly salaries.

_____ (10) Paid cash dividends, $20,000.

■ LO4     **M8–4**     **Computing Book Value (Straight-Line Depreciation)**

Calculate the book value of a three-year-old machine that cost $21,500, has an estimated residual value of $1,500, and has an estimated useful life of four years. The company uses straight-line depreciation.

■ LO4     **M8–5**     **Computing Book Value (Double-Declining-Balance Depreciation)**

Calculate the book value of a three-year-old machine that cost $21,500, has an estimated residual value of $1,500, and has an estimated useful life of four years. The company uses double-declining-balance depreciation. Round to the nearest dollar.

■ LO4     **M8–6**     **Computing Book Value (Units-of-Production Depreciation)**

Calculate the book value of a three-year-old machine that cost $21,500, has an estimated residual value of $1,500, and has an estimated useful life of 20,000 machine hours. The company uses units-of-production depreciation and ran the machine 3,000 hours in year 1, 8,000 hours in year 2, 7,000 hours in year 3, and 2,000 hours in year 4.

■ LO5     **M8–7**     **Preparing the Statement of Cash Flows**

Hansen Company had the following activities for the year ended December 31, 20B: Sold land for cash at its cost of $15,000. Purchased $80,000 of equipment, paying $75,000 in cash and the rest on a note payable. Recorded $3,000 in depreciation expense for the year. Net income for the year was $10,000. Prepare the operating and investing sections of a statement of cash flows for the year based on the data provided.

■ LO5     **M8–8**     **Computing and Evaluating the Fixed Asset Turnover Ratio**

The following information was reported by Cutter's Air Cargo Service for 1998:

| | |
|---|---|
| Net fixed assets (beginning of year) | $1,450,000 |
| Net fixed assets (end of year) | 2,250,000 |
| Net sales for the year | 3,250,000 |
| Net income for the year | 1,700,000 |

Compute the company's fixed asset turnover ratio for the year. What can you say about Cutter's ratio when compared to Delta's 1998 ratio?

■ LO6     **M8–9**     **Recording the Disposal of a Long-Lived Asset (Straight-Line Depreciation)**

As part of a major renovation at the beginning of the year, Jack's Pharmacy, Inc., sold shelving units (store fixtures) that were 10 years old for $1,400 cash. The original cost of the shelves was $6,200 and had been depreciated on a straight-line basis over an estimated useful life of 12 years with an estimated residual value of $200. Record the sale of the shelving units.

**M8–10 Computing Goodwill and Patents**

Elizabeth Pie Company has been in business for 30 years and has developed a large group of loyal restaurant customers. Bonanza Foods made an offer to buy Elizabeth Pie Company for $5,000,000. The book value of Elizabeth Pie's recorded assets and liabilities on the date of the offer is $4,400,000 with a market value of $4,600,000. Elizabeth Pie also (1) holds a patent for a pie crust fluting machine that the company invented (the patent with a market value of $200,000 was never recorded by Elizabeth Pie because it was developed internally) and (2) estimates goodwill from loyal customers to be $300,000 (also never recorded by the company). Should Elizabeth Pie Company management accept Bonanza Foods' offer of $5,000,000? If so, compute the amount of goodwill that Bonanza Foods should record on the date of the purchase.

**M8–11 Identifying Asset Impairment**

For each of the following scenarios, indicate whether an asset has been impaired (Y for yes and N for no) and, if so, how much loss should be recorded?

|  | Book Value | Estimated Future Cash Flows |
|---|---|---|
| a. Machine | $16,000 | $10,000 |
| b. Copyright | 40,000 | 41,000 |
| c. Factory building | 50,000 | 35,000 |
| d. Leasehold improvement | 30,000 | 30,000 |

# EXERCISES

**E8–1 Preparing a Classified Balance Sheet**

Hasbro, Inc.

The following is a list of account titles and amounts (in millions) reported by Hasbro, Inc., a leading manufacturer of games, toys, and interactive entertainment software for children and families:

| | | | |
|---|---|---|---|
| Buildings and improvements | $197 | Machinery and equipment | $ 296 |
| Prepaid expenses and other current assets | 319 | Accumulated depreciation | 227 |
| | | Inventories | 335 |
| Allowance for doubtful accounts | 64 | Other intangibles | 1,030 |
| Other noncurrent assets | 131 | Land and improvements | 15 |
| Accumulated amortization (other intangibles) | 192 | Accounts receivable | 1,022 |
| | | Tools, dies, and molds | 50 |
| Cash and cash equivalents | 178 | | |
| Cost in excess of net assets, net of accumulated amortization | 704 | | |

*Required:*

Prepare the asset section of the balance sheet for Hasbro, Inc., classifying the assets into Current Assets, Property, Plant, and Equipment (net), and Other Assets.

**E8–2 Computing and Recording Cost and Depreciation of Assets in a Basket Purchase (Straight-Line Depreciation)**

Hughes Company bought a building and the land on which it is located for a total cash price of $178,000. The company paid transfer costs of $2,000. Renovation costs on the building were $21,200. An independent appraiser provided market values for the building, $158,384, and land, $50,016.

*Required:*

1. Apportion the cost of the property on the basis of the appraised values. Show computations.

2. Give the journal entry to record the purchase of the property, including all expenditures. Assume that all transactions were for cash and that all purchases occurred at the start of the year.

3. Compute straight-line depreciation at the end of one year, assuming an estimated 12-year useful life and a $14,000 estimated residual value.

4. What would be the book value of the property at the end of year 2?

**LO2, 4**     **E8–3**     **Determining Financial Statement Effects of an Asset Acquisition and Depreciation (Straight-Line Depreciation)**

Flynn Company purchased a machine on March 1, 20A, at an invoice price of $20,000. On date of delivery, March 2, 20A, the company paid $8,000 on the machine, and the balance was on credit at 12 percent interest. On March 3, 20A, it paid $250 for freight on the machine. On March 5, Flynn paid installation costs relating to the machine amounting to $1,200. On October 1, 20A, the company paid the balance due on the machine plus the interest. On December 31, 20A (the end of the accounting period), Flynn recorded depreciation on the machine using the straight-line method with an estimated useful life of 10 years and an estimated residual value of $3,450.

***Required (round all amounts to the nearest dollar):***

1. Indicate the effects (accounts, amounts, and + or −) of each transaction (on March 1, 2, 3, 5, and October 1) on the accounting equation. Use the following schedule:

| Date | Assets | = | Liabilities | + | Stockholders' Equity |
|------|--------|---|-------------|---|----------------------|
|      |        |   |             |   |                      |

2. Compute the acquisition cost of the machine.

3. Compute the depreciation expense to be reported for 20A.

4. What is the impact on the cost of the machine of the interest paid on the 12 percent note? Under what circumstances can interest expense be included in acquisition cost?

5. What would be the book value of the machine at the end of 20B?

**LO2**     **E8–4**     **Evaluating the Impact of Capitalized Interest on Cash Flows and Fixed Asset Turnover from an Analyst's Perspective**

Hilton Hotels

You are a financial analyst charged with evaluating the asset efficiency of companies in the hotel industry. The financial statements for Hilton Hotels include the following note:

> **Summary of Significant Accounting Policies**
>
> *Property, Equipment and Depreciation*
>
> Property and equipment are stated at cost. Interest incurred during construction of facilities is capitalized and amortized over the life of the asset.

***Required:***

1. Assume that Hilton followed this policy for a major construction project this year. What is the sign of the effect of Hilton's policy (+ for increase, − for decrease, and NE for no effect) for the following this year (ignoring taxes)?

   *a.* Cash flows.

   *b.* Fixed asset turnover ratio.

2. Normally, how would your answer to requirement 1*b* affect your evaluation of Hilton's effectiveness in utilizing fixed assets?

3. If the fixed asset turnover ratio decreases due to interest capitalization, does this change indicate a real decrease in efficiency? Why or why not?

**LO3, 4**     **E8–5**     **Recording Depreciation and Repairs (Straight-Line Depreciation)**

Stevie-Lane Company operates a small manufacturing facility as a supplement to its regular service activities. At the beginning of 20C, an asset account for the company showed the following balances:

| | |
|---|---|
| Manufacturing equipment | $80,000 |
| Accumulated depreciation through 20B | 55,000 |

During 20C, the following expenditures were incurred for repairs and maintenance:

| | |
|---|---|
| Routine maintenance and repairs on the equipment | $ 850 |
| Major overhaul of the equipment | 10,500 |

The equipment is being depreciated on a straight-line basis over an estimated life of 15 years with a $5,000 estimated residual value. The annual accounting period ends on December 31.

*Required:*

1. Give the adjusting entry that was made at the end of 20B for depreciation on the manufacturing equipment.

2. Starting with 20C, what is the remaining estimated life?

3. Give the journal entries to record the two expenditures for repairs and maintenance during 20C.

4. Give the adjusting entry that should be made at the end of 20C for depreciation of the manufacturing equipment, assuming no change in the estimated life or residual value. Show computations.

**E8–6** **Determining Financial Statement Effects of Depreciation and Repairs (Straight-Line Depreciation)**    ■ **LO3, 4**

Refer to the information in E8–5.

*Required:*

Indicate the effects (accounts, amounts, and + or −) of

1. The adjustment for depreciation at the end of 20B.

2. The two expenditures for repairs and maintenance during 20C.

3. The adjustment for depreciation of the manufacturing equipment, assuming no change in the estimated life or residual value. Show computations and use the following format:

| Date | Assets | = | Liabilities | + | Stockholders' Equity |
|---|---|---|---|---|---|

**E8–7** **Recording and Explaining Depreciation, Extraordinary Repairs, and Changes in Estimated Useful Life and Residual Value (Straight-Line Depreciation)**    ■ **LO3, 4**

At the end of the annual accounting period, December 31, 20C, Lucy Company's records reflected the following for Machine A:

| | |
|---|---|
| Cost when acquired | $28,000 |
| Accumulated depreciation | 10,000 |

During January 20D, the machine was renovated at a cost of $11,000. As a result, the estimated life increased from five years to eight years, and the residual value increased from $3,000 to $5,000. The company uses straight-line depreciation.

*Required:*

1. Give the journal entry to record the renovation.

2. How old was the machine at the end of 20C?

3. Give the adjusting entry at the end of 20D to record straight-line depreciation for the year.

4. Explain the rationale for your entries in requirements 1 and 3.

**E8–8** **Computing Depreciation under Alternative Methods**    ■ **LO4**

Michael Paul Corporation bought a machine at the beginning of the year at a cost of $6,400. The estimated useful life was four years, and the residual value was $800. Assume that the estimated productive life of the machine is 80,000 units. Yearly production was year 1, 28,000 units; year 2, 22,000 units; year 3, 18,000 units; and year 4, 12,000 units.

*Required:*

1. Determine the amount for each cell in the following schedule. Show your computations, and round to the nearest dollar.

| | Depreciation Expense | | |
|---|---|---|---|
| Year | Straight Line | Units of Production | 200 Percent Declining Balance |
| 1 | | | |
| 2 | | | |
| 3 | | | |
| 4 | | | |
| Totals | | | |

2. Assuming that the machine was used directly in the production of one of the products that the company manufactures and sells, what factors might management consider in selecting a preferable depreciation method in conformity with the matching principle?

**LO4**      **E8–9**

**Computing the Effect of a Change in Useful Life and Residual Value on Financial Statements and Cash Flows (Straight-Line Depreciation)**

Dustin Company owns the office building occupied by its administrative office. The office building was reflected in the accounts at the end of last year as follows:

| | |
|---|---|
| Cost when acquired | $450,000 |
| Accumulated depreciation (based on straight-line depreciation, an estimated life of 30 years, and a $30,000 residual value) | 196,000 |

During January of this year, on the basis of a careful study, management decided that the total estimated useful life should be changed to 25 years (instead of 30) and the residual value reduced to $23,000 (from $30,000). The depreciation method will not change.

*Required:*

1. Compute the annual depreciation expense prior to the change in estimates.
2. Compute the annual depreciation expense after the change in estimates.
3. What will be the net effect of changing estimates on the balance sheet, net income, and cash flows for the year?

**LO4**      **E8–10**

Eastman Kodak

**Explaining Depreciation Policy**

The annual report for Eastman Kodak contained the following note:

**Significant Accounting Policies**

**Depreciation.**   Depreciation expense is provided based on historical cost and the estimated useful lives of the assets. The Company generally uses the straight-line method for calculating the provision for depreciation. For assets in the United States acquired prior to January 1, 1992, the provision for depreciation is generally calculated using accelerated methods.

*Required:*

1. Explain the term *historical cost.* What is the meaning of "provision for depreciation"?
2. Why do you think the company changed its depreciation method for assets acquired in 1992 and subsequent years? What impact did the change have on net income?

**LO4**      **E8–11**

Federal Express

**Interpreting Management's Choice of Different Depreciation Methods for Tax and Financial Reporting**

The annual report for Federal Express Corporation includes the following information:

> For financial reporting purposes, depreciation and amortization of property and equipment is provided on a straight-line basis over the asset's service life. For income tax purposes, depreciation is generally computed using accelerated methods.

*Required:*

Explain why Federal Express uses different methods of depreciation for financial reporting and tax purposes.

**E8–12** **Computing Depreciation and Book Value for Two Years Using Alternative Depreciation Methods and Interpreting the Impact on Cash Flows**

◼ **LO4, 5**

Cotton Company bought a machine for $65,000 cash. The estimated useful life was five years, and the estimated residual value was $5,000. Assume that the estimated useful life in productive units is 150,000. Units actually produced were 40,000 in year 1 and 45,000 in year 2.

*Required:*

1. Determine the appropriate amounts to complete the following schedule. Show computations, and round to the nearest dollar.

|  | Depreciation Expense for | | Book Value at the End of | |
| --- | --- | --- | --- | --- |
| Method of Depreciation | Year 1 | Year 2 | Year 1 | Year 2 |
| Straight line | | | | |
| Units of production | | | | |
| Double declining balance | | | | |

2. Which method would result in the lowest EPS for year 1? For year 2?

3. Which method would result in the highest amount of cash outflows in year 1? Why?

4. Indicate the effects of (a) acquiring the machine and (b) recording annual depreciation on the operating and investing activities on the statement of cash flows (indirect method) for year 1 (assume the straight-line method).

**E8–13** **Computing and Interpreting the Fixed Asset Turnover Ratio from a Financial Analyst's Perspective**

◼ **LO5**

Apple Computer

The following data were included in a recent Apple Computer annual report:

2000
$ 7893

316

| In millions | 1998 | 1997 | 1996 | 1995 | 1994 | 1993 | 1992 | 1991 | 1990 | 1989 |
| --- | --- | --- | --- | --- | --- | --- | --- | --- | --- | --- |
| Net sales | $5,941 | $7,081 | $9,833 | $11,062 | $9,180 | $7,977 | $7,086 | $6,309 | $5,558 | $5,284 |
| Net property, plant, and equipment | 348 | 486 | 598 | 711 | 667 | 660 | 462 | 448 | 398 | 334 |

*Required:*

1. Compute Apple's fixed asset turnover ratio for 1990, 1992, 1994, 1996, and 1998 (the even years).

2. How might a financial analyst interpret the results?

**E8–14** **Recording the Disposal of an Asset at Three Different Assumed Sale Prices**

◼ **LO6**

Federal Express

Federal Express has developed a worldwide network that delivers more than 1.7 million packages every working night. In addition to the world's largest fleet of all-cargo aircraft, the company has more than 28,000 ground vehicles that pick up and deliver packages. Assume that Federal Express sold a small delivery truck that had been used in the business for three years. The records of the company reflected the following:

| | |
|---|---|
| Delivery truck | $18,000 |
| Accumulated depreciation | 13,000 |

*Required:*

1. Give the journal entry for the disposal of the truck, assuming that the sales price was $5,000.

2. Give the journal entry for the disposal of the truck, assuming that the sales price was $5,600.

3. Give the journal entry for the disposal of the truck, assuming that the sales price was $4,600.

4. For the preceding three different situations, summarize the effects of the disposal of the asset.

**LO6**

**E8–15**

Federal Express

**Determining Financial Statement Effects of the Disposal of an Asset at Three Different Assumed Sale Prices**

Refer to the information in E8–14.

*Required:*

1. Using the following structure, indicate the effects (accounts, amounts, and plus or minus) for the disposal of the truck assuming that

   *a.* The sales price was $5,000.

   *b.* The sales price was $5,600.

   *c.* The sales price was $4,600.

| Assumption | Assets | = | Liabilities | + | Stockholders' Equity |
|---|---|---|---|---|---|

2. For the preceding three different situations, summarize the effects of the disposal of the asset.

**LO6**

**E8–16**

**Inferring Asset Age and Recording Accidental Loss on a Long-Lived Asset (Straight-Line Depreciation)**

On January 1, 20C, the records of Barken Corporation showed the following:

| | |
|---|---|
| Truck (estimated residual value, $2,000) | $12,000 |
| Accumulated depreciation (straight line, two years) | 4,000 |

On September 30, 20C, the delivery truck was a total loss as the result of an accident. The truck was insured; therefore, the company collected $5,600 cash from the insurance company on October 5, 20C.

*Required:*

1. Based on the data given, compute the estimated useful life of the truck.

2. Give all journal entries with respect to the truck on September 30 and October 5, 20C. Show computations.

**LO7**

**E8–17**

Freeport-McMoran

**Computing the Acquisition and Depletion of a Natural Resource**

Freeport-McMoran is a natural resources company involved in the exploration, development, and extraction of natural resources. Annual revenues exceed $1 billion. Assume that in February 20A, Freeport-McMoran paid $700,000 for a mineral deposit in Wyoming. During March, it spent $65,000 in preparing the deposit for exploitation. It was estimated that 900,000 total cubic yards could be extracted economically. During 20A, 60,000 cubic yards were extracted. During January 20B, the company spent another $6,000 for additional developmental work. After conclusion of the latest work, the estimated remaining recovery was increased to 1,200,000 cubic yards over the remaining life. During 20B, 50,000 cubic yards were extracted.

*Required:*

1. Compute the acquisition cost of the deposit in 20A.

2. Compute depletion for 20A.

3. Compute the acquisition cost of the deposit after payment of the January 20B developmental costs.

4. Compute annual depletion for 20B.

**E8–18** **Computing and Reporting the Acquisition and Amortization of Three Different Intangible Assets**

■ **LO7**

Wyatt Company had three intangible assets at the end of 20H (end of the accounting year):

*a.* A patent purchased from R. Jay on January 1, 20H, for a cash cost of $5,640. Jay had registered the patent with the U.S. Patent Office seven years earlier on January 1, 20A. Amortize over the remaining legal life.

*b.* A franchise acquired from the local community to provide certain services for five years starting on January 1, 20H. The franchise cost $25,000 cash.

*c.* A lease on some property for a five-year term beginning January 1, 20H. The company immediately spent $7,800 cash for long-term improvements (estimated useful life, eight years; no residual value). At the termination of the lease, there will be no recovery of these improvements.

*Required:*

1. Compute the acquisition cost of each intangible asset.

2. Compute the amortization of each intangible at December 31, 20H. The company does not use contra-accounts.

3. Show how these assets and any related expenses should be reported on the balance sheet and income statement for 20H.

**E8–19** **Recording Rent Paid in Advance, Leasehold Improvements, Periodic Rent, and Related Amortization**

■ **LO7**

Starbucks Coffee Company

Starbucks Coffee Company is a rapidly expanding retailer of specialty coffee with more than 1,650 stores. Assume that Starbucks planned to open a new store on Commonwealth Avenue near Boston University and obtained a 15-year lease starting January 1, 20D. Although a serviceable building was on the property, the company had to build an additional structure for storage. The 15-year lease required a $12,000 cash advance payment plus cash payments of $4,000 per month during occupancy. During January 20D, the company spent $60,000 cash building the structure. The new structure has an estimated life of 18 years with no residual value (straight-line depreciation).

*Required:*

1. Give the journal entries for the company to record the payment of the $12,000 advance on January 1, 20D, and the first monthly rental.

2. Give the journal entry to record the construction of the new structure.

3. Give any adjusting entries required at the end of the annual accounting period on December 31, 20D, with respect to (a) the advance payment and (b) the new structure. Show computations.

4. Compute the total amount of expense resulting from the lease for 20D.

**E8–20** **Inferring Asset Impairment**

■ **LO8**

Sunglass Hut International

Sunglass Hut International is the world's largest specialty retailer of sunglasses with stores located in a wide variety of high-traffic shopping and tourist destinations. The following note and data were reported in a recent annual report:

**NOTE 1—ORGANIZATION AND SUMMARY OF SIGNIFICANT ACCOUNTING POLICIES**

**Property and Equipment**

The Company performed an analysis of the recoverability of the net book value of property and equipment for underperforming operations. As a result of the analysis, the Company reduced property and equipment by . . .

|  | In millions |
| --- | --- |
| Cost of property and equipment (beginning of year) | $192 |
| Cost of property and equipment (end of year) | 178 |
| Capital expenditures during the year | 29 |
| Accumulated depreciation (beginning of year) | 63 |
| Accumulated depreciation (end of year) | 77 |
| Depreciation expense during the year | 27 |

*Required:*

Based on the preceding information, compute the amount of property and equipment (both cost and accumulated depreciation) that Sunglass Hut wrote off as impaired during the year. (*Hint:* Set up T-accounts.)

**LO1, 4, 6, 7, 8**    **E8–21**    **Finding Financial Information as a Potential Investor**

You are considering investing the cash gifts you received for graduation in various stocks. You have received several annual reports of major companies.

*Required:*

For each of the following, indicate where you would locate the information in an annual report (*Hint:* The information may be in more than one location):

1. The detail on major classifications of long-lived assets.

2. The accounting method(s) used for financial reporting purposes.

3. Whether the company has had any capital expenditures for the year.

4. Net amount of property, plant, and equipment.

5. Policies on amortizing intangibles.

6. Depreciation expense.

7. Any significant gains or losses on disposals of fixed assets.

8. Prior year's accumulated depreciation.

9. The amount of assets written off as impaired during the year.

## PROBLEMS

**LO1, 2**    **P8–1**    **Explaining the Nature of a Long-Lived Asset and Determining the Financial Statement Effects of Its Purchase (AP8–1)**

On January 2, 20A, Ethel Company bought a machine for use in operations. The machine has an estimated useful life of eight years and an estimated residual value of $1,500. The company provided the following expenditures:

*a.* Invoice price of the machine, $70,000.

*b.* Freight paid by the vendor per sales agreement, $800.

*c.* Installation costs, $2,000.

*d.* Payment of the $70,000 was made as follows:

On January 2:
- Ethel Company common stock, par $1; 2,000 shares (market value, $3 per share).
- Note payable, $40,000, 12 percent due April 16, 20A (principal plus interest).
- Balance of the invoice price to be paid in cash. The invoice allows for a 2 percent discount for cash paid by January 11.

On January 15:
- Ethel Company paid the balance due.

*Required:*

1. What are the classifications of long-lived assets? Explain their differences.

2. Indicate the accounts, amounts, and effects (+ for increase and − for decrease) of the purchase and subsequent cash payment on the accounting equation. Use the following structure:

| Date | Assets | = | Liabilities | + | Stockholders' Equity |
|------|--------|---|-------------|---|----------------------|

3. Explain the basis you used for any questionable items.

**P8–2** **Explaining the Nature of a Long-Lived Asset and Recording Its Purchase** (AP8–2)
Refer to the information in P8–1.

■ **LO1, 2**

*Required:*

1. What are the classifications of long-lived assets? Explain their differences.

2. Record the purchase on January 2 and the subsequent payment on January 15. Show computations.

3. Explain the basis you used for any questionable items.

**P8–3** **Analyzing the Effects of Repairs, an Addition, and Depreciation** (AP8–3)
A recent annual report for Federal Express included the following note:

■ **LO3, 4**

Federal Express

> **Property and equipment**
>
> Expenditures for major additions, improvements, flight equipment modifications and overhaul costs are capitalized. Maintenance and repairs are charged to expense as incurred.

Assume that Federal Express made extensive repairs on an existing building and added a new wing. The building is a garage and repair facility for delivery trucks that serve the Denver area. The existing building originally cost $420,000, and by the end of 20C (10 years), it was half depreciated on the basis of a 20-year estimated useful life and no residual value. Assume straight-line depreciation computed to the nearest month. During 20D, the following expenditures related to the building were made:

a. Ordinary repairs and maintenance expenditures for the year, $7,000 cash.

b. Extensive and major repairs to the roof of the building, $22,000 cash. These repairs were completed on June 30, 20D.

c. The new wing was completed on June 30, 20D, at a cash cost of $130,000. By itself, the wing had an estimated useful life of 15 years and no residual value. The company intends to sell the building and wing at the end of the building's useful life (in 9½ years from June 30, 20D).

*Required:*

1. Applying the policies of Federal Express, complete the following, indicating the effects for the preceding expenditures. If there is no effect on an account, write NE on the line:

| | Building | Accumulated Depreciation | Depreciation Expense | Repairs Expense | Cash |
|---|---|---|---|---|---|
| Balance January 1, 20D | $420,000 | _____ | _____ | | |
| Depreciation through June 30 | | _____ | _____ | | _____ |
| Balance prior to expenditures | 420,000 | _____ | _____ | | |
| Expenditure a | _____ | _____ | _____ | _____ | _____ |
| Expenditure b | _____ | _____ | _____ | _____ | _____ |
| Expenditure c | _____ | _____ | _____ | _____ | _____ |
| Depreciation July–December 31: | | | | | |
|   Existing building | | _____ | _____ | _____ | _____ |
|   Repairs and additions | | _____ | _____ | _____ | _____ |
| Balance December 31, 20D | _____ | _____ | _____ | _____ | _____ |

2. What was the book value of the building on December 31, 20D?

3. Explain the effect of depreciation on cash flows.

■ **LO2, 4**    **P8–4**

**Computing the Basket Purchase Allocation and Recording Depreciation under Three Alternative Methods** (AP8–4)

At the beginning of the year, Dittman Company bought three used machines from Hangar, Inc., for a total cash price of $38,000. Transportation costs on the machines were $2,000. The machines immediately were overhauled, installed, and started operating. The machines were different; therefore, each had to be recorded separately in the accounts. An appraiser was employed to estimate their market value at date of purchase (prior to the overhaul and installation). The book values shown on Hangar's books also are available. The book values, appraisal results, installation costs, and renovation expenditures follow:

|  | Machine A | Machine B | Machine C |
|---|---|---|---|
| Book value—Hangar | $8,000 | $12,000 | $6,000 |
| Appraisal value | 9,500 | 32,000 | 8,500 |
| Installation costs | 300 | 500 | 200 |
| Renovation costs prior to use | 2,000 | 400 | 600 |

By the end of the first year, each machine had been operating 8,000 hours.

*Required:*

1. Compute the cost of each machine by making a supportable allocation. Explain the rationale for the allocation basis used.

2. Give the entry to record depreciation expense at the end of year 1, assuming the following:

| Machine | Estimates | | Depreciation Method |
|---|---|---|---|
|  | Life | Residual Value |  |
| A | 5 | $1,500 | Straight line |
| B | 40,000 hours | 900 | Units of production |
| C | 4 | 2,000 | 200% declining balance |

■ **LO4**    **P8–5**

Reader's Digest

**Analyzing and Recording Entries Related to a Change in Estimated Life and Residual Value**

Reader's Digest is a global publisher of magazines, books, and music and video collections, and is one of the world's leading direct mail marketers. Many direct mail marketers use high-speed Didde press equipment to print their advertisements. These presses can cost more than $1 million. Assume that Reader's Digest owns a Didde press acquired at an original cost of $400,000. It is being depreciated on a straight-line basis over a 20-year estimated useful life and has a $50,000 estimated residual value. At the end of 20C, the press had been depreciated for a full eight years. In January 20D, a decision was made, on the basis of improved maintenance procedures, that a total estimated useful life of 25 years and a residual value of $73,000 would be more realistic. The accounting period ends December 31.

*Required:*

1. Compute (*a*) the amount of depreciation expense recorded in 20C and (*b*) the book value of the printing press at the end of 20C.

2. Compute the amount of depreciation that should be recorded in 20D. Show computations.

3. Give the adjusting entry for depreciation at December 31, 20D.

■ **LO4, 5**    **P8–6**

REX Stores Corporation

**Inferring Depreciation Amounts and Determining the Effects of a Depreciation Error on Key Ratios** (AP8–5)

REX Stores Corporation, headquartered in Dayton, Ohio, is one of the nation's leading consumer electronics retailers operating more than 222 stores in 35 states. The following is a note from a recent annual report:

**(1) SUMMARY OF SIGNIFICANT ACCOUNTING POLICIES—**

(e) Property and Equipment—Property and equipment is recorded at cost. Depreciation is computed using the straight-line method. Estimated useful lives are 15 to 40 years for buildings and improvements, and 3 to 12 years for fixtures and equipment. Leasehold improvements are depreciated over 10 to 12 years. The components of cost at January 31, 1999 and 1998 are as follows:

|  | 1999 | 1998 |
|---|---|---|
|  | (in thousands) | |
| Land | $ 26,716 | $ 24,779 |
| Buildings and improvements | 64,586 | 59,006 |
| Fixtures and equipment | 15,477 | 14,615 |
| Leasehold improvements | 10,217 | 9,747 |
|  | 116,996 | 108,147 |
| Less: Accumulated depreciation | (18,105) | (14,982) |
|  | $ 98,891 | $ 93,165 |

*Required:*

1. Assuming that REX Stores did not sell any property, plant, and equipment in 1999, what was the amount of depreciation expense recorded in 1999?

2. Assume that REX Stores failed to record depreciation in 1999. Indicate the effect of the error (i.e., overstated or understated) on the following ratios:

   *a.* Earnings per share.

   *b.* Fixed asset turnover.

   *c.* Assets to equity.

   *d.* Return on equity.

**P8–7** **Evaluating the Effect of Alternative Depreciation Methods on Key Ratios from an Analyst's Perspective**

Southwestern Bell provides telecommunication services to customers in Arkansas, Kansas, Missouri, Oklahoma, and Texas. The company's assets exceed $22 billion. As a result, depreciation is a significant item on Southwestern Bell's income statement. You are a financial analyst for Southwestern Bell and have been asked to determine the impact of alternative depreciation methods. For your analysis, you have been asked to compare methods based on a machine that cost $68,225. The estimated useful life is 10 years, and the estimated residual value is $2,225. The machine has an estimated useful life in productive output of 88,000 units. Actual output was 10,000 in year 1 and 8,000 in year 2.

■ **LO4, 5**

Southwestern Bell

*Required:*

1. Determine the appropriate amounts for the following table. Show your computations.

| Method of Depreciation | Depreciation Expense for | | Book Value at End of | |
|---|---|---|---|---|
|  | Year 1 | Year 2 | Year 1 | Year 2 |
| Straight line | | | | |
| Units of production | | | | |
| 200 % declining balance | | | | |

2. Evaluate each method in terms of its effect on cash flow, fixed asset turnover, and EPS. Assuming that Southwestern Bell is most interested in reducing taxes and maintaining a high EPS for year 1, what would you recommend to management? Would your recommendation change for year 2? Why or why not?

■ **LO5, 6**

Fisher-Price

**P8–8**

**Inferring Asset Age and Determining Financial Statement Effects of a Long-Lived Asset Disposal (Challenging)** (AP8–6)

Fisher-Price manufactures and markets high-quality preschool and infant toys. The company's revenues exceed $600 million. In the toy business, it is very difficult to determine the life expectancy of a product. Products that children love one year may sit on the shelf the following year. As a result, companies in the toy business often sell productive assets that are no longer needed. Assume that on December 31, 20D (after adjusting entries), Fisher-Price's records showed the following data about a machine that was no longer needed to make a toy that was popular last year:

| | |
|---|---|
| Machine, original cost | $52,000 |
| Accumulated depreciation | 27,500* |

*Based on an eight-year estimated useful life, an $8,000 residual value, and straight-line depreciation.

On April 1, 20E, the machine was sold for $26,000 cash. The accounting period ends on December 31.

*Required:*

1. How old was the machine on January 1, 20E? Show computations.

2. Indicate the effect (i.e., the amount and whether it increased or decreased) of the sale of the machine on April 1, 20E, on

   *a.* Total assets.

   *b.* Net income.

   *c.* Cash flows (by each section of the statement: Operating, Investing, and Financing Activities).

■ **LO5, 6**

Singapore Airlines

**P8–9**

**Inferring Activities Affecting Fixed Assets from Notes to the Financial Statements and Analyzing the Impact of Depreciation on Cash Flows**

Singapore Airlines reported the following information in the notes to a recent annual report (in Singapore dollars):

**SINGAPORE AIRLINES**

*Notes to the Accounts*

13. **Fixed Assets** (in $ Million)

The Company

| | Beginning of Year | Additions | Disposals/ Transfers | End of Year |
|---|---|---|---|---|
| *Cost* | | | | |
| Aircraft | 10,293.1 | 954.4 | 296.4 | 10,951.1 |
| Other fixed assets (summarized) | 3,580.9 | 1,499.1 | 1,156.7 | 3,923.3 |
| | 13,874.0 | 2,453.5 | 1,453.1 | 14,874.4 |
| *Accumulated depreciation* | | | | |
| Aircraft | 4,024.8 | 683.7 | 290.1 | 4,418.4 |
| Other fixed assets (summarized) | 1,433.4 | 158.5 | 73.8 | 1,518.1 |
| | 5,458.2 | 842.2 | 363.9 | 5,936.5 |

Singapore Airlines also reported the following cash flow details:

| Cash Flow from Operating Activities (in $ Million) | | |
|---|---|---|
| | The Company | |
| | Current Year | Prior Year |
| Operating Profit | 755.9 | 816.5 |
| Adjustments for: | | |
| Depreciation of fixed assets | 842.2 | 837.5 |
| Loss/(surplus) on sale of fixed assets | (1.3) | (0.3) |
| Other adjustments (summarized) | 82.3 | 39.4 |
| Net Cash Provided by Operating Activities | 1,679.1 | 1,693.1 |

*Required:*

1. Reconstruct the information in Note 13 into T-accounts for Fixed Assets and Accumulated Depreciation:

| Fixed Assets | | | Accumulated Depreciation | |
|---|---|---|---|---|
| Beg. balance | | | | Beg. balance |
| Acquisitions | Disposals/transfers | Disposals/transfers | | Depreciation expense |
| End. balance | | | | End. balance |

2. Compute the amount of cash the company received for disposals and transfers. Show computations.

3. Compute the percentage of depreciation expense to cash flows from operations. What do you interpret from the result?

**P8–10 Recording and Interpreting the Disposal of Three Long-Lived Assets** (AP8–7)   ■ **LO6**
During 20C, Baldwin Company disposed of three different assets. On January 1, 20C, prior to their disposal, the accounts reflected the following:

| Asset | Original Cost | Residual Value | Estimated Life | Accumulated Depreciation (straight line) |
|---|---|---|---|---|
| Machine A | $20,000 | $3,000 | 8 years | $12,750 (6 years) |
| Machine B | 42,600 | 4,000 | 10 years | 30,880 (8 years) |
| Machine C | 76,200 | 4,200 | 15 years | 57,600 (12 years) |

The machines were disposed of in the following ways:

a. Machine A: Sold on January 1, 20C, for $8,200 cash.

b. Machine B: Sold on April 1, 20C, for $10,000; received cash, $3,000, and a $7,000 interest-bearing (12%) note receivable due at the end of 12 months.

c. Machine C: On July 2, 20C, this machine suffered irreparable damage from an accident. On July 10, 20C, a salvage company removed the machine immediately at no cost. The machine was insured, and $18,500 cash was collected from the insurance company.

*Required:*

1. Give all journal entries related to the disposal of each machine.

2. Explain the accounting rationale for the way that you recorded each disposal.

**P8–11 Determining Financial Statement Effects of Activities Related to Various Long-Lived Assets** (AP8–8)   ■ **LO7**
During the 20E annual accounting period, Boyd Company completed the following transactions:

a. On January 10, 20E, paid $7,000 for a complete reconditioning of each of the following machines acquired on January 1, 20A (total cost, $14,000):

   (1) Machine A: Original cost, $26,000; accumulated depreciation (straight line) to December 31, 20D, $18,400 ($3,000 residual value).

   (2) Machine B: Original cost, $32,000; accumulated depreciation (straight line) $13,000 ($6,000 residual value).

b. On July 1, 20E, purchased a patent for $19,600 cash (estimated useful life, seven years).

c. On January 1, 20E, purchased another business for cash $60,000, including $16,000 for goodwill. The company assumed no liabilities.

d. On September 1, 20E, constructed a storage shed on land leased from A. Katz. The cost was $10,800; the estimated useful life was five years with no residual value. The company uses straight-line depreciation. The lease will expire in three years.

e. Total expenditures during 20E for ordinary repairs and maintenance were $4,800.

f. On July 1, 20E, sold Machine A for $6,000 cash.

**Required:**

1. For each of these transactions, indicate the accounts, amounts and effects (plus for increase and minus for decrease) on the accounting equation. Use the following structure:

| Date | Assets | = | Liabilities | + | Stockholders' Equity |
|------|--------|---|-------------|---|----------------------|

2. For each of these assets, compute depreciation and amortization to the nearest month to be recorded at the end of the year on December 31, 20E.

■ **LO7**
Reebok

**P8–12**  **Computing Goodwill from the Purchase of a Business and Related Depreciation and Amortization**

Reebok International is a leading worldwide designer, marketer, and distributor of sport, fitness, and lifestyle products, including footwear and apparel. The notes to a recent annual report from Reebok included the following:

**Business Acquisitions**

During the current year, the Company acquired the assets of Perfection Sport Fashions, Inc., a designer and marketer of performance apparel and accessories marketed under the *Tinley* brand name.

Assume that Reebok acquired Perfection Sport Fashions on January 5, 20A. Reebok acquired the name of the company and all of its assets, except cash, for $400,000 cash. Reebok did not assume the liabilities. The transaction was closed on January 5, 20A, at which time the balance sheet of Perfection Sport Fashions reflected the following book values and an independent appraiser estimated the following market values for the assets:

| **PERFECTION SPORT FASHIONS** January 5, 20A | Book Value | Market Value* |
|---|---|---|
| Accounts receivable (net) | $ 45,000 | $ 45,000 |
| Inventory | 220,000 | 210,000 |
| Fixed assets (net) | 32,000 | 60,000 |
| Other assets | 3,000 | 10,000 |
| Total assets | $300,000 | |
| Liabilities | $ 60,000 | |
| Stockholders' equity | 240,000 | |
| Total liabilities and stockholders' equity | $300,000 | |

*These values for the purchased assets were provided to Reebok by an independent appraiser.

*Required:*

1. Compute the amount of goodwill resulting from the purchase. (*Hint:* Assets are purchased at market value in conformity with the cost principle.)

2. Compute the adjustments that Reebok would make at the end of the annual accounting period, December 31, 20A, for

   *a.* Depreciation of the fixed assets (straight line), assuming an estimated remaining useful life of 15 years and no residual value.

   *b.* Amortization of goodwill, assuming that the maximum amortization period is used.

**P8–13 Determining the Financial Statement Effects of the Acquisition and Amortization of Three Intangibles**

■ **LO7**

Figg Company, with a fiscal year ending December 31, acquired three intangible assets during 20F. For each of the following transactions, indicate the accounts and amounts affected and the direction of the effect (+ for increase, − for decrease, and NE for no effect). Use the following headings:

| Date | Assets | = | Liabilities | + | Stockholders' Equity |
|------|--------|---|-------------|---|----------------------|

*a.* On January 1, 20F, the company purchased a patent from Ullrich, Inc., for $6,000 cash. Ullrich had developed the patent and registered it with the U.S. Patent Office on January 1, 20A.

*b.* On January 1, 20F, the company purchased a copyright for a total cash cost of $14,000; the remaining legal life was 25 years. Company executives estimated that the copyright would have no value by the end of 20 years.

*c.* The company purchased another company in January 20F at a cash cost of $120,000. Included in the purchase price was $30,000 for goodwill; the balance was for plant, equipment, and fixtures (no liabilities were assumed).

*d.* On December 31, 20F, amortize the patent over the remaining legal life.

*e.* On December 31, 20F, amortize the copyright.

*f.* On December 31, 20F, amortize the goodwill over the maximum period permitted.

**P8–14 Computing Amortization, Book Value, and Asset Impairment Related to Different Intangible Assets (AP8–9)**

■ **LO7, 8**

Warren Company has five different intangible assets to be accounted for and reported on the financial statements. The management is concerned about the amortization of the cost of each of these intangibles. Facts about each intangible follow:

*a.* *Patent.* The company purchased a patent at a cash cost of $54,600 on January 1, 20E. The patent had a legal life of 17 years from date of registration with the U.S. Patent Office, which was January 1, 20A. It is amortized over its remaining legal life.

*b.* *Copyright.* On January 1, 20E, the company purchased a copyright for $22,500 cash. The legal life remaining from that date is 30 years. It is estimated that the copyrighted item will have no value by the end of 25 years.

*c.* *Franchise.* The company obtained a franchise from Terwilliger Company to make and distribute a special item. It obtained the franchise on January 1, 20E, at a cash cost of $14,400 for a 12-year period.

*d.* *License.* On January 1, 20D, the company secured a license from the city to operate a special service for a period of five years. Total cash expended to obtain the license was $14,000.

*e.* *Goodwill.* The company started business in January 20C by purchasing another business for a cash lump sum of $400,000. Included in the purchase price was "Goodwill, $60,000." Company executives stated that "the goodwill is an important long-term asset to us." It is amortized over the maximum period permitted.

*Required:*

1. Compute the amount of amortization that should be recorded for each intangible asset at the end of the annual accounting period, December 31, 20E.

2. Give the book value of each intangible asset on January 1, 20G.

3. Assume that on January 2, 20G, the copyrighted item was impaired in its ability to continue to produce strong revenues. The other intangible assets were not affected. Warren estimated that the copyright will be able to produce future cash flows of $15,000. Compute the amount, if any, of the impairment loss to be recorded.

## ALTERNATE PROBLEMS

■ **LO1, 2**　**AP8–1**　**Explaining the Nature of a Long-Lived Asset and Determining the Financial Statement Effects of Its Purchase** (P8–1)

On June 1, 20B, the Fitzgerald Corp. bought a machine for use in operations. The machine has an estimated useful life of six years and an estimated residual value of $2,000. The company provided the following expenditures:

a. Invoice price of the machine, $60,000.

b. Freight paid by the vendor per sales agreement, $650.

c. Installation costs, $1,500.

d. Payment of the $60,000 was made as follows:

On June 1:

- Fitzgerald Corp. common stock, par $2; 2,000 shares (market value, $5 per share).
- Balance of the invoice price on a note payable, 12 percent due September 2, 20B (principal plus interest).

On September 2:

- Fitzgerald Corp. paid the balance and interest due on the note payable.

*Required:*

1. What are the classifications of long-lived assets? Explain their differences.

2. Indicate the accounts, amounts, and effects (+ for increase and − for decrease) of the purchase and subsequent cash payment on the accounting equation. Use the following structure:

| Date | Assets | = | Liabilities | + | Stockholders' Equity |
|------|--------|---|-------------|---|----------------------|

3. Explain the basis you used for any questionable items.

■ **LO1, 2**　**AP8–2**　**Explaining the Nature of a Long-Lived Asset and Recording Its Purchase** (P8–2)

Refer to the information in AP8–1.

*Required:*

1. What are the classifications of long-lived assets? Explain their differences.

2. Record the purchase on July 1 and the subsequent payment on September 2. Show computations.

3. Explain the basis you used for any questionable items.

■ **LO3, 4**　**AP8–3**　**Analyzing the Effects of Repairs, an Addition, and Depreciation** (P8–3)

AMERCO

A recent annual report for AMERCO, the holding company for U-Haul International, Inc., included the following note:

> **PROPERTY, PLANT AND EQUIPMENT**
>
> Property, plant and equipment are carried at cost and are depreciated on the straight-line and accelerated methods over the estimated useful lives of the assets. . . . Maintenance is charged to operating expenses as incurred, while renewals and betterments are capitalized. Major overhaul costs are amortized over the estimated period benefited.

AMERCO subsidiaries own property, plant, and equipment that are utilized in the manufacture, repair, and rental of U-Haul equipment and that provide offices for U-Haul. Assume that AMERCO made extensive repairs on an existing building and added a new wing. The building is a garage and repair facility for rental trucks that serve the Seattle area. The existing building originally cost $230,000, and by the end of 20F (5 years), it was one-quarter depreciated on the basis of a 20-year estimated useful life and no residual value. Assume straight-line depreciation computed to the nearest month. During 20G, the following expenditures related to the building were made:

a.  Ordinary repairs and maintenance expenditures for the year, $5,000 cash.

b.  Extensive and major repairs to the roof of the building, $17,000 cash. These repairs were completed on June 30, 20G.

c.  The new wing was completed on June 30, 20G, at a cash cost of $70,000. By itself, the wing had an estimated useful life of 15 years and no residual value. The company intends to sell the building and wing at the end of the building's useful life (in 14½ years from June 30, 20G).

*Required:*

1.  Applying the policies of AMERCO, complete the following, indicating the effects for the preceding expenditures. If there is no effect on an account, write NE on the line:

| | Building | Accumulated Depreciation | Depreciation Expense | Repairs Expense | Cash |
|---|---|---|---|---|---|
| Balance January 1, 20G | $230,000 | _____ | _____ | | |
| Depreciation through June 30 | | _____ | _____ | | _____ |
| Balance prior to expenditures | 230,000 | _____ | _____ | | |
| Expenditure a | _____ | _____ | _____ | _____ | _____ |
| Expenditure b | _____ | _____ | _____ | _____ | _____ |
| Expenditure c | _____ | _____ | _____ | _____ | _____ |
| Depreciation July–December 31: | | | | | |
| Existing building | | _____ | _____ | _____ | _____ |
| Repairs and additions | | _____ | _____ | _____ | _____ |
| Balance December 31, 20G | _____ | _____ | _____ | _____ | _____ |

2.  What was the book value of the building on December 31, 20G?

3.  Explain the effect of depreciation on cash flows.

**AP8–4** **Computing the Basket Purchase Allocation and Recording Depreciation under Three Alternative Methods (P8–4)**    ▪ **LO2, 4**

At the beginning of the year, Kohler Inc. bought three used machines from Lucas Corporation, for a total cash price of $62,000. Transportation costs on the machines were $3,000. The machines immediately were overhauled, installed, and started operating. The machines were different; therefore, each had to be recorded separately in the accounts. An appraiser was employed to estimate their market value at date of purchase (prior to the overhaul and installation). The book values shown on Lucas's books also are available. The book values, appraisal results, installation costs, and renovation expenditures follow:

| | Machine A | Machine B | Machine C |
|---|---|---|---|
| Book value—Lucas | $10,500 | $22,000 | $16,000 |
| Appraisal value | 11,500 | 32,000 | 28,500 |
| Installation costs | 800 | 1,100 | 1,100 |
| Renovation costs prior to use | 600 | 1,400 | 1,600 |

By the end of the first year, each machine had been operating 7,000 hours.

*Required:*

1.  Compute the cost of each machine by making a supportable allocation (round ratio to two decimal places). Explain the rationale for the allocation basis used.

2.  Give the entry to record depreciation expense at the end of year 1, assuming the following:

| ESTIMATES | | | |
|---|---|---|---|
| Machine | Life | Residual Value | Depreciation Method |
| A | 4 | $1,000 | Straight line |
| B | 35,000 hours | 2,000 | Units of production |
| C | 5 | 1,500 | 200% declining balance |

**LO4, 5    AP8–5**

Lechters, Inc.

### Inferring Depreciation Amounts and Determining the Effects of a Depreciation Error on Key Ratios (P8–6)

Lechters, Inc., and its subsidiaries is a specialty retailer of primarily brand-name basic and decorative housewares. As of January 30, 1999, the Company operated 578 stores in 42 states and the District of Columbia. The following is a note from a recent annual report:

**(1) SUMMARY OF SIGNIFICANT ACCOUNTING POLICIES—**

(e) Property and Equipment—Property and equipment are stated at cost. Depreciation and amortization are computed principally by the straight-line method by charges to earnings in amounts sufficient to write-off the cost of depreciable assets over their estimated lives, or where applicable, the terms of the respective leases, whichever is shorter.

The components of cost at January 30, 1999, and January 31, 1998, are as follows (in thousands):

| | 1999 | 1998 |
|---|---|---|
| Property and Equipment: | | |
| Fixtures and equipment | $ 57,678 | $ 58,403 |
| Leasehold improvements | 96,452 | 94,994 |
| | 154,130 | 153,397 |
| Less accumulated depreciation and amortization | 88,401 | 79,891 |
| Net property and equipment | $ 65,729 | $ 73,506 |

*Required:*

1. Assuming that Lechters, Inc., did not have any asset impairment write-offs and did not sell any property, plant, and equipment in 1999, what was the amount of depreciation expense recorded in 1999?

2. Assume that Lechters, Inc., failed to record depreciation in 1999. Indicate the effect of the error (i.e., overstated or understated) on the following ratios:

   *a.* Earnings per share.

   *b.* Fixed asset turnover.

   *c.* Assets to equity.

   *d.* Return on equity.

**LO5, 6    AP8–6**

Hasbro, Inc.

### Inferring Asset Age and Determining Financial Statement Effects of a Long-Lived Asset Disposal (Challenging) (P8–8)

Hasbro, Inc., designs, manufactures, and markets high-quality toys, games, and infant products. The company's revenues exceed $3.3 billion. In the toy business, it is very difficult to determine the life expectancy of a product. Products that children love one year may sit on the shelf the following year. As a result, companies in the toy business often sell productive assets that are no longer needed. Assume that on December 31, 20B (after adjusting entries), Hasbro's records showed the following data about a machine that was no longer needed to make a toy that was popular last year:

| | |
|---|---|
| Machine, original cost | $107,000 |
| Accumulated depreciation | 64,000* |

*Based on a six-year estimated useful life, an $11,000 residual value, and straight-line depreciation.

On July 1, 20C, the machine was sold for $38,000 cash. The accounting period ends on December 31.

*Required:*

1. How old was the machine on January 1, 20C? Show computations.

2. Indicate the effect (i.e., the amount and whether it increased or decreased) of the sale of the machine on July 1, 20C, on

   a. Total assets.

   b. Net income.

   c. Cash flows (by each section of the statement: Operating, Investing, and Financing Activities).

**AP8–7 Recording and Interpreting the Disposal of Three Long-Lived Assets** (P8–10)    ▇ **LO6**

During 20A, Callaway Company disposed of three different assets. On January 1, 20A, prior to their disposal, the accounts reflected the following:

| Asset | Original Cost | Residual Value | Estimated Life | Accumulated Depreciation (straight line) |
|---|---|---|---|---|
| Machine A | $24,000 | $2,000 | 5 years | $17,600 (4 years) |
| Machine B | 16,500 | 5,000 | 10 years | 8,050 (7 years) |
| Machine C | 59,200 | 3,200 | 14 years | 48,000 (12 years) |

The machines were disposed of in the following ways:

a. Machine A: Sold on January 1, 20A, for $5,750 cash.

b. Machine B: Sold on July 1, 20A, for $9,000; received cash, $4,000, and a $5,000 interest-bearing (10%) note receivable due at the end of 12 months.

c. Machine C: On October 2, 20A, this machine suffered irreparable damage from an accident. On October 10, 20A, a salvage company removed the machine immediately at no cost. The machine was insured, and $12,000 cash was collected from the insurance company.

*Required:*

1. Give all journal entries related to the disposal of each machine.

2. Explain the accounting rationale for the way that you recorded each disposal.

**AP8–8 Determining Financial Statement Effects of Activities Related to Various Long-Lived Assets** (P8–11)    ▇ **LO7**

During the 20D annual accounting period, Zhou Corporation completed the following transactions:

a. On January 1, 20D, paid $8,000 for a complete reconditioning of each of the following machines acquired on January 1, 20A (total cost, $16,000):

   (1) Machine A: Original cost, $21,500; accumulated depreciation (straight line) to December 31, 20C, $13,500 ($3,500 residual value).

   (2) Machine B: Original cost, $18,000; accumulated depreciation (straight line) to December 31, 20C, $10,200 ($1,000 residual value).

b. On July 1, 20D, purchased a license for $7,200 cash (estimated useful life, three years).    *Liab*

c. On July 1, 20D, purchased another business for cash $120,000, including $29,000 for    *+ 24000*
   goodwill. The company assumed $24,000 of liabilities from the other business.

d. On July 1, 20D, sold Machine A for $10,500 cash.

e.  On October 1, 20D, repaved the parking lot of the building leased from J. Caldwell. The cost was $7,800; the estimated useful life was five years with no residual value. The company uses straight-line depreciation. The lease will expire on December 31, 20G.

f.  Total expenditures during 20D for ordinary repairs and maintenance were $6,700.

*Required:*

1.  For each of these transactions, indicate the accounts, amounts and effects (+ for increase and − for decrease) on the accounting equation. Use the following structure:

| Date | Assets | = | Liabilities | + | Stockholders' Equity |
|------|--------|---|-------------|---|----------------------|

2.  For each of these assets, compute depreciation and amortization to the nearest month to be recorded at the end of the year on December 31, 20D.

■ **LO7, 8**    **AP8–9**    **Computing Amortization, Book Value, and Asset Impairment Related to Different Intangible Assets (P8–14)**

Bailey Corporation has five different intangible assets to be accounted for and reported on the financial statements. The management is concerned about the amortization of the cost of each of these intangibles. Facts about each intangible follow:

a.  *Patent.* The company purchased a patent at a cash cost of $18,600 on January 1, 20C. The patent had a legal life of 17 years from date of registration with the U.S. Patent Office, which was January 1, 20A. It is amortized over its remaining legal life.

b.  *Copyright.* On January 1, 20C, the company purchased a copyright for $24,750 cash. The legal life remaining from that date is 30 years. It is estimated that the copyrighted item will have no value by the end of 15 years.

c.  *Franchise.* The company obtained a franchise from Farrell Company to make and distribute a special item. It obtained the franchise on January 1, 20C, at a cash cost of $19,200 for a 12-year period.

d.  *License.* On January 1, 20B, the company secured a license from the city to operate a special service for a period of seven years. Total cash expended to obtain the license was $21,000.

e.  *Goodwill.* The company started business in January 20A by purchasing another business for a cash lump sum of $650,000. Included in the purchase price was "Goodwill, $75,000." Company executives stated that "the goodwill is an important long-term asset to us." It is amortized over the maximum period permitted.

*Required:*

1.  Compute the amount of amortization that should be recorded for each intangible asset at the end of the annual accounting period, December 31, 20C.

2.  Give the book value of each intangible asset on January 1, 20F.

3.  Assume that on January 2, 20F, the franchise was impaired in its ability to continue to produce strong revenues. The other intangible assets were not affected. Bailey estimated that the franchise will be able to produce future cash flows of $14,500. Compute the amount, if any, of the impairment loss to be recorded.

# CASES AND PROJECTS

## FINANCIAL REPORTING AND ANALYSIS CASES

■ **LO4, 5, 8**    **CP8–1**

American Eagle
Outfitters

**STANDARD
&POOR'S**

**Finding Financial Information**

Refer to the financial statements and accompanying notes of American Eagle Outfitters given in Appendix B at the end of this book, or open file AEOS10K.doc in the S&P directory on the student CD-ROM.

*Required:*

1.  What method of depreciation does the company use?

2.  What is the amount of accumulated depreciation and amortization at the end of the current year?

3. For depreciation purposes, what is the estimated useful life of fixtures and equipment?

4. What was the original cost of leasehold improvements owned by the company at the end of the current year?

5. What amount of depreciation and amortization was reported as expense for the current year?

6. What is the fixed asset turnover ratio? What does it suggest?

7. How much was the impairment loss on fixtures and leasehold improvements for the 1998 fiscal year (ended January 30, 1999)? How much was the write-off of fixed assets in the same period? Why were these amounts added back as adjustments on the statement of cash flows?

8. For each of the preceding questions, where did you locate the information?

## CP8–2 Comparing Companies within an Industry

dELiA*s Inc., which became a public company in 1996, markets apparel, accessories, and home furnishings to consumers between the ages of 10 and 24, primarily through its catalogs. In fiscal year 1998, dELiA*s expanded into the retail store trade by acquiring assets in 26 retail stores. Below is selected data from dELiA*s annual report dated January 31, 1999.

**LO4, 5, 8**

American Eagle Outfitters vs. dELiA*s

STANDARD
&POOR'S

**4. PrOPeRtY aNd eQuIPmEnT**

| Major classes of property and equipment are as follows: | Estimated Useful Lives | January 31, 1998 | January 31, 1999 |
|---|---|---|---|
| Furniture, fixtures and equipment | 5–10 years | $5,444,000 | $10,862,000 |
| Leasehold improvements | Term of lease | 1,842,000 | 4,871,000 |
| Total—at cost | | 7,286,000 | 15,733,000 |
| Less accumulated depreciation and amortization | | 1,064,000 | 3,191,000 |
| Total property and equipment— net | | $6,222,000 | $12,542,000 |

The company uses straight-line depreciation and reported the following data in the financial statements:

| | January 31, 1998 | January 31, 1999 |
|---|---|---|
| Total assets | $64,572,000 | $82,144,000 |
| | Fiscal Year Ended January 31, 1998 | Fiscal Year Ended January 31, 1999 |
| Net sales | $113,049 | $158,364 |

American Eagle Outfitters markets casual apparel, accessories, and footwear for men and women between the ages of 16 and 34, primarily through retail stores located in regional enclosed shopping malls. In 1998, American Eagle Outfitters initiated a quarterly catalog and established an internet e-commerce site offering approximately 80 percent of its merchandise. For relevant financial information, refer to the financial statements and accompanying notes of American Eagle Outfitters given in Appendix B at the end of this book, or open file CP8–2.xls in the S&P directory on the student CD-ROM. This file contains the information needed to answer the following questions for American Eagle Outfitters and dELiA*s Inc.

*Required:*

1. Compute the percentage of net fixed assets to total assets for both companies each year. Why do the companies differ?

2. Compute the percentage of the fixed assets that has been depreciated for both companies. Why do you think the percentages differ?

3. Compute the fixed asset turnover ratio for the most recent year presented for both companies. Which has a higher asset efficiency? Why?

4. What would you expect dELiA*s ratios to do (increase or decrease) over time? Why? What about American Eagle Outfitters' ratios?

**CP8–3** **Broadening Financial Research Skills: Identifying Competitors in an Industry**

MarketGuide provides lists of industries and the competitors in each at www.marketguide.com/mgi/INDUSTRY/INDUSTRY.html.

*Required:*

Using your Web browser, contact MarketGuide and identify three competitors for the following industries:

1. Airline.

2. Hotels and motels.

3. Footwear.

4. Computer hardware.

**LO8** **CP8–4** **Interpreting the Financial Press**

The October 5, 1998, edition of *Business Week* includes the article, "Earnings Hocus-Pocus." You can access the article on the Libby/Libby/Short website at www.mhhe.com/business/accounting/libby3.

*Required:*

Read pages 1 through 9 of the article (stopping at the paragraph beginning with "Meanwhile, the SEC…." Then answer the following questions:

1. What is meant by the concept that many companies take a "big bath"?

2. List several companies mentioned in the article that have taken a big bath by writing down fixed assets or intangibles. Indicate for each the nature of the earnings manipulation.

**LO4** **CP8–5** **Using Financial Reports: Analyzing the Age of Assets**

Black & Decker

A note to a recent annual report for Black & Decker contained the following information (in thousands of dollars):

|  | Current Year | Previous Year |
| --- | --- | --- |
| Land and improvements | $ 69,091 | $ 20,963 |
| Buildings | 298,450 | 160,570 |
| Machinery and equipment | 928,151 | 626,453 |
|  | 1,295,692 | 807,986 |
| Less accumulated depreciation | 468,511 | 404,591 |
|  | $ 827,181 | $403,395 |

Depreciation expense (in thousands of dollars) charged to operations was $99,234 in the current year and $81,459 in the previous year. Depreciation generally is computed using the straight-line method for financial reporting purposes.

*Required:*

1. What is your best estimate of the average expected life for Black & Decker's depreciable assets?

2. What is your best estimate of the average age of Black & Decker's depreciable assets?

**LO4** **CP8–6** **Using Financial Reports: Analyzing a Note Concerning Depreciation**

The Coca-Cola Company

A recent annual report for The Coca-Cola Company contained the following note:

Property, plant, and equipment is stated at cost, less allowance for depreciation. Depreciation expense is determined principally by the straight-line method. The annual rates of depreciation are 2 percent to 10 percent for buildings and improvements and 7 percent to 34 percent for machinery, equipment, and containers.

*Required:*

1. What is the range of expected lives for buildings and improvements?

2. Explain why Coca-Cola depreciates the cost of its containers instead of including the total in cost of goods sold in the year the product is sold.

**CP8–7 Using Financial Reports: Analyzing Fixed Asset Turnover Ratio and Cash Flows**

The Seagram Company Ltd., with headquarters in Montreal, Quebec, Canada, operates in both the beverages and entertainment industries. Seagram produces well-known spirits and wines. In June 1995, Seagram purchased an 80 percent interest in MCA, Inc., which produces and distributes motion picture, television, and home video products and recorded music; publishes books; and operates theme parks (Universal Studios) and retail stores. The purchase resulted in $2.7 billion in goodwill, which is being amortized over 40 years. Since 1995, Seagram has undertaken a number of business acquisitions and divestitures (sales of businesses) as the company expands into the entertainment industry. Selected data from a recent annual report are as follows (amounts are in millions of U.S. dollars):

■ LO4, 5, 7

The Seagram
Company Ltd.

| Property, Plan, Equipment, and Intangibles From the Consolidated Balance Sheet | Current Year | Prior Year |
|---|---|---|
| Film costs, net of amortization | $1,272 | $ 991 |
| Artists' contracts, advances, and other entertainment asset | 761 | 645 |
| Property, plant, and equipment, net | 2,733 | 2,559 |
| Excess of cost over fair value of assets acquired | 3,076 | 3,355 |
| **From the Consolidated Statement of Income** | | |
| Total revenues | $9,714 | $10,644 |
| **From the Consolidated Statement of Cash Flows** | | |
| Income from continuing operations | $ 880 | $ 445 |
| Adjustments | | |
| Depreciation and amortization of assets | 289 | 290 |
| Amortization of excess of cost over fair value of assets acquired | 208 | 165 |
| Other adjustments (summarized) | (1,618) | (256) |
| Net cash provided by continuing operations | (241) | 644 |
| **From the Notes to the Financial Statements** | | |
| Accumulated depreciation on property, plant, and equipment | $ 1,178 | $ 1,023 |

*Required:*

1. What was the approximate age of the property, plant, and equipment at the end of the current year?

2. Compute the fixed asset turnover ratio for the current year. Explain your results.

3. Compute the cost of the property, plant, and equipment at the end of the current year. Explain your answer.

4. What is Excess of cost over fair value of assets acquired? Compute an estimate of the amount to be amortized in the next year.

5. On the consolidated statement of cash flows, why are the amortization and depreciation amounts added to income from continuing operations?

**CP8–8 Using Financial Reports: Inferring the Sale of Assets**

A recent annual report for Eastman Kodak reported that the balance of property, plant, and equipment at the end of the current year was $16,774 million. At the end of the previous year, it had been $15,667 million. During the current year, the company bought $2,118 million worth of new equipment. The balance of accumulated depreciation at the end of the current year was $8,146 million and at the end of the previous year was $7,654 million. Depreciation expense for the current year was $1,181 million. The annual report does not disclose any gain or loss on the disposition of property, plant, and equipment, so you may assume that the amount was zero.

■ LO6

Eastman Kodak

*Required:*

What amount of proceeds did Eastman Kodak receive when it sold property, plant, and equipment during the current year? (*Hint:* Set up T-accounts.)

■ **LO4**
*Diageo*

**CP8–9**

### Using Financial Reports: Comparing Depreciation Methods in Different Countries

Diageo is a major international company located in London. A recent annual report contained the following information concerning its accounting policies.

**Fixed assets and depreciation**

Fixed assets are stated at cost or at professional valuation. Cost includes interest, net of any tax relief, on capital employed in major developments.

No depreciation is provided on freehold land. Other leaseholds are depreciated over the unexpired period of the lease. All other buildings, plant, equipment, and vehicles are depreciated to residual values over their estimated useful lives within the following ranges:

| | |
|---|---|
| Industrial buildings | 25 to 100 years |
| Plant and machinery | 3 to 25 years |
| Fixtures and fittings | 3 to 17 years |

*Required:*
Compare accounting for fixed assets and depreciation in England with procedures used in this country.

## CRITICAL THINKING CASES

■ **LO4**
*Amerada Hess
Corporation*

**CP8–10**

### Making a Decision as a Financial Analyst: Interpreting the Impact of the Capitalization of Interest on an Accounting Ratio

The capitalization of interest associated with self-constructed assets was discussed in this chapter. A recent annual report for Amerada Hess Corporation disclosed the following information concerning capitalization of interest:

Interest costs related to certain long-term construction projects are capitalized to comply with FAS No. 34, "Capitalization of Interest Cost." Capitalized interest in the current year amounted to $34,897,000.

The income statement for that year disclosed that interest expense was $224,200,000. A popular accounting ratio used by some analysts is the interest coverage ratio (Income ÷ Interest Expense).

*Required:*

1. Explain why an analyst would calculate this ratio.
2. Did Amerada Hess include the $34,897,000 in the reported interest expense of $224,200,000? If not, should an analyst include it when calculating the interest coverage ratio? Explain.

■ **LO4, 5**
*Ford Motor Company*

**CP8–11**

### Evaluating an Ethical Dilemma: Analyzing an Accounting Change

An annual report for Ford Motor Company included the following information:

**Note 6. Net Property, Depreciation and Amortization—Automotive**

Assets placed in service before January 1, 1993, are depreciated using an accelerated method. Assets placed in service beginning in 1993 will be depreciated using the straight-line method of depreciation. This change in accounting principle is being made to reflect improvements in the design and flexibility of manufacturing machinery and equipment and improvements in maintenance practices. These improvements have resulted in more uniform productive capacities and maintenance costs over the useful life of an asset. Straight-line is preferable in these circumstances. The change is expected to improve 1993 after-tax results by $80 to $100 million.

*Required:*

1. What was the stated reason for the change in method? What other factors do you think management considered when it decided to make this accounting change?

2. Do you think this is an ethical decision?

3. Who were affected by the change and how were they benefitted or harmed?

4. What impact did this change have on cash flows for Ford?

5. As an investor, how would you react to the fact that Ford's net income will increase by $80 to $100 million as the result of this change?

# FINANCIAL REPORTING AND ANALYSIS PROJECTS

**CP8–12 Comparing Companies across Industries**

Using your web browser, contact the websites of (1) Battle Mountain Gold (www.bmgold.com), which explores, mines, and processes gold and associated metals; (2) DaimlerChrysler (www.daimlerchrysler.com); and (3) Sprint (www.sprint.com).

■ LO4, 5

Battle Mountain Gold
vs. Sprint
vs. DaimlerChrysler

*Required:*

On the basis of the information in their latest annual reports, write a short report comparing

1. Any differences in the long-lived asset accounts used by the three companies (including intangible assets).

2. Cost allocation methods and estimates used.

3. The approximate average life of the assets.

4. The percentage of property, plant, and equipment to total assets.

5. Fixed asset turnover ratio.

6. Conclude your analysis with the reason that the companies are similar or different.

**CP8–13 Comparing Companies over Time**

Using your web browser, contact the website of Delta Air Lines (www.delta-air.com). Examine the most recent annual report.

■ LO5

Delta Air Lines

*Required:*

1. On the basis of the information, compute the fixed asset turnover ratio for each year presented.

2. Compare the ratios to those provided in the text for Delta Air Lines. What trend, if any, is suggested? What might account for the change?

**CP8–14 Team Project: Analysis of Long-Lived Assets**

MarketGuide provides lists of industries and the competitors in each at www.marketguide.com/mgi/INDUSTRY/INDUSTRY.html.
Using your web browser, contact MarketGuide. As a group, select an industry to analyze. Each team member should then, using the web browser, obtain the annual report or 10–K for one publicly traded company in the industry, with each member selecting a different company.

■ LO4, 5

*Required:*

1. On an individual basis, each team member should write a short report listing the following:

    *a.* The accounts and amounts of the company's long-lived assets (property, plant, and equipment; intangible assets; and natural resources).

    *b.* The cost allocation method(s) and estimates used for each type of long-lived asset.

    *c.* The approximate average life of the assets.

    *d.* The fixed asset turnover ratio.

2. Discuss any patterns that you as a team observe. Then, as a team, write a short report comparing and contrasting your companies according to the preceding attributes.

# Reporting and Interpreting Liabilities

## CHAPTER **NINE**

LEARNING **OBJECTIVES**

*After studying this chapter, you should be able to:*

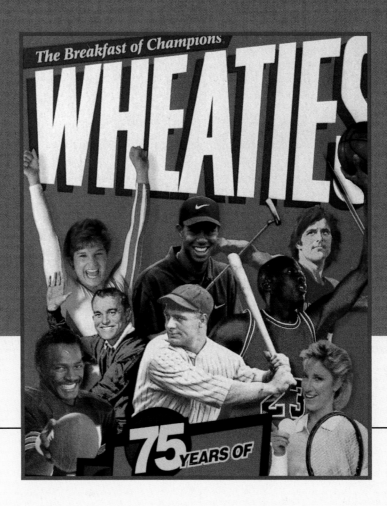

General Mills is known as a leader in the food industry. The company sells a full line of familiar breakfast cereals, numerous snack foods, and the popular Betty Crocker products. While you have grown up with a number of General Mills brands, much of the company's growth comes from innovative new products. In recent years, 27 percent of the company's growth has come from products five years old or less. New products include Scooby Doo–shaped fruit snacks and changing-flavor Fruit by the Foot Flavor Wave.

General Mills management operates the company by establishing aggressive goals. While many of these goals involve increasing sales volume and improving operating efficiencies, some focus on financial results such as achieving a 12 percent average annual growth in earnings per share and generating a minimum 25 percent return on invested capital. One of the company's financial goals pertains to the focus of this chapter:

FOCUS **COMPANY:**

# General Mills

MANAGING CAPITAL
STRUCTURE

General Mills' financial goal is to achieve performance that places us in the top 10 percent of major American companies, ranked by the combination of growth in earnings per share and return on capital over a five-year period. Our major financial targets for top-decile performance include:

* * * * * *

• Maintaining a Balance Sheet with a Strong "A" Bond Rating which will allow access to financing at reasonable costs.

**REAL WORLD EXCERPT**

*General Mills*
ANNUAL REPORT

Financial analysts consider a number of factors when they assess the strength of a balance sheet. One of the key areas they examine is how the company has financed its operations. Managing of a company's liabilities is often as important as managing its assets.

## BUSINESS BACKGROUND

Businesses finance the acquisition of their assets from two sources: funds supplied by creditors (debt) and funds provided by owners (equity). The mixture of debt and equity used by a business is called its *capital structure*. Theoretically, managers could select virtually any capital structure for their company (e.g., 60 percent debt and 40 percent equity).

The balance sheet for General Mills (Exhibit 9.1) shows that their capital structure is composed of approximately 95 percent debt and 5 percent equity. Such a low percent of equity is a little unusual and reflects the impact of a strategic decision. A few years

EXHIBIT **9.1**

**General Mills' Balance Sheet**

**REAL WORLD EXCERPT**

*General Mills*

ANNUAL REPORT

| GENERAL MILLS INC. Balance Sheet | | |
|---|---|---|
| (in millions) | May 31, 1998 | May 25, 1997 |
| **Assets** | | |
| Current Assets: | | |
| Cash and cash equivalents | $    6.4 | $    12.8 |
| Receivables, less allowance for doubtful accounts of $4.2 in 1998 and $4.1 in 1997 | 395.1 | 419.1 |
| Inventories | 389.7 | 364.4 |
| Prepaid expenses and other current assets | 107.2 | 107.3 |
| Deferred income taxes | 136.9 | 107.7 |
| Total Current Assets | 1,035,.3 | 1,011.3 |
| Land, Buildings and Equipment at cost, net | 1,186.3 | 1,279.4 |
| Other Assets | 1,639.8 | 1,611.7 |
| Total Assets | $3,861.4 | $3,902.4 |
| **Liabilities and Equity** | | |
| Current Liabilities: | | |
| Accounts payable | $  593.1 | $  599.7 |
| Current portion of long-term debt | 153.2 | 139.0 |
| Notes payable | 264.1 | 204.3 |
| Accrued taxes | 148.5 | 97.0 |
| Accrued payroll | 129.7 | 129.4 |
| Other current liabilities | 155.1 | 123.1 |
| Total Current Liabilities | 1,443.7 | 1,292.5 |
| Long-term Debt | 1,640.4 | 1,530.4 |
| Deferred Income Taxes | 284.8 | 272.1 |
| Deferred Income Taxes—Tax Leases | 129.1 | 143.7 |
| Other Liabilities | 173.2 | 169.1 |
| Total Liabilities | 3,671.2 | 3,407.8 |
| **Stockholders' Equity** | | |
| Cumulative preference stock, none issued | — | — |
| Common stock, 204.2 shares issued | 619.6 | 578.0 |
| Retained earnings | 1,622.8 | 1,535.4 |
| Less common stock in treasury, at cost, shares of 49.4 in 1998 and 44.3 in 1997 | (1,935.7) | (1,501.9) |
| Unearned compensation and other | (48.1) | (58.0) |
| Cumulative foreign currency adjustment | (68.4) | (58.9) |
| Total Stockholders' Equity | 190.2 | 494.6 |
| Total Liabilities and Equity | $3,861.4 | $3,902.4 |

ago, the Company owned the popular restaurant chains Red Lobster and Olive Garden. Management decided to focus its efforts on its core business and disposed of its restaurant operations. It did so by distributing ownership of Red Lobster and Olive Garden directly to the shareholders of General Mills. This transaction was the equivalent of a $1.3 billion dividend to shareholders. Prior to the disposal of the restaurant operations, General Mills had a capital structure that included 76 percent debt and 24 percent equity. This type of corporate restructuring is a common occurrence. General Mills sought to achieve sharper focus for its business operations to be more competitive. Financial analysts who wanted to analyze the capital structure of General Mills need to understand the nature of this corporate restructuring to evaluate the dramatic changes on the balance sheet.

The chief executive officer of General Mills, Stephen W. Sanger, explained the restructuring in the following manner:

> It is very difficult to find a single set of over-arching financial goals, themes and messages to employees and financial incentives that spread across two very different industries.

The restructuring obviously had a major impact on the capital structure of General Mills. What factors do managers consider when they select a capital structure? The answer is complex and will be discussed in great detail in your finance courses. Two key factors that are considered are risk and return. Debt capital is more risky than equity because interest payments on debt are a company's legal obligation. If a company is not able to meet a required interest payment because of a temporary cash shortage, creditors may force the company into bankruptcy and require the sale of assets to satisfy the debt obligations. In contrast, dividend payments on stock are not a legal obligation until declared by the board of directors, which means that equity offers lower risk to the issuing corporation.

Despite the risk associated with debt, most companies include borrowed funds in their capital structure because these funds can be used to earn a higher rate of return for the stockholders. The higher rate of return can be earned when it is possible to borrow money at one rate (say 6 percent) and invest at a higher rate (say 8 percent). Borrowing at one rate and investing at a different rate is called *financial leverage* and is discussed in detail in the next chapter.

Companies that include debt in their capital structure also must make strategic decisions concerning the proper balance between short-term debt and long-term debt. Financial analysts calculate a number of accounting ratios to evaluate a company's capital structure and the balance between short-term and long-term debt. In this chapter, we discuss both short-term and long-term debt. In the next chapter, we discuss a special category of long-term debt, bonds payable.

## ORGANIZATION OF THE CHAPTER

| • Liabilities Defined and Classified | • Current Liabilities | • Long-Term Liabilities | • Contingent Liabilities |
|---|---|---|---|
| Current Ratio | Accounts Payable | Long-Term Debt | Other Obligations |
| | Accounts Payable Turnover | Other Topics | |
| | Accrued Liabilities | Deferred Taxes | • Present and Future Value Concepts |
| | Deferred Revenues and Service Obligations | Accrued Retirement Benefits | Single Amount |
| | Notes Payable | | Annuities |
| | Current Portion of Long-Term Debt | | Accounting Applications |

## LIABILITIES DEFINED AND CLASSIFIED

■ **LEARNING OBJECTIVE 1**

Define, measure, and report liabilities.

**LIABILITIES** are probable future sacrifices of economic benefits that arise from past transactions.

Most people have a reasonable understanding of the definition of the word *liability*. Accountants formally define **liabilities** as probable future sacrifices of economic benefits. Liabilities arise from an entity's present obligations to transfer assets or provide services to other entities in the future as a result of past transactions or events. As shown on the balance sheet (Exhibit 9.1), as of May 31, 1998, General Mills had borrowed long-term debt of $1,640,400,000. This money was borrowed at some point in the past from a group of creditors (a past transaction). The company has a current obligation to pay cash (an asset) to those creditors at some time in the future based on the borrowing agreement. Because of this obligation, General Mills must record a long-term debt.

When a liability is first recorded, it is measured in terms of its current cash equivalent, which is the cash amount that a creditor would accept to settle the liability at the current time. General Mills borrowed $1,640,400,000 but will repay much more than that because the company must repay the money it borrowed plus interest that accrues on the debt. Interest that will be paid in the future is not included in the amount of the liability because interest accrues (and becomes a liability) with the passage of time.

Like most businesses, General Mills has several kinds of liabilities and a wide range of creditors. Users of financial statements rely on the statements for relevant information about the types and amounts of liabilities that the entity owes. The list of liabilities on the balance sheet differs for almost every company that you study because different operating activities result in different types of liabilities.

**CURRENT LIABILITIES** are short-term obligations that will be paid within the current operating cycle or one year, whichever is longer.

The liability section of the General Mills report begins with the caption Current Liabilities. **Current liabilities** are defined as short-term obligations that will be paid within the current operating cycle of the business or within one year of the balance sheet date, whichever is longer. Most companies have an operating cycle that is less than one year. In the majority of situations you encounter, current liabilities can be defined simply as liabilities that are due within one year. Noncurrent liabilities include all liabilities not properly classified as current liabilities.

# KEY **RATIO ANALYSIS:**

## CURRENT RATIO

**K**now the decision question:

Analysts often ask how liquid a company is. The word *liquid,* in this context, means the company has the ability to meet its currently maturing debts. Analysts use the *current ratio* to measure of the amount of current assets available to satisfy current liabilities. It is computed as follows:

**Current Ratio = Current Assets ÷ Current Liabilities**

The 1998 ratio for General Mills:

**$1,035.3 ÷ $1,443.7 = 0.72**

**E**xamine the ratio using two techniques:

| ① Comparisons over Time | | | ② Comparisons with Competitors | |
|---|---|---|---|---|
| **General Mills** | | | **Kellogg** | **Quaker Oats** |
| 1996 | 1997 | 1998 | 1998 | 1998 |
| 0.83 | 0.78 | 0.72 | 0.87 | 1.10 |

■ **LEARNING OBJECTIVE 2**

Use the current ratio.

**Y**ou interpret the results carefully:

**IN GENERAL** → A high ratio normally suggests good liquidity, but too high a ratio suggests inefficient use of resources.

**FOCUS COMPANY ANALYSIS** → The current ratio for General Mills is low (most companies have a current ratio between 1 and 2) and has been marginally decreasing in recent years. While this might be a concern in many circumstances, it is not in the case of General Mills. The decline is modest and the ratio is consistent with that of the rest of the industry. The notes to the financial statements indicate that the company has "bank credit lines to ensure the availability of short-term funds on an as-needed basis." Instead of borrowing money to enhance its liquidity, General Mills plans to borrow money only when it is actually needed. In this manner, the company avoids significant interest expense. Most analysts would take this borrowing arrangement into consideration when assessing a company's liquidity.

**A FEW CAUTIONS:** The current ratio as a measure of liquidity may be misleading if significant funds are tied up in assets that will not be easily converted into cash. A company with a high current ratio might still have liquidity problems if the majority of its current assets was made up of slow-moving inventory. Analysts should recognize that it is possible to manipulate the current ratio by engaging in certain transactions just before the close of the fiscal year. In most cases, for example, the current ratio can be improved by paying creditors immediately prior to the preparation of financial statements.

As you study companies, you will often hear people talk about the current ratio or a closely related concept called **working capital,** which is the dollar amount of the difference between current assets and current liabilities. The current ratio and working capital are measures of a company's liquidity.

Liabilities are very important from an analytical perspective because they affect a company's future cash flows and risk characteristics. Most analysts devote a considerable amount of time to reviewing a company's liabilities. The easiest way for us to discuss the topic of liabilities is to review them in the same order that they are listed on most balance sheets. In this manner, you will have a better understanding of the information reported on the balance sheet. We will focus on the liabilities that you have not been exposed to in previous chapters.

**WORKING CAPITAL** is the dollar difference between total current assets and total current liabilities.

# CURRENT LIABILITIES

## ACCOUNTS PAYABLE

Most companies do not produce all the goods and services that they use in their basic operating activities. Instead, they purchase these goods and services from other businesses. Typically, these transactions involve credit terms with cash payments made after the goods and services have been provided. As a result, these transactions create *accounts payable,* which are also called *trade accounts payable.* Journal entries associated with accounts payable were discussed in Chapter 7.

*Accounting Trends & Techniques* (published by the AICPA) examined the reporting practices of 600 companies and found that most companies use the term *accounts payable.**

For many companies, trade credit is a relatively inexpensive way to finance the purchase of inventory. Interest does not normally accrue on accounts payable. As an incentive to encourage more sales, some vendors offer very generous credit terms that may give the buyer the opportunity to resell merchandise and collect cash before payment must be made to the original vendor.

It may be tempting for some managers to delay payment to suppliers for as long as possible to conserve cash. This strategy normally is not advisable. Most successful companies develop positive working relationships with their suppliers to ensure quality goods and services. A positive relationship can be destroyed by slow payment of debt. Financial analysts also are concerned if a business does not meet its obligations to trade creditors on a timely basis because this slowness often indicates that the company is experiencing financial difficulties.

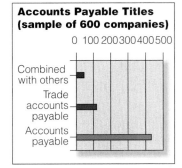

**Accounts Payable Titles
(sample of 600 companies)**

---

*Reprinted with permission from *Accounting Trends and Techniques.* Copyright © 2000 by the American Institute of Certified Public Accounts, Inc.

# KEY **RATIO ANALYSIS:**

## ACCOUNTS PAYABLE TURNOVER

**K**now the decision question:

How much time does it take for a company to meet its obligations to its suppliers? The *accounts payable turnover ratio* is a measure of how quickly management is paying trade credit. Analysts use this ratio as a measure of liquidity. It is computed as follows:

**Accounts Payable Turnover = Cost of Goods Sold ÷ Average Accounts Payable**

The 1998 ratio for General Mills:

$$\$2,389.3 \div \$596.4^* = 4.01$$

*($593.1 + $599.7) ÷ 2 = $596.4

**■ LEARNING OBJECTIVE 3**

Analyze the accounts payable turnover ratio.

**E**xamine the ratio using two techniques:

| ① Comparisons over Time | | | | ② Comparisons with Competitors | |
|---|---|---|---|---|---|
| **General Mills** | | | | **Kellogg** | **Quaker Oats** |
| 1996 | 1997 | 1998 | | 1998 | 1998 |
| 4.10 | 3.91 | 4.01 | | 9.19 | 13.20 |

**Y**ou interpret the results carefully:

**IN GENERAL** → A high ratio normally suggests that a company is paying its suppliers in a timely manner. The ratio can be stated in a more intuitive manner by dividing it into the number of days in a year:

**Average Age of Payables = 365 Days ÷ Turnover Ratio**

The 1998 ratio for General Mills:

**365 Days ÷ 4.01 = 91 Days**

**FOCUS COMPANY ANALYSIS** → The accounts payable turnover for General Mills is low compared to similar companies but is fairly stable over time. Usually, a low ratio would cause analysts to raise questions concerning a company's liquidity (or ability to meet its current obligations). It is unusual for a company to take, on average, 91 days to pay its creditors. While this might be a concern in many circumstances, it is not in the case of General Mills. Other indications of liquidity are good. It appears that the company is very aggressive in its cash management policy. By conserving cash (with slow payment to suppliers), the company is able to minimize the amount of money it must borrow (and pay interest on).

**A FEW CAUTIONS:** The accounts payable turnover ratio is an average associated with all accounts payable. The ratio might not reflect reality if a company pays some creditors on time but is late with others. The ratio is also subject to manipulation. Managers could be late with payments to creditors during the entire year but "catch up" at year-end so that the ratio is at an acceptable level. As the focus company analysis indicates, a low ratio can indicate either liquidity problems or aggressive cash management. The first is a problem; the second is a strength. Analysts would have to study other factors (such as the current ratio and the amount of cash flows generated from operating activities) to determine which is the case.

## ACCRUED LIABILITIES

**ACCRUED LIABILITIES** are expenses that have been incurred but have not been paid at the end of the accounting period.

In many situations, a business incurs an expense in one accounting period and makes cash payment for the expense in a subsequent period. **Accrued liabilities** (also called *accrued expenses*) are recorded when expenses have been incurred before the end of an accounting period but have not yet been paid. These expenses include such items as property taxes, electricity, and salaries. The balance sheet for General Mills lists both accrued taxes and accrued payroll (i.e., salaries and wages). Accrued liabilities are recorded as adjusting entries at year-end (because no exchange transaction has taken place). Adjusting entries were discussed in Chapter 4.

**Income Taxes Payable** Corporations, like individuals, must pay taxes on income they earn. Corporate tax rates are graduated with large corporations paying a top federal tax rate of 35 percent. In addition, corporations may pay state and local income taxes and in some cases, foreign income taxes. The notes to the General Mills annual report include the following information pertaining to taxes:

**REAL WORLD EXCERPT**

*General Mills*
ANNUAL REPORT

**NOTE 17—INCOME TAXES**
The components of earnings before income taxes and earnings (losses) of joint ventures and the income taxes thereon are as follows:

|  | Fiscal Year | | |
| --- | --- | --- | --- |
| In Millions | 1998 | 1997 | 1996 |
| Earnings before income taxes: | | | |
| U.S. | $688.1 | $698.5 | $744.0 |
| Foreign | (21.5) | 11.5 | 14.6 |
| Total earnings before income taxes | $666.6 | $710.0 | $758.6 |
| Income taxes: | | | |
| Current: | | | |
| Federal | $242.8 | $208.2 | $206.5 |
| State and local | 31.0 | 25.7 | 28.5 |
| Foreign | (2.6) | 3.5 | 2.0 |
| Total current | 271.2 | 237.4 | 237.0 |

Notice on the General Mills balance sheet (Exhibit 9.1) that the amount of accrued taxes for 1998 ($148.5 million) differs from the amount of taxes reported in the previous note. The amount of taxes reported in Note 17 represents the tax obligation for the year. Some of that obligation was paid in cash during the year. The amount of taxes shown on the balance sheet is the amount accrued during the year but unpaid at year-end.

**Payroll Liabilities** Liabilities associated with unpaid salaries may be reported as part of accrued liabilities or as a separate item, as is the case with General Mills (the amount shown on the balance sheet is $129.7 million). In addition to accruing salaries that have been earned but unpaid, companies also must accrue the cost of benefits, which include retirement programs, vacation time, Social Security benefits, health insurance, and many others.

All salaries and wages are taxed. The largest deductions for most people are the following two categories of taxes:

*Employee income taxes.* Federal laws (as well as many state and local laws) require the employer to deduct an appropriate amount of income tax each period from the gross earnings of each employee. The amount of income tax withheld from the employee's wages is recorded by the employer as a current liability between the date of deduction and the date the amount withheld is remitted to the government. Federal Income Tax Withheld is often referred to as FITW.

*Employee FICA taxes.* The Social Security taxes paid by the employee are called *FICA* taxes because they are required by the Federal Insurance Contributions Act. The funds that are required by the government to provide the benefits under the Social Security Act are obtained by payroll taxes, which are imposed in equal amounts on both the employee and the employer. Effective January 1, 2000, the FICA rate was 7.65 percent on the first $76,200 paid to each employee during the year. In addition, the 1.45 percent of FICA attributable to Medicare applies to income above $76,200.

The expense for employees' services is more than the salary and wage expense. This occurs because the employer must pay benefits (retirement, health care, Social Security, etc.) in addition to salary and wages that have been earned. As a result, employers often have an incentive to ask employees to work extra hours during busy times rather than hire new employees. It is often less expensive to pay overtime to a current employee than to pay wages and benefits for a new one.

Compensation expense for employee services includes all funds earned by the employee as well as funds that must be paid to others on behalf of employees (i.e., benefits). To illustrate, let's assume that General Mills accumulated the following information in its detailed payroll records for the first two weeks of June 20A:

| | |
|---|---|
| Salaries and wages earned | $1,800,000 |
| Income taxes withheld | 275,000 |
| FICA taxes (employees' share) | 105,000 |

Remember that both the employer and the employee must pay FICA taxes. As a result, the total liability associated with FICA taxes is $210,000 ($105,000 + $105,000). The entry to record the payroll and employee deduction follows:

| | | |
|---|---|---|
| Compensation expense (E) ................ | 1,905,000 | |
| Liability for income taxes withheld (L) ....... | | 275,000 |
| FICA payable (L) ...................... | | 210,000 |
| Cash (A) ............................ | | 1,420,000 |

| Assets | = | Liabilities | + | Stockholders' Equity |
|---|---|---|---|---|
| Cash −1,420,000 | | FICA payable +210,000 | | Compensation expense −1,905,000 |
| | | Liability for income taxes withheld +275,000 | | |

Notice in the journal entry that compensation expense ($1,800,000 + $105,000) includes salary and wages earned as well as the employer's share of FICA taxes because FICA is a fringe benefit earned by the employees. The cash paid to employees ($1,420,000) is not the total amount earned ($1,800,000) because the employer must withhold both income taxes ($275,000) and the employees' share of FICA taxes ($105,000). The FICA payable liability reflects both the employees' share and the employer's share.

*Accounting Trends & Techniques* found that most companies in its sample of 600 companies report employee-related liabilities.*

**Other Payroll Liabilities** Typically, businesses grant employees paid vacation time based on the number of months they have worked (e.g., one vacation day for each month). Under the matching concept, the cost of vacation time must be recorded in the year that employees perform service (i.e., help generate revenue) instead of the year that they actually take vacation. If General Mills estimated that the cost of accrued vacation time was $125,000, it makes the following adjusting entry at the end of its fiscal year:

| | | |
|---|---|---|
| Compensation expense (E) ................ | 125,000 | |
| Accrued vacation liability (L) ............. | | 125,000 |

| Assets | = | Liabilities | + | Stockholders' Equity |
|---|---|---|---|---|
| | | Vacation liability +125,000 | | Compensation expense −125,000 |

When the vacations are taken (during the next summer), the accountant records the following:

**Types of Employee-Related Liabilities (sample of 600 companies)**

0  100 200 300 400

Vacations
Benefits
Pensions
Compensation
Salaries and wages

---

*Reprinted with permission from *Accounting Trends and Techniques.* Copyright © 2000 by the American Institute of Certified Public Accounts, Inc.

| Assets | = | Liabilities | + | Stockholders' Equity |
|---|---|---|---|---|

Accrued vacation liability (L) ................ 125,000
    Cash (A) .............................          125,000

| Assets | | = | Liabilities | | + | Stockholders' Equity |
|---|---|---|---|---|---|---|
| Cash | −125,000 | | Vacation liability | −125,000 | | |

Notice that these journal entries cause the liability for vacations to be recorded in the period in which they are earned, not the period in which they are taken. Accrued vacation liabilities usually are not large relative to other liabilities, but they can be substantial in amount. In a recent statement, Eastman Kodak Company reported several hundred million dollars of liabilities related to vacation time. This amount was nearly 10 percent of the company's total liabilities. Because of the size of these liabilities, some managers try to control the amount of accrued vacation liability by requiring employees to take vacations each year. A few years ago, IBM managers offered employees an incentive to take vacation before the end of the fiscal year in an effort to reduce the amount of the accrued vacation liability reported on the balance sheet.

General Mills does not separately disclose the amount of accrued vacation liability. Instead, it is reported on the balance sheet as part of accrued payroll. Apparently, in management's opinion, the amount of accrued vacation liability is not a material factor in the analysis of General Mills. Most analysts would probably agree.

## DEFERRED REVENUES AND SERVICE OBLIGATIONS

In most business transactions, cash is paid after the product or service has been delivered. In some cases, cash is paid before delivery. You have probably paid for several magazines that you will receive at some time in the future. The publisher collects money for your subscription in advance of publishing the magazine. When a company collects cash before the related revenue has been earned, this cash is called **deferred revenues** (or *unearned revenues* or *revenues collected in advance*). Under the revenue principle, revenue cannot be recorded until it has been earned.

Deferred revenues are reported as a liability because cash has been collected but the related revenue has not been earned by the end of the accounting period. The obligation to provide the services or goods in the future exists. Accounting for deferred revenues was discussed in Chapter 6.

Another example of a liability associated with the obligation to provide a service in the future is the frequent flyer programs offered by most major airlines. Under these programs, customers earn free tickets by flying a certain number of miles or trip segments. Each year, these airlines must make an adjusting entry to record the estimated expense and related liability associated with awarding free tickets. The following note from a recent Southwest Airlines annual report illustrates this policy:

**DEFERRED REVENUES** are revenues that have been collected but not earned; they are liabilities until the goods or services are provided.

> Frequent flyer awards. The Company accrues the estimated incremental cost of providing free travel awards under its Rapid Rewards frequent flyer program.

**REAL WORLD EXCERPT**

*Southwest Airlines*
ANNUAL REPORT

Determining the amount of a future service obligation is not always easy. Notice that the amount of the liability for Southwest Airlines is the incremental cost of providing free travel, not the actual selling price of an airline ticket. Some analysts believe that the true cost of a frequent flyer program is the lost revenue associated with giving a ticket to a customer instead of selling it. These analysts believe that the liabilities reported for frequent flyer programs are severely understated. Currently, GAAP permit recording these liabilities based on incremental cost because no accurate method estimates the number of travelers who would have bought tickets if they had not earned a free award.

Many companies offer warranties on the products they sell. This is another form of future service obligation. The cost of providing repair work must be estimated and recorded as a liability (and expense) in the period in which the product is sold. General Mills, like most companies, quickly refunds money for any defective products that it sells. The company does not report a liability for this type of obligation because it estimates this amount to be immaterial.

Another type of obligation a company may face is related to the impact that its operations may have on the environment. Some companies incur significant obligations associated with the environmental impact of their operations. Freeport-McMoRan is a leading company in the production and sale of phosphate fertilizers used to grow grains. The process of extracting natural resources from the land has a major impact on the environment. Under state and federal laws, Freeport-McMoRan is obligated to restore the land once it has completed removing natural resources. The balance sheet for the company reports a $129 million liability for reclamation of land, and the notes included the following statement.

**REAL WORLD EXCERPT**

*Freeport-McMoRan*

ANNUAL REPORT

> **Environmental Remediation and Compliance.** Estimated future expenditures to restore properties and related facilities to a state required to comply with environmental and other regulations are accrued over the life of the properties. The future expenditures are estimated based on current costs, laws and regulation.

Liabilities associated with future service obligations often are based on estimates that are very difficult to develop accurately. The cost of cleaning up pollution in the future depends on a number of factors, including changing technology and federal standards. Many companies have faced bankruptcy because they underestimated the cost of environmental regulations. Managers and analysts must be very cautious in evaluating potential costs associated with activities that impact on our environment.

## NOTES PAYABLE

Most companies need to borrow money to finance their operations. When a company borrows money, a formal written document is prepared. Obligations supported by these written notes are typically called *notes payable*. A note payable specifies such items as the amount borrowed, when it must be repaid, and the interest rate associated with the borrowing.

Creditors are willing to lend cash because they will earn interest to compensate them for giving up the use of their money for a period of time. This simple concept is called the **time value of money.** The word *time* is significant because the longer borrowed money is held, the larger is the total dollar amount of interest expense. Interest for a two-year loan, at a given interest rate, is more than for a one-year loan. To the *borrower*, interest is an expense; to the *creditor*, interest is a revenue.

The **TIME VALUE OF MONEY** is interest that is associated with the use of money over time.

To calculate interest, three variables must be considered: (1) the principal (i.e., the cash that was borrowed), (2) the annual interest rate, and (3) the time period for the loan. The interest formula is

$$\textbf{Interest} = \textbf{Principal} \times \textbf{Interest Rate} \times \textbf{Time}$$

To illustrate the accounting for a note payable, assume that on November 1, 20A, General Mills borrowed $100,000 cash on a one-year, 12 percent note payable. The interest is payable on March 31, 20B, and October 31, 20B. The principal is payable at the maturity date of the note, October 31, 20B. The note is recorded in the accounts as follows:

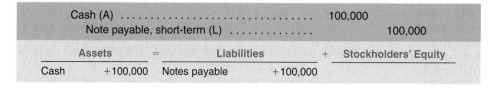

| Cash (A) ............................. | 100,000 | |
| Note payable, short-term (L) ............. | | 100,000 |

| Assets | = | Liabilities | + | Stockholders' Equity |
|--------|---|-------------|---|----------------------|
| Cash +100,000 | | Notes payable +100,000 | | |

Interest is an expense of the period when the money is used. Under the matching concept, interest expense is recorded when it is incurred rather than when the cash actually is paid. When does General Mills incur interest cost associated with the note that was recorded in the previous journal entry? Because the company uses the money for two months during 20A, it records interest expense in 20A for two months, even though cash is not paid until March 31. During 20B, the company uses the money for 10 months; therefore, it should record interest expense for 10 months in 20B.

The computation of interest expense follows:

$$\textbf{Interest} = \textbf{Principal} \times \textbf{Interest Rate} \times \textbf{Time}$$

$$\textbf{\$2,000} = \textbf{\$100,000} \times \quad \textbf{12\%} \quad \times \textbf{2/12}$$

The entry to record interest expense on December 31, 20A is

| | |
|---|---|
| Interest expense (E) . . . . . . . . . . . . . . . . . . . . . . . | 2,000 |
| Accounts payable (L) . . . . . . . . . . . . . . . . . . . | 2,000 |

| Assets | = | Liabilities | + | Stockholders' Equity |
|---|---|---|---|---|
| | | Accounts payable +2,000 | | Interest expense −2,000 |

## CURRENT PORTION OF LONG-TERM DEBT

The distinction between current and long-term debt is important for both managers and analysts because current debt must be paid within the next year. The company must have sufficient cash to repay currently maturing debt. To provide accurate information concerning current liabilities, a company must reclassify long-term debt within a year of its maturity date as a current liability. Assume that General Mills signed a note payable of $5 million on January 1, 20A. Repayment is in two installments as follows: December 31, 20D—$2.5 million and December 31, 20E—$2.5 million. The December 31, 20B, 20C, and 20D, balance sheets report the following:

| December 31, 20B | |
|---|---|
| Long-term liabilities | |
| Note payable | $5,000,000 |
| **December 31, 20C** | |
| Current liabilities | |
| Current portion of long-term note | 2,500,000 |
| Long-term liabilities | |
| Long-term note | 2,500,000 |
| **December 31, 20D** | |
| Current liabilities | |
| Current portion of long-term note | 2,500,000 |

An example of this type of disclosure can be seen in Exhibit 9.1. Notice that General Mills reported $153.2 million as the current portion of long-term debt in 1998 that will be paid in full during the following accounting period.

## FINANCIAL **ANALYSIS**

### REFINANCED DEBT: CURRENT OR NONCURRENT?

Many companies refinance their debt when it matures. Instead of repaying the debt from current cash that is available, the company either signs a new loan agreement with a new maturity date or borrows money from a new creditor and repays the original creditor. An interesting accounting question arises if a company intends to refinance debt and has the ability to do so: Should currently maturing debt that will be refinanced be classified as a current or long-term liability? Remember that analysts are interested in a company's current liabilities because these liabilities will generate cash outflows in the next accounting period. If the liability will not generate a cash outflow in the next accounting period, GAAP require that it not be classified as current. This rule can be illustrated with a note from the General Mills annual report.

**REAL WORLD EXCERPT**

*General Mills*

ANNUAL REPORT

> We have a revolving credit agreement expiring in January 2002 that provides us with the ability to refinance short-term borrowing on a long-term basis. Therefore we have reclassified a portion of our notes payable to long-term debt.

# FOCUS ON **CASH FLOWS**

**■ LEARNING OBJECTIVE 4**

Determine the impact of changes in working capital on cash flows.

## WORKING CAPITAL MANAGEMENT

Remember that the dollar difference between current assets and current liabilities is called *working capital*. Management of working capital is an important activity that can have a dramatic impact on a company's profitability and cash flows. Excess inventory or the slow collection of a customer account ties up cash and reduces profitability. The working capital accounts are closely managed by successful companies and closely watched by financial analysts.

### EFFECT ON STATEMENT OF CASH FLOWS

**IN GENERAL** → Changes in working capital accounts affect a company's cash flows as indicated in the following table:

|  | Effect on Cash Flows |
| --- | --- |
| **Operating activities** (indirect method) | |
| Net income | $xxx |
|   Adjusted for: Decreases in current assets* or increases in current liabilities | + |
|   Adjusted for: Increases in current assets* or decrease in current liabilities | − |

*Other than cash

| Selected Focus Company Comparisons: Change in Cash Flow Related to Working Capital (in millions) | |
| --- | --- |
| Home Depot | $131 |
| Wal-Mart | $1,840 |
| Harrah's | $45 |

**FOCUS COMPANY ANALYSIS** → A segment of the General Mills Statement of Cash Flows, prepared using the indirect method, follows.

The annual report for General Mills states that "continuing operations generated $181.2 million more cash in 1998 than in 1997, primarily due to strong earnings growth recorded by domestic operations and a positive impact from a change in working capital." To understand the meaning of this statement, you should reflect back on our previous discussions of the statement of cash flows. Remember that working capital accounts (i.e., current assets and current liabilities) are often related to revenues and expenses reported on the income statement. An increase in accounts receivable, for example, is associated with sales that occurred without the collection of cash. The collection of cash occurs when the customer pays the bill. An increase in accounts payable is associated with an expense that has been incurred without a cash payment. The payment of cash occurs when the account is paid.

The Statement of Cash Flows for General Mills shows that cash flows from operating activities were increased by $54.5 million as the result of changes in current assets and current liabilities. Notice the $4 million increase in cash flows for the year that occurred because of the increase in accounts payable. General Mills was able to acquire goods from suppliers but did not have to pay for them during the current accounting period.

**GENERAL MILLS INC.**
**Statement of Cash Flows**

| (in millions) | May 31, 1998 | May 25, 1997 | May 26, 1996 |
|---|---|---|---|
| Cash Flows—Operating Activities: | | | |
| Net earnings | $421.8 | $445.4 | $ 476.4 |
| Adjustments to reconcile net earnings to cash flow: | | | |
| Depreciation and amortization | 194.9 | 182.8 | 186.7 |
| Deferred income taxes | (29.3) | 20.9 | 42.4 |
| Change in current assets and liabilities, net of | | | |
| effects from business acquired | 54.5 | (86.4) | (25.9) |
| Unusual items | 166.4 | 48.4 | — |
| Other, net | (33.0) | (17.0) | (3.2) |
| Cash provided by continuing operations | 775.3 | 594.1 | 676.4 |
| Cash used by discontinued operations | (5.8) | (6.8) | (16.6) |
| Net Cash Provided by Operating Activities | 769.5 | 587.3 | 659.8 |
| Cash Flow from Changes in Current Assets and Liabilities: | | | |
| Receivables | 23.7 | (80.0) | (59.5) |
| Inventories | (26.4) | 45.0 | (23.7) |
| Prepaid expenses and other current assets | 1.6 | 2.5 | (6.3) |
| Accounts payable | 4.0 | (27.8) | 93.2 |
| Other current liabilities | 51.6 | (26.1) | (29.6) |
| Change in Current Assets and Liabilities | $ 54.5 | ($ 86.4) | ($ 25.9) |

## SELF-STUDY **QUIZ**

Earlier in this chapter, we defined the current ratio and working capital. For this quiz, assume that the current ratio for General Mills is 2.0. For each of the following events, tell whether the current ratio and working capital will increase or decrease:

1. General Mills incurs an account payable of $250,000, with no change in current assets.

2. The company borrows $1,000,000 in long-term debt.

3. The company pays taxes payable in the amount of $750,000.

4. The company finances a new building with long-term debt.

After you have completed your answers, check them with the solutions in the footnote at the bottom of this page.*

## LONG-TERM LIABILITIES

Most companies use long-term liabilities to generate funds to purchase operational assets. Long-term liabilities include long-term notes payable and bonds payable, which are contracts that specify the terms of the borrowing agreement (e.g., interest rate and repayment schedule). **Long-term liabilities** include all of the entity's obligations that are not classified as current liabilities.

To reduce risk for creditors who are willing to lend money for a long period (which, in turn, reduces the interest rate that must be paid), some companies contractually agree that specific assets will be used as security for the liability. If the liability is not satisfied, the creditor may take ownership of the asset. A liability supported by this

**LONG-TERM LIABILITIES** are all of the entity's obligations not classified as current liabilities.

---

*Current ratio     Working capital
1. Decrease      Decrease
2. Increase       Increase
3. Increase       No change
4. No change    No change

type of agreement (typically a mortgage) is called *secured debt*. An *unsecured debt* is one for which the creditor relies primarily on the borrower's integrity and general earning power.

Long-term liabilities are reported on the balance sheet immediately following current liabilities. Notice the example for General Mills in Exhibit 9.1. The accounts Long-Term Debt, Deferred Income Taxes, Deferred Income Taxes—Tax Leases, and Other Liabilities are all long-term liabilities despite the fact that no separate caption identifies them as such.

### LONG-TERM DEBT

Companies can raise long-term debt capital directly from a number of financial service organizations including banks, insurance companies, and pension plans. Raising debt from one of these organizations is known as *private placement*. This type of debt often is called a *note payable*, which is a written promise to pay a stated sum at one or more specified future dates called the *maturity dates*.

In many cases, a company's need for debt capital exceeds the financial ability of any single creditor. In these situations, the company may issue publicly traded debt called *bonds*. The bonds can be traded in established markets that provide bondholders with liquidity (i.e., the ability to sell the bond and quickly receive cash). They can sell their bonds to other investors prior to maturity if they have an immediate need for cash. Notes and bonds are very similar because both are written promises to pay a debt. Bonds will be discussed in detail in the next chapter.

# INTERNATIONAL **PERSPECTIVE**

## BORROWING IN FOREIGN CURRENCIES

Over the past years, business operations have become more global. Successful corporations market their products in many countries and locate manufacturing facilities around the world based on cost and productivity considerations. The financing of corporations also has become international, even in cases when the company does not have international operations.

Many corporations with foreign operations elect to finance those operations with foreign debt to lessen the exchange rate risk. This type of risk exists because the relative value of each nation's currency varies virtually on a daily basis because of various economic factors. As this book is being written, the British pound is worth approximately $1.65. A year earlier, it was worth $1.60. A U.S. company that owed debt denominated in pounds would experience a loss from this increase in the value of the pound.

A U.S. corporation that conducts business operations in England might decide to borrow pounds to finance its operations. The profits from the business will be in pounds, which can be used to pay off the debt, which is in pounds. If the business earned profits in pounds but paid off debt in dollars, it would be exposed to exchange rate risk because the relative value of the dollar and the pound fluctuates.

Foreign corporations face this same problem. A note to a recent annual report from Toyota (a Japanese company) stated:

**REAL WORLD EXCERPT**

*Toyota*

ANNUAL REPORT

> Earnings declined in the current year ended, as the appreciation of the yen aggravated the adverse effects of sluggish demand. . . . The movement in exchange rates reduced operating income of the company. Losses on currency exchange thus offset most of the cost savings we achieved.

Toyota has borrowed a large amount of money in the United States to lessen the exchange rate risk that it faces. The company also owns and operates many factories in this country.

Even if a company does not have international operations, it may elect to borrow in foreign markets. When a country is experiencing a recession, interest rates often are low. These situations give corporations the opportunity to borrow money at a lower cost.

Accountants must convert, or translate, foreign debt into U.S. dollars for reporting purposes. Conversion rates for all major currencies are published in most newspapers. To illustrate foreign currency translation, assume that General Mills borrowed 1 million pounds (£). For the General Mills annual report, the accountant must use the conversion rate as of the balance sheet date, which we assume was £1.00 to $1.65. The dollar equivalent of the debt is $1,650,000 (£1,000,000 × 1.65 = $1,650,000). As you can see, the dollar equivalent of foreign debt may change if the conversion rate changes even when no additional borrowings or repayments occur.

The notes to the balance sheet for General Mills indicate that the company has borrowed money primarily in the United States and Canada. In contrast, consider the following note from Toys "R" Us (in millions):

| | 1998 | 1997 |
|---|---|---|
| 7% British pound sterling loan payable | $ 49 | $ 67 |
| Japanese yen loans payable in varying amounts through 2012 | 123 | 150 |
| 8¼% sinking fund debentures, due 2017 | 89 | 89 |
| Mortgage notes payable at annual interest rates from 10% to 11% | 14 | 13 |

**REAL WORLD EXCERPT**

*Toys "R" Us*

ANNUAL REPORT

Toys "R" Us is an international company with more than 25 percent of its sales and assets located outside the United States. The company borrows heavily in international markets to minimize the risk associated with variations in exchange rates. This is typical for most large corporations and is further justification for business executives to develop an understanding of international markets.

SELF-STUDY **QUIZ**

In an earlier example, we assumed that the $100,000 note payable for General Mills required payment of interest on March 31 and October 31. Review that example and now assume that the note required the payment of interest on January 31 and July 31.

1. What adjusting entry should General Mills make at the end of its fiscal year on December 31, 20A?

2. What entry should the company make on January 31, 20B?

3. What entry should the company make on July 31, 20B?

After you have completed your answers, check them with the solutions in the footnote at the bottom of this page.*

---

| | | | |
|---|---|---|---|
| *1. | Interest expense . . . . . . . . . . . . . . . . | 2,000 | |
| | Interest payable . . . . . . . . . . . . . . | | 2,000 |
| 2. | Interest expense . . . . . . . . . . . . . . . . | 1,000 | |
| | Interest payable . . . . . . . . . . . . . . . . | 2,000 | |
| | Cash . . . . . . . . . . . . . . . . . . . . . . . | | 3,000 |
| 3. | Interest expense . . . . . . . . . . . . . . . . | 6,000 | |
| | Cash . . . . . . . . . . . . . . . . . . . . . . . | | 6,000 |

## OTHER TOPICS

Two areas of business operations may result in the creation of either an asset or a liability. These areas involve accounting for income taxes and employee retirement benefits. On most financial statements, you will see these items as liabilities, so we will discuss them along with other liabilities.

## DEFERRED TAXES

■ **LEARNING OBJECTIVE 5**

Apply deferred income tax allocation.

In previous chapters, we made simplifying assumptions concerning tax expense. We often told you the amount of tax expense (e.g., $100,000) and had you make a journal entry similar to the following:

| | | |
|---|---|---|
| Tax expense (E) ......................... | 100,000 | |
| Taxes payable (L) ...................... | | 100,000 |

| Assets | = | Liabilities | + | Stockholders' Equity | |
|---|---|---|---|---|---|
| | | Taxes payable | +100,000 | Tax expense | −100,000 |

Because separate rules govern the preparation of financial statements (GAAP) and tax returns (Internal Revenue Code), the amount of taxes based on the income before taxes reported on the income statement is normally different from the amount taxes based on taxable income computed on the tax return. This difference creates an interesting accounting problem: Should the tax liability reported on the balance sheet be the amount of taxes currently payable based on the tax return or should the liability include future tax effects that exist because of differences between GAAP and the Internal Revenue Code? Accountants have resolved this issue by recording the "economic" liability, which includes taxes currently payable adjusted for the effects of differences between GAAP and the Internal Revenue Code.

As a result of differences between GAAP and the Internal Revenue Code, the amount of *tax expense* and the amount of *taxes payable* normally differ. To have our journal entry balance, we need a new account. This new account is called *Deferred Taxes*. In practice, deferred taxes can be either assets (such as taxes related to cash collected from a customer, which is taxable before it is reported as a revenue on the income statement) or liabilities (such as taxes related to depreciation, which is reported on the tax return before it is reported on the income statement). Notice in Exhibit 9.1 that General Mills has deferred tax amounts reported as both assets and liabilities.

**DEFERRED TAX ITEMS** exist because of timing differences caused by reporting revenues and expenses according to GAAP on a company's income statement and according to the Internal Revenue Code on the tax return.

**Deferred tax items** exist because of timing differences in reporting revenues and expenses on a company's income statement and tax return. These **temporary differences** are caused by differences in GAAP that govern financial statement preparation and the Internal Revenue Code that governs the preparation of tax returns. To illustrate, let's consider one item that gives rise to deferred taxes. General Mills uses straight-line depreciation for its financial statements and accelerated depreciation for its tax return. As a result, it reports lower income on its tax return than on its income statement. Assume that General Mills computed taxes payable of $8,000,000 based on the numbers reported on the tax return and tax expense of $10,000,000 based on the income statement. The company records its tax obligation as follows:

**TEMPORARY DIFFERENCES** are timing differences that cause deferred income taxes and will reverse, or turn around, in the future.

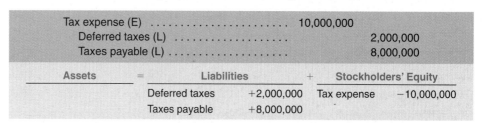

| | | |
|---|---|---|
| Tax expense (E) ...................... | 10,000,000 | |
| Deferred taxes (L) ................... | | 2,000,000 |
| Taxes payable (L) .................... | | 8,000,000 |

| Assets | = | Liabilities | + | Stockholders' Equity | |
|---|---|---|---|---|---|
| | | Deferred taxes | +2,000,000 | Tax expense | −10,000,000 |
| | | Taxes payable | +8,000,000 | | |

The deferred tax amount is paid in the future when depreciation expense "reverses." By this, we mean that at some point in the future, the accelerated depreciation recorded on the tax return will be less than the straight-line depreciation reported on the income statement (remember from Chapter 8 that accelerated depreciation causes higher depreciation expense compared to straight line in the early years of an asset's life and lower depreciation in the later years). When a temporary difference reverses, the deferred tax amount is reduced.

The computation of deferred taxes involves some complexities that are discussed in advanced accounting courses. At this point, we want you to understand that deferred tax assets and liabilities are caused by temporary differences between the income statement and the tax return. Each temporary difference has an impact on the income statement in one accounting period and the tax return in another.

## ACCRUED RETIREMENT BENEFITS

Most employers provide retirement programs for their employees. In a *defined contribution* program, the employer makes cash payments to a fund that invests the money and earns income. When employees retire, they are entitled to a portion of the fund. If the investment strategy of the fund is successful, the retirement income for the employees will be larger. If the strategy is not successful, it will be lower. The employer's only obligation is to make the required annual payments to the fund, which are recorded as pension expense.

As an alternative, some employers offer *defined benefit* programs. Under these programs, an employee's retirement benefits are based on a percentage of his or her pay at retirement or a certain number of dollars for each year of employment. The employer must record pension expense each year. Basically, the amount of pension expense that must be accrued each year is the change in the current cash value of the employee's retirement package. The current cash value changes each year for a variety of reasons. For example, it changes (1) as the employee is closer to receiving benefits, (2) as the retirement benefits increase as the result of higher pay or longer service, or (3) if the employee's life expectancy changes. The company must report a pension liability based on any portion of the current cash value of the retirement program that has not actually been funded. For example, if the company transferred $8 million to the pension fund manager but the current cash value of the pension program was $10 million, the company reports a $2 million pension liability on its balance sheet.

The financial obligation associated with defined benefit retirement programs can be very large for many corporations, especially those with unionized work forces. A recent financial statement for Ford Motor Company disclosed the following information:

**Note 2**
**Employee Retirement Benefits**
(in millions)

| Accumulated Postretirement Benefit Obligation | |
|---|---|
| Retirees | $ 7,035.0 |
| Active employees eligible to retire | 2,269.6 |
| Other active employees | 5,090.6 |
| Total accumulated obligation | $14,395.2 |

To put the size of this obligation in perspective, it represents an amount nearly equal to the company's total stockholders' equity. The retirement benefit expense for the year was $1.3 billion, which exceeded the income that Ford earned for the previous three years.

General Mills does not have a pension liability on its balance sheet because it has made cash payments to the retirement fund that are larger than the current value of the pension benefits. The notes report the following:

| Note 5 Balance Sheet Information | | |
|---|---|---|
| (in millions) | 1998 | 1997 |
| Other assets: | | |
| Prepaid pension | $471.8 | $402.5 |

This information is important to analysts who are forecasting a company's future cash flows. Ford has a much larger obligation to transfer cash to its retirement fund than does General Mills.

In recent years, employer-provided health care benefits have been the subject of a great deal of discussion. Many large companies pay for a portion of their employees' health insurance costs. The payments are recorded as an expense in the current accounting period. Some employers agree to continue to pay for health care costs after employees retire. The cost of these future benefits must be estimated and recorded as an expense in the periods when the employees perform services. The recording of future health care costs for retired employees is an excellent example of the use of estimates in accounting. Imagine the difficulty of estimating future health care costs when you do not know how long employees will live, how healthy they will be during their lives, and how much doctors and hospitals will charge for their services in the future.

Accounting for retirement benefits is a complex topic that is discussed in detail in subsequent accounting courses. This topic is introduced at this point as another example of the application of the matching concept, which requires that expenses be recorded in the year in which the benefit is received. It also illustrates how accounting avoids the creation of improper incentives for managers. If the future cost of retirement benefits were not included in the period in which work was performed, managers might have the incentive to offer employees increases in their retirement benefits instead of increases in their salaries. In this manner, managers could understate the true cost of employee services and make their companies appear more profitable. Many economists argue that the local, state, and federal governments have fallen into this trap. Government officials can give large pensions to current workers without the cost being recognized until the employee retires. By doing this, governments can appear to be very efficient when in reality they are simply deferring costs to the future.

## CONTINGENT LIABILITIES

■ **LEARNING OBJECTIVE 6**

Report contingent liabilities.

A **CONTINGENT LIABILITY** is a potential liability that has arisen as the result of a past event; not an effective liability until some future event occurs.

Each of the liabilities that we have discussed is reported on the balance sheet with a specific dollar amount. Each of these liabilities involves the *probable* future sacrifice of economic benefits. Some transactions or events create a *potential* (but not probable) future sacrifice of economic benefits. These situations create **contingent liabilities,** which are potential liabilities that have arisen as a result of a past event. The conversion of a contingent liability to a recorded liability depends on one or more future events. A situation that causes a contingent liability also causes a contingent loss.

Whether a situation causes a recorded or a contingent liability depends on the probability of the future economic sacrifice and the ability of management to estimate the amount of the liability. The following table illustrates the various possibilities:

| | Probable | Reasonably Possible | Remote |
|---|---|---|---|
| Subject to estimate | Record as liability | Disclose in note | Disclosure not required |
| Not subject to estimate | Disclose in note | Disclose in note | Disclosure not required |

The probabilities of occurrence are defined in the following manner:

1. Probable—the chance that the future event or events will occur is high.
2. Reasonably possible—the chance that the future event or events will occur is more than remote but less than likely.
3. Remote—the chance that the future event or events will occur is slight.

When recording liabilities, a company must determine whether the amount of any liability can be reasonably estimated. The general accounting guidelines are (1) a liability that is *both* probable and can be reasonably estimated must be recorded and reported on the balance sheet, (2) a liability that is reasonably possible (whether it can be estimated or not) must be disclosed in a note in the financial statements, and (3) remote contingencies are not disclosed.

The notes to General Mills' annual report include the following:

> We are contingently liable under guarantees and comfort letters for $48.3 million. The guarantees and comfort letters are issued to support borrowing arrangements primarily for our joint ventures.

**REAL WORLD EXCERPT**

*General Mills*
ANNUAL REPORT

The company did not have to record a liability on the balance sheet because the chance of having a loss from these guarantees was not probable. Harley-Davidson disclosed another contingency that is common:

> **Note 7**
> **Commitments and Contingencies**
> A state court jury in California found the Company liable for compensatory and punitive damages of $7.2 million, including interest, in a lawsuit brought by a supplier of aftermarket exhaust systems. The Company immediately appealed the verdict.

**REAL WORLD EXCERPT**

*Harley-Davidson*
ANNUAL REPORT

In this case, the existence of a liability was a reasonable possibility. As a result, GAAP required Harley-Davidson to disclose the lawsuit. The company subsequently reached an out-of-court settlement for $5 million. At that point, the loss was probable, which required recording the loss and the related liability.

*Accounting Trends & Techniques* studied the financial statements of 600 companies and found that litigation was the most common type of contingent liability.*

## OTHER OBLIGATIONS

As we have just seen with contingencies, not all financial obligations result in the recording of liabilities on the balance sheet. Another example involves situations in which an agreement is made to have an exchange in the future. Many businesses enter into labor contracts with senior executives under which they agree to pay a certain salary for a specified period of time. This financial obligation is not recorded as a liability because it involves making a payment in the future for a service that is performed in the future. Once the executive performs the service, a liability is created.

A similar situation exists when a company leases an asset. A lease contract permits a company to pay in the future for an asset that it will use in the future. As a result, many lease contracts do not create an immediate liability. Known as *operating leases,* these leases require the recording of lease expense and lease payable with the passage of time.

An underlying accounting concept requires that transactions be recorded in terms of their substance, not their form. Many corporations enter into long-term lease contracts that permit them to use an asset for its entire life. In essence, this represents the purchase and financing of an asset even though it is legally a lease agreement; such a lease

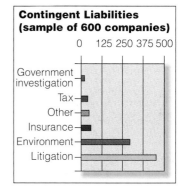

**Contingent Liabilities
(sample of 600 companies)**

0   125 250 375 500

Government investigation
Tax
Other
Insurance
Environment
Litigation

---

*Reprinted with permission from *Accounting Trends and Techniques.* Copyright © 2000 by the American Institute of Certified Public Accounts, Inc.

is called a *capital lease*. A lease that covers at least 75 percent of the life of an asset must be recorded as a capital lease (additional criteria are discussed in subsequent accounting courses). These leases are accounted for as if an asset had been purchased (an asset and a liability are recorded). The recorded value is the current cash equivalent of the lease payments. In the next section on present value concepts, we show you how this amount is actually computed.

## PRESENT AND FUTURE VALUE CONCEPTS

We have discussed the account classifications that you will encounter on most of the balance sheets that you will study. Before we leave the topic of liabilities, we want to introduce you to an important concept underlying most liabilities.

In our earlier discussion of notes payable, we looked at a very basic situation. To properly analyze more complex liabilities, you will use some relatively simple mathematics called *present* and *future value concepts*. These concepts represent an important part of our discussion of bond liabilities in the next chapter.

The concepts of future value (FV) and present value (PV) focus on the time value of money. Money received today is worth more than money received one year from today (or at any other future date) because it can be used to earn interest. If you invest $1,000 today at 10 percent, you will have $1,100 in one year. In contrast, if the $1,000 is to be received one year from today, you lose the opportunity to earn the $100 interest revenue for the year. The difference between the $1,000 and $1,100 is interest that can be earned during the year.

**PRESENT VALUE** is the current value of an amount to be received in the future; a future amount discounted for compound interest.

In some business situations, you will know the dollar amount of a cash flow that occurs in the future and will need to determine its value now. This is known as a **present value** problem. The opposite situation occurs when you know the dollar amount of a cash flow that occurs today and need to determine its value at some point in the future. This is called a **future value** problem. The value of money changes over time because money can earn interest (in other words, a dollar today is worth more than a dollar received in the future). The following illustrates the basic difference between present value and future value problems:

**FUTURE VALUE** is the sum to which an amount will increase as the result of compound interest.

|  | Now | Future |
|---|---|---|
| Present value | ? | $1,000 |
| Future value | $1,000 | ? |

In addition to the two types of business situations that you will encounter (the need to determine either a present value or a future value), there are two types of cash flows: *single payment* situations that involve one payment and *annuities* that involve a series of cash payments. This means that four different types of situations are related to the time value of money; they are identified in Exhibit 9.2. Each type of problem is based on the interest formula that was discussed earlier in this chapter:

**Interest = Principal × Interest Rate × Time**

Many inexpensive hand-held calculators can do the detailed arithmetic computations required in computing future value and present value problems. In subsequent courses and in all business situations, you will probably use a calculator to solve these problems. At this stage, we encourage you to solve problems using the tables (Tables A–1 through A–4 in Appendix A at the end of this book) that give values for each of the four types of problems for different periods of time (*n*) and at different rates of interest (*i*). We believe that use of the tables will give you a better understanding of how and why present and future value concepts apply to business problems.

| Payment or Receipt | Symbol | |
| --- | --- | --- |
| | Future Value | Present Value |
| Single amount | f | p |
| Annuity (equal payments or receipts for a series of equal time periods) | F | P |

EXHIBIT **9.2**

**Four Types of Future and Present Value Problems**

The values given in the tables are based on payments of $1. If a problem involves payments other than $1, it is necessary to multiply the value from the table by the amount of the payment.[1] We now examine each of the four types of present value and future value problems.

## FUTURE AND PRESENT VALUES OF A SINGLE AMOUNT

### FUTURE VALUE OF A SINGLE AMOUNT (f)

In future value of a single amount problems, you will be asked to calculate how much money you will have in the future as the result of investing a certain amount in the present. If you received a gift of $10,000, you might decide to put it in a savings account and use the money as a down payment on a house when you graduate from college. The future value computation will tell you how much money will be available when you graduate.

To solve a future value problem, you need to know three items: (1) the amount to be invested, (2) the interest rate ($i$) that the amount will earn, and (3) the number of periods ($n$) in which the amount will earn interest.

The future value concept is based on compound interest. Therefore, the amount of interest for each period is calculated by multiplying the principal plus any interest that accrued in prior interest periods (but was not paid out) by the interest rate.

To illustrate, assume that on January 1, 20A, you deposit $1,000 in a savings account at 10 percent annual interest, compounded annually. At the end of three years, the $1,000 originally deposited has increased to $1,331 as follows:

| Year | Amount at Start of Year | + | Interest during the Year | = | Amount at End of Year |
| --- | --- | --- | --- | --- | --- |
| 1 | $1,000 | + | $1,000 × 10% = $100 | = | $1,100 |
| 2 | 1,100 | + | 1,100 × 10% = $110 | = | 1,210 |
| 3 | 1,210 | + | 1,210 × 10% = $121 | = | 1,331 |

*1464.1*

We can avoid the detailed arithmetic by referring to Table A–1, Appendix A, Future Value of $1, f. For $i = 10\%$, $n = 3$, we find the value 1.331. We can compute the balance at the end of year 3 as $1,000 × 1.331 = $1,331. The increase of $331 is due to the time value of money. It is interest revenue to the owner of the savings account and interest expense to the savings institution. A convenient format to display the computations for this problem is

$$\$1,000 \times f_{i=10\%,n=3} \text{ (Table A–1, Appendix A, 1.3310)} = \$1,331.$$

Exhibit 9.3 summarizes this future value concept.

---

[1]Present value and future value problems involve cash flows. The basic concepts are the same for cash inflows (receipts) and cash outflows (payments). No fundamental differences exist between present value and future value calculations for cash payments versus cash receipts.

## PRESENT VALUE OF A SINGLE AMOUNT (p)

The present value of a single amount is what it is worth to you today to be able to receive that amount at some date in the future. You might be offered the opportunity to invest in a debt instrument that would pay you $10,000 in 10 years. You would want to determine the present value of the instrument before you decided whether to invest.

To compute the present value of an amount to be received in the future, the amount is subjected to discounting (which is the opposite of compounding) at $i$ interest rate for $n$ periods. In discounting, the interest is subtracted rather than added (as is the case with compounding).

To illustrate, assume that today is January 1, 20A, and you have the opportunity to receive $1,000 cash on December 31, 20C (i.e., three years from now). With an interest rate of 10 percent per year, how much is the $1,000 worth to you on January 1, 20A? You could set up a discounting computation, year by year, that would be the inverse to the tabulation shown for the future value.[2] To facilitate the computation, however, we can refer to Table A–2, Appendix A, Present Value of $1, p. For $i = 10\%$, $n = 3$, we find that the present value of $1 is 0.7513. The $1,000 to be received at the end of three years has a present value (today) of $1,000 × 0.7513 = $751.30. The difference (i.e., the discount) of $248.70 is interest. A convenient format to display the computations for this problem is

$$\$1,000 \times \text{p}_{i=10\%,n=3} \text{ (Table A–2, Appendix A, 0.7513)} = \$751.30.$$

The concept of the present value of $1 is summarized in Exhibit 9.3.

It is not difficult to learn how to compute a present value amount, but it is more important that you understand what it means. The $751.30 is the amount that you would pay to have the right to receive $1,000 at the end of three years, assuming an interest rate of 10 percent. Conceptually, you would be indifferent about having $751.30 today and having $1,000 in three years. You are indifferent because you can use financial institutions to convert dollars from the present to the future and vice versa. If you had $751.30 today but preferred $1,000 in three years, you could simply deposit the money in a savings account and it would grow to $1,000 in three years. Alternatively, if you had a contract that promised you $1,000 in three years, you could sell it to an investor for $751.30 cash today because it would permit the investor to earn 10 percent on her money.

## SELF-STUDY QUIZ

1. If the interest rate in a present value problem increases from 8 percent to 10 percent, will the present value increase or decrease?

2. What is the present value of $10,000 to be received 10 years from now if the interest rate is 5 percent compounded annually?

Check your answers in the footnote at the bottom of this page.*

---

[2]The detailed discounting is as follows:

| Periods | Interest for the Year | Present Value* |
|---|---|---|
| 1 | $1,000 − ($1,000 × 1/1.10) = $90.91 | $1,000 − $90.91 = $909.09 |
| 2 | $909.09 − ($909.09 × 1/1.10) = $82.65 | $909.09 − $82.65 = $826.44 |
| 3 | $826.44 − ($826.44 × 1/1.10) = $75.14† | $826.44 − $75.14 = $751.30 |

*Verifiable in Table A–2.

†Adjusted for rounding.

*1. The present value will be less.

2. $10,000 × 0.6139 = $6,139

EXHIBIT **9.3**

**Overview of Future and Present Value Determinations**

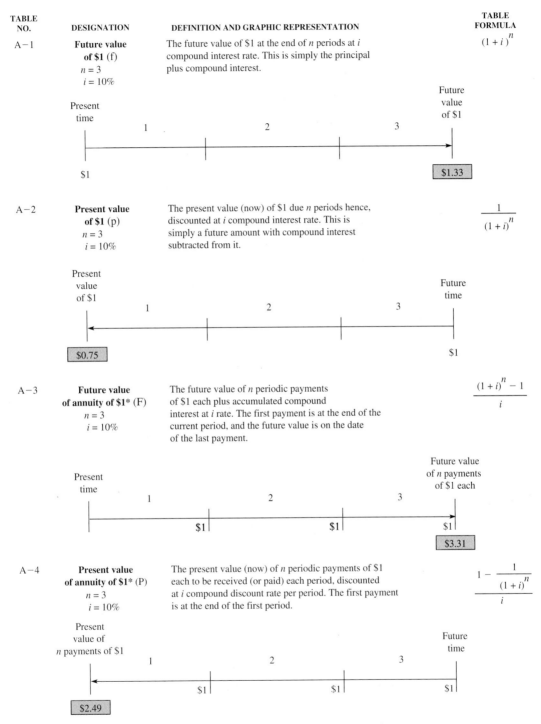

| TABLE NO. | DESIGNATION | DEFINITION AND GRAPHIC REPRESENTATION | TABLE FORMULA |
|---|---|---|---|
| A−1 | **Future value of $1** (f) $n = 3$ $i = 10\%$ | The future value of $1 at the end of $n$ periods at $i$ compound interest rate. This is simply the principal plus compound interest. | $(1 + i)^n$ |
| A−2 | **Present value of $1** (p) $n = 3$ $i = 10\%$ | The present value (now) of $1 due $n$ periods hence, discounted at $i$ compound interest rate. This is simply a future amount with compound interest subtracted from it. | $\dfrac{1}{(1 + i)^n}$ |
| A−3 | **Future value of annuity of $1*** (F) $n = 3$ $i = 10\%$ | The future value of $n$ periodic payments of $1 each plus accumulated compound interest at $i$ rate. The first payment is at the end of the current period, and the future value is on the date of the last payment. | $\dfrac{(1 + i)^n - 1}{i}$ |
| A−4 | **Present value of annuity of $1*** (P) $n = 3$ $i = 10\%$ | The present value (now) of $n$ periodic payments of $1 each to be received (or paid) each period, discounted at $i$ compound discount rate per period. The first payment is at the end of the first period. | $\dfrac{1 - \dfrac{1}{(1 + i)^n}}{i}$ |

*Notice that these are ordinary annuities; that is, they are often called end-of-period annuities. Thus, the table values for F, the future amount, are on the date of the last payment; and for P, the present value, are at the beginning of the period of the first payment. Annuities due assume the opposite; that is, they are "beginning-of-period" annuities. Ordinary annuity values can be converted to annuities due simply by multiplication of $(1 + i)$.

# FUTURE AND PRESENT VALUES OF AN ANNUITY

Many business problems involve multiple cash payments over a number of periods instead of a single payment. An **annuity** is a series of consecutive payments characterized by

An **ANNUITY** is a series of periodic cash receipts or payments that are equal in amount each interest period.

1. An equal dollar amount each interest period.
2. Interest periods of equal length (year, semiannual, quarter, or month).
3. An equal interest rate each interest period.

Examples of annuities include monthly payments on an automobile or a home, yearly contributions to a savings account, and monthly retirement benefits received from a pension fund.

### FUTURE VALUE OF AN ANNUITY (F)

If you are saving money for some purpose, such as a new car or a trip to Europe, you might decide to deposit a fixed amount of money in a savings account each month. The future value of an annuity computation will tell you how much money will be in your savings account at some point in the future.

The future value of an annuity includes *compound interest* on each payment from the date of payment to the end of the term of the annuity. Each payment accumulates less interest than the prior payments did only because the number of periods remaining to accumulate interest decreases.

Assume that you deposit $1,000 cash in a savings account each year for three years at 10 percent interest per year (i.e., a total principal of $3,000). The first $1,000 deposit is made on December 31, 20A, the second one on December 31, 20B, and the third and last one on December 31, 20C. The first $1,000 deposit earns compound interest for two years (for a total principal and interest of $1,210); the second deposit earns interest for one year (for a total principal and interest of $1,100); and the third deposit earns no interest because it was made on the day that the balance is computed. Thus, the total amount in the savings account at the end of three years is $3,310 ($1,210 + $1,100 + $1,000).

We could compute the interest on each deposit to derive the future value of this annuity. We can refer to Table A–3, Appendix A, Future Value of Annuity of $1 (F) for $i = 10\%$, $n = 3$, however, to find the value 3.3100. The total of your three deposits of $1,000 each increased to $1,000 × 3.31, or $3,310, by December 31, 20C. The increase of $310 was due to interest. A convenient format for this problem is

$$\$1,000 \times F_{i=10\%,n=3} \text{ (Table A–3, Appendix A, 3.3100)} = \$3,310.$$

This concept is summarized in Exhibit 9.3.

**The Power of Compounding**   Compound interest is a remarkably powerful economic force. The ability to earn interest on interest is the key to building economic wealth. If you save $1,000 per year for the first 10 years of your career, you will have more money when you retire than you would if you saved $15,000 per year for the last 10 years of your career. This surprising outcome occurs because the money you save early in your career will be able to earn more interest than will the money you save at the end of your career. If you start saving money now, the majority of your wealth will not be the money you saved but the interest that the saved money was able to earn. The chart illustrates the power of compounding over a brief 10-year period. In this chart, we have assumed that you deposit $1 each year in an account earning 10 percent interest. At the end of just 10 years, only 64 percent of your balance is made up of money you have saved; the rest is interest you have earned. After 20 years, only 35 percent of your balance is from saved money. The lesson associated with compound interest is clear: even though it's hard to do, you should start saving money now.

**Effects of Compound Interest**

- Deposits
- Deposits with interest

### PRESENT VALUE OF AN ANNUITY (P)

The present value of an annuity is the value now of a series of equal amounts to be received (or paid out) each period for some specified number of periods in the future. It involves discounting each of the equal periodic amounts. A good example of this type of problem is a retirement program that offers the retiree a monthly income for a period of time.

To illustrate, assume that it is now January 1, 20A, and you are to receive $1,000 cash on each December 31, 20A, 20B, and 20C. How much would the sum of these three $1,000 future amounts be worth now, on January 1, 20A, assuming an interest rate of 10 percent per year? We could use Table A–2, Appendix A values to calculate the present value as follows:

| Year | Amount | | Value from Table A–2, Appendix A, $i = 10\%$ | | Present Value |
|------|--------|---|---------------------------------------------|---|---------------|
| 1 | $1,000 | × | 0.9091 ($n = 1$) | = | $ 909.10 |
| 2 | $1,000 | × | 0.8264 ($n = 2$) | = | 826.40 |
| 3 | $1,000 | × | 0.7513 ($n = 3$) | = | 751.30 |
| | | | Total present value | = | $2,486.80 |

The present value of this annuity can be more easily computed, however, by using one present value amount from Table A–4, Appendix A as follows:

$$\$1,000 \times P_{i=10\%,n=3} \text{ (Table A–4, Appendix A, 2.4869)} = \$2,487 \text{ (rounded)}$$

This concept is summarized in Exhibit 9.3.

**Interest Rates and Interest Periods**  Notice that the preceding illustrations assumed annual periods for compounding and discounting. Although interest rates almost always are quoted on an annual basis, most interest compounding periods encountered in business are less than one year (such as semiannually or quarterly). When interest periods are less than a year, the values of $n$ and $i$ must be restated to be consistent with the length of the interest period.

To illustrate, 12 percent interest compounded annually for five years requires use of $n = 5$ and $i = 12\%$. If compounding is quarterly, the interest period is one quarter of a year (i.e., four periods per year), and the quarterly interest rate is one quarter of the annual rate (i.e., 3 percent per quarter); therefore, 12 percent interest compounded quarterly for five years requires use of $n = 20$ and $i = 3\%$.

## A QUESTION OF **ETHICS**

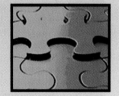

**TRUTH IN ADVERTISING**

A number of advertisements in newspapers, magazines, and on television easily can be misinterpreted if the consumer does not understand present value concepts. We discuss two examples.

Most car companies offer seasonal promotions with special financing incentives. A car dealer may advertise 4 percent interest on car loans when banks are charging 10 percent. Typically, the lower interest rate is not a special incentive because the dealer simply charges a higher price for cars that the dealership finances. It may be better to borrow from the bank and "pay cash" at the dealership to negotiate a lower price. Customers should use the present value concepts illustrated in this chapter to compare financing alternatives.

Another misleading advertisement is seen every January and promises a chance to become an instant millionaire. The fine print discloses that the winner will receive $25,000 for 40 years, which is $1,000,000 (40 × $25,000), but the present value of this annuity at 8 percent is only $298,000. Most winners are happy to get the money, but they are not really millionaires.

Some consumer advocates criticize businesses that use these types of advertisements. They argue that consumers should not have to study present value concepts to understand advertisements. Some of these criticisms may be valid, but the quality of information contained in advertisements that include interest rates has improved during the past few years.

## ACCOUNTING APPLICATIONS OF FUTURE AND PRESENT VALUES

■ **LEARNING OBJECTIVE 8**

Apply present value concepts to liabilities.

Many business transactions require the use of future and present value concepts. We illustrate two such cases so that you can test your understanding of these concepts:

**CASE A** On January 1, 20A, General Mills bought some new delivery trucks. The company signed a note and agreed to pay $200,000 for the trucks on December 31, 20B. The market interest rate for this note was 12 percent. The $200,000 represents the cash equivalent price of the trucks and the interest that will be earned for two years.

1. How should the accountant record the purchase?
*Answer:* This case requires application of the present value of a single amount. In conformity with the cost principle, the cost of the trucks is their current cash equivalent price, which is the present value of the future payment. The present value of the $200,000 is computed as follows:

$$\$200,000 \times P_{i=12\%,\, n=2} \text{ (Table A–2, Appendix A, 0.7972)} = \$159,440$$

Therefore, the journal entry is as follows:

| Delivery trucks (A) . . . . . . . . . . . . . . . . . . . . . . . . | 159,440 | |
| Note payable (L) . . . . . . . . . . . . . . . . . . . . . . | | 159,440 |

| Assets | = | Liabilities | + | Stockholders' Equity |
|---|---|---|---|---|
| Delivery trucks  +159,440 | | Note payable  +159,440 | | |

Some companies prefer to record the following journal entry:

| Delivery trucks (A) . . . . . . . . . . . . . . . . . . . . . . . . | 159,440 | |
| Discount on notes payable (XL) . . . . . . . . . . . . . | 40,560 | |
| Note payable (L) . . . . . . . . . . . . . . . . . . . . . . | | 200,000 |

| Assets | = | Liabilities | + | Stockholders' Equity |
|---|---|---|---|---|
| Delivery trucks  +159,440 | | Note payable  +200,000 | | |
| | | Discount  −40,560 | | |

The discount account is a contra-liability account that represents the interest that will accrue on the note over its life. This account will be used extensively in the next chapter during our discussion of bonds.

2. What journal entry should be made at the end of the first and second years for interest expense?
*Answer:* Each year's interest expense on the amount in the Note Payable account is recorded in an adjusting entry as follows:

| **Year 1** Interest expense (E) . . . . . . . . . . . . . . . . . . . . . . | 19,133* | |
| Note payable (L) . . . . . . . . . . . . . . . . . . . . . . | | 19,133 |
| (or Discount on note payable) | | |

*$159,440 × 12% = $19,133.

| Assets | = | Liabilities | | + | Stockholders' Equity | |
|---|---|---|---|---|---|---|
| | | Note payable | +19,133 | | Interest expense | −19,133 |

**Year 2** Interest expense (E) ..................... 21,429*
       Note payable (L) ...................... 21,429
           (or Discount on note payable)

*($159,440 + $19,133) × 12% = 21,429.

| Assets | = | Liabilities | | + | Stockholders' Equity | |
|---|---|---|---|---|---|---|
| | | Note payable | +21,429 | | Interest expense | −21,429 |

3. What journal entry should be made on December 31, 20B, to record the payment of the debt?
*Answer:* At this date the amount to be paid is the balance of Note Payable, which is the same as the maturity amount on the due date. The journal entry to record full payment of the debt follows:

Note payable (L) .......................... 200,000
    Cash (A) .............................. 200,000

| | Assets | = | Liabilities | | + | Stockholders' Equity |
|---|---|---|---|---|---|---|
| Cash | −200,000 | | Note payable | −200,000 | | |

**CASE B** On January 1, 20A, General Mills bought new printing equipment. The company elected to finance the purchase with a note payable to be paid off in three equal annual installments of $163,686. Each installment includes principal plus interest on the unpaid balance at 11 percent per year. The equal annual installments are due on December 31, 20A, 20B, and 20C.

1. What is the amount of the note?
*Answer:* The note is the present value of each installment payment, $i = 11\%$ and $n = 3$. This is an annuity because payment is made in three equal installments. The amount of the note is computed as follows:

$$\$163,686 \times P_{i=11\%,\, n=3} \text{ (Table A–4, Appendix A, 2.4437)} = \$400,000$$

The acquisition is recorded as follows:

Printing equipment (A) ..................... 400,000
    Note payable (L) ...................... 400,000

| Assets | | = | Liabilities | | + | Stockholders' Equity |
|---|---|---|---|---|---|---|
| Printing equipment | +400,000 | | Note payable | +400,000 | | |

2. What was the total amount of interest expense in dollars?
*Answer:*
$$\$163,686 \times 3 = \$491,058 - \$400,000 = \$91,058$$

3. What journal entry should be made at the end of each year to record the payment on this $400,000 note payable?
*Answer:*

Note payable (L) .......................... 119,686
Interest expense (E) ($400,000 × 11%) ........ 44,000
    Cash (A) .............................. 163,686

| | Assets | = | Liabilities | | + | Stockholders' Equity | |
|---|---|---|---|---|---|---|
| Cash | −163,686 | | Note payable | −119,686 | | Interest expense | −44,000 |

| | | |
|---|---|---|
| Note payable (L) .......................... | 132,851 | |
| Interest expense (E) | | |
| [($400,000 − $119,686) × 11%] ............. | 30,835 | |
| Cash (A) ............................... | | 163,686 |

| Assets | = | Liabilities | + | Stockholders' Equity |
|---|---|---|---|---|
| Cash    −163,686 | | Note payable    −132,851 | | Interest expense    −30,835 |

| | | |
|---|---|---|
| Note payable (L) .......................... | 147,463 | |
| Interest expense (E) ...................... | 16,223* | |
| Cash (A) ............................... | | 163,686 |

*Interest: ($400,000 − $119,686 − $132,851) × 11% = $16,223 (rounded to accommodate rounding errors).

| Assets | = | Liabilities | + | Stockholders' Equity |
|---|---|---|---|---|
| Cash    −163,686 | | Note payable    −147,463 | | Interest expense    −16,223 |

4. Prepare a debt payment schedule that shows the entry for each payment and the effect on interest expense and the unpaid amount of principal each period.

*Answer:*

**Debt Payment Schedule**

| Date | Cash Payment (Credit) | Interest Expense (Prior Balance × 11%) (Debit) | Principal Decrease (Debit) | Unpaid Principal |
|---|---|---|---|---|
| 1/1/A | | | | $400,000 |
| 12/31/A | $163,686 | $400,000 × 11% = $44,000 | $119,686[a] | 280,314[b] |
| 12/31/B | 163,686 | 280,314 × 11% = $30,835 | 132,851 | 147,463 |
| 12/31/C | 163,686 | 147,463 × 11% = $16,223* | 147,463 | 0 |
| Total | $491,058 | $91,058* | $400,000 | |

*To accommodate rounding error.
Computations:
[a]$163,686 − $44,000 = $119,686, etc.
[b]$400,000 − $119,686 = $280,314, etc.

Notice in the debt payment schedule that for each successive payment, an increasing amount is payment on principal and a decreasing amount is interest expense. This effect occurs because the interest each period is based on a lower amount of unpaid principal. When an annuity is involved, schedules such as this one often are a useful analytical tool.

In the next chapter, we will use the present value techniques that you have just learned. As you will see, present value concepts are needed to understand how bonds function in our economy.

## CHAPTER **TAKE-AWAYS**

1. **Define, measure, and report liabilities.   p. 488**
   Strictly speaking, accountants define liabilities as probable future sacrifices of economic benefits that arise from past transactions. They are classified on the balance sheet as either current or long-term. Current liabilities are short-term obligations that will be paid within the current operating cycle of the business or within one year of the balance sheet date, whichever is longer. Long-term liabilities are all obligations not classified as current.

2. **Use the current ratio.   p. 488**
   The current ratio is a comparison of current assets and current liabilities. Analysts use this ratio to assess the liquidity of a company.

3. **Analyze the accounts payable turnover ratio.   p. 490**
   This ratio is computed by dividing cost of goods sold by accounts payable. It shows how quickly management is paying its trade creditors and is considered to be a measure of liquidity.

4. **Determine the impact of changes in working capital on cash flows.   p. 496**
   Changes in working capital accounts affect cash flows from operating activities. Cash flows are increased by decreases in current assets (other than cash) or increases in current liabilities. Cash flows are decreased by increases in current assets (other than cash) or decreases in current liabilities.

5. **Apply deferred income tax allocation.   p. 500**
   Deferred tax assets or liabilities exist because of temporary (or timing) differences between the rules that govern financial statement preparation and the preparation of income tax returns. Tax expense reflects both the current obligation and the impact of any deferral.

6. **Report contingent liabilities.   p. 502**
   A contingent liability is a potential liability that has arisen as the result of a past event. Such liabilities are disclosed in a note if the obligation is reasonably possible.

7. **Apply the concepts of present and future values.   p. 504**
   These concepts are based on the time value of money. Simply stated, a dollar to be received in the future is worth less than a dollar available today (present value). Alternatively, a dollar invested today will grow to a larger amount in the future (future value). These concepts are applied either to a single payment or multiple payments called *annuities*. Either tables or calculators can be used to determine present and future values.

8. **Apply present value concepts to liabilities.   p. 510**
   Accountants use present value concepts to determine the reported amounts of liabilities. A liability involves the payment of some amount at a future date. The reported liability is not the amount of the future payment. Instead, the liability is reported at the amount of the present value of the future payment.

In this chapter, we focused on current liabilities and introduced you to present value concepts. In the next chapter, we will use present value concepts to measure long-term liabilities. We will also discuss long-term liabilities in the context of the capital structure of the company.

## Chapter Supplement A

### Federal Income Tax Concepts

A business may be organized as a sole proprietorship, partnership, or corporation. Sole proprietorships and partnerships are not required to pay federal income taxes, but their owners must report and pay taxes on their personal tax returns. Corporations, as separate legal entities, are required to pay income taxes.

Corporations must prepare a U.S. Corporate Tax Return (Form 1120), which lists revenue and expenses for the year. The amount of the tax payable is based on the taxable income reported on the tax return. As mentioned earlier, taxable income is usually different from the income reported on the income statement because the income statement is prepared in conformity with GAAP and the tax return is prepared in conformity with the Internal Revenue Code.

### CALCULATION OF TAXES PAYABLE

In most cases, a large corporation's tax obligation is determined by multiplying its taxable income by 35 percent. Rates are graduated, however, so that very small corporations pay lower rates than large corporations do. Exhibit 9.4 illustrates the calculation of taxes payable at various income levels.

Notice in Case C that a portion of the income is taxed at a rate that is actually higher than the maximum of 35 percent. The purpose of the 39 percent rate is to phase out the

EXHIBIT **9.4**

**Calculation of
Taxes Payable**

| Case A: Taxable Income | $ 90,000 |
| --- | --- |
| Computation | |
| 15% of first $50,000 | $ 7,500 |
| 25% of next $25,000 | 6,250 |
| 34% of $15,000 | 5,100 |
| Taxes payable | $ 18,850 |

| Case B: Taxable Income | $150,000 |
| --- | --- |
| Computation | |
| 15% of first $50,000 | $7,500 |
| 25% of next $25,000 | 6,250 |
| 34% of next $25,000 | 8,500 |
| 39% of $50,000 ($150,000 − $100,000) | 19,500 |
| Taxes payable | $ 41,750 |

| Case C: Taxable Income | $400,000 |
| --- | --- |
| Computation | |
| 15% of first $50,000 | $ 7,500 |
| 25% of next $25,000 | 6,250 |
| 34% of next $25,000 | 8,500 |
| 39% of next $235,000 | 91,650 |
| 34% of $65,000 ($400,000 − $335,000) | 22,100 |
| Taxes payable | $136,000 |

benefits of the lower rates that were intended to benefit only smaller corporations. The $136,000 taxes payable on taxable income of $400,000 is an effective tax rate of exactly 34 percent.

The 35 percent tax rate applies to taxable incomes higher than $10 million. A provision phases out the 34 percent tax rate for very large corporations. The tax rate from $15,000,000 to $18,333,333 is 38 percent. At higher incomes, the rate reverts to 35 percent. This results in an effective tax rate of 35 percent once a corporation earns more than $18,333,333.

## REVENUE AND EXPENSE RECOGNITION FOR INCOME TAX PURPOSES

Several differences between GAAP and the rules that govern the preparation of the federal income tax return exist. The following are common examples:

1. Interest revenue on state and municipal bonds is generally excluded from taxable income, although it is included in accounting income.

2. Revenue collected in advance (e.g., rent revenue) is included in taxable income when it is collected but it is included in accounting income when it is earned.

3. Proceeds from life insurance policies (e.g., key executive insurance) is excluded from taxable income but is included in accounting income.

4. Corporations that own less than 20 percent of another corporation's stock may exclude 70 percent of the dividends received from taxable income, although all the dividends are included in accounting income. The exclusion is 80 percent if the corporation owns more than 20 percent of the other corporation's stock.

5. Depreciation expense for tax purposes is generally based on the Accelerated Cost Recovery System (ACRS) if the assets were placed in service after 1980 but before 1987, or the Modified Accelerated Cost Recovery System (MACRS) if the assets were placed in service after 1986. These methods were discussed in Chapter 8.

## TAX MINIMIZATION VERSUS TAX EVASION

Most large corporations spend considerable time and money developing strategies that *minimize* the amount of federal income taxes that must be paid. Nothing is wrong with this approach because courts have stated that there is no legal obligation to pay more taxes than the law demands. Even if you do not major in accounting, you will probably want to take a course in federal income taxation because knowledge of the Internal Revenue Code is important for most executives. This knowledge offers opportunities to save significant amounts of money.

In contrast, tax evasion involves illegal means to avoid paying taxes that are due. Use of accelerated depreciation is an example of *tax minimization*; failure to report revenue that was collected in cash is an example of *tax evasion*. Efforts at tax minimization represent good business practice, but tax evasion is morally and legally wrong. Individuals who evade taxes run the risk of severe financial penalties and the possibility of being sent to jail.

## KEY **RATIOS**

**Current ratio** measures the ability of a company to pay its current obligations. It is computed as follows (p. 488):

$$\text{Current Ratio} = \frac{\text{Current Assets}}{\text{Current Liabilities}}$$

**Accounts payable turnover** is a measure of how quickly a company pays its creditors. It is computed as follows (p. 490):

$$\text{Accounts Payable Turnover} = \frac{\text{Costs of Goods Sold}}{\text{Average Accounts Payable}}$$

## FINDING FINANCIAL INFORMATION

### BALANCE SHEET

*Under Current Liabilities*
Liabilities listed by account title, such as
   Accounts payable
   Accrued liabilities
   Notes payable
   Current portion of long-term debt
*Under Noncurrent Liabilities*
Liabilities listed by account title, such as
   Long-term debt
   Deferred taxes
   Bonds

### INCOME STATEMENT

Liabilities are shown only on the balance sheet, never on the income statement. Transactions affecting liabilities often affect an income statement account. For example, accrued salary compensation affects an income statement account (compensation expense) and a balance sheet account (salaries payable).

### STATEMENT OF CASH FLOWS

*Under Operating Activities (indirect method)*
Net income
  + Increases in most current liabilities
  − Decreases in most current liabilities
*Under Financing Activities*
  + Increase in long-term liabilities
  − Decreases in long-term liabilities

### NOTES

*Under Summary of Significant Accounting Policies*
Description of pertinent information concerning accounting treatment of liabilities. Normally, there is minimal information.
*Under a Separate Note*
If not listed on the balance sheet, a listing of the major classifications of liabilities with information about maturities and interest rates. Information about contingent liabilities is reported in the notes.

## KEY **TERMS**

## QUESTIONS

1. Define *liability*. Differentiate between a current liability and a long-term liability.
2. How can external parties be informed about the liabilities of a business?
3. Liabilities are measured and reported at their current cash equivalent amount. Explain.
4. A *liability* is a known obligation of either a definite or an estimated amount. Explain.
5. Define *working capital*. How is it computed?
6. What is the current ratio? How is it related to the classification of liabilities?
7. Define *accrued liability*. What type of entry usually reflects an accrued liability?
8. Define *deferred revenue*. Why is it a liability?
9. Define *note payable*. Differentiate between a secured and an unsecured note.
10. Non-interest-bearing notes do not include an explicit interest rate. Differentiate between an interest-bearing note and a non-interest-bearing note.
11. Define *deferred income tax*. Explain why deferred income tax "reverses, or turns around," in subsequent periods.
12. What is a contingent liability? How is a contingent liability reported?
13. Compute 20A interest expense for the following note: face, $4,000; 12 percent interest; date of note, April 1, 20A.
14. Explain the time value of money.
15. Explain the basic difference between future value and present value.
16. If you deposited $10,000 in a savings account that earns 10 percent, how much would you have at the end of 10 years? Use a convenient format to display your computations.
17. If you hold a valid contract that will pay you $8,000 cash 10 years hence and the going rate of interest is 10 percent, what is its present value? Use a convenient format to display your computations.
18. What is an annuity?
19. Complete the following schedule:

| Table Values | | | | |
|---|---|---|---|---|
| Concept | Symbol | *n* = 4, *i* = 5% | *n* = 7, *i* = 10% | *n* = 10, *i* = 14% |
| FV of $1 | | | | |
| PV of $1 | | | | |
| FV of annuity of $1 | | | | |
| PV of annuity of $1 | | | | |

20. If you deposit $1,000 for each of 10 interest periods (ordinary annuity) that earns 8 percent interest, how much would you have at the end of period 10? Use a convenient format to display your computations.

21. You purchased an XIT auto for $18,000 by making a $3,000 cash payment and six semi-annual installment payments for the balance at 12 percent interest. Use a convenient format to display computation of the amount of each payment.

# MINI-EXERCISES

**M9–1  Computing Interest Expense**  ◼ LO1
Jacobs Company borrowed $500,000 on a 90-day note at 9 percent interest. The money was borrowed for 30 days in 20A and 60 days in 20B; the note and interest were to be paid upon maturity in 20B. How much interest expense, if any, would be reported in 20A and in 20B?

**M9–2  Recording a Note Payable**  ◼ LO1
Farmer Corporation borrowed $100,000 on November 1, 20A. The note carried a 12 percent interest rate with the principal and interest payable on June 1, 20B. Prepare the journal entry to record the note on November 1. Prepare the adjusting entry to record accrued interest on December 31.

**M9–3  Finding Financial Information**  ◼ LO1, 3, 4
For each of the following items, specify whether the information would be found in the balance sheet, the income statement, the statement of cash flows, the notes to the statements, or not at all.

1. The amount of working capital.

2. The total amount of current liabilities.

3. Information concerning company pension plans.

4. The accounts payable turnover ratio.

5. Information concerning the impact of changes in working capital on cash flows for the period.

**M9–4  Computing Measures of Liquidity**  ◼ LO2
The balance sheet for Shaver Corporation reported the following: total assets, $250,000; noncurrent assets, $150,000; current liabilities, $40,000; total stockholders' equity, $90,000. Compute Shaver's current ratio and working capital.

**M9–5  Analyzing the Impact of Transactions on Liquidity**  ◼ LO2
BSO, Inc., has a current ratio of 2.0 and working capital in the amount of $1,240,000. For each of the following transactions, determine whether the current ratio and working capital will increase, decrease, or remain the same.

*a.* Paid accounts payable in the amount of $50,000.

*b.* Recorded accrued salaries in the amount of $100,000.

*c.* Borrowed $250,000 from a local bank, to be repaid in 90 days.

*d.* Purchased $20,000 of new inventory on credit.

**M9–6  Reporting Contingent Liabilities**  ◼ LO6
Buzz Coffee Shops is famous for its large servings of hot coffee. After a famous case involving McDonald's, the lawyer for Buzz warned management (during 20A) that it could be sued if someone were to spill hot coffee and be burned; "With the temperature of your coffee, I can guarantee it's just a matter of time before you're sued for $1,000,000." Unfortunately, in 20C, the prediction came true when a customer filed suit. The case went to trial in 20D, and the jury awarded the customer $400,000 in damages, which the company immediately appealed. During 20E, the customer and the company settled their dispute for $150,000. What is the proper reporting of this liability each year?

**M9–7  Computing the Present Value of a Single Payment**  ◼ LO7
What is the present value of $500,000 to be paid in 10 years, with an interest rate of 8 percent?

**M9–8  Computing the Present Value of an Annuity**  ◼ LO7
What is the present value of 10 equal payments of $15,000, with an interest rate of 10 percent?

■ **LO7** **M9–9** **Computing the Present Value of a Complex Contract**
As a result of a slowdown in operations, Mercantile Stores is offering to employees who have been terminated a severance package of $100,000 cash; another $100,000 to be paid in one year; and an annuity of $30,000 to be paid each year for 20 years. What is the present value of the package, assuming an interest rate of 8 percent?

■ **LO7** **M9–10** **Computing the Future Value of an Annuity**
You plan to retire in 20 years. Is it better for you to save $25,000 a year for the last 10 years before retirement or $15,000 for each of the 20 years? You are able to earn 10 percent interest on your investments.

■ **LO7** **M9–11** **Making a Complex Computation of a Future Value**
You want a retirement fund of $500,000 when you retire in 20 years. You are able to earn 10 percent on your investments. How much should you deposit each year to build the retirement fund that you want?

## EXERCISES

■ **LO1, 2** **E9–1** **Computing Owners' Equity and Working Capital; Explaining the Current Ratio and Working Capital**

Flair Corporation is preparing its 20B balance sheet. The company records show the following related amounts at the end of the accounting period, December 31, 20B:

| | |
|---|---|
| Total current assets | $170,100 |
| Total all remaining assets | 525,000 |
| Liabilities: | |
| Notes payable (8%, due in 5 years) | 18,000 |
| Accounts payable | 60,000 |
| Income taxes payable | 12,000 |
| Liability for withholding taxes | 3,000 |
| Rent revenue collected in advance | 4,000 |
| Bonds payable (due in 15 years) | 100,000 |
| Wages payable | 7,800 |
| Property taxes payable | 2,000 |
| Note payable (10%; due in 6 months) | 10,000 |
| Interest payable | 400 |

⟩695100

217,200

*Required:*

1. Compute total owners' equity.

2. Compute (a) working capital and (b) the current ratio (show computations). Why is working capital important to management? How do financial analysts use the current ratio?

3. Compute the amount of interest expense for 20B on the long-term note. Assume that it was dated October 1, 20B.

■ **LO1, 4** **E9–2** **Recording a Note Payable through Its Time to Maturity with Discussion of Management Strategy**

Dayton Hudson

Many businesses borrow money during periods of increased business activity to finance inventory and accounts receivable. Dayton Hudson is one of America's largest general merchandise retailers. Each Christmas, Dayton Hudson builds up its inventory to meet the needs of Christmas shoppers. A large portion of Christmas sales are on credit. As a result, Dayton Hudson often collects cash from the sales several months after Christmas. Assume that on November 1, 20A, Dayton Hudson borrowed $4.5 million cash from Metropolitan Bank for working capital purposes and signed an interest-bearing note due in six months. The interest rate was 10 percent per annum payable at maturity. The accounting period ends December 31.

*Required:*

1. Give the journal entry to record the note on November 1.

2. Give any adjusting entry required at the end of the annual accounting period.

3. Give the journal entry to record payment of the note and interest on the maturity date, April 30, 20B.

4. If Dayton Hudson needs extra cash during every Christmas season, should management borrow money on a long-term basis to avoid the necessity of negotiating a new short-term loan each year?

**E9–3 Determining Financial Statement Effects of Transactions Involving Notes Payable**    ■ **LO1, 4**
Using the data from the previous exercise, complete the following requirements.

Dayton Hudson

*Required:*

1. Determine the financial statement effects for each of the following: (a) issuance of the note on November 1, (b) impact of the adjusting entry at the end of the accounting period, and (c ) the payment of the note and interest on April 30, 20B. Indicate the effects (e.g., cash + or −), using the following schedule:

| Date | Assets | Liabilities | Stockholders' Equity |
|------|--------|-------------|----------------------|
|      |        |             |                      |

2. If Dayton Hudson needs extra cash every Christmas season, should management borrow money on a long-term basis to avoid negotiating a new short-term loan each year?

**E9–4 Recording Payroll Costs with Discussion**    ■ **LO1**
McLoyd Company completed the salary and wage payroll for March 20A. The payroll provided the following details:

| | |
|---|---|
| Salaries and wages earned | $230,000 |
| Employee income taxes withheld | 46,000 |
| Union dues withheld | 3,000 |
| Insurance premiums withheld | 1,200 |
| FICA taxes* | 16,445 |
| FUTA taxes† | 1,610 |
| State unemployment taxes | 6,210 |

*$16,445 each for employer and employees.
†Federal unemployment taxes.

*Required:*

1. Give the journal entry to record the payroll for March, including employee deductions.

2. Give the journal entry to record the employer's payroll taxes.

3. Give a combined journal entry to show the payment of amounts owed to governmental agencies and other organizations.

4. What was the total labor cost for the company? Explain. What percentage of the payroll was take-home pay? From the employers' perspective, does an economic difference between the cost of salaries and the cost of fringe benefits exist? From the employees' perspective, does a difference exist?

**E9–5 Computing Payroll Costs; Discussion of Labor Costs**    ■ **LO1**
Town Lake Company has completed the payroll for January 20B, reflecting the following data:

| | |
|---|---|
| Salaries and wages earned | $82,000 |
| Employee income taxes withheld | 9,500 |
| Union dues withheld | 1,200 |
| FICA payroll taxes* | 6,013 |
| FUTA payroll taxes† | 589 |
| State unemployment taxes | 2,270 |

*Assessed on both employer and employee (i.e., $6,013 each).
†Unemployment taxes.

*Required:*

1. What amount of additional labor expense to the company was due to tax laws? What was the amount of the employees' take-home pay?

2. List the liabilities and their amounts that are reported on the company's January 31, 20B, balance sheet.

3. Would employers react differently to a 10 percent increase in the employer's share of FICA than to a 10 percent increase in the basic level of salaries? Would financial analysts react differently?

■ **LO1, 2**     **E9–6**

**Determining the Impact of Transaction, Including Analysis of Cash Flows**

Bryant Company sells a wide range of goods through two retail stores operated in adjoining cities. Most purchases of goods for resale are on invoices. Occasionally, a short-term note payable is used to obtain cash for current use. The following transactions were selected from those occurring during 20B:

*a.* On January 10, 20B, purchased merchandise on credit, $18,000; the company uses a periodic inventory system.

*b.* On March 1, 20B, borrowed $40,000 cash from City Bank and gave an interest-bearing note payable: face amount, $40,000, due at the end of six months, with an annual interest rate of 8 percent payable at maturity.

*Required:*

1. Describe the impact of each transaction on the balance sheet equation. Indicate the effects (e.g., cash + or −), using the following schedule:

| Date | Assets | Liabilities | Stockholders' Equity |
| --- | --- | --- | --- |

2. What amount of cash is paid on the maturity date of the note?

3. Discuss the impact of each transaction on Bryant's cash flows.

4. Discuss the impact of each transaction on the current ratio.

■ **LO1, 4, 5, 6**     **E9–7**

Ford Motor Company

**Reporting a Liability, with Discussion**

The annual report for Ford Motor Company contained the following information:

**Postretirement Health Care and Life Insurance Benefits**

The company and certain of its subsidiaries sponsor unfunded plans to provide selected health care and life insurance benefits for retired employees. The company's employees may become eligible for those benefits if they retire while working for the company. However, benefits and eligibility rules may be modified from time to time.

*Required:*

Should Ford report a liability for these benefits on its balance sheet? Explain.

■ **LO1, 4, 5, 6**     **E9–8**

American Eagle Outfitters versus Urban Outfitters

**Finding Financial Information**

Using the financial statements for American Eagle Outfitters in Appendix B and Urban Outfitters in Appendix C at the end of the book, answer the following questions. Use data for the most recent year unless instructed otherwise.

*Required:*

1. What is the amount of working capital for each company?

2. Can you determine the amount of accrued sales taxes payable for either company?

3. What amount of deferred tax liability does each company report?

4. What is the amount of long-term debt reported by each company?

5. Do the companies have any contingent liabilities?

6. Each company experienced an increase in accounts receivable during the year. Did these changes affect cash flows from operating activities? If so, how?

**E9–9** **Computing Deferred Income Tax: One Temporary Difference, with Discussion**  █ **LO5**

The comparative income statements of Martin Corporation at December 31, 20B, showed the following summarized pretax data:

|  | Year 20A | Year 20B |
|---|---|---|
| Sales revenue | $65,000 | $72,000 |
| Expenses (excluding income tax) | 50,000 | 54,000 |
| Pretax income | $15,000 | $18,000 |

Included in the 20B data is a $2,800 expense that was deductible only in the 20A income tax return (rather than in 20B). The average income tax rate was 30 percent. Taxable income from the income tax returns was 20A, $14,000, and 20B, $17,400.

*Required:*

1. For each year compute (a) income taxes payable and (b) deferred income tax. Is the deferred income tax a liability or an asset? Explain.

2. Show what amounts related to income taxes should be reported each year on the income statement and balance sheet. Assume that income tax is paid on April 15 of the next year.

3. Explain why tax expense is not simply the amount of cash paid during the year.

**E9–10** **Recording Deferred Income Tax: One Temporary Difference; Discussion of Management Strategy**  █ **LO5**

The comparative income statement for Chung Corporation at the end of December 31, 20B, provided the following summarized pretax data:

|  | Year 20A | Year 20B |
|---|---|---|
| Revenue | $80,000 | $88,000 |
| Expenses (excluding income tax) | 65,000 | 69,000 |
| Pretax income | $15,000 | $19,000 |

Included in the data is a $5,000 revenue that was taxable only in the 20A income tax return. The average income tax rate was 32 percent. Taxable income shown in the tax returns was 20A, $13,000, and 20B, $18,500.

*Required:*

1. For each year compute (a) income taxes payable and (b) deferred income tax. Is the deferred income tax a liability or an asset? Explain.

2. Give the journal entry for each year to record income taxes payable, deferred income tax, and income tax expense.

3. Show what amounts related to income taxes should be reported each year on the income statement and balance sheet. Assume that income tax is paid on April 15 of the next year.

4. Why would management want to incur the cost of maintaining separate tax and financial accounting records to defer the payment of taxes?

**E9–11** **Computing and Reporting Deferred Income Tax: Depreciation**  █ **LO5**

Amber Corporation reported the following summarized pretax data at the end of each year:

| Income Statement at December 31 | 20A | 20B | 20C |
|---|---|---|---|
| Revenues | $170,000 | $182,000 | $195,000 |
| Expenses (including depreciation)* | 122,000 | 126,000 | 130,000 |
| Pretax income | $ 48,000 | $ 56,000 | $ 65,000 |

*Depreciation expense on the income statement on a machine purchased January 1, 20A, for $75,000 was straight line. The machine has a three-year estimated life and no residual value. The company used accelerated depreciation on the income tax return as follows: 20A, $37,500; 20B, $25,000; and 20C, $12,500. The average income tax rate is 28 percent for the three years.

Taxable income from the income tax return was as follows: 20A, $32,000; 20B, $56,000; and 20C, $85,000.

*Required:*

1. For each year compute (a) income taxes payable and (b) deferred income tax. Is the deferred income tax a liability or an asset? Explain.

2. Show what amounts related to income taxes should be reported each year on the income statement and balance sheet.

**■ LO5**

Colgate-Palmolive

**E9–12** **Reporting Deferred Taxes**

The annual report for Colgate-Palmolive contains the following information (in millions):

**Income Taxes**

Differences between accounting for financial statement purposes and accounting for tax purposes result in taxes currently payable (lower) higher than the total provision for income taxes as follows:

|  | 1999 | 1998 | 1997 |
|---|---|---|---|
| Excess tax over book depreciation | $(18.0) | $(19.8) | $(18.9) |
| Other | (31.4) | 76.6 | (25.5) |
| Total | $(49.4) | $56.8 | $(44.4) |

*Required:*

1. Determine whether tax expense is higher or lower than taxes payable for each year.

2. Explain the most likely reason for tax depreciation to be higher than book depreciation.

3. Is the deferred tax liability reported on the 1999 balance sheet $49.4 million? Explain.

**■ LO6**

Carnival Cruise Lines

**E9–13** **Reporting a Liability**

Carnival Cruise Lines provides exotic vacations on board luxurious passenger ships. In 1998, the company moved its offices and included the following note in its current annual report:

**Leases**

On March 27, 1998, the Company entered into a ten-year lease for 230,000 square feet of office space located in Miami, Florida. The Company moved its operation to this location in October 1998. The total rent payable over the ten-year term of the lease is approximately $24 million.

*Required:*

Based on these facts, do you think the company should report this obligation on its balance sheet? Explain. If the obligation should be reported as a liability, how should the amount be measured?

**■ LO7**

**E9–14** **Computing Four Kinds of Present and Future Values**

On January 1, 20A, Wesley Company completed the following transactions (assume an 11 percent annual interest rate):

*a.* Deposited $12,000 in Fund A.

*b.* Established Fund B by agreeing to make six annual deposits of $2,000 each. Deposits are made each December 31.

*c.* Established Fund C by depositing a single amount that will increase to $40,000 by the end of year 7.

*d.* Decided to deposit a single sum in Fund D that will provide 10 equal annual year-end payments of $15,000 to a retired employee (payments starting December 31, 20A).

*Required (show computations and round to the nearest dollar):*

1. What will be the balance of Fund A at the end of year 9?
2. What will be the balance of Fund B at the end of year 6?
3. What single amount must be deposited in Fund C on January 1, 20A?
4. What single sum must be deposited in Fund D on January 1, 20A?

**E9–15 Computing Growth in a Savings Account: A Single Amount**  ■ **LO7**

On January 1, 20A, you deposited $6,000 in a savings account. The account will earn 10 percent annual compound interest, which will be added to the fund balance at the end of each year.

*Required (round to the nearest dollar):*

1. What will be the balance in the savings account at the end of 10 years?
2. What is the interest for the 10 years?
3. How much interest revenue did the fund earn in 20A? 20B?

**E9–16 Computing Deposit Required and Accounting for a Single-Sum Savings Account**  ■ **LO7**

On January 1, 20A, Alan King decided to deposit an amount in a savings account that will provide $80,000 four years later to send his son to college. The savings account will earn 8 percent, which will be added to the fund each year-end.

*Required (show computations and round to the nearest dollar):*

1. How much must Alan deposit on January 1, 20A?
2. Give the journal entry that Alan should make on January 1, 20A.
3. What is the interest for the four years?
4. Give the journal entry that Alan should make on (a) December 31, 20A, and (b) December 31, 20B.

**E9–17 Recording Growth in a Savings Account with Equal Periodic Payments**  ■ **LO7**

On each December 31, you plan to deposit $2,000 in a savings account. The account will earn 9 percent annual interest, which will be added to the fund balance at year-end. The first deposit will be made December 31, 20A (end of period).

*Required (show computations and round to the nearest dollar):*

1. Give the required journal entry on December 31, 20A.
2. What will be the balance in the savings account at the end of the 10th year (i.e., 10 deposits)?
3. What is the interest earned on the 10 deposits?
4. How much interest revenue did the fund earn in 20B? 20C?
5. Give all required journal entries at the end of 20B and 20C.

**E9–18 Computing Growth for a Savings Fund with Periodic Deposits**  ■ **LO7**

On January 1, 20A, you plan to take a trip around the world upon graduation four years from now. Your grandmother wants to deposit sufficient funds for this trip in a savings account for you. On the basis of a budget, you estimate that the trip currently would cost $15,000. To be generous, your grandmother decided to deposit $3,500 in the fund at the end of each of the next four years, starting on December 31, 20A. The savings account will earn 6 percent annual interest, which will be added to the savings account at each year-end.

*Required (show computations and round to the nearest dollar):*

1. How much money will you have for the trip at the end of year 4 (i.e., after four deposits)?
2. What is the interest for the four years?
3. How much interest revenue did the fund earn in 20A, 20B, 20C, and 20D?

**E9–19 Computing Value of an Asset Based on Present Value**  ■ **LO7**

You have the chance to purchase the royalty interest in an oil well. Your best estimate is that the net royalty income will average $25,000 per year for five years. There will be no residual value at that time. Assume that the cash inflow is at each year-end and that considering the uncertainty in your estimates, you expect to earn 15 percent per year on the investment. What should you be willing to pay for this investment on January 1, 20A?

# PROBLEMS

**LO1, 2, 4** **P9–1**

**Recording and Reporting Current Liabilities with Discussion of Cash Flow Effects**

Curb Company completed the following transactions during 20B. The annual accounting period ends December 31, 20B. **(AP9–1)**

| | | |
|---|---|---|
| Jan. | 8 | Purchased merchandise for resale at an invoice cost of $13,580; assume a periodic inventory system. |
| | 17 | Paid January 8 invoice. |
| Apr. | 1 | Borrowed $40,000 from National Bank for general use; executed a 12-month, 12 percent interest-bearing note payable. |
| June | 3 | Purchased merchandise for resale at an invoice cost of $17,820. |
| July | 5 | Paid June 3 invoice. |
| Aug. | 1 | Rented a small office in a building owned by the company and collected six months' rent in advance amounting to $5,100. (Record the collection in a way that will not require an adjusting entry at year-end.) |
| Dec. | 20 | Received a $100 deposit from a customer as a guarantee to return a large trailer "borrowed" for 30 days. |
| | 31 | Determined wages of $6,500 earned but not yet paid on December 31 (disregard payroll taxes). |

*Required:*

1. Prepare journal entries for each of these transactions.

2. Prepare all adjusting entries required on December 31, 20B.

3. Show how all of the liabilities arising from these transactions are reported on the balance sheet at December 31, 20B.

4. For each transaction, state whether the current ratio is increased, decreased, or remains the same.

5. For each transaction, state whether cash flow from operating activities is increased, decreased, or there is no effect.

**LO1, 2, 4** **P9–2**

**Determining Financial Effects of Transactions Affecting Current Liabilities with Discussion of Cash Flow Effects (AP9–2)**

Using data from the previous problem, complete the following requirements.

*Required:*

1. For each transaction (including adjusting entries) listed in the previous problem, indicate the effects (e.g., cash + or −), using the following schedule:

| Date | Assets | Liabilities | Stockholders' Equity |
|---|---|---|---|
| | | | |

2. For each transaction, state whether cash flow from operating activities is increased, decreased, or there is no effect.

3. For each transaction, state whether the current ratio is increased, decreased, or there is no change.

**LO1** **P9–3**

**Recording and Reporting Accrued Liabilities and Deferred Revenue, with Discussion**

During 20B, Riverside Company completed the following two transactions. The annual accounting period ends December 31.

*a.* Paid and recorded wages of $130,000 during 20B; however, at the end of December 20B, three days' wages are unpaid and unrecorded because the weekly payroll will not be paid until January 6, 20C. Wages for the three days are $3,600.

*b.* Collected rent revenue on December 10, 20B, of $2,400 for office space that Riverside rented to another party. The rent collected was for 30 days from December 10, 20B, to January 10, 20C, and was credited in full to Rent Revenue.

*Required:*

1. Give (a) the adjusting entry required on December 31, 20B, and (b) the January 6, 20C, journal entry for payment of any unpaid wages from December 20B.

2. Give (a) the journal entry for the collection of rent on December 10, 20B, and (b) the adjusting entry on December 31, 20B.

3. Show how any liabilities related to these transactions should be reported on the company's balance sheet at December 31, 20B.

4. Explain why the accrual method of accounting provides more relevant information to financial analysts than the cash method.

**P9–4 Determining Financial Statement Effects of Transactions Involving Accrued Liabilities and Deferred Revenue**

■ **LO1**

Using the data from the previous exercise, complete the following requirements.

*Required:*

1. Determine the financial statement effects for each of the following: (a) the adjusting entry required on December 31, 20B, (b) the January 6, 20C, journal entry for payment of any unpaid wages from December 20B, (c) the journal entry for the collection of rent on December 10, 20B, and (d) the adjusting entry on December 31, 20B. Indicate the effects (e.g., cash + or −), using the following schedule:

| Date | Assets | Liabilities | Stockholders' Equity |
|------|--------|-------------|----------------------|
|      |        |             |                      |

2. Explain why the accrual method of accounting provides more relevant information to financial analysts than the cash method.

**P9–5 Determining Financial Statement Effects of Various Liabilities** (AP9–3)

■ **LO1, 6**

Polaroid designs, manufactures, and markets products primarily in instant image recording. Its annual report contained the following note:

Polaroid

> **Product Warranty**
>
> Estimated product warranty costs are accrued at the time products are sold.

1. Assume that estimated warranty costs for 20A were $2 million and that the warranty work was performed during 20B. Describe the financial statement effects for each year.

Reader's Digest Association is a publisher of magazines, books, and music collections. The following note is from its annual report:

Reader's Digest
Association

> **Revenues**
>
> Sales of subscriptions to magazines are recorded as unearned revenue at the time the order is received. Proportional shares of the subscription price are recognized as revenues when the subscription is fulfilled.

2. Assume that Reader's Digest collected $10 million in 20A for magazines that will be delivered in future years. During 20B, the company delivered $8 million worth of magazines on those subscriptions. Describe the financial statement effects for each year.

Brunswick Corporation is a multinational company that manufactures and sells marine and recreational products. Its annual report contained the following information:

Brunswick
Corporation

> **Litigation**
>
> A jury awarded $44.4 million in damages in a suit brought by Independent Boat Builders, Inc., a buying group of boat manufacturers and its 22 members. Under the antitrust laws, the damage award has been trebled, and the plaintiffs will be entitled to their attorney's fees and interest.
>
> The Company has filed an appeal contending the verdict was erroneous as a matter of law, both as to liability and damages.

3. How should Brunswick account for this litigation?

The Coca-Cola Company

4. A recent annual report for The Coca-Cola Company reported current assets of $4,247,677 and current liabilities of $5,303,222. Based on the current ratio, do you think that Coca-Cola is experiencing financial difficulty?

Alcoa is involved in the mining and manufacturing of aluminum. Its products can become an advanced alloy for the wing of a Boeing 777 or a common recyclable Coca-Cola can. The annual report for Alcoa stated the following:

Alcoa

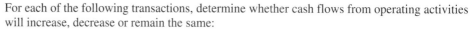

**Environmental Expenditures**

Liabilities are recorded when remedial efforts are probable and the costs can be reasonably estimated.

5. In your own words, explain Alcoa's accounting policy for environmental expenditures. What is the justification for this policy?

**LO4**    **P9–6**    **Determining Cash Flow Effects** (AP9–4)

For each of the following transactions, determine whether cash flows from operating activities will increase, decrease or remain the same:

a. Purchased merchandise on credit.

b. Paid an account payable in cash.

c. Accrued payroll for the month but did not pay it.

d. Borrowed money from the bank. The term of the note is 90 days.

e. Reclassified a long-term note as a current liability.

f. Paid accrued interest expense.

g. Recorded a contingent liability based on a pending lawsuit.

h. Paid back the bank for money borrowed in d.

i. Collected cash from a customer for services that will be performed in the next accounting period (i.e., deferred revenues are recorded).

**LO5**    **P9–7**    **Recording and Reporting Deferred Income Tax: Depreciation** (AP9–5)

At December 31, 20A, the records of Pearson Corporation provided the following information:

| Income statement | |
| --- | --- |
| Revenues | $160,000* |
| Depreciation expense (straight line) | (11,000)† |
| Remaining expenses (excluding income tax) | (90,000) |
| Pretax income | $ 59,000 |

*These revenues include $20,000 interest on tax-free municipal bonds.
†Equipment depreciated—acquired January 1, 20A, cost $44,000; estimated useful life, four years and no residual value. Accelerated depreciation is used on the tax return as follows: 20A, $17,600; 20B, $13,200; 20C, $8,800; and 20D, $4,400.

a. Income tax rate, 30 percent. Assume that 85 percent is paid in the year incurred.

b. Taxable income from the 20A income tax return, $80,000.

*Required:*

1. Compute income taxes payable and deferred income tax for 20A. Is the deferred income tax a liability or an asset? Explain.

2. Give the journal entry to record income taxes for 20A.

3. Show what amounts related to 20A income taxes should be reported on the income statement and balance sheet.

**LO7**    **P9–8**    **Computing Present and Future Values** (AP9–6)

On January 1, 20A, Plymouth Company completed the following transactions (use an 8 percent annual interest rate for all transactions):

*a.* Deposited $50,000 in a debt retirement fund. Interest will be computed at six-month intervals and added to the fund at those times (i.e., semiannual compounding). (*Hint*: Think carefully about *n* and *i*.)

*b.* Established a plant addition fund of $400,000 to be available at the end of year 5. A single sum that will grow to $400,000 will be deposited on January 1, 20A.

*c.* Established a pension retirement fund of $500,000 to be available by the end of year 6 by making six equal annual deposits each at year-end, starting on December 31, 20A.

*d.* Purchased a $180,000 machine on January 1, 20A, and paid cash, $60,000. A four-year note *payable* is signed for the balance. The note will be paid in four equal year-end payments starting on December 31, 20A.

**Required (show computations and round to the nearest dollar):**

1. In transaction *a*, what will be the balance in the fund at the end of year 4? What is the total amount of interest revenue that will be earned?

2. In transaction *b*, what single sum amount must the company deposit on January 1, 20A? What is the total amount of interest revenue that will be earned?

3. In transaction *c*, what is the required amount of each of the six equal annual deposits? What is the total amount of interest revenue that will be earned?

4. In transaction *d*, what is the amount of each of the equal annual payments that will be paid on the note? What is the total amount of interest expense that will be incurred?

**P9–9    Comparing Options Using Present Value Concepts** (AP9–7)                    ■ **LO7**
After hearing a knock at your front door, you are surprised to see the Prize Patrol from a large, well-known magazine subscription company. It has arrived with the good news that you are the big winner, having won $20 million. Later, after consulting with a lawyer, you discover that you have three options: (1) you can receive $1 million per year for the next 20 years, (2) you can have $8 million today, or (3) you can have $2 million today and receive $700,000 for each of the next 20 years. Your lawyer tells you that it is reasonable to expect to earn 10 percent on investments. Which option do you prefer? What factors influence your decision?

**P9–10    Computing Amounts for a Debt Fund with Journal Entries** (AP9–8)            ■ **LO8**
On December 31, 20A, Post Company set aside in a fund the cash to pay the principal amount of a $140,000 debt due on December 31, 20D. The company will make four equal annual deposits on each December 31 in 20A, 20B, 20C, and 20D. The fund will earn 7 percent annual interest, which will be added to the balance at each year-end. The fund trustee will pay the loan principal (to the creditor) upon receipt of the last fund deposit. The company's accounting period ends December 31.

**Required (show computations and round to the nearest dollar):**

1. How much must be deposited each December 31?

2. What amount of interest will be earned?

3. How much interest revenue will the fund earn in 20A, 20B, 20C, and 20D?

4. Give journal entries for the company on the following dates:

   *a.* For the first deposit on December 31, 20A.

   *b.* For all amounts at the end of 20B and 20C.

   *c.* For payment of the debt on December 31, 20D.

5. Show how the effect of the fund will be reported on the December 31, 20B, income statement and balance sheet.

**P9–11    Computing Equal Periodic Debt Payments and Completing a Schedule** (AP9–9)    ■ **LO8**
On January 1, 20A, you bought a new ZS238 automobile for $22,000. You made a $5,000 cash down payment and signed a $17,000 note, payable in four equal installments on each December 31, the first payment to be made on December 31, 20A. The interest rate is 12 percent per year on the unpaid balance. Each payment will include payment on principal plus the interest.

**Required:**

1. Compute the amount of the equal payments that you must make.

2. What is the interest on the installment debt during the four years?

3. Complete a schedule using the following format:

| Debt Payment Schedule | | | | |
| --- | --- | --- | --- | --- |
| Date | Cash Payment | Interest Expense | Decrease Principal | Unpaid Principal |
| 1/1/20A | | | | |
| 12/31/20A | | | | |
| 12/31/20B | | | | |
| 12/31/20C | | | | |
| 12/31/20D | | | | |
| Totals | | | | |

4. Explain why the amount of interest expense decreases each year.

# ALTERNATE PROBLEMS

■ **LO1, 4**    **AP9–1**

**Recording and Reporting Current Liabilities with Discussion of Cash Flow Effects** (P9–1)

Curb Company completed the following transactions during 20B. The annual accounting period ends December 31, 20B.

Jan.  15   Recorded tax expense for the year in the amount of $125,000. Current taxes payable were $93,000.

31   Paid accrued interest expense in the amount of $52,000.

Apr.  30   Borrowed $550,000 from Commerce Bank; executed a 12-month, 12 percent interest-bearing note payable.

June   3   Purchased merchandise for resale at an invoice cost of $75,820.

July    5   Paid June 3 invoice.

Aug.  31   Signed contract to provide security service to a small apartment complex and collected six months' fees in advance amounting to $12,000. (Record the collection in a way that will not require an adjusting entry at year-end.)

Dec.  31   Reclassified a long-term liability in the amount of $100,000 to a current liability classification.

31   Determined salary and wages of $85,000 earned but not yet paid on December 31 (disregard payroll taxes).

*Required:*

1. Prepare journal entries for each of these transactions.

2. Prepare all adjusting entries required on December 31, 20B.

3. Show how all of the liabilities arising from these transactions are reported on the balance sheet at December 31, 20B.

4. For each transaction, state whether cash flow from operating activities is increased, decreased, or there is no effect.

■ **LO1, 4**    **AP9–2**

**Determining Financial Effects of Transactions Affecting Current Liabilities with Discussion of Cash Flow Effects** (P9–2)

Using data from the previous problem, complete the following requirements.

*Required:*

1. For each transaction (including adjusting entries) listed in the previous problem, indicate the effects (e.g., cash + or −), using the following schedule:

| Date | Assets | Liabilities | Stockholders' Equity |
| --- | --- | --- | --- |

2. For each transaction, state whether cash flow from operating activities is increased, decreased, or there is no effect.

**AP9–3** **Determining Financial Statement Effects of Various Liabilities** (P9–5)

**LO1, 6**

Pulte Corporation is a national builder of homes, doing more than $2 billion in business each year. Its annual report contained the following note:

Pulte

> **Allowance for Warranties**
>
> Home purchasers are provided with warranties against certain building defects. Estimated warranty cost is provided in the period in which the sales is recorded.

1. Assume that estimated warranty costs for 20D were $8.5 million and that the warranty work was performed during 20E. Describe the financial statement effects for each year.

Carnival Cruise Lines operates cruise ships in Alaska, the Caribbean, the South Pacific, and the Mediterranean. Some cruises are brief; others can last for several weeks. The company does more than $1 billion in cruise business each year. The following note is from its annual report:

Carnival Cruise Lines

> **Revenues**
>
> Customer cruise deposits, which represent unearned revenue, are included in the balance sheet when received and are recognized as cruise revenue upon completion of voyages of duration of 10 days or less and on a pro rata basis computed using the number of days completed for voyages in excess of 10 days.

2. In your own words, explain how unearned revenue is reported in the balance sheet for Carnival. Assume that Carnival collected $19 million in 20A for cruises that will be completed in the following year. Of that amount, $4 million was related to cruises of 10 or fewer days that were not complete; $8 million to cruises more than 10 days that, on average were 60 percent complete; and $7 million was related to cruises that had not yet begun. What is the amount of unearned revenue that should be reported on the 20A balance sheet?

Sunbeam Corporation is a consumer products company that manufactures and markets a number of familiar brands including Mr. Coffee, Osterizer, First Alert, and Coleman. Annual revenues for the company exceed $2 billion. Its annual report contained the following information:

Sunbeam

> **Litigation**
>
> The Company and its subsidiaries are involved in various lawsuits arising from time to time that the Company considers to be ordinary routine litigation incidental to its business. In the opinion of the Company, the resolution of these routine matters will not have a material adverse effect upon the financial position, results of operations, or cash flows of the Company. At the end of the current year, the Company had established accruals for litigation matters of $31.2 million.
>
> In 1996, the Company recorded a $12.0 million charge related to a case for which an adverse development arose. In the fourth quarter of this year, the case was favorably resolved and, as a result, $8.1 million of the charge was reversed into income.

3. Explain the meaning of this note in your own words. Describe how litigation has affected the financial statements for Sunbeam.

4. A recent annual report for Exxon reported a current ratio of 0.90. For the previous year, the ratio was 1.08. Based on this information, do you think that Exxon is experiencing financial difficulty? What other information would you want to consider in making this evaluation?

Exxon

Brunswick Corporation is a multinational company that manufactures and sells marine and recreational products. Its annual report contained the following information:

Brunswick

> **Legal and Environmental**
>
> The company is involved in numerous environmental remediation and clean-up projects with an aggregate estimated exposure of approximately $21 million to $42 million. The Company accrues for environmental remediation-related activities for which commitments or clean-up plans have been developed and for which costs can be reasonably estimated.

5. In your own words, explain Brunswick's accounting policy for environmental expenditures. What is the justification for this policy?

**LO4**

**AP9–4    Determining Cash Flow Effects** (P9–6)

For each of the following transactions, determine whether cash flows from operating activities will increase, decrease, or remain the same:

*a.* Purchased merchandise for cash.

*b.* Paid salaries and wages for the last month of the previous accounting period.

*c.* Paid taxes to the federal government.

*d.* Borrowed money from the bank. The term of the note is two years.

*e.* Withheld FICA taxes from employees' paychecks and immediately paid to the government.

*f.* Recorded accrued interest expense.

*g.* Paid cash as the result of losing a lawsuit. A contingent liability associated with the liability had been recorded.

*h.* Paid salaries and wages for the current month in cash.

*i.* Performed services for a customer who had paid for them in the previous accounting period (i.e., deferred revenue is earned).

**LO5**

**AP9–5    Recording and Reporting Deferred Income Tax: Two Temporary Differences** (P9–7)

The records of Calib Corporation provided the following summarized data for 20D and 20E:

| **Year-End December 31** | | |
|---|---|---|
| | **20D** | **20E** |
| Income statement | | |
| Revenues | $210,000 | $218,000 |
| Expenses (excluding income tax) | 130,000 | 133,000 |
| Pretax income | $ 80,000 | $ 85,000 |

*a.* Income tax rate, 32 percent. Assume that income taxes payable are paid 80 percent in the current year and 20 percent on April 15 of the next year.

*b.* Temporary differences:

(1) The 20E expenses include an $8,000 expense that must be deducted only in the 20D tax return.

(2) 20E revenues include a $6,000 revenue that was taxable only in 20F.

*c.* Taxable income shown in the tax returns was 20D, $82,000, and 20E, $85,000.

*Required:*

1. For each year compute (a) income taxes payable and (b) deferred income tax. Is each deferred income tax a liability or an asset? Explain.

2. Give the journal entry for each year to record income taxes payable, deferred income tax, and income tax expense.

3. Show what amounts related to income taxes should be reported each year on the income statement and balance sheet.

4. As a financial analyst, would you evaluate differently a deferred tax liability compared with taxes currently payable?

**AP9–6** **Computing Present and Future Values (P9–8)**                                    ▩ LO7
On January 1, 20A, Dodge Company completed the following transactions (use a 10 percent annual interest rate for all transactions):

a.  Deposited $200,000 in a debt retirement fund. Interest will be computed at six-month intervals and added to the fund at those times (i.e., semiannual compounding). (*Hint*: Think carefully about *n* and *i*.)

b.  Established a plant addition fund of $1,000,000 to be available at the end of year 10. A single sum that will grow to $1,000,000 will be deposited on January 1, 20A.

c.  Established a pension retirement fund of $800,000 to be available by the end of year 10 by making ten equal annual deposits each at year-end, starting on December 31, 20A.

d.  Purchased a $750,000 machine on January 1, 20A, and paid cash, $400,000. A four-year note *payable* is signed for the balance. The note will be paid in four equal year-end payments starting on December 31, 20A.

*Required (show computations and round to the nearest dollar):*

1.  In transaction *a*, what will be the balance in the fund at the end of year 5? What is the total amount of interest revenue that will be earned?

2.  In transaction *b*, what single sum amount must the company deposit on January 1, 20A? What is the total amount of interest revenue that will be earned?

3.  In transaction *c*, what is the required amount of each of the ten equal annual deposits? What is the total amount of interest revenue that will be earned?

4.  In transaction *d*, what is the amount of each of the equal annual payments that will be paid on the note? What is the total amount of interest expense that will be incurred?

**AP9–7** **Comparing Options Using Present Value Concepts (P9–9)**                        ▩ LO7
After completing a long and successful career as senior vice-president for a large bank, you are preparing for retirement. After visiting the human resources office, you have found that you have several retirement options: (1) you can receive an immediate cash payment of $1 million, (2) you can receive $60,000 per year for life (you have a life expectancy of 20 years), or (3) you can receive $50,000 per year for 10 years and then $70,000 per year for life (this option is intended to give you some protection against inflation). You have determined that you can earn 8 percent on your investments. Which option do you prefer and why?

**AP9–8** **Computing Amounts for a Fund with Journal Entries (P9–10)**                     ▩ LO7
On January 1, 20A, Jalopy Company decided to accumulate a fund to build an addition to its plant. The company will deposit $320,000 in the fund at each year-end, starting on December 31, 20A. The fund will earn 9 percent interest, which will be added to balance at each year-end. The accounting period ends December 31.

*Required:*

1.  What will be the balance in the fund immediately after the December 31, 20C, deposit?

2.  Complete the following fund accumulation schedule:

| Date | Cash Payment | Interest Revenue | Fund Increase | Fund Balance |
|------|--------------|------------------|---------------|--------------|
| 12/31/19A | | | | |
| 12/31/19B | | | | |
| 12/31/19C | | | | |
| Total | | | | |

3.  Give journal entries on December 31, 20A, 20B, and 20C.

4.  The plant addition was completed on January 1, 20D for a total cost of $1,060,000. Give the entry, assuming that this amount is paid in full to the contractor.

**AP9–9** **Computing Equal Periodic Debt Payments and Completing a Schedule with Journal Entries (P9–11)**                                                                      ▩ LO8
On January 1, 20A, Idaho Company sold a new machine to U.S. Company for $80,000. U.S. Company made a cash down payment of $30,000 and signed a $50,000, 8 percent note for the balance due. The note is to be paid off in three equal installments due on December 31, 20A,

20B, and 20C. Each payment is to include principal plus interest on the unpaid balance. U.S. recorded the purchase as follows:

| | | |
|---|---|---|
| Jan. 1, 20 | A Machine ................................. 80,000 | |
| | Cash ...................................... | 30,000 |
| | Note payable ............................. | 50,000 |

*Required (show computations and round to the nearest dollar):*

1. What is the amount of the equal annual payments that U.S. Company must make?
2. What is the interest on the note?
3. Complete the following debt payment schedule:

| Date | Cash Payment | Interest Revenue | Principal Decrease | Unpaid Principal |
|---|---|---|---|---|
| 1/1/20A | | | | |
| 12/31/20A | | | | |
| 12/31/20B | | | | |
| 12/31/20C | | | | |
| Total | | | | |

4. Give the journal entries for each of the three payments.
5. Explain why interest expense decreased in amount each year.

# CASES AND PROJECTS

## FINANCIAL REPORTING AND ANALYSIS CASES

**CP9–1**  **Finding Financial Information**

Refer to the financial statements of American Eagle Outfitters given in Appendix B at the end of this book, or open file AEOS10K.doc in the S&P directory on the student CD-ROM.

*Required:*

1. What is the amount of accrued compensation and payroll taxes for the current year?
2. How did changes in accounts payable affect cash flows from operating activities in the current year?
3. What is the amount of long-term liabilities for the current year?
4. What amount of federal income taxes was deferred during the current year?
5. Does the company have a post-retirement or defined benefit program?

**CP9–2**  **Finding Financial Information**

Refer to the financial statements of Urban Outfitters given in Appendix C at the end of this book, or open file URBN10K.doc in the S&P directory on the student CD-ROM.

*Required:*

1. What is the amount of accrued compensation for the current year?
2. How did changes in payables, accrued expenses and other liabilities affect cash flows from operating activities in the current year?
3. What is the amount of long-term liabilities for the current year?
4. What are the specific components making up accrued expenses for the current year?
5. Does the company have any contingent liabilities?

**CP9–3**  **Comparing Companies within an Industry**

Refer to the financial statements of American Eagle Outfitters given in Appendix B, Urban Outfitters given in Appendix C, and the Standard and Poor's Industry Ratio Report given in Appendix D at the end of this book or open file CP9-3.xls in the S&P directory on the student CD-ROM.

*Required:*

1. Compute the current ratio for each company for each year.
2. Compare the latest year current ratio for each company to the industry average from the Standard and Poor's Industry Ratio report. Based solely on the current ratio, are these companies more or less liquid than the average company in their industry?
3. Compute the payable turnover ratio for each company for each year. What is the amount of long-term liabilities for the current year?
4. Compare the latest year payable turnover ratio for each company to the industry average from the Standard and Poor's Industry Ratio report. Are these companies doing better or worse than the average company in their industry at paying trade creditors?
5. Using this information and any other data from the annual report, write a brief assessment of the liquidity for the two companies.

STANDARD &POOR'S

**CP9–4 Explaining a Note: Accrued Liability for a Frequent Flyer Program**

LO1

Southwest Airlines

Most major airlines have frequent flyer programs that permit passengers to earn free tickets based on the number of miles they have flown. A recent Southwest Airlines annual report contained the following note:

> **Frequent Flyer Awards**
>
> The Company accrues the estimated incremental cost to provide transportation for travel awards when earned under its Company Club frequent flyer program.

The phrase *incremental cost* refers to additional expense associated with an extra passenger taking the flight (e.g., the cost of a soft drink and a snack).

*Required:*

1. What cost measures other than incremental cost could Southwest use?
2. What account should Southwest debit when it accrues this liability?

**CP9–5 Reporting Short-Term Borrowings**

LO1

PepsiCo, Inc.

PepsiCo, Inc., engages in a number of activities that are part of our daily lives. Its businesses include Pepsi-Cola, Slice, Mountain Dew, and Fritos. The company's annual revenues exceed $22 billion. A recent PepsiCo annual report contained the following information:

> At the end of the current year, $3.6 billion of short-term borrowings were classified as long-term, reflecting PepsiCo's intent and ability to refinance these borrowings on a long-term basis, through either long-term debt issuances or rollover of existing short-term borrowings. The significant amount of short-term borrowings classified as long-term, as compared to the end of the previous year when no such amounts were reclassified, primarily reflects the large commercial paper issuances in the current year, but also resulted from a refined analysis of amounts expected to be refinanced beyond one year.

*Required:*

As an analyst, comment on the company's classification of short-term borrowings as long-term liabilities. What conditions should exist to permit a company to make this type of classification?

**CP9–6 Interpreting the Financial Press**

LO6

Increasingly, companies are becoming sensitive to environmental issues surrounding their business operations. They recognize that some of their actions can have detrimental impacts on the environment in ways that may not be fully understood for years or even decades. Environmental issues present complex problems for companies that must report contingent liabilities. A related article, Munter, Sacasas, and Garcia, "Accounting and Disclosure of Enviormental Contingencies," January 1996, pp. 36–37, 50–52, from the CPA Journal (www.cpaj.com) is available on the Libby/Libby/Short website at www.mhhe.com/business/accounting/libby3. Read the article and prepare a brief memo concerning how companies should report environment issues in their financial statements.

**LO7**　**CP9–7**　**Analyzing Hidden Interest in a Real Estate Deal: Present Value**

Many advertisements contain offers that seem too good to be true. A few years ago, an actual newspaper ad offered "a $150,000 house with a zero interest rate mortgage" for sale. If the purchaser made monthly payments of $3,125 for four years ($150,000 ÷ 48 months), no interest would be charged. When the offer was made, mortgage interest rates were 12 percent. Present value for $n = 48$, and $i = 1\%$ is 37.9740.

*Required:*

1. Did the builder actually provide a mortgage at zero interest?

2. Estimate the true price of the home that was advertised. Assume that the monthly payment was based on an implicit interest rate of 12 percent.

**LO8**　**CP9–8**　**Computing the Present Value of Lease Obligations**

Exxon Corporation

A recent annual report for Exxon included the following note:

> At December 31, 1998, the corporation and its subsidiaries held noncancelable leases covering drilling equipment, tankers, service stations and other properties with minimum lease commitments as indicated in the table.
>
> | Years | Minimum Commitment (in millions ) |
> |-------|-----------------------------------|
> | 1999 | $ 864 |
> | 2000 | 713 |
> | 2001 | 564 |
> | 2002 | 488 |
> | 2003 | 373 |
> | 2004 and beyond | 1,448 |

You are a lending officer for a large commercial bank and for comparative purposes want to compute the present values of these leases.

*Required:*

Determine the present value of the minimum lease payments shown as of December 31, 1998. You may assume an interest rate of 10 percent. Identify other assumptions that you must make.

# CRITICAL THINKING CASES

**LO1, 2**　**CP9–9**　**Making Decisions as a Manager: Liquidity**

In some cases, a manager can engage in transactions that improve the appearance of financial reports without affecting the underlying economic reality. In this chapter, we discussed the importance of liquidity as measured by the current ratio and working capital. For each of the following transactions, (a) determine whether reported liquidity is improved and (b) state whether you believe that the fundamental liquidity of the company has been improved. Assume that the company has positive working capital and a current ratio of 2.

*a.* Borrowed $1 million from the bank, payable in 90 days.

*b.* Borrowed $10 million with a long-term note, payable in five years.

*c.* Reclassified current portion of long-term debt as long term as the result of a new agreement with the bank that guarantees the company's ability to refinance the debt when it matures.

*d.* Paid $100,000 of the company's accounts payable.

*e.* Entered a borrowing agreement that guarantees the ability to borrow up to $10 million when needed.

*f.* Required all employees to take accrued vacation to reduce its liability for vacation compensation.

**CP9–10 Evaluating an Ethical Dilemma: Managing Reported Results**  **LO2**
The president of a regional wholesale distribution company planned to borrow a significant amount of money from a local bank at the beginning of the next fiscal year. He knew that the bank placed a heavy emphasis on the liquidity of potential borrowers. To improve the company's current ratio, the president told his employees to stop shipping new merchandise to customers and to stop accepting merchandise from suppliers for the last three weeks of the fiscal year. Is this behavior ethical? Would your answer be different if the president had been concerned about reported profits and asked all of the employees to work overtime to ship out merchandise that had been ordered at the end of the year?

**CP9–11 Making a Decision as a Financial Analyst: Cash Flows** **LO2**
As a young analyst at a large mutual fund, you have found two companies that meet the basic investment criteria of the fund. One company has a very high current ratio but a relatively low amount of cash flow from operating activity reported on the statement of cash flows. The other company has a very low current ratio but very significant cash flows from operating activities. Which company would you tend to prefer?

**CP9–12 Making a Decision as an Auditor: Contingent Liabilities** **LO6**
For each of the following situations, determine whether the company should (a) report a liability on the balance sheet, (b) disclose a contingent liability, or (c) not report the situation. Justify and explain your conclusions.

1. An automobile company introduces a new car. Past experience demonstrates that lawsuits will be filed as soon as the new model is involved in any accidents. The company can be certain that at least one jury will award damages to people injured in an accident.

2. A research scientist determines that the company's best selling product may infringe on another company's patent. If the other company discovers the infringement and files suit, your company could lose millions.

3. As part of land development for a new housing project, your company has polluted a natural lake. Under state law, you must clean up the lake once you complete development. The development project will take five to eight years to complete. Current estimates indicate that it will cost $2 to $3 million to clean up the lake.

4. Your company has just been notified that it lost a product liability lawsuit for $1 million that it plans to appeal. Management is confident that the company will win on appeal, but the lawyers believe that it will lose.

5. A key customer is unhappy with the quality of a major construction project. The company believes that the customer is being unreasonable but, to maintain goodwill, has decided to do $250,000 in repairs next year.

**CP9–13 Assessing Contingent Liabilities** **LO6**
If a liability is both probable and subject to estimate, it must be recorded as a liability on the balance sheet. The Financial Accounting Standards Board has defined *probable* as "the future event or events are likely to occur." Working in a small group, decide on a specific probability that is appropriate for this standard. (For example, is an 80 percent chance of occurrence probable?) Be prepared to justify your determination.

**CP9–14 Evaluating an Ethical Dilemma: Fair Advertising** **LO7**
The New York State Lottery Commission ran the following advertisement in a number of New York Newspapers:

> The Lotto jackpot for Wednesday, August 25, 1999, will be $3 million including interest earned over a 20-year payment period. Constant payments will be made each year.

Explain the meaning of this advertisement in your own words. Evaluate the "fairness" of this advertisement. Could anyone be misled? Do you agree that the lottery winner has won $3 million? If not, what amount is more accurate? State any assumptions you make.

# FINANCIAL REPORTING AND ANALYSIS PROJECTS

■ **LO1, 4, 6**  **CP9–15**

**Team Project: Examining an Annual Report**
As a team, select an industry to analyze. Each team member should acquire the annual report or 10-K for one publicly traded company in the industry, with each member selecting a different company. (Library files, the SEC EDGAR service at www.sec.gov, Compustat CD, or the company itself are good sources.) On an individual basis, each team member should then write a short report answering the following questions about the selected company.

1. Review the liabilities for your company. What strategy has the company followed with respect to borrowed funds?

2. Compare the individual liability accounts over several years. How have they changed?

3. Does the company have any contingent liabilities? If so, evaluate the risk associated with the contingency.

4. Compare the company's liabilities to its assets, income, and cash flows. Do you have any concerns?

Discuss any patterns across the companies that you as a team observe. Then, as a team, write a short report comparing and contrasting your companies using these attributes. Provide potential explanations for any differences discovered.

■ **LO2, 3**  **CP9–16**

General Mills

**Comparing Companies over Time**
Using your web browser, contact General Mills at its website (www.generalmills.com). Find the latest available annual report. Compute the current ratio and the accounts payable turnover ratio. Compare the ratios to ones computed based on the financial information contained in this chapter. What conclusions do you draw concerning liquidity for General Mills? Does the comparison over time provide better information than an analysis at a single point in time?

■ **LO2, 3**  **CP9–17**

**Comparing Companies within an Industry**
Using your web browser, contact General Mills at its website (www.generalmills.com) and Kellogg at its website (www.kelloggs.com). Find the latest available annual report. Compute the current ratio and the accounts payable turnover ratio for each company and compare them. What conclusions do you draw. Do you gain additional insights by comparing ratios for two companies?

■ **LO7**  **CP9–18**

**Using Present Value Concepts**
Although it might seem early to begin your retirement planning, use the search engine on your Web browser to find a website that offers retirement planning software. Answer the questions and develop a retirement plan. Once you are finished, explain how the retirement planner used the present value concepts discussed in this chapter.

# Reporting and Interpreting Bonds

## CHAPTER **TEN**

---

LEARNING **OBJECTIVES**

*After studying this chapter, you should be able to:*

Gaming (gambling) has become big business in this country. Casinos are now just a short drive from most major cities. The most popular ones are owned and operated by major corporations whose stock is traded on the New York Stock Exchange. One of the most successful companies is Harrah's Entertainment, Inc., which operates casinos under the names Harrah's, Showboat, and Rio. Harrah's annual report states the following:

FOCUS **COMPANY:**

# Harrah's, Inc.

## FINANCING GROWTH WITH BONDS PAYABLE

"Harrah's Entertainment's strategy is different from that of our competitors. More casinos in more locations means Harrah's Entertainment has more opportunities to develop valuable relationships with more customers than any other company. Harrah's Entertainment's distribution allows us to serve customers both in their home casino markets and as they travel."

As the industry has grown and become more competitive, companies have had to invest large amounts of money to create unique gaming environments. As Harrah's annual report states, "nothing else matters if customers aren't dazzled with every encounter at every property." To illustrate the magnitude of the investment that is needed, consider the Harrah's casino in Tunica, Mississippi, 30 miles south of Memphis. The facility includes 50,000 square feet of gaming space, 1,246 slot machines, and 33 table games. To support the casino, Harrah's built a hotel with 181 rooms and 18 suites, three restaurants, a snack bar, a 250-seat showroom, a child care facility, an arcade, retail shop, 13,500 square feet of convention space, parking for 2,600 cars, and a golf course.

Because of the company's strategy of investing in large and unique casinos, Harrah's has had to raise large amounts of new capital in addition to retaining a large amount of its income. In this chapter, we will study Harrah's sale of $500 million in new bonds. We will use this bond issue to look at the question of why management decides to raise money through the sale of bonds.

## BUSINESS BACKGROUND

In Chapter 9, we introduced the term *capital structure,* which is the mixture of debt and equity that is used to finance a company's operations. Almost all companies employ some debt in their capital structure. Indeed, large corporations need to borrow billions of dollars, which makes borrowing money from individual creditors impractical for them. Instead, these corporations can issue bonds to raise debt capital.

*Bonds* are securities that corporations and governmental units issue when they borrow large amounts of money. After bonds are issued, they can be traded on established exchanges such as the New York Bond Exchange. The ability to sell a bond on the bond exchange is a significant advantage for creditors because it provides them with *liquidity,* or the ability to convert their investment into cash. If you lend money directly to a corporation for 20 years, you must wait that long to have your cash investment repaid. If you lend money by purchasing a bond, you can sell it to another creditor if you need cash before the bond matures.

The liquidity available with publicly traded bonds offers an important advantage to corporations. Because most creditors are reluctant to lend money for long periods of time with no opportunity to receive cash prior to the maturity date of the debt, they demand a higher interest rate to compensate them for long-term loans. The liquidity associated with bonds permits corporations to reduce the cost of borrowing money for long periods of time.

The use of bonds to raise long-term capital offers other significant advantages to corporations such as Harrah's:

1. Ownership and control of the company are not diluted. In contrast to stockholders, bondholders do not participate in the management (by voting) and accumulated earnings of the company.

2. Cash payments to the bondholders are limited to the specified interest payments and the principal of the debt.

**NET INTEREST COST** is interest cost less any income tax savings associated with interest expense.

3. Interest expense is a tax-deductible expense, but dividends paid to stockholders are not. The tax deductibility of interest expense reduces the net cost of borrowing. For example, if a corporation paid $100,000 interest during the year, its taxable income is $100,000 lower. If the tax rate is 35 percent, the corporation pays $35,000 less in taxes (35% × $100,000) because of the lower taxable income. Thus, the **net interest cost** is $65,000 ($100,000 − $35,000). If the corporation paid $100,000 in dividends, the net cost is $100,000 because dividends are not tax deductible.

**FINANCIAL LEVERAGE** is the use of borrowed funds to increase the rate of return on owners' equity; it occurs when the interest rate on debt is lower than the earnings rate on total assets.

4. It is often possible to borrow funds at a low interest rate and invest them at a higher rate, which is called positive **financial leverage.** To illustrate financial leverage, assume that Home Video, Inc., owns a video rental store. The company has stockholders' equity of $100,000 invested in the store and no debt. The company earns net income of $20,000 per year on the store (which is a 20 percent return on the stockholders' investment). Management plans to open a new store that will also cost $100,000 and will earn $20,000 per year. If the stockholders provide the new funds, they will still earn 20 percent on their investment ($40,000 ÷ $200,000), but if the company borrows $100,000 for the new store at a net after-tax interest cost of 8 percent, the stockholders' rate of return will actually increase. They will earn $20,000 on the first store and $12,000 on the second store ($20,000 − $8,000 interest) for a total return of $32,000. Because the company borrowed money, stockholders' equity remains at $100,000 with a rate of return of 32 percent ($32,000 ÷ $100,000).

Unfortunately, the issuance of bonds has some disadvantages. The primary disadvantages are (1) the required interest payments must be made each interest period and (2) the large principal amount must be paid at the maturity date. Interest payments to bondholders are fixed charges, which increase the risk of business. Interest payments legally must be paid each period, whether the corporation earns income or incurs a loss. In contrast, dividends usually are paid to stockholders only if earnings are satisfactory. Each year, some companies go bankrupt because of their inability to make their required interest payments to creditors. Sound business practice requires maintaining an appropriate balance between debt and equity capital.

**ORGANIZATION** OF THE CHAPTER

| • Characteristics of Bonds Payable | • Bonds Issued at Variable Interest Rate | • Long-Term Investments in Bonds |
|---|---|---|
| | Times Interest Earned | |

| • Measuring Bonds Payable and Interest Expense | • Additional Topics in Accounting for Bonds Payable | • Reporting Bond Investments Held to Maturity |
|---|---|---|
| | Effective-Interest Amortization of Bond Discounts and Premium | Bonds Purchased at Par |

| • Analyzing Bond Transactions | Early Retirement of Debt | Bonds Purchased at a Discount |
|---|---|---|
| Bonds Issued at Par | Bond Sinking Funds | |
| Bonds Issued at a Discount | | |
| Bonds Issued at a Premium | | |

KEY **RATIO ANALYSIS:**

## DEBT-TO-EQUITY

**K**now the decision question:

What is the relationship between the amount of capital provided by owners and the amount provided by creditors? The *debt-to-equity ratio* is a measure of this relationship. Analysts use this ratio to assess the debt capacity of a business. It is computed as follows:

**Debt-to-Equity Ratio = Total Liabilities ÷ Owners' Equity**

The 1998 ratio for Harrah's:

$2,434,925 ÷ $851,407 = 2.86

Examine the ratio using two techniques:

| ① Comparisons over Time | | | ② Comparisons with Competitors | |
|---|---|---|---|---|
| Harrah's | | | Mirage Resorts | Trump Casinos |
| 1996 | 1997 | 1998 | 1998 | 1998 |
| 1.63 | 1.72 | 2.86 | 1.21 | 5.33 |

You interpret the results carefully:

**IN GENERAL** → A high ratio normally suggests that a company relies heavily on funds provided by creditors. A reliance on creditors increases the risk that a company may not be able to meet its contractual financial obligations during a business down turn.

**FOCUS COMPANY ANALYSIS** → The debt-to-equity ratio for Harrah's has increased over the past few years and falls between the ratios for two major competitors. As discussed earlier, Harrah's has embarked on a strategy to create a national brand image in gaming. It is investing heavily in the acquisition of other companies and the expansion of facilities. It has recently borrowed $750 million to support this strategy. Given this context, most analysts would not be concerned about the increase in the debt-to-equity ratio over the past few years. The ratio also appears to be within the range of this ratio for major competitors.

**A FEW CAUTIONS:** The debt-to-equity ratio tells only part of the story with respect to risks associated with debt. The ratio is a good indication of debt capacity, but it does not help the analyst understand whether the company's operations can support the amount of debt that it has. Remember that debt carries with it the obligation to make cash payments for interest and principal. As a result, most analysts would evaluate the debt-to-equity ratio within the context of the amount of cash the company is able to generate from operating activities. Later in this chapter, we will introduce you to another ratio that analysts use in conjunction with the debt-to-equity ratio.

## CHARACTERISTICS OF BONDS PAYABLE

A **DEBENTURE** is an unsecured bond; no assets are specifically pledged to guarantee repayment.

The **BOND PRINCIPAL** is the amount (a) payable at the maturity of the bond and (b) on which the periodic cash interest payments are computed.

**PAR VALUE** is another name for bond principal, or the maturity amount of a bond.

**FACE AMOUNT** is another name for principal, or the principal amount of the bond.

The **STATED RATE** is the rate of cash interest per period specified in the bond contract.

Different types of bonds have different characteristics. Exhibit 10.1 summarizes many of the most common features of corporate bonds. At first, it may seem perplexing to see so many different types of bonds, but there is a solid economic reason for them. Different types of creditors have different types of risk and return preferences. A retired person, for example, may be willing to receive a lower interest rate in return for having more security. This type of creditor might want a mortgage bond that pledges a specific asset as security if the company is unable to repay the bond (called a *secured bond*). Another creditor might be willing to accept a low interest rate and an unsecured status if the company provides the opportunity to convert the bond into common stock at some point in the future if the company does very well. A bond that is not secured with the pledge of a specific asset is called a **debenture.** Companies try to design bond features that are attractive to different groups of creditors just as automobile manufacturers try to design cars that appeal to different groups of consumers.

A bond usually requires the payment of interest over its life with the repayment of principal on the maturity date. The **bond principal** is the amount (1) payable at the maturity date and (2) on which the periodic cash interest payments are computed. It does not change. The principal also is called the **par value, face amount,** and *maturity value*. All bonds have a par value, which is the amount that will be paid when the bond matures. For most bonds, the par value is $1,000, but it can be any amount.

A bond always specifies a **stated rate** of interest and when periodic cash interest payments must be paid—usually annually or semiannually. Each periodic interest payment is computed as principal times the stated interest rate. The selling price of a bond does not affect the periodic cash payment of interest. For example, a $1,000, 8 percent bond always pays cash interest of (1) $80 on an annual basis or (2) $40 on a semiannual basis.

EXHIBIT **10.1**

**Bond Characteristics and Classifications of Bonds**

| Bond Classification | Bond Characteristic |
| --- | --- |
| 1. On the basis of collateral (assets) | |
|    *a.* Unsecured bonds (often called *debentures*). | *a.* Bonds that do not include a mortgage or pledge of specific assets as a guarantee of repayment at maturity. |
|    *b.* Secured bonds (often designated on the basis of the type of asset pledged, such as a real estate mortgage). | *b.* Bonds that include the pledge of specific assets as a guarantee of repayment at maturity. |
| 2. On the basis of repayment of principal | |
|    *a.* Ordinary or single-payment bonds. | *a.* The principal that is payable in full at a single specified maturity date in the future. |
|    *b.* Serial bonds. | *b.* The principal that is payable in installments on a series of specified maturity dates in the future. |
| 3. On the basis of early retirement | |
|    *a.* Callable bonds. | *a.* Bonds that may be called for early retirement at the option of the issuer. |
|    *b.* Redeemable bonds. | *b.* Bonds that may be turned in for early retirement at the option of the bondholder. |
|    *c.* Convertible bonds. | *c.* Bonds that may be converted to other securities of the issuer (usually common stock) at the option of the bondholder. |

When Harrah's decided to issue new bonds, it prepared a bond **indenture** (bond contract) that specified the legal provisions of the bonds. These provisions include the maturity date, rate of interest to be paid, date of each interest payment, and any conversion privileges (explained later). The indenture also contains covenants designed to protect the creditors. Harrah's indenture included limitations on new debt that the company might issue in the future. Other typical covenants include limitations on the payment of dividends and required minimums of certain accounting ratios, such as the current ratio. Because they may limit future action, management prefers covenants that are least restrictive. Creditors, however, prefer more restrictive covenants, which lessen the risk of the investment. As with any business transaction, the final result is achieved through a process of negotiation. Bond covenants are typically reported in the notes to the financial statements. *Accounting Trends & Techniques* (published by the AICPA) reviewed the reporting practices of 600 companies.* The graph in the margin shows the percentage of companies that disclosed debt covenants.

Harrah's reported the following information about its debt covenants.

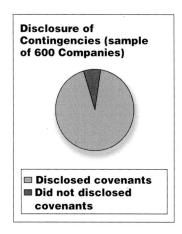

**Disclosure of Contingencies (sample of 600 Companies)**

☐ **Disclosed covenants**
■ **Did not disclosed covenants**

An **INDENTURE** is a bond contract that specifies the legal provisions of a bond issue.

**REAL WORLD EXCERPT**

*Harrah's, Inc.*
ANNUAL REPORT

> **LONG-TERM DEBT**
> Our debt agreements contain financial covenants requiring us to maintain a specific tangible net worth and to meet other financial ratios. Covenants limit our ability to pay dividends and to repurchase our outstanding shares.

Harrah's also prepared a *prospectus*, which is a legal document given to potential buyers of the bonds. The prospectus describes the company, the bonds, and how the proceeds of the bonds will be used. In the prospectus for the Harrah's bonds, we learn that the company plans to use the proceeds to reduce its outstanding debt. This debt reduction was required as part of an agreement to purchase another company (Showboat) a few months earlier.

Most companies work with an underwriter who either buys the entire issue of bonds and then resells them to individual creditors (called a *firm commitment underwriter*) or

---

*Reprinted with permission from *Accounting Trends and Techniques*. Copyright © 2000 by the American Institute of Certified Public Accounts, Inc.

simply sells the bonds without any obligation to purchase them (called a *best efforts underwriter*). The prospectus tells us that Harrah's used several underwriters (on a firm commitment basis), including Morgan Stanley Dean Witter; Bear, Stearns & Co.; and Lehman Brothers. The underwriting commission paid to these firms was $3,250,000 on a bond issue of $500 million. The cost of underwriting a new bond issue is not directly proportional to the size of the issue. A week earlier, Harrah's sold a $250 million bond issue. The underwriting costs were $2,500,000.

When a bond is issued to the investor, the person receives a **bond certificate.** All of the bond certificates for a single bond issue are identical. The face of each certificate shows the same maturity date, interest rate, interest dates, and other provisions.

An independent party, called the **trustee,** usually is appointed to represent the bondholders. A trustee's duties are to ascertain whether the issuing company fulfills all of the provisions of the bond indenture. Harrah's appointed IBJ Whitehall Bank & Trust Company to act as trustee.

As mentioned earlier, each bond issue has characteristics that are specified in the bond indenture. The issuing company often adds special characteristics to a bond to make it more attractive to investors who normally have a large number of investment alternatives from which to select.

Bonds sometimes offer different features with respect to early retirement:

**Callable bonds** may be called for early retirement at the option of the issuer.

**Redeemable bonds** may be turned in for early retirement at the option of the bondholder.

**Convertible bonds** may be converted to other securities of the issuer (usually common stock) at the option of the bondholder.

While the previous terminology is used widely, there are no accounting rules that specify consistent meaning. Notice that the Harrah's annual report mentions liabilities that are redeemable "at our option:"

**REAL WORLD EXCERPT**

*Harrah's, Inc.*

ANNUAL REPORT

The notes are redeemable, in whole or in part, at any time, and at our option, at a price equal to the greater of:
- 100% of the principal amount of the notes then outstanding, or
- the present value of the remaining payments of principal and interest discounted using the Treasury rate for securities of similar maturity plus .25%.

Bonds also differ in terms of their status in relationship to other debt:

*Senior debt* receives preference over other creditors in the event of bankruptcy or default.

*Subordinated debt* is paid off after some other group of creditors. Obviously, subordinated debt is riskier than senior debt.

Each year, corporations introduce new features that are included with their bonds. For example, The Walt Disney Company issued the first bond with a 100-year maturity. Despite an increase in unusual features, the basics that we discuss in this chapter permit you to deal with most types of bonds.

Because of the complexities associated with bonds, several agencies exist to evaluate the probability that a bond issuer will not be able to meet the requirements specified in the indenture. This risk is called *default risk.* Moody's and Standard and Poor's use letter ratings to specify the quality of a bond. Ratings above Baa/BBB are investment grade; ratings below that level are speculative and are often called *junk bonds.* Many banks, mutual funds, and trusts are permitted to invest only in bonds that are of investment grade quality.

## MEASURING BONDS PAYABLE AND INTEREST EXPENSE

When Harrah's issued its bonds, it specified two types of cash payments in the bond contract:

1. *Principal.* This is usually a single payment made when the bond matures. It is also called the *par,* or *face, value.*

2. *Cash interest payments.* These payments represent an annuity and are computed by multiplying the principal amount times the interest rate, called the *contract, stated,* or **coupon rate** of interest stated in the bond contract. The bond contract specifies whether these payments are made quarterly, semiannually, or annually.

Neither Harrah's nor the underwriter determines the price at which the bonds sell. Instead, the market determines the price using the present value concepts that were introduced in the previous chapter. To determine the present value of the bond, you compute the present value of the principal (a single payment) and the present value of the interest payments (an annuity) and add the two amounts together.

Creditors demand a certain rate of interest to compensate them for the risks related to bonds. The interest rate demanded by these creditors is the **market interest rate** (also called the **yield,** or **effective-interest rate**). The market rate is the interest rate on a debt when incurred; it should be used in computing the present value of the bond.

The present value of a bond may be the same as par, above par (**bond premium**), or below par (**bond discount**). If the stated and the market interest rates are the same, a bond sells at par; if the market rate is higher than the stated rate, a bond sells at a discount; and if the market rate is lower than the stated rate, the bond sells at a premium. These relationships can be understood in commonsense terms. If a bond pays an interest rate that is less than creditors demand, they will not buy it unless its price is reduced (i.e., a discount must be provided). If a bond pays more than creditors demand, they will be willing to pay a premium to buy it.

When a bond is issued at par, the issuer receives cash equal to its par value. When a bond is issued at a discount, the issuer receives less cash than its par value. When a bond is issued at a premium, the issuer receives more cash than the par value.

Basically, corporations and creditors do not care whether a bond is issued at par, a discount, or a premium because bonds are always priced to provide the market rate of interest. To illustrate, consider a corporation that issues three separate bonds on the same day. The bonds are exactly the same except one has a stated interest of 8 percent, another 10 percent, and a third 11 percent. If the market rate of interest was 10 percent, the first would be issued at a discount, the second at par, and the third at a premium, but a creditor who bought any one of the bonds would earn the market interest rate of 10 percent. Later in this chapter, we will use present value concepts to illustrate this point.

■ **LEARNING OBJECTIVE 2**

Report bonds payable and interest expense, with bonds sold at par, at a discount and at a premium.

The **COUPON RATE** is the stated rate of interest on bonds.

**MARKET INTEREST RATE** is the current rate of interest on a debt when incurred; also called the **YIELD,** or **EFFECTIVE-INTEREST RATE**.

**BOND PREMIUM** is the difference between the selling price and par when the bond is sold for more than par.

**BOND DISCOUNT** is the difference between the selling price and par when the bond is sold for less than par.

## FINANCIAL **ANALYSIS**

### BOND INFORMATION FROM THE BUSINESS PRESS

As mentioned earlier, bonds are widely used because they offer creditors liquidity. A creditor who needs immediate cash can sell a bond to another creditor instead of waiting until its maturity date. These transactions are between individual creditors and do not affect the financial statements of the company that issued the bonds.

Bond prices are reported each day in the business press based on transactions that occurred on the bond exchange. The following is typical of the information that you will find:

| Bond | Yield | Volume | Close | Change |
|------|-------|--------|-------|--------|
| Safeway 6.0 03 | 6.8 | 58 | 97.2 | −¼ |
| Sears 7.0 07 | 6.77 | 25 | 101.4 | −⅜ |
| Harrah's 7.5 09 | 6.9 | 580 | 104.1 | −⅞ |

This listing means that the Harrah's bond has a coupon interest rate of 7.5 percent and will mature in the year 2009. The bond currently provides a cash yield of 6.9 percent with a selling price that is 104.1 percent of par, or $1040.10. On this particular date, 580 bonds were sold and the price fell ⅞ point from the previous trading date. A point is 1 percent.

Although analysts may study the daily price changes of bonds, remember that these changes do not affect the company's financial statements. For financial reporting purposes, the company uses the interest rates that existed when the bonds were first sold to the public. Subsequent changes do not affect the company's accounting for the bonds.

## SELF-STUDY **QUIZ**

Your study of bonds will be easier if you understand the new terminology that has been introduced in this chapter. Let's review some of those terms. Define the following:

1. Market interest rate.
2. Synonyms for market interest rate.
3. Coupon interest rate.
4. Synonyms for coupon interest rate.
5. Bond discount.
6. Bond premium.

Check your answers in the footnote at the bottom of this page.*

## ANALYZING BOND TRANSACTIONS

In this section of the chapter, we illustrate three different cases of accounting for bonds payable: (1) bonds issued at par, (2) bonds issued at a discount, and (3) bonds issued at a premium. We use Harrah's for our illustration, but for the sake of simplification, we assume that the company issued bonds with a maturity value of $400,000.

### BONDS ISSUED AT PAR

Bonds sell at their par value when buyers are willing to invest in them at the interest rate stated on the bond. To illustrate, let's assume that on January 1, 20A, Harrah's issued 10 percent bonds with a par value of $400,000 and received $400,000 in cash (which means that the bonds sold at par). The bonds were dated to start interest on January 1, 20A, and will pay interest each June 30 and December 31. The bonds mature in 10 years on December 31, 20J. On the date of issuance, Harrah's records the receipt of $400,000 cash and the creation of a liability for the same amount.

---

*1. The market rate is the interest rate demanded by creditors. It is the rate used in the present value computations to discount future cash flows.

2. Market interest rate is also called *yield* or *effective-interest rate*.

3. Coupon interest rate is the stated rate on the bonds.

4. Coupon rate is also called *stated rate* and *contract rate*.

5. A bond that sells for less than par is sold at a discount. This occurs when the coupon rate is lower than the market rate.

6. A bond that sells for more than par is sold at a premium. This occurs when the coupon rate is higher than the market rate.

The creditors who bought the bonds did so with the expectation that they would earn interest over the life of the bond. Harrah's will pay interest at 5 percent (i.e., 10 percent per year) on the par value of the bonds each June 30 and December 31 until the bond's maturity date. The amount of interest each period will be $20,000 (5% × $400,000). The entry to record the interest payments follows:

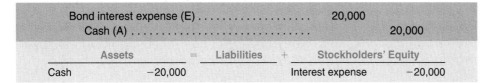

| Bond interest expense (E) . . . . . . . . . . . . . . . . . . | 20,000 | |
| Cash (A) . . . . . . . . . . . . . . . . . . . . . . . . . . . . . | | 20,000 |

| Assets | | = | Liabilities | + | Stockholders' Equity | |
|---|---|---|---|---|---|---|
| Cash | −20,000 | | | | Interest expense | −20,000 |

Bond interest payment dates rarely coincide with the last day of a company's fiscal year. Under the matching concept, interest expense that has been incurred but not paid must be accrued with an adjusting entry. If Harrah's fiscal year ended on May 31, the company would accrue interest for five months and record interest expense and interest payable.

Notice in the preceding journal entry that interest expense and cash interest paid are the same amount. This is the case when the effective interest rate and the stated rate are the same. When bonds are sold at a discount or a premium, this is not the case. We illustrate these cases later in the chapter.

The $400,000 cash that Harrah's received when the bonds were sold is the present value of the future cash flows associated with the bonds. This is computed using the present value tables contained in Appendix A:

| | Present Value |
|---|---|
| a. Principal: $400,000 × $p_{n=20, i=5\%}$ (0.3769) | $150,760 |
| b. Interest: $20,000 × $P_{n=20, i=5\%}$ (12.4622) | 249,240* |
| Issue price of Harrah's bonds | $400,000 |
| *Rounded. | |

When the effective rate of interest equals the stated rate of interest, the present value of the future cash flows associated with a bond *always* equals the bond's par amount. It is important to remember that a bond's selling price is determined by the present value of its future cash flows, not the par value. Bond liabilities also are initially recorded at the present value of future cash flows on date of issue, not par value.

## BONDS ISSUED AT A DISCOUNT

Bonds sell at a discount when the buyers are willing to invest in them only if the buyers receive the market rate of interest, which is *higher* than the stated interest rate on them. Let's now assume that the market rate of interest was 12 percent when Harrah's sold its bonds (which have a par value of $400,000). The bonds have a stated rate of 10 percent, payable semiannually, which is less than the rate demanded by the market. Therefore, the bonds sold at a discount. To compute the cash issue price of the bonds requires computation of the present value, at the *market rate of interest,* of the future cash flows specified on the bond: (1) the principal ($n = 20$, $i = 6\%$) and (2) the cash interest paid each semiannual interest period ($n = 20$, $i = 6\%$). Thus, the cash issue price of the Harrah's bonds is computed as follows:

| | Present Value |
|---|---|
| a. Principal: $400,000 × $p_{n=20, i=6\%}$ (0.3118) | $124,720 |
| b. Interest: $20,000 × $P_{n=20, i=6\%}$ (11.4699) | 229,398 |
| Issue (sale) price of Harrah's bonds | $354,118* |
| *Discount: $400,000 − $354,118 = $45,882. | |

The cash price of the bonds issued by Harrah's is $354,118. Some people refer to this price as 88.5, which means that the bonds were sold at 88.5 percent of their par value ($354,118/$400,000).

When a bond is sold at a discount, the Bonds Payable account is credited for the par amount, and the discount is recorded as a debit to Discount on Bonds Payable. The issuance of the Harrah's bonds at a discount is recorded as follows:

| Cash (A) ............................... | 354,118 | |
|---|---|---|
| Discount on bonds payable (XL) .............. | 45,882 | |
| Bonds payable (L) ..................... | | 400,000 |

| Assets | = | Liabilities | + | Stockholders' Equity |
|---|---|---|---|---|
| Cash           +354,118 | | Bonds payable      +400,000 | | |
| | | Discount on bonds   −45,882 | | |

This journal entry shows the discount in a separate contra-liability account (Discount on Bonds Payable) as a debit. The balance sheet reports the bonds payable at their book value, which is their maturity amount less any unamortized discount. In the case of Harrah's, the company does not separately disclose the amount of unamortized discount. This practice is followed by most companies when the amount of unamortized discount (or premium) is small relative to other balance sheet amounts.

The annual report for Exxon provides a good example of the reporting of a bond discount:

| | 1998 | 1997 |
|---|---|---|
| | (in millions) | |
| Exxon Corporation Notes due 2004 Face value ($1,146) net of unamortized discount | $601 | $538 |

Notice that the book value of the Exxon bonds increased from 1997 to 1998. In the next section, we see how and why this change occurs.

**Measuring and Recording Interest on Bonds Issued at a Discount**   During the 10-year term of the bonds, Harrah's must make 20 semiannual cash interest payments of $20,000 (i.e., $400,000 × 5%) and at maturity pay back the $400,000 cash principal. Therefore, in addition to the cash interest, Harrah's must repay more money than it received when it sold the bonds (i.e., it borrowed $354,118 but must repay $400,000). This extra cash that it must pay is an adjustment of interest expense that ensures that creditors earn the market rate of interest on the bonds. To adjust interest expense, the bond discount must be apportioned (*amortized*) to each semiannual interest period as an increase in interest expense. Therefore, the amortization of bond discount results in an increase in bond interest expense.

The bond discount can be allocated using two amortization methods: (1) straight line and (2) effective interest. Straight-line amortization is easy to compute. The effective-interest method is discussed later in this chapter.

**Straight-Line Amortization**   To amortize the $45,882 bond discount over the life of the Harrah's bonds using the **straight-line amortization** basis, an equal dollar amount is allocated to each interest period. Harrah's bonds have 20 six-month interest periods. Therefore, the computation is $45,882 ÷ 20 periods = $2,294 amortization on each semiannual interest date. This amount is added to the cash payment of interest ($20,000) to compute interest expense for the period ($22,294). The interest payments on Harrah's bonds each period are as follows:

| Bond interest expense (E) ................... | 22,294 | |
| Discount on bonds payable (XL) ........... | | 2,294 |
| Cash (A) ................................ | | 20,000 |

| Assets | | = | Liabilities | + | Stockholders' Equity | |
| --- | --- | --- | --- | --- | --- | --- |
| Cash | −20,000 | | Discount on bonds | +2,294 | Bond interest expense | −22,294 |

Bonds payable should be reported on the balance sheet at their *book value*; that is, the maturity amount less any unamortized bond discount (or plus any unamortized bond premium). Therefore, on June 30, 20A, the book value of Harrah's bonds is $356,412 ($354,118 + $2,294).

In each succeeding interest period, the unamortized discount decreases by $2,294; therefore, the book value of the bonds increases by $2,294 each interest period. At the maturity date of the bonds, the unamortized discount (i.e., the balance in the Discount on Bonds Payable account) is *zero*. At that time, the maturity amount of the bonds and the book value are the same (i.e., $400,000).

A note from the annual report for Ames Department Stores effectively summarizes our discussion of this point:

**REAL WORLD EXCERPT**

*Ames Department Stores*

ANNUAL REPORT

**Debt**

Debt obligations that carried face interest rates significantly less than market were discounted to their present values using estimated market rates. The discount amount will be amortized to interest expense over the term of the related obligation. The determination of appropriate interest rates was based upon evaluation of Ames' credit standing, the nature of the collateral, if any, and other terms pertaining to the debt, and the prevailing rates for similar instruments or issues with similar credit rating.

Bonds are recorded at the present value of their future cash flows using an interest rate determined by the market on the date the bonds were sold. The accounting for the bonds is not affected by subsequent changes in the market rate of interest. This interest rate is based on the terms of the debt issue and the risk characteristics of the debt.

**Zero Coupon Bonds** Some bonds do not pay periodic cash interest. These bonds are often called *zero coupon bonds* because the coupon interest rate is zero. Why would an investor buy a bond that did not pay interest? Our discussion of bond discounts has probably given you a pretty good idea of the right answer. The coupon interest rate on a bond can be virtually any amount and the price of the bond will be adjusted so that investors earn the market rate of interest. A bond with a zero coupon interest rate is simply a *deep discount bond* that will sell for substantially less than its maturity value.

Let's use the $400,000 Harrah's bond to illustrate a zero coupon. Assume that instead of paying 10 percent cash interest, the bond paid *no* cash interest. The selling price of the bond is the present value of the maturity amount because no other cash payments are made over the life of the bond:

| | Present Value |
| --- | --- |
| *a.* Principal: $400,000 × $p_{n=20, i=6\%}$ (0.3118) | $124,720 |

This zero coupon bond is recorded as follows:

| Cash (A) ............................... | 124,720 | |
| Discount on bonds payable (XL) ............. | 275,280 | |
| Bonds payable (L) ...................... | | 400,000 |

| Assets | | = | Liabilities | | + | Stockholders' Equity |
| --- | --- | --- | --- | --- | --- | --- |
| Cash | +124,720 | | Discount on bonds | −275,280 | | |
| | | | Bonds payable | +400,000 | | |

As you can see, the accounting for the zero coupon bond is no different than any bond sold at a discount. The only difference is that the amount of the discount is much larger. The annual report for General Mills contained the following information concerning zero coupon bonds:

| Note 9. Long-Term Debt (in millions) | May 31, 1998 | May 31, 1997 |
|---|---|---|
| Zero Coupon notes, yield 11.7% $63.4 due 2004 | $31.8 | $28.9 |

The note from the General Mills annual report illustrates some important points concerning zero coupon bonds. Notice that the book value of the bonds increased between 1997 and 1998. This increase occurred because of the amortization of the bond discount. The book value of the bonds was $31.8 million in 1998, but they will pay $63.4 million when they mature in 2004. The growth in value is accrued but unpaid interest. Also notice that despite the fact that these bonds do not pay cash interest, they have been priced to provide the investor with an effective interest rate of 11.7 percent.

## BONDS ISSUED AT A PREMIUM

Bonds sell at a premium when the market rate of interest is *lower* than the stated interest rate on the bonds. For example, let's assume that the market rate of interest was $8\frac{1}{2}$ percent while the Harrah's bonds paid cash interest of 10 percent. In this case, the bonds sell at a premium. The cash issue price for the Harrah's bonds when the market rate of interest was $8\frac{1}{2}$ percent is computed as follows:

|  | Present Value |
|---|---|
| *a.* Principal: $400,000 $\times$ $p_{n=20, i=41/4\%}$ (0.4350) | $174,000 |
| *b.* Interest: $20,000 $\times$ $P_{n=20, i=41/4\%}$ (13.2944) | 265,888 |
| Issue (sale) price of Harrah's bonds | $439,888 |

When a bond is sold at a premium, the Bonds Payable account is credited for the par amount, and the premium is recorded as a credit to Premium on Bonds Payable. The issuance of the bonds of Harrah's at a premium is recorded as follows:

| Cash (A) ................................ | 439,888 | |
|---|---|---|
| Premium on bonds payable (L) ............ | | 39,888 |
| Bonds payable (L) ...................... | | 400,000 |

| Assets | = | Liabilities | + | Stockholders' Equity |
|---|---|---|---|---|
| Cash +439,888 | | Premium on bonds +39,888 | | |
| | | Bonds payable +400,000 | | |

The book value of the bond is the sum of the two accounts, Premium on Bonds Payable and Bonds Payable, or $439,888.

### Measuring and Recording Interest Expense on Bonds Issued at a Premium

The premium of $39,888 recorded by Harrah's must be apportioned to each of the 20 interest periods. Using the straight-line method, the amortization of premium each semiannual interest period is $39,888 ÷ 20 periods = $1,994. This amount is subtracted from the cash interest payment ($20,000) to calculate interest expense ($18,006). Therefore, amortization of the bond premium decreases interest expense. The payment of interest on the bonds is recorded as follows:

| Bond interest expense (E) ................... | 18,006 | |
| Premium on bonds payable (L) .............. | 1,994 | |
| Cash (A) ............................ | | 20,000 |

| Assets | = | Liabilities | + | Stockholders' Equity | |
|---|---|---|---|---|---|
| Cash | −20,000 | Premium on bonds | −1,994 | Bond interest expense | −18,006 |

Notice that the $20,000 cash paid each period includes $18,006 interest expense and $1,994 premium amortization. Thus, the cash payment to the investors includes the current interest they have earned plus a return of part of the premium they paid when they bought the bonds.

The book value of the bonds is the amount in the Bonds Payable account plus any unamortized premium. On June 30, 20A, the book value of the bonds is $437,894 ($400,000 + $39,888 − $1,994).

At maturity date, after the last interest payment, the $39,888 bond premium is fully amortized, and the maturity amount of the bonds and the book value of the bonds is the same (i.e., $400,000). At maturity, December 31, 20J, the bonds are paid off in full, resulting in the same entry whether the bond was originally sold at par, a discount, or a premium.

The effect of the amortization of bond discount and bond premium on a $1,000 bond is illustrated in Exhibit 10.2.

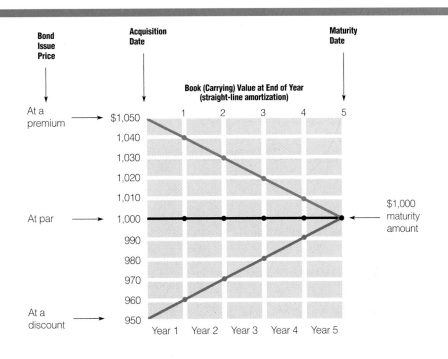

EXHIBIT **10.2**

**Amortization of Bond Discount and Premium Compared**

SELF-STUDY **QUIZ**

Assume that Harrah's issued $100,000 bonds that will mature in 10 years. The bonds pay interest twice each year at an annual rate of 9 percent. They were sold when the market rate was 8 percent. Determine the bonds' selling price.

Check your answer with the footnote at the bottom of this page.*

*$  4,500 × 13.5903 = $ 61,156
100,000 ×  0.4564 =   45,640
                      $106,796

## BONDS ISSUED AT A VARIABLE INTEREST RATE

We have discussed a number of risks associated with bonds and need to consider one more. You already have observed the impact of inflation on our economy. You may have saved up for a major purchase only to find that the item's price had increased by the time you were ready to buy it. *Inflation,* which is defined as a general rise in prices in an economy, has a powerful impact on long-term borrowing arrangements. If you lend money during a period of inflation, you will get back dollars that have less purchasing power. When people lend money, they want to be compensated both for giving up the use of their money and for any decline in the purchasing power of the dollar caused by inflation. Interest on debt has to compensate creditors for both factors. Unfortunately, it is impossible to estimate future inflation accurately. Most bonds are issued with a fixed interest rate for the life of the bond. If unexpected inflation occurs, creditors will not be adequately compensated for the declining purchasing power of the money they lent to borrowers. To compensate creditors for the effect of unexpected inflation, some debt is issued with a variable interest rate. The indenture for debt with a variable interest rate specifies an agreed upon index, such as the prime rate. When the prime rate changes, the interest rate on the debt changes. If interest rates increase, a borrower pays higher interest each period and reports higher interest expense. When rates fall, the borrower pays lower interest and reports lower expense.

# KEY **RATIO ANALYSIS:**

### TIMES INTEREST EARNED

**K**now the decision question:

Is the company generating sufficient resources from its profit-making activities to meet its current obligations associated with debt? The *times interest earned ratio* is based on a comparison of income earned and interest expense incurred. It is computed as follows:

$$\text{Times Interest Earned Ratio} = \frac{\text{Net Income} + \text{Interest Expense} + \text{Income Tax Expense}}{\text{Interest Expense}}$$

The 1998 ratio for Harrah's:

$$(\$102,024 + \$117,270 + \$74,600) \div \$117,270 = 2.51$$

**■ LEARNING OBJECTIVE 3**

Analyze the times interest earned ratio.

**E**xamine the ratio using two techniques:

| ① Comparisons over Time | | |
|---|---|---|
| Harrah's | | |
| 1996 | 1997 | 1998 |
| 3.37 | 3.12 | 2.51 |

| ② Comparisons with Competitors | |
|---|---|
| Mirage Resorts | Trump Casinos |
| 1998 | 1998 |
| 5.58 | 0.80 |

**Y**ou interpret the results carefully:

**IN GENERAL** → A high ratio is viewed more favorably than a low ratio. Basically, the ratio shows the amount of resources generated for each dollar of interest expense. A high ratio shows an extra margin of protection in case there is deterioration in profitability. Analysts are particularly interested in a company's ability to meet its required interest payments because failure to do so could result in bankruptcy.

**FOCUS COMPANY ANALYSIS** → For Harrah's, profit-making activities generated $2.51 for each dollar of interest in 1998. Harrah's income could fall substantially before the company would appear to have trouble meeting its interest obligations with resources generated by normal operations. Compare the ratio for Harrah's with the one for Trump Casinos. Notice that Trump was unable to meet its interest requirements from current operations. This would be a cause for concern for most analysts. From our earlier discussion, you may remember that Trump also had the highest debt-to-equity ratio among our three comparison companies. Clearly, Trump's ability to meet its debt obligations should be carefully reviewed.

**A FEW CAUTIONS:** The times interest earned ratio is often misleading for new or rapidly growing companies. Management of such companies often invests resources to build capacity for future operations. The times interest earned ratio reflects significant amounts of interest expense associated with the acquired capacity but current operations do not yet include the levels of expected future profitability. Analysts should be careful to understand the company's long-term strategy. While this ratio is widely used, some analysts prefer to compare interest expense to the amount of cash that a company is able to generate. They note that creditors cannot be paid with "income" that is generated; they have to be paid with cash.

## INTERNATIONAL **PERSPECTIVE**

### INTERNATIONAL FINANCIAL MARKETS

In Chapter 9, we saw that some companies borrow money in international markets, an act that may expose them to exchange rate risk. Because of the importance of international markets, U.S. institutions no longer dominate borrowing arrangements. Consider the following note from the Harrah's annual report:

> **Long-Term Debt**
> Our borrowings under our unsecured credit agreements bear interest at either the prime interest rate or the LIBOR rate.

**REAL WORLD EXCERPT**

*Harrah's, Inc.*

ANNUAL REPORT

Notice that this is a variable rate debt. Although the borrowing arrangement involved two domestic institutions, the agreement specifies an international index for determining future interest rate changes. LIBOR is an abbreviation for the London Interbank Offer Rate, which is the interest rate that international banks charge each other for overnight loans. It has become a widely accepted benchmark for determining adjustable interest rates for both corporate and government borrowers.

## FOCUS ON **CASH FLOWS**

### FINANCING ACTIVITIES

The capital structure of a corporation has a significant impact on the risk and return characteristics of a business. Because of the importance of decisions concerning capital structure, a major section of the statement of cash flows (SCF) reports transactions affecting cash flows from financing activities. The section called *Cash Flows from Financing Activities* reports both cash inflows and outflows that relate to the way that cash was obtained from external sources (owners and creditors) to finance the enterprise and its operations. An example of a cash inflow from financing activities is the issuance of a bond payable; an example of an outflow is the repayment of principal. Many students are surprised to learn that the payment of bond interest is *not* reported in the Financing Activities section of the statement of cash flows. Interest payments are directly related to earning income and are therefore reported in the *Cash Flows from Operating Activities* section of the statement of cash flows. In addition, companies are required to report the amount of cash paid for interest expense each accounting period. *Accounting Trends & Techniques* shows that companies report this information in a variety of locations.

■ **LEARNING OBJECTIVE 4**

Explain how financing activities are reported on the statement of cash flows.

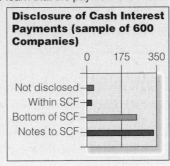

**Disclosure of Cash Interest Payments (sample of 600 Companies)**

| | 0 | 175 | 350 |
|---|---|---|---|
| Not disclosed | | | |
| Within SCF | | | |
| Bottom of SCF | | | |
| Notes to SCF | | | |

## EFFECT ON STATEMENT OF CASH FLOWS

**IN GENERAL** → As we saw in the previous chapter, transactions involving short-term creditors (e.g., accounts payable) affect working capital. Changes involving working capital accounts are reported in the operating activities section of the statement of cash flows. Cash received from long-term creditors is reported as an inflow from financing activities section. Cash payments made to long-term creditors (with the exception of interest expense) are reported as outflows from financing activities. Examples are shown in the following table:

|  | Effect on Cash Flows |
|---|---|
| Financing activities (indirect method) | |
| Issuance of bonds | + |
| Debt retirement | − |
| Repayment of bond principal upon maturity | − |

**FOCUS COMPANY ANALYSIS** → A segment of Harrah's statement of cash flows, prepared using the indirect method, follows. The first four items pertain to issues discussed in this chapter. The remaining items will be discussed in other chapters.

It might seem surprising for the company to retire $563,522,000 in old debt and issue $737,448,000 in new debt during the same accounting period. This situation illustrates that although businesses normally borrow money to finance the acquisition of long-lived assets, they also borrow to rearrange their capital structure. In the case of Harrah's, the company had outstanding debt with an interest rate of 9.25 percent. They were able to retire this debt by borrowing money at an interest rate of 7.875 percent, resulting in an annual savings of nearly $8 million in interest cost.

Analysts are particularly interested in the Financing Activities section of the statement of cash flows because it provides important insights about the future capital structure for the company. Rapidly growing companies typically report significant amounts of funds in this section of the statement of cash flows.

**REAL WORLD EXCERPT**

*Harrah's*

ANNUAL REPORT

| Statement of Cash Flows | 1998 | 1997 | 1996 |
|---|---|---|---|
| Cash flows from financing activities | | | |
| Proceeds from issuance of senior subordinated notes, net of issue costs of $12,552 | $737,448,000 | $          0 | $          0 |
| Net borrowings under Revolving Credit Facility, net of financing costs of $9,332 in 1998 and $982 in 1996 | 362,262,000 | 239,500,000 | 133,518,000) |
| Debt retirements | (563,522,000) | (202,115,000) | (2,488,000) |
| Premiums paid on early extinguishments of debt | (24,569,000) | (9,666,000) | 0 |
| Minority interests' distributions, net of contributions | (6,200,000) | (9,952,000) | (10,840,000) |
| Purchases of treasury stock | 0 | (41,022,000) | (13,014,000) |
| Other | 0 | (45,000) | 0 |
| Cash flows provided by (used in) financing activities | $505,419,000 | $(23,300,000) | $107,176,000 |

## ADDITIONAL TOPICS IN ACCOUNTING FOR BONDS PAYABLE

In the following sections, we discuss several topics commonly encountered in accounting for bonds payable: (1) effective-interest amortization of bond discounts and premiums, (2) early retirement of debt, and (3) bond sinking funds.

## EFFECTIVE-INTEREST AMORTIZATION OF BOND DISCOUNTS AND PREMIUMS

We introduced you to the straight-line method for amortizing a bond discount or premium earlier in this chapter. The only advantage of the straight-line method is the simplicity of its calculation. Under generally accepted accounting principles (GAAP), the straight-line method may be used only if the reported results are not materially different from the effective-interest method. The **effective-interest method** is a conceptually superior method to amortize a bond discount or premium. We believe it provides a better basis for understanding why the amortization of a bond discount or premium is an adjustment to interest expense.

Interest expense is the cost of borrowing money and is correctly measured by multiplying the *true* interest rate times the amount of money that was actually borrowed. The true interest rate is the rate that the market used to determine the present value of the bond. The actual amount borrowed is the cash that was received when the bond was sold, not the maturity value of the bond.

Under the effective-interest method, interest expense for a bond is computed by multiplying the current unpaid balance (i.e., the amount that was actually borrowed) times the market rate of interest that existed on the date the bonds were sold. The periodic amortization of a bond premium or discount is then calculated as the difference between interest expense and the amount of cash paid or accrued.

Earlier in this chapter, we illustrated accounting for bonds issued at a discount. Let's expand that example to see how the discount is amortized under the effective-interest method. The previous example involved 10 percent Harrah's bonds with a par value of $400,000 that were issued when the market rate was 12 percent. The issue price of the bonds was $354,118, and the bond discount was $45,882.

The first interest payment on Harrah's bonds is on June 30, 20A. The journal entry to record interest expense is basically the same as the one shown earlier in this chapter under the straight-line method. The only difference is the amount. The interest expense at the end of the first six months is calculated by multiplying the amount that was actually borrowed by the market rate of interest for six months ($354,118 × 12% × $\frac{6}{12}$ = $21,247). The amount of cash that is paid is calculated by multiplying the principal by the stated rate of interest for six months ($400,000 × 10% × $\frac{6}{12}$ = $20,000). The difference between the interest expense and the cash paid (or accrued) is the amount of discount that has been amortized ($21,247 − $20,000 = $1,247).

The amortization of the bond discount reduces the balance of the Discount on Bonds Payable account. A reduction of a contra-liability account increases the book value of the liability, as shown:

|  | January 1, 20A | June 30, 20A |
| --- | --- | --- |
| Bonds payable | $400,000 | $400,000 |
| Discount on bonds payable | 45,882 | 44,635* |
| Book value | $354,118 | $355,365 |

*$45,882 − $1,247 = $44,635.

Each period, the amortization of the bond discount increases the bond's book value (or unpaid balance). The $1,247 amortization of bond discount can be thought of as interest that was earned by the bondholders but not paid to them. During the first six months of 20A, the bondholders earned interest of $21,247 but received only $20,000 in cash. The additional $1,247 was added to the principal of the bond and will be paid when the bond matures.

Interest expense for the second six months of 20A must reflect the change in the unpaid balance of bonds payable that occurred with the amortization of the bond discount. The interest expense for the second half of 20A is calculated by multiplying the

■ **LEARNING OBJECTIVE 5**

Use the effective-interest method of amortization.

The **EFFECTIVE-INTEREST METHOD** amortizes a bond discount or premium on the basis of the effective-interest rate; theoretically preferred method.

unpaid balance on June 30, 20A, by the market rate of interest for six months ($355,365 × 12% × ⁶⁄₁₂ = $21,322). The amortization of the bond discount in the second period is $1,322.

Notice that interest expense for the second half of 20A is more than the amount for the first six months of 20A. This is logical because Harrah's effectively borrowed more money during the second half of the year (i.e., the $1,247 unpaid interest). Interest expense increases each year during the life of the bond because of the amortization of the bond discount.

An example that demonstrates both a bond premium and an adjusting entry to record accrued interest under the effective-interest amortization method is provided in the demonstration case at the end of this chapter.

Some companies use a bond amortization schedule to assist them with the detailed computations required under the effective-interest amortization method. A typical schedule follows:

| Date | (a)<br>Cash Interest | (b)<br>Interest Expense | (c)<br>Amortization | (d)<br>Unpaid Balance |
|---|---|---|---|---|
| 1/1/20A | | | | $354,118 |
| 6/30/20A | $20,000 | $21,247 | $1,247 | 355,365 |
| 12/31/20A | 20,000 | 21,322 | 1,322 | 356,687 |

**Comparisons of Amortization Methods**

- Straight-line amortization
- Effective interest amortization (discount)

Interest expense (column b) is computed by multiplying the market rate of interest by the unpaid balance at the beginning of the period (column d). Amortization is computed by subtracting cash interest (column a) from interest expense (column b). The unpaid balance (column d) is computed by adding amortization (column c) to the unpaid balance at the beginning of the period.

Under the effective-interest method, interest expense changes each accounting period as the effective amount of the liability changes. Under the straight-line method, interest expense remains constant over the life of the bond. The chart illustrates these differences.

# FINANCIAL **ANALYSIS**

## UNDERSTANDING ALTERNATIVE AMORTIZATION METHODS

Although the effective-interest method is preferred conceptually, some companies use the straight-line method because of the materiality constraint. Accounting for various transactions should conform with GAAP unless the amounts involved are immaterial and will not affect the decisions made by users of the statements. The straight-line method is permitted when the difference in periodic amortization between the two methods is not material in amount. Because differences are immaterial, most financial statements do not disclose which method the company uses. Harrah's is an exception; it indicates the following in its notes:

**REAL WORLD EXCERPT**

*Harrah's*

ANNUAL REPORT

**Summary of Significant Accounting Policies**
Original issue discount is amortized over the life of the related indebtedness using the effective interest method.

Compare the note for Harrah's to one from Kansas City Southern Industries:

**REAL WORLD EXCERPT**

*Kansas City Southern Industries*

ANNUAL REPORT

**Note 5: Debt**
Debt was issued at a discount of $1.6 million which will be amortized over the respective debt maturities on a straight line basis which is not materially different from the interest method.

Notice that in both cases, the analysts cannot quantify the impact of using one method versus the other. As a result, most analysts are not concerned about which method a company chooses.

## EARLY RETIREMENT OF DEBT

Bonds are normally issued for long periods of time, such as 20 or 30 years. As mentioned earlier in the chapter, bondholders who need cash prior to the maturity date can simply sell the bonds to another investor. This transaction does not affect the books of the company that issued the bonds.

In several situations, a corporation decides to retire a bond before its maturity date. A bond with a *call feature* may be called in for early retirement at the issuer's option. Typically, the bond indenture includes a call premium if the bonds are retired before the maturity date. This call premium often is stated as a percentage of the par value of the bonds. The prospectus for Harrah's's bonds included the following:

**■ LEARNING OBJECTIVE 6**

Report the early retirement of bonds.

**REAL WORLD EXCERPT**

*Harrah's, Inc.*

BOND PROSPECTUS

The bonds will be subject to redemption at the option of the Company, in whole or in part . . . at the redemption prices set forth below plus accrued and unpaid interest thereon:

| Year | Percentage |
|------|------------|
| 2000 | 102.775% |
| 2001 | 101.850% |
| 2002 | 100.925% |
| 2003 and thereafter | 100.000% |

Assume that in 1994, Harrah's issued 10 percent bonds in the amount of $1 million and that the bonds sold at par. If the bonds were called in 2001 with 90 days of accrued interest, Harrah's makes the following journal entry:

| | | |
|---|---|---|
| Bonds payable (L) . . . . . . . . . . . . . . . . . . . . . . . . | 1,000,000 | |
| Interest expense (E) . . . . . . . . . . . . . . . . . . . . . | 25,000* | |
| Loss on bond call (Loss) . . . . . . . . . . . . . . . . . | 18,500 | |
| Cash (A) . . . . . . . . . . . . . . . . . . . . . . . . . . . | | 1,043,500 |

*$1,000,000 × 10% × 90/360 = $25,000

| Assets | = | Liabilities | + | Stockholders' Equity | |
|--------|---|-------------|---|---------------------|---|
| Cash −1,043,500 | | Bonds payable −1,000,000 | | Interest expense | −25,000 |
| | | | | Loss | −18,500 |

The loss on bond call is the amount over par that must be paid according to the bond indenture. This amount is 1.850 percent (101.850% − 100.000%), which is multiplied by the par value of the bond to derive the expense of $18,500 (1.850% × $1,000,000). The loss on bond call is reported on the income statement as an extraordinary item.

A few years ago Southwestern Bell engaged in a transaction similar to the one just illustrated; it included the following description in the notes to its statements:

The Telephone Company reflected an extraordinary loss on the early extinguishment of debt as the result of refinancing $732,000,000 of long-term bonds. Expense associated with the refinancing, including a call premium of $67,500,000, totaled $129,300,000.

In other cases, a company may elect to retire debt early by purchasing it in the open market, just as an investor would. This approach is necessary if the bond did not have a call feature. It might also be an attractive approach if the price of the bonds fell after the date of issue.

What factors could cause the price of a bond to fall? The most common cause is a rise in interest rates. As you may have noticed during our discussion of present value concepts earlier in this chapter, bond prices move in the opposite direction of interest rates. If interest rates go up, bond prices fall, and vice versa. When interest rates have gone up, a company that wants to retire a bond before maturity may find that it is less expensive to buy the bond in the market than to pay a call premium.

Harrah's engaged in this type of transaction as described in the notes to its statement:

In the current and previous years, the Company purchased $12,096,000 and $18,460,000 face value, respectively, of the 11⅜% Mortgage-Backed Bonds Due 2002 for $11,696,000 and $12,258,000, respectively. Accordingly, the Company realized an extraordinary gain in the current year of $273,000 before income taxes of $93,000, resulting in an after-tax gain of $180,000 or $.02 per share. In the previous year, the Company realized an extraordinary gain of $6,015,000 before income taxes of $2,045,000, resulting in an after-tax gain of $3,970,000 or $.35 per share.

The note illustrates three important issues. The gain or loss on the early retirement of debt is always reported separately on the income statement as an extraordinary item. The gain from this transaction is taxable, which is an important cost for managers to consider. The amount of the gain from the early retirement of debt can be substantial. The $.35 per share gain mentioned in Harrah's note was more than 60 percent of the income reported in that year. Analysts must use caution when evaluating gains from debt retirement because these gains do not represent profits from the company's ongoing business activities.

## BOND SINKING FUNDS

**LEARNING OBJECTIVE 7**

Explain the use of bond sinking funds.

A **BOND SINKING FUND** is a cash fund accumulated for payment of a bond at maturity.

To reduce risk for bondholders, many bond indentures include the requirement that the company establish a **bond sinking fund,** which is a special cash fund to be used to meet the principal payment when the bond matures. This fund assures creditors that cash will be available for retirement of the bonds at their maturity date. Managers, on the other hand, prefer not to have a sinking fund requirement because it forces them to put cash in a special fund instead of investing it in productive assets related to the operations of the business.

Normally, cash contributions are made to the fund each year. The cash often is deposited with an independent trustee (a designated third party such as a bank or another financial institution). The trustee invests the cash and adds the earnings to the fund balance each year. Interest earned on a sinking fund is recorded as an increase in the fund balance (a debit) and as interest revenue (a credit). Thus, a bond sinking fund has the characteristics of a savings account. At the maturity date, the balance of the fund is used to pay the bondholders. Any excess cash is returned to the issuing corporation, or, in the case of a deficit, the issuer makes it up.

The purpose of a sinking fund is to reduce the risk that the issuer will not be able to meet the principal payment when bonds mature. As a result, many bond indentures permit the issuing corporation to meet sinking fund requirements either by making cash payments to a fund or by redeeming outstanding bonds. The notes to Harrah's statements indicate that "the debt will not be entitled to the benefit of any sinking fund." A note to a recent annual report for Harrow Industries illustrates a typical disclosure concerning sinking funds:

> The debentures require annual sinking fund payments of $6,500,000 beginning April 15, 1995. Sinking fund payments may be deferred to the extent that debentures purchased on the open market are tendered for cancellation. The Company has repurchased debentures totaling $26,970,000 which are available for such purpose.

**REAL WORLD EXCERPT**

*Harrow Industries*
ANNUAL REPORT

By repurchasing debentures, Harrow Industries is able to satisfy sinking fund requirements for nearly four years. As a result, it will not have to make deposits of $6.5 million for each of those years. This type of information is important to analysts who wish to project the future cash flows of a business.

A bond sinking fund normally is reported on the balance sheet as a noncurrent asset. This is done because the cash in the fund is not available for ongoing business activities or to pay current liabilities. It would be misleading for financial analysts to conclude that a bond sinking fund was part of a company's working capital.

## FINANCIAL **ANALYSIS**

### UNDERSTANDING NOTES TO FINANCIAL STATEMENTS

As mentioned earlier, features are included in bond indentures to make the bond issue more attractive to potential creditors. The wide variety of features available can make some bond contracts quite complex. Fortunately, most of the features are based on the concepts that have been discussed in this chapter. As a result, you should be able to analyze most bonds issued by corporations. To illustrate, consider the following note from the Eastman Kodak annual report:

> **Bond Liabilities**
> The zero coupon convertible subordinated debentures due in 2011 ($3,680 million face value, 6.75% yield to maturity) are convertible at the option of the holder at any time prior to maturity for the Company's common stock at a conversion rate of 5.622 shares per debenture. At the option of the holder, the debenture must be purchased by the Company at October 15, 2001 and 2006 at a price equal to the issue price plus amortized discount.

**REAL WORLD EXCERPT**

*Eastman Kodak*
ANNUAL REPORT

This note would be impossible to understand if you had not studied the chapter, but, as you can see, it includes many of the issues that we have discussed.

## SELF-STUDY **QUIZ**

Which company has the higher level of risk associated with debt—a company that has a high debt-equity ratio and a high interest coverage ratio or a company with a low debt-equity ratio and a low interest coverage ratio?

Check your answer with the footnote at the bottom of this page. *

---

\* A company can be forced into bankruptcy if it does not meet its interest obligations to creditors. Many successful companies borrow very large amounts of money without creating unreasonable risk because they generate sufficient funds from normal operations to meet their obligations. Even a small amount of debt can be a problem if a company cannot generate funds to meet current interest obligations. Usually, the company with a high debt-to-equity ratio and a high interest coverage ratio is viewed as being less risky.

# LONG-TERM INVESTMENTS IN BONDS

■ **LEARNING OBJECTIVE 8**

Report bond investments held to maturity.

To this point, we have discussed bonds from the issuer's perspective. Let's change that perspective and consider bonds from the point of view of a corporation that purchases bonds from another corporation. The only reason to invest in bonds is to earn a return on funds because bonds do not permit the holder to exert influence over another company, as is the case with an investment in common stock. Corporate bonds are riskier than government securities and savings accounts. As a result, an investment in the bonds of another corporation permits an investing corporation to earn a higher rate of return.

Bonds may be held for either short-term or long-term purposes. Short-term investments in bonds will be discussed with short-term investments in common stock in Chapter 11. In this chapter, we discuss accounting for long-term investments in bonds.

As was discussed earlier in this chapter, bonds have a fixed maturity date. This fixed maturity date offers important advantages to corporations that invest in bonds. Why would managers of a corporation invest in bonds of another corporation? A key responsibility for senior executives is cash flow management, both short term and long term. Just as a corporation must have cash on hand to meet its current obligations, it must plan to have cash available to meet its long-term needs, such as the maturity of debt or the replacement of productive assets. Bonds permit management of the investing corporation to plan future cash flows with a minimum of risk. Management that needs cash in five years can purchase bonds that mature in five years. Bonds will pay their face value on their maturity date, which permits the creditor to budget future cash flows effectively. Prior to maturity, a bond may sell for more or less than its face value, depending on interest rates in the market. If a bond must be sold prior to maturity, the amount of cash that will be available is uncertain. By holding bonds to maturity, a corporation can eliminate this uncertainty.

A **HELD-TO-MATURITY INVESTMENT** is a long-term investment in bonds that management has the ability and intent to hold until maturity.

When management plans to hold a bond until its maturity, it is reported in an account appropriately called **Held-to-Maturity Investment.** Bonds should be listed as held-to-maturity securities if management has the intent and the ability to hold them until maturity. These bonds are listed at cost (adjusted for the amortization of any bond discount or premium), not at their fair market value. Cost is considered to be a more reasonable measure of value because, by definition, the bonds will be held to maturity, at which time they will be worth face value. Unrealized gains and losses on bonds will disappear as the bonds approach their maturity date. Therefore, it is misleading to record these gains and losses during the life of the bonds.

Harrah's does not show any bond investments on its balance sheet. This probably is not surprising given the growth strategy the company adopted. Management currently wants to invest all available cash in new facilities instead of the bonds of other corporations.

Halliburton Corporation includes held-to-maturity securities on its balance sheet. Its notes to the statements indicate the following:

REAL WORLD EXCERPT

*Halliburton Corporation*
ANNUAL REPORT

**Note 1: Significant accounting policies.**
Investments classified as held-to-maturity are measured at amortized cost. This classification is based on the company's intent and ability to hold these securities to full maturity.

The annual report for JCPenney shows investments in stock and bonds of other corporations of nearly $2 billion (or approximately 10 percent of the company's assets). The majority of this investment is in bonds. Why would a retailer like JCPenney have an investment strategy that relies so heavily on bonds? The answer is related to the nature of its business. It owns an insurance subsidiary, JCPenney Direct Marketing, which sells life, health, and accident insurance. The insurance business is unusual in the sense that a company collects cash premiums months or years in advance of having to pay out policy claims. As a result, the company can earn income from two sources: (1) income it earns from selling insurance, and (2) investment income it earns on cash it holds before it has to pay out policy claims. While JCPenney wants to maximize the income it earns on investments, it would assume a large amount of risk if it invested all of its cash in the stock market. It might have difficulty in paying policy claims if stock prices were severely depressed, as was the case with the stock market crash of 1987. By investing in bonds, JCPenney Direct Marketing can match the maturity date of bonds with the actuarially determined date that it expects to pay policy claims. Through this matching process, JCPenney substantially reduces the market risk of its investments.

## REPORTING BOND INVESTMENTS HELD TO MATURITY

At the date of purchase, a bond investment that management intends to hold to maturity is recorded in conformity with the *cost principle*. The purchase cost, including all incidental acquisition costs (such as transfer fees and broker commissions), is debited to the Held-to-Maturity account. This amount may be the same as the maturity amount (if acquired at par), less than the maturity amount (if acquired at a discount), or more than the maturity amount (if acquired at a premium). Usually the premium or discount on a bond investment is not recorded in a separate account as is done for bonds payable. The investment account shows the current book value.

When discussing a bond, many analysts refer to its price as a percentage of par. *The Wall Street Journal* might report, for example, that an Exxon bond with a par value of $1,000 is selling at 82.97, which means that it would cost $829.70 (82.97 percent of $1,000) to buy the bond. Bond prices traditionally are quoted as a percentage of par, but the determination of the price is based on the present value techniques discussed earlier in this chapter. The concepts underlying accounting for bond investments are the same as accounting for bond liabilities.

### BONDS PURCHASED AT PAR

To illustrate accounting for bond investments, assume that on July 1, 20F, Harrah's invested $100,000 in 10-year, 8 percent bonds purchased in the open market. The bonds were issued originally on July 1, 20A, and mature on June 30, 20K. The 8 percent interest is paid each June 30 and December 31. Harrah's management plans to hold the bonds until maturity.

When bond investors accept a rate of interest on a bond investment that is the same as the stated rate of interest on the bonds, the bonds will sell at par (i.e., at 100). The journal entry to record the purchase of the bond follows:

| Held-to-maturity investment (A) | 100,000 | |
| Cash (A) | | 100,000 |

| Assets | | = | Liabilities | + | Stockholders' Equity |
|---|---|---|---|---|---|
| Cash | −100,000 | | | | |
| Held-to-maturity invest. | +100,000 | | | | |

If a bond investment was acquired at par, the book value remains constant over the life of the investment because no premium or discount must be amortized. In this situation, revenue earned from the investment each period is measured as the amount of cash interest collected (or accrued). The following journal entry records the receipt of interest on December 31:

| Cash (A) ($100,000 × 8% × ⁶⁄₁₂) | 4,000 | |
| Interest revenue (R) | | 4,000 |

| Assets | | = | Liabilities | + | Stockholders' Equity | |
|---|---|---|---|---|---|---|
| Cash | +4,000 | | | | Interest revenue | +4,000 |

## BONDS PURCHASED AT A DISCOUNT

If bond investors demand a rate of interest that is higher than the stated rate, bonds sell at a *bond discount*. When a bond is purchased at a discount, the investor receives the periodic interest payments stated in the bond contract plus the maturity value, which is an amount higher than the initial cash invested. As a result, the investor earns a return that is higher than the stated rate.

To illustrate accounting for a bond issued at a discount, assume that on July 1, 20F, Harrah's bought 8 percent bonds with a maturity value of $250,000 and paid $240,000 cash (the bonds sold at a discount). The bonds will mature in five years (in 20K); interest is paid each June 30 and December 31. Harrah's management intends to hold the bonds until maturity.

The purchase of the bonds is recorded as follows:

| Held-to-maturity investment (A) | 240,000 | |
|---|---|---|
| Cash (A) | | 240,000 |

| Assets | | = | Liabilities | + | Stockholders' Equity |
|---|---|---|---|---|---|
| Held-to-maturity invest. | +240,000 | | | | |
| Cash | −240,000 | | | | |

Notice that the purchase cost is recorded in the investment account. It is not necessary to record the investment at par and establish a separate bond discount account; however, it is necessary to keep track of the bond discount and amortize it over the life of the bond.

The interest earned on the bonds purchased by Harrah's will total more than the annual interest payments (8% × $250,000 × 5 years = $100,000). This is true because Harrah's will receive $250,000 when the bonds mature but paid only $240,000 when it purchased them. This extra $10,000 is additional interest revenue.

Interest revenue is recorded on December 31 as follows:

| Cash (A) ($250,000 × 8% × 6/12) | 10,000 | |
|---|---|---|
| Held-to-maturity investment (A) | 1,000 | |
| Interest revenue (R) | | 11,000 |

| Assets | | = | Liabilities | + | Stockholders' Equity | |
|---|---|---|---|---|---|---|
| Cash | +10,000 | | | | Interest revenue | +11,000 |
| Held-to-maturity invest. | +1,000 | | | | | |

The debit to the Held-to-Maturity Investment account represents amortization of the bond discount. The discount is amortized over the life of the bond; most companies use the straight-line amortization method for bond investments. The life of the bonds purchased by Harrah's is five years or 10 interest periods because the bonds pay interest every six months. The bond discount is allocated with an equal amount to each period, $10,000 ÷ 10 periods, or $1,000. Interest revenue for the period is cash received (or accrued) plus the amortization of the bond discount.

When a bond is held to maturity, a portion of the bond discount is amortized each period. Through amortization of the discount, the balance of the investment account is increased each period so that the book value will be the same as the par amount on the maturity date. In our example, the bonds purchased by Harrah's mature on June 30, 20K. At that point, the bond discount will be fully amortized and Harrah's will receive their maturity value.

Accounting for bond investments when bonds are purchased at a premium is based on the same concepts as accounting for bonds purchased at a discount. In the case of a bond premium, amortization reduces the balance of the investment account so that the book value will be the same as the par value on the maturity date.

# DEMONSTRATION **CASE**

(Try to resolve the requirements before proceeding to the suggested solution that follows.)

To raise funds to build a new plant, Reed Company management issued bonds. The board of directors approved a bond indenture. Some provisions in the bond indenture specified on the bond certificates follow:

Par value of the bonds ($1,000 bonds) $600,000.

Date of bond issue—February 1, 20A; due in 10 years on January 31, 20K.

Interest—10 percent per annum, payable 5 percent on each July 31 and January 31.

All of the bonds were sold on February 1, 20A, at 102½. The annual accounting period for Reed Company ends on December 31.

*Required:*

1. How much cash did Reed Company receive from the sale of the bonds payable on February 1, 20A? Show computations.
2. What was the amount of premium on the bonds payable? Over how many months should it be amortized?
3. Compute the amount of amortization of premium per month and for each six-month interest period; use straight-line amortization. Round to the nearest dollar.
4. Give the journal entry on February 1, 20A, to record the sale and issuance of the bonds payable.
5. Give the journal entry for payment of interest and amortization of premium for the first interest payment on July 31, 20A.
6. Give the adjusting entry required on December 31, 20A, at the end of the accounting period.
7. Give the journal entry to record the second interest payment and the amortization of premium on January 31, 20B.
8. Show how bond interest expense and bonds payable are reported on the financial statements at December 31, 20A.

## SUGGESTED SOLUTION

1. Sale price of the bonds: $600,000 × 102.5% = $615,000.
2. Premium on the bonds payable: $600,000 × 2.5% = $15,000.
   Months amortized: From date of sale, February 1, 20A, to maturity date, January 31, 20K = 120 months.
3. Premium amortization: $15,000 ÷ 120 months = $125 per month, or $750 each six-month interest period (straight line).
4. February 1, 20A (issuance date):

| | | |
|---|---|---|
| Cash (A) . . . . . . . . . . . . . . . . . . . . . . . . . . . . . . . . . . . . . . . . . . . . | 615,000 | |
|     Premium on bonds payable (L) . . . . . . . . . . . . . . . . . . . . . . . . . | | 15,000 |
|     Bonds payable (L) . . . . . . . . . . . . . . . . . . . . . . . . . . . . . . . . . | | 600,000 |
| *To record sale of bonds payable at 102½.* | | |

5. July 31, 20A (first interest payment date):

| | | |
|---|---|---|
| Bond interest expense (E) ($30,000 − $750) . . . . . . . . . . . . . . . . | 29,250 | |
| Premium on bonds payable (L) . . . . . . . . . . . . . . . . . . . . . . . . . . | 750 | |
|     Cash (A) ($600,000 × 5%) . . . . . . . . . . . . . . . . . . . . . . . . . . . | | 30,000 |
| *To record payment of semiannual interest.* | | |

6. December 31, 20A (end of the accounting period):

| | | |
|---|---|---|
| Bond interest expense (E) . . . . . . . . . . . . . . . . . . . . . . . . . . . . . . | 24,375 | |
| Premium on bonds payable (L) ($125 × 5 months) . . . . . . . . . . . | 625 | |
|     Bond interest payable (L) ($600,000 × 10% × 5/12) . . . . . . . . . | | 25,000 |
| *Adjusting entry for five months' interest accrued plus amortization of premium,* | | |
| *August 1 to December 31, 20A.* | | |

7. January 31, 20B (second interest date):

| | | |
|---|---:|---:|
| Bond interest payable (L) ................................ | 25,000 | |
| Premium on bonds payable (L) ......................... | 125 | |
| Bond interest expense (E) .............................. | 4,875 | |
|     Cash (A) ........................................... | | 30,000 |
| *To record payment of semiannual interest.* | | |

8. Interest expense reported on the 20A income statement should be for the period outstanding during the year (i.e., for 11 months, February 1 through December 31). Interest expense, per these entries, is $29,250 + $24,375 = $53,625; alternatively ($600,000 $\times$ 10% $\times$ $\frac{11}{12}$ = $55,000) − ($125 $\times$ 11 months = $1,375) = $53,625.

| | |
|---|---:|
| **Income statement for 20A:** | |
| Interest expense | $ 53,625 |
| **Balance sheet, December 31, 20A:** | |
| **Long-term liabilities:** | |
|   Bonds payable, 10% (due January 31, 20K) | 600,000 |
|   Add unamortized premium* | 13,625 |
| | $613,625 |
| *$15,000 − ($750 + $625) = $13,625. | |

## CHAPTER **TAKE-AWAYS**

1. **Describe bond characteristics and use the debt-to-equity ratio.   540**
   Bonds have a number of characteristics designed to meet the needs of the issuing corporation and the creditor. A complete listing of bond characteristics is shown in Exhibit 10.1.
   Corporations use bonds to raise long-term capital. Bonds offer a number of advantages compared to stock, including financial leverage, the tax deductibility of interest, and the fact that control of the company is not diluted. Bonds do carry additional risk because interest and principal payments are not discretionary.
   The debt-to-equity ratio compares the amount of capital supplied by creditors to the amount supplied by owners. It is a measure of a company's debt capacity. It is an important ratio because high risk is associated with debt capital because of obligatory payments.

2. **Report bonds payable and interest expense, with bonds sold at par, at a discount and at a premium.   545**
   Three types of events must be recorded over the life of a typical bond: (1) the receipt of cash when the bond is first sold, (2) the periodic payment of cash interest, and (3) the repayment of principal upon the maturity of the bond.
   Bonds are sold at a discount whenever the coupon interest rate is less than the market rate of interest. A discount is the dollar amount of the difference between the par value of the bond and its selling price. The discount is recorded as a contra-liability when the bond is sold and is amortized over the life of the bond as an adjustment to interest expense.
   Bonds are sold at a premium whenever the coupon interest rate is more than the market rate of interest. A premium is the dollar amount of the difference between the selling price of the bond and its par value. The premium is recorded as a liability when the bond is sold and is amortized over the life of the bond as an adjustment to interest expense.

3. **Analyze the times interest earned ratio.   552**
   This ratio measures the ability of a company to meet its interest obligations with resources from its profit-making activities. The ratio is computed by comparing interest expense to earnings (including net income, interest expense, and income tax expense).

4. **Explain how financing activities are reported on the statement of cash flows.   553**
   Cash flows associated with transactions involving long-term creditors are reported in the Financing Activities section of the statement of cash flows. Interest expense is reported in the Operating Activities section, however.

5. **Use the effective-interest method of amortization.**   555

   There are two methods to amortize bond discounts and premiums: (1) the straight-line method and (2) the effective-interest method. Under the effective-interest method, interest expense is computed by multiplying the current amount of the bond liability by the market rate of interest that existed when the bonds were first issued.

6. **Report the early retirement of bonds.**   557

   A corporation may retire bonds before their maturity date. The difference between the book value and the amount paid to retire the bonds is reported as a gain or loss, depending on the circumstances.

7. **Explain the use of bond sinking funds.**   558

   To reduce risk for bondholders, a bond sinking fund may be established. The issuing corporation makes periodic payments to a special cash account that is used meet the principal payment when the bond matures.

8. **Report bond investments held to maturity.**   560

   When management plans to hold a bond until maturity, it is reported as a noncurrent asset with the title *held-to-maturity investment*. Any discount or premium is amortized over the remaining life of the bond.

The capital structure of a business is made up of funds supplied by both the creditors and the owners. In this chapter, we discussed the role of bonds in the capital structure of a business. In the next chapter, we will discuss stockholders' equity.

## KEY **RATIOS**

**Debt-to-equity ratio** measures the balance between debt and equity. Debt funds are viewed as being riskier than equity funds. The ratio is computed as follows (p. 541):

$$\text{Debt-to-Equity} = \frac{\text{Total Liabilities}}{\text{Owners' Equity}}$$

**Times interest earned ratio** measures a company's ability to generate resources from current operations to meet its interest obligations. The computation of this ratio follows (p. 552):

$$\text{Times Interest Earned} = \frac{\text{Net Income} + \text{Interest Expense} + \text{Income Tax Expense}}{\text{Interest Expense}}$$

## FINDING **FINANCIAL INFORMATION**

**BALANCE SHEET**

*Under Current Liabilities*

Bonds are normally listed as long-term liabilities. An exception occurs when the bonds are within one year of maturity. Such bonds are reported as current liabilities with the following title:

Current portion of long-term debt

*Under Noncurrent Liabilities*

Bonds are listed under a variety of titles, depending on the characteristics of the bond. Titles include

   Bonds payable

   Debentures

   Convertible bonds

**INCOME STATEMENT**

Bonds are shown only on the balance sheet, never on the income statement. Interest expense associated with bonds is reported on the income statement. Most companies report interest expense in a separate category on the income statement.

**STATEMENT OF CASH FLOWS**

*Under Financing Activities*

   + Cash inflows from long-term creditors

   − Cash outflows to long-term creditors

*Under Operating Activities*

   The cash outflow associated with interest expense is reported as an operating activity.

**NOTES**

*Under Summary of Significant Accounting Policies*

   Description of pertinent information concerning accounting treatment of liabilities. Normally, there is minimal information. Some companies report the method used to amortize bond discounts and premiums.

*Under a Separate Note*

   Most companies include a separate note called "Long-Term Debt" that reports information about each major debt issue, including amount and interest rate. The note also provides detail concerning debt covenants.

## KEY **TERMS**

| | |
|---|---|
| **Bond Certificate**  p. 544 | **Financial Leverage**  p. 540 |
| **Bond Discount**  p. 545 | **Held-to-Maturity Investment**  p. 560 |
| **Bond Premium**  p. 545 | **Indenture**  p. 543 |
| **Bond Principal**  p. 542 | **Market Interest Rate**  p. 545 |
| **Bond Sinking Fund**  p. 558 | **Net Interest Cost**  p. 540 |
| **Callable Bonds**  p. 544 | **Par Value**  p. 542 |
| **Convertible Bonds**  p. 544 | **Redeemable Bonds**  p. 544 |
| **Coupon Rate**  p. 545 | **Stated Rate**  p. 542 |
| **Debenture**  p. 542 | **Straight-Line Amortization**  p. 548 |
| **Effective-Interest Method**  p. 555 | **Trustee**  p. 544 |
| **Effective-Interest Rate**  p. 545 | **Yield**  p. 545 |
| **Face Amount**  p. 542 | |

## QUESTIONS

1. What are the primary characteristics of a bond? For what purposes are bonds usually issued?
2. What is the difference between a bond indenture and a bond certificate?
3. Differentiate secured bonds from unsecured bonds.
4. Differentiate among callable, redeemable, and convertible bonds.
5. From the perspective of the issuer, what are some advantages of issuing bonds instead of issuing capital stock?
6. As the tax rate increases, the net cost of borrowing money decreases. Explain.
7. Explain financial leverage. Can it be negative?
8. At the date of issuance, bonds are recorded at their current cash equivalent amount. Explain.
9. What is the nature of the discount and premium on bonds payable? Explain.
10. What is the difference between the stated interest rate and the effective-interest rate on a bond?
11. Differentiate between the stated and effective rates of interest on a bond (a) sold at par, (b) sold at a discount, and (c) sold at a premium.
12. What is the book value of a bond payable?
13. Explain the basic difference between straight-line amortization and effective-interest methods of amortizing bond discount or premium. Explain when each method should or may be used.
14. If management plans (and has the ability) to hold a common stock investment for the long term, should it be reported in the Held-to-Maturity Investment account? Explain.

# MINI-EXERCISES

**M10–1** **Finding Financial Information**  **LO1, 2**

For each of the following items, specify whether the information would be found in the balance sheet, the income statement, the statement of cash flows, the notes to the statements, or not at all.

1. The amount of a bond liability.

2. Interest expense for the period.

3. Cash interest paid for the period.

4. Interest rates for specific bond issues.

5. The names of major holders of bonds.

6. The maturity date of specific bond issues.

**M10–2** **Computing Bond Issuance Price** **LO2**

Coopers Company plans to issue $500,000, 10-year, 10 percent bonds. Interest is payable semiannually each June 30 and December 31. All of the bonds will be sold on January 1, 20A. Determine the issuance price of the bonds, assuming a market yield of 8 percent.

**M10–3** **Computing Bond Issuance Price** **LO2**

Waterhouse Company plans to issue $300,000, 10-year, 10 percent bonds. Interest is payable semiannually each June 30 and December 31. All of the bonds will be sold on January 1, 20A. Determine the issuance price of the bonds assuming a market yield of 12 percent.

**M10–4** **Recording the Issuance of a New Bond and the Payment of Interest (Straight-Line Amortization)** **LO2**

Price Company issued $500,000, 10-year, 8 percent bonds on January 1, 20A. The bonds sold for $545,000. Interest is payable semiannually each June 30 and December 31. Record the sale of the bonds on January 1, 20A, and the payment of interest on June 30, 20A, using straight-line amortization.

**M10–5** **Recording the Issuance of a New Bond and the Payment of Interest (Effective-Interest Amortization)** **LO2, 5**

IDS Company issued $1,000,000, 10-year, 8 percent bonds on January 1, 20A. The bonds sold for $1,070,000. Interest is payable semiannually each June 30 and December 31. Record the sale of the bonds on January 1, 20A, and the payment of interest on June 30, 20A, using the effective-interest method of amortization. The yield on the bonds is 7 percent.

**M10–6** **Recording the Issuance of a New Bond and the Payment of Interest (Straight-Line Amortization)** **LO2**

Garland Company issued $600,000, 10-year, 10 percent bonds on January 1, 20A. The bonds sold for $580,000. Interest is payable semiannually each June 30 and December 31. Record the sale of the bonds on January 1, 20A, and the payment of interest on June 30, 20A, using straight-line amortization.

**M10–7** **Recording the Issuance of a New Bond and the Payment of Interest (Effective-Interest Amortization)** **LO2, 5**

Hopkins Company issued $800,000, 10-year, 10 percent bonds on January 1, 20A. The bonds sold for $753,000. Interest is payable semiannually each June 30 and December 31. Record the sale of the bonds on January 1, 20A, and the payment of interest on June 30, 20A, using effective interest amortization. The yield on the bonds is 11 percent.

**M10–8** **Determining Cash Flow Effects** **LO4**

If a company issues a bond at a discount, will interest expense each period be more or less than the cash payment for interest? If another company issues a bond at a premium, will interest expense be more or less than the cash payment for interest? Is your answer to either question affected by the method used to amortize the discount or premium?

**M10–9** **Determining Financial Statement Effects of an Early Retirement of Debt** **LO6**

If interest rates fell after the issuance of a bond and the company decided to retire the debt, would you expect the company to report a gain or loss on debt retirement? Describe the financial statement effects of a debt retirement under these circumstances.

■ **LO7**  **M10–10**  **Recording a Bond Investment**
Wall Company purchased $1,000,000, 10-year, 8 percent bonds issued by Janice Company on January 1, 20A. The purchase price of the bonds was $1,070,000. Interest is payable semiannually each June 30 and December 31. Record the purchase of the bonds on January 1, 20A .

■ **LO7**  **M10–11**  **Recording a Bond Investment and the Amortization of the Discount**
Fred Company purchased $500,000, 10-year, 8 percent bonds issued by Martin Company on January 1, 20A. The purchase price of the bonds was $530,000. Interest is payable semiannually each June 30 and December 31. Record the purchase of the bonds on January 1, 20A, and the payment of interest on June 30, 20A, using straight-line amortization.

## EXERCISES

■ **LO1, 2**  **E10–1**

Lennar Homes

**Recording Bonds Based on an Annual Report**
Lennar Homes is a nationwide builder of new homes that has constructed more than 140,000 single-family residences since its founding in 1954. The company is currently traded on the New York Stock Exchange. Lennar's annual report contained the following information (in millions):

|  | 1997 | 1996 | 1995 |
|---|---|---|---|
| Interest expense | $ 24.979 | $ 31.033 | $ 19.255 |
| Bonds payable | 661.695 | 837.498 | 635.761 |

*Required:*

1.  Record interest expense using a single journal entry for each year.

2.  Record the issuance of bonds payable, assuming that the full amount was sold during 1995.

3.  Recognizing that Lennar is a home builder, why do you think that the amounts of bonds payable fluctuated so much during this period?

■ **LO1, 2, 5**  **E10–2**

**Determining Financial Statement Effects for Bond Issue and First Interest Payment, with Premium**
Grocery Corporation sold a $250,000, 11 percent bond issue on January 1, 20A, at a market rate of 8 percent. The bonds were dated January 1, 20A, with interest to be paid each December 31; they mature 10 years from January 1, 20A.

*Required:*

1.  How are the financial statements affected by the issuance of the bonds? Describe the impact on the debt-to-equity and times interest earned ratios, if any.

2.  How are the financial statements affected by the payment of interest on December 31? Describe the impact on the debt-to-equity and times interest earned ratios, if any.

3.  Show how the bond interest expense and the bonds payable should be reported on the December 31, 20A, annual financial statements.

■ **LO1**  **E10–3**

Apple Computer

**Explaining Why Debt Is Sold at a Discount**
The annual report of Apple Computer, Inc., contained the following note:

**Long-Term Debt**
On February 10, 1994, the Company issued $300 million aggregate principal amount of its 6.5% unsecured notes. The notes were sold at 99.925% of par, for an effective yield of 6.51%. The notes pay interest semiannually and mature on February 15, 2004.

After reading this note, one student asked why Apple didn't simply sell the notes for an effective yield of 6.5 percent and avoid having to account for a very small discount over the next 10 years. Prepare a written response to this question.

**E10–4 Explaining Bond Terminology**

The balance sheet for Carnival Cruise Lines includes "zero coupon convertible subordinated notes." In your own words, explain the features of this debt. The balance sheet does not report a premium or a discount associated with this debt. Do you think it is recorded at par?

**LO1**

Carnival Cruise Lines

**E10–5 Interpreting Information Reported in the Business Press**

As this book was being written, the business press reported the following information concerning bonds issued by AT&T:

**LO1**

AT&T

| Bonds | Yield | Close |
|-------|-------|-------|
| AT&T 6.5 | 7.3 | 89.5 |

Explain the meaning of the reported information. If you bought AT&T bonds with $10,000 face value, how much would you pay (based on the preceding information reported)? Assume that the bonds were originally sold at par. What impact would the decline in value have on the financial statements for AT&T?

**E10–6 Evaluating Bond Features**

You are a personal financial planner working with a married couple in their early 40s who have decided to invest $100,000 in corporate bonds. You have found two bonds that you think will interest your clients. One is a zero coupon bond issued by PepsiCo with an effective interest rate of 9 percent and a maturity date of 2015. It is callable at par. The other is a Walt Disney bond that matures in 2093. It has an effective interest rate of 9.5 percent and is callable at 105 percent of par. Which bond would you recommend and why? Would your answer be different if you expected interest rates to fall significantly over the next few years? Would you prefer a different bond if the couple were in their late 60s and retired?

**LO1**

PepsiCo, Inc.
The Walt Disney Company

**E10–7 Computing the Issue Price of a Bond, with Discussion**

Charger Corporation issued a $150,000 bond that matures in five years. The bond has a stated interest rate of 8 percent and pays interest on February 1, May 1, August 1, and November 1. When the bond was issued, the market rate of interest was 12 percent. Record the issuance of the bond on February 1. Also record the payment of interest on May 1 and August 1. Use the straight-line method for amortization of any discount or premium. Explain why someone would buy a bond that did not pay the market rate of interest.

**LO1, 2**

**E10–8 Explaining an International Transaction**

A recent Walt Disney annual reported contained the following note:

**LO1, 2**

The Walt Disney Company

> The Company issued Yen 100 billion (approximately $920 million) of Japanese yen bonds through a public offering in Japan. The bonds are senior, unsecured debt obligations of the Company which mature in June 1999. Interest on the bonds is payable semi-annually at a fixed interest rate of 5% per year through maturity. The bonds provide for principal payments in dollars and interest payment in Japanese yen.

*Required:*

1. Describe how this bond would be reported on the balance sheet.

2. Explain why management borrowed money in this manner.

**E10–9 Analyzing Financial Ratios**

You have just started you first job as a financial analyst for a large stock brokerage company. Your boss, a senior analyst, has finished a detailed report evaluating bonds issued by two different companies. She stopped by your desk and asked for help: "I have compared two ratios for the companies and found something interesting." She went on to explain that the debt-to-equity ratio for Applied Technologies, Inc., is much lower than the industry average

**LO1, 3**

and that the one for Innovative Solutions, Inc., is much higher. On the other hand, the times interest earned ratio for Applied Technologies is much higher than the industry average, and the ratio for Innovative Solutions is much lower. Your boss then asked you to think about what the ratios indicate about the two companies so that she could include the explanation in her report. How would you respond to your boss?

■ **LO2**   **E10–10**   **Computing the Issue Price of a Bond**
Kaizen Corporation issued a $500,000 bond that matures in 10 years. The bond has a stated interest rate of 10 percent. When the bond was issued, the market rate was 10 percent. The bond pays interest twice per year. At what price was the bond issued?

■ **LO2, 4**   **E10–11**   **Computing the Issue Price of a Bond with Analysis of Income and Cash Flow Effects**

Imai Company issued a $1 million bond that matures in five years. The bond has a 10 percent stated rate of interest. When the bond was issued, the market rate was 8 percent. The bond pays interest twice per year on June 30 and December 31. Record the issuance of the bond on June 30. Notice that the company received more than $1 million when it issued the bond. How will this premium affect future income and future cash flows?

■ **LO2**   **E10–12**   **Computing Issue Prices of Bonds for Three Cases**
Thompson Corporation is planning to issue $100,000, five-year, 8 percent bonds. Interest is payable semiannually each June 30 and December 31. All of the bonds will be sold on January 1, 20A; they mature on December 31, 20E.

*Required:*

1. Compute the issue (sale) price on January 1, 20A, for each of the following independent cases (show computations):

   *par*    *a.* **Case A:** Market (yield) rate, 8 percent.
   *premium b.* **Case B:** Market (yield) rate, 6 percent.
   *discount c.* **Case C:** Market (yield) rate, 10 percent.

■ **LO2**   **E10–13**   **Recording Bond Issue and First Interest Payment with Discount**
On January 1, 20A, Seton Corporation sold a $200,000, 8 percent bond issue (9 percent market rate). The bonds were dated January 1, 20A, pay interest each December 31, and mature 10 years from January 1, 20A.

*Required:*

1. Give the journal entry to record the issuance of the bonds.
2. Give the journal entry to record the interest payment on December 31, 20A. Use straight-line amortization.
3. Show how the bond interest expense and the bonds payable should be reported on the December 31, 20A, annual financial statements.

■ **LO2**   **E10–14**   **Recording Bond Issue: Entries for Issuance and Interest**
Northland Corporation had $400,000, 10-year coupon bonds outstanding on December 31, 20A (end of the accounting period). Interest is payable each December 31. The bonds were issued (sold) on January 1, 20A. The 20A annual financial statements showed the following:

| | |
|---|---|
| **Income statement** | |
| Bond interest expense (straight-line amortization) | $ 33,200 |
| **Balance sheet** | |
| Bonds payable (net liability) | 389,200 |

*Required (show computations):*

1. What was the issue price of the bonds? Give the journal entry to record the issuance of the bonds.
2. What was the coupon rate on the bonds? Give the entry to record 20A interest.

■ **LO2, 5**   **E10–15**   **Determining Financial Statement Balance with the Effective-Interest Amortization of a Bond Discount**
Eagle Corporation issued $10,000, 10 percent bonds dated April 1, 20A. The market rate of interest was 12 percent with interest paid each March 31. The bonds mature in three years on March 31, 20D. Eagle's accounting period ends each December 31.

*Required:*

1. What amount of bond liability will be reported on April 1, 20A?

2. What amount of interest expense will be reported on December 31, 20A? The company uses the effective-interest method of amortization.

3. Show how the bonds should be reported on the balance sheet at December 31, 20A.

4. What amount of interest expense will be reported on March 31, 20B? Is this amount different than the amount of cash that is paid? If so, why?

**E10–16 Analyzing a Bond Amortization Schedule: Reporting Bonds Payable**

■ **LO2**

Stein Corporation issued a $1,000 bond on January 1, 20A. The bond specified an interest rate of 9 percent payable at the end of each year. The bond matures at the end of 20C. It was sold at a market rate of 11 percent per year. The following schedule was completed:

|  | Cash | Interest | Amortization | Balance |
|---|---|---|---|---|
| January 1, 20A (issuance) |  |  |  | $ 951 |
| End of year 20A | $90 | $105 | $15 | 966 |
| End of year 20B | 90 | 106 | 16 | 982 |
| End of year 20C | 90 | 108 | 18 | 1,000 |

*Required:*

1. What was the bond's issue price?

2. Did the bond sell at a discount or a premium? How much was the premium or discount?

3. What amount of cash was paid each year for bond interest?

4. What amount of interest expense should be shown each year on the income statement?

5. What amount(s) should be shown on the balance sheet for bonds payable at each year-end? (For year 20C, show the balance just before retirement of the bond.)

6. What method of amortization was used?

7. Show how the following amounts were computed for year 20B: (a) $90, (b) $106, (c) $16, and (d) $982.

8. Is the method of amortization that was used preferable? Explain why.

**E10–17 Preparing a Debt Payment Schedule with Effective-Interest Method of Amortization and Determining Reported Amounts**

■ **LO2, 5**

Shuttle Company issued a $10,000, three-year, 10 percent bond on January 1, 20A. The bond interest is paid each December 31. The bond was sold to yield 9 percent.

*Required:*

1. Complete a bond payment schedule. Use the effective-interest method.

2. What amounts will be reported on the financial statements at the end of 20A, 20B, and 20C?

**E10–18 Determining Effects on the Statement of Cash Flows**

■ **LO4**

A number of events over the life of a bond have effects that are reported on the statement of cash flows. For each of the following events, determine whether the event affects the statement of cash flows. If so, describe the impact and specify where on the statement the effect is reported.

1. A $1,000,000 bond is issued at a discount. The reported amount of the bond on the balance sheet is $945,000.

2. At year-end, $50,000 accrued interest is reported and $1,000 of the bond discount is amortized using the straight-line method.

3. Early in the second year, accrued interest is paid. At the same time, $8,000 interest that accrued in the second year is paid.

4. The company elects to retire the debt in the fifth year. At that time, the reported value of the bonds is $960,000 and the company reports a $25,000 gain on the early retirement of debt.

■ **LO7**          **E10–19**      **Recording Bonds Held to Maturity**

Sears, Roebuck & Co.

Sears, Roebuck & Co. is perhaps best known for its mall-based retail stores that sell apparel, home, and automotive products. The company does more than $41 billion in sales each year.

Assume that as part of its cash management strategy, Sears purchased bonds with $10 million face value for $10.5 million cash on July 1, 20A. The bonds pay 10 percent interest each June 30 and December 31 and mature in 10 years. Sears plans to hold the bonds until maturity.

*Required:*

1. Record the purchase of the bonds on July 1, 20A.

2. Record the receipt of interest on December 31, 20A.

3. Should Sears prepare a journal entry if the market value of the bonds increased to $11 million on December 31, 20A? If so, what is the entry?

■ **LO7**          **E10–20**      **Determining Financial Statement Effects for Bonds Held to Maturity**

Starbucks

Starbucks is a rapidly expanding company that provides high-quality coffee products. Assume that as part of its expansion strategy, Starbucks plans to open numerous new stores in Mexico in five years. The company has $5 million to support the expansion and has decided to invest the funds in corporate bonds until the money is needed. Assume that Starbucks purchased bonds with $5 million face value for $4.5 million cash on July 1, 20A. The bonds pay 8 percent interest each June 30 and December 31 and mature in five years. Starbucks plans to hold the bonds until maturity.

*Required:*

1. What accounts are affected when the bonds are purchased on July 1, 20A?

2. What accounts are affected when interest is received on December 31, 20A?

3. Should Starbucks prepare a journal entry if the market value of the bonds decreased to $4,000,000 on December 31, 20A? Explain.

# PROBLEMS

■ **LO1, 2**        **P10–1**      **Comparing Bonds Issued at Par, Discount, and Premium**

Sikes Corporation, whose annual accounting period ends on December 31, issued the following bonds:

> **Date of bonds: January 1, 20A.**
>
> Maturity amount and date: $100,000 due in 10 years (December 31, 20J).
>
> Interest: 10 percent per annum payable each December 31.
>
> Date sold: January 1, 20A.

*Required:*

1. Provide the following amounts to be reported on the 20A financial statements:

| | Issued at Par<br>Case A | at 96<br>Case B | at 102<br>Case C |
|---|---|---|---|
| a. Interest expense. | $ | $ | $ |
| b. Bonds payable. | | | |
| c. Unamortized premium or discount. | | | |
| d. Net liability. | | | |
| e. Stated rate of interest. | | | |
| f. Cash interest paid. | | | |

2. Explain why items *a* and *f* in requirement 1 are different.

3. Assume that you are an investment adviser and a retired person has written to you asking, "Why should I buy a bond at a premium when I can find one at a discount? Isn't that stupid? It's like paying list price for a car instead of negotiating a discount." Write a brief letter in response to the question.

**P10–2 Comparing Carrying Value and Market Value** (AP10–1)

The name Hilton is well known in the hotel industry. The Hilton annual report contained the following information concerning long-term debt:

**LO1, 6**

Hilton Hotels

> **Long-Term debt**
>
> The estimated current market value of long-term debt is based on the quoted market price for the same or similar issues. The current carrying value for long-term debt is $1,132.5 (million) and the current market value is $1,173.5 (million).

Explain why there is a difference between the carrying value and the current market value of the long-term debt for Hilton. Assume that Hilton decided to retire all of its long-term debt for cash (a very unlikely event). Prepare the journal entry to record the transaction.

**P10–3 Analyzing the Reclassification of Debt** (AP10–2)

PepsiCo, Inc., is a $25 billion company in the beverage, snack food, and restaurant businesses. PepsiCo's annual report included the following note:

**LO1**

PepsiCo, Inc.

> At year-end, $3.5 billion of short-term borrowings were reclassified as long-term, reflecting PepsiCo's intent and ability to refinance these borrowings on a long-term basis, through either long-term debt issuances or rollover of existing short-term borrowings.

As a result of this reclassification, PepsiCo's current ratio improved from 0.51 to 0.79. Do you think the reclassification was appropriate? Why do you think management made the reclassification? As a financial analyst, would you use the current ratio before the reclassification or after the reclassification to evaluate PepsiCo's liquidity?

**P10–4 Recording Bond Issuance and Interest Payment with Discussion of Management Strategy** (AP10–3)

Carter Corporation issued $400,000 in bonds that mature in 10 years. The bonds have a stated interest rate of 6 percent and pay interest on March 1 and September 1. When the bonds were sold, the market rate of interest was 8 percent. Carter uses the effective-interest method. By December 31, 20A, the market interest rate of interest had increased to 10 percent.

**LO2, 3, 5**

*Required:*

1. Record the issuance of the bond on March 1, 20A.

2. Record the payment of interest on September 1, 20A.

3. Record the adjusting entry for accrued interest on December 31, 20A.

4. As a manager of a company, would you prefer the straight-line or effective-interest method?

5. Determine the impact of these transactions at year-end on the debt-to-equity ratio and times interest earned ratio.

**P10–5 Completing Schedule Comparing Bonds Issued at Par, Discount, and Premium** (AP10–4)

Quartz Corporation sold a $500,000, 7 percent bond issue on January 1, 20A. The bonds pay interest each December 31 and mature 10 years from January 1, 20A. For comparative study and analysis, assume three separate cases. Use straight-line amortization and disregard income tax unless specifically required. Assume three independent selling scenarios: Case A, bonds sold at par; Case B, bonds sold at 98; Case C, bonds sold at 102.

**LO2**

*Required:*

1. Complete the following schedule to analyze the differences among the three cases.

| | Case A (Par) | Case B (at 98) | Case C (at 102) |
|---|---|---|---|
| *a.* Cash inflow at issue (sale) date. | | | |
| *b.* Total cash outflow through maturity date. | | | |
| *c.* Difference—total interest expense. | | | |

*Income statement for 20A*

   *d.* Bond interest expense, pretax.

*Balance sheet at December 31, 20A, Long-term liabilities*

   *e.* Bonds payable, 7 percent.

   *f.* Unamortized discount.

   *g.* Unamortized premium.

   *h.* Net liability.

   *i.* Stated interest rate.

   *j.* Total interest expense, net of income tax (25 percent tax rate).

2. For each case, explain why the amounts in items *c*, *d*, and *j* of requirement (1) are the same or different.

**■ LO2**   **P10–6**   **Recording Bond Issuance and Interest Payments** (AP10–5)

West Company issued bonds with the following provisions:

   **Maturity value: $600,000.**

   Interest: 9 percent per annum payable semiannually each June 30 and December 31.

   Terms: Bonds dated January 1, 20A, due five years from that date.

The annual accounting period ends December 31. The bonds were sold on January 1, 20A, at an 8 percent market rate.

*Required:*

1. Compute the issue (sale) price of the bonds (show computations).

2. Give the journal entry to record the issuance of the bonds.

3. Give the journal entries at the following dates (use straight-line amortization): June 30, 20A; December 31, 20A; and June 30, 20B.

4. How much interest expense would be reported on the income statement for 20A? Show how the liability related to the bonds should be reported on the December 31, 20A, balance sheet.

**■ LO2**   **P10–7**   **Completing an Amortization Schedule**

Berkley Corporation issued bonds and received cash in full for the issue price. The bonds were dated and issued on January 1, 20A. The stated interest rate was payable at the end of each year. The bonds mature at the end of four years. The following schedule has been completed (amounts in thousands):

| Date | Cash | Interest | Amortization | Balance |
|------|------|----------|--------------|---------|
| January 1, 20A |  |  |  | $6,101 |
| End of year 20A | $450 | $427 | $23 | 6,078 |
| End of year 20B | 450 | ? | ? | 6,053 |
| End of year 20C | 450 | ? | ? | ? |
| End of year 20D | 450 | ? | ? | 6,000 |

*Required:*

1. Complete the amortization schedule.

2. What was the maturity amount of the bonds?

3. How much cash was received at date of issuance (sale) of the bonds?

4. Was there a premium or a discount? If so, which and how much?

5. How much cash will be disbursed for interest each period and in total for the full life of the bond issue?

6. What method of amortization is being used? Explain.

7. What is the stated rate of interest?

8. What is the effective rate of interest?

9. What amount of interest expense should be reported on the income statement each year?

10. Show how the bonds should be reported on the balance sheet at the end of each year (show the last year immediately before retirement of the bonds).

11. Why is the method of amortization being used preferable to other methods? When must it be used?

**P10–8 Computing Amounts for Bond Issue and Comparing Amortization Methods** (AP10–6)   ■ LO2, 5

Dektronik Corporation manufactures electrical test equipment. The company's board of directors authorized a bond issue on January 1, 20A, with the following terms:

> **Maturity (par) value: $800,000.**
>
> Interest: 8 percent per annum payable each December 31.
>
> Maturity date: December 31, 20E.
>
> Effective-interest rate when sold: 12 percent.

*Required:*

1. Compute the bond issue price. Explain why both the stated and effective-interest rates are used in this computation.

2. Assume that the company used the straight-line method to amortize the discount on the bond issue. Compute the following amounts for each year (20A–E):

   *a.* Cash payment for bond interest.

   *b.* Amortization of bond discount or premium.

   *c.* Bond interest expense.

   *d.* Interest rate indicated (Item *c* ÷ $800,000).

   *e.* The straight-line rate is theoretically deficient when interest expense, *d*, is related to the net liability (i.e., book value of the debt). Explain.

3. Assume instead that the company used the effective-interest method to amortize the discount. Prepare an effective-interest bond amortization schedule similar to the one in the text (see p. 556). The effective-interest method provides a constant interest rate when interest expense is related to the net liability. Explain by referring to the bond amortization schedule.

4. Which method should the company use to amortize the bond discount? As a financial analyst, would you prefer one method over the other? If so, why?

**P10–9 Explaining Note to a Financial Statement** (AP10–7)   ■ LO6

Federal Express

Federal Express is a name synonymous with overnight delivery of important packages. The annual report for FedEx contains the following note:

> In August 1998, an agreement was executed to issue $45,000,000 of City of Indianapolis Airport Facility Refunding Bonds in September 1998. The refunding will be used to retire 11.25% Indianapolis Special Facilities Bonds, Series 1984, which were originally issued in November 1984 to finance the acquisition, construction and equipping of an express sorting hub at the Indianapolis International Airport. The refunding bonds have a maturity date of 2017 and a coupon rate of 6.85%.

*Required:*

1. In your own words, explain the meaning of this note.

2. Why did management decide to make an early retirement of this debt?

## ALTERNATE PROBLEMS

**AP10–1 Understanding the Difference between Carrying Value and Market Value** (P10–2)   ■ LO1, 6

Quaker Oats

Quaker Oats is a well-known name at most breakfast tables. The company does more than $6 billion in sales revenue each year. The Quaker annual report contained the following information concerning long-term debt:

> **Long-Term Debt**
>
> The fair value of long-term debt was $779.7 million and $730.7 million as of June 30, 1998 and 1997, respectively, which was based on market prices for the same or similar issues or on the current rates offered to the Company for similar debt of the same maturities. The carrying value of long-term debt as of June 30, 1998 and 1997 was $759.5 million and 632.6 million, respectively.

What is meant by "fair value?" Explain why there is a difference between the carrying value and the fair value of the long-term debt for Quaker Oats. Assume that Quaker Oats decided to retire all of its long-term debt for cash (a very unlikely event). Prepare the journal entry to record the transaction.

**LO1**     **AP10–2**     **Analyzing the Reclassification of Debt** (P10–3)

General Mills

General Mills is a multibillion-dollar company that makes and sells products used in the kitchens of most American homes. The Company's annual report included the following note:

> We have a revolving credit agreement expiring in two years that provides for a credit line (which permits us to borrow money when needed). This agreement provides us with the opportunity to refinance short-term borrowings on a long-term basis.

Should General Mills classify the short-term borrowing as current or noncurrent debt based on this ability to borrow money to refinance the debt if needed? If you were a member of the management team, explain what you would want to do and why. If you were a financial analyst, would your answer be different?

**LO2, 5**     **AP10–3**     **Using the Effective-Interest Method with Discussion of Management Strategy** (P10–4)

Carter Corporation issued $2,000,000 in bonds that mature in 10 years. The bonds have a stated interest rate of 8 percent and pay interest on March 1 and September 1. When the bonds were sold, the market rate of interest was 6 percent. Carter uses the effective-interest method. By December 31, 20A, the market interest rate of interest had increased to 7 percent.

*Required:*

1. Record the issuance of the bond on March 1, 20A.

2. Record the payment of interest on September 1, 20A.

3. Record the adjusting entry for accrued interest on December 31, 20A.

4. As a manager of a company, would you prefer the straight-line or effective-interest method?

5. Determine the impact of these transactions at year-end on the debt-to-equity ratio and times interest earned ratio.

**LO2, 4**     **AP10–4**     **Completing a Schedule That Involves a Comprehensive Review of the Issuance of Bonds at Par, Discount, and Premium, Including Cash Flows** (P10–5)

On January 1, 20A, Delaware Corporation sold and issued $100,000, five-year, 10 percent bonds. The bond interest is payable annually each December 31. Assume three separate and independent selling scenarios: Case A, at par; Case B, at 90; and Case C, at 110.

*Required:*

1. Complete a schedule similar to the following for each separate case assuming straight-line amortization of discount and premium. Disregard income tax. Give all dollar amounts in thousands.

2. For each separate case, calculate each of the following:

    *a.* Total pretax cash outflow.

    *b.* Total pretax cash inflow.

    *c.* Difference—net pretax cash outflow.

    *d.* Total pretax interest expense.

| | | | | | | At End of 20E | |
| --- | --- | --- | --- | --- | --- | --- | --- |
| | At Start of 20A | At End of 20A | At End of 20B | At End of 20C | At End of 20D | Prior to Payment of Principal | Payment of Principal |
| **Case A:** sold at par (100) | $ | $ | $ | $ | $ | $ | $ |
| Pretax cash inflow | | | | | | | |
| Pretax cash outflow | | | | | | | |
| Interest expense on income statement | | | | | | | |
| Net liability on balance sheet | | | | | | | |
| **Case B:** sold at a discount (90) | | | | | | | |
| Pretax cash inflow | | | | | | | |
| Pretax cash outflow | | | | | | | |
| Interest expense on income statement | | | | | | | |
| Net liability on balance sheet | | | | | | | |
| **Case C:** sold at a premium (110) | | | | | | | |
| Pretax cash inflow | | | | | | | |
| Pretax cash outflow | | | | | | | |
| Interest expense on income statement | | | | | | | |
| Net liability on balance sheet | | | | | | | |

3. *a.* Explain why the net pretax cash outflows differ among the three cases.

   *b.* For each case, explain why the net pretax cash outflow is the same as total interest expense.

**AP10–5** **Computing Issue Price of Bonds and Recording Issuance and Interest Payments** (P10–6)  ▓ **LO2**

Jacobs Company issued bonds with the following provisions:

> **Maturity value: $1,000,000.**
>
> Interest: 8 percent per annum payable semiannually each June 30 and December 31.
>
> Terms: Bonds dated January 1, 20A, due 10 years from that date.

The annual accounting period ends December 31. The bonds were sold on January 1, 20A, at 10 percent market rate.

*Required:*

1. Compute the issue (sale) price of the bonds (show computations).
2. Give the journal entry to record the issuance of the bonds.
3. Give the journal entries at the following dates (use straight-line amortization): June 30, 20A; December 31, 20A; and June 30, 20B.
4. How much interest expense would be reported on the income statement for 20A? Show how the liability related to the bonds should be reported on the December 31, 20A, balance sheet.

**AP10–6** **Straight-Line versus Effective-Interest Methods of Amortizing Bond Discount and Premium, with Discussion** (P10–8)  ▓ **LO2, 5**

United Products Corporation manufactures office equipment and supplies. The company authorized a bond issue on January 1, 20A, with the following terms:

> **Maturity (par) value: $1,200,000.**
>
> Interest: 10 percent per annum payable each December 31.
>
> Maturity date: December 31, 20E.
>
> Effective-interest rate when sold: 8 percent.

*Required:*

1. Compute the bond issue price. Explain why both the stated and effective-interest rates are used in this computation.
2. Give the entry to record this bond issue.

3. Assume that the company used the straight-line method to amortize the discount on the bond issue. Compute the following amounts for each year (20A–E):

   a. Cash payment for bond interest.

   b. Amortization of bond discount or premium.

   c. Bond interest expense.

   d. Interest rate indicated (Item $c \div \$1,200,000$).

   e. The straight-line rate is theoretically deficient when interest expense, $d$, is related to the net liability (i.e., book value of the debt). Explain.

4. Assume instead that the company used the effective-interest method to amortize the discount. Prepare an effective-interest bond amortization schedule similar to the one in the text (see p. 556). The effective-interest method provides a constant interest rate when interest expense is related to the net liability. Explain by referring to the bond amortization schedule.

5. Which method should the company use to amortize the bond discount? As a financial analyst, would you prefer one method over the other? If so, why?

**■ LO6**   **AP10–7**

AMC Entertainment, Inc.

**Understanding the Early Retirement of Debt** (P10–9)

AMC Entertainment, Inc., owns and operates 243 movie theaters with 1,617 screens in 22 states. On August 12, 1992, the company sold 11⅞ percent bonds in the amount of $52,720,000 and used the cash proceeds to retire bonds with a coupon rate of 13.6 percent. At that time, the 13.6 percent bonds had a book value of $50,000,000.

*Required:*

1. Prepare the journal entry to record the early retirement of the 13.6 percent bonds.

2. How should AMC report any gain or loss on this transaction?

3. Why did the company issue new bonds in order to retire the old bonds?

# CASES AND PROJECTS

## FINANCIAL REPORTING AND ANALYSIS CASES

**■ LO2, 4, 7**   **CP10–1**

American Eagle Outfitters

**STANDARD &POOR'S**

**Finding Financial Information**

Refer to the financial statements of American Eagle Outfitters given in Appendix B at the end of this book or open file AEOS10K.doc in the S&P directory on the student CD-ROM.

*Required:*

1. How much interest expense was paid in cash during the fiscal year ended January 30, 1999?

2. Explain why the company does not report bonds payable on its balance sheet.

3. Describe the company's established arrangements, if any, that permit it to borrow money if needed.

4. Does the company have any investments in bonds?

**■ LO2, 4, 7**   **CP10–2**

Urban Outfitters

**STANDARD &POOR'S**

**Finding Financial Information**

Refer to the financial statements of Urban Outfitters given in Appendix C at the end of this book or open file URBN10K.doc in the S&P directory on the student CD-ROM.

*Required:*

1. How much interest expense was paid in cash during the fiscal year ended January 30, 1999?

2. Explain why the company does not report bonds payable on its balance sheet.

3. Describe the company's established arrangements, if any, that permit it to borrow money if needed.

4. Does the company have any investments in bonds?

**CP10–3** **Comparing Companies within an Industry**

Refer to the financial statements of American Eagle Outfitters given in Appendix B, Urban Outfitters given in Appendix C, and the Standard and Poor's Industry Ratio Report given in Appendix D at the end of this book or open file CP10-3.xls in the S&P directory on the student CD-ROM. Most companies report some amounts of bonds payable on their balance sheets. It is somewhat surprising, therefore, that neither American Eagle or Urban Outfitters reports any bond liabilities.

LO1, 3

American Eagle
Outfitters
versus
Urban Outfitters

*Required:*

1. Based on your analysis of the reports and your understanding of the industry, explain why both companies have built these rather unusual capital structures.

2. Two financial ratios (the debt-to-equity ratio and times interest earned) are discussed in this chapter. Are they relevant for these companies? Explain.

STANDARD
&POOR'S

**CP10–4** **Analyzing Financial Leverage**

Cricket Corporation's financial statements for 20A showed the following:

LO1

| Income Statement | |
|---|---|
| Revenues | $300,000 |
| Expenses | (198,000) |
| Interest expense | (2,000) |
| Pretax income | 100,000 |
| Income tax (30%) | (30,000) |
| Net income | $ 70,000 |
| **Balance Sheet** | |
| Assets | $300,000 |
| Liabilities (average interest rate, 10%) | $ 20,000 |
| Common stock, par $10 | 200,000 |
| Retained earnings | 80,000 |
| | $300,000 |

Notice in these data that the company had a debt of only $20,000 compared with common stock outstanding of $200,000. A consultant recommended the following: debt, $100,000 (at 10 percent) instead of $20,000 and common stock outstanding of $120,000 (12,000 shares) instead of $200,000 (20,000 shares). That is, the company should finance the business with more debt and less owner contribution.

*Required (round to nearest percent):*

1. You have been asked to develop a comparison between (a) the actual results and (b) the results had the consultant's recommendation been followed. To do this, you decided to develop the following schedule:

| Item | Actual Results for 20A | Results with an $80,000 Increase in Debt |
|---|---|---|
| *a.* Total debt | | |
| *b.* Total assets | | |
| *c.* Total stockholders' equity | | |
| *d.* Interest expense (total at 10 percent) | | |
| *e.* Net income | | |
| *f.* Return on total assets | | |
| *g.* Earnings available to stockholders: | | |
|   (1) Amount | | |
|   (2) Per share | | |
|   (3) Return on stockholders' equity | | |
| *h.* Financial leverage | | |

2. Based on the completed schedule in requirement (1), provide a comparative analysis and interpretation of the actual results and the recommendation.

**LO1**

JCPenney Company

**CP10–5**

**Analyzing Zero Coupon Bonds from an Actual Company**

JCPenney Company was one of the first companies to issue zero coupon bonds. It issued bonds with a face (maturity) value of $400 million due eight years after issuance. When the bonds were sold to the public, similar bonds paid 15 percent effective interest. An article in *Forbes* magazine discussed the JCPenney bonds and stated: "It's easy to see why corporations like to sell bonds that don't pay interest. But why would anybody want to buy that kind of paper [bond]?"

*Required:*

1. Explain why an investor would buy a JCPenney bond with a zero interest rate.

2. If investors could earn 15 percent on similar investments, how much did JCPenney receive when it issued the bonds with a face value of $400 million?

**LO5**

**CP10–6**

**Explaining Bond Premiums and Effective-Interest Rate Amortization**

Times Company issued a $100,000 bond with a stated interest rate of 8 percent. When the bond was issued, the market rate was 6 percent. The bond matures in 10 years and pays interest on December 31 each year. The bond was issued on January 1, 20A.

*Required:*

1. Compute the present value of the difference between the interest paid each year ($8,000) and the interest demanded by the market ($100,000 × 6% = $6,000). Use the market rate of interest and the 10-year life of the bond in your present value computation.Discuss what this demonstrates.

2. Why does interest expense change each year when the effective-interest method is used?

3. Compute the present value of the Times Company bonds, assuming that they had a 7-year life instead of 10-year life. Compare this amount to the book value of the bond at the end of year 20C. What does this comparison demonstrate?

**LO1**

**CP10–7**

**Interpreting the Financial Press**

In this chapter, we talked about bonds primarily from the perspective of the issuing corporation. To understand bonds, it is also necessary to develop an understanding of why investors buy bonds. An article on this topic is available on the Libby/Libby/Short website at www.mhhe.com/business/accounting/libby3. You should read the article, "It's time for bonds to get some respect," January 19, 1998, and then write a short memo summarizing the article in your own words. What type of investors are interested in buying bonds? Describe the impact of inflation on bonds.

## CRITICAL THINKING CASES

**LO1**

**CP10–8**

**Making a Decision as a Financial Analyst**

You are working for a large mutual fund company as a financial analyst. You have been asked to review two competitive companies in the same industry. Both have similar cash flows and net income, but one has no debt in its capital structure and the other has a debt-to-equity ratio of 3.2. Based on this limited information, which would you prefer? Justify your conclusion. Would your preference be influenced by the companies' industry?

**LO1**

**CP10–9**

**Evaluating an Ethical Dilemma**

You work for a small company considering investing in a new Internet business. Financial projections suggest that the company will be able to earn in excess of $40 million per year on an investment of $100 million. The company president suggests borrowing the money by issuing bonds that will carry a 7 percent interest rate. He says, "This is better than printing money! We won't have to invest a penny of our own money, and we get to keep $33 million per year after we pay interest to the bondholders." As you think about the proposed transaction, you feel a little uncomfortable about taking advantage of the creditors in this fashion. You feel that it must be wrong to earn such a high return by using money that belongs to other people. Is this an ethical business transaction?

**LO1**

**CP10–10**

**Evaluating an Ethical Dilemma**

Many retired people invest a significant portion of their money in bonds of corporations because of their relatively low level of risk. During the 1980s, significant inflation caused some interest rates to rise to as high as 15 percent. Retired people who bought bonds that paid only 6 percent continued to earn at the lower rate. During the 1990s, inflation subsided and interest rates declined. Many corporations took advantage of call options on bonds and refinanced high interest rate debt with low interest rate debt. In your judgment, is it ethical for corporations to continue paying low interest rates when rates increase but to call bonds when rates decrease?

**CP10–11 Evaluating an Ethical Dilemma**

Assume that you are a portfolio manager for a large insurance company. The majority of the money you manage is from retired school teachers who depend on the income you earn on their investments. You have invested a significant amount of money in the bonds of a large corporation and have just received a call from the company's president explaining that it is unable to meet its current interest obligations because of deteriorating business operations related to increased international competition. The president has a recovery plan that will take at least two years. During that time, the company will not be able to pay interest on the bonds and, she admits, if the plan does not work, bondholders will probably lose more than half of their money. As a creditor, you can force the company into immediate bankruptcy and probably get back at least 90 percent of the bondholders' money. You also know that your decision will cause at least 10,000 people to lose their jobs if the company ceases operations. Given only these two options, what should you do?

**CP10–12 Analyzing Risk and Return**

As explained in the chapter, the use of financial leverage offers shareholders the opportunity to earn higher returns, but it also creates higher risk. Different individuals have different preferences for risk and return, so determining the optimal balance of risk and return is not an easy matter. To illustrate the problem, conduct the following exercise in a small group.

You are offered the opportunity to participate in one of the following lotteries that require an investment of $10,000:

1. There is a 100 percent probability that you will get back $10,500 at the end of one year.

2. There is a 50 percent probability that you will get back $10,000 at the end of one year and a 50 percent probability that you will get $12,000.

3. There is a 50 percent probability that you will get back $8,000 at the end of one year and a 50 percent probability that you will get $16,000.

Determine which of the three lotteries you prefer and then attempt to reach a group consensus as to which lottery the group will accept.

# FINANCIAL REPORTING AND ANALYSIS PROJECTS

**CP10–13 Project: International Financing**

Find the financial statements for a company that has borrowed money in a currency other than the dollar. (*Hint:* Look for companies with international operations.) Write a brief memo explaining why the company borrowed money in a foreign currency.

**CP10–14 Team Project: Examining an Annual Report**

As a team, select an industry to analyze. Each group member should acquire the annual report or 10-K for one publicly traded company in the industry, with each member selecting a different company. (Library files, the SEC EDGAR service at www.sec.gov, Compustat CD, and the company itself are good sources.) On an individual basis, each team member should then write a short report answering the following questions about his or her selected company.

1. Review the types of bonds issued by the company. Do you observe any unusual features?

2. Compute and analyze the debt-to-equity and times interest earned ratios.

3. Review the statement of cash flows. Has the company either issued or repaid money associated with a bond? If so, can you determine the reason?

4. Has the company issued bonds denominated in a foreign currency? Can you determine why?

5. Does the company hold any bond investments?

6. Were bonds issued at either a premium or a discount? If so, does the company use the straight-line or effective-interest amortization method?

Discuss any patterns across the companies that you as a team observe. Then, as a team, write a short report comparing and contrasting your companies using these attributes. Provide potential explanations for any differences discovered.

**LO1, 3** **CP10–15**

Harrah's Entertainment, Inc.

**Project: Using the Internet to Analyze a Company**
Using your Web browser, contact Harrah's Entertainment, Inc., homepage. This site contains a large amount of information about the company, including its annual report.

*Required:*

1. Has the company issued new bonds since this chapter was written? If so, does management explain the purpose for the new debt?

2. Compute the debt-to-equity ratio for the current year. Compare it to the ratio in this chapter. Can you explain why it has changed?

3. Compute the times interest earned ratio for the current year. Compare it to the ratio in this chapter. Can you explain why it has changed?

**LO1, 3** **CP10–16**

Harrah's Entertainment, Inc.

**Analyzing a Company over Time**
The following information was reported for Harrah's Entertainment, Inc.:

|  | 1997 | 1996 | 1995 |
|---|---|---|---|
| Times interest earned ratio | 3.32 | 3.46 | 3.05 |
| Debt-to-equity ratio | 1.26 | 1.24 | 1.29 |
| Long-term debt (in millions) | $924 | $889 | $753 |

As a financial analyst, what conclusions do you draw from this information?

**LO4** **CP10–17**

Harrah's Entertainment, Inc.

**Focus on Cash Flows: Financing Activities**
Look up Harrah's current financial statement and review the Financing Activities section of the statement of cash flows. Write a brief explanation concerning each of the items reported in this section. What insights can you gain by reviewing this information?

# Reporting and Interpreting Owners' Equity

## CHAPTER **ELEVEN**

---

LEARNING **OBJECTIVES**

*After studying this chapter, you should be able to:*

1. Explain the role of stock in the capital structure of a corporation.   p. 589

2. Describe various types of capital stock, analyze transactions affecting capital stock, and show how capital stock transactions are reported on the statement of cash flows.   p. 591

3. Explain the purpose of treasury stock and analyze transactions affecting it.   p. 598

4. Discuss dividends and analyze transactions involving common and preferred stock.   p. 599

5. Analyze the dividend yield ratio.   p. 601

6. Discuss the purpose of stock dividends, stock splits, and report transactions.   p. 604

7. Measure and report retained earnings.   p. 606

8. Analyze the dividend payout ratio.   p. 607

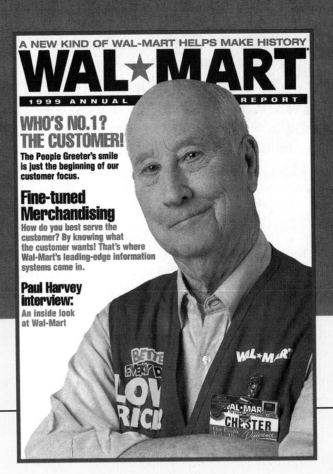

Wal-Mart is a real American success story. Today it operates nearly 2,400 discount department stores, 713 Supercenters, and 713 Sam's Clubs. The company sells more than $137 billion worth of merchandise each year (which requires more than 850,000 truck trailers to ship) and employs more than 910,000 people. To put this size in perspective, each year Wal-Mart sells 2,550,000 bicycles, 227,592,400 clothes pins, and 1,851,000,000 coffee filters. Every two seconds, it sells a Barbie doll.

FOCUS **COMPANY**:

# Wal-Mart
### FINANCING CORPORATE GROWTH WITH CAPITAL SUPPLIED BY OWNERS

Wal-Mart is international in scope with stores in Canada, Brazil, Korea, Germany, and China. It has a total of 715 international units generating more than $12 billion in sales and $500 million in profits each year. Management expects that one-third of the company's growth in sales and earnings will come from international operations.

The home office controls substantially all merchandise purchases. Approximately 77 percent of each Wal-Mart store's merchandise is shipped from one of the company's 22 distribution centers. Centralized buying is a key component of the company's strategy. The large volume of merchandise purchased by Wal-Mart permits it to negotiate aggressively with its vendors.

These cost savings permit the company to achieve its advertising slogan of "Everyday Low Price," which is critical to its large market share, rapid growth, and overall success.

Shares of Wal-Mart stock were first sold to the public in 1970 at a cost of $16.50 per share. If you had purchased one thousand shares of Wal-Mart stock in 1970 for $16,500, your investment would be worth nearly $4 million today!

In the previous chapter, we discussed the role of bonds in the capital structure of a company. In this chapter, we will focus on stock. Like bonds, stock provides many different features. Managers of businesses must identify the best mixture of features to attract investors.

## BUSINESS BACKGROUND

To some people, the words *corporation* and *business* are almost synonymous terms. You've probably heard friends refer to business careers as "the corporate world." Equating business and corporations is understandable because corporations are the dominant form of business organization in terms of volume of operations. If you were to write the names of 50 familiar companies on a piece of paper, all probably would be corporations.

The popularity of the corporate form can be attributed to a critical advantage that a corporation has over the sole proprietorship and the partnership: it is easy for individuals to participate in the ownership of corporations. This ease is related to three important factors. First, it is simple for people to become part owners by purchasing shares of stock in small amounts. You could buy a single share of Wal-Mart stock for about $52 and become one of the owners of this very successful company. Second, the corporate form facilitates the transfer of separate ownership interests because stock can be transferred easily to others by selling it on established markets such as the New York Stock Exchange. Third, corporations provide the stockholder with limited liability.[1]

The corporation is the only business form that the law recognizes as a separate entity. As a distinct entity, the corporation enjoys a continuous existence separate and apart from its owners. It may own assets, incur liabilities, expand and contract in size, sue others, be sued, and enter into contracts independently of the stockholder owners.

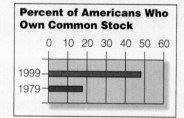

**Percent of Americans Who Own Common Stock**

Many Americans own stock, either directly or indirectly through a mutual fund or pension program (see the chart). Stock ownership offers the opportunity to earn higher returns than are available through deposits to bank accounts or investments in corporate bonds. Unfortunately, stock ownership also involves higher risk. The proper balance between risk and expected returns depends on the preferences of each individual.

Exhibit 11.1 includes consolidated statements of shareholders' equity for Wal-Mart as well as consolidated balance sheets. We use this exhibit to illustrate our discussion of stockholders' equity.

---

[1] In the case of a corporation's insolvency, the creditors have recourse for their claims only to the corporation's assets. Thus, the stockholders stand to lose, as a maximum, only their equity in the corporation. In the case of a partnership or sole proprietorship, creditors have recourse to the owners' personal assets if the assets of the business are insufficient to meet its outstanding debts.

EXHIBIT **11.1**

**Consolidated Balance Sheets and Statements of Shareholders' Equity**

**REAL WORLD EXCERPT**

*Wal-Mart Stores, Inc.*

ANNUAL REPORT

## CONSOLIDATED BALANCE SHEETS

(amounts in millions)

| January 31, | 1999 | 1998 |
|---|---|---|
| **Assets** | | |
| Current Assets: | | |
| Cash and cash equivalents | $ 1,879 | $ 1,447 |
| Receivables | 1,118 | 976 |
| Inventories | | |
| At replacement cost | 17,549 | 16,845 |
| Less LIFO reserve | 473 | 348 |
| Inventories at LIFO cost | 17,076 | 16,497 |
| Prepaid expenses and other | 1,059 | 432 |
| Total Current Assets | 21,132 | 19,352 |
| Property, Plant and Equipment, at Cost: | | |
| Land | 5,219 | 4,691 |
| Building and improvements | 16,061 | 14,646 |
| Fixtures and equipment | 9,296 | 7,636 |
| Transportation equipment | 553 | 403 |
| | 31,129 | 27,376 |
| Less accumulated depreciation | 7,455 | 5,907 |
| Net property, plant and equipment | 23,674 | 21,469 |
| Property Under Capital Lease: | | |
| Property under capital lease | 3,335 | 3,040 |
| Less accumulated amortization | 1,036 | 903 |
| Net property under capital leases | 2,299 | 2,137 |
| Other Assets and Deferred Charges | 2,891 | 2,426 |
| Total Assets | $49,996 | $45,384 |
| | | |
| **Liabilities and Shareholders' Equity** | | |
| Current Liabilities: | | |
| Accounts payable | $10,257 | $ 9,126 |
| Accrued liabilities | 4,998 | 3,628 |
| Accrued income taxes | 501 | 565 |
| Long-term debt due within one year | 900 | 1,039 |
| Obligations under capital leases due within one year | 106 | 102 |
| Total Current Liabilities | 16,762 | 14,460 |
| Long-Term Debt | 6,908 | 7,191 |
| Long-Term Obligations Under Capital Leases | 2,699 | 2,483 |
| Deferred Income Taxes and Other | 716 | 809 |
| Minority Interest | 1,799 | 1,938 |
| Shareholders' Equity | | |
| Preferred stock ($.10 par value; 100 shares authorized, none issued) | | |
| Common stock ($.10 par value; 5,500 shares authorized, 4,448 and 2,241 issued and outstanding in 1999 and 1998, respectively) | 445 | 224 |
| Capital in excess of par value | 435 | 585 |
| Retained earnings | 20,741 | 18,167 |
| Other accumulated comprehensive income | (509) | (473) |
| Total Shareholders' Equity | 21,112 | 18,503 |
| Total Liabilities and Shareholders' Equity | $49,996 | $45,384 |

EXHIBIT **11.1**
continued

## CONSOLIDATED STATEMENTS OF SHAREHOLDERS' EQUITY

| (amounts in millions except per share data) | Number of Shares | Common Stock | Other Capital in Excess of Par Value | Retained Earnings | Accumulated Comprehensive Income | Total |
|---|---|---|---|---|---|---|
| Balance—January 31, 1996 | 2,293 | $ 229 | $ 545 | $14,394 | ($ 412) | $14,756 |
| Comprehensive Income | | | | | | |
|   Net income | | | | 3,056 | | 3,056 |
|   Other accumulated comprehensive income | | | | | | |
|     Foreign currency translation adjustment | | | | | 12 | 12 |
| Total Comprehensive Income | | | | | | $3,068 |
|   Cash dividends ($.11 per share) | | | | (481) | | (481) |
|   Purchase of Company stock | (8) | | (7) | (201) | | (208) |
|   Stock options exercised and other | | (1) | 9 | | | 8 |
| Balance—January 31, 1997 | 2,285 | 228 | 547 | 16,768 | (400) | 17,143 |
| Comprehensive Income | | | | | | |
|   Net income | | | | 3,526 | | 3,526 |
|   Other accumulated comprehensive income | | | | | | |
|     Foreign currency translation adjustment | | | | | (73) | (73) |
| Total Comprehensive Income | | | | | | $3,453 |
|   Cash dividends ($.14 per share) | | | | (611) | | (611) |
|   Purchase of Company stock | (47) | (5) | (48) | (1,516) | | (1,569) |
|   Stock options exercised and other | 3 | 1 | 86 | | | 87 |
| Balance—January 31, 1998 | 2,241 | 224 | 585 | 18,167 | (473) | 18,503 |
| Comprehensive Income | | | | | | |
|   Net income | | | | 4,430 | | 4,430 |
|   Other accumulated comprehensive income | | | | | | |
|     Foreign currency translation adjustment | | | | | (36) | (36) |
| Total Comprehensive Income | | | | | | $4,394 |
|   Cash dividends ($.16 per share) | | | | (693) | | (693) |
|   Purchase of Company stock | (21) | (2) | (37) | (1,163) | | (1,202) |
|   Two-for-one stock split (announced March 4, 1999) | 2,224 | 223 | (223) | | | |
| Stock options exercised and other | 4 | | 110 | | | 110 |
| Balance—January 31, 1999 | 4,448 | $445 | $435 | $20,741 | ($ 509) | $21,112 |

## **ORGANIZATION** OF THE CHAPTER

| • Ownership of a Corporation | • Accounting for Capital Stock | • Accounting for Cash Dividends | • Retained Earnings |
|---|---|---|---|
| Authorized, Issued, and Outstanding Capital Stock | Sale and Issuance of Capital Stock | Dividends Defined | Restrictions on Retained Earnings |
| | Secondary Markets | Dividend Dates | Dividend Payout Ratio |
| | Capital Stock Sold and Issued for Noncash Assets and/or Services | Dividend Yield | |
| | Stock Options | Dividends on Preferred Stock | |

| • Types of Capital Stock | • Treasury Stock | • Accounting for Stock Dividends and Stock Splits | • Accounting and Reporting for Unincorporated Businesses |
|---|---|---|---|
| Common Stock | | Stock Dividends | |
| Preferred Stock | | Stock Splits | |

# OWNERSHIP OF A CORPORATION

When you invest in a corporation, you are known as a *stockholder* or *shareholder.* As a stockholder, you receive shares of capital stock (a stock certificate) that you can subsequently sell on established stock exchanges without affecting the corporation. The stock certificate states the name of the stockholder, date of purchase, type of stock, number of shares represented, and characteristics of the stock. The back of the certificate has instructions and a form to be completed when the shares are sold or transferred to another party.

■ **LEARNING OBJECTIVE 1**

Explain the role of stock in the capital structure of a corporation.

As an owner of common stock, you receive the following rights:

1. You may vote in the stockholders' meeting (or by proxy) on major issues concerning management of the corporation.[2]

2. You may participate proportionately with other stockholders in the distribution of the corporation's profits.

3. You may share proportionately with other stockholders in the distribution of corporate assets upon liquidation.

Owners, unlike creditors, are able to vote at the annual stockholders' meeting. The following Notice of Annual Meeting of Shareholders was recently sent to all owners of Wal-Mart stock:

**REAL WORLD EXCERPT**

*Wal-Mart Stores, Inc.*

NOTICE OF SHAREHOLDERS' MEETING

> Notice is hereby given that the annual meeting of shareholders of Wal-Mart Stores, Inc., a Delaware corporation, will be held May 27 at 10:00 A.M., in Fisher Theater in Detroit, Michigan, for the following purposes:
>
> (1) To elect directors.
> (2) To consider and act upon a proposal to ratify the adoption by the Board of Directors of the Directors Deferred Compensation Plan.
> (3) To transact other business as may properly come before the meeting or any adjournment thereof.
>
> Only shareholders of record at the close of business on April 2, are entitled to notice of and to vote at the meeting.

The notice of the annual meeting contained several pages of information concerning deferred compensation plans and the people who were nominated to be members of the board of directors. Most owners do not actually attend the annual meeting. To permit those people to vote, the notice included a proxy card, which is similar to an absentee ballot. Each owner may complete the proxy and mail it to the company. It will then be included in the votes at the annual meeting.

To protect everyone's rights, the creation and governance of corporations are tightly regulated by law. Corporations are created by making application to a specific state government (not the federal government). Each state has different laws that govern the organization of corporations created within their boundaries. Wal-Mart has its headquarters in Arkansas, but it elected to be incorporated in the state of Delaware. You will find that an unusually large number of corporations are incorporated in Delaware. The reason is simple: The state has some of the most favorable laws for establishing corporations.

To create a corporation, an application for a charter must be submitted to the appropriate state official. The application must specify the name of the corporation, the purpose (type of business), the types and amounts of capital stock authorized, and a minimum amount of capital that the owners must invest at the date of organization. Most states require a minimum of three stockholders when the corporation is formed.

---

[2]A voting proxy is written authority given by a stockholder that gives another party the right to vote the stockholder's shares in the annual meeting of the stockholders. Typically, proxies are solicited by, and given to, the president of the corporation.

Upon approval of the application, the state issues a *charter,* sometimes called the *articles of incorporation.* The governing body of a corporation is the board of directors, which the stockholders elect.

Most corporations adopt organization structures similar to the one shown in Exhibit 11.2. The actual structure depends on the nature of the company's business. Wal-Mart has seven executive vice presidents. One is responsible for each of the following areas: information systems, real estate and construction, finance and accounting, and each of the four operating divisions. This structure is unique to Wal-Mart because of the nature of its business. It might seem unusual to assign one of the most senior executives to real estate and construction, but this area is critical for Wal-Mart's strategy. Last year, for example, it opened millions of square feet of new retail space.

EXHIBIT **11.2**

**Typical Organizational Structure of a Corporation**

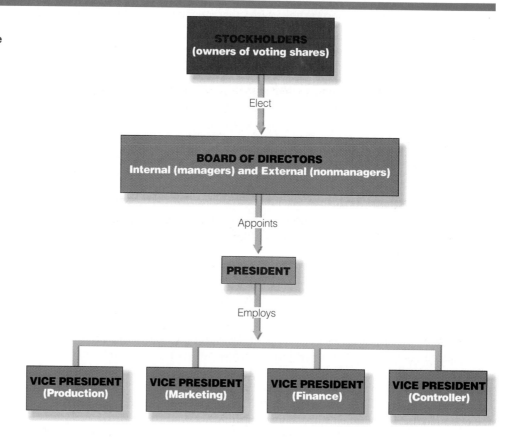

The **AUTHORIZED NUMBER OF SHARES** is the maximum number of shares of capital stock of a corporation that can be issued as specified in the charter.

**ISSUED SHARES** are the total number of shares of stock that have been issued.

**OUTSTANDING SHARES** refer to the total number of shares of stock that are owned by stockholders on any particular date.

**UNISSUED SHARES** are authorized shares of a corporation's stock that never have been issued.

## AUTHORIZED, ISSUED, AND OUTSTANDING CAPITAL STOCK

When a corporation is created, the corporate charter must specify the maximum number of shares of capital stock that it can sell to the public. This maximum is called the **authorized number of shares.** In the case of Wal-Mart, the number of authorized shares of common stock is 5,500,000,000 as shown in Exhibit 11.1. Typically, the corporate charter authorizes a larger number of shares than the corporation expects to issue initially. This strategy provides future flexibility for the issuance of additional shares without the need to amend the charter.

The number of **issued shares** and the number of **outstanding shares** are determined by the corporation's stock transactions. Authorized shares of stock that never have been sold to the public are called **unissued shares.** For Wal-Mart, the number of issued shares and of outstanding shares is the same; in 1999, this number was 4,448,000,000. The number of issued shares may differ from the number of outstanding shares if the company has bought back some of its shares from the owners so that they had been issued but were no longer outstanding. As you can see, Wal-Mart can issue more than 1,000,000,000 additional shares without exceeding the maximum authorized in its charter.

If a corporation needs to sell more shares than its charter authorizes, it must seek permission from the current stockholders to modify the charter. A few years ago, Greyhound Lines Inc. faced possible bankruptcy. The company worked out an agreement with creditors by which it would trade debt for stock, but the company did not have a sufficient number of unissued shares to complete the agreement. Management was forced to ask the stockholders to approve an increase in the number of shares authorized. As *Bloomberg Business News* reported, the vote was close:

**REAL WORLD EXCERPT**

*Bloomberg Business News*

Greyhound President Craig Lentzsch said 9.9 million of the company's 14 million outstanding shares voted in favor of the plan. Greyhound needed 9.7 million for the plan to be approved. A total of 10 million shares were voted.

Exhibit 11.3 defines and illustrates the terms usually used in respect to corporate shares.

EXHIBIT **11.3**

**Authorized, Issued, and Outstanding Shares**

| Definitions | Illustrations | |
| --- | --- | --- |
| **Authorized number of shares:** The maximum number of shares that can be issued as specified in the charter of the corporation. | Charter specifies "authorized capital stock, 100,000 shares, par value $1 per share." | |
| **Issued number of shares:** The total cumulative number of shares that the corporation has issued to date. | To date, XYZ Corporation has sold and issued 30,000 shares of its capital stock. | |
| **Unissued number of shares:** The number of authorized shares that have never been issued to date. | Authorized shares | 100,000 |
| | Issued shares | 30,000 |
| | Unissued shares | 70,000 |
| **Treasury stock:*** Shares that have been issued to investors and then reacquired by the issuing corporation. | To date, XYZ Corporation has repurchased 1,000 shares of previously issued stock. | |
| **Outstanding number of shares:** The number of shares currently owned by stockholders; that is, the number of shares authorized minus the total number of unissued shares and minus the number of treasury shares. | Authorized shares | 100,000 |
| | Treasury stock | (1,000) |
| | Unissued shares | (70,000) |
| | Outstanding shares | 29,000 |

*Treasury stock will be discussed later. Notice that when treasury stock is held, the number of shares issued and the number outstanding differ by the number of shares of treasury stock held (treasury stock is included in "issued" but not in "outstanding").

## TYPES OF CAPITAL STOCK

When people refer to *corporate stock,* they usually have in mind common stock, which all corporations must issue. Some corporations also issue preferred stock, which grants preferences that the common stock does not have. Notice in Exhibit 11.1 that Wal-Mart has authorized the issuance of preferred stock but has not issued any.

In Chapter 10, we mentioned that corporations issue many different types of bonds to appeal to the risk and return preferences of individual creditors. The same is true of stock. In this chapter, we introduce you to many features that are used to encourage investors to buy stock.

### COMMON STOCK

**Common stock** is the basic voting stock issued by a corporation. It is often called the *residual equity* because it ranks after the preferred stock for dividends and assets

■ **LEARNING OBJECTIVE 2**

Describe various types of capital stock, analyze transactions affecting capital stock, and show how capital stock transactions are reported on the statement of cash flows.

**COMMON STOCK** is the basic, normal, voting stock issued by a corporation; called *residual equity* because it ranks after preferred stock for dividend and liquidation distributions.

distributed upon liquidation of the corporation. The dividend rate for common stock is determined by the board of directors based on the company's profitability, unlike the dividend rate on preferred stock, which is fixed by contract. In the jargon of Wall Street, common stock has more "upside potential" than preferred stock and more "downside risk." This means that if the company is profitable, common stock dividends may grow to be more than preferred dividends and in fact, may increase each year (upside potential). When the company is not profitable, the board may cut or eliminate common stock dividends, but in most cases it cannot reduce preferred dividends. As a result, common stock dividends may be less than preferred stock dividends during troubled times (downside risk).

The fact that common stock dividends may increase with increases in the company's profitability helps explain why investors can make money in the stock market. Basically, you can think of the price of a share of stock as the present value of all of its future dividends. If a company's profitability improves so that it can pay out higher dividends, the present value of its common stock increases. In this situation, you would not expect the value of the preferred stock to change significantly because preferred dividends are fixed.

**PAR VALUE** is the nominal value per share of capital stock specified in the charter; serves as the basis for legal capital.

**Par Value and No-Par Value Stock**   **Par value** is a nominal value per share established in the charter of the corporation. It has no relationship to the market value of the stock. Notice in Exhibit 11.1 that Wal-Mart common stock has a par value of $0.10; the market value of the stock is several hundred times higher than its par value. Stock that is sold by the corporation to investors above par value is said to sell at a premium, whereas stock sold below par is said to sell at a discount. The initial sale of stock by the corporation to investors cannot be below par value.[3]

Most states require stock to have a par value. The original purpose of this requirement was to protect the creditors of a company, but today, the restriction has little importance to financial analysts. Par value provided protection to creditors by specifying a permanent amount of capital that the owners could not withdraw as long as the corporation existed. Thus, owners could not withdraw all of their capital in anticipation of bankruptcy and leave creditors with an empty corporate shell. This permanent amount of capital is called **legal capital.**

**LEGAL CAPITAL** is the permanent amount of capital, defined by state law, that must remain invested in the business; serves as a cushion for creditors.

Many states permit the issuance of **no-par value stock,** which does not have an amount per share specified in the charter. It may be issued at any price without a discount or premium. When a corporation issues no-par stock, the legal, or stated, capital is as defined by the state law.

**NO-PAR VALUE STOCK** is capital stock that has no par value specified in the corporate charter.

# FINANCIAL **ANALYSIS**

## PAR VALUE AND LEGAL CAPITAL

Legal capital, which usually cannot be used as the basis for dividends, represents the amount of capital that must remain invested in the corporation until it is liquidated. The definition of legal capital varies among states, but it usually is viewed as the par value of the stock outstanding. In the case of no-par stock, legal capital is viewed as either the stated value set by the company or the amount for which the stock was sold originally.

In most situations, financial analysts do not include par value and legal capital in their review of a company. Although these concepts have important legal implications, they are usually of no analytical significance.

---

[3] Our discussions concerning the sale of capital stock refer to the initial sale of the stock by the corporation rather than to later sales between investors. Because the sale of stock by a corporation at a discount no longer is legal in many states, no further discussion of it is included. The sale of stock among individuals is not recorded in the corporation's accounts.

## PREFERRED STOCK

In addition to common stock, some corporations issue **preferred stock**, which is stock with certain special rights. Some investors have risk and return preferences that can best be met by combining some of the features of bonds with some of the features of common stock. Preferred stock may be the right choice for these investors. It does not appeal to investors who want some control over the operations of the corporation because preferred stock usually does not convey voting rights. Indeed, this is one of the main reasons that some corporations issue preferred stock to raise equity capital. Preferred stock permits them to raise funds without diluting the common stockholders' control of the company. The chart in the margin shows the percentage of companies surveyed by *Accounting Trends & Techniques* utilizing preferred stock in their capital structures.

Preferred stock may be no-par value, although typically it has a par value. Most preferred stock has a fixed dividend rate. For example, "6 percent preferred stock, par value $10 per share" pays an annual dividend of 6 percent of par, or $0.60 per share. If the preferred stock is no-par value, the preferred dividend is specified as $0.60 per share.

Generally, preferred stock is less risky than common stock because of the priority it receives on dividend payments and asset distributions. We will compare common stock dividends and preferred stock dividends later in this chapter.

The priority on distribution of assets for the preferred stock occurs if the corporation goes out of business. Preferred stock usually has a specified amount per share that must be paid to the preferred stockholders upon dissolution before any assets can be distributed to the common stockholders.

**Special Features of Preferred Stock** Some corporations issue **convertible preferred stock**, which provides preferred stockholders the option to exchange their preferred shares for shares of common stock of the corporation. The terms of the conversion specify dates and a conversion ratio. The notes to the annual report for Chrysler contain typical information concerning convertible preferred stock:

> The annual dividend on convertible preferred stock is $46.25 per share. The convertible preferred stock is convertible at a rate of 27.78 shares of common stock for each share of convertible preferred, which is equivalent to a conversion price of $18.00 per share of common stock.

Some preferred stock is *callable*. At the option of the issuing corporation, holders of callable preferred stock can be required to return the shares to it for a specified amount of cash. The call price usually is higher than the par value. Creative Learning Products described its call feature in the following note to its annual report:

> The Company may, at its option, call all or a part of the preferred stock for redemption at $1.50 per share, plus all accrued but unpaid dividends.

**PREFERRED STOCK** is stock that has specified rights over common stock.

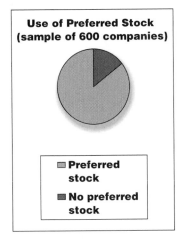

**Use of Preferred Stock (sample of 600 companies)**

■ **Preferred stock**
■ **No preferred stock**

**CONVERTIBLE PREFERRED STOCK** is preferred stock that is convertible to common stock at the option of the holder.

**REAL WORLD EXCERPT**

*Chrysler*

ANNUAL REPORT

**REAL WORLD EXCERPT**

*Creative Learning Products*

ANNUAL REPORT

## FOCUS ON CASH FLOWS

### FINANCING ACTIVITIES

Transactions involving capital stock have a direct impact on the capital structure of a business. Because of the importance of these transactions, a major section of the statement of cash flows reports both cash inflows and outflows that relate to the way that cash was obtained from external sources (owners and creditors) to finance the enterprise and its operations.

These transactions are reported in the section of the statement called *Cash Flows from Financing Activities*. Examples of cash flows associated with capital stock are included in the statement of cash flows for Wal-Mart shown in Exhibit 11.4. Notice that the company repurchased some its own stock and paid cash dividends. We will discuss both of these transactions later in this chapter.

EXHIBIT **11.4**

**Excerpt from Statement of Cash Flows for Wal-Mart**

**REAL WORLD EXCERPT**

*Wal-Mart Stores, Inc.*

ANNUAL REPORT

**CONSOLIDATED STATEMENTS OF CASH FLOWS**

(amounts in millions)

| Fiscal years ended January 31, | 1999 | 1998 | 1997 |
|---|---|---|---|
| Cash flows from financing activities | | | |
| Decrease in commercial paper | — | — | (2,458) |
| Proceeds from issuance of long-term debt | 536 | 547 | — |
| Net proceeds from formation of Real Estate Investment Trust | — | — | 632 |
| Purchase of Company stock | (1,202) | (1,569) | (208) |
| Dividends paid | (693) | (611) | (481) |
| Payment of long-term debt | (1,075) | (554) | (541) |
| Payment of capital lease obligations | (101) | (94) | (74) |
| Other financing activities | (195) | 143 | 68 |
| Net cash used in financing activities | (2,730) | (2,138) | (3,062) |

**Effect on Statement of Cash Flows**

**IN GENERAL** → Cash received from owners is reported as an inflow. Cash payments made to owners are reported as outflows. Examples are shown in the following table:

| | Effect on Cash Flows |
|---|---|
| **Financing activities** (indirect method) | |
| Issuance of capital stock | + |
| Repurchase of capital stock | − |
| Payment of cash dividends | − |

**Selected Focus Company Comparisons: Cash Flows from Financing Activities (in millions)**

| | |
|---|---|
| Dollar General | $183 |
| JCPenney | $(94) |
| Wal-Mart | $(2,730) |

**FOCUS COMPANY ANALYSIS** → Notice that for each of the last three years, Wal-Mart has repurchased significant amounts of its own capital stock (Exhibit 11.4). A company may do so for a number of reasons. Most companies issue stock options or stock to key executives. It is less expensive to use previously issued stock that has been repurchased instead of newly issued stock. Other companies buy their own stock because they believe that it is a good use of excess cash.

Wal-Mart is a very successful company and the statement of cash flows helps us understand why it is highly respected in the investment community. A rapidly growing company, last year, Wal-Mart invested nearly $4.5 billion in new property, plant and equipment. Rather than raising additional capital from financing activities, the company actually *used* more than $2 billion each year in financing activities (e.g., payment of dividends, repurchase of stock, and repayment of debt). Wal-Mart has been able to finance its rapid growth through operating activities rather than financing activities. Last year, the company generated more than $7.5 billion in cash from operating activities. Wall Street has rewarded this level of success with significant increases in the value of the company's stock.

# ACCOUNTING FOR CAPITAL STOCK

Notice the stockholders' equity section of the balance sheet for Wal-Mart shown in Exhibit 11.1. Four different stockholder equity accounts are reported on the Wal-Mart balance sheet. These accounts represent the two primary sources of stockholders' equity:

1.  *Contributed capital* from the sale of stock, which is the amount invested by stockholders through the purchase of shares of stock from the corporation. Contributed capital has two distinct components: (a) par or stated value derived from the sale of capital stock and (b) additional contributed capital in excess of par or stated value. This often is called *additional paid-in capital.* The contributed capital accounts for Wal-Mart are preferred stock, common stock, and capital in excess of par value.

2.  *Retained earnings* generated by the profit-making activities of the company. This is the *cumulative* amount of net income earned since the organization of the corporation less the cumulative amount of dividends paid by the corporation since organization.

Most companies generate a significant part of their stockholders' equity from retained earnings rather than from capital raised through the sale of stock. In the case of Wal-Mart, retained earnings generated more than 98 percent of the total stockholders' equity.

## SALE AND ISSUANCE OF CAPITAL STOCK

Two names are applied to transactions involving the initial sale of a company's stock to the public. An *initial public offering,* or *IPO,* involves the very first sale of a company's stock to the public (i.e., when the company first "goes public"). You have probably heard stories of Internet stocks that have dramatically increased in value the day of their IPO. While significant returns are sometimes earned, there are often significant risks associated with buying an IPO. Once the stock of a company is traded on established markets, the term that describes additional sales of new stock to the public is a *seasoned new issue.*

As was the case with bonds (discussed in Chapter 10), most companies use an underwriter to assist in the sale of stock. The underwriter is usually an investment bank that acts as an intermediary between the corporation and the investors. The underwriter advises the corporation on matters concerning the sale and is directly involved in the sale of shares to the public.

Most sales of stock to the public are cash transactions. To illustrate accounting for an initial sale of stock, assume that Wal-Mart sold 100,000 shares of its $0.10 par value stock for $22 per share. The company records the following journal entry:

| | | |
|---|---|---|
| Cash (A) (100,000 × $22) . . . . . . . . . . . . . . . . . . . | 2,200,000 | |
| Common stock (SE) (100,000 × $0.10) . . . . . | | 10,000 |
| Capital in excess of par value (SE) . . . . . . . . | | 2,190,000 |

| Assets | | = | Liabilities | + | Stockholders' Equity | |
|---|---|---|---|---|---|---|
| Cash | +2,200,000 | | | | Common stock | +10,000 |
| | | | | | Capital in excess of par | +2,190,000 |

The sale of common stock is reported on the balance sheet in the format shown in Exhibit 11.1.

Some corporations do not specify a par value for their stock. In these cases, depending on state law, common stock is recorded under one of the following two approaches:

1.  The corporation must specify in its bylaws a stated value per share as legal capital. This stated value is used as a substitute for par value, and the sale of common stock is recorded in a manner similar to the previous journal entry.

2. The corporation must record the total proceeds received from each sale of no-par stock as legal capital. In this case, the total proceeds are recorded in the Common Stock account; there is no account called Capital in Excess of Par.

## SECONDARY MARKETS

When a company sells stock to the public, the transaction is between the issuing corporation and the buyer. As a result, the company records the sale on its books in the manner shown earlier.

Subsequent transactions affecting the stock are between two investors and do not directly affect the corporation's accounting records. For example, if investor Jon Drago sold 1,000 shares of Wal-Mart stock to Jennifer Lea, Wal-Mart does not record a journal entry on its books. Mr. Drago received cash for the shares he sold, and Ms. Lea received stock for the cash she paid. Wal-Mart itself did not receive or pay anything because of the transaction.

Each business day, *The Wall Street Journal* reports the results of thousands of transactions between investors in the secondary markets. These markets include the New York Stock Exchange (NYSE), the American Stock Exchange (AMEX), and the over-the-counter (OTC) market.

Managers of corporations follow very closely the movements in the price of their company's stock. Stockholders expect to earn money on their investment because of dividends and increases in the price of the stock. In many instances, senior management has been replaced because of poor performance of the stock in the secondary markets. Although managers watch the stock price on a daily basis, it is important to remember that the transactions between investors do not directly affect the company's books (i.e., journal entries are not prepared to record the transactions).

# FINANCIAL **ANALYSIS**

### GOING PUBLIC

As noted, an initial public offering (IPO) is the first sale of stock to the public. Prior to that sale, the company was a private company. A company might want to go public for two common reasons. For it to grow and meet consumer demand, it must expand its productive capacity. The need for new capital may be beyond the capability of the private owners. By going public, the company can raise the funds needed to expand.

In some cases, the company may not need significant funds, but the current owners may want to create a market for its shares. Often selling shares of stock is difficult if the company is not listed on a major stock exchange. By going public, a company can increase the liquidity of its shares.

Initial public offerings often create a great deal of interest among investors. Some good opportunities are available to earn excellent returns by investing in growing companies. Substantial risk also is associated with many IPOs.

In recent years, substantial interest has surrounded Internet companies that have gone public. Virtually any company with ".Com" in its name has received significant attention from investors. There are countless stories of people in their twenties and thirties who have become instant millionaires after the IPO of a new Internet company. Less well publicized, however, are the stories of individuals who have lost money investing in new and unproven businesses.

## CAPITAL STOCK SOLD AND ISSUED FOR NONCASH ASSETS AND/OR SERVICES

Small companies are playing an increasingly important role in the U.S. economy. They created a large percentage of the new jobs that have been created in the past decade. Many of today's corporate giants were small start-up companies just a few years ago.

Companies such as Dell Computers, Microsoft, and Apple Computer began literally as basement operations in the homes of their founders.

One feature common to all start-up companies is a shortage of cash. Because these companies often cannot afford to pay cash for needed assets and services, they sometimes issue stock to people who can supply these assets and services. Indeed, many executives will join start-up companies for very low salaries because they also earn shares of stock. An executive who was given Microsoft or Amazon.com stock during its early days would be very wealthy today.

When a company issues stock to acquire assets or services, the acquired items are recorded at the *market value* of the stock issued at the date of the transaction in accordance with the *cost principle*. If the market value of the stock issued cannot be determined, the market value of the consideration received should be used.

To illustrate, assume that during its early years of operations, Wal-Mart was unable to pay cash for needed legal services. The company issued 10,000 shares of stock to the Rose law firm when the stock was selling for $15 per share. At that time, the company recorded the following journal entry:

| | | |
|---|---|---|
| Legal fees (E) .......................... | 150,000 | |
| Common stock (SE) (10,000 × $0.10) ...... | | 1,000 |
| Capital in excess of par value (SE) ........ | | 149,000 |

| Assets | = | Liabilities | + | Stockholders' Equity | |
|---|---|---|---|---|---|
| | | | | Legal fees | −150,000 |
| | | | | Common stock | +1,000 |
| | | | | Capital in excess of par | +149,000 |

Notice that the value of the legal services received is assumed to be the same as the value of the stock that was issued. This assumption is reasonable because two independent parties usually keep negotiating a deal until the value of what is given up equals the value of what is received.

## STOCK OPTIONS

One of the advantages of the corporate form is the possibility to separate management and ownership. This separation also can be a disadvantage, because some managers may not act in the owners' best interests. This problem can be overcome in a number of ways. Compensation packages can be developed to reward managers for meeting goals that are important to stockholders. Another strategy is to offer managers *stock options,* which permit them to buy stock at a fixed price. The holder of a stock option has an interest in a company's performance in the same manner as an owner. Stock option plans have become an increasingly common form of compensation over the past years. Indeed, 98 percent of the companies surveyed by *Accounting Trends & Techniques* now offer stock option plans for their employees.

The Wal-Mart annual report contains the following note:

**Note 7 Stock Option Plans**
At January 31, 1999, 131 million shares of common stock were reserved for issuance under stock option plans. The options granted under the stock option plans expire 10 years from the date of grant.

The options issued by Wal-Mart specified that stock could be bought at the stock's current market price. Granting a stock option is a form of compensation even if the grant price and the current stock price are the same. If someone gives you a stock option, you could think of it as a risk-free investment. If you hold a stock option when the stock price declines, you have lost nothing. If the price of the stock increases, you can exercise your option for the low price and sell the stock for the high price.

Stock options are a widely used form of executive compensation. Most companies offer them with a grant price equal to the current market price of the stock (as is the case with Wal-Mart). Compensation expense is reported based on the fair value of the options at the date of grant. Fair value is determined by using a complex mathematical formula called an *option pricing model* that will be discussed in advanced accounting courses.

## TREASURY STOCK

**LEARNING OBJECTIVE 3**

Explain the purpose of treasury stock and analyze transactions affecting it.

A corporation may want to purchase its own stock from existing stockholders for a number of strategic reasons. A common reason is the existence of an employee bonus plan that provides workers with shares of the company's stock as part of their compensation. Because of Securities and Exchange Commission regulations concerning newly issued shares, most companies find that it is less costly to give their employees shares of stock that were purchased from stockholders than to issue new shares.

**TREASURY STOCK** is a corporation's own stock that had been issued but was subsequently reacquired and is still being held by that corporation.

Stock that was issued to stockholders and then subsequently *reacquired* and held by that corporation is called **treasury stock.** While this stock is held by the issuing corporation, it has no voting, dividend, or other stockholder rights.

Two alternative approaches generally are used to account for treasury stock—the cost method and the par value method. We limit our discussions to the cost method because it is more widely used. The par value method is discussed in most accounting texts at the intermediate level. The recording of the purchase of treasury stock is based on the cost of the shares that were purchased. Assume that Wal-Mart bought 100,000 shares of its stock in the open market when it was selling for $22 per share. Using the cost method, the company records the following journal entry:

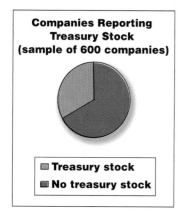

**Companies Reporting Treasury Stock (sample of 600 companies)**

☐ Treasury stock
☐ No treasury stock

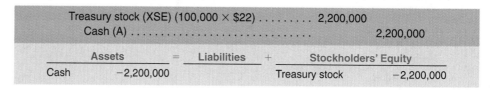

| Treasury stock (XSE) (100,000 × $22) . . . . . . . . . 2,200,000 | | |
| Cash (A) . . . . . . . . . . . . . . . . . . . . . . . . . . . . . 2,200,000 | | |

| Assets | = | Liabilities | + | Stockholders' Equity | |
| --- | --- | --- | --- | --- | --- |
| Cash | −2,200,000 | | | Treasury stock | −2,200,000 |

Intuitively, many students expect the Treasury Stock account to be reported as an asset. Such is not the case because a company cannot create an asset by investing in itself. The Treasury Stock account is actually a *contra-equity account,* which means that it is reported as a subtraction from the total stockholders' equity. This makes sense because treasury stock is stock that is no longer outstanding and, therefore, should not be included as part of stockholders' equity.

As the information in Exhibit 11.1 indicates, Wal-Mart does not report any treasury stock on its balance sheet. The company actually purchased treasury stock, but it uses an accounting alternative that treats the purchase of its own stock as a retirement of the stock. Under this alternative, the common stock account and paid-in capital accounts are reduced. If Wal-Mart had used the cost method, its stockholders' equity section would appear as follows (numbers in thousands, based on the previous example):

**WAL-MART STORES, INC.**
**Shareholders' Equity (Summarized)**

| | |
| --- | --- |
| Common stock | $ 445,000,000 |
| Capital in excess of par | 435,000,000 |
| Retained earnings | 20,741,000,000 |
| Less: Treasury stock XSE | (2,200,000) |
| Total stockholders' equity | $21,618,800,000 |

If a company eventually sells its treasury stock, it will not report an accounting profit or loss on the transaction even if it sells the stock for more or less than it paid.

GAAP do not permit a corporation to report income or losses from investments in its own stock because transactions with the owners are not considered to be normal profit-making activities. Based on the previous example, assume that Wal-Mart sold 10,000 shares of treasury stock for $30 per share. Remember that the company had purchased the stock for $22 per share. Wal-Mart records the following entry:

| | |
|---|---|
| Cash (A) (10,000 × $30) . . . . . . . . . . . . . . . . . . . . . . . . . . . . . . . 300,000 | |
|     Treasury stock (XSE) (10,000 × $22) . . . . . . . . . . . . . . . . | 220,000 |
|     Contributed capital from treasury stock transactions (SE) . . | 80,000 |

| Assets | = | Liabilities | + | Stockholders' Equity | |
|---|---|---|---|---|---|
| Cash    +300,000 | | | | Treasury stock | +220,000 |
| | | | | Contributed capital | +80,000 |

If treasury stock were sold at a price below its purchase price (i.e., an economic loss), the Contributed Capital from Treasury Stock Transactions account would be debited for the amount of the loss. Retained Earnings would be debited for some or all of the amount of the economic losses only if there were an insufficient credit balance in the Contributed Capital account.

Neither the purchase nor sale of treasury stock affects the number of shares of stock that are issued or unissued. Treasury stock affects only the number of shares of outstanding stock. The basic difference between treasury stock and unissued stock is that treasury stock has been sold at least once.

### SELF-STUDY **QUIZ**

1. Assume that Applied Technology Corporation issued 10,000 shares of its common stock, par value $2, for $150,000 cash. Prepare the journal entry to record this transaction.

2. Assume that Applied Technology purchased 5,000 shares of its stock in the open market for treasury stock when the stock was selling for $12 per share. Record this transaction using the cost method.

After you have completed your answers, check them with the solutions presented in the footnote at the bottom of this page.*

## ACCOUNTING FOR CASH DIVIDENDS

### DIVIDENDS DEFINED

Investors buy common stock because they expect a return on their investment. This return can come in two forms: stock price appreciation and dividends to owners. Some investors prefer to buy stocks that pay little or no dividends. Companies that reinvest the majority of their earnings tend to increase their future earnings potential. By increasing their future earnings potential, these companies often experience increases in their stock price. Wealthy investors in high tax brackets prefer to receive their return on stock investments in the form of higher stock prices because capital gains may be taxed at a lower rate than dividend income.

Other investors, such as retired people, prefer to receive their return on an investment in the form of dividends because they need a steady income. These people often seek stock that will pay very high dividends. Many retired people hold utility stocks because they are usually conservative investments that pay high dividends.

■ **LEARNING OBJECTIVE 4**

Discuss dividends and analyze transactions involving common and preferred stock.

| | | |
|---|---|---|
| *1. Cash | 150,000 | |
|     Common stock | | 20,000 |
|     Contributed capital in excess of par | | 130,000 |
| 2. Treasury stock | 60,000 | |
|     Cash | | 60,000 |

The board of directors must approve (i.e., declare) dividends before they can be paid. A corporation does not have a legal obligation to pay dividends. Creditors can force a company into bankruptcy if it does not meet required interest payments on debt, but stockholders do not have a similar right if a corporation is unable to pay dividends.

Without a qualifier, the term *dividend* means a cash dividend. Dividends also can be paid in assets other than cash. Some corporations issue stock dividends, which are dividend distributions of the corporation's own stock. The most common type of dividend is a cash dividend.

Although a corporation does not have a legal obligation to pay a dividend, it creates a liability once the board formally declares one. An actual press release announcing a dividend declaration for Wal-Mart contained the following information:

**DATELINE: BENTONVILLE, ARK., AUGUST 12, 1999**

The Board of Directors of Wal-Mart Stores, Inc. today declared a quarterly cash dividend on common stock of five cents ($0.05) a share, payable October 12, 1999 to shareholders of record September 17, 1999.

This declaration creates a liability. Immediately on August 12, Wal-Mart records the following journal entry to reflect the declaration of a cash dividend based on 4,448,000,000 shares outstanding ($0.05 × 4,448,000,000 = $222,400,000):

*declared*

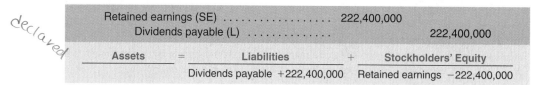

| Retained earnings (SE) | 222,400,000 | |
| Dividends payable (L) | | 222,400,000 |

| Assets | = | Liabilities | + | Stockholders' Equity |
|---|---|---|---|---|
| | | Dividends payable +222,400,000 | | Retained earnings −222,400,000 |

The subsequent payment of the liability on October 12 is recorded as follows:

*when paid*

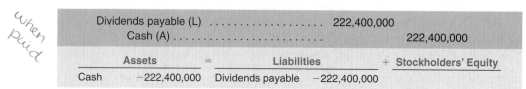

| Dividends payable (L) | 222,400,000 | |
| Cash (A) | | 222,400,000 |

| Assets | = | Liabilities | + | Stockholders' Equity |
|---|---|---|---|---|
| Cash −222,400,000 | | Dividends payable −222,400,000 | | |

Notice that the declaration and payment of a cash dividend have two impacts: they reduce assets (cash) and stockholders' equity (retained earnings) by the same amount. This observation helps us understand the two fundamental requirements for the payment of a cash dividend:

1. *Sufficient retained earnings.* The corporation must have accumulated a sufficient amount of retained earnings to cover the amount of the dividend. State incorporation laws usually place restrictions on cash dividends. For example, state laws often limit cash dividends to the balance in the Retained Earnings account.

2. *Sufficient cash.* The corporation must have access to sufficient cash to pay the dividend and to meet the continuing operating needs of the business. The mere fact that the Retained Earnings account has a large credit balance does not mean that the board of directors can declare and pay a cash dividend. The cash generated in the past by earnings represented in the Retained Earnings account may have been expended to acquire inventory, buy operational assets, and pay liabilities. Consequently, no necessary relationship exists between the balance of retained earnings and the balance of cash on any particular date (simply, retained earnings is not cash).

### DIVIDEND DATES

Refer back to the earlier example of a dividend declaration by Wal-Mart. Notice that the declaration includes three important dates:

1. **Declaration date—August 12, 1999.** The **declaration date** is the date on which the board of directors officially approved the dividend. As soon as it makes the declaration, it creates a dividend liability.

2. **Date of record—September 17, 1999.** The **record date** follows the declaration; it is the date on which the corporation prepares the list of current stockholders based on its stockholder records. The dividend is payable only to those names listed on the record date. No journal entry is made on this date.

3. **Date of payment—October 12, 1999.** The **payment date** is the date on which the cash is disbursed to pay the dividend liability. It follows the date of record as specified in the dividend announcement.

For instructional purposes, the time lag between the date of declaration and the date of payment may be ignored because it does not pose any substantive issues. When all three dates fall in the same accounting period, a single entry on the date of payment may be made in practice for purely practical reasons.

The **DECLARATION DATE** is the date on which the board of directors officially approves a dividend.

The **RECORD DATE** is the date on which the corporation prepares the list of current stockholders as shown on its records; dividends can be paid only to the stockholders who own stock on that date.

The **PAYMENT DATE** is the date on which a cash dividend is paid to the stockholders of record.

## FINANCIAL **ANALYSIS**

### IMPACT OF DIVIDENDS ON STOCK PRICE

An additional date is important in understanding dividends, but it has no accounting implications. The date two business days before the date of record is known as the *ex-dividend date.* This date is established by the stock exchanges to make certain that dividend checks are sent to the right people. If you buy stock before the ex-dividend date, you receive the dividend. If you buy the stock on the ex-dividend date or later, the previous owner receives the dividend.

If you follow the prices of some stock, you will notice that a stock's price often falls on the ex-dividend date. The reason is simple. On that date the stock is worth less because it no longer includes the right to receive the next dividend.

## KEY **RATIO ANALYSIS:**

### DIVIDEND YIELD

**K**now the decision question:
Owners of common stock expect to earn a return on their investment. A portion of this return comes in the form of dividends. The *dividend yield ratio* is a measure of the percentage return that owners are earning from the dividends they receive. Potential investors often use this ratio to help select from alternative investment opportunities. It is computed as follows:

**Dividend Yield Ratio = Dividends per Share ÷ Market Price per Share**

The 1999 ratio for Wal-Mart:

**$0.14 ÷ $52 = 0.3%**

■ **LEARNING OBJECTIVE 5**

Analyze the dividend yield ratio.

**E**xamine the ratio using two techniques:

| ① Comparisons over Time | | | | ② Comparisons with Competitors | |
|---|---|---|---|---|---|
| **Wal-Mart** | | | | **Dollar General** | **JCPenney** |
| 1997 | 1998 | 1999 | | 1999 | 1999 |
| 0.8% | 0.7% | 0.3% | | 0.4% | 6.9% |

**Y**ou interpret the results carefully:
**IN GENERAL** → Investors in common stock earn a return from dividends and capital appreciation (increases in the market price of the stock they own). Growth-oriented companies often pay out

very small amounts of dividends and rely on increases in their market price to provide a return to investors. Others pay out large dividends but have more stable market prices. Each type of stock appeals to different types of investors with different risk and return preferences.

**FOCUS COMPANY ANALYSIS** → The dividend yield for Wal-Mart is virtually immaterial in amount. This low amount and relative stability over time is a good indication that investors who need steady income from dividends should not purchase Wal-Mart stock. During the three-year comparison period, Wal-Mart stock increased by 400 percent because of significant increase in the sales and profits of the company. With this significant amount of capital appreciation, most owners would be unconcerned about the amount of dividends paid by Wal-Mart.

**A FEW CAUTIONS:** Remember that the dividend yield ratio tells only part of the return on investment story. Often, potential capital appreciation is a much more important consideration. When analyzing changes in the ratio, it is important to understand the cause. For example, a company might pay out $2 per share in dividends each year. If the market price of its stock is $100 per share, the yield is 2 percent. If the market price per share falls to $25 the following year and the company continues to pay out $2 per share in dividends, the dividend yield ratio will "improve" to 8 percent. Most analysts would not interpret this change as being favorable.

## DIVIDENDS ON PREFERRED STOCK

Investors who purchase preferred stock give up certain advantages that are available to investors in common stock. Generally, preferred stockholders do not have the right to vote at the annual meeting, nor do they share in increased earnings if the company becomes more profitable. To compensate these investors, preferred stock offers some advantages not available to common stockholders. Perhaps the most important advantage is dividend preference. You will frequently encounter the following dividend preferences:

1. Current dividend preference.
2. Cumulative dividend preference.

**CURRENT DIVIDEND PREFERENCE** is the feature of preferred stock that grants priority on preferred dividends over common dividends.

**Current Dividend Preference on Preferred Stock**   Preferred stock always carries a **current dividend preference.** It requires that the current preferred dividend be paid before any dividends are paid on the common stock. When the current dividend preference has been met and no other preference is operative, dividends can be paid to the common stockholders.

Declared dividends must be allocated between the preferred and common stock. First, the preferences of the preferred stock must be met, and then the remainder of the total dividend can be allocated to the common stock. Exhibit 11.5, Case A, illustrates the allocation of the current dividend preference under three different assumptions concerning the total amount of dividends to be paid.

**CUMULATIVE DIVIDEND PREFERENCE** is the preferred stock feature that requires specified current dividends not paid in full to accumulate for every year in which they are not paid. These cumulative preferred dividends must be paid before any common dividends can be paid.

**Cumulative Dividend Preference on Preferred Stock**   Cumulative preferred stock has a **cumulative dividend preference** that states that if all or a part of the specified current dividend is not paid in full, the unpaid amount is known as **dividends in arrears.** The amount of any cumulative preferred dividends in arrears must be paid before any common dividends can be paid. Of course, if the preferred stock is noncumulative, dividends never can be in arrears. Therefore, any dividends passed (i.e., not declared) are lost permanently by the preferred stockholders. Because preferred stockholders are not willing to accept this unfavorable feature, preferred stock is usually cumulative.

**DIVIDENDS IN ARREARS** are dividends on cumulative preferred stock that have not been declared in prior years.

Dividends are never an actual liability until the board of directors declares them. Dividends in arrears are not reported on the balance sheet but are disclosed in the notes to the statements.

The allocation of dividends between cumulative preferred stock and common stock is illustrated in Exhibit 11.5, Case B, under four different assumptions concerning the total amount of dividends to be paid. Observe that the dividends in arrears are paid first, then the current dividend preference is paid, and, finally, the remainder is paid to the common stockholders.

**Case A—Current dividend preference only**

EXHIBIT **11.5**

**Dividends on Preferred Stock**

Preferred stock outstanding, 6%, par $20; 2,000 shares = $40,000 par.

Common stock outstanding, par $10; 5,000 shares = $50,000 par.

Allocation of dividends between preferred and common stock assuming current dividend preference only:

| Assumptions | Total Dividends Paid | 6% Preferred Stock (2,000 shares at $20 par = $40,000)* | Common Stock (5,000 shares at $10 Par = $50,000) |
|---|---|---|---|
| No. 1 | $ 2,000 | $2,000 | 0 |
| No. 2 | 3,000 | 2,400 | $ 600 |
| No. 3 | 18,000 | 2,400 | 15,600 |

*Preferred dividend preference, $40,000 × 6% = $2,400, or 2,000 shares × $1.20.

**Case B—Cumulative dividend preference**

Preferred and common stock outstanding—same as in Case A. Dividends in arrears for the two preceding years.

Allocation of dividends between preferred and common stock assuming cumulative preference:

| Assumptions (dividends in arrears, 2 years) | Total Dividends Paid | 6% Preferred Stock (2,000 shares at $20 par = $40,000)* | Common Stock (5,000 shares at $10 Par = $50,000) |
|---|---|---|---|
| No. 1 | $ 2,400 | $2,400 | 0 |
| No. 2 | 7,200 | 7,200 | 0 |
| No. 3 | 8,000 | 7,200 | $ 800 |
| No. 4 | 30,000 | 7,200 | 22,800 |

*Current dividend preference, $40,000 × 6% = $2,400; dividends in arrears preference, $2,400 × 2 years = $4,800; and current dividend preference plus dividends in arrears = $7,200.

## FINANCIAL **ANALYSIS**

### IMPACT OF DIVIDENDS IN ARREARS

The existence of dividends in arrears is important information for analysts. This situation limits a company's ability to pay dividends to its common stockholders and has implications for the company's future cash flows. The following note from Lone Star Industries is typical if a company has dividends in arrears:

> The total of dividends in arrears on the $13.50 preferred stock at the end of the year was $11,670,000. The aggregate amount of such dividend must be paid before any dividends are paid on common stock.

Remember that various issues of preferred stock can offer different features. Most preferred stock has the cumulative dividend preference to provide stockholders with extra security. Companies can offer additional features to provide even more security. Many companies offer the feature described in the following note from Bally Manufacturing:

> The holders of preferred stock do not have voting rights except that the holders would have the right to elect two additional directors of Bally if dividends on the preferred stock are in arrears in an amount equal to at least six quarterly dividends.

By electing two members of the board of directors, preferred stockholders have specific individuals to represent their interests. Bally included this feature with its preferred stock to make the stock more attractive to potential stockholders.

## SELF-STUDY **QUIZ**

Answer the following questions concerning dividends:

1. On which dividend date is a liability created?
2. A cash outflow occurs on which dividend date?
3. When are dividends in arrears reported on the balance sheet as a liability?
4. What are the two fundamental requirements for the payment of a dividend?

After you have completed your answers, check them with the solutions presented in the footnote at the bottom of the page.*

## ACCOUNTING FOR STOCK DIVIDENDS AND STOCK SPLITS

### STOCK DIVIDENDS

**LEARNING OBJECTIVE 6**

Discuss the purpose of stock dividends, stock splits, and report transactions.

A **STOCK DIVIDEND** is a distribution of additional shares of a corporation's own stock.

Each year, hundreds of corporations issue stock dividends. A **stock dividend** is a distribution of additional shares of a corporation's own capital stock on a pro rata basis to its stockholders at no cost. Stock dividends usually consist of common stock issued to the holders of common stock. *Pro rata basis* means that each stockholder receives additional shares equal to the percentage of shares already held. A stockholder with 10 percent of the outstanding shares receives 10 percent of any additional shares issued as a stock dividend.

You should be careful as you read annual reports and the business press. The term *stock dividend* is sometimes ambiguous. A recent *Wall Street Journal* headline announced that a particular company had just declared a "stock dividend." A close reading of the article revealed that the company had declared a cash dividend on the stock. Just remember that a dividend paid in stock is a stock dividend and one paid in cash is a cash dividend.

The value of a stock dividend is the subject of much debate. In reality, a stock dividend has no economic value, as such. All stockholders receive a pro rata distribution of shares, which means that each owns exactly the same portion of the company both before and after the stock dividend. The value of an investment is determined by the percentage of the company that is owned, not the number of shares that are held. If you get change for a dollar, you do not have more wealth because you hold *four* quarters instead of only *one* dollar. Similarly, if you own 10 percent of a company, you do not have more wealth simply because the company declares a stock dividend and gives you (and all other stockholders) more shares of stock. At this point, you may still wonder why having extra shares of stock does not make an investor wealthier. The reason is simple: The stock market reacts immediately when a stock dividend is issued, and the stock price falls proportionally. If the stock price was $60 before a stock dividend, normally (in the absence of events affecting the company) the price falls to $30 if the number of shares is doubled. Thus, an investor could own 100 shares worth $6,000 before the stock dividend (100 × $60) and 200 shares worth $6,000 after the stock dividend (200 × $30).

In reality, the price of a stock does not fall exactly in proportion to the number of new shares that are issued. In some cases, the stock dividend makes the stock more

---

*1. Declaration date.
2. Date of payment.
3. Dividends are reported as a liability only after the date of declaration.
4. Dividends can be paid only if sufficient retained earnings and sufficient cash are both available.

attractive to new investors. Many investors prefer to buy stock in *round lots,* which are multiples of 100 shares. An investor with $10,000 might not buy a stock selling for $150 because she cannot afford to buy 100 shares. She might buy the stock, however, if the price is less than $100 as the result of a stock dividend. In other cases, stock dividends are associated with increases in cash dividends, which would be attractive to some investors. A recent press release concerning a stock dividend for Wal-Mart illustrates the simultaneous announcement of a stock dividend and an increase in the annual cash dividends.

> The Board of Directors of Wal-Mart announced a 2-1 stock split in the form of a stock dividend to be issued on August 18, 1999 to shareholders' of record as of March 19, 1999. This is the Company's 11th stock split.
>
> The stock dividend will be accompanied by a 29 percent dividend increase.

**REAL WORLD EXCERPT**

*Wal-Mart Stores, Inc.*

STOCK DIVIDEND
ANNOUNCEMENT

In this announcement, Wal-Mart uses the term "2-1 stock split." The Securities and Exchange Commission requires the use of the word *split* instead of *dividend* whenever the transaction involves 25 percent or more of the outstanding shares.

When a stock dividend occurs, the company must transfer an additional amount into the common stock account to reflect the additional shares that have been issued. The amount transferred depends on whether the stock dividend is classified as large or small. A *large* stock dividend involves the distribution of additional shares that are more than 20–25 percent of the currently outstanding shares. A *small* stock dividend involves additional shares that are less than 20–25 percent of the outstanding shares. The chart in the margin shows the size of stock dividends for 600 companies surveyed by *Accounting Trends & Techniques.*

Because the Wal-Mart stock dividend was equal to 100 percent of the outstanding shares, it should be classified as a large dividend. The company makes the following entry to record a large stock dividend:

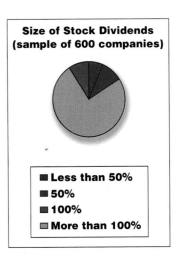

**Size of Stock Dividends
(sample of 600 companies)**

- ■ Less than 50%
- ■ 50%
- ■ 100%
- ▨ More than 100%

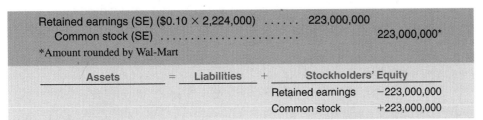

| Retained earnings (SE) ($0.10 × 2,224,000) ...... | 223,000,000 | |
| Common stock (SE) ....................... | | 223,000,000* |

*Amount rounded by Wal-Mart

| Assets | = | Liabilities | + | Stockholders' Equity | |
|--------|---|-------------|---|---------------------|--|
| | | | | Retained earnings | −223,000,000 |
| | | | | Common stock | +223,000,000 |

This journal entry moves an amount from Retained Earnings to the company's Common Stock account. The stock dividend did *not* change total stockholders' equity, it changed only the balances of some of the accounts that constitute stockholders' equity. If you examine Exhibit 11.1, you will notice that Wal-Mart actually transferred an amount from the Capital in Excess of Par account instead of Retained Earnings (as shown). The SEC permits the method used by Wal-Mart. Our journal entry is based on the method that you will more frequently encounter.

The amount transferred to the Common Stock account was based on the par value of the shares issued as a stock dividend. Par value is used when the stock dividend is classified as large. When a stock dividend is small (i.e., less than 20–25 percent), the amount transferred should be the total market value of the shares issued.

## STOCK SPLITS

Stock splits are *not* dividends. They are similar to a stock dividend but are quite different in terms of their impact on the stockholders' equity accounts. In a **stock split,** the *total* number of authorized shares is increased by a specified amount, such as a 2-for-1 split. In this instance, each share held is called in, and two new shares are issued in its place. Typically, a stock split is accomplished by reducing the par or stated value

A **STOCK SPLIT** is an increase in the total number of authorized shares by a specified ratio; does not decrease retained earnings.

per share of all authorized shares so that the total par value of all authorized shares is unchanged. If Wal-Mart executes a 2-for-1 stock split, it reduces the par value of its stock from $0.10 to $0.05 and it doubles the number of shares outstanding. In contrast to a stock dividend, a stock split does *not* result in a transfer of a dollar amount to the Common Stock account. No transfer is needed because the reduction in the par value per share compensates for the increase in the number of shares.

In both a stock dividend and a stock split, the stockholder receives more shares of stock but does not disburse any additional assets to acquire the additional shares. A stock dividend requires a journal entry; a stock split does not require one. A stock split is disclosed in the notes to the financial statements.

The comparative effects of a stock dividend versus a stock split may be summarized as follows:

| Stockholders' Equity | Before | After a 100% Stock Dividend | After a Two-for-One Stock Split |
|---|---|---|---|
| Contributed capital | | | |
| Number of shares outstanding | 30,000 | 60,000 | 60,000 |
| Par value per share | $ 10 | $ 10 | $ 5 |
| Total par value outstanding | 300,000 | 600,000 | 300,000 |
| Retained earnings | 650,000 | 350,000 | 650,000 |
| Total stockholders' equity | 950,000 | 950,000 | 950,000 |

## SELF-STUDY **QUIZ**

Barton Corporation issued 100,000 new shares of common stock (par value $10) in a stock dividend when the market value was $30 per share.

1. Record this transaction, assuming that it was a small stock dividend.

2. Record this transaction, assuming that it was a large stock dividend.

3. What journal entry is required if the transaction is a stock split?

After you have completed your answers, check them with the solutions presented in the footnote at the bottom of this page.*

## RETAINED EARNINGS

■ **LEARNING OBJECTIVE 7**

Measure and report retained earnings.

Retained earnings represents income that has been earned less dividends that have been paid out since the first day of operations for the company. In Exhibit 11.1, you can see the changes in the Wal-Mart retained earnings that took place during each of the three years covered by the statement.

Under rare circumstances, you may see a statement that includes an adjustment to the beginning balance of retained earnings. This adjustment is called a **prior period adjustment,** which is the correction of an accounting error that occurred in the financial statements of a prior period.

A **PRIOR PERIOD ADJUSTMENT** is an amount debited or credited directly to retained earnings to correct an accounting error of a prior period.

If an accounting error from a previous period is corrected by making an adjustment to the current income statement, net income for the current period is improperly

---

*1. Retained earnings           3,000,000

     Common stock                               1,000,000

     Contributed capital in excess of par        2,000,000

 2. Retained earnings           1,000,000

     Common stock                               1,000,000

 3. No journal entry is required in the case of a stock split.

measured. To avoid this problem, prior period adjustments are reported as an adjustment of the beginning balance of Retained Earnings because the incorrect amount of net income from the earlier year was closed to Retained Earnings in the year the error was made. Prior period adjustments are not reported on the current income statement.

An example of an accounting error that could result in a prior period adjustment was discussed in Chapter 7. Several years ago, the financial statements of Lafayette Radio Electronics Corporation contained the following note:

> Subsequent to the issuance of its financial statements the company discovered a computational error in the amount of $1,046,000 in the calculation of its year-end inventory which resulted in an overstatement of ending inventory.

Lafayette Radio's overstatement of inventory resulted in an overstatement of pretax income by $1,046,000. If the company corrected the error in the year it was discovered, pretax income would have been understated by $1,046,000. The incorrect measurement of income for each year could mislead some users of financial statements.

## RESTRICTIONS ON RETAINED EARNINGS

As the result of several types of business transactions, restrictions may be placed on retained earnings to limit a company's ability to pay dividends to its owners. The most typical example occurs when a business borrows money from a bank. For additional security, some banks include a loan covenant that limits the amount of dividends that a corporation can pay by placing a restriction on its retained earnings.

The *full-disclosure principle* requires restrictions on retained earnings be reported in the financial statements or in a separate note to the financial statements. Analysts are particularly interested in information concerning these restrictions because of the impact they have on the company's dividend policy.

Most companies report restrictions on retained earnings in the notes to the statements. An example of such a note from the annual report of May Department Store follows:

> Under the most restrictive covenants of long-term debt agreements, $1.2 billion of retained earnings was restricted as to the payment of dividends and/or common share repurchase.

This type of note describes any restrictions that were imposed as the result of debt covenants. These restrictions often include a limit on borrowing and required minimum balances of cash or working capital. If debt covenants are violated, the creditor can demand immediate repayment of the debt. For this reason, analysts want to review these restrictions to be sure that companies are not close to violating loan agreements.

# KEY **RATIO ANALYSIS:**

## DIVIDEND PAYOUT RATIO

**K**now the decision question:
A company can use its earnings to finance future growth or to provide a current return to its owners. The *dividend payout ratio* is the portion of current earnings that is paid to owners in the form of dividends. It is computed as follows:

$$\text{Dividend Payout Ratio} = \frac{\text{Dividends}}{\text{Net Income}}$$

The 1999 ratio for Wal-Mart:

$$\$693 \div \$4,430 = 16\%$$

■ **LEARNING OBJECTIVE 8**

Analyze the dividend payout ratio.

Examine the ratio using two techniques:

| ① Comparisons over Time | | | | ② Comparisons with Competitors | |
| --- | --- | --- | --- | --- | --- |
| **Wal-Mart** | | | | **Dollar General** | **JCPenney** |
| 1997 | 1998 | 1999 | | 1999 | 1999 |
| 16% | 18% | 16% | | 15% | 98% |

You interpret the results carefully:

**IN GENERAL** → The level of the dividend payout ratio (high or low) is not inherently good or bad; it simply gives you an insight in to the strategy of a company. Low payout ratios are typically associated with rapidly growing companies that fund much of their growth with cash generated by operating activities. Companies with high payout ratios are often in lines of business that do not offer profitable growth opportunities. Rather than investing in these opportunities, such companies distribute earnings to the owners who are free to invest them in other more profitable opportunities.

**FOCUS COMPANY ANALYSIS** → The dividend payout for Wal-Mart is a fairly low percentage of its net income. The company has maintained this low payout for a number of years. As we mentioned at the beginning of this chapter, Wal-Mart's stock price has grown rapidly over the years, as have its revenues. In the past 10 years, the sales for Wal-Mart have increased by 550 percent! It is understandable that management would want to re-invest earnings in the Company's operations. The payout ratio for Dollar General is similar to that for Wal-Mart. Dollar General has seen rapid growth in sales revenue and stock price over the past few years. In contrast, the sales revenue and stock price for JCPenney have lagged behind the industry for several years. The management of JCPenney apparently does not see attractive investment opportunities for the company and is paying out most of the company's earnings in the form of dividends.

**A FEW CAUTIONS:** Most companies try to maintain a stable or increasing amount of dividends per share instead of maintaining a fixed dividend payout ratio. This means that in an unusually profitable year, the payout ratio will be low and in a year when profits are low, the ratio could be very high and might exceed 100 percent of the current year's earnings. The advantage of maintaining level dividends is that owners are able to plan and budget for a certain amount of dividend income each year, which may be important for some investors. As a result, analysts should review this ratio over a number of years to understand management's strategy.

# ACCOUNTING AND REPORTING FOR UNINCORPORATED BUSINESSES

In this book, we emphasize the corporate form of business because it plays a dominant role in our economy. In fact, there are three forms of business organizations: corporations, sole proprietorships, and partnerships. As we have seen in this chapter, a *corporation* is a legal entity, separate and distinct from its owners. It can enter into contracts in its own name, be sued, and is taxed as a separate entity. A *sole proprietorship* is an unincorporated business owned by one individual. If you started a lawn care business in the summer by yourself, it would have been a sole proprietorship. It is not necessary to file any legal papers to create a proprietorship. A *partnership* is a business owned by two or more people. Again, it is not necessary to file legal papers to create a partnership, but it is certainly a good idea to have a lawyer draw up a contract between the partners. States have adopted the Uniform Partnership Act, which specifies certain rights and responsibilities if the partners did not enter into a formal agreement.

Neither partnerships nor proprietorships are separate legal entities. As a result, owners may be directly sued and are individually taxed on the earnings of the business.

The fundamentals of accounting and reporting for unincorporated businesses are the same as for a corporation except for owners' equity. Typical account structures for the three forms of business organizations are outlined in Exhibit 11.6.

EXHIBIT **11.6**

**Comparative Account Structure among Types of Business Entities**

| Typical Account Structure | | |
|---|---|---|
| Corporation (Stockholders' Equity) | Sole Proprietorship (Owner's Equity) | Partnership (Partners' Equity) |
| Capital Stock Contributed Capital in Excess of Par | Doe, Capital | Able, Capital Baker, Capital |
| Retained Earnings | Not used | Not used |
| Dividends Paid | Doe, Drawings | Able, Drawings Baker, Drawings |
| Revenues, expenses, gains, and losses | Same | Same |
| Asset and liabilities | Same | Same |

Accounting for sole proprietorships and partnerships is discussed in Chapter Supplement A.

## DEMONSTRATION **CASE**

(Try to resolve the requirements before proceeding to the suggested solution that follows.)

This case focuses on the organization and operations for the first year of Shelly Corporation, which was organized on January 1, 20A. The laws of the state specify that the legal capital for no-par stock is the full sale amount. The corporation was organized by 10 local entrepreneurs for the purpose of operating a business to sell various supplies to hotels. The charter authorized the following capital stock:

Common stock, no-par value, 20,000 shares.
Preferred stock, 5 percent, $100 par value, 5,000 shares (cumulative, nonconvertible, and nonvoting; liquidation value, $110).

The following summarized transactions, selected from 20A, were completed on the dates indicated:

*a.* Jan.   Sold a total of 7,500 shares of no-par common stock to the 10 entrepreneurs for cash at $52 per share. Credit the No-par Common Stock account for the total issue amount.

*b.* Feb.   Sold 1,890 shares of preferred stock at $102 per share; cash collected in full.

*c.* Mar.   Purchased land for a store site and made full payment by issuing 100 shares of preferred stock. Early construction of the store is planned. Debit Land (store site). The preferred stock is selling at $102 per share.

*d.* Apr.   Paid $1,980 cash for organization costs. Debit the intangible asset account Organization Cost.

*e.* May   Issued 10 shares of preferred stock to A. B. Cain in full payment of legal services rendered in connection with organization of the corporation. Assume that the preferred stock is selling regularly at $102 per share. Debit Organization Cost.

*f.* June   Sold 500 shares of no-par common stock for cash to C. B. Abel at $54 per share.

*g.* July   Purchased 100 shares of preferred stock that had been sold and issued earlier. The stockholder was moving to another state and needed the money. Shelly Corporation paid the stockholder $104 per share.

*h.* Aug.   Sold 20 shares of the preferred treasury stock at $105 per share.

*i.* Dec. 31   Purchased equipment for $600,000; paid cash. No depreciation expense should be recorded in 20A.

*j.* Dec. 31   Borrowed $20,000 cash from the City Bank on a one-year, interest-bearing note. Interest is payable at a 12 percent rate at maturity.

*k.* Dec. 31   Calculated the following for the year: gross revenues, $129,300; expenses, including corporation income tax but excluding amortization of organization costs, $98,000. Assume that these summarized revenue and expense transactions involved cash. Because the equipment and the bank loan transactions were on December 31, no related adjusting entries at the end of 20A are needed.

*l.* Dec. 31   Decided that a reasonable amortization period for organization costs, starting as of January 1, 20A, is 10 years. This intangible asset must be amortized to expense. Give the required adjusting entry for 20A.

*Required:*

1. Give appropriate journal entries, with a brief explanation for each of these transactions.
2. Give appropriate closing entries at December 31, 20A.
3. Prepare a balance sheet for Shelly Corporation at December 31, 20A. Emphasize full disclosure of stockholders' equity.

# SUGGESTED SOLUTION

1. Journal entries:

*a.*   Jan. 20A    Cash (A) ........................................ 390,000
            No-par common stock (7,500 shares) (SE) ...............      390,000
            *Sale of no-par common stock ($52 × 7,500 shares = $390,000).*

*b.*   Feb. 20A    Cash (A) ........................................ 192,780
            Preferred stock, 5% (par $100, 1,890 shares) (SE) .........      189,000
            Contributed capital in excess of par, preferred stock
            [1,890 shares × ($102 − $100)] (SE) .................      3,780
            *Sale of preferred stock ($102 × 1,890 shares = $192,780).*

*c.*   March 20A    Land (SE) ........................................ 10,200
            Preferred stock, 5% (par $100, 100 shares) (SE) ..........      10,000
            Contributed capital in excess of par, preferred stock (SE) ....      200
            *Purchased land for future store site; paid in full by issuance of 100 shares of preferred stock ($102 × 100 shares = $10,200.)*

*d.*   Apr. 20A    Organization cost (A) ................................ 1,980
            Cash (A) ......................................      1,980
            *Paid organization cost.*

*e.*   May 20A    Organization cost (A) ................................ 1,020
            Preferred stock 5% (par $100, 10 shares) (SE) ............      1,000
            Contributed capital in excess of par, preferred stock (SE) ....      20
            *Organization cost (legal services) paid by issuance of 10 shares of preferred stock. The implied market value is $102 × 10 shares = $1,020.*

*f.*   June 20A    Cash (A) ........................................ 27,000
            No-par common stock (500 shares) (SE) ................      27,000
            *Sold 500 shares of the no-par common stock ($54 × 500 shares = $27,000).*

*g.*   July 20A    Treasury stock, preferred (100 shares at $104) (XSE) ......... 10,400
            Cash (A) ......................................      10,400
            *Purchased 100 shares of preferred treasury stock ($104 × 100 shares = $10,400).*

*h.*   Aug. 20A    Cash (20 shares at $105) (A) .......................... 2,100
            Treasury stock, preferred (20 shares at $104) (XSE) ........      2,080
            Contributed capital from treasury stock transactions (SE) ....      20
            *Sold 20 shares of the preferred treasury stock at $105.*

*i.*   Dec. 31, 20A   Equipment (A) ..................................... 600,000
            Cash (A) ......................................      600,000
            *Purchased equipment.*

*j.*   Dec. 31, 20A   Cash (A) ........................................ 20,000
            Note payable (L) .................................      20,000
            *Borrowed on one-year, 12 percent interest-bearing note.*

*k.*   Dec. 31, 20A   Cash (A) ........................................ 129,300
            Revenues (E) ...................................      129,300
            Expenses (E) .................................... 98,000
            Cash (A) ......................................      98,000
            *To record summarized revenues and expenses.*

*l.* Dec. 31, 20A Expenses (E) ........................................ 300

Organization cost (A) ...............................      300

*Adjusting entry to amortize organization cost for one year*

*[($1,980 + $1,020) ÷ 10 years = $300].*

2. Closing entries:

*m.* Dec. 31, 20A Revenues (R) ........................................ 129,300

Retained earnings ...................................      129,300

Retained earnings ................................... 98,300

Expenses ($98,000 + $300) (E) .....................      98,300

3. Balance Sheet

**SHELLY CORPORATION**

**Balance Sheet**

**At December 31, 20A**

**Assets**

| | | |
|---|---:|---:|
| Current assets | | |
|   Cash | | $ 50,800 |
| Tangible assets | | |
|   Land | $ 10,200 | |
|   Equipment (no depreciation assumed in the problem) | 600,000 | 610,200 |
| Intangible assets | | |
|   Organization cost (cost, $3,000 less amortization, $300) | | 2,700 |
| Total assets | | $663,700 |

**Liabilities**

| | |
|---|---:|
| Current liabilities | |
|   Note payable, 12% | $ 20,000 |

**Stockholders' Equity**

| | | |
|---|---:|---:|
| Contributed capital | | |
|   Preferred stock, 5% (par value $100; authorized 5,000 shares, issued 2,000 shares of which 80 shares are held as treasury stock) | $200,000 | |
|   Common stock (no-par value; authorized 20,000 shares, issued and outstanding 8,000 shares) | 417,000 | |
|   Contributed capital in excess of par, preferred stock | 4,000 | |
|   Contributed capital from treasury stock transactions | 20 | |
|     Total contributed capital | $621,020 | |
| Retained earnings | 31,000 | |
|     Total contributed capital and retained earnings | $652,020 | |
| Less cost of preferred treasury stock held (80 shares) | (8,320) | |
|     Total stockholders' equity | | 643,700 |
| Total liabilities and stockholders' equity | | $663,700 |

## CHAPTER **TAKE-AWAYS**

1. **Explain the role of stock in the capital structure of a corporation.**   **p. 589**

   The law recognizes corporations as separate legal entities. Owners invest in a corporation and receive capital stock that can be traded on established stock exchanges. Stock provides a number of rights, including the right to receive dividends.

2. **Describe various types of capital stock, analyze transactions affecting capital stock, and show how capital stock transactions are reported on the statement of cash flows.**   **p. 591**

   Common stock is the basic voting stock issued by a corporation. Usually it has a par value, but no-par stock also can be issued. Preferred stock is issued by some corporations. This stock contains some special rights and may appeal to certain investors.

   A number of key transactions involve capital stock: (1) initial sale of stock, (2) treasury stock transactions, (3) cash dividends, and (4) stock dividends and stock splits. Each is illustrated in the chapter.

Both inflows (e.g., issuance of capital stock) and outflows (e.g., purchase of treasury stock) are reported in the Financing Activities section of the statement of cash flows. The payment of dividends is reported as an outflow in this section.

3. **Explain the purpose of treasury stock and analyze transactions affecting it.    p. 598**
Stock that was issued and subsequently reacquired is called *treasury stock*. It is recorded in a contra-equity account until resold. Gains and losses are not recorded on the sale of treasury stock. Any difference between cost and selling price is recorded in the Contributed Capital from Treasury Stock account.

4. **Discuss dividends and analyze transactions involving common and preferred stock. p. 599**
The return associated with an investment in capital stock comes from two sources: appreciation and dividends. Dividends are recorded as a liability when they are declared by the board of directors (i.e., the date of declaration). The liability is satisfied when the dividends are paid (i.e., the date of payment).

5. **Analyze the dividend yield ratio.    p. 601**
The dividend yield ratio measures the percentage of return on investment from dividends. For most companies, the return associated with dividends is very small.

6. **Discuss the purpose of stock dividends, stock splits, and report transactions.    p. 604**
Stock dividends are distributions of a company's stock to existing owners on a pro rata basis. The transaction involves transferring an additional amount in to the common stock account. A stock split also involves the distribution of additional shares to owners but no additional amount is transferred in to the common stock account. Instead, the par value of the stock is reduced.

7. **Measure and report retained earnings.    p. 606**
The retained earnings account includes income that has been earned since a company began its operations minus any dividends that have been paid. The amount of retained earnings is important because dividends normally can be paid only if there is a sufficient balance in this account (and in the cash account).

8. **Analyze the dividend payout ratio.    p. 607**
Dividends represent a distribution of the income earned by a corporation. The dividend payout ratio measures the percentage of income that is paid out each year. This percentage differs significantly among companies. Most companies that are growing rapidly pay out a small percentage of their earnings.

This chapter concludes a major section of the book. The previous several chapters have discussed individual sections of the balance sheet. We will now shift our focus to a common business transaction that will affect many accounts on each of the financial statements. For a number of strategic reasons, businesses often invest in other businesses. In the next chapter, you will see why companies invest in other companies and how these investments affect the financial statements.

## Chapter Supplement A

### Accounting for Owners' Equity for Sole Proprietorships and Partnerships

#### OWNER'S EQUITY FOR A SOLE PROPRIETORSHIP

A sole proprietorship is an unincorporated business owned by one person. The only owner's equity accounts needed are (1) a capital account for the proprietor (J. Doe, Capital) and (2) a drawing (or withdrawal) account for the proprietor (J. Doe, Drawings). The capital account of a sole proprietorship is used for two purposes: to record investments by the owner and to accumulate the periodic income or loss. Thus, the Income Summary account is closed to the capital account at the end of each accounting period. The drawing account is used to record the owner's withdrawals of cash or other assets from the business. The drawing account is closed to the capital account at the end of each accounting period. The capital account reflects the cumulative total of all investments by the owner plus all earnings of the entity less all withdrawals of resources from the entity by the owner. In most respects, the accounting for a sole proprietorship is the same as for a corporation.

Exhibit 11.7 presents the recording of selected transactions and the owner's equity section of the balance sheet of Doe Retail Store to illustrate the accounting for owner's equity for a sole proprietorship.

EXHIBIT **11.7**

**Accounting for Owner's Equity for a Sole Proprietorship**

**Selected Entries during 20A**

**January 1, 20A**

J. Doe started a retail store by investing $150,000 of personal savings. The journal entry for the business is as follows:

| Cash (A) .................................... | 150,000 | |
| J. Doe, capital (OE) ..................... | | 150,000 |

| Assets | = | Liabilities | + | Owner's Equity | |
| --- | --- | --- | --- | --- | --- |
| Cash | +150,000 | | | J. Doe, capital | +150,000 |

**During 20A**

Each month during the year, Doe withdrew $1,000 cash from the business for personal living costs. Accordingly, each month the following journal entry was made:

| J. Doe, drawings (OE) ..................... | 1,000 | |
| Cash (A) ..................................... | | 1,000 |

| Assets | = | Liabilities | + | Owner's Equity | |
| --- | --- | --- | --- | --- | --- |
| Cash | −1,000 | | | J. Doe, drawings | −1,000 |

*Note:* At December 31, 20A, after the last withdrawal, the drawings account will reflect a debit balance of $12,000.

**December 31, 20A**

Usual journal entries for the year, including adjusting and closing entries for the revenue and expense accounts, resulted in an $18,000 net income, which are closed to the capital account. The next closing entry follows:

| Individual revenue and expense accounts (R&E) . | 18,000 | |
| J. Doe, capital (OE) ..................... | | 18,000 |

| Assets | = | Liabilities | + | Owner's Equity | |
| --- | --- | --- | --- | --- | --- |
| | | | | Revenues and expenses | −18,000 |
| | | | | J. Doe, capital | +18,000 |

**December 31, 20A:**

The journal entry required on this date to close the drawings account follows:

| J. Doe, capital (OE) ..................... | 12,000 | |
| J. Doe, drawings (OE) ..................... | | 12,000 |

| Assets | = | Liabilities | + | Owner's Equity | |
| --- | --- | --- | --- | --- | --- |
| | | | | J. Doe, capital | −12,000 |
| | | | | J. Doe, drawings | +12,000 |

**Balance Sheet December 31, 20A (partial)**

| Owner's equity | |
| --- | --- |
| J. Doe, capital, January 1, 20A | $150,000 |
| Add: Net income for 20A | 18,000 |
| Total | 168,000 |
| Less: Withdrawals for 20A | (12,000) |
| J. Doe, capital, December 31, 20A | $156,000 |

A sole proprietorship does not pay income taxes. Therefore, its financial statements do not reflect income tax expense or income taxes payable. The net income of a sole proprietorship is taxed when it is included on the owner's *personal* income tax return. Because an employer/employee contractual relationship cannot exist with only one party involved, a "salary" to the owner is not recognized as an expense of a sole proprietorship. The owner's salary is accounted for as a distribution of profits (i.e., a withdrawal).

## OWNERS' EQUITY FOR A PARTNERSHIP

The Uniform Partnership Act, which most states have adopted, defines *partnership* as "an association of two or more persons to carry on as co-owners of a business for profit." Small businesses and professionals such as accountants, doctors, and lawyers use the partnership form of business. It is formed by two or more persons reaching mutual agreement about the terms of the partnership. The law does not require an application for a charter as it does in the case of a corporation. The agreement between the partners constitutes a partnership contract that should be in writing. The agreement should specify matters such as division of periodic income, management responsibilities, transfer or sale of partnership interests, disposition of assets upon liquidation, and procedures to be followed in case of the death of a partner. If the partnership agreement does not specify these matters, the laws of the resident state are binding. The primary advantages of a partnership are (1) ease of formation, (2) complete control by the partners, and (3) lack of income taxes on the business itself. The primary disadvantage is the unlimited liability of each partner for the partnership's liabilities. As a result of unlimited liability, creditors of the partnership can take the partners' personal assets if the partnership does not have sufficient assets to satisfy outstanding debt.

As with a sole proprietorship, accounting for a partnership follows the same underlying fundamentals of accounting as any other form of business organization except for those entries that directly affect owners' equity. Accounting for partners' equity follows the same pattern as illustrated earlier for a sole proprietorship except that separate partner capital and drawings accounts must be established for each partner. Investments by each partner are credited to the partner's capital account. Withdrawals from the partnership by each partner are debited to the respective drawings account. The net income for a partnership is divided between the partners in the profit ratio specified in the partnership agreement. The Income Summary account is closed to the respective partner capital accounts. The respective drawings accounts also are closed to the partner capital accounts. Therefore, after the closing process, each partner's capital account reflects the cumulative total of all investments of that individual partner plus the partner's share of all partnership earnings less all withdrawals by the partner.

Exhibit 11.8 presents selected journal entries and partial financial statements for AB Partnership to illustrate the accounting for the distribution of income and partners' equity.

---

| EXHIBIT **11.8** | **Selected Entries during 20A** |
|---|---|
| **Accounting for Partners' Equity** | **January 1, 20A**<br><br>A. Able and B. Baker organized AB Partnership on this date. Able contributed $60,000 and Baker $40,000 cash in the partnership and agreed to divide net income (and net loss) 60% and 40%, respectively. The journal entry for the business to record the investment follows: |

| | | |
|---|---|---|
| Cash (A) .................................. | 100,000 | |
| A. Able, capital (OE) .................... | | 60,000 |
| B. Baker, capital (OE) .................. | | 40,000 |

| Assets | = | Liabilities | + | Owners' Equity | |
|---|---|---|---|---|---|
| Cash   +100,000 | | | | A. Able, capital | +60,000 |
| | | | | B. Baker, capital | +40,000 |

EXHIBIT **11.8**

**continued**

**During 20A**

The partners agreed that Able would withdraw $1,000 and Baker $650 per month in cash. Accordingly, each month the following journal entry for the withdrawals was made:

| A. Able, drawings (OE) . . . . . . . . . . . . . . . . . . . . | 1,000 | |
|---|---|---|
| B. Baker, drawings (OE) . . . . . . . . . . . . . . . . . . | 650 | |
| Cash (A) . . . . . . . . . . . . . . . . . . . . . . . . . . . . . . | | 1,650 |

| Assets | | = | Liabilities | + | Owners' Equity | |
|---|---|---|---|---|---|---|
| Cash | −1,650 | | | | A. Able, drawings | −1,000 |
| | | | | | B. Baker, drawings | −650 |

**December 31, 20A**

Assume that the normal closing entries for the revenue and expense accounts resulted in a net income. The next closing entry is as follows:

| Individual revenue and expense accounts (R&E) . . | 30,000 | |
|---|---|---|
| A. Able, capital (OE) . . . . . . . . . . . . . . . . . . . . . | | 18,000 |
| B. Baker, capital (OE) . . . . . . . . . . . . . . . . . . . | | 12,000 |

| Assets | = | Liabilities | + | Owners' Equity | |
|---|---|---|---|---|---|
| | | | | Revenues and expenses | −30,000 |
| | | | | A. Able, capital | +18,000 |
| | | | | B. Baker, capital | +12,000 |

Net income is divided as follows:

| A. Able, $30,000 \times 60\%$ | $18,000 |
|---|---|
| B. Baker, $30,000 \times 40\%$ | 12,000 |
| Total | $30,000 |

**December 31, 20A**

The journal entry required to close the drawings accounts follows:

| A. Able, capital (OE) . . . . . . . . . . . . . . . . . . . . . | 12,000 | |
|---|---|---|
| B. Baker, capital (OE) . . . . . . . . . . . . . . . . . . . . | 7,800 | |
| A. Able, drawings (OE) . . . . . . . . . . . . . . . . . | | 12,000 |
| B. Baker, drawings (OE) . . . . . . . . . . . . . . . . | | 7,800 |

| Assets | = | Liabilities | + | Owners' Equity | |
|---|---|---|---|---|---|
| | | | | A. Able, capital | −12,000 |
| | | | | B. Baker, capital | −7,800 |
| | | | | A. Able, drawings | +12,000 |
| | | | | B. Baker, drawings | +7,800 |

A separate statement of partners' capital similar to the following customarily is prepared to supplement the balance sheet:

**AB PARTNERSHIP**
**Statement of Partners' Capital**
**For the Year Ended December 31, 20A**

| | A. Able | B. Baker | Total |
|---|---|---|---|
| Investment, January 1, 20A | $60,000 | $40,000 | $100,000 |
| Add: Additional investments during the year | 0 | 0 | 0 |
| Net income for the year | 18,000 | 12,000 | 30,000 |
| Totals | 78,000 | 52,000 | 130,000 |
| Less: Drawings during the year | (12,000) | (7,800) | (19,800) |
| Partners' equity, December 31, 20A | $66,000 | $44,200 | $110,200 |

The financial statements of a partnership follow the same format as those for a corporation except that (1) the income statement includes an additional section entitled Distribution of Net Income, (2) the partners' equity section of the balance sheet is detailed for each partner in conformity with the full-disclosure principle, (3) partnership has no income tax expense because partnerships do not pay income tax (each partner must report his or her share of the partnership profits on his or her individual tax return), and (4) salaries paid to partners are not recorded as expense but are treated as a distribution of earnings (withdrawals).

## KEY **RATIOS**

The **dividend yield ratio** measures the dividend return on the current price of the stock. The ratio is computed as follows (p. 601):

$$\text{Dividend Yield Ratio} = \frac{\text{Dividend per Share}}{\text{Market Price per Share}}$$

The **dividend payout ratio** measures the portion of net income that is paid to common stockholders in the form of dividends. The ratio is computed as follows (p. 607):

$$\text{Dividend Payout Ratio} = \frac{\text{Dividends}}{\text{Net income}}$$

## FINDING FINANCIAL INFORMATION

### BALANCE SHEET

*Under Current Liabilities*
Dividends, once declared by the board of directors, are reported as a liability (usually current).

*Under Noncurrent Liabilities*
Transactions involving capital stock do not generate noncurrent liabilities.

*Under Stockholders Equity*
Typical accounts include
Preferred stock
Common stock
Capital in excess of par
Retained earnings
Treasury stock

### INCOME STATEMENT

Capital stock is never shown on the income statement. Dividends paid are not an expense. They are a distribution of income and are, therefore, not reported on the income statement.

### STATEMENT OF CASH FLOWS

*Under financing activities:*
+Cash inflows from initial sale of stock
+Cash inflows from sale of treasury stock
−Cash outflows for dividends
−Cash outflows for purchase of treasury stock

### STATEMENT OF STOCKHOLDERS' EQUITY

This statement reports detailed information concerning stockholders' equity, including
(1) amounts in each equity account,
(2) number of shares outstanding,
(3) impact of transactions such as earning income, payment of dividends, and purchase of treasury stock.

### NOTES

*Under Summary of Significant Accounting Policies:*
Usually, very little information concerning capital stock is provided in this summary.

*Under a separate note:*
Most companies report information about their stock option plans and information about major transactions such as stock dividends or significant treasury stock transactions. A historical summary of dividends paid per share is typically provided.

## KEY **TERMS**

**Authorized Number of Shares**   p. 590
**Common Stock**   p. 591
**Convertible Preferred Stock**   p. 593
**Cumulative Dividend Preference**   p. 602
**Current Dividend Preference**   p. 602
**Declaration Date**   p. 601
**Dividends in Arrears**   p. 602
**Issued Shares**   p. 590
**Legal Capital**   p. 592
**No-Par Value Stock**   p. 592

**Outstanding Shares**   p. 590
**Par Value**   p. 592
**Payment Date**   p. 601
**Preferred Stock**   p. 593
**Prior Period Adjustment**   p. 606
**Record Date**   p. 601
**Stock Dividend**   p. 604
**Stock Split**   p. 605
**Treasury Stock**   p. 598
**Unissued Shares**   p. 590

## QUESTIONS

1. Define *corporation* and identify its primary advantages.
2. What is the charter of a corporation?
3. Explain each of the following terms: (a) *authorized capital stock,* (b) *issued capital stock,* (c) *unissued capital stock,* and (d) *outstanding capital stock.*
4. Differentiate between common stock and preferred stock.
5. Explain the distinction between par value stock and no-par value capital stock.
6. What are the usual characteristics of preferred stock?
7. What are the two basic sources of stockholders' equity? Explain each.
8. Owners' equity is accounted for by source. What does *source* mean?
9. Define *treasury stock.* Why do corporations acquire treasury stock?
10. How is treasury stock reported on the balance sheet? How is the "gain or loss" on treasury stock that has been sold reported on the financial statements?
11. What are the two basic requirements to support a cash dividend? What are the effects of a cash dividend on assets and stockholders' equity?
12. Differentiate between cumulative and noncumulative preferred stock.
13. Define *stock dividend.* How does it differ from a cash dividend?
14. What are the primary purposes of issuing a stock dividend?
15. Identify and explain the three important dates with respect to dividends.
16. Define *retained earnings.* What are the primary components of retained earnings at the end of each period?
17. Define *prior period adjustments.* How are they reported?
18. What does *restrictions on retained earnings* mean?

## MINI-EXERCISES

**M11–1   Evaluating Stockholders' Right**                                                     ■ LO1
Name three rights of stockholders. Which of these is most important in your mind? Why?

**M11–2   Computing the Number of Unissued Shares**                                             ■ LO1
The balance sheet for Crutcher Corporation reported 147,000 shares outstanding, 200,000 shares authorized, and 10,000 shares in treasury stock. Compute the number of unissued shares.

**M11–3   Recording the Sale of Common Stock**                                                  ■ LO2
To expand operations, Aragon Consulting issued 100,000 shares of previously unissued stock with a par value of $1. The selling price for the stock was $75 per share. Record the sale of this stock. Would your answer be different if the par value was $2 per share? If so, record the sale of stock with a par value of $2.

**M11–4   Comparing Common Stock and Preferred Stock**                                          ■ LO2
Your parents have just retired and have asked you for some financial advice. They have decided to invest $100,000 in a company very similar to Wal-Mart. The company has issued both common and preferred stock. What factors would you consider in giving them advice? Which type of stock would you recommend?

■ **LO3**   **M11–5**   **Determining the Effects of Treasury Stock Transactions**

Trans Union Corporation purchased 20,000 shares of its own stock for $45 per share. The next year, the company sold 5,000 shares for $50 per share and the following year, it sold 10,000 shares for $37 per share. Determine the impact (increase, decrease, or no change) of each of these transactions on the following classifications:

1. Total assets.
2. Total liabilities.
3. Total stockholders' equity.
4. Net income.

■ **LO4**   **M11–6**   **Determining the Amount of a Dividend**

Jacobs Company has 300,000 shares of common stock authorized, 270,000 shares issued, and 50,000 shares of treasury stock. The company's board of directors declares a dividend of 50 cents per share. What is the total amount of the dividend that will be paid?

■ **LO4**   **M11–7**   **Recording Dividends**

On April 15, 20A, the board of directors for Auction.com declared a cash dividend of 20 cents per share payable to stockholders of record on May 20. The dividends will be paid on June 14. The company has 500,000 shares of stock outstanding. Prepare any necessary journal entries for each date.

■ **LO4**   **M11–8**   **Determining the Amount of a Preferred Dividend**

Colliers, Inc., has 200,000 shares of cumulative preferred stock outstanding. The preferred stock pays dividends in the amount of $2 per share but because of cash flow problems, the company did not pay any dividends last year. The board of directors plans to pay dividends in the amount of $1 million this year. What amount will go to preferred stockholders?

■ **LO7**   **M11–9**   **Determining the Impact of Stock Dividends and Stock Splits**

Armstrong Tools, Inc., announced a 100 percent stock dividend. Determine the impact (increase, decrease, no change) of this dividend on the following:

1. Total assets.
2. Total liabilities.
3. Common stock.
4. Total stockholders' equity.
5. Market value per share of common stock.

Now assume that the company announced a 2-for-1 stock split. Determine the impact of the stock split.

■ **LO7**   **M11–10**   **Recording a Stock Dividend**

Shriver Food Systems, Inc., has issued a 50 percent stock dividend. The company has 800,000 shares authorized and 200,000 shares outstanding. The par value of the stock is $5 per share and the market value is $100 per share. Record the payment of this stock dividend.

## EXERCISES

■ **LO1, 2**   **E11–1**   **Reporting Stockholders' Equity and Determining Dividend Policy**

Sampson Corporation was organized in 20A to operate a financial consulting business. The charter authorized the following capital stock: common stock, par value $8 per share, 12,000 shares. During the first year, the following selected transactions were completed:

*a.* Sold and issued 6,000 shares of common stock for cash at $20 per share.

*b.* Issued 600 shares of common stock for a piece of land to be used for a facilities site; construction began immediately. Assume that the stock was selling at $22 per share at the date of issuance. Debit Land.

*c.* Sold and issued 2,000 shares of common stock for cash at $23 per share.

*d.* At year-end, the accounts reflected a $7,000 loss. Because a loss was incurred, no income tax expense was recorded.

*Required:*

1. Give the journal entry required for each of these transactions.

2. Prepare the stockholders' equity section as it should be reported on the year-end balance sheet.

3. Can Sampson pay dividends at this time? Explain.

**E11–2  Analyzing the Impact of Dividend Policy**

**LO4**

McDonald and Associates is a small manufacturer of electronic connections for local area networks. Consider three independent situations.

> **Case 1:** McDonald increases its cash dividends by 50 percent, but no other changes occur in the company's operations.

> **Case 2:** The company's income and cash flows increase by 50 percent but this does not change its dividends.

> **Case 3:** McDonald issues a 50 percent stock dividend, but no other changes occur.

*Required:*

1. How do you think each situation would affect the company's stock price.

2. If the company changed its accounting policies and reported higher net income, would the change have an impact on the stock price?

**E11–3  Determining the Effects of Transactions on Stockholders' Equity**

**LO1, 2**

Shelby Corporation was organized in January 20A by 10 stockholders to operate an air conditioning sales and service business. The charter issued by the state authorized the following capital stock:

> Common stock, $1 par value, 200,000 shares.

> Preferred stock, $10 par value, 6 percent, 50,000 shares.

During January and February 20A, the following stock transactions were completed:

*a.* Collected $40,000 cash from each of the 10 organizers and issued 2,000 shares of common stock to each of them.

*b.* Sold 15,000 shares of preferred stock at $25 per share; collected the cash and immediately issued the stock.

*Required:*

Net income for 20A was $40,000; cash dividends declared and paid at year-end were $10,000. Prepare the stockholders' equity section of the balance sheet at December 31, 20A.

**E11–4  Determining the Effects of the Issuance of Common and Preferred Stock**

**LO1, 2**

Kelly, Incorporated, was issued a charter on January 15, 20A, that authorized the following capital stock:

> Common stock, no-par, 100,000 shares.

> Preferred stock, 7 percent, par value $10 per share, 5,000 shares.

The board of directors established a stated value on the no-par common stock of $6 per share. During 20A, the following selected transactions were completed in the order given:

*a.* Sold and issued 20,000 shares of the no-par common stock at $18 cash per share.

*b.* Sold and issued 3,000 shares of preferred stock at $22 cash per share.

*c.* At the end of 20A, the accounts showed net income of $38,000.

*Required:*

1. Prepare the stockholders' equity section of the balance sheet at December 31, 20A.

2. Assume that you are a common stockholder. If Kelly needed additional capital, would you prefer to have it issue additional common stock or additional preferred stock? Explain.

**E11–5  Recording Stockholders' Equity Transactions, Including Noncash Consideration: Write a Brief Memo**

**LO1, 2**

Teacher Corporation obtained a charter at the start of 20A that authorized 50,000 shares of no-par common stock and 20,000 shares of preferred stock, par value $10. The corporation was organized by four individuals who "reserved" 51 percent of the common stock shares for themselves. The remaining shares were to be sold to other individuals at $40 per share on a cash basis. During 20A, the following selected transactions occurred:

a. Collected $15 per share cash from three of the organizers and received two adjoining lots of land from the fourth organizer. Issued 4,000 shares of common stock to each of the four organizers and received title to the land.

b. Sold and issued 6,000 shares of common stock to an outsider at $40 cash per share.

c. Sold and issued 8,000 shares of preferred stock at $20 cash per share.

d. At the end of 20A, the accounts reflected after-tax income of $36,000.

*Required:*

1. Give the journal entries indicated for each of these transactions.

2. Write a brief memo to explain the basis that you used to determine the cost of the land.

**LO2, 3    E11–6    Finding Amounts Missing from the Stockholders' Equity Section**

The stockholders' equity section on the December 31, 20D, balance sheet of Chemfast Corporation follows:

| Stockholders' Equity | |
| --- | --- |
| Contributed capital | |
| Preferred stock (par $20; authorized 10,000 shares, ? issued, of which 500 shares are held as treasury stock) | $104,000 |
| Common stock (no-par; authorized 20,000 shares, issued and outstanding 8,000 shares) | 600,000 |
| Contributed capital in excess of par, preferred | 14,300 |
| Contributed capital, treasury stock transactions | 1,500 |
| Retained earnings | 30,000 |
| Cost of treasury stock, preferred | 9,500 |

*Required:*

Complete the following statements and show your computations.

1. The number of shares of preferred stock issued was _____ .

2. The number of shares of preferred stock outstanding was _____ .

3. The average sale price of the preferred stock when issued was $_____ per share.

4. Have the treasury stock transactions (a) increased corporate resources _____ or (b) decreased resources _____? By how much? _____ .

5. The treasury stock transactions increased (decreased) stockholders' equity by _____ .

6. How much did the treasury stock held cost per share? $_____ .

7. Total stockholders' equity is $_____ .

8. The average issue price of the common stock was $_____ .

9. Assuming that one-fourth of the treasury stock is sold at $35 per share, the remaining balance in the Treasury Stock account is $_____.

**LO2, 3    E11–7    Finding Information Missing from an Annual Report**

Procter & Gamble

Procter & Gamble is a $38 billion company that sells products that are part of most of our daily lives, including Mr. Clean, Cheer, Crest, Vicks, Scope, Pringles, Folgers, Vidal Sassoon, Zest, and Charmin. The annual report for P&G contained the following information:

a. Retained earnings at the end of 1998 totaled $11,144 million.

b. Treasury stock amounted to $1,929 million at the end of 1998 and $2,533 million at the end of 1999.

c. Net income for 1999 was $3,763 million.

d. Stated value of the stock is $1 per share.

e. Cash dividends declared in 1999 were $1.14 per share.

f. The Common Stock, Par Value account totaled $1,320 million at the end of both 1998 and 1999.

*Required: (Assume that no other information concerning stockholders' equity is relevant.)*

1. Estimate the number of shares outstanding during 1999.

2. Estimate the amount of retained earnings at the end of 1999.

3. Did the number of shares outstanding change during 1999?

**E11–8  Recording Treasury Stock Transactions and Analyzing Their Impact**

During 20C, the following selected transactions affecting stockholders' equity occurred for Italy Corporation:

■ LO3

*a.* Feb. 1    Purchased in the open market 200 shares of the company's own common stock at $22 cash per share.

*b.* Jul. 15   Sold 100 of the shares purchased on February 1, 20C, for $24 cash per share.

*c.* Sept. 1   Sold 60 more of the shares purchased on February 1, 20C, for $20 cash per share.

*d.* Dec. 15   Sold an additional 20 of the treasury shares for $15 per share.

*Required:*

1. Give the indicated journal entries for each of the four transactions.

2. What impact does the purchase of treasury stock have on dividends paid?

3. What impact does the sale of treasury stock for an amount higher than the purchase price have on net income and the Statement of Cash Flows?

**E11–9  Computing Shares Outstanding**

The 1998 annual report for Philip Morris Companies, Inc., disclosed that 4 billion shares of common stock have been authorized. At the end of 1997, 2,805,961,317 shares had been issued and the number of shares in treasury stock was 380,474,028. During 1998, no additional shares were issued, but additional shares were purchased for treasury stock and shares were sold from treasury stock. The net change was a decrease of 5,047,286 shares. Determine the number of shares outstanding at the end of 1998.

■ LO2

Philip Morris
Companies, Inc.

**E11–10  Computing Dividends on Preferred Stock and Analyzing Differences**

The records of Hoffman Company reflected the following balances in the stockholders' equity accounts at December 31, 20H:

■ LO4

> Common stock, par $12 per share, 40,000 shares outstanding.
>
> Preferred stock, 8 percent, par $10 per share, 6,000 shares outstanding.
>
> Retained earnings, $220,000.

On September 1, 20H, the board of directors was considering the distribution of a $62,000 cash dividend. No dividends were paid during 20F and 20G. You have been asked to determine dividend amounts under two independent assumptions (show computations):

*a.* The preferred stock is noncumulative.

*b.* The preferred stock is cumulative.

*Required:*

1. Determine the total and per share amounts that would be paid to the common stockholders and to the preferred stockholders under the two independent assumptions.

2. Write a brief memo to explain why the dividends per share of common stock were less for the second assumption.

3. What factor would cause a more favorable per share result to the common stockholders?

**E11–11  Analyzing Dividends in Arrears**

Mission Critical Software, Inc., is listed on the Nasdaq and is a leading provider of systems management software for Windows NT network and Internet infrastructure. Like many start-up companies, Mission Critical struggled with cash flows as it developed new business opportunities. A student found a financial statement for Mission Critical that included the following:

■ LO4

Mission Critical
Software, Inc.

> 1998 increase in dividends in arrears on redeemable convertible preferred stock was $264,000.

The student who read the note suggested that the Mission Critical preferred stock would be a good investment because of the large amount of dividend income that would be earned when the company started paying dividends again: "As the owner of the stock, I'll get dividends for the period I hold the stock plus some previous periods when I didn't even own the stock." Do you agree? Explain.

**LO4**   **E11–12**

### Determining the Impact of Dividends

Average Corporation has the following capital stock outstanding at the end of 20B:

   Preferred stock, 6 percent, par $15, outstanding shares, 8,000.

   Common stock, par $8, outstanding shares, 30,000.

On October 1, 20B, the board of directors declared dividends as follows:

   Preferred stock: Full cash preference amount, payable December 20, 20B.

   Common stock: 10 percent common stock dividend (i.e., one additional share for each 10 held), issuable December 20, 20B.

On December 20, 20B, the market prices were preferred stock, $40, and common stock, $32.

*Required:*

Explain the overall effect of each of the dividends on the assets, liabilities, and stockholders' equity of the company.

**LO4**   **E11–13**

Sears, Roebuck and Company

### Recording the Payment of Dividends

A recent annual report for Sears, Roebuck and Co. disclosed that the company paid preferred dividends in the amount of $119.9 million. It declared and paid dividends on common stock in the amount of $2 per share. During the year, Sears had 1,000,000,000 shares of common authorized; 387,514,300 shares had been issued; 41,670,000 shares were in treasury stock. Assume that the transaction occurred on July 15.

*Required:*

Prepare a journal entry to record the declaration and payment of dividends.

**LO7**   **E11–14**

### Analyzing Stock Dividends

On December 31, 20E, the stockholders' equity section of the balance sheet of R & B Corporation reflected the following:

| | |
|---|---:|
| Common stock (par $10; authorized 60,000 shares, outstanding 25,000 shares) | $250,000 |
| Contributed capital in excess of par | 12,000 |
| Retained earnings | 75,000 |

On February 1, 20F, the board of directors declared a 12 percent stock dividend to be issued April 30, 20F. The market value of the stock on February 1, 20F, was $18 per share. The market value will be capitalized.

*Required:*

1. For comparative purposes, prepare the stockholders' equity section of the balance sheet (a) immediately before the stock dividend and (b) immediately after the stock dividend. (*Hint:* Use two amount columns for this requirement.)

2. Explain the effects of this stock dividend on the assets, liabilities, and stockholders' equity.

**LO3, 4**   **E11–15**

Winnebago

### Analyzing the Repurchase of Stock

Winnebago is a familiar name on vehicles traveling U.S. highways. The company manufactures and sells large motor homes for vacation travel. These motor homes can be quickly recognized because of the company's "flying W" trademark. A recent news article contained the following information:

> The Company's profits have been running double a year ago, revenues were up 27 percent in the May quarter and order backlog stands at 2,229 units. Those are the kind of growth statistics that build confidence in the boardroom. The Company has announced plans to spend $3.6 million to expand its manufacturing facilities and it recently authorized repurchase of $15 million worth of its own shares, the third buyback in two years. The Company's stock is now selling for $25 per share.

*Required:*

1. Determine the impact of this transaction on the financial statements.
2. Why do you think the board decided to repurchase the stock?
3. What impact will this purchase have on Winnebago's future dividend obligations?

**C11-16 Preparing a Statement of Retained Earnings and Evaluating Dividend Policy**

LO1, 4

The following account balances were selected from the records of Blake Corporation at December 31, 20E, after all adjusting entries were completed:

| | |
|---|---|
| Common stock (par $15; authorized 100,000 shares, issued 35,000 shares, of which 1,000 shares are held as treasury stock) | $525,000 |
| Contributed capital in excess of par | 180,000 |
| Bond sinking fund | 90,000 |
| Dividends declared and paid in 20E | 18,000 |
| Retained earnings, January 1, 20E | 76,000 |
| Correction of prior period accounting error (a debit, net of income tax) | 8,000 |
| Treasury stock at cost (1,000 shares) | 20,000 |
| Income summary for 20E (credit balance) | 28,000 |

Restriction on retained earnings equal to the cost of treasury stock held is required by law in this state. The stock price is currently $22.43 per share.

*Required:*

1. Prepare the statement of retained earnings for 20E.
2. Prepare the stockholders' equity section of the balance sheet at December 31, 20E.
3. Compute and evaluate the dividend yield ratio. Determine the number of shares of stock that received dividends.

**E11-17 Recording Dividends**

LO4

Black & Decker

Black & Decker is a leading global manufacturer and marketer of power tools, hardware, and home improvement products. A recent press release contained the following announcement:

> The Black & Decker Corporation announced today that its Board of Directors declared a quarterly cash dividend of 12 cents per share of the company's outstanding common stock payable December 31, 1999, to stockholders of record at the close of business on December 17, 1999.

At the time of this announcement, Black & Decker had 150,000,000 shares authorized and 87,498,000 issued and outstanding. The par value for the company's stock is $.01 per share.

*Required:*
Prepare journal entries as appropriate for each date mentioned in the note.

**E11-18 Comparing Stock Dividends and Splits**

LO4, 7

On July 1, 20B, Jones Corporation had the following capital structure:

| | |
|---|---|
| Common stock (par $1, authorized shares) | $200,000 |
| Common stock (par $1, unissued shares) | 50,000 |
| Contributed capital in excess of par | 88,000 |
| Retained earnings | 72,000 |
| Treasury stock, none | |

*Required:*

1. The number of issued shares is _____ .
2. The number of outstanding shares is _____ .

3. Total stockholders' equity is _____ .

4. Assume that the board of directors declared and issued a 10 percent stock dividend when the stock was selling at $4 per share. Give any required journal entry(ies). If none is required, explain why.

5. Disregard the stock dividend in requirement 4. Assume that the board of directors voted a 6-to-5 stock split (i.e., a 20 percent increase in the number of shares). The market price prior to the split was $4 per share. Give any required journal entry(ies). If none is required, explain why.

6. Complete the following comparative tabulation followed by comments on the comparative effects:

| Items | Before Dividend and Split | After Stock Dividend | After Stock Split |
|---|---|---|---|
| Common stock account | $ | $ | $ |
| Par per share | $    1 | $ | $ |
| Shares outstanding | # | # | # |
| Contributed capital in excess of par | $88,000 | $ | $ |
| Retained earnings | 72,000 | | |
| Total stockholders' equity | $ | $ | $ |

**■ LO4**  **E11–19**

H & R Block

### Evaluating Dividend Policy

H&R Block is a well-known name especially during income tax time each year. The company serves more than 18 million taxpayers in more than 10,000 offices in the United States, Canada, Australia, and England. A recent press release contained the following information:

> H&R Block today reported that revenues for the first quarter ended July 31, 1999, climbed 72 percent to $121 million. The company reported a first quarter net loss of $37 million, or 38 cents per share. The Board of Directors declared a quarterly dividend of 27 cents per share payable October 1, 1999, to shareholders of record on September 10, 1999.

*Required:*

1. Explain why H&R Block can pay dividends despite its loss.

2. What factors did the board of directors consider when it declared the dividends?

**■ LO5**  **E11–20**

Cinergy and Starbucks

### Evaluating the Dividend Yield Ratio

Cinergy is a utility company that provides gas and electric service in Ohio, Kentucky, and Indiana. The company's dividend yield is 6.6 percent. Starbucks, a well-known retailer of coffee products, does not pay dividends, resulting in a dividend yield of 0.0 percent. Both companies are approximately the same size with market values of $5 billion.

*Required:*

1. Based on this limited information, why do you think the dividend policies of the two companies are so different?

2. Will the two companies attract different types of investors? Explain.

**■ LO6**  **E11–21**

### Explaining Cash Flows and the Dividend Payout Ratio

You are a stockbroker for a major firm and have just received a telephone call from a major client, Bob Smith. You sent him a report about a stock you are recommending. Bob says he has one concern, "I don't understand this dividend payout ratio. You're showing me the percent of net income that is paid out but given that dividends are paid in cash, shouldn't you be calculating the percent of cash flow from operating activities that is paid out?" How do you respond to Bob's question?

# PROBLEMS

**P11–1 Finding Missing Amounts (AP11–1)**

■ LO1, 2, 3, 4, 7

At December 31, 20E, the records of Nortech Corporation provided the following selected and incomplete data:

> Common stock (par $10; no changes during 20E)
>   Shares authorized, 200,000.
>   Shares issued, ____?____; issue price $17 per share; cash collected in full, $2,125,000.
>   Shares held as treasury stock, 3,000 shares, cost $20 per share.
> Net income for 20E, $118,000.
> Dividends declared and paid during 20E, $73,200.
> Prior period adjustment, correction of 20B accounting error, $9,000 (a credit, net of income tax).
> Retained earnings balance, January 1, 20E, $155,000.
>
> State law places a restriction on retained earnings equal to the cost of treasury stock held.
> The treasury stock was acquired after the split was issued. Extraordinary gain (net of income tax), $12,000.

*Required:*

1. Complete the following tabulation:

    Shares authorized _____ .

    Shares issued _____ .

    Shares outstanding _____ .

2. The balance in the Contributed Capital in Excess of Par account appears to be $_____ .

3. EPS on net income is $_____ .

4. Dividend paid per share of common stock is $_____ .

5. Net income before extraordinary items was $_____ .

6. The prior period adjustment should be reported on the _____ as an addition of _____ or a deduction of _____ .

7. Treasury stock should be reported on the balance sheet under the major caption _____ in the amount of $_____ .

8. The amount of retained earnings available for dividends on January 1, 20E, was $_____ .

9. Assume that the board of directors voted a 100 percent stock split (the number of shares will double). After the stock split, the par value per share will be $_____ , and the number of outstanding shares will be _____ .

10. Assuming the stock split given in requirement 9, give any journal entry that should be made. If none, explain why.

11. Disregard the stock split (assumed in requirements 9 and 10). Assume instead that a 10 percent stock dividend was declared and issued when the market price of the common stock was $21. Give any journal entry that should be made.

**P11–2 Preparing the Stockholders' Equity Section of the Balance Sheet**

■ LO1, 2

Skyhawk Corporation received its charter during January 20A. The charter authorized the following capital stock:

    Preferred stock: 8 percent, par $10, authorized 20,000 shares.

    Common stock: par $8, authorized 50,000 shares.

During 20A, the following transactions occurred in the order given:

*a.* Issued a total of 40,000 shares of the common stock to the four organizers at $11 per share. The company collected cash in full from three of the organizers and received legal services from the other organizer in full payment for the shares. The stock was issued immediately.

*b.* Sold 5,000 shares of the preferred stock at $18 per share. Collected the cash and issued the stock immediately.

c. Sold 3,000 shares of the common stock at $14 per share and 1,000 shares of the preferred stock at $28. Collected the cash and issued the stock immediately.

d. Total revenues for 20A were $310,000 and total expenses (including income tax) were $262,000.

*Required:*

1. Prepare the stockholders' equity section of the balance sheet at December 31, 20A.

2. What was the average issue price of the common stock?

3. Write a brief memo explaining the basis you used to value the legal services in the first journal entry.

**LO1, 2**    **P11–3**    **Recording Transactions Affecting Stockholders' Equity (AP11–2)**

Kerr Corporation began operations in January 20A. The charter authorized the following capital stock:

Preferred stock: 9 percent, $10 par, authorized 40,000 shares.

Common stock: No-par, authorized 80,000 shares. The corporation, in conformity with state laws, established a stated value per share of $5 for the no-par common stock.

During 20A, the following transactions occurred in the order given:

a. Issued 20,000 shares of the no-par common stock to each of the three organizers. Collected $9 cash per share from two of the organizers and received a plot of land with a small building on it in full payment for the shares of the third organizer and issued the stock immediately. Assume that 30 percent of the noncash payment received applies to the building.

b. Sold 6,000 shares of the preferred stock at $18 per share. Collected the cash and issued the stock immediately.

c. Sold 500 shares of the preferred stock at $20 and 1,000 shares of the no-par common stock at $12 per share. Collected the cash and issued the stock immediately.

d. Operating results at the end of 20A were as follows:

| | |
|---|---|
| Revenue accounts | $220,000 |
| Expense accounts, including income taxes | 160,000 |

*Required:*

1. Give the journal entries indicated (including closing entries) for each of these transactions.

2. Write a brief memo explaining what you used to determine the cost of the land and the building in the first journal entry.

**LO1, 2**    **P11–4**    **Recording Transactions and Comparing Par and No-Par Stock**

McNally Company was issued a charter in January 20A, which authorized 100,000 shares of common stock. During 20A, the following selected transactions occurred in the order given:

a. Sold 9,000 shares of the stock for cash at $60 per share. Collected the cash and issued the stock immediately.

b. Acquired land to be used as a future plant site; made payment in full by issuing 600 shares of stock. Assume a market value per share of $66.

c. At the end of 20A, the Income Summary account reflected a credit balance of $48,000.

Three independent cases are assumed as follows for comparative study purposes:

**Case A:** Assume that the common stock was $25 par value per share. The state law specifies that par value is legal capital.

**Case B:** Assume that the common stock was no-par and that the total sale price is credited to the Common Stock, No-par, account because the state law specifies this amount as legal capital.

**Case C:** Assume that the common stock is no-par with a stated value, specified by the board of directors, of $15 per share.

*Required:*

1. Give the journal entries for each of the three transactions.
2. Should total stockholders' equity be the same amount among the three independent cases? Explain.
3. Should the noncash asset (land) be recorded at the same cost under each of the three independent cases? Explain.
4. Should a stockholder care whether a company issues par, no-par, or stated value stock? Explain.

**P11–5 Preparing the Stockholders' Equity Section after Selected Transactions** (AP11–3)

■ LO1, 2, 3

Worldwide Company obtained a charter from the state in January 20A, which authorized 200,000 shares of common stock, $10 par value. The stockholders were 30 local citizens. During the first year, the following selected transactions occurred in the order given:

a. Sold 60,000 shares of the common stock to the 30 stockholders at $12 per share. Collected the cash and issued the stock.
b. Purchased 2,000 shares at $15 cash per share from one of the 30 stockholders who needed cash and wanted to sell the stock back to the company.
c. Resold 1,000 of the shares of the treasury stock purchased in transaction *b* two months later to another individual at $18 cash per share.
d. Sold an additional 500 shares of the treasury stock at $14 cash per share.
e. Determined on December 31, 20A, the end of the first year of business, that the accounts reflected income of $38,200.

*Required:*

1. Prepare the stockholders' equity section of the balance sheet at December 31, 20A.
2. What dollar effect did the treasury stock transactions have on the assets, liabilities, and stockholders' equity of the company? Explain.

**P11–6 Recording Stockholder's Equity Transactions** (AP11–4)

■ LO2, 4, 7

Halliburton

Halliburton is a large multinational corporation with extensive operations in energy-related areas. The annual report for Halliburton reported the following transactions affecting stockholders' equity:

a. Purchased $3.5 million in treasury stock.
b. Declared and paid cash dividends in the amount of $254.2 million.
c. Issued 2-for-1 common stock dividend. 222.5 million additional shares were issued with a total par value of $556.3 million.

*Required:*
Prepare journal entries to record each of these transactions.

**P11–7 Analyzing Stockholders' Equity Transactions, Including Treasury Stock**

■ LO3, 4

1. Compare a stock dividend with a cash dividend.
2. Compare a large stock dividend with a small stock dividend.
3. Describe the impact of the sale of treasury stock for more than cost on the income statement and the statement of cash flows.
4. Explain why a company might purchase treasury stock.

**P11–8 Comparing Stock and Cash Dividends** (AP11–5)

■ LO4, 7

Water Tower Company had the following stock outstanding and retained earnings at December 31, 20E:

| | |
|---|---:|
| Common stock (par $8; outstanding, 30,000 shares) | $240,000 |
| Preferred stock, 7% (par $10; outstanding, 6,000 shares) | 60,000 |
| Retained earnings | 280,000 |

The board of directors is considering the distribution of a cash dividend to the two groups of stockholders. No dividends were declared during 20C or 20D. Three independent cases are assumed:

**Case A:** The preferred stock is noncumulative; the total amount of dividends is $30,000.

**Case B:** The preferred stock is cumulative; the total amount of dividends is $12,600.

**Case C:** Same as Case B, except the amount is $66,000.

*Required:*

1. Compute the amount of dividends, in total and per share, that would be payable to each class of stockholders for each case. Show computations.

2. Assume the company issued a 10 percent common stock dividend on the outstanding shares when the market value per share was $24. Complete the following comparative schedule including explanation of the comparative differences.

|  | Amount of Dollar Increase (decrease) | |
| --- | --- | --- |
| Item | Cash Dividend— Case C | Stock Dividend |
| Assets | $ | $ |
| Liabilities | $ | $ |
| Stockholders' equity | $ | $ |

**LO4**     **P11–9**

**Analyzing Dividend Policy**

Dana and David, two young financial analysts, were reviewing financial statements for Compaq, one of the world's largest manufacturers of personal computers. Dana noted that the company did not report any dividends in the financing activity section of the statement of cash flows and said, "Just a few years ago, *Forbes* magazine named Compaq as one of the best performing companies. If it's so good, I wonder why it isn't paying any dividends." David wasn't convinced that Dana was looking in the right place for dividends but didn't say anything.

Dana continued the discussion by noting, "When *Forbes* selected it as a best performing company, Compaq's sales doubled over the previous two years just as they doubled over the prior two years. Its income was only $789 million that year compared with $867 million the previous year, but cash flow from operating activities was $943 million compared to an outflow of $101 million the prior year."

At that point, David noted that the statement of cash flows reported that Compaq had invested $703 million in new property this year compared with $408 million the prior year. He also was surprised to see that inventory and accounts receivable had increased by $1 billion and nearly $2 billion, respectively, the previous year. "No wonder it can't pay dividends; it generated less than $1 billion from operating activities and had to put it all back in accounts receivable and inventory."

*Required:*

1. Correct any misstatements that either Dana or David made. Explain.

2. Which of the factors presented in the case help you understand Compaq's dividend policy?

**LO4**     **P11–10**

**Determining the Financial Statement Effects of Dividends**

Lynn Company has outstanding 60,000 shares of $10 par value common stock and 25,000 shares of $20 par value preferred stock (8 percent). On December 1, 20B, the board of directors voted an 8 percent cash dividend on the preferred stock and a 10 percent common stock dividend on the common stock. At the date of declaration, the common stock was selling at $35 and the preferred at $20 per share. The dividends are to be paid, or issued, on February 15, 20C. The annual accounting period ends December 31.

*Required:*

Explain the comparative effects of the two dividends on the assets, liabilities, and stockholders' equity (a) through December 31, 20B, (b) on February 15, 20C, and (c) the overall effects from December 1, 20B, through February 15, 20C. A schedule similar to the following might be helpful:

| | Comparative Effects Explained | |
|---|---|---|
| Item | Cash Dividend on Preferred | Stock Dividend on Common |
| 1. Through December 31, 20B: Assets, etc. | | |

**P11–11 Recording Dividends**

LO4, 7

Adobe Systems

Adobe Systems develops and markets computer software including Adobe Acrobat that enables users to access information across all print and electronic media. A recent news article contained the following information:

> September 16, 1999
>
> Adobe Systems reported record revenue and operating profit for the third quarter of fiscal 1999. The Board of Directors announced a 100% stock dividend will occur on October 26, 1999 for stockholders of record on October 4, 1999. The Board also declared this quarter's cash dividend of $0.05 per share, payable on October 12, 1999 to stockholders of record as of September 28, 1999.

*Required:*

1. Prepare any journal entries that Adobe should make as the result of information in the preceding report. Assume that the company has 1 million shares outstanding, the par value is $0.50 per share, and the market value is $40 per share.

2. What do you think happened to the company's stock price after the September 16 announcement?

3. What factors did the board of directors consider in making this decision?

**P11–12 Chapter Supplement A: Comparing Stockholders' Equity Sections for Alternative Forms of Organization**

LO1

Assume for each of the following independent cases that the annual accounting period ends on December 31, 20W, and that the Income Summary account at that date reflected a debit balance (loss) of $20,000.

**Case A:** Assume that the company is a *sole proprietorship* owned by Proprietor A. Prior to the closing entries, the capital account reflected a credit balance of $50,000 and the drawings account a balance of $8,000.

**Case B:** Assume that the company is a *partnership* owned by Partner A and Partner B. Prior to the closing entries, the owners' equity accounts reflected the following balances: A, Capital, $40,000; B, Capital, $38,000; A, Drawings, $5,000; and B, Drawings, $9,000. Profits and losses are divided equally.

**Case C:** Assume that the company is a *corporation.* Prior to the closing entries, the stockholders' equity accounts showed the following: Capital Stock, par $10, authorized 30,000 shares, outstanding 15,000 shares; Contributed Capital in Excess of Par, $5,000; Retained Earnings, $65,000.

*Required:*

1. Give all the closing entries indicated at December 31, 20W, for each of the separate cases.

2. Show how the owners' equity section of the balance sheet would appear at December 31, 20W, for each case.

## ALTERNATE PROBLEMS

**AP11–1 Finding Missing Amounts (P11–1)**

LO1. 2. 3. 4. 5

At December 31, 20C, the records of Kozmetsky Corporation provided the following selected and incomplete data:

---

Common stock (par $1; no changes during 20C)

   Shares authorized, 5,000,000.

   Shares issued, ____?___; issue price $80 per share.

   Shares held as treasury stock, 100,000 shares, cost $60 per share.

Net income for 20C, $4,800,000.

   Common stock account $1,500,000.

Dividends declared and paid during 20C, $2 per share.

Retained earnings balance, January 1, 20C, $82,900,000.

The treasury stock was acquired after the split was issued.

---

*Required:*

1. Complete the following tabulation:

   Shares issued _____ .

   Shares outstanding _____ .

2. The balance in the Contributed Capital in Excess of Par account appears to be $_____ .

3. EPS on net income is $_____ .

4. Total dividends paid on common stock during 20C is $_____ .

5. Treasury stock should be reported on the balance sheet under the major caption _____ in the amount of $_____ .

6. Assume that the board of directors voted a 100 percent stock split (the number of shares will double). After the stock split, the par value per share will be $_____ , and the number of outstanding shares will be _____ .

7. Disregard the stock split (assumed in requirements [6]). Assume instead that a 10 percent stock dividend was declared and issued when the market price of the common stock was $21. Explain how stockholders equity will change.

■ **LO1, 2**   **AP11–2**   **Recording Transactions Affecting Stockholders' Equity** (P11–3)

Arnold Company was granted a charter that authorized the following capital stock:

Common stock: No-par, 100,000 shares. Assume that the no-par stock is not assigned a stated value per share.

Preferred stock: 8 percent, par $5, 20,000 shares.

During the first year, 20A, the following selected transactions occurred in the order given:

*a.* Sold 30,000 shares of the no-par common stock at $40 cash per share and 5,000 shares of the preferred stock at $26 cash per share. Collected cash and issued the stock immediately. For the no-par stock, credit the full selling price to the common stock account.

*b.* Issued 2,000 shares of preferred stock as full payment for a plot of land to be used as a future plant site. Assume the stock was selling at $26.

*c.* Repurchased 3,000 shares of the no-par common stock sold earlier; paid cash, $38 per share.

*d.* Sold all of the treasury stock (common) purchased in (*c*). The sale price was $39 per share.

*e.* Purchased 1,000 shares of the company's own preferred stock at $28 cash per share.

*f.* At December 31, 20A, the accounts reflected income of $33,500.

*Required:*

1. Give the journal entries indicated for each of these transactions.

2. Explain the economic difference between acquiring an asset for cash compared with acquiring it by issuing stock. Is it "better" to acquire a new asset without having to give up another asset?

■ **LO1, 2, 3**   **AP11–3**   **Preparing the Stockholders' Equity Section After Selected Transactions** (P11–5)

Global Marine obtained a charter from the state in January 20A, which authorized 1,000,000 shares of common stock, $5 par value. During the first year, the following selected transactions occurred in the order given:

*a.* Sold 700,000 shares of the common stock to at $54 per share. Collected the cash and issued the stock.

*b.* Purchased 25,000 shares at $50 cash per share to use as stock incentives for senior management.

*c.* Resold 5,000 of the shares of the treasury stock purchased in transaction *b* two months later at $45 cash per share.

*d.* Declared and issued a 100 per cent stock dividend on December 1, 20A.

*e.* Determined on December 31, 20A, the end of the first year of business, that the accounts reflected income of $429,000.

*Required:*

1. Prepare the stockholders' equity section of the balance sheet at December 31, 20A.

2. What dollar effect did the treasury stock transactions have on the assets, liabilities, and stockholders' equity of the company? Explain.

**AP11–4** **Recording Stockholders' Equity Transactions (P11–6)**

LO2, 4, 7

The annual report for Kmart described the following transactions that affected stockholders' equity:

Kmart

*a.* Declared cash dividends of $0.92 per share; total dividends were $374 million.

*b.* Sold series B convertible preferred stock (no-par) in the amount of $157 million.

*c.* Sold treasury stock for $10 million; original cost was $8 million.

*d.* Issued a 100 percent stock dividend on common stock; its par value was $206 million, and the market value was $784 million.

*Required:*

Prepare journal entries to record each of these transactions.

**AP11–5** **Comparing Stock and Cash Dividends (P11–8)**

LO4, 7

Ritz Company had the following stock outstanding and retained earnings at December 31, 20D:

| | |
|---|---|
| Common stock (par $1; outstanding, 500,000 shares) | $500,000 |
| Preferred stock, 8% (par $10; outstanding, 21,000 shares) | 210,000 |
| Retained earnings | 900,000 |

The board of directors is considering the distribution of a cash dividend to the two groups of stockholders. No dividends were declared during 20B or 20C. Three independent cases are assumed:

**Case A:** The preferred stock is noncumulative; the total amount of dividends is $25,000.

**Case B:** The preferred stock is cumulative; the total amount of dividends is $25,000.

**Case C:** Same as Case B, except the amount is $75,000.

*Required:*

1. Compute the amount of dividends, in total and per share, payable to each class of stockholders for each case. Show computations.

2. Assume that the company issued a 15 percent common stock dividend on the outstanding shares when the market value per share was $50. Complete the following comparative schedule, including explanation of the comparative differences.

| | Amount of Dollar Increase (decrease) | |
|---|---|---|
| Item | Cash Dividend— Case C | Stock Dividend |
| Assets | $ | $ |
| Liabilities | $ | $ |
| Stockholders' equity | $ | $ |

# CASES AND PROJECTS

## FINANCIAL REPORTING AND ANALYSIS CASES

**■ LO1, 2,    CP11–1**
**3, 4**

American Eagle
Outfitters

**STANDARD
&POOR'S**

### Finding Financial Information

Refer to the financial statements of American Eagle Outfitters given in Appendix B at the end of this book, or open file AEOS10K.doc in the S&P directory on the student CD-ROM.

*Required:*

1. What is the number of stockholders of record as of March 1, 1999?
2. Did the company pay dividends during 1999? If so, how much per share?
3. Does the company have any treasury stock? If so, how much?
4. Has the company ever issued a stock dividend or a stock split? If so, describe.
5. What is the par value of the common stock?
6. How many shares of common stock are authorized? How many shares are outstanding?

**■ LO1, 2,    CP11–2**
**3, 4**

Urban Outfitters

**STANDARD
&POOR'S**

### Finding Financial Information

Refer to the financial statements of Urban Outfitters given in Appendix C at the end of this book, or open file URBN10K.doc in the S&P directory on the student CD-ROM.

*Required:*

1. Does the company have any treasury stock? If so, how much?
2. What was the highest price for company stock during the quarter ended January 31, 1999?
3. Did the company purchase any of its own stock during the period covered by the financial statements?
4. Describe the company's dividend policy.
5. Has the company ever issued a stock dividend or a stock split? If so, describe.
6. What is the par value of the common stock?

**■ LO4      CP11–3**

American Eagle
Outfitters versus
Urban Outfitters

**STANDARD
&POOR'S**

### Comparing Companies within an Industry

Refer to the financial statements of American Eagle Outfitters given in Appendix B, Urban Outfitters given in Appendix C, and the Standard and Poor's Industry Ratio Report given in Appendix D at the end of this book or open file CP11–3.xls in the S&P directory on the student CD-ROM.

*Required:*

1. Notice that neither company has paid cash dividends since inception and neither plans to do so in the foreseeable future. As a result, the financial ratios discussed in this chapter are not useful for analyzing the companies. Why do you think both companies have similar dividend policies?
2. Examine the Standard and Poor's Industry Ratio Report for the family clothing stores industry. Does not paying dividends appear to be the norm for the industry?
3. Notice that both American Eagle Outfitters and Urban Outfitters have split their stock. As an investor, would you buy the stock of a company that did not have plans to pay dividends in the foreseeable future?
4. Using the information from the table below, compare the dividend related industry average ratios for the family clothing store industry to the variety store industry and the natural gas distribution industry. Why do public utilities distribute more of their profits as dividends than the other two industries? What type of investor would be interested in buying stock in a public utility instead of a retail store? Why?

---

**Dividend Ratios for Various Industries**

|  | 5651—Family Clothing Stores | 5331—Variety Stores | 4924—Natural Gas Distribution |
|---|---|---|---|
| Dividend Payout | 2.49% | 7.48% | 83.73% |
| Dividend Yield | 0.09% | .38% | 4.59% |
| Example Company | The GAP | Wal-Mart | Public Service of N.C. |

**P11–4 Computing Dividends for an Actual Company**

A recent annual report for Halliburton Company contained the following information (in millions of dollars):

| Stockholders' Equity | Current Year | Previous Year |
| --- | --- | --- |
| Common stock, par value $2.50, authorized 2,000 shares | $ 298.3 | $ 298.4 |
| Paid-in capital in excess of par | 130.5 | 129.9 |
| Retained earnings | 2,080.8 | 2,052.3 |
| Less 12.8 and 13.0 treasury stock, at cost | 382.2 | 384.7 |

In the current year, Halliburton declared and paid cash dividends of $1 per share. What would be the total amount of dividends declared and paid if they had been based on the amount of stock outstanding at the end of the year?

**P11–5 Analyzing Dividend Policy**

General Mills is a very successful company with substantial growth in revenues and earnings during the past 10 years. The following information was contained in a recent annual report:

| | 1999 | 1998 | 1997 | 1996 | 1995 | 1994 | 1993 | 1992 | 1991 |
| --- | --- | --- | --- | --- | --- | --- | --- | --- | --- |
| Dividend payout ratio | 62% | 80% | 72% | 63% | 81% | 64% | 51% | 49% | 44% |
| Dividend yield ratio | 2.7% | 3.1% | 3.2% | 3.3% | 3.1% | 3.5% | 2.5% | 2.3% | 2.2% |
| Dividends per share (dollars) | 2.16 | 2.12 | 2.03 | 1.91 | 1.88 | 1.88 | 1.68 | 1.48 | 1.28 |

Based on this information, describe the dividend policy of General Mills. Assume that you are a financial analyst preparing a forecast of next year's operating results for General Mills. Net earnings for 1999 were $535 million, and the company paid out $331 million in dividends. Due to a number of factors, you believe that net income for next year will increase substantially and will be in the range of $900 to $950 million. To complete your financial forecast, you now need to estimate the total amount of dividends that General Mills will pay. What is your estimate?

**CP11–6 Inferring Financial Statement Amounts**

Dollar General is a national retailer in direct competition with Wal-Mart, the focus company of this chapter. The annual report for Dollar General contained the following information:

| Shareholders' Equity (amounts in thousands, except shares) | PREFERRED STOCK | COMMON STOCK | PAID-IN CAPITAL | RETAINED EARNINGS |
| --- | --- | --- | --- | --- |
| Balance, January 30, 1998 | $858 | $83,526 | $379,954 | $320,085 |
| (Common shares 167,052,000) | | | | |
| Net income | | | | 182,033 |
| 5-for-4 stock split | | 21,090 | | (21,090) |
| Issuance of common stock | | 1,488 | 27,523 | |

The company paid dividends in the amount of $3,497,000 to its preferred stockholders. It also paid dividends of $0.14 per share to its common stockholders. Assume that the common dividend was paid after the 5-for-4 stock split. Determine the total amount of dividends paid to common stockholders. When the annual report was issued, the common stock price was $25. Compute the dividend yield ratio and the dividend payout ratio.

**LO2, 3     CP11–7     Interpreting the Financial Press**

As discussed in the chapter, companies buy back their own stock for a number of reasons. An article on this topic is available on the Libby/Libby/Short website at www.mhhe.com/business/accounting/libby3. You should read the article, "Stock market time bomb," November 15, 1999, and then write a short memo summarizing the article. In general, do you think large stock buybacks are good for investors?

## CRITICAL THINKING CASES

**LO4, 5     CP11–8     Making a Decision as a Financial Analyst**

Assume that you are a stockbroker with two clients. One is a recent college graduate and the other is a retired couple. You have recently reviewed the annual report for Philip Morris, which sells popular tobacco and beer products along with Kraft brand foods. You were impressed with a 22 percent increase in net income for Philip Morris in 1998. You noticed that the company generated more than $8 billion in cash flows from operating activities and paid $1.68 per share in dividends. The dividend yield was 6.7 percent, one of the highest you have been able to find for large, well-known companies. Based on this information and your current knowledge of Philip Morris, would you recommend this stock for either of your clients?

**LO4, 5, 6     CP11–9     Making a Decision as an Investor**

You have retired after a long and successful career as a business executive and now spend a good portion of your time managing your retirement portfolio. You are considering three basic investment alternatives. You can invest in (1) corporate bonds currently paying 7 percent interest, (2) conservative stocks with an average dividend yield of 5 percent and dividend payout ratios in excess of 80 percent, and (3) growth-oriented technology stocks that pay no dividends. Analyze each of these alternatives and select one. Justify your selection.

**LO4, 7     CP11–10     Evaluating an Ethical Dilemma**

You are a member of the board of directors of a large company that has been in business for more than 100 years. The company is proud of the fact that it has paid dividends every year it has been in business. Because of this stability, many retired people have invested large portions of their savings in your common stock. Unfortunately, the company has struggled for the past few years as it tries to introduce new products and is considering not paying a dividend this year. The president wants to skip the dividend in order to have more cash to invest in product development: "If we don't invest this money now, we won't get these products to market in time to save the company. I don't want to risk thousands of jobs." One of the most senior board members speaks next: "If we don't pay the dividend, thousands of retirees will be thrown into financial distress. Even if you don't care about them, you have to recognize our stock price will crash when they all sell." The company treasurer proposes an alternative: "Let's skip the cash dividend and pay a stock dividend. We can still say we've had a dividend every year." The entire board now turns to you for your opinion. What should the company do?

**LO4     CP11–11     Evaluating an Ethical Dilemma**

You are the president of a very successful Internet company that has had a remarkably profitable year. You have determined that the company has more than $10 million in cash generated by operating activities not needed in the business. You are thinking about paying it out to stockholders as a special dividend. You discuss the idea with your vice president, who reacts angrily to your suggestion: "Our stock price has gone up by 200 percent in the last year alone. What more do we have to do for the owners? The people who really earned that money are the employees who have been working 12 hours a day, six or seven days a week to make the company successful. Most of them didn't even take vacations last year. I say we have to pay out bonuses and nothing extra for the stockholders." As president, you know that you are hired by the board of directors, which is elected by the stockholders. What is your responsibility to both groups? To which group would you give the $10 million?

# FINANCIAL REPORTING AND ANALYSIS PROJECTS

**CP11–12** **Comparing Companies in the Retail Industry**

LO1, 4, 5, 6, 7

Select any well-known retailer (one source of information is MarketGuide at www.marketguide.com/mgi/INDUSTRY/INDUSTRY.HTML). Go to the website for the company you select and for Wal-Mart (www.wal-mart.com). Review the annual reports for both companies as well as any recent news item related to them.

*Required:*

1. Compare the stockholders' equity section for each company. What significant differences do you observe?

2. Compute the dividend yield and dividend payout ratios for both companies. What do you conclude from this comparison.

3. Determine whether either company has had a stock split or stock dividend during the previous three years.

4. Review the business strategy and operating results for each company. Does this review help you understand any of the differences that you observed in the previous requirements?

**CP11–13** **Team Project: Evaluating Stock Compensation**

LO1

Break into two teams. One team should play the role of labor union representatives and the other the role of senior management. The labor union wants all of its employees to receive an additional 10 percent of their compensation in the form of company stock. The union president argues that the stockholders will benefit from this proposal because the employees will work harder for the company if they are also owners. Management believes that this proposal is too expensive and that the board of directors would probably fire the management team if it ever approved the proposal. Outline the points to support your position and enter a negotiation to resolve the conflict. As a team, write a final recommendation to present to the board.

**CP11–14** **Evaluating an Ethical Dilemma: Performance-Based Compensation**

LO1

Michael Eisner, CEO of Disney, made headlines a few years ago when it was announced that his compensation package included stock options worth $750 million. His compensation agreement included a bonus (paid in stock options). Eisner earned a percentage of Disney's income once the company earned an agreed-upon rate of return. Write a brief memo identifying any ethical issues you see in this type of agreement.

**CP11–15** **Evaluating an Ethical Dilemma: Treasury Stock Transactions**

LO3

You are on the board of directors of a medium-sized manufacturing company traded on the New York Stock Exchange. The president of the company has recommended that the company buy back 5 percent of its outstanding shares within the next 10 days. The buyback is being recommended because the company has a large amount of cash that it does not need in the business. Earlier in the day, you learned that within a month, the company will announce a new product improvement that will have a substantial impact on company profitability and stock price. You are concerned about the suggestion that the company should purchase large amounts of stock before an announcement is made about the new product. The president has assured the board that there is no problem because the company cannot report profits on treasury stock transactions and if there is an economic gain, it will benefit all of the stockholders. Write a brief memo to the board recommending the action that you believe is appropriate.

**CP11–16** **Team Project: Studying the Impact of Dividend Announcements**

LO4

Each member of the team should find dividend announcements for different companies. Using a source such as *The Wall Street Journal,* determine the stock price for the company for each day one week before and one week after the announcement. Using spreadsheet software, prepare a chart of the stock price movement. Compare the charts for each company.

*Required:*

The team should summarize what a comparison of the charts indicates. Review the earnings announcements. Do they help explain any of the differences observed? Write a brief statement explaining how you think the stock market reacts to earnings announcements.

■ **LO7**     **CP11–17**     **Team Project: Studying Stock Splits and Stock Dividends**

Each member of the team should find a company that has had a stock split or a stock dividend and a company in the same industry that has not. Using a source such as *The Wall Street Journal,* determine the stock price for each company at the end of each month for the previous two years. Using spreadsheet software, prepare a chart comparing the stock price movement for each company. Compare the charts for each member of the group. What do you conclude from this comparison?

■ **LO5, 8**     **CP11–18**     **Comparing Companies over Time**

Acquire the three most recent years' financial statements for Wal-Mart (contact investor relations at www.wal-mart.com or EDGAR service at www.sec.gov/cgi-bin/srch-edgar). Write a short memo comparing the company's dividend payout and dividend yield over the three years.

■ **LO1, 2**     **CP11–19**     **Comparing Companies over Time**

Acquire the three most recent years' financial statements for Wal-Mart (contact investor relations at www.wal-mart.com or EDGAR service at www.sec.gov/cgi-bin/srch-edgar). Write a short memo comparing transactions affecting stockholders' equity (e.g., stock splits, treasury stock, etc.). Explain why you think management engaged in these transactions.

# Reporting and Interpreting Investments in Other Corporations

## CHAPTER **TWELVE**

LEARNING **OBJECTIVES**

*After studying this chapter, you should be able to:*

1. Understand the three major categories of intercorporate investments. p. 640

2. Analyze and report passive investments in securities using the market value method. p. 642

3. Analyze and report investments involving significant influence using the equity method. p. 649

4. Analyze and report investments in controlling interests in subsidiaries in consolidated statements. p. 654

5. Analyze and interpret the return on assets ratio. p. 660

The name Dow Jones is best known for its index of stock prices, the Dow Jones Industrial Average. However, Dow Jones & Co. does much more. It is the largest global provider of business news and information through print and electronic publishing.

# Dow Jones & Co., Inc.
## INVESTMENT STRATEGIES IN THE MEDIA INDUSTRY

Dow Jones' flagship publication, *The Wall Street Journal,* is the country's largest daily newspaper, with circulation averaging over 1.7 million. In print publishing, Dow Jones also produces *The Wall Street Journal Europe, The Asian Wall Street Journal, The Wall Street Journal Americas* (to Central and South America), *Barron's* (a business and financial weekly publication), *Far Eastern Economic Review,* the *National Business Employment Weekly,* and various financial magazines, including *SmartMoney.* The company also owns Ottaway Newspapers, Inc., which publishes 19 general-interest community newspapers.

Dow Jones recognizes that new technologies bring increased efficiency to its operations while expanding opportunities. Production of *The Wall Street Journal,* for example, employs satellite transmission of page images to various printing plants, speeding delivery of material to the presses. Dow Jones teamed up with NBC to provide business news programming to CNBC. As part of the alliance, Dow Jones joined Microsoft Corporation and NBC to supply news and financial information to the MSNBC Internet site and the CNBC/Dow Jones

Business Video service. In addition, besides its Newswires service that provides real-time business and financial news via dedicated terminals to business professionals, Dow Jones is one of the nation's leading publishers of electronic business and financial news over the World Wide Web. Its principal products include Dow Jones Interactive (a vast news library) and The Wall Street Journal Interactive Edition (offering continuously updated news and market information).

The announcement in early 2000 of the merger of two media giants, Time Warner and America Online, brought speculation of how other media companies might respond to the changing nature of the media industry and technology. Mortimer B. Zuckerman, whose media holdings include *U.S. News & World Report,* suggested that media companies that are slow to move may find themselves with few options. "But you have to understand that a new technology is emerging that is going to be increasingly dominant in distributing that information."* Dow Jones has achieved its diversity in part by investing in the stock of other companies. To meet new challenges, the question now arises, will Dow Jones be seen "waltzing with Yahoo, AT&T, or Amazon.com?"*

*Felicity Barringer, "Media Megadeal: The Old Guard; Established Media Companies Are Nervous in Wake of Pact," *The New York Times,* January 12, 2000, p. 6, column 1.

## BUSINESS BACKGROUND

■ **LEARNING OBJECTIVE 1**

Understand the three major categories of intercorporate investments.

Many strategic factors motivate managers to invest in securities. It is easier to understand the business purpose of an investment if you first classify it in one of three categories:

- *Passive investments.* These investments are made to earn a high rate of return on funds that may be needed for short-term or long-term purposes in the future. In Chapter 10, we discussed investments in bonds. In this chapter, we focus on investments in the stock of other companies. For investments in equity securities, the investment is presumed passive if the investing company owns less than 20 percent of the outstanding voting shares of the other company.

- *Investments made with the intent of exerting significant influence over another corporation.* Significant influence is the ability of the investing company to have an important impact on the operating and financial policies of another company in which it owns shares of voting stock. Significant influence may be indicated by (1) membership on the board of directors of the other company, (2) participation in the policy-making processes, (3) material transactions between the two companies, (4) interchange of management personnel, or (5) technological dependency. In the absence of a clear-cut distinction based on these factors, significant influence is presumed if the investing company owns at least 20 percent but not more than 50 percent of the outstanding voting shares of the other company.

- *Investments made with the intent to exert control over another corporation.* Controlling another company occurs when the investing company has the ability to determine the operating and financial policies of another company in which it owns shares of the voting stock. For all practical purposes, control is presumed when the investing company owns more than 50 percent of the outstanding voting stock of the other company. In some cases, it may be possible to achieve synergy between two or more companies when the combined effectiveness of their operations is more than the sum of their individual activities. In other cases, the investing corporation may intend to exert an absolute minimum of influence. These investments can achieve diversification so that a company does not depend on the economic fortunes of a single area of business.

The 1998 balance sheet for Dow Jones & Co. is presented in Exhibit 12.1 with relevant accounts highlighted. The company has no short-term investments but does re-

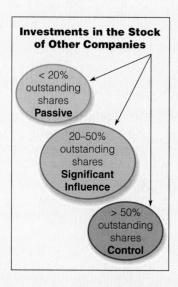

**Investments in the Stock of Other Companies**

< 20% outstanding shares
**Passive**

20–50% outstanding shares
**Significant Influence**

> 50% outstanding shares
**Control**

port long-term investments in associated companies (for influence) and other long-term investments (as passive investments). Also, the title on the balance sheet indicates that it is consolidated, suggesting the company controls other companies. In the annual report, we find that Dow Jones's significant past acquisitions include *Far Eastern Economic Review* and Ottaway Newspapers.

EXHIBIT **12.1**

**Dow Jones & Company Balance Sheet**

**DOW JONES & COMPANY**
**Consolidated Balance Sheet**
**December 31, 1998 and 1997**

| (dollars in thousands) | 1998 | 1997 | | 1998 | 1997 |
|---|---|---|---|---|---|
| **Assets:** | | | **Liabilities:** | | |
| Current Assets: | | | Current Liabilities: | | |
| Cash and cash equivalents | $ 142,877 | $ 23,763 | Accounts payable—trade | $ 75,974 | $ 147,378 |
| Accounts receivable—trade, net of | | | Accrued wages, salaries, and commissions | 52,028 | 70,011 |
| allowance for doubtful accounts of | | | Profit sharing and other retirement | | |
| $6,641 in 1998 and $16,445 in 1997 | 236,928 | 295,250 | plan contributions payable | 43,596 | 45,913 |
| Inventories | 11,386 | 13,104 | Other payables | 152,592 | 97,048 |
| Deferred income taxes | 13,992 | 16,565 | Income taxes | 37,198 | 53,895 |
| Prepaid expenses | 18,068 | 25,991 | Unearned revenue | 238,409 | 252,832 |
| Other current assets | 19,038 | 131,880 | Current maturities of long-term debt | | 5,318 |
| Total current assets | 442,289 | 506,553 | Total current liabilities | 599,797 | 672,395 |
| Investments in associated companies, | | | Long-term debt | 149,889 | 228,806 |
| at equity | 40,479 | 46,064 | Deferred compensation | 198,089 | 179,798 |
| Other investments | 223,785 | 85,290 | Other noncurrent liabilities | 34,207 | 57,913 |
| | | | Total liabilities | 981,982 | 1,138,912 |
| Plant and property, at cost: | | | **Stockholders' Equity:** | | |
| Land | 22,507 | 26,234 | | | |
| Buildings and improvements | 313,591 | 394,646 | Common stock | 81,316 | 80,621 |
| Equipment | 1,118,131 | 1,970,903 | Common stock, class B | 20,865 | 21,560 |
| Construction in progress | 121,552 | 59,806 | Additional paid-in capital | 137,479 | 136,398 |
| | 1,575,781 | 2,451,589 | Retained earnings | 624,239 | 707,539 |
| | | | Accumulated other comprehensive | | |
| Less, accumulated depreciation | 973,664 | 1,667,552 | income: | | |
| | 602,117 | 784,037 | Unrealized gain on investments | 35,775 | 3,396 |
| Goodwill, less accumulated amortization of | | | Cumulative translation adjustment | 38 | (9,540) |
| $58,610 in 1998 and $1,275,738 in 1997 | 86,554 | 387,787 | | 899,712 | 939,974 |
| Deferred income taxes | 67,171 | 93,045 | Less, treasury stock (at cost) | 390,372 | 159,152 |
| Other assets | 28,927 | 16,958 | Total stockholders' equity | 509,340 | 780,822 |
| Total assets | $1,491,322 | $1,919,734 | Total liabilities and stockholders' equity | $1,491,322 | $1,919,734 |

The accounting methods used to record investments are directly related to the purpose of the investment. A critical feature that determines the appropriate accounting method is the nature of the relationship between the investor corporation and the investee. Once you have determined the purpose of the investment (as a passive investment, for significant influence, or for control of another entity), it is easy to determine the appropriate accounting method to use for the investment. The three basic approaches are as follows:

| Category | Level of Ownership (percentage of outstanding voting shares) | Measuring and Reporting Method |
|---|---|---|
| 1. Passive | <20% | Market value method |
| 2. Significant influence | Between 20 and 50 | Equity method |
| 3. Control | >50 | Consolidated statement method |

We first discuss the market value method for measuring and reporting passive investments in trading securities and securities available for sale. Then we present the equity method of accounting for securities and related reporting requirements, followed by a discussion of accounting for the consolidation of entities.

**ORGANIZATION** OF THE CHAPTER

| • **Securities Held for Passive Investment** | • **Securities Held for Significant Influence** | • **Securities Held for Control** |
|---|---|---|
| Issues in Valuation | Classifying Investments in Associated Companies | What Are Consolidated Statements? |
| Classifying Passive Investments | Recording Investments Under the Equity Method | Methods of Acquiring a Controlling Interest |
| Recording Investments at Market Value | | Consolidated Balance Sheets |
| Comparing Trading and Available-for-Sale Securities | | Consolidated Income Statements |
| | | Return on Assets Ratio |

# SECURITIES HELD FOR PASSIVE INVESTMENT

■ **LEARNING OBJECTIVE 2**

Analyze and report passive investments in securities using the market value method.

**MARKET VALUE METHOD** reports securities at their current market value.

Among the assets and liabilities on the balance sheet, only passive investments (presumed when the investing company owns less than 20 percent of the outstanding voting stock[1]) are reported using the **market value method** on the date of the balance sheet. This is a violation of the historical cost principal.

## ISSUES IN VALUATION

Before we discuss the specific accounting for investments, we should consider two important questions:

**Why are investments accounted for under the market value method the only assets that are reported at fair market value on the balance sheet?** Two primary factors are involved in the answer to this question:

1. *Relevance.* Analysts who study financial statements often attempt to forecast a company's future cash flows. They want to know how a company can generate cash for purposes such as expansion of the business, payment of dividends, or survival during a prolonged economic downturn. One source of cash is the sale of stock from its passive investments portfolio. The best estimate of the cash that could be generated by the sale of these securities is their current market value. Notice that

---

[1]All *nonvoting* stock is accounted for under the market value method without regard to the level of ownership.

these investments are different from most assets the company holds. In the normal course of business, a company uses but does not sell productive assets such as manufacturing equipment or office buildings. Investments do not serve that same purpose. They cannot produce goods or services; their only value comes from an ability to convert them into cash.

2. *Measurability.* Accountants can record only items that can be measured in dollar terms with a high degree of reliability (an unbiased and verifiable measurement). Determining the fair market value of most assets is very difficult because they are not actively traded. The John Hancock building is an important part of the Boston skyline. John Hancock's balance sheet reports the building in terms of its original cost in part because of the difficulty in determining an objective value for it. Contrast the difficulty of determining the value of a building with the ease of determining the value of securities that John Hancock may own. It is relatively easy to use *The Wall Street Journal* to determine the current price of IBM or Exxon stock because these securities are traded each day on established stock exchanges.

**If accountants adjust the value of an investment account to reflect changes in fair market value, what other account is impacted when the asset account is increased or decreased?** At this point in our discussion, you may have anticipated this other important issue concerning investments. Under the double-entry method of accounting, every journal entry affects at least two accounts. One account is a valuation allowance that is added to the investment account to report market value. The other account affected is for **unrealized holding gains or losses** that are recorded whenever the fair market value of investments changes. These are *unrealized* because no actual sale has taken place; simply by holding the security, the value has changed. If the value of the investments increased by $100,000 during the year, an adjusting journal entry records the increase in the asset account and an unrealized holding gain for $100,000. If the value of the investments decreased by $75,000 during the year, an adjusting journal entry records the decrease in the asset and an unrealized holding loss. Recording an unrealized holding gain is a departure from the revenue principle that states that revenues and gains should be recorded when the company has completed the earnings process that generated them.

**UNREALIZED HOLDING GAINS AND LOSSES** are amounts associated with price changes of securities that are currently held.

### CLASSIFYING PASSIVE INVESTMENTS

Depending on management's intent, passive investments may be held as short- or long-term investments:

*Short-term.* Instead of leaving cash in a checking account that does not earn interest, many companies buy securities that provide a higher return, often to be used for operating purposes in the near future.

**Trading securities:** Some companies can be very aggressive with *trading securities* and actively trade them on established exchanges in an effort to maximize return. The trading securities portfolio is managed with the objective of generating profits on short-term differences in the price of the securities. The management philosophy for this portfolio is similar to the approach taken by many mutual funds. The portfolio manager actively seeks opportunities to buy and sell securities. These are classified as current assets on the balance sheet.

**TRADING SECURITIES** are all investments in stocks or bonds held primarily for the purpose of active trading (buying and selling) in the near future (classified as short term).

**Securities available for sale:** Most companies, however, invest in very low-risk securities; these investments of *securities available for sale* typically include stocks, bonds, Treasury bills (short-term debt issued by the federal government), and commercial paper (short-term debt issued by corporations). This portfolio is not as actively traded as the trading securities portfolio; its purpose is to earn a return on funds that may be required for operating purposes in the near future. These are also classified as current assets on the balance sheet.

**SECURITIES AVAILABLE FOR SALE** are all passive investments other than trading securities (classified as short or long term).

*Long-term.* The purpose of these investments is similar to the purpose of short-term investments. In this case, management invests funds that are not needed for operating purposes but may be needed for some long-term purpose.

**Securities available for sale:** Long-term investments include stocks, bonds, and Treasury notes. They are classified as long-term assets on the balance sheet based on management's intent.

## RECORDING INVESTMENTS AT MARKET VALUE

Trading securities are most commonly reported by financial institutions that actively buy and sell these short-term investments to maximize returns. Most corporations, however, invest in short- and long-term securities available for sale (SAS for short). We will focus on this latter category of investments first by analyzing investing activities for Dow Jones.

Dow Jones's Other Investments account is reported at $223,785,000 at the end of 1998 and represents 15 percent of its total assets. The notes to Dow Jones's annual report contain the following information concerning this investment portfolio:

**NOTES TO FINANCIAL STATEMENTS**

*NOTE 1. SUMMARY OF SIGNIFICANT ACCOUNTING POLICIES*

INVESTMENTS in marketable equity securities, all of which are classified as available for sale, are carried at their market value in the consolidated balance sheets. The unrealized gains or losses of these investments are recorded directly to Stockholders' Equity, net of deferred taxes. Any decline in market value below the investment's original cost that is determined to be other than temporary as well as any realized gains or losses would be recognized in income (see Note 17).

For simplification, let's assume that Dow Jones had no passive investments at the end of 1998. We will apply the accounting policy used by Dow Jones in the following illustration.

**Purchase of Securities**   At the beginning of 1999, Dow Jones purchases 10,000 shares of common stock in Internet Financial News[2] or IFN (with 100,000 outstanding shares) for $60 per share. This is a 10 percent ownership level (10,000 ÷ 100,000) and is therefore presumed to be a passive investment. Investments are recorded initially at cost:

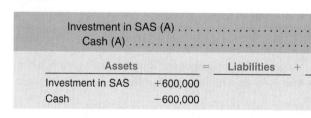

| Investment in SAS (A) . . . . . . . . . . . . . . . . . . . . . . | 600,000 | |
| Cash (A) . . . . . . . . . . . . . . . . . . . . . . . . . . . . | | 600,000 |

| Assets | = | Liabilities | + | Stockholders' Equity |
|---|---|---|---|---|
| Investment in SAS | +600,000 | | | |
| Cash | −600,000 | | | |

This entry and those that follow are illustrated in T-accounts in Exhibit 12.2.

**Receipt of Dividends**   Investments in equity securities earn a return from two sources: (1) price appreciation and (2) dividend income. Price appreciation is analyzed at year-end and when a security is sold (discussed later). Dividends earned are reported as investment income on the income statement and are included in the computation of net income for the period. Dow Jones received a $1 per share cash dividend from IFN or $10,000 ($1 × 10,000 shares).

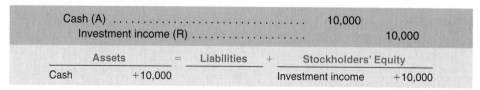

| Cash (A) . . . . . . . . . . . . . . . . . . . . . . . . . . . . | 10,000 | |
| Investment income (R) . . . . . . . . . . . . . . . . . | | 10,000 |

| Assets | = | Liabilities | + | Stockholders' Equity | |
|---|---|---|---|---|---|
| Cash | +10,000 | | | Investment income | +10,000 |

This entry is the same for dividend income earned for shares in both the trading securities and available-for-sale portfolios.

---

[2]Internet Financial News is a fictitious company.

EXHIBIT **12.2**

**T-Accounts for the Illustrated Transactions**

**Balance Sheet Accounts**

| Investment in SAS (at cost) | | | |
|---|---|---|---|
| 1/1/99 | 0 | | |
| Purchase | 600,000 | | |
| 12/31/99 | 600,000 | | |
| | | 300,000 | 2001 Sale |
| 12/31/01 | 300,000 | | |

| Valuation Allowance to Market—SAS | | | |
|---|---|---|---|
| | | 0 | 1/1/99 |
| | | 20,000 | 1999 AJE |
| | | 20,000 | 12/31/99 |
| 2000 AJE | 30,000 | | |
| 12/31/00 | 10,000 | | |
| | | 5,000 | 2001 Sale |
| | | 10,000 | 2001 AJE |
| | | 5,000 | 12/31/01 |

| Net Unrealized Loss/Gain—SAS | | | |
|---|---|---|---|
| 1/1/99 | 0 | | |
| 1999 AJE | 20,000 | | |
| 12/31/99 | 20,000 | | |
| | | 30,000 | 2000 AJE |
| | | 10,000 | 12/31/00 |
| 2001 Sale | 5,000 | | |
| 2001 AJE | 10,000 | | |
| 12/31/01 | 5,000 | | |

**Income Statement Accounts**

| Investment Income | | | |
|---|---|---|---|
| | | 10,000 | Earned |
| | | 10,000 | 12/31/99 |

| Gain on Sale of Investments | | | |
|---|---|---|---|
| | | 0 | 1/1/01 |
| | | 10,000 | 2001 Sale |
| | | 10,000 | 12/31/01 |

**Year-End Valuation** Passive investments are reported at fair market value on the balance sheet at the end of the accounting period. Assume that IFN had a $58 per share market value at the end of the year. By holding this investment for the year, Dow Jones lost value in its investment portfolio. However, since no exchange has taken place (the investment has not been sold), the holding loss is not realized. Reporting the SAS investment at market value requires adjusting it to market using a valuation allowance (a related account); the unrealized holding loss is also recorded. The following chart is used to compute any unrealized gain or loss in the SAS portfolio:

| Year | Market Value | − | Cost | = | Balance Needed in Valuation Allowance | − | Unadjusted Balance in Valuation Allowance | = | Adjustment to Valuation Allowance |
|---|---|---|---|---|---|---|---|---|---|
| 1999 | $580,000 ($58 × 10,000) | − | $600,000 | = | ($20,000) | − | $0 | = | ($20,000) An unrealized loss for the period |

The adjusting entry at the end of 1999 is as follows:

| | | |
|---|---|---|
| Net unrealized loss/gain—SAS (SE) . . . . . . . . . . . | 20,000 | |
| Valuation allowance to market—SAS (A) . . . . | | 20,000 |

| Assets | = | Liabilities | + | Stockholders' Equity |
|---|---|---|---|---|
| Valuation allowance to market—SAS  −20,000 | | | | Net unrealized loss/gain—SAS  −20,000 |

This Net Unrealized Loss/Gain—SAS account is reported in the stockholders' equity section of the balance sheet under Other Comprehensive Income. (This keeps the balance sheet in balance.) Since the SAS investment is expected to be held into the future until cash is needed, the unrealized holding gain or loss is not reported as part of net income. When the security is sold, any realized gains or losses will be included in net income.

For 1999, Dow Jones would report on the balance sheet under Other Investments its investment in securities available for sale for $580,000 ($600,000 cost less the $20,000 credit balance in the valuation allowance). It would also report under Other Comprehensive Income its net unrealized loss on securities available for sale of $20,000. The only item reported on the income statement for 1999 would be investment income of $10,000 classified under other nonoperating items.

Now let's assume that the IFN securities are held through the year 2000. At the end of 2000, the stock had a $61 per share market value. The adjustment for 2000 is computed as follows:

| Year | Market Value | – | Cost | = | Balance Needed in Valuation Allowance | – | Unadjusted Balance in Valuation Allowance | = | Adjustment to Valuation Allowance |
|---|---|---|---|---|---|---|---|---|---|
| 2000 | $610,000<br>($61 × 10,000) | – | $600,000 | = | $10,000 | – | ($20,000) | = | $30,000<br>An unrealized gain for the period |

The adjusting entry at the end of 2000 is as follows:

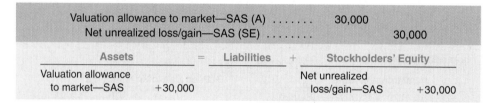

| | | |
|---|---|---|
| Valuation allowance to market—SAS (A) ....... | 30,000 | |
| Net unrealized loss/gain—SAS (SE) ........ | | 30,000 |

| Assets | | = | Liabilities | + | Stockholders' Equity | |
|---|---|---|---|---|---|---|
| Valuation allowance to market—SAS | +30,000 | | | | Net unrealized loss/gain—SAS | +30,000 |

**Sale of Securities** When securities available for sale are sold, *three* accounts on the balance sheet are affected:

- Investment in SAS.
- Valuation Allowance (to adjust the cost of the investments to market).
- Net Unrealized Loss/Gain (equal to the valuation allowance).

1998 $300,000 bought
12/31/2000 $305,000
2001 $310,000 sold

Let's assume that in 2001 Dow Jones sold half of its SAS investment in IFN for $62 per share. The company received $310,000 in cash ($62 × 5,000 shares) for stock it paid $300,000 for in 1998 ($60 × 5,000 shares). However, the investment to be sold was reported at the end of 2000 at a market value of $305,000 ($61 × 5,000 shares). Thus, the valuation allowance and its related net unrealized loss/gain account should be reduced by $5,000.

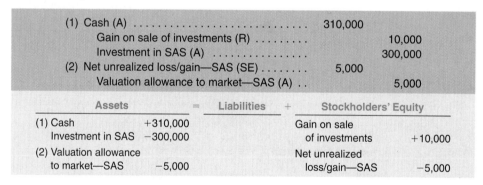

| | | |
|---|---|---|
| (1) Cash (A) ............................ | 310,000 | |
| Gain on sale of investments (R) ......... | | 10,000 |
| Investment in SAS (A) ................ | | 300,000 |
| (2) Net unrealized loss/gain—SAS (SE) ........ | 5,000 | |
| Valuation allowance to market—SAS (A) .. | | 5,000 |

| Assets | | = | Liabilities | + | Stockholders' Equity | |
|---|---|---|---|---|---|---|
| (1) Cash | +310,000 | | | | Gain on sale of investments | +10,000 |
| Investment in SAS | −300,000 | | | | | |
| (2) Valuation allowance to market—SAS | −5,000 | | | | Net unrealized loss/gain—SAS | −5,000 |

The first entry accounts for the sale of the investment as we do any asset, with gains or losses recognized as the difference between cost of the asset and cash received. The second entry eliminates the half of the valuation allowance and half of the net unrealized gain related to the securities sold.

At the end of 2001, the remaining shares in the investment portfolio are adjusted to market, $59 per share:

| Year | Market Value | – | Cost | = | Balance Needed in Valuation Allowance | – | Unadjusted Balance in Valuation Allowance | = | Adjustment to Valuation Allowance |
|---|---|---|---|---|---|---|---|---|---|
| 2001 | $295,000<br>($59 × 5,000) | – | $300,000 | = | ($5,000) | – | $5,000 | = | ($10,000)<br>An unrealized loss for the period |

The adjusting entry at the end of 2001 is as follows:

| Net unrealized loss/gain—SAS (SE) . . . . . . . . . . | 10,000 | |
|---|---|---|
| Valuation allowance to market—SAS (A) . . . . . | | 10,000 |

| Assets | | = | Liabilities | + | Stockholders' Equity | |
|---|---|---|---|---|---|---|
| Valuation allowance to market—SAS | −10,000 | | | | Net unrealized loss/gain—SAS | −10,000 |

## COMPARING TRADING AND AVAILABLE-FOR-SALE SECURITIES

The reporting impact of unrealized holding gains or losses depends on the classification of the investment:

*Available-for-sale portfolio.* Net unrealized holding gains and losses are reported as a separate component of stockholders' equity (under *other comprehensive income*). They are not reported on the income statement and do not affect net income.

*Trading securities portfolio.* Net unrealized holding gains and losses are included on the income statement and in the computation of net income. In other words, holding gains increase net income, and holding losses decrease net income. This also means that the account for net unrealized gains and losses on trading securities is closed to Retained Earnings at the end of the period. Thus, when selling a trading security, only *two* balance sheet accounts are affected: Investment in Trading Securities (TS) and the Valuation Allowance to Market for the trading securities portfolio.

Exhibit 12.3 provides comparative journal entries for the transactions illustrated for Dow Jones from 1999 to 2001.

EXHIBIT **12.3**

**Comparison of Accounting for Available-for-Sale and Trading Securities Portfolios**

| | Securities Available for Sale | | Trading Securities | |
|---|---|---|---|---|
| **1999:** | | | | |
| Purchase | Investment in SAS (A) | 600,000 | Investment in TS (A) | 600,000 |
| | Cash (A) | 600,000 | Cash (A) | 600,000 |
| Receipt of dividends | Cash (A) | 10,000 | Cash (A) | 10,000 |
| | Investment income (R) | 10,000 | Investment income (R) | 10,000 |
| Year-end adjustment to market | Net unrealized loss/gain—SAS (SE) | 20,000 | Net unrealized loss/gain—TS (E) | 20,000 |
| | Valuation allowance—SAS (A) | 20,000 | Valuation allowance—TS (A) | 20,000 |
| **2000:** | | | | |
| Year-end adjustment to market | Valuation allowance—SAS (A) | 30,000 | Valuation allowance—TS (A) | 30,000 |
| | Net unrealized loss/gain—SAS (SE) | 30,000 | Net unrealized loss/gain—TS (R) | 30,000 |
| **2001:** | | | | |
| Sale | *Three balance sheet accounts are affected* | | *Two balance sheet accounts are affected* | |
| | Cash (A) | 310,000 | Cash (A) | 310,000 |
| | Net unrealized loss/gain (SE) | 5,000 | Valuation allowance—TS (A) | 5,000 |
| | Valuation allowance—SAS (A) | 5,000 | Investment in TS (A) | 300,000 |
| | Investment in SAS (A) | 300,000 | Gain on sale of investment (R) | 5,000 |
| | Gain on sale of investment (R) | 10,000 | | |
| Year-end adjustment to market | Net unrealized loss/gain—SAS (SE) | 10,000 | Net unrealized loss/gain—TS (E) | 10,000 |
| | Valuation allowance—SAS (A) | 10,000 | Valuation allowance—TS (A) | 10,000 |
| Balance sheet reporting: | *Assets* | | *Assets* | |
| | Investment in SAS | $300,000 | Investment in TS | $300,000 |
| | Valuation allowance—SAS | (5,000) | Valuation allowance—TS | (5,000) |
| | Net investments in SAS | $295,000 | Net investments in TS | $295,000 |
| | *Stockholders' Equity* | | | |
| | Accumulated other comprehensive income: | | | |
| | Net unrealized loss—SAS | $ 5,000 | | |
| Income statement reporting: | *Other Nonoperating Items* | | *Other Nonoperating Items* | |
| | Investment income | $ 0 | Investment income | $ 0 |
| | Gain on sale of investment | 10,000 | Gain on sale of investment | 5,000 |
| | | | Net unrealized loss—TS | (10,000) |

# SELF-STUDY **QUIZ**

Now let's reconstruct the activities that Dow Jones actually undertook in 1998, assuming a few transactions. Answer the following questions, using the T-accounts to help you infer the amounts. The dollars are in thousands.

## Balance Sheet Accounts

**(In Other Investments)**
**Investment in SAS**

| | | | |
|---|---|---|---|
| 1/1/98 | 81,894 | | |
| Purchase | 118,000 | ? | Sale |
| 12/31/98 | 188,010 | | |

**Valuation Allowance to Market—SAS**

| | | | |
|---|---|---|---|
| 1/1/98 | 3,396 | | |
| | | 2,016 | Sale |
| AJE | ? | | |
| 12/31/98 | 35,775 | | |

**(In Accumulated Other Comprehensive Income)**
**Net Unrealized Loss/Gain—SAS**

| | | | |
|---|---|---|---|
| | | 3,396 | 1/1/98 |
| Sale | ? | | |
| | | ? | AJE |
| | | 35,775 | 12/31/98 |

## Income Statement Accounts

**Investment Income**

| | | | |
|---|---|---|---|
| ? | | Earned | |
| | 12,266 | 12/31/98 | |

**Loss on Sale of Investments**

| | | | |
|---|---|---|---|
| Sale | 2,384 | | |
| 12/31/98 | 2,384 | | |

| | |
|---|---|
| *a.* Purchased securities available for sale for cash. Prepare the journal entry. | |
| *b.* Received cash dividends on the investments. Prepare the journal entry. | |
| *c.* Sold SAS investments at a loss. Prepare the journal entries. | |
| *d.* At year-end, the SAS portfolio had a market value of $223,785. Prepare the adjusting entry. | |
| *e.* What would be reported on the balance sheet related to the SAS investments on December 31, 1998? On the income statement for 1998? | |
| *f.* How would year-end reporting change if the investments were categorized as trading securities instead of securities available for sale? | |

Check your responses with the answer provided in the footnote at the bottom of this page.*

---

*a.* Investments in SAS (A)      118,000

    Cash (A)      118,000

*b.* Cash (A)      12,266

    Investment income (R)      12,266

*c.* (1) Cash (A)      9,500

    Loss on sale of investment (E)      2,384

      Investment in SAS (A)      11,884

    (2) Net unrealized loss/gain—SAS (SE)      2,016

      Valuation allowance to market (A)      2,016

*d.* Valuation allowance to market (A)      34,395

    Net unrealized gains/losses (SE)      34,395

*e.* **Balance Sheet**

Assets

  Other investments      $223,785

Stockholders' Equity

  Net unrealized loss/gain      35,775

    (in Accumulated Other Comprehensive Income)

**Income Statement**

Nonoperating Items

  Loss on sale of investments      $ 2,384

  Investment income      12,266

*f.* If the securities were categorized as trading securities, there would be no net unrealized gain on the balance sheet. Therefore, when the securities were sold in *c*, there would not be a debit to the Net Unrealized Loss/Gain account and there would be a loss on the sale of $4,400 (net of the valuation allowance) reported on the income statement. Then, at year-end, the net unrealized gain of $34,395 would be reported on the income statement (not in stockholders' equity).

| Market Value | − | Cost | = | Balance Needed in Valuation Allowance | − | Unadjusted Balance in Valuation Allowance | = | Adjustment to Valuation Allowance |
|---|---|---|---|---|---|---|---|---|
| $223,785 | − | $118,010 | = | 35,775 | − | $1,380 ($3,396 − $2,016) | = | $34,395 |

# SECURITIES HELD FOR SIGNIFICANT INFLUENCE

When Dow Jones invests cash in various securities reported on its balance sheet as Other Investments, it is a passive investor. It seeks to earn a high rate of return on these investments, but it does not become involved in exerting influence over the financing and operating activities of the companies in which it invests. Accountants presume that investors are passive when they purchase less than 20 percent of the outstanding stock of another company, that is, when the market value method is used.

In many other situations, an investor may want to exert influence without becoming the majority owner (i.e., an investment in 20 to 50 percent of the outstanding stock) for a variety of long-term strategic reasons. The following are examples:

- A retailer may want to influence a manufacturer to be sure that it can obtain certain products designed to its specifications.

- A manufacturer may want to influence a computer consulting firm to ensure that it can incorporate cutting-edge technology in its manufacturing processes.

- A furniture manufacturer may recognize that a service company lacks experienced management and could prosper with additional managerial support.

Instead of applying the market value method (used for reporting passive investments), the **equity method** is used when an investor can exert significant influence over an investee which is presumed if the investor owns between 20 and 50 percent of the outstanding voting stock of the investee.

## CLASSIFYING INVESTMENTS IN ASSOCIATED COMPANIES

If management intends to exert significant influence over another company, the investment is most likely to be classified as long term. By being active in the management of another corporation, an investor may be able to earn a higher return on the investment. These are classified as long-term **investments in associated** (or **affiliated**) **companies** on the balance sheet (Investments in Associated Companies, for short).

## RECORDING INVESTMENTS UNDER THE EQUITY METHOD

Because the investing corporation can influence the operating and financing decisions of the investee, the financial effects reported by the investee affect the investor similarly:

1. If the investee reports positive net income for the year, then its net assets (Assets − Liabilities) also increase. The investor then increases its asset account (Investments in Associated Companies) and records investment income equal to its percentage share of the investee's net income. If the investee reports a net loss, the investor records the opposite effect.

2. If the investee declares and pays dividends during the year (a financing decision), its net assets are reduced. The investor then reduces its investment account and increases cash when it receives its share of the dividends. The effects are shown in the following T-account:

**Investments in Associated Companies**

| | |
|---|---|
| Beginning balance | |
| Purchases | Sales |
| (1) Company's share of investee's net income* | (2) Company's share of investee's declared dividends |
| Ending balance | |

* Or a credit if the investee reports a net loss for the period.

At the end of 1998, Dow Jones reported equity ownership in the following entities:

**LEARNING OBJECTIVE 3**
Analyze and report investments involving significant influence using the equity method.

**EQUITY METHOD** is used when an investor can exert significant influence over an investee; the method permits recording the investor's share of investee's income.

Long-term **INVESTMENTS IN ASSOCIATED (OR AFFILIATED) COMPANIES** are investments in stock held for the purpose of influencing the operating and financing strategies of the entity for the long term.

### NOTES TO FINANCIAL STATEMENTS

**NOTE 1. SUMMARY OF SIGNIFICANT ACCOUNTING POLICIES**

... The equity method of accounting is used for companies and other investments in which the company has significant influence, generally this represents common stock ownership or partnership equity of at least 20% and not more than 50% (see Note 4).

**NOTE 4. INVESTMENTS IN ASSOCIATED COMPANIES, AT EQUITY**

At December 31, 1998, the principal components of investments in associated companies, at equity were the following:

| Investment | Ownership | Description of Business |
|---|---|---|
| Business News (Asia) Private | 50% | Business and financial news television company broadcasting as CNBC Asia, in partnership with NBC |
| Business News (Europe) L.P. | 50 | Business and financial news television company broadcasting as CNBC Europe, in partnership with NBC |
| F.F. Soucy, Inc. & Partners, L.P. | 40 | Newsprint mill in Quebec, Canada |
| HB-Dow Jones S.A. | 42 | A part-owner of a publishing company in the Czech Republic |
| Interactive Video LLC | 33 | Provides Internet delivery of live and archived audio and video business and financial news, in partnership with MSNBC as CNBC/Dow Jones Business Video |
| SmartMoney | 50 | Publisher of *SmartMoney* magazine and SmartMoney.com serving the private-investor market throughout the U.S. and Canada, in partnership with Hearst Corp. |

For simplification, let's assume that Dow Jones had no long-term investments in companies in which it exerted significant influence at the beginning of 1999.

**Purchase of Equity Investments**   In 1999, Dow Jones purchased 40,000 shares of the outstanding voting common stock of Internet Financial News for $400,000 in cash. With its ownership level at 40 percent, it is presumed that Dow Jones has significant influence over IFN and must use the equity method to account for this investment. The purchase of the asset is recorded at cost.

| Investments in Associated Companies | | | |
|---|---|---|---|
| 1/1/99 | 0 | | |
| Purchase | 400,000 | | |
| Share of investee earnings | 200,000 | 80,000 | Share of investee dividends |
| 12/31/99 | 520,000 | | |

| Equity in Earnings of Associated Companies | | | |
|---|---|---|---|
| | | 0 | 1/1/99 |
| | | 200,000 | Share of investee earnings |
| | | 200,000 | 12/31/99 |

| Investments in associated companies (A) ....... | 400,000 | |
|---|---|---|
| Cash (A) ............................. | | 400,000 |

| Assets | = | Liabilities | + | Stockholders' Equity |
|---|---|---|---|---|
| Investments in associated companies (A) | +400,000 | | | |
| Cash | −400,000 | | | |

**Receipt of Dividends from Investee**   Because Dow Jones can influence the dividend policies of its long-term equity investments, any dividends it receives should not be recorded as investment income. If investment income were based on the amount of dividends paid, it would be possible for the investor to manipulate its income when significant influence existed. Instead, dividends received reduce its investment account (its asset) to reflect the effect of declaring dividends on the net assets of the investee. During 1999, IFN declared and paid a cash dividend of $2 per share to stockholders. Dow Jones received $80,000 in cash ($2 × 40,000 shares) from IFN.

| Cash (A) ............................... | 80,000 | |
| Investments in associated companies (A) .... | | 80,000 |

| Assets | | = | Liabilities | + | Stockholders' Equity |
|---|---|---|---|---|---|
| Cash | +80,000 | | | | |
| Investments in associated companies | −80,000 | | | | |

**Year-End Income** With equity investments, the investor often is actively involved in significant operating and financing decisions affecting the investee company. Because the investor participates in the process of earning income for the investee company, it is appropriate to base the investment income on the earnings of the investee company instead of the dividends it paid. At the end of 1998, IFN reported a net income of $500,000 for the year. Dow Jones's portion of the net income (that is, its percentage share of the investee's income) is $200,000 (40% × $500,000). If the investee reported a net loss for the period, the investor would record its percentage share of the loss by decreasing the investment account and recording equity in loss of associated companies (reported in Other Nonoperating Items on the income statement).

| Investments in associated companies (A) ........... | 200,000 | |
| Equity in earnings of associated companies (R) .... | | 200,000 |

| Assets | | = | Liabilities | + | Stockholders' Equity | |
|---|---|---|---|---|---|---|
| Investments in associated companies | +200,000 | | | | Equity in earnings of associated companies | +200,000 |

Based on these last two journal entries, you can see that the long-term Investments in Associated Companies account reported on the balance sheet does not reflect either cost or market. The investment account is increased for the cost of shares that were purchased and the proportionate share of the investee company's income. The account is reduced by the amount of dividends received from the investee company. At the end of the accounting period, accountants do not adjust the investment account to reflect changes in the fair market value of the securities that are held. If the securities were then sold, the difference between the cash received and the book value of the investment would be recorded as a gain or loss on sale.

**SELF-STUDY QUIZ**

Now let's reconstruct the activities that Dow Jones actually undertook in 1998 for its investments in associated companies, assuming a few transactions. Answer the following questions, using the T-accounts to help you infer the amounts. The dollars are in thousands.

**Balance Sheet Account**

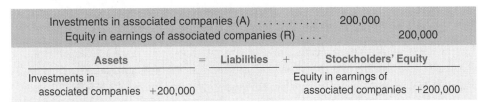

| Investments in Associated Companies (A) | | | |
|---|---|---|---|
| 1/1/98 | 46,064 | | |
| Purchase | 29,240 | 13,178 | Share of investee dividends |
| | | ? 21,647 | Share of investee net losses |
| 12/31/98 | 40,479 | | |

**Income Statement Account**

| Equity in Earnings/Losses of Associated Companies (R) | | |
|---|---|---|
| 1/1/98 | 0 | |
| Share of investee net losses | 21,653 | |
| 12/31/98 | 21,653 | |

| | |
|---|---|
| a. Purchased additional investments in associated companies for cash. Prepare the journal entry. | |
| b. Received cash dividends on the investments. Prepare the journal entry. | |
| c. At year-end, the investments in associated companies had a market value of $45,000; they also reported $50,000 in net losses for the year. Prepare the adjusting entry. | |
| d. What would be reported on the balance sheet related to the investments in associated companies on December 31, 1998?<br><br>On the income statement for 1998? | |

Check your response with the answer provided in the footnote at the bottom of this page.*

# FINANCIAL ANALYSIS

## MANAGERS' SELECTION OF ACCOUNTING ALTERNATIVES

The market value and equity methods are two alternative methods used to account for investments. The selection of a specific method is determined by the facts surrounding the investment, not by management discretion. Managers can freely choose between LIFO and FIFO or accelerated depreciation and straight-line depreciation. In the case of investments, managers may not simply choose either the market value or equity methods. Investments of less than 20 percent of the outstanding stock of a company are accounted for under the market value method, and investments of 20 percent to 50 percent are recorded under the equity method.

In some cases, managers may be able to structure the acquisition of stock in a manner that permits them to use the accounting method that they prefer. For example, a company that wants to use the market value method could purchase only 19.9 percent of the outstanding stock of another company. Why would managers want to be able to avoid using the market value method or the equity method? A typical explanation has to do with earnings volatility. Most managers prefer to minimize variations in reported earnings. If a company were going to buy stock in a firm that reported large earnings in some years and large losses in others, it might want to use the market value method. In this way, the investor would not have to report its share of the investee firm's earnings and losses. Likewise, an investor may want to use the equity method if the investee firm had relatively stable earnings but more significant variations in its stock price. By using the equity method, the investor does not have to report unrealized gains and losses on the investment.

Analysts who compare several companies must understand the way that differences in the market value and equity methods can affect earnings associated with similar investments. Analysts also should examine how management may affect reported earnings through the level of ownership that is acquired.

---

| * a. Investments in associated companies (A) | 29,240 | | d. **Balance Sheet** | | **Income Statement** | |
|---|---|---|---|---|---|---|
| Cash (A) | | 29,240 | *Assets* | | *Nonoperating Items* | |
| b. Cash (A) | 13,178 | | Investments in | | Equity in losses of | |
| Investments in associated companies (A) | | 13,178 | associated companies | $40,479 | associated companies | $21,653 |
| c. Equity in losses of associated companies (R) | 21,653 | | | | | |
| Investments in associated companies (A) | | 21,653 | | | | |

# A QUESTION OF **ETHICS**

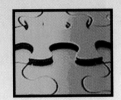

## IMPROPER INFLUENCE

A key assumption underlying accounting is that all transactions occur at "arm's length," that is, each party to the transaction is acting in his or her own self-interest. When one corporation is able to exert a significant influence over another (i.e., it owns 20 to 50 percent of the common stock), assuming that transactions between the corporations are at arm's length is unreasonable. The equity method is designed to overcome this problem.

Consider what might happen if an investor corporation could affect the dividend policy of an investee corporation. If dividends paid by the investee corporation could be reported by the investor as dividend income, the investor corporation could manipulate its income by influencing the dividend policy of the other company. In a bad year, the investor might request large dividend payments to bolster its income. In a good year, it might try to cut dividend payments to build up the investee company's retained earnings to support large dividends in the future when needed.

The equity method prevents this type of manipulation by not recognizing dividends as income. Instead, income from an investment in another company is based on a percentage of the affiliated company's reported net income.

The equity method is a good example of the way that accounting methods can affect the appearance and the reality of integrity in financial reporting.

# FOCUS ON **CASH FLOWS**

## INVESTMENTS

Many of the effects from applying the market value method to passive investments and the equity method to investments held for significant influence impact net income, but with a different, if any, cash flow effect. As you might expect, these items result in adjustments to net income on the statement of cash flows.

### Effect on Statement of Cash Flows

| IN GENERAL → | Effect on Cash Flows |
|---|---|
| **Operating Activities** | |
| Net income | $xxx |
| Adjusted for | |
|     Gains/losses on sale of investments | −/+ |
|     Equity in earnings/losses of associated companies | −/+ |
|     Dividends received from associated companies | + |
|     Net unrealized holding gains/losses on trading securities | −/+ |
| **Investing Activities** | |
|     Purchase of investments | − |
|     Sale of investments | + |

**FOCUS COMPANY ANALYSIS →** A partial statement of cash flows for Dow Jones for 1998 is presented here. Dow Jones does not invest in trading securities and will not therefore report any net unrealized holding gains or losses on the income statement. If it had, any unrealized losses would have been added and gains subtracted from net income in the Operating Activities section. However, in both investment portfolios (SAS and associated companies), Dow Jones sold and acquired securities during the year. Any gain on the sale is subtracted from net income, whereas any loss is added back in the Operating Activities section of the statement of cash flows. The cash resulting from the sale or purchase is reflected in the Investing Activities section.

The more interesting effect occurs from accounting for income under the equity method. Recall that cash dividends received from investees are not recorded as income; this amount is added to net income in the Operating Activities section. In addition, investors record as income their share of investees' earnings even though no cash is involved. This amount also needs to be adjusted; any equity in investee earnings needs to be deducted and any equity in investee losses needs to be added. Dow Jones appropriately adjusted net income for these items. In both the operating and investing activities sections, the effects related to accounting for investments have a significant impact on cash flows for Dow Jones.

Equity in losses +$21,653
Dividends + 13,178

**DOW JONES & CO. INC.**
**Consolidated Statement of Cash Flows (partial)**
**For the year ended December 31, 1998**
**(in thousands)**

**Operating Activities**

| | |
|---|---:|
| Consolidated net income | $  8,362 |
| Adjustments to reconcile net income to net cash provided by operating activities: | |
| Loss on disposition of businesses and investments | 126,085 |
| Equity in losses of associated companies, net of dividend distributions | 34,831 |
| (other adjustments—not detailed here) | 136,948 |
| Net cash provided by operating activities | **306,226** |

**Investing Activities**

| | |
|---|---:|
| Businesses and investments acquired | (55,663) |
| Disposition of businesses and investments | 478,574 |
| (other investing activities—not detailed here) | (217,250) |
| Net cash provided by investing activities | **205,661** |

# SECURITIES HELD FOR CONTROL

■ **LEARNING OBJECTIVE 4**

Analyze and report investments in controlling interests in subsidiaries in consolidated statements.

Earlier in this chapter, we discussed a number of strategic reasons for corporations to invest in other companies at a level that did not permit control (i.e., 50 percent or less ownership of the outstanding voting stock). Before we discuss financial reporting issues for situations in which a company owns more than 50 percent of the outstanding common stock of another corporation, we should consider management's reasons for acquiring this level of ownership.

The following are some of the reasons for acquiring control of another corporation:

1. *Vertical integration.* In this type of acquisition, a company acquires another at a different level in the channels of distribution. For example, Dow Jones owns a newsprint company that provides raw materials as well as a national delivery service.

2. *Horizontal growth.* These acquisitions involve companies at the same level in the channels of distribution. For example, Dow Jones has expanded internationally by creating or acquiring companies in major international markets in Asia and Europe.

3. *Synergy.* The operation of two companies together may be more profitable than the combined profitability of the companies as separate entities. Dow Jones has created or purchased a number of broadcast and internet news services. Merging and sharing news content may create more profits than operating separate entities could.

Understanding why one company has invested in other companies is a key factor in understanding the company's overall business strategy. Analysts often study recent acquisitions in an effort to predict future acquisitions. For example, if a retail company

acquires regional retailers in every region of the country except New England, it is reasonable to assume that it will seek to acquire a New England–based company. Similarly, if an internet company such as AOL buys a traditional media company such as Time Warner, analysts expect that similar acquisitions may occur between other Internet and traditional media companies. Dow Jones, which is the premier business news media company, is often discussed as a potential acquisition candidate for an Internet company.

## WHAT ARE CONSOLIDATED STATEMENTS?

Any corporate acquisition involves two companies. The **parent** is the company that gains a controlling influence over the other company. The **subsidiary** is the company that the parent acquires.

When a company acquires a controlling interest in another, **consolidated financial statements** must be presented. These statements combine the operations of two or more companies into a single set of statements. Basically, consolidated statements can be thought of as the adding together of the separate financial statements for two or more companies to make it appear as if a single company exists. Thus, the cash accounts for each company are added together as are the inventory accounts, land accounts, and others.

The notes to the Dow Jones annual report provide the following information:

> **NOTES TO FINANCIAL STATEMENTS**
>
> **NOTE 1. SUMMARY OF SIGNIFICANT ACCOUNTING POLICIES**
> THE CONSOLIDATED FINANCIAL STATEMENTS include the accounts of the company and its majority-owned subsidiaries. All significant intercompany transactions are eliminated in consolidation. . . .

As the Dow Jones note indicates, eliminating any *intercompany* items is necessary when consolidated statements are prepared. Remember that consolidated statements make it appear as if a single company exists when in fact two or more separate legal entities exist. Intercompany items would not exist for only a single corporation. For example, a debt owed by Dow Jones (the parent) to its newsprint subsidiary is not reported on a consolidated statement because a company cannot owe itself money.

## METHODS OF ACQUIRING A CONTROLLING INTEREST

From an accounting perspective, two methods are used to acquire a controlling interest. In some cases, the stock of one company, such as Internet Financial News (our fictitious example) or IFN, is acquired by exchanging shares for shares of another company, such as Dow Jones (the parent). Before the merger, the owners of IFN held shares in that company. After the merger, they hold shares in Dow Jones. If certain additional criteria are met, this type of acquisition is called a pooling of interests. To be accounted for as a pooling of interests, a transaction must meet a rigid list of criteria (discussed in advanced accounting courses). Basically, a pooling occurs when a stock-for-stock swap occurs. Under the pooling method, the assets of all of the affiliated companies are added together based on their *book value*. The assets are not revalued because a pooling is viewed as a rearrangement of ownership interest, not a purchase.

As an alternative, Dow Jones could offer cash to the owners of IFN. In that case, after the merger, the former owners of IFN hold cash but no stock in either company. This type of acquisition is known as a combination by **purchase.** Accountants view this as a *purchase/sale transaction.* As you learned in earlier chapters, assets that are purchased should be recorded in terms of their cost. Thus, there is no conceptual difference between the direct purchase of a building worth $500,000 and the purchase of a company that has a single asset, a building worth $500,000. On the acquisition date, the investment account reflects the amount paid or *market value* of the acquired shares. Recording the investment at an often higher value than original book value decreases

The **PARENT COMPANY** is the entity that gains a controlling influence over another company.

The **SUBSIDIARY COMPANY** is the entity that is acquired by the parent.

**CONSOLIDATED FINANCIAL STATEMENTS** are the financial statements of two or more companies that have been combined into a single set of financial statements as if the companies were one.

**REAL WORLD EXCERPT**

*Dow Jones & Co.*
ANNUAL REPORT

A **PURCHASE** is an acquisition that is completed by purchasing the subsidiary company's voting common stock for cash.

consolidated net income in the future when the related assets (often in the form of goodwill) expire and become expenses.

## CONSOLIDATED BALANCE SHEETS

In this chapter, we focus on the purchase method of recording business combinations because it is used most often in practice. We will review the alternative method at the end of the discussion.[3] To make the discussion a little easier, we use simplified data for Dow Jones (the parent) and IFN (the hypothetical acquired subsidiary) as shown in Exhibit 12.4.

EXHIBIT **12.4**

**Illustrative Data for Consolidation**

**DOW JONES AND IFN**
**Simplified Separate Balance Sheets**
**January 1, 20A, Immediately after Acquisition**

| (in millions) | Dow Jones | IFN |
|---|---|---|
| **Assets** | | |
| Cash and other current assets | $342 | $15 |
| Investment in IFN | 100 | |
| Plant and property (net) | 602 | 30 |
| Other assets | 447 | 45 |
| Total assets | 1,491 | 90 |
| **Liabilities and Stockholders' Equity** | | |
| Current liabilities | 600 | 10 |
| Noncurrent liabilities | 382 | |
| Stockholders' equity | 509 | 80 |
| Total liabilities and stockholders' equity | $1,491 | $90 |

**DOW JONES AND IFN**
**Simplified Separate Income Statements**
**Year ended December 31, 20A, One Year after Acquisition**

| (in millions) | Dow Jones | IFN |
|---|---|---|
| Revenues | $2,158 | $120 |
| Less: Expenses | 2,150 | 106 |
| Plus: Income from subsidiary | 14 | |
| Net income | $22 | $14 |

Let's assume that Dow Jones paid $100 (all numbers in millions) cash to buy all of IFN's stock, although the total *book value* of the stockholders' equity of IFN was only $80.[4] Thus, Dow Jones paid $20 more than book value. Why would Dow Jones pay more than book value for the investment? Actually, the answer is simple: Remember that the book value of an asset is not the same as its fair market value. Dow Jones had to pay fair market value to acquire IFN. The former owners would not have been willing to sell their stock for only book value.

In consolidation, the separate financial statements are combined into a single consolidated statement. The investment account must be eliminated to avoid double counting the subsidiary's assets and liabilities and the parent company's investment in those assets. The investment account balance of $100 on Dow Jones's books represents market value of the net assets (assets minus liabilities) at the date of acquisition. It must be eliminated against the $80 stockholders' equity of IFN, which is at *book value*

---

[3]At the time this chapter is being written, the FASB is considering eliminating pooling and requiring all acquisitions to be accounted for using the purchase method.

[4]Purchasing 100 percent of the outstanding stock results in a wholly owned subsidiary. Purchasing less than 100 percent of the stock results in *minority interest* in the subsidiary.

because the stock is no longer outstanding from a consolidated perspective. We will assume that an analysis of IFN's assets revealed the following facts:

- The book values of all assets and liabilities already on IFN's balance sheet were equal to market values.
- IFN had developed a good reputation with an important group of online investors, which increased IFN's overall value. For these reasons, Dow Jones was willing to pay $20 more than book value to acquire IFN's stock. The $20 difference between the purchase price of the company and the fair market value of its net assets (assets minus liabilities) that were acquired between the purchase cost of IFN and the market value of the investment is called **goodwill.** It may be analyzed as follows:

| | |
|---|---|
| Purchase price for 100% interest in IFN | $100 |
| Less: Net assets purchased, at market | 80 |
| Goodwill purchased | $ 20 |

**GOODWILL** is the difference between the purchase price of a company and the fair market value of the net assets (assets minus liabilities) that were acquired.

Goodwill is often attributed to the good reputation and customer appeal of an acquired company. All successful companies have some amount of goodwill, but it can be reported on the balance sheet *only* if it is acquired in a purchase transaction. Also, if the market value of IFN's assets and liabilities (e.g., property and equipment) had been different than their book values, each such item would also have been adjusted to market value.

To complete the process of consolidating Dow Jones and IFN, we want to eliminate the investment account and in its place add the assets and liabilities of IFN along with the acquired goodwill. We can accomplish this in the following four steps:

1. Subtracting the investment account balance of $100.
2. Adding the $20 goodwill purchased as an asset.
3. Subtracting the IFN stockholders' equity.
4. Adding what remains of the Dow Jones and IFN balance sheets together.

Due to the simplicity of this example, you can do the mental math to make these adjustments to the individual account balances shown in Exhibit 12.4 and then add together the amounts for each company. These adjustments and eliminations can also be entered into a spreadsheet program such as Microsoft Excel. An example of a spreadsheet is presented in Exhibit 12.5.

EXHIBIT **12.5**

**Spreadsheet for Consolidated Balance Sheet on the Date of Acquisition**

| | A | B | C | D | E |
|---|---|---|---|---|---|
| 1 | | Dow Jones | IFN | Eliminations | Consolidated |
| 2 | **ASSETS** | | | | |
| 3 | Cash and other current assets | $342 | $15 | | $357 |
| 4 | Investment in IFN | 100 | | (100) | |
| 5 | Plant and property (net) | 602 | 30 | | 632 |
| 6 | Other assets | 447 | 45 | | 492 |
| 7 | Goodwill | | | 20 | 20 |
| 8 | Total assets | 1,491 | 90 | (80) | 1,501 |
| 9 | | | | | |
| 10 | **LIABILITIES AND STOCKHOLDERS' EQUITY** | | | | |
| 11 | Current liabilities | 600 | 10 | | 610 |
| 12 | Noncurrent liabilities | 382 | | | 382 |
| 13 | Stockholders' equity | 509 | 80 | (80) | 509 |
| 14 | Total liabilities and stockholders' equity | $1,491 | $90 | (80) | $1,501 |

Microsoft Excel - Dow Jones - IFN Consolidation.xls

File Edit View Insert Format Tools Data Window Help

Sheet1 / Sheet2 / Sheet3 /

Ready

When these procedures are accomplished, the financial statement shown in Exhibit 12.6 is produced.

EXHIBIT **12.6**

**Consolidated Balance Sheet on the Date of Acquisition**

| DOW JONES AND SUBSIDIARIES | |
|---|---|
| Consolidated Balance Sheet | |
| January 1, 20A | |
| (in millions) | |
| **Assets** | |
| Cash and other current assets | $ 357 |
| Plant and property (net) | 632 |
| Other assets | 492 |
| Goodwill | 20 |
| Total assets | $1,501 |
| **Liabilities and Stockholders' Equity** | |
| Current liabilities | $ 610 |
| Noncurrent liabilities | 382 |
| Stockholders' equity | 509 |
| Total liabilities and stockholders' equity | $1,501 |

## CONSOLIDATED INCOME STATEMENTS

When we prepared the consolidated balance sheet, we combined the separate balance sheets to make it appear as if a single company exists. In consolidating the separate company income statements into a single statement, the revenues and expenses generated by the parent's own operations (excluding any investment income from the subsidiary) must be combined with the revenues and expenses of the subsidiary. The creation of goodwill (and the revaluation of assets, if any) also has implications for the consolidated income statement. This asset goodwill must be amortized in the consolidation process.

In the simple Dow Jones–IFN example, preparing the consolidated income statement then requires three steps (ignoring taxes):

1. Adding together Dow Jones's revenues from its own operations of $2,158 and IFN's revenues of $120.

2. Adding together Dow Jones's expenses related to its own operations of $2,150 and IFN's expenses of $106.

3. Adding to the expenses the $2 goodwill amortization (we assume a 10-year useful life); $20 ÷ 10 years = $2 per year.

Due to the simplicity of this example, you can directly prepare the simplified consolidated income statement in Exhibit 12.7. Complex adjustments and eliminations would normally be entered into a spreadsheet program.

EXHIBIT **12.7**

**Consolidated Income Statement**

| DOW JONES AND SUBSIDIARIES | |
|---|---|
| Consolidated Income Statement | |
| Year Ended December 31, 20A | |
| (in millions) | |
| Revenues ($2,158 + $120) | $2,278 |
| Expenses ($2,150 + $106 + $2) | 2,258 |
| Net income | $   20 |

Goodwill is created during the consolidation and is not recorded on the books of either Dow Jones or IFN. As a result, recording the amortization of goodwill as part of consolidation is necessary. Estimating the expected life of goodwill is very difficult. For some companies, goodwill may have economic value for an extremely long period. For others, it may exist for a very short time. Because of the difficulty in estimating the life of goodwill, GAAP currently require that goodwill be amortized over a realistic period not longer than 40 years.[5]

You will encounter a variety of amortization periods for goodwill. Compare the note for Dow Jones with several other notes:

GOODWILL is amortized using the straight-line method over various periods, principally forty years. The company evaluates annually whether there has been an other than temporary impairment in the value of goodwill.

*Dow Jones & Co.*
ANNUAL REPORT

Goodwill arising from business acquisitions is included in Intangible and Other Assets in the accompanying Consolidated Balance Sheets and is being amortized principally over 20 years on a straight-line basis.

*Snap On Tools*
ANNUAL REPORT

Goodwill—Goodwill is charged to net income on a straight-line basis over the periods estimated to be benefited, generally not exceeding five years.

*IBM*
ANNUAL REPORT

As a result of its investment in Infoseek, the Company recorded intangible assets of $460 million, including $421 million of goodwill, which are being amortized over an estimated useful life of two years.

*Disney*
ANNUAL REPORT

Goodwill is normally shown net of accumulated amortization on the company's balance sheet in a manner similar to the excerpt from Dow Jones's balance sheet:

*Dow Jones & Co.*
ANNUAL REPORT

|  | 1998 | 1997 |
| --- | --- | --- |
| Goodwill, less accumulated amortization of $58,610 in 1998 and $1,275,738 in 1997 | 86,554 | 387,787 |

Note that the balance in goodwill has declined because, when Dow Jones recorded the sale of its Telerate subsidiary during 1998, the associated goodwill along with its other assets and liabilities was also removed from the balance sheet.

---

[5]At the time this chapter is being written, the FASB is considering lowering that limit to 20 years with some exceptions.

# FINANCIAL **ANALYSIS**

## GOODWILL AMORTIZATION

The period over which goodwill is amortized is an important factor for analysts to consider. Goodwill can be a large portion of some companies' assets. The decision to amortize goodwill over 40 years instead of a shorter period can have a significant impact on reported earnings. When Disney purchased ABC in the mid-1990s, $16 billion of the $19 billion purchase price was allocated to the asset goodwill. The goodwill was amortized over 40 years, or $400 million per year ($16 billion ÷ 40 years). Had Disney been required to use the 20-year maximum currently proposed by the FASB and required by the International Accounting Standards Board, this amount would have risen to $800 million ($16 billion ÷ 20 years), which would have substantially reduced reported earnings over the next 20 years. Because the amortization of goodwill (like depreciation expense) is a noncash expense, decisions concerning amortization periods have no impact on cash flows from operations.

# KEY **RATIO ANALYSIS:**

## RETURN ON ASSETS (ROA)

**K**now the decision question:

How well has management used the total invested capital (provided by debt holders and stockholders) of the company during the period? It is computed* as follows:

$$\text{Return on Assets} = \frac{\text{Net Income}}{\text{Average Total Assets**}}$$

■ **LEARNING OBJECTIVE 5**

Analyze and interpret the return on assets ratio.

*In more complex return on total asset analyses, interest expense (net of tax) and minority interest are added back to net income in the numerator of the ratio, since the measure assesses return on capital independent of its source.
**Average Total Assets = (Beginning Total Assets + Ending Total Assets) ÷ 2

The 1998 ratio for Dow Jones:

$$\frac{\$8,362}{(\$1,919,734 + \$1,491,322) \div 2} = 0.005 \ (.5\%)$$

**E**xamine the ratio using two techniques:

| ① Comparisons over Time | | | | ② Comparisons with Competitors | |
|:---:|:---:|:---:|---|:---:|:---:|
| **Dow Jones** | | | | **New York Times** | **Knight-Ridder** |
| 1996 | 1997 | 1998 | | 1998 | 1998 |
| 7.1% | −34.2% | 0.5% | | 8.1% | 6.7% |

**Y**ou interpret the results carefully:

**IN GENERAL** → ROA measures how much the firm earned for each dollar of investment. It is the broadest measure of profitability and management effectiveness, independent of financing strategy. It allows investors to compare management's investment performance against alternative investment options with differing levels of risk (e.g., zero risk government treasury securities). Firms with higher ROA are doing a better job of selecting new investments, all other things equal. Company managers often compute the measure on a division-by-division basis and use it to evaluate division managers' relative performance.

**FOCUS COMPANY ANALYSIS** → ROA for the printing and publishing industry is 9.4 percent.[†]
The preceding computation indicates that Dow Jones's ROA is well below that amount. How-

| Selected Focus Company Comparisons: Return on Assets | |
|---|---|
| Harley-Davidson | 12.1% |
| Boston Beer | 6.9% |
| Papa John's | 7.1% |

---

[†]*MarketGuide* (1999).

ever, Dow Jones recorded a loss of $126.1 million on the sale of Telerate to Bridge Information Systems during the year. Without this loss, Dow Jones's ROA would have been 7.9 percent. Since the loss will not affect future periods' returns, when analysts use ROA to predict the future, they often remove such nonrecurring items. However, Dow Jones's ROA seems to be recovering from its huge loss in 1997, much of which was driven by its losses in the now-disposed-of Telerate venture.

**A FEW CAUTIONS:** Like ROE, ROA can be decomposed into its components.

$$\text{ROA} = \frac{\text{Net Profit}}{\text{Margin}} \times \text{Asset Turnover}$$

$$\frac{\text{Net Income}}{\text{Average Total Assets}} = \frac{\text{Net Income}}{\text{Net Sales}} \times \frac{\text{Net Sales}}{\text{Average Total Assets}}$$

From this, we can also see the relationship of ROA and ROE (ROE = ROA × Leverage Ratio). Like ROE, effective analysis of ROA also requires an understanding of why ROA differs from prior levels and that of its competitors. The preceding decomposition, as well as more detailed analyses of components of net profit margin and asset turnover, can provide that understanding.

## INTERNATIONAL **PERSPECTIVE**

### ALTERNATIVE METHODS OF ACCOUNTING FOR CORPORATE ACQUISITIONS

As noted earlier in the Dow Jones–IFN example, we recorded the cash acquisition as a purchase. If Dow Jones had acquired IFN in a stock-for-stock swap, the pooling of interests method could have been used. Under the pooling method, the assets of Dow Jones and IFN would have been added together based on their *book value*. The assets are not revalued and no goodwill or goodwill amortization is recorded. Thus, consolidated assets would have been $20 lower and net income would have been $2 higher. Since its denominator would be lower and the numerator would be higher, ROA would have been higher under pooling of interests.

Many managers prefer to use this method of accounting because it normally results in higher reported earnings. However many analysts believe that pooling of interests obscures the true profitability of a company. For example, analysts at Morgan Stanley Dean Witter recommend that investors go back to larger pooling acquisitions and recreate the goodwill that would have resulted.* They also note that use of pooling of interests is more limited in many other countries such as the United Kingdom, France, Japan, and Mexico, and is prohibited in Germany, Italy, the Netherlands, and Brazil.

Each year, financial markets become more international in scope. Investors and creditors who provide funds to corporations around the world must be sensitive to the range of accounting alternatives required in different countries.

---

*Trevor S. Harris, *Overcoming Accounting Differences: A Stockpickers Guide to the Numbers That Count,* Morgan Stanley Dean Witter (1998).

## SELF-STUDY **QUIZ**

Lexis Corporation purchased 100 percent of Nexis Company for $10 million and reports on a consolidated basis. On the date of acquisition, the book values of all of Nexis's assets were equal to market value, and its net book value was $6 million. Summary balance sheets for the two companies on the date of acquisition immediately after the acquisition is recorded follow:

|  | Lexis<br>(parent) | Nexis<br>(subsidiary) |
|---|---|---|
| Investment in Nexis | $10 | |
| Other Assets | 90 | $10 |
| Liabilities | 30 | 4 |
| Stockholders' Equity | 70 | 6 |

On the consolidated balance sheet, what would be the following balances?

1. Goodwill.

2. Stockholders' Equity.

3. Other Assets.

Check your answers with the answers in the footnote at the bottom of this page.*

# DEMONSTRATION **CASE A**

(Try to resolve the requirements before proceeding to the suggested solution that follows.)
Howell Equipment Corporation sells and services a major line of farm equipment. Both sales and service operations have been profitable. The following transactions affected the company during 20B:

*a.* Jan. 1   Purchased 2,000 shares of common stock of Dear Company at $40 per share. This was 1 percent of the shares outstanding. Management intends to actively trade these shares.

*b.* Dec. 28   Received $4,000 cash dividend on the Dear Company stock.

*c.* Dec. 31   Learned the current market price of the Dear stock, $39.

*Required:*

1. Prepare the journal entry for each of these transactions.
2. What accounts and amounts will be reported on the balance sheet at the end of 20B? On the income statement for 20B?

## SUGGESTED SOLUTION FOR CASE A

1.

| *a.* | Jan. 1 | Investment in trading securities (A) ................... | 80,000 | |
| | | Cash (A) ....................................... | | 80,000 |
| | | 2,000 shares × $40 per share | | |
| *b.* | Dec. 28 | Cash (A) ....................................... | 4,000 | |
| | | Investment income (R) ........................ | | 4,000 |
| *c.* | Dec. 31 | Net unrealized loss/gain on trading securities (E) ........ | 2,000 | |
| | | Valuation allowance to market (A) ................ | | 2,000 |

| Year | Market<br>Value | − | Cost | = | Balance Needed in<br>Valuation Allowance | − | Unadjusted Balance in<br>Valuation Allowance | = | Adjustment to<br>Valuation Allowance |
|---|---|---|---|---|---|---|---|---|---|
| 20B | $78,000<br>($39 × 2000<br>shares) | − | $80,000 | = | ($2,000) | − | $0 | = | ($2,000)<br>an unrealized loss<br>for the period |

---

*1. Purchase Price − Market Value of Net Assets = Goodwill   $10 − $6 = $4.

  2. The subsidiary's stockholders' equity is eliminated, leaving $70.

  3. $90 + $10 = $100.

2.  On the Balance Sheet

    *Current Assets*

    Investment in trading securities        $78,000

    On the Income Statement

    *Other Nonoperating Items*

    Investment income                                  $4,000

    Net unrealized loss on trading securities     2,000

# DEMONSTRATION **CASE B**

Assume the same facts as in Case A, except that the securities were purchased as available for sale.

*Required:*

1.  Prepare the journal entry for each of these transactions.
2.  What accounts and amounts will be reported on the balance sheet at the end of 20B? On the income statement for 20B?

## SUGGESTED SOLUTION FOR CASE B

1.

a.  Jan. 1    Investment in securities available for sale (A) . . . . . . . . . . .    80,000

              Cash (A) . . . . . . . . . . . . . . . . . . . . . . . . . . . . . . . . . . . . . .            80,000

              2,000 shares × $40 per share

b.  Dec. 28   Cash (A) . . . . . . . . . . . . . . . . . . . . . . . . . . . . . . . . . . . . . .    4,000

              Investment income (R) . . . . . . . . . . . . . . . . . . . . . . . . . . .            4,000

c.  Dec. 31   Net unrealized loss/gain on securities available for sale (SE) . .    2,000

              Valuation allowance to market (A) . . . . . . . . . . . . . . . . . . . .            2,000

| Year | Market Value | − | Cost | = | Balance Needed in Valuation Allowance | − | Unadjusted Balance in Valuation Allowance | = | Adjustment to Valuation Allowance |
|------|--------------|---|------|---|----------------------------------------|---|--------------------------------------------|---|------------------------------------|
| 20B | $78,000 ($39 × 2000 shares) | − | $80,000 | = | ($2,000) | − | $0 | = | ($2,000) an unrealized loss for the period |

2.  On the Balance Sheet

    *Current or Noncurrent Assets*

    Investment in securities

    available for sale                $78,000

    *Stockholders' Equity*

    Accumulated other comprehensive income

    Net unrealized loss on securities

    available for sale                  2,000

    On the Income Statement

    *Other Nonoperating Items*

    Investment income        $4,000

# DEMONSTRATION **CASE C**

On January 1, 20A, Connaught Company purchased 40 percent of the outstanding voting shares of London Company in the open market for $85,000 cash and exerted significant influence over London Company during the year. London declared $10,000 in cash dividends and reported net income of $60,000 for the year.

*Required:*

1.  Prepare the journal entries for 20A.
2.  What accounts and amounts were reported on Connaught's balance sheet at the end of 20A? On Connaught's income statement for 20A?

## SUGGESTED SOLUTION FOR CASE C

1. Jan. 1   Investments in associated companies (A) . . . . . . . . . . . . . . .   85,000
              Cash (A) . . . . . . . . . . . . . . . . . . . . . . . . . . . . . . . . . . . . . . . . .               85,000
   Dividends  Cash (A) [40% × $10,000]  . . . . . . . . . . . . . . . . . . . . . . . . . . .   4,000
              Investments in associated companies (A) . . . . . . . . . . . . . .                4,000
   Dec. 31   Investments in associated companies (A) [40% × $60,000] . .   24,000
              Equity in earnings of associated companies (R)  . . . . . . . . .              24,000

2. On the Balance Sheet                      On the Income Statement
   *Noncurrent Assets*                        *Other Nonoperating Items*
     Investments in associated                    Equity in earnings of
        companies            $105,000                associated companies        $24,000

# DEMONSTRATION **CASE D**

On January 1, 20A, Connaught Company purchased 100 percent of the outstanding voting shares of London Company in the open market for $85,000 cash. On the date of acquisition, the market value of London Company's operational assets was $79,000.

*Required:*
1. Was this combination by pooling of interests or by purchase? Explain.
2. Give the journal entry that Connaught Company should make at date of acquisition. If none is required, explain why.
3. Give the journal entry that London Company should make at date of acquisition. If none is required, explain why.
4. Analyze the acquisition to determine the amount of goodwill purchased.
5. Should London Company's assets be included on the consolidated balance sheet at book value or market value? Explain.

## SUGGESTED SOLUTION FOR CASE D

1. The purchase method should be used because the subsidiary's stock was acquired for cash.
2. Jan. 1, 20   Investment in subsidiary (A) . . . . . . . . . . . . . . . . . . . . . . .   85,000
                  Cash (A)  . . . . . . . . . . . . . . . . . . . . . . . . . . . . . . . . . . .               85,000
3. London Company does not record a journal entry related to the purchase of stock by Connaught Company; the transaction was between Connaught and the stockholders of London Company. The transaction did not directly involve London Company.
4. Purchase price for London Company        $85,000
   Market value of net assets purchased       79,000
   Goodwill                                  $ 6,000
5. Under the purchase method, London Company's assets should be included on the consolidated balance sheet at their market values as of the date of acquisition. The cost principle applies because a purchase/sale transaction is assumed when the combination is accounted for as a purchase. When the pooling of interests method is used, the subsidiary's assets are reported on the consolidated balance sheet at their book value.

## CHAPTER **TAKE-AWAYS**

1. **Understand the three major categories of intercorporate investments.   p. 640**
   Companies acquire stock in other companies:
   • As passive investments to earn a return on funds until the cash is needed in the short or long term (presumed if owning less than 20 percent of the outstanding voting shares of the investee).
   • To exert significant influence over the investee firm's operating and financing policies (presumed if owning between 20 and 50 percent of the outstanding voting shares of the investee).

- To control the operating and financing policies of another company (presumed if owning more than 50 percent of the outstanding voting shares of the investee).

2. **Analyze and report passive investments in securities using the market value method.   p. 642**

Passive investments may be classified as trading securities (actively traded to maximize return) or securities available for sale (earn a return but are not as actively traded), depending on management's intent. The investments are recorded at cost and adjusted to *market value* at year-end. A valuation allowance is increased or decreased to arrive at market value with the resulting unrealized holding gain or loss recorded. For trading securities, the net unrealized gains and losses are reported in net income; for securities available for sale, the net unrealized gains and losses are reported as a component of stockholders' equity in other comprehensive income. Any dividends earned are reported as revenue and any gains or losses on sales of passive investments are reported on the income statement.

3. **Analyze and report investments involving significant influence using the equity method.   p. 649**

Under the *equity method,* the investor records the investment at cost at the date of acquisition. Each period thereafter, the investment amount is increased (or decreased) by the proportionate interest in the income (or loss) reported by the investee corporation and decreased by the proportionate share of the dividends declared by the investee corporation. Each period the investor recognizes as revenue its proportionate share of the income (or loss) reported by the investee company.

The investing section of the statement of cash flows discloses purchases and sales of investments. In the operating section, net income is adjusted for any gains or losses on sales of investments, equity in the earnings of associated companies (net of dividends received), and net unrealized gains or losses on trading securities.

4. **Analyze and report investments in controlling interests in subsidiaries in consolidated statements.   p. 654**

The concept of consolidation is based on the view that a parent company and its subsidiaries constitute one economic entity. Therefore, the separate income statements, balance sheets, and statements of cash flows should be combined each period on an item-by-item basis as a single set of consolidated financial statements. Ownership of a controlling interest of another corporation may be accounted for as either a pooling of interests or a combination by purchase:

- The *pooling of interests* method usually is used when the parent company exchanges shares of its own voting stock for a controlling interest in the voting shares of the subsidiary. The book values of the two entities are added together in creating the consolidated statements.

- Under the *purchase method,* the parent company usually pays cash and/or incurs debt to acquire the voting shares of the subsidiary. In these circumstances, a purchase/sale transaction has been completed, and the acquisition is accounted for in conformity with the cost principle, with the subsidiary's assets and liabilities measured at their market values. Any amount paid above the market value of the net assets is reported as goodwill by the parent company.

5. **Analyze and interpret the return on assets ratio.   p. 660**

The return on assets ratio measures how much the company earned for each dollar of assets. It provides information on profitability and management's effectiveness, with an increasing ratio over time suggesting increased efficiency. It is computed as net income divided by average total assets.

Each year, many companies report healthy profits but file for bankruptcy. Some investors consider this situation to be a paradox, but sophisticated analysts understand how this situation can occur. These analysts recognize that the income statement is prepared under the accrual concept (revenue is reported when earned and the related expense is matched with the revenue). The income statement does not report cash collections and cash payments. Troubled companies usually file for bankruptcy because they cannot meet their cash obligations (for example, they cannot pay their suppliers or meet their required interest payments). The income statement does not help analysts assess the cash flows of a company. The statement of cash flows discussed in Chapter 13 is designed to help statement users evaluate a company's cash inflows and outflows.

## KEY **RATIO**

**Return on assets** measures how much the company earned on every dollar of assets during the period. A high or rising ratio suggests that the company is managing its assets efficiently. It is computed as follows (p. 660):

$$\text{Return on Assets (ROA)} = \frac{\text{Net Income}}{\text{Average Total Assets*}}$$

*(Beginning Total Assets + Ending Total Assets) ÷ 2

## FINDING **FINANCIAL INFORMATION**

**BALANCE SHEET**
*Current Assets*
　　Investment in trading securities (net of valuation allowance)
　　Investment in securities available for sale (net of valuation allowance)
*Noncurrent Assets*
　　Investment in securities available for sale (net of valuation allowance)
　　Investment in associated companies
*Stockholders' Equity*
　　Accumulated other comprehensive income:
　　Net unrealized loss/gain on securities available for sale

**INCOME STATEMENT**
*Other Nonoperating Items*
　　Investment income
　　Loss/gain on sale of investments
　　Net unrealized loss/gain on trading securities
　　Equity in earnings/losses of associated companies

**STATEMENT OF CASH FLOWS**
*Operating Activities*
　　Net income adjusted for:
　　　　Gains/losses on sale of investments
　　　　Equity in earnings/losses of associated companies
　　　　Dividends received from associated companies
　　　　Net unrealized gains/losses on trading securities

**NOTES**
*In various notes*
　　Accounting policies on methods for investments
　　Details on securities held as trading securities and available for sale, for significant influence, and for control (e.g., cost, market value, unrealized holding gains and losses)

## KEY **TERMS**

**Consolidated Financial Statements** p. 655

**Equity Method** p. 649

**Goodwill** p. 657

**Investments in Associated (or Affiliated) Companies** p. 649

**Market Value Method** p. 642

**Parent Company** p. 655

**Purchase** p. 655

**Securities Available for Sale** p. 643

**Subsidiary Company** p. 655

**Trading Securities** p. 643

**Unrealized Holding Gains and Losses** p. 643

## QUESTIONS

1. Explain the difference between a short-term investment and a long-term investment.
2. Explain the application of the cost principle to the purchase of capital stock in another company.
3. Under the market value method, when and how does the investor company measure revenue?

4. Under the equity method, why does the investor company measure revenue on a proportionate basis when income is reported by the investee company rather than when dividends are declared?
5. Under the equity method, dividends received from the investee company are not recorded as revenue. To record dividends as revenue involves double counting. Explain.
6. What is a parent–subsidiary relationship?
7. Explain the basic concept underlying consolidated statements.
8. What is the basic element that must be present before consolidated statements are appropriate?
9. What is pooling of interests?
10. What is a combination by purchase?
11. What are intercompany eliminations?
12. What is goodwill?

## MINI-EXERCISES

**M12–1** **Matching Ownership Levels and Measurement and Reporting Methods**   ■ **LO1**
Match the following:

| *Measurement Method* | *Level of Ownership of the Voting Capital Stock* |
|---|---|
| _____ Market value method | *a.* More than 50 percent ownership. |
| _____ Equity method | *b.* Less than 20 percent ownership. |
| _____ Consolidation | *c.* At least 20 percent but not more than 50 percent ownership. |

**M12–2** **Matching Measurement Methods and Balances in the Investment Account**   ■ **LO1**
Match the following items that relate to the long-term investment amount reported on the balance sheet of the investor company:

| *Measurement Method* | *Explanation of Balance in the Investment Account* |
|---|---|
| _____ Market value method | *a.* Current market value. |
| _____ Equity method | *b.* Original cost plus proportionate part of the income of the investee, less proportionate part of the dividends declared by investee. |

**M12–3** **Recording Trading Securities Transactions**   ■ **LO2**
During 20B, Princeton Company acquired some of the 50,000 outstanding shares of the common stock, par $10, of Cox Corporation as trading securities. The accounting period for both companies ends December 31. Give the journal entries for each of the following transactions that occurred during 20B:

| | | |
|---|---|---|
| July | 2 | Purchased 8,000 shares of Cox common stock at $28 per share. |
| Dec. | 31 | Cox Corporation declared and paid a cash dividend of $2 per share. |
| | 31 | Learned the current market price of Cox stock, $25 per share. |

**M12–4** **Recording Available-for-Sale Securities Transactions**   ■ **LO2**
Using the data in M12–3, assume that Princeton management purchased the Cox stock for the available-for-sale portfolio instead of the trading securities portfolio. Give the journal entries for each of the transactions listed.

**M12–5** **Determining Financial Statement Effects of Trading Securities Transactions**   ■ **LO2**
Using the following categories, indicate the effects of the transactions listed in M12–3. Use + for increase and − for decrease and indicate the amounts.

| | Balance Sheet | | | Income Statement | | |
|---|---|---|---|---|---|---|
| Transaction | Assets | Liabilities | Stockholders' Equity | Revenues | Expenses | Net Income |

**M12–6** **Determining Financial Statement Effects of Available-for-Sale Securities Transactions**   ■ **LO2**
Using the following categories, indicate the effects of the transactions listed above in M12–4. Use + for increase and − for decrease and indicate the amounts.

|  | Balance Sheet | | | | Income Statement | | |
| --- | --- | --- | --- | --- | --- | --- | --- |
| Transaction | Assets | Liabilities | Stockholders' Equity | | Revenues | Expenses | Net Income |

**LO3**    **M12–7**    **Recording Equity Method Securities Transactions**

On January 1, 20B, UBuy.com acquired 25 percent (10,000 shares) of the common stock of E-Net Corporation. The accounting period for both companies ends December 31. Give the journal entries for each of the following transactions that occurred during 20B:

    July    2   E-Net declared and paid a cash dividend of $3 per share.

    Dec. 31   E-Net reported net income of $200,000.

**LO3**    **M12–8**    **Determining Financial Statement Effects of Equity Method Securities**

Using the following categories, indicate the effects of the transactions listed in M12–7. Use + for increase and − for decrease and indicate the accounts affected and the amounts.

|  | Balance Sheet | | | | Income Statement | | |
| --- | --- | --- | --- | --- | --- | --- | --- |
| Transaction | Assets | Liabilities | Stockholders' Equity | | Revenues | Expenses | Net Income |

# EXERCISES

**LO1**    **E12–1**    **Comparing Primary Characteristics of Market Value and Equity Methods**

Company A purchased a certain number of Company B's outstanding voting shares at $18 per share as a long-term investment. Company B had outstanding 20,000 shares of $10 par value stock. On a separate sheet, complete the following matrix relating to the measurement and reporting by Company A after acquisition of the shares of Company B stock.

| Questions | Market Value Method | Equity Method |
| --- | --- | --- |
| a. What is the applicable level of ownership by Company A of Company B to apply the method? | Percent | Percent |
| For b, e, f, and g, assume the following: | | |
|    Number of shares acquired of Company B stock | 1,500 | 5,000 |
|    Net income reported by Company B in the first year | $60,000 | $60,000 |
|    Dividends declared by Company B in the first year | $15,000 | $15,000 |
|    Market price at end of first year, Company B stock, $15 | | |
| b. At acquisition, the investment account on the books of Company A should be debited at what amount? | $ | $ |
| c. On what basis should Company A recognize revenue earned on the stock of Company B? Explanation required. | | |
| d. After acquisition date, on what basis should Company A change the balance of the investment account in respect to the stock of Company B owned (other than for disposal of the investment)? Explanation required. | | |
| e. What is the balance in the investment account on the books of Company A at the end of the first year? | $ | $ |
| f. What amount of revenue from the investment in Company B should Company A report at the end of the first year? | $ | $ |
| g. What amount of unrealized loss should Company A report at the end of the first year? | $ | $ |

**LO2**    **E12–2**    **Recording Transactions in the Trading Securities Portfolio**

On June 30, 20A, MetroMedia, Inc., purchased 10,000 shares of Mitek stock for $20 per share. Management purchased the stock for speculative purposes and recorded the stock in the trading securities portfolio. The following information pertains to the price per share of Mitek stock:

|  | Price |
|---|---|
| 12/31/20A | $24 |
| 12/31/20B | 31 |
| 12/31/20C | 25 |

MetroMedia sold all of the Mitek stock on February 14, 20D, at a price of $23 per share. Prepare any journal entries that are required by the facts presented in this case.

**E12–3** **Recording Transactions in the Available-for-Sale Portfolio**    ▦ **LO2**

Using the data in E12–2, assume that MetroMedia management purchased the Mitek stock for the available-for-sale portfolio instead of the trading securities portfolio. Prepare any journal entries that are required by the facts presented in the case.

**E12–4** **Reporting Gains and Losses in the Trading Securities Portfolio**    ▦ **LO2**

On March 10, 20B, General Solutions, Inc., purchased 5,000 shares of MicroTech stock for $50 per share. Management purchased the stock for speculative purposes and recorded it in the trading securities portfolio. The following information pertains to the price per share of MicroTech stock:

|  | Price |
|---|---|
| 12/31/20B | $55 |
| 12/31/20C | 40 |
| 12/31/20D | 42 |

General Solutions sold all of the MicroTech stock on September 12, 20E, at a price of $39 per share. Prepare any journal entries that are required by the facts presented in this case.

**E12–5** **Reporting Gains and Losses in the Available-for-Sale Portfolio**    ▦ **LO2**

Using the data in E12–4, assume that General Solutions management purchased the MicroTech stock for the available-for-sale portfolio instead of the trading securities portfolio. Prepare any journal entries that are required by the facts presented in the case.

**E12–6** **Recording and Reporting an Equity Method Security**    ▦ **LO3**

Felicia Company acquired some of the 60,000 shares of outstanding common stock (no-par) of Nueces Corporation during 20E as a long-term investment. The annual accounting period for both companies ends December 31. The following transactions occurred during 20E:

Jan.  10  Purchased 21,000 shares of Nueces common stock at $12 per share.
Dec.  31  Received the 20E financial statement of Nueces Corporation, which reported net income of $90,000.
Dec.  31  Nueces Corporation declared and paid a cash dividend of $0.60 per share.
Dec.  31  Determined market price of Nueces stock to be $11 per share.

*Required:*

1. What accounting method should the company use? Why?

2. Give the journal entries for each of these transactions. If no entry is required, explain why.

3. Show how the long-term investment and the related revenue should be reported on the 20E financial statements of the company.

**E12–7** **Interpreting the Effects of Equity Method Investments on Cash Flow from Operations**    ▦ **LO3**

Using the data in E12–6, answer the following questions.

*Required:*

1. On the current year cash flow statement, how would the investing section of the statement be affected by the above transactions?

2. On the current year cash flow statement (indirect method), how would the equity in the earnings of the associated company and the dividends from the associated company affect the operating section? Explain the reasons for the effects.

■ **LO4**

DaimlerChrysler

**E12–8**

### Interpreting Consolidation Policy

The annual report for DaimlerChrysler includes the statement that "intercompany accounts and transactions have been eliminated in consolidation." In your own words, explain the meaning of this statement. Why is it necessary to eliminate all intercompany accounts and transactions in consolidation?

■ **LO4**

Colgate-Palmolive

**E12–9**

### Determining the Appropriate Accounting Treatment for an Acquisition

The notes to the financial statements of Colgate-Palmolive contained the following information:

> **2. Acquisitions**
>
> In March 1992, the Company acquired the Mennen Company for an aggregate price of $670 million paid with 11.6 million shares of the Company's common stock and $127 million in cash.

Should Colgate-Palmolive account for this transaction as a purchase or a pooling? Explain.

■ **LO4**

**E12–10**

### Analyzing Goodwill and Reporting the Consolidated Balance Sheet

On January 1, 20A, Company P purchased 100 percent of the outstanding voting shares of Company S in the open market for $80,000 cash. On that date (prior to the acquisition), the separate balance sheets (summarized) of the two companies reported the following book values:

|  | Immediately after the Acquisition January 1, 20A | |
| --- | --- | --- |
|  | Company P | Company S |
| Cash | $ 12,000 | $18,000 |
| Investment in Co. S (at cost) | 80,000 |  |
| Property and Equipment (net) | 48,000 | 42,000 |
| Total assets | $140,000 | $60,000 |
| Liabilities | $ 40,000 | $ 9,000 |
| Common stock: |  |  |
| Company P (no-par) | 90,000 |  |
| Company S (par $10) |  | 40,000 |
| Retained earnings | 10,000 | 11,000 |
| Total liabilities and stockholders' equity | $140,000 | $60,000 |

It was determined on the date of acquisition that the market value of the assets and liabilities of Company S were equal to their book values.

*Required:*

1. Was this a combination by pooling of interests or by purchase? Explain why.
2. Give the journal entry that Company P made at date of acquisition to record the investment. If none is required, explain why.
3. Analyze the acquisition to determine the amount of goodwill purchased.
4. Prepare a consolidated balance sheet immediately after acquisition.

■ **LO4**

**E12–11**

### Determining Consolidated Net Income

Assume that P Company acquired S Company on January 1, 20A, for $100,000 cash. At the time, the net book value of S Company was $90,000 and the market value of all of S Company's assets and liabilities equaled their book values. Any goodwill will be amortized over 10 years. During 20A, the companies reported the following results:

| | P Company | S Company |
|---|---|---|
| Revenues related to their own operations | $500,000 | $75,000 |
| Expenses related to their own operations | 350,000 | 50,000 |

Compute consolidated net income for the year ended December 31, 20A.

**E12–12 Interpreting Goodwill Accounting Policy**

Wells Fargo is one of the best-known names in banking in the United States. The company's annual report states:

> Goodwill, representing the excess of purchase price over the fair value of net assets acquired, results from acquisitions made by the Company. Substantially all of the Company's goodwill is being amortized using the straight-line method over 25 years.

Based on the discussion in this chapter, express this policy in your own words.

 **LO4**

Wells Fargo and Company

**E12–13 Interpreting Goodwill Disclosures**

Disney owns theme parks, movie studios, television and radio stations, newspapers, and television networks, including ABC and ESPN. Its balance sheet recently reported goodwill in the amount of $16 billion, which is more than 30 percent of the company's total assets. This percentage is very large compared to that of most companies. Explain why you think Disney has such a large amount of goodwill reported on its balance sheet.

**LO4**

Disney

**E12–14 Analyzing and Interpreting the Return on Assets Ratio**

Timberland is a leading designer of shoes and clothing. In a recent year, it reported the following:

**LO5**

Timberland

| | Current Year | Prior Year |
|---|---|---|
| Revenue | $862,168 | $796,458 |
| Net income | 59,156 | 47,321 |
| Total assets | 469,467 | 420,003 |
| Total stockholders' equity | 266,193 | 214,895 |

*Required:*

1. Determine the return on assets ratio for the current year.
2. Explain the meaning of the ratio.

## PROBLEMS

**P12–1 Recording Passive Investments** (AP12–1)

On March 1, 20A, HiTech Industries purchased 10,000 shares of Integrated Services Company for $20 per share. The following information applies to the stock price of Integrated Services:

**LO2**

| | Price |
|---|---|
| 12/31/20A | $18 |
| 12/31/20B | 24 |
| 12/31/20C | 30 |

*Required:*

1. Prepare journal entries to record the facts in the case, assuming that HiTech purchased the shares for the trading portfolio.
2. Prepare journal entries to record the facts in the case, assuming that HiTech purchased the shares for the available-for-sale portfolio.

**LO2**        **P12–2**    **Reporting Passive Investments** (AP12–2)

During January 20A, Crystal Company purchased the following shares as a long-term investment:

| Stock | Number of Shares Outstanding | Purchase | Cost per Share |
|---|---|---|---|
| Q Corporation Common (no-par) | 90,000 | 12,600 | $ 5 |
| R Corporation Preferred, nonvoting (par $10) | 20,000 | 12,000 | 30 |

Subsequent to acquisition, the following data were available:

| | 20A | 20B |
|---|---|---|
| Net income reported at December 31: | | |
| Q Corporation | $30,000 | $36,000 |
| R Corporation | 40,000 | 48,000 |
| Dividends declared and paid per share during the year: | | |
| Q Corporation common stock | $0.80 | $0.85 |
| R Corporation preferred stock | 0.90 | 0.90 |
| Market value per share at December 31: | | |
| Q Corporation common stock | $ 4.00 | $ 4.00 |
| R Corporation preferred stock | 29.00 | 30.00 |

*Required:*

1. What accounting method should be used for the investment in Q common stock? R preferred stock? Why?

2. Give the journal entries for the company for each year in parallel columns (if none, explain why) for each of the following:

   *a.* Purchase of the investments.

   *b.* Income reported by Q and R Corporations.

   *c.* Dividends received from Q and R Corporations.

   *d.* Market value effects at year-end.

3. For each year, show how the following amounts should be reported on the financial statements:

   *a.* Long-term investment.

   *b.* Stockholders' equity—net unrealized loss.

   *c.* Revenues.

**LO2, 3**    **P12–3**    **Recording Passive Investments and Investments for Significant Influence**

On August 4, 20A, Coffman Corporation purchased 1,000 shares of Wefald Company for $45,000. The following information applies to the stock price of Wefald Company:

| | Price |
|---|---|
| 12/31/20A | $52 |
| 12/31/20B | 47 |
| 12/31/20C | 38 |

Wefald Company declares and pays cash dividends of $2 per share on June 1 of each year.

*Required:*

1. Prepare journal entries to record the facts in the case, assuming that Coffman purchased the shares for the trading portfolio.

2. Prepare journal entries to record the facts in the case, assuming that Coffman purchased the shares for the available-for-sale portfolio.

3. Prepare journal entries to record the facts in the case, assuming that Coffman used the equity method to account for the investment. Coffman owns 30 percent of Wefald and Wefald reported $50,000 in income each year.

**P12–4** **Comparing Methods to Account for Various Levels of Ownership of Voting Stock** ■ **LO2, 3**
(AP12–3)

Company C had outstanding 30,000 shares of common stock, par value $10 per share. On January 1, 20B, Company D purchased some of these shares at $25 per share. At the end of 20B, Company C reported the following: income, $50,000, and cash dividends declared and paid during the year, $25,500. The market value of Company C stock at the end of 20B was $22 per share.

*Required:*

1. For each of the following cases (in the tabulation), identify the method of accounting that Company D should use. Explain why.

2. Give the journal entries for Company D at the dates indicated for each of the two independent cases, assuming that the investments will be held long term. If no entry is required, explain why. Use the following format:

| Tabulation of Items | Case A 3,600 Shares Purchased | Case B 10,500 Shares Purchased |
|---|---|---|

a. Entry to record the acquisition at January 1, 20B.

b. Entry to recognize the income reported by Company C for 20B.

c. Entry to recognize the dividends declared and paid by Company C.

d. Entry to recognize market value effect at end of 20B.

3. Complete the following schedule to show the separate amounts that should be reported on the 20B financial statements of Company D:

| | Dollar Amounts | |
|---|---|---|
| | Case A | Case B |
| **Balance sheet** | | |
| Investments | | |
| Stockholders' equity | | |
| **Income statement** | | |
| Investment income | | |

4. Explain why assets, stockholders' equity, and revenues for the two cases are different.

**P12–5** **Comparing the Market Value and Equity Methods** ■ **LO2, 3**

Ship Corporation had outstanding 100,000 shares of no-par common stock. On January 10, 20B, Shore Company purchased a block of these shares in the open market at $20 per share. At the end of 20B, Ship reported net income of $300,000 and cash dividends of $.60 per share. At December 31, 20B, Ship stock was selling at $18 per share. This problem involves two separate cases:

**Case A** Purchase of 10,000 shares of Ship common stock.

**Case B** Purchase of 40,000 shares of Ship common stock.

*Required:*

1. For each case, identify the accounting method that the company should use. Explain why.

2. For each case, in parallel columns, give the journal entries for each of the following (if no entry is required, explain why):

    *a.* Acquisition.

    *b.* Revenue recognition.

    *c.* Dividends received.

    *d.* Market value effects.

3. For each case, show how the following should be reported on the 20B financial statements:

    *a.* Long-term investments.

    *b.* Shareholders' equity.

    *c.* Revenues.

4. Explain why the amounts reported in requirement 3 are different for the two cases.

**LO2,3**      **P12–6**

**Determining Cash Flow Statement Effects of Passive Investments and Investments for Significant Influence**

During 20H, Russell Company purchased some of the 90,000 shares of common stock, par $8, of Sea Tuna, Inc., as a long-term investment. The annual accounting period for each company ends December 31. The following transactions occurred during 20H:

Jan.   7   Purchased 40,500 shares of Sea Tuna stock at $32 per share.

Dec. 31   Received the 20H financial statement of Sea Tuna, which reported net income of $200,000.

      31   Sea Tuna declared and paid a cash dividend of $3 per share.

      31   Learned the current market price of Sea Tuna stock, $40 per share.

Indicate how the operating activities and/or investing activities section of the cash flow statement will be affected by each transaction.

**LO4**      **P12–7**

**Analyzing Goodwill and Reporting the Consolidated Balance Sheet**

On January 4, 20A, Company P acquired all 8,000 outstanding shares of Company S for $12 cash per share. Immediately after the acquisition, the balance sheets reflected the following:

| | Balances, Jan. 4, 20A, Immediately after Acquisition | |
| --- | --- | --- |
| | Company P | Company S |
| Cash | $ 22,000 | $23,000 |
| Investment in Company S (100%), at cost | 96,000 | |
| Property and equipment (net) | 132,000 | 65,000* |
|    Total assets | $250,000 | $88,000 |
| | | |
| Liabilities | $ 27,000 | $12,000 |
| Common stock (par $5) | 120,000 | 40,000 |
| Retained earnings | 103,000 | 36,000 |
|    Total liabilities and stockholders' equity | $250,000 | $88,000 |

*Determined by Company P to have a market value of $72,000 at date of acquisition.

*Required:*

1. Was this a combination by pooling of interests or by purchase? Explain why.

2. Give the journal entry that Company P made to record the acquisition.

3. Analyze the acquisition to determine the amount of goodwill purchased.

4. Should Company S's assets be included on the consolidated balance sheet at book value or market value? Explain.

5. Prepare a consolidated balance sheet immediately after acquisition. (*Hint:* Consider your answer to requirement 4.)

# ALTERNATE PROBLEMS

**AP12–1 Recording Passive Investments (P12–1)**  ◼ **LO2**

On September 15, 20A, James Media Corporation purchased 5,000 shares of Community Broadcasting Company for $30 per share. The following information applies to the stock price of Community Broadcasting:

|  | Price |
|---|---|
| 12/31/20A | $32 |
| 12/31/20B | 24 |
| 12/31/20C | 20 |

*Required:*

1. Prepare journal entries to record the facts in the case, assuming that James Media purchased the shares for the trading portfolio.

2. Prepare journal entries to record the facts in the case, assuming that James Media purchased the shares for the available-for-sale portfolio.

**AP12–2 Reporting Passive Investments (P12–2)**  ◼ **LO2**

During January 20A, Hexagon Company purchased 12,000 shares of the 200,000 outstanding common shares (no-par value) of Seven Corporation at $30 per share. This block of stock was purchased as a long-term investment. Assume that the accounting period for each company ends December 31. Subsequent to acquisition, the following data were available:

|  | 20A | 20B |
|---|---|---|
| Income reported by Seven Corporation at December 31 | $40,000 | $60,000 |
| Cash dividends declared and paid by Seven Corporation during the year | 60,000 | 80,000 |
| Market price per share of Seven common stock on December 31 | 28 | 29 |

*Required:*

1. What accounting method should the company use? Why?

2. Give the journal entries for the company for each year (use parallel columns) for the following (if none, explain why):

   *a.* Acquisition of Seven Corporation stock.

   *b.* Net income reported by Seven Corporation.

   *c.* Dividends received from Seven Corporation.

   *d.* Market value effects at year-end.

3. Show how the following amounts should be reported on the financial statements for each year:

   *a.* Long-term investment.

   *b.* Stockholders' equity—net unrealized loss.

   *c.* Revenues.

**AP12–3 Comparing the Market Value and Equity Methods (P12–4)**  ◼ **LO2, 3**

Packer Company purchased, as a long-term investment, some of the 200,000 shares of the outstanding common stock of Boston Corporation. The annual accounting period for each company ends December 31. The following transactions occurred during 20E:

Jan.  10  Purchased shares of common stock of Boston at $15 per share as follows:

Case A—30,000 shares.
Case B—80,000 shares.

Dec. 31    Received the 20E financial statements of Boston Corporation; the reported net income was $90,000.

31    Received a cash dividend of $0.60 per share from Boston Corporation.

31    Learned the current market price of Boston stock, $9 per share.

*Required:*

1. For each case, identify the accounting method that the company should use. Explain why.

2. Give the journal entries for each case for these transactions. If no entry is required, explain why. (*Hint:* Use parallel columns for Case A and Case B.)

3. Give the amounts for each case that should be reported on the 20E financial statements. Use the following format:

|  | Case A | Case B |
|---|---|---|
| **Balance sheet** (partial) | | |
| Investments | | |
|    Investments in common stock, Boston Corporation | | |
| Stockholders' equity | | |
|    Net unrealized loss | | |
| **Income statement** (partial) | | |
|    Investment income | | |

# CASES AND PROJECTS

## FINANCIAL REPORTING AND ANALYSIS CASES

**LO2, 3, 4    CP12–1**

Urban Outfitters

STANDARD
&POOR'S

**Finding Financial Information**
Refer to the financial statements of Urban Outfitters given in Appendix C at the end of this book, or open file URBN10K.doc in the S&P directory on the student CD-ROM.

1. What types of marketable securities does Urban Outfitters report and what measurement and reporting methods are applied to them? Where did you find the information?

2. Does Urban Outfitters report the cost and market value of these securities? If so, what is the relationship of cost to market? What attributes of the securities might account for the small difference between cost and market?

3. Does Urban Outfitters operate through (a) wholly owned subsidiaries or (b) majority-owned subsidiaries? The notes indicate that the company eliminates all intercompany transactions during consolidation. Explain.

4. At the end of the current year, Urban Outfitters recorded an unrealized gain on its available for sale securities of $18,000. What effect did this have on cash flows from operations?

**LO5    CP12–2**

American Eagle
Outfitters versus
Urban Outfitters

STANDARD
&POOR'S

**Comparing Companies within an Industry**
Refer to the financial statements of American Eagle Outfitters given in Appendix B, Urban Outfitters given in Appendix C, and the Standard and Poor's Industry Ratio Report given in Appendix D at the end of this book, or open file CP12-2.xls in the S&P directory on the student CD-ROM.

*Required:*

1. Compute the return on assets ratio for both companies for the current year. What would you infer from the difference? Which company provided the higher return on its total investments during the current year?

2. Was the difference in ROA due primarily to profitability or efficiency differences? How did you know?

3. Was return on assets for American Eagle Outfitters higher or lower than the industry average? for Urban Outfitters?

**CP12–3 Using Financial Reports: Analyzing the Financial Effects of the Market Value and Equity Methods**

LO2, 3

On January 1, 20B, Woodrow Company purchased 30 percent of the outstanding common stock of Trevor Corporation at a total cost of $560,000. Management intends to hold the stock for the long term. On the December 31, 20B, balance sheet, the investment in Trevor Corporation was $720,000, but no additional Trevor stock was purchased. The company received $80,000 in cash dividends from Trevor. The dividends were declared and paid during 20B. The company used the equity method to account for its investment in Trevor. The market price of Trevor stock increased during 20B to a total value of $600,000.

*Required:*

1. Explain why the investment account balance increased from $560,000 to $720,000 during 20B.

2. What amount of revenue from the investment was reported during 20B?

3. If Woodrow used the market value method, what amount of revenue from the investment should have been reported in 20B?

4. If the market value method were used, what amount should be reported as the investment in Trevor Corporation on the December 31, 20B, balance sheet?

**CP12–4 Interpreting the Financial Press**

LO4

*The Wall Street Journal*

The FASB has issued an exposure draft financial accounting standard related to business combinations and intangible assets. A summary of the major changes included in the exposure draft as well as expert reactions to the changes are discussed in a recent article by Elizabeth McDonald, "Accounting Rule Makers Unveil Plan to Abolish Poolings of Interest for M&A," *The Wall Street Journal,* September 9, 1999, p. A4. The article is available on the Libby/Libby/Short website at www.mhhe.com/business/accounting/libby3. You should read the article and then write a short memo outlining these topics:

1. The three major changes in the new exposure draft.

2. The main reasons the FASB wants to make the changes.

3. Why some companies are opposed to the plan.

4. Why others do not believe it will affect their activities.

**CP12–5 Using Financial Reports: Interpreting International Goodwill Disclosures**

LO4

Diageo

Diageo is a major international company located in London. A recent annual report contained the following information concerning its accounting policies.

> **Acquisitions** On the acquisition of a business, including an interest in a related company, fair values are attributed to the group's share of net tangible assets and significant owned brands acquired. Where the cost of acquisition exceeds the values attributable to such net assets, the difference is treated as goodwill and is written off directly to reserves in the year of acquisition.
>
> **Intangible assets** Significant owned brands, acquired after 1st January 1985, the value of which is not expected to diminish in the foreseeable future, are recorded in the balance sheet as fixed intangible assets. No amortisation is provided on these assets but their value is reviewed annually by the directors and the cost written down as an exceptional item where permanent diminution in value has occurred.

Diageo used the word *reserves* to mean *retained earnings.* Discuss how this accounting treatment compares with procedures used in this country.

## CRITICAL THINKING CASES

**CP12–6 Evaluating an Ethical Dilemma: Using Inside Information**

Assume that you are on the board of directors of a company that has decided to buy 80 percent of the outstanding stock of another company within the next three or four months. The discussions have convinced you that this company is an excellent investment opportunity, so you decide to buy $10,000 worth of the company's stock. Is there an ethical problem with your decision? Would your answer be different if you planned to invest $500,000? Are there different ethical considerations if you don't buy the stock but recommend that your brother do so?

**LO4, 5**    **CP12–7**

**Evaluating an Acquisition from the Standpoint of a Financial Analyst**
Assume that you are a financial analyst for a large investment banking firm. You are responsible for analyzing companies in the retail sales industry. You have just learned that a large West Coast retailer has acquired a large East Coast retail chain at a price greater than the net book value of the acquired company. You have reviewed the separate financial statements for the two companies before the announcement of the acquisition. You have been asked to write a brief report explaining what will happen when the financial results of the companies are consolidated under the purchase method, including the impact on the return on assets ratio.

# FINANCIAL REPORTING AND ANALYSIS PROJECTS

**LO5**    **CP12–8**

Dow Jones

**Comparing Companies over Time**
Using your web browser, contact Dow Jones at its website (www.dowjones.com). Find the latest Dow Jones annual report. (*Note:* The necessary information also can be accessed from its Form 10-K through EDGAR at www.freeedgar.com.)

*Required:*

1. What was Dow Jones's ROA in the most recent year and how did it compare to the latest figures provided in the text? What was management's explanation for the change (if any)?
2. Compute the two components of ROA to determine what caused the bulk of the change.

**LO4**    **CP12–9**

Cisco Systems

**Project: Analysis of Acquisition Strategy**
Using your web browser, contact Cisco Systems at its website (www.cisco.com). (*Note:* The necessary information also can be accessed from its Form 10-K through EDGAR.) Find the latest annual report or Form 10-K. Write a brief report identifying the companies that Cisco acquired during the year ended June 30, 2000, the price paid for each, the purpose of each, and the accounting method applied. In terms of dollar value of acquisitions, which method was used most often, purchase or pooling? Explain why.

**LO2, 3, 4**    **CP12–10**

**Team Project: Examining an Annual Report**
As a team, select an industry to analyze. Each team member should acquire the annual report or Form 10-K for one publicly traded company in the industry, with each member selecting a different company. (Library files, the SEC EDGAR service at www.sec.gov, Compustat CD, or the company itself are good sources.) On an individual basis, each group member should then write a short report answering the following questions about his or her selected company:

1. Determine whether the company prepared consolidated financial statements. If so, did it use the purchase or pooling method?
2. Does the company use the equity method for any of its investments?
3. Does the company hold any investments in securities? If so, what is their market value? Does the company have any unrealized gains or losses?
4. Identify the company's lines of business. Why does management want to engage in these business activities?

Discuss any patterns across the companies that you as a group observe. Then, as a group, write a short report comparing and contrasting your companies using these attributes. Provide potential explanations for any differences discovered.

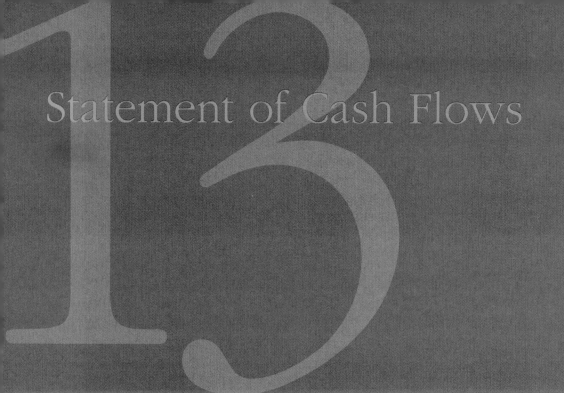

Statement of Cash Flows

## CHAPTER **THIRTEEN**

LEARNING **OBJECTIVES**

*After studying this chapter, you should be able to:*

1. Classify cash flow statement items as part of net cash flows from operating, investing, and financing activities.   p. 683

2. Report and interpret differences between net income and cash flows from operating activities.   p. 687

3. Analyze and interpret the quality of income ratio.   p. 695

4. Report and interpret cash flows from investing activities.   p. 699

5. Analyze and interpret the capital acquisitions ratio.   p. 701

6. Report and interpret cash flows from financing activities.   p. 702

7. Explain the impact of noncash investing and financing activities.   p. 704

It was no accident when 36-year-old Jim Koch, founder of Boston Beer Company, named his products for Samuel Adams, the American revolutionary who led the Boston Tea Party. When Koch delivered the first 25 cases of Samuel Adams Boston Lager to a Boston bar in 1985, he fired the first shot in a revolution that stunned the brewing industry. At that point, mega-brewers such as Anheuser-Busch and Miller dominated beer brewing; annual sales by small "craft" brewers were just over 100,000 barrels. In just ten years, craft brewers' annual sales grew to nearly 6,000,000 barrels. Boston Beer is the clear leader among craft brewers with a 21 percent market share and 1998 net income of almost $8 million.

FOCUS **COMPANY:**

# Boston Beer Company

## MANAGING PRODUCTION AND CASH FLOWS IN A SEASONAL BUSINESS

Although it may seem puzzling, growing profitable operations such as those of Boston Beer do not always ensure positive cash flow. Also, seasonal fluctuations in sales and purchases of inventory and advertising may cause high *profits* and net cash *out*flows in some quarters and *losses* and net cash *in*flows in others. As we emphasized in earlier chapters, this results because revenues and expenses are not equal to cash inflows and outflows. As a consequence, Boston Beer must carefully manage cash flows as well as profits. For the same reasons, financial analysts must consider the information provided in its cash flow statement as well as the income statement and balance sheet.

# BUSINESS BACKGROUND

Clearly, net income is an important number, but cash flow is also critical. Cash flow permits a company to expand its operations, replace needed assets, take advantage of market opportunities, and pay dividends to its owners. Some Wall Street analysts go as far as saying "cash flow is king." Both managers and analysts need to understand the various sources and uses of cash that are associated with business activity.

The cash flow statement focuses attention on a firm's ability to generate cash internally, its management of current assets and current liabilities, and the details of its investments in productive assets and external financing. It is designed to help both managers and analysts answer important cash-related questions such as these:

- Will the company have enough cash to pay its short-term debts to suppliers and others without additional borrowing?
- Is the company adequately managing its accounts receivable, inventory, and so on?
- Has the company made necessary investments in new productive capacity?
- Did the company generate enough cash flow internally to finance necessary investments, or did it rely on external financing?
- Is the company changing the makeup of its external financing?

Three main categories of activities generate and use cash: activity related to operating the business, activity related to investments in productive assets, and activity related to financing the business. The statement of cash flows is designed to provide managers and analysts with information concerning these important activities. Boston Beer is a particularly good example to illustrate the importance of the cash flow statement for two reasons. First, like all companies in its industry, Boston Beer's inventory purchases and sales vary with the seasons. This seasonal variation has surprising effects on cash flows and net income. Second, an important element of its business strategy is the outsourcing of much of its product manufacturing (called *contract brewing*). This dramatically affects its investments in plant and equipment and the need for external financing to support growth. The statement of cash flows taken from a recent quarterly report for The Boston Beer Company is shown in Exhibit 13.1. We will now discuss the information that this required statement provides.

## ORGANIZATION OF THE CHAPTER

| • Classifications on the Statement of Cash Flows | • Reporting and Interpreting Cash Flows from Operating Activities | • Reporting and Interpreting Cash Flows from Investing Activities | • Reporting and Interpreting Cash Flows from Financing Activities | • Presentation of the Statement of Cash Flows |
|---|---|---|---|---|
| Cash Flows from Operating Activities | Noncurrent Accruals | Capital Acquisitions Ratio | | Noncash Investing and Financing Activities |
| Cash Flows from Investing Activities | Changes in Current Assets and Current Liabilities | | | Supplemental Cash Flow Information |
| Cash Flows from Financing Activities | Quality of Income Ratio | | | |
| Relationships to the Balance Sheet and Income Statement | A Comparison of the Direct and Indirect Methods | | | |

# CLASSIFICATIONS OF STATEMENT OF CASH FLOWS

Basically, the statement of cash flows explains how the cash balance at the beginning of the period became the cash balance at the end of the period. For purposes of this statement, the definition of *cash* includes cash and cash equivalents. **Cash equivalents** are short-term, highly liquid investments that are both

1. Readily convertible to known amounts of cash.
2. So near their maturity that they present insignificant risk of changes in value because of changes in interest rates.

Generally, only investments with original maturities of less than three months qualify as a cash equivalent under this definition.[1] Examples of cash equivalents are Treasury bills (a form of short-term U.S. government debt), money market funds, and commercial paper (short-term notes payable issued by large corporations).

As you can see in Exhibit 13.1, the statement of cash flows reports cash inflows and outflows based on three broad categories: (1) operating activities, (2) investing activities, and (3) financing activities. To improve comparability, *FASB Statement 95* defines each category included in the required statement. These definitions (with explanations) are presented in the following sections.

■ **LEARNING OBJECTIVE 1**

Classify cash flow statement items as part of net cash flows from operating, investing, and financing activities.

A **CASH EQUIVALENT** is a short-term, highly liquid investment with an original maturity of less than three months.

EXHIBIT **13.1**

**Consolidated Statement of Cash Flows**

**REAL WORLD EXCERPT**

*Boston Beer Company*

QUARTERLY REPORT

**THE BOSTON BEER COMPANY, INC.**
**Consolidated Statement of Cash Flows**

(unaudited)

| In thousands for quarter ended | March 28, 1998 |
| --- | --- |
| Cash flows from operating activities: | |
| Net income | $2,076 |
| Adjustments to reconcile net income to net cash provided by operating activities: | |
| Depreciation and amortization | 1,225 |
| Stock option compensation expense | 59 |
| Loss on write-down of marketable equity security | 2,317 |
| Changes in assets and liabilities: | |
| Accounts receivable (net) | (3,655) |
| Inventory | 1,020 |
| Prepaid expenses | 2,699 |
| Other current assets | (38) |
| Other assets (long-term receivables) | 79 |
| Accounts payable | (1,631) |
| Accrued expenses | (2,857) |
| Net cash provided by (used in) operating activities | 1,294 |
| Cash flows for investing activities: | |
| Purchases of fixed assets | (2,198) |
| Purchases of short-term investments | (438) |
| Net cash used in investing activities | (2,636) |
| Cash flows from financing activities: | |
| Proceeds from sale of shares | 107 |
| Net borrowings under line of credit | 1,517 |
| Net cash provided by financing activities | 1,624 |
| Net increase (decrease) in cash and cash equivalents | 282 |
| Cash and cash equivalents at beginning of period | 13 |
| Cash and cash equivalents at end of period | $ 295 |
| Supplemental disclosure of cash flow information: | |
| Interest paid | 193 |
| Income taxes paid | 47 |

---

[1]*Original maturity* means original maturity to the entity holding the investment. For example, both a three-month Treasury bill and a three-year Treasury note purchased three months from maturity qualify as cash equivalents. A Treasury note purchased three years ago, however, does not become a cash equivalent when its remaining maturity is three months.

## CASH FLOWS FROM OPERATING ACTIVITIES

**Cash flows from operating activities (cash flows from operations)** are the cash inflows and cash outflows that directly relate to income from normal operations reported on the income statement. As we illustrated in Chapters 3 and 5, two alternative approaches for presenting the operating activities section of the statement are available:

1. The **direct method** reports the components of cash flows from operating activities listed as gross receipts and gross payments

| Inflows | Outflows |
|---|---|
| *Cash received from* | *Cash paid for* |
| Customers | Purchase of goods for resale and services (electricity, etc.) |
| Dividends and interest on investments | Salaries and wages |
| | Income taxes |
| | Interest on liabilities |

This method starts with cash receipts and cash expenditures to compute net cash inflow (outflow) from operating activities. The difference between the preceding inflows and outflows is called the *net cash inflow (outflow) from operating activities.* For Boston Beer, this amount was an inflow of $1,294,000 for the first quarter of 1998. The FASB recommends the direct method, but it is rarely seen in practice. Many financial executives have reported that they do not use it because it is more expensive to implement than the indirect method. This method will be illustrated briefly later in this chapter.

2. The **indirect method** adjusts net income by eliminating noncash items to compute net cash inflow (outflow) from operating activities. Boston Beer (Exhibit 13.1) and most other companies use this method. Notice in Exhibit 13.1 that in the first quarter of 1998, Boston Beer reported positive net income of $2,076,000 but generated positive cash flows from operating activities of only $1,294,000. Recall why the income of a company and its cash flows from operating activities should be so different. Remember that the income statement is prepared under the accrual concept. Revenues are recorded when earned without regard to when the related cash flows occur. Expenses are matched with revenues and recorded in the same period as the revenues without regard to when the related cash flows occur.

The statement of cash flows prepared under the indirect method starts with the net income number computed under the accrual concept and adjusts it to a cash basis. The adjustments are discussed in detail later in this chapter. By reviewing the Operating Activities section of the statement prepared under the indirect method, you can determine the specific reasons that cash flows from operating activities were lower than net income in the first quarter of 1998.

According to *Accounting Trends & Techniques,*[2] 98.3 percent of the surveyed companies use the indirect method. Because of the extensive use of this method in actual financial reporting, we emphasize it in our discussions. For now, the most important thing to remember about the two methods is that they are simply alternative ways to compute the same number. The total amount of cash flows from operating activities is *always the same* (an inflow of $1,294,000 in Boston Beer's case) regardless of whether it is computed using the direct or indirect method.

## CASH FLOWS FROM INVESTING ACTIVITIES

**Cash flows from investing activities** are cash inflows and outflows related to the purchase and disposal of productive facilities used by the company and investments in the securities of other companies. Under this classification, the cash outflows represent the

---

[2]*Accounting Trends & Techniques* (New York: American Institute of CPAs, 1998), p. 485.

entity's "investments" of cash to acquire these assets. The cash inflows occur only when cash is received from disposal (sale or collection) of the prior investments. Typical cash flows from investing activities follow:

| Inflows | Outflows |
|---|---|
| *Cash received from* | *Cash paid for* |
| Sale or disposal of property, plant, and equipment | Purchase of property, plant, and equipment |
| Sale or maturity of investments in securities | Purchase of investments in securities |

The difference between these cash inflows and outflows is called *net cash inflow (outflow) from investing activities.*

For Boston Beer, this amount was an outflow of $2,636,000 for the first quarter of 1998. The Investing Activities section of the statement shows Boston Beer's long-term investment strategy. The Management Discussion and Analysis (MD&A) section of the report indicates that the company was continuing to invest in improved packaging and brewing equipment for the new Cincinnati brewery (listed as "Purchases of fixed assets"). It is also investing excess cash in short-term investments.

## CASH FLOWS FROM FINANCING ACTIVITIES

**Cash flows from financing activities** include both cash inflows and outflows that relate to the way that cash was obtained from external sources (owners and creditors) to finance the enterprise and its operations. Under this classification, the cash inflows represent the financing activities that obtain cash from owners and creditors. The cash outflows occur only when cash is paid back to the owners and creditors for their previous cash-providing activities. Usual cash flows from financing activities include these:

**CASH FLOWS FROM FINANCING ACTIVITIES** are cash inflows and outflows related to external sources of financing (owners and creditors) for the enterprise.

| Inflows | Outflows |
|---|---|
| *Cash received from* | *Cash paid for* |
| Borrowing on notes, mortgages, bonds, etc. from creditors | Repayment of principal to creditors (excluding interest, which is an operating activity) |
| Issuing equity securities to owners | Repurchasing equity securities from owners |
| | Dividends to owners |

The difference between these cash inflows and outflows is called *net cash inflow (outflow) from financing activities.* For Boston Beer, this amount was an inflow of $1,624,000 for the first quarter of 1998. The Financing Activities section of the statement shows that Boston Beer generated much of its cash, $1,517,000, from creditors during the period and only a small amount, $107,000, from owners.

To give you a better understanding of the statement of cash flows, we now discuss in more detail Boston Beer's statement and the way that it relates to the balance sheet and income statement. As we go through the statement, we emphasize the way that each section of the statement describes a set of important decisions that Boston Beer management made. We then discuss the way that financial analysts use each section to evaluate the company.

## SELF-STUDY **QUIZ**

*Pete's Brewing Company*

Pete's Brewing Company, brewer of Pete's Wicked Ale, is the second largest craft brewer in the United States. The items included in its recent first-quarter statement of cash flows follow. Indicate whether each item is disclosed in the Operating Activities (O), Investing Activities (I), or Financing Activities (F) section of the statement. (Refer to Exhibit 13.1 as a guide.)

_____ a. Purchase of available-for-sale securities

_____ b. Net income

_____ c. Change in trade accounts receivable

_____ d. Additions to property and equipment

_____ e. Change in prepaid expenses and other current assets

_____ f. Change in inventories

_____ g. Sale of other (fixed) assets

_____ h. Depreciation and amortization

_____ i. Issuance of common shares

_____ j. Change in trade accounts payable and accrued liabilities

After you have completed your answers, check them with the solutions presented in the footnote at the bottom of this page.*

## RELATIONSHIPS TO THE BALANCE SHEET AND INCOME STATEMENT

Both preparing and interpreting the cash flow statement require analyzing the balance sheet and income statement accounts that relate to the three cash flow statement sections. As we discussed in previous chapters, companies record transactions as journal entries that are posted to T-accounts, which are used to prepare the income statement and the balance sheet. Companies cannot prepare the statement of cash flows by using amounts recorded in T-accounts because these amounts are based on accrual accounting. Instead, they must analyze numbers recorded under the accrual method and adjust them to a cash basis. To prepare the statement of cash flows, they need the following data:

1. Comparative balance sheets used in preparing the cash flows from all activities (operating, investing, and financing). To ease the preparation process, it is useful to compute the change from the beginning to the end of the period for each balance sheet item.

2. A complete income statement used primarily in preparing cash flows from operating activities.

3. Additional details concerning selected accounts that reflect several different types of transactions and events. Analysis of individual accounts is necessary because often the total change amount in an account balance during the year does not reveal the underlying nature of the cash flows.

The approach that we take to prepare and understand the cash flow statement focuses on the changes in the balance sheet accounts. It relies on a simple algebraic manipulation of the balance sheet equation

$$\textbf{Assets} = \textbf{Liabilities} + \textbf{Stockholders' Equity}$$

First, assets can be split into cash and noncash assets:

$$\textbf{Cash} + \textbf{Noncash Assets} = \textbf{Liabilities} + \textbf{Stockholders' Equity}$$

If we move the noncash assets to the right side of the equation, then

$$\textbf{Cash} = \textbf{Liabilities} + \textbf{Stockholders' Equity} - \textbf{Noncash Assets}$$

Given this relationship, the changes ($\Delta$) between the beginning and end of the period in cash must be equal to the changes ($\Delta$) between the beginning and end of the period in the amounts on the right side of the equation:

$$\Delta \textbf{ Cash} = \Delta \textbf{ Liabilities} + \Delta \textbf{ Stockholders' Equity} - \Delta \textbf{ Noncash Assets}$$

Thus, the total change in cash can be explained by the changes in the other balance sheet items.

---

* *a.* I, *b.* O, *c.* O, *d.* I, *e.* O, *f.* O, *g.* I, *h.* O, *i.* F, *j.* O.

In the next sections of the chapter, we will classify each of these other balance sheet changes as relating to operating (O), investing (I), or financing (F) activities. Each section of the cash flow statement focuses on how the related changes in the balance sheet accounts explain the change in cash.

## REPORTING AND INTERPRETING CASH FLOWS FROM OPERATING ACTIVITIES

The Operating Activities section of the cash flow statement focuses attention on the firm's ability to generate cash internally through operations and its management of current assets and current liabilities (also called *working capital*). Most analysts believe that this is the most important section of the statement because, in the long run, operations are the only source of cash. That is, investors will not invest in a company if they do not believe that it will be able to pay them dividends or make reinvestments with cash generated from operations. Similarly, creditors will not lend money if they do not believe that cash generated from operations will be available to pay back the loan.

A recent issue of *Worth* magazine[3] notes that a common rule of thumb followed by financial and credit analysts is to stay away from firms with rising net income but falling cash flow from operations. A situation in which rapidly rising inventories or receivables are the cause often predicts a future slump in profits and the need for external financing. In the first quarter of 1998, Boston Beer exhibited just such a pattern. Is this a sign of troubled waters ahead for the leader of the craft beer industry? Why, as indicated in the following chart, did net income also rise only slightly in the second quarter, but cash flow from operations rebound to all-time highs?

> **LEARNING OBJECTIVE 2**
>
> Report and interpret differences between net income and cash flows from operating activities.

|  | Net Income |  | Cash Flows from Operations |
|---|---|---|---|
| 1st quarter | $2,076 | > | $1,294 |
| 2nd quarter | $2,333 | < | $7,712 |

To answer these questions, we must carefully analyze how its operating activities are reported in the cash flow statement. At the same time, we also must learn more about the brewing industry to properly interpret this information.

Exhibit 13.2 shows Boston Beer's comparative balance sheet and income statement.[4] Preparing the operating section requires analyzing changes in the balance sheet accounts related to earning income, which we note with an O. Normally, the relevant balance sheet accounts include all *current assets other than cash and short-term investments* and all *current liabilities other than short-term debt to financial institutions* (often called *notes payable*) *and current maturities of long-term debt.*[5] The retained earnings change also is related to both the operating and financing sections; it increases by the amount of net income, which is the starting point for the Operating section (O), and it decreases by the dividends declared and paid, which is a financing outflow (noted by an F). In addition, the accumulated depreciation account (part of Equipment and Leasehold Improvements, Net) is relevant to operations because it relates to depreciation expense. As we discuss later in the chapter, assets or liabilities related to advance payment or deferral of taxes also are relevant to the cash flow from operations calculation.

---

[3]C. Willis, "How to Stay Cool in a Hot Market: Studying the Financials Can Reveal a Stock about to Stumble," *Worth*, June 1996, pp. 122–124.

[4]Note that Boston Beer reports financial statement numbers in thousands. We follow that policy in the remainder of the chapter.

[5]Current maturities of long-term debt are amounts of debt with an original term of more than one year that are due within one year of the statement date.

EXHIBIT **13.2**

**The Boston Beer Company: Comparative Balance Sheet and Current Income Statement (in thousands)**

**REAL WORLD EXCERPT**

*Boston Beer Company*

QUARTERLY REPORT

| *Related Cash Flow Section*<br>Δ in Cash | THE BOSTON BEER COMPANY, INC.<br>Consolidated Balance Sheet | | | |
|---|---|---|---|---|
| | (unaudited)<br>In Thousands | March 28,<br>1998 | December 27,<br>1997 | |
| | Assets | | | |
| | Current Assets: | | | *Change* |
| I | Cash and cash equivalents | $ 295 | $ 13 | +282 |
| O | Short-term investments | 36,132 | 38,011 | −1,879 |
| O | Accounts receivable | 20,138 | 16,483 | +3,655 |
| O | Inventories | 12,655 | 13,675 | −1,020 |
| O | Prepaid expenses | 1,645 | 4,344 | −2,699 |
| O | Deferred income taxes | 2,266 | 2,266 | 0 |
| O | Other current assets | 1,636 | 1,598 | +38 |
| | Total current assets | 74,767 | 76,390 | |
| I* | Equipment and leasehold<br>improvements, net | 29,754 | 28,781 | +973 |
| O | Other assets (long-term receivables) | 2,663 | 2,742 | −79 |
| | Total assets | $107,184 | $107,913 | |
| | Liabilities and Stockholders' Equity | | | |
| | Current Liabilities: | | | |
| O | Accounts payable | $ 7,925 | $ 9,556 | −1,631 |
| F | Bank line of credit | 1,517 | 0 | +1,517 |
| O | Accrued expenses | 10,913 | 13,770 | −2,857 |
| | Total current liabilities | 20,355 | 23,326 | |
| F | Long-term debt,<br>less current maturities | 10,000 | 10,000 | 0 |
| O | Long-term deferred taxes | 789 | 789 | 0 |
| | Stockholders' Equity: | | | |
| F | Class A Common Stock,<br>$.01 par value | 164 | 163 | +1 |
| F | Class B Common Stock,<br>$.01 par value | 41 | 41 | 0 |
| F | Additional paid-in capital | 56,188 | 56,023 | +165 |
| O and F | Retained earnings | 19,647 | 17,571 | +2,076 |
| | Total stockholders' equity | 76,040 | 73,798 | |
| | Total liabilities and stockholders' equity | $107,184 | $107,913 | |

*The accumulated depreciation account is also related to operations because it relates to depreciation.

We begin the Operating Activities section with net income of $2,076 reported on Boston Beer's income statement (see Exhibit 13.2). We then go through a two-step process to convert net income to cash flow from operations. These steps involve adjusting for the following:

1. Noncurrent accruals including expenses (such as depreciation expense) and revenues which do not affect current assets or current liabilities (also called "noncash" revenues and expenses), and gains and losses which, by definition, do not relate to normal operations (see Chapter 3).

2. Changes in each of the individual current assets (other than cash and short-term investments) and current liabilities (other than short-term debt to financial institutions and current maturities of long-term debt, which relate to financing), which reflect differences in the timing of accrual basis net income and cash flows.

EXHIBIT **13.2**

continued

**THE BOSTON BEER COMPANY, INC.**
**Consolidated Statement of Income**

| (Unaudited)<br>In Thousands Except Per Share Amounts | Quarter ended<br>March 28, 1998 |
|---|---|
| Sales | $51,660 |
| Less excise taxes | 6,412 |
| Net sales | 45,248 |
| Cost of sales | 21,428 |
| Gross profit | 23,820 |
| Operating expenses: | |
| Advertising, promotional and selling expenses | 13,540 |
| General and administrative expenses | 3,224 |
| Total operating expenses | 16,764 |
| Operating income | 7,056 |
| Other income (expense): | |
| Interest income | 466 |
| Interest expense | (170) |
| Other income (expense), net | (2,556) |
| Total other income | (2,260) |
| Income before income taxes | 4,796 |
| Provision for income taxes | 2,720 |
| Net income | $ 2,076 |

The following adjustments are the ones most frequently encountered:

| Income Statement Amounts or<br>Balance Sheet Changes | Impact on the<br>Statement of Cash Flows |
|---|---|
| Net Income | Starting point for computation |
| Depreciation expense and other noncurrent<br>   accrued expenses and losses | Added |
| Noncurrent accrued revenues and gains | Subtracted |
| Decreases in current assets | Added |
| Increases in current liabilities | Added |
| Increases in current assets | Subtracted |
| Decreases in current liabilities | Subtracted |

To keep track of all the additions and subtractions made to convert net income to cash flows from operations, it is useful to set up a schedule to record the computations. We will construct a schedule for Boston Beer in Exhibit 13.3.

## NONCURRENT ACCRUALS

**Noncurrent accruals,** such as depreciation, are reported on most income statements. Recording a noncurrent accrual does not involve either a credit or debit to cash or any other current asset or current liability. Since *noncurrent accrued expenses* have been subtracted from revenue to determine net income, we always *add them back* to income in the process of converting net income to cash flow from operations. In the case of Boston Beer, we need to add depreciation and amortization expense of $1,225 and compensation expense paid in a form of stock (called *options*) of $59 to net income to convert it to cash from operations (see Exhibit 13.3). Some companies report *noncurrent accrued revenues,* which, by the same logic, are *subtracted*. Boston Beer also recorded a write-down (loss) of a marketable equity security that had suffered a

**NONCURRENT ACCRUALS (NONCASH EXPENSES AND REVENUES)** are expenses and revenues that do not affect current assets or liabilities; for example, depreciation expense.

EXHIBIT **13.3**

**Boston Beer Company: Schedule for Net Cash Flow from Operating Activities, Indirect Method (in thousands)**

**Conversion of net income to net cash flow from operating activities:**

| Items | Amount | Explanation |
|---|---|---|
| Net income, accrual basis | $2,076 | From income statement. |
| Add (subtract) to convert to cash basis: | | |
| Depreciation and amortization | +1,225 | Add back because depreciation expense is a noncurrent accrued expense. |
| Stock option compensation expense | +59 | Add back because the expense is a noncurrent accrued expense (paid with stock). |
| Loss on write-down of marketable equity security | +2,317 | Add back because the loss is noncash and relates to investing activities |
| Accounts receivable increase | −3,655 | Subtract because cash collected from customers is less than accrual basis revenues. |
| Inventory decrease | +1,020 | Add back because cost of goods sold expense is more than purchases. |
| Prepaid expense decrease | +2,699 | Add back because accrual basis expenses are more than cash prepayments for expenses. |
| Other current assets increase | −38 | Subtract because accrual basis expenses are less than cash payments for expenses. |
| Other assets (long-term receivables) decrease | +79 | Add because cash collected from customers is more than accrual basis revenues. |
| Accounts payable decrease | −1,631 | Subtract because amounts purchased on account (borrowed from suppliers) are less than cash payments to suppliers. |
| Accrued expenses decrease | −2,857 | Subtract because accrual basis expenses are less than the cash payments for expenses. |
| Net cash inflow from operating activities | $1,294 | Reported on the statement of cash flows. |

permanent decline in value (see Chapter 12 for discussion). This loss of $2,317 related to an investing activity and did not affect cash. Thus, like noncurrent accrued expenses, this loss must also be added back to net income to convert to cash from operations. We discuss gains and losses in more detail in Chapter Supplement A.

## CHANGES IN CURRENT ASSETS AND CURRENT LIABILITIES

Each *change* in the current assets (other than cash and short-term investments) and current liabilities (other than short-term debt to financial institutions and current maturities of long-term debt, which relate to financing) causes a difference between net income and cash flow from operations. In Exhibit 13.2, these balance sheet items are noted by an O. If we understand what activities make each of these accounts change, we will see why the change must be added or subtracted in the conversion of net income to cash flows from operations.

Two simplified examples will help us understand the logic of these additions and subtractions: the effects of changes in accounts receivable and accounts payable. Consider the following T-account, which illustrates that, when credit sales are recorded, accounts receivable increases, and when cash is collected, accounts receivable decreases.

**Accounts Receivable (A)**

| | | | |
|---|---|---|---|
| Beginning balance | 16,000 | | |
| Sales revenue (on account) | 45,000 | Collections from customers | 42,000 |
| Ending balance | 19,000 | | |

In the example, sales revenue on account reported on the income statement is higher than cash collections from customers by $45,000 − $42,000 = $3,000. This shortfall in collections must be subtracted from net income to convert to cash flows from operating activities. Note that this amount is also the same as the change in the accounts receivable account (Ending balance $19,000 − Beginning balance $16,000 = $3,000). This logic leads to a general rule:

*When a current asset increases, the change is subtracted.*

*When a current asset decreases, the change is added.*

Now consider the following simplified example of a T-account for accounts payable. When purchases on account are recorded, accounts payable increases, and when cash is paid to vendors, accounts payable decreases.

**Accounts Payable (L)**

| | | | |
|---|---|---|---|
| | | Beginning balance | 17,000 |
| Payments on account | 36,000 | Purchases on account | 34,000 |
| | | Ending balance | 15,000 |

In the example, cash payments on account are higher than purchases on account by $36,000 − $34,000 = $2,000. This added payment amount must be subtracted from net income in the conversion to cash flows from operating activities. Note that this amount is also the same as the change in the accounts receivable account (Ending balance $15,000 − Beginning balance $17,000 = −$2,000). This logic leads to a general rule:

*When a current liability increases, the change is added.*

*When a current liability decreases, the change is subtracted.*

The application of this logic to the details of Boston Beer's statements is described next.

**Change in Accounts Receivable** The first operating item (O) listed on Boston Beer's Balance sheet (Exhibit 13.2) is accounts receivable. As noted in the simple preceding example, the income statement reflects sales on account and the cash flow statement must reflect collections on account. Sales on account increase the balance in accounts receivable and collections decrease the balance. So the change in accounts receivable from the beginning of the period to the end is the difference between sales and collections. As a consequence:

When a net *decrease in accounts receivable* for the period occurs, cash collected from customers is always more than accrual revenue; thus, the decrease (the extra cash collections) must be *added* in computing cash flows from operations.

When a net *increase in accounts receivable* occurs, cash collected from customers is always less than accrual sales revenue; thus, the increase (the extra accrual sales revenue) must be *subtracted* in computing cash flows from operations.

Since the balance sheet for Boston Beer Company (Exhibit 13.2) indicates an *increase* in accounts receivable of $3,655 for the period, cash collected is less than reported sales revenue.

| Section | Balance Sheet Account | March 28, 1998 | December 27, 1997 | Change | Cash Flow Effect |
|---|---|---|---|---|---|
| O | Accounts receivable, net | 20,138 | 16,483 | +3,655 | −3,655 |

Thus, to reflect the smaller cash inflow, the amount of the increase must be *subtracted* from net income to convert income to cash flow from operating activities in Exhibit 13.3. (A decrease would be added.)

# FINANCIAL **ANALYSIS**

### INCOME GROWTH AND DECLINING CASH FLOWS: A WARNING SIGN?

Managers sometimes attempt to boost declining sales by extending credit terms (for example, 30 to 60 days) or lowering credit standards (lending to riskier customers). The resulting increase in accounts receivable can cause net income to outpace cash flow from operations. As a consequence, many analysts view this pattern as a warning sign. In the first quarter of 1998, Boston Beer's net income was $2,076 (in thousands), yet it reported a cash flow from operations of $1,294, caused in part by a $3,655 increase in receivables. Does this suggest that Boston Beer may be facing more difficult times?

Analysts who cover the beverage industry know that this is a result of normal seasonal fluctuations in beer sales to distributors. First, they know that virtually all of Boston Beer's sales to distributors are on account and that it normally collects cash the month *after* sales revenue is recorded. Second, they recognize that beer sales to distributors are *low* in the last month of the fourth quarter, *December,* because of the onset of winter. As a result, the beginning balance in accounts receivable and cash collections from customers in *January* are low. Third, they recognize that sales are high at the end of the first quarter, *March,* in anticipation of spring. The higher March sales cause accounts receivable to grow, but cash is not collected based on these higher sales until *April.* As a result, cash receipts from customers in March lag behind sales revenue and accounts receivable increases between the end of the fourth quarter (December 27) and the end of the first quarter (March 28). On the cash flow statement, this results in a negative effect on cash flow from operations for the first quarter. This normal seasonal fluctuation in sales is clearly *not* a sign of problems for Boston Beer.

**Change in Inventory**   Cost of goods sold represents the cost of merchandise sold during the accounting period. It may be more or less than the amount of cash paid to suppliers during the period. Both the change in inventory and the change in accounts payable (borrowing from suppliers) determine the magnitude of this difference. It is easiest to think about the change in inventory in terms of the simple case in which the company pays cash to suppliers of inventory. We address the added complexity involved when purchases are made on account when we discuss the adjustment for the change in accounts payable.

The income statement reflects the cost of goods sold of the period, whereas the cash flow from operating activities must reflect the cash payments for purchases for the same period. Since purchases of goods increase the balance in inventory and cost of goods sold decreases the balance in inventory, the change in inventory from the beginning to the end of the period is the difference between purchases and expenses. Given this, we can generalize another rule:

> When a net *decrease in inventory* for the period occurs, cost of goods sold expense is always more than purchases of inventory; thus, the decrease (the extra cost of goods sold) must be *added* back in computing cash flows from operations.

> When a net *increase in inventory* for the period occurs, cost of goods sold expense is always less than purchases of inventory; thus, the increase (the extra purchases) must be *subtracted.*

Boston Beer's balance sheet indicates inventory decreased by $1,020.

| Section | Balance Sheet Account | March 28, 1998 | December 27, 1997 | Change | Cash Flow Effect |
|---------|-----------------------|----------------|-------------------|--------|------------------|
| O | Inventories | 12,655 | 13,675 | −1,020 | +1,020 |

Thus, to reflect the lower cash outflow (independent of the change in accounts payable, which we deal with later), the change must be *added* back to net income to convert to cash flow from operating activities in Exhibit 13.3.

FINANCIAL **ANALYSIS**

### ANALYZING INVENTORY CHANGES AND CASH FLOWS FROM OPERATIONS

An unexpected increase in inventory can be another cause for net income to outpace cash flow from operations. Such inventory growth can be a sign that planned sales growth did not materialize. A decline in inventory can be a sign that the company is anticipating lower sales in the next quarter. Should analysts be concerned by the decrease in inventory at Boston Beer?

This is a second case for which industry knowledge quickly eases any concerns. The largest component of Boston Beer's inventory is the raw material hops. This plant, which is harvested once a year in the fall, was delivered to Boston Beer during the fourth quarter. It is then used in the brewing process for the next year. This is the reason inventory decreased during the first quarter of 1998. This normal seasonal fluctuation in purchases is no cause for alarm. The obvious importance of detailed industry knowledge to accurate financial statement analysis causes most analysts to become specialists in only a few industries. For example, Skip Carpenter and Steven Somers follow Boston Beer for Donaldson, Lufkin & Jenrette. They specialize in companies in the beverages industry.

**Change in Prepaid Expenses**    Some expenses are paid for before they are recognized as expenses (e.g., prepaid rent). The income statement reflects the expenses (expiration of prepayments) of the period, whereas the cash flow from operating activities must reflect the cash prepayments for the same period. Since cash prepayments increase the balance in prepaid expenses, and expirations (expenses) decrease the balance in prepaid expenses, the change in prepaid expenses from the beginning to the end of the period is the difference between prepayments and expirations. Given this, we can generalize another rule:

When a net *decrease in a prepaid expense* or other operating asset for the period occurs, accrual basis expenses (expirations of the prepayments) are always more than the cash prepayments for the expense; thus, the decrease (the extra expense) must be *added* back in computing cash flows from operations.

When an *increase in a prepaid expense* or other operating asset occurs, accrual basis expenses (expirations of the prepayments) are always less than the cash prepayments for the expense; thus, the increase (the extra prepayments) must be *subtracted.*

Since the Boston Beer balance sheet (Exhibit 13.2) indicates a $2,699 decrease in prepaid expenses, reported expenses are more than cash payments.

| Section | Balance Sheet Account | March 28, 1998 | December 27, 1997 | Change | Cash Flow Effect |
|---------|----------------------|----------------|-------------------|--------|------------------|
| O | Prepaid expenses | 1,645 | 4,344 | −2,699 | +2,699 |

Thus, to reflect the smaller outflow, this amount must be *added* back to net income to convert income to cash flow from operating activities in Exhibit 13.3.

**Changes in Other Current Assets and Other Assets**    Other current assets usually include operating items such as interest receivable. Other assets (noncurrent) may or may not include operating items such as long-term customer receivables. When they do, as is Boston Beer's case, they must also be considered in the calculation of cash flow from operations. As with the example of accounts receivable, when these accounts for the period reflect a net increase, cash collected is always less than accrual revenue; when there is a decrease, cash collected is always more than accrual revenue.

The Boston Beer balance sheet shows an *increase* in other current assets, which indicates that cash receipts are less than revenues. Thus, the increase in other current assets of $38 must be *subtracted* from net income to convert to cash flow from operations in Exhibit 13.3. There was a *decrease* in other assets (long-term receivables), which indicates that cash received from the related sales transactions is more than accrual basis revenues. Thus, the decrease of $79 in other assets must be *added*.

| Section | Balance Sheet Account | March 28, 1998 | December 27, 1997 | Change | Cash Flow Effect |
|---------|----------------------|----------------|-------------------|--------|------------------|
| O | Other current assets | 1,636 | 1,598 | +38 | −38 |
| O | Other assets (long-term receivables) | 2,663 | 2,742 | −79 | +79 |

Had other assets included nonoperating assets such as equipment to be disposed of, its change would not be considered in the Operating section. It would affect the Investing section. *Most other noncurrent assets affect the Investing section.*

**Change in Accounts Payable**   As we noted earlier, the difference between cost of goods sold expense and cash paid to suppliers is captured in the change both in inventory and in accounts payable. Since purchases on account increase accounts payable and cash paid to suppliers decreases accounts payable, the change in accounts payable from the beginning to the end of the period is the difference between purchases on account and payments. Given this, we can generalize the rule:

When a net *increase in accounts payable* for the period occurs, purchases on account are always more than cash paid to suppliers; thus, the increase (the extra purchases) must be *added* back in computing cash flows from operations.

When a net *decrease in accounts payable* for the period occurs, purchases on account are always less than cash paid to suppliers; thus, the decrease (the extra cash payments) must be *subtracted* in computing cash flows from operations.

Accounts payable *decreased* by $1,631, which indicates that purchases are less than cash paid to suppliers.

| Section | Balance Sheet Account | March 28, 1998 | December 27, 1997 | Change | Cash Flow Effect |
|---------|----------------------|----------------|-------------------|--------|------------------|
| O | Accounts payable | 7,925 | 9,556 | −1,631 | −1,631 |

To reflect the larger cash outflow, this additional payment amount must be *subtracted* from net income in Exhibit 13.3.

**Change in Accrued Expenses**   Some expenses are paid for after they are recognized (e.g., accrued wage expense). In this case, when expenses are recorded, the balance in the liability accrued expenses increases; when payments are made, accrued expenses decrease. Thus, the change in the balance in accrued expenses from the beginning to the end of the period is the difference between expenses on the income statement and cash payments. Given this, we can generalize another rule:

When a net *increase in an accrued expense payable* for the period occurs, the recorded accrual basis expense is always more than cash paid for the expense; thus, the increase (the extra expense) must be *added* back in computing cash flows from operations.

When a net *decrease in an accrued expense payable* occurs, the recorded accrual basis expense is always less than cash paid for the expense; thus, the decrease (the extra payment) must be *subtracted* in computing cash flows from operations.

Since Boston Beer's accrued expenses on the balance sheet (Exhibit 13.2) *decreased* by $2,857 for the period, the reported expense is less than cash payments.

| Section | Balance Sheet Account | March 28, 1998 | December 27, 1997 | Change | Cash Flow Effect |
|---------|----------------------|----------------|-------------------|--------|------------------|
| O | Accrued expenses | 10,913 | 13,770 | −2,857 | −2,857 |

Thus, to reflect the larger cash outflow, the additional payment must be *subtracted* from net income to convert income to cash flow from operating activities in Exhibit 13.3.

**Summary**   We can summarize the typical additions and subtractions that are required to reconcile net income with cash flow from operating activities as follows:

| Item | Additions and Subtractions to Reconcile Net Income to Cash Flow from Operating Activities | |
|------|---|---|
| | When Item Increases | When Item Decreases |
| Depreciation, depletion, and amortization | + | |
| Accounts receivable (trade) | − | + |
| Prepaid expense assets | − | + |
| Inventory | + | |
| Other current assets | + | |
| Accounts payable (trade) | + | − |
| Accrued expense liabilities | + | − |

Notice in this table that an *increase in an asset or a decrease in a liability* is always *subtracted* to reconcile net income to cash flows from operating activities. A *decrease in an asset or an increase in a liability* is always *added* to reconcile net income to cash flows from operating activities. The cash flow statement for Boston Beer (Exhibit 13.1) shows the same additions and subtractions to reconcile net income to cash flows from operating activities described in Exhibit 13.3.

# KEY **RATIO ANALYSIS:**

## QUALITY OF INCOME RATIO

**K**now the decision question:
Are there significant differences between net income and operating cash flow? It is computed as follows:

$$\text{Quality of Income Ratio} = \frac{\text{Cash Flow from Operating Activities}}{\text{Net Income}}$$

The first quarter 1998 ratio for Boston Beer:

$$\frac{\$1,294}{\$2,076} = .623 \ (62.3\%)$$

■ **LEARNING OBJECTIVE 3**

Analyze and interpret the quality of income ratio.

**E**xamine the ratio using two techniques:

| ① Comparisons over Time | | |
|---|---|---|
| **Boston Beer (annual)** | | |
| 1996 | 1997 | 1998 |
| 1.88 | 0.92 | 2.82 |

| ② Comparisons with Competitors | |
|---|---|
| **Genesee** | **Coors** |
| 1998 | 1998 |
| 3.45 | 2.67 |

**Selected Focus Company Comparisons**

General Mills 1.28

Papa John's 1.80

Delta Air Lines 2.91

**Y**ou interpret the results carefully:

**IN GENERAL** → Quality of income ratio measures the portion of income that was generated in cash. All other things equal, a higher quality of income ratio indicates greater ability to finance operating and other cash needs from operating cash inflows.[6] A higher ratio also indicates that it is less likely that the company is using aggressive revenue recognition policies to increase net income. When this ratio does not equal 1.0, analysts must establish the source of the difference to determine the significance of the findings. There are four potential causes of any difference:

1. *The corporate life cycle (growth or decline in sales).* When sales are increasing, receivables and inventory normally increase faster than accounts payable. This often reduces operating cash flows below income, which, in turn, reduces the ratio. When sales are declining, the opposite occurs, and the ratio increases.

2. *Seasonality.* As was the case for Boston Beer, seasonal variations in sales and purchases of inventory can cause the ratio to deviate from 1.0.

3. *Changes in revenue and expense recognition.* Aggressive revenue recognition or failure to accrue appropriate expenses will inflate net income and reduce the ratio.

4. *Changes in management of operating assets and liabilities.* Inefficient management will increase operating assets and decrease liabilities, which will reduce operating cash flows and reduce the ratio. More efficient management will have the opposite effect.

**FOCUS COMPANY ANALYSIS** → Boston Beer's quality of income ratio has ranged from 0.92 to 2.82 during the last three years. As we noted earlier, the difference between net income and cash flow from operations in the case of Boston Beer for the first quarter of 1998 was not a cause for alarm. It was due to normal seasonal changes in sales and receivables. The annual results for 1998 support this conclusion, indicating the highest quality of income ratio in the prior three years. Its ratio is also quite similar to industry giant Coors Brewing. However, its ratio is lower than that of Genesee Brewing, which has diversified its operations into other food products. The wide variation in Boston Beer's ratio would prompt analysts to contact management to determine its causes.

**A FEW CAUTIONS:** The quality of income ratio can be interpreted only based on an understanding of the company's business operations and strategy. For example, a low ratio can be due simply to normal seasonal changes. However, it also can indicate obsolescent inventory, slowing sales, or failed expansion plans. Analysts often analyze this ratio in tandem with the accounts receivable turnover and inventory turnover ratios to test for these possibilities.*

*K. G. Palepu, P. M. Healy, and V. L. Bernard, *Business Analysis and Valuation Using Financial Statements,* 2e (Cincinnati, OH: South-Western, 2000)

**Additional Issues in Interpreting Cash Flows from Operations**   The reconciliation of net income to cash flow from operations may contain other adjusting items, most of which relate to topics covered in an intermediate accounting course. We describe these items briefly here.

1. *Gain or loss on sale of property, plant, and equipment.* As discussed in the next section, the total cash proceeds from the sale of property, plant, and equipment should be included in the Investing section of the statement. Since the gain or loss already

[6]When net income is negative, a more negative ratio indicates greater ability to finance the company from operations.

is included in net income, to avoid counting the effect of the gain or loss twice, it must be eliminated from the Operating section by *subtracting the gain or adding the loss.* Chapter Supplement A discusses this issue in more detail.

2. *Deferred income taxes.* Deferred taxes result from timing differences that exist between GAAP used for financial reporting and U.S. tax law that governs preparation of tax returns. An increase in a deferred tax liability is associated with an expense in the current period even though it will not cause a cash outflow until some future accounting period. Because an *increase* in a deferred tax liability does not cause a cash outflow in the current period, it is *added* to net income on the statement of cash flows. Deferred taxes always reverse at some point in the future and cause a cash outflow. When they do, the *decrease* in the liability must be *subtracted* from net income on the statement of cash flows.

3. *Equity in income or losses of unconsolidated affiliates.* When the equity method is used to account for an intercorporate investment, the investor must record in net income its share of any profits or losses generated by the affiliate. This share of profit or loss does not affect cash flows. Therefore, equity *profits* must be *subtracted* from net income because there is no cash inflow, and equity *losses* must be *added* back because there is no cash outflow.

Two additional complicating factors should be noted. Consolidated statements may include one or more subsidiaries whose statements are denominated in a currency other than the U.S. dollar (for example, the French franc). The process of translating those statements into dollars may cause the changes in the current assets and liabilities on the balance sheet not to match the changes reported on the cash flow statement.[7] Acquisitions of new subsidiaries during the period can have a similar effect.

## A QUESTION OF ETHICS

### ERRORS AND IRREGULARITIES AND CASH FLOWS FROM OPERATIONS

The cash flow statement often gives outsiders the first hint that financial statements may contain errors and irregularities. The importance of this indicator as a predictor is receiving more attention in new auditing standards, as *Business Week* reports:

> The new standard will require auditors to look for a lengthy list of "risk factors" found in previous cases of chicanery. Is management being hyperaggressive in pursuit of overly ambitious financial targets? Does a sharp mismatch exist between reported earnings and cash flow?

As noted in earlier chapters, unethical managers sometimes attempt to reach earnings targets by manipulating accruals and deferrals of revenues and expenses to inflate income. Since these adjusting entries do not affect the cash account, they have no effect on the cash flow statement. As a consequence, a growing difference between net income and cash flow from operations can be a sign of such manipulations. This early warning sign has been evident before some famous bankruptcies, such as that of W. T. Grant. This company had inflated income by failing to make adequate accruals of expenses for uncollectible accounts receivable and obsolete inventory. The growing difference between net income and cash flow from operations that resulted was noted by the more astute analysts who recommended selling the stock long before the bankruptcy.

Source: *Business Week*, December 9, 1996, p. 68.

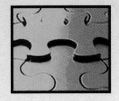

**REAL WORLD EXCERPT**

*Business Week*

---

[7]P. R. Bahnson, P. B. W. Miller, and B. P. Budge, "Nonarticulation in Cash Flow Statements and Implications for Education, Research and Practice," *Accounting Horizons,* December 1996, pp. 1–15.

## SELF-STUDY QUIZ

*Pete's Brewing Company*

Indicate which of the following items taken from Pete's Brewing Company's cash flow statement would be added (+), subtracted (−), or not included (0) in the reconciliation of net income to cash flow from operations.

_____ *a.* Increase in inventories.

_____ *b.* Net borrowings from revolving credit agreement with bank.

_____ *c.* Depreciation and amortization.

_____ *d.* Decrease in trade accounts receivable.

_____ *e.* Increase in trade accounts payable and accrued expenses.

_____ *f.* Increase in prepaid expenses and other current assets.

After you have completed your answers, check them with the solutions presented in the footnote at the bottom of this page.*

## A COMPARISON OF THE DIRECT AND INDIRECT METHODS

The indirect method of reporting cash flows from operating activities starts with net income and makes adjustments to compute net cash inflow or outflow. In contrast, the direct method accumulates all of the operating transactions that result in either a debit or a credit to cash into categories. It is important to note again that the net cash inflow or outflow is the *same* regardless of whether the direct or indirect method of presentation is used. The two methods differ only in terms of the details reported on the statement.

Exhibit 13.4 presents a comparison of these two reporting alternatives. Like most companies using the indirect method of reporting, Boston Beer does not report sufficient information to prepare the direct method presentation. Therefore, we made a number of simplifying assumptions in our computations, and the numbers do not exactly reflect Boston Beer's actual direct method cash flows.

EXHIBIT **13.4**

**Comparison of Indirect and Direct Methods**

**BOSTON BEER COMPANY**
**Statement of Cash Flows**
**(in thousands)**

Operating Activities Section of the Statement of Cash Flows Under the Indirect and Direct Methods

| Indirect Method | | Direct Method (estimated) | |
|---|---|---|---|
| Cash flows from operating activities: | | Cash flows from operating activities: | |
| Net income | $2,076 | Cash collected from customers | $41,672 |
| Adjustments to reconcile net income to net cash flow | | Cash collected for interest on investments | 212 |
| Depreciation expense | 1,225 | Cash payments to suppliers | (22,039) |
| Stock option compensation expense | 59 | Cash payments for administrative and selling expense | (18,311) |
| Loss on write-down of marketable equity security | 2,317 | Cash payments for interest | (193) |
| Accounts receivable increase | (3,655) | Cash payments for income taxes | (47) |
| Inventory decrease | 1,020 | Net cash outflow from operating activities | $ 1,294 |
| Prepaid expense decrease | 2,699 | | |
| Other current assets increase | (38) | | |
| Other assets (long-term rec.) decrease | 79 | | |
| Accounts payable decrease | (1,631) | | |
| Accrued expenses decrease | (2,857) | | |
| Net cash outflow from operating activities | $1,294 | | |

* *a.* −, *b.* 0, *c.* +, *d.* +, *e.* +, *f.* −.

The most important fact about Exhibit 13.4 to note is that *the amount reported as net cash outflow from operating activities is the same for both the direct and indirect methods of presentation.* They differ only in the method of computation. The FASB prefers but does not require the direct method because it provides to users additional information that cannot be derived from the indirect method and other statements. As noted earlier, however, because of the perceived additional costs involved, few companies use the direct method. Those that do are required to present the indirect method as an additional disclosure.

## INTERNATIONAL **PERSPECTIVE**

### AUSTRALIAN PRACTICES

Foster's Brewing is the first name in Australian beer and a major player in world beverage markets. Following Australian GAAP, which require use of the direct method of presentation, Foster's cash flow from operations is presented as follows:

| STATEMENT OF CASH FLOWS FOR THE YEAR ENDED 30 JUNE 1999 ($M) | |
|---|---:|
| **Operating Activities** | |
| Receipts from customers | 4,348.0 |
| Payments to suppliers, employees, principals | (3,806.7) |
| Dividends received | 1.8 |
| Interest received | 94.9 |
| Interest paid | (162.8) |
| Income tax paid | (129.2) |
| *Net cash flows from operating activities* | 346.0 |

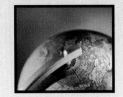

**REAL WORLD EXCERPT**

*Foster's Brewing*
ANNUAL REPORT

Note that Foster's combines payments to suppliers, employees, and principals (officers), but other companies report these items separately. Like U.S. companies that choose the direct method, Foster's reports the indirect presentation in a note to the financial statements.

## REPORTING AND INTERPRETING CASH FLOWS FROM INVESTING ACTIVITIES

This section requires analyzing the accounts related to the purchase and disposal of productive facilities used by the company, investments in the securities of other companies, and lending to other than customers. Normally, the relevant balance sheet accounts include short-term investments and long-term asset accounts such as long-term investments and property, plant, and equipment. The following relationships are the ones that you will encounter most frequently:

**■ LEARNING OBJECTIVE 4**

Report and interpret cash flows from investing activities.

| Related Balance Sheet Account(s) | Investing Activity | Cash Flow Effect |
|---|---|---|
| Property, plant, and equipment | Purchase of property, plant, and equipment for cash | Outflow |
| | Sale of property, plant, and equipment for cash | Inflow |
| Short- or long-term investments | Purchase of investment securities for cash | Outflow |
| | Sale (maturity) of investment securities for cash | Inflow |

Typical investing activities include these:

1. Cash expenditures that include the acquisition of tangible productive assets such as buildings and equipment or intangible assets such as trademarks and patents. Only purchases paid for with cash or cash equivalents are included. Purchases made using debt issued to the seller, for example, are excluded.

2. Cash proceeds from the sale of productive assets such as buildings and equipment or intangible assets such as trademarks and patents. This is the amount of cash that was received from the sale of assets, regardless of whether the assets were sold at a gain or loss.

3. Purchase of short- or long-term investments for cash. These investments can include stocks or bonds issued by other companies, bank certificates of deposit, or government securities with maturities of more than three months. (Remember that those with maturities of three months or less are cash equivalents.)

4. Cash proceeds from the sale or maturity of short- or long-term investments. Again, this is the amount of cash that was received from the sale, regardless of whether the assets were sold at a gain or loss.

In the case of Boston Beer Company, the analysis of changes in the balance sheet (shown in Exhibit 13.2) finds two noncurrent assets that have changed during the period (noted with an I). This indicates investing activities involving these two assets: Equipment and Leasehold Improvements, Net (fixed assets) and Short-Term Investments. Company records would then be searched to determine the causes of changes in these assets.

The company purchased new equipment for cash in the amount of $2,198, which is a cash outflow. It did not sell any other equipment for cash. Such sales would have resulted in a cash inflow. This item less the amount of depreciation expense added back in the Operations section, $1,225, explains the increase in Equipment and Leasehold Improvements, Net of $973.

| Section | Balance Sheet Account | March 28, 1998 | December 27, 1997 | Change |
|---------|----------------------|----------------|-------------------|--------|
| I | Equipment and leasehold improvements, net | 29,754 | 28,781 | +973 |

Cash purchases and sales of plant and equipment are listed separately on the statement of cash flows.

Boston Beer's records indicate that it also purchased an additional $438 in short-term investments during the quarter. As noted earlier in our discussion of the operating section, they also wrote down short-term investments in the amount of $2,317 and recorded the related loss. Together, they explain the $1,879 decrease (+$438 − $2,317 = −$1,879) in short-term investments reported on the balance sheet.

| Section | Balance Sheet Account | March 28, 1998 | December 27, 1997 | Change |
|---------|----------------------|----------------|-------------------|--------|
| I | Short-term investments | 36,132 | 38,011 | −1,879 |

Both of these investing items are listed in the schedule of investing activities in Exhibit 13.5. The net cash flow from investing activities that results is a $2,636 outflow.

EXHIBIT **13.5**

**Boston Beer Company:
Schedule for Net Cash Flow
from Investing Activities
(in thousands)**

| Items from Balance Sheet and Account Analysis | Cash Inflow (Outflows) | Explanation |
|---|---|---|
| Purchase of fixed assets | ($2,198) | Payment in cash for buildings and equipment. |
| Purchase of short-term investments | (438) | Payment in full for new investments. |
| Net cash inflow (outflow) from investing activities | ($2,636) | Reported on the statement of cash flows. |

# KEY **RATIO ANALYSIS:**

## CAPITAL ACQUISITIONS RATIO

**K**now the decision question:

To what degree was the company able to finance purchases of property, plant, and equipment with cash provided by operating activities? Since capital expenditures for plant and equipment often vary greatly from year to year, this ratio is often computed over longer periods of time than one year, such as three years used here. It is computed as follows:

$$\text{Capital Acquisitions Ratio} = \frac{\text{Cash Flow from Operating Activities}}{\text{Cash Paid for Property, Plant, and Equipment}}$$

The 1996 through 1998 ratio for Boston Beer:

$$\frac{\$45,120}{\$36,252} = 1.24$$

■ **LEARNING OBJECTIVE 5**

Analyze and interpret the capital acquisitions ratio.

**E**xamine the ratio using two techniques:

| ① Comparisons over Time | |
|---|---|
| Boston Beer | |
| 1993–95 | 1996–98 |
| 2.74 | 1.24 |

| ② Comparisons with Competitors | |
|---|---|
| Minnesota Brewing | Redhook Ale |
| 1996–98 | 1996–98 |
| 0.46 | 0.30 |

**Y**ou interpret the results carefully:

**IN GENERAL** → The capital acquisitions ratio reflects the portion of purchases of property, plant, and equipment financed from operating activities without the need for outside debt or equity financing or the sale of other investments or fixed assets. A high ratio indicates less need for outside financing for current and future expansion. This benefits the company because it provides the company with opportunities for strategic acquisitions, avoids the cost of additional debt, and reduces the risks of bankruptcy that come with additional leverage (see Chapter 10).

**FOCUS COMPANY ANALYSIS** → Though the ratio has declined from 2.74 to 1.24 in recent years, Boston Beer has always maintained a healthy capital acquisitions ratio. To many, the tangible nature of plant and equipment may suggest that it is a low-risk investment. When companies in an industry build more productive capacity than is necessary to meet customer demand, however, the costs of maintaining and financing idle plant can drive a company to ruin. The brewing industry currently has significant excess capacity. Boston Beer minimizes the risks of its plant and equipment investments by outsourcing a significant portion of its production to other brewers. This practice, called *contract brewing,* gives Boston Beer advantages through lower borrowing and depreciation costs and through lower costs of transportation compared to companies using a single large brewery. It also avoids the risk of excess capacity. Alternatively, Minnesota Brewing and Redhook Ale follow a strategy of building new plant and equipment. The effects of the alternative strategies are made evident by this ratio.

**Selected Focus
Company Comparisons**

Papa John's 0.98

Delta Air Lines 1.23

General Mills 2.46

**A FEW CAUTIONS:** Since the needs for investment in plant and equipment differ dramatically across industries (for example, airlines versus pizza delivery restaurants), a particular firm's ratio should be compared only with its prior years' figures or with other firms in the same industry. Also, a high ratio may indicate a failure to update plant and equipment, which can limit a company's ability to compete in the future.

# FINANCIAL **ANALYSIS**

**FREE CASH FLOW =**
Cash Flows from Operating
Activities − Dividends −
Capital Expenditures

## FREE CASH FLOW

Managers and analysts also often calculate **free cash flow** as a measure of the firm's ability to pursue long-term investment opportunities. It is normally calculated as follows:

**Free Cash Flow = Cash Flows from Operating Activities −**
**Dividends − Capital Expenditures**

Any positive free cash flow is available for additional capital expenditures, investments in other companies, and mergers and acquisitions, without the need for external financing. While free cash flow is considered a positive sign of financial flexibility, it also can represent a hidden cost to shareholders. Sometimes managers use free cash flow to pursue unprofitable investments just for the sake of growth or for perquisites for management use (such as fancy offices and corporate jets). In these cases, the shareholders would be better off if free cash flow were paid as additional dividends or used to repurchase the company's stock in the open market.

## REPORTING AND INTERPRETING CASH FLOWS FROM FINANCING ACTIVITIES

**■ LEARNING OBJECTIVE 6**

Report and interpret cash flows from financing activities.

This section reflects changes in two current liabilities, *notes payable to financial institutions* (often called *short-term debt*), *current maturities of long-term debt,* as well as changes in *long-term liabilities and stockholders' equity accounts.* These balance sheet accounts relate to the issuance and retirement of debt and stock and the payment of dividends. The following relationships are the ones that you will encounter most frequently:

| Related Balance Sheet Account(s) | Financing Activity | Cash Flow Effect |
|---|---|---|
| Short-term debt (notes payable)—bank | Issuance of bank note for cash | Inflow |
| | Repayment of principal on bank note | Outflow |
| Long-term debt | Issuance of bonds for cash | Inflow |
| | Repayment of principal on bonds | Outflow |
| Common stock and Additional paid-in capital | Issuance of stock for cash | Inflow |
| | Repurchase (retirement) of stock with cash | Outflow |
| Retained earnings | Payment of cash dividends | Outflow |

Financing activities are associated with generating capital from creditors and owners. Typical financing activities include the following:

1.  *Proceeds from issuance of short- and long-term debt.* This represents cash received from borrowing from banks and other financial institutions and issuance of bonds to the public. If the debt is issued for other than cash (for example, issued directly to a supplier of equipment to pay for a purchase), it is not included.

2. *Principal payments on short- and long-term debt.* Cash outflows associated with debt include the periodic repayment of principal as well as the early retirement of debt. As you saw in previous chapters, most debt requires periodic payments of both principal and interest. The portion of the cash payment associated with principal is listed as a cash flow from financing activities. The portion that is associated with interest is a cash flow from operating activities.

3. *Proceeds from the issuance of common stock.* This represents cash received from the sale of common stock to investors. If the stock is issued for other than cash (for example, issued directly to an employee as part of salary), it is not included.

4. *Purchase of treasury stock or retirement of stock.* This cash outflow includes cash payments for repurchase of the company's own stock from shareholders.

5. *Cash portion of dividends.* This is the amount of cash dividends paid to owners during the year. Some students wonder why cash payments made to creditors (interest) are shown as an operating activity but cash payments to owners (dividends) are shown as a financing activity. Remember that interest is reported on the income statement and is, therefore, directly associated with earning income (it is an operating activity). Dividend payments are not reported on the income statement because they represent a distribution of income. Dividends are more appropriately shown as a financing activity.

To compute cash flows from financing activities, you should review changes in debt and stockholders' equity accounts. In the case of Boston Beer Company, the analysis of changes in the balance sheet (shown in Exhibit 13.2) finds that only Bank Line of Credit and contributed capital (Class A Common Stock and Additional Paid-In Capital) changed during the period (noted with an F). Company records indicate that the change in Bank Line of Credit resulted from borrowing $1,517 in cash from its bank. This item should be listed in Exhibit 13.6. This accounts for the $1,517 increase in Bank Line of Credit.

| Section | Balance Sheet Account | March 28, 1998 | December 27, 1997 | Change |
|---------|----------------------|----------------|-------------------|--------|
| F | Bank line of credit | 1,517 | 0 | +1,517 |

The change in contributed capital resulted from an issue of common stock to employees for $107 in cash, as well as $59 in noncash compensation expense (discussed earlier). This accounts for the $166 increase in contributed capital. The $107 cash transaction should be listed in the schedule of financing activities in Exhibit 13.6. The net cash inflow from the two financing activities is $1,624.

| Section | Balance Sheet Account | March 28, 1998 | December 27, 1997 | Change |
|---------|----------------------|----------------|-------------------|--------|
| F | Class A common stock | 164 | 163 | +1 |
| F | Additional paid-in capital | 56,188 | 56,023 | +165 |

| Items from Balance Sheet and Account Analysis | Cash Inflow (Outflows) | Explanation |
|-----------------------------------------------|------------------------|-------------|
| Borrowing under line of credit | $1,517 | Proceeds from borrowing from bank on short-term note payable |
| Issuance of stock | 107 | Proceeds from issue of common stock |
| Net cash inflow (outflow) from financing activities | $1,624 | Reported on the statement of cash flows. |

EXHIBIT **13.6**

**Boston Beer Company: Schedule for Net Cash Flow from Financing Activities (in thousands)**

When Boston Beer pays back the bank debt (principal only) or retires some of its own stock, it will report them as cash outflows in the Financing section for that period. Should Boston Beer ever decide to pay dividends, it would also list them as financing cash outflows.

## FINANCIAL ANALYSIS

### FINANCING GROWTH

The long-term growth of a company is normally financed from three sources: internally generated funds (cash from operating activities), the issuance of stock, and money borrowed on a long-term basis. As we discussed in Chapter 10, companies can adopt a number of different capital structures (the balance of debt and equity). The financing sources that management uses to fund growth will have an important impact on the firm's risk and return characteristics. The statement of cash flows shows how management has elected to fund its growth. This information is used by analysts who wish to evaluate the capital structure and growth potential of a business.

## SELF-STUDY QUIZ

*Pete's Brewing Company*

Indicate which of the following items taken from Pete's Brewing Company's cash flow statement would be reported in the Investing section (I) or Financing section (F) and whether the amount would be an inflow (+) or an outflow (−).

_____ *a.* Net payments on revolving credit agreement with bank.

_____ *b.* Additions to property and equipment (for cash).

_____ *c.* Additions to other (intangible) assets.

_____ *d.* Proceeds from sale (issuance) of common shares.

After you have completed your answers, check them with the solutions presented in the footnote at the bottom of this page.*

## PRESENTATION OF THE STATEMENT OF CASH FLOWS

The formal statement of cash flows for Boston Beer Company is shown in Exhibit 13.1. As you can see, it is a simple matter to construct the statement after the detailed analysis of the accounts and transactions has been completed (shown in Exhibits 13.3, 13.5, and 13.6). As you would expect, the preparation of the statement for a larger, more complex company is more difficult than was the case for Boston Beer. Despite the added complexity, the preparation of the statement for all companies is based on the same analytical approach that we have just discussed. Companies also must provide two other disclosures related to the cash flow statement.

**■ LEARNING OBJECTIVE 7**

Explain the impact of noncash investing and financing activities.

**NONCASH INVESTING AND FINANCING ACTIVITIES** are transactions that do not have direct cash flow effects; they are reported as a supplement to the statement of cash flows in narrative or schedule form.

### NONCASH INVESTING AND FINANCING ACTIVITIES

Certain transactions are important investing and financing activities but have no cash flow effects. These are called **noncash investing and financing activities.** For example, the purchase of a $100,000 building with a $100,000 mortgage given by the former owner does not cause either the inflow or the outflow of cash. As a result, these noncash activities are not listed in the three main sections of the cash flow statement. *FASB Statement 95* requires supplemental disclosure of these transactions in either narrative or schedule form. Boston Beer's statement of cash flows does not list any noncash investing and financing activities. The following schedule from the annual report of U•S Airways illustrates the significance and diversity of these noncash transactions.

---

\* *a.* F−, *b.* I−, *c.* I−, *d.* F+.

| U•S Airways | (in thousands) | | |
|---|---|---|---|
| | 1998 | 1997 | 1996 |
| Noncash investing and financing activities | | | |
| Net unrealized gain on available-for-sale securities, | | | |
| net of income tax effect | $73 | $104 | — |
| Reduction of aircraft-related purchase deposits | $61 | — | — |
| Reduction of parent company receivable-assignment | | | |
| of aircraft purchase rights by parent company | $22 | — | — |
| Issuances of debt-refinancing of debt secured by aircraft | — | — | $160 |
| Reductions of debt-refinancing of debt secured by aircraft | — | — | $154 |
| Reduction of parent company debt-aircraft acquisitions | — | — | $ 69 |
| Issuances of debt-aircraft acquisitions | — | — | $ 29 |

## SUPPLEMENTAL CASH FLOW INFORMATION

Companies such as Boston Beer that use the indirect method of presenting cash flows from operations also must provide two other figures: cash paid for interest and cash paid for income taxes. These are normally listed at the bottom of the statement or in the notes.

## EPILOGUE

Our more detailed analysis of Boston Beer's first-quarter cash flow indicates that the difference between net income and cash flows in the first quarter was not a cause for alarm. In fact, it was a normal consequence of seasonal variations in sales, purchases of raw materials, and advertising expenditures. On the income statement, lower sales in the first quarter are usually more than offset by the decline in advertising in the same period, resulting in strong earnings. The upsurge in sales in March, however, causes receivables to rise, resulting in lower cash flow from operations. Collections of these receivables in the second quarter account for much of the upsurge in cash flows from operations in that quarter. Our further analysis of Boston Beer's investing and financing indicates that the cash needs to continue its investment strategy should be more than met by operations.

In fact, the year ended December 26, 1998, was one of record cash flow from operations for Boston Beer, $22,374. In his most recent report on Boston Beer,[8] K. Timothy Swanson of A.G. Edwards does not see any problems related to cash flow. He sees a tough competitive environment and continuing tough times for the whole craft beer segment in 1999. In the longer term, though, he believes that Boston Beer will be among the growth leaders in the segment. Successful competition for retail shelf space and new product introductions will be keys to Boston Beer's future growth.

## DEMONSTRATION **CASE**

*Redhook Ale Brewery*

(Try to resolve the requirements before proceeding to the suggested solution that follows.)

During a recent year (ended December 31, 20A), Redhook Ale Brewery, a Seattle-based craft brewer, reported net income of $3,182 (all numbers in thousands) and cash and cash equivalents at the beginning of the year of $472. It also engaged in the following activities:

a. Paid $18,752 in principal on debt.
b. Received $46,202 in cash from initial public offering of common stock.
c. Incurred other noncurrent accrued operating expenses of $857.
d. Paid $18,193 in cash for purchase of fixed assets.
e. Accounts receivable increased by $881.

---

[8]Dated May 1, 1998.

f. Borrowed $16,789 from various lenders.

g. Refundable deposits payable increased by $457.

h. Inventories increased by $574.

i. Made cash deposits on equipment of $5,830.

j. Income tax refund receivable decreased by $326.

k. Sold (issued) stock to employees for $13 in cash.

l. Accounts payable decreased by $391.

m. Received $4 from other investing activities.

n. Accrued expenses increased by $241.

o. Prepaid expenses increased by $565.

p. Recorded depreciation of $1,324.

q. Paid $5 cash in other financing activities.

*Required:*

Based on this information, prepare the cash flow statement using the indirect method.

## SUGGESTED SOLUTION

**REDHOOK ALE BREWERY**
**Statement of Cash Flows**
**For the Year Ended December 31, 20A**
**(in thousands)**

| | |
|---|---:|
| Operating activities | |
| Net income | $ 3,182 |
| Adjustments | |
| Depreciation | 1,324 |
| Other noncurrent accrued expenses | 857 |
| Change in accounts receivable | (881) |
| Change in inventories | (574) |
| Change in income taxes receivable | 326 |
| Change in prepaid expenses | (565) |
| Change in accounts payable | (391) |
| Change in accrued expenses | 241 |
| Change in refundable deposits payable | 457 |
| Net cash flow from operating activities | 3,976 |
| Investing activities | |
| Expenditures for fixed assets | (18,193) |
| Deposits on equipment | (5,830) |
| Other | 4 |
| Net cash flow from investing activities | (24,019) |
| Financing activities | |
| Proceeds from debt | 16,789 |
| Repayment of debt | (18,752) |
| Proceeds from sale of stock (IPO) | 46,202 |
| Proceeds from sale of stock (options) | 13 |
| Other | (5) |
| Net cash flow from financing activities | 44,247 |
| Increase in cash and cash equivalents | 24,204 |
| Cash and cash equivalents: | |
| Beginning of year | 472 |
| End of year | $24,676 |

## Chapter Supplement A

### Adjustment for Gains and Losses

As noted earlier, the operating activities section of the statement may include an adjustment for gains and losses reported on the income statement. The transactions that cause gains and losses should be classified on the cash flow statement as operating, investing, or financing activities, depending on their dominant characteristics. For example, if the sale of a productive asset (e.g., a delivery truck) produced a gain, it would be classified as an investing activity.

An adjustment must be made in the Operating Activities section to avoid double counting the gain or loss. To illustrate, consider the following entry for Boston Beer to record the disposal of a delivery truck:

| Cash (A) ................................ | 8,000 | |
| Accumulated depreciation (XA) .............. | 4,000 | |
|     Property, plant, and equipment (A) ........ | | 10,000 |
|     Gain on disposal (R) .................... | | 2,000 |

| Assets | | = | Liabilities | + | Stockholders' Equity | |
| --- | --- | --- | --- | --- | --- | --- |
| Cash | +8,000 | | | | Gain on disposal | +2,000 |
| Accumulated depreciation | +4,000 | | | | | |
| Property, plant, and equipment | −10,000 | | | | | |

The inflow of cash was $8,000, but only the reported gain of $2,000 was shown on the income statement. This transaction should be reported on the statement of cash flows as an investing activity with a cash inflow of $8,000. Because the gain was included in the computation of income, it is necessary to remove (subtract) the $2,000 gain from the Operating Activities section of the statement to avoid double counting. If we avoid the double counting by reporting only $6,000 cash inflow from investing activities, we misstate the actual effects of the transaction.

When a loss is reported on the income statement, it also must be removed when preparing the cash flow statement. Consider the following entry to record the sale of assets:

| Cash (A) ................................ | 41,000 | |
| Accumulated depreciation (XA) .............. | 15,000 | |
| Loss on disposal (E) ...................... | 12,000 | |
|     Property, plant, and equipment (A) ........ | | 68,000 |

| Assets | | = | Liabilities | + | Stockholders' Equity | |
| --- | --- | --- | --- | --- | --- | --- |
| Cash | +41,000 | | | | Loss on disposal | −12,000 |
| Accumulated depreciation | +15,000 | | | | | |
| Property, plant, and equipment | −68,000 | | | | | |

On the cash flow statement, the loss of $12,000 must be removed (added back) in the computation of cash from operating activities, and the total cash collected of $41,000 must be shown in the investing activities section of the statement.

## Chapter Supplement B

### Spreadsheet Approach—Statement of Cash Flows: Indirect Method

As situations become more complex, the analytical approach that we used to prepare the statement of cash flows for Boston Beer Company becomes cumbersome and inefficient. In actual practice, most companies use a spreadsheet approach to prepare the statement of cash flows. The spreadsheet is based on the same logic that we used in our previous illustration. The spreadsheet's primary advantage is that it offers a more systematic way to keep track of data. You may find it useful even in simple situations because it minimizes the possibility of errors.

Exhibit 13.7 shows Boston Beer Company's spreadsheet, which is organized as follows:

1. Four columns to record dollar amounts are established. The first column is for the beginning balances for items reported on the balance sheet; the next two columns reflect debit and credit changes to those balances; the final column contains the ending balances for the balance sheet accounts.

2. On the far left of the top half of the spreadsheet, each account name from the balance sheet is entered.

3. On the far left of the bottom half of the spreadsheet, the name of each item that will be reported on the statement of cash flows is entered.

*Changes* in the various balance sheet accounts are analyzed in terms of debits and credits in the top half of the spreadsheet with the offsetting debits and credits being recorded in the bottom half of the spreadsheet in terms of their impact on cash flows. Each change in the noncash balance sheet accounts explains part of the change in the Cash account. To illustrate, let's examine each of the entries on the spreadsheet for Boston Beer Company shown in Exhibit 13.7. You will note that they follow each of the items presented in the schedule to prepare the cash flow statement shown in Exhibits 13.3, 13.5, and 13.6.

a. This entry is used to start the reconciliation; net income is shown as an inflow in the Operating Activities section to be reconciled by the noncash reconciling entries. The credit to Retained Earnings reflects the effects of the original closing entry. This is the starting point for the reconciliation.

b. Depreciation expense is a noncurrent accrued expense. It is added back to net income because this type of expense does not cause a cash outflow when it is recorded. The credit to Accumulated Depreciation reflects the effects of the original entry to record depreciation.

c. Stock option compensation expense is a noncurrent accrued expense (an expense paid with common stock). It is added back to net income because this type of expense does not cause a cash outflow when it is recorded. The credit to Additional Paid-In Capital (and Common Stock of an amount less than $1) reflects the original entry for the issuance of the stock.

d. The write-down (loss) of a marketable security that had suffered a permanent decline in value relates to an investing activity and did not affect cash. Like noncurrent accrued expenses, this loss is added back to net income because it does not cause a cash outflow when it is recorded. The credit to short-term investments reflects the effects of the original entry to record the loss.

e. This entry reconciles the change in accounts receivable during the period with net income. It is subtracted from net income because cash collections from customers totaled less than sales revenue.

f. This entry reconciles the purchases of inventory with cost of goods sold. It is added to net income because less inventory was purchased than was sold.

g. This entry reconciles the prepayment of expenses with their expiration. It is added to net income because cash payments for new prepayments are less than the amounts that expired and were recorded on the income statement during the period.

h. This entry reconciles payments for purchases of other current assets and their expiration. It is subtracted from net income because cash payments for new other current assets are more than the amounts that expired and were recorded on the income statement during the period.

EXHIBIT **13.7**

**Spreadsheet to Prepare Statement of Cash Flows, Indirect Method**

**BOSTON BEER COMPANY**
**Quarter Ended March 28, 1998**
**(in thousands)**

| | Beginning Balances, 12/27/1997 | Analysis of Change Debit | | Analysis of Change Credit | | Ending Balances, 3/28/1998 |
|---|---|---|---|---|---|---|
| **Items from Balance Sheet** | | | | | | |
| Cash and cash equivalents | 13 | (p) | 282 | | | 295 |
| Short-term investments | 38,011 | (m) | 438 | (d) | 2,317 | 36,132 |
| Accounts receivable, net | 16,483 | (e) | 3,655 | | | 20,138 |
| Inventories | 13,675 | | | (f) | 1,020 | 12,655 |
| Prepaid expenses | 4,344 | | | (g) | 2,699 | 1,645 |
| Deferred income taxes | 2,266 | | | | | 2,266 |
| Other current assets | 1,598 | (h) | 38 | | | 1,636 |
| Equipment and leasehold improvements | 39,652 | (l) | 2,198 | | | 41,850 |
| Accumulated depreciation | (10,871) | | | (b) | 1,225 | (12,096) |
| Other assets (long-term receivables) | 2,742 | | | (i) | 79 | 2,663 |
| Accounts payable | 9,556 | (j) | 1,631 | | | 7,925 |
| Bank line of credit | 0 | | | (o) | 1,517 | 1,517 |
| Accrued expenses | 13,770 | (k) | 2,857 | | | 10,913 |
| Long-term debt, less current maturities | 10,000 | | | | | 10,000 |
| Long-term deferred taxes | 789 | | | | | 789 |
| Class A common stock | 163 | | | (n) | 1 | 164 |
| Class B common stock | 41 | | | | | 41 |
| Additional paid-in capital | 56,023 | | | (c) | 59 | 56,188 |
| | | | | (n) | 106 | |
| Retained earnings | 17,571 | | | (a) | 2,076 | 19,647 |

| | | Inflows | | Outflows | | Subtotals |
|---|---|---|---|---|---|---|
| **Statement of Cash Flows** | | | | | | |
| Cash flows from operating activities: | | | | | | |
| Net income | | (a) | 2,076 | | | |
| Adjustments to reconcile net income to net cash provided by operating activities: | | | | | | |
| Depreciation and amortization | | (b) | 1,225 | | | |
| Stock option compensation expense | | (c) | 59 | | | |
| Loss on write-down of marketable equity security | | (d) | 2,317 | | | |
| Changes in assets and liabilities: | | | | | | |
| Accounts receivable (net) | | | | (e) | 3,655 | |
| Inventory | | (f) | 1,020 | | | |
| Prepaid expenses | | (g) | 2,699 | | | |
| Other current assets | | | | (h) | 38 | |
| Other assets (long-term receivables) | | (i) | 79 | | | |
| Accounts payable | | | | (j) | 1,631 | |
| Accrued expenses | | | | (k) | 2,857 | |
| | | | | | | 1,294 |
| Cash flows for investing activities: | | | | | | |
| Purchases of fixed assets | | | | (l) | 2,198 | |
| Purchases of short-term investments | | | | (m) | 438 | |
| | | | | | | (2,636) |
| Cash flows from financing activities: | | | | | | |
| Proceeds from sale of shares | | (n) | 107 | | | |
| Net borrowings under line of credit | | (o) | 1,517 | | | |
| | | | | | | 1,624 |
| Net increase in cash and cash equivalents | | | | (p) | 282 | |
| | | | 22,198 | | 22,198 | 282 |

*i.* This entry reconciles cash received from long-term receivables and accrual basis revenues. It is added because more cash is received than revenues recorded.

*j.* This entry reconciles cash paid to suppliers with purchases on account. It is subtracted because more cash was paid than was borrowed during the period.

*k.* This entry reconciles the accrual of expenses with payments for these expenses. It is subtracted because cash payments for expenses are more than new accruals.

*l.* This entry records the purchases of new plant and equipment (fixed assets) for cash.

*m.* This entry records the purchases of investments for cash.

*n.* This entry records the cash received from the issuance of stock. The credits to Common Stock and Additional Paid-In Capital reflect the original entry to record the issuance.

*o.* This entry records the cash received from new borrowing from the bank.

*p.* This entry shows that the net increase or decrease reported on the statement of cash flows is the same as the change in the cash balance on the balance sheet during the period.

The preceding entries complete the spreadsheet analysis because all accounts are reconciled. The accuracy of the analysis can be checked by adding the two analysis columns to verify that Debits = Credits. The formal statement of cash flows can be prepared directly from the spreadsheet.

Preparing a statement of cash flows is more difficult than preparing an income statement or a balance sheet. To develop the statement of cash flows, it is necessary to analyze changes in various accounts to determine the cash flow effects. The other statements can be prepared easily by taking the balances from various accounts in the ledger.

The analytical technique that you have learned for preparing the statement of cash flows will help you deal with other significant business problems. For example, this type of analysis is useful for developing cash budgets for a business. Many small businesses that experience rapid sales growth get into serious financial difficulties because they did not forecast the cash flow effects associated with credit sales and large increases in inventory.

## CHAPTER **TAKE-AWAYS**

1. **Classify cash flow statement items as part of net cash flows from operating, investing, and financing activities.   p. 683**

   The statement has three main sections: Cash Flows from Operating Activities, which are related to earning income from normal operations; Cash Flows from Investing Activities, which are related to the acquisition and sale of productive assets; and Cash Flows from Financing Activities, which are related to external financing of the enterprise. The net cash inflow or outflow for the year is the same amount as the increase or decrease in cash and cash equivalents for the year on the balance sheet. Cash equivalents are highly liquid investments with original maturities of less than three months.

2. **Report and interpret differences between net income and cash flows from operating activities.   p. 687**

   The indirect method for reporting cash flows from operating activities reports a conversion of net income to net cash flow from operating activities. The conversion involves additions and subtractions for (1) noncurrent accruals including expenses (such as depreciation expense) and revenues which do not affect current assets or current liabilities and (2) changes in each of the individual current assets (other than cash and short-term investments) and current liabilities (other than short-term debt to financial institutions and current maturities of long-term debt, which relate to financing), which reflect differences in the timing of accrual basis net income and cash flows.

3. **Analyze and interpret the quality of income ratio. p. 697**

   Quality of income ratio (Cash Flow from Operating Activities ÷ Net Income) measures the portion of income that was generated in cash. A higher quality of income ratio indicates greater ability to finance operating and other cash needs from operating cash inflows. A higher ratio also indicates that it is less likely that the company is using aggressive revenue recognition policies to increase net income.

4. **Report and interpret cash flows from investing activities. p. 699**

   Investing activities reported on the cash flow statement include cash payments to acquire fixed assets and short- and long-term investments and cash proceeds from the sale of fixed assets and short- and long-term investments.

5. **Analyze and interpret the capital acquisitions ratio. p. 701**

   The capital acquisitions ratio (Cash Flow from Operating Activities ÷ Cash Paid for Property, Plant, and Equipment) reflects the portion of purchases of property, plant, and equipment financed from operating activities without the need for outside debt or equity financing or the sale of other investments or fixed assets. A high ratio benefits the company because it provides the company with opportunities for strategic acquisitions.

6. **Report and interpret cash flows from financing activities. p. 702**

   Cash inflows from financing activities include cash proceeds from issuance of short- and long-term debt and common stock. Cash outflows include cash principal payments on short- and long-term debt, cash paid for the repurchase of the company's stock, and cash dividend payments. Cash payments associated with interest are a cash flow from operating activities.

7. **Explain the impact of noncash financing and investing activities. p. 704**

   Noncash investing and financing activities are investing and financing activities that do not involve cash. They include, for example, purchases of fixed assets with long-term debt or stock, exchanges of fixed assets, and exchanges of debt for stock. These transactions are disclosed only as supplemental disclosures to the cash flow statement.

Throughout the preceding chapters, we emphasized the conceptual basis of accounting. An understanding of the rationale underlying accounting is important for both preparers and users of financial statements. In Chapter 14, we bring together our discussion of the major users of financial statements and how they analyze and use them. We discuss and illustrate many widely used analytical techniques discussed in earlier chapters, as well as additional techniques. As you study Chapter 14, you will see that an understanding of accounting rules and concepts is essential for effective analysis of financial statements.

## KEY **RATIOS**

**Quality of income ratio** indicates what portion of income was generated in cash. It is computed as follows (p. 695):

$$\text{Quality of Income Ratio} = \frac{\text{Cash Flow from Operating Activities}}{\text{Net Income}}$$

**Capital acquisitions ratio** measures the ability to finance purchases of plant and equipment from operations. It is computed as follows (p. 701):

$$\text{Capital Acquisitions Ratio} = \frac{\text{Cash Flow from Operating Activities}}{\text{Cash Paid for Property, Plant, and Equipment}}$$

## FINDING FINANCIAL INFORMATION

| | |
|---|---|
| **BALANCE SHEET**<br>*Changes in Assets, Liabilities, and Stockholders' Equity* | **INCOME STATEMENT**<br>*Net Income and Noncurrent Accruals* |
| **STATEMENT OF CASH FLOWS**<br>*Cash Flows from Operating Activities*<br>*Cash Flows from Investing Activities*<br>*Cash Flows from Financing Activities*<br>*Separate schedule (or note):*<br>    Noncash investing and financing activities<br>    Interest and taxes paid | **NOTES**<br>*Under Summary of Significant Accounting Policies*<br>    Definition of cash equivalents<br>*Under Separate Note*<br>    If not listed on cash flow statement:<br>        Non-cash investing and financing<br>          activities<br>        Interest and taxes paid |

## KEY TERMS

**Cash Equivalent** p. 683

**Cash Flows from Financing Activities** p. 685

**Cash Flows from Investing Activities** p. 684

**Cash Flows from Operating Activities (Cash Flows from Operations)** p. 684

**Direct Method** p. 684

**Free Cash Flow** p. 702

**Indirect Method** p. 684

**Noncash Investing and Financing Activities** p. 704

**Noncurrent Accruals (Noncash Expenses and Revenues)** p. 689

## QUESTIONS

1. Compare the purposes of the income statement, the balance sheet, and the statement of cash flows.
2. What information does the statement of cash flows report that is not reported on the other required financial statements? How do investors and creditors use that information?
3. What are cash equivalents? How are purchases and sales of cash equivalents reported on the statement of cash flows?
4. What are the major categories of business activities reported on the statement of cash flows? Define each of these activities.
5. What are the typical cash inflows from operating activities? What are the typical cash outflows from operating activities?
6. Under the indirect method, depreciation expense is added to net income to report cash flows from operating activities. Does depreciation cause an inflow of cash?
7. Explain why cash paid during the period for purchases and for salaries is not specifically reported on the statement of cash flows, indirect method, as cash outflows.
8. Explain why a $50,000 increase in inventory during the year must be included in developing cash flows for operating activities under both the direct and indirect methods.
9. Compare the two methods of reporting cash flows from operating activities in the statement of cash flows.
10. What are the typical cash inflows from investing activities? What are the typical cash outflows from investing activities?
11. What are the typical cash inflows from financing activities? What are the typical cash outflows from financing activities?
12. What are noncash investing and financing activities? Give two examples. How are they reported on the statement of cash flows?
13. How is the sale of equipment reported on the statement of cash flows using the indirect method?

# MINI-EXERCISES

**M13–1  Matching Items Reported to Cash Flow Statement Categories (Indirect Method)**

LO1

Adolph Coors

Adolph Coors Company, founded in 1873, is the third largest U.S. brewer. Its tie to the magical appeal of the Rocky Mountains is one of its most powerful trademarks. Some of the items included in its recent annual consolidated statement of cash flows presented using the *indirect method* are listed here. Indicate whether each item is disclosed in the Operating Activities (O), Investing Activities (I), or Financing Activities (F) section of the statement or (NA) if the item does not appear on the statement. (*Note:* This is the exact wording used on the actual statement.)

_____  1.  Proceeds from sale of properties.

_____  2.  Purchase of stock. [This involves repurchase of its own stock.]

_____  3.  Depreciation, depletion, and amortization.

_____  4.  Accounts payable (decrease).

_____  5.  Inventories (decrease).

_____  6.  Principal payment on long-term debt.

**M13–2  Determining the Effects of Account Changes on Cash Flow from Operating Activities (Indirect Method)**

LO2

Indicate whether each item would be added (+) or subtracted (−) in the computation of cash flow from operating activities using the indirect method.

_____  1.  Depreciation, depletion, and amortization.

_____  2.  Inventories (increase).

_____  3.  Accounts payable (decrease).

_____  4.  Accounts receivable (decrease).

_____  5.  Accrued expenses (increase).

**M13–3  Analyzing the Quality of Income Ratio**

LO3

Lisa K. Corporation reported net income of $80,000, depreciation expense of $3,000, and cash flow from operations of $60,000. Compute the quality of income ratio. What does the ratio tell you about the company's ability to finance operating and other cash needs from operating cash inflows?

**M13–4  Computing Cash Flows from Investing Activities**

LO4

Based on the following information, compute cash flows from investing activities.

| Cash collections from customers | $800 |
|---|---|
| Sale of used equipment | 250 |
| Depreciation expense | 100 |
| Purchase of short-term investments | 300 |

**M13–5  Computing Cash Flows from Financing Activities**

LO6

Based on the following information, compute cash flows from financing activities.

| Purchase of short-term investments | $ 250 |
|---|---|
| Dividends paid | 800 |
| Interest paid | 400 |
| Additional short-term borrowing from bank | 1,000 |

**M13–6  Reporting Noncash Investing and Financing Activities**

LO7

Which of the following transactions qualify as noncash investing and financing activities?

_____  Purchase of equipment with short-term investments

_____  Dividends paid in cash

_____  Purchase of building with mortgage payable

_____  Additional short-term borrowing from bank

# EXERCISES

■ **LO1**          **E13–1**     **Matching Items Reported to Cash Flow Statement Categories (Indirect Method)**

*Nike*

Nike, Inc., is the best-known sports shoe, apparel, and equipment company in the world because of its association with sports legends such as Michael Jordan, teams such as the Michigan Wolverines, and events such as the Olympics. Some of the items included in its recent annual consolidated statement of cash flows presented using the *indirect method* are listed here.

Indicate whether each item is disclosed in the Operating Activities (O), Investing Activities (I), or Financing Activities (F) section of the statement or (NA) if the item does not appear on the statement. (*Note:* This is the exact wording used on the actual statement.)

_____  1.  Depreciation.

_____  2.  Additions to property, plant, and equipment.

_____  3.  Increase (decrease) in notes payable. (The amount is owed to financial institutions.)

_____  4.  (Increase) decrease in other current assets.

_____  5.  Disposal of property, plant, and equipment.

_____  6.  Reductions in long-term debt including current portion.

_____  7.  Repurchase of stock.

_____  8.  (Increase) decrease in inventory.

_____  9.  Net income.

_____  10.  Additions to long-term debt.

■ **LO1**          **E13–2**     **Determining Cash Flow Statement Effects of Transactions**

*Stanley Furniture*

Stanley Furniture Company is a Virginia-based furniture manufacturer. For each of the following first-quarter transactions, indicate whether *net cash inflows (outflows)* from operating activities (NCFO), investing activities (NCFI), or financing activities (NCFF) are affected and whether the effect is an inflow (+) or outflow (−), or (NE) if the transaction has no effect on cash. (*Hint:* Determine the journal entry recorded for the transaction. The transaction affects net cash flows if and only if the account Cash is affected.)

_____  1.  Paid cash to purchase new equipment.

_____  2.  Purchased raw materials inventory on account.

_____  3.  Collected payments on account from customers.

_____  4.  Recorded an adjusting entry to record an accrued salaries expense.

_____  5.  Recorded and paid interest on debt to creditors.

_____  6.  Repaid principal on revolving credit loan from bank.

_____  7.  Prepaid rent for the following period.

_____  8.  Sold used equipment for cash at book value.

_____  9.  Made payment to suppliers on account.

_____  10.  Declared and paid cash dividends to shareholders.

■ **LO1**          **E13–3**     **Determining Cash Flow Statement Effects of Transactions**

*Compaq Computer*

Compaq Computer Corporation is a leading manufacturer of personal computers and servers for the business and home markets. For each of the following recent transactions, indicate whether *net cash inflows (outflows)* from operating activities (NCFO), investing activities (NCFI), or financing activities (NCFF) are affected and whether the effect is an inflow (+) or outflow (−), or (NE) if the transaction has no effect on cash. (*Hint:* Determine the journal entry recorded for the transaction. The transaction affects net cash flows if and only if the account Cash is affected.)

_____  1.  Recorded and paid income taxes to the federal government.

_____  2.  Issued common stock for cash.

_____  3.  Prepaid rent for the following period.

_____  4.  Recorded an adjusting entry for expiration of a prepaid expense.

_____  5.  Paid cash to purchase new equipment.

_____ 6. Issued long-term debt for cash.

_____ 7. Collected payments on account from customers.

_____ 8. Purchased raw materials inventory on account.

_____ 9. Recorded and paid salaries to employees.

_____ 10. Purchased new equipment by signing a three-year note.

## E13–4 Interpreting Noncurrent Accruals from a Management Perspective ▓ LO2

QuickServe, a chain of convenience stores, was experiencing some serious cash flow difficulties because of rapid growth. The company did not generate sufficient cash from operating activities to finance its new stores, and creditors were not willing to lend money because the company had not produced any income for the previous three years. The new controller for QuickServe proposed a reduction in the estimated life of store equipment to increase depreciation expense; thus, "we can improve cash flows from operating activities because depreciation expense is added back on the statement of cash flows." Other executives were not sure that this was a good idea because the increase in depreciation would make it more difficult to have positive earnings: "Without income, the bank will never lend us money."

*Required:*
What action would you recommend for QuickServe? Why?

## E13–5 Comparing the Direct and Indirect Methods ▓ LO2

To compare statement of cash flows reporting under the direct and indirect methods, enter check marks to indicate which items are used with each method.

| | Statement of Cash Flows Method | |
|---|---|---|
| Cash Flows (and Related Changes) | Direct | Indirect |
| 1. Revenues from customers | | |
| 2. Accounts receivable increase or decrease | | |
| 3. Payments to suppliers | | |
| 4. Inventory increase or decrease | | |
| 5. Accounts payable increase or decrease | | |
| 6. Payments to employees | | |
| 7. Wages payable, increase or decrease | | |
| 8. Depreciation expense | | |
| 9. Net income | | |
| 10. Cash flows from operating activities | | |
| 11. Cash flows from investing activities | | |
| 12. Cash flows from financing activities | | |
| 13. Net increase or decrease in cash during the period | | |

## E13–6 Reporting Cash Flows from Operating Activities (Indirect Method) ▓ LO2

The following information pertains to Day Company:

| | | |
|---|---|---|
| Sales | | $80,000 |
| Expenses | | |
| Cost of goods sold | $50,000 | |
| Depreciation expense | 6,000 | |
| Salaries expense | 12,000 | 68,000 |
| Net income | | $12,000 |
| Accounts receivable increase | $ 5,000 | |
| Merchandise inventory decrease | 8,000 | |
| Salaries payable increase | 500 | |

*Required:*

Present the Operating Activities section of the statement of cash flows for Day Company using the indirect method.

■ **LO2**    **E13–7**    **Reporting and Interpreting Cash Flows from Operating Activities from an Analyst's Perspective (Indirect Method)**

Kane Company completed its income statement and balance sheet for 20D and provided the following information:

| | | |
|---|---:|---:|
| Service revenue | | $50,000 |
| Expenses | | |
| Salaries | $42,000 | |
| Depreciation | 7,000 | |
| Amortization of copyrights | 300 | |
| Utilities | 7,000 | |
| Other expenses | 1,700 | 58,000 |
| Net loss | | ($ 8,000) |
| Decrease in accounts receivable | $12,000 | |
| Bought a small service machine | 5,000 | |
| Increase in salaries payable | 9,000 | |
| Decrease in service revenue collected in advance | 4,000 | |

*Required:*

1. Present the Operating Activities section of the statement of cash flows for Kane Company using the indirect method.
2. What were the major reasons that Kane was able to report a net loss but positive cash flow from operations? Why are the reasons for the difference between cash flow from operations and net income important to financial analysts?

■ **LO2**    **E13–8**    **Reporting and Interpreting Cash Flows from Operating Activities from an Analyst's Perspective (Indirect Method)**

*Sizzler International, Inc.*

Sizzler International, Inc., operates 700 family restaurants around the world. The company's recent annual report contained the following information (in thousands):

| | 20C |
|---|---:|
| Net loss | $(9,482) |
| Depreciation and amortization | 33,305 |
| Increase in receivables | 170 |
| Decrease in inventories | 643 |
| Increase in prepaid expenses | 664 |
| Decrease in accounts payable | 2,282 |
| Decrease in accrued liabilities | 719 |
| Increase in income taxes payable | 1,861 |
| Reduction of long-term debt | 12,691 |
| Additions to equipment | 29,073 |

*Required:*

1. Based on this information, compute cash flow from operating activities using the indirect method.
2. What were the major reasons that Sizzler was able to report a net loss but positive cash flow from operations? Why are the reasons for the difference between cash flow from operations and net income important to financial analysts?

■ **LO2**    **E13–9**    **Inferring Balance Sheet Changes from the Cash Flow Statement**

*Colgate-Palmolive*

A recent statement of cash flows for Colgate-Palmolive reported the following information (in millions):

| Operating Activities | 20B |
|---|---|
| Net income | $477.0 |
| Depreciation | 192.5 |
| Cash effect of changes in | |
| Receivables | (38.0) |
| Inventories | 28.4 |
| Other current assets | 10.6 |
| Payables | (10.0) |
| Other | (117.8) |
| Net cash provided by operations | $542.7 |

*Required:*

Based on the information reported on the statement of cash flows for Colgate-Palmolive, determine whether the following accounts increased or decreased during 20B: Receivables, Inventories, Other Current Assets, and Payables.

**E13–10 Inferring Balance Sheet Changes from the Cash Flow Statement**

A recent statement of cash flows for Apple Computer contained the following information (in thousands):

■ **LO2**

Apple Computer, Inc.

| Operations | 20D |
|---|---|
| Net income | $310,178 |
| Depreciation | 167,958 |
| Changes in assets and liabilities | |
| Accounts receivable | (199,401) |
| Inventories | 418,204 |
| Other current assets | 33,616 |
| Accounts payable | 139,095 |
| Income taxes payable | 50,045 |
| Other current liabilities | 39,991 |
| Other adjustments | (222,691) |
| Cash generated by operations | $736,995 |

*Required:*

For each of the asset and liability accounts listed on the statement of cash flows, determine whether the account balances increased or decreased during 20D.

**E13–11 Analyzing Cash Flows from Operating Activities; Interpreting the Quality of Income Ratio**

A recent annual report for PepsiCo contained the following information for 20C (in millions):

■ **LO3**

PepsiCo

| | |
|---|---|
| Net income | $1,587.9 |
| Depreciation and amortization | 1,444.2 |
| Increase in accounts receivable | 161.0 |
| Increase in inventory | 89.5 |
| Decrease in prepaid expense | 3.3 |
| Increase in accounts payable | 143.2 |
| Decrease in taxes payable | 125.1 |
| Decrease in other current liabilities | 96.7 |
| Cash dividends paid | 461.6 |
| Treasury stock purchased | 463.5 |

*Required:*

1. Compute cash flows from operating activities for PepsiCo using the indirect method.

2. Compute the quality of income ratio.

3. What were the major reasons that Pepsi's quality of income ratio did not equal 1.0?

■ **LO4, 6**        **E13–12**

Rowe Furniture

**Reporting Cash Flows from Investing and Financing Activities**

Rowe Furniture Corporation is a Virginia-based manufacturer of furniture. In a recent quarter, it reported the following activities:

| | |
|---|---:|
| O Net income | $ 4,135 |
| I● Purchase of property, plant, and equipment | − 871 |
| F Borrowings under line of credit (bank) | +1,417 |
| F Proceeds from issuance of stock | +11 |
| O Cash received from customers | +29,164 |
| F Payments to reduce long-term debt | −46 |
| I Sale of marketable securities | +134 |
| I Proceeds from sale of property and equipment | +6,594 |
| F Dividends paid | −277 |
| O Interest paid | −90 |
| F Purchase of treasury stock (stock repurchase) | −1,583 |

*Required:*

Based on this information, present the Cash Flow from Investing and Financing Activities sections of the cash flow statement.

■ **LO4, 6**        **E13–13**

Gibraltar Steel

**Reporting and Interpreting Cash Flows from Investing and Financing Activities with Discussion of Management Strategy**

Gibraltar Steel Corporation is a Buffalo, New York–based manufacturer of high-value-added cold-rolled steel products. In a recent year, it reported the following activities:

| | |
|---|---:|
| Net income | $ 5,213 |
| Purchase of property, plant, and equipment | 10,468 |
| Payments of notes payable (bank) | 8,598 |
| Net proceeds of initial public offering | 26,061 |
| Depreciation and amortization | 3,399 |
| Long-term debt reduction | 17,832 |
| Proceeds from sale of marketable securities | 131 |
| Proceeds from sale of property, plant, and equipment | 1,817 |
| Proceeds from long-term debt | 10,242 |
| Decrease in accounts receivable | 1,137 |
| Proceeds from notes payable (bank) | 3,848 |

*Required:*

1. Based on this information, present the Cash Flow from Investing and Financing Activities sections of the cash flow statement.

2. What do you think was Gibraltar management's plan for the use of the cash generated by the initial public offering of stock?

■ **LO5**        **E13–14**

Pete's Brewing

**Analyzing and Interpreting the Capital Acquisitions Ratio**

A recent annual report for Pete's Brewing Company contained the following data for the three most recent years:

| | (in thousands) | | |
|---|---:|---:|---:|
| | **20C** | **20B** | **20A** |
| Cash flow from operation activities | $  821 | $1,460 | $619 |
| Cash flow from investing activities | (1,404) | (1,315) | (862) |
| Cash flow from financing activities | 42,960 | 775 | 360 |

Assume that all investing activities involved acquisition of new plant and equipment.

*Required:*

1. Compute the capital acquisitions ratio for the three-year period in total.

2. What portion of Pete's investing activities was financed from external sources or preexisting cash balances during the three-year period?

3. What do you think is the likely explanation for the dramatic increase in cash flow from financing activities during 20C?

**E13–15** **Reporting Noncash Transactions on the Statement of Cash Flows; Interpreting the Effect on the Capital Acquisitions Ratio**

■ **LO7**

An analysis of Martin Corporation's operational asset accounts provided the following information:

a. Acquired a large machine that cost $26,000, paying for it by giving a $15,000, 12 percent interest-bearing note due at the end of two years and 500 shares of its common stock, with a par value of $10 per share and a market value of $22 per share.

b. Acquired a small machine that cost $8,700. Full payment was made by transferring a tract of land that had a book value of $8,700.

*Required:*

1. Show how this information should be reported on the statement of cash flows.

2. What would be the effect of these transactions on the capital acquisitions ratio? How might these transactions distort interpretation of the ratio?

**E13–16** **Determining Cash Flows from the Sale of Property (Supplement A)**

AMC Entertainment

AMC Entertainment is the second-largest motion picture exhibitor in the United States. The following was abstracted from the company's statement of cash flows (in thousands):

|  | 1993 | 1992 | 1991 |
|---|---|---|---|
| Cash flows from operating activities |  |  |  |
| Gain on sale of property | (9,638) | (7,314) | — |
| Cash flows from investing activities |  |  |  |
| Proceeds from disposition of property | 14,768 | 11,623 | 1,797 |

*Required:*

Determine the cash flow from the sale of property for each year for AMC.

**E13–17** **Determining Cash Flows from the Sale of Equipment (Supplement A)**

During 20F, English Company sold some excess equipment at a loss. The following information was collected from the company's accounting records:

| From the Income Statement |  |
|---|---|
| Depreciation expense | $   700 |
| Loss on sale of equipment | 3,000 |
| From the Balance Sheet |  |
| Beginning equipment | 12,500 |
| Ending equipment | 8,000 |
| Beginning accumulated depreciation | 2,000 |
| Ending accumulated depreciation | 2,400 |

No new equipment was bought during 20F.

*Required:*

For the equipment that was sold, determine its original cost, its accumulated depreciation, and the cash received from the sale.

**E13–18** **Preparing a Statement of Cash Flows, Indirect Method: Complete Spreadsheet (Supplement B)**

An analysis of accounts follows:

a. Purchased an operational asset, $20,000, and issued capital stock in full payment.

b. Purchased a long-term investment for cash, $15,000.

c. Paid cash dividend, $12,000.

d. Sold operational asset for $6,000 cash (cost, $21,000, accumulated depreciation, $19,000).

e. Sold capital stock, 500 shares at $12 per share cash.

| Items from Balance Sheet | Beginning Balances, 12/31/20A | Analysis of Changes | | Ending Balances, 12/31/20B |
|---|---|---|---|---|
| | | Debit | Credit | |
| Income statement items | | | | |
| Sales | | | $140,000 | |
| Cost of goods sold | | $59,000 | | |
| Depreciation | | 7,000 | | |
| Wage expense | | 28,000 | | |
| Income tax expense | | 9,000 | | |
| Interest expense | | 5,000 | | |
| Remaining expenses | | 15,800 | | |
| Gain on sale of operational asset | | | 4,000 | |
| Net income | | 20,200 | | |
| Balance sheet items | | | | |
| Cash | $ 20,500 | | | $ 19,200 |
| Accounts receivable | 22,000 | | | 22,000 |
| Merchandise inventory | 68,000 | | | 75,000 |
| Investments, long-term | | | | 15,000 |
| Operational assets | 114,500 | | | 113,500 |
| Total debits | $225,000 | | | $244,700 |
| | | | | |
| Accumulated depreciation | $ 32,000 | | | $ 20,000 |
| Accounts payable | 17,000 | | | 14,000 |
| Wages payable | 2,500 | | | 1,500 |
| Income taxes payable | 3,000 | | | 4,500 |
| Bonds payable | 54,000 | | | 54,000 |
| Common stock, no par | 100,000 | | | 126,000 |
| Retained earnings | 16,500 | | | 24,700 |
| Total credits | $225,000 | | | $244,700 |
| | | Inflows | Outflows | |
| Statement of cash flows | | | | |
| Cash flows from operating activities: | | | | |
| Cash flows from investing activities: | | | | |
| Cash flows from financing activities: | | | | |
| Net increase (decrease) in cash | | | | |
| Totals | | | | |

**Required:**

Complete the spreadsheet for the statement of cash flows, indirect method.

## PROBLEMS

**P13–1**    **Using Schedule Approach to Prepare the Statement of Cash Flows (Indirect Method)**
(AP13–1)

The income statement of Frank Corporation follows on the next page.

*Analysis of Selected 20B Account Balances and Transactions:*

*a.* Purchased investment securities for $5,000 cash.

*b.* Borrowed $15,000 on a two-year, 8 percent interest-bearing note.

*c.* During 20B, sold machinery for its net book value; received $11,000 in cash.

*d.* Purchased machinery for $50,000; paid $9,000 in cash and signed a four-year note payable to the dealer for $41,000.

*e.* At December 31, 20B, declared and paid a cash dividend of $10,000.

*f.* Cash balance on December 31, 20A was $21,000.

---

**FRANK CORPORATION**

**Income Statement**

**For the Year Ended December 31, 20B**

**Accrual Basis**

| | | |
|---|---|---|
| Sales revenue (one-fourth on credit; <u>accounts</u> receivable at year's end 20A, $12,000; 20B, $17,000) | | 400,000 |
| Cost of goods sold (one-third on credit; accounts payable at year's end 20A, $10,000; 20B, $7,000; inventory at year's end—20A, $60,000; 20B, $52,000) *inventory* | | 268,000 |
| Expenses | | |
| Salaries and wages (including accrued wages payable at at year's end—20A, $1,000; 20B, $800) | $51,000 | |
| Depreciation expense | 9,200 | |
| Rent expense (no accruals) | 5,800 | |
| Interest expense (no accruals) | 12,200 | |
| Income tax expense (income taxes payable at year's end— 20A, $3,000; 20B, $5,000) | $11,800 | |
| Total expenses | | 90,000 |
| Net income | | $ 42,000 |

*Required:*

Prepare a statement of cash flows, indirect method, using the schedule approach. Include any additional required note disclosures.

**P13–2 Using Schedule Approach to Prepare the Statement of Cash Flows (Indirect Method)**
Rocky Mountain Chocolate Factory manufactures an extensive line of premium chocolate candies for sale at its franchised and company-owned stores in malls throughout the United States. Its balance sheet for the first quarter of 1996 is presented along with an analysis of selected accounts and transactions:

■ **LO1, 2, 4, 6**

Rocky Mountain
Chocolate Factory

**ROCKY MOUNTAIN CHOCOLATE FACTORY, INC.**

**Balance Sheets**

| Assets | May 31, 1996 (Unaudited) | February 29, 1996 |
|---|---|---|
| **CURRENT ASSETS** | | |
| Cash and cash equivalents | $ 921,505 | $ 528,787 |
| Accounts and notes receivable—trade, less allowance for doubtful accounts of $43,196 at May 31 and $28,196 at February 29 | 1,602,582 | 1,463,901 |
| Inventories | 2,748,788 | 2,504,908 |
| Deferred tax asset | 59,219 | 59,219 |
| Other | 581,508 | 224,001 |
| Total current assets | 5,913,602 | 4,780,816 |
| PROPERTY AND EQUIPMENT—AT COST | 14,010,796 | 12,929,675 |
| Less accumulated depreciation and amortization | −2,744,388 | −2,468,084 |
| | 11,266,408 | 10,461,591 |
| **OTHER ASSETS** | | |
| Notes and accounts receivable due after one year | 100,206 | 111,588 |
| Goodwill, net of accumulated amortization of $259,641 at May 31 and $253,740 at Feb. 29 | 330,359 | 336,260 |
| Other | 574,130 | 624,185 |
| | 1,004,695 | 1,072,033 |
| | $18,184,705 | $16,314,440 |

*continued*

| | May 31, 1996 (Unaudited) | February 29, 1996 |
|---|---|---|
| **Liabilities and Equity** | | |
| CURRENT LIABILITIES | | |
| Short-term debt | $ 0 | $1,000,000 |
| Current maturities of long-term debt | 429,562 | 134,538 |
| Accounts payable—trade | 1,279,455 | 998,520 |
| Accrued liabilities | 714,473 | 550,386 |
| Income taxes payable | 11,198 | 54,229 |
| Total current liabilities | 2,434,688 | 2,737,673 |
| LONG-TERM DEBT, less current maturities | 4,193,290 | 2,183,877 |
| DEFERRED INCOME TAXES | 275,508 | 275,508 |
| **Stockholders' Equity** | | |
| Common stock—authorized 7,250,000 shares, $.03 par value; issued 3,034,302 shares at May 31 and at Feb. 29 | 91,029 | 91,029 |
| Additional paid-in capital | 9,703,985 | 9,703,985 |
| Retained earnings | 2,502,104 | 2,338,267 |
| | 12,297,118 | 12,133,281 |
| Less common stock held in treasury, at cost— 129,153 shares at May 31 and at February 29 | 1,015,899 | 1,015,899 |
| | 11,281,219 | 11,117,382 |
| | $18,184,705 | $16,314,440 |

The accompanying notes are an integral part of these statements.

### Analysis of Selected Accounts and Transactions

*a.* Net income was $163,837. Notes and accounts receivable due after one year relate to operations.

*b.* Depreciation and amortization totaled $282,205.

*c.* No "other" noncurrent assets (which relate to investing activities) were purchased this period.

*d.* No property, plant, and equipment were sold during the period. No goodwill was acquired or sold.

*e.* Proceeds from issuance of long-term debt were $4,659,466 and principal payments were $2,355,029. (Combine the current maturities with the long-term debt in your analysis.)

*f.* No dividends were declared or paid.

### Required:
Prepare a statement of cash flows, indirect method, using the schedule approach.

■ **LO2**    **P13–3**    **Comparing Cash Flows from Operating Activities (Direct and Indirect Methods)**
Beta Company's accountants just completed the income statement and balance sheet for the year and have provided the following information (in thousands):

| Income Statement | | |
|---|---|---|
| Sales revenue | | $20,600 |
| Expenses | | |
| Cost of goods sold | $9,000 | |
| Depreciation expense | 2,000 | |
| Salaries expense | 5,000 | |
| Rent expense | 2,500 | |
| Insurance expense | 800 | |
| Utilities expense | 700 | |
| Interest expense on bonds | 600 | |
| Loss on sale of investments | 400 | 21,000 |
| Net loss | | $ (400) |

| Selected Balance Sheet Accounts | | |
| --- | --- | --- |
| | 20A | 20B |
| Merchandise inventory | $ 60 | $ 82 |
| Accounts receivable | 450 | 380 |
| Accounts payable | 210 | 240 |
| Salaries payable | 20 | 29 |
| Rent payable | 6 | 2 |
| Prepaid rent | 7 | 2 |
| Prepaid insurance | 5 | 14 |

*Other Data:*
The company issued $20,000, 8 percent bonds payable during the year.

*Required:*

1. Prepare the Cash Flows from Operating Activities section of the statement of cash flows using the direct method.
2. Prepare the Cash Flows from Operating Activities section of the statement of cash flows using the indirect method.

**P13–4 Preparing Statement of Cash Flows Spreadsheet, Statement of Cash Flows, and Schedules Using Indirect Method (Supplement B)** (AP13–2)

Hunter Company is developing its annual financial statements at December 31, 20B. The statements are complete except for the statement of cash flows. The completed comparative balance sheets and income statement are summarized:

| | 20A | 20B |
| --- | --- | --- |
| Balance sheet at December 31 | | |
| Cash | $ 18,000 | $ 44,000 |
| Accounts receivable | 29,000 | 27,000 |
| Merchandise inventory | 36,000 | 30,000 |
| Fixed assets (net) | 72,000 | 75,000 |
| | $155,000 | $176,000 |
| Accounts payable | $ 22,000 | $ 25,000 |
| Wages payable | 1,000 | 800 |
| Note payable, long-term | 48,000 | 38,000 |
| Common stock, no par | 60,000 | 80,000 |
| Retained earnings | 24,000 | 32,200 |
| | $155,000 | $176,000 |
| Income statement for 20B | | |
| Sales | | $100,000 |
| Cost of goods sold | | (61,000) |
| Expenses | | (27,000) |
| Net income | | $ 12,000 |

*Additional Data:*

a. Bought fixed assets for cash, $9,000.
b. Paid $10,000 on the long-term note payable.
c. Sold unissued common stock for $20,000 cash.
d. Declared and paid a $3,800 cash dividend.
e. Incurred expenses that included depreciation, $6,000; wages, $10,000; taxes, $3,000; other, $8,000.

*Required:*

1. Prepare a statement of cash flows spreadsheet using the indirect method to report cash flows from operating activities.
2. Prepare the statement of cash flows.
3. Prepare a schedule of noncash investing and financing activities if necessary.

# ALTERNATE PROBLEMS

**LO1, 2, 4, 6, 7**

**AP13–1**

**Using Schedule Approach to Prepare the Statement of Cash Flows (Indirect Method)** (P13–1)

Stonewall Company was organized on January 1, 20A. During the year ended December 31, 20A, the company provided the following data:

| Income Statement | |
|---|---:|
| Sales revenue | $ 80,000 |
| Cost of goods sold | (35,000) |
| Depreciation expense | (4,000) |
| Remaining expenses | (32,000) |
| Net income | $  9,000 |
| **Balance Sheet** | |
| Cash | $ 48,000 |
| Accounts receivable | 18,000 |
| Merchandise inventory | 15,000 |
| Machinery (net) | 25,000 |
| Total assets | $106,000 |
| Accounts payable | $ 10,000 |
| Accrued expenses payable | 21,000 |
| Dividends payable | 2,000 |
| Note payable, short-term | 15,000 |
| Common stock | 54,000 |
| Retained earnings | 4,000 |
| Total liabilities and stockholders' equity | $106,000 |

### Analysis of Selected Accounts and Transactions:

a.  Sold 3,000 shares of common stock, par $10, at $18 per share; collected cash.

b.  Borrowed $15,000 on a one-year, 8 percent interest-bearing note; the note was dated June 1, 20A.

c.  During 20A, purchased machinery; paid $29,000.

d.  Purchased merchandise for resale at a cost of $50,000 (debited Inventory because the perpetual system is used); paid $40,000 cash, balance credited to Accounts Payable.

e.  Exchanged plant machinery with a book value of $2,000 for office machines with a market value of $2,000.

f.  At December 31, 20A, declared a cash dividend of $5,000; paid $3,000 in December 20A; the balance will be paid March 1, 20B.

g.  Because this is the first year of operations, all account balances are zero at the beginning of the year; therefore, the changes in the account balances are equal to the ending balances.

### Required:

Prepare a statement of cash flows, indirect method, using the schedule approach.

**AP13–2**

**Preparing Statement of Cash Flows Spreadsheet and Statement of Cash Flows Using Indirect Method: Includes Noncash Investing and Financing Activity and Sale of an Asset at Book Value (Supplement B)** (P13–4)

Ellington Company is developing its 20B annual report. The following information is provided:

|                                      | 20A      | 20B      |
|--------------------------------------|----------|----------|
| Cash                                 | $21,000  | $22,400  |
| Accounts receivable                  | 18,000   | 21,000   |
| Inventory                            | 35,000   | 32,000   |
| Prepaid insurance                    | 2,400    | 1,400    |
| Investments, long-term               | 12,500   | 9,300    |
| Fixed assets (net)                   | 31,100   | 59,600   |
| Patent                               | 2,000    | 1,500    |
| Accounts payable                     | 27,000   | 15,000   |
| Wages payable                        | 4,000    | 1,000    |
| Income taxes payable                 | 2,000    | 2,200    |
| Note payable, long-term              | 20,000   | 10,000   |
| Common stock ($10 par)               | 50,000   | 80,000   |
| Contributed capital in excess of par | 3,000    | 6,000    |
| Retained earnings                    | 16,000   | 33,000   |

*Other Information:*

a.  Sold long-term investment at book value, $3,200. Purchased fixed assets by issuing 3,000 shares of common stock; market value of common stock, $11 per share.

b.  Revenues, $150,000.

c.  Expenses: depreciation, $4,500; patent amortization, $500; insurance, $2,000; wages, $48,500; income taxes, $7,000; and cost of goods sold, $62,000.

*Required:*

1.  Prepare a statement of cash flows spreadsheet using the indirect method to report cash flows from operating activities.

2.  Prepare the statement of cash flows.

3.  Prepare a schedule of noncash investing and financing activities.

# CASES AND PROJECTS

## FINANCIAL REPORTING AND ANALYSIS CASES

**CP13–1  Finding Financial Information**

Refer to the financial statements of American Eagle Outfitters given in Appendix B at the end of this book, or open file AEOS10K.doc in the S&P directory on the student CD-ROM.

*Required:*

1.  Which of the two basic reporting approaches for the cash flows from operating activities did the company adopt?

2.  What amount of tax payments did the company make during the current year?

3.  Explain why "Restricted stock compensation" and "Loss on impairment and write-off of fixed assets" were added back in the reconciliation of net income to net cash provided by operating activities.

4.  What was free cash flow for the year ended January 30, 1999?

5.  Has the company paid cash dividends during the last three years? How did you know?

**LO2, 4, 6**

American Eagle
Outfitters

STANDARD
&POOR'S

**CP13–2  Finding Financial Information**

Refer to the financial statements of Urban Outfitters given in Appendix C at the end of this book, or open file URBN10K.doc in the S&P directory on the student CD-ROM.

**LO2, 4, 6**

Urban Outfitters

STANDARD
&POOR'S

*Required:*

1. What were the three largest "Adjustments to reconcile net income to net cash provided by operating activities"? Explain the direction of the effect of each in the reconciliation.

2. What have been Urban Outfitters' major uses of cash over the past three years? What have been its major sources of cash for these activities? What are the company's plans for financing future expenditures? How did you know?

3. What was free cash flow for the year ended January 31, 1999? What does this imply about the company's financial flexibility?

■ **LO3, 5**    **CP13–3**

American Eagle
Outfitters Versus
Urban Outfitters

**STANDARD
&POOR'S**

**Comparing Companies within an Industry**

Refer to the financial statements of American Eagle Outfitters given in Appendix B, Urban Outfitters given in Appendix C, and the Standard and Poor's Industry Ratio Report given in Appendix D at the end of this book or open file CP13-3.xls in the S&P directory on the student CD-ROM.

*Required:*

1. Compute the quality of income ratio for both companies for the current year. How might the difference in their sales growth rates explain the difference in the ratio? Sales Growth Rate = (Current Year's Sales − Prior Year's Sales) ÷ Prior Year's Sales.

2. Compare the quality of income ratio for both companies to the industry average. Are these companies producing more or less cash from operating activities relative to net income than the average company in the industry? Does comparing the sales growth rate for these two companies to the industry average help explain why their quality of income ratio is above or below the industry average? Explain.

3. Compute the capital acquisitions ratio for both companies for the current year. Compare their abilities to finance purchases of property, plant, and equipment with cash provided by operating activities.

4. Compare the capital acquisitions ratio for both companies to the industry average. How do these two companies' abilities to finance the purchase of property, plant, and equipment with cash provided by operating activities compare to the industry?

■ **LO1, 2**    **CP13–4**

Scottish & Newcastle

**Using Financial Reports: Analyzing a U.K. Cash Flow Statement**

Scottish & Newcastle serves up Courage by the pint. The U.K.'s largest brewer, it makes a number of popular beers, including Courage, John Smith's, Newcastle, and McEwan's. It also makes licensed brands such as Foster's, Kronenbourg, and Miller. As do all U.K. companies, the Edinburgh-based company follows U.K. generally accepted accounting principles. Its cash flow statement prepared according to those principles follows, along with one of the related notes.

*Required:*

1. Which of the two basic reporting approaches for the statement of cash flows did the company adopt?

2. Compare Scottish & Newcastle's statement with that of Boston Beer presented in Exhibit 13.1. What differences do you see in the U.S. and U.K. versions of the statement?

**SCOTTISH & NEWCASTLE PLC**
**Group Cash Flow Statement**
**Year ended 2 May 1999**

| | Notes | 1999 (52 weeks) £m | £m | 1998 (53 weeks) £m | £m |
|---|---|---|---|---|---|
| Net cash inflow from operating activities | 32 | | 542.7 | | 565.0 |
| Dividends from joint ventures | | | 7.7 | | 2.5 |
| Returns on investments and servicing of finance | | | | | |
| Interest received | | 3.0 | | 3.1 | |
| Interest paid | | (71.0) | | (59.0) | |
| Preference dividends paid | | (0.7) | | (1.1) | |
| Net cash outflow for returns on investments and servicing of finance | | | (68.7) | | (57.0) |
| Taxation | | | (88.2) | | (82.5) |
| Capital expenditure and financial investment | | | | | |
| Purchase of tangible fixed assets | | (374.0) | | (314.2) | |
| Purchase of investments | | (45.0) | | (67.0) | |
| Sale of tangible fixed assets | | 108.5 | | 43.0 | |
| Realisation of investments | | 55.4 | | 67.4 | |
| Net cash outflow for capital expenditure and financial investment | | | (255.1) | | (270.8) |
| Acquisition and disposals | | | | | |
| Purchase of businesses | | — | | (225.0) | |
| New Overdraft acquired with businesses | | — | | (1.0) | |
| Disposal of investment in joint venture | | — | | 2.2 | |
| Net cash outflow for acquisitions and disposals | | | — | | (223.8) |
| Equity dividends paid | | | (148.8) | | (135.8) |
| Net cash outflow before use of liquid resources and financing | | | (10.4) | | (202.4) |
| Management of liquid resources | | | | | |
| Movement in short-term deposits with banks | | | 14.4 | | (2.9) |
| Financing | | | | | |
| Issues of ordinary share capital | | 7.2 | | 8.0 | |
| Proceeds of loan capital | | 314.2 | | 388.5 | |
| Repayment of loan capital | | (284.7) | | (123.0) | |
| Net cash inflow from financing | | | 36.7 | | 273.5 |
| Increase in cash in the period | 33 | | 40.7 | | 68.2 |

Liquid resources comprise term deposits of less than one year.

**NOTE 32: NET CASH INFLOW FROM OPERATING ACTIVITIES**

| | 1999 £m | 1998 £m |
|---|---|---|
| Group operating profit | 399.4 | 470.5 |
| Exceptional charges against operating profit | 63.5 | — |
| Depreciation-normal | 133.0 | 123.8 |
| Provisions against investments | 3.1 | 2.3 |
| Decrease in stocks | 14.0 | 4.6 |
| Decrease in debtors | 7.9 | 2.6 |
| Decrease in creditors | (23.6) | (10.5) |
| Net cash inflow from ordinary operating activities | 597.3 | 593.3 |
| Reorganisation costs | (15.7) | (14.3) |
| Utilisation of acquisition and pensions provisions | (38.9) | (14.0) |
| Net cash inflow from operating activities | 542.7 | 565.0 |

# CRITICAL THINKING CASES

■ **LO2**     **CP13–5**

Carlyle Golf, Inc.

**Making a Decision as a Financial Analyst: Analyzing Cash Flow for a New Company**
Carlyle Golf, Inc., was formed in September 1992. The company designs, contracts for the manufacture of, and markets a line of men's golf apparel. A portion of the statement of cash flows for Carlyle follows:

|  | 1993 |
|---|---|
| Cash flows from operating activities |  |
| Net income | $(460,089) |
| Depreciation | 3,554 |
| Noncash compensation (stock) | 254,464 |
| Deposits with suppliers | (404,934) |
| Increase in prepaid assets | (42,260) |
| Increase in accounts payable | 81,765 |
| Increase in accrued liabilities | 24,495 |
| Net cash flows | $(543,005) |

Management expects a solid increase in sales in the near future. To support the increase in sales, it plans to add $2.2 million to inventory. The company did not disclose a sales forecast. At the end of 1993, Carlyle had less than $1,000 in cash. It is not unusual for a new company to experience a loss and negative cash flows during its start-up phase.

*Required:*
As a financial analyst recently hired by a major investment bank, you have been asked to write a short memo to your supervisor evaluating the problems facing Carlyle. Emphasize typical sources of financing that may or may not be available to support the expansion.

# FINANCIAL REPORTING AND ANALYSIS PROJECTS

■ **LO4, 6**     **CP13–6**

**Comparing Cash Flow from Investing and Financing Activities within Industries**
Acquire the cash flow statements from the annual reports or 10-Ks of two companies from the same industry. (Library files, the SEC EDGAR service at www.sec.gov/cgi-bin/srch-edgar, Compustat, or the companies themselves are good sources.) Write a short report indicating any differences in the investing and financing activities of the two companies over the last three years. Indicate what differences in business strategy the documents indicate.

■ **LO2, 3**     **CP13–7**

 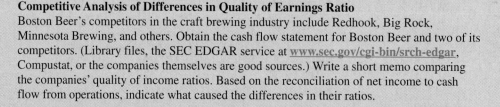

**Competitive Analysis of Differences in Quality of Earnings Ratio**
Boston Beer's competitors in the craft brewing industry include Redhook, Big Rock, Minnesota Brewing, and others. Obtain the cash flow statement for Boston Beer and two of its competitors. (Library files, the SEC EDGAR service at www.sec.gov/cgi-bin/srch-edgar, Compustat, or the companies themselves are good sources.) Write a short memo comparing the companies' quality of income ratios. Based on the reconciliation of net income to cash flow from operations, indicate what caused the differences in their ratios.

■ **LO3**     **CP13–8**

  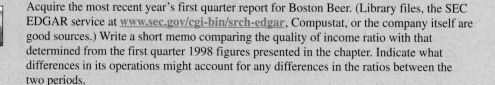

**Financial Analysis Update**
Acquire the most recent year's first quarter report for Boston Beer. (Library files, the SEC EDGAR service at www.sec.gov/cgi-bin/srch-edgar, Compustat, or the company itself are good sources.) Write a short memo comparing the quality of income ratio with that determined from the first quarter 1998 figures presented in the chapter. Indicate what differences in its operations might account for any differences in the ratios between the two periods.

**CP13–9  Ethics Project: Analyzing Irregularities in Revenue Recognition**

LO1, 2

Obtain a recent news story outlining an accounting irregularity related to accounts receivable or inventories. (Library files, *Wall Street Journal* Index, *Dow Jones Interactive*, and *Bloomberg Business News* are good sources. Search for the term *accounting irregularities*.) Examine the company's cash flow statements for the three years prior to disclosure of the irregularity. Write a short memo outlining the nature of the irregularity and whether there were indications of the pending problem in the company's cash flow statements.

**CP13–10  Broadening Financial Research Skills: Earnings Conference Calls on the Web**

LO1

Yahoo!Broadcast is the leading source of multimedia company information. Contact it at www.broadcast.com/business/. Look under "corporate earnings," where you will see a list of recent company conference calls with financial analysts. Choose a listed company and listen to the call from the archive. Prepare an outline of the major points made in the company presentation. Then listen to the questions from the analysts noting any questions related to the cash flow statement.

**CP13–11  Team Project: Analyzing Cash Flows**

LO1, 2, 3, 4, 5, 6

As a team, select an industry to analyze (industry lists can be found at www.marketguide.com/mgi/INDUSTRY/INDUSTRY.html and www.hoovers.com; click on companies and industries). Each team member should acquire the annual report or 10-K for one publicly traded company in the industry, with each member selecting a different company. (Library files, the SEC EDGAR service at www.sec.gov cgi-bin/srch-edgar, Compustat CD, or the company itself are good sources.) On an individual basis, each team member should then write a short report answering the following questions about their selected company.

1. Which of the two basic reporting approaches for cash flows from operating activities did the company adopt?

2. What is the quality of earnings ratio for the most current year? What were the major causes of differences between net income and cash flow from operations?

3. What is the capital acquisitions ratio for the three-year period presented in total? How is the company financing its capital acquisitions?

4. What portion of the cash from operations in the current year is being paid to stockholders in the form of dividends?

Discuss any patterns across the three companies that your team observes. Then, as a team, write a short report comparing and contrasting your companies using these attributes. Provide potential explanations for any differences discovered.

# Analyzing Financial Statements

## CHAPTER **FOURTEEN**

LEARNING **OBJECTIVES**

*After studying this chapter, you should be able to:*

1. Discuss how analysts use financial statements.   p. 734

2. List five major categories of accounting ratios.   p. 740

3. Identify and compute widely used accounting ratios.   p. 740

4. Interpret accounting ratios.   p. 755

The history of Home Depot is an unusual success story. Founded in 1978 in Atlanta, Home Depot has grown to be America's largest home improvement retailer and, according to *Fortune* magazine, ranks among the nation's 30 largest retailers. Financial statements for Home Depot are presented in Exhibit 14.1.

FOCUS **COMPANY:**

# Home Depot

FINANCIAL ANALYSIS:

BRINGING IT ALL

TOGETHER

As you can see, Home Depot is continuing its rapid growth. Sales revenue for the year ended January 31, 1999, was 55 percent higher than in 1997, and the company's net earnings increased by more than 72 percent.

Despite this rapid growth, financial analysts offer a variety of recommendations concerning Home Depot's stock. Merrill Lynch does not currently recommend buying it, noting that the "stock has performed like a passbook savings account. Over the past four years, the company has generated an average annual return of just 2 percent. This lackluster performance has occurred despite strong earnings."

Another investment analyst, Smith Barney, recommends buying the stock, concluding that "Home Depot's lackluster stock performance represents an attractive buying opportunity. The company's operating profit margins are beginning to rise, which could lead to a higher stock price."

Given this conflicting advice, would you want to buy Home Depot stock? To make a rational decision, you would want to consider more factors than just the company's rapid growth in profitability and the recommendation of a financial analyst. The information contained in Home Depot's financial statements and the analytical tools discussed in this chapter provide an important basis to help you decide whether to invest in Home Depot stock.

EXHIBIT **14.1**

**Home Depot Financial Statements**

**REAL WORLD EXCERPT**

*Home Depot*

ANNUAL REPORT

**THE HOME DEPOT, INC. AND SUBSIDIARIES**
**Consolidated Balance Sheets**
**(amounts in millions, except share data)**

| | January 31, 1999 | February 1, 1998 |
|---|---|---|
| **Assets** | | |
| Current Assets: | | |
| Cash and Cash Equivalents | $ 62 | $ 172 |
| Short-Term Investments, including current maturities of long-term investments | — | 2 |
| Receivables, Net | 469 | 556 |
| Merchandise Inventories | 4,293 | 3,602 |
| Other Current Assets | 109 | 128 |
| Total Current Assets | 4,933 | 4,460 |
| Property and Equipment, at cost: | | |
| Land | 2,739 | 2,194 |
| Buildings | 3,757 | 3,041 |
| Furniture, Fixtures, and Equipment | 1,761 | 1,370 |
| Leasehold Improvements | 419 | 383 |
| Construction in Progress | 540 | 336 |
| Capital Leases (notes 2 and 5) | 206 | 163 |
| | 9,422 | 7,487 |
| Less Accumulated Depreciation and Amortization | 1,262 | 978 |
| Net Property and Equipment | 8,160 | 6,509 |
| Long-Term Investments | 15 | 15 |
| Notes Receivable | 26 | 27 |
| Cost in Excess of the Fair Value of Net Assets Acquired, net of accumulated amortization of $24 at January 31, 1999 and $18 at February 1, 1998 | 268 | 140 |
| Other | 63 | 78 |
| | $13,465 | $11,229 |
| **Liabilities and Stockholders' Equity** | | |
| Current Liabilities | | |
| Accounts Payable | $ 1,586 | $ 1,358 |
| Accrued Salaries and Related Expenses | 395 | 312 |
| Sales Taxes Payable | 176 | 143 |
| Other Accrued Expenses | 586 | 530 |
| Income Taxes Payable | 100 | 105 |
| Current Installments of Long-Term Debt (notes 2 and 5) | 14 | 8 |
| Total Current Liabilities | 2,857 | 2,456 |
| Long-Term Debt, excluding current installments (notes 2 and 5) | 1,566 | 1,303 |
| Other Long-Term Liabilities | 208 | 178 |
| Deferred Income Taxes (note 3) | 85 | 78 |
| Minority Interest (note 10) | 9 | 116 |
| **Stockholders' Equity** (notes 2, 4 and 6) | | |
| Common Stock, par value $0.05. Authorized: 2,500,000,000 shares; issued and outstanding— 1,475,452,000 shares at January 31, 1999 and 1,464,216,000 shares at February 1, 1998 | 74 | 73 |
| Paid-in Capital | 2,854 | 2,626 |
| Retained Earnings | 5,876 | 4,430 |
| Accumulated Other Comprehensive Income | (61) | (28) |
| | 8,743 | 7,101 |
| Less: Shares Purchased for Compensation Plans (notes 4 and 6) | 3 | 3 |
| Total Stockholders' Equity | 8,740 | 7,098 |
| Commitments and Contingencies (notes 5 and 9) | | |
| | $13,465 | $11,229 |

EPS

See accompanying notes to consolidated financial statements.

EXHIBIT **14.1**

continued

## THE HOME DEPOT, INC. AND SUBSIDIARIES
### Consolidated Statements of Earnings
### (amounts in millions, except share data)

| | Fiscal Year Ended | | |
|---|---|---|---|
| | January 31, 1999 (52 weeks) | February 1, 1998 (52 weeks) | February 2, 1997 (53 weeks) |
| Net Sales | $30,219 | $24,156 | $19,535 |
| Cost of Merchandise Sold | 21,614 | 17,375 | 14,101 |
| Gross Profit | 8,605 | 6,781 | 5,434 |
| Operating Expenses: | | | |
| Selling and Store Operating | 5,341 | 4,303 | 3,529 |
| Pre-Opening | 88 | 65 | 55 |
| General and Administrative | 515 | 413 | 324 |
| Non-Recurring Charge (note 8) | — | 104 | — |
| Total Operating Expenses | 5,944 | 4,885 | 3,908 |
| Operating Income | 2,661 | 1,896 | 1,526 |
| Interest Income (Expense): | | | |
| Interest and Investment Income | 30 | 44 | 25 |
| Interest Expense (note 2) | (37) | (42) | (16) |
| Interest, net | (7) | 2 | 9 |
| Earnings Before Income Taxes | 2,654 | 1,898 | 1,535 |
| Income Taxes (note 3) | 1,040 | 738 | 597 |
| Net Earnings | $ 1,614 | $ 1,160 | $ 938 |
| Basic Earnings Per Share (note 7) | $1.10 | $ 0.80 | $ 0.65 |
| Weighted Average Number of Common Shares Outstanding | 1,471 | 1,459 | 1,438 |
| Diluted Earnings Per Share (note 7) | $ 1.06 | $ 0.78 | $ 0.65 |
| Weighted Average Number of Common Shares Outstanding Assuming Dilution | 1,547 | 1,524 | 1,464 |

See accompanying notes to consolidated financial statements.

## THE HOME DEPOT, INC. AND SUBSIDIARIES
### Consolidated Statements of Cash Flows
### (amounts in millions)

| | Fiscal Year Ended | | |
|---|---|---|---|
| | January 31, 1999 (52 weeks) | February 1, 1998 (52 weeks) | February 2, 1997 (53 weeks) |
| Cash Provided from Operations: | | | |
| Net Earnings | $1,614 | $1,160 | $938 |
| Reconciliation of Net Earnings to Net Cash Provided by Operations: | | | |
| Depreciation and Amortization | 373 | 283 | 232 |
| Deferred Income Tax Expense (Benefit) | 7 | (28) | 29 |
| Decrease (Increase) in Receivables, net | 85 | (166) | (58) |
| Increase in Merchandise Inventories | (698) | (885) | (525) |
| Increase in Accounts Payable and Accrued Expenses | 423 | 577 | 434 |
| Increase in Income Taxes Payable | 59 | 83 | 25 |
| Other | 54 | 5 | 25 |
| Net Cash Provided by Operations | $1,917 | 1,029 | 1,100 |

*continued*

EXHIBIT **14.1**
concluded

| | January 31, 1999 (52 weeks) | February 1, 1998 (52 weeks) | February 2, 1997 (53 weeks) |
|---|---|---|---|
| **Cash Flows from Investing Activities:** | | | |
| Capital Expenditures, net of $41, $44 and $54 of non-cash expenditures in fiscal 1998, 1997, and 1996, respectively | (2,059) | (1,481) | (1,194) |
| Purchase of Remaining interest in The Home Depot Canada | (261) | — | — |
| Proceeds from Sales of Property and Equipment | 45 | 85 | 22 |
| Proceeds from Sales of Investments | — | — | 41 |
| Purchases of Investments | (2) | (194) | (409) |
| Proceeds from Maturities of Investments | 4 | 599 | 27 |
| Repayment of Advances Secured by Real Estate, net | 2 | 20 | 6 |
| Net Cash used in Investing Activities | (2,271) | (971) | (1,507) |
| **Cash Flows from Financing Activities:** | | | |
| Issuance of (Repayments of) Commercial Paper Obligations, net | 246 | — | (620) |
| Proceeds from Long-Term Borrowings, net | — | 15 | 1,093 |
| Repayments of Notes Receivable from ESOP | — | — | 17 |
| Principal Repayments of Long-Term Debt | (8) | (40) | (3) |
| Proceeds from Sale of Common Stock, net | 167 | 122 | 104 |
| Cash Dividends Paid to Stockholders | (168) | (139) | (110) |
| Minority Interest Contributions to Partnership | 11 | 10 | 19 |
| Net Cash Provided by (Used in) Financing Activities | 248 | (32) | 500 |
| Effect of Exchange Rate Changes on Cash and Cash Equivalents | (4) | — | — |
| (Decrease) Increase in Cash and Cash Equivalents | (110) | 26 | 93 |
| Cash and Cash Equivalents at Beginning of Year | 172 | 146 | 53 |
| Cash and Cash Equivalents at End of Year | $ 62 | $ 172 | $ 146 |
| **Supplemental Disclosure of Cash Payments Made For:** | | | |
| Interest, net of interest capitalized | $ 36 | $ 42 | $ 3 |
| Income Taxes | $ 940 | $ 685 | $ 548 |

## BUSINESS BACKGROUND

In the United States, companies spend billions of dollars each year preparing, auditing, and publishing their financial statements. These statements are mailed to current and prospective investors. Each year Home Depot sends out more than 66,000 copies of its financial statements to current stockholders. Most companies also make financial information available on the Internet. Home Depot has a particularly interesting home page (http://www.homedepot.com) that contains current financial statements, recent news articles about the company, and a variety of relevant information.

The reason that Home Depot spends so much money to provide information to investors is simple: Financial statements help people make better economic decisions. Two broad groups of people use financial statements. One group is the management of the business; it relies on accounting data to make important operating decisions, such as the pricing of products or expansion of productive capacity. The second group is external decision makers. This group consists primarily of investors (both present and potential owners), investment analysts, creditors, governmental units, labor organizations, and the public.

Users of financial statements are interested in three types of information:

1. *Information about past performance.* Information concerning items such as income, sales volume, cash flows, and return earned on the investment helps assess the success of the business and the effectiveness of its management. Such information also helps the decision maker compare one company with others.

2. *Information about the present condition of a business.* This type of information helps answer questions such as these: What types of assets are owned? How much debt does the business owe, and when is it due? What is its cash position? What are its EPS, return on investment, and debt-to-equity ratios? What is the inventory position? Answers to these and similar questions help people assess the successes and failures of the past; more important, they provide information useful in assessing the cash flow and profit potentials of the business.

3. *Information about the future performance of the business.* Decision makers select from among several alternative courses of action. All decisions are future oriented. As you know, financial statements report on the past and cannot predict the future. Nevertheless, reliable measurements of what has happened in the past are an important part of predicting what will happen in the future. For example, the recent sales and earnings trends of a business are good indicators of what might be expected in the future. In other words, you must know where you are in order to plan where you are able to go.

**ORGANIZATION** OF THE CHAPTER

| • Understanding a Company's Strategy | • Finanacial Statement Analysis | • Ratio and Percentage Analyses |
|---|---|---|
| | | Component Percentages |

| • Commonly Used Ratios | • Tests of Profitability | • Tests of Liquidity |
|---|---|---|
| | 1. Return on Equity (ROE) | 8. Cash Ratio |
| | 2. Return on Assets (ROA) | 9. Current Ratio |
| | 3. Financial Leverage Percentage | 10. Quick Ratio (Acid Test) |
| | 4. Earnings per Share (EPS) | 11. Receivable Turnover |
| | 5. Quality of Income | 12. Inventory Turnover |
| | 6. Profit Margin | |
| | 7. Fixed Asset Turnover Ratio | |

| • Tests of Solvency and Equity Position | • Market Tests | • Miscellaneous Ratio |
|---|---|---|
| 13. Times Interest Earned Ratio | 16. Price/Earnings (P/E) Ratio | 18. Book Value per Share |
| 14. Cash Coverage Ratio | 17. Dividend Yield Ratio | |
| 15. Debt-to-Equity Ratio | | |

| • Other Analytical Considerations | • Interpreting Ratios | • Impact of Accounting Alternatives on Ratio Analysis |
|---|---|---|
| | | Information in an Efficient Market |

## THE INVESTMENT DECISION

Perhaps the single largest group of people who use financial statements is composed of investors including current owners, potential owners, and investment analysts (because they advise investors). Investors purchase stock with the expectation of earning a return on their investment. The return on a stock investment has two components: (1) dividend revenue during the investment period and (2) increases in the market value of the shares owned.

When considering a stock investment, the investor should evaluate the future income and growth potential of the business on the basis of three factors:

1. *Economywide factors.* Often the overall health of the economy has a direct impact on the performance of an individual business. Investors should consider data such as the gross national product, productivity, unemployment rate, general inflation rate, and changes in interest rates. For example, increases in interest rates often slow economic growth because consumers are less willing to buy merchandise on credit when interest rates are high.

2. *Industry factors.* Certain events have a major impact on each company within an industry but have only a minor impact on other companies. For example, a major drought may be devastating for food-related industries but may have no effect on the electronics industry.

3. *Individual company factors.* To properly analyze a company, you should get to know as much as you can about it. Good analysts do not rely only on the information contained in the financial statements. They visit the company, buy its products, and read about it in the business press. If you evaluate McDonald's, it is equally important to assess the quality of its balance sheet and the quality of its Big Mac. The importance of nonquantitative information can be illustrated by a research report on Home Depot written by Salomon Brothers, a large investment banking firm:

**REAL WORLD EXCERPT**

*Home Depot*

SALOMON BROTHERS
RESEARCH REPORT

We believe that the company's strong culture—which focuses on employee empowerment and customer service—is the key reason that it has become the nation's largest home center chain in only 12 years and that it will be able to dramatically expand its national market share over the next several years, as it expands its presence across the country and around the world.

## UNDERSTANDING A COMPANY'S STRATEGY

Financial statement analysis involves more than just "crunching numbers." Before you start looking at numbers, you should know what you are looking for.

A number of accounting ratios can be computed. A useful starting point was introduced in Chapter 5. The return on equity (ROE) profit driver analysis (or DuPont analysis) shows a logical relationship among several ratios and demonstrates that ratio analysis provides useful insights into the strategy of a business. The basic ROE model is as follows:

$$\text{ROE} = \frac{\text{Net Profit}}{\text{Margin}} \times \frac{\text{Asset}}{\text{Turnover}} \times \frac{\text{Financial}}{\text{Leverage}}$$

$$\frac{\text{Net Income}}{\text{Average Stockholders' Equity}} = \frac{\text{Net Income}}{\text{Net Sales}} \times \frac{\text{Net Sales}}{\text{Average Total Assets}} \times \frac{\text{Average Total Assets}}{\text{Average Stockholders' Equity}}$$

A goal for any business is to earn a high return for the owners (i.e., a high ROE). As you review the model, you can see that a number of potential strategies result in a high ROE. Two fundamental strategies follow:

1. *Product differentiation.* Under this strategy, companies offer products that are unique in some manner, such as being high quality or offering unusual features or style. This allows companies to charge higher prices. In general, higher prices result in a higher profit margin, which the ROE model tells us will lead to a higher ROE.

2. *Cost advantage.* Under this strategy, companies attempt to operate more efficiently than competitors. This efficiency permits these companies to offer lower prices to attract customers. The efficient use of resources is captured in the asset turnover ratio. The ROE model tells us that higher efficiency (i.e., high asset turnover) leads to higher ROE.

You can probably think of a number of companies that have followed one of these two basic strategies. In the auto industry, Cadillac and Mercedes are examples of products that have been differentiated based on quality. The Ford Escort and the Dodge Neon are products that appeal to consumers because they offer a cost advantage. Similarly, in the retail industry, Nordstrom and Tiffany have differentiated themselves as stores that offer high-quality merchandise. Wal-Mart and Kmart offer different shopping experiences and lower-quality merchandise at much lower prices.

The best place to start your analysis is with a solid understanding of a company's business strategy. To evaluate how a company is doing, you must know what it is trying to do. You can learn a great deal about a company's strategy by reading its complete annual report, especially the letter from the president. It also is useful to read articles about the company in the business press.

Home Depot's business strategy is described by Salomon Brothers as follows:

**REAL WORLD EXCERPT**

*Home Depot*

SALOMON BROTHERS
RESEARCH REPORT

> The Home Depot successful formula combines the low everyday prices of a large store, "category killer" retailer, with the service usually found only in a small, local hardware store. Few if any of its competitors are able to duplicate both of these customer driven strategies.

This strategy has several implications for our analysis of Home Depot:

1. Cost control is critical. Home Depot must be able to purchase merchandise at low prices to beat competitors.

2. Stores must be able to generate high volume to cover the cost of operating large stores.

3. Employee compensation and training costs are higher than competitors' costs to offer a high level of service. This puts pressure on Home Depot to control costs in other areas.

By understanding the company's strategy, the analyst is able to attach more meaning to the information contained in the financial statements.

## FINANCIAL STATEMENT ANALYSIS

Financial statements include a large volume of quantitative data supplemented by disclosure notes. It is impossible to analyze financial data without a basis of comparison. For example, would you be impressed with a company that earned $1 million last year? You probably answered the question by thinking, "It depends." A $1 million profit might be very good for a company that lost money the year before but not good for a company that made $500 million during the previous year; it might be good for a small company but not good for a very large company; it might be good if all the other companies in the industry lost money but not good if they all earned much larger profits. As you can see from this simple example, financial results cannot be evaluated in isolation. You must develop appropriate comparisons to properly analyze the information reported in financial statements. Finding an appropriate benchmark requires judgment and is not always an easy task. For this reason, financial analysis is a sophisticated skill instead of a mechanical process.

The two types of benchmarks for making financial comparisons are as follows:

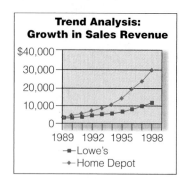

**Trend Analysis: Growth in Sales Revenue**

— Lowe's
— Home Depot

1. *Time series analysis.* In this type of analysis, information for a single company is compared over time. For example, a company may have a current ratio (current assets divided by current liabilities) of 1.2. Without additional information, this ratio does not tell us very much. Time series analysis might tell you that the ratio has declined each year for the past five years, from a high of 2. This time series information might cause you to do further study concerning the factors that caused a steady deterioration of this ratio in the recent past.

   Home Depot is viewed as a growth company. Times series analysis gives us a good feel for this growth when sales data are presented in graphic form. The accompanying chart compares the growth in sales revenue for Home Depot compared to Lowe's, a main competitor.

2. *Comparison with similar companies.* Financial results often are affected by industry and economywide factors. By comparing a company with another one in the same line of business, the analyst can get better insights concerning specific company performance. An analyst would be concerned if General Motors' sales revenue fell by 2 percent in a given year. The analyst might be less concerned if for the same period Ford experienced a 10 percent decline and Chrysler had a 16 percent decline. This comparison would indicate that the entire automobile industry had a bad year but that General Motors had done well compared to its major domestic competitors.

Finding comparable companies often is very difficult. American Brands is a well-known company that sells tobacco, distilled spirits, life insurance, home improvement products, office products, and golf equipment. No other company sells exactly that group of products. Care must be exercised when selecting comparable companies from the same basic industry. Days Inn, La Quinta, Hilton, Four Seasons, Marriott, and Mirage Resorts are all in the hotel industry but not all could be considered comparable companies for purposes of financial analysis.

The federal government has established *standard industrial classification (SIC) codes* that are used to report economic data (as this book is being written, SIC codes are scheduled to be replaced by The North American Industry Classification System). Analysts often use these four-digit codes to make industry comparisons for various companies. Financial information services, such as Robert Morris Associates, provide averages for many common accounting ratios for various industries as defined by the standard industrial classification codes. Because of the diversity of companies included in each industry classification, you should use these data with great care. Some analysts prefer to compare two companies that are very similar instead of using industry-wide comparisons.

## RATIO AND PERCENTAGE ANALYSES

**RATIO (PERCENTAGE) ANALYSIS** is an analytical tool designed to identify significant relationships; it measures the proportional relationship between two financial statement amounts.

All financial analysts use **ratio analysis,** or **percentage analysis,** when they review companies. A ratio or percentage expresses the proportionate relationship between two different amounts. A ratio or percentage is computed by dividing one quantity by another quantity. For example, the fact that a company earned net income of $500,000 assumes greater significance when net income is compared with the stockholders' investment in the company. Assuming that stockholders' equity is $5 million, the relationship of earnings to stockholder investment is $500,000 ÷ $5,000,000 = 10 percent. This measure indicates a different level of performance than would be the case if stockholders' equity were $50 million. Ratio analysis helps decision makers identify significant relationships and compare companies more realistically than if only single amounts were analyzed.

Ratios may be computed using amounts within one statement, such as the income statement, or between different statements, such as the income statement and the balance sheet. The current ratio (current assets divided by current liabilities) is based on information from a single statement. Return on assets (net income divided by total assets) is based on information from the income statement and the balance sheet.

Financial statement analysis is a judgmental process. No single ratio can be identified as appropriate to all situations. Each analytical situation may require the calculation of several ratios. We will discuss several ratios that are appropriate to many situations.

## COMPONENT PERCENTAGES

**Component percentages** are used to express each item on a particular statement as a percentage of a single *base amount*, the denominator of the ratio. To compute component percentages for the income statement, the base amount is net sales revenue. Each expense is expressed as a percentage of net sales revenue. On the balance sheet, the base amount is total assets. The percentages are derived by dividing each balance sheet account by total assets.

Discerning important relationships and trends in the Home Depot income statement shown in Exhibit 14.1 is difficult without using component percentages. Income increased by more than 70 percent between 1997 and 1999, which is obviously very good, but it is difficult for an analyst to evaluate the operating efficiency of Home Depot based on the reported numbers on the income statement.

Exhibit 14.2 shows a component analysis for Home Depot's income statement (from Exhibit 14.1). If you simply reviewed the dollar amounts on the income statement, you might be concerned about several significant differences. For example, cost of goods sold increased by more than $4 million between 1998 and 1999. Is this increase reasonable? Should you be concerned as an analyst? By reviewing the component analysis, you quickly see that cost of goods sold for each year is approximately 72 percent of sales revenue. In other words, cost of goods sold has increased primarily because of the increase in sales revenue.

Many analysts use graphics software in their study of financial results. Graphic representation is especially useful when communicating findings during meetings or in printed form. A graphic summary of key 1999 data from Exhibit 14.2 is shown along with a comparison to data from Lowe's, a key competitor.

The component analysis for Home Depot (in Exhibit 14.2) helps highlight several additional issues:

1. Income for Home Depot increased by $676 million between 1997 and 1999. A portion of this increase can be attributed to an increase in sales revenue but a significant portion is attributable to increased efficiency in operations. Both operating costs and cost of goods sold as a percentage of sales decreased during the period.

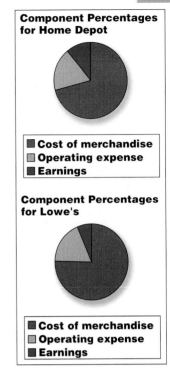

**Component Percentages for Home Depot**

■ Cost of merchandise
■ Operating expense
■ Earnings

**Component Percentages for Lowe's**

■ Cost of merchandise
■ Operating expense
■ Earnings

A **COMPONENT PERCENTAGE** expresses each item on a particular financial statement as a percentage of a single base amount.

|  | **Component Percentages** | | |
|---|---|---|---|
| **Income Statement** | **1999** | **1998** | **1997** |
| Net sales | 100.0% | 100.0% | 100.0% |
| Cost of merchandise sold | 71.6 | 71.9 | 72.2 |
| Gross profit | 28.4 | 28.1 | 27.8 |
| Operating expenses |  |  |  |
|   Selling and store operating | 17.6 | 17.8 | 18.0 |
|   Pre-opening | 0.3 | 0.3 | 0.3 |
|   General and administrative | 1.7 | 1.7 | 1.7 |
| Total operating expenses | 19.6 | 19.8 | 20.0 |
| Operating income | 8.8 | 8.3 | 7.8 |
| Interest income | 0.1 | 0.2 | 0.1 |
| Interest expense | (0.1) | (0.2) | 0.0 |
| Interest, net | 0.0 | 0.0 | 0.1 |
| Earnings, before taxes | 8.8 | 8.3 | 7.9 |
| Income taxes | 3.4 | 3.1 | 3.0 |
| Net earnings | 5.4 | 5.2 | 4.9 |

EXHIBIT **14.2**

**Component Percentages for Home Depot**

2. Some of the changes in percentages may seem immaterial, but they involve very significant amounts of money. The improvement in the ratio of selling and store operating as a percentage of sales from 1997 to 1999 added $120 million to earnings before taxes.

3. Cost of goods sold as a percentage of sales declined consistently between 1997 and 1999. As we mentioned earlier, a key part of the strategy for Home Depot is selling merchandise at low prices. This improvement in the ratio of cost of goods sold to sales revenue is a very positive indication of the successful implementation of the company's strategy.

4. Significant stability in all of the income statement relationships indicates a well-run company. Notice that all of the individual income statement items changed by less than one percentage point over a three-year period.

5. Analysts are primarily concerned with the continuing operations of a company because they want to make decisions about future events. Notice that the income statement for 1998 includes at item called Non-recurring charge. This expense relates to the settlement of a major lawsuit, a one-time event. It explains why total operating expense increased in 1998, but it would not be a factor in predicting the future operating efficiency of the company.

## COMMONLY USED RATIOS

**LEARNING OBJECTIVE 2**

List five major categories of accounting ratios.

In addition to component percentages, analysts use a large number of ratios to compare related items from the financial statements. You were introduced to many of these ratios earlier in this book. For example, the current ratio compares current assets and current liabilities. This comparison is widely used as a measure of liquidity, or the ability of a company to pay its short-term debt. The comparison makes sense because current liabilities may be paid with current assets.

Numerous ratios can be computed from a single set of financial statements, but only a selected number may be useful in a given situation. It is never useful to compare cost of goods sold to property, plant, and equipment because these items have no natural relationship. A common approach is to compute certain widely used ratios and then decide which additional ratios are relevant to the particular decision. For example, research and development costs as a percentage of sales is not a common ratio, but it is useful in some special situations. You would want to look at that ratio if you were evaluating companies that depended on new products, such as manufacturers of drugs or computers.

When you compute ratios, it is important to remember a basic fact about financial statements. Balance sheet amounts relate to one instant in time, and income statement amounts relate to a period of time. Therefore, when an income statement account is compared with a balance sheet amount, a balance sheet *average amount* should be used to reflect changes in the balance sheet amounts. The selected balance sheet amount usually is computed as the average of the amounts shown on the beginning and ending balance sheets. In many cases, analysts simply use data from the ending balance sheet. This approach is appropriate only if no significant changes in balance sheet amounts have occurred. For consistency, we always use average amounts.

Commonly used financial ratios can be grouped into the five categories shown in Exhibit 14.3.

## TESTS OF PROFITABILITY

**LEARNING OBJECTIVE 3**

Identify and compute widely used accounting ratios.

Profitability is a primary measure of the overall success of a company. Indeed, it is a necessary condition for survival. Investors and creditors prefer a single measure of profitability that is meaningful in all situations. Unfortunately, no single measure can be devised to meet this comprehensive need. Tests of profitability focus on measuring the adequacy of income by comparing it with one or more primary activities or factors

| Ratio | Basic Computation | EXHIBIT **14.3** |
|---|---|---|
| | | **Widely Used Accounting Ratios** |

**Tests of Profitability**

1. Return on equity (ROE)

$$\frac{\text{Income}}{\text{Average Owners' Equity}}$$

*Measures return earned for owners based upon their investment (including retained earnings) in the business*

2. Return on assets (ROA)

*Net profit margin ratio × total asset turnover ratio*
*NI/sales × sales/Avg total assets*

$$\frac{\text{Income} + \text{Interest Expense (net of tax)}}{\text{Average Total Assets}}$$
*Net Income*

*Measures the entity's performance in using total resources (total assets) available to it*

3. Financial leverage percentage
*can be 0, neg, pos.*

Return on Equity − Return on Assets

*Advantage to be gained by investors when the interest rate (net of tax) is less than rate earned on investment*

4. Earnings per share

$$\frac{\text{Income}}{\text{Average Number of Shares of Common Stock Outstanding}}$$
*Net*

*Tends to measure return earned on each share of common stock outstanding*

5. Quality of income
*>1 ⇒ high quality*
*<1 ⇒ low quality*

$$\frac{\text{Cash Flows from Operating Activities}}{\text{Net Income}}$$

*A measure of whether reported earnings are supported by cash flows*

6. Profit margin

$$\frac{\text{Income (before extraordinary items)}}{\text{Net Sales Revenue}}$$

*Indicates % of each sales dollar that was represented by income*

7. Fixed asset turnover ratio
*PPE - long term assets*

$$\frac{\text{Net Sales Revenue}}{\text{Net Fixed Assets}}$$

*An indication of how efficiently mgmt is using fixed assets*

**Tests of Liquidity**

8. Cash ratio

$$\frac{\text{Cash} + \text{Cash Equivalents}}{\text{Current Liabilities}}$$

*The most stringent test of liquidity; it measures the amount of cash available to pay current liab*

9. Current ratio
*CA/CL = working capital*
*↑ ratio ⇒ good liquidity*
*most bt wn 1 & 2*

$$\frac{\text{Current Assets}}{\text{Current Liabilities}}$$

*Tends to measure the adequacy of working capital by relating total current assets to total current liabilities*

10. Quick ratio *or acid test*
*all assets listed above inventory*

$$\frac{\text{Quick Assets}}{\text{Current Liabilities}}$$

*A severe test of liquidity by relating quick assets to total current liabilities*

11. Receivable turnover
*Avg. collection period -*
*365 ÷ 3.75 = 97.3 days   Avg. # of days to collect*

$$\frac{\text{Net Credit Sales}}{\text{Average Net Trade Receivables}}$$

*Tends to measure effectiveness of credit granting + collection of receivables*

12. Inventory turnover
*how many times a year*
*Days supply  365 ÷ 2.9 = 186 days*

$$\frac{\text{Cost of Goods Sold}}{\text{Average Inventory}}$$

*Tends to indicate the velocity w/ which merchandise flows through the business*

**Tests of Solvency and Equity Position**

13. Times interest earned
*compares amt of income in current period to interest obligation for same period*

$$\frac{\text{Net Income} + \text{Interest} + \text{Income Tax Expense}}{\text{Interest Expense}}$$

*A measure of the amount of earnings available to cover interest expense*

14. Cash coverage

$$\frac{\text{Cash Flows from Operating Activities (before interest and tax expense)}}{\text{Interest Paid}}$$

*amount of cash flow from operating activities available to cover interest expense*

*creditors/owners*
*A   L*
*SE*

15. Debt-to-equity ratio
*measures portion of company financed w/ debt as opposed to equity*

$$\frac{\text{Total Liabilities}}{\text{Owners' Equity}}$$
*Total*

*measures relationship between resources provided by creditors vs. resources owned by owners*

**Market Tests**

16. Price/earnings ratio
*Multiple ↑ ratio ⇒ significant growth potential*

$$\frac{\text{Current Market Price per Share}}{\text{Earnings per Share}}$$

*measures earnings of the company that may benefit directly to indirectly the investor. It's the ratio of income to the current market price of the stock*

17. Dividend yield ratio
*investors return < dividend / growth*

$$\frac{\text{Dividends per Share}}{\text{Market Price per Share}}$$

*measures cash return to the stockholder from dividends in relationship to the current market price of the stock*

**Miscellaneous Ratio**
*measures relationship btwn dividends per share pd. & the current price of the stock.*
*2 returns when investors buy stock*
*- price appreciations*
*- dividend yields*

18. Book value per share

$$\frac{\text{Common Stock Equity}}{\text{Number of Shares of Common Stock Outstanding}}$$

that are measured in the financial statements. Several different tests of profitability are commonly used.

*19. Dividend payout ratio*
$$\frac{\text{Dividends}}{\text{Net income}}$$
*portion of NI pd to common stockholders*

## 1. RETURN ON EQUITY (ROE)
*20. Gross profit percentage ratio*
$$\frac{\text{Gross profit}}{\text{Net sales}}$$
*measures ability to charge premium prices + produce goods + services @ a lower cost*

*Return on equity* (also called *return on owners' investment* or $ROI_O$) is a fundamental test of profitability. It relates income to the investment that was made by the owners to earn income. It reflects the simple fact that investors expect to earn more money if they invest more money. Two investments that offer a return of $10,000 are not comparable if one requires a $100,000 investment and the other requires a $250,000 investment. The return on equity ratio is computed as follows:[1]

$$\textbf{Return on Equity} = \frac{\textbf{Income*}}{\textbf{Average Owners' Equity}}$$

$$\textbf{Home Depot 1999} = \frac{\textbf{\$1,614}}{\textbf{\$7,919}\dagger} = \textbf{20.4\%}$$

*Income **before** extraordinary items should be used.
†Average owners' equity is preferable when available. For Home Depot, it is computed as ($8,740 + $7,098) ÷ 2 = $7,919.

Home Depot earned 20.4 percent, after income taxes, on the investment provided by the owners. Is this return good or bad? The question can be answered only by comparing its ROE with the ROE of similar companies. The return on equity for three of Home Depot's competitors follows:

| | |
|---|---|
| Lowe's | 15.4% |
| Payless Cashways | NM |
| Home Depot | 20.4 |

Payless Cashways reported a loss in 1999, which makes its ROE not meaningful (we have included this comparison to illustrate the difficulty in finding comparable companies; even though Payless is a direct competitor, it is not possible to make some comparisons). Home Depot is doing very well in relationship to major competitors.

## 2. RETURN ON ASSETS (ROA)

Another view of the return on investment concept relates income to total assets (i.e., total investment) used to earn income. Many analysts consider the *return on assets ratio* (also called the *return on total investment ratio, $ROI_T$*) to be a better measure of management's ability to effectively utilize assets independent of how the assets were financed. The return on equity could be very large for a company that was highly leveraged (i.e., employed a large amount of debt) even though management earned a low rate of return on total assets. Return on assets is computed as follows:

$$\textbf{Return on Assets} = \frac{\textbf{Income* + Interest Expense (net of tax)}}{\textbf{Average Total Assets}}$$

$$\textbf{Home Depot 1999} = \frac{\textbf{\$1,614 + (\$37 × 66\%)}}{\textbf{\$12,347}\dagger} = \textbf{13.3\%}$$

*Income before extraordinary items should be used. This illustration uses a corporate tax rate of 34 percent.
†Average total assets should be used. For Home Depot that is ($13,465 + $11,229) ÷ 2 = $12,347.

Home Depot earned 13.3 percent on the total resources it used during the year. Under the ROA concept, investment is the amount of resources provided by both owners and creditors. Notice that the measure of return includes the return to both owners and creditors. To compute return on assets, interest expense (net of income tax) is added back to income because interest is the return on the creditors' investment. It must be added back because it was previously deducted to compute net income. The denominator represents total investment; therefore, the numerator (income) must include the total return that was available to the suppliers of funds. Interest expense is measured

---

[1]The figures for Home Depot used throughout the following ratio examples are taken from the financial statements in Exhibit 14.1.

net of income tax because it represents the net cost to the corporation for the funds provided by creditors.

As you would expect, return on assets usually is smaller than return on equity. The return on assets for Home Depot's competitors is shown here. Each of these ratios is less than the return on equity ratio shown earlier.

| | |
|---|---|
| Lowe's | 7.6% |
| Payless Cashways | NM |
| Home Depot | 13.3 |

## 3. FINANCIAL LEVERAGE PERCENTAGE

*Financial leverage percentage* is the advantage, or disadvantage, that occurs as the result of earning a return on equity that is different from the return earned on assets (i.e., ROE − ROA). Most companies have positive leverage. Positive leverage occurs when the rate of return on a company's assets is higher than the average after-tax interest rate on borrowed funds. Basically, the company borrows at one rate and invests at a higher rate of return.

In the Dupont model discussed earlier in this chapter, we saw that financial leverage is the proportion of assets acquired with funds supplied by owners. Some analysts use the term financial leverage percentage to describe the relationship between the return on equity and the return on assets. Under this concept, financial leverage percentage can be measured by comparing the two return on investment ratios as follows:

$$\text{Financial Leverage} = \frac{\text{Return on}}{\text{Equity}} - \frac{\text{Return on}}{\text{Assets}} = \text{(positive leverage)}$$

$$\text{Home Depot 1999} = 20.4\% - 13.3\% = 7.1\%$$

When a company is able to borrow funds at an after-tax interest rate and invest those funds to earn a higher after-tax rate of return, the difference accrues to the benefit of the owners. The notes to Home Depot's annual report indicate that the company has borrowed money at rates ranging from 3.25 percent to 10.5 percent and invested this money in assets earning 13.3 percent. The difference between the money that the company earns and the amount that it pays out in interest to creditors is available for the owners of Home Depot. Financial leverage is the primary reason that most companies obtain a significant amount of resources from creditors rather than obtaining resources only from the sale of their capital stock. Notice that financial leverage can be enhanced either by investing effectively (i.e., earning a high return on investment) or borrowing effectively (i.e., paying a low rate of interest).

## 4. EARNINGS PER SHARE (EPS)

Some analysts are critical of the return on investment ratios because they are based on historical cost data. The amount of owners' investment represents their original investment plus retained earnings, not the current market value of that investment. The same concern applies to the return on assets.

*Earnings per share* is based on the number of shares outstanding instead of dollar amounts reported on the balance sheet. Investors easily can interpret EPS in terms of their personal circumstances. An investor with 1,000 shares of stock can quickly compute the return on his or her investment using EPS. The investor would not be able to compute his or her return with only the information that the company had earned 20.4 percent on equity. Basically, EPS is computed as follows:

$$\text{Earnings per Share} = \frac{\text{Income}}{\text{Average Number of Shares of Common Stock Outstanding}}$$

$$\text{Home Depot 1999} = \frac{\$1,614}{\$1,470^*} = \$1.10 \text{ per share}$$

*Average number of shares is (1,475 + 1,464) ÷ 2 = 1,470

This simplified computation of EPS may produce a result that is different from the amount actually reported on the income statement. A difference is caused by some additional complexities in the computation of EPS that are discussed in advanced accounting courses.

Earnings per share is probably the single most widely watched ratio. Companies' announcement of their EPS each quarter during the fiscal year is normally reported in the business press. The following report concerning Home Depot appeared in Reuters News Service at the end of 1999:

Home Depot's third-quarter earnings beat expectations with a 31 percent increase in profit. The company's stock rose 50 cents to $47.87 on the announcement. The reported profit was 26 cents per share against 20 cents in the year-ago period. The company was expected to earn 25 cents per share according to the average estimate determined by a survey of financial analysts.

## 5. QUALITY OF INCOME

As you saw in earlier chapters, some accounting procedures (e.g., accelerated depreciation, LIFO) are considered conservative because they tend to produce lower reported earnings compared to less conservative procedures. Financial analysts often talk about the *quality* of a company's earnings. These analysts are concerned with the issue of whether a company's earnings are generated by its operations or the aggressive use of liberal accounting policies. A measure of the *quality of income* is computed as follows:

$$\text{Quality of Income} = \frac{\text{Cash Flows from Operating Activities}}{\text{Net Income}}$$

$$\text{Home Depot 1999} = \frac{\$1,917}{\$1,614} = 1.19$$

A ratio higher than 1 is considered to indicate higher-quality earnings because each dollar of income is supported by at least one dollar of cash flow. A ratio below 1 represents lower-quality earnings.

## 6. PROFIT MARGIN

The *profit margin* percentage is based on two income statement amounts. It is computed as follows:

$$\text{Profit Margin} = \frac{\text{Income (before Extraordinary Items)}}{\text{Net Sales Revenue}}$$

$$\text{Home Depot 1999} = \frac{\$1,614}{\$30,219} = 5.3\%$$

This profitability measurement represents the percentage of each sales dollar, on the average, that is profit. For Home Depot, each dollar of sales generated 5.3 cents of profit. Care must be used in analyzing the profit margin because it does not consider the amount of resources employed (i.e., total investment) to earn income. For example, the hypothetical income statements of Home Depot and Lowe's might show the following:

|  | Home Depot | Lowe's |
|---|---|---|
| a. Sales revenue | $100,000 | $150,000 |
| b. Income | $ 5,000 | $ 7,500 |
| c. Profit margin (b ÷ a) | 5% | 5% |
| d. Total investment | $50,000 | $125,000 |
| e. Return on total investment* (b ÷ d) | 10% | 6% |

*Assuming no interest expense.

In this example, both companies reported the same profit margin (5 percent). Home Depot, however, appears to be performing much better because it is earning a 10 percent return on the total investment versus the 6 percent earned by Lowe's. The profit margin percentages do not reflect the effect of the $50,000 total investment in Home Depot compared to the $125,000 total investment in Lowe's. The effect of the different amounts of investment in each company is reflected in the return on investment (ROI) percentages. Thus, the profit margin omits one of the two important factors that should be used in evaluating return on the investment.

Comparing profit margins for companies in different industries is difficult. For example, profit margins in the food industry are low while profit margins in the jewelry business are large. Both types of businesses can be quite profitable because they differ in terms of the sales volume that can be generated from a given level of investment. Grocery stores have small margins but generate a large sales volume from relatively inexpensive stores and inventory. Jewelry stores earn more profit from each sales dollar but require a large investment in luxury stores and very expensive inventory. This relationship between profit margin and sales volume can be stated in very simple terms: Would you prefer to have 5 percent of $1,000,000 or 10 percent of $100,000? As you can see, a larger percentage is not always better.

The operating strength of Home Depot comes more clearly into focus when you compare its profit margin with that of major competitors:

| Lowe's | 3.9% |
|---|---|
| Payless Cashways | NM |
| Home Depot | 5.3 |

## 7. FIXED ASSET TURNOVER RATIO

A key indication of management effectiveness is its ability to effectively utilize available resources. The *fixed asset turnover ratio* measures management's ability to generate sales given an investment in fixed assets. The term *fixed assets* is synonymous with *property, plant, and equipment*. The ratio is computed as follows:

$$\text{Fixed Asset Turnover} = \frac{\text{Net Sales Revenue}}{\text{Net Fixed Assets}}$$

$$\text{Home Depot 1999} = \frac{\$30,219}{\$7,334*} = 4.12$$

*Average net fixed assets are ($8,160 + $6,509) ÷ 2 = $7,334.

The fixed asset turnover ratio for Home Depot is better than Lowe's (3.69). In simple terms, this means that Home Depot has a competitive advantage over Lowe's in terms of its ability to effectively utilize its fixed assets to generate revenue. For each dollar Home Depot has invested in property, plant, and equipment, it is able to earn $4.12 in sales revenue. Lowe's can earn only $3.69. This comparison is extremely important because it indicates that management of Home Depot is able to operate more efficiently than the company's main competitor.

The fixed asset turnover ratio is widely used to analyze capital-intensive companies such as airlines and electric utilities. Analysts often calculate a different turnover ratio for companies that have large amounts of inventory and accounts receivable. The asset turnover ratio is based on total assets:

$$\text{Asset Turnover} = \frac{\text{Net Sales Revenue}}{\text{Total Assets}}$$

$$\text{Home Depot 1999} = \frac{\$30,219}{\$12,347^*} = 2.45$$

*Average total assets are ($13,465 + $11,229) ÷ 2 = $12,347.

This ratio shows the analyst that Home Depot was able to generate $2.45 in revenue for each dollar invested in the company's assets. This ratio compares to Lowe's ratio of $2.11. Remember that the fixed asset ratio for Home Depot was better than the one for Lowe's. These comparisons show that Home Depot is able to generate more sales dollars than Lowe's from its investments in inventory, accounts receivable, and fixed assets.

As we showed with the ROE model earlier in this chapter, one strategy to improve return on equity is to generate more sales dollars from the company's assets. Home Depot has shown consistent improvement in its asset turnover ratio each year. Many analysts consider this type of improvement to be an important indication of the quality of its management.

## SELF-STUDY **QUIZ**

Show how to compute the following ratios:

1.   Return on equity =

2.   Return on assets =

3.   Profit margin =

After you have completed your answers, check them with the solutions presented in the footnote at the bottom of this page.*

## TESTS OF LIQUIDITY

**TESTS OF LIQUIDITY** are ratios that measure a company's ability to meet its currently maturing obligations.

*Liquidity* refers to a company's ability to meet its currently maturing debts. **Tests of liquidity** focus on the relationship between current assets and current liabilities. A company's ability to pay its current liabilities is an important factor in evaluating its short-term financial strength. For example, a company that does not have cash available to pay for purchases on a timely basis will lose its cash discounts and run the risk of having its credit discontinued by vendors. Three ratios are used to measure liquidity: the cash ratio, the current ratio, and the quick ratio. Recall that *working capital* is the dollar difference between total current assets and total current liabilities.

### 8. CASH RATIO

Cash is the lifeblood of a business. Without cash, a company cannot pay its employees or meet obligations to its creditors. In other words, a business will fail without suffi-

---

*1.    $\dfrac{\text{Income}}{\text{Average Owners' Equity}}$

2.   $\dfrac{\text{Income} + \text{Interest Expense (net of tax)}}{\text{Average Total Assets}}$

3.   $\dfrac{\text{Income (before extraordinary items)}}{\text{Net Sales Revenue}}$

cient cash. A measure of the adequacy of available cash is called the *cash ratio*. It is computed as follows:

$$\text{Cash Ratio} = \frac{\text{Cash} + \text{Cash Equivalents}}{\text{Current Liabilities}}$$

$$\text{Home Depot 1999} = \frac{\$62}{\$2,857} = 0.022 \text{ to } 1$$

Analysts often use this ratio to compare comparable companies. The cash ratio for Lowe's is 0.13, which indicates that it has a larger cash reserve compared to its current liabilities. Would analysts be concerned about the lower ratio for Home Depot? Probably not. The statement of cash flows for Home Depot shows that the company generates a very large amount of cash from operating activities each year. As a result, it does not have to keep a large amount of cash on reserve to meet unexpected needs. Indeed, most analysts believe that companies should be careful not to have a cash ratio that is too high because holding excess cash usually is uneconomical. It is far better to invest the cash in productive assets or reduce debt.

Another appropriate use of this ratio is to compare it over time for a single company. The cash ratio for Home Depot has decreased over recent years. In most cases, this deterioration might be a cause for concern. It could be an early warning that the company was experiencing financial difficulty. Given the strong performance of Home Depot, the deterioration in the cash ratio is more likely the result of an aggressive strategy by management to minimize the amount of cash that is used to operate the business.

Some analysts do not use this ratio because it is very sensitive to small events. The collection of a large account receivable, for example, may have a significant impact on the cash ratio. The current ratio and the quick ratio are much less sensitive to the timing of certain transactions.

## 9. CURRENT RATIO

The *current ratio* measures the relationship between total current assets and total current liabilities at a specific date. It is computed as follows:

$$\text{Current Ratio} = \frac{\text{Current Assets}}{\text{Current Liabilities}}$$

$$\text{Home Depot 1999} = \frac{\$4,933}{\$2,857} = 1.73 \text{ to } 1$$

At year-end, current assets for Home Depot were 1.73 times current liabilities or, for each $1 of current liabilities, there was $1.73 of current assets. The current ratio measures the cushion of working capital maintained to allow for the inevitable unevenness in the flow of funds through the working capital accounts. Because the current ratio measures the adequacy of working capital, it sometimes is called the *working capital ratio*.

To properly use the current ratio, analysts must understand the nature of a company's business. Most companies have developed sophisticated systems to minimize the amount of inventory they must hold. These systems are called *just-in-time inventory* and are designed to have an inventory item arrive just as it is needed. These systems work well in manufacturing processes, but they do not work as well in retailing. Customers expect to find merchandise when they want it, and it has proven difficult to precisely forecast consumer behavior. As a result, most retailers carry large inventories and, therefore, have high current ratios. To illustrate this issue, Home Depot maintains an inventory of 45,000 different products in each store.

Analysts consider a current ratio of 2 to be conservative. Indeed, most companies have current ratios that are less than 2. The optimal level for a current ratio depends on the business environment in which a company operates. If cash flows are predictable and stable (a utility company, for example), the current ratio can be just a little higher than 1. For a business with highly variable cash flows (such as an airline), a current ratio closer to 2 may be desirable.

Most analysts would judge the current ratio for Home Depot to be very strong, given the company's ability to generate cash.

It is possible to have a current ratio that is too high. It is normally considered to be inefficient to tie up too much money in inventory or accounts receivable. If a Home Depot store sells 100 hammers a month, there is no reason to have 1,000 in stock. A very high current ratio may indicate serious operating difficulties.

### 10. QUICK RATIO (ACID TEST)

The *quick ratio* is similar to the current ratio except that it is a more stringent test of short-term liquidity. It is computed as follows:

$$\text{Quick Ratio} = \frac{\text{Quick Assets}}{\text{Current Liabilities}}$$

$$\text{Home Depot 1999} = \frac{\$531}{\$2,857} = 0.19 \text{ to } 1$$

Quick assets are readily convertible into cash at approximately their book values. Quick assets include cash, short-term investments, and accounts receivable (net of the allowance for doubtful accounts). Inventories usually are omitted from quick assets because of the uncertainty of when cash will be received from the sale of inventory in the future. Prepaid expenses also are excluded from quick assets. Thus, the quick, or acid test, ratio is a more severe test of liquidity than is the current ratio.

The quick ratio tells us that Home Depot has 19 cents in cash and near cash assets for every $1 in current liabilities. This is a relatively low margin of safety but should not be a concern to analysts because of the large amount of cash that is generated from operating activities. By comparison, the quick ratio for Lowe's is 0.21 to 1.

### 11. RECEIVABLE TURNOVER

Short-term liquidity and operating efficiency can be measured in terms of *turnover* of certain current assets. Two additional ratios that measure nearness to cash are receivable turnover and inventory turnover.

*Receivable turnover* is computed as follows:

$$\text{Receivable Turnover} = \frac{\text{Net Credit Sales*}}{\text{Average Net Trade Receivables}}$$

$$\text{Home Depot 1999} = \frac{\$30,219}{\$512†} = 59 \text{ Times}$$

*When the amount of credit sales is not known, total sales may be used as a rough approximation.
†($469 + $556) ÷ 2 = $512

This ratio is called a *turnover* because it reflects how many times the trade receivables were recorded, collected, and then recorded again during the period (i.e., "turnover"). Receivable turnover expresses the relationship of the average balance in Accounts Receivable to the transactions (i.e., credit sales) that created those receivables. This ratio measures the effectiveness of the company's credit-granting and collection activities. A high receivable turnover ratio suggests effective collection activities. Granting credit to poor credit risks and making ineffective collection efforts cause this ratio to be low. A very low ratio obviously is a problem, but a very high ratio also can be a problem. A very high ratio may indicate an overly stringent credit policy that could cause lost sales and profits.

The receivable turnover ratio often is converted to a time basis known as the *average age of receivables*. The computation is as follows:

$$\text{Average Age of Trade Receivables} = \frac{\text{Days in a Year}}{\text{Receivable Turnover}}$$

$$\text{Home Depot 1999} = \frac{365}{59} = 6.2 \text{ Average Days to Collect}$$

The effectiveness of credit and collection activities sometimes is judged by the rule of thumb that the average days to collect should not exceed 1½ times the credit terms. For example, if the credit terms require payment in 30 days, the average days to collect should not exceed 45 days (i.e., not more than 15 days past due). Like all rules of thumb, this one has many exceptions.

When you evaluate financial statements, you should always think about the reasonableness of the numbers you compute. We computed the average age of receivables for Home Depot as 6.2 days. Is that number reasonable? Probably not. It is very unlikely that Home Depot collects cash from its credit customers on average in just 6.2 days. Remember that we do not know the amount of credit sales for Home Depot and had to use total sales as an approximation. Think about the last time you were in a retail store and watched a customer buying merchandise on credit. In most case, the customer used a bank credit card such as MasterCard and Visa. A sales transaction involving a bank credit card is recorded virtually the same as cash sale from the perspective of the seller. In other words, a credit sale involving a bank credit card does not create an account receivable on the books of the seller. The account receivable is on the books of the credit card company. In practice, Home Depot relies on bank credit cards for the majority of its credit sales. As a result, the accounts receivable turnover ratio is not meaningful for Home Depot.

## 12. INVENTORY TURNOVER

*Inventory turnover* measures the liquidity of the inventory. It reflects the relationship of the inventory to the volume of goods sold during the period. The computation is as follows:

$$\textbf{Inventory Turnover} = \frac{\textbf{Cost of Goods Sold}}{\textbf{Average Inventory}}$$

$$\textbf{Home Depot 1999} = \frac{\$21,614}{\$3,948^*} = \textbf{5.5 Times}$$

*($4,293 + $3,602) ÷ 2 = $3,948.

The inventory for Home Depot "turned over" 5.5 times during the year. Because profit normally is realized each time the inventory is sold (i.e., turned over), an increase in the ratio is usually favorable. If the ratio is too high, however, sales may be lost because of items that are out of stock.

The inventory turnover ratio is critical for companies that have adopted the Home Depot strategy. They want to be able to offer the customer the right product when it is needed at a price that beats the competition. If they do not effectively manage their inventory levels, they will incur extra costs that must be passed on to the customer. Let's compare the Home Depot inventory turnover to that of its major competitors:

| | |
|---|---|
| Lowe's | 6.4 |
| Payless Cashways | 3.7 |
| Home Depot | 5.5 |

As you can see, Home Depot has a significant competitive advantage over Payless Cashways in terms of inventory turnover but not over Lowe's. As recently as the early 1990s, inventory turnover for Home Depot was as high as 6.3. Home Depot recently spent $9 million to upgrade computer systems in all of its stores and is now transmitting data via satellite. One of the announced goals of this investment is to increase inventory turnover. Management and analysts will watch closely to see whether inventory turnover improves.

The turnover ratio often is converted to a time-basis expression called *the average days' supply in inventory*. The computation is

$$\text{Average Days' Supply in Inventory} = \frac{\text{Days in Year}}{\text{Inventory Turnover}}$$

$$\text{Home Depot 1999} = \frac{365}{5.5}$$

$$= 66 \text{ Average Days' Supply in Inventory}$$

Turnover ratios vary significantly by industry classification. Companies in the food industry (grocery stores and restaurants) have high inventory turnover ratios because their inventory is subject to rapid deterioration in quality. Companies that sell expensive merchandise (automobile dealers and high-fashion clothes) have much lower ratios because sales of these items are infrequent but customers want to have a selection to choose from when they do buy.

## SELF-STUDY **QUIZ**

Show how to compute the following ratios:

1. Quality of income =

2. Quick ratio =

3. Cash ratio =

After you have completed your answers, check them with the solutions presented in the footnote at the bottom of this page.*

## TESTS OF SOLVENCY AND EQUITY POSITION

*Solvency* refers to a company's ability to meet its long-term obligations on a continuing basis. **Tests of solvency** measure a company's ability to meet these obligations. Certain critical relationships can be identified by analyzing the way that a company has financed its assets and activities.

**TESTS OF SOLVENCY** are ratios that measure a company's ability to meet its long-term obligations.

### 13. TIMES INTEREST EARNED RATIO

Interest payments are a company's fixed obligation. Failure to make required interest payments may result in creditors forcing the company into bankruptcy. Because of the importance of interest payments, analysts often compute a ratio called *times interest earned:*

$$\text{Time Interest Earned} = \frac{\text{Net Income} + \text{Interest Expense} + \text{Income Tax Expense}}{\text{Interest Expense}}$$

$$\text{Home Depot 1999} = \frac{\$1,614 + \$37 + \$1,040}{\$37} = 72.7 \text{ Times}$$

This ratio compares the amount of income that has been generated in the current period to the interest obligation for the same period. It represents the margin of protection for the creditors. Home Depot generated more than $72 in income for each $1 of interest expense. This is a very high ratio and, therefore, a very secure position for creditors. Some analysts prefer to calculate this ratio including all contractually re-

---

*1. $\dfrac{\text{Cash Flows from Operating Activities}}{\text{Net Income}}$

2. $\dfrac{\text{Quick Assets}}{\text{Current Liabilities}}$

3. $\dfrac{\text{Cash + Cash Equivalents}}{\text{Current Liabilities}}$

quired payments. These include principal payments and rent obligations under lease contracts. Other analysts believe that this ratio is flawed because interest expense and other obligations are paid in cash, not with net income. They prefer to compute the cash coverage ratio.

## 14. CASH COVERAGE RATIO

Given the importance of cash flows and required interest payments, it is easy to understand why the *cash coverage ratio* is important. It is computed as follows:

$$\text{Cash Coverage} = \frac{\text{Cash Flows from Operating Activities}}{\text{before Interest and Taxes}}$$
$$\frac{}{\text{Interest Paid (from statement of cash flows)}}$$

$$\text{Home Depot 1999} = \frac{\$1,917 + \$37 + \$1,040}{\$37} = 80.9$$

The cash coverage ratio for Home Depot shows that the company generated nearly $81 in cash for every $1 of interest expense. This is strong coverage. Notice that in the denominator of the ratio, we used interest payments reported on the statement of cash flows instead of interest expense. The cash coverage ratio compares the cash generated with the cash obligations of the period. Remember that analysts are concerned about a company's ability to make required interest payments. Accrued interest and interest payments normally are similar in amount each period, but not always. Consider a company that has a 20-year, zero coupon bond. The company reports accrued interest each period, but it does not have to make an interest payment until the bond matures in the 20th year. In this case, interest payments are a better measure of the company's current obligation than is accrued interest expense.

## 15. DEBT-TO-EQUITY RATIO

The *debt-to-equity ratio* expresses the proportion between debt and owners' equity.[2] It is computed as follows:

$$\text{Debt-to-Equity Ratio} = \frac{\text{Total Liabilities (i.e., creditors' equity)}}{\text{Owners' Equity}}$$

$$\text{Home Depot 1999} = \frac{\$4,725}{\$8,740} = 0.54 \text{ (or } 54\%)$$

This ratio means that for each $1 of owners' equity, there were 54 cents of liabilities. Debt is risky for a company because it imposes important contractual obligations. There are (1) specific maturity dates for the principal amounts and (2) specific interest payments that must be made. Debt obligations are enforceable by law and do not depend on the company's earnings. In contrast, dividends for stockholders are always at the discretion of the company and are not legally enforceable until declared by the board of directors. Owners' equity is "permanent" capital that does not have a maturity date. Thus, equity capital usually is seen as much less risky than debt for a company.

Despite the risk associated with debt, most companies obtain significant amounts of resources from creditors because of the advantages of financial leverage discussed earlier in this chapter. In addition, interest expense is a deductible expense on the income

---

[2]The relationship between debt and owners' equity alternatively may be calculated with the following two ratios:

$$\text{Owners' Equity to Total Equities} = \frac{\text{Owners' Equity}}{\text{Total Equity}}$$

$$\text{Home Depot 1999} = \frac{\$8,740}{\$13,465} = 64.9\%$$

$$\text{Creditors' Equity to Total Equities} = \text{Creditors' Equity}$$

$$\text{Home Depot 1999} = \frac{\$4,725}{\$13,465} = 35.1\%$$

tax return. When selecting a capital structure, a company must balance the higher returns that are available with leverage against the higher risk associated with debt. Because of the importance of this risk-and-return relationship, most analysts consider the debt-to-equity ratio to be a key part of any company evaluation.

## MARKET TESTS

Several ratios measure the "market worth" of a share of stock. These **market tests** relate the current market price of a share of stock to an indicator of the return that might accrue to the investor. The tests focus on the current market price of the stock because that is the amount the buyer would invest. Two market test ratios used by analysts and investors are the price/earnings ratio and the dividend yield ratio.

### 16. PRICE/EARNINGS (P/E) RATIO

The *price/earnings (P/E) ratio* measures the relationship between the current market price of the stock and its earnings per share. A recent price for Home Depot stock was $62 per share. The EPS for Home Depot calculated earlier was $1.10. The P/E ratio for the company is computed as follows:

$$\text{Price/Earnings Ratio} = \frac{\text{Current Market Price per Share}}{\text{Earnings per Share}}$$

$$\text{Home Depot 1999} = \frac{\$62}{\$1.10} = 56.4$$

Home Depot stock was selling at 56.4 times the EPS. The P/E ratio often is referred to as the *multiple*, as in price/earnings multiple. The P/E ratio is used as an indicator of the future performance of the stock. A high price/earnings multiple indicates that the market expects earnings to grow rapidly. The P/E ratio for Home Depot is high compared to its major competitors:

| | |
|---|---|
| Lowe's | 38.3 |
| Payless Cashways | NM |
| Home Depot | 56.4 |

The P/E ratio for Home Depot is high compared to that of its competitors and most other companies. It is currently more than twice the average for companies included in the S&P 500 stock index. Furthermore, the ratio for Home Depot has increased significantly over the past three years. When the P/E ratio was in the low 30s, one analyst focused on the P/E ratio as an explanation for Home Depot's poor stock performance during the period:

> The lackluster performance has occurred despite strong earnings because of a declining price earnings multiple. We think the decline in the multiple during the past four years partly reflects a growing awareness about the Company's sensitivity to macroeconomic issues. The multiple could continue declining if the company's growth rate keeps on moderating. However, we think a large competitive shakeout will occur soon and the multiple could rally.

Since that report was written, Home Depot's earnings have increased significantly and its P/E multiple has doubled. The analyst's assessment was very accurate. Two major competitors (Hechinger's and Builders Square) filed for bankruptcy, and Payless Cashways is currently operating at a loss. The improvement in both the P/E ratio and the earnings of the company has resulted in an increase of more than 300 percent in the price of Home Depot stock since the analyst report was published.

Sometimes the components of the P/E ratio are inverted, giving the *capitalization rate*. This is the rate at which the stock market apparently is capitalizing the current earnings. Computation of the capitalization rate on current earnings per share for Home Depot is $1.09 ÷ $62 = 1.8 percent.

A high P/E ratio is usually associated with companies that have significant growth potential. The value of a stock is related to the present value of its future earnings. A company that expects to increase its earnings in the future is worth more than one that cannot grow its earnings (assuming other factors to be the same). Currently, many new Internet companies have high stock prices despite the fact that they have never earned any money. Clearly, the market is valuing their stock based on an assessment of future earnings growth.

## 17. DIVIDEND YIELD RATIO

When investors buy stock, they expect returns from two sources: price appreciation and dividend income. The *dividend yield ratio* measures the relationship between the dividends per share paid and the current market price of the stock. Home Depot paid dividends of 23 cents per share when the market price per share was $62. The dividend yield ratio for Home Depot is computed as follows:

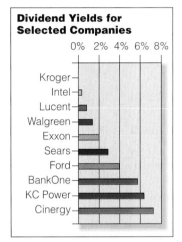

**Dividend Yields for Selected Companies**

$$\text{Dividend Yield Ratio} = \frac{\textbf{Dividend per Share}}{\textbf{Market Price per Share}}$$

$$\text{Home Depot 1999} = \frac{\$0.23}{\$62} = .37\%$$

It might seem surprising that the dividend yield for Home Depot is below 1 percent, given that an investor could earn more than 5 percent in a federally insured savings account. The dividend yield for most stocks is not very high compared to alternative investments. Investors are willing to accept low dividend yields when they expect that the price of the stock will increase while they own it. Clearly, investors who buy Home Depot stock do so with the expectation that the price of the stock will increase. The current dividends are probably a very small factor in their decisions. Stocks with low growth potential often offer much higher dividend yields than do stocks with high growth potential. These stocks often appeal to investors who are retired and need current income rather than future growth potential. The accompanying chart presents some examples of dividend yields.

## MISCELLANEOUS RATIO

### 18. BOOK VALUE PER SHARE

The *book value per share* of stock measures the owners' equity in terms of each share of common stock outstanding. In the case of a simple capital structure, with *only* common stock outstanding, the computation of book value per share is not difficult. The computation of book value per share is

$$\text{Book Value per Common Share} = \frac{\textbf{Total Owners' Equity}}{\textbf{(applicable to common shares)}} \Big/ \textbf{Common Shares Outstanding}$$

$$\text{Home Depot 1999} = \frac{\$8,740}{1,475 \text{ shares}} = \$5.93$$

Notice that book value per share has no relationship to market value. The book value of a share of Home Depot stock was $5.93 when the market value was $62. For most companies, book value per share is less than the market value. Some analysts compute a price/book value ratio that compares the current market value of the stock (i.e., selling price) with the book value. Higher ratios are typically associated with companies that have good growth potential. The price/book ratio for Home Depot is $62 ÷ $5.93 = 10.5. Over the past five years, this ratio has ranged from a low of 2.9 to a high of 12. The ratio for Home Depot is another indication that it is a company with good growth potential.

## SELF-STUDY **QUIZ**

Show how to compute the following ratios:

1.  Current ratio =

2.  Inventory turnover =

3.  Price/earnings ratio =

After you have completed your answers, check them with the solutions presented in the footnote at the bottom of this page.*

## OTHER ANALYTICAL CONSIDERATIONS

The ratios that we have discussed so far are general-purpose ratios that are useful in most analytical considerations. Each company is different, and your evaluation of each company should be different.

To illustrate, let's look at some special factors that might affect our analysis of Home Depot.

1.  *Rapid growth.* In some cases, a company that opens many new stores each year may obscure the fact that existing stores are not meeting customer needs and are experiencing declining sales. In other words, growth in total sales volume does not always indicate that a company is successful. The family pizza chain Chuck-E-Cheese reported rapid growth in total sales revenue for a number of years, but it was generated by opening new stores. New stores initially generated very large sales volumes because they were very popular with families with young children. Unfortunately, the novelty of the Chuck-E-Cheese stores proved to be short-lived fads, and same-store sales volume fell quickly. The company was forced to reorganize. In contrast, the annual report for Home Depot shows that the company has had same-store sales increases ranging from 3 percent to 15 percent in each of the previous 10 years, which indicates that it is able to generate increases in sales volume from both new and existing stores.

2.  *Uneconomical expansion.* Some growth-oriented companies open stores in less desirable locations once all the good locations have been taken. These poor locations can cause the stores' average productivity to decline. One measure of productivity in the retail industry is sales volume per square foot of selling space. For Home Depot, productivity results are mixed:

| Year | Sales per Square Foot |
|------|-----------------------|
| 1999 | $410 |
| 1998 | 406 |
| 1997 | 398 |
| 1996 | 390 |
| 1995 | 404 |

*1.  $\dfrac{\text{Current Assets}}{\text{Current Liabilities}}$

2.  $\dfrac{\text{Cost of Goods Sold}}{\text{Average Inventory}}$

3.  $\dfrac{\text{Current Market Price per Share}}{\text{Earnings per Share}}$

The sales per square foot for Home Depot have stabilized in recent years after rapid growth in the early 90s when the figure increased by more than $100 per square foot. Management explains that this has occurred as the direct result of its strategy:

> We continue our cannibalization strategy, whereby we take the pressure off a busy store by opening another one nearby. While some challenge this approach because it tends to lower sales productivity, this strategy results in better service and greater customer satisfaction, which ultimately translates into higher sales and profits.

**REAL WORLD EXCERPT**

*Home Depot*

ANNUAL REPORT

3. *Subjective factors.* It is important to remember that vital information about a company is not contained in the annual report. We discussed earlier that a strategy of Home Depot is to be a price leader. The best way to evaluate that strategy is to visit the stores of Home Depot and of several competitors. The analyst who studied Home Depot for Salomon Brothers did exactly that:

> On July 15, we surveyed the Boca Raton, Florida market. The Home Depot store is about two years old and was particularly impressive with respect to its in-stock position, customer service and total store presentation. We were able to compare Home Depot's pricing on 20 sample items. Our price analysis revealed that Home Depot is the price leader in the market by an average of 11 percent below the average total price of our 20-item market basket. Given the Home Depot's low cost structure, we believe that it will remain the price leader in this important market.

**REAL WORLD EXCERPT**

*Home Depot*

SALOMON BROTHERS
RESEARCH REPORT

As these examples illustrate, no single approach can be used to analyze all companies. Furthermore, effective analysis requires going beyond the information contained in an annual report.

## INTERPRETING RATIOS

The computation of any particular ratio is not standardized. Neither the accounting profession nor security analysts have prescribed the manner in which a ratio must be computed (except for earnings per share). Thus, users of financial statements should compute the various ratios in accordance with their decision objectives. Before using ratios computed by others, the analyst should determine the computational approach that was used.

To interpret a ratio, it should be compared with some standard that represents an optimal or desirable value. For example, the return on investment ratio may be compared with alternative investment opportunities. Some ratios, by their characteristics, are unfavorable if they are either too high or too low. For example, analysis may indicate that a current ratio of approximately 2:1 may be considered optimal for a company. In this situation, a ratio of 1:1 may indicate the danger of being unable to meet maturing debts. A ratio of 3:1 may indicate that excess funds are being left idle rather than being employed profitably. Furthermore, an optimal ratio for one company often is not the optimal ratio for another company. Comparisons of ratios for different companies are appropriate only if the companies are indeed comparable. Noteworthy differences in industry, nature of operations, size, and accounting policies can make the value of many comparisons questionable.

Most ratios represent averages. Therefore, they may obscure underlying factors that are of interest to the analyst. To illustrate, a current ratio of 2:1 may be considered optimal in a given industry. But even an optimal current ratio may obscure a short-term liquidity problem if the company has a very large amount of inventory and a minimal amount of cash with which to pay debts as they mature. Careful analysis can uncover this liquidity problem. In other cases, careful analysis cannot uncover obscured problems. For example, consolidated statements include financial information about the

■ **LEARNING OBJECTIVE 4**

Interpret accounting ratios.

parent and its subsidiaries. The parent company may have a high current ratio and the subsidiary a low ratio. When the statements are consolidated, the current ratio (in effect, an average of the parent and the subsidiary) may be within an acceptable range. Obscured is the fact that the subsidiary may have a serious liquidity problem.

Despite limitations, ratio analysis is a useful analytical tool. Financial ratios are effective for predicting bankruptcy. Exhibit 14.4 gives the current and debt-to-equity ratios for Braniff International Corporation for each year before it filed for bankruptcy. Notice the deterioration of these ratios each year. Analysts who studied the financial ratios probably were not surprised by Braniff's bankruptcy. After selling many of its assets and undergoing a complete financial restructuring, Braniff was able to resume limited flight operations but was forced to file for bankruptcy for a second time after additional financial difficulty.

EXHIBIT **14.4**

Selected Financial Ratios for
Braniff International

| | Years before Bankruptcy | | | | |
| --- | --- | --- | --- | --- | --- |
| | 5 | 4 | 3 | 2 | 1 |
| Current ratio | 1.20 | 0.91 | 0.74 | 0.60 | 0.49 |
| Debt-to-equity ratio | 2.03 | 2.45 | 4.88 | 15.67 | N/A* |

*In the year before bankruptcy, Braniff reported negative owners' equity as the result of a large net loss that produced a negative balance in retained earnings. Creditors' equity exceeded total equities.

## IMPACT OF ACCOUNTING ALTERNATIVES ON RATIO ANALYSIS

Financial statements provide information for the average investor. Users who understand basic accounting are able to more effectively analyze the information contained in financial statements. While studying this book, you have developed an understanding of the accounting vocabulary. A knowledge of this vocabulary is necessary to understand financial statements.

Familiarity with the underlying accounting concepts also is essential for proper analysis of statements. Some unsophisticated users do not understand the cost principle and believe that assets are reported on the balance sheet at their fair market value. We have stressed accounting concepts throughout the book because it is impossible to interpret accounting numbers without an understanding of the concepts that were used to develop the numbers.

When comparing companies, you will find that they rarely use exactly the same accounting policies. If the comparisons are to be useful, the analyst must understand the impact of various accounting alternatives. One company may use conservative accounting alternatives such as accelerated depreciation and LIFO while another may use income-maximizing alternatives such as straight-line depreciation and FIFO. Users who do not understand the effects of accounting methods may misinterpret financial results. Perhaps the most important first step in analyzing financial statements is a review of the accounting policies that the company has selected. This information must be disclosed in a note to the statements.

# A QUESTION OF **ETHICS**

### INSIDER INFORMATION

Financial statements are an important source of information for investors. Announcement of an unexpected earnings increase or decrease can cause a substantial movement in the price of a company's stock.

Accountants for a company may become aware of important financial information before it is made available to the public. This type of data is called *insider information*. It might be tempting for some people to buy or sell stock based on insider information, but to do so is a serious criminal offense. The Securities and Exchange Commission has brought a number of cases against individuals who traded on insider information, which resulted in large fines and time in jail.

In some cases, it may be difficult to decide whether something is insider information. An individual may simply overhear a comment made in the company elevator by two executives. A well-respected Wall Street investment banker gave good advice: "If you are not sure if something is right or wrong, apply the newspaper headline test. Ask yourself how you would feel to have your family and friends read about what you had done in the newspaper." Interestingly, many people who spent time in jail and lost small fortunes in fines because of insider trading convictions say that the most difficult part of the process was telling their families.

To uphold the highest ethical standard, many public accounting firms have rules that prevent members of their professional staff from investing in companies that the firm audits. These rules are designed to ensure that the company's auditors cannot be tempted to engage in insider trading.

## INFORMATION IN AN EFFICIENT MARKET

Considerable research has been performed on how the stock markets react to new information. Much of this evidence supports the view that the markets react very quickly to new information in an unbiased manner (the market does not systematically overreact or underreact to new information). A market that reacts to information in this manner is called an **efficient market.** In an efficient market, the price of a security fully reflects all available information.

**EFFICIENT MARKETS** are securities markets in which prices fully reflect available information.

It is not surprising that the stock markets react quickly to new information. Many professional investors manage stock portfolios valued in the hundreds of millions of dollars. These investors have a large financial incentive to find new, relevant information about a company and to trade quickly based on that information.

The research on efficient markets has important implications for financial analysis. It probably is not beneficial to study old information (say an annual report that was released six months earlier) to identify a stock that has been undervalued by the market. In an efficient market, the price of the stock reflects all of the information contained in the report shortly after it was released.

In an efficient market, we expect that it is not possible for a company to manipulate the price of its stock by manipulating accounting policy. The market should be able to differentiate a company with increasing earnings due to improved productivity from one that has increased earnings by changing from conservative to liberal accounting policies.

## CHAPTER **TAKE-AWAYS**

1. **Discuss how analysts use financial statements.** 737

    Analysts use financial statements to understand present conditions and past performance as well as to predict future performance. Financial statements provide important information to help users understand and evaluate corporate strategy. The data reported on statements can be used for either time-series analysis (evaluating a single company over time) or in comparison with similar companies at a single point in time. Most analysts compute component percentages and ratios when using statements.

2. **List five major categories of accounting ratios.** 740

    The following are the five categories:
    *a.* Tests of profitability.
    *b.* Tests of liquidity.
    *c.* Tests of solvency and equity position.
    *d.* Market tests.
    *e.* Miscellaneous.

3. **Identify and compute widely used accounting ratios.** 740

   A large number of ratios can be computed from a financial statement. The appropriate set of ratios depends on the company being analyzed and the decision that must be made. Exhibit 14.3 lists widely used ratios and shows how to compute them.

4. **Interpret accounting ratios.** 755

   Interpretation of a ratio involves comparing it with some standard that is considered optimal or desirable. Most analysts compare ratios over time to measure improvement or deterioration. Analysts also compare ratios for one company to industry averages or other similar companies. It is often difficult to identify companies that are sufficiently similar to provide meaningful comparisons. Analysts must understand accounting differences among companies whenever they attempt to compare them.

## FINDING FINANCIAL INFORMATION

**BALANCE SHEET**

Ratios are not reported on the balance sheet, but analysts use balance sheet information to compute many ratios. Most analysts use an average of the beginning and ending amounts for balance sheet accounts when comparing the account to an income statement account.

**INCOME STATEMENT**

Earnings per share is the only ratio that is required to be reported on the financial statements. It is usually reported at the bottom on the income statement.

**STATEMENT OF CASH FLOWS**

Ratios are not reported on this statement, but some ratios use amounts from this statement.

**STATEMENT OF STOCKHOLDERS' EQUITY**

Ratios are not reported on this statement, but some ratios use amounts from this statement.

**NOTES**

*Under Summary of Significant Accounting Policies*

This note has no information pertaining directly to ratios, but it is important to understand accounting differences if you are comparing two companies.

*Under a Separate Note*

Most companies include a 10-year financial summary as a separate note. These summaries include data for significant accounts, some accounting ratios, and nonaccounting information.

## KEY **TERMS**

**Component Percentage**  p. 739

**Efficient Markets**  p. 757

**Market Tests**  p. 752

**Ratio (Percentage) Analysis**  p. 738

**Tests of Liquidity**  p. 746

**Tests of Solvency**  p. 750

## QUESTIONS

1. What are three fundamental uses of external financial statements by decision makers?
2. What are some of the primary items on financial statements about which creditors usually are concerned?
3. Explain why the notes to the financial statements are important to decision makers.
4. What is the primary purpose of comparative financial statements?
5. Why are statement users interested in financial summaries covering several years? What is the primary limitation of long-term summaries?
6. What is *ratio analysis?* Why is it useful?
7. What are *component percentages?* Why are they useful?
8. Explain the two concepts of return on investment.
9. What is *financial leverage?* How is it measured as a percentage?
10. Is profit margin a useful measure of profitability? Explain.
11. Compare and contrast the current ratio and the quick ratio.

12. What does the debt-to-equity ratio reflect?
13. What are market tests?
14. Identify two factors that limit the effectiveness of ratio analysis.

# MINI-EXERCISES

**M14–1** **Inferring Financial Information Using Component Percentages**                          ▒ **LO3**
A large retailer reported revenue of $1,680,145,000. The company's gross profit percentage
was 55.9 percent. What amount of cost of goods sold did the company report?

**M14–2** **Inferring Financial Information Using Component Percentages**                          ▒ **LO3**
A consumer products company reported a 6.8 percent increase in sales from 20A to 20B. Sales
in 20A were $20,917. In 20B, the company reported cost of goods sold in the amount of
$9,330. What was the gross profit percentage in 20B?

**M14–3** **Computing the Return on Owners' Investment Ratio**                                    ▒ **LO3**
Compute the return on equity ratio for 20B given the following data:

|                      | 20B         | 20A         |
| -------------------- | ----------- | ----------- |
| Net income           | $  185,000  | $  160,000  |
| Stockholders' equity | 1,000,000   | 1,200,000   |
| Total assets         | 2,400,000   | 2,600,000   |
| Interest expense     | 40,000      | 30,000      |

**M14–4** **Inferring Financial Information Using Component Percentages**                          ▒ **LO3**
Compute financial leverage percentage for 20B given the following data:

|                  | 20B  | 20A  |
| ---------------- | ---- | ---- |
| Return on equity | 22%  | 24%  |
| Return on assets | 8    | 6    |
| Profit margin    | 12   | 10   |

**M14–5** **Analyzing the Inventory Turnover Ratio**                                              ▒ **LO3, 4**
A manufacturer reported an inventory turnover ratio of 8.6 during 20A. During 20B,
management introduced a new inventory control system that was expected to reduce average
inventory levels by 25 percent without affecting sales volume. Given these circumstances,
would you expect the inventory turnover ratio to increase or decrease during 20B? Explain.

**M14–6** **Inferring Financial Information Using a Ratio**                                       ▒ **LO3**
Scruggs Company reported total assets of $1,200,000 and noncurrent assets of $480,000. The
company also reported a current ratio of 1.5. What amount of current liabilities did the
company report?

**M14–7** **Analyzing Financial Relationships**                                                  ▒ **LO4**
Doritos Company has prepared draft financial results now being reviewed by the accountants.
You notice that the financial leverage percentage is negative. You also note that the current
ratio is 2.4 and the quick ratio is 3.7. You remember that these financial relationships are
unusual. Does either imply that a mistake has been made? Explain.

**M14–8** **Inferring Financial Information Using a Ratio**                                       ▒ **LO3**
In 20A, Drago Company reported earnings per share of $8.50 when its stock was selling for
$212.50. In 20B, its earnings increased by 20 percent. If all other relationships remain
constant, what is the price of the stock? Explain.

**M14–9** **Inferring Financial Information Using a Ratio**                                       ▒ **LO3**
An Internet company earned $5 per share and paid dividends of $2 per share. The company
reported a dividend yield of 5 percent. What was the price of the stock?

■ **LO4**    **M14–10**    **Analyzing the Impact of Accounting Alternatives**

Lexis Corporation is considering changing its inventory method from FIFO to LIFO and wants to determine the impact on selected accounting ratios. In general, what impact would you expect on the following ratios: profit margin, fixed asset turnover, current ratio, and quick ratio?

# EXERCISES

■ **LO3**    **E14–1**    **Matching Each Ratio with Its Computational Formula**

Match each ratio or percentage with its computation by entering the appropriate letters in the blanks.

| Ratios or Percentages | Definitions |
|---|---|
| _____ 1. Profit margin | A. Income (before extraordinary items) ÷ Net Sales. |
| _____ 2. Inventory turnover ratio | B. Days in Year ÷ Receivable Turnover. |
| _____ 3. Average collection period | C. Income ÷ Average Owners' Equity. |
| _____ 4. Creditors' equity to total equities | D. Income ÷ Average number of Shares of Common Stock Outstanding. |
| _____ 5. Dividend yield ratio | |
| _____ 6. Return on equity | E. Return on Equity − Return on Assets. |
| _____ 7. Current ratio. | F. Quick Assets ÷ Current Liabilities. |
| _____ 8. Debt-to-equity ratio | G. Current Assets ÷ Current Liabilities. |
| _____ 9. Price/earnings ratio | H. Cost of Goods Sold ÷ Average Inventory. |
| _____ 10. Financial leverage percentage | I. Net Credit Sales ÷ Average Net Trade Receivables. |
| _____ 11. Receivable turnover ratio | |
| _____ 12. Average days' supply of inventory | J. Creditors' Equity (debt) ÷ Total Equities. |
| _____ 13. Owners' equity to total equities | K. Days in Year ÷ Inventory Turnover. |
| _____ 14. Earnings per share | L. Total Liabilities ÷ Owners' Equity. |
| _____ 15. Return on assets | M. Dividends per Share ÷ Market Price per Share. |
| _____ 16. Quick ratio | N. Owners' Equity ÷ Total Equities. |
| _____ 17. Book value per share | O. Current Market Price per Share ÷ Earnings per Share. |
| _____ 18. Times interest earned | |
| _____ 19. Cash coverage ratio | P. Owners' Equity ÷ Shares Outstanding. |
| _____ 20. Fixed asset turnover | Q. Income + Interest Expense (net of tax) ÷ Average Total Assets. |
| | R. Cash from Operating Activities (before interest and taxes) ÷ Interest Paid. |
| | S. Net Sales Revenue ÷ Net Fixed Assets. |
| | T. (Net Income + Interest Expense + Income Tax Expense) ÷ Interest Expense. |

■ **LO3**    **E14–2**    **Preparing a Schedule Using Component Percentages**

Walgreens

Walgreens is one of the fastest-growing retailers in the United States. It claims to lead the chain drugstore industry in sales and profits. Complete component percentage analysis on the company's income statement that follows. Discuss any insights provided by this analysis.

| Walgreens | 1999 | 1998 |
|---|---|---|
| **Income Statement (amounts in millions)** | | |
| Net sales | $17,838.8 | $15,306.6 |
| Cost sales | 12,978.6 | 11,139.4 |
| Selling, occupancy and administration | 3,844.8 | 3,332.0 |
| Interest expense | .4 | 1.1 |
| Interest income | 12.3 | 5.6 |
| Gain on sale of long-term assets | | 37.4 |
| Income tax expense | 403.2 | 339.9 |
| Change in accounting method | | (26.4) |
| Net earnings | 624.1 | 510.8 |

**E14–3**   **Analyzing the Impact of Selected Transactions on the Current Ratio**

■ **LO3**

Current assets totaled $54,000, and the current ratio was 1.8. Assume that the following transactions were completed: (1) purchased merchandise for $6,000 on short-term credit and (2) purchased a delivery truck for $10,000, paid $1,000 cash, and signed a two-year interest-bearing note for the balance.

*Required:*
Compute the cumulative current ratio after each transaction.

**E14–4**   **Analyzing the Impact of Selected Transactions on the Current Ratio**

■ **LO3, 4**

Sunbeam

Sunbeam is a leading designer, manufacturer, and marketer of branded consumer products, including Mr. Coffee, Osterizer, First Alert, and Coleman camping gear. Recently, the company has experienced significant financial difficulties and has been named in a number of lawsuits alleging material misstatements in its financial statements. The company's financial statements acknowledge that actions pending against the company "could have a material adverse impact on the Company's financial position." As a result, management must pay close attention to the impact that each operating decision has on the company's liquidity. In the most recent statement, Sunbeam reported current assets of $1,090,068,000 and current liabilities of $602,246,000. Determine the impact of the following transactions on the current ratio for Sunbeam: (1) sold long-term assets that represented excess capacity, (2) accrued severance pay and fringes for employees who will be terminated, (3) wrote down the carrying value of certain inventory items that were deemed to be obsolete, and (4) acquired new inventory; supplier was not willing to provide normal credit terms, so an 18-month interest-bearing note was signed.

**E14–5**   **Analyzing the Impact of Selected Transactions on Accounts Receivable and Inventory Turnover**

■ **LO3, 4**

Procter & Gamble

Procter & Gamble is a multinational corporation that manufactures and markets many products that are probably in your home. Last year, sales for the company were $38,125 (all amounts in millions). The annual report did not disclose the amount of credit sales, so we will assume that 30 percent of sales was on credit. The average gross margin rate was 45 percent on sales. Account balances follow:

|  | Beginning | Ending |
|---|---|---|
| Accounts receivable (net) | $2,940 | $2,781 |
| Inventory | 3,380 | 3,284 |

*Required:*
Compute the turnover for the accounts receivable and inventory, the average age of receivables, and the average days' supply of inventory.

**E14–6**   **Computing Financial Leverage**

■ **LO3**

Motorola

Motorola is a global leader in providing integrated communications and electronic solutions for businesses. Its financial statements reported the following at year-end (in millions):

| | |
|---|---|
| Total assets | $28,728 |
| Total debt (average 8% interest) | 16,506 |
| Net income (average tax rate 30%) | 1,180 |

*Required:*
Compute the financial leverage percentage. Was it positive or negative?

**E14–7**   **Analyzing the Impact of Selected Transactions on the Current Ratio**

■ **LO3, 4**

Current assets totaled $100,000, and the current ratio was 1.5. Assume that the following transactions were completed: (1) paid $6,000 for merchandise purchased on short-term credit, (2) purchased a delivery truck for $10,000 cash, (3) wrote off a bad account receivable for $2,000, and (4) paid previously declared dividends in the amount of $25,000.

*Required:*
Compute the cumulative current ratio after each transaction.

**■ LO3**     **E14–8**     **Inferring Financial Information**

Dollar General
Corporation

Dollar General Corporation operates general merchandise stores that feature quality merchandise at low prices to meet the needs of middle-, low-, and fixed-income families. All stores are located in the United States, predominantly in small towns in 24 midwestern and southeastern states. In a recent year, the company reported average inventories of $721,843,000 and an inventory turnover of 3. Average total fixed assets were $283,142,000, and the fixed asset turnover ratio was 11.4. Determine the gross margin for Dollar General.

**■ LO3**     **E14–9**     **Computing Selected Ratios**

Sales for the year were $600,000, of which one-half was on credit. The average gross margin rate was 40 percent on sales. Account balances follow:

|  | Beginning | Ending |
|---|---|---|
| Accounts receivable (net) | $40,000 | $60,000 |
| Inventory | 70,000 | 30,000 |

*Required:*
Compute the turnover for the accounts receivable and inventory, the average age of receivables, and the average days' supply of inventory.

**■ LO3, 4**     **E14–10**     **Analyzing the Impact of Selected Transactions on the Current Ratio**

Current assets totaled $500,000, the current ratio was 2.0, and the company uses the periodic inventory method. Assume that the following transactions were completed: (1) sold $12,000 in merchandise on short-term credit, (2) declared but did not pay dividends of $50,000, (3) paid prepaid rent in the amount of $12,000, (4) paid previously declared dividends in the amount of $50,000, (5) collected an account receivable in the amount of $12,000, and (6) reclassified $40,000 of long-term debt as a short-term liability.

*Required:*
Compute the cumulative current ratio after each transaction.

**■ LO3**     **E14–11**     **Computing Liquidity Ratios**

Cintas

Cintas designs, manufactures, and implements corporate identity uniform programs that it rents or sells to customers throughout the United States and Canada. The company's stock is traded on the NASDAQ and has provided investors with significant returns over the past few years. Selected information from the company's balance sheet follows. The company reported sales revenue of $1,751,568,000 and cost of goods sold of $1,066,706,000.

| Cintas | 1999 | 1998 |
|---|---|---|
| **Balance Sheet (amounts in thousands)** | | |
| Cash | $ 15,803 | $ 13,423 |
| Marketable securities | 72,315 | 88,154 |
| Accounts receivable, less allowance of $8,754, $7,987 | 202,079 | 185,938 |
| Inventories | 137,983 | 129,655 |
| Prepaid expense | 6,151 | 5,524 |
| Accounts payable | 46,783 | 54,275 |
| Accrued compensation | 25,521 | 21,470 |
| Deferred income taxes | 40,214 | 43,745 |
| Long-term debt due within one year | 16,370 | 11,741 |

*Required:*
Compute the current ratio, quick ratio, inventory turnover, and accounts receivable turnover (assuming that 60 percent of sales was on credit).

**E14–12** **Using Financial Information to Identify Mystery Companies**     ▇ **LO3, 4**

The following selected financial data pertain to four unidentified companies:

| | Companies | | | |
|---|---|---|---|---|
| | 1 | 2 | 3 | 4 |
| **Balance Sheet Data** | *[handwritten: Probably Car]* | *[handwritten: Probably Candy]* | *[handwritten: Probably fur]* | *[handwritten: Advertising agency]* |
| (component percentage) | | | | |
| Cash | 3.5 | 4.7 | 8.2 | 11.7 |
| Accounts receivable | 16.9 | 28.9 | 16.8 | 51.9 |
| Inventory | 46.8 | 35.6 | 57.3 | 4.8 |
| Property and equipment | 18.3 | 21.7 | 7.6 | 18.7 |
| **Income Statement Data** | | | | |
| (component percentage) | | | | |
| Gross profit | 22.0 | 22.5 | 44.8 | N/A* *[handwritten: – no COGS, service co.]* |
| Profit before taxes | 2.1 | 0.7 | 1.2 | 3.2 |
| **Selected Ratios** | | | | |
| Current ratio | 1.3 | 1.5 | 1.6 | 1.2 |
| Inventory turnover | 3.6 | 9.8 | 1.5 | N/A |
| Debt-to-equity | 2.6 | 2.6 | 3.2 | 3.2 |
| *N/A = Not applicable | | | | |

This financial information pertains to the following companies:

*a.* Retail fur store

*b.* Advertising agency

*c.* Wholesale candy company

*d.* Car manufacturer

*Required:*

Match each company with its financial information.

**E14–13** **Using Financial Information to Identify Mystery Companies**     ▇ **LO3, 4**

The following selected financial data pertain to four unidentified companies:

| | Companies | | | |
|---|---|---|---|---|
| | 1 | 2 | 3 | 4 |
| **Balance Sheet Data** | | | | |
| (component percentage) | | | | |
| Cash | 7.3 | 21.6 | 6.1 | 11.3 |
| Accounts receivable | 28.2 | 39.7 | 3.2 | 22.9 |
| Inventory | 21.6 | 0.6 | 1.8 | 27.5 |
| Property and equipment | 32.1 | 18.0 | 74.6 | 25.1 |
| **Income Statement Data** | | | | |
| (component percentage) | | | | |
| Gross profit | 15.3 | N/A* | N/A | 43.4 |
| Profit before taxes | 1.7 | 3.2 | 2.4 | 6.9 |
| **Selected Ratios** | | | | |
| Current ratio | 1.5 | 1.2 | 0.6 | 1.9 |
| Inventory turnover | 27.4 | N/A | N/A | 3.3 |
| Debt-to-equity | 1.7 | 2.2 | 5.7 | 1.3 |
| *N/A = Not applicable | | | | |

This financial information pertains to the following companies:

a. Travel agency

b. Hotel

c. Meat packer

d. Drug company

**Required:**
Match each company with its financial information.

**LO3, 4**   **E14–14**   **Using Financial Information to Identify Mystery Companies**

The following selected financial data pertain to four unidentified companies:

| | Companies | | | |
|---|---|---|---|---|
| | 1 | 2 | 3 | 4 |
| **Balance Sheet Data** | | | | |
| (component percentage) | | | | |
| Cash | 5.1 | 8.8 | 6.3 | 10.4 |
| Accounts receivable | 13.1 | 41.5 | 13.8 | 4.9 |
| Inventory | 4.6 | 3.6 | 65.1 | 35.8 |
| Property and equipment | 53.1 | 23.0 | 8.8 | 35.7 |
| **Income Statement Data** | | | | |
| (component percentage) | | | | |
| Gross profit | N/A* | N/A | 45.2 | 22.5 |
| Profit before taxes | 0.3 | 16.0 | 3.9 | 1.5 |
| **Selected Ratios** | | | | |
| Current ratio | 0.7 | 2.2 | 1.9 | 1.4 |
| Inventory turnover | N/A | N/A | 1.4 | 15.5 |
| Debt-to-equity | 2.5 | 0.9 | 1.7 | 2.3 |
| *N/A = Not applicable | | | | |

This financial information pertains to the following companies:

a. Cable TV company

b. Grocery store

c. Accounting firm

d. Retail jewelry store

**Required:**
Match each company with its financial information.

**LO3, 4**   **E14–15**   **Using Financial Information to Identify Mystery Companies**

The selected financial data on the following page pertain to four unidentified companies:

This financial information pertains to the following companies:

a. Full-line department store

b. Wholesale fish company

c. Automobile dealer (both new and used cars)

d. Restaurant

**Required:**
Match each company with its financial information.

|  | Companies | | | |
|---|---|---|---|---|
|  | 1 | 2 | 3 | 4 |
| **Balance Sheet Data** | | | | |
| (component percentage) | | | | |
| Cash | 11.6 | 6.6 | 5.4 | 7.1 |
| Accounts receivable | 4.6 | 18.9 | 8.8 | 35.6 |
| Inventory | 7.0 | 45.8 | 65.7 | 26.0 |
| Property and equipment | 56.0 | 20.3 | 10.1 | 21.9 |
| **Income Statement Data** | | | | |
| (component percentage) | | | | |
| Gross profit | 56.7 | 36.4 | 14.1 | 15.8 |
| Profit before taxes | 2.7 | 1.4 | 1.1 | 0.9 |
| **Selected Ratios** | | | | |
| Current ratio | 0.7 | 2.1 | 1.2 | 1.3 |
| Inventory turnover | 30.0 | 3.5 | 5.6 | 16.7 |
| Debt-to-equity | 3.3 | 1.8 | 3.8 | 3.1 |

# PROBLEMS

**P14–1** **Analyzing Comparative Financial Statement Using Percentages** (AP14–1)      ■ **LO3**

The comparative financial statements prepared at December 31, 20B, for Goldfish Company showed the following summarized data:

*Common size income stment*
*20B        20A*

|  | 20B | 20A | | |
|---|---|---|---|---|
| **Income Statement** | | *divide everything by sales* | 100% | 100% |
| Sales revenue | $180,000* | $165,000 | 61% | 61% |
| Cost of goods sold | 110,000 | 100,000 | 39% | 39% |
| Gross margin | 70,000 | 65,000 | 31% | 32% |
| Operating expenses and interest expense | 56,000 | 53,000 | 8% | 7% |
| Pretax income | 14,000 | 12,000 | 2% | 2% |
| Income tax | 4,000 | 3,000 | 6% | 5% |
| Net income | $ 10,000 | $ 9,000 | | |
| **Balance Sheet** | | | | |
| Cash | $ 4,000 | $ 8,000 | | |
| Accounts receivable (net) | 14,000 | 18,000 | | |
| Inventory | 40,000 | 35,000 | | |
| Operational assets (net) | 45,000 | 38,000 | | |
|  | $103,000 | $ 99,000 | | |
| Current liabilities (no interest) | $ 16,000 | $ 19,000 | | |
| Long-term liabilities (10% interest) | 45,000 | 45,000 | | |
| Common stock (par $5) | 30,000 | 30,000 | | |
| Retained earnings† | 12,000 | 5,000 | | |
|  | $103,000 | $ 99,000 | | |

*One-third was credit sales.
†During 20B, cash dividends amounting to $9,000 were declared and paid.

*Required:*

1. Complete the following columns for each item in the preceding comparative financial statements:

|  | Increase (Decrease) 20B over 20A | |
|---|---|---|
|  | Amount | Percent |
|  |  |  |

2. Respond to the following.

    *a.* Compute the percentage increase in sales revenue, net income, cash, inventory, liabilities, and owners' equity.

    *b.* By what amount did working capital change?

    *c.* What was the percentage of change in the average income tax rate?

    *d.* What was the amount of cash inflow from revenues for 20B?

    *e.* What was its percentage of change for the average markup realized on goods sold?

    *f.* How much did the book value per share change?

■ **LO3**     **P14–2**     **Analyzing Comparative Financial Statements Using Percentages and Selected Ratios** (AP14–2)
Use the data given in P14–1 for Goldfish Company.

*Required:*

1. Present component percentages for 20B only.

2. Respond to the following for 20B:

    *a.* What was the average percentage markup on sales?

    *b.* What was the average income tax rate?

    *c.* Compute the gross profit margin. Was it a good or poor indicator of performance? Explain.

    *d.* What percentage of total resources was invested in operational assets?

    *e.* Compute the debt-to-equity ratio. Does it look good or bad? Explain.

    *f.* What was the return on equity?

    *g.* What was the return on assets?

    *h.* Compute the financial leverage percentage. Was it positive or negative? Explain.

    *i.* What was the book value per share of common stock?

■ **LO3, 4**     **P14–3**     **Analyzing a Financial Statement Using Several Ratios**
Use the data in P14–1 for Goldfish Company. Assume a stock price of $28 per share. Compute appropriate ratios and explain the meaning of each.

■ **LO3, 4**     **P14–4**     **Analyzing Ratios** (AP14–3)

Sears, Roebuck and JCPenney

Sears, Roebuck and JCPenney are two giants of the retail industry. Both offer full lines of moderately priced merchandise. Annual sales for Sears total $41 billion. JCPenney is somewhat smaller with $30 billion in revenues. Compare the two companies as a potential investment based on the following ratios:

| Ratio | Sears | JCPenney |
|---|---|---|
| P/E | 8.1 | 9.7 |
| Gross profit margin | 33.5 | 23.1 |
| Profit margin | 3.6 | 1.7 |
| Quick ratio | 0.1 | 0.6 |
| Current ratio | 2.2 | 1.6 |
| Debt-to-equity | 2.8 | 1.4 |
| Return on equity | 23.5 | 7.5 |
| Return on assets | 4.1 | 3.2 |
| Dividend yield | 3.0% | 5.9% |
| Dividend payout ratio | 24.0% | 118.0% |

**P14–5** **Analyzing a Financial Statement Using Several Ratios**

Summer Corporation has just completed its comparative statements for the year ended December 31, 20B. At this point, certain analytical and interpretive procedures are to be undertaken. The completed statements (summarized) are as follows:

| | 20B | 20A |
|---|---|---|
| **Income Statement** | | |
| Sales revenue | $450,000* | $420,000* |
| Cost of goods sold | 250,000 | 230,000 |
| Gross margin | 200,000 | 190,000 |
| Operating expenses (including interest on bonds) | 167,000 | 168,000 |
| Pretax income | 33,000 | 22,000 |
| Income tax | 10,000 | 6,000 |
| Net income | $ 23,000 | $ 16,000 |
| **Balance Sheet** | | |
| Cash | $ 6,800 | $ 3,900 |
| Accounts receivable (net) | 42,000 | 28,000 |
| Merchandise inventory | 25,000 | 20,000 |
| Prepaid expenses | 200 | 100 |
| Operational assets (net) | 130,000 | 120,000 |
| | $204,000 | $172,000 |
| Accounts payable | $ 17,000 | $ 18,000 |
| Income taxes payable | 1,000 | 2,000 |
| Bonds payable (10% interest rate) | 70,000 | 50,000 |
| Common stock (par $5) | 100,000† | 100,000 |
| Retained earnings | 16,000‡ | 2,000 |
| | $204,000 | $172,000 |

*Credit sales totaled 40 percent.
†The market price of the stock at the end of 20B was $18 per share.
‡During 20B, the company declared and paid a cash dividend of $40,000.

*Required:*

1. Compute appropriate ratios and explain the meaning of each.

2. Respond to the following for 20B:

    *a.* Evaluate the financial leverage. Explain its meaning using the computed amount(s).

    *b.* Evaluate the profit margin amount and explain how a stockholder might use it.

    *c.* Explain to a stockholder why the current ratio and the quick ratio are different. Do you observe any liquidity problems? Explain.

    *d.* Assuming that credit terms are 1/10, n/30, do you perceive an unfavorable situation for the company related to credit sales? Explain.

**P14–6** **Identifying Companies Based on the Price/Earnings Ratio**

The price/earnings ratio provides important information concerning the stock market's assessment of the growth potential of a business. The following are price/earnings ratios for selected companies as of the date this book was written. Match the company with its ratio and explain how you made your selections. If you are not familiar with a company, you should contact its website.

| Company | Price/Earnings Ratio |
|---|---|
| 1. Commerce Bank | A. 55 |
| 2. Cinergy Gas and Electric | B. 12 |
| 3. Compaq Computers | C. 26 |
| 4. Home Depot | D. not applicable (no earnings) |
| 5. Motorola | E. 10 |

| Company | Price/Earnings Ratio |
|---|---|
| 6. Starbucks | F. 143 |
| 7. America Online | G. 108 |
| 8. Amazon.com | H. 65 |
| 9. Pepsi | I. 82 |

■ **LO3, 4**   **P14–7**   **Comparing Alternative Investment Opportunities** (AP14–4)

The 20B financial statements for Armstrong and Blair companies are summarized here:

|  | Armstrong Company | Blair Company |
|---|---|---|
| **Balance Sheet** | | |
| Cash | $ 35,000 | $ 22,000 |
| Accounts receivable (net) | 40,000 | 30,000 |
| Inventory | 100,000 | 40,000 |
| Operational assets (net) | 140,000 | 400,000 |
| Other assets | 85,000 | 308,000 |
| Total assets | $400,000 | $800,000 |
| Current liabilities | $100,000 | $50,000 |
| Long-term debt (10%) | 60,000 | 70,000 |
| Capital stock (par $10) | 150,000 | 500,000 |
| Contributed capital in excess of par | 30,000 | 110,000 |
| Retained earnings | 60,000 | 70,000 |
| Total liabilities and stockholders' equity | $400,000 | $800,000 |
| **Income Statement** | | |
| Sales revenue (⅓ on credit) | $450,000 | $810,000 |
| Cost of goods sold | (245,000) | (405,000) |
| Expenses (including interest and income tax) | (160,000) | (315,000) |
| Net income | $ 45,000 | $ 90,000 |
| **Selected data from the 20A statements** | | |
| Accounts receivable (net) | $ 20,000 | $ 38,000 |
| Inventory | 92,000 | 45,000 |
| Long-term debt | 60,000 | 70,000 |
| **Other data** | | |
| Per share price at end of 20B (offering price) | $    18 | $    15 |
| Average income tax rate | 30% | 30% |
| Dividends declared and paid in 20B | $ 36,000 | $150,000 |

The companies are in the same line of business and are direct competitors in a large metropolitan area. Both have been in business approximately 10 years, and each has had steady growth. The management of each has a different viewpoint in many respects. Blair is more conservative, and as its president said, "We avoid what we consider to be undue risk." Neither company is publicly held. Armstrong Company has an annual audit by a CPA but Blair Company does not.

*Required:*

1. Complete a schedule that reflects a ratio analysis of each company. Compute the ratios discussed in the chapter.

2. A client of yours has the opportunity to buy 10 percent of the shares in one or the other company at the per share prices given and has decided to invest in one of the companies. Based on the data given, prepare a comparative written evaluation of the ratio analyses (and any other available information) and give your recommended choice with the supporting explanation.

■ **LO3, 4**   **P14–8**   **Analyzing the Impact of Alternative Inventory Methods on Selected Ratios**

Company A uses the FIFO method to cost inventory, and Company B uses the LIFO method. The two companies are exactly alike except for the difference in inventory costing methods.

Costs of inventory items for both companies have been rising steadily in recent years, and each company has increased its inventory each year. Each company has paid its tax liability in full for the current year (and all previous years), and each company uses the same accounting methods for both financial reporting and income tax reporting.

*Required:*

Identify which company will report the higher amount for each of the following ratios. If it is not possible, explain why.

1. Current ratio.

2. Quick ratio.

3. Debt-to-equity ratio.

4. Return on equity.

5. Earnings per share.

**P14–9  Analyzing a Financial Statement Using Appropriate Ratios** (AP14–5)

Lands' End is a direct merchant offering traditionally styled casual clothing and accessories through catalogs and the Internet. The following information was reported in a recent annual statement. For the current year, compute the ratios discussed in this chapter. If there is not sufficient information, describe what is missing and explain what you would do.

■ **LO3**

Lands' End

| LANDS' END, INC. & SUBSIDIARIES<br>Consolidated Statement of Operations<br>(in thousands, except per share data) | | | |
|---|---|---|---|
| For the period ended | January 29,<br>1999 | January 30,<br>1998 | January 31,<br>1997 |
| Net sales | $1,371,375 | $1,263,629 | $1,118,743 |
| Cost of sales | 754,661 | 675,138 | 609,168 |
| Gross profit | 616,714 | 588,491 | 509,575 |
| Selling, general and administrative expenses | 544,446 | 489,923 | 424,390 |
| Non-recurring charge | 12,600 | — | — |
| Charge from sale of subsidiary | — | — | 1,400 |
| Income from operations | 59,668 | 98,568 | 83,785 |
| Other income (expense): | | | |
| Interest expense | (7,734) | (1,995) | (510) |
| Interest income | 16 | 1,725 | 1,148 |
| Gain on sale of subsidiary | — | 7,805 | — |
| Other | (2,450) | (4,278) | 496 |
| Total other income (expense), net | (10,168) | 3,257 | 1,134 |
| Income before income taxes | 49,500 | 101,825 | 84,919 |
| Income tax provision | 18,315 | 37,675 | 33,967 |
| Net income | $    31,185 | $    64,150 | $    50,952 |

| LANDS' END, INC. & SUBSIDIARIES<br>Consolidated Balance Sheets | | |
| --- | --- | --- |
| (in thousands) | January 29,<br>1999 | January 30,<br>1998 |
| **Assets** | | |
| Current assets: | | |
| Cash and cash equivalents | $ 6,641 | $ 6,338 |
| Receivables, net | 21,083 | 15,443 |
| Inventory | 219,686 | 241,154 |
| Prepaid advertising | 21,357 | 18,513 |
| Other prepaid expenses | 7,589 | 5,085 |
| Deferred income tax benefits | 17,947 | 12,613 |
| Total current assets | 294,303 | 299,146 |
| Property, plant and equipment, at cost: | | |
| Land and buildings | 102,018 | 81,781 |
| Fixtures and equipment | 154,663 | 118,190 |
| Leasehold improvements | 5,475 | 5,443 |
| Construction in progress | — | 12,222 |
| Total property, plant and equipment | 262,156 | 217,636 |
| Less-accumulated depreciation and amortization | 101,570 | 84,227 |
| Property, plant and equipment, net | 160,586 | 133,409 |
| Intangibles, net | 1,030 | 917 |
| Total assets | $455,919 | $433,472 |
| **Liabilities and shareholders' investment** | | |
| Current liabilities: | | |
| Lines of credit | $ 38,942 | $ 32,437 |
| Account payable | 87,922 | 83,743 |
| Reserve for returns | 7,193 | 6,128 |
| Accrued liabilities | 54,392 | 34,942 |
| Accrued profit sharing | 2,256 | 4,286 |
| Income taxes payable | 14,578 | 20,477 |
| Total current liabilities | 205,283 | 182,013 |
| Deferred income taxes | 8,133 | 8,747 |
| **Shareholders' investment** | | |
| Common stock, 40,221 shares issued | 402 | 402 |
| Donated capital | 8,400 | 8,400 |
| Additional paid-in capital | 26,994 | 26,457 |
| Deferred compensation | (394) | (1,047) |
| Accumulated other comprehensive income | 2,003 | 875 |
| Retained earnings | 406,396 | 375,211 |
| Treasury stock, 10,317 and 9,281 shares at cost, respectively | (201,298) | (167,586) |
| Total shareholders' investment | 242,503 | 242,712 |
| Total liabilities and shareholders' investment | $455,919 | $433,472 |

■ **LO3, 4**     **P14–10**

**Analyzing an Investment by Comparing Selected Ratios** (AP14–6)

You have the opportunity to invest $10,000 in one of two companies from a single industry. The only information you have follows. The word *high* refers to the top third of the industry; *average* is the middle third; *low* is the bottom third. Which company would you select? Write a brief paper justifying your recommendation.

| Ratio | Company A | Company B |
|-------|-----------|-----------|
| Current | High | Average |
| Quick | Low | Average |
| Debt-to-equity | High | Average |
| Inventory turnover | Low | Average |
| Price/earnings | Low | Average |
| Dividend yield | High | Average |

**P14–11 Analyzing and Investment by Comparing Selected Ratios** (AP14–7)

■ **LO3, 4**

You have the opportunity to invest $10,000 in one of two companies from a single industry. The only information you have is shown here. The word *high* refers to the top third of the industry; *average* is the middle third; *low* is the bottom third. Which company would you select? Write a brief paper justifying your recommendation.

| Ratio | Company A | Company B |
|-------|-----------|-----------|
| Current | Low | Average |
| Quick | Average | Average |
| Debt-to-equity | Low | Average |
| Inventory turnover | High | Average |
| Price/earnings | High | Average |
| Dividend yield | Low | Average |

## ALTERNATE PROBLEMS

**AP14–1 Analyzing a Financial Statement Using Ratios and Percentage Changes** (P14–1)

■ **LO3**

Taber Company has just prepared the following comparative annual financial statements for 20B:

| TABER COMPANY | | |
|---|---|---|
| Comparative Income Statement | | |
| For the Years Ended December 31, 20B, and 20A | | |
| | **20B** | **20A** |
| Sales revenue (one-half on credit) | $110,000 | $99,000 |
| Cost of goods sold | 52,000 | 48,000 |
| Gross margin | $ 58,000 | $51,000 |
| Expenses (including $4,000 interest expense each year) | 40,000 | 37,000 |
| Pretax income | $ 18,000 | $14,000 |
| Income tax on operations (30%) | 5,400 | 4,200 |
| Income before extraordinary items | $ 12,600 | $ 9,800 |
| Extraordinary loss $2,000 | | |
| Less income tax saved 600 | 1,400 | |
| Extraordinary gain | | $3,000 |
| Applicable income tax | | 900  2,100 |
| Net income | $ 11,200 | $11,900 |

*income for ratio analysis* (handwritten annotation)

**TABER COMPANY**
**Comparative Balance Sheet**
**At December 31, 20B, and 20A**

| | 20B | 20A |
|---|---|---|
| **Assets** | | |
| Cash | $ 49,500 | $ 18,000 |
| Accounts receivable (net; terms 1/10, n/30) | 37,000 | 32,000 |
| Inventory | 25,000 | 38,000 |
| Operational assets (net) | 95,000 | 105,000 |
| Total assets | $206,500 | $193,000 |
| **Liabilities** | | |
| Accounts payable | $ 42,000 | $ 35,000 |
| Income taxes payable | 1,000 | 500 |
| Note payable, long-term | 40,000 | 40,000 |
| **Stockholders' equity** | | |
| Capital stock (par $10) | 90,000 | 90,000 |
| Retained earnings | 33,500 | 27,500 |
| Total liabilities and stockholders' equity | $206,500 | $193,000 |

*Required (round percentage and ratios to two decimal places):*

1. For 20B, compute the tests of (a) profitability, (b) liquidity, (c) solvency, and (d) market. Assume that the quoted price of the stock was $23 for 20B. Dividends declared and paid during 20B were $6,750.

2. Respond to the following for 20B:

   a. Compute the percentage changes in sales, income before extraordinary items, net income, cash, inventory, and debt.

   b. What appears to be the pretax interest rate on the note payable?

3. Identify at least two problems facing the company that are suggested by your responses to requirements 1 and 2.

■ **LO3, 4** **AP14–2** **Using Ratios to Analyze Several Years of Financial Data** (P14–2)
The following information was contained in the annual financial statements of Pine Company, which started business January 1, 20A (assume account balances only in Cash and Capital Stock on this date; all amounts are in thousands of dollars).

| | 20A | 20B | 20C | 20D |
|---|---|---|---|---|
| Accounts receivable (net; terms n/30) | $11 | $12 | $18 | $ 24 |
| Merchandise inventory | 12 | 14 | 20 | 30 |
| Net sales (¾ on credit) | 44 | 66 | 80 | 100 |
| Cost of goods sold | 28 | 40 | 55 | 62 |
| Net income (loss) | (8) | 5 | 12 | 11 |

*Required (show computations and round to two decimal places):*

1. Complete the following tabulation

| Items | 20A | 20B | 20C | 20D |
|---|---|---|---|---|
| a. Profit margin—percentage | | | | |
| b. Gross margin—ratio | | | | |
| c. Expenses as percentage of sales, excluding cost of goods sold | | | | |
| d. Inventory turnover | | | | |
| e. Days supply in inventory | | | | |
| f. Receivable turnover | | | | |
| g. Average days to collect | | | | |

2. Evaluate the results of the related ratios *a, b,* and *c* to identify the favorable or unfavorable factors. Give your recommendations to improve the company's operations.

3. Evaluate the results of the last four ratios (*d, e, f,* and *g*) and identify any favorable or unfavorable factors. Give your recommendations to improve the company's operations.

**AP14–3 Analyzing Ratios** (P14–4)

Coke and Pepsi are well-known international brands. Coca-Cola sells more than $13 billion worth of beverages each year while annual sales of Pepsi products exceed $22 billion. Compare the two companies as a potential investment based on the following ratios:

**LO3, 4**

Coca-Cola and PepsiCo

| Ratio | Coca-Cola | PepsiCo |
|---|---|---|
| P/E | 65.0 | 26.5 |
| Gross profit margin | 69.3 | 58.4 |
| Profit margin | 12.2 | 8.8 |
| Quick ratio | 0.4 | 0.7 |
| Current ratio | 0.6 | 1.1 |
| Debt-to-equity | 0.7 | 0.4 |
| Return on equity | 27.4 | 29.1 |
| Return on assets | 28.0 | 16.6 |
| Dividend yield | 1.0% | 1.6% |
| Dividend payout ratio | 65.0% | 41.0% |

**AP14–4 Comparing Loan Requests from Two Companies Using Several Ratios** (P14–7)

The 20B financial statements for Rand and Tand companies are summarized here:

**LO3, 4**

|  | Rand Company | Tand Company |
|---|---|---|
| **Balance Sheet** | | |
| Cash | $ 25,000 | $ 45,000 |
| Accounts receivable (net) | 55,000 | 5,000 |
| Inventory | 110,000 | 25,000 |
| Operational assets (net) | 550,000 | 160,000 |
| Other assets | 140,000 | 57,000 |
| Total assets | $880,000 | $292,000 |
| Current liabilities | $ 120,000 | $ 15,000 |
| Long-term debt (12%) | 190,000 | 55,000 |
| Capital stock (par $20) | 480,000 | 210,000 |
| Contributed capital in excess of par | 50,000 | 4,000 |
| Retained earnings | 40,000 | 8,000 |
| Total liabilities and stockholders' equity | $880,000 | $292,000 |
| **Income Statement** | | |
| Sales revenue (on credit) | (½) $800,000 | (¼) $280,000 |
| Cost of goods sold | (480,000) | (150,000) |
| Expenses (including interest and income tax) | (240,000) | (95,000) |
| Net income | $ 80,000 | $ 35,000 |
| **Selected Data from the 20A Statements** | | |
| Accounts receivable, net | $ 47,000 | $ 11,000 |
| Long-term debt (12%) | 190,000 | 55,000 |
| Inventory | 95,000 | 38,000 |
| **Other Data** | | |
| Per share price at end of 20B | $14.00 | $11.00 |
| Average income tax rate | 30% | 30% |
| Dividends declared and paid in 20B | $20,000 | $9,000 |

These two companies are in the same line of business and in the same state but in different cities. Each company has been in operation for about 10 years. Rand Company is audited by one of the national accounting firms; Tand Company is audited by a local accounting firm. Both companies received an unqualified opinion (i.e., the independent auditors found nothing wrong) on the financial statements. Rand Company wants to borrow $75,000 cash, and Tand Company needs $30,000. The loans will be for a two-year period and are needed for "working capital purposes."

**Required:**

1. Complete a schedule that reflects a ratio analysis of each company. Compute the ratios discussed in the chapter.

2. Assume that you work in the loan department of a local bank. You have been asked to analyze the situation and recommend which loan is preferable. Based on the data given, your analysis prepared in requirement 1, and any other information, give your choice and the supported explanation.

■ **LO3**

**AP14–5**

Payless ShoeSource

**Analyzing a Financial Statement Using Appropriate Ratios** (P14–9)

Payless ShoeSource is a footwear retailer that sells affordable footwear for women, men, and children under the brand names Payless ShoeSource and Parade of Shoes. Annual revenues exceed $2 billion. The following information was reported in a recent annual statement. Compute the ratios discussed in this chapter. If there is not sufficient information, describe what is missing and explain what you would do.

**Consolidated Statement of Earnings**
**(dollars in millions, except per share data)**

|  | 1998 | 1997 | 1996 |
|---|---|---|---|
| Net Retail Sales | $2,615.5 | $2,566.9 | $2,333.7 |
| Cost of sales | 1,798.9 | 1,799.4 | 1,663.5 |
| Selling, general and administrative expenses | 599.2 | 562.1 | 497.3 |
| Interest (income) expense, net | (7.1) | (8.9) | (6.2) |
| Total cost of sales and expenses | 2,391.0 | 2,352.6 | 2,154.6 |
| Earnings before income taxes | 224.5 | 214.3 | 179.1 |
| Provision for income taxes | 89.5 | 85.4 | 71.4 |
| Net Earnings | $135.0 | $128.9 | $107.7 |

**Consolidated Balance Sheet**
**(dollars in millions, except per share data)**

|  | January 30, 1999 | January 31, 1998 |
|---|---|---|
| **Assets** | | |
| Current assets: | | |
|   Cash and cash equivalents | $ 123.5 | $210.0 |
|   Merchandise inventories | 342.1 | 324.6 |
|   Current deferred income taxes | 14.2 | 16.9 |
|   Other current assets | 16.0 | 11.4 |
| Total current assets | 495.8 | 562.9 |
| Property and equipment: | | |
|   Land | 6.3 | 4.3 |
|   Buildings and leasehold improvements | 594.8 | 559.3 |
|   Furniture, fixtures and equipment | 284.2 | 279.7 |
|   Property under capital leases | 7.6 | 7.5 |
| Total property and equipment | 892.9 | 850.8 |
|   Accumulated depreciation and amortization | (400.1) | (364.1) |
| Property and equipment, net | 492.8 | 486.7 |
| Deferred income taxes | 25.8 | 19.9 |
| Other assets | 3.5 | 3.5 |
| Total assets | $1,017.9 | $1,073.0 |

| | January 30, 1999 | January 31, 1998 |
|---|---|---|
| **Liabilities and Shareholders' Equity** | | |
| Current liabilities: | | |
| Current maturities of long-term debt | $ 1.5 | $ 1.4 |
| Accounts payable | 75.5 | 63.8 |
| Accrued expenses | 117.9 | 112.9 |
| Total current liabilities | 194.9 | 178.1 |
| Long-term debt | 72.0 | 6.5 |
| Other liabilities | 48.2 | 52.0 |
| Shareowners' Equity: | | |
| Preferred stock, $.01 par value; 25,000,000 shares authorized; none issued | | |
| Common stock, $.01 par value; 240,000,000 shares authorized; 36,924,127 and 41,000,000 issued in 1998 and 1997, respectively; 32,453,406 and 37,332,068 shares outstanding in 1998 and 1997, respectively | 0.3 | 0.4 |
| Additional paid-in capital | 35.0 | 21.0 |
| Unearned restricted stock | (3.3) | (7.6) |
| Retained earnings | 670.8 | 822.6 |
| Total shareowners' equity | 702.8 | 836.4 |
| Total liabilities and shareowners' equity | $1,017.9 | $1,073.0 |

**AP14–6  Analyzing an Investment by Comparing Selected Ratios** (P14–10)   **LO3, 4**

You have the opportunity to invest $10,000 in one of two companies from a single industry. The only information you have is shown here. The word *high* refers to the top third of the industry; *average* is the middle third; *low* is the bottom third. Which company would you select? Write a brief paper justifying your recommendation.

| Ratio | Company A | Company B |
|---|---|---|
| EPS | High | Low |
| ROA | Low | High |
| Debt-to-equity | High | Average |
| Current | Low | Average |
| Price/earnings | Low | High |
| Dividend yield | High | Average |

**AP14–7  Analyzing an Investment by Comparing Selected Ratios** (P14–11)   **LO3, 4**

You have the opportunity to invest $10,000 in one of two companies from a single industry. The only information you have is shown here. The word *high* refers to the top third of the industry; *average* is the middle third; *low* is the bottom third. Which company would you select? Write a brief paper justifying your recommendation.

| Ratio | Company A | Company B |
|---|---|---|
| ROA | High | Average |
| Profit margin | High | Low |
| Financial leverage | High | Low |
| Current | Low | High |
| Price/earnings | High | Average |
| Debt-to-equity | High | Low |

# CASES AND PROJECTS

## FINANCIAL REPORTING AND ANALYSIS CASES

**■ LO3**    **CP14–1**

American Eagle
Outfitters

STANDARD
&POOR'S

### Analyzing Financial Statements

Refer to the financial statements of American Eagle Outfitters given in Appendix B at the end of this book, or open file AEOS10K.doc in the S&P directory on the student CD-ROM. From the list of ratios that were discussed in this chapter, select and compute the ratios that help you evaluate the Company's operations.

**■ LO3**    **CP14–2**

Urban Outfitters

STANDARD
&POOR'S

### Analyzing Financial Statements

Refer to the financial statements of Urban Outfitters given in Appendix C at the end of this book, or open file URBN10K.doc in the S&P directory on the student CD-ROM. From the list of ratios that were discussed in this chapter, select and compute the ratios that help you evaluate the Company's operations.

**■ LO3**    **CP14–3**

### Inferring Information from the ROE Model

In this chapter, we discussed the ROE profit driver (or DuPont model). Using that framework, find the missing amount in each case below:

**Case 1:** ROE is 10 percent, net income is $200,000; asset turnover is 5, and net sales are $1,000,000. What is the amount of average stockholders' equity?

**Case 2:** Net income is $1,500,000; net sales are $8,000,000; average stockholders' equity is $12,000,000; ROE is 22 percent and asset turnover is 8. What is the amount of average total assets?

**Case 3:** ROE is 15 percent; net profit margin is 10 percent; asset turnover is 5; and average total assets are $1,000,000. What is the amount of average stockholders' equity?

**Case 4:** Net income is $500,000; ROE is 15 percent; asset turnover is 5; net sales are $1,000,000; and financial leverage is 2. What is the amount of average total assets?

**■ LO3, 4**    **CP14–4**

### Interpreting Financial Results Based on Corporate Strategy

In this chapter, we discussed the importance of analyzing financial results based on an understanding of the company's business strategy. Using the ROE model, we illustrated how different strategies could earn high returns for investors. Assume that two companies in the same industry adopt fundamentally different strategies. One manufactures high-quality consumer electronics. Its products employ state-of-the-art technology, and the company offers a high level of customer service both before and after the sale. The other company emphasizes low cost with good performance. Its products utilize well-established technology but are never innovative. Customers buy these products at large, self-service warehouses and are expected to install the products using information contained in printed brochures. Which of the ratios discussed in this chapter would you expect to differ for these companies as a result of their different business strategies?

**■ LO3, 4**    **CP14–5**

Nordstrom and
JCPenney

### Interpreting Financial Results Based on Corporate Strategy

In this chapter, we discussed the importance of analyzing financial results based on an understanding of the company's business strategy. Using the ROE model, we illustrated how different strategies could earn high returns for investors. Both Nordstrom and JCPenney are in the retail industry. Nordstrom is a specialty apparel retailer operating in 23 states. Annual revenues exceed $5 billion. The store is well know for high-quality merchandise and a high level of customer service. JCPenney is a full-line retailer appealing to middle income shoppers. Its merchandise is moderately priced, and customers receive a lower level of service. The following are several ratios from each company. Identify which company is Nordstrom and which is JCPenney. Which of these ratios do you think are affected by the different strategies? Explain.

| Ratio | Company A | Company B |
|---|---|---|
| Gross margin | 34.4 | 23.1 |
| Profit margin | 4.0 | 1.7 |
| Current ratio | 1.8 | 1.6 |
| Debt-to-equity | 0.8 | 1.4 |
| Return on equity | 15.9 | 7.5 |
| Return on assets | 6.5 | 2.3 |
| Dividend payout | 22.1 | 117.0 |
| Price/earnings | 15.3 | 9.3 |

**CP14–6  Interpreting Financial Publications**

■ **LO3, 4**

Home Depot

An important source of information for most investors is the analyst report published by all large investment firms. A professional analyst report* for Home Depot is available on the Libby/Libby/Short website at www.mhhe.com/business/accounting/libby3. You should read this report and then write a short memo discussing the use of financial information in the report.

*Copyright Reuters Limited 1998.

# CRITICAL THINKING CASES

**CP14–7  Analyzing the Impact of Alternative Depreciation Methods on Ratio Analysis**

■ **LO3, 4**

Speedy Company uses the sum-of-years'-digits method to depreciate its property, plant, and equipment, and Turtle Company uses the straight-line method. Both companies use 175 percent declining-balance depreciation for income tax purposes. The two companies are exactly alike except for the difference in depreciation methods.

*Required:*

1. Identify the financial ratios discussed in this chapter that are likely to be affected by the difference in depreciation methods.

2. Which company will report the higher amount for each ratio that you have identified? If you cannot be certain, explain why.

**CP14–8  Determining the Impact of Selected Transactions on Measures of Liquidity**

■ **LO3, 4**

Three commonly used measures of liquidity are the current ratio, the quick ratio, and working capital. For each of the following transactions, determine whether the measure will increase, decrease, or not change. You should assume that both ratios are higher than 1 and that working capital is positive.

*a.* The company purchased $100,000 of inventory on credit.

*b.* Merchandise, which cost $35,000, was sold on credit for $50,000. The company uses the periodic inventory method.

*c.* Previously declared dividends are paid in cash.

*d.* Depreciation expense is recorded.

*e.* A customer pays money on his account receivable.

**CP14–9  Evaluating an Ethical Dilemma**

■ **LO4**

Almost Short Company requested a sizable loan from First Federal Bank to acquire a large tract of land for future expansion. Almost Short reported current assets of $1,900,000 ($430,000 in cash) and current liabilities of $1,075,000. First Federal denied the loan request for a number of reasons, including the fact that the current ratio was below 2:1. When Almost Short was informed of the loan denial, the comptroller of the company immediately paid $420,000 that was owed to several trade creditors. The comptroller then asked First Federal to reconsider the loan application. Based on these abbreviated facts, would you recommend that First Federal approve the loan request? Why? Are the comptroller's actions ethical?

**CP14–10  Making a Decision as a Stockholder**

■ **LO3, 4**

You have recently been hired as a stockbroker with a major national firm. Your first client is a retired school teacher who is 72 years old. He lives on a small pension and has less than $100,000 available to invest. He wants to invest $25,000 of this money in a single stock.

Using Internet resources, identify a stock that you think would be appropriate for him. Write a brief report justifying your recommendation.

■ **LO3, 4** **CP14–11**

**Making a Decision as a Stockbroker**
You have recently been hired as a stockbroker with a major national firm. Your first client is a young couple saving for their first house, which they hope to buy within five years. They both work and have a combined income of $55,000. They received almost $15,000 in cash for wedding gifts and want to invest this money in a single stock. Using Internet resources, identify a stock that you think would be appropriate for your client. Write a brief report justifying your recommendation.

■ **LO3, 4** **CP14–12**

**Making a Decision as a Stockbroker**
You have recently been hired as a stockbroker with a major national firm. Your first client is a single woman, age 37. She is currently saving a large portion of her income with the goal of retiring at the earliest possible time. She has indicated that she will retire as soon as she has an investment portfolio worth at least $1 million. Your client wants to invest $50,000 of this money in a single stock and has indicated that if you do well, she will let you manage her entire portfolio. Using Internet resources, identify a stock that you think would be appropriate for your client. Write a brief report justifying your recommendation.

## FINANCIAL REPORTING AND ANALYSIS PROJECTS

■ **LO3, 4** **CP14–13**
American Eagle
Outfitters

**Comparing Companies in the Retail Industry**
Select any well-known retailer (one source of information is MarketGuide at www.marketguide.com/mgi/INDUSTRY/INDUSTRY.HTML). Go to the home page for the company you select and American Eagle Outfitters. Review the annual reports for both companies and any recent news items. Compute appropriate accounting ratios for each company and compare the two companies.

■ **LO3, 4** **CP14–14**
Home Depot

**Analyzing Financial Results**
Go to the web page for Home Depot (www.homedepot.com) and review the current financial statements as well as other company information. The text describes recent investment performance as "lackluster" and notes that investment analysts have mixed recommendations for the stock. Write a brief report comparing the company's current performance to the results described in this chapter. Your report should include a specific recommendation concerning whether this stock should be bought at this time.

■ **LO3, 4** **CP14–15**

**Determining Quality of Earnings**
Using library resources or the Internet, identify one company with a low quality of income and another with a high quality of income. Review the financial statements for both companies to determine reasons that help explain the difference in their quality of income (e.g. different accounting methods). Write a brief report explaining why the quality of earnings for the two is different.

■ **LO3, 4** **CP14–16**

**Analyzing Financial Results to Predict Bankruptcy**
Using library resources or the Internet, identify a company that has filed for bankruptcy. Locate financial information for the company for at least four years prior to the announced bankruptcy. Compute the ratios discussed in this chapter to determine whether any provided an early warning of impending bankruptcy. Write a brief report to identify the ratios that you believe are useful in predicting bankruptcy and justify your conclusion.

■ **LO3, 4** **CP14–17**

**Team Project: Examining an Annual Report**
As a team, select an industry to analyze. Each team member should acquire the annual report or 10-K for one publicly traded company in the industry, with each member selecting a different company. (Library files, the SEC EDGAR service at www.sec.gov, Compustat CD, or the company itself are good resources.) On an individual basis, each team member should write a brief report analyzing his or her company using the techniques discussed in this chapter.

Discuss any patterns across the companies that you as a team observe. Then, as a team, write a short report comparing and contrasting your companies. Provide potential explanations for any difference discovered.

**CP14–18  Finding Comparison Companies**

To properly evaluate accounting ratios, most analysts make a comparison to either industry average or comparable companies. Due to the diverse nature of business operations, it is often difficult to find comparable companies. Using Internet sources (a good starting point is MarketGuide at www.marketguide.com/mgi/INDUSTRY/INDUSTRY.HTML), select a company that is comparable to IBM. Justify your selection.

LO3, 4

**CP14–19  Using Electronic Data Sources**

Go to the website for Quicken (www.quicken.com). This site provides a variety of financial information. Using this source, review information concerning Home Depot. Write a brief memo evaluating the usefulness of the information provided by Quicken. You should consider such issues as whether adequate information is provided and whether secondary sources such as Quicken are more efficient to use than a company's financial statements.

LO4

Quicken and Home Depot

# Appendix A

**Future Value of $1, F = (1 + i)^n$**

| Periods | 2% | 3% | 3.75% | 4% | 4.25% | 5% | 6% | 7% | 8% |
|---|---|---|---|---|---|---|---|---|---|
| 0 | 1. | 1. | 1. | 1. | 1. | 1. | 1. | 1. | 1. |
| 1 | 1.02 | 1.03 | 1.0375 | 1.04 | 1.0425 | 1.05 | 1.06 | 1.07 | 1.08 |
| 2 | 1.0404 | 1.0609 | 1.0764 | 1.0816 | 1.0868 | 1.1025 | 1.1236 | 1.1449 | 1.1664 |
| 3 | 1.0612 | 1.0927 | 1.1168 | 1.1249 | 1.1330 | 1.1576 | 1.1910 | 1.2250 | 1.2597 |
| 4 | 1.0824 | 1.1255 | 1.1587 | 1.1699 | 1.1811 | 1.2155 | 1.2625 | 1.3108 | 1.3605 |
| 5 | 1.1041 | 1.1593 | 1.2021 | 1.2167 | 1.2313 | 1.2763 | 1.3382 | 1.4026 | 1.4693 |
| 6 | 1.1262 | 1.1941 | 1.2472 | 1.2653 | 1.2837 | 1.3401 | 1.4185 | 1.5007 | 1.5869 |
| 7 | 1.1487 | 1.2299 | 1.2939 | 1.3159 | 1.3382 | 1.4071 | 1.5036 | 1.6058 | 1.7138 |
| 8 | 1.1717 | 1.2668 | 1.3425 | 1.3686 | 1.3951 | 1.4775 | 1.5938 | 1.7182 | 1.8509 |
| 9 | 1.1951 | 1.3048 | 1.3928 | 1.4233 | 1.4544 | 1.5513 | 1.6895 | 1.8385 | 1.9990 |
| 10 | 1.2190 | 1.3439 | 1.4450 | 1.4802 | 1.5162 | 1.6289 | 1.7908 | 1.9672 | 2.1589 |
| 20 | 1.4859 | 1.8061 | 2.0882 | 2.1911 | 2.2989 | 2.6533 | 3.2071 | 3.8697 | 4.6610 |

| Periods | 9% | 10% | 11% | 12% | 13% | 14% | 15% | 20% | 25% |
|---|---|---|---|---|---|---|---|---|---|
| 0 | 1. | 1. | 1. | 1. | 1. | 1. | 1. | 1. | 1. |
| 1 | 1.09 | 1.10 | 1.11 | 1.12 | 1.13 | 1.14 | 1.15 | 1.20 | 1.25 |
| 2 | 1.1881 | 1.2100 | 1.2321 | 1.2544 | 1.2769 | 1.2996 | 1.3225 | 1.4400 | 1.5625 |
| 3 | 1.2950 | 1.3310 | 1.3676 | 1.4049 | 1.4429 | 1.4815 | 1.5209 | 1.7280 | 1.9531 |
| 4 | 1.4116 | 1.4641 | 1.5181 | 1.5735 | 1.6305 | 1.6890 | 1.7490 | 2.0736 | 2.4414 |
| 5 | 1.5386 | 1.6105 | 1.6851 | 1.7623 | 1.8424 | 1.9254 | 2.0114 | 2.4883 | 3.0518 |
| 6 | 1.6771 | 1.7716 | 1.8704 | 1.9738 | 2.0820 | 2.1950 | 2.3131 | 2.9860 | 3.8147 |
| 7 | 1.8280 | 1.9487 | 2.0762 | 2.2107 | 2.3526 | 2.5023 | 2.6600 | 3.5832 | 4.7684 |
| 8 | 1.9926 | 2.1436 | 2.3045 | 2.4760 | 2.6584 | 2.8526 | 3.0590 | 4.2998 | 5.9605 |
| 9 | 2.1719 | 2.3579 | 2.5580 | 2.7731 | 3.0040 | 3.2519 | 3.5179 | 5.1598 | 7.4506 |
| 10 | 2.3674 | 2.5937 | 2.8394 | 3.1058 | 3.3946 | 3.7072 | 4.0456 | 6.1917 | 9.3132 |
| 20 | 5.6044 | 6.7275 | 8.0623 | 9.6463 | 11.5231 | 13.7435 | 16.3665 | 38.3376 | 86.7362 |

**Present Value of $1, p = 1/(1 + i)^n$**

| Periods | 2% | 3% | 3.75% | 4% | 4.25% | 5% | 6% | 7% | 8% |
|---|---|---|---|---|---|---|---|---|---|
| 1 | 0.9804 | 0.9703 | 0.9639 | 0.9615 | 0.9592 | 0.9524 | 0.9434 | 0.9346 | 0.9259 |
| 2 | 0.9612 | 0.9426 | 0.9290 | 0.9246 | 0.9201 | 0.9070 | 0.8900 | 0.8734 | 0.8573 |
| 3 | 0.9423 | 0.9151 | 0.8954 | 0.8890 | 0.8826 | 0.8638 | 0.8396 | 0.8163 | 0.7938 |
| 4 | 0.9238 | 0.8885 | 0.8631 | 0.8548 | 0.8466 | 0.8227 | 0.7921 | 0.7629 | 0.7350 |
| 5 | 0.9057 | 0.8626 | 0.8319 | 0.8219 | 0.8121 | 0.7835 | 0.7473 | 0.7130 | 0.6806 |
| 6 | 0.8880 | 0.8375 | 0.8018 | 0.7903 | 0.7790 | 0.7462 | 0.7050 | 0.6663 | 0.6302 |
| 7 | 0.8706 | 0.8131 | 0.7728 | 0.7599 | 0.7473 | 0.7107 | 0.6651 | 0.6227 | 0.5835 |
| 8 | 0.8535 | 0.7894 | 0.7449 | 0.7307 | 0.7168 | 0.6768 | 0.6274 | 0.5820 | 0.5403 |
| 9 | 0.8368 | 0.7664 | 0.7180 | 0.7026 | 0.6876 | 0.6446 | 0.5919 | 0.5439 | 0.5002 |
| 10 | 0.8203 | 0.7441 | 0.6920 | 0.6756 | 0.6595 | 0.6139 | 0.5584 | 0.5083 | 0.4632 |
| 20 | 0.6730 | 0.5534 | 0.4789 | 0.4564 | 0.4350 | 0.3769 | 0.3118 | 0.2584 | 0.2145 |

| Periods | 9% | 10% | 11% | 12% | 13% | 14% | 15% | 20% | 25% |
|---|---|---|---|---|---|---|---|---|---|
| 1 | 0.9174 | 0.9091 | 0.9009 | 0.8929 | 0.8850 | 0.8772 | 0.8696 | 0.8333 | 0.8000 |
| 2 | 0.8417 | 0.8264 | 0.8116 | 0.7972 | 0.7831 | 0.7695 | 0.7561 | 0.6944 | 0.6400 |
| 3 | 0.7722 | 0.7513 | 0.7312 | 0.7118 | 0.6931 | 0.6750 | 0.6575 | 0.5787 | 0.5120 |
| 4 | 0.7084 | 0.6830 | 0.6587 | 0.6355 | 0.6133 | 0.5921 | 0.5718 | 0.4823 | 0.4096 |
| 5 | 0.6499 | 0.6209 | 0.5935 | 0.5674 | 0.5428 | 0.5194 | 0.4972 | 0.4019 | 0.3277 |
| 6 | 0.5963 | 0.5645 | 0.5346 | 0.5066 | 0.4803 | 0.4556 | 0.4323 | 0.3349 | 0.2621 |
| 7 | 0.5470 | 0.5132 | 0.4817 | 0.4523 | 0.4251 | 0.3996 | 0.3759 | 0.2791 | 0.2097 |
| 8 | 0.5019 | 0.4665 | 0.4339 | 0.4039 | 0.3762 | 0.3506 | 0.3269 | 0.2326 | 0.1678 |
| 9 | 0.4604 | 0.4241 | 0.3909 | 0.3606 | 0.3329 | 0.3075 | 0.2843 | 0.1938 | 0.1342 |
| 10 | 0.4224 | 0.3855 | 0.3522 | 0.3220 | 0.2946 | 0.2697 | 0.2472 | 0.1615 | 0.1074 |
| 20 | 0.1784 | 0.1486 | 0.1240 | 0.1037 | 0.0868 | 0.0728 | 0.0611 | 0.0261 | 0.0115 |

## TABLE **A.3**

Future Value of Annuity of $1 (ordinary), $F = \frac{(1 + i)^n - 1}{i}$

| Periods* | 2% | 3% | 3.75% | 4% | 4.25% | 5% | 6% | 7% | 8% |
|---|---|---|---|---|---|---|---|---|---|
| 1 | 1. | 1. | 1. | 1. | 1. | 1. | 1. | 1. | 1. |
| 2 | 2.02 | 2.03 | 2.0375 | 2.04 | 2.0425 | 2.05 | 2.06 | 2.07 | 2.08 |
| 3 | 3.0604 | 3.0909 | 3.1139 | 3.1216 | 3.1293 | 3.1525 | 3.1836 | 3.2149 | 3.2464 |
| 4 | 4.1216 | 4.1836 | 4.2307 | 4.2465 | 4.2623 | 4.3101 | 4.3746 | 4.4399 | 4.5061 |
| 5 | 5.2040 | 5.3091 | 5.3893 | 5.4163 | 5.4434 | 5.5256 | 5.6371 | 5.7507 | 5.8666 |
| 6 | 6.3081 | 6.4684 | 6.5914 | 6.6330 | 6.6748 | 6.8019 | 6.9753 | 7.1533 | 7.3359 |
| 7 | 7.4343 | 7.6625 | 7.8386 | 7.8983 | 7.9585 | 8.1420 | 8.3938 | 8.6540 | 8.9228 |
| 8 | 8.5830 | 8.8923 | 9.1326 | 9.2142 | 9.2967 | 9.5491 | 9.8975 | 10.2598 | 10.6366 |
| 9 | 9.7546 | 10.1591 | 10.4750 | 10.5828 | 10.6918 | 11.0266 | 11.4913 | 11.9780 | 12.4876 |
| 10 | 10.9497 | 11.4639 | 11.8678 | 12.0061 | 12.1462 | 12.5779 | 13.1808 | 13.8164 | 14.4866 |
| 20 | 24.2974 | 26.8704 | 29.0174 | 29.7781 | 30.5625 | 33.0660 | 36.7856 | 40.9955 | 45.7620 |

| Periods* | 9% | 10% | 11% | 12% | 13% | 14% | 15% | 20% | 25% |
|---|---|---|---|---|---|---|---|---|---|
| 1 | 1. | 1. | 1. | 1. | 1. | 1. | 1. | 1. | 1. |
| 2 | 2.09 | 2.10 | 2.11 | 2.12 | 2.13 | 2.14 | 2.15 | 2.20 | 2.25 |
| 3 | 3.2781 | 3.3100 | 3.3421 | 3.3744 | 3.4069 | 3.4396 | 3.4725 | 3.6400 | 3.8125 |
| 4 | 4.5731 | 4.6410 | 4.7097 | 4.7793 | 4.8498 | 4.9211 | 4.9934 | 5.3680 | 5.7656 |
| 5 | 5.9847 | 6.1051 | 6.2278 | 6.3528 | 6.4803 | 6.6101 | 6.7424 | 7.4416 | 8.2070 |
| 6 | 7.5233 | 7.7156 | 7.9129 | 8.1152 | 8.3227 | 8.5355 | 8.7537 | 9.9299 | 11.2588 |
| 7 | 9.2004 | 9.4872 | 9.7833 | 10.0890 | 10.4047 | 10.7305 | 11.0668 | 12.9159 | 15.0735 |
| 8 | 11.0285 | 11.4359 | 11.8594 | 12.2997 | 12.7573 | 13.2328 | 13.7268 | 16.4991 | 19.8419 |
| 9 | 13.0210 | 13.5975 | 14.1640 | 14.7757 | 15.4157 | 16.0853 | 16.7858 | 20.7989 | 25.8023 |
| 10 | 15.1929 | 15.9374 | 16.7220 | 17.5487 | 18.4197 | 19.3373 | 20.3037 | 25.9587 | 33.2529 |
| 20 | 51.1601 | 57.2750 | 64.2028 | 72.0524 | 80.9468 | 91.0249 | 102.4436 | 186.6880 | 342.9447 |

*There is one payment each period.

## TABLE **A.4**

Present Value of Annuity of $1, $P = \frac{1 - 1/(1 + i)^n}{i}$

| Periods* | 2% | 3% | 3.75% | 4% | 4.25% | 5% | 6% | 7% | 8% |
|---|---|---|---|---|---|---|---|---|---|
| 1 | 0.9804 | 0.9709 | 0.9639 | 0.9615 | 0.9592 | 0.9524 | 0.9434 | 0.9346 | 0.9259 |
| 2 | 1.9416 | 1.9135 | 1.8929 | 1.8861 | 1.8794 | 1.8594 | 1.8334 | 1.8080 | 1.7833 |
| 3 | 2.8839 | 2.8286 | 2.7883 | 2.7751 | 2.7620 | 2.7232 | 2.6730 | 2.6243 | 2.5771 |
| 4 | 3.8077 | 3.7171 | 3.6514 | 3.6299 | 3.6086 | 3.5460 | 3.4651 | 3.3872 | 3.3121 |
| 5 | 4.7135 | 4.5797 | 4.4833 | 4.4518 | 4.4207 | 4.3295 | 4.2124 | 4.1002 | 3.9927 |
| 6 | 5.6014 | 5.4172 | 5.2851 | 5.2421 | 5.1997 | 5.0757 | 4.9173 | 4.7665 | 4.6229 |
| 7 | 6.4720 | 6.2303 | 6.0579 | 6.0021 | 5.9470 | 5.7864 | 5.5824 | 5.3893 | 5.2064 |
| 8 | 7.3255 | 7.0197 | 6.8028 | 6.7327 | 6.6638 | 6.4632 | 6.2098 | 5.9713 | 5.7466 |
| 9 | 8.1622 | 7.7861 | 7.5208 | 7.4353 | 7.3513 | 7.1078 | 6.8017 | 6.5152 | 6.2469 |
| 10 | 8.9826 | 8.5302 | 8.2128 | 8.1109 | 8.0109 | 7.7217 | 7.3601 | 7.0236 | 6.7101 |
| 20 | 16.3514 | 14.8775 | 13.8962 | 13.5903 | 13.2944 | 12.4622 | 11.4699 | 10.5940 | 9.8181 |

| Periods* | 9% | 10% | 11% | 12% | 13% | 14% | 15% | 20% | 25% |
|---|---|---|---|---|---|---|---|---|---|
| 1 | 0.9174 | 0.9091 | 0.9009 | 0.8929 | 0.8550 | 0.8772 | 0.8696 | 0.8333 | 0.8000 |
| 2 | 1.7591 | 1.7355 | 1.7125 | 1.6901 | 1.6681 | 1.6467 | 1.6257 | 1.5278 | 1.4400 |
| 3 | 2.5313 | 2.4869 | 2.4437 | 2.4018 | 2.3612 | 2.3216 | 2.2832 | 2.1065 | 1.9520 |
| 4 | 3.2397 | 3.1699 | 3.1024 | 3.0373 | 2.9745 | 2.9137 | 2.8550 | 2.5887 | 2.3616 |
| 5 | 3.8897 | 3.7908 | 3.6959 | 3.6048 | 3.5172 | 3.4331 | 3.3522 | 2.9906 | 2.6893 |
| 6 | 4.4859 | 4.3553 | 4.2305 | 4.1114 | 3.9975 | 3.8887 | 3.7845 | 3.3255 | 2.9514 |
| 7 | 5.0330 | 4.8684 | 4.7122 | 4.5638 | 4.4226 | 4.2883 | 4.1604 | 3.6046 | 3.1611 |
| 8 | 5.5348 | 5.3349 | 5.1461 | 4.9676 | 4.7988 | 4.6389 | 4.4873 | 3.8372 | 3.3289 |
| 9 | 5.9952 | 5.7590 | 5.5370 | 5.3282 | 4.1317 | 4.9464 | 4.7716 | 4.0310 | 3.4631 |
| 10 | 6.4177 | 6.1446 | 5.8892 | 5.6502 | 5.4262 | 5.2161 | 5.0188 | 4.1925 | 3.5705 |
| 20 | 9.1285 | 8.5136 | 7.9633 | 7.4694 | 7.0248 | 6.6231 | 6.2593 | 4.8696 | 3.9539 |

*There is one payment each period.

# AE Annual Report 98

 AMERICAN EAGLE
OUTFITTERS

Shop In Your Underwear℠ 24 hours a day,
7 days a week @ www.ae.com

AE Annual Report 98

## Selected Consolidated Financial Data

*(Dollars in thousands, except per share amounts and square foot data)*

| | For the Years Ended | | | | |
|---|---|---|---|---|---|
| | January 30, 1999 | January 31, 1998 | February 1, 1997 | February 3, 1996 (2) (Unaudited) | July 29, 1995 |
| Net sales *(1)* | $587,600 | $405,713 | $326,404 | $340,323 | $296,563 |
| Operating income (loss) *(1)* | $87,053 | $31,120 | $8,859 | ($1,073) | $12,043 |
| Net income (loss) | $54,118 | $19,537 | $5,925 | ($1,334) | $6,765 |
| Basic earnings (loss) per share *(3)* | $1.20 | $0.44 | $0.13 | ($0.03) | $0.15 |
| Diluted earnings (loss) per share *(3)* | $1.13 | $0.43 | $0.13 | ($0.03) | $0.15 |
| Total assets | $210,948 | $144,795 | $110,438 | $95,363 | $134,484 |
| Working capital | $94,753 | $48,486 | $34,378 | $24,775 | $19,264 |
| Stockholders' equity | $151,197 | $90,808 | $71,056 | $63,796 | $57,932 |
| Average return on stockholders' equity | 44.7% | 24.1% | 8.8% | (2.3%) | 12.5% |
| Current ratio | 2.59 | 1.90 | 1.87 | 1.78 | 1.25 |
| Long-term debt | — | — | — | — | — |
| Total stores at year-end | 386 | 332 | 303 | 273 | 297 |
| Comparable stores sales increase (decrease) | 32.1% | 15.1% | (1.8%) | 6.6% | 2.9% |
| Net sales per average selling square foot *(4)* | $497 | $391 | $340 | $381 | $351 |
| Total selling square feet at end of period | 1,276,889 | 1,080,657 | 990,980 | 916,796 | 1,001,262 |
| Net sales per average gross square foot *(4)* | $388 | $303 | $261 | $288 | $264 |
| Total gross square feet at end of period | 1,624,933 | 1,393,361 | 1,285,598 | 1,200,816 | 1,317,857 |

(1) The prior year amounts have been reclassified to conform to the January 30, 1999 classifications.

(2) The 53-weeks ended February 3, 1996 includes 9 months of sales, or $21.5 million, from outlet stores sold in October 1995. It also includes 6 months of operations from the year ended July 29, 1995, representing $113.7 million of net sales, $13.7 million of operating loss, and $8.4 million of net loss.

(3) Earnings (loss) per share has been restated for the January 1998 and May 1998 three-for-two stock splits, the May 1999 two-for-one stock split, and for the effect of Financial Accounting Standards Board Statement No. 128, Earnings per Share. See Notes 2 and 12 to the Consolidated Financial Statements.

(4) Average net sales per square foot is calculated using sales for the period divided by the straight average of the beginning and ending square footage for the period.

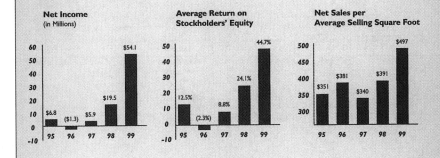

## Letter to Our Stockholders

Fiscal 1998 was a year of important milestones for American Eagle Outfitters. Among the 1998 achievements we are pleased to report:

- *Record* Sales of $587.6 million versus $405.7 million, an increase of 44.8%
- *Record* Same Store Sales increase of 32.1% versus 15.1% in 1997
- *Record* Net Income of $54.1 million, or $1.13 per diluted share versus $19.5 million last year, or $0.43 per diluted share
- *Record* Return on Average Stockholders' Equity of 44.7%

The strength of our 1998 operating performance is clearly reflected in our balance sheet. Our cash and investment position grew to $85 million, from $48 million a year ago. Our working capital needs and capital expenditures of nearly $25 million in 1998 were financed entirely through operating cash flow. We continue to maintain no debt. Our inventory productivity, as measured by average inventory turnover, improved for the fourth consecutive year, increasing to 4.1 times. We have achieved these results through better sell-through of our merchandise, improved merchandise planning and supply chain efficiencies, aimed at speeding the flow of our merchandise to our stores.

In 1998, we continued to build upon the strength of the AE brand. Our merchandise assortment offers quality apparel, footwear and accessories at affordable prices and is highly focused on the active lifestyle of our 16-34 year old target customer. More and more young men and women are choosing to shop at American Eagle Outfitters as evidenced by the strong increase of our unit sales, which on a comparable store basis increased by 18.1% in 1998.

We believe the opportunities for continued growth of our brand are excellent, especially given the demographic outlook for the population segment that includes our target customer base. It is estimated that the teenage population will grow at a rate nearly double that of the overall U.S. population through 2005. We have made a significant investment in our brand through advertising and co-marketing opportunities and we will continue to do so. Our goal is to build recognition of the AE brand and to continue to distinguish our company from our competition.

We opened 56 new stores across the country in 1998, including locations in important new markets on the West Coast. We are very pleased with our initial performance in the Seattle market, where we opened three stores in Fiscal 1998 and plan to open two additional locations in Fiscal 1999. We also opened new stores in Utah and Idaho. For Fiscal 1999, we plan to enter California, which we believe offers tremendous opportunity to reach our 16-34 year old target customer and expand our AE brand. We expect to open approximately 80 stores in 1999, increasing our store base by over 20%.

Adding to our list of 1998 accomplishments was the establishment of two new and important businesses, e-commerce and our quarterly catalog, *AE Magazine*, currently reaching a circulation of over 500,000 per issue. We launched e-commerce in April 1998 through *ae-outfitters.com*, but recently changed our internet address to the shorter and more easily found domain name of *ae.com*. Although still a relatively small part of our retail sales, internet and catalog sales are growing rapidly and we are optimistic about the future growth of our merchandise sales through these distribution channels.

Our internet site, *ae.com*, is a comfortable electronic extension of the AE lifestyle that we convey in our stores and catalog. While offering approximately 80% of our product on the internet site, we also provide movie and music clips, horoscopes, and book selections, all carefully selected and edited for our target customer. We believe more and more customers will take advantage of the opportunity to *Shop In Your Underwear*[SM] at *ae.com*.

During 1998 we continued to invest in our distribution infrastructure. We invested $6 million in our distribution center, primarily upgrading our existing sorting systems to improve our processing efficiencies. This helped to drive our unit processing costs down 8% compared to the prior year. These enhancements considerably improved our processing time for new orders and replenishment. It is part of our immediate plan to increase our capacity to handle the distribution needs for 700 stores. To accomplish this goal, we are adding 120,000 square feet to our distribution and office facilities during Spring 1999. We are also researching additional locations for distribution as we expand our store base. As part of this strategy, we have opened a 42,000 square foot distribution facility in Mexico from which we expect to ship 5 million T-shirts annually.

We believe the current store design in the majority of our stores is effective, meeting the needs of our target customer. However, we understand that we must evolve and react quickly to the rapidly changing retail environment. Accordingly, we are in the final stages of an AE store format re-design, which we will be testing in June 1999. We feel that this enhanced format will improve the overall shopping experience of our customers through improved design and the incorporation of the latest store technologies.

In order to organize the charitable endeavors of our organization, we have recently established the American Eagle Outfitters Foundation, which will focus on working with organizations that reflect our brand strategy and reach our targeted customers. The foundation will include involvement of our many associates and business partners, nationally and worldwide.

We are committed to increasing our stockholder value, and to that end announced a two-for-one stock split on March 30, 1999, which will be distributed on May 3, 1999. We are proud of our accomplishments this past year, but realize that many challenges lie ahead. We are committing the resources to building and improving the technological infrastructure of our business to support the demands that will be placed on our organization. Our management team is committed to achieving even greater future success as we are all enormously enthusiastic about our opportunities. We thank all of our associates and business partners who contributed to our success in 1998 and add sincere thanks to you, our stockholders, for your continued support.

Jay L. Schottenstein
Chairman of the Board and Chief Executive Officer

George Kolber
Vice Chairman and Chief Operating Officer

Roger S. Markfield
President and Chief Merchandising Officer

Where do you wear yours?℠

Laid-back, Casual and Cool...

Our target customer is family and career-oriented. He or she is a participant in life, not a spectator, and actively supports common sense causes like literacy and hunger. The target customer had a job in high school and may have a job now to help pay for college. A typical weekend for our target customer might involve mountain biking, going to a diner for breakfast with friends, work, and a movie or video. He or she is not trendy, but fashionable and aware of new music and movies. The race and ethnic background of our target customer is as varied and different as America itself. Given the choice, they would prefer to wear something like jeans and a T-shirt every day of the week.

 **AMERICAN EAGLE** OUTFITTERS | Shop In Your Underwear℠ 24 hours a day. 7 days a week @e www.ae.com | **AE Annual Report 98** | 5

# Store Locations By State

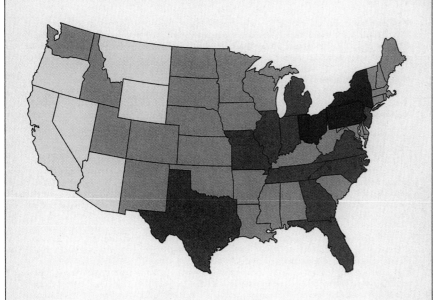

| ■ 21-30 Stores | ■ 1-10 Stores |
| ■ 11-20 Stores | ■ Growth Opportunities |

**Alabama**
10 stores

**Arkansas**
3 stores

**Colorado**
3 stores

**Connecticut**
8 stores

**Delaware**
1 store

**Florida**
18 stores

**Georgia**
14 stores

**Idaho**
1 store

**Illinois**
20 stores

**Indiana**
11 stores

**Iowa**
10 stores

**Kansas**
5 stores

**Kentucky**
6 stores

**Louisiana**
6 stores

**Maine**
1 store

**Maryland**
10 stores

**Massachusetts**
12 stores

**Michigan**
19 stores

**Minnesota**
9 stores

**Mississippi**
5 stores

**Missouri**
11 stores

**Nebraska**
3 stores

**New Hampshire**
4 stores

**New Jersey**
13 stores

**New Mexico**
2 stores

**New York**
26 stores

**North Carolina**
16 stores

**North Dakota**
2 stores

**Ohio**
24 stores

**Oklahoma**
4 stores

**Pennsylvania**
29 stores
★ National
   Headquarters

**South Carolina**
7 stores

**South Dakota**
2 stores

**Tennessee**
14 stores

**Texas**
17 stores

**Utah**
1 store

**Vermont**
2 stores

**Virginia**
19 stores

**Washington**
3 stores

**West Virginia**
6 stores

**Wisconsin**
9 stores


**Total Stores: 386**

**For the nearest AE store, call toll-free 1-888-AEAGLE-5**
**Cyberspace @ℯ www.ae.com**

## Management's Discussion and Analysis of Financial Condition and Results of Operations

### Overview

We achieved record sales and earnings for the year ended January 30, 1999 ("Fiscal 1998"). The improved sales and profitability resulted from our focus on several operating goals and merchandise strategies developed to improve operating performance, enhance brand image, and differentiate us from our competition. We emphasized these merchandising strategies:

- focus our merchandise assortment to support the American Eagle Outfitters® brand and to appeal to our target customer,
- commit to key merchandise items, and
- execute an in-season, regionally based merchandise strategy.

Our strategic marketing initiatives focused on efforts to expand the non-store distribution of our merchandise through providing commerce opportunities on our Internet web site, *ae.com*, and through catalog promotions. Our operating initiatives included the addition of 54 new stores, net of closings, the upgrade of 16 locations to our newest store design, and continued focus on inventory productivity to improve merchandise flow and increase inventory turns. We also improved our distribution center facility productivity through a $6.0 million upgrade of the facility during Fiscal 1998. We believe this upgrade, together with a planned expansion in Fiscal 1999, will continue to improve replenishment and processing of new orders and increase the capacity of our facility to 700 stores.

As a result of these initiatives, our sales for Fiscal 1998 increased to $587.6 million compared to $405.7 million for the year ended January 31, 1998 ("prior year" or "Fiscal 1997"), an increase of 44.8%. Comparable store sales achieved record levels for Fiscal 1998, increasing 32.1% compared to the prior year. We achieved this increase primarily through an 18.1% increase over last year in the number of merchandise units sold in comparable stores. Our net sales per average selling square foot increased to $497 for Fiscal 1998 from $391 for Fiscal 1997, a 27.1% increase. Additionally, gross profit increased to $234.5 million, or 39.9% of sales, for Fiscal 1998, compared to $137.0 million, or 33.8% of sales for the prior year. The increased gross profit reflected implementation of our strategic initiatives, resulting in improved merchandise mark-ons, decreased markdowns as a percent of sales, and improved leveraging of buying, occupancy and warehousing costs.

We continued our focus on improving inventory productivity, which is reflected in inventory turnover of 4.1 times in Fiscal 1998 versus 3.6 times in the prior year. Our liquidity, as measured by the current ratio, improved to 2.59 as of January 30, 1999 compared to 1.90 at the end of the prior year.

Fiscal 1998's higher gross profit translated into significantly improved operating profit and net income. Operating profit for Fiscal 1998 increased nearly 180% to $87.1 million compared to $31.1 million in the prior year. Net income for Fiscal 1998 was $54.1 million, or $1.13 per share on a diluted basis, compared to $19.5 million, or $0.43 per share on a diluted basis, in the prior year. Our strong operating performance for the year as well as continued inventory productivity allowed us to fund working capital requirements entirely through cash flow. No borrowings were required under our $75.0 million credit facility.

Our balance sheet improved as a result of the operating performance achieved in Fiscal 1998. As of January 30, 1999, cash and cash equivalents, including short-term investments, increased by approximately 76% to $85.3 million from $48.4 million in the prior year as a result of cash provided by operating activities. Inventory was $49.7 million compared with $36.3 million in the prior year, and increased 18.2% on a per store basis reflecting earlier receipt of Spring 1999 merchandise. Stockholders' equity increased almost 67% to $151.2 million, or $3.28 per share, in Fiscal 1998 compared to $90.8 million, or $2.02 per share, at the end of the prior period. Average return on stockholders' equity was 44.7% for Fiscal 1998, compared with 24.1% for Fiscal 1997.

## Results of Operations

This table shows, for the periods indicated, the percentage relationship to net sales of the listed items included in our Consolidated Statements of Operations.

| | For the Fiscal Years Ended | | |
| --- | --- | --- | --- |
| | January 30, 1999 | January 31, 1998 | February 1, 1997 |
| Net sales | 100.0% | 100.0% | 100.0% |
| Cost of sales, including certain buying, occupancy and warehousing expenses | 60.1 | 66.2 | 69.7 |
| Gross profit | 39.9 | 33.8 | 30.3 |
| Selling, general and administrative expenses | 23.6 | 24.3 | 25.7 |
| Depreciation and amortization | 1.5 | 1.8 | 1.9 |
| Operating income | 14.8 | 7.7 | 2.7 |
| Interest income, net | 0.4 | 0.3 | 0.3 |
| Income before income taxes | 15.2 | 8.0 | 3.0 |
| Provision for income taxes | 6.0 | 3.2 | 1.2 |
| Net income | 9.2% | 4.8% | 1.8% |

### Comparison of Fiscal 1998 to Fiscal 1997

Net sales increased 44.8% to $587.6 million from $405.7 million. The increase includes:

- $127.3 million from comparable store sales, representing a 32.1% increase over the prior year, and
- $54.6 million from new and non-comparable store sales, and non-store sales.

The increase resulted from an increase of 31.6% in units sold, as well as an 8.8% increase in prices. We operated 386 stores at the end of Fiscal 1998, compared to 332 stores at the end of Fiscal 1997.

Gross profit increased to $234.5 million from $137.0 million. Gross profit as a percent of net sales increased to 39.9% from 33.8%. The increase in gross profit as a percent of net sales, was attributable to a 3.6% increase in merchandise margins as well as a 2.5% improvement in buying, occupancy, and warehousing costs. The increase in merchandise margins resulted from a decrease in markdowns as a percent of sales, and improved mark-ons. This improvement in buying, occupancy and warehousing costs reflects improved leveraging achieved through comparable store sales growth.

Selling, general and administrative expenses increased to $138.8 million from $98.5 million. As a percent of net sales, these expenses decreased to 23.6% from 24.3%. The $40.3 million increase includes:

- $16.9 million in compensation costs to support increased sales and new incentive programs,
- $9.0 million for general services purchased, supplies, and other expenses,
- $7.8 million in store operating expenses to support new store growth,
- $5.4 million for increased promotional advertising, direct mail, catalog and Internet development costs, and
- $1.2 million related to costs in connection with the Natco merger. (See Note 3 of the Consolidated Financial Statements.)

Depreciation and amortization expense increased to $8.6 million from $7.3 million. As a percent of net sales, these expenses decreased to 1.5% from 1.8%.

Interest income increased to $2.4 million from $1.2 million because of higher cash reserves available for investment. No borrowings were required under the terms of our line of credit during the current or prior period.

Income before income taxes increased to $89.5 million from $32.3 million. As a percent of net sales, income before income taxes increased to 15.2% from 8.0%. The increase in income before income taxes as a percent of sales was attributable to the factors noted above.

## Comparison of Fiscal 1997 to Fiscal 1996

Net sales increased 24.3% to $405.7 million from $326.4 million. The increase includes:

- $47.5 million from comparable store sales, representing a 15.1% increase over the prior year, and
- $31.8 million from new and non-comparable stores, offset by closed store sales.

The total increase in net sales resulted primarily from an increase of 28.2% in units sold. We operated 332 stores at the end of Fiscal 1997, compared to 303 stores at the end of Fiscal 1996.

Gross profit increased to $137.0 million from $98.8 million. Gross profit as a percent of net sales increased to 33.8% from 30.3%. The increase was attributable to a 2.0% increase in merchandise margins and a 1.5% improvement in buying, occupancy, and warehousing costs. The increase in merchandise margins resulted primarily from improved mark-ons and decreased markdowns as a percent of sales. This improvement in buying, occupancy, and warehousing costs reflects improved leveraging of these expenses.

Selling, general and administrative expenses increased to $98.5 million from $83.8 million. As a percent of net sales, these expenses decreased to 24.3% from 25.7%. The $14.7 million increase includes:

- $6.9 million in compensation costs to support increased sales, new incentive programs, and the increase in the minimum wage effective September 1, 1997,
- $4.3 million in store operating expenses to support new store growth, and
- $3.5 million for increased promotional advertising and general services purchased.

Depreciation and amortization expense increased to $7.3 million from $6.1 million. As a percent of net sales, these expenses decreased to 1.8% from 1.9%.

Interest income increased to $1.2 million from $1.0 million primarily due to interest earned on the short-term note receivable from Azteca Production International. No borrowings were required under the terms of our line of credit during the current or prior period.

Income before income taxes increased to $32.3 million from $9.8 million. As a percent of net sales, income before income taxes increased to 8.0% from 3.0%. The increase was attributable to the factors noted above.

## Liquidity and Capital Resources

Our primary source of cash in Fiscal 1998 was from operations. Our primary use of cash of $24.9 million was invested in capital expenditures. Additionally, $13.4 million was used to support inventory increases for anticipated sales growth and new stores. Working capital at year-end was $94.8 million for Fiscal 1998, $48.5 million for Fiscal 1997, and $34.4 million for Fiscal 1996. Fiscal 1998's increase resulted primarily from the increase in cash provided by operating activities.

For Fiscal 1998, the source of the $59.8 million of cash provided by operating activities was net income adjusted for non-cash charges for depreciation and amortization. A portion of the cash flow provided by operating activities was used to fund new store expansion, remodel existing stores, and other capital expenditures discussed below. Also, we used $13.4 million to purchase short-term investments with original maturities of six months to one year. These investments can be sold at any time. The remainder of the cash flow provided by operating activities is being retained to fund new store growth, remodelings, future system enhancements, and other capital expenditures. We fund merchandise purchases through operating cash flow.

At January 30, 1999, we had an unsecured demand lending arrangement with a bank to provide a $75.0 million line of credit at either the lender's prime lending rate (7.75% at January 30, 1999) or a negotiated rate such as LIBOR. The facility has a limit of $40.0 million to be used for direct borrowing. No borrowings were required against the line during Fiscal 1998. At January 30, 1999, letters of credit in the amount of $39.2 million were outstanding, leaving a remaining available balance on the line of $35.8 million.

Capital expenditures, net of construction allowances, totaled $24.9 million for Fiscal 1998. These expenditures included:

- the addition of 56 new stores totaling $9.5 million,
- 16 remodeled locations totaling $3.5 million,
- $6.0 million in improvements to our distribution center,
- $1.9 million in fixture and leasehold retrofits to existing stores, and
- $4.0 million in other capital expenditures.

We expect capital expenditures for Fiscal 1999 to total approximately $40 million. We plan to open approximately 80 stores during Fiscal 1999 at an estimated cost of $19.0 million. This forward-looking statement will be influenced by our financial position, consumer spending, and the number of acceptable mall store leases that may become available. Additionally, we have selected approximately 22 locations to upgrade to our newest store design in Fiscal 1999 for an estimated cost of $6.6 million. These locations were selected based upon sales performance and lease terms. Additionally, we plan to spend approximately $3.0 million to review and upgrade existing systems. We plan to spend approximately $5.0 million for fixtures and equipment upgrades in our distribution center facility to improve operating efficiencies and accommodate new store growth.

Our growth strategy includes the possibility of growth through acquisitions. We periodically consider and evaluate acquisitions and opportunities to support future growth, and may undertake acquisitions in 1999. At this time we have not committed to any material future acquisitions. In the event we did pursue material future acquisitions, any such acquisitions could require additional equity or debt financing, which we would seek to obtain as required. There can be no assurance that we will be successful in closing any potential acquisition transaction, or that any acquisition we undertake will increase our profitability.

**Income Taxes**

At year-end, we had deferred tax assets of $10.4 million for Fiscal 1998 and $7.6 million for Fiscal 1997, which result from financial and tax accounting differences. We have had taxable income during each of the past three tax years and anticipate that future taxable income will be able to recover the full amount of the deferred tax asset. Assuming a 40% effective tax rate, we will need to recognize pre-tax net income of $26 million to recover existing deferred tax amounts. See Note 8 "Income Taxes" in the Notes to Consolidated Financial Statements.

**Impact of Inflation**

We do not believe that the relatively modest levels of inflation which have been experienced in the United States in recent years have had a significant effect on our net sales or our profitability. Substantial increases in cost, however, could have a significant impact on us and the industry in the future.

## Impact of Year 2000

The Year 2000 issue is the result of computer programs being written using two digits rather than four to define the applicable year. Any of our computer programs or hardware that have date-sensitive software or embedded chips may recognize a date using "00" as the year 1900 rather than the year 2000.

*State of Readiness:* Our plan to resolve the internal Year 2000 issue involves two major phases: detection and correction. The detection phase includes planning, inventory, triage, and detailed assessment. We took an inventory of all our information technology and non-information technology systems to determine which of our systems were not Year 2000 compliant. We also implemented procedures to review the Year 2000 readiness in all new equipment acquired by us. Next, we prioritized our Year 2000 problems based upon their potential impact on us. This detailed assessment of the problems and a plan to correct these problems were completed in October 1998.

The correction phase includes repair and resolution and testing and implementation. We have four mission critical systems: distribution center systems, point of sale systems, merchandising software, and financial software. A portion of the packing systems in our distribution center are not Year 2000 compliant. We are implementing a software upgrade to make the packing system Year 2000 compliant. The point of sale register systems need to have a BIOS upgrade and a minor software upgrade. We are working with our outside vendors to complete these repairs in each store location. Additionally, our point of sale store polling system is not Year 2000 compliant and is being replaced with a Year 2000 compliant system. Our merchandise software needs a version upgrade in order to make it Year 2000 compliant. We are working to make the necessary upgrades by May 1999. Our financial software is Year 2000 compliant. We are internally reviewing and testing all mission critical systems and major systems components for Year 2000 compliance and plan to complete such tests by June 1999. We believe that all mission critical systems will be Year 2000 compliant.

With respect to suppliers and business partners, we have sent letters to approximately 1,800 parties in an attempt to determine the possible impact of failure of third parties to be Year 2000 compliant. Approximately 75% of the parties contacted have returned our questionnaire. We have had discussions with our major suppliers and continue to follow up with third parties to ensure that they remain on schedule with their Year 2000 compliance. We plan to visit our major suppliers to review their Year 2000 readiness. We have determined that approximately 10% of our vendors will not be Year 2000 compliant. However, none of these third parties are critical to our continuing operations. We believe that all of our major suppliers and business partners will be Year 2000 compliant.

*Costs to Address Our Year 2000 Issues:* The total cost of the Year 2000 project is estimated at $2.1 million and is being funded through cash flows from operations. To date, we have incurred approximately $1.2 million of which $0.3 million relates to hardware and software which was capitalized. The remaining costs were expensed as incurred and include salaries, incentive compensation and third party consulting services. Of the total remaining project costs, approximately $0.3 million is attributable to the purchase of new software and hardware, which will be capitalized. There can be no guarantee that these estimates will be achieved and actual results could differ materially from these plans.

*Risks of Our Year 2000 Issues:* We are dependent on our suppliers and business partners. If efforts on our part, our customers' part, our suppliers and business partners' part, or the part of public utilities or the government fail to adequately address the relevant Year 2000 issues, the most likely worst case scenario would be possible delays in the delivery of merchandise to our stores. We do not currently believe that any such delay will cause a material adverse effect on us.

*Our Contingency Plans:* While we anticipate that all of our major suppliers and business partners will be Year 2000 compliant, we are developing a contingency plan which will allow the continuation of business operations in the event that we or any of our significant suppliers or business partners do not properly address Year 2000 issues. We will obtain early delivery of some merchandise from suppliers in an attempt to mitigate any Year 2000 issues that may arise. We are also looking for alternative vendors to supply products and services in the event that some of our current non-mission critical vendors are unable to perform because of Year 2000 problems. Further, we are searching for ways that we can support our current vendors who may have Year 2000 problems. We cannot assure you that our efforts will prevent all consequences. There may be undetermined future costs due to business disruption that may be caused by suppliers, transportation disruptions, or unforeseen circumstances.

## Safe Harbor Statement, Seasonality and Business Risks

This report contains various "forward-looking statements" within the meaning of Section 27A of the Securities Act of 1933, as amended, and Section 21E of the Securities Exchange Act of 1934, as amended, which represent our expectations or beliefs concerning future events, including the following:

- the possibility of growth through acquisitions,
- the planned opening of approximately 80 stores in Fiscal 1999,
- the selection of approximately 22 stores for remodeling,
- the planned upgrade and expansion of our distribution center facilities,
- the planned review and upgrade of existing systems, and
- the completion of modifications to computer systems to enable the processing of transactions in the year 2000 and beyond.

We caution that these statements are further qualified by factors that could cause actual results to differ materially from those in the forward-looking statements, including without limitation, the following:

- our ability to successfully acquire and integrate other businesses,
- decline in demand for our merchandise,
- the ability to obtain suitable sites for new stores at acceptable costs,
- the hiring and training of qualified personnel,
- the integration of new stores into existing operations,
- the expansion of buying and inventory capabilities,
- the availability of capital,
- our ability to anticipate and respond to changing consumer preferences and fashion trends in a timely manner,
- the effect of economic conditions, and
- the effect of competitive pressures from other retailers.

Results actually achieved may differ materially from expected results in these statements.

Historically, our operations have been seasonal, with a disproportionate amount of net sales and a majority of net income occurring in the fourth fiscal quarter, reflecting increased demand during the year-end holiday selling season and, to a lesser extent, the third quarter, reflecting increased demand during the back-to-school selling season. As a result of this seasonality, any factors negatively affecting us during the third and fourth fiscal quarters of any year, including adverse weather or unfavorable economic conditions, could have a material adverse effect on our financial condition and results of operations for the entire year. Our quarterly results of operations also may fluctuate based upon such factors as the timing of certain holiday seasons, the number and timing of new store openings, the amount of net sales contributed by new and existing stores, the timing and level of markdowns, store closings, refurbishments and relocations, competitive factors, weather and general economic conditions.

AMERICAN EAGLE
OUTFITTERS

Shop In Your Underwear℠ 24 hours a day,
7 days a week @e www.ae.com

**AE Annual Report 98**   12

## American Eagle Outfitters, Inc.
## Consolidated Balance Sheets

*(Dollars in thousands)*

| | January 30, 1999 | January 31, 1998 | February 1, 1997 |
|---|---|---|---|
| **Assets** | | | |
| Current assets: | | | |
| Cash and cash equivalents | $71,940 | $48,359 | $34,326 |
| Short-term investments | 13,360 | — | — |
| Merchandise inventory | 49,688 | 36,278 | 27,117 |
| Accounts and note receivable, including related party | 8,560 | 7,647 | 3,556 |
| Prepaid expenses and other | 2,757 | 5,388 | 4,381 |
| Deferred income taxes | 8,199 | 4,801 | 4,380 |
| Total current assets | 154,504 | 102,473 | 73,760 |
| Fixed assets: | | | |
| Fixtures and equipment | 36,307 | 25,842 | 23,118 |
| Leasehold improvements | 46,996 | 35,978 | 32,671 |
| | 83,303 | 61,820 | 55,789 |
| Less: Accumulated depreciation and amortization | 29,933 | 23,273 | 21,598 |
| Net fixed assets | 53,370 | 38,547 | 34,191 |
| Other assets | 3,074 | 3,775 | 2,487 |
| Total assets | $210,948 | $144,795 | $110,438 |
| **Liabilities and stockholders' equity** | | | |
| Current liabilities: | | | |
| Accounts payable | $18,551 | $24,606 | $20,430 |
| Accrued compensation and payroll taxes | 17,739 | 9,227 | 4,926 |
| Accrued rent | 13,042 | 7,909 | 6,006 |
| Accrued income and other taxes | 3,208 | 8,738 | 5,478 |
| Other liabilities and accrued expenses | 7,211 | 3,507 | 2,542 |
| Total current liabilities | 59,751 | 53,987 | 39,382 |
| Stockholders' equity | 151,197 | 90,808 | 71,056 |
| Total liabilities and stockholders' equity | $210,948 | $144,795 | $110,438 |

*See Notes to Consolidated Financial Statements*

## American Eagle Outfitters, Inc.
## Consolidated Statements of Operations

*(In thousands, except per share amounts)*

| | For the Years Ended | | |
|---|---|---|---|
| | January 30, 1999 | January 31, 1998 | February 1, 1997 |
| Net sales | $587,600 | $405,713 | $326,404 |
| Cost of sales, including certain buying, occupancy and warehousing expenses | 353,089 | 268,746 | 227,648 |
| Gross profit | 234,511 | 136,967 | 98,756 |
| Selling, general and administrative expenses | 138,847 | 98,529 | 83,810 |
| Depreciation and amortization | 8,611 | 7,318 | 6,087 |
| Operating income | 87,053 | 31,120 | 8,859 |
| Interest income, net | 2,436 | 1,158 | 973 |
| Income before income taxes | 89,489 | 32,278 | 9,832 |
| Provision for income taxes | 35,371 | 12,741 | 3,907 |
| Net income | $54,118 | $19,537 | $5,925 |
| Basic earnings per common share | $1.20 | $0.44 | $0.13 |
| Diluted earnings per common share | $1.13 | $0.43 | $0.13 |
| Weighted average common shares outstanding – basic | 45,281 | 44,181 | 43,899 |
| Weighted average common shares outstanding – diluted | 47,952 | 45,633 | 45,388 |

*See Notes to Consolidated Financial Statements*

## American Eagle Outfitters, Inc.
## Consolidated Statements Of Stockholders' Equity

*For the Years Ended January 30, 1999, January 31, 1998 and February 1, 1997*

*(In thousands)*

| | Shares (1) | Common Stock | Contributed Capital | Retained Earnings | Treasury Stock | Deferred Compensation Expense | Stockholders' Equity |
|---|---|---|---|---|---|---|---|
| Balance at February 3, 1996 | 9,875 | $99 | $56,670 | $11,194 | ($1,516) | ($2,651) | $63,796 |
| Net income | — | — | — | 5,925 | — | — | 5,925 |
| Exercise and cancellation of stock options and restricted stock | 43 | — | 356 | — | (109) | 53 | 300 |
| Tax benefit realized on exercised stock options and vested restricted stock | — | — | 44 | — | — | — | 44 |
| Restricted stock and stock option compensation | — | — | — | — | — | 991 | 991 |
| Restricted stock grant | — | — | 1,229 | — | — | (1,229) | — |
| Balance at February 1, 1997 | 9,918 | 99 | 58,299 | 17,119 | (1,625) | (2,836) | 71,056 |
| Net income | — | — | — | 19,537 | — | — | 19,537 |
| Exercise of stock options | 115 | 1 | 973 | — | — | — | 974 |
| Tax benefit realized on exercised stock options and vested restricted stock | — | — | 277 | — | — | — | 277 |
| Investment in Prophecy, Ltd. | — | — | (1,350) | (900) | — | — | (2,250) |
| Restricted stock and stock option compensation | — | — | 370 | — | — | 844 | 1,214 |
| Three-for-two stock split- January 5, 1998 | 4,978 | 50 | (50) | — | — | — | — |
| Balance at January 31, 1998 | 15,011 | 150 | 58,519 | 35,756 | (1,625) | (1,992) | 90,808 |
| Net income | — | — | — | 54,118 | — | — | 54,118 |
| Exercise of stock options | 426 | 4 | 1,776 | — | — | — | 1,780 |
| Tax benefit realized on exercised stock options and vested restricted stock | — | — | 2,255 | — | — | — | 2,255 |
| Restricted stock and stock option compensation | — | — | — | — | — | 1,336 | 1,336 |
| Restricted stock grant | 64 | 1 | 1,417 | — | 345 | (1,763) | — |
| Merger costs incurred by Natco | — | — | 900 | — | — | — | 900 |
| Three-for-two stock split- May 8, 1998 | 7,554 | 76 | (76) | — | — | — | — |
| Two-for-one stock split May 3, 1999 | 23,055 | 230 | (230) | — | — | — | — |
| Balance at January 30, 1999 | 46,110 | $461 | $64,561 | $89,874 | ($1,280) | ($2,419) | $151,197 |

*(1) 125 million authorized, 46 million issued (adjusted for the January 1998, May 1998, and May 1999 stock splits) $.01 par value common stock at January 30, 1999, January 31, 1998, and February 1, 1997.*

*See Notes to Consolidated Financial Statements*

### American Eagle Outfitters, Inc.
### Consolidated Statements Of Cash Flows

*(In thousands)*

| | For the Years Ended | | |
|---|---|---|---|
| | January 30, 1999 | January 31, 1998 | February 1, 1997 |
| **Operating activities:** | | | |
| Net income | $54,118 | $19,537 | $5,925 |
| Adjustments to reconcile net income to net cash provided by operating activities: | | | |
| Depreciation and amortization | 8,611 | 7,318 | 6,087 |
| Loss on impairment and write-off of fixed assets | 1,467 | 2,292 | 2,067 |
| Restricted stock compensation | 1,336 | 1,214 | 991 |
| Deferred income taxes | (2,753) | (496) | (1,898) |
| Merger costs incurred by Natco | 900 | — | — |
| Changes in assets and liabilities: | | | |
| Merchandise inventory | (13,410) | (8,903) | (3,723) |
| Receivables | (913) | (2,611) | 2,055 |
| Prepaid and other | 2,445 | (1,578) | (400) |
| Receivables from officers | — | 376 | (30) |
| Accounts payable | (5,400) | (1,657) | 4,018 |
| Accrued liabilities | 13,420 | 10,676 | 3,489 |
| Total adjustments | 5,703 | 6,631 | 12,656 |
| Net cash provided by operating activities | 59,821 | 26,168 | 18,581 |
| **Investing activities:** | | | |
| Capital expenditures | (24,919) | (12,646) | (10,540) |
| Net purchase of short-term investments | (13,360) | — | — |
| Investment in Prophecy, Ltd. | — | (900) | — |
| Proceeds from sale of assets | 6 | 54 | 5,874 |
| Net cash used for investing activities | (38,273) | (13,492) | (4,666) |
| **Financing activities:** | | | |
| Net proceeds from stock options exercised | 2,033 | 1,357 | 425 |
| Net cash provided by financing activities | 2,033 | 1,357 | 425 |
| Net increase in cash and cash equivalents | 23,581 | 14,033 | 14,340 |
| Cash and cash equivalents – beginning of period | 48,359 | 34,326 | 19,986 |
| Cash and cash equivalents – end of period | $71,940 | $48,359 | $34,326 |

*See Notes to Consolidated Financial Statements*

## Notes to Consolidated Financial Statements
*Year Ended January 30, 1999*

### 1. Business Operations and Basis of Presentation

American Eagle Outfitters, Inc. (the "Company") is a specialty retailer of all-American casual apparel, accessories, and footwear for men and women between the ages of 16 and 34. The Company designs, markets, and sells its own brand of versatile, relaxed, and timeless classics like AE dungarees, khakis, and T-shirts, providing high quality merchandise at affordable prices. The Company operates retail stores located primarily in regional enclosed shopping malls. The Consolidated Financial Statements include the accounts of the Company and its wholly-owned royalty and investment and sourcing subsidiaries. All inter-company transactions have been eliminated.

The following table sets forth the approximate percentage of net sales attributable to each merchandise group for each of the periods indicated:

|  | For the Years Ended | | |
|---|---|---|---|
|  | January 30, 1999 | January 31, 1998 | February 1, 1997 |
| Mens apparel | 40% | 41% | 36% |
| Womens apparel | 52% | 50% | 47% |
| Footwear and accessories | 8% | 9% | 17% |
| Total | 100% | 100% | 100% |

Effective May 4, 1997, the Company acquired the operations of Prophecy, Ltd. partnership ("Prophecy"), a New York-based production and sourcing company. The majority partner of Prophecy was a related party. The goals of the acquisition were to leverage the talent and expense of the Company's New York design office and to use Prophecy's production and sourcing expertise and manufacturing relationships to shorten product delivery cycles and enable the Company to improve product quality and value. The terms of the acquisition included a cash payment of $0.9 million at closing as well as the assumption of net liabilities of approximately $2.7 million. The

acquisition was accounted for as a purchase; however, the assets acquired and the liabilities assumed have been recorded at historic carrying value because Prophecy was under common control with the Company. The premium in excess of Prophecy's book value was recorded as a reduction to equity. The results of operations of Prophecy are included in the accompanying Consolidated Financial Statements from the date of acquisition.

Prior to the consummation of the Company's initial offering, the existing stockholders contributed 1,171,124 shares of common stock to the Company which in turn, issued the common stock to officers, directors and other individuals performing services for the Company. Pursuant to the April 13, 1994 restricted stock agreements, this common stock was issued without cash consideration and vests over five years.

### 2. Summary of Significant Accounting Policies

*Fiscal Year*

The Company's financial year is a 52/53 week year that ends on the Saturday nearest to January 31. For tax purposes, the Company reports on a July year-end. As used herein, "Fiscal 1998," "Fiscal 1997" and "Fiscal 1996" refer to the twelve month periods ended January 30, 1999, January 31, 1998 and February 1, 1997, respectively. "Fiscal 1999" refers to the twelve month period ending January 29, 2000.

AMERICAN EAGLE OUTFITTERS    Shop In Your Underwear℠ 24 hours a day, 7 days a week @ www.ae.com    AE Annual Report 98    16

*Estimates*

The preparation of financial statements in conformity with generally accepted accounting principles requires management to make estimates and assumptions that affect the reported amounts of assets and liabilities and disclosure of contingent assets and liabilities at the date of the financial statements and the reported amounts of revenues and expenses during the reporting period. Actual results could differ from those estimates. On an ongoing basis, management reviews its estimates based on currently available information. Changes in facts and circumstances may result in revised estimates.

*Recent Financial Accounting Standards Board Pronouncements*

*FASB 130 Reporting Comprehensive Income*

In 1997, the Financial Accounting Standards Board (FASB) issued Statement of Financial Accounting Standards No. 130, "Reporting Comprehensive Income," which establishes standards for the reporting and display of comprehensive income and its components in financial statements. This standard is effective for Fiscal 1998, however, it does not have any impact on the financial statement disclosures because the Company does not currently have any elements of comprehensive income.

*FASB 131 Disclosures about Segments of an Enterprise*

In 1997, the FASB issued Statement of Financial Accounting Standards No. 131, "Disclosures about Segments of an Enterprise," which establishes standards for the disclosure of selected information about reportable segments, disclosures about products and services, geographic areas, and major customers in financial statements. This standard is effective for Fiscal 1998, however, it does not currently have a significant impact on financial statement disclosures of the Company.

*FASB 132 Disclosures about Pensions and Other Post-retirement Benefits*

In 1998, the FASB issued Statement of Financial Accounting Standards No. 132, "Disclosures about Pensions and Other Post-retirement Benefits," which modifies established standards for disclosures related to pensions and other post-retirement benefits. This standard is effective for Fiscal 1998. The Company does not maintain any post-retirement or defined benefit plans. Therefore, this statement does not have any impact on financial statement disclosures.

*FASB 133 Accounting for Derivative Instruments and Hedging Activities*

In 1998, the FASB issued Statement of Financial Accounting Standards No. 133, "Accounting for Derivative Instruments and Hedging Activities," which establishes standards for the recognition and measurement of derivatives and hedging activities. This standard is effective for Fiscal 2000. The Company does not currently engage in these types of risk management or investment activities. This statement is not anticipated to have any impact on the Company's financial statements.

*Cash and Cash Equivalents*

Cash includes cash equivalents. The Company considers all highly liquid investments purchased with a maturity of three months or less to be cash equivalents.

*Short-Term Investments*

Cash in excess of operating requirements is invested in marketable equity or government debt obligations. As of January 30, 1999, short-term investments include investments with an original maturity of greater than three months (averaging approximately 10 months) and consist of tax-exempt municipal bonds classified as available for sale. These investments are recorded at cost and approximate market value.

## Merchandise Inventory

Merchandise inventory is valued at the lower of average cost or market, utilizing the retail method. Average cost includes merchandise design and sourcing costs and related expenses.

The Company reviews its inventory levels in order to identify slow-moving merchandise and generally uses markdowns to clear merchandise. Markdowns may occur when inventory exceeds customer demand for reasons of style, seasonal adaptation, changes in customer preference, lack of consumer acceptance of fashion items, competition, or if it is determined that the inventory in stock will not sell at its currently ticketed price. Such markdowns may have an adverse impact on earnings, depending on their extent and amount of inventory affected.

## Fixed Assets

Fixed assets are recorded on the basis of cost with depreciation and amortization computed utilizing the straight-line method over the estimated useful lives. Estimated useful lives range from three to ten years. Depreciation and amortization expense is summarized as follows:

*(Dollars in thousands)*

| | For the Years Ended | | |
|---|---|---|---|
| | January 30, 1999 | January 31, 1998 | February 1, 1997 |
| Depreciation expense | $8,215 | $6,943 | $5,933 |
| Amortization expense | 396 | 375 | 154 |
| Total | $8,611 | $7,318 | $6,087 |

In accordance with FASB Statement No. 121, "Accounting for the Impairment of Long-Lived Assets and for Long-Lived Assets to Be Disposed Of," impairment losses are recorded on long-lived assets used in operations when events and circumstances indicate that the assets might be impaired and the undiscounted cash flows estimated to be generated by those assets are less than the carrying amounts of those assets.

## Stock Option Plan

In October 1995, the FASB issued Statement No. 123, "Accounting for Stock-Based Compensation," which establishes financial accounting and reporting standards for stock-based employee compensation plans. The Company continues to account for its stock-based employee compensation plan using the intrinsic value method under Accounting Principles Board Opinion No. 25. See pro forma disclosures required under FASB Statement No. 123 in Note 10.

## Income Taxes

Income taxes are accounted for using the liability method. Under this method, the deferred taxes are determined based on the differences between the financial statement and tax basis of assets and liabilities at enacted tax rates in effect for the years in which the differences are expected to reverse.

## Preopening Expenses and Closing Costs

Expenditures of a noncapital nature incurred prior to the opening of a new store are charged to operations as incurred. Costs of closing a store are recognized when, in management's judgment, it is probable that the store will be closed.

## Advertising Costs

Advertising costs are expensed as incurred. Advertising expense is summarized as follows:

*(Dollars in thousands)*

| | For the Years Ended | | |
|---|---|---|---|
| | January 30, 1999 | January 31, 1998 | February 1, 1997 |
| Advertising expense | $16,431 | $10,067 | $8,501 |

*Supplemental Disclosures of Cash Flow Information*

*(Dollars in thousands)*

|  | For the Years Ended | | |
|---|---|---|---|
|  | January 30, 1999 | January 31, 1998 | February 1, 1997 |
| Cash paid during the periods for: | | | |
| Income taxes | $41,706 | $9,675 | $4,420 |
| Interest | $   — | $   — | $   — |

*Earnings Per Share*

The Company adopted Financial Accounting Standards Board issued Statement No. 128, "Earnings per Share," (FASB 128) in Fiscal 1997. Earnings per share amounts for all periods have been restated to give effect to the application of FASB No. 128. The effect of the restatement on earnings per share for the restated periods is immaterial.

The following table shows the amounts used in computing earnings per share and the effect on income and the weighted average number of shares of dilutive potential common stock.

*(Dollars in thousands)*

|  | For the Years Ended | | |
|---|---|---|---|
|  | January 30, 1999 | January 31, 1998 | February 1, 1997 |
| Net income used in basic EPS | $54,118 | $19,537 | $5,925 |
| Weighted average number of common shares used in basic EPS | 45,281 | 44,181 | 43,899 |
| Effect of dilutive stock options and non-vested restricted stock | 2,671 | 1,452 | 1,489 |
| Weighted average number of common shares and dilutive potential common stock used in diluted EPS | 47,952 | 45,633 | 45,388 |

*Reclassification*

Certain reclassifications have been made to the Consolidated Financial Statements for prior periods in order to conform to the Fiscal 1998 presentation.

AMERICAN EAGLE OUTFITTERS          Shop In Your Underwear℠ 24 hours a day, 7 days a week @ www.ae.com          **AE Annual Report 98**    19

## 3. Related Party Transactions

The Company has various transactions with related parties. The nature of the relationship is primarily through common ownership. The Company has an operating lease for its corporate headquarters and distribution center with an affiliate. The lease, which was entered into on January 1, 1996, and expires on December 31, 2010 provides for annual rental payments of approximately $1.2 million through 2001, $1.6 million through 2006, and $1.8 million through the end of the lease.

In addition, the Company and its subsidiaries purchase merchandise from and sell merchandise to various related parties and use the services of a related importing company. During 1998, the Company advanced funds to the importing company for estimated expenses incurred on behalf of the Company, but not billed. As of January 30, 1999, these advances exceeded the billings for goods in-transit in the amount of $1.9 million and are included in accounts and note receivable on the Consolidated Balance Sheet.

During Fiscal 1997, the Company provided a short-term loan in the amount of $3.0 million to Azteca Production International, a related party vendor. The terms of the note included annual interest at 7% plus a margin defined as the difference between 8.5% and National City Bank's prime lending rate. The note receivable outstanding balance at January 31, 1998 was approximately $1.3 million. The loan was paid off in April 1998.

The Company has entered into a Plan of Reorganization and Agreement and Plan of Merger with Natco Industries, Inc. ("Natco") and Thorn Hill Acquisition Corp. ("Newco"), a wholly owned subsidiary of Natco, with the Company surviving the merger and becoming a wholly owned subsidiary of Natco. Natco is related to the Company through common controlling stockholders. This merger was completed by the Company to (i) eliminate Natco's potential conflicts of interest as to the financial objectives of the Company, (ii) obtain the benefits of the holding company structure arising from the reorganization and merger, and (iii) reduce the concentration of ownership of the Company providing the opportunity to increase liquidity in the market and enhance the Company's long-term ability to raise capital. During Fiscal 1998, $0.9 million in costs were incurred by Natco in connection with the merger which are reflected in selling, general, and administrative expenses in the Consolidated Statements of Operations. In addition, during Fiscal 1998, the Company incurred approximately $0.3 million in costs in connection with the merger, which are also included in selling, general, and administrative expenses. The net assets of Natco primarily consist of approximately 30% ownership of the Company's common stock. The transaction did not have a significant impact on the Company's existing financial statements.

Related party amounts follow:

*(Dollars in thousands)*

| | For the Years Ended | | |
|---|---|---|---|
| | January 30, 1999 | January 31, 1998 | February 1, 1997 |
| Merchandise purchases through a related party importer | $79,852 | $65,192 | $42,629 |
| Accounts payable | $1,237 | $7,826 | $7,068 |
| Accounts and note receivable | $2,829 | $3,755 | $1,334 |
| Rent expense | $1,548 | $1,549 | $1,407 |
| Merchandise sales | $3,289 | $8,669 | $2,812 |

The Company provided loans to certain officers and other individuals to pay the taxes on the restricted stock that vests each year. These loans have been paid off and there was no receivable balance outstanding as of January 30, 1999 or January 31, 1998. As of February 1, 1997, the outstanding value of these loans, including interest at 6.8%, approximated $376,000.

### 4. Accounts Receivable

Accounts receivable is comprised of the following:

*(Dollars in thousands)*

| | For the Years Ended | | |
|---|---|---|---|
| | January 30, 1999 | January 31, 1998 | February 1, 1997 |
| Accounts receivable – construction allowances | $4,008 | $1,518 | $1,336 |
| Related party accounts and note receivable | 2,829 | 3,755 | 1,334 |
| Accounts receivable – other | 1,723 | 2,374 | 886 |
| Total | $8,560 | $7,647 | $3,556 |

### 5. Notes Payable

The Company has an unsecured demand lending arrangement with a bank to provide a $75 million line of credit at either the lender's prime lending rate (7.75% at January 30, 1999) or a negotiated rate such as LIBOR. This reflects a $15 million increase in line availability for letters of credit which occurred in July 1998. Because there were no borrowings in Fiscal 1998, there were no amounts paid for interest. The facility has a limit of $40 million to be used for direct borrowing. No borrowings were outstanding as of January 30, 1999, January 31, 1998, and February 1, 1997. The Company had letters of credit of approximately $39.2 million outstanding at January 30, 1999, which were primarily related to the purchase of inventory. The remaining balance which could be borrowed under this lending arrangement was $35.8 million at January 30, 1999.

### 6. Impairment of Assets

In accordance with FASB No. 121, "Accounting for the Impairment of Long-Lived Assets and for Long-Lived Assets to Be Disposed Of," management evaluates the ongoing value of leasehold improvements and store fixtures associated with retail stores which have been open longer than one year. Based on these evaluations, the Company determined that assets with a net carrying amount of approximately $2.2 million at January 30, 1999, compared with $2.3 million at January 31, 1998 were impaired. The expense included in selling, general and

administrative expenses for Fiscal 1998, and Fiscal 1997 was $0.2 million and $1.7 million, respectively. Fair value was based on management's estimate of the potential future benefits of such assets.

### 7. Lease Commitments

All store operations are conducted from leased premises. These leases generally provide for base rentals and the payment of a percentage of sales as additional rent when sales exceed specified levels. Minimum rentals relating to these leases are recorded on a straight-line basis. In addition, the Company is typically responsible under its leases for common area maintenance charges, real estate taxes and certain other expenses. These leases are classified as operating leases.

Rent expense charged to operations, including amounts paid under short-term cancelable leases, was as follows:

*(Dollars in thousands)*

| | For the Years Ended | | |
|---|---|---|---|
| | January 30, 1999 | January 31, 1998 | February 1, 1997 |
| Minimum rentals | $53,482 | $47,421 | $42,738 |
| Contingent rentals | 6,177 | 1,725 | 674 |
| Total | $59,659 | $49,146 | $43,412 |

The table below summarizes future minimum lease obligations under operating leases in effect at January 30, 1999:

*(Dollars in thousands)*

| Fiscal years: | Future Minimum Lease Obligations |
|---|---|
| 1999 | $38,523 |
| 2000 | 36,857 |
| 2001 | 34,669 |
| 2002 | 32,646 |
| 2003 | 32,573 |
| Thereafter | 82,921 |
| Total | $258,189 |

The Company is contingently liable for the rental payments totaling approximately $3.2 million for the outlet stores which were sold in October 1995.

## 8. Income Taxes

The significant components of the Company's deferred tax assets (there are no deferred tax liabilities) were as follows:

*(Dollars in thousands)*

| | January 30, 1999 | January 31, 1998 | February 1, 1997 |
|---|---|---|---|
| **Current:** | | | |
| Inventories | $2,826 | $1,297 | $1,326 |
| Accrued rent | 3,375 | 2,545 | 2,015 |
| Salaries and compensation | 1,274 | 743 | 773 |
| Other | 724 | 216 | 266 |
| | 8,199 | 4,801 | 4,380 |
| **Long Term:** | | | |
| Basis differences in fixed assets | 2,200 | 2,790 | 1,391 |
| Other | — | 55 | — |
| | 2,200 | 2,845 | 1,391 |
| Total | $10,399 | $7,646 | $5,771 |

Significant components of the provision for income taxes are as follows:

*(Dollars in thousands)*

| | January 30, 1999 | January 31, 1998 | February 1, 1997 |
|---|---|---|---|
| **Current:** | | | |
| Federal | $31,819 | $12,366 | $4,709 |
| State | 6,305 | 2,250 | 1,096 |
| Total current | 38,124 | 14,616 | 5,805 |
| **Deferred:** | | | |
| Federal | (2,298) | (1,733) | (1,584) |
| State | (455) | (142) | (314) |
| Total deferred | (2,753) | (1,875) | (1,898) |
| Provision for income taxes | $35,371 | $12,741 | $3,907 |

A tax benefit has been recognized as contributed capital, in the amount of $2,255,000 for the year ended January 30, 1999, $277,000 for the year ended January 31, 1998 and $44,000 for the year ended February 1, 1997, resulting from additional tax deductions related to vested restricted stock grants and stock options exercised.

A reconciliation between the statutory federal income tax and the effective tax rate follows:

| | For the Years Ended | | |
|---|---|---|---|
| | January 30, 1999 | January 31, 1998 | February 1, 1997 |
| Federal income tax rate | 35% | 35% | 35% |
| State income taxes, net of federal income tax effect | 4 | 4 | 4 |
| Other items, net | 1 | 1 | 1 |
| | 40% | 40% | 40% |

### 9. Profit Sharing Plan and Employee Stock Purchase Plan

The Company maintains a 401(k) retirement plan and contributory profit sharing plan. Full-time employees who have attained twenty-one years of age and have completed one year of service can contribute up to 15% of their salaries to the 401(k) plan on a pre-tax basis, subject to IRS limitations. The Company will match up to 3% of the participants' eligible compensation. Contributions to the profit sharing plan, as determined by the Board of Directors, are discretionary, but generally may not exceed 15% of defined annual compensation paid to all participating employees. The Company recognized $2,885,000, $1,242,000 and $669,000 in expense during Fiscal 1998, Fiscal 1997 and Fiscal 1996, respectively, in connection with these plans.

The Employee Stock Purchase Plan (ESPP), effective on April 1, 1996, covers employees who are at least 20-1/2 years old, have one year of service, and work at least 1,000 hours. Contributions are determined by the employee with a maximum of $1,248 annually with the Company matching 15% of the investment. These contributions are used to purchase shares of Company stock in the open market.

### 10. Stock Option Plan and Restricted Stock Agreements

The Company has elected to follow Accounting Principles Board Opinion No. 25 (APB 25), "Accounting for Stock Issued to Employees" and related interpretations in accounting for its employee stock options because, as discussed below, the alternative fair value accounting provided for under FASB Statement No. 123 (FASB 123), "Accounting for Stock-Based Compensation," requires the use of option valuation models that were not developed for use in valuing employee stock options. Under APB 25, because the exercise price of the Company's employee stock options equals the market price of the underlying stock on the date of grant, no compensation expense is recognized.

On February 10, 1994, the Company's Board of Directors adopted the American Eagle Outfitters, Inc. 1994 Stock Option Plan (the "Plan"). The Plan provides for the grant of 2,700,000 incentive or non-qualified options to purchase common stock. On June 3, 1996, the Plan was amended to provide for the grant of an additional 1,350,000 shares for which options may be granted under the Plan. On May 7, 1997, the Plan was further amended to provide for the grant of an additional 1,350,000 shares for which options may be granted under the Plan. Additionally, the amendment provided that the maximum number of options which may be granted to one individual may not exceed 1,800,000 shares. All full-time employees and selected related party consultants to the Company are eligible to receive options which are approved by a committee of the Board of Directors. These options primarily vest over five years and are exercisable for a ten-year period from the date of grant. Directors who are not officers or employees of the Company were previously granted options for 11,250 shares of stock annually at fair value, which vest one year after the date of grant. On September 11, 1996, the Plan was amended to grant 4,500 shares of stock at fair value to the members of the Board of Directors who are not officers or employees of the Company on the first trading day of each fiscal quarter of the Company which vest one year after the date of grant and are exercisable for a ten-year period from the date of grant. This provision became effective for the third quarter of Fiscal 1996.

Pro forma information regarding net income and earnings per share is required by FASB 123, which also requires that the information be determined as if the Company has accounted for its employee stock options granted beginning in the fiscal year subsequent to December 31, 1994 under the fair value method of that Statement. The fair value for these options was estimated at the date of grant using a Black-Scholes option pricing model with the following weighted-average assumptions for Fiscal 1998: risk-free interest rates of 5%; no dividend yield; volatility factors of the expected market price of the Company's common stock of .678; weighted -average expected life of the option of 6 years; and an expected forfeiture rate of approximately 12%. The assumptions for Fiscal 1997 included risk-free interest rates of 6%; no dividend yield; volatility factors of the expected market price of the Company's common stock of .644; weighted-average expected life of the option of 6 years; and an expected forfeiture rate of approximately 13%. The assumptions for Fiscal 1996 included risk-free interest rates of 5%; no dividend yield; volatility factors of the expected market price of the Company's common stock of .7384; weighted-average expected life of the option of 5 years; and an expected forfeiture rate of approximately 15%.

The Black-Scholes option valuation model was developed for use in estimating the fair value of traded options which have no vesting restrictions and are fully transferable. In addition, option valuation models require the input of highly subjective assumptions including the expected stock price volatility. Because the Company's employee stock options have characteristics significantly different from those of traded options, and because changes in the subjective input assumptions can materially affect the fair value estimate, in management's opinion, the existing models do not necessarily provide a reliable single measure of the fair value of its employee stock options.

For purposes of pro forma disclosures, the estimated fair value of the options is amortized to expense over the options' vesting period. The Company's pro forma information follows:

| (In thousands, except earnings per share) | January 30, 1999 | January 31, 1998 | February 1, 1997 |
|---|---|---|---|
| Pro forma net income | $52,467 | $19,060 | $5,354 |
| Pro forma net income per share | | | |
| Basic | $1.16 | $0.43 | $0.12 |
| Diluted | $1.09 | $0.42 | $0.12 |

A summary of the Company's stock option activity follows:

| | **For the Years Ended** | | | | | |
| | January 30, 1999 (2) | | January 31, 1998 (2) | | February 1, 1997 (2) | |
| | Options | Weighted-Average Exercise Price | Options | Weighted-Average Exercise Price | Options | Weighted-Average Exercise Price |
|---|---|---|---|---|---|---|
| Outstanding – beginning of year | 3,356,238 | $2.11 | 2,843,552 | $1.98 | 1,601,774 | $2.94 |
| Granted (Exercise Price equal to Fair Value) | 1,236,152 | $11.16 | 1,035,000 | $2.63 | 2,132,776 | $2.12 |
| Granted (Exercise Price less than Fair Value) | — | — | — | — | 526,500 | $1.50 |
| Exercised (1) | (950,606) | $1.88 | (442,214) | $2.21 | (193,274) | $1.58 |
| Cancelled | (115,354) | $6.19 | (80,100) | $2.27 | (1,224,224) | $3.33 |
| Outstanding – end of year (3) | 3,526,430 | $5.21 | 3,356,238 | $2.11 | 2,843,552 | $1.98 |
| Exercisable – end of year (4) | 553,224 | $2.37 | 664,424 | $1.63 | 474,434 | $1.72 |
| Weighted average fair value of options granted during the year | | $6.91 | | $1.46 | | $1.66 |

(1) Options exercised during Fiscal 1998 ranged in price from $1.39 - $6.45 with an average of $1.88.

(2) As of January 30, 1999, January 31, 1998 and February 1, 1997, the Company had 287,472 shares, 1,408,276 shares and 1,013,174 shares available for grant, respectively.

(3) As of January 30, 1999, the exercise price of 1,996,178 options outstanding ranged between $1.39 and $2.78 with weighted average remaining contractual lives between approximately 7 and 8 years. The exercise price of 1,232,252 options outstanding ranged between $3.84 and $8.92 with weighted average remaining contractual lives between approximately 7 and 9 years.

(4) As of January 30, 1999, the exercise price of 517,924 options exercisable ranged between $1.39 and $3.88.

The Company maintains a restricted stock plan for compensating certain employees and selected related party consultants. At January 30, 1999, 1,256,938 shares of restricted stock were outstanding at grant prices ranging from $3.56 to $24.92, with 906,150 shares vested. During Fiscal 1998, 128,000 shares of restricted stock were granted ranging in price from $8.92 to $24.92.

For Fiscal 1998, Fiscal 1997, and Fiscal 1996, the Company recorded $1,336,156, $1,214,167, and $990,050 in compensation expense, respectively, on restricted stock and certain stock options granted during Fiscal 1996 where the exercise price is less than fair value of the underlying stock, and certain options granted to non-employees. Assuming no acceleration of vesting, the Company will record $1,401,172 per year in compensation expense during the remaining vesting periods.

## 11. Quarterly Financial Information – Unaudited

*(In thousands, except earnings per share)* — **Quarters Ended**

| | May 2, 1998 | August 1, 1998 | October 31, 1998 | January 30, 1999 |
|---|---|---|---|---|
| Net sales | $99,694 | $125,731 | $149,068 | $213,107 |
| Gross profit | 37,217 | 49,063 | 60,420 | 87,811 |
| Income before provision for income taxes | 9,561 | 15,738 | 22,685 | 41,505 |
| Net income | 5,805 | 9,553 | 13,871 | 24,889 |
| Basic earnings per common share (1) | $0.13 | $0.21 | $0.31 | $0.55 |
| Diluted earnings per common share (1) | $0.12 | $0.20 | $0.29 | $0.52 |

| | May 3, 1997 | August 2, 1997 | November 1, 1997 | January 31, 1998 |
|---|---|---|---|---|
| Net sales | $60,952 | $86,159 | $104,902 | $153,700 |
| Gross profit | 14,253 | 25,053 | 38,654 | 59,007 |
| Income (loss) before provision for income taxes | (5,996) | 1,878 | 10,339 | 26,057 |
| Net income (loss) | (3,619) | 1,120 | 6,276 | 15,760 |
| Basic earnings (loss) per common share (1) | ($0.08) | $0.03 | $0.14 | $0.35 |
| Diluted earnings (loss) per common share (1) | ($0.08) | $0.02 | $0.14 | $0.34 |

(1) Per share amounts have been restated to reflect the adoption of FASB 128, the three-for-two stock splits, and the two-for-one split.

## 12. Subsequent Events

On March 17, 1999, the Company's Board of Directors approved a two-for-one stock split to be distributed on May 3, 1999, to stockholders of record on April 23, 1999. All share amounts and per share data have been restated to reflect this stock split.

The Natco merger discussed in Note 3 was approved by the stockholders on March 29, 1999, and became effective on April 7, 1999. In connection with the merger, the Company increased its authorized shares of common stock to 125,000,000 and authorized 5,000,000 shares of preferred stock. These shares have $.01 par value.

## Market Price Information

Our stock is traded on The Nasdaq National Market under the symbol "AEOS." The following table sets forth the high and low sales prices of the common stock as reported on The Nasdaq National Market during the periods indicated. As of March 1, 1999, there were 110 stockholders of record. The following information reflects the January 1998, May 1998, and May 1999 stock splits.

| For the Quarters Ended | Market Price | |
| --- | --- | --- |
| | High | Low |
| April 1997 | $2.78 | $1.81 |
| July 1997 | $3.72 | $2.24 |
| October 1997 | $6.45 | $3.45 |
| January 1998 | $8.98 | $6.56 |
| April 1998 | $20.79 | $7.75 |
| July 1998 | $26.75 | $16.57 |
| October 1998 | $27.31 | $14.13 |
| January 1999 | $34.19 | $21.88 |

We have never paid cash dividends and presently anticipate that all of our future earnings will be retained for the development of our business and do not anticipate paying cash dividends in the foreseeable future.

The payment of any future dividends will be at the discretion of our Board of Directors and will be based on future earnings, financial condition, capital requirements and other relevant factors.

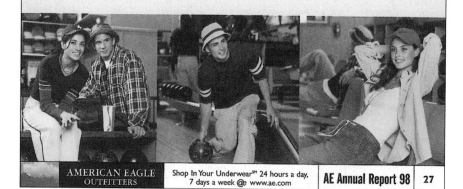

AMERICAN EAGLE OUTFITTERS    Shop In Your Underwear℠ 24 hours a day, 7 days a week @ www.ae.com    **AE Annual Report 98**    27

## Management Responsibility for Financial Reporting

The integrity and objectivity of the financial statements and related financial information in this report are the responsibility of the management of the Company. The financial statements have been prepared in conformity with generally accepted accounting principles and include, when necessary, the best estimates and judgements of management.

We maintain a system of internal accounting controls designed to provide reasonable assurance, at appropriate cost, that assets are safeguarded, transactions are executed in accordance with our authorization, and the accounting records provide a reliable basis for the preparation of the financial statements. The system of internal accounting controls is continually reviewed by management and improved and modified as necessary in response to changing business conditions and recommendations of the Company's independent auditors.

The Audit Committee of the Board of Directors, consisting of outside directors, meets periodically with management and independent auditors to review matters relating to our financial reporting, the adequacy of internal accounting controls and the scope and results of audit work.

Ernst & Young LLP, Certified Public Accountants, are engaged to audit our consolidated financial statements. Their Independent Auditors' Report, which is based on an audit made in accordance with generally accepted auditing standards, expresses an opinion as to the fair presentation of these financial statements.

## Report of Independent Auditors

To the Board of Directors and Stockholders
American Eagle Outfitters, Inc.

We have audited the accompanying consolidated balance sheets of American Eagle Outfitters, Inc. as of January 30, 1999, January 31, 1998 and February 1, 1997 and the related consolidated statements of operations, stockholders' equity, and cash flows for the years then ended. The financial statements are the responsibility of the Company's management. Our responsibility is to express an opinion on these financial statements based on our audits.

We conducted our audits in accordance with generally accepted auditing standards. Those standards require that we plan and perform the audit to obtain reasonable assurance about whether the financial statements are free of material misstatement. An audit includes examining, on a test basis, evidence supporting the amounts and disclosures in the financial statements. An audit also includes assessing the accounting principles used and significant estimates made by management, as well as evaluating the overall financial statement presentation. We believe that our audits provide a reasonable basis for our opinion.

In our opinion, the consolidated financial statements referred to above present fairly, in all material respects, the consolidated financial position of American Eagle Outfitters, Inc. at January 30, 1999, January 31, 1998 and February 1, 1997 and the consolidated results of its operations and its cash flows for the years then ended, in conformity with generally accepted accounting principles.

Ernst & Young LLP

Pittsburgh, Pennsylvania
February 26, 1999
except for Note 12, as to which the date is
April 7, 1999

## Directors and Officers

### Directors

Jay L. Schottenstein
Chairman of the Board and
Chief Executive Officer

Saul Schottenstein
Vice Chairman

George Kolber
Vice Chairman and
Chief Operating Officer

Roger S. Markfield
President and
Chief Merchandising Officer

Ari Deshe
Chairman and Chief Executive Officer of
Safe Auto Insurance Company

Jon P. Diamond
President and Chief Operating Officer of
Safe Auto Insurance Company

Martin P. Doolan
President and Chief Executive Officer of
Value City Department Stores, Inc.

Gilbert W. Harrison
Chairman of Financo, Inc.

### Directors

Michael G. Jesselson
President of Jesselson Capital Corporation

Thomas R. Ketteler
Vice President of Finance and Chief
Operating Officer of Schottenstein Stores
Corporation

John L. Marakas
Retired President of Nationwide
Corporation

David W. Thompson
President of Value City Furniture

Gerald E. Wedren
President of Craig Capital Co.

### Executive Officers

Jay L. Schottenstein
Chairman of the Board and
Chief Executive Officer

George Kolber
Vice Chairman and
Chief Operating Officer

Roger S. Markfield
President and
Chief Merchandising Officer

Laura A. Weil
Executive Vice President and
Chief Financial Officer

Joseph E. Kerin
Executive Vice President and
Director of Store Operations

Dale E. Clifton
Vice President, Controller, and
Chief Accounting Officer

William P. Tait
Vice President, Secretary and
Treasurer

### Corporate Officers

Steven Baum
Vice President – Director of Design

Michael E. Bergdahl
Vice President – Human Resources

Andrew M. Calogero
President – Prophecy Company

Michael J. Fostyk
Vice President – Distribution

Frederick W. Grover
Vice President – General Merchandising
Manager

Howard Landon
Vice President – Production
and Sourcing

Michael J. Leedy
Vice President – Marketing and
E–Commerce

Susan P. Miller
Vice President – General Merchandising
Manager

## Stockholder Information

We will supply to any stockholder, upon written request to Laura A. Weil, at our address, and without charge, a copy of the Report on Form 10-K for the period ended January 30, 1999, which has been filed with the Securities and Exchange Commission.

**Legal Counsel**
Porter, Wright, Morris & Arthur
41 South High Street
Columbus, OH 43215-6194

**Independent Auditors**
Ernst & Young LLP
One Oxford Centre
Pittsburgh, PA 15219-6403

**Registrar and Transfer Agent**
National City Bank
Stock Transfer Department
P.O. Box 92301
Cleveland, OH 44193-0900
(800) 622-6757

**Common Shares Listed**
NASDAQ Symbol: AEOS

**Investor Contact**
Laura A. Weil
Executive Vice President and Chief
Financial Officer
(724) 776-4857

**Headquarters of the Company**
150 Thorn Hill Drive
Warrendale, PA 15086-7528
(724) 776-4857

**For the nearest AE store**
call toll free 1-888-AEAGLE-5

**Check out the AE online store**
Shop In Your Underwear[SM]
@e www.ae.com

**To request a catalog,**
call toll free 1-888-232-4535

OVERVIEW
<URBAN OUTFITTERS>

# SELECTED FINANCIAL DATA

*(In thousands, except share and per share data)*

The following table sets forth selected consolidated income statement and balance sheet data for the periods indicated. The selected consolidated balance sheet and income statement data at the fiscal year end for each of the five fiscal years presented below are derived from the consolidated financial statements of the Company. The data presented below should be read in conjunction with the consolidated financial statements of the Company, including the related notes thereto, included elsewhere in this document.

| *Fiscal Year Ended January 31,* | 1999 | 1998 | 1997 | 1996 | 1995 |
|---|---|---|---|---|---|
| **Income Statement Data:** | | | | | |
| Net sales | $208,969 | $173,121 | $156,414 | $133,036 | $110,121 |
| Gross profit | 79,344 | 60,562 | 57,087 | 49,158 | 42,866 |
| Income from operations | 25,117 | 22,062 | 21,356 | 19,867 | 17,576 |
| Net income | $ 15,760 | $ 13,880 | $ 13,260 | $ 12,308 | $ 10,817 |
| Net income per common share | $ 0.89 | $ 0.79 | $ 0.76 | $ 0.72 | $ 0.64 |
| Weighted average common shares outstanding | 17,702,922 | 17,576,203 | 17,429,375 | 17,028,856 | 16,790,740 |
| Net income per common share— assuming dilution | $ 0.88 | $ 0.78 | $ 0.75 | $ 0.70 | $ 0.62 |
| Weighted average common shares outstanding— assuming dilution | 17,929,109 | 17,843,873 | 17,722,629 | 17,487,673 | 17,407,608 |
| **Balance Sheet Data:** | | | | | |
| Working capital | $ 47,527 | $ 52,133 | $39,239 | $36,487 | $26,872 |
| Total assets | 133,363 | 107,424 | 89,675 | 71,117 | 56,766 |
| Total liabilities | 28,069 | 16,766 | 13,983 | 11,665 | 10,015 |
| Long-term debt, excluding current maturities | — | — | — | — | — |
| Total shareholders' equity | 105,294 | 90,658 | 75,692 | 59,452 | 46,751 |

**99** |ₗᵤₗₗₗₗᵤₗₗₗᵤₗₗₗₗₗᵤₗₗₗᵤₗₗₗₗₗₗₗ
51270653001264634209¹ 5
**URBAN OUTFITTERS**
ᴄᴏᴅᴇ

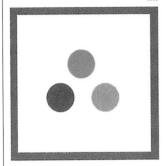

*Urban Outfitters, Inc.*  *is an international merchandising company with two retail divisions and one wholesale division.*

OVERVIEW
<URBAN OUTFITTERS>
# COMPANY PROFILE

*Urban Outfitters Retail* ● *offers lifestyle merchandise to an 18-30 year old customer. There are thirty-three Urban retail stores in major metropolitan areas across the United States, Canada, and the United Kingdom.*

*Anthropologie Retail* ● *provides an eclectic mix of home and soft goods to a 30-45 year old female customer. There are fourteen store locations across the United States plus a direct response catalog and website.*

*Urban Wholesale* ● *designs and sells women's apparel under three brand labels—Bulldog, Free People, and Co-op. These brands are sold to better retail stores throughout the United States, Canada and Japan.*

1999 Annual REPORT
<URBAN OUTFITTERS>

# CONTENTS—*EDITORIAL SECTIONS*

*The Annual Meeting of Shareholders will be held on
Tuesday, May 18, 1999, at 10:30 am at the National
Society of the Colonial Dames of America, 1630
Latimer Street, Philadelphia, PA.*

**1999 Annual REPORT**
**<URBAN OUTFITTERS, INC.>**

*Urban Outfitters, Inc.*  *Net sales have grown at a 20% compounded annual rate over the past 5 years. During that same time, shareholders' equity has increased 200%.*

# NET SALES **209**.0     SHAREHOLDERS' EQUITY **105**.3

| | | | | |
|---|---|---|---|---|
| 1999 | 209.0 | | 1999 | 105.3 |
| 1998 | 173.1 | | 1998 | 90.7 |
| 1997 | 156.4 | | 1997 | 75.7 |
| 1996 | 133.0 | | 1996 | 59.5 |
| 1995 | 110.1 | | 1995 | 46.8 |

(IN MILLIONS)                    (IN MILLIONS)

**SALES**

+20
%

**CAGR**

**EQUITY**

+24
%

**CAGR**

DIR. N°

OVERVIEW
<URBAN OUTFITTERS>

# SHAREHOLDERS' LETTER

**DEAR SHAREHOLDERS:**

*Last year I outlined the steps the Company would take over the next few years in order to help us produce faster top and bottom line growth. These steps included investing in the design, production and purchasing departments of both retail groups to achieve better comparable store sales, accelerating the rate of new store openings, launching new concepts such as the Anthropologie catalog and web site, and expanding existing concepts into new markets. I am pleased to report that we have made excellent progress in all of these areas and that the Company's growth rate has indeed accelerated.*

*For the fiscal year ending January 31, 1999, the Company's net sales increased by 21% over the prior year to a record $209 million. This compares favorably with the 11% revenue growth booked in Fiscal 1998. And net income, also a record at $15.8 million, rose 14% in Fiscal 1999 versus 5% the prior year. The yearly growth rates, however, tell only part of the story since the increase in rates of both revenue and profit growth on a quarterly basis reveal a steady sharp rise as Fiscal 1999 progressed. In the fourth quarter of Fiscal 1999 net sales were up 32% and net income was up 36% compared to the same period in Fiscal 1998. This positive momentum augurs well for Fiscal 2000.*

### Growth in the Retail Divisions

*Both retail divisions achieved banner results in Fiscal 1999 with revenue growth coming from new stores and greater productivity in existing ones. Comparable store sales, a measure of that productivity, advanced 11% in Fiscal 1999 after being flat the prior year. This resulted primarily from the considerable human and technological investments the Company made during the past two years in the design, production and purchasing departments.*

*The Company also successfully accelerated its rate of new store openings, more than doubling the number of stores opened in any prior fiscal year. Eleven new stores were opened during the year, bringing the total number of stores for Urban Retail to 32 and Anthropologie to 14. The increased rate of openings was made possible by staff additions in the development area. The Company intends to continue to open a similar number of new stores during the current fiscal year.*

### New Concepts

*The Company tested an Anthropologie catalog in the Spring of 1998. Based on the success of that test, the business was launched during the second half of the year. For both the Fall and Holiday books, customer demand, based upon order dollars per catalog mailed, exceeded plan considerably. The Company believes that the catalog investment, which significantly reduced earnings per share in Fiscal 1999, should generate a direct monetary return in the near future and produce an ongoing secondary benefit of increasing in-store sales through heightened brand awareness. During the current fiscal year, circulation of the Anthropologie catalog will more than double to approximately eight million.*

*Anthropologie.com was set up in August 1998 to handle catalog requests. Then, in response to customer demand, the site began accepting merchandise orders in December. Site hits and orders continue to be well above planned levels and, as a result the Company intends to invest additional amounts in e-commerce during the current fiscal year.*

### New Markets

In June 1998, Urban Outfitters opened its first retail store in Europe. The 16,000 square foot shop on Kensington High Street in London was an immediate success, attracting both Londoners and tourists into its cavernous multi-level environment. In addition to offering the product categories carried in the U.S. Urban Retail stores, the London shop also houses a café and music center. Ranked by sales, the London store is consistently one of the best in the Urban Retail group. Lease negotiations are currently underway to open more outlets in the British Isles.

### Wholesale Division

The Wholesale division had a very difficult year in Fiscal 1999. Several large customers decreased their orders significantly, and there were also some quality and delivery problems in the Spring offering. As a result, net sales slowed by a third from the previous year. In response, the design and production staffs were reorganized and enlarged and the brands were repositioned to achieve a tighter and more focused offering. These changes have worked. Customer response to the new lines has been very positive, and the quality and delivery problems have been significantly diminished. Sales for the current year are projected to increase slightly.

### Conclusion

Last year I proposed a very ambitious plan to accelerate the Company's growth. We succeeded in implementing all of the components of that plan: increasing comparable store sales, significantly raising the rate of new store openings, launching a direct response business, and successfully expanding our Urban Retail concept into Europe. Accomplishing any one of these objectives would be noteworthy; achieving all four is exceptional and I thank all of our dedicated employees for their considerable efforts in realizing those goals.

The cornerstone for growth is now firmly established; the current year will be dedicated to maintaining and building upon that foundation. We will endeavor to sustain positive comparable store sales and the increased number of store openings. We plan to expand the customer catalog database and continue to invest in electronic commerce and other new-media opportunities. We will continue to rebuild the wholesale business, with a view toward focused branding.

I am confident that the resources are in place to make this strategic vision a tactical plan. Our sound capital base, our solid corporate infrastructure, and our extraordinary people convince me that Fiscal Year 2000 will be a very successful year for the Company and the shareholders.

*Richard A. Hayne*

Richard A. Hayne
March 19, 1999

URBAN OUTFITTERS
CODE

1999 *Annual* REPORT
<URBAN OUTFITTERS>

# MANAGEMENT'S DISCUSSION AND ANALYSIS
# OF FINANCIAL CONDITION AND RESULTS OF OPERATIONS

The following discussion of the Company's historical results of operations and of its liquidity and capital resources should be read in conjunction with the selected financial data and the consolidated financial statements of the Company and related notes thereto appearing elsewhere in this Annual Report.

### GENERAL
The Company's fiscal year ends on January 31. All references in this discussion to fiscal years of the Company refer to the fiscal years ended on January 31 in those years. For example, the Company's 1999 Fiscal year ended on January 31, 1999. The comparable store net sales data presented in this discussion are calculated based on the net sales of all stores open at least twelve full months at the beginning of the period for which such data is presented.

The Company operates two business segments—a lifestyle-oriented general merchandise retailing segment and a wholesale apparel business ("Wholesale"). The retailing segment operates through retail stores and through direct response, including a catalog and a website. The two retail concepts are Urban Outfitters ("Urban Retail") and Anthropologie. Urban Retail is the larger of the two and generates most of the Company's revenues and profits. Urban Retail had 32 stores open at January 31, 1999 and 26 at January 31, 1998. The Company's first Anthropologie store opened in October 1992. Anthropologie had 14 stores open at January 31, 1999 and 9 at January 31, 1998. The Company has plans to open six Urban Retail stores and five Anthropologie stores in Fiscal 2000. An Anthropologie catalog was tested in the first half of Fiscal 1999 and, based upon the success of the test, was launched during the second half of the year. To support the catalog, a website was established in August 1998. In response to

customer requests, the site began accepting orders in December 1998. The direct response operation incurred a loss for the year, and management expects the catalog and the Company's "e-commerce" efforts to also incur a loss for Fiscal 2000.

Fiscal 1999 and 1998 continued as profitable years for Urban Outfitters with earnings to net sales of 7.6% and 8.0%, respectively, as well as return on beginning shareholders' equity of 17.4% and 18.3%, respectively. The slight contraction of earnings as a percent of sales in Fiscal 1999 and the reduction in return on shareholders' equity in that year resulted primarily from the start-up costs of the catalog effort and the 35% decrease in sales by Wholesale to unrelated entities. The Wholesale company had recorded sales growth of 8% in Fiscal 1998. The Wholesale company is anticipated to grow at a modest rate in Fiscal 2000.

The Company previously established a European subsidiary—Urban Outfitters (U.K.) Ltd.—and opened its first Urban Retail store in London in June 1998. The success of the London store opening enabled the subsidiary to make a small profit during Fiscal 1999.

### RESULTS OF OPERATIONS
The following tables set forth, for the periods indicated, the percentage of the Company's net sales represented by certain income statement data and the growth of certain income statement data from period to period. The Company has revised its manner of reporting gross profit to group certain buying, distribution and occupancy costs with cost of goods sold in order to enhance the comparability of its results with other specialty apparel retailers. Prior period amounts have been reclassified to conform to the current year's presentation.

1999 Annual REPORT
<URBAN OUTFITTERS>

# MANAGEMENT'S DISCUSSION AND ANALYSIS

*(continued)*

| Fiscal Year Ended January 31, | 1999 | 1998 | 1997 |
|---|---|---|---|
| **As a Percentage of Net Sales** | | | |
| Net sales .............................. | 100.0% | 100.0% | 100.0% |
| Cost of goods sold, including certain buying, distribution and occupancy costs ........ | 62.0 | 65.0 | 63.5 |
| Gross profit ...................... | 38.0 | 35.0 | 36.5 |
| Selling, general and administrative expenses ... | 26.0 | 22.3 | 22.8 |
| Income from operations ... | 12.0 | 12.7 | 13.7 |
| Net interest and other expenses (income) .......... | (0.8) | (1.0) | (0.8) |
| Income before income taxes ................ | 12.8 | 13.7 | 14.5 |
| Income tax expense ............. | 5.2 | 5.7 | 6.0 |
| Net income ...................... | 7.6% | 8.0% | 8.5% |
| **Period over Period Dollar Growth** | | | |
| Net sales .............................. | 20.7% | 10.7% | 17.6% |
| Gross profit .......................... | 31.0% | 6.1% | 16.1% |
| Income from operations ........ | 13.8% | 3.3% | 7.5% |
| Net income .......................... | 13.5% | 4.7% | 7.7% |

## FISCAL 1999 COMPARED TO FISCAL 1998

Net sales in Fiscal 1999 increased to $209.0 million from $173.1 million in the prior fiscal year, a 20.7% increase. The $35.9 million increase was attributable to a combination of comparable store net sales increases of $15.1 million, net sales increases of $25.6 million from stores opened during Fiscal 1998 and Fiscal 1999, and catalog and e-commerce revenues of $5.7 million, offset in part by a decrease of $10.5 million from the Wholesale company.

In Fiscal 1999, increases in the number of transactions in comparable stores and an increase in average sales prices resulting from the lower proportion of markdowns accounted for the comparable store sales dollar increase. Eleven new stores were opened in Fiscal 1999 and three new stores were opened in Fiscal 1998. The Wholesale sales decrease reflected lower purchases by larger retail chains, as well as customer issues regarding quality, delivery and fashion which have been addressed by management.

Gross profit margins increased to 38.0% of sales in Fiscal 1999 from 35.0% of sales in Fiscal 1998. This increase is attributable to higher initial mark-ups and lower markdown percentages in the Urban Retail and Anthropologie stores. Comparable store sales increases in existing stores offset the higher occupancy costs of noncomparable and new stores. Reduced sales in the Wholesale segment necessitated an increased proportion of merchandise to be sold in the "off-price" sector, offsetting in part, the higher retail segment performance.

Selling, general and administrative expenses increased to 26.0% of sales in Fiscal 1999 from 22.3% of sales in Fiscal 1998 due to the costs incurred for the start-up of the catalog and European operations as well as the substantial negative leverage associated with the decline in Wholesale segment sales. The increase in dollars in selling, general and administrative expenses is attributable to the opening of additional stores as well as the catalog start-up.

URBN

1999 Annual REPORT
<URBAN OUTFITTERS>

# MANAGEMENT'S DISCUSSION AND ANALYSIS

*(continued)*

### FISCAL 1998 COMPARED TO FISCAL 1997

Net sales in Fiscal 1998 increased to $173.1 million from $156.4 million in the prior fiscal year, a 10.7% increase. The $16.7 million increase was attributable to a combination of comparable store net sales decreases of $1.6 million, net sales increases of $16.1 million from stores opened or enlarged during Fiscal 1997 and Fiscal 1998 and net sales increases of $2.2 million from the Wholesale company.

The decrease in comparable store sales of 1% or $1.6 million resulted primarily from one merchandise division that did not perform to prior year levels. Average selling prices were not a significant determinant of Fiscal 1998 sales levels. New and enlarged stores included seven stores opened in Fiscal 1997 and three opened in Fiscal 1998. The Company believes increased net sales from the Wholesale subsidiary during Fiscal 1997 and Fiscal 1998 were attributable to increased orders and order size due to the popularity of its product lines.

The Company's gross profit margin declined from 36.5% in Fiscal 1997 to 35.0% in Fiscal 1998 due to higher cost of goods sold and higher occupancy costs. The primary contributor to the cost of goods sold increase was higher markdowns in the retail segment. Markdowns were triggered by lower than planned comparable store sales. Occupancy costs as a percentage of sales increased due to the impact of new stores and the comparable store sales decline.

Selling, general and administrative expenses grew to $38.5 million in Fiscal 1998 from $35.7 million in the prior fiscal year, a 7.7% increase. As a percentage of net sales, selling, general and administrative costs decreased from 22.8% of sales in Fiscal 1997 to 22.3% of sales in Fiscal 1998. The increase in dollars is due to the opening of new stores during Fiscal 1997 and Fiscal 1998. The decrease in such expenses as a percentage of sales was attributable to cost containment measures at store level.

### LIQUIDITY AND CAPITAL RESOURCES

During the last three years, the Company has satisfied its cash requirements through cash flow from operations. The Company's primary uses of cash have been to open new stores and purchase inventories. Most recently, the Company invested in the Anthropologie direct response effort and in a new European subsidiary. An investment has also been made in a direct response company aimed at teen shoppers (see "HMB Publishing" below). In addition to cash generated from operations, sources of cash have included the net proceeds from the exercise of certain employee stock options in each of Fiscal 1999, 1998 and 1997. Over the next few years, the Company expects to incur capital expenditures in support of its expansion program. Accumulated cash and future cash from operations are expected to fund such expansion-related uses of cash, including additional investments in the direct response operations.

Although the Company has not borrowed short-term or long-term funds during the last five fiscal years, it maintains a line of credit of $16.2 million, all of which is available for cash borrowings or for the issuance of letters of credit. The line is unsecured and any cash borrowings under the line would accrue interest upon an as-offered basis not to exceed LIBOR plus ½ of 1 percent. The Company uses letters of credit primarily to purchase private label and Wholesale merchandise from offshore suppliers. Outstanding balances of letters of credit at January 31, 1999 and 1998 were $4.1 million and $4.7 million, respectively. There were no short-term or long-term borrowings outstanding at January 31, 1999 or at January 31, 1998. The Company expects that accumulated cash and cash from operations will be sufficient to meet the Company's cash needs for at least the next three years.

1999 Annual REPORT
<URBAN OUTFITTERS>

# MANAGEMENT'S DISCUSSION AND ANALYSIS
*(continued)*

### OTHER MATTERS

**Year 2000**  The Year 2000 problem concerns the inability of information and technology–based operating systems to function properly after December 31, 1999. This could result in system failures and miscalculations which may cause business disruptions.

The Company does not generally sell products that must be brought into Year 2000 compliance. However, the Company does rely upon many vendors and suppliers for their products and services, as well as utilities, financial institutions and governmental entities that provide critical services to the Company and to its customers. The Company has conducted a comprehensive review of its computer systems to identify the systems that could be affected by the Year 2000 issue. Based on the review, the Company's major information technology systems ("IT") that would be adversely affected by Year 2000 dates will be upgraded or replaced through the normal course of business prior to December 31, 1999. Internal resources will be used in a timely manner to evaluate, modify and test the Company's less critical systems that are not scheduled to be upgraded or replaced through the normal course of business. The Company's core merchandising and financial system upgrades and the store register system upgrades have been completed; testing of these upgrades is substantially complete. In addition, the Company is in the process of completing the inventory and assessment of its non-information technology systems ("non-IT"), including those with embedded processor chips—heating, ventilation and air conditioning systems, elevators, etc.

The Company has also reviewed and continues to monitor the implemented changes or planned changes of its major suppliers that management believes could be affected by Year 2000 dates. The Company is evaluating key vendor preparedness by conducting interviews, obtaining compliance representation letters and, if deemed necessary, conducting comprehensive tests.

The Company expects to complete its Year 2000 compliance evaluation program by June 30, 1999. At this time, management continues to believe that the incremental costs associated with major system upgrades and/or replacements, as well as internal efforts to evaluate, modify and test the Company's other systems to ensure Year 2000 compliance will not be material to the Company.

There can be no guarantee, however, that the Company's efforts will prevent Year 2000 issues from having a material adverse impact on its results of operations, financial condition and cash flows. The possible consequences to the Company if its vendors and suppliers are not fully Year 2000 compliant (including the global banking systems, communications and other public utilities and the transportation industry) include temporary store closings and delays in the receipt of key merchandise. Accordingly, the Company is in the process of developing contingency plans to mitigate the potential disruptions that may result from the Year 2000 issue. Such plans may include earlier receipt of key merchandise, preparing alternative merchandise delivery methodologies and securing alternative suppliers. It is anticipated that these contingency plans to manage identified IT and non-IT areas of high risk will be completed by June 30, 1999. There can be no guarantee, however, that any contingency plans developed by the Company will prevent such material adverse effects.

1999 Annual REPORT
<URBAN OUTFITTERS>

# MANAGEMENT'S DISCUSSION AND ANALYSIS

(continued)

**Recent Accounting Pronouncements** In June 1998, the Financial Accounting Standards Board issued Statement of Financial Accounting Standards No. 133, "Accounting for Derivative Instruments and Hedging Activities" ("SFAS No. 133") which is required to be adopted in fiscal years beginning after June 15, 1999. The Company plans to adopt SFAS No. 133 effective February 1, 2000. The Company currently enters into short-term foreign currency forward exchange contracts to manage exposures related to its Canadian dollar denominated investments and anticipated cash flow. The amounts of the contracts and related gains and losses have not been material. The adoption of SFAS No. 133 is not expected to have a significant effect on the financial position or results of operations of the Company.

**Market Risks** The Company is exposed to the following types of market risks – fluctuations in the purchase price of merchandise, as well as other goods and services; the value of foreign currencies in relation to the U.S. dollar; and changes in interest rates. Due to the Company's inventory turn and its historical ability to pass through the impact of any generalized changes in its cost of goods to its customers through pricing adjustments, commodity and other product risks are not expected to be material. The Company purchases substantially all its merchandise in U.S. dollars, including a portion of the goods for its stores located in Canada and the United Kingdom. As explained in the section above on "Recent Accounting Pronouncements," the market risk is further limited by the Company's purchase of foreign currency forward exchange contracts.

Since the Company has not been a borrower, its exposure to interest rate fluctuations is limited to the impact on its marketable securities portfolio. This exposure is minimized by the limited investment maturities and "put" options available to the Company as explained in the notes to the financial statements appearing elsewhere in this report. The impact of a hypothetical two percent increase or decrease in prevailing interest rates would not materially affect the Company's consolidated financial position or results of operations.

**HMB Publishing, Inc.** On February 5, 1998 the Company entered into an agreement with HMB Publishing, Inc. ("HMB") for the purchase of securities convertible into a minority interest in the company through Series B Convertible Preferred Stock ("Series B Preferred") and certain convertible debentures. The agreement called for additional investments and ownership if HMB met certain performance milestones. HMB is a development stage company that publishes *mXg*™, a combination magazine and catalog and operates a website—www.mXgonline.com—that caters to teenage girls. The original business plan contemplated substantial losses in the first two fiscal years.

As of January 31, 1999, the Company has invested approximately $2.0 million in the Series B Preferred and an additional $1.75 million in the convertible debentures. Since January 31, 1999, the Company has advanced an additional $1.1 million to fund further marketing efforts and additional development of the website and, together with additional investors, will seek to position HMB for more rapid expansion. The Company expects to realize a return on its investment, and it is the Company's intent to maintain an equity interest following any public offering by HMB.

**Subsequent Event** In accordance with its previously announced stock buyback program that authorized the Company to repurchase up to 800,000 of its shares, the Company has repurchased 279,000 shares of its common stock at a cost of $3.7 million during the period from February 1, 1999 through March 12, 1999 in a series of individual open market transactions.

Our discussions in this and other sections of this Annual Report contain "forward-looking statements" that are based upon our best estimate of the trends we know about or anticipate. Actual results may be different from our estimates. We have described the factors that could change these forward-looking statements in our 1999 Annual Report on Form 10-K.

1999 Annual REPORT
<URBAN OUTFITTERS>

# MANAGEMENT'S DISCUSSION AND ANALYSIS

*(continued)*

### SEASONALITY AND QUARTERLY RESULTS

While Urban Outfitters has been profitable in each of its last 36 operating quarters, its operating results are subject to seasonal fluctuations. The Company's highest sales levels have historically occurred during the five-month period from August 1 to December 31 of each year (the "Back-to-School" and Holiday periods). Sales generated during these periods have traditionally had a significant impact on the Company's results of operations. Any decreases in sales for these periods or in the availability of working capital needed in the months preceding these periods could have a material adverse effect on the Company's results of operations. The Company's results of operations in any one fiscal quarter are not necessarily indicative of the results of operations that can be expected for any other fiscal quarter or for the full fiscal year.

The Company's results of operations may also fluctuate from quarter to quarter as a result of the amount and timing of expenses incurred in connection with, and sales contributed by, new stores, store expansions and the integration of new stores into the operations of the Company or by the size and timing of mailings of the Company's Anthropologie catalog. Fluctuations in the bookings and shipments of the Wholesale products between quarters can also have positive or negative effects on earnings during the quarters.

The following tables, which are unaudited, set forth the Company's net sales, gross profit, net income and income per share for each quarter during the last three fiscal years and the amount of such net sales and net income, respectively, as a percentage of annual net sales and annual net income. The Company has revised its manner of reporting gross profit to group certain buying, distribution and occupancy costs with cost of goods sold in order to enhance the comparability of its results with other specialty apparel retailers. Prior period amounts have been reclassified to conform to the current year's presentation.

URBN

1999 Annual REPORT
<URBAN OUTFITTERS>

# MANAGEMENT'S DISCUSSION AND ANALYSIS

*(continued) (Dollars in thousands, except per share data)*

### SEASONALITY AND QUARTERLY RESULTS (CONTINUED)

| Fiscal 1997 Quarter Ended | April 30, 1996 | July 31, 1996 | Oct. 31, 1996 | Jan. 31, 1997 |
|---|---|---|---|---|
| Net sales | $33,635 | $35,898 | $44,884 | $41,997 |
| Gross profit | 12,235 | 13,368 | 16,809 | 14,675 |
| Net income | 2,927 | 2,849 | 4,632 | 2,852 |
| Net income per share—assuming dilution | $ 0.17 | $ 0.16 | $ 0.26 | $ 0.16 |
| As a Percentage of Fiscal Year: | | | | |
| Net sales | 21% | 23% | 29% | 27% |
| Net income | 22% | 21% | 35% | 22% |

| Fiscal 1998 Quarter Ended | April 30, 1997 | July 31, 1997 | Oct. 31, 1997 | Jan. 31, 1998 |
|---|---|---|---|---|
| Net sales | $37,197 | $41,316 | $48,373 | $46,235 |
| Gross profit | 12,674 | 14,091 | 17,575 | 16,222 |
| Net income | 2,423 | 2,855 | 4,783 | 3,819 |
| Net income per share—assuming dilution | $ 0.14 | $ 0.16 | $ 0.27 | $ 0.21 |
| As a Percentage of Fiscal Year: | | | | |
| Net sales | 21% | 24% | 28% | 27% |
| Net income | 17% | 21% | 34% | 28% |

| Fiscal 1999 Quarter Ended | April 30, 1998 | July 31, 1998 | Oct. 31, 1998 | Jan. 31, 1999 |
|---|---|---|---|---|
| Net sales | $39,384 | $48,068 | $60,462 | $61,055 |
| Gross profit | 13,974 | 17,758 | 23,520 | 24,092 |
| Net income | 2,100 | 3,440 | 5,035 | 5,185 |
| Net income per share—assuming dilution | $ 0.12 | $ 0.19 | $ 0.28 | $ 0.29 |
| As a Percentage of Fiscal Year: | | | | |
| Net sales | 19% | 23% | 29% | 29% |
| Net income | 13% | 22% | 32% | 33% |

# CONSOLIDATED STATEMENTS OF INCOME

*(in thousands, except share and per share data)*

| Fiscal Year Ended January 31, | 1999 | 1998 | 1997 |
|---|---|---|---|
| Net sales | $208,969 | $173,121 | $156,414 |
| Cost of sales, including certain buying, distribution and occupancy costs | 129,625 | 112,559 | 99,327 |
| Gross profit | 79,344 | 60,562 | 57,087 |
| Selling, general and administrative expenses | 54,227 | 38,500 | 35,731 |
| Income from operations | 25,117 | 22,062 | 21,356 |
| Interest income | 2,126 | 1,772 | 1,506 |
| Other expenses, net | (531) | (209) | (193) |
| Income before income taxes | 26,712 | 23,625 | 22,669 |
| Income tax expense | 10,952 | 9,745 | 9,409 |
| Net income | $ 15,760 | $ 13,880 | $ 13,260 |
| Net income per common share: | | | |
| Basic | $ 0.89 | $ 0.79 | $ 0.76 |
| Diluted | $ 0.88 | $ 0.78 | $ 0.75 |
| Weighted average common shares outstanding: | | | |
| Basic | 17,702,922 | 17,576,203 | 17,429,375 |
| Diluted | 17,929,109 | 17,843,873 | 17,722,629 |

*See accompanying notes.*

URBN

1999 Annual REPORT
<URBAN OUTFITTERS>

# CONSOLIDATED BALANCE SHEETS

*(in thousands, except share and per share data)*

| January 31, | 1999 | 1998 |
|---|---|---|
| **Assets** | | |
| Current assets: | | |
| Cash and cash equivalents | $ 25,165 | $ 26,712 |
| Marketable securities *investment* | 13,032 | 10,865 |
| Accounts receivable, net of allowance for doubtful accounts of $603 and $616 at January 31, 1999 and 1998, respectively | 4,824 | 4,497 |
| Inventory | 21,881 | 17,128 |
| Prepaid expenses and other current assets | 4,729 | 4,662 |
| Deferred taxes | 1,924 | 1,929 |
| Total current assets | 71,555 | 65,793 |
| Property and equipment, less accumulated depreciation and amortization | 43,066 | 26,893 |
| Marketable securities *investment* | 12,218 | 11,993 |
| Other assets | 6,524 | 2,745 |
| | $133,363 | $107,424 |
| **Liabilities and Shareholders' Equity** | | |
| Current liabilities: | | |
| Trade accounts payable | $ 14,763 | $ 10,386 |
| Income taxes payable | 1,300 | 366 |
| Current portion of capital lease obligations | 88 | — |
| Accrued compensation | 2,011 | 1,024 |
| Accrued expenses and other current liabilities | 5,866 | 1,884 |
| Total current liabilities | 24,028 | 13,660 |
| Capital lease obligations, net of current portion | 185 | — |
| Accrued rent and other liabilities | 3,856 | 3,106 |
| Total liabilities | 28,069 | 16,766 |
| Commitments and contingencies | | |
| Shareholders' equity: | | |
| Preferred shares; $.0001 par, 10,000,000 authorized, none issued | — | — |
| Common shares; $.0001 par, 50,000,000 shares authorized, 17,639,754 and 17,649,360 issued at January 31, 1999 and 1998, respectively | 2 | 2 |
| Additional paid-in capital | 20,825 | 21,482 |
| Retained earnings | 84,934 | 69,174 |
| Accumulated other comprehensive income (loss) | (467) | — |
| Total shareholders' equity | 105,294 | 90,658 |
| | $133,363 | $107,424 |

*See accompanying notes.*

1999 Annual REPORT
<URBAN OUTFITTERS>

# CONSOLIDATED STATEMENTS OF SHAREHOLDERS' EQUITY

*(in thousands; except share data)*

| | Comprehensive Income (Loss) | Common Shares Number of Shares | Par Value | Additional Paid-in Capital | Retained Earnings | Accumulated Other Comprehensive Income (Loss) | Total |
|---|---|---|---|---|---|---|---|
| Balances at January 31, 1996 | | 17,080,372 | $ 1 | $17,417 | $42,034 | $ — | $ 59,452 |
| Net income | $13,260 | — | — | — | 13,260 | — | 13,260 |
| Foreign currency translation | — | — | — | — | — | — | — |
| Comprehensive income | $13,260 | | | | | | |
| Exercise of stock options | | 448,326 | — | 806 | — | — | 806 |
| Tax effect of exercises | | — | — | 2,173 | — | — | 2,173 |
| Effect of stock split | | — | 1 | — | — | — | 1 |
| Balances at January 31, 1997 | | 17,528,698 | 2 | 20,396 | 55,294 | — | 75,692 |
| Net income | $13,880 | — | — | — | 13,880 | — | 13,880 |
| Foreign currency translation | — | — | — | — | — | — | — |
| Comprehensive income | $13,880 | | | | | | |
| Exercise of stock options | | 120,662 | — | 558 | — | — | 558 |
| Tax effect of exercises | | — | — | 528 | — | — | 528 |
| Balances at January 31, 1998 | | 17,649,360 | 2 | 21,482 | 69,174 | — | 90,658 |
| Net income | $15,760 | — | — | — | 15,760 | — | 15,760 |
| Foreign currency translation | (467) | — | — | — | — | (467) | (467) |
| Comprehensive income | $15,293 | | | | | | |
| Exercise of stock options | | 157,594 | — | 688 | — | — | 688 |
| Tax effect of exercises | | — | — | 909 | — | — | 909 |
| Purchase and retirement of common shares | | (167,200) | — | (2,254) | — | — | (2,254) |
| Balances at January 31, 1999 | | 17,639,754 | $ 2 | $20,825 | $84,934 | $(467) | $105,294 |

*See accompanying notes.*

1999 Annual REPORT
<URBAN OUTFITTERS>

# CONSOLIDATED STATEMENTS OF CASH FLOWS

*(in thousands)*

| *Fiscal Year Ended January 31,* | 1999 | 1998 | 1997 |
|---|---|---|---|
| **Cash flows from operating activities:** | | | |
| Net income | $ 15,760 | $ 13,880 | $ 13,260 |
| Adjustments to reconcile net income to net cash provided by operating activities: | | | |
| Depreciation and amortization | 5,621 | 4,588 | 3,461 |
| Provision for deferred income taxes | (561) | (794) | (705) |
| Provision for losses (recovery) of accounts receivable | (13) | (27) | 112 |
| Changes in assets and liabilities: | | | |
| Increase in receivables | (314) | (1,643) | (1,366) |
| Increase in inventory | (4,753) | (163) | (6,488) |
| Decrease (increase) in prepaid expenses and other assets | 474 | 249 | (1,549) |
| Increase in payables, accrued expenses and other liabilities | 11,030 | 2,783 | 2,318 |
| Net cash provided by operating activities | 27,244 | 18,873 | 9,043 |
| **Cash flows from investing activities:** | | | |
| Capital expenditures | (21,521) | (6,272) | (11,980) |
| Purchases of marketable securities held-to-maturity | (11,068) | (9,333) | (20,522) |
| Purchases of marketable securities available-for-sale | (3,110) | (8,075) | (2,425) |
| Sales of marketable securities available-for-sale | 1,900 | 6,100 | 5,035 |
| Maturities of marketable securities held-to-maturity | 9,886 | 9,752 | 12,356 |
| Purchase of investment | (3,754) | — | — |
| Net cash used in investing activities | (27,667) | (7,828) | (17,536) |
| **Cash flows from financing activities:** | | | |
| Exercise of stock options | 1,597 | 1,086 | 2,979 |
| Purchases and retirement of common stock | (2,254) | — | — |
| Net cash (used in) provided by financing activities | (657) | 1,086 | 2,979 |
| Effect of exchange rate changes on cash and cash equivalents | (467) | — | — |
| Increase (decrease) in cash and cash equivalents | (1,547) | 12,131 | (5,514) |
| Cash and cash equivalents at beginning of period | 26,712 | 14,581 | 20,095 |
| Cash and cash equivalents at end of period | $ 25,165 | $ 26,712 | $ 14,581 |

*See accompanying notes.*

1999 Annual REPORT
<URBAN OUTFITTERS>

# NOTES TO CONSOLIDATED FINANCIAL STATEMENTS

*(Dollars in thousands, except per share data)*

### NOTE 1. SIGNIFICANT ACCOUNTING POLICIES

***Principles of Consolidation*** The consolidated financial statements include the accounts of Urban Outfitters, Inc. and its wholly owned subsidiaries. All significant intercompany transactions have been eliminated in consolidation. The principal business activity of the Company is the operation of a general consumer product retail business through retail stores, a catalog and a website. In addition, the Company engages in the wholesale distribution of apparel to over 1,300 better specialty stores worldwide.

***Cash and Cash Equivalents*** Cash and cash equivalents are defined as cash and highly liquid investments with original maturities of less than three months. They are carried at amortized cost, which approximates fair value because of the short maturity of these instruments.

***Marketable Securities*** The Company's debt and equity securities are classified as either held-to-maturity or available-for-sale. Held-to-maturity securities represent those securities that the Company has both the positive intent and ability to hold to maturity and are carried at amortized cost. Interest on these securities as well as amortization is included in interest income. Available-for-sale securities represent those securities that do not meet the classification of held-to-maturity, are not actively traded and are carried at fair value. Unrealized gains and losses on these securities are excluded from earnings and should be reported as a separate component of shareholders' equity, net of applicable taxes, until realized. Gross unrealized gains and losses, net of the related deferred taxes, have not been material. When available-for-sale securities are sold, the cost of the securities is specifically identified and is used to determine the realized gain or loss. These amounts have not been material.

***Concentration of Credit Risk*** Financial instruments that potentially subject the Company to concentrations of credit risk consist principally of cash equivalents and investments. The Company manages the credit risk associated with cash equivalents and investments by investing with high-quality institutions and, by policy, limiting the amount of credit exposure to any one institution.

***Inventories*** Inventories, which consist of general consumer merchandise held for sale, are valued at the lower of cost or market. The cost is determined on the first-in, first-out method.

***Depreciation and Amortization*** Property and equipment are stated at cost. Depreciation and amortization are computed using the straight-line method over five years for furniture and fixtures, "life of lease" for leasehold improvements and three to ten years for other operating equipment. The Company reviews long-lived assets for possible impairment whenever events or changes in circumstances indicate the carrying amount may not be recoverable. This determination includes evaluation of factors such as current market value, future asset utilization and future net undiscounted cash flows expected to result from the use of the assets.

***Income Taxes*** The Company utilizes the asset and liability method of accounting for income taxes. Under this method, deferred tax assets and liabilities are recognized for the expected future tax consequences of temporary differences between the carrying amounts and the tax bases of assets and liabilities.

***Net Income Per Share*** Basic earnings per share are based upon the weighted average number of common shares outstanding. Diluted earnings per share are based upon the weighted average number of common shares outstanding and the potential dilution that could occur if stock options were exercised.

***Accounting Estimates*** The preparation of financial statements in conformity with generally accepted accounting principles requires management to make estimates and assumptions that affect the reported amounts of assets, liabilities and disclosure of contingencies at the date of the financial statements and the reported amounts of net sales and expenses during the reporting period. Differences from those estimates, if any, are recorded in the period they become known.

***Accounting for Stock-Based Compensation*** In October 1995, the Financial Accounting Standards Board issued Statement of Financial Accounting Standards No. 123, "Accounting for Stock-Based Compensation" ("SFAS No. 123"). SFAS No. 123 defines a fair value-based method of accounting for employee stock options or other similar equity instruments. Companies must either adopt the new method or disclose the pro forma income statement effects in their financial statements. The Company has chosen to disclose the pro forma income statement effects of SFAS No. 123 only.

1999 Annual REPORT
<URBAN OUTFITTERS>

# NOTES

*(continued)*

**Advertising** The Company expenses the costs of advertising when the advertising occurs, except for direct response advertising, which is capitalized and amortized over its expected period of future benefit. Advertising costs reported as prepaid expenses are not material. Advertising expense was $4,486 for the fiscal year ended January 31, 1999. Advertising expenses incurred for the fiscal years ended January 31, 1998 and January 31, 1997 were immaterial.

**Foreign Currency Translation** The financial statements of the Company's foreign operations are translated into U.S. dollars. Assets and liabilities are translated at current exchange rates while income and expense accounts are translated at the average rates in effect during the year. Translation adjustments are not included in determining net income but are included in accumulated other comprehensive income within shareholders' equity.

**Recent Accounting Pronouncements** In June 1998, the Financial Accounting Standards Board issued Statement of Financial Accounting Standards No. 133, "Accounting for Derivative Instruments and Hedging Activities" ("SFAS No. 133") which is required to be adopted in fiscal years beginning after June 15, 1999. The Company plans to adopt SFAS No. 133 effective February 1, 2000. The Company currently enters into short-term foreign currency forward exchange contracts to manage exposures related to its Canadian dollar denominated investments and anticipated cash flow. The amounts of these contracts and related gains and losses have not been material. The adoption of SFAS No. 133 is not expected to have a significant effect on the financial position or results of operations of the Company.

**Reclassifications** Certain reclassifications of prior years' data have been made to conform to the Fiscal 1999 presentation.

## NOTE 2. MARKETABLE SECURITIES

The amortized cost and estimated fair value of the marketable securities are as follows:

| | January 31, 1999 | | January 31, 1998 | |
|---|---|---|---|---|
| | Amortized Cost | Fair Value | Amortized Cost | Fair Value |
| **Current portion** | | | | |
| Held-to-maturity | | | | |
| Tax-exempt municipal securities | $ 9,206 | $ 9,273 | $ 7,272 | $ 7,294 |
| U.S. government securities | — | — | 1,318 | 1,318 |
| Total current held-to-maturity | 9,206 | 9,273 | 8,590 | 8,612 |
| Available-for-sale | | | | |
| Tax-exempt municipal securities, putable | 3,826 | 3,844 | 2,275 | 2,275 |
| Total current marketable securities | 13,032 | 13,117 | 10,865 | 10,887 |
| **Noncurrent portion** | | | | |
| Held-to-maturity | | | | |
| Tax-exempt municipal securities | 12,218 | 12,367 | 11,993 | 12,111 |
| U.S. government securities | — | — | — | — |
| Total noncurrent held-to-maturity | 12,218 | 12,367 | 11,993 | 12,111 |
| Total marketable securities | $25,250 | $25,484 | $22,858 | $22,998 |

1999 Annual REPORT
<URBAN OUTFITTERS>
# NOTES
*(continued)*

The noncurrent portion of investments held-to-maturity has contractual maturities of one to four years. The investments available-for-sale have a contractual maturity of greater than five years. Actual maturities may differ from contractual maturities as a result of put and call options that enable either the Company and/or the issuer to redeem particular securities at an earlier date. The fair value of the securities is determined based upon market prices.

## NOTE 3. INVENTORY
Inventory is summarized as follows:

| January 31, | 1999 | 1998 |
| --- | --- | --- |
| Work-in-progress | $ 711 | $ 861 |
| Finished goods | 21,170 | 16,267 |
| Total | $21,881 | $17,128 |

## NOTE 4. PROPERTY AND EQUIPMENT
Property and equipment is summarized as follows:

| January 31, | 1999 | 1998 |
| --- | --- | --- |
| Land | $ 543 | $ 543 |
| Furniture and fixtures | 17,901 | 13,739 |
| Leasehold improvements | 45,045 | 28,267 |
| Other operating equipment | 2,888 | 2,034 |
| | 66,377 | 44,583 |
| Accumulated depreciation and amortization | (23,311) | (17,690) |
| Total | $ 43,066 | $ 26,893 |

## NOTE 5. ACCRUED EXPENSES
Accrued expenses consist of the following:

| January 31, | 1999 | 1998 |
| --- | --- | --- |
| Accrued sales taxes | $ 956 | $ 489 |
| Accruals for construction in progress | 1,223 | — |
| Other current liabilities | 3,687 | 1,395 |
| Total | $5,866 | $1,884 |

The reported amounts approximate fair value because of the short maturity of these obligations.

## NOTE 6. LINE OF CREDIT
The Company has available a $16,200 revolving line of credit to facilitate letter of credit transactions and cash advances. Interest on outstanding balances is payable monthly based on an "as offered" rate not to exceed the London Interbank Offered Rate (LIBOR) plus ½%. No principal amounts were outstanding under this line at January 31, 1999 and 1998. Outstanding letters of credit totaled $4,096 and $4,706 as of January 31, 1999 and 1998, respectively. These letters of credit, which have terms from one month to one year, collateralize the Company's obligation to third parties for the purchase of inventory. The fair value of these letters of credit is estimated to be the same as the contract values.

## NOTE 7. SEGMENT REPORTING
In June 1997, the Financial Accounting Standards Board issued Statement of Financial Accounting Standards No. 131, "Disclosures about Segments of an Enterprise and Related Information" ("SFAS No. 131"). The adoption of SFAS No. 131 has no impact on the Company's consolidated results of operations, financial position or cash flows. Its effect is limited to the disclosures contained in the financial statements.

Urban Outfitters is a national retailer of general consumer products through 46 stores operating under the retail names "Urban Outfitters" and "Anthropologie," and through a catalog and website. Sales from this retail segment account for over 90% of total consolidated sales for the fiscal year ended January 31, 1999. The remainder is derived from a wholesale division that manufactures and distributes apparel to the retail segment and to over 1,300 better specialty stores worldwide.

99

| 8340 5431 00 |

URBN

1999 Annual REPORT
<URBAN OUTFITTERS>
# NOTES
(continued)

The Company has aggregated its operations into these two reportable segments based upon their unique management, customer base and economic characteristics. Reporting in this format provides management with the financial information necessary to evaluate the success of the segments and the overall business.

The Company evaluates the performance of the segments based on the net sales and pre-tax income from operations (excluding intercompany royalty and interest charges) of the segment. Corporate expenses include expenses incurred in and directed by the corporate office that are not allocated to segments.

The principal identifiable assets for each operating segment are inventory and fixed assets. Other assets are comprised primarily of general corporate assets, which principally consist of cash and cash equivalents, marketable securities and other assets.

Intersegment sales were immaterial in each of the last three fiscal years. The Company accounts for intersegment sales and transfers as if the sales and transfers were made to third parties making similar volume purchases.

Both the retail and wholesale segments are highly diversified. No customer comprises more than 10% of sales. Foreign operations are immaterial relative to the overall Company.

The accounting policies of the operating segments are the same as the policies described above in Note 1, "Significant Accounting Policies". A summary of the information about the Company's operations by segment is as follows:

| Fiscal Year | 1999 | 1998 | 1997 |
|---|---|---|---|
| **Operating revenues** | | | |
| Retail operations | $189,034 | $142,638 | $128,081 |
| Wholesale operations | 23,652 | 35,343 | 31,944 |
| Intersegment elimination | (3,717) | (4,860) | (3,611) |
| Total net sales | $208,969 | $173,121 | $156,414 |
| **Income from operations** | | | |
| Retail operations | $ 25,886 | $ 17,600 | $ 16,104 |
| Wholesale operations | 985 | 5,397 | 5,995 |
| Total segment operating income | 26,871 | 22,997 | 22,099 |
| General corporate expenses | (1,754) | (935) | (743) |
| Total income from operations | $ 25,117 | $ 22,062 | $ 21,356 |
| **Depreciation and amortization expense** | | | |
| Retail operations | $ 5,409 | $ 4,382 | $ 3,400 |
| Wholesale operations | 211 | 205 | 60 |
| Corporate | 1 | 1 | 1 |
| Total depreciation and amortization expense | $ 5,621 | $ 4,588 | $ 3,461 |
| **Inventory** | | | |
| Retail operations | $ 19,397 | $ 14,353 | $ 13,323 |
| Wholesale operations | 2,484 | 2,775 | 3,642 |
| Total inventory | $ 21,881 | $ 17,128 | $ 16,965 |
| **Net fixed assets** | | | |
| Retail operations | $ 42,230 | $ 25,993 | $ 24,736 |
| Wholesale operations | 835 | 898 | 471 |
| Corporate | 1 | 2 | 2 |
| Total net fixed assets | $ 43,066 | $ 26,893 | $ 25,209 |
| **Capital expenditures** | | | |
| Retail operations | $ 21,373 | $ 5,640 | $ 11,935 |
| Wholesale operations | 148 | 632 | 45 |
| Total capital expenditures | $ 21,521 | $ 6,272 | $ 11,980 |

1999 Annual REPORT
&lt;URBAN OUTFITTERS&gt;

# NOTES

*(continued)*

### NOTE 8. PROFIT-SHARING PLAN

The Company has a profit-sharing plan that covers all employees who are at least 18 years of age and have completed at least one thousand hours of service. Plan contributions are at the discretion of management but may not exceed 15% of qualified employee earnings.

A contribution of $198 was made by the Company for the fiscal year ended January 31, 1999; no contributions were made by the Company for the fiscal years ended January 31, 1998 or January 31, 1997.

### NOTE 9. INCOME TAXES

Income tax expense consists of:

| Fiscal Year Ended January 31, | 1999 | 1998 | 1997 |
|---|---|---|---|
| Current: | | | |
| Federal | $ 9,069 | $8,433 | $8,041 |
| State and local | 1,955 | 2,106 | 2,073 |
| Foreign | 489 | — | — |
| Deferred: | | | |
| Federal | (494) | (499) | (613) |
| State and local | (98) | (32) | (92) |
| Foreign | 31 | (263) | — |
| Total | $10,952 | $9,745 | $9,409 |

The effective tax rate was different than the statutory U.S. federal income tax rate for the following reasons:

| Fiscal Year Ended January 31, | 1999 | 1998 | 1997 |
|---|---|---|---|
| Expected provision at federal statutory rate | 35% | 35% | 35% |
| State and local income taxes, net of federal tax benefit, and other | 6 | 6 | 7 |
| Effective rate | 41% | 41% | 42% |

The significant components of deferred tax assets and liabilities at January 31, 1999 and 1998 are as follows:

| | 1999 | 1998 |
|---|---|---|
| Deferred tax liability: | | |
| Prepaid expenses | $ (303) | $ (242) |
| Deferred tax assets: | | |
| Depreciation and lease transactions | 2,640 | 2,221 |
| Inventory | 1,687 | 1,328 |
| Accounts receivable | 461 | 533 |
| Loss carryforwards | 232 | 263 |
| Accrued salaries and benefits | 91 | 145 |
| Other | 16 | 15 |
| Net deferred tax assets | $4,824 | $4,263 |

At January 31, 1999, the Company had net operating loss carryforwards for tax purposes of approximately $750 in the United Kingdom that do not expire. At January 31, 1999 and 1998, a deferred tax asset of $2,900 and $2,334, respectively, is included in Other assets.

The cumulative amount of the Company's share of undistributed earnings of non-U.S. subsidiaries for which no deferred taxes have been provided was $804 as of January 31, 1999. These earnings are deemed to be permanently reinvested to finance growth programs.

### NOTE 10. LEASES

The Company leases its stores and certain warehouse space under noncancelable operating leases. The following is a schedule by year of the future minimum lease payments for operating leases with terms in excess of one year:

1999 Annual REPORT
‹URBAN OUTFITTERS›
# NOTES
(continued)

| Fiscal Year | |
|---|---|
| 2000 | $ 15,686 |
| 2001 | 15,960 |
| 2002 | 15,913 |
| 2003 | 15,118 |
| 2004 | 14,178 |
| Thereafter | 62,650 |
| Total minimum lease payments | $139,505 |

Certain store leases provide for predetermined escalations in future minimum annual rentals. The pro rata portions of future minimum rent escalations, amounting to $3,856 and $3,095, at January 31, 1999 and 1998, respectively, have been included in Other liabilities in the accompanying consolidated balance sheets. Subsequent to year end, the Company entered into leases for additional locations. Commitments related to these leases are included in the above.

The store leases provide for payment of direct operating costs including real estate taxes. Certain store leases provide for contingent rentals when sales exceed specified levels.

Rent expense consisted of the following:

| Fiscal Year Ended January 31, | 1999 | 1998 | 1997 |
|---|---|---|---|
| Minimum rentals | $14,110 | $11,631 | $ 9,946 |
| Contingent rentals | 484 | 380 | 599 |
| Total | $14,594 | $12,011 | $10,545 |

During the year ended January 31, 1999, the Company entered into a three-year capitalized lease for certain computer equipment. The capital lease obligation of $273 was recorded as a liability, and the offsetting asset is being amortized over the lease period. Remaining principal payments for the next three fiscal years are $88, $91 and $94, respectively.

## NOTE 11. CONTINGENCIES
The Company is party to various legal proceedings arising from normal business activities. Management believes that the ultimate resolution of these matters will not have an adverse material effect on the Company's financial condition or results of operations.

## NOTE 12. STOCK OPTION PLANS
The 1997 Stock Option Plan authorizes up to an aggregate of 1,250,000 common shares which can be granted as either incentive stock options or nonqualified stock options. The vesting period for this Plan can range from one to ten years. This 1997 Plan replaced the previous 1987, 1992 and 1993 Plans which were precluded from making additional grants due either to expiration or insufficiently available shares. Individual grants outstanding under certain of the superseded plans, however, have expiration dates which extend into the year 2008.

The Company has adopted the disclosure-only provisions of Statement of Financial Accounting Standards No. 123, "Accounting for Stock-Based Compensation" ("SFAS No. 123"). Accordingly, no compensation cost has been recognized for the stock option plans. Had compensation cost for the Company's four stock option plans been determined based on the fair value provisions of SFAS No. 123 at the grant date for awards during Fiscal 1999, 1998 and 1997, the Company's net earnings and earnings per share would have been reduced to the pro forma amounts indicated below:

| Fiscal Year Ended January 31, | 1999 | 1998 | 1997 |
|---|---|---|---|
| Net income—as reported | $15,760 | $13,880 | $13,260 |
| Net income—pro forma | $14,412 | $12,693 | $12,649 |
| Net income per share— assuming dilution— as reported | $ 0.88 | $ 0.78 | $ 0.75 |
| Net income per share— assuming dilution— pro forma | $ 0.80 | $ 0.72 | $ 0.72 |

The pro forma results may not be representative of the effects on reported operations for future years.

1999 Annual REPORT
<URBAN OUTFITTERS>

# NOTES

*(continued)*

The fair value of each option grant is estimated on the date of grant using the Black-Scholes option-pricing model with the following weighted average assumptions:

|  | 1999 | 1998 | 1997 |
|---|---|---|---|
| Expected life (years) | 7.0 | 6.7 | 5.7 |
| Risk-free interest rate | 5.8% | 6.9% | 6.1% |
| Volatility | 50.0% | 50.7% | 49.5% |
| Dividend rate | 0% | 0% | 0% |

Information regarding these option plans for Fiscal 1999, 1998, and 1997 is as follows:

|  | FY 1999 | | FY 1998 | | FY 1997 | |
|---|---|---|---|---|---|---|
| *Fixed Options* | Shares | Weighted Average Exercise Price | Shares | Weighted Average Exercise Price | Shares | Weighted Average Exercise Price |
| Options outstanding at beginning of year | 1,305,094 | $10.60 | 1,010,756 | $ 9.50 | 1,274,582 | $ 5.99 |
| Options granted | 545,500 | 15.10 | 415,000 | 11.54 | 185,000 | 15.02 |
| Options exercised | (157,594) | 4.37 | (120,662) | 4.62 | (448,326) | 1.80 |
| Options canceled | (10,500) | 12.61 | — | n/a | (500) | 15.19 |
| Options outstanding at end of year | 1,682,500 | $12.63 | 1,305,094 | $10.60 | 1,010,756 | $ 9.50 |
| Options exercisable at end of year | 614,999 |  | 603,426 |  | 472,920 |  |
| Weighted average fair value of grants per share | $8.49 |  | $6.89 |  | $7.99 |  |

The following table summarizes information concerning currently outstanding and exercisable options:

|  | Options Outstanding | | | Options Exercisable | |
|---|---|---|---|---|---|
| *Range of Exercise Prices* | Amount Outstanding at 1/31/99 | Wtd. Avg. Remaining Contractual Life | Wtd. Avg. Exercise Price | Amount Exercisable at 1/31/99 | Wtd. Avg. Exercise Price |
| $ 8.35–$10.44 | 227,000 | 1.9 | $ 9.19 | 160,332 | $ 9.27 |
| $10.44–$12.53 | 737,000 | 4.9 | $11.00 | 320,000 | $11.15 |
| $12.53–$14.61 | 350,000 | 9.7 | $14.02 | 40,000 | $13.25 |
| $14.61–$16.70 | 243,500 | 7.5 | $15.92 | 52,667 | $15.34 |
| $16.70–$20.88 | 125,000 | 8.6 | $18.25 | 42,000 | $20.72 |

URBN

1999 Annual REPORT
<URBAN OUTFITTERS>
# NOTES
*(continued)*

### NOTE 13. NET INCOME PER SHARE (EPS)

The following is a reconciliation of the denominators of the net income per share and net income per share – assuming dilution ("EPS") computations:

*(in shares)*

| Fiscal Year Ended January 31, | 1999 | 1998 | 1997 |
|---|---|---|---|
| Net income per share | 17,702,922 | 17,576,203 | 17,429,375 |
| Effect of dilutive options | 226,187 | 267,670 | 293,254 |
| Net income per share— assuming dilution | 17,929,109 | 17,843,873 | 17,722,629 |

Options to purchase 40,000 shares at $20.88 per share and 10,000 shares at $17.69 per share, were outstanding during Fiscal 1999, but were not included in the computation of diluted EPS because the options' exercise price was greater than the average market price of the common shares. Options to purchase 40,000 shares at $20.88 per share, 10,000 shares at $17.69 per share, 35,000 shares at $16.88 per share and 69,500 shares at $15.19 per share were outstanding during Fiscal 1998, but were not included in the computation of diluted EPS because the options' exercise price was greater than the average market price of the common shares.

### NOTE 14. ACCUMULATED OTHER COMPREHENSIVE INCOME (LOSS)

In June, 1997, the Financial Accounting Standards Board issued Statement of Financial Accounting Standards No. 130, "Reporting Comprehensive Income" ("SFAS No. 130") that the Company adopted in the first quarter of Fiscal 1999. SFAS No. 130 requires presentation of comprehensive income and its components in the financial statements. Comprehensive income includes charges and credits to equity that are not the result of transactions with shareholders. Comprehensive income is comprised of two subsets–net income and other comprehensive income. All amounts in Accumulated Other Comprehensive Income (Loss) relate to foreign currency translation adjustments. The foreign currency translation adjustments are not adjusted for income taxes since these adjustments related to indefinite investments in non-U.S. subsidiaries.

### NOTE 15. SUPPLEMENTAL CASH FLOW INFORMATION

| Fiscal Year Ended January 31, | 1999 | 1998 | 1997 |
|---|---|---|---|
| Cash paid during the year for: | | | |
| Interest | $ 6 | $ 29 | $ 28 |
| Income taxes | $8,843 | $9,668 | $8,260 |

### NOTE 16. STOCK SPLIT

During 1996, the Board of Directors Inc. declared a two-for-one stock split in the form of a stock dividend for shareholders of record on June 1, 1996.

### NOTE 17. INVESTMENT IN HMB PUBLISHING, INC.

On February 5, 1998 the Company entered into an agreement with HMB Publishing, Inc. ("HMB") for the purchase of securities convertible into a minority interest in the company through Series B Convertible Preferred Stock ("Series B Preferred") and certain convertible debentures. The agreement called for additional investments and ownership if HMB met certain performance milestones. HMB is a development stage company which publishes *mXg*,™ a combination magazine and catalog and operates a website—www.mXgonline.com— which caters to teenage girls. The original business plan contemplated substantial losses in the first two fiscal years and a public offering as soon as feasible.

As of January 31, 1999, the Company has invested approximately $2,000 in the Series B Preferred and an additional $1,750 in the convertible debentures. Since January 31, 1999, the Company has advanced an additional $1,100 to fund further marketing efforts and additional development of the website and, together with additional investors, will seek to position HMB for more rapid expansion. It is the Company's intent to maintain an equity interest following any public offering by HMB.

### NOTE 18. SUBSEQUENT EVENT

In accordance with its previously announced stock buyback program that authorized the Company to repurchase up to 800,000 of its shares, the Company has repurchased 279,000 shares of its common stock at a cost of $3,729 during the period from February 1, 1999 through March 12, 1999 in a series of individual open market transaction.

## REPORT OF INDEPENDENT ACCOUNTANTS

*To the Board of Directors and Shareholders of*
*Urban Outfitters, Inc.*

In our opinion, the accompanying consolidated balance sheets
and the related consolidated statements of income, shareholders'
equity and cash flows present fairly, in all material respects, the
financial position of Urban Outfitters, Inc. and its subsidiaries
at January 31, 1999 and 1998, and the results of their operations
and their cash flows for each of the three years in the period
ended January 31, 1999, in conformity with generally accepted
accounting principles. These financial statements are the
responsibility of the Company's management; our responsibility
is to express an opinion on these financial statements based
on our audits. We conducted our audits of these statements in
accordance with generally accepted auditing standards which
require that we plan and perform the audit to obtain reasonable
assurance about whether the financial statements are free
of material misstatement. An audit includes examining, on
a test basis, evidence supporting the amounts and disclosures
in the financial statements, assessing the accounting principles
used and significant estimates made by management, and
evaluating the overall financial statement presentation. We
believe that our audits provide a reasonable basis for the
opinion expressed above.

*PricewaterhouseCoopers LLP*

Philadelphia, Pennsylvania
March 12, 1999

1999 Annual REPORT
<URBAN OUTFITTERS>

# MARKET INFORMATION

The Company's common shares are traded on the NASDAQ National Market System under the symbol "URBN." The following table sets forth the high and low bid prices for the Company's common shares during the period indicated as reported by NASDAQ. The Company has not paid any cash dividends since its inception and does not anticipate paying any in the foreseeable future. On April 2, 1999 the Company had approximately 1,800 shareholders.

| Market Prices ($)* | High Bid Price | Low Bid Price |
|---|---|---|
| **Fiscal 1997** | | |
| Quarter ended April 30, 1996 | 16¹⁵⁄₁₆ | 12 |
| Quarter ended July 31, 1996 | 27⅜ | 14¾ |
| Quarter ended October 31, 1996 | 24¾ | 13⅝ |
| Quarter ended January 31, 1997 | 17 | 10½ |
| **Fiscal 1998** | | |
| Quarter ended April 30, 1997 | 14 | 10½ |
| Quarter ended July 31, 1997 | 18½ | 12 |
| Quarter ended October 31, 1997 | 19¾ | 15⅛ |
| Quarter ended January 31, 1998 | 19 | 14½ |
| **Fiscal 1999** | | |
| Quarter ended April 30, 1998 | 24¾ | 15¾ |
| Quarter ended July 31, 1998 | 20 | 14½ |
| Quarter ended October 31, 1998 | 17 | 11 |
| Quarter ended January 31, 1999 | 18 | 11⁹⁄₁₆ |

*Post June 1, 1996 2-for-1 stock split

**STORE LOCATIONS**

LOCATIONS
*Urban Outfitters Stores*

*UNITED KINGDOM*

London, England
36-38 Kensington High Street

*UNITED STATES*
(EAST)

New York, NY
628 Broadway

New York, NY
374 Avenue of Americas

New York, NY
127 East 59th Street

New York, NY
162 2nd Avenue

Philadelphia, PA
1801 Walnut Street

Philadelphia, PA
110 South 36th Street

Boston, MA
361 Newbury Street

Cambridge, MA
11 J.F. Kennedy Street

Washington, DC
3111 M Street, N.W.

Miami Beach, FL
653 Collins Ave.

Burlington, VT
81 Church Street (4/99)

(MIDWEST)

Chicago, IL
2352 N. Clark Street

Chicago, IL
935 N. Rush Street

Ann Arbor, MI
231 S. State Street

Minneapolis, MN
3006 Hennepin Ave., S.

Madison, WI
604 State Street

Boulder, CO
934 Pearl Street

Bloomington, IN
530 E. Kirkwood Ave.

Columbus, OH
1782 N. High Street

(WEST)

San Francisco, CA
80 Powell Street

Berkeley, CA
2590 Bancroft Way

Seattle, WA
401 Broadway, East

Portland, OR
2320 N.W. Westover Road

Pasadena, CA
139 W. Colorado Blvd.

Santa Monica, CA
1440 Third Street Promenade

Costa Mesa, CA
2930 Bristol Street

San Diego, CA
665 Fifth Avenue

Los Angeles, CA
7650 Melrose Avenue

(SOUTHWEST)

Tempe, AZ
545 South Mill Ave.

Austin, TX
2406 Guadalupe Street

Houston, TX
2501 University Blvd.

*CANADA*

Montreal, PQ
1246 Ste. Catherine Street, W.

Toronto, ON
235 Yonge Street

LOCATIONS
*Anthropologie Stores*

*UNITED STATES*
(EAST)

Boston, MA
799 Boylston Street

Westport, CT
1365 Post Road, East

SoHo, NY
375 West Broadway

Greenvale, NY
9 Northern Blvd.

Wayne, PA
201 W. Lancaster Ave.

Rockville, MD
11500 Rockville Pike

(MIDWEST)

Chicago, IL
1120 N. State Street

Highland Park, IL
1780 Green Bay Road

Birmingham, MI
214 West Maple Road

(WEST)

Seattle, WA
2520 NE University Village, #120

Santa Monica, CA
1402 Third Street Promenade

Beverly Hills, CA
320 N. Beverly Drive

Newport Beach, CA
823 Newport Center Drive

Santa Barbara, CA
901 State Street

COMPANY INFORMATION

MANAGEMENT

**Richard A. Hayne**
Chairman of the Board of Directors and President

**Stephen A. Feldman**
Chief Financial Officer and Treasurer

**Glen A. Bodzy**
Secretary and General Counsel

**Michael A. Schultz**
President, Urban Outfitters
Wholesale, Inc.

**Glen T. Senk**
President, Anthropologie, Inc.

BOARD OF DIRECTORS

**Scott A. Belair**
Director

**Harry S. Cherken, Jr.**
Director

**Kenneth K. Cleeland**
Director

**Richard A. Hayne**
Director

**Joel S. Lawson III**
Director

**Burton M. Sapiro**
Director

HOME OFFICES

Urban Outfitters, Inc.
1809 Walnut Street
Philadelphia, PA 19103
215.564.2313

Anthropologie, Inc.
235 South 17th Street
Philadelphia, PA 19103
215.564.2313

To request a catalog, please visit:
www.anthropologie.com

TRANSFER AGENT

StockTrans, Inc.
7 East Lancaster Avenue
Ardmore, PA 19003
610.649.7300

INDEPENDENT ACCOUNTANTS

PricewaterhouseCoopers LLP
30 South Seventeenth Street
Philadelphia, PA 19103

CONCEPT + DESIGN
Tolleson Design SF/CA

## STANDARD & POOR'S INDUSTRY RATIO REPORT
### SIC* 5651, Family Clothing Stores

| (Ratio, except as noted) | |
| --- | --- |
| **Liquidity** | |
| Current ratio | 2.26 |
| Quick ratio | 0.74 |
| **Activity** | |
| Inventory turnover | 4.67 |
| Receivables turnover | 72.51 |
| Average collection period (days) | 5.00 |
| Accounts payable turnover | 8.20 |
| Fixed asset turnover | 12.79 |
| Total asset turnover | 2.55 |
| Days to sell inventory | 92.00 |
| Operating cycle (days) | 98.00 |
| **Profitability** | |
| Gross profit margin (%) | 36.48 |
| Operating profit margin (%) | 7.73 |
| Net profit margin (%) | 4.15 |
| Return on equity (%) | 27.39 |
| Return on assets (%) | 10.58 |
| Quality of income | 2.19 |
| **Leverage** | |
| Times interest earned | 62.28 |
| Interest coverage ratio | 100.97 |
| Total debt/Total equity | 1.59 |
| Total assets/Total equity | 2.59 |
| **Dividends** | |
| Dividend payout (%) | 2.49 |
| Dividend yield (%) | 0.09 |
| **Other** | |
| Advertising-to-sales (%) | 2.26 |
| Sales growth (%) | 16.15 |
| Capital acquisitions ratio | 1.79 |
| Price/Earnings | 26.13 |

### COMPANIES USED IN INDUSTRY ANALYSIS

| Company Name | Ticker Symbol |
| --- | --- |
| Abercrombie & Fitch | ANF |
| American Eagle Outfitters Inc. | AEOS |
| Big Dog Holdings Inc. | BDOG |
| Buckle Inc. | BKE |
| Burlington Coat Factory Warehouse | BCF |
| Designs Inc. | DESI |
| Factory 2-U Inc. | FTUS |
| Filenes Basement Corp. | BSMT |
| Gadzooks Inc. | GADZ |
| Gap Inc. | GPS |
| Goodys Family Clothing Inc. | GDYS |
| Harolds Stores Inc. | HLD |
| Iturf Inc. | TURF |
| Jacobs (Jay) Inc. | 3JAYJ |
| Lamonts Apparel Inc. | 3LMNT |
| Nordstrom Inc. | JWN |
| Pacific Sunwear California Inc. | PSUN |
| Ross Stores Inc. | ROST |
| Stage Stores Inc. | SGE |
| Stein Mart Inc. | SMRT |
| Syms Corp. | SYM |
| TJX Companies Inc. | TJX |
| Urban Outfitters Inc. | URBN |

*SIC = Standard Industrial Classification Code. A four-digit code used to identify the business activities of a company. Developed by the U.S. Department of Commerce, it is being replaced by a new six-digit coding system, the North American Industry Classification System (NAICS).

Industry Return on Equity (ROE) profit driver analysis

ROE = Net Profit Margin $\times$ Asset Turnover $\times$ Financial Leverage
$27.39 = 4.15 \times 2.55 \times 2.59$

# Glossary

**Accelerated Depreciation** Methods that result in higher depreciation expense in the early years of an asset's life and lower expense in the later years. (434)

**Account** A standardized format that organizations use to accumulate the dollar effects of transactions on each financial statement item. (59)

**Account form** lists assets on the left, liabilities and stockholders' equity on the right (79)

**Accounting** A system that collects and processes (analyzes, measures, and records) financial information about an organization and reports that information to decision makers. (5)

**Accounting Cycle** The recordkeeping process used during and at the end of the accounting period that results in financial statements. (166)

**Accounting Entity** The organization for which financial data are to be collected. (8)

**Accounting Period** The time period covered by the financial statements. (12)

**Accounts Receivable (Trade Receivables, Receivables)** Open accounts owed to the business by trade customers. (310)

**Accrual Basis Accounting** Records revenues when earned and expenses when incurred, regardless of the timing of cash receipts or payments. (114)

**Accruals** Revenues that have been earned and expenses that have been incurred by the end of the current accounting period but that will not be collected or paid until a future accounting period. (174)

**Accrued Liabilities** Expenses that have been incurred but have not been paid at the end of the accounting period. (490)

**Accrued Revenues** and **Accrued Expenses** Revenues that have been earned and expenses that have been incurred by the end of the current accounting period but that will not be collected or paid until a future accounting period. (171)

**Accumulated Other Comprehensive Income** Net unrealized gains or losses on securities, net minimum pension liability adjustments, and net foreign currency translation adjustment, which are directly credited or debited to the stockholders' equity account. (254)

**Acquisition Cost** Net cash equivalent amount paid or to be paid for the asset. (425)

**Additions** Extensions to or enlargements of existing assets that increase the cost of the existing asset. (429)

**Adjusting Entries** Entries necessary at the end of the accounting period to measure income properly, correct errors, and provide for adequate valuation of balance sheet accounts. (170)

**Aging of Accounts Receivable Method** Estimates uncollectible accounts based on the age of each account receivable. (314)

**Allowance for Doubtful Accounts (Allowance for Bad Debts, Allowance for Uncollectible Accounts)** Contra-asset account containing the estimated uncollectible accounts receivable. (311)

**Allowance Method** Bases bad debt expense on an estimate of uncollectible accounts. (311)

**Amortization** Systematic and rational allocation of the acquisition cost of an intangible asset over its useful life. (448)

**Annuity** A series of periodic cash receipts or payments that are equal in amount each interest period. (508)

**Assets** Probable future economic benefits owned by the entity as a result of past transactions. (55)

**Audit** An examination of the financial reports to ensure that they represent what they claim and conform with generally accepted accounting principles. (25)

**Authorized Number of Shares** Maximum number of shares of capital stock of a corporation that can be issued as specified in the charter. (590)

**Bad Debt Expense (Doubtful Accounts Expense, Uncollectible Accounts Expense, Provision for Uncollectible Accounts)** Expense associated with estimated uncollectible accounts receivable. (311)

**Balance Sheet (statement of financial position)** Reports the financial position (assets, liabilities, and stockholders' equity) of an accounting entity at a point in time. (8)

**Bank Reconciliation** Process of verifying the accuracy of both the bank statement and the cash accounts of the business. (321)

**Bank Statement** Monthly report from a bank that shows deposits recorded, checks cleared, other debits and credits, and a running bank balance. (321)

**Basic Accounting Equation (Balance Sheet Equation)** Assets = Liabilities + Stockholders' Equity. (10)

**Basket Purchase** Acquisition of two or more assets in a single transaction for a single lump sum. (426)

**Bond Certificate** The bond document that each bondholder receives. (544)

**Bond Discount** The difference between selling price and par when a bond is sold for less than par. (545)

**Bond Premium** The difference between selling price and par when a bond is sold for more than par. (545)

**Bond Principal** The amount (a) payable at the maturity of the bond and (b) on which the periodic cash interest payments are computed. (542)

**Bond Sinking Fund** A cash fund accumulated for payment of a bond at maturity. (558)

**Book Value (Net Book Value, Carrying Value)** of an asset is the acquisition cost of the asset less accumulated depreciation, depletion, or amortization (169, 430)

**Callable Bonds** Bonds that may be called for early retirement at the option of the issuer. (544)

**Capital Expenditures** Expenditures that provide future benefits and are recorded as increases in asset accounts, not as expenses. (428)

**Capital in Excess of Par (Additional Paid-in Capital, Contributed Capital in Excess of Par, Paid-in Capital)** The amount of contributed capital less the par value of the stock. (254)

**Capitalized Interest** Interest expenditures included in the cost of a self-constructed asset. (426)

**Cash** Money and any instrument that banks will accept for deposit and immediately credit to the company's account, such as a check, money order, or bank draft. (319)

**Cash Basis Accounting** Records revenues when cash is received and expenses when paid. (113)

**Cash Equivalents** Short-term investments with original maturities of three months or less that are readily convertible to cash and whose value is unlikely to change. (319, 683)

**Cash Flows from Financing Activities** Cash inflows and outflows related to external sources of financing (owners and creditors) for the enterprise. (685)

**Cash Flows from Investing Activities** Cash inflows and outflows related to the acquisition or sale of productive facilities and investments in the securities of other companies. (684)

**Cash Flows from Operating Activities (Cash Flows from Operations)** Cash inflows and outflows directly related to earnings from normal operations. (684)

**Closing Entries** Made at the end of the accounting period to transfer balances in temporary accounts to Retained Earnings and to establish a zero balance in each of the temporary accounts. (192)

**Common Stock** The basic, normal, voting stock issued by a corporation; called *residual equity* because it ranks after preferred stock for dividend and liquidation distributions. (591)

**Comparable Information** Information that can be compared across businesses because similar accounting methods have been applied. (246)

**Completed Contract Method** Records revenue when the completed product is delivered to the customer. (328)

**Component Percentage** Expresses each item on a particular financial statement as a percentage of a single base amount. (739)

**Comprehensive Income** Net income plus unrealized gain or loss on securities, minimum pension liability adjustment, and foreign currency translation adjustment. (260)

**Conservatism** Suggests that care should be taken not to overstate assets and revenues or understate liabilities and expenses. (264)

**Consistent Information** Information that can be compared across businesses because similar accounting methods have been applied. (246)

**Consolidated Financial Statements** The financial statements of two or more companies that have been combined into a single set of financial statements as if the companies were one. (655)

**Contingent Liability** Potential liability that has arisen as the result of a past event; not an effective liability until some future event occurs. (502)

**Continuity (Going-Concern) Assumption** States that businesses are assumed to continue to operate into the foreseeable future. (54)

**Contra-Account** An account that is an offset to, or reduction of, the primary account. (169)

**Contributed Capital** Results from owners providing cash (and sometimes other assets) to business owners. (57)

**Convertible Bonds** Bonds that may be converted to other securities of the issuer (usually common stock). (544)

**Convertible Preferred Stock** Preferred stock that is convertible to common stock at the option of the holder. (593)

**Goods Available for Sale** The sum of beginning inventory and purchases (or transfers to finished goods) for the period. (367)

**Copyright** Exclusive right to publish, use, and sell a literary, musical, or artistic work. (450)

**Cost-Benefit Constraint** Suggests that the benefits of accounting for and reporting information should outweigh the costs. (246)

**Cost of Goods Sold Equation** BI + P − EI = CGS. (367)

**Cost Principle** Requires assets to be recorded at the historical cash-equivalent cost, which on the date of the transaction is cash paid plus the current dollar value of all noncash considerations also given in the exchange. (57)

**Coupon Rate** The stated rate of interest on bonds. (545)

**Credit** The right side of an account. (66)

**Credit Card Discount** Fee charged by the credit card company for its services. (305)

**Cumulative Dividend Preference** Preferred stock feature that requires specified current dividends not paid in full to accumulate for every year in which they are not paid. These cumulative preferred dividends must be paid before any common dividends can be paid. (602)

**Cumulative Effects of Changes in Accounting Methods** Amounts reflected on the income statement for adjustments made to balance sheet accounts when applying different accounting principles. (259)

**Current Assets** Assets that will be used or turned into cash within one year. Inventory is always considered a current asset regardless of the time needed to produce or sell it. (55)

**Current Dividend Preference** The feature of preferred stock that grants priority on preferred dividends over common dividends. (602)

**Current Liabilities** Short-term obligations that will be paid in cash (or other current assets) or satisfied by providing service within the coming year. (488)

**D**

**Debenture** An unsecured bond; no assets are specifically pledged to guarantee repayment. (542)

**Debt** The left side of an account. (66)

**Declaration Date** The date on which the board of directors officially approves a dividend. (601)

**Declining-Balance Depreciation** The method that allocates the cost of an asset over its useful life based on a multiple of (often two times) the straight-line rate. (435)

**Deferrals** Previously recorded assets, liabilities, revenues, or expenses that need to be adjusted at the end of the period to reflect earned revenues or incurred expenses. (176)

**Deferred Revenues** and **Deferred Expenses** Previously recorded assets, liabilities, revenues, or expenses that need to be adjusted at the end of the period to reflect earned revenues or incurred expenses. (170)

**Deferred Tax Items** Timing differences caused by reporting revenues and expenses according to GAAP on a company's income statement and according to the Internal Revenue Code on the tax return. (500)

**Depletion** Systematic and rational allocation of the cost of a natural resource over the period of exploitation. (446)

**Depreciation** Systematic and rational allocation of the cost of property, plant, and equipment (but not land) over their useful lives. (430)

**Direct Labor** The earnings of employees who work directly on the products being manufactured. (365)

**Direct Method** The method of presenting the operating activities section of the statement of cash flow statement reports components of cash flows from operating activities as gross receipts and gross payments. (684)

**Discontinued Operations** Financial results from the disposal of a major segment of the business and are reported net of income tax effects. (258)

**Dividend Dates**

**Declaration Date** Date on which the board of directors officially approves a dividend. (601)

**Payment Date** Date on which a cash dividend is paid to the stockholders of record. (601)

**Record Date** Date on which the corporation prepares the list of current stockholders as shown on its records; dividends can be paid only to the stockholders who own stock on that date. (601)

**Dividends in Arrears** Dividends on cumulative preferred stock that have not been declared in prior years. (602)

**E**

**Earnings Forecasts** Predictions of earnings for future accounting periods. (241)

**Effective-Interest Method** Amortizes a bond discount or premium on the basis of the effective-interest rate; theoretically preferred method. (555)

**Effective-Interest Rate** Another name for the market rate of interest on a bond. (545)

**Efficient Markets** Securities markets in which prices fully reflect available information. (757)

**Equity Method** Used when an investor can exert significant influence over an investee. It permits recording of investor's share of investee's income. (649)

**Estimated Useful Life** Expected service life of an asset to the present owner. (431)

**Expenses** Decreases in assets or increases in liabilities to generate revenues during the period. (112)

**Extraordinary Items** Gains and losses that are both unusual in nature and infrequent in occurrence; they are reported net of tax on the income statement. (259)

**Extraordinary Repairs** Expenditures for major, high-cost, long-term repairs that increase the economic usefulness of the asset. (429)

**F**

**Face Amount** Another name for principal or the principal amount of a bond. (542)

**Factory Overhead** Manufacturing costs that are not raw material or direct labor costs. (365)

**Financial Accounting Standards Board (FASB)** The private sector body given the primary responsibility to work out the detailed rules that become generally accepted accounting principles. (22)

**Financial Leverage** Use of borrowed funds to increase the rate of return on owners' equity; occurs when the interest rate on debt is lower than the earnings rate on total assets. (540)

**Finished Goods Inventory** Manufactured goods that are completed and ready for sale. (365)

**First-In, First-Out (FIFO) Method** Assumes that the oldest units costs are the first units sold. (372)

**Form 8-K** The report used by publicly traded companies to disclose any material event not previously reported. (250)

**Form 10-K** The annual report that publicly traded companies must file with the SEC. (250)

**Form 10-Q** The quarterly report that publicly traded companies must file with the SEC. (250)

**Franchise** A contractual right to sell certain products or services, use certain trademarks, or perform activities in a geographical region. (450)

**Future Value** The sum to which an amount will increase as the result of compound interest. (504)

**G**

**Gains** Increases in assets or decreases in liabilities from peripheral transactions. (112)

**Generally Accepted Accounting Principles (GAAP)** The measurement rules used to develop the information in financial statements. (21)

**Goods Available for Sale** The sum of beginning inventory and purchases (or transfers to finished goods) for the period. (367)

**Goodwill** The difference between the purchase price of a company and the fair market value of the net assets (assets minus liabilities) that were acquired. (657)

**Goodwill (Cost in Excess of Net Assets Acquired)** For accounting purposes, the excess of the purchase price of a business over the market value of the business's assets and liabilities. (448)

**Gross Profit (Gross Margin)** Net sales less cost of goods sold. (257)

**H**

**Held-to-Maturity Investment** A long-term investment in bonds that management has the ability and intent to hold until maturity. (560)

**I**

**Income before Income Taxes (Pretax Earnings)** Revenues less all expenses except income tax expense. (257)

**Income from Operations (Operating Income)** Equal net sales less cost of goods sold and other operating expenses. (257)

**Income Statement (Statement of Income, Statement of Earnings, Statement of Operations)** Reports the revenues less the expenses of the accounting period. (12)

**Income Summary** A temporary account used only during the closing process to facilitate the closing of revenues and expenses. (192)

**Indenture** A bond contract that specifies the legal provisions of a bond issue. (543)

**Indirect Method** The method of presenting the operating activities section of the statement of cash flows that adjusts net income to compute cash flows from operating activities. (684)

**Installment Method** Recognizes revenue on the basis of cash collection after the delivery of goods. (328)

**Institutional Investors** Managers of pension, mutual, endowment, and other funds that invest on the behalf of others. (245)

**Intangible Assets** Assets that have special rights but not physical substance. (424)

**Internal Controls** Processes by which the company's board of directors, management, and other personnel provide reasonable assurance regarding the reliability of the company's financial reporting, the effectiveness and efficiency of its operations, and its compliance with applicable laws and regulations. (326)

**Inventory** Tangible property held for sale in the normal course of business or used in producing goods or services for sale. (364)

**Issued Shares** Total number of shares of stock that have been issued; shares outstanding plus treasury shares held. (590)

## J

**Journal Entry** An accounting method for expressing the effects of a transaction on accounts in a debits-equal-credits format. (67)

## L

**Last-In, First-Out (LIFO) Method** Assumes that the most recently acquired units are sold first. (372)

**Leaseholds** Rights granted to a lessee under a lease contract. (450)

**Legal Capital** The permanent amount of capital defined by state law that must remain invested in the business; serves as a cushion for creditors. (592)

**Lenders (Creditors)** Suppliers and financial institutions that lend money to companies. (245)

**Liabilities** Probable debts or obligations of the entity that result from past transactions, which will be paid with assets or services. (56, 488)

**LIFO Liquidation** A sale of a lower-cost inventory item from beginning LIFO inventory. (392)

**LIFO Reserve** A contra-asset for the excess of FIFO over LIFO inventory. (378)

**Long-Lived Assets** Tangible and intangible resources owned by a business and used in its operations over several years. (424)

**Long-Term Liabilities** All of the entity's obligations that are not classified as current liabilities. (497)

**Losses** Decreases in assets or increases in liabilities from peripheral transactions. (113)

**Lower of Cost or Market (LCM)** Valuation method departing from the cost principle that recognizes a loss when replacement cost or net realizable value drops below cost. (384)

## M

**Market Interest Rate** Current rate of interest on a debt when incurred; also called *yield* or *effective-interest rate.* (545)

**Market Tests** Ratios that tend to measure the market worth of a share of stock. (752)

**Market Value Method** Reports securities are at their current market value. (642)

**Matching Principle** Requires that expenses recorded when incurred in earning revenue. (117)

**Material Amounts** Amounts that are large enough to influence a user's decision. (264)

**Merchandise Inventory** Goods held for resale in the ordinary course of business. (364)

## N

**Natural Resources** Assets occurring in nature, such as mineral deposits, timber tracts, oil, and gas. (446)

**Net Interest Cost** Interest cost less any income tax savings associated with interest expense. (540)

**Net Realizable Value** The expected sales price less selling costs (e.g., repair and disposal costs). (385)

**Noncash Investing and Financing Activities** Transactions that do not have direct cash flow effects; reported as a supplement to the statement of cash flows in narrative or schedule form. (704)

**Noncurrent Accurals (Noncash Expenses and Revenues)** Expenses and revenues that do not affect current assets or liabilities; for example, depreciation expense. (689)

**No-Par Value Stock** Capital stock that has no par value specified in the corporate charter. (592)

**Notes Receivable** Written promises that requires another party to pay the business under specified conditions (amount, time, interest). (310)

**Notes (Footnotes)** Provide supplemental information about the financial condition of a company, without which the financial statements cannot be fully understood. (18)

## O

**Operating Cycle (Cash-to-Cash Cycle)** The time it takes for a company to purchase goods or services from suppliers, sell those goods and services to customers, and collect cash from customers. (109)

**Ordinary Repairs and Maintenance** Expenditures for the normal operating upkeep of long-lived assets. (429)

**Outstanding Shares** Total number of shares of stock that are owned by stockholders on any particular date. (590)

## P

**Parent Company** The entity that gains a controlling influence over another company (the subsidiary). (655)

**Par Value** A legal amount per share established by the board of directors; it establishes the minimum amount a stockholder must contribute and has no relationship to the market price of the stock. Also, another name for bond principal or the maturity amount of a bond. (254, 542)

**Patent** Granted by the federal government for an invention; gives the owner the exclusive right to use, manufacture, and sell the subject of the patent. (449)

**Payment Date** The date on which a cash dividend is paid to the stockholders of record. (601)

**Percentage of Completion Method** Records revenue based on the percentage of work completed during the accounting period. (328)

**Percentage of Credit Sales Method** Bases bad debt expense on the historical percentage of credit sales that result in bad debts. (313)

**Periodic Inventory System** Ending inventory and cost of goods sold determined at the end of the accounting period based on a physical inventory count. (386)

**Permanent (Real) Accounts** The balance sheet accounts that carry their ending balances into the next accounting period. (192)

**Perpetual Inventory System** A detailed inventory record maintained recording each purchase and sale during the accounting period. (386)

**Post-Closing Trial Balance** Should be prepared as the last step in the accounting cycle to check that debits equal credits and all temporary accounts have been closed. (193)

**Preferred Stock** Stock that has specified rights over common stock. (593)

**Present Value** The current value of an amount to be received in the future; a future amount discounted for compound interest. (504)

**Press Release** A written public news announcement normally distributed to major news services. (247)

**Primary Objective of External Financial Reporting** Provides useful economic information about a business to help external parties make sound financial decisions. (53)

**Prior Period Adjustment** Amount debited or credited directly to retained earnings to correct an accounting error of a prior period. (606)

**Private Investors** Individuals who purchase shares in companies. (245)

**Purchase** An acquisition that is completed by purchasing the subsidiary company's voting common stock for cash. (655)

**Purchase Discount** Cash discount received for prompt payment of an account. (395)

**Purchase Returns and Allowances** A reduction in the cost of purchases associated with unsatisfactory goods. (394)

## R

**Ratio (Percentage) Analysis** An analytical tool designed to identify significant relationships; measures the proportional relationship between two financial statement amounts. (738)

**Raw Materials Inventory** Items acquired for the purpose of processing into finished goods. (364)

**Record Date** The date on which the corporation prepares the list of current stockholders as shown on its records; dividends can be paid only to the stockholders who own stock on that date. (601)

**Redeemable Bonds** Bonds that may be turned in for early retirement at the option of the bondholder. (544)

**Relevant Information** Information that can influence a decision; it is timely and has predictive and/or feedback value. (246)

**Reliable Information** Information that is accurate, unbiased, and verifiable. (246)

**Replacement Cost** The current purchase price for identical goods. (384)

**Report forms** Lists assets on top, liabilities and stockholders' equity on the bottom. (79)

**Report of Independent Accountants (Audit Report)** Describes the auditors' opinion of the fairness of the financial statement presentations and the evidence gathered to support that opinion. (25)

**Report of Management** Indicates management's primary responsibility for financial statement information and the steps to ensure the accuracy of the company's records. (24)

**Residual (or Salvage) Value** Estimated amount to be recovered, less disposal costs, at the end of the company's estimated useful life of an asset. (431)

**Retained Earnings** Cumulative earnings of a company that are not distributed to the owners and are reinvested in the business. (57)

**Revenue Expenditures** Expenditures that provide benefits during the current accounting period only and are recorded as expenses. (428)

**Revenue Principle** Revenues are recognized (recorded) when the earnings process is complete or nearly complete, an exchange has taken place, and collection is probable. (114)

**Revenues** Increases in assets or settlements of liabilities from ongoing operations. (111)

## S

**Sales (or Cash) Discount** Cash discount offered to encourage prompt payment of an account receivable. (305)

**Sales Returns and Allowances** Reduction of sales revenues for return of or allowances for unsatisfactory goods. (307)

**Securities and Exchange Commission (SEC)** The U.S. government agency that determines the financial statements that public companies must provide to stockholders and the measurement rules that they must use in producing those statements. (22)

**Securities Available for Sale** All passive investments other than trading securities (classified as either short-term or long-term). (643)

**Separate-Entity Assumption** States that business transactions are separate from the transactions of the owners. (54)

**Specific Identification Method** Identifies the cost of the specific item that was sold. (373)

**Stated Rate** The rate of cash interest per period specified in the bond contract. (542)

**Statement of Cash Flows** Reports inflows and outflows of cash during the accounting period in the categories of operating, investing, and financing. (16)

**Statement of Retained Earnings** Reports the way that net income and the distribution of dividends affected the financial position of the company during the accounting period. (15)

**Stock Dividend** Distribution of additional shares of a corporation's own stock. (604)

**Stockholders' Equity (Owners' Equity or Shareholders' Equity)** The financing provided by the owners and the operations of the business. (57)

**Stock Split** An increase in the total number of authorized shares by a specified ratio; does not decrease retained earnings. (605)

**Straight-Line Amortization** Simplified method of amortizing a bond discount or premium that allocates an equal dollar amount to each interest period. (548)

**Straight-Line Depreciation** Method that allocates the cost of an asset in equal periodic amounts over its useful life. (432)

**Subsidiary Company** The entity that is acquired by the parent company. (655)

**T**

**T-account** A tool for summarizing transaction effects for each account, determining balances, and drawing inferences about a company's activities. (68)

**Tangible Assets (or fixed assets)** Assets that have physical substance. (424)

**Temporary (Nominal) Accounts** Income statement (and sometimes dividends declared) accounts that are closed to Retained Earnings at the end of the accounting period. (192)

**Temporary Differences** Timing differences that cause deferred income taxes and will reverse, or turn around, in the future. (500)

**Tests of Liquidity** Ratios that measure a company's ability to meet its currently maturing obligations. (746)

**Tests of Solvency** Ratios that measure a company's ability to meet its long-term obligations. (750)

**Time Period Assumption** The long life of a company can be reported in shorter time periods. (111)

**Time Value of Money** Interest that is associated with the use of money over time. (494)

**Trademark** An exclusive legal right to use a special name, image, or slogan. (449)

**Trading Securities** All investments in stocks or bonds that are held primarily for the purpose of active trading (buying and selling) in the near future (classified as short-term). (643)

**Transaction** (1) An exchange between a business and one or more external parties to a business or (2) a measurable internal event such as *adjustments* for the use of assets in operations. (58)

**Transaction Analysis** The process of studying a transaction to determine its economic effect on the business in terms of the accounting equation. (61)

**Treasury Stock** A corporation's own stock that has been issued but was subsequently reacquired and is still being held by that corporation. (598)

**Trial Balance** A list of all accounts with their balances to provide a check on the equality of the debits and credits. (168)

**Trustee** An independent party appointed to represent the bondholders. (544)

**U**

**Unissued Shares** Authorized shares of a corporation's stock that never have been issued. (590)

**Unit-of-Measure Assumption** States that accounting information should be measured and reported in the national monetary unit. (54)

**Units-of-Production Depreciation** Method that allocates the cost of an asset over its useful life based on its periodic output related to its total estimated output. (433)

**Unqualified (Clean) Audit Opinion** Auditors' statement that the financial statements are fair presentations in all material respects in conformity with GAAP. (240)

**Unrealized Holding Gains and Losses** Amounts associated with price changes of securities that are currently held. (643)

**W**

**Weighted Average Method** The weighted average unit cost of the goods available for sale for both cost of goods sold and ending inventory. (373)

**Working Capital** The dollar difference between total current assets and total current liabilities. (489)

**Work in Process Inventory** Goods in the process of being manufactured. (365)

# Illustration Credits

# Business Index

# Subject Index